A HISTORY OF

The Modern World

A HISTORY OF
THE
Modern World

by

R. R. PALMER
PRINCETON UNIVERSITY

Second Edition, Revised with the Collaboration of

JOEL COLTON
DUKE UNIVERSITY

Alfred · A · Knopf : New York

1962

ACKNOWLEDGMENT *is hereby made for permission to quote from the following works:*

Lenin: A Biography, by David Shub. Copyright, 1948, by David Shub and reprinted by permission of Doubleday & Company, Inc.

The Growth of the American Republic, by S. E. Morison and H. S. Commager. Copyright, 1932, 1937, 1942, by Oxford University Press, Inc.

"The White Man's Burden" from *The Five Nations* by Rudyard Kipling. Copyright, 1903, by Rudyard Kipling, reprinted by permission of Mrs. George Bambridge, Methuen & Company, and Doubleday & Company, Inc.

Three Who Made a Revolution, by Bertram D. Wolfe, by permission of the Dial Press, Inc. Copyright, 1948, by Bertram D. Wolfe.

World Population, by A. N. Carr-Saunders. Clarendon Press, Oxford.

L.C. catalog card number: 56–5395

© *Alfred A. Knopf, Inc.. 1956*

THIS IS A BORZOI BOOK
PUBLISHED BY ALFRED A. KNOPF, INC.

PUBLISHED JULY 24, 1950. REPRINTED SEVEN TIMES

SECOND EDITION, REVISED, RESET, AND PRINTED FROM NEW PLATES,

WITH NEW MAPS, 1956

REPRINTED 1956, 1957, 1958, 1959 (2), 1960 (2), 1961 (2), 1962

Preface

to the Second Edition

━━━

]I T IS A pleasure after six years to be able to offer a revised edition of *A History of the Modern World*. I am fortunate in having secured the collaboration of Dr. Joel Colton of the Duke University History Department. He has used the book as a text at Duke for several years, and so brings much practical experience to the problem of revision. Since most of the labor has been his, I can say without hesitation that I think the book much improved; but we have worked closely together, and are both responsible for the new edition as it now stands.

In character and contents the book remains much the same, but changes have been made throughout. We have reviewed every word, and have occasionally simplified the language. Subheadings have been added as an aid in comprehension. Treatment of a few matters has been shortened. The former Chapters VI and VII have been transposed in order to integrate more closely the analysis of intellectual developments in the seventeenth and eighteenth centuries. The internal history of Great Britain, France and Germany from 1870 to 1914 has been somewhat amplified. The greatest change is in the more extended account of contemporary history since the end of the First World War. In this expanded portion, the Second World War and its aftermath, formerly compressed into an epilogue, are now set forth as a full chapter on a scale commensurate with the rest of the work. Since the new edition is slightly longer than the original one, we have saved space by compressing the bibliography, which, however, still lists and classifies about two thousand items.

Mr. Theodore R. Miller has redesigned and redrawn the maps, and

added a number of new ones. Maps and accompanying captions have been
planned to fit closely with the text. The same is true of the illustrations, in
which, as in the first edition, we have sought significance rather than numbers.

For those who may wish to use it with students, Professor Colton has
prepared a separate workbook drawn from his own experience in the class-
room.

We are indebted for ideas to many of Mr. Colton's colleagues at
Duke, and to mine at Princeton. We wish also to express our thanks to many
others, in other colleges and universities, who have made suggestions or
called attention to errors in the first edition. We have tried to act in each
case according to our best judgment. Without the efforts of Messrs. J. T.
Hawes, T. A. Bledsoe and Sidney R. Jacobs and Miss Zita de Schauensee of
Alfred A. Knopf, Inc., the new edition could not have come into being.
Lastly we owe more than a word of appreciation to our wives, without whose
aid and tolerance the work would not have been possible at all.

R. R. PALMER

Princeton, N.J.

Preface

to the First Edition

~~~~~~

A READER approaching a volume of almost a thousand pages may appreciate a hint as to its contents, which at the beginning the author is best able to supply.

Like others, I have tried to rethink the record of our troubled civilization. By enlarging on some points, and condensing others, I have sought to present what is most useful and enlightening for people who must live in the present and impending future.

The book is designed to set forth the modern history of Europe and European civilization as a unit, and in its later chapters attempts to tell the story of an integrated, or at least interconnected, world. Emphasis falls on situations and movements of international scope, or on what Europeans and their descendants have done and faced in common. National histories are therefore somewhat subordinated, and in each national history the points of contact with a larger civilization are most fully treated. Historic regional differences within Europe, as between East and West, are brought out, and the history of the Americas is woven into the story at various points, as are developments of the last century in Asia and Africa. A good deal of institutional history is included. There is not much on the fine arts, imaginative literature, or pure philosophy, but considerable space is given to the history of ideas, not only in special sections devoted to ideas, but throughout the book in close connection with the account of institutions and events. Social and economic development bulks rather large. Since our own age is one in which much depends on political decision, I have thought of this volume as political history in the broadest sense—in that matters of many kinds, such as religion, economics, welfare, and international relations, have presented themselves as public questions requiring public action by responsible citizens or public persons. Nor have I hesitated, living in the present age, to dwell at some length on war and revolution. The greater wars and revolutions have perhaps had more profound consequences than are generally acknowledged. In any event, they are good examples of movements that transcend individual nations and affect the course of modern history as a whole.

The illustrations are reproductions of paintings, most of them well known, dating from the fifteenth century to the twentieth. They are chosen, not so much to illustrate art as art, as to give life and body to certain general ideas that recur in the text. For example, the idea of "class" and of the landed aristocracy, middle class, laboring class, and peasantry, is conveyed in four paintings of women, by Gainsborough, Copley, David, and Millet.

In writing the book I have drawn heavily on the French series, *Peuples et civilisations,* edited by Halphen and Sagnac, and especially on the works in that series written by MM. Hauser, Lefebvre, Weill, Pouthas, Baumont, and Renouvin. My indebtedness to these superb volumes is so great that I hereby acknowledge it with pleasure and without reservation. I have also made liberal use of the series entitled the *Rise of Modern Europe,* edited by W. L. Langer, and most especially of the volumes by W. L. Dorn and the late R. C. Binkley.

I am indebted to many of my colleagues in the Department of History at Princeton, especially to Professors T. E. Mommsen, C. E. Black, E. H. Harbison, and Jerome Blum, each of whom has read and advised me on one or more chapters. Mr. Blum likewise gave me the benefit of his judgment on the maps. Professor Donald D. Egbert of the Department of Art and Archaeology at Princeton helped with the selection of illustrations. The bibliography is the work of Mr. Fredrick Aandahl, Jr., to whom its merits are entirely due. Various parts of the book have been read by Professors John B. Wolf of the University of Minnesota, Franklin C. Palm and Raymond J. Sontag of the University of California, George L. Mosse of the University of Iowa, Walter L. Dorn of the Ohio State University, Leland H. Carlson of Northwestern University, Leo Gershoy of New York University, and Geoffrey Bruun of Ithaca, N.Y. To all these friends and professional colleagues I owe and hereby express my thanks for their criticisms; but they are in no way responsible for errors of fact or judgment which other readers may discover.

I should like to express the hope that the book may prove useful for the person for whom it was written, namely the reader.

R. R. PALMER

Princeton, N.J.

Contents

Illustrations

Maps

BY THEODORE R. MILLER

A HISTORY OF

The Modern World

CHAPTER I

The Rise of Europe

1. Ancient Times: Greece, Rome, and Christianity
2. The Early Middle Ages: The Formation of Europe
3. The High Middle Ages: Secular Civilization
4. The High Middle Ages: The Church

T HE modern world in the second half of the twentieth century is a large and complicated affair. The whole earth is included in it, for few mountain valleys are so secluded, or few islands so remote, as to be untouched by the spreading forces of modern civilization. Persons of all colors and creeds proceed by boat or plane to sit down at the same conferences, or at times to fight in the same wars. A Moslem religious leader, the Aga Khan, presides at the League of Nations, sees his son wedded to (and divorced from) a Hollywood actress, and lives habitually on the French Riviera, spending lavishly on the wares of France and the West the money flowing to him from India and East Africa. A young African chief, studying at Oxford, rocks both the black world and the white by marrying a London typist. The people of Java issue postage stamps bearing portraits of Washington and Jefferson. The likeness of Karl Marx is paraded in Peiping.

It might therefore seem that a history of the modern world, such as this book professes to be, should relate the history of all the world's peoples alike. The reader will discover, however, that the book is in the main a history of Europe. Why is this?

It is in part because the author and most of his readers are transplanted Europeans, and because Americans in view of their own history have a special reason for trying to understand Europe. But there are better and less self-centered explanations. There are reasons why even the Aga Khan or the young African chief, by understanding Europe better, might better understand the world of which they are a part. The main reason is that modern civilization has been formed by the expansion of ideas, institutions, and industries that originated in Europe. Europe itself, to be sure, has always received much from others—from the calendar and Christianity to the use of cotton and potatoes. Europe itself, moreover, became "modernized" by the effects upon it of its growing contacts with the earth as a whole, especially after the discovery of America and the ocean trade routes in the days of Columbus. But in the last few centuries Europe has had more of an influence on the rest of the world than the rest of the world has had upon Europe. The last few centuries may in fact be called the European Age, and while this age is probably now closing, it has produced the world as we know it today.

The modern world has become increasingly an interlocking unity. Events on one side of the globe have immediate repercussions on the other. It is a world characterized by modern science, by modern industry and machines, modern sources of energy, modern transport and communications, modern medicine, sanitation, and methods of raising food. It is filled with states and nations that call themselves Powers, which have fought wars by advanced technical methods and negotiate or maintain peace by certain practices of diplomacy. It is a world knitted by finance and trade, loans and debts, investments and bank accounts. It is a world that seeks for democracy, for more equality, for self-government and representative institutions, for an enlargement of individual liberty and extension of individual well being. It is a world in which common men begin to sense the attractions of a higher standard of living, of better food and housing in return for less laborious and spirit-killing work, to see their ancestral religions and historic rulers in a new light, to shake loose from the past, to form new political parties, to favor revolutionary movements which may be either slow and gradual or abrupt and catastrophic. It is a troubled world, at once materialistic and possessed by new ideals, both dynamic and hard to move, both ruthless and humane.

All these indexes of modernity, if such they may be called, appeared first in the history of Europe, or of the European world in the extended sense in which the United States is included. The present book deals mainly with the growth of European society and civilization, with an increasing attention, in the later chapters, to the earth as a whole.

As for the time-span, the term "modern" is purely relative, but it is generally agreed that modern times began in Europe about the year 1500. Modern times were preceded by a period of a thousand years called the Middle Ages, which set in about A.D. 500, and which were in turn preceded by another thousand years of classical Greco-Roman civilization. Before that reached the long histories of Egypt and Mesopotamia, and, further east, of the Indus Valley and of China. All times prior to the European Middle Ages are commonly called "ancient." But the whole framework—ancient, medieval, and modern—is largely a matter of words and convention, without meaning except for Europe, and even for Europe not always more significant than the words Tuesday, Wednesday, and Thursday. We shall begin our history with a running start, and slow down the pace, surveying the scene more fully, in proportion as the times grow more "modern."

1. Ancient Times: Greece, Rome, and Christianity

BEFORE THE GREEKS: THE NEAR EAST

Europeans were by no means the pioneers of human civilization. Half of man's recorded history had passed before anyone in Europe could read or write. The priests of Egypt began to keep written records between 4000 and 3000 B.C., but more than two thousand years later the poems of Homer were still being circulated in the Greek city-states by word of mouth. Shortly after 3000 B.C., while the pharaohs were building the first pyramids, Europeans were creating nothing more distinguished than huge garbage heaps. Ironically, like the pyramids, they still endure and are known to archaeologists as "kitchen middens." At the time when the Babylonian king Hammurabi, about 2000 B.C., caused the laws of a complex society to be carved on stone, the most advanced Europeans were peoples like the Swiss Lake Dwellers, simple agriculturists who lived in shelters built over the water to protect themselves from beasts and men. In a word, until after 2000 B.C., Europe was in the Neolithic or New Stone Age. This was in truth a great age in man's history, the age in which men learned to make and use sharp tools, weave cloth, build living quarters, domesticate animals, plant seeds, harvest crops and sense the returning cycles of the months and years. But the Near East—Egypt, the Euphrates and Tigris valley, the island of Crete and the shores of the Aegean Sea (which belonged more to Asia than to Europe)—had reached and passed the Neolithic two thousand years before Europe. By about 4000 B.C. the Near East had already moved on into the Bronze Age.

After about 2000 B.C., in the dim dark continent that Europe then was, there began to be great changes that are now difficult to trace. The new elements came from Asia, or from Africa by way of Gibraltar. Europeans, too, learned how to smelt and forge metals, with the Bronze Age setting in about 2000 and the Iron Age about 1000 B.C. The new knowledge passed from tribe to tribe, from east to west. The Iron Age, for example, began in Asia Minor about 1400 B.C., in what is now Austria about 1000 B.C., in England about 400 B.C. At the same time there was a steady infusion of new peoples into Europe. They probably came from Asia, for they spoke languages related to languages now spoken in India and Persia. All these languages (whose interconnection was not known until the nineteenth century) are now referred to as Indo-European, and the people who spoke them, merging with and imposing their speech upon older European stocks, became the ancestors both of the classical Greeks and Romans and of the Europeans of modern times.

All European languages today are Indo-European with the exception of Basque, which is thought to be a survival from before the Indo-European invasion, and of Finnish and Hungarian, which were brought into Europe from Asia some centuries later. All that is known of these invading Indo-Europeans is that they diffused over Europe the kind of speech from which the Latin, Greek, Germanic, Slavic, Celtic, and Baltic languages were later derived. What racial or cultural contribution they may have made is most unclear.[1]

THE GREEK WORLD

The first Indo-Europeans to emerge into the clear light of history, in what is now Europe, were the Greeks. They filtered down through the Balkan peninsula to the shores of the Aegean Sea, where they undermined and ruined the very ancient Cretan civilization. The newcomers were composed of many separate barbaric tribes, and their occupation of what has ever since been called Greece was completed about 1000 B.C. The *Iliad* and the *Odyssey*, written down about 800 B.C., but composed and recited much earlier, probably refer to wars between Greek invaders and the earlier inhabitants with their higher urban civilization, of which one center was at Troy in Asia Minor. The siege of Troy by the Greeks, as related in the *Iliad*, is thought to have occurred about 1200 B.C.

The Greeks soon proved to be as gifted a people as mankind has ever produced. In four centuries, from about 900 to 500 B.C., they passed from barbarism to the peak of civilization, from illiteracy to supreme heights in thought and letters. They absorbed the knowledge of the to them mysterious East, the mathematical lore of the ancient Chaldeans, the arts and crafts that they found in Asia Minor and on voyages to Egypt. They added immediately to everything that they learned. It was the Greeks of the fifth and fourth centuries B.C. who first became fully conscious of the powers of the human mind, who discovered what the Western world has meant by the beautiful, and who first speculated on political freedom.

As they settled down, the Greeks formed tiny city-states, all independent and often at war with one another, each comprising only a few hundred square miles, and typically including a coastal city and its adjoining farmlands. Athens, Corinth, Sparta were such city-states. Many were democratic; all citizens (*i.e.*, all grown men except slaves and "metics" or outsiders) congregated in the market place to elect officials and discuss their public business.

wwwwwwwwwwwwww

[1] Formerly the term Aryan was sometimes used to denote Indo-European. In Germany, under Adolf Hitler, much nonsense was written about an Aryan race, and the term Aryan was made in practice to mean simply non-Jewish. The grain of truth in all this was simply that Hebrew is not an Indo-European but a Semitic language, closely related to Arabic (which is also Semitic) and less closely to the language of the ancient Egyptians. There is no Indo-European (Aryan) or Semitic "race"; persons speaking these languages no more had to be of one physical descent than are persons who speak English today.

Politics was turbulent in the small Greek states. Democracy alternated with aristocracy, oligarchy, despotism, and tyranny. From this rich fund of experience was born systematic political science as set forth in the unwritten speculations of Socrates and in the *Republic* of Plato and the *Politics* of Aristotle in the fourth century before Christ. The Greeks also were the first to write history as a subject distinct from myth and legend. Herodotus, "the Father of History," traveled throughout the Greek world and far beyond, ferreting out all he could learn of the past; and Thucydides, in his account of the wars between Athens and Sparta, presented history as a guide to enlightened citizenship and constructive statecraft.

Perhaps because they were a restless and vehement people, the Greeks came to prize the "classical" virtues, which they were the first to define. For them, the ideal lay in moderation, or a golden mean. They valued order, balance, symmetry, clarity, and control. Their statues revealed their conception of what man ought to be—a noble creature, dignified, poised, unterrified by life or death, master of himself and of his feelings. Their architecture, as in the Parthenon, made use of exactly measured angles and rows of columns. The classical "order," or set of carefully wrought pillars placed in a straight line at specified intervals, represented the firm impress of human reason on the brute materials of nature. The same sense of form was thrown over the torrent of human words. Written language became contrived, carefully planned, organized for effect. The epic poem, the lyric, the drama, the oration, along with history and the philosophic dialogue, each with its own rules and principles of composition, became the "forms" within which, in Western civilization, men long continued to express their thoughts.

Reflecting on the world about them, the Greeks concluded that some-

---

Europe: Physical (map on following pages)

Topographically Europe is a peninsula jutting off from Asia. It is notable for the great number of its sub-peninsulas, inland seas, and off-shore islands. The south is generally mountainous, with the ranges running from east to west, and enclosing occasional pockets of flat land, as in the Ebro, Po, and middle Danube valleys; but the only point at which one may go from the Mediterranean to the North without climbing mountains is in France, which is the only country that clearly belongs both to the Mediterranean and to the North. A great plain, with branches in England and Sweden, runs from northern France through northern Germany, Poland, and Russia and on into Asia. The plain is barely interrupted by the Ural Mountains, which, though conventionally the boundary between Europe and Asia, are too low and gradual to form an actual barrier. In any case, the Urals stop five hundred miles north of the Caspian Sea, leaving a broad lowland called the Caspian Gate. One might draw a straight line from Amsterdam eastward through the Caspian Gate as far as the borders of western China; and although this line would reach the distance from New York to a point five hundred miles west of San Francisco, one would never in traveling along it be higher above sea level than the top of the Empire State Building. Europe, including the Russian plain, is about as large as the United States together with the inhabited regions of Canada. It comprises only one fifteenth of the earth's land surface. Nevertheless, in the past century, a quarter of the human race has lived in it.

EUROPE
PHYSICAL

AREAS
BELOW SEA LEVEL

500 MILES

thing more fundamental existed beyond the world of appearances, that true reality was not what met the eye. With other peoples, and with the Greeks themselves in earlier times, this same realization had led to the formation of myths, dealing with invisible but mighty beings known as gods, and with faraway places on the tops of mountains, beneath the earth, or in a world that followed death. Greek thinkers set to criticizing the web of myth. They looked for rational or natural explanations of what was at work behind the variety and confusion that they saw. Some, observing human sickness, said that disease was not a demonic possession, but a natural sequence of conditions in the body, which could be identified, understood, foreseen, and even treated in a natural way. Others, turning to physical nature, said that all matter was in reality composed of a very few things—of atoms or elements—which they usually designated as fire, water, earth, and air. Some said that change was a kind of illusion, all basic reality being uniform; some, that only change was real, and that the world was a flux. Some, like Pythagoras, found the enduring reality in "number" or mathematics. The Greeks, in short, laid the foundations for science. Studying also the way in which the mind worked, or ought to work if it was to reach truthful conclusions, they developed the science of logic. The great codifier of Greek thought on almost all subjects in the classical period was Aristotle, who lived in Athens from 384 to 322 B.C.

Greek influence spread widely and rapidly. Hardly were some of the city-states founded when their people, crowded within their narrow bounds, sent off some of their number with equipment and provisions to establish colonies. In this way Greek cities were very early established in south Italy, in Sicily, and even in the western Mediterranean, where Marseilles was founded about 600 B.C. Later the Greek city-states, unable to unite, succumbed to conquest by Philip of Macedon, who came from the relatively crude northern part of the Greek world, and whose son, Alexander the Great (356–323 B.C.), led a phenomenal and conquering march into Asia, across Persia and on as far as India itself. Alexander's empire did not hold together, but Greek civilization, after having penetrated the raw world of the western Mediterranean, now began to revivify the ancient peoples of Egypt and the Near East. Greek thought, Greek art, and the Greek language spread far and wide. The most famous "Greeks" after the fourth century B.C. and on into the early centuries of the Christian era usually did not come from Greece but from the Hellenized Near East, and especially from Alexandria in Egypt. Among these later Greeks were the great summarizers or writers of encyclopedias in which ancient science was passed on to later generations—Strabo in geography, Galen in medicine, Ptolemy in astronomy. All three lived in the first and second centuries after Christ.

THE ROMAN WORLD

In 146 B.C. the Greeks of Greece were conquered by a new people, the Romans. The Romans, while keeping their own Latin language, rapidly absorbed what they could of the intellectual and artistic culture of the Greeks. Over a period of two or three centuries they assembled an empire in which the whole world of ancient civilization (west of Persia) was included. Egypt, Greece, Asia Minor, Syria all became Roman provinces, but in them the Romans had hardly any deep influence except in a political sense. In the West, in what are now Tunisia, Algeria, Morocco, Spain, Portugal, France, Switzerland, Belgium, and England, the Romans, though ruthless in their methods of conquest, in the long run acted as civilizing agents, transmitting to these hitherto backward countries the age-old achievements of the East and the more recent culture of Greece and of Rome itself. So thorough was the Romanization that in the West Latin even became the currently spoken language. It was later wiped out in Africa by Arabic, but survives to this day, transformed by time, in the languages of France, Spain, Italy, and Portugal.

In the Roman Empire, which lasted with many vicissitudes from about 31 B.C. to the latter part of the fifth century A.D., virtually the entire civilized world of the ancient West was politically united and enjoyed generations of internal peace. Rome was the center, around which in all directions lay the "circle of lands," the *orbis terrarum*, the known world. The Empire consisted essentially in the coasts of the Mediterranean Sea, which provided the great artery of transport and communication, and from which no part of the Empire, except northern Gaul (France), Britain, and the Rhineland, was more than a couple of hundred miles away. Civilization was uniform; there were no distinct nationalities; the only significant cultural difference was that east of Italy the predominant language was Greek, in Italy and west of it, Latin. Cities grew up everywhere, engaged in a busy commercial life and exchange of ideas with one another. They remained most numerous in the East, where most of the manufacturing crafts and the densest population were still concentrated, but they sprang up also in the West—indeed, most of the older cities of France, Spain, England, and western and southern Germany boast of some kind of origin under the Romans.

The distinctive aptitude of the Romans lay in organization, administration, government, and law. Never before had armies been so systematically formed, maintained over such long periods, despatched at a word of command over such distances, or maneuvered so effectively on the field of battle. Never had so many peoples been governed from a single center. The Romans had at first possessed self-governing and republican institutions, but they lost them in the process of conquest, and the governing talents which they displayed in the days of the Empire were of an authoritarian character—talents, not for self-government, but for managing, co-ordinating and ruling the manifold and scattered parts of one enormous system. Locally, cities and city-states enjoyed a good deal of autonomy. But above them all rose a pyramid of imperial officials and provincial governors, culminating in the Emperor at the top. The Empire kept peace, the *pax Romana,* and even provided a certain justice as between its many peoples. Lawyers worked on the body of principles known ever afterwards as Roman Law.

Roman judges had somehow to settle disputes between persons of different regions, with conflicting local customs, for example two merchants of Spain and Egypt. The Roman law came therefore to hold that no custom is necessarily right, that there is a higher or universal law by which fair decisions may be made, and that this higher, universal, or "natural" law, or "law of nature," will be understandable or acceptable to all men, since it arises from human nature and reason. Here the lawyers drew on Greek philosophy for support. They held also that law derives its force from being enacted by a proper authority (not merely from custom, usage, or former legal cases); this authority to make law they called *majestas* or sovereign power, and they attributed it to the Emperor. Thus the Romans emancipated the idea of law from mere custom on the one hand, and mere caprice on the other; they regarded it as something to be formed by enlightened intelligence, consistently with reason and the nature of things; and they associated it with the solemn action of official power. It must be added that Roman law favored the State, or the public interest as seen by the government, rather than the interests or liberties of individual persons. These principles, together with more specific ideas on property, debt, marriage, wills, *etc.*, were in later centuries to have a great effect in Europe.

THE COMING OF CHRISTIANITY

The thousand years during which Greco-Roman civilization arose and flourished were notable in another way even more momentous for all the later history of mankind. It was in this period that the great world religions came into being. Within the time-bracket 700 B.C.–A.D. 700 the lives of Confucius and Buddha, of the major Jewish prophets and of Mohammed are all included. At the very midpoint (probably about 4 B.C.), in Palestine in the Roman Empire, was born a man named Jesus believed by his followers to be the Son of God. The first Christians were Jews; but both under the impulse of its own doctrine, which held that all men were alike in spirit, and under the strong leadership of Paul, a man of Jewish birth, Roman citizenship, and Greek culture, Christianity began to make converts without regard to former belief. There were certainly a few Christians in Rome by the middle of the first century. Both Paul and the elder apostle, Peter, according to church tradition, died as martyrs at Rome in the time of the Emperor Nero about A.D. 67.

The Christian teaching spread at first among the poor, the people at the bottom of society, those whom Greek glories and Roman splendors had passed over or enslaved, and who had the least to delight in or to hope for in the existing world. Gradually it reached other classes; a few classically educated and well-to-do people became Christians; in the second century Christian bishops and writers were at work publicly in various parts of the Empire. In the third century the Roman government, with the Empire falling into turmoil, and blaming the social troubles on the Christians, subjected them to wholesale persecution. In the fourth century (possibly in A.D. 312) the Em-

peror Constantine was converted to Christianity. By the fifth century the
entire Roman world was formally Christian; no other religion was officially
tolerated; and the deepest thinkers were also Christians, men who combined
Christian beliefs with the now thousand-year-old tradition of Greco-Roman
thought and philosophy.

It is impossible to exaggerate the importance of the coming of Christianity. It brought with it, for one thing, an altogether new sense of human
life. Where the Greeks had shown man his mind, the Christians showed him
his soul; and they taught that in the sight of God all souls were equal, that
every human life was sacrosanct and inviolate, and that all worldly distinctions of greatness, beauty, and brilliancy were in the last analysis superficial.
Where the Greeks had identified the beautiful and the good, had thought
ugliness to be bad, and had shrunk from disease as an imperfection and from
everything misshapen as horrible and repulsive, the Christians resolutely saw
a spiritual beauty even in the plainest or most unpleasant exterior, and sought
out the diseased, the crippled, and the mutilated to give them help. Love, for
the ancients, was never quite distinguished from Venus; for the Christians,
who held that God was love, it took on deep overtones of sacrifice and compassion. Suffering itself was proclaimed by Christians to be in a way divine,
since God himself had suffered on the Cross in human form. A new dignity
was thus found for suffering that the world could not cure. At the same time
the Christians worked to relieve suffering as none had worked before. They
protested against the massacre of prisoners of war, against the mistreatment
and degradation of slaves, against the sending of gladiators to kill each other
in the arena for another's pleasure. In place of the Greek and pagan self-
satisfaction with human accomplishments they taught humility in the face
of an almighty Providence, and in place of proud distinctions between high
and low, slave and free, civilized and barbarian, they held that all men were
brothers because all were children of the same God.

On an intellectual level Christianity also marked a revolution. It was
Christianity, not rational philosophy, that dispelled the swarm of greater and
lesser gods and goddesses, the blood sacrifices and self-immolation, the frantic
resort to magic, fortune-telling and divination, or grim resignation in the
temples of Fate and Fortune. The Christians taught that since there was only
one God, the pagan gods must be at best lesser demons, and even this idea
was gradually given up. The pagan conception of local, tribal, or national
gods disappeared. It was now held that for all the world there was only one
God, one plan of Salvation, and one Providence, and that all mankind took
its origin from one source. The idea of the world as one thing, a "universe,"
was thus affirmed with a new depth of meaning. The very intolerance of
Christianity (which was new to the ancient world) came from this overwhelming sense of human unity, in which it was thought that all men should
have, and deserved to have, the one true and saving religion.

It was for their political ideas that the Christians were most often
denounced and persecuted. The Roman Empire was a world state; there was
no other state but it; no living human being except the Emperor was sover-

eign; no one anywhere on earth was his equal. Between gods and men, in the pagan view, there was moreover no clear distinction. Some gods behaved much like men, and some men were more like gods than others. The Emperor was held to be veritably a god, *divus Caesar, semper Augustus*. A cult of Caesar was established, regarded as necessary to maintain the state, which was the world itself. All this the Christians firmly refused to accept. It was because they would not worship Caesar that the Roman officials regarded them as monstrous social incendiaries who must be persecuted and stamped out.

The Christian doctrine on this point went back to the saying gathered from Jesus, that one should render to Caesar the things that were Caesar's, and to God those that were God's. The same dualism was presented more systematically by St. Augustine about A.D. 420 in his *City of God*, than which few books have been more influential in shaping the later development of Western civilization.

The "world," the world of Caesar, in the time of St. Augustine, was going to ruin. Rome itself was plundered in 410 by heathen barbarians. Augustine wrote the *City of God* with this event obsessing his imagination. He wrote to show that though the world itself perished there was yet another world that was more enduring and more important.

There were, he said, really two "cities," the earthly and the heavenly, the temporal and the eternal, the city of man and the City of God. The earthly city was the domain of state and empire, of political authority and political obedience. It was a good thing, as part of God's providential scheme for human life, but it had no inherently divine character of its own. The Emperor was a man. The state was not absolute; it could be judged, amended, or corrected from sources outside itself. It was, for all its majesty and splendor, really subordinate in some way to a higher and spiritual power. This power lay in the City of God. By the City of God Augustine meant many things, and all sorts of meanings were found by readers in later ages. The heavenly city might mean heaven itself, the abode of God and of blessed spirits enjoying life after death. It might mean certain elect spirits of this world, the good people as opposed to the bad. It might, more theoretically, be a system of ideal values or ideal justice, as opposed to the crude approximations of the actual world. Or it was later thought, by some, to mean the organized church and its clergy.

In any case, with this Christian dualism the Western world escaped from what is called Caesaropapism, the holding by one man of the powers of ruler and of pontiff. The spiritual and the political power were held to be separate and independent. In later times, popes and kings often quarreled with each other; the clergy often struggled for worldly power, and governments at various times (including the twentieth century with its totalitarian systems) have attempted to dictate what men should believe, or love, or hope for. But speaking in general of European history neither side has ever won out, and in the sharp distinction between the spiritual and the temporal has lain the germ of many liberties in the West. At the same time, the idea that no ruler, no government, and no institution is too mighty to rise above moral criticism has opened the way to a dynamic and progressive way of living in the West.

As for Augustine himself, he lived to see the world grow worse. He died in A.D. 430. In 429 the Roman province of Africa, where he had been a bishop, was pillaged by a wild Germanic tribe called the Vandals.

2. The Early Middle Ages: The Formation of Europe

There was really no Europe in ancient times. In the Roman Empire we may see a Mediterranean world, or even a West and an East in the Latin- and Greek-speaking portions. But the West included parts of Africa as well as of Europe, and Europe as we know it was divided by the Rhine-Danube frontier, south and west of which lay the civilized provinces of the Empire, and north and east the "barbarians" of whom the civilized world knew almost nothing. To the Romans "Africa" meant Tunisia-Algeria, "Asia" meant the Asia Minor peninsula; and the word "Europe," since it meant little, was scarcely used by them at all. It was in the half-millennium from the fifth to the tenth centuries that Europe as such for the first time emerged with its peoples brought together in a life of their own, clearly set off from that of Asia or Africa.

THE DISINTEGRATION OF THE ROMAN EMPIRE

First of all the Roman Empire went to pieces, especially in the West. The Christianizing of the Empire did nothing to impede its decline. The Emperor Constantine, who in embracing Christianity undoubtedly hoped to strengthen the imperial system, also took one other significant step. In A.D. 330 he founded a new capital at the old Greek city of Byzantium, which he renamed Constantinople. Thereafter the Roman Empire had two capitals, Rome and Constantinople, and was administered in two halves. Increasingly the center of gravity moved eastward, as if returning to the more ancient centers in the Near East, as if the "modern" experiment of civilizing the West were to be given up as a failure.

Throughout its long life the Empire had been surrounded on almost all sides by barbarians, wild Celts in Wales and Scotland, Germans in the heart of Europe, Persians or Parthians in the East ("barbarian" only in the ancient sense of speaking neither Greek nor Latin), and, in the southeast, the Arabs. (In the South the Empire simply faded off into the Sahara.) These barbarians, always with the exception of Persia, had never been brought within the pale of ancient civilization. They remained illiterate, unsettled, townless, more or less nomadic, and frequently bellicose. Somewhat like the Chinese, who about 200 B.C. built the Great Wall to solve the same problem, the Romans simply drew a line beyond which they themselves rarely ventured, and would not allow the barbarians to pass. Nevertheless the barbarians filtered in. As early as the third century A.D. emperors and generals recruited bands of them to serve in the Roman armies. Their service over, they would receive farmlands, settle down, marry and mingle with the population. By the fourth and fifth centuries a good many individuals of barbarian birth were even reaching high positions of state. At the same time, in the West, for reasons that are not fully understood, the activity of the Roman cities began to falter, commerce began to decay, local governments became paralyzed, taxes became more ruinous, and free farmers were bound to the soil. The army seated and unseated emperors. Rival generals fought with each other. Gradually the West fell into decrepitude and an internal barbarization so that the old line between the Roman provinces and the barbarian world made less and less difference.

The barbarians themselves, after some centuries of relative stability, rather suddenly began to move. Sometimes they first sought peaceable access to the Empire, pushed by other peoples from behind, or attracted by the warmer Mediterranean climate, or desiring with a child-like eagerness to share in the advantages of Roman civilization. More often, tribes consisting of a few tens of thousands, men, women, and children, moved swiftly and by force, plundering, fighting, and killing as they went. At first most of the barbarians threatening the Empire were Germanic, going under many names. The Angles and Saxons overran Britain about 450, the Franks invaded Gaul at the same time, the Vandals reached as far as Roman Africa in 429, the East Goths appeared in Asia Minor in 382 and in Italy in 493, the West Goths lunged toward Constantinople about 380, tore through Greece in 396, sacked Rome itself in 410, and reached Spain about the year 420. In 476 the last Roman Emperor in the West was deposed by a barbarian chieftain. Sometimes in the general upheaval wild Turkman peoples fresh from Asia were intermixed. Of these the most famous were the Huns, who cut through central Europe and France about 450 under their leader Attila, the "scourge of God"—and then disappeared. Nor were these invasions all. Two centuries later new irruptions burst upon the Greco-Roman world on its opposite side, where hitherto outlying peoples poured in from the Arabian deserts. The Arabs, aroused by the new faith of Islam (Mohammed died in 632), fell as conquerors upon Syria, Mesopotamia, Persia; occupied Egypt about 640, the old Roman Africa about 700, and in 711 reached Spain, where they destroyed the Germanic kingdom set up there by the West Goths.

Beneath these blows the old unity of the Greco-Roman or Mediter-

---

Mediterranean World about 400, 800, and 1250 A.D.

The unified world of Mediterranean civilization, as it existed under the Roman Empire, broke apart into three segments in the early Middle Ages. Each segment developed its own type of life. Each segment also expanded beyond the limits of the ancient Mediterranean civilization. Latin Christendom reached to the Baltic and beyond, Greek Christendom penetrated north of the Black Sea, and the Moslem world spread into inner Asia and to the borders of Negro Africa. In 1250, and until 1492, the Moslems, or Moors, still held the southern tip of Spain.

MEDITERRANEAN
WORLD
ABOUT
400 A.D.

PAGANS

PAGANS

ABOUT
800 A.D.

BARBARIANS

THE
ROMAN
EMPIRE

BARBARIANS

PAGANS

LATIN
CHRISTIANS

GREEK
CHRISTIANS

MOSLEMS

PAGANS

ABOUT
1250 A.D.

PAGANS

TRM

ranean world was broken. The "circle of lands" divided into three segments. Three types of civilization now confronted each other across the inland sea.

THE BYZANTINE WORLD, THE ARABIC WORLD,
AND THE WEST ABOUT A.D. 700

One was the Eastern Roman, Later Roman, Greek, or Byzantine Empire (all names for the same thing) with its capital at Constantinople, and now including only the Asia Minor peninsula, the Balkan peninsula, and parts of Italy. It represented the most direct continuation of the immemorial civilization of the Near East. It was Christian in religion and Greek in culture and language. Its people felt themselves to be the truest heirs both of early Christianity and of the Greeks of the golden age. Art and architecture, trades and crafts, commerce and navigation, thought and writing, government and law, while not so creative or flexible as in the classic age, were still carried on actively in the Eastern Empire, on much the same level as in the closing centuries of ancient times. For all Christians, and for heathen barbarians in Europe, the Emperor of the East stood out as the world's supreme ruler, and Constantinople as the world's pre-eminent and almost fabulous city.

The second segment, and the most extensive, was the Arabic and Mohammedan. It reached from the neighborhood of the Pyrenees through Spain and all north Africa into Arabia, Syria, and the East. Arabic was its language; it became, and still remains, the common speech from Algeria to the Persian Gulf. Islam was its religion. It was organized in the caliphate in which all Moslems were included, and the caliph was regarded as the true religious and military successor to Mohammed himself. The Arabic world, like the Byzantine, built directly upon the heritage of the Greco-Romans. In religion, the early Moslems regarded themselves as successors to the Jewish and Christian traditions. They considered the line of Jewish prophets to be spokesmen of the true God, and they put Jesus in this line. But they added that Mohammed was the last and greatest of the prophets, that the Koran set forth a revelation replacing that of the Jewish Bible, that the New Testament of the Christians was mistaken because Christ was not divine, and that the Christian belief in a Trinity was erroneous because there was in the strictest and most rigid sense only One True God. To the Moslem Arabs, therefore, all Christians were contemptible infidels.

In mundane matters, the Arabs speedily took over the civilization of the lands they conquered. In the caliphate, as in the Byzantine empire, the civilization of the ancient world went its way without serious interruption. Huge buildings and magnificent palaces were constructed; ships plied the Mediterranean; merchants ventured over the deserts and traversed the Indian Ocean; holy or learned men corresponded over thousands of miles; taxes were collected, laws were enforced, and provinces were kept in order. In the sciences the Arabs not only learned from but went beyond the Greeks. The Greek scientific literature was translated; some of it is known today only through these medieval Arabic versions. Arab geographers had a wider knowledge of the world than anyone had possessed up to their time. Arab mathematicians developed algebra so far beyond the Greeks as almost to be its creator ("algebra" is an Arabic word), and in introducing the "Arabic" numerals (through their contacts with India) they made arithmetic, which in Roman numerals had been a formidably difficult science, into something that every schoolchild can be taught.

The third segment, about A.D. 700, did not look very promising. It was what was left over from the other two—what the Byzantines were unable to hold, and the Arabs unable to conquer. It included only Italy (shared in part with the Byzantines), France, Belgium, the Rhineland, and Britain. Barbarian kings were doing their best to rule small kingdoms, but in truth all government had fallen to pieces. Strange and uncouth peoples milled about. Usually the invading barbarians remained a minority, eventually to be absorbed. Only in England, and in the region immediately west of the Rhine, did the Germanic element obliterate the older Celtic and Latin. But the presence of the invaders, armed and fierce amid peasants and city-dwellers reduced to passivity by Roman rule, together with the disintegration of Roman institutions that had gone on even before the invasions, left this region in chaos.

The Western barbarians, as has been said, were Germanic; and the Germanic influence was to be a distinctive contribution to the making of Europe. With a few exceptions, the Germans were illiterate and heathen when they burst upon the West. Their languages had not been written down, but they possessed an intricate folk-lore and a weird religion, in which fighting and heroic valor were much esteemed. Though now in a migratory phase, they were an agricultural people who knew how to work iron, and they had a rudimentary knowledge of the crafts of the Romans. They were organized in small tribes, and had a strong sense of tribal kinship, which (as with many primitive peoples) dominated their ideas of leadership and law. They enjoyed more freedom in their affairs than did the citizens of the Roman Empire. Many of the tribes were rough democracies in that all free men, those entitled to bear arms, met in open fields to hold council; and often the tribe itself elected its leader or king. They had a strong sense of loyalty to persons, of fealty to the acknowledged king or chief; but they had no sense of loyalty to large or general institutions. They had no sense of the state—of any distant, impersonal, and continuing source of law and rule. Law they regarded as the inflexible custom of each tribe. In the absence of abstract jurisprudence or trained judges, they settled disputes by rough and ready methods. In the ordeal, for example, a person who obstinately floated when thrown into water was adjudged guilty. In trial by battle, the winner of a kind of ritualistic duel was regarded as innocent. The gods, it was thought, would not allow wrong to prevail.

The Germans who overran the old Roman provinces found it difficult to maintain any political organization at more than a local level. Security and civil order all but disappeared. Peasant communities were at the mercy of wandering bands of habitual fighters. Fighters often captured peasant villages, took them under their protection, guarded them from further marauders, and lived off their produce. Sometimes the same great fighting man came to possess many such villages, moving with his retinue of horsemen from one village to another to support himself throughout the year. Thus originated a new distinction between lord and servant, noble and commoner, martial and menial class. Life became local and self-sufficient. People ate, wore, used, and dwelled in only what they themselves and their neighbors could produce. Trade died down, the cities became depopulated, money went out of circulation, almost nothing was bought or sold. The Roman roads fell into neglect; people often used them as quarries for ready-cut building blocks for their own crude purposes. The West not only broke up into localized villages, but also ceased to have habitual contacts across the Mediterranean. It became isolated from the Eastern centers from which its former civilization had always been drawn. The West was reverting. From roughly 500 A.D. on, Europe was in the "Dark Ages."

THE CHURCH AND THE RISE OF THE PAPACY

Only one organized institution maintained a tie with the civilized past. Only one institution, reaching over the whole West, could receive news or dispatch its agents over the whole area. This institution was the Christian Church. Its framework still stood; its network of bishoprics, as built up in late Roman times, remained intact except in places like England where the barbarian conquest was complete.

In addition, a new type of religious institution was rapidly spreading with the growth of monasteries. The serious and the sensitive, both men and women (though not together, to be sure), rejected the savagery about them and retired into communities of their own. Usually they were left unmolested by rough neighbors who held them in religious awe. In a world of violence they formed islands of quiet and of peace. In a society of burly barbarians they lived the life of contemplation. Their prayers, it was believed, were of use to all the world, and their example might at the least arouse in obstreperous worldlings the pangs of shame. The monastic houses generally adopted the rule of St. Benedict (c. 480–543), and were generally governed by an abbot. Dedicated to the same ideals, they formed unifying filaments throughout the chaos of the Latin West.

Bishops, abbots, and monks looked with veneration to Rome as the spot where St. Peter, the first apostle, had been martyred. The bishop of Rome corresponded with other bishops, sent out missionaries (to England, for example), gave advice on doctrine when he could, and attempted to keep in mind the situation throughout the Latin world as a whole. Moreover, with no emperor any longer in Rome, the bishop took over the government and public affairs of the city. Thus the bishop of Rome, while claiming a primacy over all Christians, was not dominated by any secular power. In the

East the great church functionaries, the patriarchs, fell under the influence of the emperor who continued to rule at Constantinople, so that a tradition of Caesaropapism grew up in the East; but in the West the independence of the bishop of Rome now confirmed in practice a principle always maintained by the great churchmen of the West—the independence of the spiritual power from the political or temporal.

In this way was built up the authority of the popes. It was fortified by various arguments. St. Peter, it was held, had imparted the spiritual authority given to him by Christ himself to the Roman bishops who were his successors. This doctrine of the "Petrine supremacy" was based on two verses in the Bible, according to which Christ designated Peter as the head of the Church, giving him the "power of the keys," to open and close the doors of eternal salvation.[2] As for the pope's temporal rule in Rome, it was affirmed that the Emperor Constantine had endowed the bishop with the government of the city. This "Donation of Constantine" was accepted as historical fact from the eighth century to the fifteenth,when it was proved to be a forgery.

It was the Church which incorporated the barbarians into a higher way of life, and when a barbarian embraced a more civilized way of living it was the Church that he entered. As early as about A.D. 340, the Church sent out Ulfilas to convert the Goths; his translation of the Bible represents the first writing down of any Germanic language. About 496 the king of the Franks, Clovis, was converted to Christianity. A hundred years later, in 596, the king of Kent in southeast England yielded to the persuasions of Augustine of Canterbury, a missionary dispatched from Rome, and the Christianization of the Anglo-Saxons gradually followed. Missionaries from Ireland also, to which Christians of the Roman Empire had fled before the heathen barbarians, now returned to both Britain and the Continent to spread the gospel. By some such year as A.D. 700, after three centuries of turmoil, the borders of Christianity in the West were again roughly what they had been in late Roman times. Then in 711, as we have seen, the Arabs conquered Spain. They crossed the Pyrenees and raced toward Central Europe, but were stopped by a Christian and Frankish army in 732 at Tours on the river Loire. Islam was not destined to reach beyond Spain.

THE EMPIRE OF CHARLEMAGNE, A.D. 800

Among the Franks, in what is now northern France and the German Rhineland, there had meanwhile arisen a line of capable rulers of whom the greatest was Charlemagne. The Frankish kings made it their policy to co-

vvvvvvvvvvvvvvvvvvvv

2 "Thou art Peter, and upon this rock I will build my church; and the gates of hell shall not prevail against it. And I will give unto thee the keys of the kingdom of heaven, and whatsoever thou shalt bind on earth shall be bound in heaven; and whatsoever thou shalt loose on earth shall be loosed in heaven." Matthew xvi, 18–19. In Greek the name Peter meant a "rock"; a play upon words was involved. The pun is still evident in some modern languages, as in French, where *pierre*, a rock, is the same as *Pierre*, Peter.

operate with the pope. The pope needed a protector against depredations by his barbarian neighbors, and against the political claims of the Byzantine Empire upon the city of Rome. The Frankish kings, in return for protection thus offered, won papal support to their side. This made it easier for them to control their own bishops, who were more often seen on horseback than in the episcopal chair, and was of use in pacifying their own domains and in wars of conquest against the heathen. In the year 800, in Rome, the pope crowned Charlemagne as Emperor of the West. Frankish king and Roman bishop both believed that if only the Roman Empire could be restored peace and order might once more reign. Church and Empire, the spirit and the state, were to be as two mighty swords employed in the same holy cause.

Charlemagne crossed the Pyrenees and won back the northeastern corner of Spain to Christian rule. He overthrew and subordinated the barbarian kings who had set themselves up in Italy. He sent forces down the Danube, penetrated into Bohemia, and proceeded against some of the still heathen Germans (the Saxons) who lived along the river Elbe, and whom he either massacred or converted to Christianity. All these regions he brought within his new empire. Except for England and Ireland, which remained outside, the borders of his empire were co-extensive with those of the Latin Christian world.

Once more, to a degree, the West was united. But a momentous change had occurred. Its capital was now not Rome, and did not lie in the ancient world of the Mediterranean. Its capital was at Aix-la-Chapelle, or Aachen, near the mouth of the Rhine. Its ruler, Charlemagne, was a German of an ethnical group which ancient civilization had left outside. Its people were Germans, French, and Italians, or the ancestors from whom these nationalities were to be developed. In the Greco-Roman world the north had always been at best provincial. Now the north became a center in its own right. Charlemagne dispatched embassies to the emperor at Constantinople, and to Harun al-Rashid, the great caliph at Bagdad. In intellectual matters, too, the north now became a capital. Centuries of violence and confusion had left ignorance very widespread. Charlemagne himself, though he understood Latin, could barely read and never learned to write. He used his authority to revive the all but forgotten ancient learning and to spread education at least among the clergy. To his palace school came scholars from England, Germany, France, Italy, Spain. They wrote and spoke in Latin, the only Western language in which any complicated ideas could at the time be expressed. Disintegrating ancient manuscripts were copied, and then again copied to assure a more abundant supply for study—always by hand, but in a more rapid script than had before been used, the so-called Carolingian minuscule, from which come the small letters of the modern western alphabet, only the capitals being Roman. Commerce also, which had virtually disappeared, Charlemagne undertook to foster. He created a new and more reliable coinage, which was based on silver, the gold coins of the Roman Empire having long since vanished. A pound of silver was divided into 20 *solidi* and 240 pennies. This scheme of values, though long used in many parts

of Europe, survives today only in the country that remained outside Charlemagne's empire, namely in England, in its pound sterling of 20 shillings each
containing twelve pence.

NINTH-CENTURY INVASIONS; EUROPE BY A.D. 1000

It is in Charlemagne's empire that we can first see the shape of Europe, as a unit of society and culture distinct from the Mediterranean world
of antiquity. The Empire did not last. The troubled era was not yet over.
New hordes of barbarians assailed Western Christendom in the ninth century. The Magyars (called in Latin "Hungarians") terrified various parts of
Europe until they settled down on the middle Danube about the year 900.
New Germanic tribes uprooted themselves, coming this time from Scandinavia, and variously known as Norsemen, Vikings, or Danes. Bursting out in
all directions, they founded Kiev in Russia in 864, reached Iceland in 874,
and even touched America in 1000. In the Christian world they assaulted the
coasts and pushed up the rivers, but settled in considerable numbers only in
the Danelaw in England and in Normandy in France. Meanwhile the Arabs
raided the shores of France and Italy, and occupied Sicily. Nowhere was the
power of government strong enough to ward off such attacks. Everywhere the
harassed local population found its own means of defense, or, that failing,
was slaughtered, robbed, or carried off into slavery.

Gradually the second wave of barbarians was incorporated as the first
had been, by the same process of conversion to Christianity. By the year
1000 the process was nearly complete. In 1001 the pope sent a golden crown
to the Magyars to crown St. Stephen as their first king, thus bringing Hungary within the orbit of the Latin West. Poland, Bohemia, and the Scandinavian homelands of the Norsemen were being rapidly Christianized. In
older Christian countries, such as France, the last remote and isolated rustics
—the "heathen" who lived in the "heath"—were finally ferreted out by
missionaries and brought within the Christian fold. In Christian countries
Christianity now permeated to every corner, and the historic peoples of
western Europe had come together within the spreading system of the Latin
Church.

Meanwhile West and East continued to drift apart. The refusal of
Greek patriarchs at Constantinople to recognize the claims to primacy of the
bishop of Rome, whom they regarded as a kind of western barbarian, and
the refusal of the Roman pontiff to acknowledge the political pretensions of
the Byzantine empire, led to the Great Schism of East and West. This
schism, after developing for three centuries, became definite in 1054. It divided the Christian world into the Latin or Roman Catholic and the Greek
Orthodox Churches. It was from Constantinople that Christianity reached
the peoples of Russia. The Russians, like the Balkan peoples, remained out
of contact with the West during the centuries when spiritual and intellectual
contacts were carried through the clergy. They believed, indeed, that the

Latin West was evil, heretical, contumacious, and unholy. The Latin West, at the same time, by the schism, cut one more of its ties with antiquity, and emerged the more clearly as an independent center of its own civilization.

By the year 1000, or soon thereafter, the entity that we call Europe had been brought into existence. From the turbulence that followed the collapse of the Greco-Roman civilization had issued the peoples and the countries of modern Europe. A kingdom of France was in being, adjoining the great ill-defined bulk of Germany to the east. There were small Christian kingdoms in northern Spain and a number of city-states in the Italian peninsula. In the north there were now a kingdom of England and a kingdom of Scotland, and Denmark, Norway, and Sweden had taken form. In the east rose the three great kingdoms of Poland, Bohemia, and Hungary, the first two predominantly Slavic, Hungary predominantly Magyar, but all Latin and Catholic in culture and religion, and western in orientation. The east Slavs, or Russians, and the Slavs and other peoples of the Balkan peninsula, also formed kingdoms of their own. Their way was diverging from the West. Christianized by Byzantine missionaries, they were Greek and Orthodox in culture and religion, and oriented toward Constantinople.

The civilization of the West, in the year 1000, was still not much to boast of in the more polished circles of Byzantium or Bagdad. It might still seem that the West would suffer more than the East from their separation. But the West began at this time to experience a remarkable activity, ushering in the European civilization of the High Middle Ages.

3. The High Middle Ages: Secular Civilization

EMERGENCE FROM THE DARK AGES

Some historical periods are so dynamic that a person who lives to be fifty years old can remember sweeping changes that have come in his own lifetime. Such a time has been the last century of the modern age. Such a time, also, began in Europe in the eleventh century. A man could see new towns rise and grow before his eyes. He could observe new undertakings in commerce or government. It is hardly too much to say that all the cities that Europe was to know before the modern industrial era sprang up between about 1050 and 1200. The population of western Europe, which had been sparse even in Roman days, and even more so during the Dark Ages, suddenly began to grow more dense about the year 1000, expanded steadily for two or three hundred years, and then, from the fourteenth century, did not again abruptly increase until after 1800. The people of the High Middle Ages did not develop the conception of progress, because their minds were set upon timeless values and personal salvation in another world, but the period was nevertheless one of rapid progress in non-religious or "secular" things. It was a period in which much was created that remained fundamental far into modern times.

It is by no means clear how Europe pulled itself out of the Dark Ages. For one thing, about A.D. 1000, there began to be more security of life and limb. The farmer could plant with more confidence that he would reap. A man could build a house and expect to live his life in it and pass it on to his children. Hence there was more planting and building. One reason for the new personal security was that, after the Norse and Magyar inroads, Europe was spared the assaults of barbarians. Moreover, the church persuaded warring nobles to moderate their quarrelsome habits. In the Peace of God, instituted in the eleventh century, the bishops and magnates of a locality joined together to repress violence and levied fines on offenders. Thirdly, peace and personal security were advanced by the growth of institutions that we know as "feudalism."

Feudalism was intricate and diverse, but in essence it was a means of carrying on some kind of government on a local basis where no organized state existed. After the collapse of Charlemagne's empire the real authority fell into the hands of persons who were most often called "counts." The count was the most important man of a region covering a few hundred square miles. To build up his own position, and strengthen himself for war against other counts, he tried to keep the peace and maintain control over the lesser lords in his county, those whose possessions extended over a few hundred or a few thousand acres. These lesser lords accepted or were forced to accept his protection. They became his vassals, and he became their "lord." The lord-and-vassal relation was one of reciprocal duties. The lord protected the vassal and assured him justice and firm tenure of his land. If two vassals of the same lord disputed the possession of the same village, the lord decided the case, sitting in council (or "court") with all his vassals assembled, and judging according to the common memory of customary law of the district. If a vassal died young, leaving only small children, the lord took the family under his "wardship" or guardianship, guaranteeing that the rightful heirs would inherit in due time. Correspondingly the vassal agreed to serve the lord as a fighting man for a certain number of days in the year. From other "unauthorized" fighting and squabbling the vassal was supposed to refrain. The vassal also owed it to the lord to attend and advise him, to sit in his court in the judging of disputes. Usually he owed no money or material payment; but if the lord had to be ransomed from captivity, or when his children married, the vassal paid a fee. The vassal also paid a fee on inheriting an estate, and the income of estates under wardship went to the lord. Thus the lord collected sporadic revenues with which to finance his somewhat primitive government.

This feudal scheme, which probably originated locally, gradually spread. Lords at the level of counts became in turn the vassals of dukes. In the year 987 the great lords of France chose Hugh Capet as their king, and became his vassals. The kings of France enjoyed little real power for another two hundred years, but the descendants of Hugh occupied their throne for eight centuries, until the French Revolution. Similarly the magnates of Germany elected a king in 911; in 962 the German king was crowned Emperor, as Charlemagne had been before him; thus originated the Holy Roman Empire of which much will be heard in the following chapters.

To England, in these formative centuries, it was not given to choose a king by election. England was conquered in 1066 by the Duke of Normandy, William. The Normans (the old Norsemen re-shaped by a century of Christian and French influence) imposed upon England a centralized and efficient type of feudalism which they had developed in Normandy. In England, from an early date, the king and his central officials therefore had considerable power. In England there was more civil peace and personal security than on the Continent. Within its strong monarchy self-governing institutions could eventually develop with a minimum of disorder.

The notable feature of feudalism was its mutual or reciprocal character. In this it differed from the old Roman imperial principle, by which the emperor had been a majestic and all-powerful sovereign. Under feudalism no one was sovereign. King and people, lord and vassal, were joined in a kind of contract. Each owed something to the other. If one defaulted, the obligation ceased. If a vassal refused his due services, the king had the right to enforce compliance. If the king violated the rights of the vassal, the vassals could join together against him. The king was supposed to act with the advice of the vassals, who formed his council or court. If the vassals believed the king to be exceeding his lawful powers, they could impose terms upon him. It was out of this mutual or contractual character of feudalism that ideas of constitutional government later developed.

Feudalism applied in the strict sense only to the military or noble class. Below the feudal world lay the vast mass of the peasantry. Here, in the village, the lowliest vassal of a higher noble was lord over his own subjects. The village, with its people and surrounding farmlands, constituted a "manor," the estate of a lord. In the eleventh century most people of the manor were serfs. They were "bound to the soil" in that they could not leave the manor without the lord's permission. Few wanted to leave anyway, at a time when the world beyond the village was unknown and dangerous, and filled at best only with other similar manors in which opportunities were no different. The lord, for his part, could not expropriate the villagers or drive them away. He owed them protection and the administration of justice. They in turn worked his fields, and gave him part of the produce of their own. No money changed hands, because there was virtually no money in circulation. The manorial system was the agricultural base on which a ruling class was supported. It supported also the clergy, for the church held much land in the form of manors. It gave the protection from physical violence, and the framework of communal living, without which the peasants could not grow their crops or tend their livestock.

There had been important innovations in agriculture during the obscure centuries of the Dark Ages. Sometime before the year 1000 a heavier plow had been invented, which cut a deeper furrow. Better methods of harnessing horses had been found than the ancients had ever known. The Romans had continued simply to throw a yoke over a horse's neck, so that the animal in pulling a weight easily choked. Europeans, before the year 1000, began to use a horse collar that rested on the animal's shoulders. The single horse could pull a greater load, or several horses could now for the first time be hitched in tandem. The amount of available animal power was thus multiplied, at a time when animals were the main source of power other than human muscle. Probably windmills, unknown to the ancients, were developed in the Low Countries about this time. They too offered a new source of power. Thus, at the very beginning of a specifically "European" history, one may detect a characteristic of European civilization—a faculty for invention, a quest for sources of power other than man's muscle. With such labor-saving devices men continued to work very hard, but they obtained more results by their efforts. Probably the use of such new inventions, together with the influence of the Christian clergy, accounts for the gradual disappearance of slavery from Europe, and its replacement by the less abject and less degrading status of serfdom. Medieval Europe was the first complex human society not to have slavery at its base.

Better ways of using land were introduced in the "three-field" system, which spread almost everywhere where cereal crops were the staple. In this "system" the peasant village divided its arable fields into three parts. In a given year one part was sown with one crop, such as wheat, a second part with another, such as barley, and the third was left to lie fallow. The three parts were rotated from year to year. Formerly, to avoid soil exhaustion, half or less of the available fields had been cultivated at any one time. With the three-field system two-thirds of the land came into annual use. This fact, reinforced by better plowing and more effective employment of animals, led to a huge increase in the supply of food.

Many consequences flowed from this rise of agricultural productivity. Lords and even a few peasants could produce a surplus, which they might sell if only they could find a market. The country was able to produce enough food for a town population to live on. And since population grew with the increase of the food supply, and since not all the new people were needed in agriculture, a surplus of population also began to exist. Restless spirits among the peasants now wanted to get away from the manor. And many went off to the new towns.

THE RISE OF TOWNS AND COMMERCE

We have seen how the ancient cities had decayed. In the ninth and tenth centuries, with few exceptions, there were none left in western Europe. Here and there one would find a cluster of population around the headquarters of a bishop, a great count, or a king. But there were no commercial centers. There was no merchant class. The simple crafts—weaving, metal working, harness making—were carried on locally on the manors. Rarely, an itinerant trader might appear with such semi-precious goods as he could carry for long distances on donkeys—Eastern silks, or a few spices for Europe's upper class. Among these early traders Jews were often important, because Judaism, penetrating the Byzantine and Arabic worlds as well as the Western, offered one of the few channels of distant communication that were open.

Long-distance trading was the first to develop. The city of Venice was founded about A.D. 570 when refugees from the barbarians settled in its islands. The Venetians, as time went on, brought Eastern goods up the Adriatic and sold them to traders coming down from central Europe. In Flanders in the north, in what is now Belgium, there developed manufacturers of woollen cloth. Flemish woollens were of a unique quality, owing to peculiarities of the atmosphere and the skill of the weavers. They could not be duplicated elsewhere. Nor could Eastern goods be procured except through the Venetians— or the Genoese or Pisans. Such goods could not possibly be produced locally, yet they were in demand wherever they became known. Merchants traveled in increasing numbers to disseminate them. Money came back into more general circulation; where it came from is not quite clear, since there was little mining of gold or silver in the Middle Ages. Merchants began to establish permanent headquarters, settling within the deserted walls of ghostly Roman towns, or near the seat of a lord or ecclesiastic, whose throngs of retainers might become customers. Craftsmen moved from the over-populated manors to these same growing centers, where they might produce wares that the lords or merchants would wish to buy. The process once started tended to snowball: the more people settled in such an agglomeration the more they needed food brought to them from the country, and the more craftsmen left the villages the more the country people, lords and serfs, had to obtain clothing and simple tools and utensils from the towns. Hence a busy local trade developed also.

By 1100, or not long thereafter, such centers existed all over Europe, from the Baltic to Italy, from England as far east as Bohemia. Usually there was one about every twenty or thirty miles. The smallest towns had only a few hundred inhabitants, the larger ones two or three thousand, or sometimes more. Each carried on a local exchange with its immediate countryside and purveyed goods of more distant origin to local consumers. But their importance was by no means merely economic. What made them "towns" in the full sense of the word was their acquisition of political rights.

The merchants and craftsmen who lived in the towns did not wish to remain, like the country people, subject to neighboring feudal lords. At worst, the feudal lords regarded merchants as fat possessors of ready money; they might hold them up on the road, plunder their mule trains, collect tolls at river crossings, or extort cash by offering "protection." At best, the most well meaning feudal lord could not supervise the affairs of merchants, for the feudal and customary law knew nothing of commercial problems. The traders in the course of their business developed a "law merchant" of their own, having to do with money and money changing, debt and bankruptcy, contracts, invoices, and bills of lading. They wished to have their own means of apprehending thieves, runaway debtors or sellers of fraudulent goods. They strove, therefore, to get recognition for their own law, their own courts, their own judges and magistrates. They wished, too, to govern their towns themselves, and to avoid payment of fees or taxes to near-by nobles.

Everywhere in Latin Christendom, along about 1100, the new towns struggled to free themselves from the encircling feudalism and to set themselves up as self-governing little republics. Where the towns were largest and closest together—along the highly urbanized arteries of the trade routes, in north Italy, on the upper Danube and Rhine rivers, in Flanders, or on the Baltic coast—they emancipated themselves the most fully. Venice, Genoa, Pisa, Florence, Milan became virtually independent city-states, each governing a substantial tract of its surrounding country. In Flanders also, towns like Bruges and Ghent dominated their localities. Along the upper Danube, the Rhine, the North Sea, the Baltic, many towns became imperial free cities within the Holy Roman Empire, each a kind of small republic owing allegiance to no one except the distant and usually ineffectual emperor. Nuremberg, Frankfurt, Augsburg, Strasburg, Hamburg, Lübeck were free cities of this kind. In France and England, where the towns in the twelfth century were somewhat less powerful, they obtained less independence but received charters of liberties from the king. By these charters they were assured the right to have their own town governments and officials, their own courts and law, and to pay their own kind of taxes to the king in lieu of ordinary feudal obligations.

Often towns formed leagues or urban federations, joining forces to repress banditry or piracy, or to deal with ambitious monarchs or predatory nobles. The most famous such league was the Hanse; it was formed mainly of German towns, fought wars under its own banner, and dominated the commerce of the North Sea and the Baltic until after 1300. Similar tendencies of the towns to form political leagues, or to act independently in war and diplomacy, were suppressed by the kings in England, France, and Spain.

The fact that Italy, Germany, and the Netherlands were commercially more advanced than the Atlantic countries in the Middle Ages, and so had a more intensive town life, was to be one cause (out of many) preventing political unification. Not until 1860 or 1870 were nation-wide states created in this region. In the west, where towns also grew up, but where more of a balance was kept between town and country, the towns were absorbed into nation-wide monarchies that were arising under the kings. This difference between central and western Europe was to shape all the subsequent history of modern times.

The liberties won by the towns were corporate liberties. Each town was a collective thing. The townsman did not possess individual rights, but only the rights which followed from being a resident of his particular town. Among these were personal liberty; no townsman could be a serf, and fugitive serfs who lived over a year in a town were generally deemed to be free. But no townsman wanted individual liberty in the modern sense. The world was still too unsettled for the individual to act alone. The citizens wanted to join together in a compact body, and to protect themselves by all sorts of regulations and controls. The most obvious evidence of this communal solidarity was the wall within which most towns were enclosed. The citizens in time of trouble looked to their own defense. As the towns grew they built new walls farther out. Today, in Paris or Cologne, one may still see remains of different walls in use from the tenth to the thirteenth centuries.

Economic solidarity was of more day-to-day importance. The towns required neighboring peasants to sell foodstuffs only in the town market place. They thus protected their food supply against competition from other towns. Or they forbade the carrying on of certain trades in the country; this was to oblige peasants to make purchases in town, and protect the jobs and livelihood of the town craftsmen. They put up tariffs and tolls on the goods of other towns brought within their own walls. Or they levied special fees on merchants from outside who did business in the town. In Italy and Germany they often coined their own money; and the typical town fixed the rates at which various moneys should exchange. The medieval towns, in short, at the time of their greatest liberty, followed in a local way the same policies of protectionism and exclusiveness which national governments were generally to follow in modern times.

Within each town, merchants and craftsmen formed associations or "gilds" for collective supervision of their affairs. Merchants formed a merchant gild. Stonemasons, carpenters, barbers, dyers, goldsmiths, coppersmiths, weavers, hatters, tailors, shoemakers, grocers, apothecaries, *etc.* formed craft gilds of their own. The gilds served a public purpose, for they provided that work should be done by reliable and experienced persons, and so protected people from the pitfalls of shoddy garments, clumsy barbers, poisonous drugs, or crooked and flimsy houses. They also provided a means of vocational education and marked out a career for young men. Typically a boy became an apprentice to some master, learned the trade, and lived with and was supported by the master's family for a term of years, such as seven. Then he became a journeyman, a qualified and recognized worker, who might work for any master at a stated wage. Lastly, he might become a master himself, open his own shop, hire journeymen, and take apprentices. So long as the towns were growing, careers remained open, and a boy could reasonably expect to become a master himself; but as early as 1300 many gilds were becoming frozen, and the masters were increasingly chary of admitting new persons to their own status. From the beginning, in any case, it was an important function of the gilds to protect their own members. The masters, assembled together, preserved their reputation by regulating the quality of their product. They divided work among themselves, fixed the terms of apprenticeship, the wages to be paid to journeymen, and the prices at which their goods must be sold. Or they took collective steps to meet or keep out the competition of the same trade in near-by towns.

Whether among individuals within the town itself, or as between town

and country, or between town and town, the spirit of the medieval economy
was to prevent competition. Risk, adventure, and speculation were not
wanted. Almost no one thought it proper to work for monetary profit. The
few who did, big merchants trading over large areas, met with suspicion and
disapproval wherever they went.

The towns, although in many ways they tried to subject the peasants'
interests to their own, nevertheless had an emancipating influence on the
country. A rustic by settling in town might escape from serfdom. But the
town influence was more widespread, and far out of proportion to the relatively small number of people who could become town dwellers. The growth
of towns increased the demand for foods. Lords began to clear new lands.
All western Europe set about developing a kind of internal frontier. Formerly
villages had been separated by dark tracts of roadless woods, in which wolves
roamed freely, shadowed by the gnomes, elves, and fairies of popular folklore.
Now pioneers with axes cleared farmlands and built villages in these immemorial forests. The lords who usually supervised such operations (since
their serfs were not slaves, and could not be moved at will) offered freer terms
to entice peasants to go and settle on the new lands. It was less easy for the
lord of an old village to hold his people in serfdom when in an adjacent village, within a few hours' walk, the people were free. The peasants, moreover,
were now able to obtain a little money by selling produce in town. The lords
now wanted money because the towns were producing more articles which
money could buy. It became very common for peasants to obtain personal
freedom, holding their own lands, in return for an annual money payment
to the lord for an indefinite period into the future. As early as the twelfth
century serfdom began to disappear in northern France and southern England, and by the fifteenth century it had disappeared from most of western
Europe. The peasant could now, in law, move freely about. But the manorial
organization remained; the peasant owed dues and fees to the lord, and was
still under his legal jurisdiction.

THE GROWTH OF NATIONAL MONARCHIES

Meanwhile the kings were busy, each trying to build his kingdom into
an organized monarchy that would outlast his life.[3] Monarchy became
hereditary; the king inherited his position like any other feudal lord or possessor of an estate. Inheritance of the crown made for peace and order, for
elections under conditions of the time were usually turbulent and disputed,
and where the older Germanic principle of elective monarchy remained alive,
as in the Holy Roman Empire, there was periodic commotion. The kings
sent out executive officers to supervise their interests throughout their kingdoms. The kings of England sent a sheriff into each of the forty shires; the
kings of France created similar officers who were called bailiffs. The kings

[3] See pp. 23–4.

likewise instituted royal courts, under royal justices, to decide property disputes and repress crime. This assertion of legal jurisdiction, together with the
military force to enforce judgments upon obstinate nobles, became a main
pillar of the royal power. In England especially, and in lesser degree elsewhere, the kings required local inhabitants to assist royal judges in the discovery of relevant facts in particular cases. They put men on oath to declare
what they knew of events in their own neighborhood. It is from this enforced
association of private persons with royal officers that the jury developed.

The kings needed money to pay for their governmental machinery or
to carry on war with other kings. Taxation, as known in the Roman Empire,
was quite unknown to the Germanic and feudal tradition. In the feudal
scheme each person was responsible only for the customary fees which arose
on stated occasions. The king, like other lords, was supposed to live on his
own income—on the revenue of manors that he owned himself, the proceeds
of estates temporarily under his wardship, or the occasional fees paid to him
by his vassals. No king, even for the best of reasons, could simply decree a new
tax and collect it. At the same time, as the use of money became more common, the kings had to assure themselves of a money income. In England, in
the twelfth century, the customary obligation of the vassal to render military
service to the king was converted into a money payment, called "scutage" or
shield money. As the towns grew up, with a new kind of wealth and a new
source of money income, they agreed to make certain payments in return for
their royal charters.

The royal demands for money, the royal claims to exercise jurisdiction,
were regarded as innovations. They were constantly growing and sometimes
were a source of abuse. They met with frequent resistance in all countries. A
famous case historically (though somewhat commonplace in its own day)
was that of Magna Carta in England in 1215, when the English lords and
high churchmen, joined by representatives of the city of London, required
King John to confirm and guarantee their historic liberties.

The king, as has been said, like any lord, was supposed to act in council or "court" with his vassals. The royal council became the egg out of which
departments of government were hatched—such as the royal judiciary, exchequer, and military command. From it also was hatched the institution of
parliaments. The kings had always, in a rough sort of way, held great parleys
or "talks" (the Latin *parliamentum* meant simply a "talking") with their
chief retainers. In the twelfth and thirteenth centuries the growth of towns
added a new element to European life. To the lords and bishops was now
added a burgher class, which, if of far inferior dignity, was too stubborn, free-
spirited, and well furnished with money to be overlooked. When representatives of the towns began to be normally summoned to the king's great "talks,"
along with lords and clergy, parliaments may be said to have come into being.

Parliaments, in this sense, sprouted all over Europe in the thirteenth
century. Nothing shows better the similarity of institutions in Latin Christendom, or the inadequacy of tracing the history of any one country by itself.
The new assemblies were called *cortes* in Spain, diets in Germany, estates-

general in France, parliaments in the British Isles. Usually they are referred to generically as "estates," the word "parliament" being reserved for Britain, but in origin they were all essentially the same.

The kings called these assemblies as a means of publicizing and strengthening the royal rule. They found it more convenient to explain their policies, or to ask for money, to a large gathering brought together for that purpose than to have a hundred officials make local explanations and strike local bargains in a hundred different places. The kings did not recognize, nor did the assemblies claim, any right of the parliament to dictate to the king and his government. But usually the king invited the parliament to state grievances; his action upon them was the beginning of parliamentary legislation.

The parliaments were considered to represent not the "nation" nor "people" nor yet the individual citizen, but the "estates of the realm," the great collective interests of the country. The first and highest estate was the clergy, the second the landed or noble class; to these older ruling groups were added, as a "third estate," the burghers of the chartered towns. Quite commonly these three types of people sat separately as three distinct chambers. But the pattern varied from country to country. In England, Poland, and Hungary the clergy as a whole ceased to be represented; only the bishops came, sitting with lay magnates in an upper house. Eventually the burghers dropped out in Poland, Bohemia, and Hungary, leaving the landed aristocracy in triumph in Eastern Europe. In Castile and Würtemberg, on the other hand, the noble estate eventually refused to attend parliament, leaving the townspeople and clergy in the assemblies. In some countries—in Scandinavia, Switzerland, and in the French Estates General—even peasants were allowed to have delegates.

In England, almost from the beginning, the parliament developed in a distinctive way. There came to be only two houses, the Lords and the Commons. The Lords, as in Hungary or Poland, included both great prelates and great lay magnates. The House of Commons was more unique. In England overt class distinctions were already blurred, and the lesser landholders, the people who elsewhere counted as small nobles, sat in the same House of Commons with representatives of the towns. The Commons was made up of "knights and burgesses," or gentry and townsmen together, a fact which greatly added to its strength, for the middle class of the towns long remained too weak to act alone. The mingling of classes in England, the willingness of townsmen to follow the leadership of the gentry, and of the gentry to respect the interests of townsmen, helped to root representative institutions in England more deeply than in other countries, in many of which the parliaments tended to die out in later times, in part because of class conflict. Moreover, England was a small country in the Middle Ages, even smaller than it looked on the map because the north was almost wild. There were no provincial or local parliamentary bodies (as in France, the Holy Roman Empire, or Poland), which might jealously cut into the powers of the central body, or with which the king could make local arrangements without violating the principle of representative government. And finally, as a reason for the strength of Parliament in England, the elected members of the House of Commons very early obtained the power to *commit* their constituents. If they voted a tax, those who elected them had to pay it. The king, in order to get matters decided, insisted that the votes be binding. Constituents were not allowed to repudiate the vote of their deputy, nor to punish or harass him when he came home, as often happened in other countries. Parliament thus exercised power as well as rights.

In summary, the three centuries of the High Middle Ages laid foundations both for order and for freedom. Slavery was defunct and serfdom expiring. Politically, the multitude of free chartered towns, the growth of juries in some places, the rise of parliaments everywhere, provided means by which peoples could take some part in their governments. The ancient civilizations had never created a free political unit larger than the city-state. The Greeks had never carried democracy beyond the confines within which people could meet in person, nor had the Romans devised means by which, in a large state, the governed could share any responsibilities with an official bureaucracy. The ancients had never developed the idea of representative government, or of government by duly elected and authorized representatives acting at a distance from home. The idea is by no means as obvious or simple as it looks. It first appeared in the medieval monarchies of the West.

4. The High Middle Ages: The Church

So far in our account of the High Middle Ages we have told the story of Hamlet without speaking of the Prince of Denmark, for we have left aside the Church, except, indeed, when some mention of it could not be avoided. In the real life of the time the Church was omnipresent. Religion permeated every pore. In feudalism, the mutual duties of lord and vassal were confirmed by religious oaths, and bishops and abbots, as holders of lands, became feudal personages themselves. In the monarchies, the king was crowned by the chief churchman of his kingdom, adjured to rule with justice and piety, and anointed with holy oils. In the towns, gilds served as lay religious brotherhoods; each gild chose a patron saint and marched in the streets on holy days. For amusement the townsmen watched religious dramas, the morality and miracle plays in which religious themes were enacted. The rising town, if it harbored a bishop, took especial care to erect a new cathedral. Years of effort and of religious fervor produced the Gothic cathedrals which still stand as the best known memorials of medieval civilization.

THE DEVELOPMENT OF THE MEDIEVAL CHURCH AND PAPACY

If, however, we turn back to the tenth century, the troubled years before 1000, we find the Church in as dubious a condition as everything else.

The church reflected the life about it. It was fragmented and localized. Every bishop went his own way. Though the clergy was the only literate class, many of the clergy themselves could not read and write. Christian belief was mixed with the old pagan magic and superstition. The monasteries were in decay. Priests often lived in a concubinage that was generally condoned. It was customary for them to marry, so that they had recognized children, to whom they intrigued to pass on their churchly position. Often rough laymen dominated their ecclesiastical neighbors, with the big lords appointing the bishops, and the little ones the parish priests. When people thought about Rome at all, they sensed a vague respect for something legendary and far away; but the bishop of Rome, or pope, had no influence and was treated in unseemly fashion in his own city. The popes of the tenth century were the creatures of the unruly Roman nobles. Marozia, daughter of a Roman "senator," became the mistress of one pope, by whom she had a son who became pope in turn, until she imprisoned him so that another son, by another father, could claim the papacy also.

The Roman Catholic Church is in fact unrecognizable in the jumble of the tenth century. So far at least as human effort was concerned, it was virtually created in the eleventh century along with the other institutions of the High Middle Ages.

The impulse to reform came from many quarters. Sometimes a secular ruler undertook to correct conditions in his own domains. For this purpose he asserted a strict control over his clergy. In 962 the Holy Roman Empire was proclaimed. This Empire, like the Carolingian and Roman Empires which it was supposed to continue, was in theory coterminous with Latin Christendom itself, and endowed with a special mission of preserving and extending the Christian faith. Neither in France nor in England (nor, when they became Christian states, in Spain, Hungary, Poland, or Scandinavia) was this claim of the Holy Roman Empire ever acknowledged. But the Empire did for a time embrace Italy as well as Germany. The first emperors, in the tenth and eleventh centuries, denouncing the outrageous conditions in Rome, strove to make the pope into their appointee.

At the same time a reform movement arose from spiritual sources. Serious Christians took matters into their own hands. They founded a new monastery at Cluny in France, which soon had many daughter houses. It was their purpose to purify monastic life and to set a higher Christian ideal to which all clergy and laity might look up. To rid themselves of immediate local pressures, the greed, narrowness, ignorance, family ambition, and self-satisfied inertia that were the main cause of corruption, the Cluniacs refused to recognize any authority except that of Rome itself. Thus, at the very time when conditions in Rome were at their worst, Christians throughout Europe built up the prestige of Rome, of the idea of Rome, as a means to raise all Latin Christendom from its depths.

As for the popes in Rome, those who preserved any independence of judgment or respect for their own office, it was their general plan to free themselves from the Roman mobs and aristocrats without falling into dependence upon the Holy Roman Emperor. In 1059 Pope Nicholas II issued a decree providing that future popes should be elected by the cardinals. The cardinals, at that time, were the priests of churches in the city of Rome, or bishops of neighboring dioceses. By entrusting the choice of future popes to them, Pope Nicholas hoped to exclude all influence from outside the clergy itself. Popes have been elected by cardinals ever since, though not always without influence from outside.

One of the first popes so elected was Gregory VII, known also as Hildebrand, a dynamic and strong-willed man who was pope from 1073 to 1085. He had been in touch with the Cluniac reformers, and dreamed of a reformed and reinvigorated Europe under the universal guidance of the Roman pontiff.

To understand what followed, the reader must exert his imagination. In his mind's eye he must see a world in which all political barriers have dropped away. In this world people have no nationality. They do not live in the state, as in modern times; they live in the church. Society itself is a great religious community. Its leaders are the clergy, to which all educated persons belong. The public personage with whom people come into most frequent contact is the priest, and the most important public official is the bishop. The chief public buildings are churches, abbeys, and cathedrals. Secular interests, those of kings and dukes, of merchants and artisans, are earthbound and shortsighted. All persons, even kings, in addition to secular interests, have a higher concern. All are living in the religious community and preparing their souls for eternal life. The religious community, or church, reaches in principle as far as the borders of the known world. It is universal, for all men must be saved. At its head stands the bishop of Rome, the Vicar of Christ, the successor to Peter, the keeper of the keys, the *servus servorum Dei*, the servant of the servants of God.

Some such vision filled the mind of Hildebrand, and with it he founded the papal supremacy of the High Middle Ages. He believed that the church should stand apart from worldly society, that it should judge and guide all human actions, and that a pope could judge and punish kings and emperors if he deemed them sinful. His ideal was not a "world state," but its spiritual counterpart, a world church officered by a single-minded and disciplined clergy, centralized under a single authority. He began by insisting that the clergy free itself of worldly involvements. He required married priests to put aside their wives and families. Celibacy of the clergy, never generally established in the Greek Orthodox Church, and later rejected by Protestants in the West, became and remained the rule for the Roman Catholic priesthood. Gregory insisted also that no ecclesiastic might receive office through appointment by a layman. In his view only clergy might institute or influence clergy, for the clergy must be independent and self-contained.

Hildebrand soon faced a battle with that other aspirant to universal supremacy and a sacred mission, the Holy Roman Emperor, who at this time was Henry IV. In Germany the bishops and abbots possessed a great deal of the land, which they held and governed under the emperor as feudal magnates in their own right. To the emperor it was vitally important to have his own men, as reliable vassals, in these great positions. Hence in Germany "lay investiture" had become very common. "Lay investiture" meant the practice by which a layman, the emperor, conferred upon the new bishop the signs of his spiritual authority, the ring and the staff. Gregory prohibited lay investiture. He supported the German bishops and nobles when they rebelled against Henry. Henry proving obstinate, Gregory excommunicated him, *i.e.*, outlawed him from Christian society by forbidding any priest to give him the sacraments. Henry, baffled, sought out the pope at Canossa in Italy to do penance. "To go to Canossa" in later times became a byword for submission to the will of Rome.

In 1122, after both original contenders had died, a compromise on the matter of lay investiture was effected by which bishops recognized the emperor as their feudal head but looked to Rome for spiritual authority. But the struggle between popes and emperors went on unabated. The magnates of Germany, lay lords as well as bishops, often allied with the pope to preserve their own feudal liberties from the emperor. The emperor in Germany was never able to consolidate his domains as did the kings in England and France. In Italy, too, the popes and emperors quarreled, the foes of each commonly siding with the other. The unwillingness of lords and churchmen (and of towns also, as we have seen) to let the emperors build up an effectual government left its mark permanently upon Europe in two ways. It contributed to the centralization of Latin Christendom under Rome, and it blocked national unity in central Europe.

The height of the medieval papacy came with Innocent III, whose pontificate lasted from 1198 to 1216. Innocent virtually realized Gregory's dream of a unified Christian world. He intervened in politics everywhere. He was recognized as a supreme arbiter. At his word, a king of France took a wife, a king of England accepted an unwanted archbishop, a king of Leon put aside the cousin whom he had married, and a claimant to the crown of Hungary deferred to his rival. Innocent advised the kings of Bohemia, Poland, and Denmark on weighty matters, and the kings of England, Aragon, and Portugal acknowledged him as feudal overlord within their realms. Huge revenues now flowed to Rome from all over Latin Christendom, and an enormous bureaucracy worked there to dispatch the voluminous business of the papal court. As kings struggled to repress civil rebellion, so Innocent and his successors struggled to repress heresy, which, defined as doctrine at variance with that of the church at large, was becoming alarmingly common among the Albigensians of southern France.

In 1215 Innocent called a great church council, the greatest since antiquity, attended by five hundred bishops and even by the patriarchs of Constantinople and Jerusalem. The council labored at the perplexing task of keeping the clergy from worldly temptations. By forbidding priests to officiate at ordeals or trials by battle, it put an end to these survivals of barbarism. It attempted to regularize belief in the supernatural by controlling the superstitious traffic in relics. It declared the sacraments to be the channel of God's saving grace and defined them authoritatively.[4] In the chief sacrament, the Eucharist or Mass, it promulgated the dogma of transubstantiation, which holds that, in the Mass, the priest converts the substance of bread and wine into the substance of Christ's body and blood. Except for heretics, who were suppressed, the acts of the Fourth Lateran Council were accepted with satisfaction throughout Latin Europe.

INTELLECTUAL LIFE: THE UNIVERSITIES, SCHOLASTICISM

Under the auspices of the Church, as rising governments gave more civil security, and as the economy of town and country became able to support men devoted to a life of thought, the intellectual horizon of Europeans began to open. The twelfth and thirteenth centuries saw the founding of the first universities. These originated in the natural and spontaneous coming together of teachers and pupils which had never wholly disappeared even in the Dark Ages. By 1200 there was a center of medical studies at Salerno in south Italy, of legal studies at Bologna in north Italy, of theological studies at Paris. Oxford was founded about 1200 by a secession of disgruntled students and professors from Paris, Cambridge shortly thereafter. By 1300 there were a dozen such universities in Latin Europe, by 1500 almost a hundred.

As the early agglomerations of traders developed into organized towns, so the informal concourses of students and teachers developed into organized institutions of learning, receiving the sharp corporate stamp that was characteristic of the High Middle Ages. It was in having this corporate identity that medieval universities resemble our own, and differed from the schools of Athens or Alexandria in ancient times. A university, the early University of Paris, for example, was a body of men, young and old, interested in learning and endowed by law with a communal name and being. It possessed definite liberties under some kind of charter, regulated its own affairs through its own officials, and kept its own order among its often boisterous population. It gave, and even advertised, courses and lectures, and it decided collectively which professors were the best qualified to teach. It might consist of distinct schools or "faculties"—the combination of theology, law, and medicine, as at Paris, was the most usual. It held examinations and awarded degrees, whose meaning and value were recognized throughout the Latin West. The degree, which originated as a license to teach, admitted its holder to certain honors or privileges such as those of a craft gild. With it, a professor might readily move from one

---

[4] A sacrament is understood to be the outward sign of an inward grace. In Catholic doctrine the sacraments were and are seven in number: baptism, confirmation, penance, the Eucharist, extreme unction, marriage, and holy orders. Except for baptism, a sacrament may be administered only by a priest. A dogma is the common belief of the church, in which all the faithful share and must share so long as they are members of the church. Dogmas are regarded as implicitly the same in all ages; they cannot be invented or developed, but may from time to time be clarified, defined, promulgated, or proclaimed.

university to another. Students moved easily also, the language being everywhere Latin and the curriculum much the same. The university, moreover, though typically it began in poverty, was as a corporate body capable of holding property of its own; and the benefactions of pious donors, as the years went on, often built up substantial endowments in lands and manors. So organized, free from outside control, and enjoying property of its own, the university lived on as an institution beyond the lifetime of all living men, through good times and bad, through civil war or disorder, through dreary years when students were few or professors undistinguished, always to some extent fulfilling its role of conserving or diffusing knowledge, and always ready for a periodic wave of reform.

The queen of the sciences was theology, the intellectual study of religion. Many in Europe, by the eleventh century, were beginning to reflect upon their beliefs. They continued to believe, but could no longer believe with naive or unthinking acceptance. It was accepted as a fact, for example, that the Son of God had been incarnated as a man in Jesus Christ. But in the eleventh century an Italian named Anselm, who became archbishop of Canterbury, wrote a treatise called *Cur Deus Homo?* —"Why did God become Man?"—giving reasoned explanations to show why God had taken this means to save mankind. Soon afterwards Abelard, who taught at Paris, wrote his *Sic et non*—"Yes and No" or "Pro and Con"—a collection of inconsistent statements made by St. Augustine and other Fathers of the Church. Abelard's purpose was to apply logic to the inherited mass of patristic writings, show wherein the truth of Christian doctrine really lay, and so make the faith consistent with reason and reflection.

Meanwhile, in the twelfth century a great stream of new knowledge poured into Europe, bringing about a veritable intellectual revolution. It was derived from the Arabs, with whom Christians were in contact in Sicily and Spain. The Arabs, as has been seen, had taken over the ancient Greek science, translated Greek writings into Arabic, and in many ways added further refinements of their own. Bilingual Christians (assisted by numerous learned Jews who passed readily between the Christian and Moslem worlds) translated these works into Latin. Above all, they translated Aristotle, the great codifier of Greek knowledge who had lived and written in the fourth century B.C. The Europeans, barely emerging from barbarism, were overwhelmed by this sudden disclosure of an undreamed of universe of knowledge. Aristotle became The Philosopher, the unparalleled authority on all branches of knowledge other than religious.

The great problem for Europeans was now to digest the gigantic bulk of Aristotle, or, in more general terms, to assimilate or reconcile the body of Greek and Arabic learning to the Christian faith. The universities, with their "scholastic" philosophers or "schoolmen," performed this useful social function. Most eminent of scholastics was Thomas Aquinas (1225–74), the Angelic Doctor, known also to his own contemporaries as the Dumb Ox from the slow deliberation of his speech. His chief work, appropriately called the *Summa Theologica*, was a survey of all knowledge. The thought of Aquinas, as recently as 1879, was pronounced by Pope Leo XIII to be the foundation of official Catholic philosophy.

The chief accomplishment of Thomas Aquinas was his demonstration that faith and reason could not be in conflict. By reason he meant a severely logical method, with exact definition of words and concepts, deducing step by step what follows and must follow if certain premises are accepted. His philosophy is classified as a form of "realism." It holds, that is, that the general idea is more "real" than the particular—that "man" is more real than this or that man or woman, that "law" as such is more real and binding than this or that particular law. He derived his philosophy from what he took to be the nature of God, of man, of law, of reason, of beings in general. He taught a hierarchic view of the universe and of society, of which God was the apex, and in which all things and all men were subordinated to God in a descending order, each bound to fulfill the role set by its own place and nature. It was the emphasis on the superior reality of abstractions that enabled men in the Middle Ages to believe steadfastly in the church while freely attacking individual churchmen, to have faith in the papacy while denouncing the popes as scoundrels—or to accept without difficulty the mystery of transubstantiation, which declared that what admittedly looked and tasted like bread and wine was, in real inner substance, the body of Christ.[5]

The scholastic philosophy, as perfected by Thomas Aquinas, was not very favorable to the growth of natural science, because, in its emphasis

[5] See also the illustration following and the caption below.

The Meeting of St. Anthony and St. Paul
BY SASSETTA (ITALIAN, 1392–1450)

Here we can see something of the medieval way of thinking. The picture tells a religious story. St. Anthony appears in three places, walking alone, converting a centaur, and meeting and embracing St. Paul. There is no attempt to present him as a unique individual person; his head and features disappear behind those of St. Paul in the principal scene. The picture gives the "idea" of the story. The two figures are typical saints, with the haloes which conventionally designated sacred persons. The artist has painted the "idea" or "essence" of a forest, i.e., many trees; he has not shown the actual appearance of a particular forest, with underbrush, shadows, trees of different sizes and foliage of different kinds. His hills are hills in general, i.e., mounds of earth; his cave is a cave in general, i.e., a dark hole. When the two saints embrace, their arms and legs are placed where the mind knows that they ought to be, not where the eye would see them concretely in any particular situation. The picture thus illustrates, on a simple level, what is meant by the abstractness or "realism" (the realism of ideas) of medieval thought. A child today, or an artistically untrained adult, draws in the same way, portraying the idea rather than the physical actuality. The idea of a forest is, after all, "many trees"; all else is special or incidental, not of the essence. Courtesy of the National Gallery, Washington, D.C. (Kress Collection).

on an inner reality, it drew attention away from the actual details and behavior of concrete things. On the other hand, the scholastic philosophy laid foundations on which later European thought was to be reared. It habituated Europeans to great exactness, to careful distinctions, even to the splitting of hairs. It called for disciplined thinking. And it made the world safe for reason. If any historical generalization may be made safely, it may be safely said that any society that believes reason to threaten its foundations will suppress reason. In Thomas's time, there were some who said that Aristotle and the Arabs were infidels, dangerous influences that must be silenced. Any reasoning about the faith, they warned, was a form of weakness. Thomas's doctrine that faith could not be endangered by reason gave a freedom to thinkers to go on thinking. Here Latin Christendom may be contrasted with the Moslem world. It was ruled, in about the time of Thomas Aquinas, that valid interpretation of the Koran had ended with the Four Great Doctors of early Islam. As Moslems said, the Gate was closed. Arabic thought, so brilliant for several centuries, withered away.

THE CRUSADES; NEW INVASIONS; EUROPE BY 1300

Meanwhile, the West was expanding. Europe in the eleventh century took the offensive against Islam. All Latin Christendom went on the Crusades. War itself was subordinated to the purposes of religion.

The most ambitious, best remembered, and least successful of such expeditions were the Crusades to win back the Holy Land. The First Crusade was preached in 1095 by Pope Urban II, who hoped thereby to ad-

---

Magdalene at the Foot of the Cross

BY SANDRO BOTTICELLI (ITALIAN, 1447?–1510)

Botticelli, in his love of the human form, was a typical painter of the Italian Renaissance (see pp. 49–56). But the carrying over of medieval attitudes is also evident in his work. The painting reproduced here is a mysterious one. Its setting is clearly in the natural world, with the city of Florence recognizably in the background, standing in actual space against hills and sky. But the mood is sombre. Some have called it a picture of abject grief, in the figure of the woman prostrate at the foot of the cross. Others find the main theme in the avenging angel. Indeed, the painting has been known also under the title of "The Punishment of Heaven for the Murder of Savonarola." Savonarola was a religious leader who in 1494 aroused a strong moral reaction at Florence against the more pagan aspects of the Renaissance. In 1498 he was put to death. Botticelli was his follower. It seems likely that this painting contains an allegory. The angel is represented as scourging a lion cub (the lion was the heraldic device of the city of Florence), while fiendish figures appear darkly through the smoke, and other angels approach from the heavens. There is no exuberance of the Renaissance here, but rather a tragic brooding on wrongs that cannot be undone. Courtesy of the Fogg Art Museum, Harvard University.

vance the Peace of God by draining off belligerent nobles to fight the
infidels, and to build up the leadership of Rome, just asserted by Gregory VII, through raising a universal cause of which the pope might be the
head. Crusades to the Holy Land, with varying success, and sometimes
departing woefully from their religious aims, went on intermittently
for two hundred years. It was the growth of Italian shipping in the
Mediterranean, the rise of more orderly feudal monarchies, the increasing sense of a Europe-wide common purpose, that made possible the
assembly and transport of considerable forces over a great distance. It is
sometimes said that the Crusades, by bringing contacts with the East,
stimulated the development of civilization in the West, but it seems
more likely that, as Europe's counterthrust against Islam, the Crusades
were the consequence of Europe's own growing strength. For a century
the Latin Christians occupied parts of Palestine and Syria. But in the

Medieval Christendom expanded geographically until about A.D. 1250.
Shaded regions are those Christianized shortly before and after A.D. 1000. *Arrows
indicate organized military-religious expeditions. Dates are rounded and very
rough.*

thirteenth century they had to withdraw, and the Moslems remained in possession.

Other crusades (for such they were) had more lasting results. A party of Normans won Sicily from the Arabs about 1100. Iberian Christians, descending from the mountains of northern Spain, carried on a *reconquista* of two centuries against the Moors. By 1250 they had staked out the Christian kingdoms of Portugal, Leon, Castile, Aragon, and Valencia, leaving the Moslems only Granada in the extreme south, which was conquered much later, in 1492. An Albigensian crusade in the thirteenth century put down the heretics, those born in the faith but erring from it. Against remaining European heathen, those born in ignorance of the faith, of whom a few were still found along the Baltic coast, crusading expeditions were also launched. The Teutonic Order, a military-religious society of knights founded originally to fight in the Holy Land, transferred its operations to the north. Christianity, and with it the civilization of the Latin West, was brought by the sword to primitive Prussia and the east Baltic regions.

About the year 1250 there developed a new threat of invasion from Asia. As the Huns had burst out of Asia in the fifth century, and the Magyars in the ninth, so now the Tartars appeared in the thirteenth century, to be followed in the fourteenth by the Ottoman Turks. The Tartars (or Mongols) overran and conquered Russia and defeated Polish and Hungarian armies in 1241. But powerful as they were, they penetrated no farther into the Latin West. About 1350, the Moslem Ottoman Turks filtered into the Balkan peninsula and subdued what would today be the whole region from Rumania to Greece. In 1453 Constantinople itself fell to the conquering Turks, ending the thousand-year-old Roman Empire in the East. With the Turks in possession of the Balkan peninsula and Constantinople, and the Tartars (who adopted Islam) controlling the Russian plain, the world of Eastern or Greek Orthodox Christianity now passed completely under the political domination of Moslem overlords.

The great struggle between Latin Christendom and Islam was not over. We shall see how the Turks long continued to press upon Central Europe.[6] But, on the whole, by the thirteenth century, Europe was capable of resistance. Always until then it had lain open, an outlying, backward, thinly populated protuberance from the Eurasian land-mass. It had lain open in the remote past to wandering Indo-Europeans, then to Roman imperial conquerors, to Germanic barbarians, to Huns, Magyars, and, in part, the Arabs. All these were assimilated. The blood of all flowed in European veins. In spirit all were assimilated by the Roman Church, the Latin language, the common institutions of feudalism, monarchy, a free town life, parliamentary assemblies, scholastic learning, which ran as an almost seamless web from England to Sicily and from Portugal to Poland.

· · ·

[6] See pp. 72, 187, and the index under Ottoman Empire.

By 1300 the "rise of Europe" was an accomplished fact. The third of the three segments into which the Greco-Roman world had divided, the one which in A.D. 700 had been the most barbarous, now some six hundred years later had a civilization of its own. It had geographically filled out the contours of what we know as Europe, and was able to stand against further penetration from outside. It is not possible to make sweeping comparisons of whole civilizations. In all respects except political unity, however, the Europe of 1300 probably surpassed the Roman empire. It compared well enough, for the first time, with the older civilizations of the East. It was not in its material culture, in the technical crafts, in the arts of building, in the distances traveled by its merchants, nor in the mere size or magnificence of its cities that Europe in 1300 surpassed the Arabic, Byzantine, Indian, or Chinese civilizations of that time. If it surpassed them at all, if it had any secret that the others did not know, its uniqueness lay in the realm of intangibles. Europe had a political system that blended freedom with more general order; a labor system in which no one was totally enslaved; a spiritual outlook producing a restless activity, because nothing that actually existed was ever believed to be perfect; an intellectual outlook not averse to the new, yet incorporating the old; a diversity of many nations which yet somehow were all the same. The Arabs inherited Greco-Roman civilization, and the Byzantines inherited Christianity as well. In Europe some third element was added in the Middle Ages, something that neither the Greco-Romans nor ancient Christianity had alone supplied, something that cannot be characterized in a few words nor even in many, and yet was decisive in the making of modern Europe.

CHAPTER II

The Revolution in the Christian Church, 1300-1560

I N THE light of world history, as we see it today, one of the most momentous experiences that can befall any civilization is for it to break loose from its religious base. Today we can observe this process at work everywhere: the Chinese reconsider the age-old teachings of Confucius, the Moslems enter into wider activities than those known to the Koran, the peoples of India attempt to found a society in which neither historic Hindu practices, nor the historic split between Hindu and Moslem, shall form the dominant pattern. It is not, in most cases, that peoples reject their ancestral religion. On the contrary, they often reaffirm it; but they try also to modernize it, to adapt it, to make room for new and non-religious interests, to bring it about that religion, instead of being the womb or matrix from which all else comes, shall be one interest among many.

Latin Christendom was the first modern society to embark on the momentous, troublesome, and long drawn out process of "secularization." In 1300 Europe was still primarily a religious community. The clergy were the prestige-enjoying class. All else was somehow oriented to or pervaded by religious belief. Three centuries later religion was one interest among many. The church itself was divided. The Christian faith still stood; indeed it was purified and reaffirmed both by those who became Protestant and by those who remained Catholic. But other interests made equal claims upon men's attention. Government, law, philosophy, science, the arts, material and economic activities were pursued without regard to Christian values. Power, order, beauty, wealth, knowledge, control of nature were all accepted as desirable in themselves.

It is this process of secularization that gives unity to the intricate history set forth in the present chapter.

5. The Decline of the Church

At the close of the thirteenth century the church of the High Middle Ages, centralized in the papacy, stood at its zenith. But the church (as good Catholics always remind us) was staffed by mortal men who were no different from others. The church faced the danger that besets every successful institution—a form of government, an army or navy, a business corporation, a labor union, a university, to choose modern examples—the danger of believing that the institution exists for the benefit of those who conduct its affairs. The papacy, being at the top, was the most liable to this danger. The papacy became "corrupt," set in its ways, absorbed by the possession of wealth and authority, afflicted by a self-perpetuating bureaucracy, out of touch with public opinion, more concerned with maintaining papal grandeur than with spiritual religion, unable to reform itself, and unwilling to let anyone else reform it. At the same time, forces quite outside the papacy or the church, forces which had been growing up for generations before 1300, became too strong after 1300 to be held in the old containers, asserted themselves with ever more insistence, and clashed with the official clergy of the international church. Such forces, especially, were the new national monarchies and the commercial classes in the towns.

THE PAPACY DIVIDED

The decline of the papacy can be readily dated, from the time when Pope Boniface VIII ran into trouble with the kings of England and of

France. These two kings, needing money for war, undertook to tax the clergy in their respective kingdoms, in both of which the clergy were substantial owners of land. Boniface prohibited the taxation of clergy by the civil ruler. In the ensuing altercation, in 1302, he issued the famous bull *Unam Sanctam*,[1] the most extreme of all assertions of papal supremacy, declaring that outside the Roman church there was no salvation, and that "every human creature" was "subject to the Roman pontiff." The French king, Philip the Fair, retorted by sending soldiers to arrest Boniface, who soon died. French influence in the college of cardinals brought about the election of a pope who was subservient to Philip, and who took up his residence, with his court and officials, at Avignon on the lower Rhone river, on the then borders of France. Thus began the "Babylonian Captivity" of the church. The rest of Europe regarded the popes at Avignon throughout the century as tools of France. The prestige of the papacy as a universal institution was badly dimmed.

Attempts to correct the situation made matters worse. In 1378 the college of cardinals, torn by French and anti-French factions within it, elected two popes. Both were equally legitimate, being chosen by the cardinals, but one lived at Rome, one at Avignon, and neither would resign. The French and their supporters recognized the Avignon pope, England and most of Germany, the Roman. For forty years both lines were perpetuated. There were now two papacies, estranged by the Great Schism of the West, and it seemed as if the schism might become permanent, as the earlier schism between Rome and Constantinople had proved to be. All agreed that the situation was scandalous and must be ended, but no one in influential position would make the sacrifice necessary to put it to an end.

Never had the papacy been so externally magnificent as in the days of the Captivity and the Schism. The papal court at Avignon surpassed the courts of kings in splendor. The papal officialdom grew in numbers, ignoring the deeper problems while busily transacting each day's business. Papal revenues mounted, and new papal taxes were devised, for example the "annates," by which every bishop or abbot in Christendom had to transmit to Rome most of the first year's income of his office. In the continuing movement of funds from all over Europe to the papal court, from the thirteenth century on, a new class of international bankers rose and prospered.

But the papacy, never so sumptuous, had never since the tenth century rested on such shaky foundations. People pay willingly for institutions in which they believe, and admire magnificence in leaders whom they respect. But before 1378, with the pope submissive to France, and after 1378, with two popes and two papacies to support, there was growing com-

---

[1] Bulls are known by their first one or two Latin words, which in this case mean "one holy (Catholic Church)"; a "bull," while the most solemn form of papal edict, does not as such embody a dogma, and it is not Catholic practice today to affirm this policy of Boniface VIII.

plaint at the extravagance and worldliness of papal rule. The most pious Christians were the most shocked. To them the behavior of the cardinals was disgraceful. Earnest souls were worried in conscience. To obtain God's grace was to them of all things the most vital, but with two churches under two popes, each claiming to hold the keys of Peter, how could anyone be certain that his church gave him true salvation? In a society that was still primarily a religious community, this sense of religious insecurity was a source of unutterable uneasiness and dread.

UNSETTLED SOCIAL CONDITIONS AFTER 1300

Social conditions in the fourteenth century, and on into the fifteenth, were most unsettled. Journeymen in the gilds were turning into life-long wage-workers without a future. The spread of the money economy in the countryside led to peasant restlessness and rebellion, as in Wat Tyler's rebellion in England in 1381. Such rebellions were forcibly suppressed by the upper classes, but the disturbing question ran through men's minds:

> *When Adam delved, and Eve span,*
> *Who was then the gentleman?*

After 1300 for a long time the royal governments developed their organization very slowly. More power fell into the hands of parliaments, diets, and estates, so that the old feudal classes enjoyed a resurgence, and many countries fell into a chronic anarchy of "barons' wars." England and France became locked in the Hundred Years' War (1337–1453), in which bands of destructive English soldiery roamed back and forth across a France divided within itself. Germany and Central Europe also were rocked by civil turmoil. To all this were added the horrors of plague. The Black Death, or bubonic plague, swept over Europe from east to west, beginning in 1347. In some places half or more of the population, suddenly and within a few months, died in the squalor and misery of the pesthouse. The plague kept recurring, striking blindly and inexorably, for fifty years.

The old moorings were weakened, the old certainties lost, the wrath of God seemed to be raining upon mankind, and no one had the slightest notion of how the world was going to turn out. Symptoms of mass neurosis appeared. Some people sought refuge in a hectic merriment or brief sensual self-indulgence. Others became preoccupied with grisly subjects. Some frantically performed the Dance of Death in the cemeteries, others furtively celebrated the Black Mass, parodying religion in a mad desire to appease the devil. The Order of Flagellants grew up; its members went through the streets, two by two, beating each other with chains and whips. It was at this time that the great witchcraft delusion, which was to reach its height in the fifteenth and sixteenth centuries, first became important. In a century like the thirteenth, people had believed in witches, but had not worried about them because they felt secure in the protection of God's church. Now witches were feared, hunted out, prosecuted, and disposed of by burning alive, a form of punishment which also now became more common than in former times. Nor was the belief entirely unfounded, for there was in fact a social phenomenon of diabolism. Some people actually thought they were in a compact with the devil, and, if they did not thereby become witches, they were nevertheless, in many cases, anti-social beings who meant no good to their neighbors.

It was widely agreed, in this afflicted society, that the true church must be restored in its purity. Led by men like the Italian Marsiglio of Padua, or the Englishmen Ockham and Wycliff, reformers declared that the church consisted in the whole body of the faithful, not merely or even primarily in the clergy. If the clergy, they said, were not performing their spiritual duties to the laity, then either a secular ruler or a general council representing the whole church might enforce reform upon the clergy, and even upon the pope. John Wycliff went even further. He taught, about 1380, that no visible church was needful for salvation, that ordinary persons might obtain divine grace by reading the Bible, without the ministrations of any clergy whatsoever. This doctrine, which, if pursued far enough, would explode any church as an authoritative institution, was promptly branded as heresy. Wycliff nevertheless won many adherents. In England itself they were mostly "poor men," called Lollards, who sought escape from all forms of established authority. In Bohemia, John Huss took up Wycliff's ideas, and here the doctrine became a national movement. The Hussites were both a religious party and at the same time a Slavic or Czech party protesting against the supremacy of the Germans who lived in Bohemia. The Hussite wars ravaged central Europe for decades in the early part of the fifteenth century.

THE CONCILIAR MOVEMENT AND ITS FAILURE

Settled, influential, educated, and established persons did not turn to heresy, nor yet to witchcraft or flagellation. Their answer to the needs of the day was the conciliar movement. Professors at the universities, advisers to kings, enlightened bishops, thoughtful burghers, about 1400, believed the pope (or rather, popes) to be incapable of reforming existing abuses. They demanded a great Europe-wide council of the entire church at which all the gravest matters that were troubling Christendom might be discussed and decided. They would introduce into the church, that is to say, the type of parliamentary institutions which at this time were functioning in the civil affairs of almost all countries.

In 1409 such a church council met at Pisa. All parts of the Latin West were represented. The council declared both reigning popes deposed, and obtained the due election of another, but since the first two refused to resign there were now three. In 1414 an even greater and more fully attended council met at Constance. Its aims were three: to end the now threefold schism, to extirpate heresy, and to reform the church "in head and members," or from top to bottom. Not much was accomplished in reform. To discourage heresy, John Huss was interrogated, condemned, and burned at the stake. The schism was ended. All three popes were at last persuaded or compelled to withdraw, and another, Martin V, was elected. The unity of the church, under the papacy, was at last restored.

The majority at the Council of Constance wished to make general councils part of the permanent apparatus of the church for all time in the future. They regarded the pope as, so to speak, a constitutional monarch, and the general body of the faithful as self-governing in religious matters. In its decree *Sacrosancta*, the Council solemnly declared that a council was superior to a pope, and, in the decree *Frequens*, that councils should be assembled every ten years in the future.

Martin V, however, no sooner elected pope, reaffirmed the prerogatives of the papal office. He dissolved the Council of Constance, and repudiated its decrees. The next thirty years saw a continuing tug of war between successive popes and successive councils. On the one hand, with the pope, stood the papal court and central bureaucracy, supported by the monastic orders, and by scattered individuals for various reasons. On the other, with the councils, stood most Catholic bishops from all countries (outside of Italy), together with representatives of the Emperor and the kings. Popes argued that theirs was the true apostolic authority derived from Peter, and that in any case to entrust power to the territorial bishops, exposed as they were to local pressure from kings and princes, would endanger the unity and independence of the church. Councils argued that the bishop of Rome was fundamentally only a bishop like any other; that the authority of Christ was vested in the whole church as a collective body, over which the pope was no more than a symbolic or merely administrative head.

In this acrimonious battle for jurisdiction few reforms could be adopted, and fewer still enforced. Increasingly the life of the church was corrupted by money. No one believed in bribery; but everyone knew that many high churchmen (like many high civil officials of the day) could be bribed. To buy or sell a church office was a crime in the canon law, known as "simony"; but it was a crime which in the fifteenth century could not be suppressed. For churchmen to live with mistresses was considered understandable, if unseemly; the standards of laymen in such matters were not high; but for a bishop or other ecclesiastic to give lucrative church positions to his own children (or other relatives) was the abuse known as nepotism, and it, too, could not be eradicated. To sell divine grace for money, all agreed, was not only wrong but impossible. In 1300 Boniface VIII had devised a new kind of sacred writ called an "indulgence." A person, if properly confessed, absolved, and truly repentant, might, by obtaining an indulgence, be spared certain of the temporal punishments of purgatory. One obtained such an indulgence, almost always, in turn for a donation of money. Indulgences were never "sold," but many unenlightened persons thought they were; and a protest arose all over Europe, among both laity and clergy, that the abuse of indulgences was discrediting the sacraments and undermining common morals. But to raise money in this way was fatally easy, and this practice, too, could not be stopped.

The councils insisted that such conditions be reformed, to which popes replied, while agreeing in principle, that the papal authority must be upheld first. Gradually the popes prevailed. The conciliar movement, for Christendom as a whole, was greatly weakened when the powerful French element secured its aims by a local national arrangement. In the Pragmatic Sanction of Bourges, in 1438, the Gallican (or French) church affirmed the supremacy of councils over popes, declared its administrative independence from the Holy See, suppressed the payment of annates to Rome, and forbade papal intervention in the appointment of French prelates. The papacy thus lost influence in France, but the conciliarists themselves were divided. In 1449, with the dissolution of the Council of Basel, the conciliar movement came to an end. In 1450 a great Jubilee was held to celebrate the papal triumph.

The papacy, its prestige and freedom of action thus secured, now passed into the hands of a series of cultivated gentlemen, men of the world, men of "modern" outlook in tune with their times—the famous popes of the Renaissance. Some, like Nicholas V (1447–55) or Pius II (1458–64) were accomplished scholars and connoisseurs of books. Some were like Innocent VIII (1484–92), a pleasant man who was the first pope to dine in public with ladies. Alexander VI (1492–1503) exploited his office in the vain attempt to gratify his avaricious relatives who swarmed from Spain. He schemed also to make his son Caesar Borgia the ruler of all Italy. Julius II (1503–13) was a capable general, and Leo X (1513–21) a superb patron of the arts. But we must now describe the Italian Renaissance, in which worthies of this type were elevated to the see of Peter and the vicariate of Christ.

6. The Renaissance in Italy

The Renaissance first received its name, which means a "rebirth," from those who thought of the Middle Ages as a dark and trance-like period from which the human spirit had to be awakened. It was called a rebirth in the belief that men in the fifteenth century, after a long interruption, took up and resumed the civilization of the Greco-Romans. It was at the same time, in the Renaissance itself, that the Middle Ages began to be thought of as in the "middle." Hence the Renaissance is often regarded as the beginning of "modern" times. Nowadays the Middle Ages are not regarded as dark, at least after the year 1000 or 1100, nor is it clear that any curtain ever suddenly went up on "modern" times. One useful distinction can be made. The basic institutions, the great framework of collective action by which Europe continued to live far into the modern centuries, all originated in the Middle Ages. But the Renaissance marked a new era in thought and feeling, by which Europe and its institutions were in the long run to be transformed. It was in the Italy of the Quattrocento (as Italians call the fifteenth century) that an almost purely secular attitude first appeared. Nor was any institution more secular, as has been intimated, than the Renaissance church itself.

THE ITALIAN CITIES AND THE NEW CONCEPTION OF MAN

The towns of Italy, so long as trade converged in the Mediterranean, were the biggest and most bustling of all the towns that rose in Europe in the Middle Ages. The crafts of Italy included many refined trades such as those of the goldsmith or stone-carver, which were so zealously pursued that artisanship turned into art, and a delight in the beautiful became common among all classes. Merchants made fortunes in commerce; they lent their money to popes or princes, and so made further fortunes as bankers. They bought the wares of the craftsmen-artists. They rejoiced, not so much in money or the making of money, as in the beautiful things and psychological satisfactions that money could buy; and if they forgot the things which money could not buy, this is only to say again that their outlook was "secular." Politically, since no general government grew up in Italy, and the towns became independent city-states, the merchant oligarchies had an unhampered stage on which to display other talents—talents for getting and holding office, for charming the populace, for works of public munificence, for making alliances, hiring armies, outwitting rivals, and conducting the affairs of state. In short, Italy offered an environment in which many facets of human personality could be richly developed.

For illustration, one may cite the Medici family. The founder of its fortunes was Giovanni (d. 1429), a merchant and banker of Florence. His son, Cosimo de' Medici (1389–1464), allying himself with the popular element against the ruling families of the republic, soon became unofficial ruler himself. Cosimo's grandson, Lorenzo the Magnificent (1449–92), also used his great wealth to govern, but is chiefly remembered as a poet, connoisseur, and lavish benefactor of art and learning. After Lorenzo's death Tuscany became a grand duchy, of which the Medici were hereditary grand dukes until

---

Portrait of a Condottiere

BY GIOVANNI BELLINI (ITALIAN, 1430–1516)

An emphatic portrayal of Renaissance individualism. Note the artist's ability to present a concrete human being, one who is not merely an abstract type. For the condottieri see p. 55. The name of this particular condottiere is not known. But the hard expression and set features, the firm lines about the mouth and chin, the bull neck and the unflinching gaze, suggest an aggressive character of considerable virtù. The face is thoughtful and intelligent but devoid of spirituality. The man is clearly in the habit of depending on himself alone. The artist has heightened the sense of his subject's independence and self-sufficiency by making him stand out from a dark and entirely vacant background. Courtesy of the National Gallery, Washington, D.C. (Kress Collection).

the family died out in 1735. Thus established, they furnished numerous cardinals and two popes to the church, and two Medici women became queens of France.

What arose in Italy, in these surroundings, was no less than a new conception of man himself. The world was so exciting that a next world need not be thought of. It seemed very doubtful whether a quiet, cloistered, or celibate life was on a higher plane than an active, gregarious, or even promiscuous life. It was hard to believe that clergy were any better than laity, or that life led to a stern divine judgment in the end. That man's will and intelligence might mislead him seemed a gloomy doctrine. That man was a frail creature, in need of God's grace and salvation, though perhaps said with the lips, was not felt in the heart. Instead, what captivated the Italians of the Renaissance was a sense of man's tremendous powers, the rich potentialities of human nature, the free and unfettered creative play of human talent in every field.

Nor was it merely "man" in general that so fascinated them; it was the great individual person. In the Middle Ages the individual soul had received much attention, and, as in all ages, many men had shown strong individual character; but it was supposed that all persons fitted somehow into a hierarchy, each having his place in some estate or corporate body, united with others in some kind of communion, of which the highest was the church. Renaissance individualism gloried in emancipation. The great individual stood out from others. He shook off all restraints. He was free in mind and spirit. He shaped his own destiny. He had *virtù*. *Virtù* had little to do with "virtue." It was the quality of being a man (*vir*, "man") in the sense of successfully demonstrating human powers. A man of *virtù*, in the arts, in war or statecraft, was a man who knew what he was doing, who, from resources within himself, made the best use of his opportunities, hewing his way through the world, and excelling in all he did.

The growing preoccupation with things human can be traced in the sculpture, the architecture, and the music of the Renaissance but perhaps most clearly in the Renaissance painters, even though painting remained in its choice of subjects the most religious of the arts. With the invention of painting in oils, and the steady demand of merchants and ecclesiastics for pictures, painting made rapid progress. Working out the mathematics of

---

Erasmus of Rotterdam

BY HANS HOLBEIN, THE YOUNGER (GERMAN, 1497–1543)

The classic portrayal of humanism at its best. The portrait was painted in 1523, when Eramus was fifty-six, and the Lutheran Reformation and Peasant Rebellion were raging in Germany. Holbein has conveyed the mood of tight-lipped calm, or of saddened humanity, felt by a life-long reforming writer who has lived to see violent revolution. The face, finely delineated, and high-lighted against the deeper tones of the cap and cloak, is concentrated upon Erasmus' only weapon, the pen. The picture captures the life of thought; it is a picture of the human mind, as Bellini's Condottiere *is a picture of the will. Courtesy of the Louvre.*

perspective, painters placed their human figures against more realistic backgrounds, thus locating them in a specific world of time and space. Making a close study of anatomy, they drew people in living attitudes. Faces took on more expression; individual personality was depicted. Differences among men were shown, not merely abstract characteristics that all men or certain kinds of men, such as kings or saints, had in common. Painting became less symbolic, less an intimation of general truths, more a portrayal of concrete realities as they met the eye. In the accompanying portrait by Bellini of a *condottiere* the reader can see for himself, though who the man was is not known, how a strong, real, and vivid personality looks out from the canvas. Similarly, the great religious paintings were peopled by human beings. In Leonardo da Vinci's *Last Supper* Christ and his disciples are seen as a group of men each with his own characteristics, Raphael's Madonnas seem to be young Italian women, and in the mighty figures of Michelangelo the attributes of humanity invade heaven itself.[2]

HUMANISM AND THE CULT OF ANTIQUITY

The literary movement in Renaissance Italy is called "humanism," because the principal writers made a veritable cult of humanity and human powers. They found humanity at its best among the ancients. The leading authors of antiquity had been known and read in the Middle Ages but mainly in order to reconcile them with Christian theology as the scholastic philosophers had done.[3] In the Renaissance the ancient writers were approached in a new spirit, and with tremors of excitement. The excitement grew, when, about 1400, it became common for the first time for Italians to learn Greek. Why did the works of Plato and Homer, Horace and Cicero, now produce such thrills?

It was in part because the Italian humanists, as a group, were among the first European writers who were not members of the clergy. They were mostly laymen, and in the Greeks and Romans they saw laymen, too. The humanists, on the whole, were interested only in "literary" writings. To them the Middle Ages were a blur, because there was no great body of medieval literary writing, at least for any date before 1300. Antiquity, on the other hand, through the pages of Livy or Cicero, seemed to them to be wonderfully clear-cut and distinct. Here was a world of light, a world neither supernatural nor mysterious, untroubled by church or clergy or petty monkish quarrels, a world in which men acted, like Julius Caesar, from rational and understandable motives, or, like Cicero, wrote in a reasonable and human way on philosophical topics. It was a world in which the secular spirit felt at ease. The Greeks and Romans, moreover, unquestionably had style—a sense of form, a taste for the elegant and the epigrammatic. Here too, the Italian humanists

[2] On Leonardo see also p. 261.
[3] See pp. 37–8.

sensed a kindred spirit. A rage spread throughout Italy to hunt for unknown manuscripts of Greek and Roman authors. Many were found—they had, of course, been copied and stored away by monkish toilers of the Middle Ages.

The humanists not only steeped themselves in antiquity. They even tried to dress, talk, and comport themselves like the noble Romans. They disdained to write in Italian, as earlier writers like Dante and Boccaccio had done. They scoffed at the current Latin used in the church and the universities, a Latin which had changed with the times and adopted new words for things unknown to the Romans. Medieval Latin had departed from classical Latin (and anticipated the modern languages) in other significant ways, for medieval Latin poems and hymns used a rhythm that modern ears could hear, and they also rimed. But all medieval Latin was dismissed by the humanists as barbarous and corrupted. It was only with the vocabulary and style of a Cicero or a Vergil that the humanists would consent to write. We hear of one churchman who made a habit of washing his mouth after saying mass, because he considered the Latin of the mass to be so debased. In their effort to write exactly like ancients, the humanists naturally made it impossible for themselves to treat most contemporary questions. They sacrificed matter to manner, and content to verbal effects. They astonished each other with feats of stylistic *virtù*, but they seemed never to learn what seems so obvious: that the Greeks and Romans had not been simply mere imitators, and that the classic virtues have never included imitation, however ingenious.

Exceptions there were, indeed; for among all these eager authors there were some who had something to say. One was Lorenzo Valla, a scholar who was a founder of the modern science of textual criticism. He showed conclusively, from the language used in the document, that the Donation of Constantine, on which the papacy then based its temporal claims, could not have been written in Constantine's time and so was a forgery.[4] Another was Pico della Mirandola, who, with others at the Academy of Florence, took a serious interest in the study of Plato. Pico, however, revealed the weakness of the humanist movement, when, in 1486, at the age of twenty-three, he offered to expatiate publicly on all human knowledge in nine hundred theses. It was in ancient books—those of "the Chaldaic, Arabic, Hebrew, Grecian, Egyptian, and Latin sages," as Pico put it—that the humanists thought truth was to be found. Nor was it supposed that any very laborious effort was needed to master them.

After 1500, when Italian writers began again to write in Italian and so to communicate with the public, works of more significance were produced. Ariosto in his *Orlando Furioso*, and Tasso in his *Jerusalem Delivered*, wrote epics that were long widely read. Italian taste and the Italian love of good workmanship exerted a strong influence upon northern Europe for two hundred years. Of Machiavelli, the most significant of Italian Renaissance writers for our purposes, more will be said very shortly.

The Renaissance was a movement of the elite. It was not exactly aris-

---

[4] See p. 19.

tocratic, because aristocracy implies a concern with birth and background to which Italians of the Renaissance were largely indifferent; but it was exclusive in spirit, affecting a small group of acutely self-conscious persons at the top of society, or those who by their *virtù* might reach the top. Renaissance individualism was the individualism of the dazzling few. The pomposities of the humanists were mocked by the populace in their own day. The humanists, by insisting on an artificial elaborateness, made writing a new kind of mystery of which they alone were the masters. When printing, invented in Germany about 1450, began to spread into Italy the Italian humanists received it with indignation. Printed books seemed a cheap substitute for their beloved manuscripts, nor did they wish any enlargement of the reading public to include persons without taste. Taste, style, manner, correctitude, *aplomb* were set above more substantial attainments.

The Renaissance invented the "gentleman." Books of etiquette began to appear, of which the most successful was Castiglione's *Book of the Courtier.* Hitherto Europeans had been like big children in their manners: they spat, belched, hiccuped, and blew their noses without inhibition, snatched at food with their fingers, bawled at each other when aroused, or sulked when their feelings were offended. Castiglione issued a new code of refinement. The "courtier," according to Castiglione, should be a man of good birth but is chiefly the product of training. His education in youth, and his efforts in mature years, should be directed toward mixing agreeably in the company of his equals. His clothes should be neat, his movements graceful, his approach to other people perfectly poised. He must converse with facility, be proficient in sports and arms, and know how to dance and appreciate music. He should know Latin and Greek. With literary and other subjects he should show a certain familiarity, but never become too engrossed. For the well-bred man speaks with "a certain carelessness, to hide his art, and show that what he says or does comes from him without effort or deliberation." Pedantry and heaviness must yield to a certain air of effortless superiority, so that even if the "courtier" knows or does something seriously, he must treat it lightly as one of many accomplishments. At its best, the code taught a certain considerateness for the feelings of others. Castiglione's book was translated into numerous languages, and a hundred editions were printed before 1600. Its ideal was inculcated for centuries by private tutors and in the schools. The conception of the gentleman helped to tame and civilize Europe's upper classes, and in the end all classes so far as they imitated their social betters. But politeness, though of real historical importance as a means of smoothing human relationships, was hardly a sufficient answer to the problems affecting Europe.

POLITICS AND THE ITALIAN RENAISSANCE

The Italian Renaissance produced no institution or great idea by which men living in society could be held together. Indeed, the greatest of

Europe's institutions, the Roman church, in which Europeans had lived for centuries, and without which they did not see how they could live at all, fell into sheer neglect under the Renaissance popes. For decades after breaking the conciliar movement the triumphant papacy made no attempts at reform. Nor did Italy develop any effectual political institutions. The fat merchants and aesthetic enthusiasts who controlled the city-states could not fight for themselves, nor arouse their citizens to fight for them. They therefore hired professional fighting men, *condottieri*, private leaders of armed bands, who contracted with the various city-states to carry on warfare, and often raised their price or changed sides during hostilities. Italian politics became a tangled web, a labyrinth of subterfuge and conspiracy, a platform on which great individuals might exhibit their *virtù*. "Italian cunning" became a byword throughout Europe. Power in Italy made no pretense to legitimacy, to represent any moral idea, or to further any social good. Dictators rose and fell. The old republican spirit evaporated; the Medici became dukes in Florence, the Sforza in Milan, while in Venice and Genoa, where the republics were kept, narrow oligarchies held the rule. These states, along with the States of the Church, jockeyed about like pugilists in a ring, held within an intricate, shifting, and purely local balance of power.

Italy was the despair of its patriots, or of such few as remained. One of these was Niccolò Machiavelli, who, in *The Prince* (1513), wrote the one really lasting work of the Italian Renaissance. He wrote in Italian, but he resembled the other humanists in his dislike of the church and his yearning to live imaginatively in the world of the ancients. He dreamed of the day when the citizens of his native Florence, or indeed of all Italy, should behave like early Romans—show virility in their politics, fight in citizen armies for patriotic causes, and uphold their dignity before Europe. It was outside Italy, in Kings Ferdinand of Aragon, Louis XI of France, Henry VII of England, that Machiavelli was obliged to find his heroes. He admired them because they were successful builders of states. In *The Prince* he produced a handbook of statecraft which he hoped Italy might find useful. He produced also the first purely secular treatise on politics.

Medieval writings on politics, those of Thomas Aquinas or Marsiglio of Padua, for example, had always talked of God's will for the government of men, with such accompanying matters as justice and right, or divine and natural law. All this Machiavelli put aside. He "emancipated" politics from theology and moral philosophy. He undertook to describe simply what rulers actually did, and thus anticipated what was later called the scientific spirit, in which questions of good and bad are ignored, and the observer attempts to discover only what really happens. What really happens, said Machiavelli, is that effective rulers and governments act only in their own political interest. They keep faith or break it, observe treaties or repudiate them, are merciful or ruthless, forthright or sly, peaceable or aggressive, according as they estimate their own political needs. Machiavelli was prepared to admit that such behavior was bad; he only insisted that it was in this way, however regrettably, that successful rulers behaved. He was thought unduly cynical even in an age not characterized by political delicacy. He had nevertheless diagnosed the new era with considerable insight. It was an age when politics was in fact becoming more secular, breaking off from religion, with the building up of states and of state-authority emerging as a goal requiring no other justification.

But the most successful states of the time, as Machiavelli saw, were not in Italy. They were what history knows as the New Monarchies, and they owed their strength to something more than princely craft, for they enjoyed a measure of spontaneous loyalty from their own peoples. Italy was politically helpless. Politics in Italy was not about anything vital; it was an affair of *virtù*; and the people of Italy lost interest in politics, as they did in war, becoming "effeminate" in the eyes of outsiders.

So Italy, the sunny land of balmy Mediterranean skies, rich in the busy life of its cities, its moneyed wealth, its gorgeous works of art, lay helplessly open to the depredations of less easy-going peoples, from Spain and the north, who possessed institutions in which men could act together in large numbers. In a new age of rising national monarchies the city-states of Italy could not compete. In 1494 a French army crossed the Alps. Italy became a bone of contention between France and Spain. In 1527 a horde of undisciplined Spanish and German mercenaries, joined by foot-loose Italians, fell upon Rome itself. Never, not even from the Goths of the fifth century, had Rome experienced anything so horrible and degrading. The city was sacked, thousands were killed, soldiers milled about for a week in an orgy of rape and loot, the pope was imprisoned, and cardinals were mockingly paraded through the streets facing backward on the backs of mules. By this time religious passions were aroused; we are encroaching on the story of the Reformation.

After the sack of Rome the Renaissance faded away. Politically, for over three hundred years, Italy remained divided, the passive object of the ambitions of outside powers.

7. The Renaissance outside Italy

Outside Italy people were much less conscious of any sudden break with the Middle Ages. Developments north of the Alps, and in Spain, were more of an outgrowth of what had gone before. There was indeed a Renaissance in the Italian sense, shown in a great outburst of painting and in a movement of literary humanism emphasizing a neoclassical Latin style. But the northern Renaissance was more a blend of old and new. Above all, it was more religious.

RELIGIOUS SCHOLARSHIP AND SCIENCE

It is customary to distinguish between the "pagan" humanism of Italy and the Christian humanism of the north. In the north, Christian humanists studied the Hebrew and Greek texts of the Bible and read the Church Fathers, both Latin and Greek, in order to deepen their understanding of Christianity and to restore its moral vitality. Among lesser people, too, without pretense to humanistic learning, religion remained a force. Medieval intellectual interests persisted. This is apparent from the continuing foundation of universities. The humanists generally regarded universities as centers of a pedantic, monkish, and "scholastic" learning. Concentrating upon theology, or upon medicine and law, the universities gave little encouragement to experimental science and still less to purely literary studies. In Italy in the fifteenth century no new universities were established. But in Spain, in France, in Scotland, in Scandinavia, and above all in Germany, new universities sprouted up. Between 1386 and 1506 no less than fourteen universities were established in Germany. At one of the newest, Wittenberg, founded in 1502, Martin Luther was to launch the Protestant Reformation.

Germany at this time, on the eve of the great religious upheaval, and before the shift of the commercial artery from central Europe to the Atlantic seaboard, was a main center of European life. Politically, the German-speaking world was an ill-defined and ill-organized region, composed of many diverse parts, from which the Netherlands and Switzerland were not yet differentiated. Parts of it were infested by robber knights, picturesque in legend, but unpleasant for those who had to live with them in reality. Economically, nevertheless, western and southern Germany enjoyed a lead; the towns traded busily, and German banking families, like the famous Fugger, controlled more capital than any others in Europe. Technical inventiveness was alive; mining was developing; and it was in the Rhineland, at Mainz, that Gutenberg, about 1450, produced the first books printed with movable type. In painting, the western fringe of the Germanic world produced the Flemish masters, and south Germany gave birth to Dürer and the Holbeins.

Intellectually, Germany shared in the Latin culture of Europe, a fact often obscured by the Latinizing of German names. Regiomontanus (the Latin name of Johann Müller of Königsberg) laid the foundations during his short lifetime (1436–76) for a mathematical conception of the universe. He was probably the most influential scientific worker of the fifteenth century, especially since Leonardo da Vinci's scientific labors remained unknown. Nicholas of Cusa (1401?–64) was a churchman whose mystical philosophy entered into the later development of mathematics and science. From such a background of mathematical interests came Copernicus (Nikolaus Koppernigk, 1473–1543), who believed that the earth moved about the sun; he was a Pole, but was born and spent most of his life in the mixed German-Polish region of East Prussia.[5] Fortified by the same mathematical interests, Europe's best known cartographers were also Germans, such as Behaim and Schöner, whose world maps the reader may see on p. 275. Paracelsus (Latin for Hohenheim) undertook to revolutionize medicine at the University of Basel. His wild prophecies made him a mixture of scientist and charlatan; but, in truth,

〰〰〰〰〰〰〰〰〰

[5] On Copernicus, and the rise of modern science in general, see below, Chapter VII.

science was not yet clearly distinguished from the occult, with which it shared the idea of control over natural forces. A similar figure, remembered in literature and the arts, was the celebrated Dr. Faustus. In real life Faust, or Faustus, was perhaps a learned German of the first part of the sixteenth century. He was rumored to have sold his soul to the devil in return for knowledge and power. The Faust story was dramatized in England as early as 1593 by Christopher Marlowe, and, much later, by Goethe in poetry and by Gounod in the opera. In the legend of Faust later generations were to see a symbol of the inordinate striving of modern man.

The idea of man's powers to understand and control physical nature, as developed most especially north of the Alps, corresponded in many ways to the more purely Italian and humanistic idea of the infinite richness of human personality. Together, they constituted the new Renaissance spirit, for both emphasized the emancipation of humanity's limitless potentialities. The two ideas constantly interacted; in fact, most of the scientific workers just mentioned—Regiomontanus, Nicholas of Cusa, Copernicus—spent many years in Italy, receiving the stimulus of Italian thought.

MYSTICISM AND LAY RELIGION

In the north a genuine religious impulse, in addition to religious humanistic scholarship, also remained alive. Where in Italy the religious sense, if not extinct, seemed to pass into the aesthetic, into a joyous and public cult in which God was glorified by works of art, in the north it took on a more mystical or a more soberly moral tone. Germany in the fourteenth century produced a series of mystics. The mystic tendencies of Nicholas of Cusa have been mentioned. More typical mystics were Meister Eckhart (d. 1327) and Thomas à Kempis (d. 1471), author of the *Imitation of Christ*. The essence of mysticism lay in the belief, or experience, that the individual soul could in perfect solitude commune directly with God. The mystic had no need of reason, nor of words, nor of joining with other people in open worship, nor even of the sacraments administered by the priests—nor even of the church. The mystics did not rebel against the church; they accepted its pattern of salvation; but at bottom they offered, to those who could follow, a deeper religion in which the church as a social institution had no place. All social institutions, in fact, were transcended in mysticism by the individual soul; and on this doctrine, both profound and socially dangerous, Martin Luther was later to draw.

For the church, it was significant also that religion was felt deeply outside the clergy. Persons stirred by religion, who in the Middle Ages would have taken holy orders, now frequently remained laymen. In the past the church had often needed reform. But in the past, in the bad times of the tenth century, for example, the church had found reformers within itself. The church had thus been repeatedly reformed and renewed without revolution. Now, in the fifteenth and early sixteenth centuries an ominous line seemed to be increasingly drawn: between the clergy as an established interest, inert and set in its ways, merely living, and living well, off the church; and groups of people outside the clergy—religious laymen, religiously inclined humanists and writers, impatient and headstrong rulers—who were more influential than ever before, and more critical of ecclesiastical abuses.

Lay religion was especially active in the Netherlands. A lay preacher, Gerard Groot, attracted followers by his sermons on spiritual regeneration. About 1400 these men began to live together, sharing their goods, and electing a rector. They called themsleves Brothers of the Common Life. Soon they had branch houses in various parts of the Rhineland and Germany. It was in much this same way, in medieval times, that new religious orders like the Franciscans or Dominicans had originated, but such earlier groups had applied for recognition by the pope and had organized themselves within the old monastic framework. The Brothers of the Common Life asked for no ecclesiastical recognition. They took no binding religious vows. They remained laymen. They opened many schools, in which they taught, besides reading and writing and such elementary subjects, a Christian ideal of character and conduct. They paid little attention to systematic doctrine, but emphasized instead such personal qualities as humility, tolerance, reverence, love of one's neighbor, and conscientiousness in the performance of duty. This Modern Devotion, as it was called, spread very widely in the Netherlands. By the close of the fifteenth century thousands of laymen throughout the Rhine valley and Germany had received their schooling from the Brothers. The Brothers of the Common Life, while critical of worldliness in the clergy, never opposed the organized church. They simply found that it did not meet their religious needs.

ERASMUS OF ROTTERDAM

In this atmosphere grew up the greatest of all the northern humanists, and indeed the most notable figure of the entire humanist movement, Erasmus of Rotterdam (1466–1536). Like all the humanists, Erasmus chose to write in a "purified" and usually intricate Latin style. He regarded the Middle Ages as benighted, ridiculed the scholastic philosophers, and studied deeply the classical writers of antiquity. He had the strength and the limitations of the pure man of letters. To the hard questions of serious philosophy he was largely indifferent; he feared the unenlightened excitability of the common people, and he was almost wholly unpolitical in his outlook. He rarely thought in terms of worldly power or advantage, and made too little allowance for those who did. An exact contemporary to the most notorious of the worldly Renaissance popes, Erasmus was keenly aware of the need of a reform of the clergy. He put his faith in education, enlightened discussion, and gradual moral improvement. He led no burning crusade, and counseled against all violence or fanaticism. He prepared new Greek and Latin editions of the New Testament. Urging also the reading of the New Testament in the vernacular languages, he hoped that with a better understanding of Christ's teaching people might turn from their evil ways. In his *Praise of Folly* he satirized all worldly pretensions and ambitions, those of the clergy most emphatically. In his *Handbook of a Christian Knight* he showed how a man might take part in the affairs of the world while remaining a devout Christian. Mildness, reasonableness, tolerance, restraint, scholarly understanding, a love of peace, a critical and reforming zeal which, hating nobody, worked through trying to make men think, a subdued and controlled tone from which shouting or bad temper were always excluded—such were the Erasmian virtues.[6]

Erasmus achieved an international eminence such as no man of purely intellectual attainments has ever enjoyed. He corresponded with the great of Europe. He lectured at Cambridge, and edited books for a publisher at Basel. The king of Spain named him a councillor, the king of France called him to Paris, Pope Leo X assisted him when he was in trouble. Theologians found fault with Erasmus's ideas (in which, indeed, the supernatural had little importance), but among the chief practical men of the church, the popes and prelates, he had many admirers. Erasmus, it must be noted, attacked only the abuses in the church, the ignorance or sloth of the clergy, the moral or financial corruption of their lives. The essence and principle of the Roman Catholic Church he never called into question. Whether the Erasmian spirit, so widely diffused about 1520, would have sufficed to restore the church without the revolutionary impact of Protestantism is one of the many unanswerable questions of history.

8. The New Monarchies

Meanwhile, in Europe outside Italy, kings were actively building up the institutions of the modern state. It was these states, more than any other single thing, that were to determine the course of the religious revolution. Whether a country turned Protestant, or remained Catholic, or was divided into separate religious communities, was to depend very largely upon political considerations.

CENTRALIZATION UNDER THE NEW MONARCHIES

War, civil war, class war, feudal rebellion, and plain banditry afflicted a good deal of Europe in the middle of the fifteenth century. All this formless violence, which presented itself to contemporaries simply as a series of calamities, goes historically under many names: the Hundred Years' War between England and France (ended in 1453), the Hussite wars in Germany and Bohemia (ended 1436), Jack Cade's rebellion in England in 1450, the

---

[6] See the portrait by Hans Holbein facing p. 5.

Wars of the Roses in England (ended 1485), peasant uprisings or *jacqueries* in France, social restlessness in the cloth towns of Flanders. Central governments were weak or almost nonexistent. The parliamentary bodies, whose establishment at the close of the Middle Ages were noted in the last chapter, enjoyed great influence over the kings. Constitutionally, it was the "golden age" of medieval parliaments. In social reality, since the predominance of these assemblies meant the predominance of feudal nobles and of narrowly localistic towns, it was an age of insecurity and confusion. Even at best, under peaceable conditions, medieval institutions had been either localistic or universal—centered on the one hand in the manor, town, or province, and on the other in the Roman church and Latin culture of Western Christendom as a whole. To the medieval man the intermediate level, that of the nation, was the least real.

With the middle of the fifteenth century appeared a group of kings known as the New Monarchs, who attempted to put down violence, enforce domestic peace, and curb the power of the feudal nobles. The New Monarchs laid the foundations for national, or at least territorial, states. They were not altogether new, for in placing royal authority over feudal authority they resumed the interrupted labors of kings of the High Middle Ages, and they succeeded in laying a basis for national states only where medieval developments had already pointed in this direction, as in England and France and to a lesser degree in Spain.[7]

The New Monarchs offered the institution of monarchy as a guarantee of law and order. They aroused latent sentiments of loyalty to the reigning dynasty, which in most countries was now centuries old. They proclaimed that hereditary monarchy was the legitimate form of public power, which all should accept without turmoil or resistance. They especially enlisted the support of middle class people in the towns, who were tired of the private wars and marauding habits of the feudal nobles. The middle class was willing to pay taxes in return for peace. They were willing to let parliaments be dominated or even ignored by the king, for parliaments had proved to be too often strongholds of the noble class, or too often had merely accentuated class conflict. The king, receiving money in taxes, was able to organize armies with which to put down the nobles. The use of the pike and the long-bow, which enabled the foot soldier to stand against the horseman, was here of great potential value. The king, if only he could get his monarchy sufficiently organized, and his finances into reliable order, could hire great numbers of foot soldiers, who generally came from the endless ranks of plebeians, unlike the knightly horsemen. But to organize his monarchy, the king had to break down the mass of feudal, inherited, customary or "common" law in which the rights of the feudal classes were entrenched. For this purpose, the New Monarch made use of Roman law, which was now actively studied in the universities.[8] He called himself a "sovereign"—it was at this time that kings began to be addressed as "majesty." The king, said the experts in Roman

[7] See pp. 23–4, 29–32.
[8] See pp. 9–10.

law, incorporated the will and welfare of the people in his own person—and they would cite the principle *salus populi suprema lex,* "the welfare of the people is the highest law." The king, they added, could *make* law, enact it by his own authority, regardless of previous custom or even of historic liberties— and they would quote, *quod principi placuit legis habet vigorem,* or "what pleases the prince has the force of law."

THE NEW MONARCHY IN ENGLAND, FRANCE AND SPAIN

The New Monarchy came to England with the dynasty of the Tudors (1485–1603), whose first king, Henry VII (1485–1509), combined the claims of previous contenders for the throne, and put an end to the civil turbulence of the Wars of the Roses. In these wars the great English baronial families had largely decimated each other, to the great convenience of the king and the bulk of the citizenry. Henry VII passed laws against "livery and mainte- nance," the practice by which great lords maintained private armies wearing their own livery or insignia. Since the common law had recently failed to give security, witnesses being afraid to testify and juries afraid to offend the mighty, Henry VII instituted a new type of court to deal with property dis- putes and infractions of the public peace. It met in a room decorated with stars, whence its name, the Star Chamber. It acted upon Roman principles, represented the king's authority only, used Roman rules of evidence, and dispensed with a jury. Later denounced as an instrument of despotism, it was popular enough at first, because it preserved order and rendered substantial justice. Henry VII, though miserly and unpleasant in person, was accepted as a good ruler. National feeling in England consolidated around the House of Tudor.

In France the New Monarchy was represented by Louis XI (1461–83), of the Valois line, and his successors. In the five centuries since the first French king had been crowned, the royal domain had steadily expanded from its original small nucleus around Paris through a combination of in- heritance, marriage, war, intrigue, and conquest. Louis XI continued to round out the French borders. Internally, he built up a royal army, suppressed brigands, and subdued rebellious nobles. He acquired far greater powers than the English Tudors to raise taxation without parliamentary consent. The Estates-General of France met only once in his reign. On that occasion, remembering the anarchy of the past, they requested the king to govern with- out them in the future. The king proceeded to legislate on his own, reinforced the prestige of his officials *vis-à-vis* local magnates in various parts of the country, and broke down the chartered rights and localistic self-regarding attitudes of the numerous towns. Over the first estate of the realm, namely the clergy, the French monarchy asserted extensive powers. We have seen how, by the Pragmatic Sanction of 1438, the Gallican church had won con- siderable national independence.[9] In 1516 King Francis I reached an agree-

[9] See p. 49.

ment with Pope Leo X, the Concordat of Bologna. By this agreement the Pragmatic Sanction was rescinded; the pope received his "annates," or money income, from French ecclesiastics; the king appointed the bishops and abbots. The fact that, after 1516, the kings of France already controlled their own national clergy was one reason why, in later years, they were never tempted to turn Protestant.

Strictly speaking, there was no kingdom of Spain. Various Spanish kingdoms had combined into two, Aragon and Castile. To Aragon, which lay along the Mediterranean side of the peninsula, belonged the Balearic Islands, Sardinia, Sicily, and the south Italian kingdom of Naples. To Castile, after 1492, belonged the newly discovered Americas. The two were joined in a personal union by the marriage of Ferdinand of Aragon and Isabella of Castile in 1469. The union was personal only; that is, both kingdoms recognized the two monarchs, but they had no common political, judicial, or administrative institutions. There was little or no Spanish national feeling; indeed, the Catalans in northern Aragon spoke a language quite different from Castilian Spanish. The common feeling throughout Spain was the sense of belonging to the Spanish Catholic Church. The common memory was the memory of the Christian crusade against the Moors. The one common institution, whose officials had equal authority and equal access to all the kingdoms, was a church court, the Inquisition. The church in Spain was in vigorous condition. Cardinal Ximenes, shortly before 1500, managed to rid it of the abuses and the inertia which debilitated the church in the rest of Europe. The *reconquista* was at last completed. In 1492 Granada, the southern tip of Spain, was conquered from the Moors. Its annexation added to the heterogeneous and undigested character of the Spanish dominions.

In these circumstances the New Monarchy in Spain followed a religious bent. Unification took place around the church. The rulers, though they made efforts at political centralization, worked largely through facilities offered by the church, notably the Inquisition. They insisted on religious conformity. National feeling was church feeling; the sense of "Spanishness" was a sense of Catholicity. Formerly the Spanish had been among the most tolerant of Europeans; Christians, Moslems, and Jews had managed to live together. But in the wave of national (or religious) excitement that accompanied the conquest of Granada both the Jews and the Moors were expelled.[10]

ᴧᴧᴧᴧᴧᴧᴧᴧᴧᴧᴧᴧᴧᴧᴧᴧᴧ

[10] The expulsion of the Jews by the decree of 1492 was actually a sign of former toleration in Spain; for the Jews had been expelled from England in 1290 and from France in 1306, nor were they again allowed in England until the mid-seventeenth century, nor in France (with great exceptions) until the French Revolution. It would appear that, in the history of many European peoples, the attainment of a certain degree of national self-consciousness brought a dislike of the Jews as "outsiders." The Jews who left Spain (the Sephardic Jews) went to the Near East, and, in smaller numbers, to the Netherlands and even to southwestern France (one of the exceptions noted above). The Jews who earlier left England and France generally went to Germany, the great center of Ashkenazic Jewry in the Middle Ages. Driven from Germany in the fourteenth century they concentrated in Poland, which remained the great center of European Jewry until the Nazi massacres of the 1940's.

All persons in Spain were now supposed to be Christians. In fact, however, Spain was the one country in Europe where a person's Christianity could not be taken for granted, because many Spanish families had been Jewish or Moslem for centuries, and had only accepted Christianity to avoid expulsion. Hence arose a fear of false Christians, of an unassimilated element secretly hostile to the foundations of Spanish life. It was feared that Moriscos (Christians of Moorish background) and Marranos (Christians of Jewish background) retained a clandestine sympathy for the religion of their forebears. A distaste for eating pork, or an inclination not to work on Saturday, was enough to arouse suspicion. Thousands of such persons were hailed before the Inquisition, where, as in the civil courts under Roman procedure, torture could be employed to extort confessions. Spanish life became rigidly and ostentatiously orthodox. It was safest to be profuse in one's external devotions. It was the way of proving oneself to be a good Spaniard. The national and the Catholic were fused.

The life of Spain remained a great crusade, a crusade within Spain against Moriscos and Marranos, a crusade carried against the Moors into Africa itself, which the Spanish invaded immediately after the conquest of Granada. The crusade crossed the ocean into the Americas, where the Spanish Church set about gathering the Indians into the fold. And it was soon to spread to Europe also. Spain was ready, before Protestantism ever appeared, to play its role in the Reformation, to be the avenging angel to extirpate heresy, and the stern apostle demanding Catholic reform.

THE HOLY ROMAN EMPIRE AND THE HAPSBURG SUPREMACY

Ideas of the New Monarchy were at work even in Germany, which is to say, in the Holy Roman Empire. There were three kinds of states in the Empire. There were the princely states—duchies, margraviates, etc.—each a little hereditary dynastic monarchy in itself, such as Saxony, Brandenburg, or Bavaria. There were ecclesiastical states—bishoprics, abbacies, etc.—in which the bishop or abbot, whose rule was of course not hereditary, conducted the government. A large portion of the area of the empire consisted in these church states, as may be seen from the map on pp. 66–7. Thirdly, there were the imperial free cities, some fifty in number; their collective area was not large, but they dominated the commercial and financial life of the country. There was in truth also a fourth category, made up of some thousands of imperial knights, noblemen of minor consequence who possessed a few manors, but who belonged to no state, recognizing the supremacy of none but the emperor. The various states, over the centuries, had prevented the emperor from infringing upon their local liberties. They had taken care to keep the emperorship an elective office, so that with each election local liberties could be reaffirmed. After 1356 the right of electing an emperor was vested in seven Electors—namely, four of the princely lords, the Count Palatine, Duke of Saxony, Margrave of Brandenburg, and King of Bohemia (the one king in the Empire), and in three ecclesiastical lords, the Archbishops of Mainz, Trier, and Cologne. In 1438 the Electors chose the Archduke of Austria to be emperor. His family name was Hapsburg. The Hapsburgs, by using the resources of their hereditary possessions in Austria (and later elsewhere) and by delicately balancing and bribing the numerous political forces within Germany, managed to get themselves consistly re-elected to the Holy Roman Emperorship in every generation, with one exception, from 1438 until 1806.

The principles of New Monarchy were successful mainly in the hereditary princely states of reasonable size. Here the rulers went through the familiar process of quelling their own feudal subordinates, increasing their revenues, enforcing local peace, and letting their own parliamentary bodies fall into abeyance. Thus Brandenburg, Saxony, Bavaria, Würtemberg, and a few others, though small, began to take on the semblance of modern states.

The Hapsburg emperors also tried to introduce the centralizing principles of the New Monarchy in the empire as a whole. Under Maximilian I (1493–1519) there seemed to be progress in this direction: the empire was divided into administrative "circles," and an Imperial Chamber and Council were created, but they were all doomed to failure before the immovable obstacle of states' rights. Maximilian was the author of the Hapsburg family fortunes in a quite different way. *Bella gerunt alii; tu, felix Austria, nubes—* "where others have to fight wars, you, fortunate Austria, marry!" Maximilian himself married the heiress of the dukes of Burgundy, who, over the past century, had acquired a number of provinces in the western extremities of the Empire—the Netherlands and the Free County of Burgundy, which bordered upon France. Maximilian by this marriage had a son Philip, whom he married to Joanna, heiress to Ferdinand and Isabella of Spain. Philip and Joanna produced a son Charles. Charles combined the inheritances of his four grandparents: Austria from Maximilian, the Netherlands and Free County from Mary of Burgundy, Castile and Spanish America from Isabella, Aragon and its Mediterranean and Italian possessions from Ferdinand. In addition, in 1519, he was elected Holy Roman Emperor, and so became the symbolic head of all Germany.

Charles V of the empire (he was known as Charles I in Spain) was thus beyond all comparison the most powerful ruler of his day. But still other

---

Europe, 1526 (map on following pages)

The main feature of the political map of Europe about 1526 is the predominance of the house of Hapsburg. Much of Europe was ruled by the Hapsburg Emperor Charles V, who was at the same time King Charles I of Spain. As is explained in this and the following chapter, Charles left his possessions in Austria, Hungary and Bohemia to his brother, those in Spain, the Netherlands, Italy and America to his son. He thus established the Austrian and Spanish branches of the Hapsburg dynasty. France was nearly encircled by Hapsburg dominions, and habitually formed alliances with various German princes and with Sweden, Poland and Turkey. The Hapsburgs remained the principal power in Europe until after the Thirty Years' War, which ended in 1648.

EUROPE
1526

■ HAPSBURG
  DOMINIONS

░ CHURCH
  LANDS

SHETLAND IS.

NORWAY

Bergen

Oslo

ORKNEY IS.

SCOTLAND

NORTH
SEA

DENMARK

Edinburgh

THE HEBRIDES

IRELAND

York

Hamburg

Dublin

ENGLAND

WALES

DUTCH
NETH.

Leyden

Münster

A T L A N T I C

London

Canterbury

BELGIAN
NETH.

Antwerp

Brussels

Cologne

Schmolkalden

SAX

Calais
(BR)

LUX.

Trier

ENGLISH CHANNEL

Rouen

Worms

PALATINATE

Metz

Ratisbon

O C E A N

St. Malo

Paris

Strasburg

BAVARIA

Augsburg

Munich

Orléans

FR. COMTÉ

Basel

SWISS
CONFED.

TYROL

Bourges

D. OF
BURGUNDY

FRANCE

Geneva

Milan

Trent

Angoulême

SAVOY

Parma

Venice

Bordeaux

DAUPHINE

Genoa

Bayonne

Avignon

Florence

Santiago

Marseilles

Burgos

NAVARRE

PYRENEES

CORSICA
(GENOA)

Rome

Oporto

PORTUGAL

Valladolid

ARAGON

CATALONIA

Escorial

Madrid

Barcelona

Lisbon

Toledo

SPAIN

SARDINIA

Valencia

BALEARIC IS.

MAJORCA

Seville

Granada

GRANADA

Cadiz

Algiers

Tunis

Melilla
(SP)

SULTANATE OF
FEZ

SULTANATE OF
ALGIERS

SULTANATE OF
TUNIS

B A R B A R Y   S T A T E S

fortunes awaited the House of Hapsburg. The Turks, who had occupied Constantinople in 1453, were at this time pushing through Hungary and menacing central Europe. In 1526 they defeated the Hungarians at the battle of Mohacs. The parliaments of Hungary, and of the adjoining kingdom of Bohemia, hoping to gain allies in the face of the Turkish peril, thereupon elected Charles V's brother Ferdinand as their king. The Hapsburg family was now entrenched in central Europe, in the Netherlands, in Spain, in the Mediterranean, in south Italy, in America. No one since Charlemagne had stood so far above all rivals. Contemporaries cried that Europe was threatened with "universal monarchy," with a kind of world-state in which no people could preserve its independence.

The reader who wishes to understand the religious revolution, and consequent emergence of Protestantism, to which we shall now turn, must bear in mind the extraordinarily intricate interplay of the factors that have now been outlined: the decline of the church, the growth of secular and humanistic feeling, the spread of lay religion outside the official clergy, the rise of monarchs who wished to control everything in their kingdoms, including the church, the resistance of feudal elements to these same monarchs, the lassitude of the popes and their fear of church councils, the atomistic division of Germany, the Turkish peril, the zeal of Spain, the pre-eminence of Charles V, and the fears felt in the rest of Europe, especially in France, of absorption or suffocation by the amazing empire of the Hapsburgs.

9. Protestantism

It is always misleading to read history backwards, and especially the history of the Reformation. Seen in retrospect, since northern Europe became Protestant while the south remained Catholic, it looks as if the north had broken off in a body from a once solid Roman church. The reality was not so simple. Let us for the moment put aside the term "Protestant," and call the adherents of the new religion religious revolutionaries.[11] These revolutionaries were active for a time in almost all parts of Europe. The new ideas leaped over every frontier. It was the entire or "universal" church that the revolutionaries intended to reform. Their aim was not to be let alone to follow their own religion in their own country, but to purify the whole church of Christ itself. Everywhere adherents of the old faith remained active also. No one thought that people should be free to believe individually as they chose. No one regarded religion as a mere opinion. For all parties the issue lay between God's true word and abominable misconceptions, and all saw in the

~~~~~~~~~~~~~~~~~~~~

[11] The word "Protestant" arose as an incident in the struggle, at first denoting certain Lutherans who drew up a formal protest against an action of the diet of the Empire in 1529. Only very gradually did the various groups of anti-Roman reformers think of themselves as collectively Protestant, and in recent times some High Church Anglicans, while anti-Roman, have refused to be called Protestant.

church the supreme institution in which men lived. All maintained (isolated exceptions were few and unimportant) that in so vital a matter as religion people who lived together must believe alike.

For years many thought that old and new ideas of the church might be combined. Many deplored the extremes, but gradually in the heat of struggle had to choose one side or the other. The issues became drawn; and each side long aspired to destroy its adversary. For over a century the revolutionaries maintained the hope that "popery" would everywhere fall. For over a century the upholders of the old order worked to annihilate or re-convert their opponents. Only very slowly did Catholics and Protestants come to accept each other's existence as an established fact of European society. Though the religious frontier that was to prove permanent appeared as early as 1560, it was not generally accepted until after the Thirty Years' War, which closed in 1648, and in Hungary the Protestant-Catholic war may be said to have lasted until after 1700.

The Protestant doctrines were revolutionary because they held, not merely that "abuses" in the church must be corrected, but that the Roman church itself, even if perfect by its own ideals, was wrong in principle. The Protestants aimed not to restore the medieval church but to overthrow it. In its place they meant to put a church founded on principles drawn from the Bible.

LUTHER AND LUTHERANISM

The first to formulate the Protestant principles was Martin Luther. He was a monk, a vehement and spiritually uneasy man, with many dark and introspective recesses in his personality, terrified by the thought of the awful omnipotence of God, distressed by his own littleness, apprehensive of the devil, and suffering from the chronic conviction that he was damned. The means offered by the church to allay such spiritual anguish—the sacraments, prayer, attendance at Mass—gave him no satisfaction. From a reading and pondering of St. Paul (Romans, i, 17)—"the just shall live by faith"—there dawned upon him a new realization and sense of peace. He developed the doctrine of justification by faith alone. This held that what "justifies" a man is not what the church knew as "works" (prayer, alms, the sacraments, holy living) but "faith alone," an inward bent of spirit given to each soul directly by God. Good works, Luther thought, were the consequence and external evidence of this inner grace, but in no way its cause. A man did not "earn" grace by doing good; he did the good because he possessed the grace of God. With this idea Luther for some years lived content. Even years later some high-placed churchmen believed that in Luther's doctrine of justification by faith there was nothing contrary to the teachings of the Catholic Church.

Luther, now a professor at Wittenberg, was brought out of seclusion by an incident of 1517. A friar named Tetzel was traveling through Germany distributing indulgences, authorized by the pope to finance the building of

St. Peter's in Rome.[12] In return for them the faithful paid certain stipulated sums of money. Luther thought that people were being deluded, that no one could in this way obtain grace for himself, or ease the pains of relatives in purgatory, as was officially claimed. In the usual academic manner of the day, he posted ninety-five theses on the door of the castle church at Wittenberg. In them he reviewed the Catholic sacrament of penance. Luther held that, after confession, the sinner is freed of his burden not by the priest's absolution, but by inner grace and faith alone. Increasingly, it seemed that the priesthood performed no necessary function in the relation between man and God.

Luther at first appealed to the pope, Leo X, to correct the abuse of indulgences in Germany. When the pope refused action Luther (like many before him) urged the assembly of a general church council as an authority higher even than the pope. He was obliged, however, to admit in public debate that even the decision of a general council might be mistaken. The council of Constance, he said, had in fact erred in its condemnation of John Huss. But if neither the pope, nor yet a council, had authority to define true Christian belief, where was such authority to be found? Luther's answer was, in effect: There is no such authority. He held that each individual might read the Bible and freely make his own interpretation according to his own conscience. It was the doctrine of the priesthood of all believers. It was as revolutionary, for the church, as would be the assertion today that neither the Supreme Court nor any other body may authoritatively interpret or enforce the constitution of the United States, since each citizen may interpret the constitution in his own way.

From his first public appearance Luther won ardent supporters, for there was a good deal of resentment in Germany against Rome. In 1519 and 1520 he rallied public opinion in a series of tracts, setting forth his main beliefs. He declared that the claim of the clergy to be different from the laity was an imposture. He urged people to find Christian truth in the Bible for themselves, and in the Bible only. He denounced the reliance on fasts, pilgrimages, saints, and masses. He rejected the belief in purgatory. He reduced the seven sacraments to two—baptism and the communion, as he called the mass. In the latter he repudiated the new and "modern" doctrine of transubstantiation, while affirming that God was still somehow mysteriously present in the bread and wine.[13] He declared that the clergy should marry, upbraided the prelates for their luxury, and demanded that monasticism be eliminated. To drive through such reforms, while depriving the clergy of their pretensions, he called upon the temporal power, the princes of Germany. He thus issued an invitation to the state to assume control over religion, an invitation which, in the days of the New Monarchy, a good many rulers were enthusiastically willing to accept.

Threatened by a papal bull with excommunication unless he recanted, Luther solemnly and publicly burned the bull. Excommunication followed.

---

[12] On indulgences see pp. 48–9.
[13] See pp. 36, 38.

To the Emperor, Charles V, now fell the duty of apprehending the heretic and repressing the heresy. Luther was summoned to appear before a diet of the Empire, held at Worms. He declared that he could be convinced only by Scripture or right reason, otherwise—"I neither can nor will recant anything, since it is neither right nor safe to act against conscience. God help me! Amen." He was placed under the ban of the Empire. But the Elector of Saxony and other north German princes took him under their protection. In safe seclusion, he began to translate the Bible into German.

Luther's excitable obstinacy, intemperate language, and sweeping repudiation of existing authorities antagonized many who had at first looked upon him with favor, and who still hoped for a reform of the church without revolution. Among these was Erasmus, who, as often happens to those who find themselves in the middle, was in his last years looked upon by both sides, Lutheran and Catholic, as a meddlesome friend of the opposition.

Lutheranism, or at least anti-Romanism, swept over Germany, assuming the proportions of a national upheaval. It became mixed with all sorts of political and social revolution. A league of imperial knights, adopting Lutheranism, attacked their neighbors, the church states of the Rhineland, hoping by annexations to enlarge their own meager territories. In 1524 the peasants of a large part of Germany revolted. They were stirred by new religious ideas, worked upon by preachers who went beyond Luther in asserting that any man could see for himself what was right. Their aims, however, were social and economic; they demanded a regulation of rents and security of common village rights, and complained of exorbitant exactions and oppressive rule by their manorial overlords. Luther repudiated all connection with the peasants, called them filthy swine, and urged the princes to suppress them by the sword. The peasants were unmercifully put down, but popular unrest continued to stir the country, expressing itself, in a religious age, in various forms of extreme religious frenzy. Various leaders had various followings, known collectively as Anabaptists. Some said that all the world needed was love, some that Christ would soon come again, some that they were saints and could do no wrong, and some that infant baptism was useless, immersion of full-grown adults being required, as described in the Bible. The roads of Germany were alive with obscure zealots, of whom some tens of thousands converged in 1534 on the city of Münster. There they proclaimed the reign of the saints, abolished property, and introduced polygamy as authorized in the Old Testament. A Dutch tailor, John of Leyden, claimed authority from God himself, and, hemmed in by besieging armies, ruled Münster by a revolutionary terror. Luther advised his followers to join even with Catholics to repress such an appalling menace. After a full year Münster was relieved. The "saints" were pitilessly rooted out; John of Leyden died in torture.

Luther, horrified at the way in which religious revolution passed into social revolution, defined his own position more conservatively. He qualified his idea of the priesthood of all believers, restricted, while never denying, the right of private judgment in matters of conscience, and made a larger place for an established clergy, Lutheranized, to be sure, but still established as teachers over the laity. Always well disposed to temporal rulers, having called upon the princes to act as religious reformers, he was thrown by the peasant and Anabaptist uprisings into an even closer alliance with them. Lutheranism took on a character of submissiveness to the state. Christian liberty, Luther insisted, was an internal freedom, purely spiritual, known only to God. In worldly matters, he said, the good Christian owed perfect obedience to established authority. Lutheranism, more than Catholicism and more than the Calvinism which soon arose, came to hold the state in a kind of religious awe as an institution almost sacred in its own right.

In the revolution that was rocking Germany it was not the uprising of imperial knights, nor that of peasants or tailors and journeymen that was successful, but the rebellion of the higher orders of the empire against the Emperor. Charles V, as Holy Roman Emperor, was bound to uphold Catholicism because only in a Catholic world did the Holy Empire have any meaning. The states of the empire, always fearing the loss of local liberty, saw in Charles' efforts to repress Luther a threat to their own freedom. Many imperial free cities, and most of the dynastic states of north Germany, now insisted on adding to their other rights and liberties the right, or liberty, to determine their own religion. The *ius reformandi*, they said, the right or power to reform, belonged to member states, not to the Empire itself. They became Lutheran, locally, introducing Lutheran bishops, doctrines, and forms of worship. Where a state turned Lutheran it usually "secularized" (*i.e.*, confiscated) the church properties within its borders, a process which considerably enriched some of the Lutheran princes, and gave them a strong material interest in the success of the Lutheran movement. In most of the church states, since the Catholic archbishop or bishop was himself the government, Catholicism prevailed. But a few church states turned Lutheran. A good example of the secularization of a church state was afforded in East Prussia, just outside the Empire. This territory belonged to the Teutonic Order, a Catholic organization of which the grand commander, an elective official, was at this time Albert of Brandenburg. In 1525 Albert declared for Luther and converted East Prussia into a secular duchy, of which he and his descendants became hereditary dukes.

Against the Emperor, a group of Lutheran princes and free cities formed the League of Schmalkald. The king of France, Francis I, though a Catholic in good standing, allied with and supported the League. Political interests overrode religious ones. Against the "universal monarchy" of the swollen Hapsburgs the French found alliances where they could, allying with the Turks as with the Lutherans, building up a balance of power against their mighty foe. It became the studied policy of Catholic France to maintain the religious division of Germany.

Charles V strove to find some basis of agreement by which the permanent religious division of Germany could be avoided. He was at war with France over certain disputed territories and with the Turks, who in 1529 besieged Vienna itself. Though the Lutheran princes did render a little help at the last moment, it seemed on the whole that the infidels might overrun Germany before the German states would yield their liberties to their own Emperor.

Charles appealed to the pope, urging him to assemble a Europe-wide council in which all disputed matters could be considered, the Protestants heard, compromises effected, and church unity and German unity (such as it was) restored. The king of France schemed at Rome to prevent the pope from calling any such council. The kings of both France and England urged national councils instead, in which religious questions could be settled on a national basis. Pope after pope delayed. The papacy feared that a council of all Latin Christendom might get out of control, since Catholics as much as Protestants demanded reform. At the very rumor of a council the price of salable offices in Rome abruptly fell. To the papacy, remembering the Council of Constance, nothing was more upsetting than the thought of a council, not even the Protestants, not even the Turks. So the popes procrastinated, no council met, years passed, and a new generation grew up in Lutheranism. Desperately, in 1548, Charles tried to settle matters himself, issuing the *Interim*, to guide religion in all Germany until a general church council could complete its work. The *Interim* upheld the main Catholic doctrines, but, to attract the Protestants, allowed marriage of the clergy and one or two other minor concessions. Neither side would accept it: Protestants found that it gave too little, and Catholics refused to have their religion tampered with by the temporal power.

Meanwhile the Schmalkaldic League, allied with France, had actually gone to war with the Emperor in 1546. Germany fell into an anarchy of civil struggle between Catholic and Protestant states, the latter aided by France. The war was ended by the Peace of Augsburg of 1555.

The terms set at Augsburg signified a complete victory for the cause of Lutheranism and states' rights. Each state of the empire received the liberty to be either Lutheran or Catholic as it chose—*cuius regio eius religio*, "whose the region, his the religion." No individual freedom of religion was permitted; if a ruler decided for Lutheranism then all his subjects had to be Lutheran. Similarly in Catholic states all had to be Catholic. The churches were state churches, rather more so in the Lutheran than in the Catholic territories, since Lutheranism was set up and maintained in each case by the individual states, while Catholicism retained its connection with Rome and with the Catholic world beyond each state's borders. The Peace of Augsburg provided also, by the so-called Ecclesiastical Reservation, that any Catholic bishop or other churchman who turned Lutheran in the future (or who had turned Lutheran as recently as 1552) should not carry his territory with him, but should turn Lutheran as an individual and move away, leaving his land and its inhabitants Catholic. Since the issues in Germany were still far from stabilized, this proviso was often disregarded in later years.

The Peace of Augsburg was thus, in religion, a great victory for Protestantism, and at the same time, in German politics and constitutional matters, a step in the disintegration of Germany into a mosaic of increasingly separate states. Lutheranism prevailed in the north, and in the south in the duchy of Würtemberg and various detached islands formed by Lutheranized free cities. Catholicism prevailed in the south (except in Würtemberg and certain cities), in the Rhine valley, and in the direct possessions of the House of Hapsburg, which in 1555 reached as far north as the Netherlands. The Germans, because of conditions in the Holy Roman Empire, were the one large European people to emerge from the religious conflict almost evenly divided between Catholic and Protestant.

No rights were granted by the Peace of Augsburg to another group of religious revolutionaries which neither Lutherans nor Catholics were willing to tolerate, namely the followers of John Calvin.

Lutheranism, it must be pointed out, was adopted by the kings of Denmark and Sweden as early as the 1520's. Since Denmark controlled Norway, and Sweden ruled Finland and the eastern Baltic, all Scandinavia and the Baltic regions became, like north Germany, Lutheran. Beyond this area Lutheranism failed to take root. Like Anglicanism in England (to be described shortly) Lutheranism was too closely associated with established states to spread easily as an international movement. The most successful international form of the Protestant movement was Calvinism.

CALVIN AND CALVINISM

John Calvin was a Frenchman, born Jean Cauvin, who called himself Calvinus in Latin. Born in 1509, he was a full generation younger than Luther. He was trained both as a priest and as a lawyer, and had a humanist's knowledge of Latin and Greek, as well as Hebrew. At the age of twenty-four, experiencing a sudden conversion, or fresh insight into the meaning of Christianity, he joined forces with the religious revolutionaries of whom the best known was then Luther. Three years later, in 1536, he published, in the international language, Latin, his *Institutes of the Christian Religion*. Where Luther had aimed much of his writing either at the existing rulers of Germany, or at the German national feeling against Rome, Calvin addressed his *Institutes* to all the world. He seemed to appeal to human reason itself; he wrote in the severe, logical style of the trained lawyer; he dealt firmly, lucidly, and convincingly with the most basic issues. In the *Institutes* men in all countries, if dissatisfied with the existing Roman church (as many in all countries were), could find cogent expression of universal propositions, which they could apply to their own local circumstances as they required.

With Luther's criticisms of the Roman church, and with most of Luther's fundamental religious ideas, such as justification by faith and not by works, Calvin agreed. In what they retained of the Catholic mass, the communion or Lord's Supper as they called it, they developed certain doctrinal differences; both rejected transubstantiation, but where Luther insisted that God was somehow actually present in the bread and wine used in the service ("consubstantiation"), Calvin and his followers tended more to regard it as a pious act of symbolic or commemorative character.

The chief differences between Calvin and Luther were two. Calvin made far more of the idea of predestination. Both, drawing heavily on St. Augustine, held that man by his own actions could earn no merit in the sight of divine justice, that any grace which a man possessed came from the free action of God alone. God, being Almighty, knew and willed in advance all things that happened, including the way in which every life would turn out. He knew and willed, from all eternity, that some were saved and some were damned. Calvin, a severe critic of human nature, felt that those who had grace were relatively few. They were the "elect," the "godly," the little band chosen without merit of their own, from all eternity, for salvation. A person could feel in his own mind that he was among the saved, God's chosen few, if throughout all trials and temptations he persisted in a saintly life. Thus the idea of predestination, of God's omnipotence, instead of turning to fatalism and resignation, became a challenge to unrelenting effort, a sense of burning conviction, a conviction of having a mission, of doing battle for the Lord, of being on the side of that Almighty Power which must in the end be everlastingly triumphant. It was the most resolute spirits that were attracted to Calvinism. Calvinists, in all countries, were militant, uncompromising, perfectionist—or Puritan, as they were called first in England and later in America.

The second way in which Calvinism differed from Lutheranism was in its attitude to society and to the state. Calvinists refused to recognize the subordination of church to state, or the right of any government—king, parliament, or civic magistracy—to lay down laws for religion. On the contrary, they insisted that true Christians, the elect or godly, should Christianize the state. They wished to remake society itself into the image of a religious community, with all people living stern, disciplined, and saintly lives, and kings themselves doing the Lord's work. They rejected the institution of bishops (which both the Lutheran and Anglican churches retained), and provided instead that the church should be governed by presbyteries, elected bodies made up of ministers and devout laymen. By thus bringing an element of lay control into church affairs, they broke the monopoly of priestly power and so promoted secularization. On the other hand, they were the reverse of secular, for they wished to Christianize all society.

Calvin, called in by earlier reformers who had driven out their bishop, was able to set up his model Christian community at Geneva in Switzerland. A body of ministers ruled the church; a consistory of ministers and elders ruled the town. The rule was strict; all loose, light, or frivolous living was suppressed; disaffected persons were driven into exile. The form of worship was severe, and favored the intellectual rather than the emotional or the aesthetic. The service was devoted largely to long sermons elucidating Christian doctrine, and all appeals to the senses—color, music, incense—were rigidly subdued. The black gown of Geneva replaced brighter clerical vestments. Images, representing the saints, Mary, or Christ, were taken down and destroyed. Candles went the way of incense. Chanting was replaced by the singing of hymns. Instrumental music was frowned upon, and many Calvinists thought even bells to be a survival of "popery." In all things Calvin undertook to regulate his church by the Bible. Nor was he more willing than Luther to countenance any doctrine more radical than his own. When a Spanish refugee, Michael Servetus, who denied the Trinity, *i.e.*, the divinity of Christ, sought asylum at Geneva, Calvin pronounced him a heretic and burned him at the stake.

To Geneva flocked reformers of all nationalities, Englishmen, Scots, Frenchmen, Netherlanders, Germans, Poles, and Hungarians, to see and study a true scriptural community so that they might reproduce it in their own countries. Geneva became the Protestant Rome, the one great international center of Reformed doctrine. Everywhere Calvinists made their teachings heard (even in Spain and Italy in isolated cases), and everywhere, or almost everywhere, little groups which had locally and spontaneously broken with the old church found in Calvin's *Institutes* a reasoned statement of doctrine and a suggested method of organization. Thus Calvinism spread, or was adopted, very widely. In Hungary and Bohemia large elements turned Protestant, and usually Calvinist, partly as a way of opposing the Hapsburg rule. In Poland there were many Calvinists, along with less organized Anabaptists and Unitarians, or Socinians as those who denied the Trinity were then called. Calvinists spread in Germany, where, opposing both Lutheran and Catholic churches as ungodly impositions of worldly power, they were disliked equally by both. In France the Huguenots were Calvinist, as were the Protestants of what are now Belgium and Holland. John Knox in the 1550's brought Calvinism to Scotland, where Presbyterianism became and remained the established religion. At the same time Calvinism began to penetrate England, from which it was later to reach British America, giving birth to the Presbyterian and Congregationalist churches of the United States.

Calvinism was far from democratic in any modern sense, being rather of an almost aristocratic outlook, in that those who sensed themselves to be God's chosen few felt free to dictate to the common run of mankind. Yet in many ways Calvinism entered into the development of what became democracy. For one thing, Calvinists never venerated the state; they always held that the sphere of the state and of public life was subject to moral judgment. For another, the Calvinist doctrine of the "calling" taught that a man's labor had a religious dignity, and that any form of honest work was pleasing in the sight of God. In the conduct of their own affairs Calvinists developed a type of self-government. They formed "covenants" with one another, and devised machinery for the election of presbyteries. They refused to believe that authority was transmitted downward through bishops or through kings. They were inclined also to a democratic outlook by the circumstance that in most countries they remained an unofficial minority. Only at Geneva, in the Dutch Netherlands, in Scotland and in New England (and for a few years in England in the seventeenth century) were Calvinists ever able to prescribe the mode of life and religion of a whole country. In England, in France, in Germany, in Eastern Europe Calvinists remained in opposition to the established authorities of church and state, and hence disposed to favor limitations upon established power.

THE REFORMATION IN ENGLAND

England was peculiar in that its government broke with the Roman church before adopting any Protestant principles. Henry VIII (1509–47) in fact prided himself on his orthodoxy. When a few obscure persons, about 1520, began to whisper Luther's ideas in England, Henry himself wrote a *Defense of the Seven Sacraments* in refutation, for which a grateful pope conferred upon him the title of "Defender of the Faith." But the king had no male heir. Recalling the anarchy from which the Tudor dynasty had extricated England, and determined as a New Monarch to build up a durable monarchy, he felt, or said, that before all else he must have a son. In order to remarry, he requested the pope to annul his existing marriage to Catherine of Aragon. Popes in the past had obliged monarchs similarly pressed. The pope now, however, was embarrassed by the fact that Catherine, who objected, was the aunt of the Emperor Charles V, whom the pope was in no position to offend. Henry, not a patient man, drove matters forward. He put in a new Archbishop of Canterbury, repudiated the Roman connection, and married the buxom Anne Boleyn. The fact that only three years later he put to death the unfortunate Anne, and thereafter in quick succession married four more wives, for a total of six, threw considerable doubt on the original character of his motives.

Henry acted through Parliament, believing, as he said, that a king was never stronger than when united with representatives of his kingdom. In 1534 Parliament passed the Act of Supremacy, which declared the English king to be the "Protector and Only Supreme Head of the Church and Clergy of England." All subjects were required, if asked, to take the oath of supremacy acknowledging the religious headship of Henry and rejecting that of the pope. For refusing this oath Sir Thomas More, a statesman and humanist best known as the author of *Utopia*, was executed for treason. He received a somewhat delayed reward four centuries later when the Roman Church pronounced him to be a saint. Henry, in the next few years, closed all the monasteries in England. The extensive monastic lands, accumulated by never dying corporations from gifts made over the centuries, were seized by the king, who passed them out to numerous followers, thus strengthening and reconstituting a landed aristocracy which had been seriously weakened in the Wars of the Roses. The new landed gentry remained firm supporters of the House of Tudor and the English national church, whatever its doctrines.

It was Henry's intent not to change the doctrines at all. He simply wished to be the supreme head of an English Catholic Church. On the one hand, in 1536, he forcibly suppressed a Catholic rebellion, and on the other, in 1539, through the Six Articles, required everybody to believe in transubstantiation, the celibacy of the clergy, the need of confession, and a few other test items of Catholic faith and practice. But it proved impossible to maintain this position, for a great many people in England began to favor one or another of the ideas of Continental Reformers, and a small minority were willing to accept the entire Protestant position.

For three decades the government veered about. Henry died in 1547, and was succeeded by his ten-year-old son, Edward VI, under whom the Protestant party came to the fore. But Edward died in 1553, and was succeeded by his much older sister, Mary, the daughter of Catherine of Aragon and a devout Roman Catholic whose whole life had been embittered by the break with Rome. Mary tried to re-Catholicize England; but she actually made Catholicism more unpopular with the English. She married the king of Spain, Philip II, who became king of England, but in name only. The English did not like Philip, nor the Spanish, nor the intense Spanish Catholicism that Philip represented. Under Mary, moreover, some three hundred persons were burned at the stake, as heretics, in public mass executions. It was the first (and last) time that such a thing had happened in England, and it set up a wave of horror. In any event, Mary did not live long. She was succeeded in 1558 by Henry's younger daughter, Elizabeth, the child of Anne Boleyn. Whatever Elizabeth's real views in religion might be (she was rumored to have none, and concealed them successfully) she could not be a Roman Catholic. For Catholics she was illegitimate, and so unable to be queen.

Under Elizabeth the English became Protestant, gradually and in their own way. The Church of England took on a form of its own. Organizationally, it resembled a Lutheran church. It was a state church, for its existence and doctrines were determined by the temporal power, in this case the monarch acting through Parliament. All English subjects were obliged to belong to it, and laws were passed against "recusants," a term used to cover both the Roman Catholics and the more advanced Calvinists who refused to acknowledge it. With the exception of monasteries and certain other church foundations, the Church of England retained the physical possessions, buildings, and internal organization of the medieval church—the bishops and the archbishops, who continued to sit in the House of Lords, the episcopal courts with their jurisdiction over marriage and wills, the tithes or church-taxes paid by all landowners, the parish structure, the universities of Oxford and Cambridge. In religious practice, the Church of England was definitely Protestant: English replaced Latin as the language of the liturgy, there was no cult of the saints, and the clergy married, though Elizabeth confessed to some embarrassment at the thought of an archbishop having a wife. In doctrine, it was Elizabeth's policy to make the dogmas broad and ambiguous, so that persons of all shades of belief could be more readily accommodated. The Thirty-nine Articles (1563), composed by a committee of bishops, defined the creed of the Anglican Church. In the light of the burning issues of the day many of the articles were evasive, though Protestant in tone. All but one of the Anglican bishops had been newly appointed by Elizabeth at her accession; many had lived in exile among Continental Protestants in the reign of Mary Tudor; and except on the matter of church government through bishops (known as episcopacy) a strong Calvinist impress was set upon Anglican belief in the time of Elizabeth. Anglicans, for a century or more, generally considered themselves closer to Geneva than to Rome, the seat of "popery," and regarded Lutherans as "semi-papist." There remained, however, a High Church element, emphasizing the Catholic rather than the Protestant character of Anglicanism.

The same ecclesiastical settlement was prescribed for Ireland, where a replica of the Church of England was established, called the Church of Ireland, which took over the properties and position of the Roman church in the lesser island. The native Irish remained almost solidly Roman Catholic. As in Hungary or Bohemia people who resented the Hapsburgs were likely to turn Protestant rather than share in the ruler's religion, so in Ireland the fact that the ruling English were Protestant only confirmed the Irish in their attachment to the Roman church. The Catholic priests, deprived of status, income, and church buildings, and often in hiding, became national leaders of a discontented people.

THE RELIGIOUS SITUATION BY 1560

Neither in England, nor in Germany, nor in a Europe at large penetrated by international Calvinism were the issues regarded as settled in 1560. Nor had the Roman church accepted the new situation. But by 1560 the chief Protestant doctrines had been affirmed, and geographically Protestantism had made many conquests. The spiritual unity of Latin Christendom had been broken. Even without Protestantism the unity of the late medieval church had been badly disjointed, in recurring conflicts between conciliarists and upholders of papal power, and in the tendency of Catholic clergy and Catholic monarchs to assert national autonomy for their churches, as seen most especially in France. But whatever spiritual or administrative unity might still have been derived from the Roman supremacy was now lost by the Protestant revolt. Christendom was disintegrating into a purely intangible ideal. A world of separate states and nations was taking its place.

Protestants differed with one another, yet there was much that all had in common. All rejected the papal authority. None participated in any effective international organization; the ascendancy of Geneva was spiritual only, and proved to be temporary. All Protestants rejected the special, sacerdotal, or supernatural character of the priesthood; indeed, the movement was perhaps most fundamentally a revolt against the medieval position of the clergy. Protestants called their clergy ministers, not priests. All Protestant clergy were entitled to marry. There were no Protestant monks, nuns, or friars. All Protestant churches replaced Latin with the vernacular in religious services—

English, French, German, Czech as the case might be. All Protestants reduced the number of sacraments, usually to two or three; such sacraments as they retained they regarded more as symbols than as actual carriers of divine grace; all believed, in one way or another, in justification by faith. All denied transubstantiation, or the miracle of the Mass. All gave up the obliga-

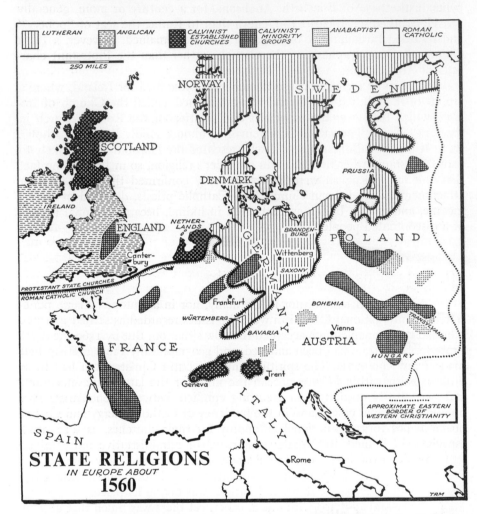

STATE RELIGIONS
IN EUROPE ABOUT
1560

It is not possible to draw a religious map of Europe during the Reformation, because persons of different religious belief were intermixed, and each group still labored to convert others to its position. Legally, however, by 1560 or 1570, the churches were as indicated above. Many Catholics lived north of the heavy line, especially in Ireland, and many Protestants south of it, especially in France, Bohemia, and Hungary. The Germans, because of political disunity within the Holy Roman Empire, were the one large people of Europe to emerge from the Reformation almost evenly divided. In the other large countries one side or the other, Protestant or Catholic, was ultimately reduced to a small minority.

tory confessional, and with it priestly absolution. All gave up the idea of purgatory as a kind of temporal zone between heaven and hell, and hence abandoned the practice of saying prayers and masses for the dead. It need hardly be added that nothing like indulgences remained. All gave up the cult of the saints and of the Virgin Mary, whose intercession in heaven was no longer expected. All declared that the one true source of Christian belief was the Holy Scripture; all denied any such authority to church tradition, *i.e.*, to the cumulative religious development that had occurred between ancient times and their own. And while all established Protestant churches, in the sixteenth century, insisted on conformity to their own doctrines, allowing no individual freedom, all Protestants still had some small spark of the spirit first ignited by Luther, so that none flatly, formally, or positively repudiated the right of private judgment in matters of conscience.

In recent times it has often been maintained that one of the motivations in Protestantism was economic—that a new acquisitive, aggressive, dynamic, progressive, capitalistic impulse shook off the restrictions imposed by medieval religion. The fact that Protestant England and Holland soon underwent a rapid capitalistic development gives added likelihood to this idea. The alacrity with which Protestant governments confiscated church lands shows a keen material interest; but in truth, both before and since the Reformation, governments confiscated church properties without breaking with the Roman church. That profound economic changes were occurring at the time will become apparent in the following chapter. Yet it seems that economic conditions were far less decisive than religious convictions and political circumstances. Calvinism appealed, not only to the economically advanced, but to the economically backward, as the Scots then were, and as the Poles and Hungarians long remained. Lutheranism spread more successfully in the economically retarded north Germany than in the busy south. The English were for years no more inclined to Protestantism than the French, and in France, while many lords and peasants turned Protestant, Paris and many other towns remained as steadfastly Catholic. It is possible that Protestantism, by casting a glow of religious righteousness over a man's daily business and material prosperity, later contributed to the economic success of Protestant peoples, but it does not seem that economic forces were of any distinctive importance in the first stages of Protestantism.

10. Catholicism Reformed and Reorganized

The Catholic movement corresponding to the rise of Protestantism is known as the Catholic Reformation or the Counter-Reformation, the former term being preferred by Catholics, the latter by Protestants. Both are applicable. On the one hand the Catholic church underwent a genuine reform, which would probably have worked itself out in one way or another even if the stimulus of revolutionary Protestantism had been absent. On the other hand the character of the reform, the decisions made, and the measures adopted were shaped by the need of responding explicitly to the Protestant challenge; and certainly, also, there was a good deal of purely "counter" activity aimed at the elimination of Protestantism as such.

The demand for reform was as old as the abuses against which it was directed. Characteristically, it had expressed itself in the demand for a general or ecumenical church council. The conciliar movement, defeated by the popes about 1450, showed signs of revival after 1500.[14] But it was almost as hard, even then, to assemble a general council as it is today to create an international body possessing any effective authority.

Several years before Luther had been heard of, Europe's two most important secular rulers, the king of France and the Holy Roman emperor, jointly convened on their own authority a council at Pisa in 1511. It was their purpose to force reforms upon Pope Julius II, and if necessary depose him. But no delegates from other countries attended; the five cardinals and handful of bishops who came to Pisa were regarded as minions of the two rulers who sent them; the council lacked moral authority, no one listened to it, and it accomplished nothing, never even attaining historically the name of a council. The pope, however, to ward off the danger of a council under secular auspices, himself assembled the Fifth Lateran Council at Rome in 1512. It was supposed to be general, ecumenical, Europe-wide, representing that "spiritual unity" sometimes imagined to have existed in Europe before Luther. In fact, few took it seriously, because it was composed mainly of Italian prelates, who began by denouncing the doctrines of the Council of Constance, and ended by making a few tame resolutions on miscellaneous topics.

Then came the Lutheran upheaval, and the attempts of Charles V, in the interests of German unity, to persuade the pope to assemble a true and adequately empowered council, so that removal of abuses in the church, which no one really defended, would take away the grounds upon which many Germans were turning to Lutheranism. But meanwhile the king of France found reason to favor the pope and to oppose the emperor. The French king, Francis I (1515–47), could support the pope because he had obtained from the papacy what he wanted, namely control over the Gallican Church, as acquired in the Concordat of Bologna of 1516.[15] And he had reason to oppose Charles V, because Charles V ruled not only in Germany but in the Netherlands, Spain, and much of Italy, thus encircling France and threatening Europe with what contemporaries called "universal monarchy." Francis I therefore actively encouraged the Protestants of Germany as a means of maintaining dissension there, and used his influence at Rome against the calling of a council by which the troubles of the Catholic world might be relieved. The pope was afraid to summon a council against the wishes of Francis I, for fear that Francis, if angered, might take the Gallican Church entirely outside the Roman fold as Henry VIII had already taken

[14] On the conciliar movement see pp. 47–9.
[15] See p. 63.

the Anglican. On so little did the religious destiny of nations seem to depend! Gradually, in the curia, there arose a party of reforming cardinals who concluded that the need of reform was so urgent that all dangers of a council must be risked. The pope summoned a council to meet in 1537, but the wars between France and the Empire forced its abandonment. Then a council was called for 1542, but no one came except a few Italians so that it had to be suspended. Finally, in 1545, a council did assemble and begin operations. It met at Trent, on the Alpine borders of Germany and Italy. The Council of Trent, which shaped the destiny of all modern Catholicism, sat at irregular intervals for almost twenty years—in 1545–47, 1551–52, 1562–63.

THE COUNCIL OF TRENT

The Council was troubled by difficulties of a political nature, which seemed to show that under modern conditions an international council was no longer a suitable means of regulating Catholic affairs. For one thing, it was poorly attended. Where at the Fourth Lateran Council of 1215, and at Constance in 1415, some five hundred prelates had assembled, the attendance at Trent was never nearly so great; it sometimes fell as low as twenty or thirty, and the important decree on "justification," the prime issue raised by Luther, and one on which some good Catholics had until then believed a compromise to be possible, was passed at a session where only sixty prelates were present. The most regular in attendance were the Italians and Spanish; French and Germans came erratically and in smaller numbers. Even with the small attendance, the old conciliar issue was raised. A party of bishops believed that the bishops of the Catholic Church, when assembled in council from all parts of the Catholic world, collectively constituted an authority superior to that of the pope. To stave off this "episcopal" movement was one of the chief duties of the cardinal legates deputed by the pope to preside over the sessions. Moreover, the great Catholic states showed little friendliness. In 1547, the imperial diet of the Holy Roman Empire, in which Catholics still had a majority despite the spread of Lutheranism, requested a "free" council in which bishops should be free from the pope's direction, and urged that the decrees thus far enacted at Trent be reconsidered, since they were making the religious gulf in Germany impossible to bridge. In 1551, the French king announced that France would not be bound by the council at all. In 1562 the emperor Ferdinand, successor to Charles V, issued a reform program, in which he urged the council, then nearing its end, to reassert the supremacy of council over pope, and impose further controls on the papacy, the cardinals, and the curia.

Thus, to the end of the council, the idea persisted of limiting the papal power. The popes, however, managed successfully to resist, and in the end triumphed, through a final ruling, voted by the council, that no act of the council should be valid unless accepted by the Holy See. It is possible that had the conciliar theory won out, the Catholic Church might have become

as disunited in modern times as the Protestant. It was clear, at Trent, that
the various bishops tended to see matters in a national way, in the light of
their own problems at home, and to be frequently under strong influence
from their respective secular monarchs. In any case, the papal party prevailed, which is to say that the centralizing element, not the national, triumphed. The Council of Trent in fact marked an important step in the
movement which issued, three hundred years later, in the promulgation of
the infallibility of the pope in matters of faith and morals. And the only
council that has met since 1563 was the Vatican Council of 1870 at which
this papal infallibility was proclaimed.[16] The Council of Trent thus preserved
the papacy as a center of unity for the Catholic Church and helped prevent
the very real threat of its dissolution into state churches. Even so, the Council's success was not immediate, for in every important country the secular
rulers at first accepted only what they chose of its work, and only gradually
did its influence prevail.

Questions of national politics and of church politics apart, the Council
of Trent addressed itself to two kinds of labors, to a statement of Catholic
doctrine, and to a reform of abuses in the church. When the council began
to meet, in 1545, the Protestant movement had already gone so far that any
reconciliation was probably impossible—Protestants, especially Calvinists,
simply did not wish to belong to the church of Rome under any conditions.
In any case, the Council of Trent made no concessions.

It declared justification to be by works and faith combined, enumerated the seven sacraments and defined them exactly, affirmed a sacrament to
be a vehicle of grace independent of the spiritual state of him who received
it, reaffirmed transubstantiation, and declared the priesthood to be a special
estate set apart from the laity by the sacrament of holy orders, and endowed
with a supernatural power transmitted from Christ and the apostles. As
sources of Catholic faith, the Council put Scripture and Tradition on an
equal footing. It thus rejected the Protestant claim to find true faith in the
Bible alone, and reaffirmed the validity of church development since New
Testament times. The Vulgate, a translation into Latin made by St. Jerome
in the fourth century, was declared to be the only version of the Bible on
which authoritative teaching could be based. The right of individuals to
believe that their own interpretation of Scripture was more true than that
of church authorities (private judgment) was denied. Latin (as against the
national languages) was prescribed as the language of religious worship.
Celibacy of all clergy was maintained. Monasticism was upheld. The existence of purgatory was reaffirmed. The theory and correct practice in the grant
of indulgences were restated. The veneration of saints, the cult of the Virgin,
the use of images, relics, and pilgrimages were approved as spiritually useful
and pious actions.

It was easier for a council to define doctrines than to reform abuses,
since the latter consisted in the rooted habits of thousands and millions of

[16] See p. 604.

people's lives. The council decreed, however, a drastic reform of the monastic orders. It acted against the abuse of indulgences while upholding the principle. It ruled that bishops should reside habitually in their dioceses and attend more carefully to their proper duties. It gave bishops more administrative control over clergy in their own dioceses, such as mendicant friars, who in the past had been exempt from episcopal jurisdiction, and whose presence had often caused disturbance, or indeed scandal, among the local people. The abuse by which one man had held numerous church offices at the same time (pluralism) was checked, and steps were taken to assure that church officials should be competent. The council ordered, to provide an educated clergy, that a seminary should be set up in each diocese for the training of priests.

THE COUNTER-CRUSADE

As laws in general have little force unless sustained by opinion, so the reform decrees of the Council of Trent would have remained ineffectual had not a renewed sense of religious seriousness been growing up at the same time. Herein lay the inner force of the Catholic Reform. Men of a new type came forward. In Italy, as the Renaissance became more undeniably pagan, and as the sack of Rome, in 1527, showed the depths of hatred felt even by Catholics toward the Roman clergy, the voices of severer moralists began to be heeded. The line of Renaissance popes was succeeded by a line of reforming popes, of whom the first was Paul III (1534–49). The reforming popes insisted on the primacy of the papal office, but they regarded this office, unlike their predecessors, as a moral and religious force. In many bishoprics, in many countries, bishops began on their own initiative to be more strict. The new Catholic religious sense, unlike the Protestant, and more than in the Middle Ages, centered in a profound reverence for the sacraments, particularly the Mass, as the main avenue of the religious life, and a mystical awe for the church itself as a divine institution which no human sinfulness had ever polluted, and which extended as a seamless web throughout the ages and among all peoples, even those by whom it was flouted. Missionary fervor became more characteristic of Catholics than of Protestants. In Europe it expressed itself as an intense desire to reconvert the Protestant heretics. It showed itself, too, in missions among the poor, as in the work of St. Vincent de Paul among the human wreckage of Paris, for which the established Protestant churches failed to produce anything comparable. In America, as colonies developed in the sixteenth and seventeenth centuries, the Protestant clergy tended to take the layman's view of the Indians, while Catholic clergy labored to convert and preserve them; and the Catholic Church generally worked to mitigate the brutality of Negro slavery, to which the pastors in English and Dutch colonies, perhaps because they were less independent of the laity, remained largely indifferent, when, indeed, they did not positively declare that black men had no souls at all.

We have seen how in Spain, where the Renaissance had never taken much hold, the very life of the country was a boundless Christian crusade. It was in Spain that much of the new Catholic feeling first developed, and from Spain that much of the missionary spirit first went out. It was Spain that gave birth to St. Ignatius Loyola (1491–1556). A soldier in youth, he too, like Luther and Calvin, had a religious "experience" or "conversion," which occurred in 1521, before he had heard of Luther, and while Calvin was still a boy. It was by reading the life of Christ that he was converted, but his evangelizing zeal proved very different from that of either the Protestants or of the Catholic mystics who, in the North, had founded the lay Brothers of the Common Life.

Loyola resolved to become a soldier of the church, a militant crusader for the pope and the Holy See. On this principle he established the Society of Jesus, commonly known as the Jesuits. Authorized by Paul III in 1541, the Jesuits constituted a monastic order of a new type, less attached to the cloister, more directed toward active participation in the affairs of the world. Only men of proven strength of character and intellectual force were admitted. Each Jesuit had to undergo an arduous and even horrifying mystical training, set forth by Loyola in his *Spiritual Exercises*. The order was ruled by an iron discipline, which required each member to see in his immediate superior the infallibility of Holy Church. If, said Loyola, the church teaches to be black what the eye sees as white, the mind will believe it to be black. Aside from demanding absolute submission in matters of faith, the Jesuits generally favored rationality and a measure of liberty in the religious life. For two hundred years they were the chief schoolmasters of Catholic Europe, eventually conducting some five hundred schools for boys of the upper and middle classes. In them they taught, besides the faith, the principles of gentlemanly deportment (their teaching of dancing and dramatics became a scandal to more puritanical Catholics), and they carried over the Renaissance and humanist idea of the Latin classics as the main substance of adolescent education. The Jesuits made a specialty of work among the ruling classes. They became confessors to kings, and hence involved in political intrigue. In an age when Protestants subordinated the organized church either to the state or to the individual conscience, and when even Catholics frequently thought of the church within a national framework, the Jesuits seemed almost to worship the church itself as a divine institution, the Church Militant and the Church Universal, internationally organized and governed by the Roman pontiff. All full-fledged Jesuits took a special vow of obedience to the pope. Jesuits in the later sessions of the Council of Trent fought obstinately, and successfully, to uphold the position of Rome against that of the national bishops. The high papalism of the Jesuits (later called "ultramontanism") for centuries made them as obnoxious to many Catholics as they were to the Protestants.

By 1560 the Catholic Church, renewed by a deepening of its religious life, and by an uncompromising restatement of its dogmas and discipline, had devised also the practical machinery for a counter-offensive against Protestantism. The Jesuits acted as an international missionary force. They

recruited members from all countries, including those in which the governments had turned Protestant. English Catholics, for example, trained as
Jesuits on the Continent, returned to England to overthrow the heretic
usurper, Elizabeth, seeing in the universal church a higher cause than national independence in religion. Jesuits poured also into the most hotly
disputed regions where the issue still swayed in the balance—France, Germany, Bohemia, Poland, Hungary. As after every great revolution, many
people after an initial burst of Protestantism were inclined to turn back to
the old order, especially as the more crying evils within the Catholic church
were corrected. The Jesuits reconverted many who thus hesitated.

For the more recalcitrant other machinery was provided. All countries
censored books; Protestant authorities labored to keep "papist" works from
the eyes of the faithful, and Catholic authorities took the same pains to
suppress all knowledge of "heretics." All bishops, Anglican, Lutheran, and
Catholic, regulated reading matter within their dioceses. In the Catholic
world, with the trend toward centralization under the pope, a special importance attached to the list published by the bishop of Rome, the papal Index
of Prohibited Books. Only with special permission, granted to reliable persons for special study, could Catholics read books listed on the Index (or can
they today); on it most of the significant works written in Europe since the
Reformation have been included.

All countries, Protestant and Catholic, also set up judicial and police
machinery to enforce conformity to the accepted church. In England, for
example, Elizabeth established the High Commission to bring "recusants"
into the Church of England. All bishops, Protestant and Catholic, likewise
possessed machinery of enforcement in their episcopal courts. But no court
made itself so dreaded as the Inquisition. In reality two distinct organizations
went under this name, the word itself being simply an old term of the Roman
law, signifying a court of inquest or inquiry. One was the Spanish Inquisition,
established originally, about 1480, to ferret out Jewish and Moslem survivals
in Spain. It was then introduced into all countries ruled by the Spanish
Crown and employed against Protestantism, particularly in the Spanish
Netherlands, which was an important center of Calvinism. The other was
the Roman or papal Inquisition, established at Rome in 1542 under a permanent committee of cardinals called the Holy Office; it was in a sense a revival
of the famous medieval tribunal established in the thirteenth century for
the detection and repression of heresy. Both the Spanish and the Roman
Inquisition employed torture, for heresy was regarded as the supreme crime,
and all persons charged with crime could be tortured, in civil as well as
ecclesiastical courts, under the existing laws. In the use of torture, as in the
imposition of the harshest sentence, burning alive, the Roman Inquisition
was milder than the Spanish. With the growth of papal centralization the
Roman Inquisition in principle offered a court to protect purity of faith in all
parts of the Catholic world. But the national resistance of Catholic countries
proved too strong; few Catholics wished the agents of Rome inquiring locally
into their opinions; and the Roman Inquisition never functioned for any

length of time outside of Italy. In France no form of the Inquisition was admitted either then or later.

In the "machinery" of enforcing religious belief, however, no engine was to be so powerful as the apparatus of state, of political sovereignty. Where Protestants won control of government, peoples became Protestant. Where Catholics retained control of governments, Protestants became in time small minorities. And it was in the clash of governments, which is to say in war, for about a century after 1560, that the fate of European religion was worked out. In 1560 the strongest powers of Europe—Spain, France, Austria—were all officially Catholic. The Protestant states were all small or at most middle-sized. The Lutheran states of Germany, like all German states, were individually of little weight. The Scandinavian monarchies were far away. England, the most considerable of Protestant kingdoms, was a country of only four million people, with an independent and hostile Scotland to the north, and with no sign of colonial empire yet in existence. In the precedence of monarchs, as arranged in the earlier part of the century, the king of England ranked just below the king of Portugal, and next above the king of Sicily. Clearly, had a great combined Catholic crusade ever developed, Protestantism could have been wiped out. To launch such a crusade was the dream of the king of Spain. It never succeeded; why, will be seen in the next chapter.

The Wars of Religion, 1560-1648

IT IS convenient, when we wish a single phrase, to think of the period of almost a century following 1560 as the age of the Wars of Religion. France, England, the dominions of the king of Spain, and the Holy Roman Empire were all torn by civil struggles in which religion was an issue, and all these powers, with Denmark and Sweden in addition, at one time or another fought international wars in which religion was at stake. Religion was by no means the sole motivating force or cause of conflict. It may even be that the term Wars of Religion is a misnomer. The wars involved political, constitutional, economic, and social issues as well as religious. Often the ideological line became blurred, with Catholics lending aid to Protestants, or vice versa. Nevertheless, the "ideological" element was always important: had the Spanish Armada landed in England, for example, it is entirely conceivable that Catholicism might have been restored there. The wars of the time may be called Wars of Religion somewhat as the wars of our own century might be called, by some future historian, Wars of Social Doctrine—wars in which the "ideology" of democracy, autocracy, capitalism, or communism is an actual issue, and wars in which the social character of many countries has been profoundly affected, yet in which ideology has been mixed with national interest, political security, political expansionism, or economic need—or greed. So it was with the "ideology" of religion in the Wars of Religion.

But before going farther it is necessary to describe basic changes in the economic and social foundation of the European countries.

11. The Opening of the Atlantic

Always until about 1500 the Atlantic Ocean had been a barrier, an end. About 1500 it became a bridge, a starting place. In the Middle Ages, and even in Roman times, small craft had groped from port to port on Europe's Atlantic coast. In 1317 the Venetians established the Flanders galleys, commercial flotillas which regularly made the passage between the Adriatic and the North Sea. In the fifteenth century, with further improvements in shipbuilding, in the rigging and manipulation of sails, and with the adoption of the mariner's compass, it became feasible to sail in the open ocean out of sight of land. It was the Portuguese who first made use of this opportunity. They were perhaps mainly drawn by the simple lure of exploration, but they were certainly tempted, on the material level, by the thought of trading directly with Asia.

For centuries, Asia had been a source for Europe of many highly valued commodities, partly manufactures in which Europe could not compete, such as silk and cotton fabrics, rugs, jewelry, porcelains, and fine steel, and partly raw or semi-manufactured drugs and foodstuffs, such as sugar and above all spices. The latter—pepper, cinnamon, cloves, ginger, nutmeg, and many less common ones—were of more importance then than now. They were used in pharmacy, and in the preservation of meat, as in the making of sausages. They added palatability to fresh meats and other foods which easily spoiled in the absence of refrigeration. Europeans had never themselves gone to the sources of supply of Eastern goods. Somewhere, east of Suez, barely known to Europeans, was another world of other merchants, mainly Arabs, who moved the wares of China, India, and the East Indies spice islands by caravan over land and by boat through the Red Sea or Persian Gulf to the markets of the eastern Mediterranean. Traders of the two worlds met and did business at such thriving centers as Alexandria or Beirut or Constantinople.

THE PORTUGUESE IN THE EAST

For some time the Portuguese royal house had sponsored and encouraged exploration of the Atlantic. In 1498 the Portuguese navigator

Vasco da Gama, having rounded Africa in the wake of other intrepid explorers, found himself in the midst of the unknown world of Arab commerce. He landed on the Malabar Coast (the southwest coast of India), where he found a busy commercial population of heterogeneous religious background. These people knew at least as much about Europe as Europeans did about India (one Jew was able to act as da Gama's interpreter) and they realized that the coming of the Portuguese would disturb their established channels of commerce. Da Gama, playing upon local rivalries, was able to load his ships with the coveted wares, but on his second voyage, in 1502, he came better prepared, bringing a fighting fleet of no less than twenty-one vessels. A ferocious war broke out between the Portuguese and Arab merchants, the latter supported in one way or another by the Egyptians, the Turks, and even the distant Venetians, all of whom had an interest in maintaining the old routes of trade. For the Portuguese, trained like the Spaniards in long wars against the Moors at home, no atrocities were too horrible to commit against the infidel competitors whom they found at the end of their heroic quest. Cities were devastated, ships burned at their docks, prisoners butchered and their dismembered hands, noses, and ears sent back as derisive trophies. One Brahmin, mutilated in this way, was left alive to bear them to his people. Such, unfortunately, was India's introduction to the West.

In the following years, under the first governor-general, Albuquerque, the Portuguese built permanent fortified stations at Goa on the Malabar coast, at Aden near the mouth of the Red Sea, at Ormuz near the mouth of the Persian Gulf, and in East Africa. In 1509 they reached Malacca, near the modern Singapore, from which they passed northward into China itself, and eastward to Amboina, the heart of the Spice Islands, just west of New Guinea. Thus an empire was created, the first of Europe's commercial-colonial empires, maintained by superiority of firearms and sea power and with trade alternating with war and plunder. Albuquerque died in 1515, dreaming grandiose and preposterous dreams—to deflect the course of the Nile and so destroy Egypt and Egyptian commerce, and to capture Mecca and exchange it for the Holy Land. It should be added that bold Jesuits soon arrived, led by St. Francis Xavier, who, by 1550, had baptized thousands of souls in India, Indonesia, and even Japan.

By the new route the cost of Eastern goods for Europeans was much reduced, for the old route had involved many transshipments, unloadings, and re-loadings, movements by sea and by land, through the hands of many merchants. In 1504 spices could be bought in Lisbon for only a fifth of the price demanded in Venice. The Venetians (who in their desperation even talked of digging a Suez canal) were hopelessly undersold; their trade thereafter was confined to products of the Near East itself. As for the Portuguese, never was a commercial monopoly built so fast. The lower prices added enormously to European demand and consumption. Beginning in 1504, only five years after da Gama's first return, an average of twelve ships a year left Lisbon for the East.

THE DISCOVERY OF AMERICA

Meanwhile, as every American schoolchild can tell, the same quest for
a route to the East had led to the somewhat disappointing discovery of
America. Like most such discoveries, this was no chance hit of a queer or
isolated genius. Behaim's globe, constructed in 1492,[1] the very year of Columbus's first voyage, could hardly fail to suggest the idea of sailing westward.
Nevertheless, it was Christopher Columbus who had the persistence and
daring to undertake the unprecedented westward voyage. Before the invention of sufficiently accurate clocks (in the eighteenth century) mariners had
no way of determining longitude, *i.e.*, their east-west position; and learned
geographers, as may be seen from Behaim's map, greatly underestimated the
probable distance from Europe westward to Asia. When Columbus struck
land, he naturally supposed it to be an outlying part of the Indies. The people
were soon called Indians, and the islands where Columbus landed, the West
Indies.

Columbus had sailed with the backing of Queen Isabella of Castile,
and the new lands became part of the composite dominions of the crown of
Spain. The Spaniards, hoping to beat the Portuguese to the East (which da
Gama had not yet reached), received Columbus' first reports with enthusiasm.
For his second voyage they gave him seventeen ships, filled with 1,500 workmen and artisans. Columbus himself, until his death in 1506, kept probing
about in the Caribbean, baffled and frustrated, hoping to find something that
looked like the fabulous East. Others were more willing to accept the new
land for what it was. Churchmen, powerful in Spain, regarded it as a new
field for crusading and conversion. The government saw it as a source of gold
and silver for the royal exchequer. Foot-loose gentry of warlike habits, left
idle by the end of war with the Moors, turned to it to make their fortunes.
The *conquistadores* fell upon the new lands. Cortés conquered the Aztecs in
Mexico, Pizarro the Incas in Peru. They despoiled the native empires. Mines
for precious metals were opened almost immediately. The Indians were put
to forced labor, in which many died. The attempts of the church to protect
its Indian converts, and restrictions set by the royal authorities on their exploitation, led almost immediately to the importation of African slaves, of
whom, it was estimated, 100,000 had been brought to America by 1560.

Explorers began to feel their way along the vast dim bulk that barred
them from Asia. A Spanish expedition, led by Magellan, found a southwestern
passage in 1520, sailed from the Atlantic into the Pacific, crossed the Pacific,
discovered the Philippine Islands, and fought its way through hostile Portuguese across the Indian Ocean back to Spain. The globe was thus circum-
navigated for the first time, and an idea of the true size and interconnection
of the oceans was brought back to Europe. Geographical experts immediately
incorporated the new knowledge, as in the map drawn by Schöner in 1523.[2]

[1] See p. 275.
[2] See p. 275.

Meanwhile others sailing for Spain, the Cabots sailing for England, Jacques Cartier for France began the long and fruitless search for a northwest passage. An English expedition, looking for a northeast passage, discovered the White Sea in 1553. English merchants immediately began to take the ocean route to Russia. Archangel became an ocean port.

For a century it was only the Spanish and Portuguese who followed up the new ocean routes to America and the East. These two peoples, accepting the arbitration of the pope, divided the globe between them. The Philippines, because of Magellan's discovery, went to Spain; Brazil, because it had been discovered by Cabral in 1500, to Portugal. Otherwise Spain received all America, and Portugal all rights of trade in Asia and the East Indies.

THE SPANISH EMPIRE IN AMERICA

In the populous and civilized East the Portuguese were never more than a handful of transients who could not impose their language, their religion, or their way of life. In America, after the first fiendishness of the *conquista*, the Spanish established their own civilization. In Protestant countries, and also in France, as the years went on, there arose an extremely unfavorable idea of the Spanish regime in America, where, it was noted, the Inquisition was presently established and the native peoples were reduced to servitude by the conquerors. The Spanish themselves came to dismiss this grim picture as a Black Legend concocted by their rivals. The true character of the Spanish empire in America is not easy to portray. The Spanish government (like the home governments of all colonial empires until the American Revolution, and even later) regarded its empire as existing for the benefit of the mother country. The Indians were put into servitude, to work in mines or in agriculture. The government introduced the *encomienda*, a kind of distant analogue to the European manor. The "lord" of the *encomienda* controlled the labor of his Indians, but according to law he could not deprive an Indian of his own parcel of land, and he must make Indians work for him no more than four days a week, leaving them two days to work on their parcels. Such conditions corresponded very closely to those in which the white masses of Eastern Europe lived until the nineteenth century. How much the royal regulations were enforced in remote *encomiendas* is another question, on which answers vary. Negro slavery never assumed the importance in Spanish America that it later assumed in the Dutch, French, and English colonies, and Negro slaves generally received protection and status not accorded them in the northern colonies. The white population remained small. Castilian Spaniards looked down on American-born whites, or creoles. Since few women emigrated from Spain, there arose a large class of *mestizos*, of mixed white and Indian descent.

The *mestizos*, along with pure Indians in the towns and *encomiendas*, adopted the Spanish language and the faith of the Spanish Church. The Indians, while unfree, had usually been unfree under their own tribal chiefs;

they were spared from tribal war; and the rigors of the Inquisition were mild compared with the sheer physical cruelty of the Aztecs or Incas. The printing press was brought to Mexico in 1544. By the middle of the sixteenth century Spanish America consisted of two great vice-royalties, those of Mexico and Peru, with twenty-two bishoprics, and with a university in each vice-royalty, the University of Lima established in 1551, that of Mexico in 1553. When Harvard college was founded in New England (in 1636) there were five universities on the European model in Spanish America. In sum, it may be observed not only that the Spanish empire let the Indians survive, but that in all the long record of European expansion the Spanish are the only people, along with the Portuguese in Brazil, who have ever really "Europeanized" a large non-European mass in its own native environment.

In 1545 a great discovery was made, the prodigiously rich silver deposits at Potosí in Peru. Almost simultaneously, better methods of extracting silver from the ore by the use of mercury were developed. American production of precious metals shot up suddenly and portentously. For years, after the mid-century, half a million pounds of silver flowed annually from America to Spain, and ten thousand pounds of gold. A price revolution followed in Europe. The riches of Potosí financed the European projects of the king of Spain. Peruvian ores, Indian labor, and Spanish management combined to make possible the militant and anti-Protestant phase of the Counter-Reformation.

The opening of the Atlantic reoriented Europe. In an age of oceanic communications Europe became a center from which America, Africa, and Asia could all be reached. In Europe itself, the Atlantic coast enjoyed great advantages over the center. No sooner did the Portuguese begin to bring spices from the East Indies than Antwerp began to flourish as the point of redistribution for northern Europe. But for a century after the great discoveries the northern peoples did not take to the oceans. French corsairs did indeed put out from Bayonne or St. Malo, and Dutch prowlers and English "sea dogs" followed at the close of the century, all bent upon plundering the Iberian treasure ships. Still the Spanish and Portuguese kept their monopoly. No organized effort, backed by governments, came from the north until about 1600. For it is by no means geography alone that sets the fate of peoples, and the English, Dutch, and French could not make use of the opportunities with which the opening of the Atlantic provided them until they had cleared up domestic troubles at home, and survived the perils and hazards of the Wars of Religion.

12. The Commercial Revolution

In the period under discussion a great economic readjustment was taking place in Europe in which the opening of ocean trade routes was an important but by no means the only factor. The changes about to be described are usually summarized under the term Commercial Revolution, which in general signifies the rise of a capitalistic economy and the transition from a town-centered to a nation-centered economic system. This "revolution" was an exceptionally slow and protracted one, for it began at least as early as the fourteenth century and lasted into the eighteenth century.

CHANGES IN COMMERCE AND PRODUCTION

In the Middle Ages the town and its adjoining country formed an economic unit.[3] Craftsmen, organized in gilds, produced common articles for local use. Peasants and lords sold their agricultural products to the local town, from which they bought manufactures. The town protected itself by its own tariffs and regulations. In the workshop the master both owned his "capital"—his house, workbench, tools, and materials—and acted as a workman himself along with half a dozen journeymen and apprentices. The masters owned a modest capital, but they were hardly capitalists. They produced only upon order, or at least for customers whose tastes and number were known in advance. There was little profit, and little risk of loss. There was much social mobility; the journeymen could expect to become a master, and the apprentice might even marry the master's daughter. Journeymen as well as masters could generally vote for town officials.

All this changed with the widening of the trading area, or market. Even in the Middle Ages, as we have seen, there was a certain amount of long-distance trading in articles that could not be produced as well in one place as in another. Gradually more articles came within this category. Where goods were produced to be sold at some time in the future, in far away places, to persons unknown, the local gildmaster could not manage the operation. He lacked the money (or "capital") to tie up in stocks of unsold wares; he lacked the knowledge of what distant customers wanted, or where, in what quantities, and at what price people would buy. In this type of business a new type of man developed. Economists call him the "enterpriser" or *entrepreneur*. He usually started out as a merchant working in an extensive market, and ended up as a banker. The Italian Medici family has been mentioned.[4] Equally typical were the German Fuggers.

The first of this family, Johann Fugger, a small town weaver, came to Augsburg in 1368. He established a business in a new kind of cloth, called fustian, in which cotton was mixed, and which had certain advantages over the woollens and linens in which people then clothed themselves. He thus enjoyed a more than local market, and made trips to Venice to obtain the cotton imported from the Near East. Gradually the family began to deal also in spices, silks, and other Eastern goods obtained at Venice. They made large profits, which were invested in other enterprises, notably mining. They lent

---

[3] See p. 28.
[4] See pp. 50–1.

money to the Renaissance popes. They lent Charles V the money which he spent to obtain election as Holy Roman Emperor in 1519. They became bankers to the Hapsburgs in both Germany and Spain. Together with other German and Flemish bankers, the Fuggers financed the Portuguese trade with Asia, either by outright loans, or by providing in advance, on credit, the cargoes which the Portuguese traded for spices. Portugal was not a very productive country, nor did Asian peoples want European manufactures. The Portuguese ships went out loaded mainly with metals, both precious and common, gold, silver, copper, lead, and mercury, produced mainly in Germany and controlled by German capital. The Fuggers, and others like them, through branches established at Lisbon and Antwerp, likewise controlled the distribution in Europe of wares that the Portuguese ships brought back. The wealth of the Fuggers became proverbial, and declined only through repeated Hapsburg bankruptcies, and with the general economic decline that beset Germany in the sixteenth century.

Other dealers in cloth, less spectacular than the first Fugger, broke away from the town-and-gild framework in other ways. England until the fifteenth century was an exporter of raw wool and an importer of finished woollens from Flanders. In the fifteenth century certain Englishmen began to develop the spinning, weaving and dyeing of wool in England. To avoid the restrictive practices of the towns and gilds they "put out" the work to people in the country, providing them with looms and other equipment for the purpose, of which they generally retained the ownership themselves. This "putting out" or "domestic" system spread very widely. In France, the cloth dealers of Rouen, feeling the competition of the new silk trade, developed a lighter, cheaper, and more simply made type of woollen cloth. Various gild regulations in Rouen, to protect the workers there, prohibited the manufacture of this cheaper cloth. The Rouen dealers, in 1496, took the industry into the country, installed looms in peasant cottages, and farmed out the work to the peasants.

This domestic system, or system of rural household industry, remained typical of production in many lines (cloth, hardware, *etc.*) in Western Europe until the introduction of factories in the late eighteenth century. It was clearly capitalistic. On the one hand were the workers, people who worked as the employer needed them, received wages for what they did, and had no interest in or knowledge of more than their own task. Living both by agriculture and by cottage industry, they formed an expansible labor force, available when labor was needed, left to live by farming or local charity when times were bad. On the other hand was the man who managed the whole affair. He had no personal acquaintance with the workers. Estimating how much of his product, let us say woollens, he could sell in a national or even international market, he purchased the needed raw materials, passed out wool to be spun by one group of peasants, took the yarn to another group for weaving, collected the cloth and took it still elsewhere to be dyed, paying wages on all sides for services rendered, while retaining ownership of the materials and the equipment and keeping the coordination and management of the whole enterprise in his own head. Much larger business enterprises could be established in this way than within the municipal framework of gild and town. Indeed, the very master weavers of the gilds often sank to the status of sub-contractors, hardly different from wage employees, of the great "clothiers" and "drapers" by whom the business was dominated. The latter, with the widening market, became personages of national or even international repute. And, of course, the bigger the business the more of a capital investment it represented.

Certain other industries, new or virtually new in the fifteenth and sixteenth centuries, could by their nature never fit into a town-centered system and were capitalistic from the start, in that they required a large initial outlay before any income could be received. One such was mining. Another was printing and the book trade; books had a national and even international market, being mainly in Latin; and no ordinary craftsman could afford the outlay required for a printing press, for fonts of type, supplies of paper, and stocks of books on hand. Printers therefore borrowed from capitalists, or shared with them an interest in business. Shipbuilding was so stimulated by the shift to the oceans as almost to be a new industry, and still another was the manufacture of cannons and muskets. For the latter the chief demand came from the state, from the New Monarchies which were organizing national armies. In the rise of capitalism the needs of the military were in fact fundamentally important. Armies, which started out by requiring thousands of weapons, in the seventeenth century required thousands of uniforms, and in the eighteenth century many solidly built barracks and fortifications. These were the first demands for mass production; and where governments themselves did not take the initiative, capitalists stepped in as middlemen between these huge impersonal requirements and the myriads of small handicraft workers by whom, before the industrial age, the actual product was still manufactured.

The new sea route to the East and the discovery of America brought a vast increase in trade not only of luxury items but of bulk commodities like rice, sugar, tea, and other consumer goods. Older commercial activities were transformed by the widening of markets. Spain increasingly drew cereals from Sicily. The Netherlands was fed from Poland, the French wine districts lived on food brought from northern France. With the growth of shipping, the timber, tar, pitch and other "naval stores" of Russia and the Baltic came upon the commercial scene. There was thus an ever growing movement of heavy staple commodities, in which again only men controlling large funds of capital could normally take part.

Not all capital was invested; some was simply lent, either to the church, or to governments, or to impecunious nobles, or, though perhaps this was the least common type of lending in the sixteenth century, to persons engaged in trade and commerce. Bankers and others who lent money expected to receive back, after a time, a larger sum than that of the loan. They expected "interest"; and they sometimes received as much as 30 per cent a year. In the Middle Ages the taking of interest had been frowned upon as usury, denounced as avarice, and forbidden in the canon law. It was still frowned upon in the sixteenth century by almost all but the lenders themselves. The Catholic Church maintained its prohibitions. The theologians of the University of Paris ruled against it in 1530. Luther, who hated "Fuggerism," continued to preach against usury. Calvin made allowances, but as late as 1640, in capitalist Holland itself, the stricter Calvinist ministers still denounced lending at interest. Nothing could stop the practice. Borrowers compounded with lenders to evade prohibitions, and theologians of all churches began to distinguish between "usury" and a "legitimate return." Gradually, as interest rates fell, as banking became more established, and as loans were made for economically productive uses rather than to sustain ecclesiastics, princes, and nobles in their personal habits, the feeling against a "reasonable" interest died down, and interest became an accepted feature of capitalism. The Bank of Amsterdam, in the seventeenth century, because depositors knew that their money was safe and could be withdrawn at will, was able to attract deposits from all countries by offering a very low rate of interest, which enabled it in turn to make loans, at a low rate, to finance commercial activities.

The net effect of all these developments was a "commercialization of industry." The great man of business was the merchant. Industry, the actual processes of production, remaining in an essentially handicraft stage, was subordinate to the buyers and sellers. Producers—weavers, hatters, metal workers, gunsmiths, glass workers, etc.,—worked to fill orders of the merchants, and often with capital which the merchants supplied and owned. The man who knew where the article could be sold prevailed over the man who simply knew how to produce it. This commercial capitalism remained the typical form of capitalism until after 1800, when, with the introduction of power machinery, it yielded to industrial capitalism, and merchants became dependent on those who owned, understood, and organized the machines. Meanwhile, of all middle-class or non-noble people, the merchant, along with the banker, enjoyed the highest social prestige and political influence.

THE PRICE REVOLUTION

With these more purely commercial changes went a monetary revolution that in many ways was even more far-reaching, since all classes of society were affected by it. Shiploads of precious metal poured into Spain, especially after the discoveries at Potosí. The Spaniards used it to finance economic wants or political objectives in the rest of Europe. The amount of metal in circulation rose much faster than the volume of goods or services produced, and as a result the value of metal declined, which is to say that prices rose. For a century and a half after the discovery of America, Europe experienced a steady inflation. It was most rapid in the second half of the sixteenth century. It varied from one country to another, but, roughly speaking, prices be-

tween 1550 and 1600 approximately doubled, and by 1650 they were more
than three times higher than in 1500. In 1500 an Englishman with an annual
income of fifty pounds sterling was well-to-do, but in 1650 he was barely
middle-class. Wheat and hay sold in the Paris market, in 1650, for fifteen
times the price of 1500. So it went everywhere. The persistent inflation had
the effects that inflation always has: persons whose income was fixed in
money value suffered, because the money always bought less; persons whose
debts and obligations were fixed in money value benefited, because as years
passed the same sum of money was easier to obtain and less of a burden to
pay. Or as a Frenchman observed in 1620: "The debtor gains what the
creditor has lost."

Governments were caught between fixed income and mounting expenses. The idea persisted, carried over from the Middle Ages, that kings
should normally live "on their own," from the income of the manors and
other properties in their crown domain, and from feudal payments or customary taxes, such as import and export duties, whose amount had usually
been fixed in money value in the past.[5] At the same time kings were maintaining larger armies and fighting frequent wars, of which the costs were
always rising. Various kings adopted various expedients. They might simply
borrow, as the Hapsburgs did from the Fuggers. Often they "devalued" their
money or "debased" their coinage, simply declaring that a given weight of
silver or gold should be worth a larger number of *livres*, or *reals*, or florins.
This practice, while temporarily raising a king's income, in the long run
added to the inflation. Others, especially in France, sold government offices
in return for cash. Or they sold monopolies, or the exclusive privilege of
doing a certain kind of business in a certain place or in the country as a
whole. Or they encroached on the rights of towns, requiring money payments
in return for confirmation of town charters. Or they quarreled with their
parliaments, notably in England but also elsewhere, demanding assent to new
taxes which parliaments were either unwilling to grant or willing to grant
only in return for political concessions. Thus the monetary crisis helped to
precipitate a constitutional crisis, with the king increasingly at odds with
representative bodies. Out of this constitutional crisis, in the seventeenth
century, came the triumph of Parliament in England and of royal absolutism
almost everywhere else.

In the towns, inflation accentuated the class differences that were also
arising from other causes. Generally it benefited the merchants. The wealth
of the merchants was in goods whose value, measured in money, was rising.
Merchants and others who owned urban real estate benefited from the increase of rents. Merchants who bought ships or dyeing vats or copper mines
found their investment automatically increasing in value as time went by.
On the other hand the town wage-earners, the journeymen, were consistently
worse off because wages rarely rose as fast as prices. Thus the journeyman,
whose position had deteriorated in any case for quite different reasons, who

[5] See p. 30.

could no longer aspire to become an independent master, who competed
with peasants under the growing system of domestic industry and who increasingly worked simply as an occasional employee of the merchant, was in
addition pinched by purely monetary developments. Journeymen formed
mysterious organizations of their own, outside the gilds, and to which the
masters of the gilds were not admitted; these were the first true labor unions,
and they sometimes conducted strikes to obtain better wages. Governments
tried to suppress them, but in many places they persisted in secrecy.

Towns everywhere divided into an upper or "bourgeois" and a lower
or laboring class. The journeymen lost their voice in civic affairs, and the
nearly universal suffrage of townsmen of the Middle Ages gave way to rule
by a bourgeois patriciate, oligarchy, or "corporation." The laboring class lived
in slums, often in the very buildings built in the thirteenth or fourteenth
century. The merchants and bourgeois lived in substantial new houses of
brick or stone. In England they began to consider themselves gentlemen; in
Holland they ruled the country; in France they called themselves *honnêtes
hommes* and on their tombstones left the epitaph that they had "lived
nobly."

SOCIAL DEVELOPMENTS IN WESTERN AND EASTERN EUROPE

But it was chiefly in the country that the price revolution had its most
sweeping effects, especially when it is remembered that all parts of Europe
remained overwhelmingly agricultural. The effects worked inversely in western and in eastern Europe. In the west, the peasant went up and the lord
went down in general position. In the east, the peasant went down and the
lord went up.

In western Europe, as early as the fourteenth century, the peasants
had very commonly secured manorial lands for themselves by agreeing to
pay the lords a set annual sum of money in perpetuity into the future.[6] The
sum so set, while not changing in amount, was in real value much less in
1600 than in 1300 or 1400 because of the inflation. Peasants, selling their
own farm products, benefited from rising prices and received a higher money
income, yet they owed the lord only the same old amount. Peasants, therefore, were proportionately far better off. It was from such peasant dues and
fees that, in western Europe, the bulk of the old feudal class, the small
nobles, gentry or landed aristocracy, drew most of its income. These lords of
manors were usually not farmers themselves; they did not raise and sell agricultural products on their own account; most of the area of their manors was
let out to peasants on perpetual and hereditary leaseholds in return for the
payments just mentioned. Most nobles and gentry were thus receivers of
fixed income, and as such they were faced with ruin.

The period, in the west, was one of a distressed landed aristocracy, of

[6] See p. 29.

impoverished *hidalgos* in Spain, *hoberaux* in France, squires in England, who met their problem in different ways. Sometimes they borrowed from bankers or merchants, and then lost their lands when unable to pay their debts. Sometimes they sold lands and manors outright to affluent merchants, who thereupon moved into the country, where they "lived nobly," or "like gentlemen." The real noble, the noble of blood and birth, thus losing his patrimony, or unable to live from it if he kept it, drifted off to one kind of activity or another. The large number of uprooted minor nobles, to whom war was the one honorable occupation, made a restless element from which all sides were recruited in the civil struggles of the Wars of Religion. Spanish *hidalgos* went off to America. In all countries there were many who took service with the king. In England some went into trade, thus further blurring the class boundaries in England. In England, however, the landed gentry, enriched by farmlands that had formerly belonged to the monasteries, and turning to sheep raising to meet the growing demand for wool, was less hard hit by economic changes than was the corresponding lesser nobility of other countries.

In eastern Europe, it was the lords who benefited from rising prices and the growing market for grain and forest products. Here too the institution of the manor existed; but the peasant land-tenures were more precarious than in the west, more dependent on accidents of death or on the wishes of the lord, and the lord worked a larger part of the manor with his own workmen for his own use or profit. The rise of prices and expansion of the Baltic trade gave the lord an incentive to increase his output. In northeast Germany (where such lords were called *Junkers*), in Poland, in the Baltic region, and as time went on in Russia, and also in Bohemia and Hungary, beginning in the sixteenth century and continuing into the eighteenth, there set in a vast process by which the mass of the peasantry sank into serfdom. It was hastened in many regions by the violence and insecurity of the religious wars. Typically, the peasant lost his parcel of land, or received it back on condition that he render unpaid labor services to the lord. Usually the peasant owed three or four days a week of such forced labor (called *robot* in Bohemia and adjoining territories), remaining free to work during the remainder of the week on his own parcel. Often the number of days of *robot* exacted by the lord was greater, since in eastern Europe, where central monarchy was weak and centralized legal systems almost unknown, the lord himself was the final court of appeal for his people. His people were in fact his "subjects." Serfdom in Germany was not called serfdom, an ill-sounding word, but "hereditary subjection." The serf, or hereditary subject of the manorial lord, by whatever name called throughout eastern Europe, could not leave the manor, marry, or learn a trade without the lord's express permission. The lord, drawing on this large reserve of compulsory labor, using most of it for agriculture but teaching some quick-minded youths the various handcrafts that were needed on the estate, worked the land as his own venture, sold the produce, and retained the profit.

Thus in the east, at the beginning of modern times, the rural masses lost personal freedom and lived in a poverty unknown to the peasants of the west, poor as the latter were. In the west the peasants were already on the way to becoming small farmers. They were free men in the law. They could migrate, marry, and learn trades as opportunity offered. Those who held land could defend it in royal courts, and they raised crops and took part in the market economy on their own account. They owed the lord no forced labor—or virtually none, for the ten days a year of *corvée* still found in parts of France hardly compared with the almost full-time *robot* of the peasant of eastern Europe.

The landlord, in the east, from the sixteenth century onward, was solidly entrenched in his own domain, monarch of all he surveyed, with no troublesome bourgeoisie to annoy him (for towns were few), and with kings and territorial rulers solicitous of his wishes. Travelers from the west were impressed with the lavishness of great Polish and Lithuanian magnates, with their palatial homes, private art galleries, well stocked libraries, collections of jewels, swarms of servants, trains of dependent lesser gentry, gargantuan dinners, and barbaric hospitality. The *Junkers* of northeast Germany lived with more modesty, but enjoyed the same kind of independence and social superiority. The importance of all this will become evident when, in later chapters, we turn to Prussia, Poland, Russia, and the Austrian lands.

MERCANTILISM

There was still another aspect of the Commercial Revolution, namely the various government policies that go historically under the name of mercantilism. Rulers, as we have seen, were hard pressed for money, and needed more of it as it fell in value. The desire of kings and their advisers to force gold and silver to flow into their own kingdoms was one of the first impulses leading to mercantilist regulation. Gradually this "bullionist" idea was replaced by the more general idea of building up a strong and self-sufficient economy. The means adopted, in either case, was to "set the poor on work," as they said in England, to turn the country into a hive of industry, to discourage idleness, begging, vagabondage and unemployment, to introduce new crafts and manufactures, to give favors to merchants who kept "the poor" occupied and who sold the country's products abroad, to raise the export of finished goods and reduce the export of unprocessed raw materials, to curtail all imports except of needed raw materials, and thus obtain a "favorable" balance of trade so that other countries would have to pay their debts in bullion. Since all this was done by a royal or nation-wide system of regulations, mercantilism became in the economic sphere what the state-building of the New Monarchies was in the political, signifying the transition from town to national units of social living.[7]

Mercantilists frowned upon the gilds, with their localistic and con-

---

[7] On the New Monarchies see pp. 60–5.

servative outlook. In England the gilds ceased to have any importance. Parliament, in the time of Elizabeth, did on a national scale what gilds had once done locally when it enacted the Statute of Artificers of 1563, regulating the admission to apprenticeship and level of wages in various trades. In France the royal government kept the gilds in being, because they were convenient bodies to tax, but it deprived them of most of their old independence, and used them as organizations through which royal control of industry could be enforced. In both countries, the government assisted merchants who wished to set up domestic or cottage industry in the country, against the protests of the town gilds, which in their heyday had forbidden rural people to engage in crafts. Governments generally tried to suppress idleness, especially in Protestant countries where begging was out of favor, and where it was thought unwise to give alms without asking questions. The famous English Poor Law of 1601 (which remained in effect, with amendments, until 1834) was designed both to force people to work and to relieve absolute destitution.

Governments likewise took steps to introduce new industries. The silk industry was brought from Italy to France under royal protection, to the dismay of French woollen and linen interests. The English government assisted in turning England from a producer of raw wool into a producer of finished woollens, supervising the immigration of skilled Flemish weavers, and even fetching from faraway Turkey, about 1582, two youths who understood the more advanced dyeing arts of the Near East. Generally, under mercantilism, governments fought to steal skilled workers from each other while prohibiting or discouraging the emigration of their own skilled workers, who might take their trade secrets and "mysteries" to foreign parts.

By such means governments helped to create a national market and an industrious nation-wide labor supply for their great merchants, and without such government support the great merchants, such as the drapers or clothiers, could never have risen and prospered. The same help was given to merchants operating in foreign markets. Henry VII of England in 1496 negotiated a commercial treaty with Flanders, known as the Intercursus Magnus; and in the next century the kings of France signed a number of treaties with the Ottoman Empire by which French merchants obtained privileges in the Near East. A merchant backed by a national monarchy was in a much stronger position than one backed merely by a city, such as Augsburg or Venice. This backing on a national scale was again given when national governments subsidized exports, paying bounties for goods whose production they wished to encourage, or when they erected tariff barriers against imports to protect their own producers from competition. Thus a national tariff system was superimposed on the old network of provincial and municipal tariffs. These latter were now thought of as "internal tariffs," and mercantilists usually wished to abolish them, in order to create an area of free trade within the state as a whole. But local interests were so strong, and a sense of interprovincial and inter-town unity was so slow to develop, that for centuries they were unable to get rid of local tariffs except in England.

In wild or distant parts of the world, or in exotic regions nearer home, such as the Moslem Near East or Russia, it was not possible for individual merchants to act by merely private initiative. Merchants trading with such countries needed a good deal of capital, they often had to obtain special privileges and protection from native rulers, and they had to arm their ships against Barbary or Malay pirates or against hostile Europeans. Merchants and their respective governments came together to found official companies for the trans-ocean trade. In England, soon after the English discovery of the White Sea in 1553, a Russia Company was established. A Turkey Company soon followed. Shortly after 1600 a great many such companies were operating out of England, Holland, and France. The most famous of all were the East India Companies, the English founded in 1600, the Dutch in 1602, the French not until 1664. Each of these companies was a state-supported organization, with special rights. Each was a monopoly in that only merchants who belonged to the company could legally engage in trade in the region for which the company had a charter. Each was expected to find markets for the national manufactures, and of most of them it was hoped that they would bring home gold or silver. With these companies the northern peoples began to encroach on the Spanish and Portuguese monopoly in America and the East. With them new commercial-colonial empires were to be launched. But, as has been already observed, before this could happen it was necessary for certain domestic and purely European conflicts and controversies to be settled.

13. The Crusade of Catholic Spain: The Dutch and English

THE AMBITIONS OF PHILIP II

Charles V, having tried in vain for thirty-five years to preserve religious unity in Germany, abdicated his many crowns and retired to a monastery in 1556, the year after the Peace of Augsburg.[8] He left Austria, Bohemia, and Hungary (or the small part of it not occupied by the Turks) to his brother Ferdinand, who was soon elected Holy Roman Emperor.[9] All his other possessions Charles left to his son Philip, who became Philip II of Spain. The Hapsburg dynasty remained thereafter divided into two branches, the Austrian and the Spanish. The two cooperated in European affairs. The Spanish for a century was the more important. Philip II (1556–98) not only possessed the Spanish kingdoms but in 1580 inherited Portugal, so that the whole Iberian peninsula was brought under his rule. He possessed the seventeen provinces of the Netherlands and the Free County of Burgundy, which were member states of the Holy Roman Empire, lying on its western border,

ᴧᴧᴧᴧᴧᴧᴧᴧᴧᴧᴧᴧᴧᴧᴧᴧ

[8] See pp. 72–5.
[9] See map, pp. 66–7.

adjacent to France. Milan in north Italy and Naples in the south belonged to
Philip, and since he also held the chief islands, as well as Tunis, he enjoyed a
naval ascendancy in the Western Mediterranean which was threatened only
by the Turks. For five years, until 1558, he was titular king of England, and
in 1589, in the name of his daughter, he laid claim to the throne of France.
All America belonged to Philip II, and after 1580 all the Portuguese empire
as well, so that except for a few nautical daredevils all ships plying the open
ocean were the Spanish king's.

Philip II therefore naturally regarded himself as an international figure,
and the more so because he thought in terms not of nationality but of religion. Before all else he was a Catholic, fervid and fanatical, committed to
upholding the sway of the Universal Church, within which all nations were
no more than minorities and all heretics no more than rebels. A grave and
sober man, of abstemious personal habits, sharing in the moral severity of
the Catholic Reform, and in the dark, brooding, and tormented inner world
of the Spanish mystics, he took upon himself the headship of a far-flung
Catholic counteroffensive, into which he was willing to pour with grim persistence the blood and treasure of all his kingdoms. To economic and material interests he gave no thought, and in such matters Spanish society began
to deteriorate in his reign; but for all material problems the wealth of Potosí
provided a facile solution, and meanwhile Spain entered upon the Golden
Age of its culture.

In this period, the *siglo de oro*, running in round dates from 1550 to
1650, Cervantes wrote his *Don Quixote* and Lope de Vega his seven hundred
dramas, while El Greco, Murillo, and Velasquez painted their pictures, and
the Jesuit Suarez composed works on philosophy and law that were read
even in Protestant countries. But the essence of Spanish life was its peculiarly
intensive Catholicism. The church was vitally present at every social level,
from the Archbishop of Toledo, who ranked above grandees and could address the king as an equal, down to a host of penniless and mendicant friars,
who mixed with the poorest and most disinherited of the people. It is said
that about 1600 a third of the population of Spain was in one way or another
in the service of the church. Spain, whose whole history had been a crusade,
was ideally suited to be Philip's instrument in the re-Catholicizing of
Europe.[10]

Philip II built himself a new royal residence ("palace" is hardly the
word), the Escorial, which well expressed in solid stone its creator's inner
spirit. Madrid itself was a new town, merely a government center, far from
the worldly distractions of Toledo or Valladolid. But it was thirty miles from
Madrid, on the bleak arid plateau of central Castile, overlooked by the jagged
Sierra, that Philip chose to erect the Escorial. He built it in honor of St.
Lawrence, on whose day he had won a battle against the French. The great
pile of connecting buildings was laid out in the shape of a grill, since according to martyrologists St. Lawrence, in the year 258, had been roasted

[10] See pp. 63–4.

alive on a grill over burning coals. Somber and vast, angular and unrelieved, made of blocks of granite meant to last forever, and with its highest spire rising three hundred feet from the ground, the Escorial was designed not only as a palace but as a monastery and a mausoleum. The monks moved in before the king, who, when he installed himself, brought with him eight coffins, those of his father, his dead wives and his children, to remind him of his own. Here, in an atmosphere that could be painted only by El Greco, the king of Spain worked and lived, a slim figure dressed almost like a monk himself, always industrious, avid for detail, despatching his couriers to Mexico, to Manila, to Vienna, to Milan, his troops and his bars of bullion to Italy and the Netherlands, his diplomats to all courts, and his spies to all countries, wholly and utterly absorbed in his one consuming project.

Let us try to see the events of the time internationally, for though it may be confusing to try to see all nations together, it is distorting to look at only one of them alone. The first years of Philip's reign were also the first years of Elizabeth's reign in England, where the religious issue was still in flux; they were years in which Calvinism agitated the Netherlands, and when France, ruled by teen-age boys, fell apart into implacable civil war. Religious loyalties that knew no frontiers overlapped all political boundaries. Everywhere there were people who looked for guidance outside their own countries. Calvinists in England, France, and the Netherlands felt closer to one another than to their own monarchs or their own neighbors. Zealous Catholics, in all three countries, welcomed the support of international Catholic forces—the Jesuits, the king of Spain, the pope. National unity threatened to dissolve, or was not yet formed. The mere unity of juxtaposition, the sense of mutual trust between people who live side by side, was eaten away; and people who lived not only in the same country, but in the same town, the same street or even the same house, turned against each other in the name of a higher cause.

For about five years, beginning in 1567, it seemed that the Catholic cause might prevail. The great crusade took the offensive on all fronts. In 1567 Philip sent a new and firmer governor-general to the Netherlands, the Duke of Alva, with 20,000 Spanish soldiers; the duke proceeded to suppress religious and political dissidents by establishing a Council of Troubles. In 1569 Philip put down a revolt of the Moriscos in Spain. In the same year the Catholics of northern England, led by the Duke of Norfolk, and sewing the cross of crusaders on their garments, rose in armed rebellion against their heretic queen. In the next year, 1570, the pope excommunicated Elizabeth, and absolved her subjects from allegiance to her, so that English Catholics, if they wished, could henceforth in good conscience conspire to overthrow her. In 1571 the Spanish won a great naval battle against the Turks, at Lepanto off the coast of Greece; on their sails they wove the same cross that had been raised at the other corner of Europe, by the Duke of Norfolk in England; and they themselves believed that they were carrying on the crusades of the Middle Ages. In the next year, 1572, the Catholic leaders of France, with the advice of the pope and of Philip II, decided to make an end of the Huguenots, or French Protestants. Over three thousand were seized and put to death on the eve of St. Bartholomew's Day in Paris alone; and this massacre was followed by lesser liquidations throughout the provinces. At the news of St. Bartholomew Philip II is reported to have laughed aloud, and the pope, Gregory XIII, declaring it "more agreeable than fifty Lepantos," had the scenes in Paris painted by the Italian artist Vasari, and issued a medal, *Ugonotorum strages,* "Destruction of the Huguenots."

But none of these victories proved enduring. The Turkish power was not seriously damaged at Lepanto. In fact, the Turks took Tunis from Philip two years later. The Moriscos were not assimilated. The English Catholic rebellion was stamped out; eight hundred persons were put to death by Elizabeth's government. The revolt in the Netherlands remained very much alive, as did the French Huguenots. Twenty years later England was Protestant, the Dutch were winning independence, a Huguenot had become king of France, and the Spanish fleet had gone to ruin in northern waters. Let us see how these events came to pass.

THE REVOLT OF THE NETHERLANDS

The Netherlands, or Low Countries (they had no other name), roughly comprised the area of the modern kingdoms of the Netherlands and Belgium and the grand duchy of Luxembourg. They consisted of seventeen provinces, which in the fifteenth century, one by one, had been inherited, purchased, or conquered by the dukes of Burgundy, from whom they were inherited by Charles V and his son Philip II. In the mid-sixteenth century neither a Dutch nor a Belgian nationality yet existed. In the northern provinces the people spoke German dialects; in the southern provinces they spoke dialects of French, but neither here, nor elsewhere in Europe, was it felt that language boundaries had anything to do with political borders. The southern provinces had for centuries been busy commercial centers, and we have seen how Antwerp, having once flourished on trade with Venice, now flourished on trade with Lisbon. The northern provinces, or rather the two of them which were most open to the sea, the counties of Holland and Zealand, had developed rapidly in the fifteenth century. They had a popular literature of their own, written in their own kind of German, which came to be called Dutch. The lay piety of the Brothers of the Common Life had originated in this region, and here Erasmus of Rotterdam had been born. The wealth of the northern provinces was drawn from deep-sea fishing. Holland, observed one traveler, had no vineyards, yet nowhere was wine more bibulously consumed; it had neither wool nor flax, yet all the world knew its woollen and linen fabrics. Wines, wool, and flax all came originally to Holland in exchange for fish. Amsterdam was said to be built on herringbones, and the Dutch, when they added trading to fishing, still lived by the sea.

The northern provinces felt no tie with each other, and no sense of difference from the southern. Each of the seventeen provinces was a small state or country in itself. Each province enjoyed typical medieval liberties, privileges, and immunities, including the right to preserve its own law and consent to its own taxes. This constitution of the Netherlands, for such it was, went under the name of the *Joyeuse Entrée*, from the "joyous entry" made by the reigning duke into Brussels in 1355 after a solemn promise to recognize the liberties of the province of Brabant. The common bond of all seventeen provinces was simply that beginning with the dukes of Burgundy they had the same ruler; but since they had the same ruler they were called upon from time to time to send delegates to an Estates-General, and so developed an embryonic sense of federal collaboration. The feeling of Netherlandish identity was heightened with the accession of Philip II, for Philip unlike his father, was thought of as foreign, a Spaniard who lived in Spain; and after 1560 Spanish governors-general, Spanish officials and Spanish troops were seen more frequently in the Netherlands. Moreover, since the Netherlands was the crossroads of Europe, with a tradition of earnestness in religion, Protestant ideas took root very early, and after 1560, when the religious wars began in France, a great many French Calvinists fled across the borders. At first, there were probably more Calvinists in the southern provinces than in the northern, more among the people that we now call Belgians than among those that we now call Dutch.

The revolt against Philip II was inextricably political and religious at the same time, and it became increasingly an economic struggle as the years went by. It began in 1566, when some two hundred nobles of the various provinces founded a league to check the "foreign" or Spanish influence in the Netherlands. The league, to which both Catholic and Protestant nobles belonged, petitioned Philip II not to introduce the Spanish Inquisition into the Netherlands. They feared the trouble it would stir up; they feared it as a foreign court; they feared that in the enforcement of its rulings the liberties of their provinces would be crushed. Philip's agents in the Netherlands refused the petition. A mass revolt now broke out. Within a week fanatical Calvinists pillaged four hundred churches, pulling down images, breaking stained-glass windows, defacing paintings and tapestries, making off with gold chalices, destroying with a fierce contempt the symbols of "popery" and "idolatry." The fury spread from town to town, to Antwerp, to Amsterdam, to Armentières (now in France, but then in the Netherlands); it was chiefly journeymen wage-earners, numerous in the industrial Netherlands, and aroused by social and economic grievances as well as religious belief, who formed the rank-and-file for these anti-Catholic and anti-Spanish demonstrations. Before such vandalism many of the petitioning nobles recoiled; the Catholics among them, as well as less militant Protestants, unable to control their revolutionary followers, began to look upon the Spanish authorities with less disfavor.

Philip II, appalled at the sacrilege, forthwith sent in the Inquisition, the Duke of Alva, and reinforcements of Spanish troops. Alva's Council of Troubles, nicknamed the Council of Blood, sentenced some thousands to death, levied new taxes, and confiscated the estates of a number of important nobles. These measures united people of all classes in opposition; and what might have been primarily a class conflict took on the character of a national opposition. At its head emerged one of the noblemen whose estates had been confiscated, William of Orange (called William the Silent), Philip II's "stadholder" or lieutenant in the County of Holland. Beginning to claim the authority of a sovereign, he issued letters of marque, or authorizations to ship captains—Dutch, Danes, Scots, English—to make war at sea. Fishing crews, "sea dogs" and downright pirates began to raid the small port towns of the Netherlands and France, descending upon them without warning, desecrating the churches, looting, torturing and killing, in a wild combination of religious rage, political hatred, and lust for booty. The Spanish reciprocated by renewing their confiscations, their inquisitorial tortures, and their burnings and hangings. The Netherlands was racked by anarchy, revolution, and civil war. No lines were clear, either political or religious. But in 1576 the anti-Spanish feeling prevailed over religious difference when representatives of all seventeen provinces, putting aside the religious question, formed a union to drive out the Spanish at any cost.

THE INVOLVEMENT OF ENGLAND

But the Netherlands revolution, though it was a national revolution with political independence as its first aim, was only part of the international politico-religious struggle. All sorts of other interests became involved in it. Queen Elizabeth of England lent aid to the Netherlands, though for many years surreptitiously, not wishing to provoke a war with Spain, in which it was feared that English Catholics might side with the Spaniards Elizabeth was troubled by having on her hands an unwanted guest, Mary Queen of Scots, a Catholic who had been queen of France until her husband's premature death, and queen of Scotland until driven out by irate Calvinist lords, and who—if the pope, the king of Spain, the Society of Jesus and many English Catholics were to have their way—would also be queen of England instead of the usurper Elizabeth.[11] Elizabeth under these circumstances kept Mary Stuart imprisoned. Many intrigues were afoot to put Mary on the English throne, some with, and some without, Mary's knowledge.

In 1576 Don Juan, the hero of Lepanto, and brother of Philip II, became governor-general of the embattled Netherlands. It was his grandiose idea, formed after consultations in Rome, not merely to subdue the Netherlands but to use that country as a base for an invasion of England, and after overthrowing Elizabeth with Spanish troops to put Mary Stuart on the throne, marry her himself, and so become king of a re-Catholicized England. Thus the security of Elizabethan and Protestant England was coming to depend on the outcome of fighting in the Netherlands. Elizabeth signed an

ᴧᴧᴧᴧᴧᴧᴧᴧᴧᴧᴧᴧᴧᴧᴧᴧᴧ

[11] Mary Stuart was the next lawful heir to the English throne after Elizabeth, since Elizabeth had no children, and Mary Stuart was a great-granddaughter of Henry VII

alliance with the Netherlands patriots, and countered with another intrigue. The Virgin Queen, throughout her long reign, used the approaches of suitors to political advantage, and it now happened that certain French Huguenots hoped to marry the Duke of Alençon to Elizabeth. Alençon had already led a French force into the Netherlands to assist the anti-Spanish revolutionaries in that country; and his followers believed that, as husband to the Queen of England, he would receive enough support from her to set up a Protestant kingdom in the seventeen provinces, with himself as king. Elizabeth gave him grounds for hope, enough to keep him in the field against the Spanish; but in the end rejected his highly political courtship, having no intention of becoming too involved on the Continent.

Don Juan died in 1578, and was succeeded as governor-general of the Netherlands by the Prince of Parma. A diplomat as well as a soldier, Parma broke the solid front of the seventeen provinces by a mixture of force and persuasion. He promised that the historic liberties of the *Joyeuse Entrée* would be respected, and he appealed not only to the more zealous Catholics but to moderates who were wearying of the struggle and repelled by mob violence and religious vandalism. On this basis he rallied the southernmost provinces to his side. The seven northern provinces, led by Holland and Zealand, responded by forming the Union of Utrecht in 1579. In 1581 they formally declared their independence from the king of Spain, calling themselves the United Provinces of the Netherlands. Thus originated what was more commonly called the Dutch Republic, or simply "Holland" in view of the predominance of that county among the seven. The great Flemish towns, Antwerp, Ghent, and Bruges, at first sided with the Union.

Where formerly all had been turmoil, a geographical line was now drawn. A south rallied to Philip II now faced a still rebellious north. But neither side accepted any such partition. Parma still fought to reconquer the north, and the Dutch, led by William the Silent, still struggled to clear the Spanish out of all seventeen provinces. Meanwhile the two sides fought to capture the intermediate Flemish cities. When Parma moved upon Antwerp, still the leading port of the North Sea, and one from which an invasion of England could best be mounted, Elizabeth at last openly entered the war on the side of the rebels, sending six thousand English troops to the Netherlands under the Earl of Leicester in 1585.

England was now clearly emerging as the chief bulwark of Protestantism and of anti-Spanish feeling in northwestern Europe. In England itself, the popular fears of Spain, the popular resentment against Catholic plots revolving about Mary Stuart, the popular indignation at "foreign" and "outside" meddling in English matters, produced an unprecedented sense of national solidarity. The country rallied to Protestantism and to Elizabeth, and even the Catholic minority for the most part disowned the conspiracies against her. The English were now openly and defiantly allied with the Protestant Dutch. Not only were they fighting together in the Netherlands, but both English and Dutch sea-raiders fell upon Spanish shipping, captured the treasure ships, and even pillaged the Spanish Main, the mainland coast of northern South America. The Dutch were beginning to penetrate East Indian waters. Elizabeth was negotiating with Scotland, with German Calvinists and French Huguenots. At the Escorial it was said that the Netherlands could only be re-won by an invasion of England, that the queen of the heretics must be at last dethroned, that in any case it was cheaper to launch a gigantic attack upon England than to pay the cost of protecting Spanish galleons, year after year, against the depredations of piratical sea dogs.

Philip II therefore prepared to invade England. The English retorted with vigor. Mary Stuart, after twenty years' imprisonment, was put to death in 1587; an aroused Parliament, more than Elizabeth herself, demanded her life on the eve of foreign attack. Sir Francis Drake, most spectacular of the sea dogs, sailed into the port of Cadiz and burnt the very ships assembling there to join the Armada. This was jocosely described as singeing the beard of the king of Spain.

The great Armada, the *armada católica*, was ready early in 1588. With crosses on the sails, and banners bearing the image of the Holy Virgin, it went forth as to a new Lepanto against the Turks of the north. It consisted of 130 ships, weighing 58,000 tons, carrying 30,000 men and 2,400 pieces of artillery, the most prodigious assemblage of naval power that the world had ever seen. In Spain only the pessimistic observed that its commander was no seaman, that some of its ships were too cumbersome, and some too frail, to weather the gales of the north, that orders had to be issued to its crews in six languages, and the antagonisms of Portuguese, Catalans, Castilians, Irishmen, and émigré English Catholics somehow appeased. The plan was for the fleet to sail to the Netherlands, from which it was to escort the Prince of Parma's army across the straits to the English Coast. In the Channel the Armada was met by some two hundred English vessels, commanded, under a noble figurehead, by Sir Francis Drake. The English craft, lighter, smaller, and faster, though well furnished with guns, harried the lumbering mass of the Armada, broke up its formations, attacked its great vessels one by one. It found no refuge at Calais, where English fireships drove it out again to sea. Then arose a great storm, the famous "Protestant wind," which blew the broken Armada northward, into seas that to southerners seemed almost polar, around the tip of Scotland, the Orkneys, the Hebrides, and northern Ireland, forbidding coasts which the Spaniards had to skirt without charts or pilots, and which they strewed with their wreckage and their bones.

THE RESULTS OF THE STRUGGLE

The war went on for several years. Philip died in 1598, after a long and horrible illness, a frustrated and broken man. In the wars with Spain the English had, above all else, assured their national independence. They had acquired an intense national spirit, a love of "this other Eden, demi-paradise," "this precious stone set in the silver sea," as Shakespeare wrote; and they had become more solidly Protestant, almost unanimously set against "popery."

With the ruin of the Armada, they were more free to take to the sea; we have seen how the English East India Company was founded in 1600.

In the Netherlands, the battle-lines swayed back and forth until 1609. In that year a Twelve Years' Truce was agreed to. By this truce the Netherlands were partitioned. The line of partition ran somewhat farther north than in Parma's time, for the Spaniards had retaken Antwerp and other cities in the middle zone. The seven provinces north of the line, those that had formed the Union of Utrecht in 1579, were henceforth known as Dutch. The ten provinces south of the line were known as the Spanish Netherlands. Protestants in the south either became Catholics or fled to the north, so that the south (the modern Belgium) became solidly Catholic, while the number of Protestants in the north was increased. Even so, the Dutch were not a completely Protestant people, for probably as many as a third of them remained Catholic. Calvinism was the religion of most Dutch burghers, and the religion favored by the state; but in the face of an exceptionally large religious minority the Dutch Netherlands adopted a policy of toleration. The southern Netherlands were ruined by almost forty years of war. The Dutch, moreover, occupied the mouth of the Scheldt, and refused to allow ocean-going vessels to proceed upstream to Antwerp or to Ghent. The Scheldt remained "closed" for two centuries, and the Flemish cities never recovered their old position. Amsterdam became the commercial and financial center of northern Europe; it retained its commercial supremacy for a century, and its financial supremacy for two centuries. For the Dutch, as for the English, the weakening of Spanish naval power opened the way to the sea. The Dutch East India Company was organized in 1602. Both Dutch and English began to found overseas colonies. Englishmen settled in Virginia in 1607, Dutchmen at New York in 1612.

As for Spain, while it remained the most formidable military power of Europe for another half-century, its internal decline had already begun. At the death of Philip II the monarchy was living from hand to mouth, habitually depending on the next arrival of treasure from the Indies. The productive forces of the country were weakened by inflation, by taxation, by emigration, by depopulation. At Seville, for example, only 400 looms were in operation in 1621, where there had been 16,000 a century earlier. Spain suffered from the very circumstances that made it great. The qualities most useful in leading the Counter-Reformation were not those on which a modern society could most easily be built. The generations of crusading against infidels, heathen, and heretics had produced an exceptionally large number of minor aristocrats, chevaliers, dons, and *hidalgos*, who as a class were contemptuous of work, content with small incomes, and generally idle, and who were numerous enough and close enough to the common people to impress their haughty indifference upon the country as a whole. The wealth of America gave the government and some of the upper classes an easy income, leaving them without incentive to encourage commerce or manufacturing and in any case ignorant of real economic questions. With the extreme concentration on religion the ablest men entered the church, and so great was the popular admiration for saints and mystics, missionaries and crusaders, theologians, archbishops, ascetics, and begging friars, that more secular activities offered little psychological satisfaction or reward.

The very unity accomplished under Ferdinand and Isabella threatened to dissolve. After more than a century of the Inquisition people were still afraid of false Christians and crypto-Moslems. The question of the Moriscos rose again in 1608.[12] The Moriscos included some of the best farmers and most skilled artisans in the country. They lived in almost all parts of Spain; they were in no sense a "foreign" element; they were simply the descendants of those Spaniards who, in the Moslem period, which had begun nine hundred years before, had adopted the Moslem religion and Arabic language and culture. They were now supposedly Christian, but the true and pure Christians accused them of preserving in secret the rites of Islam and of sympathy for the Barbary pirates. They were thought to be clannish, marrying among themselves; and they were so efficient, sober, and hard working that they outdistanced other Spaniards in competition. In 1609 some 150,000 Moriscos were driven out of Valencia; in 1610 some 64,000 were driven from Aragon; in 1611 an unknown number were expelled from Castile. All were simply put on boats and sent off with what they could carry. Spain, whose total population was rapidly falling in any case, thus lost one of the most socially valuable, if not religiously orthodox, of all its minorities.

Nor could the Christian kingdoms hold peaceably together. In 1640 Portugal, which had been joined to the Spanish crown since 1580 when its own ruling line had run out, re-established its independence. That same year Catalonia rose in open rebellion. The Catalan war, in which the French streamed across the Pyrenees to aid the rebels, lasted for almost twenty years. Catalonia was at last reconquered, but it managed to preserve its old privileges and separate identity. Catalan and Castilian viewed each other with increased repugnance. The Spanish kingdoms were hardly more unified, in spirit or in institutions, than in the days of Isabella and Ferdinand. They suffered, too, during the seventeenth century from a line of kings whose mental peculiarities reached the point of positive imbecility. Meanwhile, however, the might of Spain was still to be felt in both Germany and France.

14. The Disintegration and Reconstruction of France

Both France and Germany, in the so-called Wars of Religion, fell into an advanced state of decomposition, France in almost forty years of civil war between 1562 and 1598, Germany in a long period of civil troubles culminating in the Thirty Years' War between 1618 and 1648. From this decomposition France recovered in the seventeenth century, but Germany did not.

wwwwwwwwwwwww

[12] See p. 64.

POLITICAL AND RELIGIOUS DISUNITY

The Wars of Religion in France, despite the religious ferocity shown by partisans of both sides, were no more religious than they were political, and were essentially a new form of the old phenomenon of feudal rebellion against a higher central authority. "Feudal," when the word is used of the sixteenth, seventeenth, or eighteenth centuries, generally refers not to nobles only, but to all sorts of component groups having rights within the state, and so including towns and provinces, and even craft gilds and courts of law, in addition to the church and the noble class. It remained to be seen whether all these elements could be welded into one body politic. If the reader will recall how hard it is in the twentieth century to unify an army, navy, and air force, or form a tariff union between two sovereign states, not to mention the problem of international government, he may be less puzzled as to why the history of Europe, for centuries, seems to consist of struggles between "feudal decentralization" and the "central power."

In France the New Monarchy, resuming the work of medieval kings, had imposed a certain unity on the country.[13] Normally, or apart from civil war, the country acted as a unit in foreign affairs. The king alone made treaties, and in war his subjects all fought on his side, if they fought at all. Internally, the royal centralization was largely administrative; that is, the king and those who worked for him dealt with subordinate bodies of all kinds, while these subordinate bodies remained in existence with their own functions and personnel. France by the ideas of the time was a very large country. It was three times as large as England, and five times as populous. At a time when the traveler could move hardly thirty miles a day it took three weeks of steady plodding to cross the kingdom. Local influence was therefore very strong. Beneath the platform of royalty there was almost as little substantial unity in France as in the Holy Roman Empire. Where the Empire had three hundred "states," France had some three hundred areas with their own legal systems. Where the Empire had free cities, France had *bonnes villes,* the king's "good towns," each with its stubbornly defended corporate rights. Where the Empire had middle-sized states like Bavaria, France had provinces as great as some European kingdoms—Brittany, Burgundy, Provence, Languedoc—each ruled by the French king, to be sure, but each with its own identity, autonomy, laws, courts, tariffs, taxes and parliament or Provincial Estates. To all this diversity, in France as in Germany, was now added diversity of religion. Calvin himself was by birth and upbringing a Frenchman. Calvinism spread in France very rapidly. The difference between Calvinism and Catholicism, let it be repeated, was not a mere difference of opinion, involving only freedom of "thought"; it was a difference on the nature and function of the church, which was still the principal public institution, and it manifested itself in the outward habits of daily life.

ᴧᴧᴧᴧᴧᴧᴧᴧᴧᴧᴧᴧᴧᴧᴧᴧᴧ

[13] See p. 62.

France was not much attached to a papal, Rome-centered, or international Catholicism. The French clergy had long struggled for its national or Gallican liberties; the French kings had dealt rudely with popes, ignored the Council of Trent, and allied for political reasons with both the Lutherans and the Turks. Since 1516 the king of France had the right to nominate the French bishops. The fact that both the monarchy and the clergy felt already independent of Rome, and so had less sense of grievance against Rome than was common in Germany in Luther's day, held them back from the revolutionary solutions of Protestantism. The Protestantism which did spread in France was of the most clear-cut and radical kind, namely Calvinism, which preached at kings, attacked bishops, and smashed religious images and desecrated the churches. Even in countries that became Protestant—England, north Germany, even the Netherlands—this extreme Protestantism was the doctrine of a minority. In France there was no middle-of-the-road Protestantism, no broad and comfortable Anglicanism, no half-way Lutheranism inspired by governments, and in the long run, as will be seen, the middle of the road was occupied by the Catholics.

At first, however, the Huguenots, as the French Calvinists were called, though always a minority, were neither a small one nor modest in their demands. In a class analysis, it is clear that it was chiefly the nobility that was attracted to Protestantism, though of course it does not follow that most French Protestants were nobles, since the nobility was a small class. More than a third, and possibly almost a half, of the French nobility was Protestant in the 1560's or 1570's. Frequently the *seigneur*, or lord of one or more manors, believed that he should have the *ius reformandi*, or right to regulate religion on his own estates, as the princes of Germany decided the religion of their own territories. It thus happened that a lord might defy the local bishop, put a Calvinist minister in his village church, throw out the images, simplify the sacraments, and have the service conducted in French. In this way peasants also became Huguenots. Occasionally peasants turned Huguenot without encouragement by the lord. It was chiefly in southwestern France that Protestantism spread as a general movement affecting whole areas. But in all parts of the country, north as well as south, many towns converted to Protestantism. Usually this meant that the bourgeois oligarchy, into whose hands town government had generally fallen, went over to Calvinism and thereupon banned Catholic services, of which the sequel might be either that the journeymen wage-earners followed along, or that, estranged by the class differences whose development has been described above, they remained attached to their old priests.[14] In general, the unskilled laboring mass probably remained the least touched of all classes by Calvinist doctrine.

Both Francis I and Henry II opposed the spread of Calvinism—as did Lutheran and Anglican rulers—for Calvinism, a kind of grass-roots movement in religion, rising spontaneously among laity and reforming ministers, seemed to threaten not only the powers of monarchy but the very idea of a

---

[14] See pp. 99–100.

nationally established church. The fact that in France the nobility, a traditionally ungovernable class, figured prominently in the movement only made it look the more like political or feudal rebellion. Persecution of Huguenots, with burnings at the stake, began in the 1550's.

Then in 1559 King Henry II was accidentally killed in a tournament. He left three sons, of whom the eldest in 1559 was only fifteen. Their mother, Henry's widow, was Catherine de Médicis, an Italian woman who brought to France some of the polish of Renaissance Italy, along with some of its taste for political intrigue and inclination to vices both natural and unnatural, all of which, for thirty years, she exploited in the attempt to govern a distracted country for her royal sons. (Their names were Francis II, who died in 1560, Charles IX, who died in 1574, and Henry III, who lasted until 1589.) The trouble was that, with no firm hand in control of the monarchy, the country fell apart, and that in the ensuing chaos various powerful factions tried to get control of the youthful, effeminate, and entirely ineffectual monarchs for their own purposes. Among these factions were both Huguenots and Catholics. The Huguenots, under persecution, were too strong a minority to go into hiding. Counting among their number a third or more of the professional warrior class, the nobles, they took naturally and aggressively to arms.

THE CIVIL AND RELIGIOUS WARS

Exact history distinguishes no less than nine civil wars in the concluding four decades of the sixteenth century in France, but in this history they will be telescoped together. They were not civil wars of the kind where one region of a country takes up arms against another, each retaining some apparatus of government, as in the American Civil War or the civil wars of the seventeenth century in England. They were civil wars of the kind fought in the absence of government. Roving bands of armed men, without territorial base or regular means of subsistence, wandered about the country, fighting and plundering, joining or separating from other similar bands, in shifting hosts that were quickly formed or quickly dissolved. The underlying social conditions, the incessant rise of prices, detached many people from their old routines, made it impossible for small gentry or wage workers to live on their incomes and threw them into a life of adventure. The more prominent leaders could thus easily obtain followers, and at the coming of such cohorts the peasants usually took to the woods, while bourgeois would lock the gates of their cities. Or else peasants would form protective leagues, like vigilantes; and even small towns maintained diminutive armies.

The Huguenots were led by various personages of rank, such as Admiral de Coligny and Henry of Bourbon, king of Navarre, a small independent kingdom at the foot of the Pyrenees between Spain and France. A pronounced Catholic party arose under the Guise family, headed by the Duke of Guise and the Cardinal of Lorraine. Catherine de Médicis was left in the middle, opposed like all monarchs to Calvinism, but unwilling to fall under the domination of the Guises. While the Guises wished to extirpate heresy they wished even more to govern France. Among the Huguenots, some fought for local liberties in religion, while the more ardent spirits hoped to drive "idolatry" and "popery" out of all France, and indeed out of the world itself. Catherine de Médicis for a time tried to play the two parties against each other. But in 1572, fearing the growing influence of Coligny over the king, and taking advantage of a great concourse of leading Huguenots in Paris to celebrate the marriage of Henry of Navarre, she decided to rid herself of the heads of the Huguenot party at a single blow. In the resulting massacre of St. Bartholomew some thousands of Huguenots were dragged from their beds after midnight and unceremoniously murdered. Coligny was killed; Henry of Navarre escaped by temporarily changing his religion.

This outrage only aroused Huguenot fury, and led to a renewal of civil war, with mounting atrocities committed by both sides. The armed bands slaughtered each other and terrorized non-combatants. Both parties hired companies of mercenary soldiers, mainly from Germany. Spanish troops invaded France at the invitation of the Guises. Protestant towns, like Rouen and La Rochelle, appealed to Elizabeth of England, reminding her that kings of England had once reigned over their parts of France, inviting English invasion and a renewal of the horrors of the Hundred Years' War; but Elizabeth was too preoccupied with her own problems to give more than very sporadic and insignificant assistance. Neither side could subdue the other, and hence there were numerous truces, during which fighting still flared up, since no one had the power to impose peace. The truces usually acknowledged the *status quo*, allowing Protestant worship locally in places where it was actually going on; but the Protestants felt no security in such terms, nor were Catholics satisfied at such recognition of heresy, so that each truce expired in further war.

Gradually, mainly among the more perfunctory Catholics, but also among moderate Protestants, there developed still another group, who thought of themselves as the "politicals" or *politiques*. The *politiques* were men who concluded that too much was being made of religion, that no doctrine was important enough to justify everlasting war, that perhaps after all there might be room for two churches, and that what the country needed above all else was civil order. Theirs was the secular not the religious view. They believed that men lived primarily in the state, not in the church. They were willing to overlook a man's ideas if only he would obey the king and go peaceably about his business. To escape anarchy they put their hopes in the institution of monarchy. Henry of Navarre, now again a Protestant, was at heart a *politique*. Another was the political philosopher Jean Bodin (1530–96), the first thinker to develop the modern theory of sovereignty. He held that in every society there must be one power strong enough to give law to all others, with their consent if possible, without their consent if necessary. Thus, from the disorders of the religious wars in France was germinated the idea of royal absolutism and of the sovereign state.

THE END OF THE WARS: RECONSTRUCTION UNDER HENRY IV

In 1589 both Henry III, the reigning king, and Henry of Guise, the Catholic party chief who was trying to depose him, were assassinated, each by a partisan of the other. The throne now came by legal inheritance to the third of the three Henrys, Henry of Navarre, the Huguenot chieftain. He reigned as Henry IV. Most popular and most amiably remembered of all French kings, except for medieval St. Louis, he was the first of the Bourbon dynasty, which was to last until the French Revolution.

The civil wars did not end with the accession of Henry IV. The Catholic party refused to recognize him, set up a pretender against him, and called in the Spaniards. Henry, the *politique*, sensed that the majority of the French people were still Catholic, and that the Huguenots were not only a minority but after thirty years of civil strife an increasingly unpopular minority kept going as a political party by obstinate nobles. Paris especially, Catholic throughout the wars, refused to admit the heretic king within its gates. Supposedly remarking that "Paris is well worth a mass," Henry IV in 1593 abjured the Calvinist faith, and subjected himself to the elaborate processes of papal absolution. Thereupon the *politiques* and less excitable Catholics consented to work with him. The Huguenots, at first elated that their leader should become king, were now not only outraged by Henry's abjuration but alarmed for their own safety. They demanded not only religious liberty, but positive guarantees.

Henry IV in 1598 responded by issuing the Edict of Nantes. The Edict granted to every *seigneur*, or noble who was also a manorial lord, the right to hold Protestant services in his own household. It allowed Protestantism in towns where it was in fact the prevailing form of worship, and in any case in one town of each *baillage* (a unit corresponding somewhat to the English shire) throughout the country; but it barred it from Catholic episcopal towns and from a zone surrounding and including the city of Paris. It promised that Protestants should enjoy the same civil rights as Catholics, the same chance for public office, and access to the Catholic universities. In certain of the superior law courts it created "mixed chambers" of both Protestants and Catholics—somewhat as if a stated minority representation were to be legally required in United States federal courts today. The Edict also gave Protestants their own means of defense, granting them about a hundred fortified towns to be held by Protestant garrisons under Protestant command.

The Huguenot minority, reassured by the Edict of Nantes, became less of a rebellious element within the state. The majority of the French people viewed the Edict with suspicion. The *parlements*, or supreme law courts, of Paris, Bordeaux, Toulouse, Aix, and Rennes all refused to recognize it as the law of the land. It was the king who forced toleration upon the country. He silenced the *parlements*, and subdued Catholic opposition by doing favors for the Jesuits. France's chief minority was thus protected by the central government, not by popular wishes. Where in England the Catholic minority had no rights at all, and in Germany the religious question was settled only by cutting the country into small and hostile fragments, in France a compromise was effected, by which the Protestant minority had both individual and territorial rights. A considerable number of French statesmen, generals, and other important persons in the seventeenth century were Protestants.

Henry IV, having appeased the religious controversy, did everything that he could to let the country gradually recover, to re-plant, rebuild, transact business and rediscover the arts of peace. His ideal, as he breezily put it, was a "chicken in the pot" for every Frenchman. He worked also to put the ruined government back together, to collect taxes, pay officials, discipline the army, and supervise the administration of justice. Roads and bridges were repaired, new manufactures were introduced under mercantilist principles, and the export of grain was legalized so that peasant landowners would have a better market. Never throughout his reign of twenty-one years did he summon the Estates-General. A country that had just hacked itself to pieces in civil war was scarcely able to govern itself, and so, under Henry IV, the foundations of the later royal absolutism of the Bourbons were laid down.

Henry IV was assassinated in 1610 by a crazed fanatic who believed him a menace to the Catholic church. Under his widow, Marie de Médicis, the nobility and upper Catholic clergy again grew restless, and forced the summoning of the Estates-General, in which so many conflicting and mutually distrustful interests were represented that no program could be adopted, and Marie dismissed them in 1615 to the general relief of all concerned. No Estates-General of the kingdom as a whole thereafter met until the French Revolution. National government was to be conducted by and through the king.

CARDINAL RICHELIEU

In the name of Marie de Médicis and her young son, Louis XIII, the control of affairs gradually came into the hands of an ecclesiastic, Cardinal Richelieu. In the preceding generation Richelieu might have been called a *politique*. It was the state, not the church, whose interests he worked to further. He tried to strengthen the state economically by mercantilistic edicts. He attempted to draw impoverished gentlemen into trade by allowing them to engage in maritime commerce without loss of noble status. For wholesale merchants, as an incentive, he made it possible to become nobles, in return for payments into the royal exchequer. He founded and supported many commercial companies on the Anglo-Dutch model.

For a time it seemed that civil war might break out again. Nobles still feuded with each other and evaded the royal jurisdiction. Richelieu prohibited private warfare and ordered the destruction of all fortified castles not manned and needed by the king himself. He even prohibited dueling, a custom much favored by the d'Artagnans of the day, but regarded by Riche-

lieu as a mere remnant of private war. The Huguenots, too, with their own
towns and their own armed forces under the Edict of Nantes, had become
something of a state within the state. In 1627 the Duke of Rohan led a
Huguenot rebellion, based on the city of La Rochelle, which received military support from the English. Richelieu after a year suppressed the rebellion,
and in 1629, by the Peace of Alais, amended the Edict of Nantes. For this
highly secularized cardinal of the Catholic church it was agreeable for the
Protestants to keep their religion, but not for them to share in the instruments of political power. The Huguenots lost, in 1629, their fortified cities,
their Protestant armies, and all their military and territorial rights, but in
their religious and civil rights they were not officially molested for another
fifty years.

The French monarchy no sooner re-established itself after the civil
wars than it began to recur to the old foreign policy of Francis I, who had
opposed on every front the European supremacy of the House of Hapsburg.[15]
The Spanish power still encircled France at the Pyrenees, in the Mediterranean, in the Free County of Burgundy, and in Belgium. The Austrian
branch had pretensions to supremacy in Germany and all Central Europe.
Richelieu found his opportunity to assail the Hapsburgs in the civil struggles
which now began to afflict Germany.

15. The Thirty Years' War, 1618–48: The Disintegration
of Germany

The Holy Roman Empire extended from France on the west to Poland
and Hungary on the east. It included the Czechs of Bohemia, and sizable
French-speaking populations in what are now Belgium, Lorraine, eastern
Burgundy, and western Switzerland; but with these exceptions the empire
was made up of Germans.[16] Language, however, was far less important than
religion as the tie which people felt to be basic to a community; and in religion the empire was almost evenly divided. Where in England, after stabilization set in, Roman Catholics sank to a minority of some three per cent,
and in France the Huguenots fell to not much over five per cent, in Germany
there was no true minority, and hence no majority, and religion gave no
ground for national concentration. Possibly there were more Protestants
than Catholics in the empire in 1600, for not only was Protestantism the
state religion in many of the three hundred states, but individual Protestants
were exceedingly numerous in the legally Catholic states of the Austrian
Hapsburgs. Bohemia had a Protestant majority, rooted in the Czech people,
and even in Austria, in meetings of the estates, the Protestants sometimes
prevailed. Farther east, outside the Holy Roman Empire, the Hungarian

~~~~~~~~~~~~~~~~~~~~~~

[15] See map, pp. 66–7; and p. 72.
[16] See maps, pp. 66–7, 128–9.

nobles were mainly Protestant, and Transylvania, in the elbow of the Carpathian mountains, was an active center of Calvinism.

In 1500 Germany had led in the life of Europe, but in 1600 it showed evidences of backwardness and provincialism. Literature had declined, and the language itself became barbarized and ungainly. Where both Catholics and Calvinists recognized international affiliations, and read with interest books written in other countries, Lutherans were suspicious of the world outside the Lutheran states of Germany and Scandinavia, and hence suffered from a cultural isolation. The German universities, both Lutheran and Catholic, attracted fewer students than formerly, and their intellectual effort was consumed in combative dogmatics, each side demonstrating the truth of its own ideas. Nowhere was superstition so rife as in Germany. More witches were burned there than elsewhere, the popular fairy tales were more gruesome, and the educated were more fascinated by astrology. The commerce of south Germany and the Rhineland was in decay, both because of the shift of trade to the Atlantic and because the Dutch controlled the mouth of the Rhine in their own interests. The Baltic trade was rapidly growing, but it was not the old German Hanseatic towns that benefited. The king of Denmark controlled the Sound, or mouth of the Baltic, and the king of Sweden most of its shores; these two rulers opened the Baltic to the Dutch and English, and the old German trading towns could not compete with merchants who had the backing of national monarchs. German bankers, such as the Fuggers, were of slight importance after 1600. It was now in the West that capital was being formed.

BACKGROUND OF THE THIRTY YEARS' WAR

The Peace of Augsburg in 1555, with its principle of *cuius regio eius religio*, had provided that in each state the government could prescribe the religion of its subjects.[17] In some states an abbot or an archbishop or bishop himself constituted the government. In these cases, whenever an incumbent died, there was a race to name his successor, to secure the territory as Lutheran or Catholic. In 1593 a small war was fought for the control of Aix-la-Chapelle, in 1600 another for the control of Cologne. In general, in the decades following the Peace of Augsburg, the Lutherans made considerable gains, putting Lutheran administrators into the church states, or "secularizing" them and converting them into lay principalities. The Catholics did not accept this constant attrition, which violated the Ecclesiastical Reservation of the Peace of Augsburg. In addition, Calvinism spread into Germany. Though Calvinists had no rights under the Peace of Augsburg, a number of states became Calvinist. One of these was the Palatinate, important because it was strategically placed across the middle Rhine, and because its ruler, the Elector Palatine, was one of the seven persons who elected the Holy Roman

〰〰〰〰〰〰〰〰〰

[17] See p. 73.

Emperor. In 1608 the Protestant states, urged on by the Elector Palatine, formed a Protestant union to defend their gains. To obtain support, they negotiated with the Dutch, with the English, and with Henry IV of France. In 1609 a league of Catholic German states was organized by Bavaria. It looked for help from Spain.

The Germans were thus falling apart, or rather coming together, into two parties in anticipation of a religious war, and each party solicited foreign assistance against the other. Other issues were also maturing. The Twelve Years' Truce between Spain and the Dutch, signed in 1609, was due to expire in 1621. The Spanish (whose military power was still unaffected by internal decline) were again preparing to crush the Dutch Republic, or, at the very least to open the mouth of the Scheldt and to get Dutch traders out of the East Indies. Since the Dutch insisted on independence, and were in any case unwilling to leave the Indies or to remove their stranglehold on the port of Antwerp, a renewal of the Dutch-Spanish war appeared to be inevitable. The Spanish also wished to consolidate the Hapsburg position in Central Europe. From Milan in north Italy they proposed to build up a fork of territory, one of whose prongs would lead through the easternmost of the Swiss cantons direct to Hapsburg Austria, the other through the westernmost Swiss cantons to the valley of the Rhine. There, on and near the Rhine, if they could conquer a few states like the Calvinistic Palatinate, they might join the Netherlands and Franche-Comté (the Free County of Burgundy, ruled by Spain) into a large and continuous territorial block.[18] These Spanish designs in the Rhineland and Switzerland naturally aroused the opposition of France. Moreover, the Austrian branch of the Hapsburg family was slowly bestirring itself to eradicate Protestantism in its own domains, and even to turn the Holy Roman Empire into a more modern and national type of state. The idea of a strong power in Germany was abhorrent to the French. France, through opposition to the Hapsburgs, was again put in the position of chief protector of Protestantism. France, as we have observed, was a giant of Europe, five times as populous as England, over ten times as populous as Sweden or the Dutch Republic, incomparably more populous than any single German state. And France after 1600 was at last unified within—at least relatively. As a French writer has observed, speaking of these years, the appearance of the fleur-de-lis upon the Rhine would tumble to the ground the vast projects of the Counter Reformation.

The Thirty Years' War, resulting from all these pressures, was therefore exceedingly complex. It was a German civil war fought over the Catholic-Protestant issue. It was also a German civil war fought over constitutional issues, between the emperor striving to build up the central power of the empire and the member states struggling to maintain independence. These two civil wars by no means coincided, for Catholic and Protestant states were alike in objecting to imperial control. It was also an international war, between France and the Hapsburgs, between Spain and the Dutch, with the

---

[18] See map, pp. 128–9.

kings of Denmark and Sweden and the prince of Transylvania becoming involved, and with all these outsiders finding allies within Germany, on whose soil most of the battles were fought. The wars were further complicated by the fact that many of the generals were soldiers of fortune, who aspired to create principalities of their own, and who fought or refused to fight to suit their own convenience. Allies became fearful of each other's successes, and so changed their aims while operations were still in progress. The powers which sought to crush each other were themselves highly vulnerable; France, Spain, and the Austrian realms were all weakened by collusion of their own subjects with the enemy during hostilities. The whole struggle, resembling nothing so much as the croquet game in *Alice in Wonderland* where the players used the necks of flamingoes for mallets and hedgehogs for balls, was too fluctuating, oblique, contradictory, and protracted to be recounted in any detail. Yet it was the greatest of all European wars before the time of the French Revolution.

THE FOUR PHASES OF THE WAR

The fighting began in Bohemia. It is in fact customary to divide the war into four phases, the Bohemian (1618–25), the Danish (1625–29), the Swedish (1630–35), and the Swedish-French (1635–48).

In 1618 the Bohemians, or Czechs, fearing the loss of their Protestant liberties, dealt with two emissaries from the Hapsburg Holy Roman Emperor, Ferdinand II (who was also their king), by a method occasionally used in that country—throwing them out of the window. After this "defenestration of Prague" Ferdinand sent troops to restore his authority, whereupon the Bohemians deposed him and elected a new king. For this honor, in order to obtain Protestant assistance, they chose the Calvinist Elector Palatine, the head of the Protestant Union. This young man proceeded to Bohemia, where he assumed the title of Frederick V. He brought aid to the Bohemians from the Protestant Union, the Dutch sent money, and the prince of Transylvania harried the Hapsburg rear. The emperor Ferdinand, assisted by money subsidies from the pope, by Spanish troops sent up from Milan, and by the forces of Catholic Bavaria, and benefiting from the fears felt by Lutherans in the Protestant Union for the radical Calvinism that broke out in Bohemia, managed to overwhelm the Bohemians at the battle of the White Mountain in 1620. Frederick fled, jeered or pitied as the "winter king." His ancestral domains in the Palatinate were overrun by the Spaniards.

Two facts emerged in consequence of the Bohemian war. First, the Spaniards were entrenching themselves in the Rhineland, building up their position against the French and the Dutch. Second, Bohemia was reconquered and revolutionized by the Hapsburgs. Ferdinand got himself elected again as king. He confiscated the estates of some half the Bohemian nobles. He granted these lands as endowments for Catholic churches, orders, and monasteries, or gave them out to a swarm of adventurers of all nationalities who had entered his service, and who now became the new landed aristocracy of Bohemia. Jesuits streamed in, and through missions and schools, as well as court proceedings and executions, the re-Catholicization of Bohemia began. In Austria also, which had at first joined Bohemia in rebellion, Protestantism was stamped out.

With Protestant fortunes at a low ebb, and the Protestant Union itself dissolved in 1621, the lead in Protestant affairs was now taken by the King of Denmark, who was also Duke of Holstein, a state of the Holy Roman Empire. His aims were well mixed with politics, for he hoped by acquiring a few bishoprics in Germany to construct a kingdom for his younger son. With a little aid from the Dutch and English, and with promises from Richelieu, he entered the fray. Against him the emperor Ferdinand raised another army, or, rather, commissioned Albert of Wallenstein to raise one on his own private initiative. Wallenstein assembled a force of professional fighters, of all nationalities, who lived by pillage rather than by pay. His army was his personal instrument, not the Emperor's, and he therefore followed a policy of his own, which was so tortuous and well concealed that the name of Wallenstein has always remained an enigma. Possibly he dreamed of a united empire and a revived Germany from which foreigners should be expelled; certainly he dreamed of creating a sizable principality for himself. Wallenstein and other Imperial generals soon defeated the King of Denmark, reached the Baltic coast and even invaded the Danish peninsula.

The full tide of the Counter Reformation now flowed over Germany. Not only was Catholicism again seeping into the Palatinate, and again flooding Bohemia, but it rolled northward into the inner recesses of the Lutheran states. By the Edict of Restitution, in 1629, the Emperor declared all church territories secularized since 1552 automatically restored to the Catholic church. Two archbishoprics, twelve bishoprics, and over a hundred small territories formerly belonging to monasteries and religious orders were involved. Some, like the bishopric of Lübeck, were as far north as the Baltic. Some had been Protestant since the oldest person could remember. Terror swept over Protestant Germany. It seemed that the whole Protestant Reformation, now a century old, might be undone. In addition, the Emperor showed signs of wishing to create a Hapsburg monarchy over the whole Empire. He talked of holding the seacoast and of putting Germany on the seas, discussed prospects for a Flemish-Spanish-German commercial company to compete with the Danes, Dutch and English, and endowed Wallenstein, who was besieging the coastal city of Stralsund, with the magniloquent title of Admiral of the Oceanic and Baltic Seas.

Among those to be alarmed were the French and the Swedes. Richelieu, however, was still putting down fractious nobles and Huguenots. He had not yet consolidated France to his satisfaction, and believed that France, without fighting itself, could counter the Hapsburg ambitions through the use of allies. He sent diplomats to help extricate the king of Sweden from a war with Poland, and he promised him financial assistance, which soon rose to a million *livres* a year in return for the maintenance in Germany of 40,000

Swedish troops. The Dutch subsidized the Swedes with some 50,000 florins a month.

The king of Sweden was Gustavus Adolphus, a ruler of superlative ability, who had conciliated all parties in Sweden, worked harmoniously with his Estates-General, and thus created a base from which he could safely conduct oversea operations. He had extended Swedish holdings on the east shore of the Baltic. Using Dutch and other military experts, he had created the most modern army of the times, noted for its firm discipline, high courage and mobile cannon. Himself a religious man, he had his troops march to battle singing Lutheran hymns. He was ideally suited to be the Protestant champion, a role he now willingly took up, landing in Germany in 1630. Richelieu, besides giving financial help, negotiated with the Catholic states of Germany, playing on their fears of imperial centralization, and so sowing discord among German Catholics and isolating the Emperor, against whom the Swedish war machine was now hurled.

The Swedes, with military aid from Saxony, won a number of spectacular victories, at Breitenfeld in 1631 and Lützen in 1632, where, however, Gustavus Adolphus was killed. His chancellor, Oxenstierna, carried on. The Swedish army penetrated into Bohemia, and as far south as the Danube. What those in the higher counsels of Sweden were aiming at is not clear. Perhaps they dreamed of a great federal Protestant empire, to include Scandinavia and north Germany, a Lutheran empire confronting a Catholic and Hapsburg empire in the south. But the brilliant Swedish victories came to little. Both sides were weakened by disagreement. Wallenstein, who disliked the Spanish influence in Germany, virtually ceased to fight the Swedes and Saxons, with whom he even entered into private talks, hoping to create an independent position for himself. He was finally disgraced by the Emperor, and assassinated by one of his own staff. On the Swedish-Saxon side, the Saxons decided to make a separate peace. Saxony therefore signed with the Emperor the Peace of Prague of 1635. The other German Protestant states concurred in it, and withdrew their support from the Swedes. The Emperor, by largely annulling the Edict of Restitution, allayed Protestant apprehensions. The Swedes were left isolated in Germany. It seemed that the German states were coming together, that the religious wars might be nearing an end. But, in fact, in 1635, the Thirty Years' War was only well begun. Neither France nor Spain wished peace or reconciliation in Germany.

Richelieu renewed his assurances to the Swedes, paid subsidies even to the wealthy Dutch, hired a German princeling, Bernard of Saxe-Weimar, to maintain an army of Germans in the French service, and, cardinal of the Roman Church though he was, at last came out openly and plainly in favor of the German Protestants.

So the fleur-de-lis at last moved toward the Rhine, though not at first with the success for which Frenchmen or Protestants might hope. The Spanish, from their bases in Belgium and Franche-Comté, drove instead deep into France. Champagne and Burgundy were ravaged, and Paris itself was seized with panic. The Spanish also raided the south. The French had a taste of the plunder, murder, burnings, and stealing of cattle by which Germany had been afflicted. But the French soon turned the tables. When Portugal and Catalonia rebelled against Philip IV, France immediately recognized the independence of Portugal under the new royal house of Braganza—as did England, Holland, and Sweden with equal alacrity. French troops streamed over the Pyrenees into Catalonia, spreading the usual devastation. Richelieu even recognized a Catalan republic.

In Germany the last or Swedish-French phase of the war was not so much a civil war among Germans as an international struggle on German soil. Few German states now sided with the French and Swedes. A feeling of national resentment against foreign invasion even seemed to develop, and the Emperor had as allies not only Catholic Bavaria but Lutheran Saxony. But these states regarded themselves emphatically as the Emperor's allies, not his subordinates. They were willing to negotiate separately with the enemy and even make a separate peace. No centralized German authority or unity of action could be built up. Spanish, French, and Swedish armies cut wide swaths across the country. The Empire had as much to fear from its friends, the Spanish, as from its declared enemies. The Spanish still fought to subdue the Dutch, and to consolidate, within the Empire, a belt of Spanish territory from Milan to the Netherlands. The French, Swedes, and Dutch—not to mention the Hungarians, Portuguese, Catalans, and a good many Germans intriguing behind the scenes—while pursuing different and often contradictory aims had one aim in common, to smash the Hapsburgs both Spanish and Austrian.

THE PEACE OF WESTPHALIA, 1648

Peace talks began in 1644 in Westphalia, at the two towns of Münster and Osnabrück. The German states were crying for peace, for a final religious settlement, and for "reform" of the Holy Roman Empire. France and Sweden insisted that the German states should individually take part in the negotiations, a disintegrating principle that the German princes eagerly welcomed and which the Emperor vainly resisted. To Westphalia, therefore, hundreds of diplomats and negotiators now repaired, representing the Empire, its member states, Spain, France, Sweden, the Dutch, the Swiss, the Portuguese, the Venetians, many other Italians, and the pope. There had been no such European congress since the Council of Constance, and the fact that a European assemblage had in 1415 dealt with affairs of the church, and now in the 1640's dealt with affairs of state, war and power, was a measure of the secularization that had come over Europe. The papal nuncio, it may be remarked, was barely listened to at Westphalia, and the pope never signed the treaties.

The negotiations dragged on, because the armies were still fighting, and after each battle one side or the other raised its terms. France and Spain refused to make peace with each other at all, and in fact remained at war until 1659. But for the Holy Roman Empire a settlement was agreed to, incorporated in 1648 in the two treaties of Münster and Osnabrück, and commonly known as the Peace of Westphalia.

The Peace of Westphalia represented a general checkmate to the Counter Reformation in Germany. It not only renewed the terms of the Peace of Augsburg, granting each German state the right to determine its own religion, but it added Calvinism to Lutheranism and Catholicism as an acceptable faith. On the controversial issue of church territories secularized after 1552 the Protestants won a complete victory. These lands were to remain in the possession of those who held them in 1624, before the Edict of Restitution. The right of the Austrian Hapsburg ruler to reconquer and re-Catholicize his own direct possessions, namely Austria and Bohemia, was not questioned; here as elsewhere the principle of *cuius regio eius religio* prevailed; and in the Austrian Hapsburg lands the Counter Reformation went forward successfully.

The dissolution of the Holy Roman Empire, which had been advanced by the drawing of internal religious frontiers in the days of Luther, was now confirmed in politics and international law. Borderlands of the Empire fell away. The Dutch and Swiss ceased to belong to it, both the United Provinces and Swiss cantons (or Helvetic Body) being recognized as sovereign and independent. The Dutch, in addition, were confirmed in their conquest of both banks of the lower Scheldt, the closure of that river to ocean-going vessels, and hence the commercial destruction of Antwerp. They likewise received, from Portugal, the right to have outposts in Brazil and Indonesia.

From the disintegrating western frontier of the Holy Empire the French cut off small pieces, receiving the sovereignty over three Lorraine bishoprics, which they had occupied for a century, and certain rights in Alsace which were so confused that they later led to trouble. The king of Sweden received the bishoprics of Bremen and Verden and the western half of Pomerania, including the city of Stettin. Sweden thus added to its trans-Baltic possessions. The mouths of the imperial rivers were now controlled by non-Germans, the Oder, Elbe, and Weser by Sweden, the Rhine and the Scheldt by the Dutch. In the interior of the Empire Brandenburg received eastern Pomerania, the large archbishopric of Magdeburg and two smaller bishoprics, while Bavaria also increased its stature, obtaining part of the Palatinate and a seat in the Electoral College, so that the Empire now had eight Electors.

Europe, 1648 (map on following pages)

The map shows the European states at the time of the Peace of Westphalia. The main feature of the Peace of Westphalia was that the threat of domination of Europe by the Catholic Hapsburgs was averted. A plurality of independent sovereign states was henceforth considered normal. The plurality of religions was also henceforth taken for granted for Europe as a whole, though each state continued to require, or at least to favor, religious uniformity within its own borders. By weakening the Hapsburgs, and furthering the disintegration of Germany, the Peace of Westphalia opened the way for the political ascendancy of France.

EUROPE
1648

Legend:
- AUSTRIAN HAPSBURGS
- SPANISH MONARCHY
- SWEDISH DOMINIONS
- BRANDENBURG-PRUSSIA
- CHURCH LANDS

SHETLAND IS.

ORKNEY IS.

Bergen

NORWAY

SCOTLAND

KINGDOM OF
DENMARK
AND
NORWAY

Edinburgh

NORTH SEA

DENMARK

Belfast

IRELAND

ENGLAND

COMMONWEALTH,
1649-1660
UNITED KINGDOM,
1707

SCHLESWIG

Dublin

Liverpool

BOUNDARY OF
HOLY ROMAN
EMPIRE

HOLSTEIN

(SW)

Lübeck

Hamburg

UNITED
PROVINCES

Bremen

HANOVER

London

Bristol

Amsterdam
Ryswick

Utrecht

Münster

Leipzig

ATLANTIC

ENGLISH CHANNEL

Brussels
SPAN.

NETH.

Cologne

MINOR
GERMAN
STATES

RHINE

Rouen

Paris

Trier
Metz PALAT.
LORRAINE

Mainz

Strasburg

BAVARIA

Rennes

Nantes

Orleans

ALSACE

Augsburg

OCEAN

FRANCE

FRANCHE
COMTE

SWISS
CANTONS

Bordeaux

Lyons

SAVOY

PIEDMONT

REP.
OF
VENICE

Milan

Parma

Genoa

Florence

Montauban

Avignon

Marseilles

TUSCANY

Corunna

León

NAVARRE

PYRENEES

Oporto

PORTUGAL
TO SPAIN, 1580-1640

Valladolid

Saragossa

ARAGON

CATALONIA

Barcelona

CORSICA
(GENOA)

Rome

Lisbon

Escorial Madrid

Toledo

SPAIN

Mérida

Valencia

Seville

Murcia

BALEARIC IS.

MINORCA

MAJORCA

SAR-
DINIA

Málaga

Cadiz

MEDITERRANEAN

Tangier
(PORT.)

GIBRALTAR
Ceuta
(SP.)

Oran (SP.)

Algiers

Tunis

FEZ
AND
MOROCCO

ALGERIA
(TURKISH)

TUNISIA
(TURKISH)

BARBARY STATES

TRM

SWEDEN

FINLAND

Helsingfors

INGRIA

Stockholm

ESTONIA

LIVONIA

Riga

COURLAND

BRANDENBURG-
PRUSSIA

Stralsund
(SW.)
POMERANIA

Danzig

EAST
PRUSSIA

Stettin

BRANDEN-
BURG
Berlin

GREAT
POLAND

Warsaw

VISTULA R.

LITTLE
POLAND

LITHUANIA

Minsk

POLAND

Kiev

SAXONY

Breslau

SILESIA

Cracow

Lemberg

GALICIA

PODOLIA

DNIESTER R.

BOHEMIA

Prague

Dresden

MORAVIA

CARPATHIAN

AUSTRIA

Vienna

HUNGARY

Budapest

TRANSYLVANIA

MOLDAVIA

BESSARABIA

YEDISAN

CRIMEA

SLAVONIA

DANUBE R.

WALLACHIA

DOBRUJA

BLACK SEA

BOSNIA

Belgrade

SERBIA

Bucharest

DANUBE R.

PAPAL
STATES

Zara

ADRIATIC SEA

OTTOMAN

BULGARIA

EMPIRE

Aquila

MONTE-
NEGRO

Constantinople

NAPLES

Naples

Bari

ALBANIA

RUMELIA

Salonica

KINGDOM OF THE
TWO SICILIES

IONIAN
IS.
(VENICE)

GREECE

AEGEAN
SEA

Smyrna

SICILY

Athens

RHODES
(TURKISH)

CYPRUS
(TURKISH)

MALTA
(SP.)

MEDITERRANEAN SEA

CRETE
(VENICE)

500 MILES

RUSSIA
(MUSCOVY)

LOW
COUNTRIES
1648

UNITED
PROVINCES
INDEP. 1572, 1609, 1648

FINLAND

IJSSEL
MEER

OVERIJSSEL

The Hague

Ryswick

Amsterdam

Utrecht

HOLLAND

Münster

SPANISH
(BELGIAN)
NETHERLANDS

ZEELAND

THE
GENERALITY

Calais

Bruges

Ghent

Antwerp

FLANDERS

BRABANT

Brussels

Liège

Cologne

Lille

ARTOIS

SCHELDT R.

HAINAULT

Aix-
la-Ch.

RHINE R.

FRANCE

LUXEMBURG

Trier

50 MILES

It was in the new constitution of the Empire itself, not in territorial changes, that the greatest victory of the French and their Swedish and Dutch allies was to be found. The German states, over three hundred in number, became virtually sovereign. Each received the right to conduct diplomacy and make treaties with foreign powers. The Peace of Westphalia further stipulated that no laws could be made by the Empire, no taxes raised, no soldiers recruited, no war declared or peace terms ratified except with the consent of the imperial estates, the three-hundred-odd princes, ecclesiastics, and free cities in the Reichstag assembled. Since it was well known that agreement on any such matters was impossible, the principle of self-government, or of medieval constitutional liberties, was used to destroy the Empire itself as an effective political entity. While most other European countries were consolidating under royal absolutism, Germany sank back into "feudal chaos." A constitution for Germany was written into an international treaty. As people then said, the "German liberties," or German states' rights, became part of the public law of Europe. France and Sweden were made guarantors of the Peace of Westphalia. Though Sweden presently became too weak to exercise this right effectively, France for a century and a half enjoyed a legal basis for intervention in Central Europe.

Not only did the Peace of Westphalia block the Counter Reformation, and not only did it frustrate the Austrian Hapsburgs and forestall for almost two centuries any movement toward German national unification, but it also marked the advent in international law of the modern European *Staatensystem* or system of sovereign states. The diplomats who assembled at Westphalia represented independent powers which recognized no superior or common tie. No one any longer pretended that Europe had any significant unity, religious, political, or other. Statesmen delighted in the absence of any such unity, in which they sensed the menace of "universal monarchy." Europe was understood to consist in a large number of unconnected sovereignties, free and detached atoms, or states, which moved about according to their own laws, following their own political interests, forming and dissolving alliances, exchanging embassies and legations, alternating between war and peace, shifting position with a shifting balance of power.

Physically Germany was wrecked by the Thirty Years' War. Cities were sacked by mercenary soldiers with a rapacity that their commanders could not control, or the commanders themselves, drawing no supplies from their home governments, systematically looted whole areas to maintain their armies. Magdeburg was besieged ten times, Leipzig five. In one woollen town of Bohemia, with a population of 6,000 before the wars, the citizens fled and disappeared, the houses collapsed, and eight years after the peace only 850 persons were found there. On the site of another small town Swedish cavalry found nothing but wolves. The peasants, murdered, put to flight or tortured by soldiers to reveal their few valuables, ceased to give attention to farming; agriculture was ruined, so that starvation followed, and with it came pestilence. Even revised modern estimates allow that in many extensive parts of Germany as much as a third of the population may have perished. The effects of fire, disease, undernourishment, homelessness, and exposure in the seventeenth century were the more terrible because of the lack of means to combat them. People lived in piles of debris and ransacked dumps to find food, as they did after the Second World War. But even the Second World War, in sheer depopulation, was not as devastating for Germany as was the Thirty Years' War. It is quite possible for human beings to die like flies without benefit of scientific destruction. The horrors of modern war are not wholly different from horrors that men and women have experienced in the past.

Germany as such, physically wrecked, and politically cut into small pieces, ceased for a long time to play any part in European affairs. A kind of political and cultural vacuum existed in Central Europe. On the one hand, the western or Atlantic peoples—French, English, Dutch—began in the seventeenth century to take the lead in European affairs. On the other hand, in eastern Germany, around Berlin and Vienna, new and only half-German power-complexes began to form. These themes will be traced in the two following chapters.

With the close of the Thirty Years' War the Wars of Religion came to an end. While in some later wars, as in Hungary or in the British Isles, religion remained an issue, it was never again an important issue in the political affairs of Europe as a whole. In general, by the close of the seventeenth century, the division between Protestant and Catholic had become stabilized. Neither side any longer expected to make territorial gains at the expense of the other. Both the Protestant and the Catholic Reformations were accomplished facts. Seen in the long view, each had succeeded, but each also had failed, for Protestants had not freed the whole Christian world of "idolatry," nor had Catholics been able to exterminate "heresy." A compromise was in the end accepted. Latin Christendom was partitioned. The breaking up of the medieval church, with the accompanying break-up of the medieval view of life and of the world—a process that may be said to have lasted from 1300 to 1650, and was as slow and deeply disrupting as a geological upheaval—perhaps came as near as anything in European history to breaking up Europe itself; but after about 1650 such troubles became past history, and Europe entered upon a new age.

CHAPTER IV

The Establishment of West-European Leadership

‸‸

16. The Grand Monarque and the Balance of Power
17. The Dutch Republic
18. Britain: The Puritan Revolution
19. Britain: The Triumph of Parliament
20. The France of Louis XIV, 1643–1715: The Triumph of Absolutism
21. The Wars of Louis XIV: The Peace of Utrecht, 1713

_____

‏‎F THE reader were to take a map of Europe, set one leg of a pair of dividers on the city of Paris, and with the other leg describe a circle having a radius of five hundred miles, he would mark out a zone from which, since about the year 1650, a great deal of modern or "western" civilization has radiated. The circle would not constitute Western Europe in a strict geographical sense, since the extreme western parts of Europe—Ireland, Portugal, and Spain—would be left mainly outside it. But it might with considerable accuracy be equated with modern Western Europe in a cultural sense.

For the zone so traced out, including all of France, England, the Low Countries, and Switzerland, and reaching into Lowland Scotland, western and central Germany and northern Italy, for over two hundred years beginning in the seventeenth century, was the earth's principal center of what anthropologists might call cultural diffusion. Leadership in Europe, in those aspects of civilization deemed worthy of imitation by other Europeans, became concentrated along the Atlantic seaboard north of the Pyrenees, and as Europeans increasingly penetrated the overseas world it was the west-Europeans who did so. Eastern Europe, the Iberian peninsula, colonial America, all in various ways "borrowed" from the zone of greater advancement. A secular society, modern natural science, a highly developed capitalism, the centralized state, parliamentary government in its modern form, democratic ideas, machine industry—and much else—if they did not exactly originate, received their first full development or expression in the zone described by the reader's imaginary dividers.

This leadership of Western Europe became established in the half-century following the Peace of Westphalia. The fading out of the Italian Renaissance, the subsiding of religious wars, the ruin of the Holy Roman Empire and the decay of Spain all cleared the stage on which the Dutch, English, and French were to be the principal actors. But the Dutch were few in number, and the English during most of the seventeenth century were weakened by domestic discord. It was France that for a time played the most imposing role. The whole half-century following the Peace of Westphalia is in fact often called the Age of Louis XIV.

16. The Grand Monarque and the Balance of Power

This king of France inherited his throne in 1643 at the age of five, assumed the personal direction of affairs in 1661 at the age of twenty-three, and reigned for seventy-two years until his death in 1715. No one else in modern history has held so powerful a position for so long a time. Louis XIV was more than a figurehead. For over half a century, during his whole adult life, he was the actual and working head of the French government. Inheriting the achievement of Richelieu,[1] he made France the strongest country in Europe. Using French money, by bribes or other inducements, he built up a pro-French interest in virtually every country from England to Turkey. His policies and the counter-policies that others adopted against him set the pace of public events, and his methods of government and administration, war and diplomacy, became a model for other rulers to copy. During his time the French language, French thought and literature, French architecture and landscape gardens, French styles in clothes, cooking, and etiquette became the accepted standard for Europe. France seemed to be the land of light, and

⁓⁓⁓⁓⁓⁓⁓⁓⁓⁓⁓⁓⁓

[1] See pp. 119–20.

Louis XIV was called by his fascinated admirers Louis the Great, the *Grand Monarque*, and the Sun King. To the internal achievements of France we shall shortly return.

Internationally, the consuming political question of the last decades of the seventeenth century (at least in Western Europe—Eastern Europe we shall reserve for the next chapter) was the fate of the still vast possessions of the Spanish crown. Spain was what Turkey was later called, "the sick man of Europe." To its social and economic decline[2] was added hereditary physical deterioration of its rulers. In 1665 the Spanish throne was inherited by Charles II, an unfortunate afflicted by many ills of mind and body, impotent, even imbecile, the pitiable product of generations of inbreeding in the Hapsburg house. His rule was irresolute and feeble. It was known from the moment of his accession that he could have no children, and that the Spanish branch of the Hapsburg family would die out with his own death. The whole future not only of Spain but of the Spanish Netherlands, the Spanish holdings in Italy and all Spanish America was therefore in question. Charles II dragged out his miserable days until 1700, the object of jealousy and outright assault during his lifetime, and precipitating a new European war by his death.

Louis XIV, who in his youth married a sister of Charles II, intended to benefit from the debility of his royal brother-in-law. His expansionist policies followed two main lines. One was to push the French borders eastward to the Rhine, annexing the Spanish Netherlands (or Belgium) and the Franche-Comté or Free County of Burgundy, a French-speaking region lying between ducal Burgundy and Switzerland.[3] Such a policy involved the further dismemberment of the Holy Roman Empire. The other line of Louis XIV's ambitions, increasingly clear as time went on, was his hope of obtaining the entire Spanish inheritance for himself. By combining the resources of France and Spain he would make France supreme in Europe, in America, and on the sea. To promote these ends Louis XIV intrigued with the smaller and middle-sized powers of Europe. He took various princes of Germany, and for a time a king of England, into his pay. He supported, with complete disregard of ideology, the republicans in Holland against their prince, and the royalists in England against the Parliamentary opposition, knowing that in Holland it was the republicans, and in England the partisans of high monarchy, who were most dependent on foreign assistance and most likely to follow his wishes.

Were Louis XIV to succeed in his aims, he would create the "universal monarchy" dreaded by diplomats, that is to say, a political situation in which one state might subordinate all others to its will. The technique used against universal monarchy was the balance of power. Universal monarchy had formerly been almost achieved by the Austro-Spanish Hapsburgs. The Hapsburg supremacy had been blocked mainly by a balance of power headed

[2] See pp. 112–13.
[3] See map, pp. 128–9.

by France, and of which the Thirty Years' War and the Peace of Westphalia were the outstanding triumphs. Now the danger of universal monarchy came from France, and it was against France that the balance of power was directed.

THE IDEA OF THE BALANCE OF POWER

It will be useful to explain what a balance of power was and was not meant to be. The phrase itself, which came into general use at this time, has been employed ever since in different though related senses. In one sense it refers to a condition of equilibrium, or of even balance, in which power is distributed among many separate states. The second sense arises when this equilibrium is disturbed. If one state preponderates, and if others then form a coalition against it, then the coalition itself may be called the "balance," though it is actually the counterweight by which balance or equilibrium is to be restored. In a third sense one speaks of "holding" or "controlling" the balance of power; here the balance refers to that decisive increment of weight or power which one state may bring to bear. Thus if a state is a vitally necessary member of a coalition, more needed by its allies than it is in need of them, it may be said to "hold" the balance. Or if it belongs to no coalition at all, but tries to keep all other states in a condition of equilibrium, so that its own intervention on one side or the other would be decisive, it may also be said to "hold" the balance, although strictly speaking not participating in the balance at all.

The aim of statesmen pursuing policies of balance of power in the seventeenth and eighteenth centuries was generally to preserve their own independence of action to the utmost. Hence the basic rule was to ally against any state threatening domination. If one state seemed to dictate too much, others would shun alliance with it unless they were willing (from ideological sympathy or other reasons) to become its puppets. They would seek alliance with the other weaker states instead. They would thus create a balance or counterweight, or "restore the balance," against the state whose ascendancy they feared. Another more subtle reason for preferring alliance with the weak rather than with the strong was that in such an alliance each member could feel his own contribution to be necessary and valued, hence could preserve his own dignity and prestige, and by threatening to withdraw his support could win consideration of his own policies. Indeed, the balance of power may be defined as a system in which each state tends to throw its weight where it is most needed, so that its own importance may be enhanced.

The purpose of balance-of-power politics was not to preserve peace, but to preserve the sovereignty and independence of the states of Europe, or the "liberties of Europe," as they were called, against potential aggressors. The system was effective as a means to this end in the seventeenth and eighteenth centuries. Combinations were intricate, and alliances were readily made and unmade to deal with emerging situations. One reason for the effectiveness of the system lay in the great number of states capable of pursuing an independent foreign policy. These included not only the greater and middle-sized states of Austria, Spain, France, England, Holland, Sweden, and Bavaria, but a great number of small independent states, such as Denmark, the German principalities, Portugal after 1640, and Savoy, Venice, Genoa, and Tuscany. States moved easily from one alliance to another, or from one side of the balance to another. They were held back by no ideologies or sympathies, especially after the religious wars subsided, but could freely choose or reject allies, aiming only to protect their own independence or enlarge their own interests. Moreover, owing to the military technology of the day, small states might count as important military partners in an alliance. By controlling a strategic location, like the king of Denmark, or by making a contribution of ships or money, like the Dutch Republic, they might add just enough strength to an alliance to balance and overbalance the opposing great power and its allies.

As the ambitions of Louis XIV became bolder, and as the capacity of Spain to resist them withered away, the prevention of universal monarchy under France depended increasingly on combining the states of Europe into a balance of power against him. The balance against Louis XIV was engineered mainly by the Dutch. The most tireless of his enemies, and the man who did more than any other to checkmate him, was the Dutchman William III, the Prince of Orange, who in his later years was king of England and Scotland as well.

Let us, after first surveying the Dutch in the seventeenth century, turn to the British Isles, where a momentous conflict occurred between Parliament and king. We shall then examine the French absolute monarchy under Louis XIV and conclude the present chapter with the wars of Louis XIV, particularly the War of the Spanish Succession, in which the great international issues of the time conflicted and were resolved.

17. The Dutch Republic

DUTCH CIVILIZATION AND GOVERNMENT

The ambassadors of kings, strolling beside a canal at the Hague, might on occasion observe a number of burghers in plain black garments step out of a boat and proceed to make a meal of cheese and herring on the lawn, and they would recognize in these portly figures Their High Mightinesses the Estates-General of the United Provinces, as the Dutch government was known in the diplomatic language of the day. Though noblemen lived in the country, the Dutch were the most bourgeois of all peoples. They were not the only republicans in Europe, since the Swiss cantons, Venice, Genoa, and even England for a few years were republics, but of all republics the United Provinces was by far the most wealthy, the most flourishing and the most pre-eminently civilized.

The Dutch acquired a nationality of their own in the long struggle against Spain, and with it a pride in their own freedom and independence. In the later phases of the war with Spain, notably during the 'Thirty Years' War, they were able to rely more on their wealth, ready money, shipping, and diplomacy than on actual fighting, so that during the whole seventeenth century they enjoyed a degree of comfort, and of intellectual, artistic, and commercial achievement unexcelled in Europe. The classic Dutch poets and dramatists wrote at this time, making a literary language of what had formerly been a dialect of Low German. Hugo Grotius produced, in his *Law of War and Peace*, a pioneering treatise on international law. Baruch Spinoza, of a family of refugee Portuguese Jews, quietly turned out works of philosophy, examining the fundamentals of reality, of human conduct, and of church and state. Spinoza made his living by grinding lenses; there were many other lens grinders in Holland; some of them developed the microscope, and some of these, in turn, Leeuwenhoek, Swammerdam and others, peering through their microscopes and beholding for the first time the world of microscopic life, became founders of modern biological science. The greatest Dutch scientist was Christian Huyghens (1629–95), who worked mainly in physics and mathematics; he improved the telescope (a Dutch invention), made clocks move with pendulums, discovered the rings of Saturn, and launched the wave theory of light. A less famous writer, Balthasar Bekker, in his *World Bewitched* (1691) delivered a decisive blow against the expiring superstition of witchcraft.

But the most eternally fresh of the Dutch creations, suffering from no barrier of time or language, were the superb canvases of the painters. Frans Hals produced bluff portraits of the common people. Jan Vermeer threw a spell of magic and quiet dignity over men, and especially women, of the burgher class. Rembrandt conveyed the mystery of human consciousness itself. In Rembrandt's *Masters of the Cloth Hall* (see illustration) we face a group of men who seem about to speak from the canvas, inclined slightly forward, as intent on their business as judges on the proceedings in a courtroom; men of the kind who conducted the affairs of Holland, in both commerce and government; intelligent men, calculating but not cunning, honest but determined to drive a hard bargain, stern rather than mild; and the sober black cloaks, with the clean white collars, set against the carved woodwork and rich table-covering of the Cloth Hall, seem to suggest that personal vanity must yield to collective undertakings, and personal simplicity be maintained in the midst of material opulence. And in Vermeer's *Geographer*, painted in 1669 (also reproduced as an illustration in this book) there appears not only an immaculately scrubbed and dusted Dutch interior, but something of a symbol of the modern world in its youth—the pale northern sunlight streaming through the window, the globe and the map, the dividers in the scholar's right hand, instrument of science and mathematics, the tapestry flung over the table (or is it an Oriental rug brought from the East?), the head lifted in thought and eyes resting on an invisible world of fresh discoveries and opening horizons.

In religion, after initial disputes, the Dutch Republic adopted toleration. Early in the seventeenth century the Dutch Calvinists divided. One group favored a modification of Calvinism, with a toning down of the doctrine of absolute and unconditional predestination; it drew its main support from the comfortable burghers and its doctrines from a theologian of Leyden named Arminius. To deal with this Arminian heresy a great international Calvinist synod met in 1618 at Dordrecht in Holland. Of the hundred delegates almost a third came from Scotland, England, Germany, Switzerland, and France. The orthodox party won out at the synod; one old man was put to death; the philosopher Grotius fled to France for safety. But beginning in 1632 the Arminians were tolerated. Rights were granted to the large Catholic minority. Jews had long been welcomed in the republic; and Christian sects despised everywhere else, such as the Mennonites, found a refuge in it. Although none of these people had as many political or economic rights as the Calvinists, the resulting mixture stimulated both the intellectual life and the commercial enterprise of the country.

The Dutch as early as 1600 had 10,000 ships, and throughout the seventeenth century they owned most of the shipping of northern Europe. They were the carriers between Spain, France, England, and the Baltic. Much coastwise shipping between ports of France was in Dutch hands. They settled in Bordeaux to buy wines, lent money to vintners, and soon owned many vineyards in France itself. They sailed on every sea. They explored the waters around Spitzbergen and almost monopolized Arctic whaling. They entered the Pacific by way of South America, where they rounded Cape Horn and named it after Hoorn in Holland. Organized in the East India Company of 1602, their merchants increasingly replaced the Portuguese in India and the Far East. In Java, in 1619, they founded the city of Batavia—the Latin name for Holland. Finding some Englishmen in 1623 at Amboina, in the midst of the Spice Islands, they tortured and killed them—the Dutch remained in Indonesia, and the English did not return until the days of Napoleon. Not long after 1600 the Dutch reached Japan. But the Japanese, fearing the political consequences of Christian penetration, in 1641 expelled all other Europeans, and confined the Dutch to limited operations on an island near Nagasaki. The Dutch remained for over two centuries the sole link of the West with Japan. In 1612 the Dutch founded a New Amsterdam

---

The Masters of the Cloth Hall

BY REMBRANDT VAN RIJN (DUTCH, 1606–69)

For the subject of the painting see p. 137. These men are "clothiers" or "drapers" such as are described on pp. 96–7 as characteristic of the Commercial Revolution. Rembrandt was not only the greatest but also the most productive of Dutch artists. Though he never traveled more than twenty miles from his native Leyden, he drew and painted all types of persons that streamed into the Netherlands, and conveyed all types of experience, from the commercial practicality of the present group to the deeply mystical and the religious. Courtesy of the Rijksmuseum, Amsterdam.

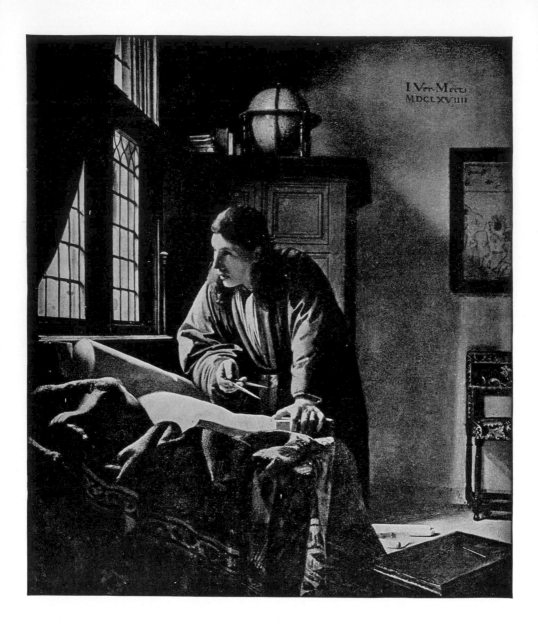

on Manhattan Island, and in 1621 they established a Dutch West India Company to exploit the loosely held riches of Spanish and Portuguese America. They founded colonies at Pernambuco and Bahia in Brazil (lost soon thereafter) and at Caracas, Curaçao, and in Guiana in the Caribbean. In 1652 the Dutch captured the Cape of Good Hope in South Africa from the Portuguese. Dutch settlers soon appeared—men, women, and children. It is here alone, among the modern Afrikaner people, that a kind of overseas Holland, Dutch in language and culture, persists to this day.

In 1609 the Dutch founded the Bank of Amsterdam. European money was a chaos; coins were minted not only by great monarchs but by small states and cities in Germany and Italy, and even by private persons. In addition, under inflationary pressures, kings and others habitually debased their coins by adding more alloy, while leaving the old coins in circulation along with the new. Anyone handling money thus accumulated a miscellany of uncertain value. The Bank of Amsterdam accepted deposits of such mixed money from all persons and from all countries, assessed the gold and silver content, and, at rates of exchange fixed by itself, allowed depositors to withdraw equivalent values in gold florins minted by the Bank of Amsterdam. These were of known and unchanging weight and purity. They thus became an internationally sought money, an international measure of value, acceptable everywhere. Depositors were also allowed to draw checks against their accounts. These conveniences, plus a safety of deposits guaranteed by the Dutch government, attracted capital from all quarters and made possible loans for a wide range of purposes. Amsterdam remained the financial center of Europe until the French Revolution.

Under their republican government the Dutch enjoyed great freedom, but it can hardly be said that their form of government met all the requirements of a state. Their High Mightinesses (the *Hooge Moogende*), who made up the Estates-General, were only delegates from their respective seven provinces, and could act only as the estates of the provinces gave instructions. The seven provinces, like the states of the Holy Roman Empire in which they had originated, were jealous of their own independence. Each province had, as its executive, an elected stadholder, but there was no stadholder for the United Provinces as a whole. This difficulty was overcome by the fact that most of the various provinces usually elected the same man as stadholder. The stadholder in most provinces was usually the head of the house

---

The Geographer

BY VERMEER (DUTCH, 1632–75)

Vermeer's work is notable for a certain purity and quietude, a burgherlike Dutch tidiness and an extraordinary luminosity of rather mild colors. In this picture he has captured the spirit of seventeenth-century science, in which Dutch physicists, cartographers, navigators, and instrument-makers played a leading role. For other meanings that may be seen in the picture see p. 137. Courtesy of the Städelsches Kunstinstitut, Frankfurt.

of Orange, which since the days of William the Silent and the wars for independence had enjoyed exceptional prestige in the republic. The Prince of Orange, apart from being stadholder, was simply one of the feudal noblemen of the country, for the United Provinces had a landed feudal aristocracy which was represented in the seven provincial estates. But the aristocratic class had been outdistanced by the commercial, and affairs were generally managed by the burghers. The burghers, intent on making money and enjoying comfort, rarely worried over military questions, and hated taxes.

Politics in the Dutch Republic was a see-saw between the burghers, pacifistic and absorbed with business, and the Princes of Orange, to whom the country owed most of its military security. When foreigners threatened invasion, the power of the stadholder increased. When all was calm, the stadholder could do little. The Peace of Westphalia produced a mood of confidence in the burghers, followed by a constitutional crisis, in the course of which the stadholder William II died, in 1650. No new stadholder was elected for twenty-two years. The burgher, civilian, and decentralizing tendencies prevailed.

In 1650, eight days after his father's death, was born the third William of the house of Orange, seemingly fated never to be stadholder and to pass his life as a private nobleman on his own estates. William III grew up to be a grave and reserved young man, small and rather stocky, with thin compressed lips and a determined spirit. He learned to speak Dutch, German, English, and French with equal facility, and to understand Italian, Spanish, and Latin. He observed the requirements of his religion, which was Dutch Calvinism, with sober regularity. He had a strong dislike, Dutch and Calvinistic, for everything magnificent or pompous; he lived plainly, hated flattery, and took no pleasure in social conversation. In these respects he was the opposite of his life-long enemy the Sun King, whom he resembled only in his diligent preoccupation with affairs. In 1677 he married the king of England's brother's daughter, Mary.

FOREIGN AFFAIRS: CONFLICT WITH THE ENGLISH AND FRENCH

Meanwhile matters were not going too favorably for the Dutch Republic. In 1651 the revolutionary government then ruling England passed a Navigation Act. This act may be considered the first of a long series of political measures by which the British colonial empire was built up. It was aimed against the Dutch carrying trade. It provided that goods imported into England and its dependencies must be brought in English ships, or in ships belonging to the country exporting the goods. Since the Dutch were too small a people to be great producers and exporters themselves, and lived largely by carrying the goods of others, they saw in the new English policy a threat to their economic existence. The English likewise, claiming sovereignty of the "narrow seas," demanded that Dutch ships salute the English flag in the Channel. Three wars between the Dutch and English followed, running with interruptions from 1652 to 1674 and generally indecisive, though the English annexed New York.

While thus assaulted at sea by the English, the Dutch were menaced on land by the French. Louis XIV made his first aggressive move in 1667, claiming the Spanish Netherlands and Franche-Comté by alleging certain rights of his Spanish wife, and overrunning the Spanish Netherlands with his army. The Dutch, to whom the Spanish Netherlands were a buffer against France, set into motion the mechanism of the balance of power. Dropping temporarily their disputes with the English, they allied with them instead; and since they were able also to secure the adherence of Sweden, the resulting Triple Alliance was sufficient to give pause to Louis XIV, who withdrew from the Spanish Netherlands, made peace, and renounced his claims, though keeping a few towns in Flanders. It was soon evident that Louis XIV had been only temporarily halted, and that the next time he would pass straight through the Spanish Netherlands into the Dutch provinces themselves. He broke up the Triple Alliance, detaching Sweden from Holland, and secretly sending funds to the king of England, who at this time preferred to depend on the king of France rather than on his own Parliament for his income. The Dutch, still under their burgher government, were slow to take alarm and did nothing to strengthen their army. In 1672 Louis XIV rapidly crossed the Spanish Netherlands, attacked with forces five times as large as the Dutch, and occupied three of the seven Dutch provinces.

A popular clamor now arose among the Dutch for William of Orange, demanding that the young prince, who was now twenty-two years of age, be installed in the old office of stadholder, in which his ancestors had defended them against Spain. He was duly elected stadholder in six provinces. In 1673 these six provinces voted to make the stadholderate hereditary in the house of Orange. William, during his whole tenure or "reign" in the Netherlands, attempted to centralize and consolidate his government, put down the feudal liberties of the provinces and free himself from constitutional checks, moving generally in the direction of absolute monarchy, which by the tests of power and under French example was the successful form of government at the time. He was unable, however, to go far in this course, and the United Provinces remained a republic until 1795 under the hereditary stadholderate of William's descendants. Meanwhile, to stave off the immediate menace of Louis XIV, William resorted to a new manipulation of the balance of power. He formed an alliance this time with the minor powers of Denmark and Brandenburg (the German margraviate around Berlin) and with the Austrian and Spanish Hapsburgs. Nothing could indicate more clearly the new balance of power precipitated by the rise of France than this coming over of the Dutch to the Hapsburg side. The alliance was successful to the extent at least of wearying Louis XIV of the war. Peace was signed in 1678 (treaty of Nimwegen), but only at the expense of Spain and the Holy Roman Empire, from which Louis XIV took the long coveted Franche-Comté, together with another batch of towns in Flanders. The Dutch preserved their territory intact.

In the next ten years came the great windfall of William's life. In 1689 he became king of England. He was now able to bring the British Isles into his perpetual combinations against France. Since the real impact of France was yet to be felt, and the real bid of Louis XIV for universal monarchy was yet to be made, and since the English at this time were rapidly gaining in strength, the entrance of England was a decisive addition to the balance formed against French expansion. In this way the constitutional troubles of England, by bringing a determined Dutchman to the English throne, entered into the general stream of European affairs, and helped to assure that western Europe and its overseas offshoots should not be dominated totally by France.

18. Britain: The Puritan Revolution

After the defeat of the Spanish Armada and recession of the Spanish threat the English were for a time less closely involved with the affairs of the Continent. They played no significant part in the Thirty Years' War, and were almost the only European people, west of Poland, who were not represented at the Congress of Westphalia. At the time of the Westphalia negotiations in the 1640's they were in fact engaged in a civil war of their own. This English civil war was a milder variant of the Wars of Religion which desolated France, Germany and the Netherlands. It was fought, not between Protestants and Catholics as on the Continent, but between the more extreme or Calvinistic Protestants called Puritans and the more moderate Protestants, or Anglicans, adhering to the established Church of England. As in the wars on the Continent, religious differences were mixed indistinguishably with political and constitutional issues. As the Huguenots represented to some extent feudal rebelliousness against the French monarchy, as German Protestants fought for states' rights against imperial centralization, and the Calvinists of the Netherlands for provincial liberties against the king of Spain, so the Puritans asserted the rights of Parliament against the mounting claims of royalty in England.

The civil war in England was relatively so mild that England itself can be said to have escaped the horrors of the Wars of Religion. The same was not true of the British Isles as a whole. After 1603 the kingdoms of England and Scotland, while otherwise separate, were ruled by the same king; the kingdom of Ireland remained, as before, a dependency of the English crown. Between England and Presbyterian Scotland there was constant friction, but the worst trouble was between England and Catholic Ireland, which was the scene of religious warfare as savage as that of the Continent.

ENGLAND IN THE SEVENTEENTH CENTURY

For the English the seventeenth century was an age of great achievement, during which they made their debut as one of the chief peoples of modern Europe. In 1600 only four or five million persons, in England and lowland Scotland, spoke the English language. The number did not rise rapidly for another century and a half. But the population began to spread. Religious discontents, reinforced by economic pressures, led to considerable emigration. Twenty thousand Puritans settled in New England between 1630 and 1640, and about the same number went to Barbados and other West India islands during the same years. A third stream, again roughly of the same size, but made up mainly of Scotch Presbyterians, settled in northern Ireland under government auspices, driving away or expropriating the native Celts. English Catholics were allowed by the home government to settle in Maryland. A great many Anglicans went to Virginia in the mid-century, adding to the small settlement made at Jamestown in 1607. Except for the movement to northern Ireland, called the "plantation of Ulster," these migrations took place without much attention on the part of the government, through private initiative organized in commercial companies. After the middle of the century the government began deliberately to build an empire. New York was conquered from the Dutch, Jamaica from the Spanish, and Pennsylvania and the Carolinas were established. All the Thirteen Colonies except Georgia were founded before 1700, and there were at that time perhaps half a million people in British North America. Relatively to the home population, it was as if the United States should in three generations build up a distant colonial appendage with fifteen million inhabitants.

The English also, like the Dutch, French and Spanish at the time, were creating their national culture. Throughout Western Europe the national languages, encroaching upon international Latin on the one hand and local dialects on the other, were becoming adequate vehicles for the expression of thought and feeling. Shakespeare and Milton projected their mighty conceptions with overwhelming power of words, not since equaled in English or in any other tongue. The English classic literature, rugged in form but deep in content, vigorous yet subtle in insight, majestic, abundant and sonorous in expression, was almost the reverse of French classical writing, with its virtues of order, economy, propriety and graceful precision. The English could never thereafter quite yield to French standards, nor be dazzled or dumbfounded, as some peoples were, by the cultural glories of the Age of Louis XIV. In the arts other than literature, except in architecture, the English showed no conspicuous talent in the seventeenth century. There were no painters at all comparable to those on the Continent.

Economically the English were enterprising and affluent, though in 1600 far outdistanced by the Dutch. They had a larger and more productive country than the Dutch, and were therefore not as limited to purely mercantile and seafaring occupations. Coal was mined around Newcastle, and was increasingly used, but was not yet a leading source of English wealth. The great industry was the growing of sheep and manufacture of woollens, which were the main export. Weaving was done to a large extent in the country, under the putting-out system, and organized by merchants according to the methods of commercial capitalism.[4] Since 1553 the English had traded with Russia by way of the White Sea; they were increasingly active in the Baltic and eastern Mediterranean; and with the founding of the East India Company, in 1600, they competed with the Dutch in assaulting the old Portuguese monopoly in India and the Far East. But profitable as such overseas operations were, the main wealth of England was still in the land. The richest men were not merchants but landlords, and the landed aristocracy formed the richest class.

BACKGROUND TO THE CIVIL WAR: THE CONFLICT
BETWEEN PARLIAMENT AND THE STUART KINGS

In England, as elsewhere in the seventeenth century, the kings clashed with their old medieval representative bodies. In England the old body, Parliament, won out against the king. But this was not the unique feature in the English development. In Germany the estates of the Holy Roman Empire triumphed against the Emperor, and much the same thing, as will be seen, occurred in Poland. But on the Continent the triumph of the old representative bodies generally meant political dissolution or even anarchy. Successful governments were generally those in which kingly powers increased; this was the strong tendency of the time, evident even in the Dutch Republic after 1672 under William of Orange. The unique thing about England was that Parliament, in defeating the king, arrived at a workable form of government. Government remained strong, but came under Parliamentary control. This determined the character of modern England, and launched into the history of Europe and of the world the great movement of liberalism and representative institutions.

What happened was somewhat as follows. In 1603, on the death of Queen Elizabeth, the English crown was inherited by the son of Mary Stuart, James VI of Scotland, who became king of England also, taking there the title of James I. James was a philosopher of royal absolutism. He had even written a book on the subject, *The True Law of Free Monarchy*. By a "free" monarchy James meant a monarchy free from control by Parliament, churchmen, or laws and customs of the past. It was a monarchy in which the king, as father to his people, looked after their welfare as he saw fit, standing above all parties, private interests, and pressure groups. He even declared that kings drew their authority from God, and were responsible to God alone. The doctrine which he represented is known as the divine right of kings.[5]

Probably any ruler succeeding Elizabeth would have had trouble with Parliament, which had shown signs of restlessness in the last years of her reign, but had deferred to her as an aging woman and a national symbol. She had maintained peace within the country and fought off the Spaniards, but

wwwwwwwwwwwwww

[4] See pp. 96–7.
[5] See pp. 158–9, 284–5.

these very accomplishments persuaded many people that they could safely bring their grievances into the open. James I was a foreigner, a Scotchman, who lacked the touch for dealing with the English, and who was moreover a royal pedant, the "wisest fool in Christendom," as he was uncharitably called. Not content with the actualities of control, as Elizabeth had been, he read the Parliament tiresome lectures on the royal rights. He also was in constant need of money. He was far from economical, and in any case, in an age of rising prices, he could not live within the fixed and customary revenues of the English crown. These were of a medieval character, increasingly quaint under the new conditions—rights of wardship and marriage, escheats, franc-fiefs and fees for the distraint of knighthood, together with "tunnage and poundage," or rights given to the king by Parliament at his accession (and normally unchanged during his reign) to collect specified duties on exports and imports, according to quantity, not value, and hence inflexible in a period of inflation.

Neither to James I nor to his son Charles I, who succeeded him in 1625, would Parliament grant adequate revenue, because it distrusted them both. Many members of Parliament were Puritans, dissatisfied with the organization and doctrine of the Church of England.[6] Elizabeth had tried to hush up religious troubles, but James threatened to "harry the Puritans out of the land," and Charles supported the Anglican hierarchy which, under Archbishop Laud, sought to enforce religious conformity. Many members of Parliament were also lawyers, who feared that the common law of England, the historic or customary law, was in danger. They disliked the prerogative courts, the Star Chamber set up by Henry VII, the High Commission set up by Elizabeth.[7] They heard with trepidation the modern doctrine that the sovereign king could make laws and decide cases at his own discretion.[8] Last but not least, practically all members of Parliament were property-owners. Landowners, supported by the merchants, feared that if the king succeeded in raising taxes on his own authority their wealth would be insecure. Hence there were strong grounds for resistance.

In England the Parliament was so organized as to make resistance effective.[9] There was only one Parliament for the whole country. There were no provincial or local estates, as in the Dutch Republic, Spain, France, Germany, and Poland. Hence all parliamentary opposition was concentrated in one place. In this one place, the one and only Parliament, there were only two houses, the House of Lords and the House of Commons. The landed interest dominated in both houses, the noblemen in the Lords and the gentry in the Commons. In the Commons the gentry, who formed the bulk of the aristocracy, mixed with representatives of the merchants and the towns. Indeed the towns frequently chose country gentlemen to represent them.

wwwwwwwwwwwwww

[6] See pp. 75–9.
[7] See pp. 62, 87.
[8] See pp. 61–2.
[9] See pp. 31–2.

Hence the houses of Parliament did not accentuate, as did the estates on the Continent, the class division within the country. Nor was the Church present in Parliament as a separate force. Before Henry VIII's break with Rome the bishops and abbots together had formed a large majority in the House of Lords. Now there were no abbots left, for there were no monasteries. The House of Lords was now predominantly secular; in the first Parliament of James I there were eighty-two lay peers and twenty-six bishops. The great landowners had captured the House of Lords. The smaller landowners of the Commons had been enriched by receiving former monastic lands, and had prospered by raising wool. The merchants had likewise grown up under mercantilistic protection. Parliament was strong not only in organization but in the social interests and wealth that it represented. No king could long govern against its will.

In 1629 king and Parliament came to a deadlock. Charles I attempted to rule without Parliament, which could legally meet only at the royal summons. He intended to give England a good and efficient government. Had he succeeded, the course of English constitutional development would have paralleled that of France. But by certain reforms in Ireland he antagonized the English landlords who had interests in that country. By supporting the high Anglicans he made enemies of the Puritans. By attempting to modernize the navy with funds raised without parliamentary consent (called "ship money") he alarmed all property-owners, whose opposition was typified in the famous lawsuit of a country gentleman, John Hampden, in 1637.

The ship-money case illustrates the best arguments of both sides. It was the old custom in England for coastal towns to pay a tax, called ship money, for the arming of ships in time of war. Charles I wished to maintain a navy in time of peace, and to have ship money paid by the country as a whole, including the inland counties. In the old or medieval view it was the function of the towns which were directly affected to maintain a fleet. In the new view, sponsored by the king, the whole nation was the unit on which a navy should be based. The country gentlemen whom Parliament mainly represented, and most of whom lived in inland counties, neither wished to pay new taxes, nor to depart from old customs which worked in their favor, nor even to maintain a navy in which they saw little advantage to themselves. It was the king who, in the ship-money case, represented the more modern ideas of government and the needs of state. The Parliamentary class represented the idea, derived from the Middle Ages, that new taxes must be authorized by Parliament. John Hampden lost his case in court, but he won the sympathy of the politically significant classes of the country. Until the king could govern with the confidence of Parliament, or until Parliament itself was willing, not merely to keep down taxes, but to assume the responsibilities of government under modern conditions, neither a navy nor any effectual government could be maintained.

The Scotch were the first to rebel. In 1637 they rioted in Edinburgh against attempts to impose the Anglican religion in Scotland. Charles, to raise funds to put down the Scottish rebellion, convoked the English Parlia-

ment in 1640, for the first time in eleven years. When it proved hostile to
him he dissolved it and called for new elections. The same men were returned. The resulting body, since it sat theoretically for twenty years without
new elections, from 1640 to 1660, is known historically as the Long Parliament. Its principal leaders—men like John Hampden, John Pym and Oliver
Cromwell, were small or moderately well-to-do landowning gentry. The merchant class, while furnishing no leaders, lent its support.

The Long Parliament, far from assisting the king against the Scots,
used the Scottish rebellion as a means of pressing its own demands. These
were revolutionary from the outset. Parliament insisted that the chief royal
advisers be not merely removed but impeached and put to death. It abolished
the Star Chamber and the High Commission. The most extreme Calvinist
element, the "root and branch" men or "radicals," drove through a bill for
the abolition of bishops, revolutionizing the Anglican Church. In 1642
Parliament and king came to open war, the king drawing followers mainly
from the north and west, the Parliament from the commercially and agri-
culturally more advanced counties of the south and east. During the war, as
the price of support from the Scottish army, Parliament adopted the Solemn
League and Covenant. This prescribed that religion in England, Scotland
and Ireland should be made uniform "according to the word of God and the
example of the best reformed churches." Thus Presbyterianism became the
established legal religion of the three kingdoms.

THE EMERGENCE OF CROMWELL

The Parliamentary forces, called Roundheads from the close haircuts
favored by Puritans, gradually defeated the royalists. The wars brought a
hitherto unknown gentleman named Oliver Cromwell to the foreground. A
devout Puritan, he organized a new and more effective military force, the
Ironsides, in which extreme Protestant exaltation provided the basis for
morale, discipline, and the will to fight. Parliament had no sooner defeated
the king than it fell out with its own army. The army, in which a lower
economic class was represented than in the Parliament, became the center
of advanced democratic ideas. Many of the soldiers objected to Presbyterianism as much as to Anglicanism. They were Independents, favoring little
congregations of like-minded spirits subject to no superior church organization of any kind.

Cromwell concluded that the defeated king, Charles I, could not be
trusted, that "ungodly" persons of all kinds put their hopes in him (what
later ages would call counter-revolution), and that he must be put to death.
Since Parliament hesitated, Cromwell with the support of the army broke
Parliament up. The Long Parliament, having started in 1640 with some five
hundred members, had sunk by 1649 to about a hundred and fifty (for this
revolution, like others, was pushed through by a minority); of these Cromwell now drove out almost a hundred, leaving a Rump of fifty or sixty. This

operation was called Pride's Purge, after the Colonel Pride who commanded the soldiers by which Parliament was intimidated; and in subsequent revolutions such excisions have been commonly known as purges, and the residues, sometimes, as rumps. The Rump put King Charles to death on the scaffold in 1649.

England, or rather the whole British Isles, was now declared a republic. It was named the Commonwealth. Cromwell tried to govern as best he could. Religious toleration was decreed except for unitarians and atheists on the one hand, and except for Roman Catholics and the most obstinate Anglicans on the other—a considerable exception. Cromwell had to subdue both Scotland and Ireland by force. In Scotland the execution of the king, violating the ancient national Scottish monarchy of the Stuarts, had swung the country back into the royalist camp. Cromwell crushed the Scots in 1650. Meanwhile the Protestant and Calvinist fury swept over Ireland. A massacre of newly settled Protestants in Ulster in 1641 had left bitter memories which were now avenged. The Irish garrisons of Drogheda and Wexford were defeated and massacred. Thousands of Catholics were killed; priests were put to the sword, and women and small children despatched in cold blood. Where formerly, in the "plantation" of Ulster, a whole Protestant population had been settled in northern Ireland, bodily replacing the native Irish, now Protestant landlords were scattered over the country as a whole, replacing the Catholic landlords, and retaining the Catholic peasantry as their tenants. What now happened in Ireland was a close parallel to what had happened thirty years before in Bohemia, except that Protestant and Catholic roles were reversed.[10] For the Irish, as for the Czechs, the native religion and clergy were driven underground, a foreign and detested church was established, and a new and foreign landed aristocracy, originally recruited in large measure from military adventurers, was settled upon the country, in which, as soon as it assured the payment of its rents, it soon ceased to reside.

In England itself Cromwell ruled with great difficulty. In external affairs his regime was successful enough, for he not only completed the subjugation of Ireland, but in the Navigation Act of 1651 [11] he opened the English attack on the Dutch maritime supremacy, and in a war with Spain, in which the English acquired Jamaica, he opened the English bidding for the inheritance of the Spanish Hapsburgs. But he failed to make himself loved by a majority of the English. He was pressed by the extreme democrats, variously called Levellers, Diggers, or Fifth Monarchy Men, because they favored a "leveling" between rich and poor, or because they "dug" for themselves in common lands or the land of others, or because they believed in that Fifth Monarchy when Jesus would reign on earth, as prophesied in the Book of Revelations. Some of these elements, particularly in the army, carried on advanced political debates in which they spoke of their natural rights and their rights as Englishmen and even voiced demands for a written constitu-

---

[10] See pp. 123–4, 191–2.
[11] See p. 140.

tion and for a democratic suffrage. All established persons in society were alarmed by such agitation, which Cromwell himself did not favor. On the other hand, he could not conciliate the landed and Anglican interests, nor even the predominantly middle-class Presbyterians. Unable to agree even with the Rump, he abolished it also in 1653, and thereafter vainly attempted to govern, as Lord Protector, through representative bodies devised by himself and his followers, under a written constitution, the *Instrument of Government*. Actually, he was driven to place England under military rule, the regime of the "major-generals." These officials, each in his district, repressed malcontents, vagabonds, and "bandits," closed ale-houses, and prohibited cock-fighting, in a mixture of moral puritanism and political dictatorship. Cromwell died in 1658; and his son was unable to maintain the Protectorate. Two years later, with all but universal assent, royalty was restored. Charles II, son of the dead Charles I, became king of England and of Scotland.

    Cromwell, by beheading a king and keeping his successor off the throne for eleven years, had left a lesson which was not forgotten. Though he professed a belief in constitutional and parliamentary government and had granted a measure of religious toleration, he had ruled as a dictator in behalf of a stern Puritan minority. The English people now began to blot from their memories the fact that they had ever had a real revolution. The fervid dream of a "godly" England was dissipated forever. What was remembered was a nightmare of standing armies and major-generals. The English lower classes, for whom politics could still take only a religious form, ceased to have any political consciousness for almost two centuries.

    Democratic ideas in the full sense, the Levellers' demand that every man should have the vote, the principle of natural and equal human rights, the doctrine that government should be established by a written constitution drawn up by the people, were generally abandoned in England after 1660, or were cherished by obscure individuals who could not make themselves heard. Such ideas, indeed, had a more continuous history in the English colonies in America, in which some leaders of the discredited revolution took refuge.

19. Britain: The Triumph of Parliament

THE RESTORATION, 1660–88: THE LATER STUARTS

    What was restored in 1660 was not only the monarchy, in the person of Charles II, but also the Church of England and the Parliament. Everything, legally, was supposed to be as it had been in 1640. The difference was that Charles II, knowing the fate of his father, was careful not to provoke Parliament to extremes, and that the classes represented in Parliament, frightened by the disturbances of the past twenty years, were for some time more warmly loyal to the king than they had been before 1640, and more willing to uphold the established church.

Parliament during the Restoration enacted some far-reaching legislation. It changed the basis of land tenure, abolishing certain old feudal payments owed by landholders to the king. It thus turned the possession of land into private property of modern type, and the landowning class more definitely into a propertied aristocracy. In place of the feudal dues to the king, which had been automatically payable, Parliament arranged for the king to receive income in the form of taxation, which Parliament could raise or reduce in amount. This gave a new power to Parliament, and a new flexibility to government. The aristocracy, in short, cleared their property of customary restrictions and obligations, and at the same time undertook to support the state by imposing taxes on themselves. The English aristocracy proved more willing than the corresponding classes on the Continent to pay a large share of the expenses of government. Its reward was that, for a century and a half, it virtually ran the government to the exclusion of everyone else. Landowners in this period directed not only national affairs through Parliament, but also local affairs as justices of the peace. The justices, of whom there were about a dozen or so for each county, decided small lawsuits, punished misdemeanors, and supervised the parish officials charged with poor relief and care of the roads. The regime of the landlord-justices came to be called the "squirearchy."

Other classes drew less immediate advantage from the Restoration. The Navigation Act of 1651 was renewed and even added to, so that commercial, shipping, and manufacturing interests were well protected. But in other ways the landed classes now in power showed themselves unsympathetic to the business classes of the towns. Many people in the towns were Dissenters, of the element formerly called Puritan, and now refusing to accept the restored Church of England. Parliament excluded Dissenters from the town corporations, forbade any dissenting clergymen to teach school or come within five miles of an incorporated town, and prohibited all religious meetings, called "conventicles," not held according to the forms and by the authority of the Church of England. The effect was that many middle-class townspeople found it difficult or impossible to follow their preferred religion, to obtain an education for their children, either elementary or advanced (for Oxford and Cambridge were a part of the established church), to take part in local affairs through the town corporations, or to sit in the House of Commons, since the corporations in many cases chose the burgesses who represented the towns. The lowest classes, the very poor, were discouraged by the same laws from following sectarian and visionary preachers. Another enactment fell upon them alone, the Act of Settlement of 1662, which decentralized the administration of the Poor Law, making each parish responsible only for its own paupers. Poor people, who were very numerous, were condemned to remain in the parishes where they lived. A large section of the English population was immobilized.

But it was not long after the Restoration that Parliament and king were again at odds. The issue was again religion. There was at this time a tendency throughout Europe for Protestants to return voluntarily to Roman

Catholicism, a tendency naturally dreaded by the Protestant churches. It was most conspicuously illustrated when the daughter of Gustavus Adolphus himself, Queen Christina of Sweden, to the consternation of the Protestant world, abdicated her throne and was received into the Roman Church. In England the national feeling was excitedly anti-Catholic. No measures were more popular than those against "popery"; and the squires in Parliament, stiffly loyal to the Church of England, dreaded papists even more than Dissenters. The king, Charles II, was personally inclined to Catholicism. He admired the magnificent monarchy of Louis XIV, which he would have liked to duplicate, so far as possible, in England. At odds with his Parliament, Charles II made overtures to Louis XIV. The secret treaty of Dover of 1670 was the outcome. Charles hereby agreed to join Louis XIV in his expected war against the Dutch; and Louis agreed to pay the king of England three million *livres* a year during the war, and two million more whenever Charles II found it opportune to rejoin the Roman Church.

While these arrangements were unknown in detail in England, it was known that Charles II was well disposed to the French and to Roman Catholicism. England went to war again with the Dutch. The king's brother and heir, James, Duke of York, publicly announced his conversion to Rome. Charles II, in a "declaration of indulgence," announced the nonenforcement of laws against Dissenters. The king declared that he favored general toleration, but it was rightly feared that his real aim was to promote Roman Catholicism in England, and that his policy might be the opening wedge for the Counter Reformation, which had already swept Protestantism out of Bohemia and Poland, and was at this very moment menacing it in France. Parliament retorted in 1673 by passing the Test Act, which required all office-holders to take communion in the Church of England. The Test Act renewed the legislation against Dissenters and also made it impossible for Catholics to serve in the government or in the army and navy. The Test Act remained on the statute books until 1828.

While Charles's pro-French and pro-Catholic policies were extremely unpopular, both among the country gentry who disliked Frenchmen from prejudice, and the merchants who found in them increasingly pressing competitors, still the situation might not have come to a head except for the avowed Catholicism and French orientation of Charles's brother James, due to be the next king since Charles had no legitimate children. A strong movement developed in Parliament to exclude James by law from the throne. The exclusionists—and those generally who were most suspicious of king, Catholics, and Frenchmen—received the nickname of Whigs. The king's supporters were popularly called Tories. The Whigs, while backed by the middle class and merchants of London, drew their main strength from the upper aristocracy, especially certain great noblemen who might expect, if the king's power were weakened, to play a prominent part in ruling the country themselves. The Tories were the party of the lesser aristocracy and gentry, those who were suspicious of the "moneyed interest" of London, and felt a strong loyalty to church and king. These two parties became permanently established in English public life. But all the Whigs and Tories together, at this time, did not number more than a few thousand persons.

THE REVOLUTION OF 1688

James II, despite Whig vexation, became king in 1685. He soon antagonized even the Tories. The Tories were strong Anglicans or Church of England men. As landowners they appointed most of the parish clergy, who imparted Tory sentiments to the rural population, and from their ranks were drawn the bishops, archdeacons, university functionaries and other higher personnel of the Church. The laws keeping Dissenters and Catholics from office had given Anglicans a monopoly in local and national government and in the army and navy. James II acted as if there were no Test Act, claiming the right to suspend its operation in individual cases, and appointed a good many Catholics to influential and lucrative positions. He offered a program, as his brother had done, of general religious toleration, to allow Protestant Dissenters as well as Roman Catholics to participate in public life. Such a program, whether frankly meant as a secularizing of politics or indirectly intended as favoritism to Catholics, was equally repugnant to the Church of England. Seven bishops refused to endorse it. They were prosecuted for disobedience to the king but were acquitted by the jury. James, by these actions, violated the liberties of the established church, threatened the Anglican monopoly of church and state, and aroused the popular terrors of "popery." He was also forced to take the position philosophically set forth by his grandfather James I, that a king of England could make and unmake the law by his own will. The Tories joined the Whigs in opposition. In 1688, a son was born to James II and baptized into the Catholic faith. The prospect now opened up of an indefinite line of Catholic rulers in England. Leading men of both parties thereupon abandoned James II. They offered the throne to his grown daughter Mary, born and brought up a Protestant before her father's conversion to Rome.

Mary was the wife of William of Orange. William, it will be recalled, had spent his adult life in blocking the ambitions of the king of France, who, it should be recalled likewise, threatened Europe with a "universal monarchy" by absorbing or inheriting the world of Spain. To William III it would be a mere distraction to be husband to a queen of England, or even to be king in his own name, unless he could use England for his own purposes. He was immutably Dutch; his purpose was to save Holland and hence to ruin Louis XIV. His only interest in England was to bring the English into his balance of power against France. Since the English were generally anti-French, and had chafed under the pro-French tendencies of their kings, William without difficulty reached an understanding with the discontented Whigs and Tories. Protected by a written invitation from prominent Englishmen he invaded England with a considerable army. James II fled, and William was proclaimed co-ruler with Mary over England and Scotland. In the next year, 1690, at the Boyne river in Ireland, a motley army of Dutchmen, Germans, Scotch, and French Huguenots under William III defeated a French and Irish force led by James II. Thus the liberties of England were saved. James II fled to France.

Louis XIV of course refused to recognize his inveterate enemy as ruler of England. He maintained James at the French court with all the honors due the English king. It was thereafter one of his principal war aims to restore the Catholic and Stuart dynasty across the Channel. The English, contrariwise, had added reason to fight the French. French victory would mean counter-revolution and royal absolutism in England. The whole revolution of 1688 was at stake in the French wars.

In 1689, Parliament enacted a Bill of Rights, stipulating that no law could be suspended by the king (as the Test Act had been), no taxes raised or army maintained except by Parliamentary consent, and no subject (however poor) arrested and detained without legal process. William III accepted these articles as conditions to receiving the crown. Thereafter the relation between king and people was a kind of contract. It was further provided, by the Act of Settlement of 1701, that no Catholic could be king of England; this excluded the descendants of James II, known in the following century as the Pretenders. Parliament also passed the Toleration Act of 1689, which allowed Protestant Dissenters to practice their religion, but still excluded them from political life and public service. Since ways of evading these restrictions were soon found, and since even Catholics were not molested unless they supported the Pretenders, there was thereafter no serious trouble over religion in England and Lowland Scotland.

The English Parliament could make no laws for Scotland, and it was to be feared that James II might some day be restored in his northern kingdom. The securing of the Parliamentary revolution in England, and of the island's defenses against France, required that the two kingdoms be organically joined. There was little sentiment in Scotland, however, for a merger with the English. The English tempted the Scotch with economic advantages. The Scotch still had no rights in the English East India Company, nor in the English colonies, nor within the English system of mercantilism and Navigation Acts. They obtained such rights by consenting to a union. In 1707 the United Kingdom of Great Britain was created. The Scotch retained their own legal system and established Presbyterian church, but their government and parliament were merged with those of England. The term "British" came into use to refer to both English and Scotch.

As for Ireland, feared as a center of Stuart and French intrigue, its Catholicism hated by the English, it fared badly by the revolution of 1688. To the burden of an alien church and absentee landlordism was now added the "penal code." Catholic clergy were banished, and Catholics were forbidden to vote or to sit in the Irish parliament. Catholic teachers were forbidden to teach, and Catholic parents were forbidden to send children overseas to be educated in Catholic schools. Catholic Irishmen were forbidden to purchase land, to lease it for more than thirty-one years, to inherit it from a Protestant, or to own a horse worth more than £5. A Catholic whose son turned Protestant found his own property rights limited in his son's favor. Catholics were forbidden to be attorneys, to serve as constables, or, in most trades, to have more than two apprentices. Irish shipping was excluded from the British colonies, nor could the Irish import colonial goods except through England. Export of Irish woollens and glass manufactures was prohibited. No import tariff on English manufactures could be levied by the Irish parliament. About all that was left to the Irish, in international trade, was the export of agricultural produce; and the foreign exchange acquired in this way went very largely to pay the rents of absentee landlords. The purpose of the penal code was to destroy the economic life of Ireland and to demoralize and enfeeble the people. In this it was successful; it is unfortunately quite possible to degrade a people by legislation, especially when maintained, as in the case of Ireland, for over a hundred years. The Irish emerged from these seventeenth-century events as probably the most thoroughly repressed people of Western Europe.

England, immediately after the expulsion of James II, joined William III's coalition against France. To the alliance England brought a highly competent naval force, together with very considerable wealth. William's government, to finance the war, borrowed £1,200,000 from a syndicate of private lenders, who in return for holding government bonds were given the privilege of operating a bank. Thus originated, in 1694, both the Bank of England and the British national debt. Owners of liquid assets, merchants of London and Whig aristocrats with fat rent-rolls, having lent their money to the new regime had a compelling reason to defend it against the French and James II. And having at last a government whose policies they could control, they were willing to entrust it with money in large amounts. The national debt rapidly rose, while the credit of the government held consistently good; and for many years the Continent was astonished at the wealth that the British government could tap at will, and the quantities of money that it could pour into the wars of Europe.

The events of 1688 came to be known to the English as the Glorious Revolution. The Revolution was considered to have vindicated the principles of parliamentary government, the rule of law, and even the right of rebellion against tyranny. It has often been depicted as the climax in the growth of English constitutional self-government. Political writers like John Locke, shortly after the events, helped to give wide currency to these ideas.[12] There was in truth some justification for these views even though in more recent times some writers have "deglorified" the revolution of 1688. They point out that it was a class movement, promoted and maintained by the landed aristocracy. The Parliament which boldly asserted itself against the king was at the same time closing itself to large segments of the people. Where in the Middle Ages members of the House of Commons had usually received

[12] On John Locke and the philosophy of the Glorious Revolution see pp. 285-7.

pay for their services, this custom disappeared in the seventeenth century, so that thereafter only men with independent incomes could sit. After the Parliamentary triumph of 1688 this tendency became a matter of law. An act of 1710 required members of the House of Commons to possess private incomes corresponding to some $15,000 a year in the United States today. This income had to come from the ownership of land. England from 1688 to 1832 was the best example in modern times of a true aristocracy, *i.e.*, of a country in which the aristocratic landowning class not only enjoyed privileges but also conducted the government. But the landowning interest was then the only class sufficiently wealthy, numerous, educated and self-conscious to stand on its own feet. The rule of the "gentlemen of England" was within its limits a regime of political liberty.

20. The France of Louis XIV, 1643–1715: The Triumph of Absolutism

FRENCH CIVILIZATION IN THE SEVENTEENTH CENTURY

Having travelled in the outer orbits of the European political system, we come now to its radiant and mighty center, the domain of the Sun King himself, the France against which the rest of Europe felt obliged to combine, and on whose push and pull depended the course of the lesser bodies—the future of the Spanish possessions, the independence of Holland, the maintenance in England of the Parliamentary revolution. The France of Louis XIV owed much of its ascendancy to the quantity and the quality of its population. With 21,000,000 inhabitants in 1700 it was four times as populous as England and twice as populous as Spain; and its people were among the most industrious, thrifty, and generally proficient in Europe. Its fertile soil, in an agricultural age, made it exceptionally wealthy; and it also had a great many cities with a busy commercial and capitalistic class, so much so that the French term for the upper elements of townspeople, the *bourgeoisie*, came later to designate this class in all countries. The French in the seventeenth century began trading in India and Madagascar, founded Canada, penetrated the Great Lakes and the Mississippi Valley, set up plantations in the West Indies, expanded their ancient commerce with the Levant, enlarged their mercantile marine and for a time had the leading navy of Europe.

The dominance of France meant the dominance not merely of power, but of a people generally admitted to be in the forefront of civilization. They carried over the versatility of the Italy of the Renaissance. In Poussin and Claude Lorrain they produced a notable school of painters, their architecture was emulated throughout Europe, and they excelled in military fortification and general engineering. Much of their literature, though often written by bourgeois writers, was designed for an aristocratic and courtly audience, which had put aside the uncouth manners of an earlier day and prided itself on the refinement of its tastes and perceptions. Corneille and Racine wrote austere tragedies on the fundamental situations of human life. Molière, in his comedies, ridiculed bumbling doctors, new-rich bourgeois, and foppish aristocrats, making the word "marquis" almost a joke in the French language. La Fontaine gave the world his animal fables, and La Rochefoucauld, in his witty and sardonic maxims, a great nobleman's candid judgment on human nature. In Descartes the French produced a great mathematician and scientific thinker, in Pascal a scientist who was also a profound spokesman for Christianity, in Bayle the father of modern skeptics. It was French thought and the French language, not merely the armies of Louis XIV, which in the seventeenth century were sweeping the European world.

THE DEVELOPMENT OF ABSOLUTISM IN FRANCE

This ascendancy of French culture went along with a regime in which political liberties were at a discount. It was an embellishment to the absolute monarchy of Louis XIV. France had a tradition of political freedom in the feudal sense. It had the same kind of background of feudal liberties as did the other countries of Europe. It had an Estates-General, which had not met since 1615 but was not legally abolished. In some regions Provincial Estates, still meeting frequently, retained a measure of self-government and of power over taxation. There were about a dozen bodies known as parliaments,[13] which, unlike the English Parliament, had developed as courts of law, each being the supreme court for a certain area of the country. The parliaments upheld certain "fundamental laws" which they said the king could not overstep, and they often refused to enforce royal edicts which they declared to be unconstitutional. We have already observed how France, beneath the surface, was almost as composite as Germany.[14] French towns had won charters of acknowledged rights, and many of the great provinces enjoyed liberties written into old agreements with the Crown. These local liberties were the main reason for a good deal of institutional complication. There were some three hundred "customs" or regional systems of law; it was observed that a traveller sometimes changed laws more often than he changed horses. Internal tariffs ran along the old provincial borders. Tolls were levied by manorial lords. The king's taxes fell less heavily on some regions than on others. Neither coinage nor weights and measures were uniform throughout the country. France was a bundle of territories held together by allegiance to the king.

This older kind of freedom discredited itself in France at the very time when by triumphing in Germany it pulled the Holy Roman Empire to pieces, and when in England it successfully made the transition to a more modern form of political liberty, embodied in the Parliamentary

[13] Often spelled *parlements*, as in French, to distinguish from the English Parliament.

[14] See p. 114 and map, p. 161.

though aristocratic state. In France the old medieval, feudal or local type of liberty became associated with disorder. It has already been related how after the disorders of the sixteenth-century religious wars people had turned with relief to the monarchy and how Henry IV and then Richelieu had begun to make the monarchy strong.[15] The troubles of the Fronde provided additional incentive for absolutism in France.

The Fronde broke out immediately after the Peace of Westphalia, while Louis XIV was still a child, and was directed against Cardinal Mazarin, who was governing in his name. It was an abortive revolution, led by the same elements, the parliaments and the nobility, which were to precipitate the great French Revolution in 1789. The parliaments, especially the Parliament of Paris, insisted in 1648 on their right to pronounce certain edicts unconstitutional. Barricades were thrown up and street fighting broke out in Paris. The nobility rebelled, as often in the past. Leadership was assumed by certain prominent noblemen who, roughly like the great Whigs of England, had enough wealth and influence to believe that, if the king's power were kept down, they might govern the country themselves. The nobility demanded a calling of the Estates-General, expecting to dominate over the bourgeoisie and the clergy in that body. Armed bands of soldiers, unemployed since the Peace of Westphalia and led by nobles, roamed about the country terrorizing the peasants. If the nobles had their way, it was probable that the manorial system would fall on the peasants more heavily, as in Eastern Europe, where triumphant lords were at this very time exacting increased labor services from the peasants. Finally the rebellious nobles called in Spanish troops, though France was at war with Spain. By this time the bourgeoisie, represented in the parliaments, had withdrawn support from the rebellious nobles. The agitation subsided in total failure, because bourgeoisie and aristocracy could not work together, because the nobles outraged the loyalty of many Frenchmen by joining with a power with which France was at war, and because the *frondeurs*, especially after the parliaments deserted them, had no systematic or constructive program, aiming only at the overthrow of the unpopular Cardinal Mazarin, and at obtaining offices and favors for themselves.

After the Fronde, as after the religious wars, the bourgeoisie and peasantry of France, to protect themselves against the claims of the aristocracy, were in a mood to welcome the exercise of strong power by the kings. And in the young Louis XIV they had a man more than willing to grasp all the power he could get. Louis, on Mazarin's death in 1661, announced that he would govern the country himself. He was the third king of the Bourbon line. It was the Bourbon tradition, established by Henry IV and by Richelieu, to draw the teeth from the feudal aristocrats, and this tradition Louis XIV followed. He was not a man of any transcendent abilities, though he had the capacity, often found among successful executives, of learning a good deal from conversation with experts. His education was not

[15] See pp. 119–20.

very good, having been made purposely easy; but he had the ability to see and stick to definite lines of policy, and he was extremely methodical and industrious in his daily habits, scrupulously loading himself with administrative business throughout his reign. He was extremely fond of himself and his position of kingship, with an insatiable appetite for admiration and flattery; he loved magnificent display and elaborate etiquette, though to some extent he simply adopted them as instruments of policy rather than as a personal whim.

With the reign of Louis XIV the "state" in its modern form took a long step forward. The state in the abstract has always seemed theoretical to the English-speaking world. Let us say, for simplicity, that the state represents a fusion of justice and power. A sovereign state possesses, within its territory, a monopoly over the administration of justice and the use of force. Private persons neither pass legal judgments on others, nor control private armies of their own. For private and unauthorized persons to do so, in an orderly state, constitutes rebellion. This was in contrast to the older feudal practice, by which feudal lords maintained manorial courts and led their own followers into battle. Against these feudal practices Louis XIV energetically worked, though not with complete success, claiming to possess in his own person, as sovereign ruler, a monopoly over the law-making processes and the armed forces of the kingdom. This is the deeper meaning of his reputed boast, L'état, c'est moi—"the state is myself." In the France of the seventeenth century, divided by classes and by regions, there was in fact no means of consolidating the powers of state except in a single man.

The state, however, while representing law and order within its borders, has generally stood in a lawless and disorderly relation to other states, since no higher monopoly of law and force has existed. Louis XIV, personifying the French state, had no particular regard for the claims of other states or rulers. He was constantly either at war or preparing for war with his neighbors. The modern state, indeed, was created by the needs of peace at home and war abroad. Machinery of government, as devised by Louis XIV and others, was a means of giving order and security within the territory of the state, and of raising, supporting and controlling armies for use against other states.

The idea that law and force within a country should be monopolized by the lawful king was the essence of the seventeenth century doctrine of absolutism. Its principal theorist in the time of Louis XIV was Bishop Bossuet. Bossuet advanced the old Christian teaching that all power comes from God, and that all who hold power are responsible to God for the way they use it. He held that kings were God's representatives in the political affairs of earth. Royal power, according to Bossuet, was absolute but not arbitrary: not arbitrary because it must be reasonable and just, like the will of God which it reflected; absolute in that it was free from dictation by parliaments, estates or other subordinate elements within the country. Law, therefore, was the will of the sovereign king, so long as it conformed to the higher law which was the will of God. This doctrine, affirming the divine right of kings, was popularly held in France at the time, and was taught in the churches. It was fortified by the principles of Roman law, which also held that laws could be made and unmade, modified and amended, by act of the sovereign power. In addition, the authority of Louis XIV rested on purely practical considerations. Experience showed absolutism to be the corrective to anarchy, and the king was widely believed to represent the interests of the country better than anyone else.

GOVERNMENT AND ADMINISTRATION

Possibly the most fundamental step taken by Louis XIV was to assure himself of control of the army. Armed forces had formerly been almost a private enterprise. Specialists in fighting, leading their own troops, worked for governments more or less as they chose, either in return for money or to pursue political aims of their own. This was especially common in Central Europe, but even in France great noblemen had strong private influence over the troops, and in times of disorder nobles led armed retainers about the country. Colonels were virtually on their own. Provided with a general commission and with funds by some government, they recruited, trained and equipped their own regiments, and likewise fed and supplied them, often by preying upon bourgeois and peasants in the vicinity. In these circumstances it was often difficult to say on whose side soldiers were fighting. It was hard for governments to set armies into motion, and equally hard to make them stop fighting, for commanders fought for their own interests and on their own momentum. War was not a "continuation of policy"; it was not an act of the state; it easily degenerated, as in the Thirty Years' War, into a kind of aimless and perpetual violence.

Louis XIV made war an activity of state. He saw to it that all armed persons in France fought only for him. This produced peace and order in France, while strengthening the fighting power of France against other states. Under the older conditions there was also little integration among different units and arms of the army. Infantry regiments and troops of horse went largely their own way, and the artillery was supplied by civilian technicians under contract. Louis XIV created a stronger unity of control, put the artillery organically into the army, systematized the military ranks and grades, and clarified the chain of command, placing himself at the top. The government supervised recruiting, required colonels to prove that they were maintaining the proper number of soldiers, and assumed most of the responsibility for equipping, provisioning, clothing and housing the troops. Higher officers, thus becoming dependent on the government, could be subjected to discipline. The soldiers were put into uniforms, taught to march in step, and housed in barracks; thus they too became more susceptible to discipline and control. Armed forces became less of a terror to their own people, and a more effective weapon in the hands of the government. They were employed usually against other governments, but if necessary to suppress rebellion at home.

Louis XIV also increased the French army in size, raising it from about 100,-
000 to about 400,000. These changes, both in size and in degree of government control, were made possible by the growth of a large civilian administration. The heads of this administration under Louis XIV were civilians.
They were in effect the first ministers of war, and their assistants, officials, inspectors, and clerks constituted the first organized war ministry.

Louis XIV was not only a vain man, but made it a political principle
to overawe the country with his own grandeur. He built himself a whole
new city at the old village of Versailles about ten miles from Paris. Where
the Escorial had the atmosphere of a monastery, Versailles was a monument
to worldly splendor. Tremendous in size alone, fitted out with polished mirrors, gleaming chandeliers, and magnificent tapestries, opening on to a formal
park with fountains and shaded walks, the palace of Versailles was the marvel
of Europe and the envy of lesser kings. It was virtually a public building,
much of it used for government offices, and with nobles, churchmen, notable
bourgeois, and servants milling about on the king's affairs. The more exclusive
honors of the château were reserved for the higher aristocrats. The king surrounded his daily routine of rising, eating, and going to bed (known as the
lever, dîner, and *coucher*) with an infinite series of ceremonial acts, so minute
and so formalized that there were, for example, six different entries of persons
at the *lever,* and a certain gentleman at a specified moment held the right
sleeve of the king's nightshirt as he took it off. The most exalted persons
thought themselves the greater for thus waiting on so august a being. In this
way, and by more material favors, many great lords were induced to live
habitually at court. Here, under the royal eye, they might engage in palace
intrigue, but were kept away from real political mischief. Versailles completed
the political and moral ruin of the French aristocracy as a class. The king
himself was one of the few who could proceed through such rounds of elaborate living and still be able to attend regularly to public affairs. Neither the
nobles whom he kept about him, nor his own successors Louis XV and
Louis XVI, were able to carry the burden.

For positions in the government, as distinguished from his personal
entourage, Louis XIV preferred to use men of the bourgeois class, who were
dependent on him for salaries and careers, and who unlike noblemen could
aspire to no independent political influence of their own. He never called the
Estates-General, which in any case no one except some of the nobility
wanted. Some of the Provincial Estates, because of local and aristocratic
pressures, he allowed to remain functioning. He temporarily destroyed the
independence of the parliaments, commanding them to accept his orders, as
Henry IV had commanded them to accept the Edict of Nantes.[16] He stifled
the old liberties of the towns, turning their civic offices into empty and
purchasable honors, and likewise regulating the operation of the gilds. He
developed a strong system of administrative coordination, centering in a
number of councils of state, which he attended in person, and in "intendants"

〰〰〰〰〰〰〰〰〰

[16] See p. 118.

who represented these councils throughout the country. Councillors of state and intendants were generally of bourgeois origin. Each intendant, within his district, embodied all aspects of the royal government, supervising the

FRANCE TO **1789**

FROM THE *LAST YEARS OF LOUIS* XIV
TO THE REVOLUTION OF *1789*

AUSTRIAN NETHERLANDS

GERMAN STATES

Arras
8
58

• Rouen

13

Metz

60 27 • Nancy

◉
Paris

Colmar

2

Rennes

3 60

Dijon • Besançon

61 15

SWITZ-
ERLAND

60

7

61

9

7

10

10

30 Grenoble

ITALY

• Bordeaux

TO THE
POPE

9

30

Aix

7

30

• Toulouse

25

3 • Pau

Perpignan

S P A I N

20

PAYS D'ÉTAT

COLBERT'S TARIFF UNION

AREA REMAINING ENTIRELY OUTSIDE
THE FRENCH TARIFF SYSTEM

• SEATS OF PARLIAMENTS OR
SUPREME COURTS OF LAW

NUMERALS INDICATE THE PRICE OF SALT,
I.E., THE AMOUNT OF SALT TAX

150 MILES

TRM

    The map gives an idea of the diversity of law and administration before the Revolution. Shaded areas are pays d'état, *provinces in which representative bodies ("estates") continued to meet. Cities named are the seats of what the French called parliaments (see p. 156). The barred line encloses Colbert's tariff union, the Five Great Farms (see p. 163). The area marked with crosshatching remained outside the French tariff system entirely; it continued to trade with the states of the Holy Roman Empire (from which it had been annexed) without interference by the French government. Numerals indicate the price of salt, i.e., the amount of the salt tax, in various regions. In general, it will be seen that regions farthest from Paris enjoyed the most "privileges" or "liberties," preserving their legal and judicial identity, provincial estates, local tariffs, and a favored position in national taxation.*

flow of taxes and recruiting of soldiers, keeping an eye on the local nobility, dealing with towns and gilds, controlling the more or less hereditary office-holders, stamping out bandits, smugglers and wolves, policing the market places, relieving famine, watching the local law courts and often deciding cases himself. In this way a firm and uniform administration was superimposed upon the heterogeneous mass of the old France. In contrast to England, all local questions were handled by agents of the central government, usually honest and often efficient, but essentially bureaucrats constantly instructed by, and referring back to, their superiors at Versailles.

ECONOMIC AND FINANCIAL POLICIES: COLBERT

To support the reorganized and enlarged army, the panoply of Versailles, and the growing civil administration the king needed a good deal of money. Finance was always the weak spot in the French monarchy. Methods of collecting taxes were costly and inefficient. Direct taxes passed through the hands of many intermediate officials; indirect taxes were collected by private concessionnaires called tax-farmers, who made a substantial profit. The state always received far less than what the taxpayers actually paid. But the main weakness arose from an old bargain between the French crown and nobility; the king might raise taxes without consent if only he refrained from taxing the nobles. Only the "unprivileged" classes paid direct taxes, and these came almost to mean the peasants only, since many bourgeois in one way or another obtained exemptions. The system was outrageously unjust in throwing the tax burden on the poor and helpless. It was ruinous to the government, since the government could never raise enough money, however hard it taxed the poor, being unable to tap the real source of ready wealth, namely the wealthier people. It was ruinous also to the French nobility, who in paying no direct taxes lost their hold over the government, lacked incentive to interest themselves in public affairs, and were unable to assume leadership of the bulk of the population. Louis XIV was willing enough to tax the nobles, but was unwilling to fall under their control, and only toward the close of his reign, under extreme stress of war, was he able, for the first time in French history, to impose direct taxes on the aristocratic elements of the population. This was a great step toward equality before the law and toward sound public finance, but so many concessions and exemptions were won by nobles and bourgeois that the reform lost much of its value.

Like his predecessors, Louis resorted to all manner of expedients to increase his revenues. He raised the tax-rates, always with disappointing results. He devaluated the currency. He sold patents of nobility to ambitious bourgeois. He sold government offices, judgeships, and commissions in the army and navy. For both financial and political reasons the king used his sovereign authority to annul the town charters, then sell back reduced rights at a price; this produced a little income but demoralized local government and civic spirit. The need for money, arising from the fundamental inability to tax the wealthy, which in turn reflected the weakness of absolutism, of a government which would not or could not share its rule with the propertied classes, corrupted much of the public life and political aptitude of the French people.

Louis XIV wished, if only for his own purposes, to make France economically powerful. His great minister Colbert worked for twenty years to do so. Colbert went beyond Richelieu in the application of mercantilism, aiming to make France a self-sufficing economic unit and to increase the wealth from which taxes were drawn.[17] He managed to abolish local tariffs in a large part of Central France, where he set up a tariff-union oddly entitled the Five Great Farms (since the remaining tolls were collected by tax-farmers); and although vested interests and provincial liberties remained too strong for him to do away with all internal tariffs, the area of the Five Great Farms was in itself one of the largest free-trade areas in Europe, being about the size of England. For the convenience of business men Colbert promulgated a Commercial Code, replacing much of the local customary law, and long a model of business practice and business regulation. He improved communications by building roads and canals, of which the most famous was one joining the Bay of Biscay with the Mediterranean. Working through the gilds, he required the handicraft manufacturers to produce goods of specified kind and quality, believing that foreigners, if assured of quality by the government, would purchase French products more freely. He gave subsidies, tax exemptions, and other privileges to expand the manufacture of silks, tapestries, glassware, and woollens. He helped to found colonies, built up the navy, and established the French East India Company. Export of some goods, notably foodstuffs, was forbidden, for the government wished to keep the populace quiet by holding down the price of bread. Export of other goods, mainly manufactures, was encouraged, partly as a means of bringing money into the country, where it could be funneled into the royal treasury. The growth of the army, and the fact that under Louis XIV the government clothed and equipped the soldiers, and hence placed unprecedentedly large orders for uniforms, overcoats, weapons, and ammunition, greatly stimulated the employment of weavers, tailors and gunsmiths, and advanced the commercial capitalism by which such labors were organized. In general, trade and manufacture developed in France under more direct government guidance than in England. They long gave the English an extremely brisk competition. Not until the age of iron and coal did France begin economically to lag.

RELIGION: THE REVOCATION OF THE EDICT OF NANTES, 1685

The consolidation of France under Louis XIV reached its high point in his policies toward religion. Toward Rome Louis backed the old claims of the Gallican Church to enjoy a certain national independence of policy. He repressed the movement known as Jansenism, a kind of Calvinism within

—————————————

[17] On mercantilism in general, see pp. 102–4.

the Catholic Church, which persisted for almost two centuries. But it was the Protestants who suffered most.

France, in the early years of Louis XIV's reign, still allowed more religious toleration than any other large state in Europe. The Huguenots had lost their separate political status under Richelieu, but they continued to live in relative security and contentment, protected by the Edict of Nantes of 1598.[18] From the beginning, however, toleration had been a royal rather than a popular policy, and under Louis XIV the royal policy changed. The fate of Catholics at the hands of a triumphant Parliament in England suggests that the Protestants in France would have been no better off under more popular institutions.

Bending all else to his will, Louis XIV resented the presence of heretics among his subjects. He considered religious unity necessary to the strength and dignity of his rule. He perhaps envied the right claimed by most governments at the time, Protestant as well as Catholic, to determine the religion of their respective peoples. He fell under the influence of certain Catholic advisers, who, not content with the attrition by which some Protestants were turning back to Catholicism in any case, wished to hasten the process to the greater glory of themselves. Systematic conversion of Huguenots was begun. Life for Protestant families was gradually made unbearable. Finally they were literally "dragooned," mounted infantrymen being quartered in Huguenot homes to reinforce the persuasions of missionaries. In 1685 Louis revoked the Edict of Nantes. During the persecutions a good many Protestants left France, migrating to Holland, Germany, and America. Their loss was a blow to French economic life, for although Protestants were found in all levels of French society, those of the commercial and industrial classes were the most mobile. With the revocation of the Edict of Nantes France embarked on a century of official intolerance (slowly mitigated in practice), under which Protestants in France were in much the same position as Catholics in the British Isles. The fact that a hundred years later, when Protestants were again tolerated, many of them were found to be both commercially prosperous and politically loyal indicates that they fared far better than the Catholic Irish.

All things considered, the reign of Louis XIV brought considerable advantages to the French middle and lower classes. His most bitter critics, with the natural exception of Protestants, were disgruntled nobles such as the Duke of Saint-Simon. His use of bourgeois in influential positions, and willingness to issue patents of nobility in return for money, while disgusting to the old aristocracy, were gratifying to the middle class. For the common people he did less, but he did save them from falling under the control of the lords. The intendants were assiduous enemies of the manorial courts; they did everything possible to keep the peasants under royal, not feudal, jurisdiction. Hence the French peasantry was kept free from the burden of serfdom that was rising in eastern Europe, and from the submission to rural

---

[18] See pp. 118–20.

squires that prevailed in England after the Restoration. Louis XIV, at a heavy and indeed prohibitive cost of privileges to the nobles, yet accomplished something for the cause of equality in France. He was generally popular, and even loved. What finally turned a good many Frenchmen against him in his last years was the strain brought by incessant wars.

21. The Wars of Louis XIV: The Peace of Utrecht, 1713

BEFORE 1700

From the outset of his reign Louis pursued a vigorous foreign policy. The quarrel between the House of France and the House of Hapsburg had gone on for more than a century. The Austrian branch of the Hapsburgs had been checkmated at the Peace of Westphalia. With the Spanish branch the French remained at war for another decade, until the Peace of the Pyrenees in 1659. When, two years later, Louis XIV assumed his personal rule, Spanish territories still faced France on three sides, northeast, east, and south; but so weakened was Spain that this fact was no longer a menace to France so much as a temptation to French expansion. Louis XIV could count on popular national feeling to support him, for the dream of a frontier on the Rhine and the Alps was captivating to Frenchmen. He struck in 1667. (The war was called the "War of Devolution," from a legal term used in the preliminary demands.) He was blocked, as noted above, by a Triple Alliance engineered by the Dutch.[19] With strength renewed by reforms at home, and in alliance with Charles II of England, he struck again in 1672 (the "Dutch War"), invading the Dutch provinces on the lower Rhine, and this time raising up his great adversary and inveterate enemy, the Prince of Orange.[20] William III, bringing the Austrian and Spanish Hapsburgs, Brandenburg and Denmark into alliance with the Dutch Republic, forced Louis to sign the treaty of Nimwegen in 1678. The French gave up their ambitions against Holland, but took from Spain the rich province of Franche-Comté, which outflanked Alsace on the south, and brought French power to the borders of Switzerland.

In the very next year, 1679, Louis further infiltrated the dissolving frontier of the Holy Roman Empire, this time in Lorraine and Alsace. By the Peace of Westphalia the French king had rights in this region, but the terms of that treaty were so ambiguous, and the local feudal law so confusing, that claims could be made in contrary directions. Louis XIV now set up *chambres de réunion*, as he called them, law courts in which French judges examined the claims to various parcels of territory and pronounced in favor of the king of France. French troops thereupon moved in. In 1681 French troops occupied the city of Strasburg, which, as a free city of the Holy Roman

[19] See p. 141.
[20] See pp. 141–2, 153.

Empire, regarded itself as an independent little republic. A protest went up over Germany against this undeclared invasion. But Germany was not a political unity. Since 1648 each German state conducted its own foreign policy, and at this very moment, in 1681, Louis XIV had an ally in the Elector of Brandenburg (forerunner of the kings of Prussia); and the Electors of the Rhineland church-states—the archbishops of Cologne, Trier, and Mainz— were on the French payroll, receiving "subsidies" from the French king. The diet of the Holy Roman Empire was divided between an anti-French and a pro-French party. The Emperor, Leopold I, was distracted by developments in the East. The Hungarians, incited and financed by Louis XIV, were again rebelling against the Hapsburgs. They appealed to the Turks, and the Turks in 1683 moved up the Danube and actually besieged Vienna—as in 1529. Louis XIV, if he did not on this occasion positively assist the Turks, ostentatiously declined to join the proposed crusade against them.

The Emperor, with Polish assistance, succeeded in getting the Turkish host out of Austria.[21] Returning to western problems, observing the western border of the Empire constantly crumbling, Franche-Comté already lost, the Spanish Netherlands constantly threatened, Lorraine and Alsace absorbed bit by bit, and the Rhineland archbishops reduced to the status of French puppets, and not forgetting that Louis XIV had designs on the whole of Hapsburg Spain, the Emperor Leopold gathered the Catholic powers into a combination against the French. The Protestant states at the same time, aroused by Louis' revocation of the Edict of Nantes in 1685 and by Huguenot émigrés who called down the wrath of God on the perfidious Sun King, began to ally the more readily with William of Orange. Catholic and Protestant enemies of Louis XIV came together in 1686 in the League of Augsburg, which comprised the Holy Roman Emperor, the Kings of Spain and of Sweden, the Electors of Bavaria, Saxony, and the Palatinate, and the Dutch Republic. In 1686 the King of England was still a protégé of France, but three years later, when William became king in England, that country too joined the League.

The War of the League of Augsburg broke out in 1688. The French armies won battles, but could not drive so many enemies from the field. The French navy could not overmaster the combined fleets of the Dutch and English. Louis XIV found himself badly strained (it was at this time that he first imposed direct taxes on the French nobles), and finally made peace at Ryswick in the Netherlands in 1697. The Peace of Ryswick, terminating the long "War of the League of Augsburg," left matters about where they had been when the war began.

In all the warring and negotiating, in the plans of the Augsburg allies and in the maneuvers of Louis XIV, the question had not been merely the fate of this or that piece of territory, nor even the French thrust to the east, but the eventual disposition of the whole empire of Spain. The Spanish king, Charles II, prematurely senile, momentarily expected to die, yet lived on

[21] See pp. 189–90.

year after year. He was still alive at the time of the Peace of Ryswick. The greatest diplomatic issue of the day was still unsettled.

THE WAR OF THE SPANISH SUCCESSION

The War of the Spanish Succession lasted eleven years, from 1702 to 1713. It was less destructive than the Thirty Years' War, for armies were now supplied in more orderly fashion, subject to more orderly discipline and command, and could be stopped from fighting at the will of their governments. Except for the effects of civil war in Spain and of starvation in France, the civilian populations were generally spared, and in this respect the war foreshadowed the typical warfare of the eighteenth century, fought by professional armies rather than by whole peoples. Among wars of the largest scale, the War of the Spanish Succession was the first in which religion counted for little, the first in which commerce and sea power were the principal stakes, the first in which English money was liberally used in Continental politics, and the first that can be called a "world war" in involving the overseas world together with the leading powers of Europe.

The struggle had long been foreseen. The two main aspirants to the Spanish inheritance were the King of France and the Holy Roman Emperor, each of whom had married a sister of the perpetually moribund Charles II, and each of whom could hope to place a younger member of his family on the throne of Spain. During the last decades of the seventeenth century the powers had made various treaties agreeing to "partition" the Spanish possessions. The idea was, by dividing the Spanish heritage between the two claimants, to preserve the balance of power in Europe.[22] But when Charles II finally died, in 1700, it was found that he had made a will, in which he stipulated that the world of Spain should be kept intact, that all Spanish territories without exception should go to the grandson of Louis XIV, and that if Louis XIV refused to accept in the name of his five-year-old grandson, the entire inheritance should pass to the son of the Hapsburg emperor in Vienna. Louis XIV decided to accept. With Bourbons reigning in Versailles and Madrid, even if the two thrones were never united, French influence would run from Belgium to the Straits of Gibraltar, and from Milan to Mexico and Manila. At Versailles the word went out: "The Pyrenees exist no longer."

Never, at least in almost two centuries, had the political balance within Europe been so threatened. Never had the other states faced such a prospect of relegation to the sidelines. William III acted at once; he gathered the stunned or hesitant diplomats into the last of his coalitions, the Grand Alliance of 1701. He died the next year, before hostilities began, and with Louis XIV at the seeming apex of his grandeur, but he had in fact launched the engine that was to crush the Sun King. The Grand Alliance included England, Holland, and the Emperor, supported by Brandenburg and eventu-

---

[22] On the idea of the balance of power see pp. 135–6.

ally by Portugal and the Italian duchy of Savoy. Louis XIV could count on Spain, which was generally loyal to the late king's will. Otherwise his only ally was Bavaria, whose rivalry with Austria made it a habitual satellite of France. The Bavarian alliance gave the French armies an advanced position toward Vienna, and maintained that internal division, balance of power, or cancellation of forces within Germany which was fundamental to the politics of the time, and of a long time to come.

The war was long, mainly because each side no sooner gained a temporary advantage than it raised its demands on the other. The English, though they sent relatively few troops to the Continent, produced in John Churchill, Duke of Marlborough, a pre-eminent military commander for the Allied forces. The Austrians were led by Prince Eugene of Savoy. The Allies won notable battles at Blenheim in Bavaria (1704), and at Ramillies (1706), Oudenarde (1708) and Malplaquet (1709) in the Spanish Netherlands. The French were routed; Louis XIV asked for peace, but would not make it because the Allied terms were so enormous. Louis fought to hold the two crowns, to conquer Belgium, to get French merchants into Spanish America, and at the worst in self-defense. After minor successes in 1710 he again insisted on controlling the crown of Spain. The Spanish fought to uphold the will of the deceased king, the unity of the Spanish possessions, and even the integrity of Spain itself—for the English moved in at Gibraltar and made a menacing treaty with Portugal, while the Austrians landed at Barcelona and invaded Catalonia, which (as in 1640) again rose in rebellion, recognizing the Austrian claimant, so that all Spain fell into civil war.

The Austrians fought to keep Spain in the Hapsburg family, to crush Bavaria, and to carry Austrian influence across the Alps into Italy. The Dutch fought as always for their security, to keep the French out of Belgium, and to close the river Scheldt. The English fought for these same reasons, and also to keep the French-supported Catholic Stuarts out of England and preserve the revolution of 1688. It was to be expected that the Stuarts, if they returned, would ruin the Bank of England and repudiate the National Debt. Both maritime powers, England and Holland, fought to keep French merchants out of Spanish America, and to advance their own commercial position in America and the Mediterranean. These being the war aims, the Whigs were the implacable war party in England, the vaguely pro-Stuart and anti-commercial Tories being quite willing to make peace at an early date. As for the minor allies, Brandenburg and Savoy, their rulers had simply entered the alliance to gain such advantages as might turn up.

THE PEACE OF UTRECHT

Peace was finally made at the treaties of Utrecht and Rastadt of 1713 and 1714. So fierce was the Whig war spirit in England that ratification of the treaty of Utrecht incidentally marked a step in English constitutional history. The Whigs thought the treaty insufficiently favorable to England.

The Tories, pledged to peace, had won the House of Commons in 1710, but the Whigs continued to control the House of Lords. Queen Anne, at the request of Tory leaders and in the interests of peace, raised twelve Tory commoners to the peerage, the number required to give a Tory majority in the

THE
ATLANTIC WORLD
AFTER THE PEACE OF UTRECHT
1713

The map shows the partitioning of the Spanish empire and the rise of the British. Spain and its American possessions went to the Bourbon Philip V; the European possessions of Spain—the Netherlands, Milan, Naples and Sicily— went to the Hapsburgs. Britain meanwhile was strengthened by the union of England and Scotland, the acquisition of Minorca, Gibraltar and the commercial privilege of the asiento from Spain, and of Newfoundland and Nova Scotia from France. (See also map, pp. 304–5.)

Lords, and hence to obtain ratification of the treaty. This established itself as a precedent; it became an unwritten article of the British constitution that when the Lords blocked the Commons on an issue of fundamental importance, enough new Lords of appropriate views would be created to make a majority in that House.[23]

The treaty of Utrecht, with its allied instruments, in fact partitioned the world of Spain. But it did not divide it between the two legal claimants only. The British remained at Gibraltar, to the great irritation of the Spaniards, and likewise annexed the island of Minorca. The Duke of Savoy was granted the former Spanish island of Sardinia in return for his contribution to the Allied cause.[24] The rest of the Spanish Mediterranean holdings— Milan, Naples, and Sicily—passed to the Austrian Hapsburgs, as did the Spanish Netherlands (or Belgium), subsequently referred to as the Austrian Netherlands—except that the tiny region of Spanish Guelderland was handed over to the Elector of Brandenburg for his pains. In Spain itself, shorn of its European possessions but retaining America, the grandson of Louis XIV was confirmed as king (Philip V of Spain), on the understanding that the French and Spanish thrones should never be inherited by the same person. The Bourbons reigned in Spain, with interruptions, from Philip V to the republican revolution of 1931. French influence was strong in the eighteenth century, for a good many French courtiers, advisers, administrators, and business men crossed the Pyrenees with Philip V. They helped somewhat to revive the Spanish monarchy by applying the methods of Louis XIV, and they passed a swelling volume of French manufactures through Seville into Spanish America.

The old objective of William III, to prevent domination by France, was realized at last. The war itself was the main cause of French loss of strength. It produced poverty, misery, and depopulation, exposed Louis XIV to severe criticism at home, and led to a revival of aristocratic and parliamentary opposition. By the peace treaties the French abandoned, for the time being, their efforts to conquer Belgium. They ceased to recognize the Stuart pretender as king of Great Britain. They surrendered to the British two of their colonies, Newfoundland and Nova Scotia (called Acadia), and recognized British sovereignty in the disputed American northwest, known as the Hudson's Bay territory. But the French were only checked, not downed. They retained the conquests of Louis XIV in Alsace and the Franche-Comté. Their influence was strong in Spain. Their deeper strength and capacity for recovery were soon evident in renewed economic expansion. Their language and civilization continued to spread throughout Europe.

The Dutch received guarantees of their security. They were granted

ᴧᴧᴧᴧᴧᴧᴧᴧᴧᴧᴧᴧᴧᴧᴧᴧᴧᴧ

[23] The precedent was invoked in 1832 and 1911, but never since 1713 have the Lords allowed themselves to be swamped by newcomers. They have yielded at the threat.

[24] By the terms of 1713 Sardinia was awarded to Austria and Sicily to Savoy, but Sardinia and Sicily were exchanged in 1720. The kingdom of the Two Sicilies (Naples and Sicily) was thereby reconstituted. Savoy came to be called "Sardinia."

the right to garrison the "Dutch Barrier," a string of forts in Belgium on the side toward France. With Belgium transferred to Austria, which was not expected to stimulate Belgian commerce, and with the closure of the river Scheldt reconfirmed at Utrecht, the Dutch could comfortably expect a minimum of competition from their southern neighbors. But the Dutch, strained by the war and outdistanced by England, never again played a primary role in European political affairs. Two other small states ascended over the diplomatic horizon, Savoy and Brandenburg. The rulers of both, for having sided with the victors, were recognized as "kings" by the treaty of Utrecht. Savoy came to be known as "Sardinia," and Brandenburg as "Prussia." More is said of Prussia in the next chapter.

The greatest winners were the British. Great Britain made its appearance as a great power. Union of England and Scotland had taken place during the war. Based at Gibraltar and Minorca, Britain was now a power in the Mediterranean. Belgium, the "pistol pointed at the heart of England," was in the innocuous hands of the Austrians. The Austrians had not especially wanted Belgium; it was too distant from Vienna and too likely to embroil them with France; they had taken it largely at the instigation of the maritime states, Britain and Holland, which saw in transfer to Austria a good solution to the problem. The British added to their American holdings at the expense of France. Far more valuable than Newfoundland or Nova Scotia, won from France, was the *asiento* extorted from Spain. The *asiento* granted the lucrative privilege (which the French had sought) of providing Spanish America with African slaves. Much of the wealth of Bristol and Liverpool in the following decades was to be built upon the slave trade. The *asiento*, by permitting one shipload of British goods to be brought each year to Porto Bello in Panama, also provided opportunities for illicit trade in nonhuman cargoes. The Spanish empire was pried open, and British merchants entered on an era of wholesale smuggling into Spanish America, competing strenuously with the French, who because of their favored position in Spain were usually able to go through more legal channels. Moreover the British, by defeating France, assured themselves of a line of Protestant kings, and of the maintenance of constitutional and Parliamentary government. The landed aristocracy and their merchant allies could now govern as they saw fit. The result was a rapid increase of wealth in England, precipitating within a few generations a veritable Industrial Revolution.

Except for the addition of England, the same powers were parties to the treaty of Utrecht in 1713 as to the Peace of Westphalia in 1648, and they now confirmed the system of international relations established by Westphalia. The powers accepted each other as members of the European system, recognized each other as sovereign states connected only by free negotiation, war, and treaty, and adjusted their differences through rather facile exchanges of territory, made in the interests of a balance of power, and without regard to the nationality or presumed wishes of the peoples affected. With Germany still in its "feudal chaos," Italy negligible, and Spain subordinated to France, the treaty of Utrecht left France and Great Britain as the two most vigorous powers of Europe, and as the two principal carriers and exporters of the type of civilization most characteristic of the modern world. In the next chapter we turn to central and eastern Europe, to see how these regions developed along lines of their own, though under strong influence from the West.

CHAPTER V

The Transformation of Eastern Europe, 1648-1740

URING the century after the Peace of Westphalia of 1648 a development of permanent importance for the modern world took place in central and eastern Europe, the appearance of three new powers—Prussia, Austria, and Russia. The three new states grew at the expense of three older political organizations that were in decay—the Holy Roman Empire, the Republic of Poland, and the empire of the Ottoman Turks.[1] By overrunning the intermediate ground of Poland in the eighteenth century the new states came to adjoin one another and to cover all Eastern Europe except the Balkans. It

---

[1] See map, p. 179.

was in this same period that Russia expanded territorially, adopted some of the civilization of the West, and became a power in the affairs of Europe.

East and West are of course relative terms. For the Russians Germany and even Poland were "western." But for Europe as a whole a real though indefinite line ran along the Elbe and the Bohemian mountains to the head of the Adriatic Sea. East of this line towns were fewer than in the West, human labor less productive, the middle classes less strong. Above all, the peasants were governed by their landlords.[2] From the sixteenth to the eighteenth century, in Eastern Europe in contrast to what happened in the West, the peasant mass increasingly lost its freedom. The commercial revolution and widening of the market, which in the West raised up a strong merchant or bourgeois class and tended to turn working people into a legally free and mobile labor force, in Eastern Europe strengthened the great landlords who produced for export, and who secured their labor force by the institutions of serfdom and "hereditary subjection." The main social unit was the agricultural estate, which the lord exploited with uncompensated compulsory labor (or *robot*) furnished by his people, who could neither migrate, marry, nor learn a trade except as he permitted, and who, until the eighteenth century, had no legal protector or court of appeal other than himself. In the East, therefore, the landlords were exceedingly powerful. They were the only significant political class. And the three new states that grew up—Prussia, Austria, Russia—were alike in being landlord states.

22. Three Aging Empires

In 1648 the whole mainland of Europe from the French border almost to Moscow was occupied by the three large and loosely built structures that have been mentioned—the Holy Roman Empire, the Republic of Poland, and the empire of the Ottoman Turks.[3] The Turkish power reached to about fifty miles from Vienna, extended over what is now Rumania, and prevailed over the Tartars on the north shore of the Black Sea. Even so, its European holdings were but a projection from the main mass in Asia and Africa. Poland

[2] See pp. 101–2.
[3] See maps, pp. 175 and 179.

Central and Eastern Europe, 1660–1795

The "three aging empires" of central and eastern Europe in the seventeenth century are shown in simplified form on p. 179. The present map, besides giving other regional details, shows the border between the eastern and western agrarian zones, running from the mouth of the Elbe river into central Germany and down to Trieste. East of this line, from the sixteenth to the eighteenth centuries, the mass of people sank into a kind of serfdom in which they rendered forced labor to their lords on large farms. West of the line the peasants owed little or no forced labor, and tilled small farms which they owned or rented. This line is one of the most important sociological boundaries in the history of modern Europe.

CENTRAL AND EASTERN EUROPE

HOLY ROMAN EMPIRE
BORDER BETWEEN AGRARIAN ZONES
CHURCH LANDS

1660

1795

250 MILES

TRM

extended roughly from a hundred miles east of Berlin to a hundred miles west of Moscow, and virtually from "sea to sea" in the old phrase of its patriots, from the Baltic around Riga almost to the Black Sea coast, which, however, was held by Tartar Khans under the overlordship of the Turkish Sultan at Constantinople. The Holy Roman Empire extended from Poland and Hungary to the North Sea.

These three empires were by no means alike. The Holy Empire bore some of the oldest traditions of Christendom. Poland too had old connections with the West. Turkey was a Moslem power, strange to Europe and contemptuous of it. Yet in some ways the three resembled each other. In all of them central authority had become weak, consisting largely of understandings between a nominal head and outlying dignitaries or potentates. All lacked efficient systems of administration and government. All were being put out of date by newer types of state of which France was the leading example. All, but especially Poland and Turkey, were made up of diverse populations, the actual distribution of ethnic or language groups being about as they are today. None of these peoples, nor any combination of them—neither the dominant Germans, Poles, and Turks, nor the submerged Lithuanians, White Russians, Ukrainians, Czechs, Slovaks, Rumanians, Croats, Magyars, Serbs, Bulgars, or Greeks—had been formed into a compact organization. The whole immense area was politically soft. It was malleable in the hands of whoever might become a little stronger than his neighbor. We must try to see in what this softness consisted, and then how newer and harder "state-forms" (as the Germans would say) were created.

THE HOLY ROMAN EMPIRE AFTER 1648

With the Holy Roman Empire the reader is already familiar.[4] It was an empire, especially after the Peace of Westphalia, with next to no army, revenues, or working organs of government. Voltaire called it neither holy, Roman nor an empire. As the seventeenth-century German jurist Pufendorf put it, it was somewhat of an abortion and a monstrosity. Created in the Middle Ages, it was Roman in that it was then believed to continue the imperial sway of the Rome of antiquity, and it was holy in being the secular counterpart to the spiritual empire of the Pope. It had been ruined by the Reformation, which left the Germans divided almost evenly between Protestant and Catholic, with each side thereafter demanding special safeguards against the other. The Empire continued, however, to be universal in principle, having no relation to nationality, and theoretically being a form of government suitable to all peoples, although it had never made good this theoretical claim, and had shown no expansionist tendency since the Middle Ages. In actuality, the Empire was very roughly coterminous with the German states and the region of the German language, except that it excluded after 1648

[4] See pp. 20, 24, 33, 64–5, 126–30.

the Dutch and Swiss, who no longer considered themselves German; and it likewise excluded those Germans who since the fourteenth century had settled along the eastern shores of the Baltic.

The Thirty Years' War subjected the Empire to almost unimaginable devastation. We have seen how a large fraction of the people perished. The war broke up commercial connections, wasted away savings and capital, and produced a pervading insecurity of property and life. The burgher class, its ambitions blocked, lost much of its old vitality. No overseas colonies could be founded, for want of strong enough government backing, as was shown when a colonial venture of Brandenburg came to nothing. There was no stock exchange in Germany until one was established at Vienna in 1771, half a century after those of London, Paris, and Amsterdam. Laws, tariffs, tolls, and coinage were more variegated than in France. Even the calendar varied. It varied, indeed, throughout Europe as a whole, since Protestant states long declined to accept the corrected calendar issued by pope Gregory XIII in 1582, but in parts of divided Germany the holidays, the date of the month, and the day of the week changed every few miles. The arts and letters, flourishing in western Europe as never before, were at a low ebb in Germany in the seventeenth century. In science the Germans during and after the Thirty Years' War did less than the English, Dutch, French, or Italians, despite the great mathematician and philosopher Leibnitz, one of the great minds of the age. Only in music, as in the work of the Bach family, did the Germans at this time excel. But music was not then much heard beyond the place of its origin. Germany for the rest of the world was a mute country, a vacuum in the higher civilization of Europe.

The low state of Germany was due mainly to old political evils. After the Thirty Years' War each state had sovereign rights. These "states" numbered some three hundred or two thousand, depending on how they were counted. The higher figure included the "knights of the Empire," found in south Germany and the Rhineland. They were persons who acknowledged no overlordship except that of the Emperor himself. The knights had tiny estates of their own, averaging not over a hundred acres apiece, consisting of a castle and a manor or two, enclosed by the territory of a larger state but not forming a part of it. These free knights had arisen in various ways; in Würtemberg, for example, the lords simply ceased to attend the diet, won exemption from the duke's jurisdiction, and retired to their own domains, leaving the surface of Würtemberg pock-marked with small units politically independent of it. It was as if, in England, the peers had lost interest in the House of Lords and had set up independently, each on his own estates. Since the Emperor, whom the knights regarded as their only superior, had in fact no authority, the knights were in effect private persons enjoying sovereign status—the last anomaly of bizarre neo-feudalism and distorted freedom.

But even without the knights there were about three hundred states capable of some independence of action—free cities, abbots without subjects, archbishops and bishops ruling with temporal power, landgraves, margraves and dukes, and one king, the King of Bohemia. The highest ranking were called Electors, who had the privilege of electing the Emperor. By the Golden Bull of 1356 there were seven Electors—three ecclesiastics, the archbishops of Cologne, Mainz, and Trier—and four laymen, the Count Palatine of the Rhine, the Duke of Saxony, the Margrave of Brandenburg, and the King of Bohemia. Bavaria was made an electorate at the Peace of Westphalia, and Hanover at the end of the century, so that finally there were nine electors. The fact that nearly half the electors were Protestants after the Reformation, whereas the Holy Empire had meaning only in a Catholic world, added to the internal confusion and general oddity of the system.

All these states were intent on preserving what were called the "Germanic liberties." They were gladly assisted by outside powers, notably but not exclusively France. The Germanic liberties meant freedom of the member states from control by Emperor or Empire. The Electors, at each election of an Emperor, required the candidate to accept certain "capitulations," in which he promised to safeguard all the privileges and immunities of the states. The Hapsburgs, though consistently elected after 1438, had none of the advantages of hereditary rulers, each having to bargain away in turn any gains made by his predecessor. The elective principle meant that imperial power could not be accumulated and transmitted from one generation to the next. It opened the doors to foreign intrigue, the Electors being willing to consider whatever candidate would promise them most. The French repeatedly supported a rival candidate to the Hapsburgs. After 1648 they had a party in the electoral college, Bavaria and Cologne being the most consistently pro-French. Cardinal Mazarin in 1658 even entertained the thought of making the young Louis XIV Holy Roman Emperor. He had to accept election of a Hapsburg, despite liberal use of French money, but the new Emperor, Leopold I, undertook not to engage the Empire in any war supporting the Spanish Hapsburgs against France. In 1742 the French obtained the elevation of their Bavarian ally to the imperial throne. The office of emperor became the political football of Germans and non-Germans working together.

Nor would the German states, after the Thirty Years' War, allow any authority to the imperial diet. The diet possessed the power to raise troops

---

Aging Empires and New Powers

The upper panel shows the "three aging empires" which occupied much of central and eastern Europe in the seventeenth century. (See pp. 174–87.) Though maintaining themselves with growing difficulty under modern conditions, the Polish Republic lasted until 1795, the Holy Roman Empire until 1806, the Ottoman Empire until 1923. Meanwhile, beginning in the seventeenth century, the political leadership in this area was assumed by three states of more modern type, organized around the institutions of monarchy, the standing army and the professional bureaucracy or civil service—the reorganized Austrian empire of the Hapsburgs, the Hohenzollern kingdom of Prussia and the Russian empire of the Romanovs. These are shown in the lower panel. All three figured prominently in the affairs of Europe for over two hundred years; all perished in the First World War, 1914–1918.

NORTH
SEA

BALTIC SEA

@Moscow

Berlin

Warsaw

REPUBLIC OF
POLAND

HOLY

ROMAN

EMPIRE

Vienna

Budapest

KINGDOM OF
HUNGARY

ADRIATIC SEA

OTTOMAN

BLACK SEA

Constantinople

1660
"THREE AGING
EMPIRES"
AND.....

EMPIRE

.....THE POWERS
THAT GREW AT
THEIR EXPENSE
1795

BALTIC SEA

Moscow

Berlin

PRUSSIA

Warsaw

RUSSIAN

EMPIRE

HOLY ROMAN
EMPIRE

Vienna

AUSTRIAN

Budapest

MONARCHY

ADRIATIC SEA

OTTOMAN

BLACK SEA

Constantinople

EMPIRE

300 MILES

TRM

and taxes for the whole Empire, but the power remained unused. On matters affecting religion, after 1648, either Protestants or Catholics could demand the *ius eundi in partes*, or "right of sitting apart." Each religious group then constituted itself as a chamber, Protestant or Catholic, and since agreement of the two was required, each possessed a veto. The deliberations of the diet became notorious for their wordiness and futility. Many sessions were spent for example, in attempts to fix for all Germany a common date of Easter, on which the whole calendar depended. In 1663 a diet met to consider measures against a new Turkish advance on the Danube. It was the last diet ever to be convoked, for it lasted "forever," *i.e.*, until the end of the Holy Empire in 1806. It became the "perpetual diet" of Regensburg, never dismissed or renewed, unresponsive to events or issues, the states simply replacing their representatives individually, generation after generation, as at an endless congress of diplomats.

The states which insisted with such obstinacy on their liberties from the Empire gave few liberties to their subjects. The free cities were closed oligarchies, as indeed were most cities in other countries, but in Germany the burgher oligarchs of the free cities were virtually sovereign also. Most of the other states, large or small, developed in the direction of absolutism. Absolutism was checked for Germany as a whole, only to reappear in miniature in hundreds of different places. Each ruler thought himself a little Louis XIV, each court a small Versailles. The rulers raised diminutive standing armies developed their corps of officials, superintended their churches, planned and regulated economic life within their restricted frontiers. The local princes in many cases gave seed to the peasants and rebuilt villages and towns after the Thirty Years' War. Operating over a small area and a small population, absolutism became more personal and paternalistic than in France, more concerned with and more easily informed of the minutest details in the lives of the people. Subjects became attached by ties of sentiment to their rulers, who almost always lived in the neighborhood and could be readily seen by passers-by. People liked the little courts, the toy armies, the gossipy politics, and the familiar officials of their tiny states. Such localism perhaps gave the Germans a taste for personal and immediate government.

The Empire, for all its faults, had the merit of holding this conglomeration of states in a lawful relation to one another. It was a kind of miniature league of nations. For a century and a half after the Peace of Westphalia infinitesimally small states existed alongside larger ones, or often totally enclosed within them, without serious fear for their security and without losing their independence. Only in power politics and in European or world affairs was the Empire a shadow. For the Germans it was a reality, a world in itself, a thing of sublime tradition and rich and colorful associations, which no one for a long time dreamed of violating or even reforming, for its existence assured a way of life which most Germans were glad to keep.

Yet there were many ambitious rulers in Germany after the Peace of Westphalia. The princes were "on the make." They had won recognition of their sovereignty in 1648. They were busily building absolutist monarchies over their subjects. They aspired also to extend their dominions and cut a greater figure in the world. There were other ways of doing this than by devouring their smaller neighbors outright. One was by marriage and inheritance. The Empire in this respect was a paradise of fortune hunters; the variety of possible marriages was enormous because of the great number of ruling families; and legal claims to inheritance could be pushed in every direction, because territories had shifted back and forth for twenty generations. Another outlet for ambition lay in the high politics of the Empire. The Wittelsbach family, which ruled in Bavaria, managed to win an electorate in the Thirty Years' War; they consistently placed members of the family as Archbishop of Cologne and in the other great Rhineland sees, and with the interest thus built up were able to sell their influence to France, which in turn backed them against the Hapsburgs. The Guelph family, ruling in Hanover, schemed for years to obtain an electorate, which they finally extorted from the Emperor in 1692; in 1714 they inherited the throne of Great Britain, preferred by the British as Protestants to their Catholic Stuart cousins. Two electors of Saxony in these years got themselves crowned king of Poland. The Hohenzollerns, electors of Brandenburg, were extremely fortunate in the seventeenth century in inheriting territories as far apart as the Rhine and the Vistula. The Hapsburgs, hereditary rulers in Austria, a mere archduchy, not even an electorate, were confirmed by the Peace of Westphalia as hereditary kings of Bohemia, where they had formerly depended on election.

The half century after the Peace of Westphalia was a highly critical period in central Europe. The situation in Germany was fluid. No one could tell which, if any, of the half-dozen chief German states would emerge in the lead. Nothing was crystallized; anything might happen. Germany and central Europe, politically chaotic, were a tempting field for dynastic ambition, political calculation, and military adventure. The politics of the Empire was a web zealously woven by half a dozen sizable states and three hundred small ones, many of them with foreign connections, and with foreigners constantly interfering in their own interest; a complex mass of family arrangements, private understandings, petty intrigue, and abstruse legal argument harking back to the Middle Ages; a strange contest in which the stakes were sometimes substantial, involving the whole European balance of power, sometimes only archaic titles and obsolete dignities; an abyss which the most expert political observers could study for a lifetime and still not altogether fathom. Two states definitely came forward after 1700, built by the skill and persistence of their rulers—Austria and Prussia. It is a curious and revealing fact that neither really had a name of its own. They were for a long time known most commonly as "houses"—the house of Austria or Hapsburg and the house of Brandenburg or Hohenzollern. Each house put together a certain combination of territories. Each would have been as willing to possess any other combination had the course of events been different. By extension of meaning, one came to be called "Austria," which for centuries had been simply an archduchy on the upper Danube, and the other "Prussia," which for centuries had meant only a certain stretch of the Baltic coast. To the development of these two states we shall shortly turn.

THE REPUBLIC OF POLAND ABOUT 1650

Running almost a thousand miles eastward from the Holy Roman Empire in the middle of the seventeenth century lay the vast tract of the Republic of Poland, called a republic because its king was elected, and because the political classes took pride in their constitutional liberties. Its vast size was one cause of its internal peculiarities. No administrative system could have kept up with the expansion of its frontiers, so that a large degree of freedom had always been left to outlying lords. In addition, the population was heterogeneous.

The Polish state was a far more recent and less substantial creation than the Holy Roman Empire. It was made up of two main parts, Poland proper in the west and the Grand Duchy of Lithuania in the east, the two having been joined by a union of their crowns.[5] Only in the extreme west, in the valley of the Vistula river, was there a mass of Polish population. East Prussia, a fief of the Polish crown, was peopled by Germans. Further east a White Russian and Ukrainian peasantry was presided over by a scattering of Polish and Lithuanian landlords. Even in Poland itself the urban population was not generally Polish, the townspeople being largely Germans and Jews. The latter spoke Yiddish, a dialect basically German, and were very numerous because a king of Poland, in the later Middle Ages, had welcomed Jewish settlers fleeing from Germany.[6] The Jews did not adopt the Polish language. They were confined to ghettoes, and were in any case obliged by their religion to live in separate communities, islands of Orthodox Jewish life in the Gentile ocean. The Germans too held aloof, resisting assimilation to their less advanced surroundings. An unsurpassable barrier thus existed between town and country. There was no national middle class. The towns were in any case not as flourishing as in the Middle Ages, the old commerce between the Black and Baltic seas having declined. The landlords, the dominant element, lived in most parts of the country as conquerors settled on an alien land, which they felt they had redeemed from occupation by the Turks and Tartars. The official and political language was Latin. Roman Catholicism was the leading religion. There was little literature in the Polish language, and the native arts remained at the level of folk productions.

Poland is interesting as the region in which the landed aristocracy won over all other groups in the country, neither allowing the consolidation of the state on absolutist lines, as happened in France, the German principalities and even Sweden and Denmark in the seventeenth century, nor yet creating an effective constitutional or parliamentary government, as was done in

~~~~~~~~~~~~~~~~~

[5] See maps, pp. 175 and 179.
[6] See p. 63, note.

England. The Polish aristocracy, or *szlachta,* made up some eight per cent of the population, a far higher proportion than the aristocracy of any country of western Europe. On this ground the old Polish kingdom has sometimes been considered, especially by modern Polish nationalists, as the possessor of an early form of democracy. The aristocracy were sticklers for their liberties, called the "Polish liberties," and resembling the German liberties in consisting largely of a fierce suspicion of central authority and in being a perpetual invitation to foreign interference. As in the Holy Roman Empire, the monarchy was elective, and the king upon election had to accept certain contractual agreements, which, like the German "capitulations," made impossible the accumulation of authority by the crown. As in the Empire, the royal elections were a cockpit of foreign influence, bribery, and intrigue. The Poles were too factious to accept one of their own number as king. They were divided into pro-French, pro-Swedish, pro-Russian, and other parties. From 1572 to the extinction of Poland over two centuries later there were only two native Polish kings who reigned for any length of time, and one of these was the discarded lover of a Russian empress. The other was the national hero John Sobieski, whose decisive action against the Turks is noted below.

As in Germany, also, the central diet was ineffective and the nuclei of political action were local. There were no organized states or governments, as in the Empire, but the aristocracy met in fifty or sixty regional diets, turbulent assemblages of warlike gentry, in which the great lords used the little ones for their own purposes. The central diet, from which the towns were excluded, was a periodic meeting of emissaries, under binding instructions, from the regional diets. It came to be recognized, as one of the liberties of the country, that the central diet could take no action to which any member objected. Any member, by stating his unalterable opposition, could oblige a diet to disband. This was the famous *liberum veto,* the free veto, and to use it to break up a diet was called "exploding" the diet. The first diet was exploded in 1652. Of fifty-five diets held from that year to 1764, forty-eight were exploded. Since parliamentary methods were thus unworkable, a right of "confederation" was recognized, by which individuals might band together and take up arms to force acceptance of their program. This procedure, often justified as the right of resistance to oppression, or on the ground of bringing a stubborn minority to reason, was itself often resorted to by minority factions, sometimes supported by foreign powers.

Government became a fiasco. The monopoly of law and force, characteristic of the modern state, failed to develop in Poland. The king of Poland had practically no army, no law courts, no officials, and no income. The nobility paid no taxes. By 1750 the revenues of the king of Poland were about one-thirteenth those of the tsar of Russia and one seventy-fifth those of the king of France. Armed force was in the hands of a dozen or so aristocratic leaders, who also conducted their own individual foreign policies, pursuing their own adventures against the Turks, or bringing in Russians, French, or Swedes to help them against other Poles. The landlords became local monarchs on their manorial estates, and the mass of the rural population fell deeper into a serfdom scarcely different from slavery, bound to compulsory labor on estates resembling plantations, with police and disciplinary powers in the hands of the lords, and with no outside legal or administrative system to set the limits of exploitation. Some Polish aristocrats, hiring architects or buying libraries from Germany and western Europe, traveling with trains of servants to Italy or France, masters of many languages and habitually associating with the great, became among the most accomplished and cosmopolitan people in Europe. A great Polish nobleman could boast of more territory and subjects, and of more international consideration, than many a sovereign princeling of Germany. But the mass of the aristocracy became an impoverished, ill-educated, and unruly body of decayed gentry, dependent on their connections with the powerful families, and indifferent to western Europe.

The huge expanse comprised under the name of Poland was, in short, in modern parlance, a power vacuum, an area of low political pressure; and as centers of higher pressure developed, notably around Berlin and Moscow, the push against the Polish frontiers became steadily stronger. It was facilitated by the centrifugal habits of the Poles themselves. The Polish nobles lacked the means, and their neighbors the will, to preserve the integrity of their sprawling empire. As early as 1660 the East Prussian fief became independent of the Polish crown. As early as 1667 the Muscovites reconquered Smolensk and Kiev. Already there was confidential talk of partitioning Poland, which, however, was deferred for a century. The history of the world would have been different had the Poland of the seventeenth century held together. There would have been no kingdom of Prussia, and no Prussian influence in Germany; nor would Russia have become the chief Slavic power, or reached so far into central Europe. Such speculations are rather futile, since it is hard to see, in the circumstances, how the great Poland of the seventeenth century could have been maintained; but they do suggest the gravity of the issues at stake, and the full significance of what actually happened.

THE OTTOMAN EMPIRE ABOUT 1650

The Ottoman state, the third of the three empires which together spread over so much of Europe, was larger than either of the others, and in the seventeenth century was more solidly organized. In 1529 the Turks had attacked Vienna and seemed about to burst into Germany.[7] To the Christian world the Turks were a mystery as well as a terror, not only ferocious and merciless fighters but fanatics of a wicked religion, sunk in polygamy and fornication (it being popularly believed that all Turks had several wives), and led by a sultan or Grand Turk whose government was known as the

---

[7] See pp. 41, 68, 72.

Sublime Porte (French for "lofty gate"), and who ruled through horse-tailed pashas, the number of horse-tails carried before a dignitary being a badge of his rank.

The Ottoman Turks were in truth among the rougher of the Moslem peoples. They had erupted from central Asia only a few centuries before, and owed most of their higher civilization to the Arabs and the Persians. They were within Islam what the Romans had been in the ancient world, a military and conquering people, who subjected but also learned from their more civilized neighbors. In addition, after conquering Constantinople, they fell heir to some traditions of the Christian Byzantine empire. Their dominions extended, about 1650, from the Hungarian plain and the south Russian steppes as far as Algeria, the upper Nile and the Persian Gulf. The empire was based to a large degree on military proficiency. Long before Europe the Turks had a standing army, of which the main striking force was the janissaries. The janissaries were originally recruited from Christian children taken from their families in early childhood, brought up as Moslems, reared in military surroundings, and forbidden to marry; without background or ties, interests, or ambition outside the military organization to which they belonged, they were an ideal fighting material in the hands of political leaders. The Turkish forces were long as well equipped as the Christian, being especially strong in heavy artillery. But by the mid-seventeenth century they were falling behind. They had changed little, or for the worse, since the days of Suleiman the Magnificent a century before, whereas in the better organized Christian states discipline and military administration had been improved, and firearms, land-mines, and siegecraft had become more effective.

The comparison of the Turkish empire to the Roman, more or less valid in the matter of army organization and conquest, is in some other ways entirely fallacious. The Turks, unlike the Romans, had no special aptitude for law, and no conception of a universal or natural law applying to all peoples and persons. And they cared little about assimilating subject peoples to their language or institutions. Law was religious law derived from the Koran. Law-courts and judges were hard to distinguish from religious authorities, for there was no separation between religious and secular spheres. The Sultan was also the caliph, the commander of the faithful, and while on the one hand there was no clergy in the European sense, on the other hand religious influences affected all aspects of life. The Turks, for the most part, applied the Moslem law only to Moslems. Non-Moslems, mostly Christians, remained outside this law, having no rights against true believers, disdainfully regarded as "cattle," bearing the burden of the taxes and subject to various forms of extortion.

The Ottoman government left its non-Moslem subjects to settle their own affairs in their own way, not according to nationality, which was generally indistinguishable, but according to religious groupings. The Greek Orthodox Church, to which most Christians in the empire belonged, thus became an almost autonomous intermediary between the Sultan and a large fraction of his subjects. Armenian Christians and Jews formed other separate bodies. Except in the western Balkans (Albania and Bosnia) there was no general conversion of Christians to Islam during the Turkish rule, although there were many individual cases of Christians turning Moslem to obtain the privileges of the ruling faith. North of the Danube the Christian princes of Transylvania, Wallachia and Moldavia (later combined in the modern Rumania) continued to rule over Christian subjects. They were kept in office for that purpose by the Sultan, to whom they paid tribute. In general, since their subjects were more profitable to them as Christians, the Turks were not eager to proselytize for Islam.

The Ottoman empire was therefore a relatively tolerant empire, far more so than the states of Europe. Christians in the Turkish empire fared better than Moslems would have fared in Christendom, or than the Moors had in fact fared in Spain. Christians were better off in Turkey than were Protestants in France, after 1685, or Catholics in the British Isles. The empire was tolerant because it was composite, an aggregation of peoples, religions, and laws, having no drive, as did the western states, toward internal unity and complete legal sovereignty. The same was evident in the attitude toward foreign merchants.

The king of France had had treaty arrangements with Turkey since 1535, and many traders from Marseilles had spread over the port towns of the Near East. They were exempted by treaty from the laws of the Ottoman empire and were liable to trial only by their own judges, who though residing in Turkey were appointed by the king of France. They were free to exercise their Roman Catholic religion, and if disputes with Moslems arose, they appeared in special courts where the word of an infidel received equal weight with that of a follower of the Prophet. Similar rights in Turkey were obtained by other European states. Thus began "extra-territorial" privileges of the kind obtained by Europeans in later centuries in China and elsewhere. wherever the local laws were regarded as backward. To the Turks of the seventeenth century there was nothing exceptional about such arrangements, and nothing insulting to the dignity of the Sublime Porte. Only much later, under western influence, did the Turks learn to resent these "capitulations" as impairments of their own sovereignty.

Yet the Turkish rule was oppressive, and the "terrible Turk" was with reason the nightmare of Eastern Europe. Ottoman rule was oppressive to Christians if only because it relegated them to a despised position, and because everything they held holy was viewed by the Turks with violent contempt. But it was oppressive also in that it was arbitrary, and brutal even by the none too sensitive standards of Europeans. It was worse in these respects in the seventeenth century than formerly, for the central authority of the sultans had become corrupt, and the outlying governors, or pashas, had a virtually free hand with their subjects. The sultans, once virile leaders of armies, now lived in seclusion and self-indulgence in their harems, surrounded by jealous women and eunuchs, fearful of being deceived by their grand viziers, whom therefore they made and unmade, appointed and executed with disconcerting vacillation. They were fearful even of the stability of their own thrones—one Sultan about the year 1600 put to death his nineteen brothers to secure himself against rivals. The pashas, never knowing how long they might remain in their governorships, made haste to get rich by the quickest means. From the grand viziers, dependent for life itself on the whims of a morally undisciplined sultan, down through all levels and grades of office the functionaries were exposed to the caprice of those above them, and protected themselves by erratic demands on those below. The powers of office were too often used to intimidate people and then make them pay for protection. Persons of influence had to receive money before they would use it. The whole regime became riddled with what American slang knows as the shake-down. The burden was ultimately borne by those at the bottom, the Christian peasants of Bulgaria or the Moslem peasants of Egypt.

Those parts of the Ottoman empire which adjoined the Christian states were among the least firmly attached to Constantinople. The Tartar Khans of south Russia, like the Christian princes of the Danubian principalities, were simply protégés who paid tribute. Hungary was occupied, but was more a battlefield than a province. These regions were disputed by Germans, Poles, and Russians. It seemed in the middle of the seventeenth century as if the grip of the Turks might be relaxing. But a dynasty of unusually capable grand viziers, the Kiuprilis, came to power, and retained it contrary to Turkish customs for fifty years. Under them the empire again put forth a mighty effort. By 1663 the janissaries were again mobilizing in Hungary. Tartar horsemen were on the move. Central Europe again felt the old terror. The pope feared that the dreaded enemy might break into Italy. Throughout Germany by the Emperor's order special "Turk bells" sounded the alarm. The states of the Empire assembled in 1663 as a diet at Regensburg. They voted to raise a small imperial army. The Holy Empire, even in its senility, bestirred itself temporarily against the historic enemy of the Christians. But it was not the Empire, but the House of Austria, under whose auspices the Turks were to be repelled.

23. The Formation of an Austrian Monarchy

Having now surveyed the three very different empires whose occupancy of most of Europe from France to Muscovy kept the whole area politically malleable and soft, we turn to the three new states which consolidated themselves in this region, namely Austria, Prussia, and Russia.

THE RECOVERY AND GROWTH OF HAPSBURG

POWER, 1648–1740

The Austria which appeared by 1700 was in truth a new creation, though not as obviously so as the two others. The Austrian Hapsburgs had long enjoyed an eminent role. Formerly their position had rested on their headship of the Holy Roman Empire, and on their family connection with the more wealthy Hapsburgs of Spain. In the seventeenth century these two supports collapsed. The hope for an effective Hapsburg empire in Germany disappeared in the Thirty Years' War. The connection with Spain lost its value as Spain declined, and vanished when in 1700 Spain passed to the

GROWTH OF **AUSTRIAN MONARCHY,** 1521–1772

The map shows the main body of the Austrian monarchy as it came to be in the eighteenth century, and continued until the collapse of the empire in 1918. There were three main parts: (1) a nucleus, composed of Austria and adjoining duchies, often called the Hereditary Provinces; (2) the lands of the Bohemian crown, which became Hapsburg in 1526, and where the Hapsburgs reasserted their power during the Bohemian phase of the Thirty Years' War; and (3) the lands of the Hungarian crown, where at first the Hapsburgs held only the segment called Imperial Hungary, the rest remaining Turkish until reconquered by the Hapsburgs in 1699. In the First Partition of Poland the Hapsburgs annexed Galicia. Silesia was lost to Prussia in 1740. Outlying parts of the empire in the eighteenth century, not shown on the map, were most of what is now Belgium (then the Austrian Netherlands) and the duchy of Milan in Italy. The Italian duchy of Tuscany, where the Medici family died out in 1737, was ruled as a separate state by a Hapsburg archduke.

House of France. The Austrian family in the latter half of the seventeenth century stood at the great turning point of its fortunes. It successfully made a difficult transition, emerging from the husk of the Holy Empire and building an empire of its own. At the same time the Hapsburgs continued to be Holy Roman Emperors and remained active in German affairs, using resources drawn from outside Germany to maintain their influence over the German princes. The relation of Austria to the rest of Germany became a political conundrum, forcibly solved by Bismarck in 1866 by the exclusion of Austria, only to be raised again by Adolf Hitler in the twentieth century.

The dominions considered by the House of Austria to be its own direct possessions were in three parts. The oldest were the "hereditary provinces"— Upper and Lower Austria, with the adjoining Tyrol, Styria, Carinthia, and Carniola. Secondly, there was the kingdom of Bohemia—Bohemia, Moravia, and Silesia joined under the Crown of St. Wenceslas. Thirdly, there was the kingdom of Hungary—Hungary, Transylvania, and Croatia joined under the Crown of St. Stephen. Nothing held all these regions together except the fact that the Austrian Hapsburg dynasty, in the seventeenth century, reaffirmed its grip upon them all. The Thirty Years' War, a calamity to the Austrian Hapsburgs from their older point of view, in that they failed to re-Catholicize Germany or to maintain the authority of the Holy Empire, was from the newer point of view, that of a new Hapsburg monarchy in process of formation, a notable success. During the war the dynasty rooted Protestantism and feudal rebelliousness out of Austria and the hereditary provinces. It reconquered and re-Catholicized Bohemia, with whose rebellion the Thirty Years' War had begun. And in the following decades it conquered Hungary also.

Since 1526 most of Hungary had been occupied by the Turks. For generations the Hungarian plain was a theater of intermittent warfare between the armies of Vienna and Constantinople. The struggle flared up again in 1663, when the Kiuprili vizier started Turkish armies moving up the Danube. A mixed force assembled from the Empire and from all Christendom, forcing the Turks in 1664 to accept a twenty-year truce. But Louis XIV, who in these years was busily dismembering the western frontier of the Empire, stood to profit greatly from a diversion on the Danube; he incited the Turks (old allies of France through common hostility to the Hapsburgs) to resume their assaults, which they did as the twenty-year truce came to a close.

In 1683 a vast Turkish host, including some Hungarian and Rumanian Christians, reached the city of Vienna and besieged it. The Turks again, as in 1529, peered into the very inner chambers of Europe. The garrison and people of Vienna, greatly outnumbered, held off the besiegers for two months, enough time for another international force to reach the spot. The decisive weight was brought by the king of Poland, John Sobieski, who, resisting the pressure of French agents in Poland, personally led a large army to relieve the city. It was the last great military effort of the dying Republic of Poland, and it saved Europe from the incalculable consequences of a Turkish foothold in Germany. The Turks withdrew, and a general counter-offensive against them developed, in which forces of the pope, Poland, Russia and the Republic of Venice joined with the Hapsburgs. It was in this war, in fighting between Turks and Venetians, that the Parthenon at Athens, which had survived for two thousand years but was now used as an ammunition dump by the Turks, was blown into ruins.

The Hapsburgs, whose luck was proverbial, fighting now on two fronts against Turks and French, had the good fortune to obtain the services of a man of remarkable talent, Prince Eugene of Savoy. Eugene, like many other servants of the Austrian house, was not Austrian at all; he was in fact French by origin and education, but like many of the aristocratic class of the time was an international personage. More than anyone else he was the founder of the modern Austrian state. Distinguished both as a military administrator and as a commander in the field, he reformed the supply, equipment, training, and command of the Hapsburg forces, along lines laid out by Louis XIV, and in 1697 he won the battle of Zenta, driving the Turks out of Hungary. The English and Dutch offered mediation, since their commerce in the Mediterranean was disturbed by the war, and since they desired Austria to concentrate against France. At the Peace of Karlowitz (1699) the Turks yielded most of Hungary, together with Transylvania and Croatia, to the Hapsburg house.

The Hapsburgs were now free to pursue their designs in the west. They entered the War of the Spanish Succession to win the Spanish crown, but although an Austrian archduke campaigned in Spain for years, assisted by the English, they had to content themselves at the treaty of Rastadt in 1714 with the old Spanish Netherlands, and with Milan and Naples. Prince Eugene, freed now in the west, again turned eastward. Never before or afterwards were the Austrians so brilliantly successful. Eugene captured Belgrade and pushed through the Iron Gate into Wallachia. For a generation the Austrians held what are now western Rumania and central Yugoslavia. Eugene's dream of reaching the Black Sea and Aegean seemed on the point of realization. But Austria was preoccupied elsewhere, nor were the Turks yet helpless; and by the Peace of Belgrade (1739) a frontier was drawn which on the Austrian side remained unchanged until the twentieth century. The Turks continued to hold Rumania and the whole Balkan peninsula except Catholic Croatia, which, incorporated in the Hapsburg empire, was again faced toward Europe. The Hapsburg government, to open a window on the Mediterranean, developed a seaport at Trieste.

THE AUSTRIAN MONARCHY BY 1740

Thus the House of Austria, in two or three generations after its humiliation at the Peace of Westphalia, acquired a new empire of very considerable proportions. Though installed in Belgium and Italy, it was essentially an empire of the middle Danube, with its headquarters at Vienna in Austria proper, but possessing the sizable kingdoms of Hungary and Bohemia, and so filling the basin enclosed by the Alpine, Bohemian, and Carpathian mountain systems. Though German influence was strong, the empire was international or non-national. At the Hapsburg court, and in the Hapsburg government and army, the names of Czech, Hungarian, Croatian, and Italian noblemen were very common. It is hard today to see this empire as it was, because it is hard to see it except through the eyes of its enemies. It made enemies of all Protestants. Democrats came to hate it. When the nationalistic movement swept over Europe in the nineteenth century, the empire was denounced as tyrannical by Hungarians, Croats, Serbs, Rumanians, Czechs, Poles, Italians, and even some Germans, whose national ambitions were blocked by its existence. Today, disillusioned by nationalism in central and eastern Europe, some tend to romanticize unduly the old Danubian monarchy, noting that it had at least the merit of holding many discordant peoples together.

The empire was from the first international, based on a cosmopolitan aristocracy of landowners who felt closer to each other, despite difference of language, than to the laboring masses who worked on their estates. Not for many years, until after 1848, did the Hapsburg government really touch these rural masses; it dealt with the landed class and with the relatively few cities, and left the landlords to control the peasants. The old diets remained in being in Bohemia, Hungary, and the Austrian provinces. No diet was created for the empire as a whole. The diets were essentially assemblages of landlords; and though they no longer enjoyed their medieval freedom, they retained certain powers over taxation and administration, and a sense of constitutional liberty against the crown, like the Provincial Estates in France. So long as they produced taxes and soldiers as needed, and accepted the wars and foreign policy of the ruling house, no questions were asked at Vienna. The peasants remained in, or reverted to, serfdom. The law allowed the lord to exact three days a week of *robot* from his peasants.[8] In France, by way of contrast, where the monarchy checked the feudal interest, the royal courts generally limited such peasant service for the lord to twelve days a year.

The Hapsburgs were determined to make their new empire unmistakably hereditary and Catholic. It is understandable that the Austrian house, together with its officials, should have acquired a strong distaste for both Protestantism and elective monarchy. These were the two biggest rocks on which Hapsburg ambitions in the Holy Roman Empire had been sunk. In addition the Hapsburgs of Austria, like those of Spain, were usually somewhat stodgily pious, and often under the influence of Jesuits, who saw in every realm only a province of the Universal Faith.

The first to feel the blow had been Bohemia. The Czech rebellion had been crushed, as we have seen, at the battle of the White Mountain in 1620.[9] This ended, until 1918, the national independence of a people who

wwwwwwwwwwwwww

[8] See pp. 101–2.
[9] See pp. 123–4.

had greatly prospered in the Middle Ages. The reigning Hapsburg, Ferdinand II, abrogated the elective Bohemian monarchy and declared the kingdom hereditary. He poured Catholic missionaries into the country. He confiscated the estates of the rebel nobles, and granted them to a host of adventurers of many nationalities, mostly colonels and generals of the Thirty Years' War, who were ignorant of the language or customs of the people, and who owed their position entirely to the Hapsburgs. Yet even under these circumstances he could not rule unconditionally. In 1627 he issued a new charter or constitution to Bohemia, or rather to the pro-Hapsburg aristocracy whom he installed there. By this charter the new landlords received considerable liberties, the right to meet in a diet, raise taxes, supervise administration, and conduct the affairs of Bohemia in their own way. Bohemia remained an entirely separate kingdom. Its new aristocracy, while remaining apart from the native peasantry and the towns, soon developed, as the ruling element of the country, a sense of Bohemian autonomy and a desire to be let alone by the central government at Vienna.

Somewhat the same happened in Hungary after its reconquest from the Turks in 1699. Protestantism was widespread in Hungary, where it formed part of the famous Hungarian liberties. Every Hungarian magnate, like princes of the Holy Roman Empire, possessed the *ius reformandi*, or right to reform religion on his own estates. There was thus religious disorder, and religion and politics were mixed. The Turks, during their occupation, favored the Protestants, knowing that Protestants would have no longing for a Catholic Hapsburg king. In Hungary, therefore, as in Bohemia, the first step following the reconquest was to repress Protestantism, which was not only detested as heretical but feared as pro-Turkish. The elective monarchy was done away with; the Crown of St. Stephen [10] became the hereditary possession of the Hapsburgs. The Hungarian nobles lost their constitutional right of armed rebellion. German veterans were settled in the country, the Croats given privileges, and even Serbs imported from across the Danube, all to weaken the grip of the Magyar aristocracy; the effect was to scramble the nationalities in an already heterogeneous region. Hardly had Eugene's armies entered Turkish Hungary when a rebellion against the Hapsburgs broke out in 1703, led by Prince Francis Rakoczy, whose name is known to the world through the traditional march bearing his name, and which originated at this time as a patriotic song of the rebels. Rakoczy received help from Louis XIV, but was finally crushed by 1711, and spent the rest of his life in France and Turkey. The Hungarians, proud and stubborn, became nationalistic before the era of nationalism. And for all that the Hapsburgs could do, Hungary remained a distinct kingdom, and the magnates of Hungary remained the freest-handed aristocracy in Europe, except for the Poles.

Thus, despite the efforts of the Hapsburgs, the Austrian monarchy remained a collection of territories held together by a personal union. Inhabitants of Austria proper considered their ruler as archduke, Bohemians

wwwwwwwwwwwww

[10] See p. 21.

saw in him the king of Bohemia, Magyars the Apostolic king of Hungary. Each country retained its own law, diet, and political life. No feeling in the people held these regions together, and even the several aristocracies were joined only by common service to the House. For the empire to exist, all crowns had to be inherited by the same person.

After the reconquest of Hungary the king-archduke, Charles VI (1711–40) devised a form of insurance to guarantee such an undivided succession. This took the form of a document called the Pragmatic Sanction, first issued in 1713. By it every diet in the empire, and the various archdukes of the Hapsburg family, were to agree to regard the Hapsburg territories as indivisible, and to recognize only one specified line of heirs. The matter became urgent when it developed that Charles would have no children except a daughter, Maria Theresa, and that the direct male line of the Austrian Hapsburgs, as of the Spanish a few years before, was about to become extinct. Charles VI gradually won acceptance of the Pragmatic Sanction by all parts of his empire and all members of his family. He then set about having foreign powers guarantee it, knowing that Bavaria, Prussia, or others might well put in claims for this or that part of the inheritance. This process took years, and was accomplished at the cost of many damaging concessions. Charles VI had attempted, for example, to revive Belgium commercially by founding an overseas trading company at Ostend. The British government, before agreeing to guarantee the Pragmatic Sanction, demanded and obtained the abandonment of this commercial project. Finally all powers signed. Charles VI died in 1740, having done all that could be done, by domestic law and international treaty, to assure the continuation of the Austrian empire.

He was scarcely dead when armed "heirs" presented themselves. A great war broke out to partition the Austrian empire, as the Spanish empire had been partitioned shortly before. Bohemia threw off its allegiance. Hungary almost did the same. But these events belong later in the story.[11] At the moment it is enough to know that by 1740 a populous empire, of great military strength, had been founded on the Danube.

24. The Formation of Prussia

Nothing is more characteristic of the seventeenth century than the way in which very small states were able to play an influential part in European affairs, seemingly out of all proportion to their size. That small population was no barrier to the attainment of a high level of wealth, comfort, and intellectual and artistic activity is perhaps not surprising. Of such high civilization among a small people the Dutch were the conspicuous example. It is more surprising that small population, and even relative economic back-

ᴧᴧᴧᴧᴧᴧᴧᴧᴧᴧᴧᴧᴧᴧᴧ

[11] See pp. 245–58.

wardness, presented no insuperable barrier to military and political strength.

The main reason why small states could act as great powers was that armies were small and weapons simple. Difficulties of supply and communications, the poor state of the roads, the lack of maps, the absence of general staffs, together with many other administrative and technical difficulties, held down the number of soldiers who could be successfully managed in a campaign. The battles of the Thirty Years' War, on the average, were fought by armies of less than 20,000 men. And while Louis XIV, by the last years of his reign, built up a military establishment aggregating some 400,000, the actual field armies in the wars of Louis XIV did not exceed, on the average, 40,000. Armies of this size were well within the reach of smaller powers. If especially well trained, disciplined, and equipped, and if ably commanded and economically employed, the armies of small powers could defeat those of much larger neighbors. On this fact, fundamentally, the German state of Prussia was to be built. But Prussia was not the first to exploit the opportunity with spectacular consequences. The first, it may be said, was Sweden.

SWEDEN'S SHORT-LIVED EMPIRE

Sweden almost, but not quite, formed an empire out of the malleable matter of central and eastern Europe in the seventeenth century. The population of Sweden at the time was not over a million; it was smaller than that of the Dutch Republic. But the Swedes produced a line of extraordinary rulers, ranging from genius in Gustavus Adolphus (1611–32) to the verge of madness in Charles XII (1697–1718). The elective Swedish kingship was made definitely hereditary, the royal power freed from control by the estates, craftsmen and experts brought from the west, notably Holland, war industries subsidized by the government, and an army created with many novel features in weapons, organization, and tactics.

With this army Gustavus Adolphus crossed the Baltic in the Thirty Years' War, made alliances with Protestant German princes, cut through the yielding mass of the Holy Roman Empire, and helped to ward off unification of Germany by the Hapsburgs.[12] The Swedish crown, by the Peace of Westphalia, received certain coastal regions of Germany—western Pomerania including the city of Stettin, and the former bishoprics of Bremen and Verden on the North Sea. Subsequently, in a confused series of wars, in which a Polish king claimed to be king of Sweden, and a Swedish king claimed to be king of Poland, the Swedes won control of virtually all the shores and cities of the Baltic. Only Denmark at the mouth of that sea and the territories of the House of Brandenburg, which had almost no ports, remained independent. For a time the Baltic was a Swedish lake. The Russians were shut off

〰〰〰〰〰〰〰〰〰〰〰

[12] See pp. 124–30.

from it, and the Poles and even the Germans, who lived on its shores, could reach it only on Swedish terms.

The final Swedish effort was made by the meteoric Charles XII, a young man crazed by military ambition, who led an army for years back and forth across the plains of Poland and Russia, only to be ruined in the end by the Russians, and spend more long years as a guest and protégé of the Turks.[13] With the death of Charles XII in 1718 the Swedish sphere contracted to Sweden itself, except that Finland and reduced holdings in northern Germany remained Swedish for a century more. The Swedes in time proved themselves exceptional among European peoples in not harping on their former greatness. They successfully and peaceably made the transition from the role of a great power to that of a small one.

THE TERRITORIAL GROWTH OF BRANDENBURG-PRUSSIA

In the long run it was to be Prussia that dominated this part of Europe, and through its later influence on Germany was to play a momentous part in the modern world. The south coast of the Baltic, where Prussia was to arise, was an unpromising site for the creation of a strong political power. It was an uninviting country, thinly populated, with poor soil and without mineral resources, more backward than Saxony or Bohemia, not to mention the busy centers of south Germany and western Europe. It was a flat open plain, merging imperceptibly into Poland, without prominent physical features or natural frontiers.[14] The coastal region directly south from Sweden was known as Pomerania. Inland from it, shut off from the sea, was the electoral margraviate of Brandenburg, centering about Berlin. In 1417 the Hohenzollern family had come to rule Brandenburg, which was to be the nucleus of modern Prussia. Brandenburg had been founded in the Middle Ages as a "mark" or "march" of the Holy Roman Empire, to fight the battles of the Holy Empire against the then heathen Slavs. All Germany east of the Elbe represented a medieval conquest by the German-speaking peoples—the German *Drang nach Osten,* or drive to the East. From the Elbe to Poland, German conquerors and settlers had replaced the primitive Slavs, eliminating them or absorbing them by intermarriage.

Extending eastward from Brandenburg and Pomerania, and outside the Holy Roman Empire, stretched the region then known as Prussia, named after an aboriginal people called Prussians or Borussians, who had been related to the Lithuanians, but who had disappeared under the impact of Germans and Poles. Western Prussia was part of Poland; this region separated Brandenburg and Pomerania from East Prussia. East Prussia, or the duchy of Prussia, was the historic land of the Teutonic Knights, a military crusading order which had conquered and Christianized the native peoples in the thirteenth century.[15] The duchy of Prussia, except for its seacoast on

[13] See pp. 212–14.
[14] See maps, pp. 6–7 and 175.
[15] See p. 41.

the Baltic, was totally enclosed by the Polish kingdom. The language and culture of ducal Prussia were German. To the north of Prussia, on the Baltic, as far as the Gulf of Finland, German minorities lived among undeveloped Lithuanians, Letts, and Estonians. The towns were German, founded as German commercial colonies in the Middle Ages, and many of the landlords were German also, descendants of the Teutonic Knights, and later known as the "Baltic barons." These Germans at that time, since nationalist sentiment scarcely existed, felt no affiliation with the main block of Germans farther west, but they retained their German language and traditions.

Modern Prussia appeared in the seventeenth century when a number of territories came together in the hands of the Hohenzollerns of Brandenburg, who, we have noted, had ruled in Brandenburg since 1417. In 1618 the Elector of Brandenburg inherited the duchy of Prussia (East Prussia). Prussia had belonged to the Teutonic Knights until the Protestant Reformation, at which time it so happened that the grand master of the Teutonic Order was a member of the Hohenzollern family, who turned Protestant and "secularized" the lands of the Order, making himself hereditary duke under Polish overlordship.[16] The ducal family died out after a few generations, leaving the duchy in 1618 to the elder or Brandenburg branch of the Hohenzollerns. This was the first significant step in the territorial growth of Brandenburg-Prussia. Another important development occurred when the old ruling line expired in Pomerania during the Thirty Years' War. Although the Swedes succeeded in taking the better part of Pomerania, including the city of Stettin, the Elector of Brandenburg received at the Peace of Westphalia eastern or Farther Pomerania. Barren, rural, and harborless though it was, it at least had the advantage of connecting Brandenburg with the Baltic. The Hohenzollerns no sooner obtained it than they began to dream of joining it to the duchy of Prussia, a task which required the absorption of western Prussia which was in Polish hands, and which was not to be accomplished until 1772.

Had East Prussia and Farther Pomerania been the only acquisitions of the Hohenzollerns, their state would have been oriented almost exclusively toward eastern Europe. But at the Peace of Westphalia they received, in addition to Farther Pomerania, the large bishopric of Halberstadt and the still larger archbishopric of Magdeburg, which lay on the west bank of the Elbe. Moreover, through the play of inheritance so common in the Holy Roman Empire, the Hohenzollerns had earlier fallen heir, in 1614, to the small state of Cleves on the Rhine at the Dutch border and a few other small territories also in western Germany. These were separated from the main mass around Brandenburg by many intermediate German principalities. But they gave the Hohenzollerns a direct contact with the more advanced regions of western Europe, and a base from which larger holdings in the Rhineland were eventually to be built up.

In the seventeenth century, meanwhile, the dominions of the House of

wwwwwwwwwwwww

[16] See p. 72.

Brandenburg were in three disconnected masses. The main mass was Brandenburg, with the adjoining Pomerania and Elbe bishoprics. There was a detached eastern mass in ducal Prussia, and a small detached western mass on and near the Rhine. The middle and western masses were within the Holy Roman Empire. The eastern mass was outside the Empire, and until 1660, a fief of Poland. To connect and unify the three masses became the underlying long-range policy of the Brandenburg house.

THE MAKING OF THE PRUSSIAN STATE

In the midst of the Thirty Years' War, in 1640, a young man of twenty, named Frederick William, succeeded to these diverse possessions. Known later as the Great Elector, he was the first of the men who made modern Prussia. He had grown up under trying conditions. Brandenburg was one of the parts of Germany to suffer most heavily from the war. Its location made it the stamping ground of Swedish and Hapsburg armies. In 1640, in the twenty-two years since the beginning of the war, the population of Berlin had fallen from about 14,000 to about 6,000, that of Frankfurt-on-the-Oder perhaps from 12,000 to 2,000. Hundreds of villages had been wiped out. Wolves roamed over the countryside.

Frederick William concluded that in his position, ruling a small and open territory, without natural frontiers or possibility of defense in depth, surrounded by hard-pressing and much more powerful neighbors, he must put his main reliance in a competent army. With an effective army, even if small, he could oblige the stronger states to take him into their calculations, and so could enter with some hope of advantage into the politics of the balance of power. This long remained the program of the Brandenburgers—to have an army but not to use it, to conserve it with loving and even miserly care, to keep an "army in being," and to gain their ends by diplomatic maneuver. Frederick William liquidated the mercenary adventurers employed by his predecessor. By the end of the Thirty Years' War he had a small army of 8,000 men under his own control. He was able thus to get a

---

Growth of Prussia, 1417–1918 (map on following pages)

The maps on the two following pages give a conspectus of Prussian history from the time when Brandenburg began to expand in the seventeenth century. One may see, by looking at all the panels together, how Prussia was really an East European state until 1815; its center of gravity shifted westward, in significant degree, only in the nineteenth century. Panel 2 shows the early formation of three unconnected masses; Panel 3, the huge bulk of Silesia relative to the small kingdom that annexed it (p. 248); Panel 4, the fruits of the Partitions of Poland (p. 220). Napoleon pared Prussia down (p. 383). The main crisis at the Congress of Vienna, and its resolution, are shown in Panels 6 and 7 (pp. 417–18). Bismarck's enlargement of Prussia appears in Panel 8 (pp. 522–4). The boundaries established by Bismarck remained unchanged until the fall of the Prussian monarchy in 1918.

GROWTH
OF
PRUSSIA
1417-1918

100 MILES

① THE NUCLEUS
1417-1614

BRANDENBURG
1417

ACQUISITIONS
1462-1614

Berlin

KROSSEN
1482

1462

BEUTHEN
1603, 07

NIEMEN R.

ELBE R.

ODER R.

VISTULA R.

② AT THE DEATH OF
THE GREAT ELECTOR
BY 1688

BRANDENBURG
1614

BRANDENBURG-
PRUSSIA
1618

EAST
PRUSSIA
1618

FARTHER
POMERANIA
1648

RAVENSBURG
1614

CLEVES
1614

MARK
1614

MAGDEBURG
1648

Berlin

NIEMEN R.

ELBE R.

RHINE R.

ODER R.

VISTULA R.

③ THE CONQUEST OF
SILESIA
BY 1748

PRUSSIA
1688

ACQUISITIONS
1715-1748

EAST
FRIESLAND
1744

GUELDERS
1715

Berlin

SILESIA
FROM AUSTRIA
1740

NIEMEN R.

ELBE R.

RHINE R.

ODER R.

VISTULA R.

④ POLISH
ACQUISITIONS
1772-1807

PRUSSIA
1748

ACQUISITIONS
1748-1772

TEMPORARY
ACQUISITIONS
1793-1795,
TO 1807

WEST
PRUSSIA
1772

DANZIG
1793

NEW
EAST
PRUSSIA
1795

MANSFELD
1780

Berlin

SOUTH
PRUSSIA
1793

NIEMEN R.

ELBE R.

RHINE R.

ODER R.

VISTULA R.

TRM

5 CUT DOWN BY NAPOLEON 1807-1814

TERRITORY LOST IN 1807
PRUSSIA 1807-1814

NIEMEN R.
ELBE R.
Berlin
VISTULA R.
RHINE R.
ODER R.
LOST TO GRAND DUCHY OF WARSAW AND TO RUSSIA 1807
LOST TO RHINE CONFEDERATION STATES AND TO FRANCE 1807

6 RUSSO-PRUSSIAN PROPOSALS 1814

PRUSSIA 1814
PROPOSED TERRITORIAL CHANGES 1814

ELBE R.
Berlin
VISTULA R.
RHINE R.
SAXONY (TO PRUSSIA)
POLAND (TO RUSSIA)
ODER R.

7 AGREED AT CONGRESS OF VIENNA 1815

PRUSSIA 1814
RECOVERED OR ACQUIRED 1815

NIEMEN R.
SWEDISH POMERANIA
ELBE R.
Berlin
POSEN
VISTULA R.
RHINE R.
PART OF SAXONY
RHINELAND
ODER R.

8 BISMARCK'S CONQUESTS 1866

PRUSSIA 1863
ACQUISITIONS 1866

SCHLESWIG
HOLSTEIN
NIEMEN R.
HANOVER
ELBE R.
Berlin
VISTULA R.
RHINE R.
HESSE
ODER R.

PRUSSIA 1866-1918
GERMAN EMPIRE 1871-1918

TRM

hearing at the Peace of Westphalia, and to prevent the Swedes from annexing all Pomerania. But even with all its accessions of territory, since north Germany was thinly populated and had been ravaged by war, the Brandenburgers at the death of the Great Elector (in 1688) had fewer than 1,500,000 subjects —less than the Dutch, and not a twelfth as many as the king of France. Brandenburg-Prussia was still a small power, one of half a dozen rising creations in Germany.

The foreign policy of the Great Elector and his successors was like that of the rival German princes after the Peace of Westphalia, that is to say, tortuous in the extreme and forever in search of lucky windfalls. In the south the Brandenburgers played off France against the Hapsburgs, to the disadvantage of the Holy Roman Empire, for a pro-French phase in Brandenburg policy made it easier for Louis XIV to absorb Alsace in the 1680's.[17] In the north they played off Sweden against Poland. The Great Elector aspired to make himself sovereign in East Prussia by ridding himself of feudal dependence on Poland. First he combined with Sweden, signing a secret treaty for a partition of Poland; then, when the Poles defeated these projects, he allied with the Poles against Sweden, demanding as the price of his aid, and obtaining it, the recognition of his sovereignty over ducal Prussia in 1660.

The next step was to become not only sovereign duke of Prussia, but king. This step was successfully taken by the Great Elector's successor, Frederick I. Various German princes were trying to make themselves kings. Since except for Bohemia, which was a special case, there could be no kingdoms in the Holy Roman Empire, aspirants to royal honors had to cast their hopes outside it. By 1700 the elector of Saxony was king of Poland, the elector of Hanover was in line to be king of England, the elector of Bavaria was intriguing avidly to obtain any crown he could get, and the archduke of Austria had confirmed his position as king of both Hungary and Bohemia. The Brandenburgers were fearful of being outdistanced. In 1701 the Hapsburg Emperor was preparing to enter the War of the Spanish Succession. He wanted the support of 8,000 Brandenburg troops. The Elector named his price: recognition of himself, by the Emperor, as king in Prussia. The Emperor yielded; the title, at first explicitly limited to the less honorable king *in* Prussia, soon became king *of* Prussia. Another rent was made in the old fabric of the Holy Empire. There was now a German king above all the other German princes, for where the union between Hanover and England, or between Saxony and Poland, remained a purely personal tie, Brandenburg and Prussia became institutionally joined as a German state. East Prussia remained outside the Holy Roman Empire, but was fused with the Hohenzollern dominions within the Empire. All the scattered Hohenzollern possessions, from the Rhine to the Lithuanian border, came to be known as the kingdom of Prussia.

wwwwwwwwwwwwww

[17] See pp. 165–6.

THE KINGDOM OF PRUSSIA: THE ROLE OF THE ARMY

The new kingdom of Prussia was still the most insignificant kingdom in Europe, with the exception of Savoy in Italy, a state much like Prussia in its ambitions and methods, and whose duke was recognized as king at about the same time. Weak and small, Prussia was created by policy. It let others do its fighting; its efficient new army was seldom risked. In 1720, for example, the king of Prussia won Stettin and part of western Pomerania from the Swedes. But it was Peter the Great of Russia and a Russian force that carried on most of the military operations. The Prussian king gained this service from the tsar by diplomatic jockeying, in which he used Prussian troops very sparingly. Until late in its history Prussia was militaristic but not warlike. It was ambitious, but not belligerent. It was far more reluctant to be involved in actual fighting than were its wealthier and stronger neighbors. It was less bellicose than Austria, France, or Great Britain. Yet it was more militaristic than any of these states, for its very essence was its army.

The preoccupation of Prussia with its army was unquestionably defensive in origin, arising from the horrors of the Thirty Years' War. But it outlasted its cause, and became the settled habit and character of the country. Prussia was not unique, in a world of Bourbons and Hapsburgs, Swedes, Russians, Turks, and the growing British navy, in the attention it paid to its armed forces. The unique thing about Prussia was the disproportion between the size of the army and the size of the resources on which the army was based. The government, to maintain the army, had to direct and plan the life of the country for this purpose. Nor was Prussia the originator of the "standing" army, kept active in time of peace, and always preparing for war. Most governments imitated Louis XIV in establishing standing armies, not merely to promote foreign ambitions, but to keep armed forces out of the hands of nobles and military adventurers, and under control by the state.

But Prussia was unique in that, more than in any other country, the army developed a life of its own, almost independent of the life of the state. It was older than the Prussian state. In 1657 the Great Elector fought a great battle at Warsaw with soldiers from all parts of his dominions. It was the first time that men from Cleves, Brandenburg, and ducal Prussia had ever done anything together. The army was the first "all-Prussian" institution. Institutions of civilian government, common to all Prussia, developed later and largely to meet the needs of the army. And in later generations the army proved more durable than the state. When Prussia collapsed before Napoleon in 1806, the spirit and morale of the Prussian army carried on; and when the Hohenzollern empire finally crashed in 1918, the army still maintained its life and traditions on into the Republic, which again it survived.[18]

In all countries, to some extent, the machinery of the modern state

---

[18] See pp. 406-7, 687-9, 760.

developed as a means of supporting armed forces, but in Prussia the process was exceptionally clear and simple. In Prussia the rulers drew roughly half their income from the crown domain, and only about half from taxes. The crown domain, consisting of manors and other productive enterprises owned directly by the ruler as lord, was in effect a kind of government property, for the Prussian rulers used their income almost entirely for state purposes, being personally men of simple and even Spartan habits. The rulers of Prussia, until a century after the accession of the Great Elector, were able to pay the whole cost of their civil government from their own income, the proceeds of the crown domain. To maintain an army, they had to supplement the remaining income from the domain with new income derived from taxes. To develop the domain, increase its productivity, account for and transfer the funds, they created a large body of civilian officials. The domain bulked so large that much of the economy of the country was not in private hands but consisted of enterprises owned and administered by the state. For additional income the Great Elector introduced taxes of the kind used in France, such as excise taxes on consumers' goods, and a government monopoly on the sale of salt. These taxes, together with the old land tax, began to be collected during the disorders of the Thirty Years' War by war commissars, later organized into a general commissariat. In effect, the army itself collected the taxes and determined the purposes for which the funds should be spent. All taxes, for a century after the accession of the Great Elector, were levied for the use of the army.

Economic life grew up under government sponsorship, rather than by the enterprise of a venturesome business class. This was because, for a rural country to maintain an organized army, productive and technical skills had to be imported, mainly from the West. The Great Elector in his youth spent a number of years in Holland, where he was impressed by the wealth and prosperity that he saw. After becoming Elector he settled Swiss and Frisians in Brandenburg (the Frisians were almost Dutch); he welcomed Jews from Poland; and when Louis XIV began to persecute the French Protestants, he provided funds and special officials to assist the immigration of 20,000 Huguenots to Brandenburg. Frenchmen for a time formed a sixth of the population of Berlin, and were the most advanced element of that comparatively primitive city. The government, as in France under Colbert, initiated and helped to finance various industries; but the importance of such government participation was greater than in France, because the amount of privately owned capital available for investment was incomparably less. Military needs, more than elsewhere, dominated the market for goods, because civilian demand, in so poor a country, was relatively low; so that the army, in its requirements for food, uniforms, and weapons, was a strong force in shaping the economic growth of the country. For all its scraping thrift and careful planning, the government depended on outside financial assistance from Western Europe. The Great Elector, for example, in the last fifteen years of his reign, received (as subsidies requiring no repayment) 973,000 thalers from the Empire, 912,000 from the Dutch, 503,000 from France,

467,000 from Spain, and 57,000 from Denmark. With money from France the Great Elector attempted to enter the overseas world, founding a Brandenburg colony in West Africa; but this venture was financially dependent from the beginning, and was liquidated as a useless expense by his successor.

The army had a profound effect also on the social development and class structure of Prussia. It became the policy of the rulers to absorb practically the whole landed aristocracy, the *Junkers*, into military service. They used the army, with conscious purpose, as a means of implanting an "all-Prussian" psychology in the landed families of Cleves, Brandenburg, Pomerania, and the former dominions of the Teutonic Knights. The sense of service to the king or state was exalted as the supreme human virtue. The fact that Prussia was a very recent and artificial combination of territories, so that loyalty to it was not at first a natural sentiment, made it all the more necessary to instil it by obvious and martial means. Emphasis on duty, obedience, service, and sacrifice, morally the best side of the army code, was probably encouraged in Prussia by the Lutheran religion, which, as has been seen, was strongly inclined to teach that Christian freedom was a matter of the inner spirit, and that in earthly affairs men owed a willing obedience to their princes.[19] That military virtues became characteristic of the whole Prussian aristocracy was also due, like so much else, to the small size of the population. In France, for example, with perhaps 50,000 male adult nobles, only a small minority served habitually as army officers. In Prussia there were few *Junker* families that did not have some of their members in uniform.

Moreover, the Great Elector and his successors, like all absolutist rulers, repressed the estates or parliamentary assemblages in which the landed aristocracy was the main element. To mollify the squires, the rulers promised commissions in the army to men of their class. They promised them also a free hand over their peasants. The Prussian monarchy was largely based on an understanding between the ruler and the landlord gentry—the latter agreed to accept the ruler's government and to serve in his army, in return for holding their own peasants in hereditary subjection. Serfdom spread in Prussia as elsewhere in eastern Europe.[20] In East Prussia the condition of the peasants became as deplorable as in Poland.

The Prussian rulers believed that the *Junkers* made better army officers because they were brought up in the habit of commanding their own peasants. Bourgeois officers, a minority in all armies, were of the utmost rarity in Prussia. To preserve the officer class, legislation forbade the sale of "noble" lands, *i.e.*, manors, to persons not noble. In France, again by way of contrast, where manorial rights had become simply a form of property, bourgeois and even peasants could legally acquire manors and enjoy a lordly or "seigneurial" income. In Prussia this was not possible; classes were frozen by owning non-exchangeable forms of property. It was thus harder for middle class persons to enter the aristocracy by setting up as landed gentry. The

[19] See pp. 71–2.
[20] See pp. 101–2, 174, 183–4, 191, 209.

bourgeois class in any case had little spirit of independence. Few of the old towns of Germany were in Prussia. The Prussian middle class was not wealthy. It was not strong by the possession of private property. The typical middle-class man was an official, who worked for the government as an employee or lease-holder of the large crown domain, or in an enterprise subsidized by the state. The civil service in Prussia, from the days of the Great Elector, became notable for its honesty and efficiency. But the middle class, more than else-where, deferred to the nobles, served the state, and stood in awe of the army.

These peculiar features of Prussia developed especially under Frederick William I, who was king from 1713 to 1740. He was an earthy, uncouth man, who, were the matter less serious, might almost be regarded as a comical character. He disdained whatever savored of "culture," to which his father and grandfather (the Great Elector) and also his son (Frederick the Great) were all strongly attracted. He begrudged every penny not spent on the army. He cut the expense of the royal household by three-fourths. On his corona-tion journey to Königsberg he spent 2,547 thalers, where his father had spent five million. He ruled the country in a fatherly German way, supervising it like a private estate, prowling the streets of Berlin in an old seedy uniform, and disciplining negligent citizens with blows of his walking-stick. He worked all the time, and expected everyone else to do likewise. He loved the army, which all his policies were designed to serve. He was the first Prussian king to appear always in uniform. He rearranged the order of courtly precedence, pushing army officers up and civilians down. His love of tall soldiers is famous; he collected a special unit, men between six and seven feet high, from all over Europe, and indeed Peter the Great sent him some from Asia. He devised new forms of discipline and maneuver, founded a cadet corps to train the sons of the *Junkers,* and devised a new system of recruiting and replacement (the canton system, long the most effective in Europe), by which each regiment had a particular district or canton assigned to it as a source of soldiers. He raised the size of the army from 40,000 at his acces-sion to 83,000 at his death. During his reign Berlin grew to be a city of 100,000, of whom 20,000 were soldiers, a proportion probably matched in no other city of Europe. He likewise left to his successor (for he fought prac-tically no wars himself) a war chest of 7,000,000 thalers.

With this army and war chest Frederick II, later called the Great, who became king in 1740, startled Europe. Charles VI of Austria had just died. His daughter Maria Theresa entered upon her manifold inheritance. All Europe was hedging on its guarantee of the Pragmatic Sanction. While others waited, Frederick struck. Serving no notice, he moved his forces into Silesia, to which the Hohenzollerns had an old though doubtful claim. Silesia was a part of the kingdom of Bohemia on the side toward Poland, lying in the upper valley of the Oder River, and adjoining Brandenburg on the north. The addition of Silesia to the kingdom of Prussia almost doubled the popu-lation and added valuable industries, so that Prussia now, with 6,000,000 people and an army which Frederick raised to 200,000, at last established itself as a great power. But Frederick, as will be seen, had to fight repeatedly to retain Silesia. Having made his great conquest by sudden aggression, and spent his father's war chest, he soon came up against the fundamental problem of Prussia, its relative poverty, and relapsed into the cautious program of his forebears.[21] Only at the beginning was the career of Frederick the Great an exception to the picture of Prussia here set forth—that it was a militaristic but unwarlike and even timid state, preferring to secure its ends by threats, machinations, balance of power policies, and intrigue. It must be added that, judged simply as a human accomplishment, Prussia was a remarkable creation, a state made on a shoestring, a triumph of work and duty.

25. The "Westernizing" of Russia

The affairs of central and eastern Europe, from Sweden to Turkey and from Germany to the Caspian Sea, were profoundly interconnected. The underlying theme of the present chapter, it may be recalled, is that this whole great area was fluid, occupied by the flabby bodies of the Holy Roman Empire, Poland, and Turkey, and that in this fluid area three harder masses developed—the modern Austrian monarchy, the kingdom of Prussia, and the Russian empire. All, too, in varying degree, were modernized by borrowings from the West.

In the century after 1650 the old tsardom of Muscovy turned into modern Russia. Moving out from the region around Moscow, the Russians not only established themselves across northern Asia, reaching the Bering Sea about 1700, but also entered into closer relations with Europe, undergoing especially in the time of Tsar Peter the Great (1682–1725) a rapid process of Europeanization. To what extent Russia became truly European has always been an open question, disputed both by western Europeans and by Russians themselves. In some ways the Russians have been European from as far back as Europe itself can be said to have existed, *i.e.*, from the early Middle Ages. Ancient Russia had been colonized by Vikings, and the Russians had become Christians long before the Swedes, the Lithuanians, or the Finns. But Russia had not been part of the general development of Europe for a number of reasons. For one thing, Russia had been converted to the Greek Orthodox branch of Christianity; therefore, the religious and cultural influence of Constantinople, not of Rome, had predominated. Secondly, the Mongol invasions and conquest about 1240 had kept Russia under Asiatic domination for about two hundred and fifty years, until 1480 when a grand duke of Muscovy, Ivan III (1462–1505) was able to throw off the Mongol overlordship and cease payment of tribute.[22] Lastly, Russian geography, especially the lack of warm-water or ice-free seaports had made commerce and communication with the West difficult. For these reasons

wwwwwwwwwwwwwww

[21] See pp. 245–6, 311.
[22] See pp. 21–2, 41.

Russia had not shared in the general European development after about 1100, and the changes that took place in the seventeenth and eighteenth centuries may accurately be called Europeanization, or at least a wholesale borrowing of the apparatus of civilization from the West. The Europeanizing or westernizing of Russia was by no means a unique thing. It was a step in the expansion of the European type of civilization, and hence in the formation of the modern world as we have known it in the last three hundred years.

In some ways the new Russian empire resembled the new kingdom of Prussia. Both took form in the great plain which runs uninterruptedly from the North Sea into inner Asia. Both lacked natural frontiers, and grew by addition of territories to an original nucleus. In both countries the state arose primarily as a means of supporting a modern army. In both the government developed autocratically, in conjunction with a landlord class which was impressed into state-service and which in turn held the peasantry in serfdom. Neither Russia nor Prussia had a native commercial class of any political importance. In neither country could the modern state and army have been created without the importation of skills from western Europe. Yet Prussia, with its German connections, its Protestant religion, its universities and its nearness to the busy commercial artery of the Baltic, was far more "European" than Russia, and the Europeanization of Russia may perhaps better be compared with the later westernization of Japan.[23] In the Russia of 1700, as in the Japan of 1870, the main purpose of the westernizers was to obtain scientific, technical, and military knowledge from the West, in part with a view to strengthening their own states against penetration or conquest by Europeans. Yet here too the parallel must not be pushed too far. Russia became more fully Europeanized than did the peoples of Asia. In time, its upper classes intermarried with Europeans, and Russian music and literature became part of the culture of Europe. Russia developed a unique blend of European and non-European traits.

RUSSIA BEFORE PETER THE GREAT

The Russians in the seventeenth century, as today, were a medley of peoples distinguished by their language, which was of the Slavic family, of the great Indo-European language group.[24] The Great Russians or Muscovites lived around Moscow. Moving out from that area, they had penetrated the northern forests and had also settled in the southern steppes and along the Volga, where they had assimilated various Asiatic peoples known as Tartars. After two centuries of expansion, from roughly 1450 to 1650, the Russians had almost but not quite reached the Baltic and the Black Seas. The Baltic shore was held by Sweden. The Black Sea coast was still held by Tartar khans under the protection of Turkey. In the rough borderlands between Tartar

[23] See pp. 548–54.
[24] See p. 4; see also map, Languages of Europe, p. 437.

and Russian lived the semi-independent cowboy-like Cossacks, largely recruited from migratory Russians. West of Muscovy were the White Russians (or Bielorussians) and southwest of Muscovy the Little Russians (or Ruthenians or Ukrainians), both in the seventeenth century under the rule of Poland, which was then the leading Slavic power.

The energies of the Great Russians were directed principally eastward. They conquered the Volga Tartars in the sixteenth century, thus reaching the Ural Mountains, which they immediately crossed. Muscovite pioneers, settlers, and townbuilders streamed along the river-systems of Siberia, felling timber and trading in furs as they went. In the 1630's, while the English founded Boston and the Dutch New York, the Russians were establishing towns in the vast Asiatic stretches of Siberia, reaching to the Pacific itself. A whole string of settlements, remote, small, and isolated—Tomsk and Tobolsk, Irkutsk and Yakutsk—extended for five thousand miles across northern Asia.

It was toward the vast heartland of central Asia that Muscovy really faced, looking out upon Persia and China across the deserts. The bazaars of Moscow and Astrakhan were frequented by Persians, Afghans, Kirghiz, Indians, and Chinese. The Caspian Sea, into which flowed the Volga, the greatest of Russian rivers, was better known than was the Baltic. Europe as sensed from Moscow was in the rear. During most of the seventeenth century even Smolensk and Kiev belonged to Poland. And, as has been noted, while the Swedes blocked the Russians from access to the Baltic, the Tartars and Turks barred them from the Black Sea and the Mediterranean. Poles and Swedes, on various occasions, actually discouraged the passage of Europeans into Great Russia, fearing the consequences should their monstrous eastern neighbor acquire western arts. Yet the Russians were not totally shut off from Europe. In 1552, when Ivan the Terrible conquered Kazan from the Tartars, he had a German engineer in his army. In the next year, 1553, Richard Chancellor arrived in Moscow from England by the roundabout way of Archangel on the White Sea.[25] Thereafter trade between England and Muscovy was continuous. The tsars valued Archangel as their only inlet from the West, through which military materials could be imported. The English valued it as a means of reaching the wares of Persia.

Russia in the seventeenth century reflected its long estrangement from Europe, and its long association with some of the more barbarous peoples of Asia. Women of the upper classes were secluded and often wore veils. Men wore beards and skirted garments that seemed exotic to Europeans. Customs were crude, wild drunkenness and revelry alternating with spasms of repentance and religious prostration. Dwarfs and fools, no longer the fashion in the West, still amused the tsar and his retainers. Superstition infected the highest classes of church and state. Life counted for little; murder, kidnapping, torture, and elaborate physical cruelty were common. The Russian church supported no such educational or charitable institutions

wwwwwwwwwwwwww
[25] See p. 93.

as did the Catholic and Protestant Churches of Europe, and had developed no such respect for learning or sentiments of humanity. Churchmen feared the incipient Western influences. "Abhorred of God," declared a Russian bishop, "is any who loves geometry; it is a spiritual sin." Even arithmetic was hardly understood in Russia. Arabic numerals were not used, and merchants computed with the abacus. The calendar was dated from the creation of the world. Ability to predict an eclipse seemed a form of magic. Clocks, brought in by Europeans, seemed as wonderful in Russia as they did in China, where they were brought in by Jesuits at about the same time. The principal Russian art was the painting of icons. There was no literature in the Russian language, which was scarcely a written language at all. A few annals, tales, and translations from Greek ecclesiastical literature were written in Slavonic, an artificial, learned language used in the churches. The most notable writer to live in Moscow in the seventeenth century was not a Russian but a Croatian, Yury Krizhanich (who wrote in Latin), founder of the idea that all Slav peoples should act together, and who went all the way to Moscow to win support for his Pan-Slav dream. But the Muscovites were not yet ready for his doctrine. They exiled him to Tobolsk, in Siberia.

Yet this great barbarous Russia, which fronted on inner Asia, was European in some of its fundamental social institutions. It possessed a variant of the manorial and feudal systems. It felt the same wave of constitutional crises that was sweeping over Europe at the same time. Russia had a Duma or council of retainers and advisers to the tsar, and the rudiments of a national assembly corresponding to meetings of the estates in western Europe. In Russia as in Europe the question was whether power should remain in the hands of these bodies or become concentrated in the hands of the ruler. Ivan the Terrible, who ruled from 1533 to 1584 and was the first grand duke of Muscovy to assume the title of tsar,[26] was a shrewd observer of contemporary events in Poland. He saw the dissolution that was overtaking the Polish state and was determined to avoid it in Muscovy. His ferocity toward those who opposed him made him literally terrible, but though his methods were not used in Europe, his aims were the aims of his European contemporaries. Not long after his death Russia passed into a period known as the Time of Troubles (1604–13), during which the Russian nobles elected a series of tsars, and demanded certain assurances of their own liberties. But the country was racked by contending factions and civil war, in which, as in the religious wars in France or the Thirty Years' War in central Europe at approximately the same time, the issue lay between feudal independence and a more modern centralization.

In 1613 a national assembly, hoping to settle the troubles, elected a seventeen-year-old boy as tsar, or emperor, believing him young enough to

[26] The Slavic word *tsar*, like the German *Kaiser*, derives from *Caesar*, a title used as a synonym for *emperor* in the Roman, the Holy Roman and the Byzantine (or Eastern Roman) empires. The spelling *czar*, formerly more common in English, reveals the etymology and the current English-language pronunciation, which is *zar*.

have no connection with any of the warring factions. The new boy tsar was Michael Romanov, of a gentry family, related by marriage to the old line of Ivan the Terrible. Thus was established, by vote of the political classes of the day, the Romanov dynasty which ruled in Russia until 1917. The early Romanovs, aware of the fate of elective monarchy in Poland and elsewhere, soon began to repress the representative institutions of Russia and set up as absolute monarchs. Here again, though they were more lawless and violent than any European king, they followed the general pattern of contemporary Europe.

Nor can it be said that the main social development of the seventeenth century in Russia, the sinking of the peasantry into an abyss of helpless serfdom, was exclusively a Russian phenomenon. The same generally took place in eastern Europe.[27] Serfdom had long been overtaking the older free peasantry of Russia. In Russia, as in the American colonies, land was abundant and labor scarce. The natural tendency of labor was to migrate over the great plain, to run off to the Cossacks, or to go to Siberia. In the Time of Troubles, especially, there was a good deal of moving about. The landlords wished to assure themselves of their labor force. To this end they obtained the support of the Romanov tsars. The manor, or what corresponded to it in Russia, came to resemble the slave plantation of the New World.[28] Laws against fugitive serfs were strengthened; lords won the right to recover fugitives up to fifteen years after their flight, and finally the time limit was abolished altogether. Peasants came to be so little regarded that a law of 1625 authorized anyone killing another man's peasant simply to give him another peasant in return. Lords exercised police and judicial powers. By a law of 1646 landowners were required to enter the names of all their peasants in government registers; peasants once so entered, together with their descendants, were regarded as attached to the estate on which they were registered. Thus the peasant lost the freedom to move at his own will. For a time he was supposed to have secure tenure of his land; but a law of 1675 allowed the lords to sell peasants without the land, and thus to move peasants like chattels at the will of the owner. This sale of serfs without land, which made their condition almost indistinguishable from slavery as practiced in America, became indeed a distinctive feature of serfdom in Russia, since in Poland, Prussia, Bohemia, and other regions of serfdom, the serf was generally regarded as "bound to the soil," inseparable from the land.

Against the loss of their freedom the rural population of Russia protested as best it could, murdering landlords, fleeing to the Cossacks, taking refuge in a vagrant existence, countered by wholesale government-organized manhunts and by renewed and more stringent legislation. A tremendous uprising was led in 1667 by Stephen Razin, who gathered a host of fugitive serfs, Cossacks, and adventurers, outfitted a fleet on the Caspian Sea, plundered Russian vessels, defeated a Persian squadron, and invaded Persia itself.

---

[27] See pp. 101–2, 174, 203.
[28] See p. 230.

He then turned back, ascended the Volga, killing and burning as he went and proclaiming a war against landlords, nobles, and priests. Cities opened their gates to him; an army sent against him went over to his side. He was caught and put to death in 1671. The consequence of the rebellion, for over a century, was that serfdom was clamped on the country more firmly than ever. But the memory of Razin lived in the folklore of Russian peasants. A hill near the lower Volga was named for him. The legend grew that whoever climbed Razin's hill at night would learn his secret—and that this secret was class war.

Even from the church the increasingly wretched rural people drew little comfort. The Russian Orthodox Church at this same time went through a great internal crisis, and ended up as hardly more than a department of the tsardom, useful to the government in instilling a superstitious reverence for Holy Russia. The Russian Church had historically looked to the Patriarch of Constantinople as its head. But the conquest of Constantinople by the Turks made the head of the Greek Orthodox Church a merely tolerated inferior to the Moslem sultan-caliph, so that the Russians in 1589 set up an independent Russian patriarch of their own. In the following generations the Russian patriarchate first became dependent on, then was destroyed by, the tsarist government.

In the 1650's the Russian patriarch undertook certain church reforms, mainly to correct mistranslations in Russian versions of the Bible and other sacred writings. The changes aroused the horror and indignation of the general body of believers. Superstitiously attached to the mere form of the written word, believing the faith itself to depend on the customary spelling of the name of Jesus, the malcontents saw in the reformers a band of cunning Greek scholars perpetrating the work of Antichrist and the devil. The patriarch and higher church officials forced through the reforms, but only with the help of the government and the army. Those who rejected the reforms came to be called Old Believers. More ignorant and fanatical than the established church, agitated by visionary preachers, dividing into innumerable sects, the Old Believers became very numerous, especially among the peasants. Old Believers were active in Stephen Razin's rebellion and in all the sporadic peasant uprisings that followed. The peasants, already put by serfdom outside the protection of law, were also largely estranged from the established religion. A distrust of all organized authority settled over the Russian masses, to whom both church and government seemed mere engines of repression. The Russian Orthodox Church meanwhile maintained its position only by support of the tsar.

But while willing enough to modernize to the extent of correcting mistranslations from the Greek, the church officials resisted the kind of modernization that was coming in from western Europe. They therefore opposed Peter the Great at the end of the century. After 1700 no new patriarch was appointed. Peter put the church under a committee of bishops called the Holy Synod, and to the Synod he attached a civil official called the Procurator of the Holy Synod, who was not a churchman but head of a government

bureau, and whose task was to see that the church did nothing displeasing to
the tsar. Peter thus secularized the church, making himself in effect its head.
But while the consequences were more extreme in Russia than elsewhere, it
must again be noted that this action of Peter's followed the general pattern
of Europe. Secular supervision of religion had become the rule almost everywhere, especially in Protestant countries. Indeed an Englishman of the time
thought that Peter the Great, in doing away with the patriarchate and putting the church under his own control, was wisely imitating England, which
he visited in his youth.

PETER THE GREAT: FOREIGN AFFAIRS AND
TERRITORIAL EXPANSION

The Russia in which Peter the Great became tsar, in 1682, was in short
fundamentally European in some ways, and had in any case been in
contact with Westerners for over a century. Without Peter, Russia would
have developed its European connections more gradually. Peter, by his
tempo and methods, made the process a social revolution.

Peter obtained his first knowledge of the West in Moscow itself, where
a part of the city known as the German quarter was inhabited by Europeans
of various nationalities, whom Peter often visited as a boy. Peter also in his
early years mixed with Westerners at Archangel, still Russia's only port, for
he was fascinated by the sea, and took lessons in navigation on the White
Sea from Dutch and English ship captains. Like the Great Elector of Brandenburg, Peter as a young man spent over a year in western Europe, especially
Holland and England, where he was profoundly impressed with the backwardness of his own country. He had considerable talents as a mechanic
and organizer. He labored with his own hands as a ship's carpenter in Amsterdam, and talked with political and business leaders on means of introducing
western organization and technology into Russia. He visited workshops,
mines, commercial offices, art galleries, hospitals, and forts. Europeans saw
in him a barbarian of genius, a giant of a man standing a head above most
others, bursting with physical vitality and plying all he met with interminable
questions on their manner of working and living. He had neither the refinement nor the pretension of Western monarchs; he mixed easily with workmen and technical people, dressed cheaply and carelessly, loved horseplay
and crude practical jokes, and dismayed his hosts by the squalid disorder in
which he and his companions left the rooms put at their disposal. A man of
acute practical mind, he was as little troubled by appearances as by moral
scruples.

Peter on his visit to Europe in 1697–8 recruited almost a thousand experts for service in Russia, and many more followed later. He cared nothing
for the civilization of Europe except as a means to an end, and this end was
to create an army and a state which could stand against those of the West.

His aim from the beginning was in part defensive, to ward off the Poles, Swedes, and Turks who had long pushed against Russia; and in part expansionist, to obtain seaports or "windows on the West," warm-water ports on the Baltic and Black seas, free from the shortcomings of Archangel, which was frozen a good part of the year and in any case offered only a roundabout route to Europe. For all but two years of his long reign Peter was at war.

The Poles were a receding danger. A Polish prince had indeed been elected tsar of Muscovy during the Time of Troubles, and for a while the Poles aspired to conquer and Catholicize the Great Russians, but in 1667 the Russians had regained Smolensk and Kiev, and the growing anarchy in Poland made that country no longer a menace, except as the Swedes or others might install themselves in it. The Turks and their feudatories the Tartars, though no longer expanding, were still obstinate foes. Peter before going to Europe managed in 1696 to capture Azov at the mouth of the Don, but he was unable to hold any of the Black Sea coast, and learned in these campaigns to know the inferiority of the Russian army. The Swedes were the main enemy of Russia. Their army, for its size, was still probably the best in Europe. By occupying Finland, Karelia, and Livonia they controlled the whole eastern shore of the Baltic including the Gulf of Finland. In 1697, the Swedish king having died, Peter entered into an alliance with Poland and Denmark to partition the overseas posessions of the Swedish house.

The new king of Sweden, the youthful Charles XII, though descended from civilized enough forebears, was in some ways as crude as Peter (as an adolescent he had sheep driven into his rooms in the palace in order to enjoy the warlike pleasure of killing them), but he proved also to have remarkable aptitude as a general. In 1700, at the battle of Narva, with an army of 8,000 men, he routed Peter's 40,000 Russians. The tsar thus learned another lesson on the need of westernizing his state and army. Fortunately for the Russians Charles XII, instead of immediately pressing his advantage in Russia, spent the following years in furthering Swedish interests in Poland, where he forced the Poles to elect the Swedish candidate as their king. Peter meanwhile, with his imported officers and technicians, reformed the training, discipline, and weapons of the Russian army. Finally Charles XII invaded Russia with a large and well prepared force. Peter used against him the strategy later used

---

The Growth of Russia in the West

At the accession of Peter the Great in 1682 the Russian Empire, expanding from the old grand duchy of Muscovy, had almost but not quite reached the Black and Baltic seas. Most of Peter's conquests were in the Baltic region, where he pushed back the Swedes and built St. Petersburg. Under Catherine the Great (1762–96) Russia took part in the three partitions of Poland, and also reached the Black Sea. The tsar Alexander (1801–25), thanks largely to the Napoleonic wars, was able to acquire still more of Poland, and annex Finland and Bessarabia; he also made conquests in the Caucasus. In the nineteenth century the western boundary of Russia remained stabilized, but additional gains were made in the Caucasus.

Russia also spread over northern Asia in the seventeenth century, first reaching the Pacific as early as 1630. (See also map, pp. 730–1.)

THE GROWTH OF **RUSSIA** IN THE WEST

500 MILES

1

SWEDEN

WHITE SEA
•Archangel

BALTIC SEA

•Moscow

•Warsaw
POLAND

OTTOMAN EMPIRE

Azov
Astrakhan

VOLGA R.

CASPIAN SEA

BLACK SEA
Constantinople

MUSCOVY IN 1462
ACQUISITIONS 1462-1682

2

SWEDEN

WHITE SEA
•Archangel

INGRIA AND LIVONIA, 1720

BALTIC SEA

St.Petersburg

•Moscow

•Warsaw
POLAND

OTTOMAN EMPIRE

Azov
Astrakhan

VOLGA R.

CASPIAN SEA

CAUCASUS

BLACK SEA
Constantinople

RUSSIA IN 1682
ACQUISITIONS OF PETER THE GREAT, 1682-1725

3

SWEDEN

WHITE SEA
•Archangel

FINLAND 1808

BALTIC SEA

St.Petersburg

•Moscow

1772
•Warsaw
1815 1795 1793
POLAND

BESSARABIA 1812

JEDISAN 1792
KRIM TARTARS 1783
Constantinople
MINGRELIA 1803

Azov Astrakhan

VOLGA R.

CASPIAN SEA

BLACK SEA

GEORGIA 1801

DAGHESTAN 1813

OTTOMAN EMPIRE

RUSSIA IN 1725
ACQUISITIONS, 1725-1815

4

SWEDEN

WHITE SEA
•Archangel

FINLAND

BALTIC SEA

St.Petersburg

•Moscow

•Warsaw
POLAND

Azov Astrakhan

VOLGA R.

CASPIAN SEA

CIRCASSIA 1829

BLACK SEA
Constantinople

KARS 1878

CAUCASUS

DAGHESTAN

OTTOMAN EMPIRE

RUSSIA IN 1815
ACQUISITIONS, 1815-1914

TRM

by the Russians against Napoleon and Adolf Hitler; he drew the Swedes into the endless plains, exposing them to the Russian winter, which happened to be an exceptionally severe one, and in 1709, at Poltava in south Russia, he met and overwhelmed the demoralized remainder. The entire Swedish army was destroyed at Poltava, only the king and a few hundred fugitives managing to escape across the Turkish frontier. Peter in the next years conquered Livonia and part of eastern Finland. He landed troops near Stockholm itself. He campaigned in Pomerania almost as far west as the Elbe. Never before had Russian influence reached so deeply into Europe. Prussia, as we have seen, rose with the rise of Russia, receiving Stettin and most of western or Swedish Pomerania through an understanding with Peter and without serious commitment of its own forces. The imperial day of Sweden was now over, terminated by Russia. Peter had won for Russia the Baltic shore and with it warm-water outlets. These significant developments ending the great Northern War (1709–21) were confirmed in the treaty of Nystadt in 1721.

War is surely not the father of all things, as has been sometimes claimed, but these wars did a good deal to father imperial Russia. The army was transformed from an Asiatic horde into a professional force of the kind maintained by Sweden, France, or Prussia. The elite of the old army had been the *streltsi*, a kind of Moscow guard, composed of nobles and constantly active in politics. A rebellion of the *streltsi* in 1698 had cut short Peter's tour of Europe; he had returned and quelled the mutiny by ferocious use of torture and execution, killing five of the rebels with his own hands. The *streltsi* were liquidated only two years before the great Russian defeat at Narva. Peter then rebuilt the army from the ground up. He employed European officers of many nationalities, paying them half again as much as native Russians of the same grades. He filled his ranks with soldiers supplied by districts on a territorial basis, somewhat as in Prussia. He put the troops into uniforms resembling those of the West, and organized them in regiments of standardized composition. He armed them with muskets and artillery of the kind used in Europe, and tried to create a service of supply. With this army he had not only driven the Swedes back into Sweden, but also dominated Russia itself. At the very time of the Swedish invasion large parts of the country were in rebellion, as in the days of Stephen Razin, for the whole middle and lower Volga, together with the Cossacks of the Don and Dnieper, rose against the tsar and rallied behind slogans of class war and hatred of the tsar's foreign experts. Peter crushed these disturbances with the usual ruthlessness. The Russian empire, loose and heterogeneous, was held together by military might.

While the war was still in progress, even before the decisive battle of Poltava, Peter laid the foundations of a wholly new city in territory conquered from the Swedes and inhabited not by Russians but by various Baltic peoples. This city is now called Leningrad. Peter named it St. Petersburg after himself and his patron saint. From the beginning it was more truly a city than Louis's spectacular creation at Versailles established at almost the same time. Standing at the head of the Gulf of Finland, it was Peter's chief window on the west. Here he established the offices of government, required noblemen to build town houses, and gave favorable terms to foreign merchants and craftsmen to settle. Peter meant to make St. Petersburg a symbol of the new Russia, a new city facing toward Europe and drawing the minds of the Russians westward, replacing the old capital, Moscow, which faced toward Asia and was the stronghold of opposition to his westernizing program. St. Petersburg soon became one of the leading cities of northern Europe. It remained the capital of Russia until the revolution of 1917 when Moscow resumed its old place.

INTERNAL CHANGES UNDER PETER THE GREAT

The new army, the new city, the new and expanding government offices all required money, which in Russia was very scarce. Taxes were imposed on an inconceivable variety of objects—on heads, as poll taxes; on land; on inns, mills, hats, leather, cellars, and coffins; on the right to marry, sell meat, wear a beard, or be an Old Believer. The tax burden fell mainly on the peasants; and to assure the payment of taxes the mobility of peasants was further restricted, and borderline individuals were classified as peasants in the government records, so that serfdom became both more onerous and more nearly universal. To raise government revenues and to stimulate production Peter adopted the mercantilist policies exemplified by Colbert in France. He encouraged exports, built a fleet on the Baltic, and developed mining, metallurgy, and textiles, which were indispensable to the army. He organized mixed groups of Russians and foreigners into commercial companies, provided them with capital from government funds (little private capital being available), and gave them a labor supply by assigning them the use of serfs in a given locality. Serfdom, in origin mainly an agricultural institution, began to spread in Russia as an industrial institution also. The fact that serf-owners obtained the right to sell serfs without land, or to move them from landed estates into mines or towns, made it easier for industry in Russia to develop on the basis of unfree labor. Nor were the employers of serfs, in these government enterprises, free to modify or abandon their projects at will. They too were simply in the tsar's service. The economic system rested largely on impressment of both management and labor, not on private profit and wages as in the increasingly capitalistic West. In this way Peter's efforts to force Russia to a European level of material productivity widened the gap between Russia and western Europe.

To oversee and operate this system of tax-collecting, recruiting, economic controls, serf-hunting, and repression of internal rebellion Peter created a new administrative system. The old organs of local self-government wasted away. The Duma and the national assembly, decadent anyway in that they could not function without disorder, disappeared. In their place Peter put a "senate" dependent on himself, and ten territorial areas called "governments" or *gubernii*—the very words were not Slavic but Latin, and showed imitation of the West. The Church he ruled through his Procurator of the Holy Synod.[29] At the top of the whole structure was himself, an absolute ruler, tsar and autocrat of all the Russias. Before his death, dissatisfied with his son, he abolished the rule of hereditary succession to the tsardom, claiming the right for each tsar to name his own successor. Transmission of supreme power was thus put outside the domain of law, and in the following century the accession of tsars and tsarinas was marked by strife, conspiracy, and assassination. The whole system of centralized absolutism, while in form resembling that of the West, notably France, was in fact significantly different, for it lacked legal regularity, was handicapped by the insuperable ignorance of many officials, and was imposed on a turbulent and largely unwilling population. The empire of the Romanovs has been called a state without a people.

Peter, to assure the success of his westernizing program, developed what was called "state-service," which had been begun by his predecessors. Virtually all land-owning and serf-owning aristocrats were required to serve in the army or civil administration. Offices were multiplied to provide places for all. In the state-service birth counted for nothing. Peter used men of all classes; Prince Dolgoruky was of the most ancient nobility, Prince Menshikov had been a cook, the tax administrator Kurbatov was an ex-serf, and many others were foreigners of unknown background. Status in Peter's Russia depended, not on inherited rank which Peter could not control, but on rank in his state-service, civilian grades being equated with military, and all persons in the first eight grades being considered gentry. "History," wrote a Scotsman serving in Peter's army, "scarcely affords an example where so many people of low birth have been raised to such dignities as in tsar Peter's reign, or where so many of the highest birth and fortune have been leveled to the lowest ranks of life." In this respect especially Peter's program resembled a true social revolution. It created a new governing element in place of the old, almost what in modern parlance would be called a party, a body of men working zealously for the new system with a personal interest in its preservation. These men, during Peter's lifetime and after his death, were the bulwarks against an anti-Western reaction, the main agents in making Peter's revolution stick. In time the new families became hereditary themselves. The priority of state-service over personal position was abandoned a generation after Peter's death. Offices in the army and government were filled by men of property and birth. After Peter's revolution, as after some others, the new upper class became merged with the old.

Revolutionary also, suggesting the great French Revolution or the Russian revolution of 1917, were Peter's unconcealed contempt for everything reminiscent of the old Russia, and his zeal to re-educate his people in the new ways. He required all gentry to put their sons in school. He sent many abroad to study. He simplified the Russian alphabet. He edited the first newspaper to appear in Russia. He ordered the preparation of the first Russian

[29] See pp. 210–11.

book of etiquette, teaching his subjects not to spit on the floor, scratch themselves or gnaw bones at dinner, to mix socially with women, take off their hats, converse pleasantly, and look at people while talking. The beard he took as a symbol of Muscovite backwardness; he forbade it in Russia, and himself shaved a number of men at his court. He forced people to attend evening parties to teach them manners. He had no respect for hereditary aristocracy, torturing or executing the highborn as readily as the peasants. As for religion, we are told that he was a pious man and enjoyed singing in church, but he was contemptuous of ecclesiastical dignity, and in one wild revel paraded publicly with drunken companions clothed in religious vestments and mocking the priests. Like most great revolutionists since his time, he was aggressively secular.

THE RESULTS OF PETER'S REVOLUTION

Peter's tactics provoked a strong reaction. Some adhered strictly to the old ways, others simply thought that Peter was moving too fast and too indiscriminately toward the new. Many Russians resented the inescapable presence of foreigners, who often looked down on Russians as savages, and who enjoyed special privileges such as the right of free exit from Russia and higher pay for similar employments. One center around which malcontents rallied was the church. Another was Peter's son Alexis, who declared that when he became tsar he would put a stop to the innovations and restore respect for the customs of old Russia. Peter, after some hesitation, finally put his own son to death. He ruled that each tsar should choose his own successor. He would stop at nothing to remake Russia in his own fashion.

Peter died in 1725, proclaimed "the Great" in his own lifetime by his admiring Senate. Few men in all history have exerted so strong an individual influence, which has indirectly become more far-reaching as the stature of Russia itself has grown. Though the years after Peter's death were years of turmoil and vacillation, his revolutionary changes held firm against those who would undo them. It is not simply that he Europeanized Russia and conquered a place on the Baltic; these developments would probably have come about in any case. It is by the methods he used, his impatient forcing of a new culture on Russia, that he set the future character of his empire. His methods fastened autocracy, serfdom, and bureaucracy more firmly upon the country. They perhaps associated the idea of civilization with the idea of force, and they provoked a reaction in which western Europe was viewed with accentuated dislike and distrust. He was able, for all his efforts, to reach only the upper classes. Many of these became more Europeanized than he could dream, habitually speaking French and living spiritually in France or in Italy. But as time went on many upper-class Russians, because of their very knowledge of Europe, became impatient of the stolid immovability of the peasants around them, sensed themselves as strangers in their own country, or were troubled by a guilty feeling that their position rested on the degradation and enslavement of human beings. Russian psychology, always mysterious to the West, could be explained in part by the violent paradoxes set up by rapid Europeanization. As for the peasant masses, they remained outside the system, egregiously exploited, estranged except by force of habit from their rulers and their social superiors, regarded by them as brutes or children, never sharing in any comparable way in their Europeanized civilization. These facts worked themselves out in later times. As for Peter's own time, Russia by his efforts came clearly out of its isolation, its vast bulk was now organized to play a part in international affairs, and its history thenceforward was a part of the history of Europe and increasingly of the world. Russia, like Prussia and the Austrian monarchy, was to be counted among the powers of Europe.

26. The Partitions of Poland

The fate of Poland in the eighteenth century reaches beyond the time limits of the present chapter, but it illustrates and brings together many of the strands traced in the preceding pages, so that a few words on it at this point may be useful. Poland in the eighteenth century, if Russia is considered non-European, was still by far the largest European state. It still reached from the Baltic almost to the Black Sea, and extended eastward for eight hundred miles across the north-European plain. But it was the classic example, along with the Holy Roman Empire, of an older political structure which failed to develop modern organs of government.[30] It fell into ever deeper anarchy and confusion. Without army, revenues, or administration, internally divided among parties forever at cross purposes, with many Poles more willing to bargain with foreigners than to work with each other, the country was a perpetual theater for diplomatic maneuvering and was finally absorbed by its growing neighbors.

It will be recalled that King John Sobieski, in 1683, drove the Turks from Vienna.[31] The Polish relief of Vienna, the last great effort of the decaying Republic, initiated the general crusade against Turkey of the following years, in which the Hapsburgs conquered Hungary and pushed their frontiers temporarily into the Balkans. For Poland itself this turn of affairs was not altogether beneficial. The Turks were the historic enemy of the Poles, and the weaker the historic enemy became the less there was to hold the Polish nobles together. Sobieski, though a national hero, spent his last years in disillusionment at the progressive disorders in his country. He died in 1696.

The Polish royal elections in the eighteenth century were as usual an international auction and the royal election of 1733 actually precipitated a general European war known as the War of the Polish Succession, which

---

[30] See pp. 182–4 and map, p. 179.
[31] See p. 189.

lasted in some areas of the fighting until 1739. The war resulted in the confirmation of the Russian candidate Augustus III as king and also in several territorial adjustments in Europe. France, for example, which had backed Louis XV's father-in-law Stanislas for the Polish throne was compensated for the French loss of standing in Poland by the acquisition of Lorraine.

Not long thereafter, by the middle of the eighteenth century, a reforming movement began to gather strength in Poland. Polish patriots hoped to do away with the *liberum veto* and other elements in the constitution which made government impossible. Their efforts were repeatedly frustrated by foreign influence, notably that of Catherine II, tsarina of Russia (1762–96), who preferred a Poland in which she could intervene at will. On the death of Augustus III in 1763 Catherine strengthened her hold over the country by obtaining the election of another Russian puppet, a Polish nobleman named Stanislas Poniatowski, her former lover, as king. She declared herself protector of the Polish liberties. It was to the Russian advantage to maintain the existing state of affairs in Poland, which enabled Russian influence to pervade the whole country, rather than to divide the country with neighbors who might exclude Russian influence from their own spheres. The Prussians, however, long awaiting the day when by annexing West Prussia they might join East Prussia and Brandenburg-Pomerania into one continuous territory, were more willing to entertain the prospect of a partition of Poland. It was the fundamental policy of Prussia to absorb territory without the risk of war. In the War of the Polish Succession, which had involved most of the powers of Europe, the eccentric and army-loving Frederick William had remained quiet, making no overt move to snatch the coveted West Prussia. His successor, Frederick the Great, though he had gone to war for Silesia, likewise hoped to obtain West Prussia by diplomatic means. The opportunity finally presented itself in connection with another war between Russia and Turkey, which threw the whole situation in eastern Europe into question. The Turkish empire was now at last showing signs of unmistakable weakness. It too, like Poland, offered the prospect of partition or of control from outside. The Republic of Poland and the Ottoman Empire were in the cauldron together, ready to be melted down and fused with their stronger neighbors. The Russians were successful in the Turkish war which began in 1768. Their troops overran the north coast of the Black Sea and poured into the Danubian principalities, occupying Bucharest. They were in a position, for all the Turks might do, to cross the Danube and stream into the Balkans to Constantinople itself.

What saved Turkey and condemned Poland was the play of the balance of power. The Russians hesitated to cross the Danube, fearing that the Austrians would fall upon their flank, for they knew that the Austrians, too, had designs upon Turkey and would not permit them a monopoly of the spoils. Prussia meanwhile viewed with concern the prospects of a war that might result in a Russian and Austrian partition of the Turkish territories. Such an eventuality would result in an aggrandizement of the other two east-European states to the disadvantage of Prussia and would upset the balance of power in eastern Europe. The Prussians, therefore, came forward with a proposal. It was a proposal designed to prevent an Austro-Russian war and to preserve the east-European balance of power unchanged by leaving Turkey more or less intact but by having all three powers take territory from Poland instead. The proposition was accepted by the three parties.

The Russians called off their war with Turkey. They evacuated the Danubian principalities and most of the Black Sea coast. They did not, indeed, allow the Turkish empire to escape intact. The sultan was obliged to renounce his suzerainty over the Black Sea Tartars, to admit Russian shipping to the Black Sea and the Straits, and to recognize the Russian government as "protector" of Christian interests at Constantinople. These terms were written into the treaty of Kuchuk Kainarji of 1774, a great turning point in the expansion of Russia southward. The Russians soon used the advantage thus gained to absorb the north coast of the Black Sea, to continue their interference in Turkey, and to send naval vessels into the Mediterranean.

Poland was meanwhile sacrificed. By the first partition, in 1772, its outer territories were cut away. Russia took an eastern slice, around the city of Vitebsk. Austria took a southern slice, the region known as Galicia. Prussia took West Prussia, the region later called the Polish corridor. The Prussians thus at last realized their old ambition. Prussia now reached continuously as a solid block from the Elbe to the borders of Lithuania.[32] The partition sobered the Poles, who renewed their efforts at a national revival, hoping to create an effective sovereignty which could secure the country against outsiders. But the Polish movement lacked deeper strength, for it was confined mainly to the nobles, who had themselves brought the country to ruin. The mass of the serf population, and the Jews in the towns, did not care whether they were governed by Poles, Russians, or Germans. In addition, the Polish national revival was persistently blocked by the three neighboring powers. In 1792, when Europe was again at war in consequence of the great French Revolution, the three eastern powers seized the opportunity to finish with

[32] See map, pp. 198–9, panel 4.

Poland Since the Eighteenth Century

The top panel shows, in simplified form, the ethnic composition of the area included in the great Poland of 1772. In addition to languages shown, Yiddish was spoken by the large scattered Jewish population. Note how the line set in 1795 as the western boundary of Russia persists through later transformations. It reappears as the eastern border of Napoleon's Grand Duchy (p. 389), and of Congress Poland (p. 418). After the First World War the victorious Allies contemplated much this same line as Poland's eastern frontier (the dotted line in the fourth panel, known as the Curzon Line); but the Poles in 1920–1 conquered territory farther east (p. 726). After the Second World War the Russians pushed the Poles back to the same basic line, but compensated Poland with territory taken from Germany, as far west as the river Oder. If the reader will compare the position of Warsaw in each panel he will see how Poland has been shoved westward.

POLAND
SINCE THE EIGHTEENTH CENTURY

200 MILES

LANGUAGES

- POLISH
- LITHUANIAN
- LETTISH
- WHITE RUSSIAN
- UKRAINIAN
- GERMAN

Smolensk
Stettin
Warsaw
BALTIC SEA

THE THREE PARTITIONS
1772-1795

	1772	1793	1795
TO RUSSIA			
TO PRUSSIA			
TO AUSTRIA			

PRUSSIA
EAST PRUSSIA
Stettin
1772
1795
1793
Warsaw
1795
1793 1795 1793 1772
RUSSIA
Smolensk
1795
AUSTRIA
1772
1660 BOUNDARY
BALTIC SEA

DURING AND AFTER THE NAPOLEONIC ERA
1808-1831

- GRAND DUCHY OF WARSAW, 1808-1814
- CONGRESS POLAND, 1815-1831

BALTIC SEA
P R U S S I A
Stettin
Warsaw
Smolensk
RUSSIA
AUSTRIA
1772 BOUNDARY

AFTER WORLD WAR I
1922-1939

- POLAND, 1922-1939
- CURZON LINE, 1919

BALTIC SEA
Stettin
GERMANY
Warsaw
Smolensk
SOVIET UNION
CZECHOSL.
1772 BOUNDARY

AFTER WORLD WAR II

- POLAND AFTER WORLD WAR II

BALTIC SEA
Stettin
EAST GERMANY
Warsaw
Smolensk
SOVIET UNION
CZECHOSL.
1772 BOUNDARY

TRM

Poland. By the second and third partitions, in 1793 and 1795, they absorbed all the remaining Polish territory. Thereafter there was no really independent Polish state until 1918.

The three partitioning powers extenuated their conduct on various grounds. They even took pride in it as a diplomatic achievement, accomplished without war between the partitioners, and preserving the balance of power in eastern Europe. What seemed to be robbery was justified by the argument that the gains were equal; this was the diplomatic doctrine of "compensation." It was argued also that the partitions of Poland put an end to an old cause of international rivalry and war, replacing anarchy with solid government in a large area of eastern Europe. It is a fact that Poland was scarcely more independent before the partitions than after. It is to be noted also, though nationalist arguments were not much used at the time, that on national grounds the Poles themselves had no claim to large parts of the old Poland. The regions taken by Russia, in all three partitions, were inhabited overwhelmingly by White Russians and Ukrainians, among whom the Poles were mainly a landlord class. Russia, even in the third partition, reached only to the true ethnic border of Poland. But later, after the fall of Napoleon, by general international agreement, the Russian sphere was extended deep into the territory inhabited by Poles.

The partitions of Poland, however extenuated, were nevertheless a great shock to the old system of Europe. Many advanced thinkers of the day praised the partitions as a triumph of enlightened rulers, putting an end to an old nuisance. But Edmund Burke, in England, prophetically saw in the first partition the crumbling of the old international order. His diagnosis was a shrewd one. The principle of the balance of power had been historically invoked to preserve the independence of European states, to secure weak or small ones against Universal Monarchy. It was now used to destroy the independence of a weak but ancient kingdom. Not that Poland was the first to be "partitioned"; the Spanish and Swedish empires had been partitioned, and during the eighteenth century, as will be seen, there were attempts to partition Prussia and the Austrian empire also. But Poland was the first to be partitioned without war, and the first to disappear totally. That Poland was partitioned without war, a source of great satisfaction to the partitioning powers, was still a very unsettling fact. It was alarming for a huge state to vanish simply by cold diplomatic calculation. It seemed that no established rights were safe even in peacetime. The partitions of Poland showed that in a world where great powers had arisen, controlling modern apparatus of state, it was dangerous not to be strong. They suggested that any area failing to develop a sovereign state capable of keeping out foreign infiltration, and so situated as to be reached by the great powers of Europe, was unlikely to retain its independence. In this way they anticipated, for example, the partitions of Africa a century later, when Africa too, lacking strong governments, was almost totally divided, without war, among half a dozen states of Europe.

Moreover the partitions of Poland, while maintaining the balance in eastern Europe, profoundly changed the balance of Europe as a whole. The disappearance of Poland was a blow to France, which had long used Poland, as it had used Hungary and Turkey, as an outpost of French influence in the east. The three new eastern powers, especially Prussia and Russia, expanded their territory materially, while France enjoyed henceforth no permanent growth. Eastern Europe bulked larger than ever before in the affairs of Europe in general. Likewise in Germany, a kind of Europe in miniature, the eastern Germans, the Prussians and Austrians, bulked larger than ever in purely German affairs. Prussia, Russia, and the Austrian empire became contiguous by the partitions of Poland. They had an interest in common, the repression of Polish resistance to their rule. Polish resistance, dating from before the partitions and continuing after them, was the earliest example of modern revolutionary nationalism in Europe. The independence of Poland, and of other submerged nationalities, became in time a cause much favored in Western Europe, while the three great monarchies of Eastern Europe were drawn together in common opposition to nationalist programs; and this fact, plus the fact that the eastern monarchies were primarily landlord states, accentuated the characteristic division of Europe, in the nineteenth century, between a West that inclined to be liberal and an East that inclined to be reactionary. But these ideas anticipate a much later part of the story.

CHAPTER VI

The Struggle for Wealth and Empire

~~~~~~

27. The Global Economy of the Eighteenth Century
28. Western Europe after Utrecht, 1713–40
29. The Great War of the Mid-Eighteenth Century:
The Peace of Paris, 1763

IN THE preceding chapters we have followed the political history of western Europe through the War of the Spanish Succession, terminated in 1713–14 by the treaties of Utrecht and Rastadt. Affairs of Germany have been traced to 1740. In that year the new kingdom of Prussia and the new or renovated Austrian monarchy each passed into the hands of a new ruler and stood on the eve of a struggle with one another for ascendancy in central Europe, a struggle that merged with the world-wide contest of the mid-eighteenth century between the French and the British for world empire and for commercial supremacy. As for Eastern Europe, we have observed the Europeanizing and the expansion of the Russian Empire, and seen how the vast area called Poland ceased to form an independent state. Before turning to the great international issues of the mid-eighteenth century, we must first describe the important economic and social developments taking place in Europe and the expanding European world.

27. The Global Economy of the Eighteenth Century

The opening of the Atlantic in the sixteenth century, it will be recalled, had reoriented Europe. In an age of oceanic communications Europe became a center from which America, Asia, and Africa could all be reached. A global economy had been created. The first to profit had been the Portuguese and the Spanish, and they had retained their monopoly through most of the sixteenth century, but the decline of the Portuguese and Spanish had paved the way for the triumph of the British, the French, and the Dutch. In the eighteenth century the outstanding economic development was the expansion of the global economy and the fact that Europe, or at least the Atlantic region north of Spain, became incomparably wealthier than any other part of the world. The new wealth, in the widest sense, meaning conveniences in every form, was produced by increasing scientific and technical knowledge, which in turn it helped to produce; and the two together, more wealth and more knowledge, helped to form one of the most far-reaching ideas of modern times, the idea of progress. To the increase in scientific knowledge, the idea of progress, and other intellectual developments of this age, we shall return in the chapters that follow.

COMMERCE AND INDUSTRY IN THE EIGHTEENTH CENTURY

The new wealth of Europe was not like the age-old wealth of the gorgeous East, said by Milton to "shower on her kings barbaric pearl and gold." It consisted of gold, to be sure, but even more of bank deposits and facilities for credit, of more and better devices for mining coal, casting iron, and spinning thread, more productive agriculture, better and more comfortable houses, a wider variety of diet on the table, more and improved sailing ships, warehouses, and docks; more books, more newspapers, more medical instruments, more scientific equipment; greater government revenues, larger armies, and more numerous government employees. In the wealthy European countries, and because of the growing wealth, more people were freed from the necessity of toiling for food, clothing, and shelter, and were enabled to devote themselves to all sorts of specialized callings in government, management, finance, war, teaching, writing, inventing, exploring, and researching, and in producing the amenities rather than the barest necessities of life.

The increase of wealth was brought about by the methods of commercial capitalism and handicraft industry. Only at the close of the eighteenth century, and not really until the nineteenth century, did the use of steam engines and power-driven machinery, and the growth of large factories and great manufacturing cities, begin to bring about the conditions of modern industrialism. The economic system of the eighteenth century, while it contained within itself the seeds of later industrialism, represented the flowering of the older merchant capitalism, domestic industry and mercantilist government policies which had grown up since the sixteenth century and which have been already described.[1]

Most people in the eighteenth century lived in the country. Agriculture was the greatest single industry and source of wealth. Cities remained small. London and Paris, the largest of Europe, each had a population of 600,000 or 700,000, but the next largest cities did not much exceed 200,000, and in all Europe at the time of the French Revolution (in 1789) there were only fifty cities with as many as 50,000 people. Urbanization, however, was no sign of industrial advancement. Spain, Italy, and even the Balkan peninsula, according to an estimate made in the 1780's, each had more large cities (over 50,000) than did Great Britain. Urbanization did not equate with industry because most industry was carried on in the country, by peasants and part-time agricultural workers who worked for the merchant capitalists of the towns. Thus, while it is true to say that most people still lived in the country, it would be false to say that their lives and labors were devoted to agriculture exclusively. One English estimate, made in 1739, held that there were 4,250,000 persons "engaged in manufactures" in the British Isles, a figure that included women and children, and comprised almost half the entire population. These people worked characteristically in their own cottages, employed as wage earners by merchant capitalists under the "domestic" system.[2] Almost half of them, about 1,500,000, were engaged in the weaving and processing of woollens. Others were in the copper, iron, lead, and tin manufactures; others in leather goods; much smaller were the paper, glass, porcelain, silk, and linen trades; and smallest of all, in 1739, was the manufacture of cotton cloth, which accounted for only about 100,000 workers. The list suggests the importance of non-agricultural occupations in the preindustrial age.

England, even with half its population engaged at least part of the time in manufactures, was not yet the unrivaled manufacturing country that it was to become after 1800. England in the eighteenth century produced no more iron than Russia, and no more manufactures than France. The population of England was still small; it began to grow rapidly about 1760, but as late as 1800 France was still twice as populous as England and Scotland together. France, though less intensively developed than England, with probably far less than half its people "engaged in manufactures," nevertheless, because of its greater size, remained the chief industrial center of Europe.

Although foreign and colonial trade grew rapidly in the eighteenth century, it is probable that, in both Great Britain and France, the domestic or internal trade was greater in volume and occupied more people. Great Britain, with no internal tariffs, with an insignificant gild system, and with no monopolies allowed within the country except to inventors, was the largest area of internal free trade in Europe. France, or at least Colbert's Five Great

[1] See pp. 94–104.
[2] See p. 96.

Farms,[3] offered a free-trading internal market hardly less great. A great deal of economic activity was therefore domestic, consisting of exchange between town and town or between region and region. The proportions between domestic and international trade cannot be known. But foreign trade was important in that the largest enterprises were active in it, the greatest commercial fortunes were made in it, and the most capital was accumulated from it. And it was the foreign trade that led to international rivalry and war.

THE WORLD ECONOMY: THE DUTCH, BRITISH, AND FRENCH

In the international economic scene a great part was still played by the Dutch. After the Peace of Utrecht the Dutch ceased to be a great political power, nor did they become a great economic power in the sense of being an industrial center, for their country was too small to sustain manufactures in any great amount. But their role in commerce, shipping, and finance remained undiminished, or diminished only relatively by the continuing commercial growth of France and Great Britain. They were still the middlemen and common carriers for other peoples. Their freight rates remained the lowest of Europe. They continued to grow rich on imports from the East Indies. To a large extent also, in the eighteenth century, the Dutch simply lived on their investments. The capital they had accumulated over two hundred years they now lent out to French or British or other *entrepreneurs*. Dutch capital was to be found in every large commercial venture of Europe, and was lent to governments far and wide. A third of the capital of the Bank of England in the mid-eighteenth century belonged to Dutch shareholders. The Bank of Amsterdam remained the chief clearing-house and financial center of Europe. Its supremacy ended only with the invasion of Holland by a French Revolutionary army in 1795.

The Atlantic trade routes, leading to America, to Africa, and to Asia, tempted the merchants of many nationalities in Europe. A great many East India Companies were established—usually to do business in America as well as the East, for the "Indies" at the beginning of the eighteenth century was still a general term for the vast regions overseas. Both the English and the French East India Companies were reorganized, with an increased investment of capital, shortly after 1700. A number of others were established—by the Scotch, the Swedes, the Danes, the imperial free city of Hamburg, the republic of Venice, Prussia, and the Austrian monarchy. But, with the exception of the Danish company which lasted some sixty years, they all failed after only a few years, either for insufficiency of capital or because they lacked strong diplomatic, military, and naval support. Their failure showed that, in the trans-ocean trade, unassisted business enterprise was not enough. Merchants to succeed in this sphere needed strong national backing. Neither

[3] See p. 163.

free city, nor small kingdom, nor tiny republic, nor the amorphous Austrian empire provided a firm enough base.

It was the British and French who won out in the commercial rivalry of the eighteenth century. Britain and France were alike in having, besides a high level of industrial production at home, governments organized on a national scale and able to protect and advance, under mercantilist principles, the interests of their merchants in distant countries. For both peoples the eighteenth century—or the three quarters of a century between the end of the War of the Spanish Succession in 1713 and the beginning of the French Revolution in 1789—was an age of spectacular enrichment and commercial expansion.

Although the trade figures are difficult to arrive at, French foreign and colonial trade may well have grown even more rapidly than the British in the years between the 1720's and the 1780's. In any event, by the 1780's, the two countries were about equal in their total foreign and colonial trade. Of the areas with which they carried on their trade, the British in the 1780's enjoyed proportionately more than the French of the trade with overseas America and Asia; the French enjoyed considerably more of the trade with the rest of Europe and the Near East. The contest for markets played an important part in the colonial and commercial wars between Britain and France all through the eighteenth century and on into the final and climactic struggle, and British triumph, in the time of Napoleon.

ASIA, AMERICA, AND AFRICA IN THE GLOBAL ECONOMY

In the expanding global economy of the eighteenth century each continent played its special part. The trade with Asia was subject to an ancient limitation. Asia was almost useless as a market for European manufactures. There was much that Europeans wanted from Asia, but almost nothing that Asiatics wanted from Europe. The peoples of Chinese, Indian, and Malay culture had elaborate civilizations with which they were content; they lacked the dynamic restlessness of Europeans, and the masses were so impoverished (more so even than in Europe) that they could buy nothing anyway. Europeans found that they could send little to Asia except gold. The drain of gold from Europe to Asia had gone on since ancient times, and, accumulating over the centuries, was one source of the fabulous treasures of Oriental princes. To finance the swelling demand for Asiatic products it was necessary for Europeans constantly to replenish their stocks of gold. The British found an important new supply in Africa along the Gulf of Guinea, where one region is still called the Gold Coast. The word "guinea" became the name of a gold coin minted in England from 1663 to 1813, and is still used as a fashionable way of saying twenty-one shillings.

What Europeans sought from Asia was still in part spices—pepper and ginger, cinnamon and cloves—now brought in mainly by the Dutch from their East India islands. But they wanted manufactured goods also. Asia was still in some lines superior to Europe in technical skill. It is enough to mention rugs, chinaware, and cotton cloth. The very names by which cotton fabrics are known in English and other European languages reveal the places from which they were thought to come. "Madras" and "calico" refer to the Indian cities of Madras and Calicut, "muslin" to the Arabic city of Mosul. "Gingham" comes from a Malay word meaning "striped"; "chintz," from a Hindustani word meaning "spotted." Most of the Eastern manufactures were increasingly imitated in the eighteenth century in Europe. Axminister and Aubusson carpets competed with Oriental rugs. In 1709 a German named Boettcher discovered a formula for making a vitreous and translucent substance comparable to the porcelain of China; this European "china," made at Sèvres, Dresden, and in England, soon competed successfully with the imported original. Cotton fabrics were never produced in Europe at a price to compete with India until after the introduction of power machinery, which began in England about 1780. Before that date the demand for Indian cotton goods was so heavy that the woollen, linen, and silk interests became alarmed. They could produce nothing like the sheer muslins and bright calico prints which caught the public fancy, and many governments, to protect the jobs and capital involved in the old European textile industries, simply forbade the import of Indian cottons altogether. But it was a time of many laws and little enforcement, the forbidden fabrics continued to come in, and Daniel Defoe observed in 1708 that, despite the laws, cottons were not only sought as clothing by all classes, but "crept into our houses, our closets and bedchambers; curtains, cushions, chairs and at last beds themselves were nothing but calicoes or Indian stuffs." Gradually, in the face of tariff protection for "infant industries" in Europe, and the rapid growth of European cotton manufactures, import of cottons and other manufactures from Asia declined. After about 1770 most of the imports of the British East India Company consisted in tea, which was brought from China.

America in the eighteenth century bulked larger than Asia in the trade of western Europe. The American trade was based overwhelmingly on one commodity—sugar. Sugar had long been known in the East, and in the European Middle Ages little bits of it had trickled through to delight the palates of lords and prelates. About 1650 sugar cane was brought from the East and planted in the West Indies by Europeans. A whole new economic system arose in a few decades. It was based on the "plantation." A plantation was an economic unit consisting of a considerable tract of land, a sizable investment of capital, often owned by absentees in France or England, and a force of impressed labor, supplied by Negroes brought from Africa as slaves. Sugar, produced in quantity with cheap labor at low cost, proved to have an inexhaustible market. The eighteenth century was the golden age, economically speaking, of the West Indies. From its own islands alone, during the eighty years from 1713 to 1792, Great Britain imported a total of £162,000,000 worth of goods, almost all sugar; imports from India and China, in the same eighty years, amounted to only £104,000,000. The little islands of Jamaica, Barbados, St. Kitts, and others, as suppliers of Europe, not only dwarfed the whole mainland of British America but the whole mainland of Asia as well. For France, less well established than Britain on the American mainland and in Asia, the same holds with greater force. The richest of all the sugar colonies, San Domingo, now called Haiti, belonged to France.

The plantation economy, first established in sugar, and later in cotton (after 1800), brought Africa into the foreground. Slaves had been obtained from Negro Africa from time immemorial, both by the Roman Empire and by the Moslem world, both of which, however, enslaved blacks and whites indiscriminately. After the European discovery of America Negroes were taken across the Atlantic by the Spanish and Portuguese. Dutch traders landed Negroes in Virginia in 1619, a year before the arrival of the Pilgrim Fathers in Massachusetts. But slavery in the Americas before 1650 may be described as occasional. With the rise of the plantation economy after 1650, and especially after 1700, it became a fundamental economic institution. Slavery now formed the labor supply of a very substantial and heavily capitalized branch of world production. About 610,000 Negroes were landed from Africa in the island of Jamaica alone between 1700 and 1786. Total figures are hard to give, but it is certain that, until well after 1800, far more Africans than Europeans made the voyage to the Americas. The transatlantic slave trade in the eighteenth century was conducted mainly by English-speaking interests, principally in England but also in New England, followed as closely as they could manage it by the French. Yearly export of merchandise from Great Britain to Africa, used chiefly in exchange for slaves, increased tenfold between 1713 and 1792. As for merchandise coming into Britain from the British West Indies, virtually all produced by slaves, in 1790 it constituted almost a fourth of all British imports. If we add British imports from the American mainland, including what in 1776 became the United States, the importance of Negro labor to the British economic system will appear still greater, since a great part of exports from the mainland consisted in agricultural products, such as tobacco and indigo, produced partly by slaves. It can scarcely be denied that the phenomenal rise of British capitalism in the eighteenth century was based to a considerable extent on the enslavement of Africans. The town of Liverpool, an insignificant place on the Irish Sea in 1700, built itself up by the slave trade and the trade in slave-produced wares to a busy transatlantic commercial center, which in turn, as will be seen later, stimulated the "industrial revolution" in Manchester and other neighboring towns.[4]

The west-European merchants, British, French, and Dutch, sold the products of America and Asia to their own peoples and those of central and eastern Europe. Trade with Germany and Italy was fairly stable. With Russia it enormously increased. To cite the British record only, Britain imported fifteen times as much goods from Russia in 1790 as in 1700, and sold the Russians six times as much. The Russian landlords, as they became Europeanized, desired western manufactures and the colonial products such as

[4] See pp. 424–30.

sugar, tobacco, and tea which could be purchased only from western Europeans. They had grain, timber, and naval stores to offer in return. Similarly, landlords of Poland and north Germany, in the seventeenth and eighteenth centuries, found themselves increasingly able to move their agricultural products out through the Baltic, and hence increasingly able to buy the products of western Europe, America, and Asia in return. Landlords of eastern Europe thus had an incentive to make their estates more productive. "Big" agriculture spread, developing in Eastern Europe a system not unlike the plantation economy of the New World. It had many effects. It contributed, along with political causes, to reducing the bulk of the east-European population to serfdom. It helped to civilize and refine, in a word to "Europeanize," the upper classes. And it helped to enrich the merchants of western Europe.

THE WEALTH OF WESTERN EUROPE: SOCIAL CONSEQUENCES

The wealth which accumulated along the Atlantic seaboard of Europe was, in short, by no means produced by the efforts of western Europeans only. All the world contributed to its formation. The natural resources of the Americas, the resources and skills of Asia, the gold and manpower of Africa, all alike went into producing the vastly increased volume of goods moving in world commerce. Europeans directed the movement. They supplied capital; they contributed technical and organizing abilities; and it was the demand of Europeans, at home in Europe and as traders abroad, that set increasing numbers of Indians to spinning cotton, Chinese to raising tea, Malays to gathering spices, and Africans to the tending of sugar cane. A few non-Europeans might benefit in the process—Indian or Chinese merchants who dealt locally with Europeans, Indian potentates "subsidized" by the East India companies, African chiefs who captured slaves from neighboring tribes and sold them to Europeans. But the profits of the world economy really went to Europe. The new wealth, over and above what was necessary to keep the far-flung and polyglot labor force in being, and to pay other expenses, piled up in Britain, Holland, and France.

Here it was owned by private persons. It accumulated within the system of private property, and as part of the institutions of private enterprise or private capitalism. Governments were dependent on these private owners of property, for governments, in western Europe, had almost no source of revenue except loans and taxes derived from their peoples. When the wealth-owners gave their support, the government was strong and successful, as in England. When they withdrew support, the government collapsed, as it was to collapse in France in the Revolution of 1789.

In a technical sense there were many "capitalists" in western Europe, persons who had a little savings which they used to buy a parcel of land or a loom, or entrusted to some other person to invest at interest. And in a general sense the new wealth was widely distributed; the standard of living rose in western Europe in the eighteenth century. Tea, for example, which cost as much as £10 a pound when introduced into England about 1650, was an article of common consumption a hundred years later. But wealth used to produce more wealth, *i.e.*, capital, was owned or controlled in significant amounts by relatively few persons. In the eighteenth century some people became unprecedentedly rich (including some who started quite poor, for it was a time of open opportunity); the great intermediate layers of society became noticeably more comfortable; and the people at the bottom, such as the serfs of eastern Europe, the Irish peasantry, the dispossessed farm workers in England, the poorest peasants and workmen of France, were worse off than they had been before. The poor continued to live in hovels. The prosperous created for themselves that pleasant world of the eighteenth century that is still admired, a world of well-ordered Georgian homes, closely cropped lawns and shrubs, furniture by Chippendale or *à la* Louis XV, coaches-and-four, family portraits, high chandeliers, books bound in morocco, and a staff of servants "below stairs."

Families enriched by commerce, and especially the daughters, mixed and intermarried with the old families which owned land. The merchant in England or France no sooner became prosperous than he bought himself a landed estate. In France he might also purchase a government office or patent of nobility. Contrariwise, the landowning gentleman, especially in England, no sooner increased his landed income than he invested the proceeds in commercial enterprise or government bonds. The two forms of property, bourgeois and aristocratic, tended to merge. Until toward the end of the century the various propertied interests worked harmoniously together, and the unpropertied classes were of no political consequence. Hence the period, though one of commercial expansion, was an age of considerable social stability in western Europe.

The foregoing might be illustrated from the lives of thousands of men and women. Two examples are enough, one English and one French. They

---

The Hon. Mrs. Graham

BY THOMAS GAINSBOROUGH (ENGLISH, 1727–88)

The meaning of aristocracy is abundantly evident in this picture of a young gentlewoman, whose title, "The Honorable" is still used in Great Britain for the daughters of viscounts and barons. Wealth is apparent in the brooch, the plumes, the silks, bows and ruffles, and in the pearls which are both worn in strings and sewn on the hat and garments. The meticulous coiffure and complexities of dress suggest the constant attentions of lady's maids. The tall stature, delicate hands, refined mouth and haughty expression all reveal high breeding, and the classical colonnade on which the lady so casually rests her arm lends an air of familiarity with magnificent surroundings. Perhaps the aristocrats of the eighteenth century did not often look like this, but this is the way they liked to imagine themselves and to be portrayed for posterity. In Gainsborough, Sir Joshua Reynolds, and Sir Thomas Lawrence, England had an unparalleled group of artists who specialized in painting the upper class. Courtesy of the National Gallery of Scotland.

show the working of the world economic system, the rise of the commercial class in western Europe, and the role of that class in the political life of the western countries.

Thomas Pitt, called "Diamond" Pitt, was born in 1653, the son of a parish clergyman in the Church of England. He went to India in 1674. Here he operated as an "interloper," trading in defiance of the legal monopoly of the East India Company. Returning to England, he was prosecuted by the Company and fined £400, but was rich enough to buy the manor of Stratford and with it the borough of Old Sarum, a rotten borough which gave him a seat in the House of Commons without the trouble of an election. He soon returned to India, again as an interloper, where he competed so successfully with the Company that it finally took him into its own employment. He traded on his own account, as well as for the Company, sent back some new chintzes to England, and defended Madras against the nawab of the Carnatic, buying off the nawab with money. In 1702, though his salary was only £300 a year, he purchased a 410-carat uncut diamond for £20,400. He bought it from an Indian merchant who had himself bought it from an English skipper, who in turn had stolen it from the slave who had found it in the mines, and who had concealed it in a wound in his leg. Back in Europe, Pitt had his diamond cut at Amsterdam and sold it in 1717 to the regent of France for £135,000. The regent put it in the French crown; it was appraised at the time of the French Revolution at £480,000. A daughter of "Diamond" Pitt became the Countess of Stanhope, one of his sons the Earl of Londonderry. Another son became father to the William Pitt who guided Britain through the Seven Years' War with France, and who was raised to the peerage as the Earl of Chatham. After this Pitt the city of Pittsburgh was named, so that a fortune gained in the East gave its name to a frontier settlement in the interior of America. Chatham's younger son, the second William Pitt, became prime minister at twenty-four. The younger Pitt guided Britain through another and greater war with France, until his death in 1805 during the high tide of the Napoleonic empire.

Jean-Joseph Laborde was born in 1724, of a bourgeois family of south-

---

Mrs. Seymour Fort

BY JOHN SINGLETON COPLEY (AMERICAN, 1737–1815)

Mrs. Fort may be contrasted with the Hon. Mrs. Graham. Mrs. Fort, a New England woman, may have belonged to the aristocracy of colonial America, but in the larger sphere of European civilization she would count as middle-class. Whatever Mrs. Fort in real life may have been like, the picture may be taken to typify, in its portrayal of a middle-aged woman, the bourgeois family background from which came most of the leadership of the American and French revolutions. It was generally a background of substance, comfort, and hard work. The lady in the picture has chosen to be represented at her needlework, erect in her chair. Her expression is between the prim and the pleasant. She is neither fashionable nor elegant, but she clearly represents, and expects from others, a settled standard of behavior and decorum. Courtesy of the Wadsworth Atheneum, Hartford.

ern France. He went to work for an uncle who had a business at Bayonne trading with Spain and the East. From the profits he built up vast plantations and slave-holdings in San Domingo. His ships brought sugar to Europe, and returned with prefabricated building materials, each piece carefully numbered, for his plantations and refineries in the West Indies. He became one of the leading bankers in Paris. His daughter became the Countess de Noailles. He himself received the title of marquis, which he did not use. He bought a number of manors and chateaux near Paris. As a real estate operator he developed that part of Paris, then suburban, now called the Chaussée d'Antin. During the Seven Years' War he was sent by the French government to borrow money in Spain, where he was told that Spain would lend nothing to Louis XV, but would gladly lend him personally 20,000,000 *reals*. In the War of American Independence he raised 12,000,000 *livres* in gold for the government, to help pay the French army and navy, thus contributing to the success of the American Revolution. He acted as investment agent for Voltaire, gave 24,000 *livres* a year to charity, and subscribed 400,000 *livres* in 1788 toward building new hospitals in Paris. In July 1789 he helped to finance the insurrection which led to the fall of the Bastille and the Revolution. His son, in June 1789, took the Oath of the Tennis Court, swearing to write a constitution for France. He himself was guillotined in 1794. His children turned to scholarship and the arts.

28. Western Europe after Utrecht

The Peace of Utrecht registered the defeat of French ambitions in the wars of Louis XIV. The French move toward "universal monarchy" had been blocked. The European state system had been preserved. Europe was to consist of a number of independent and sovereign states, all legally free and equal, continuously entering or leaving alliances along the principles of the balance of power. More specifically, the peace settlement of 1713–14 placed the Bourbon Philip V on the Spanish throne, but partitioned the Spanish empire.[5] Spain itself, with Spanish America and the Philippines, went to Philip V. Of the remaining Spanish possessions, Belgium, Milan, and Naples-Sicily went to the Austrian Hapsburgs, Sardinia ultimately to the Duke of Savoy, Minorca and Gibraltar to Great Britain. Britain likewise took from France Newfoundland, Nova Scotia, and the Hudson Bay region. Great Britain, consolidated during the wars as a combined kingdom of England and Scotland, installed as a naval power in the Mediterranean, winning territory from France and Spain, and receiving trading rights within the hitherto closed domain of Spanish America, emerged as the most dynamic of the Atlantic powers.

wwwwwwwwwwww

[5] See pp. 168–72 and map, p. 169.

SPAIN AND THE LESSER WESTERN POWERS AFTER 1713

For a time Europe was troubled by the unwillingness of many in Spain to accept the treaty. The Spanish queen, an Italian woman named Elizabeth Farnese, went to great lengths to acquire a kingdom in Italy for her younger son, an operation characteristic enough of the international politics of the day, and one in which she found much support in Spain among patriots who resented the loss of Spanish holdings in Italy and the Mediterranean. A minor war over this matter broke out in 1719. In the 1730's France and Spain fought Austria in the War of the Polish Succession.[6] As a result of the war Austria ceded the kingdom of the Two Sicilies to the Spanish on condition that it never be joined to Spain. A separate Bourbon monarchy was thus established in south Italy, and there were now three Bourbon kingdoms, France, Spain, and the Two Sicilies. In general the period from 1713 to 1740 was one of relative peace in western Europe. Not until after 1740 were the full efforts of the western peoples again engaged in a military struggle.

Men in authority turned to repairing the damages of war. Spain was somewhat rejuvenated by the French influence under its new Bourbon house. The drift and decadence that had set in under the last Hapsburgs were at least halted. The Spanish monarchy was administratively strengthened. Its officials followed the absolutist government of Louis XIV as a model. The estates of the east-Spanish kingdoms, Aragon and Valencia, ceased to meet, going like the Estates-General of France into the limbo of obsolete institutions. They had chosen the losing side in the Spanish civil war that accompanied the War of the Spanish Succession, and their disappearance in the reign of Philip V removed a source of the localism and cross purposes which afflicted Spain. On the whole the French influence in eighteenth-century Spain was intangible. Nothing was changed in substance, but the old machinery functioned with more precision. Administrators were better trained and took a more constructive attitude toward government work; they became more aware of the world north of the Pyrenees, and recovered confidence in their country's future. They tried also to tighten up the administration of their American empire. More revenue officers and coast guards were introduced in the Caribbean, whose zeal led to repeated clashes with smugglers, mainly British. Friction on the Spanish Main, reinforced by Spanish dislike for British occupation of Gibraltar, kept Spain and Britain in a continual ferment of potential hostility.

The Dutch after Utrecht receded from the political stage, though their alliance was always sought because of the huge shipping and financial resources they controlled. The Swiss also became important in banking and financial circles. The Belgians founded an overseas trading company in 1723 on the authority of their new Austrian ruler; this "Ostend Company" sent out six voyages to China, which were highly profitable, but the commercial

---

[6] See pp. 218–19.

jealousy of the Dutch and British obliged the Austrian emperor to withdraw his support, so that the enterprise soon came to an end. The Scotch began at about this time to play their remarkable role of energizing business affairs in many countries. Union with England gave them access to the British empire and to the numerous commercial advantages won by the English. John Law, the financial wizard of France, was a Scotsman, as was William Paterson, one of the chief founders of the Bank of England.

FRANCE AND BRITAIN AFTER 1713

Our main attention falls on Britain and France. Though one was the victor and the other the vanquished in the wars ended in 1713, and though one stood for absolutism and the other for constitutionalism in government, their development in the years after Utrecht was in some ways surprisingly parallel. In both countries for some years the king was personally ineffective, and in both the various propertied interests therefore gained many advantages. Both enjoyed the commercial expansion described above. Both went through a short period of financial experimentation and frantic speculation in stocks, the bubble bursting in each case in 1720. Each was thereafter governed by a statesman, Cardinal Fleury in France and Robert Walpole in England, whose policy was to keep peace abroad and conciliate all interests at home. Fleury and Walpole held office for about two decades, toward the end of which the two countries again went to war. But the differences are at least as instructive as the parallels.

In France the new king was a child, Louis XV, the great-grandson of Louis XIV, and only five years old when he began to reign in 1715. The government was entrusted to a regent, the Duke of Orleans, an elder cousin of the young king. Orleans, lacking the authority of a monarch, had to admit the aristocracy to a share in power. Most of the nobles had never liked the absolutism of Louis XIV, and there was much dissatisfaction with absolutism among all classes, because of the ruin and suffering brought by Louis XIV's wars.

The nobles, ousted by Louis XIV, now reappeared in the government. For a time Orleans worked through committees of noblemen, roughly corresponding to ministries, a system lauded by its backers as a revival of political freedom; but the committees proved so incompetent that they were soon abandoned. The old parliaments of France,[7] and especially the Parliament of Paris, which Louis XIV had reduced to silence, vigorously reasserted themselves after his death. The parliaments were primarily law courts, originally composed of bourgeois judges; but Louis XIV and his predecessors, to raise money, had made the judgeships into salable offices, to which they attached titles of nobility to increase the price. Hence in the time of the Regency the judges of the parliaments had bought or inherited their seats, and were almost

[7] See pp. 156–7, 160.

all nobles. Because they had property rights in their offices, they could not be removed by the king. The Regent conceded much influence to the Parliament of Paris, utilizing it to modify the will of Louis XIV. The parliaments broadened their position, claiming the right to assent to legislation and taxes, through refusing to enforce what they considered contrary to the unwritten constitution or fundamental laws of France. They managed to exercise this right, off and on, from the days of the Regency until the great Revolution of 1789. The eighteenth century, for France, was a period of absolutism checked and balanced by organized privileged groups. It was an age of aristocratic resurgence, in which the nobles won back many powers of which Louis XIV had tried to deprive them.

In Great Britain the Parliament was very different from the French parliaments, and the British aristocracy was more politically competent than the *noblesse* of France. Parliament proved an effective machine for the conduct of public business. The House of Lords was hereditary, with the large exception of the bishops, who were appointed by the government and made up about a quarter of the active members of the upper house. The House of Commons was not at all representative of the country according to modern ideas. Only the wealthy, or those patronized by the wealthy, could sit in it,[8] and they were chosen by diverse and eccentric methods, in counties and towns, almost without regard to the size or wishes of the population. Some boroughs were owned outright, like the Old Sarum of the Pitt family. But through the machinations of bosses, or purchase of seats, all kinds of interests managed to get representatives into the Commons. Some members spoke for the "landed interest," others for the "funded interest" (mainly government creditors), others for the "London interest," the "West India interest," the "East India interest" and others. All politically significant groups could expect to have their desires heeded in Parliament, and all therefore were willing to go through parliamentary channels. Parliament was corrupt, slow, and expensive, but it was effective. For Parliament was not only a roughly representative body; it could also act, having acquired, in practice, a sovereign power of legislation.

Queen Anne, the last reigning Stuart, died in 1714. She was succeeded by George I, Elector of Hanover, as provided for by Parliament in the Act of Settlement of 1701.[9] George I was the nearest relative of the Stuarts who was also a Protestant. A heavy middle-aged German who spoke no English, he continued to spend much of his time in Germany, and he brought with him to England a retinue of German ministers and favorites and two ungainly mistresses, dubbed in England the "Elephant and the Maypole." He was never popular in England, where he was regarded as at best a political convenience. He was in no position to play a strong hand in English public life, and during his reign Parliament gained much independence from the crown.

〰〰〰〰〰〰〰〰〰

[8] See pp. 154–5.
[9] See p. 153.

The main problem was still whether the principles of the revolution of 1688 should be maintained.[10] The agreement of parties which had made that revolution relatively bloodless proved to be temporary. The Whigs, who considered the revolution as their work, long remained a minority made up of a few great landowning noblemen, wealthy London merchants, lesser business people, and Non-conformists in religion. The Whigs generally controlled the House of Lords, but the House of Commons was more uncertain; at the time of the Peace of Utrecht its majority was Tory. We have already noted the significance for English constitutional development of the conflict at that time between the pro-war Whig majority in the House of Lords and the Tory majority in Commons, and how the conflict was resolved to help establish the primacy of the House of Commons.[11] For half a century after 1714 the House of Commons was in Whig hands. The bulk of the country, however, probably long remained Tory in sympathy. Gentry and yeomen of the shires and byways, and the populace of London, were easily aroused against the great noblemen and men of money who led the Whigs. In the established Anglican church the lesser clergy were often Tory, though the bishops were mostly Whigs. Outside the official church were a group of Anglican clergy who refused the oath of loyalty after 1688 and were called Non-Jurors; they held that the church must not be controlled by the state, and kept alive a shadow-church until 1805. In Scotland also, the ancestral home of the Stuarts, many were disaffected with the new regime.

Tories, Non-Jurors, and Scots made up a milieu after 1688 in which what would now be called counter-revolution might develop. Never enthusiastic for the "Whig wars" against France,[12] critical of the mounting national debt which the wars created, distrustful of the business and moneyed interests, they began to look wistfully to the exiled Stuarts. After 1701, when James II died in France, the Stuart claims devolved upon his son, whose birth in 1688 had precipitated the revolution, and who lived until 1766, scheming time and again to make himself king of England. His partisans were known as Jacobites, from *Jacobus*, the Latin for James; they regarded him as "James III," where others called him the Pretender. The Jacobites felt that, at least if he would give up his Catholic religion, he should be accepted as Britain's rightful king. To strengthen his claims they kept agitating the theory of divine right.

The Whigs could not tolerate a return of the Stuarts. The restoration of "James III" and his divine-right partisans would undo the principles of the Glorious Revolution—limited monarchy, constitutionalism, Parliamentary supremacy, the rule of law, the toleration of dissenting Protestants, in short all that was summarized and defended in the writings of John Locke.[13] Moreover, those who held stock in the Bank of England or who had lent their money to the government would be ruined, since "James III" would surely

---

[10] See pp. 152–5.
[11] See pp. 168–70.
[12] See pp. 168–70.
[13] See pp. 285–7.

repudiate a debt contracted by his foes. The Whigs were bound to support the Hanoverian George I. And George I was bound to look for support in a strange country among the Whigs.

George lacked personal appeal even for his English friends. To his enemies he was ridiculous and repulsive. The successful establishment of his dynasty would ruin the hopes of Tories and Jacobites. In 1715 the Pretender landed in Scotland, gathered followers from the Highlands, and proclaimed a rebellion against George I. Civil war seemed to threaten. But the Jacobite leaders bungled, and many of their followers proved to be undecided. They were willing enough to toast the "king over the water" in protest against the Whigs, but not willing in a showdown to see the Stuarts, with all that went with them, again in possession of the crown of England. The Fifteen, as the revolt came to be called, petered out. But thirty years later came the Forty-five. In 1745, during war with France, the Pretender's son, "Bonnie Prince Charlie" or the "Young Pretender," again landed in Scotland and again proclaimed rebellion. This time, though almost no one in England rallied, the uprising was more successful. A Scottish force penetrated to within eighty miles of London, and was driven back and crushed with the help of Hanoverian regiments rushed over from Germany. The government set out to destroy Jacobitism in the Highlands. The social system of the Highlands was wiped out; the clans were broken up; McDuffs and McDougals were forcibly reorganized according to modern notions of property and of landlord and tenant.[14]

The Jacobite uprisings confirmed the old reputation of England in the eyes of Europe, namely, as Voltaire said, that its government was as stormy as the seas which surrounded it. To partisans of monarchy on the Continent they illustrated the weaknesses of parliamentary government. But their ignominious collapse actually strengthened the parliamentary regime in England. They left little permanent mark, and soon passed into an atmosphere of romantic legend. Many Tories, however, continued to believe in the value of a strong and independent ruler. For example, Henry St. John, Viscount Bolingbroke, a Jacobite until after 1715, published in 1749 his *Idea of a Patriot King*, in which he argued that the king should be a popular leader, balancing the interest of the whole country against the special interests of the propertied classes. These views influenced George III, who acceded in 1760, and who, as is well known to Americans, by his efforts to "be a king" provoked the rebellion of the American colonists.[15]

THE "BUBBLES" AND THEIR EFFECTS

Meanwhile, immediately after the Peace of Utrecht, the problem of dealing with a post-war economic situation had to be faced in both England and France. In both countries it meant finding a way to carry the greatly

[14] See pp. 248, 321–2.
[15] See pp. 320–7.

swollen government debt. Organized permanent public debt was new at the time. The possibilities and limitations of large-scale banking, paper money, and credit were not clearly seen. In France there was much amazement at the way in which England and Holland, though smaller and less wealthy than France, had been able to maximize their resources through banking and credit and even to finance the alliance which had eclipsed the Sun King. In addition there was much private demand for both lending and borrowing money. Private persons all over western Europe were looking for enterprises in which to invest their savings. And promoters and organizers, anticipating a profit in this or that line of business, were looking for capital with which to work. Out of this whole situation grew the "South Sea bubble" in England and the "Mississippi bubble" in France. Both bubbles broke in 1720, and both had important long-range effects.

A close tie between government finance and private enterprise was usual at the time, under mercantilist ideas of government guidance of trade. In England, for example, a good deal of the government debt was held by companies organized for that purpose. The government would charter a company, strengthen it with a monopoly in a given line of business, and then receive from the company, after the stockholders had bought up the shares, a large sum of cash as a loan. Much of the British debt, contracted in the wars from 1689 to 1713, was held in this way by the Bank of England, founded in 1694; [16] by the East India Company, reorganized in 1708 in such a way as to provide funds for the government; and by the South Sea Company, founded in 1713. The Bank enjoyed a legal monopoly over certain banking operations in London, the East India Company over trade with the East, the South Sea Company for exploiting the *asiento* [17] and other commercial privileges extorted from Spain. The companies were owned by private investors. Savings drawn from trade and agriculture, put into shares in these companies, became available both for economic reinvestment and for use of the government in defraying the costs of war.

In 1716 the Prince Regent of France was attracted to a Scotch financier, John Law, reputedly by Law's remarkable mathematical system in gambling at cards. Law founded a much needed French central bank. In the next year, 1717, he organized a *Compagnie d'Occident*, popularly called the Mississippi Company, which obtained a monopoly of trade with Louisiana, where it founded New Orleans in 1718. This Company, under Law's management, soon absorbed the French East India, China, Senegal, and African companies. It now enjoyed a legal monopoly of all French colonial trade. Law then proposed, and was authorized by the Regent, to assume the entire government debt. The Company received from individuals their certificates of royal indebtedness or "bonds," and gave them shares of Company stock in

[16] See p. 154.
[17] See p. 171.

return. It proposed to pay dividends on these shares, and to extinguish the debt, from profits in the colonial trade and from a monopoly over the collection of all indirect taxes in France. The project carried with it a plan for drastic reform of the whole taxation system, to make taxes both more fair to the taxpayer and more lucrative to the government. Shares in the Mississippi Company were gobbled up by the public. There was a frenzy of speculation, a wild fear of not buying soon enough. Quotations rose to 18,000 livres a share. But the Company rested only on unrealized projects. Shareholders began to fear for their money. They began to unload. The market broke sharply. Many found their life savings gone. Others lost ancestral estates on which they had borrowed in the hope of getting rich. Those, however, who had owned shares in the Company before the rise, and who had resisted the speculative fever, lost nothing by the bursting of inflated prices, and later enjoyed a gilt-edged commercial investment.

Much the same thing happened in England, where it was thought by many that Law was about to provide a panacea for France. The South Sea Company, outbidding the Bank of England, took over a large fraction of the public debt by receiving government "bonds" from their owners in return for shares of its stock. The size and speed of profits to be made in Spanish America were greatly exaggerated, and the market value of South Sea shares rose rapidly for a time, reaching £1050 for a share of £100 par value. Other schemes abounded in the passion for easy money. Promoters organized mining and textile companies, as well as others of more fanciful or bolder design: a company to bring live fish to market in tanks, an insurance company to insure female chastity, a company "for an undertaking which shall in due time be revealed." Shares in such enterprises were snatched at mounting prices. But in September 1720 the South Sea stockholders began to sell, doubting whether operations would pay dividends commensurate to £1000 a share. They dragged down the whole unstable structure. As in France, many people found that their savings or their inheritances had disappeared.

Indignation in both countries was extreme. Both governments were implicated in the scandal. John Law fled to Brussels. The Regent was discredited; he resigned in 1723, and French affairs were afterwards conducted by Cardinal Fleury. In England there was a change of ministers. Robert Walpole, a country gentleman of Whig persuasion, who had long sat in the Commons, and who had warned against the South Sea scheme from the beginning, became the principal minister to George I.

Britain recovered from the crisis more successfully than France. Law's bank, a useful institution, was dissolved in the reaction against him. France lacked an adequate banking system during the rest of the century. French investors developed a morbid fear of paper securities, and a marked preference for putting their savings into land. Commercial capitalism and the growth of credit institutions in France were retarded. In England the same fears were felt. Parliament passed the "Bubble Act," forbidding all companies except those specifically chartered by the government to raise capital by the sale of stock. In both countries the development of joint-stock financing along the lines of the modern corporation was slowed down for over a century. Business enterprises continued to be typically owned by individuals and partnerships, which expanded by reinvestment of their own profits, and so had another reason to keep profits up and wages down. But in England Walpole managed to save the South Sea Company, the East India Company, and the Bank, all of which were temporarily discredited in the eyes of the public. England continued to perfect its financial machinery.

The credit of the two governments was also shaken by the "bubbles." Much of the French war debt was repudiated in one way or another. Repudiation was in many cases morally justifiable, for many government creditors were unscrupulous war profiteers, but financially it was disastrous, for it discouraged honest people from lending their money to the state. Nor was much accomplished toward reform of the taxes. The nobles continued to evade the taxes imposed on them by Louis XIV, John Law's plans for taxation evaporated with the rest of his project, and when in 1726 a finance minister tried to levy a two per cent tax on all property, the vested interests, led by the Parliament of Paris, annihilated this proposal also. Lacking an adequate revenue, and repudiating its debts, the French monarchy had little credit. The conception of public or national debt hardly developed in France in the eighteenth century. The debt was considered to be the king's debt, for which no one except a few ministers felt any responsibility. The Bourbon government in fact often borrowed through the church, the provincial estates, or the city of Paris, which lenders considered to be better financial risks than the king himself. The government was severely handicapped in its foreign policy and its wars. It could not fully tap the wealth of its own subjects.

In England none of the debt was repudiated. Walpole managed to launch and keep going the system of the sinking fund, by which the government regularly set aside the wherewithal to pay interest and principal on its obligations. The credit of the British government became absolutely firm. The debt was considered a national debt, for which the British people itself assumed the responsibility. Parliamentary government made this development possible. In France no one could tell what the king or his ministers might do, and hence everyone was reluctant to trust them with his money. In England the people who had the money could also, through Parliament, determine the policies of state, decide what the money should be spent for, and levy enough taxes to maintain confidence in the debt. Similarities to France there were; the landowners who controlled the British Parliament, like those who controlled the Parliament of Paris, resisted direct taxation, so that the British government drew two-thirds or more of its revenues from indirect taxes paid by the mass of the population. Yet landowners, even dukes, did pay important amounts of taxes. There were no exemptions by class or rank, as in France. All propertied interests had a stake in the government. The wealth of the country stood behind the national debt. The national credit seemed inexhaustible. This was the supreme trump card of the British in their wars with France from the founding of the Bank of England in 1694 to the fall of Napoleon a hundred and twenty years later. And it was the political freedom of England that gave it its economic strength.

FLEURY IN FRANCE; WALPOLE IN ENGLAND

Fleury was seventy-three years old when he took office, and ninety when he left it. He was not one to initiate programs for the distant future. Louis XV, as he came of age, proved to be indolent and selfish. Public affairs drifted, while France grew privately more wealthy, especially the commercial and bourgeois classes. Walpole likewise kept out of controversies. His motto was *quieta non movere,* "let sleeping dogs lie." It was to win over the Tory squires to the Hanoverian and Whig regime that Walpole kept down the land taxes; this policy was successful, and Jacobitism quieted down. Walpole supported the Bank, the trading companies, and the financial interests, and they in turn supported him. It was a time of political calm, in which the lower classes were quiet and the upper classes not quarreling, favorable therefore to the development of parliamentary institutions.

Walpole is usually called the first prime minister and the architect of cabinet government, a system in which the ministers, or executives, are also members of the legislative body. He saw to it, by careful rigging, that a majority in the Commons always supported him. He avoided issues on which his majority might be lost. He thus began to acknowledge the principle of cabinet responsibility to a majority in Parliament, which was to become an important characteristic of cabinet government. And by selecting colleagues who agreed with him, and getting rid of those who did not, he advanced the idea of the cabinet as a body of ministers bound to each other and to the prime minister, obligated to follow the same policies and to stand or fall as a group. Thus Parliament was not only a representative or deliberative body like the diets and estates on the Continent, but one that developed an effective executive organ, without which neither representative government nor any government could survive.

To assure peace and quiet in domestic politics the best means was to avoid raising taxes. And the best way to avoid taxes was to avoid war. Fleury and Walpole both tried to keep at peace. They were not in the long run successful. Fleury was drawn into the War of the Polish Succession in 1733. Walpole kept England out of war until 1739. He always had a war party to contend with, and the most bellicose were those interested in the American trade—the slave trade, the sugar plantations, and the illicit sale of goods in the Spanish empire. The British official figures show that while trade with Europe, in the eighteenth century, was always less in war than in peace, trade with America always increased during war, except, indeed, during the War of American Independence.

In the 1730's there were constant complaints of indignities suffered by sturdy Britons on the Spanish Main. The war party produced a Captain Jenkins, who carried with him a small box containing a withered ear, which he said had been cut from his head by the outrageous Spaniards. Testifying in the House of Commons, where he "commended his soul to God and his cause to his country," he stirred up a commotion which led to war. So in 1739, after twenty-five years of peace, England plunged with wild enthusiasm into the War of Jenkins' Ear. "They are ringing the bells now," said Walpole; "they will soon be wringing their hands." The war soon became merged in a conflict involving Europeans and others in all parts of the world.

29. The Great War of the Mid-Eighteenth Century

The fighting lasted until 1763, with an uneasy interlude between 1748 and 1756. It went by many names. The opening hostilities between England and Spain were called, by the English, the War of Jenkins' Ear. The Prussians spoke of three "Silesian" wars. The struggle on the Continent in the 1740's was often known as the War of the Pragmatic Sanction. British colonials in America called the fighting of the 1740's King George's War, or used the term "French and Indian Wars," for the whole sporadic conflict. Disorganized and nameless struggles at the same time shook the peoples of India. The names finally adopted by history were the War of the Austrian Succession for operations between 1740 and 1748, and the Seven Years' War for those between 1756 and 1763. The two wars were really one. They involved the same two principal issues, the duel of Britain and France for colonies, trade, and sea power, and the duel of Prussia and Austria for territory and military power in central Europe.

EIGHTEENTH-CENTURY WARFARE

Warfare at the time was in a kind of classic phase, which strongly affected the development of events. It was somewhat slow, formal, elaborate, and indecisive. The enlisted ranks of armies and navies were filled with men considered economically useless, picked up by recruiting officers among unwary loungers in taverns or on the wharves. All governments protected their productive population, peasants, mechanics, and bourgeois, preferring to keep them at home, at work, and paying taxes. Soldiers were a class apart, enlisted for long terms, paid wages, professional in their outlook, and highly trained. They lived in barracks or great forts, and were dressed in bright uniforms (like the British "redcoats"), which, since camouflage was unnecessary, they wore even in battle. Weapons were not destructive; infantry was predominant, and was armed with the smooth-bore musket, to which the bayonet could be attached. In war the troops depended on great supply depots built up beforehand, which were practically immovable with the transportation available, so that armies, at least in central and western Europe, rarely operated more than a few days' march from their bases. Soldiers fought methodically for pay. Generals hesitated to risk their troops, which took years to train and equip, and were very expensive. Strategy took the form, not of seeking out the enemy's main force to destroy it in battle, but of maneuvering for advantages of position, applying a cumulative and subtle pressure somewhat as in a game of chess.

There was little national feeling, or feeling of any kind. The Prussian army recruited half or more of its enlisted personnel outside Prussia; the British army was largely made up of Hanoverian or other German regiments; even the French army had German units incorporated in it. Deserters from one side were enlisted by the other. War was between governments, or between the oligarchies and aristocracies which governments represented, not between whole peoples. It was fought for power, prestige, or calculated practical interests, not for ideologies, moral principles, world conquest, national survival, or ways of life. Popular nationalism had developed farthest in England, where "Rule Britannia" and "God Save the King," both breathing a low opinion of foreigners, became popular songs during these mid-eighteenth-century wars.

Civilians were little affected, except in India or the American wilderness where European conditions did not prevail. In Europe, a government aspiring to conquer a neighboring province did not wish to ruin or antagonize it beforehand. The fact that the west-European struggle was largely naval kept it well outside civilian experience. Never had war been so harmless, certainly not in the religious wars of earlier times, or in the national wars initiated later. This was one reason why governments went to war so lightly. On the other hand governments also withdrew from war much more readily than in later times. Their treasuries might be exhausted, their trained soldiers used up; only practical or rational questions were at stake; there was no war hysteria or pressure of mass opinion; the enemy of today might be the ally of tomorrow. Peace was almost as easy to make as war. Peace treaties were negotiated, not imposed. So the eighteenth century saw a series of wars and treaties, more wars, treaties and rearrangements of alliances, all arising over much the same issues, and with exactly the same powers present at the end as at the beginning.

THE WAR OF THE AUSTRIAN SUCCESSION, 1740–48

The War of the Austrian Succession was started by the king of Prussia. Frederick II, or the "Great," was a young man of twenty-eight when he became king in 1740. His youth had not been happy; he was temperamentally incompatible with his father. His tastes as a prince had run to playing the flute, corresponding with French men of letters, and writing prose and verse in the French language. His father, the sober Frederick William I,[18] thought him frivolous and effeminate, and dealt with him so clumsily that at the age

[18] See p. 204.

of eighteen he tried to escape from the kingdom. Caught and brought back, he was forced to witness the execution, by his father's order, of the friend and companion who had shared in his attempted flight. Frederick changed as the years passed from a jaunty youth to an aged cynic, equally undeceived by himself, his friends, or his enemies, and seeing no reason to expect much from human nature. Though his greatest reputation was made as a soldier, he retained his literary interests all his life, became a historian of merit, and is perhaps of all modern monarchs the only one who would have a respectable standing if considered only as a writer. An unabashed free thinker, like many others of his day, he considered all religions ridiculous and laughed at the divine right of kings; but he would have no nonsense about the rights of the House of Brandenburg, and he took a solemn view of the majesty of the State.

Frederick, in 1740, lost no time in showing a boldness which his father would have surely dreaded. He decided to conquer Silesia,[19] and on December 16, 1740, he invaded that province, a region adjoining Prussia, lying in the upper valley of the Oder, and belonging to the kingdom of Bohemia and hence to the Danubian empire of the Hapsburgs. The Pragmatic Sanction, a general agreement signed by the European powers, including Prussia, had stipulated that all domains of the Austrian Hapsburgs should be inherited integrally by the new heiress, Maria Theresa.[20] The issue was between law and force. Frederick in attacking Silesia could invoke nothing better than "reason of state," the welfare and expansion of the state of which he was ruler. But he was not mistaken in the belief that if he did not attack the Austrians some one else soon would.

The Pragmatic Sanction was universally disregarded. All turned against Maria Theresa. Bavaria and Saxony put in claims. Spain, still hoping to revise the Peace of Utrecht, saw another chance to win back former Spanish holdings in Italy. The decisive intervention was that of France. It was the fate of France to be torn between ambitions on the European continent and ambitions on the sea and beyond the seas. Economic and commercial advantage might dictate concentration on the impending struggle with Britain. But the French nobles were less interested than the British aristocrats in commercial considerations. They were influential because they furnished practically all the army officers and diplomats. They saw in Austria the traditional enemy, in Europe the traditional field of valor, and in Belgium, which now belonged to the Austrians, the traditional object for annexation to France. Cardinal Fleury, much against his will and judgment, found himself forced into war against the Hapsburgs.

Maria Theresa was at this time a young woman of twenty-three. She proved to be one of the most capable rulers ever produced by the House of Hapsburg. She made full use of her feminine qualities. Graceful and attrac-

---

[19] See map, pp. 198–9, panel 3.
[20] See p. 193.

tive as a young woman, buxom and motherly as she grew older, she commanded an affectionate loyalty from her assistants such as few male rulers ever obtained. She was fond of her husband, bore ten children, and set a model of conscientious family living at a time of much indifference to such matters among the upper classes. She was as devout and as earnest as Frederick of Prussia was irreligious and seemingly flip. She dominated her husband and her grown sons as she did her kingdoms and her duchies. With a good deal of practical sense, she reconstructed her empire without having any doctrinaire program, and she accomplished more in her methodical way than more brilliant contemporaries with more spectacular projects of reform. She knew how to use so-called feminine wiles, charms, moods, and even outbursts or tears to gain her ends. She once remarked to her husband, Francis of Lorraine, that the singer they had just heard at the opera was the greatest actress that ever lived. "Except yourself, Madam," he replied, with a freedom permitted to the husbands even of queens.

She was pregnant when Frederick invaded Silesia, giving birth to her first son, the future emperor Joseph II, in March 1741. She then turned her attention to politics. Her dominions were assailed by half a dozen outside powers, and were also quaking within, for her two kingdoms of Hungary and Bohemia (both of which had accepted the Pragmatic Sanction) were slow to see which way their advantage lay. She betook herself to Hungary to be crowned with the crown of St. Stephen—and to rally support. The Hungarians were still in a grumbling frame of mind, as in the days of the Rakoczy rebellion forty years before.[21] She made a carefully arranged and dramatic appearance before them, implored them to defend an outraged woman, swore to uphold the liberties of the Hungarian nobles and the separate constitution of the kingdom of Hungary. All Europe told how the beautiful young queen, by raising aloft the infant Joseph at a session of the Hungarian parliament, had thrown the dour Magyars into paroxysms of chivalrous resolve. The story was not quite true, but it is true that she made an eloquent address to the Magyars, that she took her baby with her and proudly exhibited him, and that she probably gained more by being a woman than a male Hapsburg could possibly have received. The Hungarian magnates pledged their "blood and life," and delivered a hundred thousand soldiers.

The war, as it worked out in Europe, was reminiscent of the struggles of the time of Louis XIV, or even of the Thirty Years' War now a century in the past. It was, again, a kind of civil struggle within the Holy Roman Empire, in which a league of German princes banded together against the monarchy of Vienna. This time they included the new kingdom of Prussia. It was, again, a collision of Bourbons and Hapsburgs, in which the French pursued their old policy of maintaining division in Germany, by supporting the German princes against the Hapsburgs. The basic aim of French policy, according to instructions given by the French foreign office to its ambassador

〰〰〰〰〰〰〰〰〰〰

[21] See p. 192.

in Vienna in 1725, was to keep the Empire divided by the principles of the Peace of Westphalia,[22] preventing the union of German powers into "one and the same body, which would in fact become formidable to all the other powers of Europe." This time the Bourbons had Spain on their side. Maria Theresa was supported only by Britain and Holland, which subsidized her financially, but which had inadequate land forces. The Franco-German-Spanish combination was highly successful. In 1742 Maria Theresa, hard pressed, accepted the proposals of Frederick for a separate peace. She temporarily granted him Silesia, and he temporarily slipped out of the war which he had been the first to enter. The French and Bavarians moved into Bohemia and almost organized a puppet kingdom with the aid of Bohemian nobles. The French obtained the election of their Bavarian satellite as Holy Roman Emperor, Charles VII. In 1745 the French won the battle of Fontenoy in Belgium, the greatest battle of the war; they dominated Belgium, which neither the Dutch nor British were able to defend. In the same year they fomented the Jacobite rebellion in Scotland.

But the situation overseas offset the situation in Europe. It was America that tilted the balance. The French fortress of Louisburg on Cape Breton Island was captured by an expedition of New Englanders in conjunction with the British navy. British warships drove French and Spanish shipping from the seas. The French West Indies were blockaded. The French government, in danger of losing the wealth and taxes drawn from the sugar and slave trades, announced its willingness to negotiate.

Peace was made at Aix-la-Chapelle in 1748. It was based on an Anglo-French agreement in which Maria Theresa was obliged to concur. Britain and France arranged their differences by a return to the *status quo ante bellum*. The British restored Louisburg despite the protests of the Americans, and relaxed their stranglehold on the Caribbean. The French restored Madras, which they had captured, and gave up their hold on Belgium. The Atlantic powers recognized Frederick's annexation of Silesia, and required Maria Theresa to cede some Italian duchies—Parma and Piacenza—to a Spanish Bourbon. Belgium was returned to Maria Theresa at the especial insistence of Britain and the Dutch. She and her ministers were very dissatisfied. They would infinitely have preferred to lose Belgium and keep Silesia. They were required, in the interest of a European or even intercontinental balance of power, to give up Silesia and to hold Belgium for the Dutch against the French.

The war had been more decisive than the few readjustments of the map seemed to show. It proved the weakness of the French position, straddled as it was between Europe and the overseas world. Maintaining a huge army for use in Europe, the French could not, like Britain, concentrate upon the sea. On the other hand, because vulnerable on the sea, they could not hold their gains in Europe or conquer Belgium. The Austrians, though bitter, had reason for satisfaction. The war had been a war to partition the Hapsburg

---

[22] See pp. 127–30.

empire. The Hapsburg empire still stood. Hungary had thrown in its lot with Vienna, a fact of much subsequent importance. Bohemia was won back. In 1745, when Charles VII died, Maria Theresa got her husband elected Holy Roman Emperor, a position for which she could not qualify because she was a woman. But the loss of Silesia was momentous. Silesia was as populous as the Dutch Republic, almost purely German, and industrially the most advanced region east of the Elbe. Prussia by acquiring it doubled its population and more than doubled its resources. Prussia with Silesia was unquestionably a great power. Since Austria was still a great power there were henceforth two great powers in the vague world known as "Germany," a situation which came to be known as the German dualism. But the transfer of Silesia, which doubled the number of Germans ruled by the king of Prussia, made the Hapsburg empire less German, more Slavic and Hungarian, more Danubian and international. Silesia was the keystone of Germany. Frederick was determined to hold it, and Maria Theresa to win it back. A new war was therefore foreseeable in Central Europe. As for Britain and France, the peace of Aix-la-Chapelle was clearly only a truce.

The next years passed in a busy diplomacy, leading to what is known as the "reversal of alliances" and Diplomatic Revolution of 1756. The Austrians set themselves to nipping off the growth of Prussia. Maria Theresa's foreign minister, Count Kaunitz, perhaps the most artful diplomat of the century, concluded that the time had come to abandon ideas that were centuries old. The rise of Prussia had revolutionized the balance of power. Kaunitz, reversing traditional policy, proposed an alliance between Austria and France—between the Hapsburgs and the Bourbons. He encouraged French aspirations for Belgium in return for French support in the destruction of Prussia. The overtures between Austria and France obliged Britain, Austria's former ally, to reconsider its position in Europe; the British had Hanover to protect, and were favorably impressed by the Prussian army. An alliance of Great Britain and Prussia was concluded in January, 1756. Meanwhile Kaunitz consummated his alliance with France. One consequence was to marry the future Louis XVI to one of Maria Theresa's daughters, Marie Antoinette, the "Austrian woman" of Revolutionary fame. The Austrian alliance was never popular in France. Some Frenchmen thought that the ruin of Prussia would only enhance the Austrian control of Germany, and so undo the fundamental "Westphalia system." The French progressive thinkers, known as *philosophes*, believed Austria to be priest-ridden and backward, and were for ideological reasons admirers of the free-thinking Frederick II. Dissatisfaction with its foreign policy was one reason for the growth of a revolutionary attitude toward the Bourbon government.

In any case, when the Seven Years' War broke out in 1756, though it was a continuation of the preceding war in that Prussia fought Austria, and Britain France, the belligerents had all changed partners. Great Britain and Prussia were now allies, as were, more remarkably, the Hapsburgs and the Bourbons. In addition, Austria had concluded a treaty with the Russian empire for the annihilation of Prussia.

THE SEVEN YEARS' WAR, 1756–63: IN EUROPE AND AMERICA

The Seven Years' War began in America. Let us turn, however, to Europe first. Here the war was another war of "partition." As a league of powers had but recently attempted to partition the empire of Maria Theresa, and a generation before had in fact partitioned the empires of Sweden and Spain, so now Austria, Russia, and France set out to partition the newly created kingdom of Prussia. Their aim was to relegate the Hohenzollerns to the margraviate of Brandenburg. Prussia, even with Silesia, had less than 6,000,000 people; each of its three principal enemies had 20,000,000 or more. But war was less an affair of peoples than of states and standing armies, and the Prussian state and Prussian army were the most efficient in Europe. Frederick fought brilliant campaigns, won victories as at Rossbach in 1757, moved rapidly along interior lines, eluded, surprised and re-attacked the badly coordinated armies opposed to him. He proved himself the great military genius of his day. But genius was scarcely enough. Against three such powers, reinforced by Sweden and the German states, and with no ally except Great Britain (and Hanover) whose aid was almost entirely financial, the kingdom of Prussia by any reasonable estimate had no chance of survival. There were times when Frederick believed all to be lost, yet he went on fighting, and his strength of character in these years of adversity, as much as his ultimate triumph, later made him a hero and symbol for the Germans. His subjects, *Junkers* and even serfs, advanced in patriotic spirit under pressure. The coalition tended to fall apart. The French lacked enthusiasm; they were fighting Britain, the Austrian alliance was unpopular, Kaunitz would not plainly promise them Belgium. The Russians found that the more they moved westward the more they alarmed their Austrian allies. In 1762 the tsarina Elizabeth died; her successor, Peter III, a somewhat infantile admirer of the soldierly Frederick, immediately called off hostilities—an event often called the "miracle of the House of Brandenburg." Frederick was left to deal only with the implacable Austrians, for whom he was more than a match. By the peace of Hubertusburg in 1763 not only did he lose nothing; he retained Silesia.

For the rest, the Seven Years' War was a phase in the long dispute between France and Great Britain. Its stakes were supremacy in the growing world economy, control of colonies, and command of the sea. The two empires had been left unchanged in 1748 by the peace of Aix-la-Chapelle. Both held possessions in India, in the West Indies, and on the American mainland.[23] In India both British and French possessed only disconnected commercial establishments on the coast, infinitesimal specks on the giant body of India. Both also traded with China at Canton. Both occupied way stations on the route to Asia, the British in St. Helena and Ascension Island in the south Atlantic, the French in the much better islands of Mauritius and

‸‸‸‸‸‸‸‸‸‸‸‸‸‸‸‸‸‸

[23] See maps, pp. 169, 257.

Reunion in the Indian Ocean. Frenchmen were active also on the coasts of Madagascar. The greatest way station, the Cape of Good Hope, belonged to the Dutch. In the West Indies the British plantations were mainly in Jamaica, Barbados, and some of the Leeward Islands; the French in San Domingo, Guadeloupe, and Martinique. All were supported by the booming slave trade in Africa.

On the American mainland the French had more territory, the British more people. In the British colonies from Georgia to Nova Scotia lived perhaps two million whites, predominantly English but with strong infusions of Scotch-Irish, Dutch, Germans, French, and Swedes. Philadelphia, with some 40,000 people, was as large as any city in England except London. The colonies, in population, bulked about a quarter as large as the mother country. But they were provincial, locally minded, incapable of concerted action. In 1754 the British government called a congress at Albany in New York, hoping that the colonies would assume some collective responsibility for the coming war. The congress adopted an "Albany plan of union" drawn up by Benjamin Franklin, but the colonial legislatures declined to accept it, through fear of losing their independence. The colonials were willing, in a politically immature way, to rely on Britain for military action against France.

The French were still in possession of Louisburg on Cape Breton Island, a stronghold begun by Louis XIV, located in the Gulf of St. Lawrence. It was designed for naval domination of the American side of the north Atlantic, and to control access to the St. Lawrence river, the Great Lakes and the vast region now called the Middle West. Through all this tract of country Frenchmen constantly came and went, but there were sizable French settlements only around New Orleans in the south and Quebec in the north. One source of French strength was that the French were more successful than the British in gaining the support of the Indians. This was probably because the French, being few in numbers, did not threaten to expropriate the Indians from their lands, and also because Catholics at this time were incomparably more active than Protestants in Christian missions among non-European peoples.

Both empires, French and British, were held together by mercantilist regulations framed mainly in the interest of the home countries. In some ways the British empire was more liberal than the French; it allowed local self-government, and permitted immigration from all parts of Europe. In other ways the British system was more strict. British subjects, for example, were required by the Navigation Acts to use empire ships and seamen— English, Scotch, or colonial—whereas the French were more free to use the carrying services of other nations. British sugar planters had to ship raw sugar to the home country, there to be refined and sold to Europe, whereas French planters were free to refine their sugar in the islands. The mainland British colonials were forbidden to manufacture ironware and numerous other articles for sale; they were expected to buy such objects from England. Since the British sold little to the West Indies, where the slave population had no income with which to buy, the mainland colonies, though less valued as a source of wealth, were a far more important market for British goods. The colonials, though they had prospered under the restrictive system, were beginning to find much of it irksome at the time of the Seven Years' War, and indeed evaded it when they could.

Fighting was endemic even in the years of peace in Europe. Nova Scotia was a trouble spot. French in population, it had been annexed by Britain at the Peace of Utrecht. Its proximity to Louisburg made it a scene of perpetual agitation. The British government in 1755, foreseeing war with France, bodily removed about 7,000 of its people, who called themselves Acadians, scattering them in small numbers through the other mainland colonies. But the great disputed area was the Alleghenies. British colonials were beginning to feel their way westward through the mountains. French traders, soldiers, and empire builders were moving eastward toward the same mountains from points on the Mississippi and the Great Lakes. In 1749, at the request of Virginia and London capitalists, the British government chartered a land-exploitation company, the Ohio company, to operate in territory claimed also by the French. The French threw up a fort at the point where the Ohio river is formed by the junction of two smaller streams—Fort Duquesne, later called Pittsburgh. A force of colonials and British regular troops, under General Braddock, started through the wilderness to dislodge the French. It was defeated in July 1755, perhaps through its commander's unwillingness to take advice from the colonial officers, of whom one was George Washington.

A year later France and Britain declared war. The British were brilliantly led by William Pitt, subsequently the Earl of Chatham, a man of wide vision and superb confidence. "I know that I can save the country," he said, "and I know that no one else can." He concentrated British effort on the navy and colonies, while subsidizing Frederick of Prussia to fight in Europe, so that England, as he put it, might win an empire on the plains of Germany. Only the enormous credit of the British government made such a policy feasible. In 1758 British forces successfully took Fort Duquesne. Louisburg fell again in the same year. Gaining entry to the St. Lawrence, the British moved upstream to Quebec, and in 1759 a force under General Wolfe, stealthily scaling the heights, appeared by surprise on the Plains of Abraham outside the fortress, forcing the garrison to accept a battle, which the British won. With the fall of Quebec no further French resistance was possible on the American mainland. The British also, with superior naval power, occupied Guadeloupe and Martinique and the French slave stations in Africa.

THE SEVEN YEARS' WAR, 1756–63: IN INDIA

Both British and French interests were meanwhile profiting from disturbed conditions in India. As large as Europe without Russia, India was a congested country of impoverished masses, speaking hundreds of languages and following many religions and sub-religions, the two greatest being the

Hindu and the Moslem. Waves of invasion through the northwest frontier since the Christian year A.D. 1001 had produced a Moslem empire, whose capital was at Delhi and which for a short time held jurisdiction over most of the country. These Moslem emperors were known as Great Moguls. The greatest was Akbar, who ruled from 1556 to 1605, built roads, reformed the taxes, patronized the arts, and attempted to minimize religious differences among his peoples. The Moslem artistic culture flourished for a time after Akbar. One of his successors, Shah Jehan (1628–1658), built the beautiful Taj Mahal near Agra, and at Delhi the delicately carved alabaster palace of the Moguls, in which he placed the Peacock Throne, made of solid gold and studded with gems.

But meanwhile there was restlessness among the Hindus. The Sikhs, who had originated in the fifteenth century as a reform movement in Hinduism, went to war with the Mogul emperor in the seventeenth century. They became one of the most ferociously warlike of Indian peoples. Hindu princes in central India formed a "Mahratta confederacy" against the Moslem emperor at Delhi. Matters were made worse when Aurungzeb, the last significant Mogul emperor (1658–1707), adopted repressive measures against the Hindus. After Aurungzeb, India fell into political dissolution. Many of the modern princely states originated or became autonomous at this time. Hindu princes rebelled against the Mogul. Moslems, beginning as governors or commanders under the Mogul, set up as rulers in their own right. Thus originated Hyderabad, which included the fabulous diamond mines of Golconda, and whose ruler long was called the wealthiest man in the world. Princes and would-be princes fought with each other and with the emperor. New Moslem invaders also poured across the northwest frontier. In 1739 a Persian force occupied Delhi, slaughtered thirty thousand people and departed with the Peacock Throne. Between 1747 and 1761 came a series of forays from Afghanistan, which again resulted in the looting of Delhi and the massacre of uncounted thousands.

The situation in India resembled, on a larger and more frightful scale, what had happened in Europe in the Holy Roman Empire, where also irreconcilable religious differences (of Catholics and Protestants) had torn the country asunder, ambitious princes and city-states had won a chaotic independence, and foreign armies appeared repeatedly as invaders. India, like central Europe, suffered chronically from war, intrigue, and rival pretensions to territory; and in India, as in the Holy Roman Empire, outsiders and ambitious insiders benefited together.

The half-unknown horrors in the interior had repercussions on the coasts. Here handfuls of Europeans were established in the coastal cities. By the troubles in the interior the Indian authorities along the coasts were reduced, so to speak, to a size with which the Europeans could deal. The Europeans—British and French—were agents of their respective East India companies. The companies built forts, maintained soldiers, coined money, and entered into treaties with surrounding Indian powers, under charter of their home governments, and with no one in India to deny them the exercise of such sovereign rights. Agents of the companies, like Indians themselves, ignored or respected the Mogul emperor as suited their own purpose. They were, at first, only one of the many elements in the flux and reflux of Indian affairs.

Neither the British nor the French government, during the Seven Years' War, had any intention of territorial conquest in India, their policy in this respect differing radically from policy toward America. Nor were the two companies imperialistic. The company directors, in London and Paris, disapproved of fantastic schemes of intervention in Indian politics, insisted that their agents should attend to business only, and resented every penny and every sou not spent to bring in commercial profit. But it took a year or more to exchange messages between Europe and India, and company representatives in India, caught up in the Indian vortex, and overcome by the chance to make personal fortunes or by dreams of empire, acted very much on their own, committing their home offices without compunction. Involvement in Indian affairs was not exactly new. We have seen how "Diamond" Pitt, in 1702, purchased the good will of the nawab of the Carnatic, when the nawab threatened, by military force, to reduce the English traders at Madras to submission.[24] But the first European to exploit the possibilities of the situation was the Frenchman Dupleix. Dupleix felt that the funds sent out by the company in Paris, to finance trade in India, were insufficient. His idea seems to have been, not empire-building, but to make the company into a local territorial power, in order that, from taxes and other political revenues, it might have more capital for its commercial operations. In any case, during the years of peace in Europe after 1748, Dupleix found himself with about 2,000 French troops in the Carnatic, the east coast around Madras. He lent them out to neighboring native rulers in return for territorial concessions. The first to drill native Indians by European methods, he was the originator of the "sepoys." Following a program of backing claimants to various Indian thrones, he built up a clientele of native rulers under obligation to himself. He was very successful, for a few European troops or sepoys could overcome hordes of purely Indian forces in pitched battle. But he was recalled to France in 1754, the company becoming apprehensive of war with Britain and other trouble; and he died in disgrace.

When war came, in 1756, British interests in India were advanced chiefly by Robert Clive. He had come out many years before as a clerk for the company, but had shown military talents and an ability to comprehend Indian politics. He had maneuvered, with little success, against Dupleix in the Carnatic in the 1740's. In 1756, on hearing the news of war in Europe, he shifted his attention to Bengal, hoping to drive the French from their trading stations there. The French were favored in Bengal by the local Moslem ruler, Suraja Dowla, who proceeded to anticipate Clive's arrival by expelling the British from Calcutta. Capturing the city, he shut up one hundred and forty-six Englishmen in a small room without windows (soon known as

---

[24] See p. 233

the "Black Hole of Calcutta"), and kept them there all night, during which most of them died of suffocation. Clive, soon appearing with a small force of British and sepoys, routed Suraja Dowla at the battle of Plassey in 1757. He put his own puppet on the Bengal throne, and extorted huge reparations both for the company and for himself. Back in England he was received with mixed feelings, and again, in India, strove to purify the almost incredible corruption of company employees there, men normal enough but demoralized by irresistible chances for easy riches. Finally he committed suicide in 1774.

It was British sea power, more fundamentally than Clive's tactics, that assured the triumph of British over French ambitions in the East. The British government still had no intention of conquest in India, but it could not see its East India Company forced out by agents of the French company in collaboration with Indian princes. Naval forces were therefore dispatched to the Indian Ocean, and they not only allowed Clive to shift from Madras to Calcutta at will, but gradually cut off the French posts in India from Europe and from each other. By the end of the war all the French establishments in India, as in Africa and America, were at the mercy of the British. The French overseas lay prostrate, and France itself was again detached from the overseas world on which much of its economy rested. In 1761 France made an alliance with Spain, which was alarmed for the safety of its own American empire after the British victories at Quebec and in the Caribbean. But the British also defeated Spain.

THE PEACE SETTLEMENT OF 1763

The British armed forces had been spectacularly successful. Yet the peace treaty, signed at Paris in February 1763, five days before the Austro-Prussian peace of Hubertusburg, was by no means unfavorable to the defeated. The French Duke of Choiseul was a skillful and single-minded negotiator. The British, Pitt having fallen from office in 1761, were represented by a confused group of Parliamentary favorites of the new king, George III. France ceded to Britain all French territory on the North American mainland east of the Mississippi. Canada thereby became British, and the colonials of the Thirteen Colonies were relieved of the French presence beyond the Alleghenies. To Spain, in return for aid in the last days of the war, France ceded all holdings west of the Mississippi and at its mouth. France thereby abandoned the North American continent. But these almost empty regions were of minor commercial importance, and the French, in return for surrendering them, retained many economically more valuable establishments elsewhere. In the West Indies the British planters, and in England the powerful "West India interest," feared competition from the French sugar islands, which produced more cheaply, and wanted them left outside the protected economic system of the British empire. France therefore received back Guadeloupe and Martinique, as well as most of its slave stations in Africa. In India, the French remained in possession of their commercial installations—offices, warehouses, and docks—at Pondicherry and other towns. They were forbidden to erect fortifications or pursue political ambitions among Indian princes—a practice which neither the French nor the British government had hitherto much favored in any case.

The treaties of Paris and Hubertusburg, closing the prolonged war of the mid-century, made the year 1763 a memorable turning point. Prussia was to continue in being. The dualism of Germany was to be lasting; Austria and Prussia eyed each other as rivals. Frederick's aggression of 1740 was legalized, and even moralized by the heroic defense that had proved necessary to retain the plunder. Frederick himself, from 1763 until his death in 1786, was a man of peace, philosophical and even benign. But the German crucible had boiled, and out of it had come a Prussia harder and more metallic than ever, more disposed, by its escape from annihilation, to glorify its army as the steel framework of its life.

The Anglo-French settlement was far-reaching and rather curious. Although the war was won overwhelmingly by the British, it resulted in no commercial calamity to the French. French trade with America and the East grew as rapidly after the Seven Years' War as before it, and in 1785 was double what it had been in 1755. For England the war opened up new commercial channels. British trade with America and the East probably tripled between 1755 and 1785.[25] But the outstanding British gains were imperial and strategic. The European balance of power was preserved, the French had been kept out of Belgium, British subjects in North America seemed secure, and Britain had again vindicated its command of the sea. British sea power implied, in turn, that British seaborne commerce was safe in peace or war, while the seaborne commerce of the French, or of any others, depended ultimately on the political requirements of the British. But the French still had a few cards to play, and were to play them in the American and French Revolutions.

For America and India the peace of 1763 was decisive. America north of Mexico was to become part of an English-speaking world. In India the British government was drawn increasingly into a policy of territorial occupation; a British "paramount power" eventually emerged in place of the empire of the Moguls. British political rule in India stimulated British busi-

〰〰〰〰〰〰〰〰〰〰

[25] See p. 228.

The World in 1763

   At the Peace of Paris of 1763 the British overseas empire triumphed over the French. The French ceded their holdings on the North American mainland east of the Mississippi to Britain, those west of the Mississippi to Spain. Britain also took Florida from Spain in 1763, but lost it, returning it to Spain in 1783, at the close of the War of American Independence. The French retained their sugar islands in the West Indies, and their trading stations in India; they were stopped from empire building, but did not greatly suffer commercially from the Seven Years' War. The British proceeded to build their empire in India. (See also map, pp. 304–5.)

WORLD IN 1763

"EAST INDIA"

"WEST INDIA"

ness there, until in the greatest days of British prosperity India was one of the main pillars of the British economic system, and the road to India became in a real sense the lifeline of the British empire. But in 1763 this state of affairs was still in the future, and was to be reached by many intermediate steps.

CHAPTER VII

The Scientific View
of the World

THE seventeenth century has been called the century of genius. One reason is that it was the age when science became "modern." It was the great age of Galileo and Sir Isaac Newton, whose combined lifetimes spanned the century, with Galileo dying and Newton born in the year 1642. When Galileo was young those who probed into the secrets of nature still labored largely in the dark, isolated from one another and from the general public, working oftentimes by methods of trial and error, not altogether clear on what they were trying to do, with their thinking still complicated by ideas not nowadays considered scientific. They had nevertheless accomplished a good deal. Discoveries had been made, and ideas developed, without which the intellectual revolution of the seventeenth century would not have occurred. But in a way all scientific investigators before Galileo seem to be precursors, patient workers destined never to enter into the world toward which they labored. In 1727, when Newton died, all was changed. Scientific men were in continual touch with one another, and science was recognized as one of the principal enterprises of European society. Scientific methods of inquiry had been defined.

The store of factual knowledge had become very large. The first modern scientific synthesis, or coherent theory of the physical universe, had been presented by Newton. Scientific knowledge was applied increasingly to navigation, mining, agriculture, and many branches of manufacture. Science and invention were joining hands. Science was accepted as the main force in the advancement of civilization and progress. And science was becoming popularized; many people who were not themselves scientists "believed" in science, and attempted to apply scientific habits of thought to diverse problems of man and society.

The history of science is too great a story to be told in this book, but there are a few ideas about it which even a book of this kind must attempt to make clear. First, science, purely as a form of thought, is one of the supreme achievements of the human mind, and to have a humanistic understanding of man's powers one must sense the importance of science, as of philosophy, literature, or the arts. Second, science has increasingly affected practical affairs, entering into the health, wealth, and happiness of mankind. It has changed the size of populations and the use of raw materials, revolutionized methods of production, transport, business, and war, and so helped to formulate political and economic questions. This is especially true of modern civilization since the seventeenth century. Third, in the modern world ideas have had a way of passing over from science into other domains of thought. Many people today, for example, in their notions of themselves, their neighbors, or the meaning of life, are influenced by ideas which they believe to be those of Freud or Einstein—they talk of repressions or relativity without necessarily knowing much about them. Ideas derived from biology and from Darwin—such as evolution and the struggle for existence—have likewise spread far and wide. Similarly the scientific revolution of the seventeenth century had repercussions far beyond the realm of pure science. It changed ideas of religion and of God and man. And it helped to spread certain very deep-seated beliefs, such as that the physical universe in which man finds himself is essentially orderly and harmonious, that the human reason is capable of understanding and dealing with it, and that man can conduct his own affairs by methods of peaceable exchange of ideas and rational agreement. Thus was laid a foundation for belief in free and democratic institutions.

The purpose of this chapter is to sketch the rise of modern science in the seventeenth century and the emergence of the scientific view of the world and of human affairs. The chapter that follows will describe the popularization and application of these ideas in the eighteenth century, in the era generally known as the Age of Enlightenment.

30. Prophets of a Scientific Civilization: Bacon and Descartes

SCIENCE BEFORE THE SEVENTEENTH CENTURY

The scientific view became characteristic of European society about the middle of the seventeenth century. There had, indeed, been a few in earlier times who caught glimpses of a whole civilization reared upon science. To us today the most famous of these is Leonardo da Vinci (1452–1519) the universal genius of the Italian Renaissance, who had been artist, engineer, and scientific thinker all in one. Leonardo, by actual dissection of dead bodies, had obtained an accurate knowledge of human anatomy; he had conceived of the circulation of the blood and the movement of the earth about the sun; and he had drawn designs for submarines and airplanes, and speculated on the use of parachutes and poison gases. But Leonardo had not published his scientific ideas. He was known almost exclusively as an artist. His work in science remained outside the stream of scientific thought, without influence on its course. It was not even known until the discovery of his private note-books in recent years. Leonardo thus figures in the history of science as an isolated genius, a man of brilliant insights and audacious theories, which died with their author's death, whereas science depends on a transmission of ideas in which men build upon one another's discoveries, test one another's experiments, and fill in the gaps in one another's knowledge.

A century after the death of Leonardo da Vinci educated Europeans were by no means scientifically minded. Among thoughtful persons many currents were stirring. On the one hand there was a great deal of skepticism, a constantly doubting frame of mind, which held that no certain knowledge is possible for human beings at all, that all beliefs are essentially only customs, that some people believe one thing and some another, and that there is no sound way of choosing between them. This attitude was best expressed by the French essayist Montaigne (1533–92), whose thought distilled itself into an eternal question, *Que sais-je?* "What do I know?" with the always implied answer, "Nothing." Montaigne's philosophy led to a tolerant, humane, and broad-minded outlook; but as a system of thought it was not otherwise very constructive. On the other hand, there was also a tendency to over-belief, arising from the same inability to distinguish between true and false. There was no accepted line between chemistry and alchemy, or between astronomy and astrology; all alike were regarded as ways of penetrating the "secrets" of nature. The sixteenth century had been a great age of charlatans, such as Nostradamus and Paracelsus, some of whom, notably Paracelsus, mixed magic and valid science in a way hardly understandable to us today.[1] As late as the seventeenth century, especially in Central Europe where the Thirty Years' War produced chaos and terror, kings and generals kept private as-

[1] See pp. 57–8.

trologers to divine the future. The two centuries from about 1450 to about 1650 were also the period when fear of witches was at its height. The witchcraft panic lasted longest in Germany and Central Europe, probably kept alive by the insecurities engendered by the Thirty Years' War. But about twenty persons were hanged as witches in Massachusetts as late as 1692, for the English colonies, as a remote and outlying part of the European world, were among the last to feel some of the waves originating in Europe. It was in Scotland, another outlying region of Europe, that the last known execution for witchcraft took place, in 1722.

It was by no means clear, in the early part of the seventeenth century, which way Europe was going to develop. It might conceivably have fallen into a kind of chaos, as India did at about this time. We have seen that much of Europe was wracked by chronic and marauding violence, to which an end was put by the consolidation of the modern state and the conversion of armed bands into organized and disciplined armies. Similarly, in things of the mind, there was no settled order. Doubt went with superstition, indifference with persecution. Science in time provided Europe with a new faith in itself. The rise of science in the seventeenth century possibly saved European civilization from petering out in a long post-medieval afterglow, or from wandering off into the diverse paths of a genial skepticism, ineffectual philosophizing, desultory magic, or mad fear of the unknown.

BACON AND DESCARTES

Two men stand out as prophets of a world reconstructed by science. One was the Englishman Francis Bacon (1561–1626), the other the Frenchman René Descartes (1596–1650). Both published their most influential books between 1620 and 1640. Both addressed themselves to the problem of knowledge. Both asked themselves how it is possible for human beings to know anything with certainty, or to have a reliable, truthful, and usable knowledge of the world of nature. Both shared in the doubts of their day. They branded virtually all beliefs of preceding generations (outside religion) as worthless. Both ridiculed the tendency to put faith in ancient books, to cite the writings of Aristotle or others, on questions having to do with the workings of nature. Both attacked earlier methods of seeking knowledge; they rejected the methods of the "schoolmen" or "scholastics," the thinkers in the academic tradition of the universities founded in the Middle Ages. On the whole, medieval philosophy had been rationalistic and deductive.[2] That is, its characteristic procedure was to start with definitions and general propositions, and then discover what further knowledge could be logically deduced from the definitions thus accepted. Or it proceeded by affirming the nature of an object to be such-and-such (*e.g.*, that "man is a political animal") and then describing how objects of such a nature do or should behave. These

[2] See pp. 37–9.

methods, which owed much to Aristotle and other ancient codifiers of human thought, had generally ceased to be fruitful in discovery of knowledge of nature. Bacon and Descartes held that the medieval (or Aristotelian) methods were backwards. They held that truth is not something that we postulate at the beginning, and then explore in all its ramifications, but that it is something which we find at the end, after a long process of investigation, experiment, or intermediate thought.

Bacon and Descartes thus went beyond mere doubt. They offered a constructive program, and though their programs were different, they both became heralds or philosophers of a scientific view. They maintained that there was a true and reliable method of knowledge. And they maintained in addition that once this true method was known and practiced, once the real workings of nature were understood, men would be able to use this knowledge for their own purposes, control nature in their own interests, make undreamed of useful inventions, improve their mechanical arts, and add generally to their wealth and comfort. Bacon and Descartes thus announced the advent of a scientific civilization.

Francis Bacon planned a great work in many volumes, to be known as the *Instauratio Magna* or "Great Renewal," calling for a complete new start in science and civilization. He completed only two parts. One, published in 1620, was the *New Organon*, or new method of acquiring knowledge. Here he insisted on *inductive* method. An inductive method is one in which we proceed from the particular to the general, from the concrete to the abstract. For example, in the study of leaves, if we begin with a general idea of what we think a leaf is, and then examine millions of actual leaves to see whether they correspond to this idea, we are following a *deductive* method; we learn no more of the "nature" of a leaf than what we knew or thought we knew at the beginning. If, on the other hand, we start with innumerable actual leaves, of all sizes and shapes, and if we assemble, observe, and compare them with minute scrutiny, then we are using an inductive method in the sense meant by Bacon, and if successful we may finally arrive at a knowledge, based on observed facts, of the general nature of a leaf as such. Bacon advised men to put aside all traditional ideas, to rid themselves of prejudices and preconceptions, to look at the world with fresh eyes, to observe and study the innumerable things that are actually perceived by the senses. He thus became a leading philosopher of empiricism. This philosophy, together with the philosophy of purely inductive method, has always proved a useful safeguard against fitting facts into preconceived patterns. It demands that we let the patterns of our thought be shaped by actual facts as we observe them.

The other completed part of Bacon's great work, published in 1623, was called in its English translation *The Advancement of Learning*. Here Bacon developed the same ideas, and especially insisted that true knowledge was useful knowledge. He put these ideas in more popular form in *The New Atlantis* (1627), portraying a kind of scientific utopia in which men enjoyed a perfect society through their knowledge and command of nature. The idea of the usefulness of knowledge became the other main element in the

Baconian tradition. In this view there was no sharp difference between pure science and applied science, or between the work of the purely scientific investigator and that of the mechanic or inventor who in his own way probed into nature and devised instruments or machines for putting natural forces to work. The fact that knowledge could be used for practical purposes became a sign or proof that it was true knowledge. For example, the fact that men could aim their cannon and hit their targets more accurately in the seventeenth century became a proof of the theory of ballistics which had been scientifically worked out. Enthusiastic Baconians believed that knowledge was power. True knowledge could be put to work, if not immediately at least in the long run, after more knowledge was discovered. It was useful to mankind, unlike the "delicate learning" of the misguided scholastics. In this coming together of knowledge and power arose the far-reaching modern idea of progress. And in it arose many of the problems of modern men, since the power given by scientific knowledge can be either bad or good.

But Bacon, though a force in redirecting the European mind, never had much influence on the development of actual science. Kept busy as Lord Chancellor of England and in other government duties, he was not even fully abreast of the most advanced scientific thought of his day. Like the public generally of his lifetime, he was undisturbed by the new theories of astronomers holding the earth to move about the sun. Bacon's greatest weakness was his failure to understand the role of mathematics. Mathematics, dealing with pure abstractions and proceeding deductively from axioms to theorems, was not an empirical or inductive method of thought such as Bacon demanded. Yet science in the seventeenth century went forward most successfully in subjects where mathematics could be applied. Even today the degree to which a subject is truly scientific depends on the degree to which it can be made mathematical. We have pure science where we have formulas and equations, and the scientific method itself is both inductive and deductive.

Descartes was a great mathematician in his own right. He is considered the inventor of co-ordinate geometry. He showed that by use of co-ordinates (or graph paper, in simple language) any algebraic formula could be plotted as a curve in space, and contrariwise that any curve in space, however complex, could be converted into algebraic terms and thus dealt with by methods of calculation. And one effect of his general philosophy was to create belief in a vast world of nature that could be reduced to mathematical form.

Descartes set forth his ideas in his *Discourse on Method,* in 1637, and in many more technical writings. He advanced the principle of systematic doubt. He began by trying to doubt everything that could reasonably be doubted, thus sweeping away past ideas and clearing the ground for his own "great renewal," to use Bacon's phrase. He held that he could not doubt his own existence as a thinking and doubting being (*cogito ergo sum,* "I think, therefore I exist"); he then deduced, by systematic reasoning, the existence of God and much else. He arrived at a philosophy of dualism, the famous "Cartesian dualism," which held that God has created two kinds of fundamental reality in the universe. One was "thinking substance"—mind, spirit, consciousness, subjective experience. The other was "extended substance"—everything outside the mind and hence objective. Of everything except the mind itself the most fundamental and universal quality was that it occupied a portion of space, minute or vast. Space itself was conceived as infinite, and everywhere geometric.

This philosophy had profound and long-lasting effects. For one thing, the seemingly most real elements in human experience, color and sound, joy and grief, seemed somehow to be shadowy and unreal, or at least illusive, with no existence outside the mind itself. But all else was quantitative, measurable, reducible to formulas or equations. Over all else, over the whole universe or half-universe of "extended substance," the most powerful instrument available to the human understanding, namely mathematics, reigned supreme. "Give me motion and extension," said Descartes, "and I will build you the world."

Descartes also, with French genius, expressed the Baconian idea. Instead of the "speculative philosophy of the schools," he wrote in the *Discourse on Method*, men might discover a "practical philosophy by which, understanding the forces and action of fire, water, air, the stars and heavens and all other bodies that surround us, as distinctly as we understand the mechanical arts of our craftsmen, we can use these forces in the same way for all purposes for which they are appropriate, and so make ourselves the masters and possessors of nature. And this is desirable not only for the invention of innumerable devices by which we may enjoy without trouble the fruits of the earth and the conveniences it affords, but mainly also for the preservation of health, which is undoubtedly the principal good and foundation of all other good things in this life."

31. The Road to Newton: The Law of Universal Gravitation

SCIENTIFIC ADVANCES

Meanwhile actual scientific discovery was advancing on many fronts. It did not advance on all with equal speed. Some of the sciences were, and long remained, dependent mainly on the collection of specimens. Botany was one of these; Europe's knowledge of plants expanded enormously with the explorations overseas, and botanical gardens and herb collections in Europe became far more extensive than ever before, bringing important enlargements in the stock of medicinal drugs. Other sciences drew their impetus from intensive and open-minded observation. The Flemish Vesalius, by a book published in 1543, *The Structure of the Human Body*, renewed and modernized the study of anatomy. Formerly anatomists had generally held that the writings of Galen, dating from the second century A.D., contained an authoritative description of all human muscles and tissues.[3] They had indeed dissected cadavers, but had dismissed those not conforming to Galen's description as somehow abnormal or not typical. Vesalius put Galen behind him, and based his general description of the human frame on actual bodies as he found them. In physiology also, dealing with the functioning rather than the structure of living bodies, there was considerable progress. Here the method of laboratory experiment could be profitably used. William Harvey, after years of laboratory work, including the vivisection of animals, published in 1628 a book *On the Movement of the Heart and Blood.* Here he set forth the doctrine, confirmed by evidence, of the continual circulation of the blood through arteries and veins. The Italian Malpighi, using the newly invented microscope, confirmed Harvey's findings by the discovery of capillaries in 1661. The Dutch Leeuwenhoek, also by use of the microscope, was the first to see blood corpuscles, spermatozoa, and bacteria, of which he left published drawings.

These sciences, and also chemistry, although work in them went continually on, did not come fully into their own until after 1800. They were long overshadowed by astronomy and physics. Here mathematics could be most fully applied, and mathematics underwent a rapid development in the seventeenth century. Decimals came into use to express fractions, the symbols used in algebra were improved and standardized, and in 1614 logarithms were invented by the Scotchman John Napier. Co-ordinate geometry was mapped out by Descartes, the theory of probabilities developed by Pascal, and calculus invented simultaneously in England by Newton and in Germany by Leibnitz. These advances made it more generally possible to think about nature in purely quantitative terms, to measure with greater precision, and to perform complex and laborious computations. Physics and astronomy were remarkably stimulated, and it was in this field that the most astonishing scientific revolution of the seventeenth century took place.

THE SCIENTIFIC REVOLUTION: COPERNICUS TO GALILEO

From time immemorial, since the Greek Ptolemy had codified ancient astronomy in the second century A.D.,[4] educated Europeans had held a conception of the cosmos which we call Ptolemaic. The cosmos in this view was a group of concentric spheres, a series of balls within balls each having the same center. The innermost ball was the earth, made up of hard, solid, earthy substance such as men were familiar with underfoot. The other spheres, encompassing the earth in series, were all transparent. They were the "crystalline spheres" made known to us by the poets; their harmony was the "music of the spheres." These spheres all revolved about the earth, each sphere containing, set in it as a jewel, a luminous heavenly body or orb which moved about the earth with the movement of its transparent sphere. Nearest to the

[3] See p. 8
[4] See p. 8.

earth was the sphere of the moon; then, in turn, the spheres of Mercury and Venus, then the sphere of the sun, then those of the outer planets. Last came the outermost sphere containing all the fixed stars studded in it, all moving majestically about the earth in daily motion, but motionless with respect to each other because held firmly in the same sphere. Beyond the sphere of the fixed stars, in general belief, lay the "empyrean," the home of angels and immortal spirits; but this was not a matter of natural science.

A man standing on the earth, and looking up into the sky, thus felt himself to be enclosed by a dome of which his own position was the center. In the blue sky of day he could literally see the crystalline spheres; in the stars at night he could behold the orbs which these spheres carried with them. All revolved about him, presumably at no very alarming distance. The celestial bodies were commonly supposed to be of different material and quality from the earth. The earth was of heavy dross; the stars and planets and the sun and moon seemed made of pure and gleaming light, or at least of a bright ethereal substance almost as tenuous as the crystal spheres in which they moved. The cosmos was a hierarchy of ascending perfection. The heavens were purer than the earth.

This system corresponded to actual appearances, and except for scientific knowledge would be highly believable today. It was formulated also in rigorous mathematical terms. Ever since the Greeks, and becoming increasingly intricate in the Middle Ages, a complex geometry had grown up to explain the observed motion of the heavenly bodies. The Ptolemaic system was a mathematical system. And it was for purely mathematical reasons that it first came to be reconsidered. There was a marked revival of mathematical interest at the close of the Middle Ages, in the fourteenth and fifteenth centuries, a renewed concentration on the philosophic traditions of Pythagoras and Plato. In these philosophies could be found the doctrine that number might be the final key to the mysteries of nature. With them went a metaphysical belief that simplicity was more likely to be a sign of truth than complication, and that a simpler mathematical formulation was better than a more complex one.

These ideas motivated Nicholas Copernicus, born in Poland of German and Polish background, who, after study in Italy, wrote his epochal work *On the Revolutions of the Heavenly Orbs*. In this book, published in 1543 after his death, he held the sun to be the center of the solar system and fixed stars, and the earth to be one of the planets revolving in space around it. This view had been entertained by a few isolated thinkers before. Copernicus gave a mathematical demonstration. To him it was a purely mathematical problem. With increasingly detailed knowledge of the actual movement of the heavenly bodies it had become necessary to make the Ptolemaic system more intricate by the addition of new "cycles" and "epicycles," until, as John Milton expressed it later, the cosmos was

With Centric and Concentric scribbled o'er,
Cycle and Epicycle, Orb in Orb.

Copernicus needed fewer such hypothetical constructions to explain the known movements of the heavenly bodies. The heliocentric or sun-centered theory was mathematically a little simpler than the geocentric or earth-centered theory hitherto held.

The Copernican doctrine long remained a hypothesis known only to experts. Most astronomers for a time hesitated to accept it, seeing no need, from the evidence yet produced, of so overwhelming a readjustment of current ideas. Tycho Brahe (1546–1601), the greatest authority on the actual positions and movements of the heavenly bodies in the generations immediately after Copernicus, never accepted the Copernican system in full. But his assistant and follower, John Kepler (1571–1630), not only accepted the Copernican theory but carried it further.

Kepler, a German, was a kind of mathematical mystic, part-time astrologer, and scientific genius. He felt ecstasy at the mysterious harmonies of mathematical forms. He built upon the exact observations of Tycho Brahe. Copernicus had believed the orbits of the planets about the sun to be perfect circles. Tycho showed that this belief did not fit the observable facts. Kepler discovered that orbits of the planets were ellipses. The ellipse, like the circle, is an abstract mathematical figure with knowable properties. Kepler demonstrated that, as a planet moves in its elliptical path about the sun, the straight line connecting it with the sun sweeps through an area of space proportional to the time taken by the planet's motion; that is, that a planet sweeps equal areas in equal times; or, more simply, that the closer a planet is to the sun in its elliptical orbit, the faster it moves. Kepler further showed that the length of time in which the several planets revolve about the sun varies proportionately with their distance from the sun: the square of the time is proportional to the cube of the distance.

It is not possible for most people to understand the mathematics involved, but it is possible to realize the astounding implications of Kepler's laws of planetary motion. Kepler showed that the actual world of stubborn facts, as observed by Tycho, and the purely rational world of mathematical harmony, as surmised by Copernicus, were not really in any discrepancy with each other; that they really corresponded exactly. Why they should he did not know; it was the mystery of numbers. He digested an overwhelming amount of hitherto unexplained information into a few brief statements. He showed a cosmic mathematical relationship between space and time. And he described the movement of the planets in explicit formulas, which any competent person could verify at will.

The next step was taken by Galileo (1564–1642). So far the question of what the heavenly bodies were made of had hardly been affected. Indeed, they were not thought of as bodies at all, but rather as orbs. Only the sun and moon had any dimension; stars and planets were only points of light; and the theories of Copernicus and Kepler, like those of Ptolemy, might apply to insubstantial luminous objects in motion. In 1609 Galileo built a telescope. Turning it to the sky, he perceived that the moon had a rough and apparently mountainous surface, as if made of the same kind of material as the earth. Seeing clearly the dark side of the moon in its various phases, and noting that in every position it only reflected the light of the sun, he concluded that the moon was not itself a luminous object, another indication that it might be made of earth-like substance. He saw spots on the sun, as if the sun were not pure and perfect. He found that the planets had visible breadth when seen in the telescope, but that the fixed stars remained only points of light, as if incalculably further away. He discovered also that Jupiter had satellites, moons moving around it like the moon around the earth. These discoveries reassured him of the validity of the Copernican theory, which he had in any case already accepted. They suggested also that the heavenly bodies might be of the same substance as the earth, masses of matter moving in space. Contrariwise, it became easier to think of the earth as itself a kind of heavenly body revolving about the sun. The difference between the earth and the heavens was disappearing. This struck a terrifying blow at all earlier philosophy and theology. Some professors were afraid to look through the telescope, and Galileo was condemned and forced to an ostensible recantation by his Church.

Moreover, where Kepler had found mathematical laws describing the movement of planets, Galileo found mathematical laws describing the movement of bodies on the earth. Formerly it had been thought that some bodies were by nature heavier than others, and that heavier bodies fell to the ground faster than light ones. Galileo in 1591, according to the story, dropped a ten-pound and a one-pound weight simultaneously from the top of the Leaning Tower of Pisa. The truth of this story has been questioned, but in any case Galileo showed that despite all previous speculation on the subject two bodies of different weights, when allowance was made for differences in air resistance due to differences of size or shape, struck the ground at the same time. His further work in dynamics, or the science of the motion of bodies, took many years to accomplish. He had to devise more refined means for measuring small intervals of time, find means of estimating the air resistance, friction, and other impediments which always occur in nature, and conceive of pure or absolute motion, and of force and velocity, in abstract mathematical terms. He arrived at the conception of inertia, holding that motion and rest are equally natural states of matter. Only *change* in motion, he thought, required physical explanation, for bodies in motion would move forever in a straight line at the same speed except as acted on by an external force. This dispensed with the need of an Unmoved Mover felt in the older philosophy. Of bodies moving on the earth, Galileo discovered that when falling freely they fall with a velocity that increased according to mathematical formula.

THE ACHIEVEMENT OF NEWTON: THE PROMISE OF SCIENCE

It was the supreme achievement of Newton to bring Kepler and Galileo together, that is, to show that Kepler's laws of planetary motion and Galileo's laws of terrestrial motion were two aspects of the same laws. Galileo's findings, holding that moving bodies move uniformly in a straight line unless deflected by a definite force, made it necessary to explain why the planets, instead of flying off in straight lines, tend to fall toward the sun, the result being their elliptical orbits—and why the moon, similarly, tends to fall toward the earth. Newton seems early to have suspected that the answer would be related to Galileo's laws of falling bodies—that is, that gravity, or the pull of the earth upon objects on earth, might be a form of a universal gravitation, or similar pull characterizing all bodies in the solar system. Great technical difficulties stood in the way, but finally, after inventing calculus, and using a new measurement of the size of the earth made by a Frenchman, and experiments with circular motion made by the Dutch Huyghens on the pendulum, Newton was able to bring his calculations to fruition, and to publish, in 1687, his *Mathematical Principles of Natural Philosophy*.

This stupendous book showed that all motion that could then be timed and measured, whether on the earth or in the solar system, could be described by the same mathematical formulas. All matter moved as if every particle attracted every other particle with a force proportional to the product of the two masses, and inversely proportional to the square of the distance between them. This "force" was universal gravitation. What it was Newton did not pretend to explain. For two hundred years the law stood unshaken, always verified by every new relevant discovery. Only in the last fifty years have its limitations been found; it does not hold good in the infinitesimal world of subatomic structure, or in the macrocosm of the whole physical universe as now conceived.

With Newton's work (which affected other fields than are here mentioned) the promise of science seemed fulfilled. Even in purely practical affairs conveniences followed, as anticipated by the Baconians. The tides could now be understood and predicted by the gravitational interplay of earth, moon, and sun. Exact mathematical knowledge of the solar system was of great help to navigation. In the eighteenth century chronometers were developed, making possible the finding of precise longitude at sea. Merchant ships and naval squadrons could thus operate with more assurance. Better determination of longitude, at sea and on land, was of great value to cartography, the science of map-making. Eighteenth-century Europeans were the first human beings to have a fairly accurate idea of the shapes and sizes of continents and oceans. Or again, mathematical advance, including the development of calculus, which allowed an exact treatment of curves and trajectories, reinforced by technical discoveries in the working of metals, led to an increased use of artillery. Armies in 1750 used twice as many cannon per soldier as in 1650. Naval ordnance also improved. These were items making armed forces more expensive to maintain, requiring governments to increase their taxes, and hence producing constitutional crises. Improved firearms likewise heightened the advantage of armies over insurrectionists or private fighting bands, thus strengthening the sovereignty of the state. They gave Europeans the military advantage over other peoples, in America, India, or elsewhere, on which the world ascendancy of Europe in the European age was built. This example, chosen somewhat at random, suggests the almost inconceivable ramifications of the practical consequences of science.

The instance of the steam engine may also be cited. Steam power was eventually almost literally to move the world. In 1700 it was a cloud no bigger than a man's hand. Yet it was in sight on the horizon. A Frenchman, Denis Papin, in 1681 invented a device in which steam moved a piston, but it produced so little power that it was used only in cooking. British scientists turned their minds to it. Robert Boyle, discoverer of "Boyle's law" on the pressure of gases, studied the problem; scientists, mechanics, and instrument makers collaborated. In 1702 Thomas Newcomen, a man without scientific training but associated with scientists, produced the steam engine known thereafter as Newcomen's engine, from which, as will be seen, James Watt developed the steam engine as we know it. Newcomen's engine was primitive according to later ideas. It burnt so much fuel that it could be used only in coal mines. But it was used. Not long after 1700 it was widely employed to pump water from the coal pits. It saved labor, cheapened production, and opened hitherto unusable deposits to exploitation. It was the first application of steam to an economic purpose.

The faith in natural knowledge was becoming institutionalized. Organized bodies of men, possessing equipment and funds, were engaged in scientific study. Most notable of these were the Royal Society of London, founded in 1662, and the Academy of Sciences in France, founded in 1666. Both originated when earlier and informal groups, usually gentlemen of the landed classes, received charters from their governments to pursue scientific interests. Scientific periodicals began to be published. Scientific societies provided the medium for prompt interchange of ideas indispensable to the growth of scientific knowledge. They published articles not only on the natural sciences and mathematics, but also on paleography, numismatics, chronology, legal history, and natural law. The work of the learned had not yet yielded to specialization. All felt a common interest in the advance of all fronts of knowledge. It is to be noted also how the scientific movement was an international one, shared in by all central and western Europe except Portugal and Spain. Men of many nationalities constantly made use of each other's hypotheses or discoveries. Many or even most of the books written in this age were first published in Latin, still the international language of science and learning, and many articles in the new scientific journals were written in Latin also.

THE SCIENTIFIC REVOLUTION AND THE WORLD OF THOUGHT

It was perhaps in the world of thought that the revolution accomplished from Copernicus to Newton was most profound. It has been called the greatest spiritual readjustment that men have been required to make.

The old heavens were exploded. Man was no longer the center of creation. The luminaries of the sky no longer shone to light his way or to give him beauty. The sky itself was an illusion, its color a thing in the mind only, for when a man now looked upwards he was really looking only into the darkness of endless space. The old cosmos, comfortably enclosed and ranked in an ascending order of purity, gave way to a new cosmos which seemed to consist in an infinite emptiness through which particles of matter were distributed. Man was the puny denizen of a material object swinging in space along with other very distant material objects of the same kind. About the physical universe there was nothing especially Christian, nothing that the God portrayed in the Bible would be likely to have made. The gap between Christianity and natural science, always present yet always bridged in the Middle Ages, now opened wider than ever. It was felt with anguish by some in the seventeenth century, notably by the Frenchman Blaise Pascal, a considerable scientist, pre-eminent mathematician, and deep and troubled Christian believer. He left a record of his state of mind in his *Pensées* or *Thoughts,* jottings from which he hoped some day to write a great book on the Christian faith. "I am terrified," he said in one of these jottings, "by the eternal silence of these infinite spaces."

But on the whole the reaction was more optimistic. Man might be merely a reed, as Pascal said, but Pascal added, "a thinking reed." Man might be no longer the physical center of the world. But it was man's mind that had penetrated the world's laws. The Newtonian system, as it became popularized, a process which took about fifty years, led to a great intellectual complacency. Never had confidence in human powers been so high. As Alexander Pope put it,

> Nature and nature's laws lay hid in night;
> God said, "Let Newton be," and all was light.

Or, according to another epigram on the subject, there was only one universe to discover, and this universe had been discovered by Newton. Everything seemed possible to the human reason. The old feeling of dependency upon God lost much of its force, or became something to be discussed by clergymen in church on Sunday. Man was not really a little creature, a wayfarer in a world that was alien to him, yearning for the reunion with God that would bring him peace. Man was a dignified creature, one of great capacity in his own right, living in a world that was understandable and manageable by him, and in which he might install himself with quite adequate comfort. These ideas contributed greatly to the secularizing of European society, pushing religion and churches to the sidelines.

The scientific discoveries also reinforced the old philosophy of natural law. This philosophy, developed by the Greeks and renewed in the Middle Ages, held that the universe is fundamentally orderly, and that there is a natural rightness or justice, universally the same for all people, and knowable by reason. It was very important in political theory, where it stood out against arbitrariness and the mere claims of power. The laws of nature as discovered by science were somewhat different, but they taught the same lesson, namely the orderliness and minute regularity of the world. It was reassuring to feel that everywhere throughout an infinite space, whether or not yet discovered and probed by man, every particle of matter was quietly attracting every other particle by a force proportionate to the product of the masses and inversely proportional to the square of the distance. The physical universe laid bare by science—orderly, rational, balanced, smoothly running, without strife or rivalry or contention—became a model on which many thinkers, as time went on, hoped to refashion human society. They hoped to make society also fulfill the rule of law.

In some ways it would be possible to exaggerate the impact of pure science. Scientists themselves did not usually apply their scientific ideas to religion and society. Few suffered the spiritual torment of Pascal. Both Descartes and Newton wrote placid tractates arguing for the truth of certain ecclesiastical doctrines. Bacon and Harvey were conservative politically, upholders of king against Parliament. The Englishman Joseph Glanvill, in the 1660's, used the Cartesian dualism to demonstrate the probable existence of witches. Descartes, despite his systematic doubt, held that the customs of one's country were to be accepted without question. Natural science, in the pure sense, was not inherently revolutionary or even upsetting. If Europeans in the seventeenth century began to waiver in many old beliefs it was not only because of the stimulus of pure science, but also because of an increasing knowledge and study of man himself.

32. New Knowledge of Man and Society

Here one of the most potent forces at work was the discovery and exploration of the world overseas. Europe was already becoming part of the world as a whole, and could henceforth understand itself only by comparison with non-European regions. Great reciprocal influences were at work. The influences of European expansion on other parts of the world are easily seen: the Indian societies of America were transformed or extinguished, the Negro societies of Africa were dislocated and many of their members enslaved and transported; in the long run even the ancient societies of Asia were to be undermined. From the beginning the counter-influence of the rest of the world upon Europe was equally great. It took the form not only of new medicines, new diseases, new foods, new and exotic manufactures brought to Europe, and the growth of material wealth in west-European countries. It affected European thinking also. It undermined the old Europe and its ideas, just as Europe was undermining the old cultures beyond the oceans. Vast new horizons opened before Europeans in the sixteenth and seventeenth centuries. Europeans of this period were the first men to whom it was given to know the globe as a whole, or to realize the variety of the human race and its multifarious manners and customs.

THE CURRENT OF SKEPTICISM

This realization was very unsettling. The realization of human differences had the effect, in Europe, of breaking what anthropologists call the
"cake of custom." A new sense of the relative nature of social institutions
developed. It became harder to believe in any absolute rightness of one's own
ways. Montaigne, already mentioned, expressed the relativist outlook clearly,
and nowhere more clearly than in his famous essay on cannibals. The cannibals, he said humorously, did in fact eat human flesh; that was their custom,
and they have their customs as we have ours; they would think some of our
ways odd or inhuman; peoples differ, and who are we to judge? Travelers'
books spread the same message increasingly through the seventeenth century.
As one of them observed (whether or not rightly), in Turkey it was the custom to shave the hair and wear the beard, in Europe to shave the beard and
wear the hair; what difference does it really make? That the ways of non-
Europeans might be good ways was emphasized by Jesuit missionaries. Writing from the depths of the Mississippi Valley or from China, the Jesuit
fathers often dwelt on the natural goodness and mental alertness of the native
peoples they encountered, perhaps hoping in this way to gain support in
Europe for their missionary labors. Sometimes strange people appeared in
Europe itself. In 1684 a delegation of aristocratic Siamese arrived in Paris,
followed by another in 1686. The Parisians went through a fad for Siam; they
recounted how the king of Siam, when asked by a missionary to turn Christian, replied that divine Providence, had it wished a single religion to prevail
in the world, could easily have so arranged it. The Siamese seemed civilized,
wise, philosophic; they allowed Christians to preach in their own country,
whereas it was well known what would happen to a Siamese missionary who
undertook to preach in Paris. China also was seen through an ideal glow. By
1700 there were even professors of Arabic, at Paris, Oxford, and Utrecht, who

---

The Growth of Geographical Knowledge

The four maps show the best scientific knowledge at their respective dates.
Behaim has no inkling of the existence of America, and has filled in the hemisphere opposite to Europe with a mass of islands, representing what he has heard
of the East Indies and Japan. He knows pretty well the limits of Africa. Schöner in
1523 fills in America and even distinguishes two American continents. He knows
of the Gulf of Mexico, but fails to realize the narrowness of the Isthmus of Panama. He knows of the Straits of Magellan (but not Cape Horn) and hopefully fills
in a corresponding Northwest Passage in the north. His conception of the Indian
Ocean is quite accurate. To Homan, two centuries later, the size and shapes of
oceans and continents are well known, but he believes New Guinea joined to Australia and is frankly ignorant of the northwest coast of North America, representing it by a straight line. D'Anville in 1761 has no island of Tasmania, does not
understand that Alaska is a peninsula, and believes the American polar regions to
be impassable by sea. Otherwise his map is indistinguishable from one on the same
scale today.

THE GROWTH OF
GEOGRAPHICAL KNOWLEDGE

1492
BEHAIM

1523
SCHÖNER

1716
HOMAN

1761
D'ANVILLE

TRM

said that Mohammedanism was a religion to be respected, as good for Mohammedans as Christianity was for Christians.

Thus was created a strong current of skepticism, holding that all beliefs are relative, varying with time and place. Its greatest spokesman at the end of the century was Pierre Bayle (1647–1706). Bayle was influenced by the scientific discoveries also; not exactly that he understood them, for he was an almost purely literary scholar, but he realized that many popular beliefs were without foundation. Between 1680 and 1682 a number of comets were seen. The one of 1682 was studied by a friend of Newton's, Edmund Halley, the first man to predict the return of a comet. He identified the one of 1682 with the one observed in 1302, 1456, 1531, and 1607, and predicted its reappearance in 1757 (it appeared in 1759); it was last seen in 1910 and is still called Halley's comet. In the 1680's people were talking of comets excitedly. Some said that comets emitted poisonous exhalations, others that they were supernatural omens of future events. Bayle, in his *Thoughts on the Comet*, argued at great length that there was no basis for any such beliefs except human credulity. In 1697 he published his *Historical and Critical Dictionary*, a tremendous repository of miscellaneous lore, conveying the message that what is called truth is often mere opinion, that most people are amazingly gullible, that many things firmly believed are really ridiculous, and that it is very foolish to hold too strongly to one's own views. Bayle's *Dictionary* remained a reservoir on which skeptical writers continued to draw for generations. Bayle himself, having no firm basis in his own mind for settled judgment, mixed skepticism with an impulse to faith. Born a Protestant, he was converted to Rome, then returned to his Calvinist background. In any case his views made for toleration in religion. For Bayle, as for Montaigne, no opinion was worth burning your neighbor for.

THE NEW SENSE OF EVIDENCE

But in the study of man, as in the study of physical nature, Europeans of the seventeenth century were not generally content with skepticism. They were not possessed by a mere negative and doubting mood, important and salutary as such an attitude was. In the subjects collectively called the humanities, as in pure science, they were looking not for disbelief but for understanding. They wanted new means of telling the true from the false, a new method for arriving at some degree of certainty of conviction. And here, too, a kind of scientific view of the world arose, if that term be understood in a general sense. It took the form of a new sense of evidence. Evidence is that which allows one to believe a thing to be true, or at least truer than something else for which the evidence is weaker. And if to believe without evidence is the sign of primitive or irrational thinking, to require evidence before believing is in a way to be scientific, or at least to trust and use the power of human intelligence.

The new sense of evidence, and of the need of evidence, revealed itself in many ways. One of the clearest was in the law. The English law of evidence, for example, began to take on its modern form at the close of the seventeenth century. Previously the belief had been that the more atrocious the crime the less evidence should be necessary in arriving at a verdict of guilty; this was thought necessary to protect society from the more hideous offenses. From the end of the seventeenth century, in English law, the judge lost his power of discretion in deciding what should constitute evidence, and the same rules of evidence were applied in all forms of accusation, the essential question being recognized as always the same—did such-and-such a fact (however outrageous) occur or did it not? After 1650 mere hearsay evidence, long vaguely distrusted, was ruled definitely out of court. After 1696 even persons charged with felony were allowed legal counsel.

The new sense of evidence was probably the main force in putting an end to the delusions of witchcraft. What made witchcraft so credible and so fearsome was that many persons confessed themselves to be witches, admitting to supernatural powers and to evil designs upon their neighbors.[5] Many or most such confessions were extracted under torture. Reformers urged that confessions obtained under torture were not evidence, that people would say anything to escape unbearable pain, so that no quantity of such confessions offered the slightest ground for believing in witches. As for the voluntary confessions, and even the boastings of some people of their diabolical powers, it was noted that such statements often came from half-demented old women, or from persons who would today be called hysterical or psychotic. Witches came to be regarded as self-deluded. Their ideas of themselves were no longer accepted as evidence. But it must be added that, except in England, the use of legal torture lasted on through most of the eighteenth century, in criminal cases in which the judge believed the accused to be guilty.

HISTORY AND HISTORICAL SCHOLARSHIP

What are called the historical sciences also developed rapidly at this time. History, like the law, depends on the finding and using of evidence. The historian and the judge must answer the same kind of question—did such-and-such a fact really occur? All knowledge of history, so far as it disengages itself from legend and wishful thinking, rests ultimately on pieces of evidence, written records and other works of man created in the past and surviving in some form or other in the present. On this mass of material the vast picture of the past is built, and without it men would be ignorant of their own antecedents, or would have only folk tales and tribal traditions.

There was much skepticism about history in the seventeenth century. Some said that history was not a form of true knowledge because it was not mathematical. Others said that it was useless because Adam, the perfect man, had neither had nor needed any history. Many felt that what passed for

[5] See pp. 46–7.

history was only a mass of fables. History was distrusted also because historians were often pretentious, claiming to be high-flying men of letters, writing for rhetorical or inspirational appeal or for argumentative reasons, disdaining the hard labor of actual study. History was losing the confidence of thinking people. How was it possible, they asked, to feel even a modicum of certainty about alleged events that had happened long before any living person had been born?

This doubting attitude itself arose from a stricter sense of evidence, or from a realization that there was really no proof for much of what was said about the past. But scholars set to work to assemble what evidence there was. They hoped to create a new history, one that should contain only reliable statements. Europe was littered with old papers and parchments. Abbeys, manor houses, royal archives were full of written documents, many of them of unknown age or unknown origin, often written in a handwriting which people could no longer read. Learned and laborious enthusiasts set to work to explore this accumulation. They added so much to the efforts of their predecessors as virtually to create modern critical scholarship and erudition. The French Benedictine monk Jean Mabillon, in 1681, in his book *On Diplomatics* (referring to ancient charters and "diplomas") established the science of paleography, which deals with the deciphering, reading, dating, and authentication of manuscripts. The Frenchman DuCange in 1688 published a dictionary of medieval Latin which is still used. Others, like the Italian Muratori, spent whole lifetimes exploring archives, collecting, editing, or publishing masses of documents, comparing manuscript copies of the same text and trying to discover what the author had really said, rejecting some as fabrications or forgeries, pronouncing others to be genuine pieces of historical evidence. Others made themselves experts in ancient coins, many of which were far more ancient than the oldest manuscripts; they founded the science of numismatics. Still others, or indeed the same ones, turned to a critical examination of the incriptions on old buildings and ruins.

Another important but little known historical "science," namely chronology, was greatly stimulated also. Chronology deals with the age of the world, and with finding a common denominator between the dating systems of various peoples. Probably it is not natural for the human mind to think in terms of dates at all. For simple people it is enough to know that some things happened "long ago," and even the learned do not commonly remember the dates of incidents in their own lives, or think of their lives as flowing along a numerical scale. In the seventeenth century the new interest in numbers, evident in physical science, turned also to the human past. Archbishop James Usher, an Anglican prelate of Ireland, after much study of the Bible, announced the date 4004 B.C. as that of the creation of the world. His chronological system was later printed in the margins of the Authorized Version of the English Bible, and is still adhered to by some fundamentalists as if part of the Bible itself. But Usher's system was not accepted by scholars even in his own time. Geographical knowledge was revealing China and its dynasties to Europe; historical knowledge was beginning to discover ancient Egypt. The Chinese and Egyptian records claimed a greater antiquity for their countries than the Old Testament seemed to allow for the human race. There was much crudite conjecture; one scholar about 1700 counted seventy estimates of the age of the world, ranging as high as 170,000 years, a figure which then seemed fantastic and appalling.

The difficulty was not only in the language of the Old Testament. It was in finding the correspondence between the chronological systems of different peoples. A Chinese system of dating by dynasties might be coherent within itself, but how could it be equated with the European system of dating from the birth of Christ, a date as unknown to the Chinese as the date of Wu Wang was to Europeans? Even European records presented the same difficulty; the Romans counted by consulships, or from the supposed year of the founding of Rome; many medieval documents told only the year of some obscure ruler's reign. Only infinite patience, interminable research, and endless calculation could reduce such a jumble to the simple system of modern textbooks. This is of more importance than may be at first thought. A common system of dating is a great aid to thinking of human history as an interconnected whole. An over-all conception of the human race is made easier by the dating of all events according to the Christian era. This itself, it may be pointed out, is an arbitrary and conventional scale, since Christ is now thought to have been born, not in A.D. 1, but in 4 B.C.

Common dating was of importance is practical affairs as well as in historical knowledge. Europe was disunited even on the Christian calendar. Protestant and some Orthodox countries followed the old or Julian calendar, Catholic countries the corrected or Gregorian calendar, issued in the sixteenth century under authority of Pope Gregory XIII. The two calendars varied in the seventeenth century by ten days. Only gradually was the Gregorian calendar accepted, by England in 1752, by Russia in 1918. Most other peoples today, in China, India, the Arabic world, and elsewhere, use or recognize the Gregorian calendar. Without a uniform way of specifying days and years it would be less easy to transact international affairs, hold international conferences, make plans, or pay and receive money. This common dating, easily taken for granted, is a consequence of the predominance of Europe in modern times. It is a sign of growing unity in world civilization.

THE QUESTIONING OF TRADITIONAL BELIEFS

The historical sciences provided a foundation on which a knowledge of man's activities in the past could be reared, and the growing geographical knowledge spread a panorama of man's diverse activities and peculiarities in the present. This new knowledge of man shared with natural science, and probably derived from it, or from philosophers of science like Descartes and Bacon, the view that many traditional ideas were erroneous, but that much could be known by a disciplined use of the human mind. The humanities and the sciences were alike in demanding evidence for belief and in trusting to the power of reason. In their impact on the old certainties of European life, the studies of man exerted possibly a greater direct force than those of nature. Pascal, in his attempt to defend the Christian faith, feared the spirit of Montaigne, the mood of skepticism and denial, which he felt himself, more than he feared the findings of mathematical and physical science. And the movement of historical thought, with its insistence on textual criticism, threw doubt on much of the Christian religion, or at least on the sacred history related in the Bible, which was considered to be part and parcel of religion itself.

In 1678 a French priest, Richard Simon, published a pioneering work in Biblical criticism, his *Critical History of the Old Testament.* Though his book was condemned both by the Church and by the government of Louis XIV, Richard Simon always felt himself to be orthodox; Catholic faith, he insisted, depended more on church tradition than on the literal statements of the Bible. He simply applied to the Old Testament the methods of textual criticism which others were applying to secular documents. He concluded that the Old Testament, as known, rested on medieval manuscripts many of which were of unknown or doubtful origin, that monkish copyists had brought in errors and corruptions, and that the books thought to have been written by Moses could not have been written by him, since they contained obvious contradictions and matter clearly inserted after his death. Others went further, questioning not merely the evidence of the Biblical text, but the very possibility of some events that it related. From the scientific idea of the absolute regularity of nature on the one hand, and from a strong sense of human credulity on the other, they denied that miracles had ever occurred, and looked upon oracles and prophecies, among either the Greeks or the Hebrews, with a dubious eye.

The most profoundly disturbing of all thinkers of the time was Baruch Spinoza (1632–77), the lens-grinder of Amsterdam, a Jew who was excommunicated by his own synagogue and who refused a professorship at the University of Heidelberg, craving only the quiet to think in peace. Spinoza drew on both the scientific and humanistic thought of his day. He arrived at a philosophy holding that God had no existence apart from the world, that everything was itself an aspect of God, a philosophy technically called pantheism but considered by many to be really atheistic. He denied the inspiration of the Bible, disbelieved in miracles and the supernatural, rejected all revelation and revealed religion, Jewish or Christian, and held that few if any governments of the day were really just. He taught a pure, stern, and intellectual ethical code, and one which had few consolations for the average man. His name became a byword for impiety and horrendous unbelief. People were literally afraid to read his works, even when they could find them, which was not often because of the censorship. His influence spread slowly, through the mediation of other writers.

More widely read, less abstruse, more reassuring, dwelling on the merits of common sense, were the writings of the Englishman John Locke (1632–1704), who summarized many of the intellectual trends of his lifetime, and exerted a strong influence for the following hundred years. He combined practical experience and theoretical interests. Educated in medicine, he kept in touch with the sciences, and was acquainted with Newton. He was associated with the great Whig noblemen who were the main authors of the English revolution in 1688. For political reasons he spent several years in the 1680's in the Netherlands, where he became familiar with thought on the Continent. He wrote on many subjects—finance, economics, education, religious policy, political theory, general philosophy—always with an engaging directness and sober air of the sensible man of the world. In his *Letter on Toleration* (1689) he advocated an established church, but with toleration of all except Roman Catholics and atheists; these he held to be dangerous to society, the former because of a foreign allegiance, the latter because they lacked a basis of moral responsibility. In his *Reasonableness of Christianity* he argued that Christianity, rightly considered, is after all a reasonable form of religion; this softened the friction between religion and natural knowledge, but tended to shut out the supernatural and merge religious feeling into an unruffled common sense.

Locke's deepest book was his *Essay Concerning the Human Understanding* (1690). Here he faced the great problem of the day, the problem of knowledge; he asked what it was possible for men to know with certainty, and how certain knowledge was arrived at. His answer was that true or certain knowledge is derived from experience—from perceptions of the sense organs and reflection of the mind on these perceptions. Locke at the end of the century thus echoed Bacon at the beginning; they became the two great pillars of empirical philosophy, insisting on experience and observation as the source of truth. Locke denied Descartes' doctrine of innate ideas, or inevitable disposition of the human mind to think in certain ways. He held that the mind at birth is a blank tablet or *tabula rasa*, and that what a man comes to think or believe depends on the environment in which he lives. Locke's environmentalist philosophy became fundamental to liberal and reforming thought in later years. It seemed that false ideas or superstitions were the result of bad environment and bad education. It seemed that the evil in human actions was due to bad social institutions, and that an improvement in human society would improve human behavior. This philosophy, whether or not wholly true in the final analysis, was largely true with respect to many practical conditions. It gave confidence in the possibility of social progress, and turned attention to a sphere in which planned and constructive action was possible, namely the sphere of government, public policy and legislation. Here we touch on political theory, to which Locke contributed *Two Treatises of Government*. These are discussed below.

33. Political Theory: The School of Natural Law

Political theory can never be strictly scientific. Science deals with what does exist or has existed. It does not tell what ought to exist. To tell what society and government ought to be like, in view of man's nature and his capacity to be miserable or contented, is a main purpose of political theory. Political theory is in a sense more practical than science. It is the scientists and scholars who are most content to observe facts as they are. Practical men, and scientists and scholars so far as they have practical interests, must always ask themselves what ought to be done, what policies ought to be adopted, what measures taken, what state of affairs maintained or brought about. Conservatives and radicals, traditionalists and innovators, are alike in this respect. It is impossible in human affairs to escape the word "ought."

But political theory was affected by the scientific view. The Renaissance Italian, Niccolò Machiavelli (1469–1527), had opened the way in this direction.[6] Machiavelli too had his "ought"; he preferred a republican form of government in which citizens felt a patriotic attachment to their state. But in his book, *The Prince*, he disregarded the question of the best form of government, a favorite question of Christian and scholastic philosophers of the Middle Ages. He separated the study of politics from theology and moral philosophy. He undertook to describe how governments and rulers actually behaved. He observed that successful rulers behaved as if holding or increasing power were their only object, that they regarded all else as means to this end. Princes, said Machiavelli, kept their promises or broke them, they told the truth or distorted or colored it, they sought popularity or ignored it, they advanced public welfare or disrupted it, they conciliated their neighbors or destroyed them, depending merely on which course of action seemed the best means of advancing their political interests. All this was bad, said Machiavelli; but that was not the question, for the question was to find out what rulers really did. Machiavelli, in *The Prince*, chose to be non-moral in order to be scientific. To most readers he seemed to be simply immoral. Nor was it possible to draw the line between *The Prince* as a scientific description of fact and *The Prince* as a book of maxims of conduct. In telling how successful rulers obtained their successes, Machiavelli also suggested how rulers *ought* to proceed. And though governments did in fact continue to behave for the most part as Machiavelli said, most people refused to admit that they ought to.

NATURAL RIGHT AND NATURAL LAW

Political theory in the seventeenth century did not embrace the cynicism attributed to Machiavelli. Nor did it fall into the skepticism of those who said that the customs of one's country should be passively accepted, or that one form of government was about as good as another. It directly faced the question, What is right? The seventeenth century was the classic age of the philosophy of natural right or of natural law.

The idea of natural law has underlain a good deal of modern demo-

───────────

[6] See pp. 55–6.

cratic development, and its decline in the last century has been closely connected with many of the troubles of recent times. It is not easy to say in
what the philosophy of natural law essentially consisted. It held that there is,
somehow, in the structure of the world, a law that distinguishes right from
wrong. It held that right is "natural," not a mere invention of men. This
right is not determined, for any country, by its heritage, tradition, or customs,
nor yet by its actual laws (called "positive" laws) of the kind that are enforced in the law courts. All these may be unfair or unjust. We detect un-
fairness or injustice in them by comparing them with natural law as we
understand it; thus we have a basis for saying that cannibalism is bad, or that
a law requiring forced labor from orphan children is unjust. Nor is natural
law, or the real rightness of a thing, determined by the authority of any person or people. No king can make right that which is wrong. No people, by
its will as a people, can make just that which is unjust. Right and law, in the
ultimate sense, exist outside and above all peoples. They are universal, the
same for all. No one can make them up to suit himself. A good king, or a
just people, are a king or people whose actions correspond to the objective
standard. But how, if we cannot trust our own positive laws or customs, or
our leaders or even our collective selves, can we know what is naturally right?
How do we discover natural law? The answer, in the natural law philosophy,
is that we discover it by reason. Man is considered to be a rational animal.
And all men are assumed to have, at least potentially and when better enlightened, the same powers of reason and understanding—Germans or English, Siamese or Europeans. This view favored a cosmopolitan outlook, and
made international agreement and general world progress seem realizable
goals. As time went on, the premises of this philosophy came to be questioned. By the twentieth century it was widely thought that man was not an
especially rational being, but was motivated by drives or urges or instincts,
and that human differences were so fundamental that men of different nationalities or classes could never expect to see things in the same way. When
this happened the older philosophy of natural law lost its hold on many
minds.

In the seventeenth and eighteenth centuries it was generally accepted.
Some, carrying over the philosophy of the Middle Ages, thought of natural
law as an aspect of the law of God. Others, more secular in spirit, held that
the natural law stood of itself. These included even some churchmen; a
group of theologians, mainly Jesuits, were condemned by the pope in 1690
for holding that universal right and wrong might exist by reason only, whether
God existed or not. The idea of natural law and the faith in human reason
went side by side, and both were fundamental in the thought of the time.
They were to be found everywhere in Europe, in their religious or their
secular form.

On the basis of natural law some thinkers tried to create an international law or "law of nations," to bring order into the maze of sovereign territorial states, great and small, that was developing in Europe. Hugo Grotius,
in 1625, published the first great book devoted exclusively to this subject, his

Law of War and Peace. Samuel Pufendorf followed with his *Law of Nature and of Nations* in 1672. Both held that sovereign states, though bound by no positive law or authority, should work together for the common good, that there was a community of nations as of individuals, and that in the absence of a higher international sovereignty they were all still subordinate to natural reason and justice. Certain concrete doctrines, such as the freedom of the seas or the immunity of ambassadors, were put forward. The principles of international law remained those of natural law. The content came to include specific agreements between governments, certain kinds of admiralty and maritime law, and the terms of treaties such as the treaties of Westphalia, Utrecht, and others. The means of enforcement, to be sure, remained weak or non-existent in crises.

HOBBES AND LOCKE

In domestic affairs the philosophy of natural law, though it rather favored constitutionalism, was used to justify both constitutional and absolutist governments. Right itself was held to be in the nature of things, beyond human power to change. But forms of government were held to be means to an end. No philosopher at the time thought the state to have an absolute value in itself. The state had to be "justified," made acceptable to the moral consciousness or the reason. There were, indeed, important competing philosophies. On the side of absolutism was the doctrine of the divine right of kings. On the side of constitutionalism were arguments based on heritage or custom, emphasizing the charters, bulls, or compacts of former times and the historic powers of parliaments and estates. But neither the supernatural argument of the divine right of kings, nor the historical argument pointing back to liberties of the Middle Ages, was entirely satisfactory in the scientific atmosphere of the seventeenth century. Neither carried complete conviction to the reason or moral sense of the most acute thinkers. Both were reinforced by arguments of natural law. Two Englishmen stand out above all others in this connection. Absolutism was philosophically justified by Thomas Hobbes, constitutionalism by John Locke.

Hobbes (1588–1679) followed the scientific and mathematical discoveries of his time with more than an amateur interest. In philosophy he held to a materialistic and even atheistic system. In English politics he sided with king against Parliament; he disliked the disorder and violence of the civil war of the 1640's, and the unstable conditions of the English republic of the 1650's.[7] He concluded that men have no capacity for self-government. His opinion of human nature was low; he held that men in the "state of nature," or as imagined to exist without government, were quarrelsome and turbulent, forever locked in a war of all against all. In his famous phrase, life in the state of nature was "solitary, poor, nasty, brutish and short." From fear of

[7] See pp. 147–9.

each other, to obtain order, and enjoy the advantages of law and right, men came to a kind of agreement or "contract" by which they surrendered their freedom of action into the hands of a ruler. It was necessary for this ruler to have unrestricted or absolute power. Only thus could he maintain order. It was intolerably dangerous, according to Hobbes, for anyone to question the actions of government, for such questioning might reopen the way to chaos. Government must in fact be a kind of Leviathan (the monster mentioned in the Bible, Job 41); and it was by the word *Leviathan* that Hobbes entitled his principal book, published in 1651, two years after the execution of King Charles I.

By this book Hobbes became the leading secular exponent of absolutism, and one of the principal theorists of the unlimited sovereignty of the state. His influence on later thinkers was very great. He accustomed political theorists to the use of purely natural arguments. He quoted freely from the Bible, but the Bible had no influence on his thought. After Hobbes, all advanced political theorists regarded government as a thing created by human purpose. It was no longer considered, except popularly and except by professional theologians, as part of a divine dispensation of God to man. Hobbes also affected later theorists by his arguments for a sovereign authority, and, more negatively, by obliging them to refute his idea of an unlimited personal sovereign. But he was never a popular writer. In England the cause which he favored was lost. In those continental countries where royal absolutism prevailed his arguments were received with secret gratification, but his irreligion was too dangerous to make public, and the absolutist argument, on the popular level, remained that of the divine right of kings. In any case Hobbes's arguments were in some ways insufficient for real monarchs. Hobbes abhorred struggle and violence. His case for absolutism required absolutism to produce civil peace, individual security, and a rule of law. He also held that absolute power depended on, or had at least originated in, a free and rational agreement by which people accepted it. An absolute monarchy that flagrantly violated these conditions could with difficulty be justified even by the doctrines of Hobbes. It is in these respects that Hobbes differs from totalitarian theorists of recent times. For Hobbes, in the final analysis, absolute power was an expedient to promote individual welfare. It was a means necessary to the realization of natural law.

John Locke (1632–1704), as has been seen, also stood in the main current of scientific thought and discovery. But in his political philosophy he carried over many ideas of the Middle Ages, as formulated in the thirteenth century by St. Thomas Aquinas,[8] and kept alive in England by successive thinkers of the Anglican church. Medieval philosophy had never favored an absolute power. With Hobbes, Locke shared the idea that good government is an expedient of human purpose, neither provided by divine Providence nor inherited by a national tradition. He held, too, like Hobbes and the whole school of natural law, that government was based on a kind of contract, or

---

[8] See pp. 37–9.

rational and conscious agreement between ruler and ruled. In contrast to Hobbes, he sided with Parliament against king in the practical struggles of politics. After the Parliamentary revolution of 1688, by which William III was called to the English throne, he published *Two Treatises of Government* (1690), in which he justified what had already occurred.[9]

Locke took a more genial view of human nature than Hobbes. As he showed in his other books, he believed that a moderate religion was a good thing, and above all that men could learn from experience and hence could be educated to an enlightened way of life. These ideas favored a belief in self-government. Locke declared (in contradiction to Hobbes) that men in the "state of nature" were reasonable and well disposed, willing to get along with one another though handicapped by the absence of public authority. Men likewise had a moral sense, quite independently of government; and they also possessed by nature certain rights, quite apart from the state. These rights were the rights to life, liberty, and property. Locke threw very heavy emphasis on the right of property, by which he usually meant the possession of land. His philosophy can in fact be regarded as an expression of the landed classes of England in their claims against the king; it should be noted that land ownership in England was more widespread in 1690 than it later became. Men, as individuals in the state of nature, are not altogether able, according to Locke, to win general respect for their individual natural rights. They cannot by their own efforts protect what is "proper" to them, *i.e.*, their property. They agree to set up government to enforce observance of the rights of all. Government is thus created by a contract, but the contract is not unconditional, as claimed by Hobbes. It imposes mutual obligations. The people must be reasonable; only rational beings can be politically free. Liberty is not an anarchy of undisciplined will; it is the freedom to act without compulsion by another. Only rational and responsible creatures can exercise true freedom; but adult human beings, according to Locke, are or can be educated to be rational and responsible. They therefore can and should be free. On government, also, certain conditions and obligations are imposed. If a government breaks the contract, if it threatens the natural rights which it is the sole purpose of government to protect, if for example it takes away a man's property without his consent, then the governed have a right to reconsider what they have done in creating the government, and may even in the last extremity rebel against it. The right to resist government, Locke admits, is very dangerous, but it is less dangerous than its opposite, which would lead to enslavement; and in any case we are talking about reasonable and responsible people.

If Locke's ideas seem familiar, especially to Americans, it is because of the wide popularizing of his philosophy in the century after his death. Nowhere was his influence greater than in the British colonies. The authors of the American Declaration of Independence and of the Constitution of the United States knew the writings of Locke very thoroughly. Some phrases

[9] See pp. 152–5.

of the Declaration of Independence echo his very language. In Great Britain also, and in France and elsewhere, in the course of time, Locke's influence was immense.

What Locke did was to convert an episode in English history into an event of universal meaning. In England, in 1688, certain great lords, winning the support of the established church, gentry and merchants, put out one king and brought in another. On the new king they imposed certain obligations, specified in the Bill of Rights of 1689, and all dealing with legal or technical interpretations of the English constitution. The revolution of 1688 was a very English affair. England in 1688 was still little known to the rest of Europe. The proceedings in England, so far as known, might seem no different from a rebellion of the magnates of Hungary. Locke, in arguing that Parliament had done right to eject James II, put the whole affair on a level of reason, natural right, and human nature. It thus came to have meaning for everyone. At the same time, Locke made the English revolution a sign of progress rather than reaction. The new and modern form of government in 1690 was royal absolutism, with its professional bureaucracy and corps of paid officials. Almost everywhere there was resistance to the kings, led by landed interests and harking back to earlier freedoms. Such resistance seemed to many Europeans to be feudal and medieval. Locke made the form taken by such resistance in England, namely the revolution of 1688 against James II, into a modern and forward-looking move. He checked the prestige of absolutism. He gave new prestige to constitutional principles. He carried over, in modified form, many ideas from the scholastic philosophers of the Middle Ages, who had generally maintained that kings had only a relative and restricted power, and were responsible to their peoples. To these ideas he added the force of the newer scientific view of the world. He did not rest his case on supernatural or providential arguments. He did not say that constitutional government was the will of God. He said that it rested on experience and observation of human nature, on recognition of certain individual rights and especially the right of property, and on the existence of a purely natural law of reason and justice. He was an almost entirely secular thinker.

One must not claim too much for Locke, or for any writer. England was in fact, in 1688, more modern in many ways than other countries in Europe. The Glorious Revolution was in fact not exactly like uprisings of the landed and propertied classes elsewhere. England in the following century did in fact create a form of parliamentary government that was unique. But facts go together with the theories that give them an understandable meaning. Events in England, as explained by Locke, and as seen in other countries and even in England and its colonies through Locke's eyes, launched into the main stream of modern history the superb tradition of constitutional government, which has been one of the main themes in the history of the modern world ever since.

By 1700, at the close of the "century of genius," some beliefs that were to be characteristic of modern times had clearly taken form, notably a faith in science, in human reason, in natural human rights, and in progress. The following period, generally known as the Age of Enlightenment, was to be a time of clarifying and popularizing ideas which the more creative seventeenth century had produced. These ideas were eventually to revolutionize Europe, America, and the world. They were also in subsequent years to be modified, amended, challenged, and even denied. But they are still very much alive today.

The Age
of Enlightenment

‸‸

T H E eighteenth century, or at least the years of that century preceding the French Revolution of 1789, is commonly known as the Age of Enlightenment, and though that name has more than the usual difficulties by which such sobriquets are always attended, still there is no other that describes so many features of the time so well. People strongly felt that theirs was an enlightened age, and it is from their own evaluation of themselves that our term Age of Enlightenment is derived. Everywhere there was a feeling that Europeans had at last emerged from a long twilight. The past was regarded as a time of barbarism and darkness. The sense of progress was all but universal among the educated classes. It was the belief both of the forward-looking thinkers and writers known as the *philosophes* and of the forward-looking kings and empresses, the "enlightened despots," together with their ministers and officials.

34. The Philosophes

THE ENLIGHTENMENT SPIRIT: THE IDEA OF PROGRESS

The spirit of the eighteenth-century Enlightenment was drawn from the scientific and intellectual revolution of the seventeenth century. The Enlightenment carried over and popularized the ideas of Bacon and Descartes, of Bayle and Spinoza, and, above all, of Locke and Newton. It carried over the philosophy of natural law and of natural right. Never was there an age so skeptical toward tradition, so confident in the powers of human reason and of science, so firmly convinced of the regularity and harmony of nature, and so deeply imbued with the sense of civilization's advance and progress.

The idea of progress is often said to be the dominant or characteristic idea of European civilization from the seventeenth century to the twentieth. It is a belief, a kind of non-religious faith, that the conditions of human life become better as time goes on, that in general each generation is better off than its predecessors and will contribute by its labors to an even better life for generations to come, and that in the long run all mankind will share in the same advance. All the elements of this belief had been present by 1700. It was after 1700, however, that the idea of progress became explicit. In the seventeenth century it had shown itself in a more rudimentary way, in a sporadic dispute, among men of letters in England and France, known as the quarrel of Ancients and Moderns. The Ancients held that the works of the Greeks and Romans had never been surpassed. The Moderns, pointing to science, art, literature, and invention, declared that their own time was the best, that it was natural for men of their time to do better than the ancients because they came later and built upon their predecessors' achievements. The quarrel was never exactly settled, but a great many people in 1700 were Moderns. Europeans had always felt themselves better off than the ancients in being Christians where the ancients were pagans. Now, for the first time in the history of Europe, a great many Europeans felt that in purely worldly ways they had outdone the noble Greeks and Romans. And many felt that this progress need never cease.

Far-reaching also was the faith of the age in the natural faculties of the human mind. Pure skepticism, the negation of reason, was overcome. Nor were the educated, after 1700, likely to be superstitious, terrified by the unknown, or addicted to magic. The witchcraft mania abruptly died. Indeed all sense of the supernatural became dim. "Modern" people not only ceased to fear the devil; they ceased also to fear God. They thought of God less as a Father than as a First Cause of the physical universe. There was less sense of a personal God, or of the inscrutable imminence of divine Providence, or of man's need for saving grace. God was less the God of Love; He was the inconceivably intelligent being who had made the amazing universe now discovered by man's reason. The great symbol of the Christian God was the Cross, on which a divine being had suffered in human form. The symbol which occurred to people of scientific view was the Watchmaker. The intricacies of the physical universe were compared to the intricacies of a watch, and it was argued that just as a watch could not exist without a watchmaker, so the universe as discovered by Newton could not exist without a God who created it and set it moving by its mathematical law. It was almighty intelligence that was thought divine.

All this promoted the spirit of secularism in Europe. Intellectual developments reinforced social and economic causes in turning people away from the old religion. Churches and churchmen lost out in leadership and prestige. Economics and politics, business and the state, were no longer subordinated to religious ends. They threw off the restraints imposed by moral or religious judgments. At the same time religious toleration spread. Persecution of religious minorities became less common. In any case, in their attempts to enforce acceptance of religious doctrine, churches no longer used the barbaric methods of former times, such as the fagot and the stake. Barbaric methods as used by the state, against persons suspected or convicted of crimes or political offenses, also came increasingly into disrepute.

THE PHILOSOPHES

It was through the *philosophes* that the ideas of the Enlightenment were spread. The *philosophes* were not essentially philosophers in the usual sense of the word. They were rather popularizers or publicists. They read the great books which most people did not read and reworded the ideas in such a way as to hold the interest of the average reader. They were primarily "men of letters." Formerly authors had generally been gentlemen of leisure, or talented protégés of aristocratic or royal patrons, or professors or clerics supported by the income from religious foundations. In the Age of Enlightenment a great many were free-lancers, grub-streeters, or journalists. They wrote for "the publick."

The reading public had greatly expanded. The educated middle class, commercial and professional, was much larger than ever before. Country gentlemen were putting off their rustic habits and even noblemen wished to keep informed. Newspapers and magazines multiplied, and people who could not read them at home could read them in coffee-houses or in reading-rooms organized for that purpose. There was a great demand also for dictionaries, encyclopedias, and surveys of all fields of knowledge. The new readers wanted matters made interesting and clear. They appreciated wit and lightness of touch. From such a public, literature itself greatly benefited. The style of the eighteenth century became admirably fluent, clear, and exact, neither ponderous on the one hand nor frothy on the other. And from writings of this kind the readers benefited also, from the interior of Europe to the America of Benjamin Franklin. The bourgeois middle class was becoming not only educated but thoughtful. But the movement was not a class movement only.

There was another way in which writings of the day were affected by social conditions. They were all written under censorship. The theory of censorship was to protect people from harmful ideas as they were protected from shoddy merchandise or dishonest weights and measures. In England the censorship was so mild as to have little effect. Other countries, such as Spain, had a powerful censorship but few original writers. France, the center of the Enlightenment, had both a complicated censorship and a large reading and writing public. The church, the Parliament of Paris, the royal officials, and the printers' gilds all had a hand in the censoring of books. French censorship, however, was very loosely administered, and after 1750 writers were disturbed by it very little. It cannot be compared to censorship in some countries in the twentieth century. Yet in one way it had an unfavorable effect on French thought and letters. It discouraged writers from addressing themselves, in a common-sense way, to a serious consideration of concrete public questions. Legally forbidden to criticize church or state, they threw their criticisms on an abstract level. Debarred from attacking things in particular, they tended to attack things in general. Or they talked of the customs of the Persians and the Iroquois but not the French. Their works became full of double meanings, sly digs, innuendoes, and jokes, by which an author, if questioned, could declare that he did not mean what all the world knew he did mean. As for readers, they developed a taste for forbidden books, which were always easy enough to obtain through illicit channels. No one wanted to read merely authorized literature, and Parisians who heard that a book was frowned upon by the archbishop or the Parliament could hardly wait to read it and talk about it. Ideas were prized because they were daring, or even merely naughty. French thought was made more radical by the half-way measures used to control it.

Paris was the heart of the movement. There ladies in their *salons* held evening parties at which wits, men of letters, and people of society talked brilliantly on many topics. In Paris, too, was published the most serious of all *philosophe* enterprises, the *Encyclopédie*, edited by Denis Diderot in seventeen large volumes and completed over the years 1751 to 1772. It was a great compendium of scientific, technical, and historical knowledge, carrying a strong undertone of criticism of existing society and institutions, and epitomizing the skeptical, rational, and scientific spirit of the age. It was not the first encyclopedia, but it was the first to have a distinguished list of contributors or to be conceived as a positive force for social progress. Virtually all the French *philosophes* contributed—Voltaire, Montesquieu, Rousseau, d'Alembert (who assisted in the editing), Buffon, Turgot, Quesnay, and many others, all sometimes collectively called the Encyclopedists.

Another group of thinkers was the Physiocrats, whom their critics called "economists," a word originally thought to be mildly insulting. They included Quesnay, physician to Louis XV, Turgot, minister to Louis XVI, and Dupont de Nemours, founder of the industrial family of the Du Ponts in the United States. The Physiocrats concerned themselves with fiscal and tax reform, and with measures to increase the national wealth of France.

The first to use the term *laissez faire* ("let things alone"), they believed that wealth would increase if there were greater freedom for investment and for the trade and circulation of goods, though they insisted on the planning authority of an "enlightened" government.

Men and women who considered themselves *philosophes*, or close to the *philosophes* in spirit, were found all over Europe. Frederick the Great was an eminent *philosophe*; not only was he the friend of Voltaire and host to a circle of literary and scientific men at Potsdam, but he himself wrote epigrams, satires, dissertations, and histories, as well as works on military science, and he had a gift of wit, a sharp tongue, and a certain impishness toward the traditional and the pompous. Catherine the Great, empress of Russia, was also a *philosophe* for much the same reasons. Maria Theresa, of Austria, was not a *philosophe*; she was too religious and too little concerned with general ideas. Her son Joseph, on the other hand, as we shall see, proved to be a *philosophe* enthroned. In England Bishop Warburton was considered by some of his friends as a *philosophe*; he held that the Church of England of his day, as a social institution, was exactly what pure reason would have invented. The Scottish skeptical philosopher David Hume counted as a *philosophe*, as did Edward Gibbon, who shocked the pious by his attacks on Christianity in his famous *Decline and Fall of the Roman Empire*. Dr. Samuel Johnson was not a *philosophe*; he worried over the supernatural, adhered to the established church, deflated pretentious authors, and even declared that Voltaire and Rousseau were bad men who should be sent "to the plantations." There were also Italian and German *philosophes*, like the Marquis di Beccaria who sought to humanize the criminal law, or Baron Grimm who sent a literary newsletter from Paris to his many subscribers.

MONTESQUIEU, VOLTAIRE, AND ROUSSEAU

Most famous of all *philosophes* were the French trio, Montesquieu (1689–1755), Voltaire (1694–1778), and Rousseau (1712–78). They differed vehemently with each other. All were hailed as literary geniuses in their own day. All turned from pure literature to works of political commentary and social protest. All thought that the existing state of society could be improved.

Montesquieu, twice a baron, was a landed aristocrat, *seigneur* or manorial lord of southern France. He inherited from his uncle a seat in the Parliament of Bordeaux, and sat actively in that parliament in the days of the Regency.[1] He was part of the noble resurgence which followed the death of Louis XIV and continued on through the eighteenth century. Although he shared many of the ideas in the stream of aristocratic and anti-absolutist thought, he went beyond a mere self-centered class philosophy. In his great work, *The Spirit of Laws*, published in 1748, he developed two

---

[1] See pp. 236–7.

principal ideas. One was that forms of government varied according to climate and circumstances, for example that despotism was suited only to large empires in hot climates, and that democracy would work only in small city-states. His other great doctrine, aimed against royal absolutism in France (which he called "despotism"), was the separation and balance of powers. In France he believed that power should be divided between the king and a great many "intermediate bodies"—parliaments, provincial estates, organized nobility, chartered towns, and even the church. It was natural for him, a judge in parliament, a provincial and a nobleman, to favor the first three, and reasonable for him to recognize the position of the bourgeoisie of the towns; as for the church, he observed that, while he took no stock in its teachings, he thought it useful as an offset to undue centralization of government. He greatly admired the English constitution as he understood it, believing that England carried over, more successfully than any other country, the feudal liberties of the early Middle Ages. He thought that in England the necessary separation and balance of powers was obtained by an ingenious mixture of monarchy, aristocracy, and democracy (king, lords, and commons) and by a separation of the functions of the executive, legislature, and judiciary. This doctrine had a wide influence, and was well known to the Americans who in 1787 wrote the constitution of the United States. Montesquieu's own *philosophe* friends thought him too conservative, and even tried to dissuade him from publishing his ideas. He was, indeed, technically a reactionary, favoring a scheme of things that antedated Louis XIV, and he was unusual among contemporaries in his admiration of the "barbarous" Middle Ages.

Voltaire was born in 1694 into a comfortable bourgeois family and christened Francois-Marie Arouet; "Voltaire," an invented word, is simply the most famous of all pen-names. Until he was over forty he was known only as a smart writer of epigrams, tragedies in verse, and an epic. Thereafter he turned increasingly to philosophical and public questions. His strength throughout lay in the facility of his pen. He is the easiest of all great writers to read. He was always trenchant, logical, and incisive, sometimes scurrilous; mocking and sarcastic when he wished, equally a master of deft irony and of withering ridicule. However serious in his purpose, he achieved it by creating a laugh.

In his youth Voltaire spent eleven months in the Bastille for what was considered to be impertinence to the Regent, who, however, in the next year rewarded him with a pension for one of his dramas. He was again arrested after a fracas with a nobleman, the Chevalier de Rohan. He remained an incorrigible bourgeois, while never deeply objecting to the aristocracy on principle. Through his admirer Mme. de Pompadour (another bourgeois, though the king's favorite) he became a gentleman of the bedchamber and royal historian to Louis XV. These functions he fulfilled *in absentia*, when at all, for Paris and Versailles were too hot for him. He was the personal friend of Frederick the Great, with whom he lived for about two years at Potsdam. The two finally quarreled, for no stage was big enough to hold two such prima donnas for very long. Voltaire made a fortune from his writings, pensions, speculations, and practical business sense. In his later years he purchased a manor at Ferney near the French frontier. Here he became, as he said, the "hotel keeper of Europe," receiving the streams of distinguished admirers, favor hunters, and distressed persons who came to seek him out. He died at Paris in 1778, at the age of eighty-four, by far the most famous man of letters in Europe. His collected writings fill over seventy volumes.

Voltaire was mainly interested in the freedom of thought. Like Montesquieu, he was an admirer of England. He spent three years in that country, where, in 1727, he witnessed the State funeral accorded to Sir Isaac Newton and his burial in Westminster Abbey. Voltaire's *Philosophical Letters on the English* (1733) and *Elements of the Philosophy of Newton* (1738) not only brought England increasingly before the consciousness of the rest of Europe, but also popularized the new scientific ideas—the inductive philosophy of Bacon, the physics of Newton, and the sensationalist psychology of Locke,[2] whose doctrine that all true ideas arose from sense experience undercut the authority of religious belief. What Voltaire mainly admired in England was its religious liberty, its relative freedom of the press, and the high regard paid to men of letters like himself. Political liberty concerned him much less than it did Montesquieu. Louis XIV, a villain for Montesquieu and the neo-aristocratic school, was a hero for Voltaire, who wrote a laudatory *Age of Louis XIV* (1751) praising the Sun King for the splendor of art and literature in his reign. Voltaire likewise continued to esteem Frederick the Great, though he quarreled with him personally. Frederick was in fact almost his ideal of the enlightened ruler, a man who sponsored the arts and sciences, recognized no religious authority, and granted toleration to all creeds, welcoming Protestants and Catholics on equal terms if only they would be socially useful.

After about 1740 Voltaire became more definitely the crusader, preaching the cause of religious toleration. He fought to clear the memory of Jean Calas, a Protestant put to death on the charge of murdering a son to prevent his conversion to Rome. He wrote also to exonerate a youth named La Barre, who had been executed for defiling a wayside cross. *Ecrasez l'infâme!* became the famous Voltairean war cry—"crush the infamous thing!" The *infâme* for him was bigotry, intolerance, and superstition, and behind these the power of an organized clergy. He assaulted not only the Catholic Church but the whole traditional Christian view of the world. He argued for "natural religion" and "natural morality," holding that belief in God and the difference between good and evil arose from reason itself. This doctrine had in fact long been taught by the Catholic Church. But Voltaire insisted that no supernatural revelation in addition to reason was desirable or necessary, or rather, that belief in a special supernatural revelation made men intolerant, stupid, and cruel. He was the first to present a purely secular conception of world history. In his *Essai sur les moeurs*, or "Universal History," he began with ancient China and surveyed the great civilizations in

[2] See p. 281.

turn. Earlier writers of world history had put human events within a Christian framework. Following the Bible, they began with the Creation, proceeded to the Fall, recounted the rise of Israel and so on. Voltaire put Judeo-Christian history within a sociological framework. He represented Christianity and all other organized religions as social phenomena or mere human opinions. Spinoza had said as much; Voltaire spread these ideas through Europe.

In matters of politics and self-government Voltaire was neither a liberal nor a democrat. His opinion of the human race was about as low as his friend Frederick's. If only a government was enlightened he did not care how powerful it was. By an enlightened government he meant one that fought against sloth and stupidity, kept the clergy in a subordinate place, allowed freedom of thought and religion, and advanced the cause of material and technical progress. He had no developed political theory, but his ideal for large civilized countries approached that of enlightened or rational despotism. Believing that only a few could be enlightened, he thought that these few, a king and his advisers, should have the power to carry their program against all opposition. To overcome ignorance, habit, credulity, and priestcraft it was necessary for the state to be strong. It may be said that what Voltaire most desired was liberty for the enlightened.

Jean-Jacques Rousseau was very different. Born in Geneva in 1712, he was a Swiss, a Protestant, and almost of lower-class origin. He never felt at ease in France or in Paris society. Neglected as a child, a runaway at sixteen, he lived for years by odd jobs, such as copying music, and not until the age of forty did he have any success as a writer. He was always the little man, the outsider. In addition, his sex life was unsatisfactory; he finally settled down with an uneducated girl named Thérèse Levasseur, and with her mother, who kept interfering with his affairs. By Thérèse he had five children, whom he deposited at an orphanage. He had no social status, no money, and no sense of money, and after he became famous he lived largely by the generosity of his friends. He was pathetically and painfully maladjusted. He came to feel that he could trust no one, that those who tried to befriend him were deriding or betraying him behind his back. He suffered from what would now be termed complexes; possibly he was paranoiac. He talked endlessly of his own virtue and innocence, and complained bitterly that he was misunderstood.

But unbalanced though he was, he was possibly the most profound writer of the age, and was certainly the most permanently influential. Rousseau felt, from his own experience, that in society as it existed a good man could not be happy. He therefore attacked society, declaring that it was artificial and corrupt. He even attacked reason, calling it a false guide when followed alone. He felt doubts on all the progress and civilization which gave such satisfaction to his contemporaries. In his two "discourses," one on the *Arts and Sciences* (1750), the other on the *Origin of Inequality among Men* (1753), he argued that civilization made men evil and that life in the "state of nature" was much better. As Voltaire told him, when Rousseau sent him a copy of his second discourse (Voltaire who relished civilization in every form), it made him "feel like going on all fours." To Rousseau the best traits of human character, such as kindness, unselfishness, honesty, and true understanding, were products of nature. Deep below reason, he sensed the presence of feeling. He delighted in the warmth of sympathy, the quick flash of intuition, the clear message of conscience. He was religious by temperament, for though he believed in no church, no clergy, and no revelation he had a respect for the Bible, a reverent awe toward the cosmos, a love of solitary meditation, and a belief in a God who was not merely a "first cause" but also a God of love and beauty. Rousseau thus made it easier for serious-minded people to slip away from orthodoxy and all forms of churchly discipline. He was feared by the churches as the most dangerous of all "infidels," and was condemned both in Catholic France and at Protestant Geneva.

In general, in most of his books, Rousseau, unlike so many of his contemporaries, gave the impression that impulse is more reliable than considered judgment, spontaneous feeling more to be trusted than critical thought. Mystical insights were for him more truthful than rational or clear ideas. He became the "man of feeling," the "child of nature," the forerunner of the coming age of romanticism, and an important source of all modern emphasis on the non-rational and the subconscious.

In the *Social Contract* (1762) Rousseau seemed to contradict all this. In it he held, somewhat like Hobbes,[3] that the "state of nature" was a brutish condition without law or morality. In other works he had held that the badness of men was due to the evils of society. He now held that good men could be produced only by an improved society. Earlier thinkers, for example both Locke and Hobbes, had thought of the "contract" as an agreement between a ruler and a people. Rousseau thought of it as an agreement among the people themselves. It was a social, not merely a political, contract. Organized civil society, *i.e.*, the community, rested upon it. It was an understanding by which all individuals surrendered their natural liberty to each other, fused their individual wills into a combined General Will, and agreed to accept the rulings of this General Will as final. This General Will was the sovereign; and true sovereign power, rightly understood, was "absolute," "sacred," and "inviolable." Government was secondary; kings, officials or elected representatives were only delegates of a sovereign people. Rousseau devoted many difficult and abstruse pages to explaining how the *real* General Will could be known. It was not necessarily determined by vote of a majority. "What generalizes the will," he said, "is not the number of voices but the common interest that unites them." He said little of the mechanism of government, and had no admiration for parliamentary institutions. He was concerned with something deeper. Maladjusted outsider that he was, he craved a commonwealth in which every person could feel that he belonged. He wished a state in which all persons had a sense of membership and participation.

[3] See pp. 284–5.

By these ideas Rousseau made himself the prophet of both democracy and nationalism. Indeed, in his *Considerations on Poland*, written at the request of Poles who were fighting against the partitions, Rousseau applied the ideas of the *Social Contract* in more concrete form, and became the first systematic theorist of a conscious and calculated nationalism.[4] In writing the *Social Contract* he had in mind a small city-state like his native Geneva. But what he did, in effect, was to generalize and make applicable to large territories the psychology of small city republics—the sense of membership, of community and fellowship, of responsible citizenship and intimate participation in public affairs—in short, of common will. All modern states, democratic or undemocratic, strive to impart this sense of moral solidarity to their peoples. Whereas in democratic states the General Will can in some way be identified with the sovereignty of the people, in dictatorships it becomes possible for individuals (or parties) to arrogate to themselves the right to serve as spokesmen and interpreters of the General Will. Both totalitarians and democrats have regarded Rousseau as one of their prophets.

The *Social Contract* was little read and almost unknown in its own time. Rousseau's influence on his contemporaries was spread by his other writings and especially his novels, *Émile* (1762) and the *Nouvelle Héloïse* (1760). The novels were widely read in all literate classes of society, especially by the women, who made a kind of cult of Jean-Jacques, while he was living and after his death, which occurred in 1778. He was a literary master, able to evoke shades of thought and feeling that no writer had touched before, and by his literary writings he spread in the highest circles a new respect for the comman man, a love of common things, an impulse of human pity and compassion, a sense of artifice and superficiality in aristocratic life. Women took to nursing their own babies. Even men spoke of the delicacy of their sentiments. Tears became the fashion. The queen, Marie-Antoinette, built herself a village in the gardens at Versailles where she pretended to be a simple milkmaid. In all this there was much that was ridiculous or shallow. Yet it was the wellspring of modern humanitarianism, the force leading to a new sense of human equality. Rousseau estranged the French upper classes from their own mode of life. He made many of them lose faith in their own superiority. That was his main direct contribution to the French Revolution.

MAIN CURRENTS OF ENLIGHTENMENT THOUGHT

It is clear that the currents of thought in France and Europe were divergent and inconsistent. Most people believed in progress, reason, science, and civilization. Rousseau had his doubts, and praised the beauties of character. Montesquieu thought the church useful, but did not believe in religion; Rousseau believed in religion, but saw no need of any church. Montesquieu was concerned over practical political liberty; Voltaire would sur-

⁴ See pp. 222–3.

render political liberty in return for guarantees of intellectual freedom; Rousseau wanted emancipation from the trivialities of society, and sought the freedom that consists in merging willingly with nature and with one's fellows. Most *philosophes* were closest to Voltaire.

The most active center of ideas in the Age of Enlightenment, it has become clear, was France. French *philosophes* traveled all over Europe. Frederick II and Catherine II invited French thinkers to their courts. French was the language of the academies of St. Petersburg and Berlin. Frederick wrote his own works in the French language. There was a uniform, cosmopolitan culture among the upper classes of most of Europe, and this culture was predominantly French. But England was important also. Hitherto somewhat on the outer fringes of the European consciousness, England now moved closer to the center. Montesquieu and Voltaire may be said to have "discovered" England to Europe. Through them the ideas of Bacon, Newton, and Locke, and the whole theory of English law and parliamentary government became matters for general discussion and comment. The rise of Britain in wealth and empire gave irresistible prestige to these ideas. And as English families grew more affluent their sons increasingly made the "grand tour" on the Continent, until the *milords anglais* became familiar figures to Europeans, never quite understood but often secretly envied. All such influences, French and English, added to the leadership of western Europe in modern civilization.

The thought of the Enlightenment was completely secular. The church was considered, at most, a socially useful institution. To the more militant it was a survival of barbarism. Churchmen themselves, in the established churches, often looked with distrust on the religious zeal that did appear. For everywhere, it is true, there were religious stirrings, forms of revivalist religion, urging a new and fresh realization of gospel teachings: Jansenism continued in France, Pietism developed in Germany, the Methodist movement began in England, the "great awakening" took place in the Anglo-American colonies. But these revivalist movements had their greatest success among the least comfortable classes. The official churches, Anglican, Lutheran, Catholic, did not wish to be disturbed. Bishops were cultivated and enlightened gentlemen of the age, and reasoned like enlightened gentlemen.

By intellectual leaders all churches were pushed aside. Toleration in religion, or even indifference, became the mark of progress. The older Christian view seemed no longer to be necessary. Thinkers provided theories of society, world history, human destiny, and of the nature of good and evil in which Christian explanations had no part. Old Christian virtues, such as humility, chastity, or the patient bearing of pain and sorrow, ceased to be regarded as significant (except in some ways by Rousseau). Christian love was transformed and secularized into humanitarian good will. The most important virtue was to be socially useful. The progress of society, from generation to generation, toward a more comfortable and decent life on earth, became the dominant idea that gave meaning to the history and destiny of mankind. It was a faith summarized by one of the later *philosophes*, the

Marquis de Condorcet, when he wrote, shortly before committing suicide in the French Revolution, his *Outline of the Progress of the Human Mind*.

The main instrument of progress was thought to be the state. Whether in the form of limited monarchy on the English model favored by Montesquieu, or of the enlightened despotism preferred by Voltaire, or of the ideal republican commonwealth portrayed by Rousseau, the rightly ordered society was considered the best guarantee of social welfare. It was to the enlightened state that people now looked for salvation, and all hope of progress rested upon political reform, education, and the creation of an enlightened environment.

Though they thought in terms of reform by the state, the thinkers of the time were not nationalists but "universalists." They believed in the unity of mankind, and held that all men subsisted under the same natural law of right and reason. In this they carried over the classical and Christian outlook in a new way. They supposed that all men would participate alike in the same progress, that in the long run all men would agree, and that the outcome of history would be one uniform civilization in which all peoples and races would share equally. No nation was thought to have a peculiar message. French ideas enjoyed a wide currency, but no one thought of them as peculiarly French, arising from a French "national character." It was simply thought that the French at the time, as the most civilized people, had most fully developed the capacities of the human mind. Never since the Age of Enlightenment has there been such unquestioning belief in the potential similarity of all human beings.

All the thinking of the time was designed to make men free. All thought of the Enlightenment, in one way or another, was concerned with the problem of liberty. Montesquieu wanted guarantees against despotism. Rousseau wanted freedom from the artificialities and restraints of society as he knew it. For Voltaire and most of the *philosophes*, liberty meant freedom from the church and from intolerance, freedom of the mind, freedom from misconception and ignorance, the most insidious of all forms of enslavement. To clear the ground, to shake people out of the habits of ages, to repress the forces which he believed to endanger this liberation of the spirit, Voltaire and others were willing to trust to a powerful and well-disposed government, *i.e.*, to an "enlightened despot." Enlightened despotism, somewhat in the manner favored by Voltaire and most of the *philosophes*, became the characteristic tone of government in Europe after about 1740.

35. Enlightened Despotism: France, Austria, Prussia

THE MEANING OF ENLIGHTENED DESPOTISM

Enlightened despotism is hard to define, because it grew out of the earlier absolutism represented by Louis XIV or Peter the Great. Characteristically, the enlightened despots drained marshes, built roads and bridges, codified the laws, repressed provincial autonomy and localism, curtailed the independence of church and nobles, and built up a trained and salaried officialdom. All these things had been done by kings before. The typical enlightened despot differed from his "unenlightened" predecessor mainly in attitude and tempo. He said little of a divine right to his throne. He might even not emphasize his hereditary or dynastic family right. He justified his authority on grounds of usefulness to society, calling himself, as Frederick the Great did, the "first servant of the state."

Enlightened despotism was secular; it claimed no mandate from heaven and recognized no especial responsibility to God or church. The typical enlightened despot consequently favored toleration in religion, and this was an important new emphasis after about 1740; but here again there was precedent in the older absolutism, for the rulers of Prussia had been inclined toward toleration long before Frederick, and even the French Bourbons had recognized a degree of religious liberty for almost a century following the Edict of Nantes.[5] The secular outlook of the enlightened governments is again seen in the common front they adopted against the Jesuits. High papalists and ultramontanes,[6] affirming the authority of a universal church, and at the same time intellectually and in other ways the strongest religious order in the Catholic world, the Jesuits were distasteful to the enlightened monarchs and their civil officials, and in the 1760's were expelled from almost all Catholic countries. In 1773 the pope was persuaded to dissolve the Society of Jesus entirely. The various governments concerned, in France, Austria, Spain, Portugal, and Naples, confiscated the Jesuit property and took over the Jesuit schools. Not until 1814 was the order reconstituted.

Enlightened despotism was also rational and reformist. The typical despot set out to reconstruct his state by the use of reason. Sharing the current view of the past as benighted, he was impatient of custom and of all that was imbedded in custom or claimed as a heritage from the past, such as systems of customary law and the rights and privileges of church, nobles, towns, gilds, provinces, assemblies of estates, or, in France, the judicial bodies called parliaments. The complex of such institutions was disparagingly referred to as "feudalism." Monarchs had long struggled against feudalism in this sense, but in the past they had usually compromised. The enlightened despot was less willing to compromise, and herein lay the difference in tempo. The new despot acted abruptly, desiring quicker results.

Enlightened despotism, in short, was an acceleration of the old institution of monarchy, which now put aside the quasi-sacred mantle in which it had clothed itself, and undertook to justify itself in the cold light of reason and secular usefulness. In theory even the dynastic claim was awkward, for it rested on inheritance from the past. Under enlightened despotism the idea of the state itself was changing, from the older notion of an estate belonging

---

[5] See pp. 118, 120, 163–4.
[6] See p. 86.

by a kind of sanctified property right to its ruler, to a newer notion of an abstract and impersonal authority exercised by public officers, of whom the king was simply the highest.

The trend to enlightened despotism after 1740 owed a great deal to writers and *philosophes*, but it arose also out of a very practical situation, namely the great war of the mid-eighteenth century.[7] War, in modern history, has usually led to concentration and rationalizing of government power, and the wars of 1740–48 and 1756–63 were no exception. Under their impact even governments where the rulers were not considered by *philosophes* to be enlightened, notably those of Louis XV and Maria Theresa, and even the government of Great Britain, which was certainly not despotic, embarked on programs which all bear features in common. They attempted to augment their revenues, devise new taxes, tax persons or regions hitherto more or less tax-exempt, limit the autonomy of outlying political bodies, and centralize and renovate their respective political systems. The workings of enlightened despotism might be seen in many states, in Hapsburg Tuscany under Leopold, in Bourbon Naples and Spain under Charles III, in Portugal under the minister Pombal, in Denmark under Struensee. But it seems best to consider only the more important countries at some length—France and Austria, Prussia and Russia—and then the rather different, yet not wholly different, course of events in the British empire.

THE FAILURE OF ENLIGHTENED DESPOTISM IN FRANCE

It was in France that enlightened despotism had the least success. Louis XV, who had inherited the throne in 1715 and lived until 1774, though by no means stupid, was indifferent to most serious questions, absorbed in the daily rounds at Versailles, disinclined to make trouble for people that he saw personally, and interested in government only by fits and starts. His remark, *après moi le déluge*, whether or not he really said it, sufficiently characterizes his personal attitude to conditions in France. Yet the French government was not unenlightened, and many capable officials carried on its affairs all through the century. These men generally knew what the basic trouble was. All the practical difficulties of the French monarchy could be traced to its system of taxation. The most important impost, the *taille*, a kind of land tax, was generally paid only by the peasants. Nobles were exempt from it on principle, and office-holders and bourgeois, for one reason or another, were generally exempt also. In addition, the church, which owned between five and ten per cent of the land of the country, insisted that its property was not taxable by the state; it granted to the king a periodic "free gift" which, though sizable, was less than the government might expect from direct taxation. The consequence of the tax exemptions was that, although France itself was wealthy and prosperous, the government was chronically poor, because the social classes which enjoyed most of the wealth and pros-

[7] See pp. 244–55.

perity did not pay taxes corresponding to their incomes. Louis XIV, under pressure of war, had tried to tax everybody alike by creating new levies, the *capitation* or poll tax and the *dixième* or tenth, both of which were assessed in proportion to income; but these taxes had been widely evaded. A similar effort was made in 1726, but it too had failed. The propertied classes resisted taxation because they thought it degrading. France had succumbed to the appalling principle that to pay direct taxes was the sure mark of inferior status. Nobles, churchmen, and bourgeois also resisted taxation because they were kept out of policymaking functions of government, and so had no sense of political responsibility or control. There were good historical reasons for this, but the result was financially ruinous.[8]

In 1748, under pressure of the heavy war costs, and at the prompting of Mme. de Pompadour, Louis XV bestirred himself to appoint a controller-general of finance who devised a tax to be paid by all persons receiving income from property—land, manorial rights, business investments, and offices such as parliamentary judgeships—irrespective of class status, provincial liberties, or previous exemptions of any kind. A clamor arose from the Parliament of Paris, the eleven provincial parliaments, the estates of Brittany, and the Church. All these were dominated by noblemen, and because of the aristocratic resurgence that had begun with the Regency, were politically stronger than in the days of Louis XIV. They could also now cite Montesquieu to justify their opposition to the crown. The Parliament of Paris ruled the new tax unconstitutional, or incompatible with the laws of France and liberties of Frenchmen. The estates of Brittany, and of other *pays d'états*, i.e., provinces having assemblies of estates, declared that their customary and historic liberties were being outraged. The Church protested with vehemence. After several years of wrangling, Louis XV decided to push the matter no further; he withdrew his support from his finance minister, and the whole project collapsed.

The 1750's and 1760's saw continued friction between the ministry and the various semi-autonomous bodies within the country. Meanwhile came the enormous costs and humiliating reverses of the Seven Years' War. The government renewed its determination to win effective centralized control. It was decided to eliminate the parliaments as a political force, and for this purpose, in 1768, Louis XV called to the chancellorship a man named Maupeou, who simply abrogated the old parliaments and set up new ones in their place. Maupeou had the sympathy of Voltaire and most of the *philosophes*. In the "Maupeou parliaments" the judges had no property rights in their seats, but became salaried officials appointed by the crown with

[8] See pp. 62, 157, 162–3.

Europe, 1740 (map on following pages)

Boundaries are as of 1740. Thereafter, until the wars of the French Revolution began in 1792, there were no major changes except the transfer of Silesia from Austria to Prussia, and the First Partition of Poland. France obtained Corsica in 1768.

EUROPE
1740

SCOTLAND
Edinburgh

NORTH
SEA

IRELAND
Dublin

Liverpool

WALES
ENGLAND

London

GREAT
BRITAIN

BOUNDARY OF
HOLY ROMAN EMPIRE

UNITED
PROVINCES

Amsterdam

Utrecht

AUSTRIAN
NETH.

Antwerp Cologne
Oudenarde
Ramillies

ENGLISH   CHANNEL

CAPE
DE LA HOGUE
CHANNEL IS.
(BR.)

Malplaquet

Rouen

Reims

Metz

ATLANTIC

SEINE R.

Paris

LORRAINE
(FR. 1766)

Quiberon

Orléans

LOIRE R.

Tours

Besançon

FRANCE

Geneva

OCEAN

Limoges

Lyons

RHÔNE R.

Bordeaux

GARONNE R.

Avignon

Marseilles

Toulon

Santiago

León

Toulouse

Pamplona

EBRO R.

Burgos

ARAGON

CATALONIA

Barcelona

PORTUGAL

Madrid

Lisbon

TAGUS R.

Toledo

SPAIN

BALEARIC   IS.

MINORCA
(BR.)

MAJORCA
(SP.)

Almanza

GUADALQUIVIR R.

Seville

Granada

Cadiz

BOURBON
DOMINIONS

GIBRALTAR (BR.)

Tangier

Algiers

MOROCCO
(INDEP.)

ALGERIA
(TURK.)

TRM

assurances of secure tenure, and they were forbidden to reject government edicts or to pass on their constitutionality, being confined to purely judicial functions. Maupeou likewise proposed to make the laws and judicial procedure more uniform throughout the whole country. Meanwhile, with the old parliaments out of the way, another attempt was made to tax the privileged and exempted groups.

But Louis XV died in 1774. His grandson and successor, Louis XVI, though far superior in personal habits to his grandfather, and possessed by a genuine desire to govern well, resembled Louis XV in that he lacked sustained will power, and could not bear to offend the people who could get to see him personally. In any case he was only twenty in 1774. The kingdom resounded with outcries against Maupeou and his colleagues as minions of despotism, and with demands for the immediate restoration of the old Parliament of Paris and the others. Louis XVI, fearful of beginning his reign as a "despot," therefore recalled the old parliaments and abolished those of Maupeou. The abortive Maupeou parliaments represented the farthest step taken by enlightened despotism in France. It was arbitrary, high-handed, and despotic for Louis XV to destroy the old parliaments, but it was certainly enlightened in the sense then connoted by the word, for the old parliaments were strongholds of aristocracy and privilege, and had for decades blocked programs of reform.

Louis XVI, in recalling the old parliaments in 1774, began his reign by pacifying the privileged classes. At the same time he appointed a reforming ministry. At its head was Turgot, a *philosophe* and Physiocrat and a widely experienced government administrator. Turgot undertook to suppress the gilds, which were privileged municipal monopolies in their several trades. He allowed greater freedom to the internal commerce in grain. He planned to abolish the royal *corvée* (a requirement that certain peasants labor on the roads a few days each year), replacing it by a money tax which would fall on all classes. He began to review the whole system of taxation, and was known even to favor the legal toleration of Protestants. The Parliament of Paris, supported by the provincial estates and the church, vociferously opposed him, and in 1776 he resigned. Louis XVI, by recalling the parliaments, had made reform impossible. In 1778 France again went to war with Britain. The same cycle was repeated: war costs, debt, deficit, new projects of taxation, resistance from the parliaments and other semi-autonomous bodies. In the 1780's the clash led to revolution.[9]

AUSTRIA: THE REFORMS OF MARIA THERESA (1740–80) AND OF JOSEPH (1780–90)

For Maria Theresa the war of the 1740's proved the extraordinary flimsiness of her empire.[10] Had the Continental allies won a more smashing

[9] See pp. 337–41.
[10] See pp. 245–8.

victory not only would Silesia have been lost to Prussia, but Belgium would have gone to France, Bohemia and Austria to the Elector of Bavaria supported by France, and the emperorship of the Holy Roman Empire, long a source of prestige to the Hapsburgs, would have passed permanently in all probability to a Bavarian or other pro-French German prince. Maria Theresa would have become queen of Hungary only. Nor did her subjects show much inclination to remain together under her rule. In Breslau, the capital of Silesia, after the Prussian attack of 1740, the citizens stood so stubbornly by their town liberties that they would not admit her army within their walls. In Bohemia almost half the nobles welcomed the invading Franco-Bavarians. In Hungary Maria Theresa won support, but only by confirming the historic Hungarian liberties. The empire was only a loose bundle of territories, without common purpose or common will. The Pragmatic Sanction devised by Charles VI, it should be recalled, had been meant not only to guarantee the Hapsburg inheritance against foreign attack, but also to secure the assent of the several parts of the empire to remain united under the dynasty.[11]

The war of the 1740's led to internal consolidation. The reign of Maria Theresa set the course of all later development of the Austrian empire, and hence of the many peoples who lived within its borders. She was aided by a notable team of ministers, whose origin illustrated the non-national character of the Hapsburg system. Her most trusted adviser in foreign relations, the astute Kaunitz,[12] was a Moravian; her main assistants in domestic affairs were a Silesian and a Bohemian-Czech. They worked smoothly with the German archduchess-queen, and with German officials in Vienna. Their aim was primarily to prevent dissolution of the monarchy by enlarging and guaranteeing the flow of taxes and soldiers. This involved breaking the local control of territorial nobles in their several diets, which corresponded somewhat to the French provincial estates. Hungary, profoundly separatist, was let alone. But the Bohemian and Austrian provinces were welded together. The kingdom of Bohemia, in 1749, lost the constitutional charter which it had received in 1627.[13] The several Bohemian and Austrian diets lost their right to consent to taxes. The separate offices, or "chancelleries," by which their affairs had been separately handled at Vienna, were abolished. Formerly local affairs, recruiting, and tax collecting had been dominated by committees of the diets, made up of landed noblemen of the neighborhood, gentlemen amateurs who were often negligent or indifferent, and who, since they served without pay, were impervious to official discipline, reprimand, or coordination. They were replaced by salaried administrators. Bureaucracy took the place of local self-government. Officials (following a form of mercantilist doctrine called "cameralism" in central Europe) planned to augment the economic strength of the empire by increasing production. They checked the local gild monopolies, suppressed brigandage on the roads, and in 1775 pro-

[11] See pp. 193, 246–7.
[12] See p. 249.
[13] See p. 192.

duced a tariff union of Bohemia, Moravia, and the Austrian duchies. This region became the largest area of free trade on the European continent, since even France was still divided by internal tariffs. Bohemia, industrially the most advanced part of the empire, benefited substantially; one of its cotton manufacturing plants, at the end of Maria Theresa's reign, employed 4,000 persons.

The great social fact, both in the Hapsburg lands and in all eastern Europe, was the serfdom into which the rural masses had progressively fallen during the past two hundred years.[14] Serfdom meant that the peasant belonged more to his landlord than to the state. The serf owed labor to his lord, often unspecified in amount or kind. The tendency, so long as the landlords ruled locally through their diets, was for the serf to do six days a week of forced labor on the lord's land. Maria Theresa, from humane motives, and also from a desire to lay hands on the manpower from which her armies were recruited, launched a systematic attack on the institutions of serfdom, which meant also an attack on the landed aristocracy of the empire. With the diets reduced in power, the protests of the nobles were less effective; still, the whole agricultural labor system of her territories was involved, and Maria Theresa proceeded with caution. Laws were passed against abuse of peasants by lords or their overseers. Other laws regularized the labor obligations, requiring that they be publicly registered, and usually limiting them to three days a week. The laws were often evaded. But the peasant was to some extent freed from arbitrary exactions of the lord. Maria Theresa accomplished more to alleviate serfdom than any other ruler of the eighteenth century in eastern Europe, with the single exception of her own son, Joseph II.

The great archduchess-queen died in 1780, having reigned for forty years. Her son, who had been co-regent with his mother since 1765, had little patience with her methods. Maria Theresa, though steady enough in aim, had always been content with partial measures. Instead of advertising her purposes by philosophic generalization she disguised or understated them, never carrying matters to the point of arousing an unmanageable reaction, or of uniting against her the vested interests that she undermined. She backed and filled, watched and waited. Joseph II would not wait. Though he thought the French *philosophes* frivolous, and Frederick of Prussia a mere clever cynic, he was himself a pure representative of the Age of Enlightenment, and it is in his brief reign of ten years that the character and the limitations of enlightened despotism can best be seen. He was a solemn, earnest, good man, who sensed the misery and hopelessness of the lowest classes. He believed existing conditions to be bad, and he would not regulate or improve them; he would end them. Right and reason, in his mind, lay with the views which he himself adopted; upholders of the old order were self-seeking or mistaken, and to yield to them would be to compromise with evil.

"The state," said Joseph, anticipating the Philosophical Radicals in England, meant "the greatest good for the greatest number." He acted ac-

[14] See pp. 101–2, 174, 191, 203.

cordingly. His ten years of rule passed in a quick succession of decrees. Maria Theresa had regulated serfdom. Joseph abolished it. His mother had collected taxes from nobles as well as peasants, though not equally. Joseph decreed absolute equality of taxation. He insisted on equal punishment for equal crimes whatever the class status of the offender; an aristocratic army officer, who had stolen 97,000 gulden, was exhibited in the pillory, and Count Podstacky, a forger, was made to sweep the streets of Vienna chained to common convicts. At the same time many legal punishments were made less physically cruel. Joseph granted complete liberty of the press. He ordered toleration of all religions, except for a few popular sects which he thought too ignorant to allow. He granted equal civic rights to the Jews, and equal duties, making Jews liable, for the first time in Europe, to service in the army. He even made Jewish nobles, an amazing phenomenon to those of aristocratic "blood." He clashed openly and rudely with the pope, supporting a movement called Febronianism which urged more national independence from Rome for German Catholic prelates, on the model of the French Gallican liberties. He demanded increased powers in the appointment and supervision of bishops, and he suppressed a good many monasteries, using their property to finance secular hospitals in Vienna, and thus laying the foundations of Viennese excellence as a medical center. He attempted also to develop the empire economically, and built up the port of Trieste, where he even established an East India Company, which soon failed for obvious reasons—neither capital nor naval support being forthcoming from central Europe. His attempts to reach the sea commercially through Belgium, like those of his grandfather at the time of the Ostend company, were blocked by the Dutch and British interests.

To force through his program Joseph had to centralize his state, like earlier rulers, except that he went farther. Regional diets and aristocratic self-government fared even worse than under his mother. Where she had always sagaciously let Hungary go its own way, he applied most of his measures to Hungary also—what was right must be right everywhere. His ideal was a perfectly uniform and rational empire, with all irregularities smoothed out as if under a steam-roller. He thought it reasonable to have a single language for administration, and naturally chose German; this led to a program of Germanizing the Czechs, Poles, Magyars, and others, which in turn aroused their nationalistic resistance. Using the German language, pushing the emperor's program against regional and class opposition, was a hard pressed, constantly growing, and increasingly disciplined body of officials. Bureaucracy became recognizably modern, with training courses, promotion schedules, retirement pensions, efficiency reports, and visits by inspectors. The clergy likewise were employed as mouthpieces of the state to explain new laws to their parishioners and teach due respect for the government. To watch over the whole structure Joseph created a secret police, whose agents, soliciting the confidential aid of spies and informers, reported on the performance of government employees, or the ideas and actions of nobles, clergy, or others from whom trouble might be expected. The police state, so infamous to the liberal world, was first systematically built up under Joseph as an instrument of enlightenment and reform.

Joseph II, the "revolutionary emperor," anticipated much that was done in France by the Revolution and under Napoleon. He could not abide "feudalism" or "medievalism"; he personally detested the nobility and the church. But few of his reforms proved lasting. He died prematurely in 1790, at the age of forty-nine, disillusioned and broken-hearted. Hungary and the Belgian provinces were in revolution against him. They held that their old constitutional liberties had been outraged—that they were being governed without their consent. In Hungary all the good will won by Maria Theresa seemed to be lost; in Belgium, the provinces stood stubbornly by the same medieval privileges, the old *Joyeuse Entrée*, which they had vindicated two hundred years before against the king of Spain.[15] Noble landlords throughout the Hapsburg empire, having lost their control over labor by the abolition of serfdom, and their caste status by legal and fiscal reforms, naturally were indignant. The church believed itself to be prostituted and despoiled. The peasants were grateful for their new personal liberty, but balked at the official attitude of condescending uplift, and often, in real life, sympathized with their priests and their gentlefolk. The officials were unequal to the task demanded of them. There were too few bourgeois in most parts of the empire to staff the civil service, so that many functionaries were members of the landowning nobility which Joseph humiliated; and in any case they frequently found the directives that flowed from Vienna impossible to enforce or even to understand. Joseph was a revolutionist without a party. He failed because he could not be everywhere and do everything himself. His reign demonstrated the limitations of a merely despotic enlightenment. It showed that a legally absolute ruler could not really do as he pleased. It suggested that drastic and abrupt reform could only come with a true revolution, on a wave of public opinion, and under the leadership of men who shared in a coherent body of ideas.

Joseph was succeeded by his brother Leopold, one of the ablest rulers of the century, who for many years as grand duke of Tuscany had given that country the best government known in Italy for generations, and who now, in 1790, was plagued by outcries from his sister, Marie-Antoinette, caught in the toils of a real revolution in France.[16] He refused to interfere in French affairs; in any case, he was busy dealing with the uproar left by Joseph. He abrogated most of Joseph's edicts, but he did not yield entirely. The nobles did not win back full powers in their diets. The peasants were not wholly consigned to the old serfdom; Joseph's efforts to provide them with land and to rid them of forced labor had to be given up, but they remained personally free, in law, to migrate, marry, or choose an occupation at will. Leopold died in 1792, and was followed by his son Francis II. Under Francis the aristocratic and clerical reaction gathered strength, terrified by the memory of Joseph II

[15] See pp. 108, 110.
[16] See p. 353.

and by the spectacle of revolutionary France, with which Austria went to war soon after Leopold's death.

PRUSSIA UNDER FREDERICK THE GREAT (1740–86)

In Prussia, Frederick the Great continued to reign for twenty-three years after the close of the Seven Years' War. "Old Fritz," as he was called, spent the time peaceably, writing memoirs and histories, rehabilitating his shattered country, promoting agriculture and industry, replenishing his treasury, drilling his army, and assimilating his huge conquest of Silesia, and, after 1772, that part of Poland which fell to him in the first partition. Frederick's fame as one of the most eminent of enlightened despots rests, however, not so much on his actual innovations as on his own intellectual gifts, which were considerable, and on the admiring publicity which he received from such literary friends as Voltaire. "My chief occupation," he wrote to Voltaire, "is to fight ignorance and prejudices in this country. . . . I must enlighten my people, cultivate their manners and morals, and make them as happy as human beings can be, or as happy as the means at my disposal permit." He did not conceive that sweeping changes were necessary to happiness in Prussia. The country was docile, for its Lutheran church had long been subordinate to the state, its relatively few burghers were largely dependents of the crown, and the independence of the *Junker* landlords, as expressed in provincial diets, had been curtailed by Frederick's predecessors.[17] Frederick simplified and codified the many laws of the kingdom, and made the law courts cheaper, more expeditious, and more honest. He kept up a wholesome and energetic tone in his civil service. He gave religious freedom, and he decreed, though he did not realize, a modicum of elementary education for all children of all classes. Prussia under Frederick was attractive enough for some 300,000 immigrants to seek it out.

But society remained stratified in a way hardly known in western Europe. Nobles, peasants, and burghers lived side by side in a kind of segregation. Each group paid different taxes and owed different duties to the state, and no person could buy property of the type pertaining to one of the other two groups. Property was legally classified, as well as persons; there was little passing from one group to another. The basic aim of these policies was military, to preserve, by keeping intact their respective forms of property, a distinct peasant class from which to draw soldiers and a distinct aristocratic class from which to draw officers. The peasants, except in the western extremities of the kingdom, were serfs holding patches of land on precarious terms in return for obligations to labor on the estates of the lords. They were likewise considered the lord's "hereditary subjects," and were not free to leave the lord's estate, to marry, or to learn a trade except with his permission. Frederick in his early years considered steps to relieve the burden of serfdom.

[17] See pp. 203–4.

He did relieve it on his own manors, those belonging to the Prussian crown domain, which comprised a quarter of the area of the kingdom. But he did nothing for serfs belonging to the private landlords or *Junkers*. No king of Prussia could fundamentally antagonize the *Junker* class which commanded the army. On the other hand, even in Prussia, the existence of a monarchical state was of some advantage to the common man; the serf in Prussia was not so badly off as in adjoining areas—Poland, Livonia, Mecklenburg, or Swedish Pomerania—where the will of the landlords was the law of the land, and which therefore have not inaptly been called *Junker* republics. In these countries cases came to light in which owners sold their serfs as movable property, or gambled or gave them away, breaking up families in the process, as Russian landlords might do with their serfs or American plantation-owners with their slaves. Such abuses were unknown in Prussia.

Frederick's system was centralized not merely at Potsdam but in his own head. He himself attended to all business, and made all important decisions. None of his ministers or generals ever achieved an independent reputation. As he said of his army, "no one reasons, everyone executes"—that is, no one reasoned except the king himself. Or again, as Frederick put it, if Newton had had to consult with Descartes he would never have discovered the law of universal gravitation. To have to take account of other people's ideas, or to entrust responsibilities to men less capable than himself, seemed to Frederick wasteful and anarchic. He died in 1786, after ruling forty-six years, and having trained no successors. Twenty years later Prussia was all but destroyed by Napoleon.[18] It was not surprising that Napoleon should defeat Prussia, but Europe was amazed, in 1806, to see Prussia collapse totally and abruptly. It was then concluded, in Prussia and elsewhere, that government by a master-mind working in lofty and isolated superiority did not offer a viable form of state under modern conditions.

36. Enlightened Despotism: Russia

The Russian empire has long been out of sight in the preceding pages. There are reasons for its absence, for it played no part in the intellectual revolution of the seventeenth century, and its role in the struggle for wealth and empire which reached a climax in the Seven Years' War was somewhat incidental. In the Age of Enlightenment the role of Russia was passive. No Russian thinker was known to Europe. But European thinkers were well known in Russia. The French-dominated cosmopolitan culture of the European upper classes spread to the upper classes of Russia. The Russian court and aristocracy took over French as their common conversational language. With French (German was also known, and sometimes English, for the Russian aristocrats were remarkable linguists) all the ideas boiling up in west-

[18] See pp. 383, 406.

ern Europe streamed into Russia. The Enlightenment, if it did not affect Russia profoundly, yet affected it significantly. It continued the westernization so forcibly pushed forward by Peter, and carried further the estrangement of the Russian upper classes from their own people and their own native scene.

RUSSIA AFTER PETER THE GREAT

Peter the Great died in 1725.[19] To secure his revolution he had decreed that each tsar should name his successor, but he himself had named none, and had put to death his own son Alexis to prevent social reaction. Peter was succeeded by his wife, a woman of peasant origin, who reigned for two years as Catherine I. Then came the boy Peter II, son of Alexis and grandson of Peter I. Peter II reigned only from 1727 to 1730. He was followed by Anna, 1730–40; in her reign the old native Russian party, in an attempt to undo the Petrine revolution, tried to surround the tsardom with various constitutional checks. They failed; Anna was followed by Ivan VI, who was tsar for a few months only, during which his mother, a German woman, ran affairs according to the views of the German party in Russia, which was indispensable to the westernization program and was resented by the Russian nativists. A palace revolution in 1741 brought to the throne Peter the Great's daughter, Elizabeth, who managed to hold power until her death twenty-one years later. She was so ignorant that she thought England could be reached by land, but in her reign the military power of Russia expanded, and she entered into European diplomacy and joined in the Seven Years' War against Prussia, fearing that the continued growth of Prussia would endanger the new Russian position on the Baltic. It was Elizabeth's death in 1762 that so decisively relieved the pressure on Frederick.[20] Her nephew, Peter III, was so odd that at twenty-six he still played with paper soldiers, and is said to have solemnly tried and hanged a rat which gnawed some of them during the night. Peter III, soon after making peace with Prussia, was dethroned and probably assassinated by a group acting in the name of his wife Catherine, who was proclaimed the empress Catherine II and is called "the Great." She enjoyed a long reign from 1762 to 1796, during which she acquired a somewhat exaggerated reputation as an enlightened despot.

The names of the tsars and tsarinas between Peter I and Catherine II are of slight importance. But their violent and rapid sequence tells a story. With no principle of succession, dynastic or other, the empire fell into a lawless struggle of parties, in which plots against rulers while living alternated with palace revolutions upon their death. The underlying issue was always the westernizing revolution of Peter—whether it should be repudiated or maintained, and, if maintained, by what party, German or native Russian or

---

[19] See pp. 217–18.
[20] See p. 250.

a faction or sub-grouping of these. To western Europe Russia still seemed Byzantine and barbaric.

CATHERINE THE GREAT (1762–96): DOMESTIC PROGRAM

Catherine the Great was a German woman, of a small princely house of the Holy Roman Empire. She had gone to Russia at the age of fifteen to be married. She had immediately cultivated the good will of the Russians, learned the language, and embraced the Orthodox Church. Early in her married life, disgusted with her moronic husband, she foresaw the chance of becoming empress herself. She was nothing like her feminine contemporary Maria Theresa, except possibly in having much the same practical sense. Mannish, hearty, and boisterous, she wore out a long succession of many lovers, mixing them freely with politics and using them in positions of state. When she died at the age of sixty-seven, of a stroke of apoplexy, she was still living with the last of these venturesome paramours. Her intellectual powers were as remarkable as her physical vigor; even after becoming empress she often got up at five in the morning, lighted her own fire, and turned to her books, making a digest, for example, of Blackstone's *Commentaries on the Laws of England*, published in 1765. She corresponded with Voltaire, and invited Diderot, editor of the Encyclopedia, to visit her at St. Petersburg, where, she reported, he thumped her so hard on the knee in the energy of his conversation that she had to put a table between them. She bought Diderot's library, allowing him to keep it during his lifetime, and in other ways won renown by her benefactions to the *philosophes*, whom she probably regarded as useful press agents for Russia. Her gifts to them were substantial, though dwarfed by the £12,000,000 she is estimated to have bestowed on her lovers.

When she first came to power she publicized an intention to make certain enlightened reforms. She summoned a kind of constitutional convention, called a Legislative Commission, which met in the summer of 1767. Nothing much came of its deliberations, though it sat for a year and a half, except that Catherine obtained a good deal of information on conditions in the country, and concluded, from the profuse loyalty exhibited by the deputies, that though a usurper and a foreigner she possessed a strong hold upon Russia. The reforms which she subsequently enacted consisted in a measure of legal codification, restrictions on the use of torture, and a certain support of religious toleration, though she would not allow Old Believers to build their own chapels. Such innovations were enough to raise an admiring chorus from the *philosophes*, who saw in her, as they saw retrospectively in Peter the Great, the standard-bearer of civilization among a backward people. Like other enlightened despots, Catherine turned assiduously to administrative questions also. Consolidating the machinery of state, she replaced Peter's ten *gubernii* with fifty, each subdivided into districts, and all equipped with appropriate sets of governors and officials.

Whatever ideas Catherine may conceivably have at first had, as a

thoughtful and progressive young woman, on the fundamental subject of reforming serfdom in Russia, did not long outlast her experience as empress,
and dissolved with the great peasant insurrection of 1773, known as Pugachev's rebellion. The condition of the Russian serfs was deteriorating. Serf-
owners were increasingly selling them apart from land, breaking up families,
using them in mines or manufactures, disciplining and punishing them at
will, or exiling them to Siberia. The serf population was restless, worked upon
by Old Believers and cherishing distorted popular memories of the mighty
hero, Stephen Razin, who a century before had led an uprising against the
landlords.[21] Class antagonism, though latent, was profound, nor was it made
less when the rough *moujik*, in some places, heard the lord and his family
talking French so as not to be understood by the servants, or saw them wearing European clothes, reading European books, and adopting the manners
of a foreign and superior way of life. Hope stirred among the peasants at the
convocation of the Legislative Commission, in which even serfs were represented, and at which the problem of serfdom was thoroughly discussed. Yet
nothing happened.

In 1773 a Don Cossack, Emelian Pugachev, a former soldier, appeared
at the head of an insurrection in the Urals. Following an old Russian custom,
he announced himself as the true tsar, Peter III (Catherine's deceased husband), now returned after long travels in Egypt and the Holy Land. He surrounded himself with duplicates of the imperial family, courtiers, and even a
secretary of state. He issued an imperial manifesto proclaiming the end of
serfdom, and of taxes and military conscription. Tens and hundreds of thousands, in the Urals and Volga regions, Tartars, Kirghiz, Cossacks, agricultural
serfs, servile workers in the Ural mines, fishermen in the rivers and in the
Caspian Sea, flocked to Pugachev's banner. The great host surged up the
Volga, capturing town after town, burning and pillaging, killing priests and
landlords. The upper classes in Moscow were terrified; a hundred thousand
serfs lived in the city as domestic servants or industrial workers, and their
sympathies went out to Pugachev and his horde. Armies were at first unsuccessful. But famine along the Volga in 1774 dispersed the rebels. Pugachev,
betrayed by some of his own followers, was brought to Moscow in an iron
cage. Catherine forbade the use of torture at his trial, but he was executed by
the drawing and quartering of his body, a punishment, it should perhaps be
noted, used at the time in western Europe in cases of flagrant treason.

Pugachev's rebellion was the most violent peasant uprising in the history of Russia, and the most formidable mass upheaval in Europe in the century before 1789. Catherine replied to it by repression. She conceded more
powers to the landlords. The nobles shook off the last vestiges of the compulsory state-service to which Peter had bound them. The peasants were henceforth the only bound or unfree class. As in Prussia, the state came more than
ever to rest on an understanding between ruler and gentry, by which the
gentry accepted the monarchy, with its laws, officials, army, and foreign pol-

∿∿∿∿∿∿∿∿∿∿∿∿

[21] See pp. 209–10.

icy, and received from it, in return, the assurance of full authority over the rural masses. Government reached down through the aristocracy and the scattered towns, but it stopped short at the manor; there the lord took over, and was himself a kind of government in his own person. Under these conditions the number of serfs increased, and the load on each became more heavy. Catherine's reign saw the culmination of Russian serfdom, which now ceased to differ in any important respect from the chattel slavery to which Negroes were subject in the Americas. One might read in the Moscow *Gazette* such advertisements as the following: "For sale, two plump coachmen; two girls eighteen and fifteen years, quick at manual work. Two barbers: one, twenty-one, knows how to read and write and play a musical instrument; the other can do ladies' and gentlemen's hair."

CATHERINE THE GREAT: FOREIGN AFFAIRS

Territorially Catherine was one of the main builders of Russia. When she became tsarina in 1762 the empire reached to the Pacific and into central Asia, and it touched upon the Gulf of Riga and the Gulf of Finland on the Baltic, but westward from Moscow one could go only two hundred miles before reaching Poland, and no one standing on Russian soil could see the waters of the Black Sea.[22] Russia was separated from central Europe by a wide band of loosely organized domains, extending from the Baltic to the Black Sea and the Mediterranean, and nominally belonging to the Polish and Turkish states. Poland was an old enemy, which had once threatened Muscovy, and both in Poland and in the Ottoman Empire there were many Greek Orthodox Christians, with whom Russians felt an ideological tie, and whose stories of mistreatment, directed in Poland against Roman Catholics, and in Turkey against Moslems, always aroused a crusading spirit in Russia. In western Europe the disposal of the whole Polish-Turkish tract, which stretched over into Asia and Africa, came to be called the Eastern Question. Though the name went out of use after 1900, the question itself has never ceased to exist.

Catherine's supreme plan was to penetrate the entire area, Turkish and Polish alike. If successful, she would reach into Europe as far as Silesia and the Adriatic. We have already seen what happened to this plan.[23] In 1763 Catherine put a discarded lover, Stanislas Poniatowski, on the Polish throne. This led to armed disputes among the Poles, some of whom favored Russia, some Prussia, some Austria, some France, and some even Turkey. In 1768 the Turkish sultan went to war with Russia. Catherine retorted with her "Greek project," a scheme looking to no less than the overthrow of the Ottoman government and revival of the medieval Greek or Byzantine empire, in which the "Greeks," *i.e.*, members of the Greek Orthodox Church, would replace the Moslems as the ruling element in the Near East. Since these "Greeks" would

ᴧᴧᴧᴧᴧᴧᴧᴧᴧᴧᴧᴧᴧᴧᴧᴧᴧᴧ

[22] See map, p. 213.
[23] See pp. 219–20.

be guided and counseled from Holy Russia, Russian supremacy would be established at Constantinople and run through the Balkans, the eastern Mediterranean, and the Levant. In the war which began in 1768 the Russians overcame all Turkish opposition. Catherine seemed about to dominate Turkey as she did Poland.

But the European balance of power now lumbered into play. Catherine could hardly expect such a gigantic aggrandizement without war with Austria or even with Europe. Frederick II, seeing a chance to win West Prussia without risk, and playing on Catherine's disinclination for a general war, proposed that in return for letting Turkey off lightly she annex a portion of Poland, and that, to keep the proper balance in eastern Europe, Prussia and the Austrian monarchy absorb parts of Poland also. The partition was effected in 1772. Frederick took West Prussia, Catherine parts of White Russia, Maria Theresa, Galicia.[24] Frederick digested his portion with relish, realizing an old dream of the Brandenburg house; Catherine swallowed hers with somewhat less appetite, since she had satisfactorily controlled the whole of Poland before; to Maria Theresa the dish was distasteful, and even shocking, but she could not see Russia and Prussia go ahead without her, and she shared in the feast by suppressing her moral scruples. "She wept," said Frederick cynically, "but she kept on taking." Catherine, in 1774, signed a peace treaty with the defeated Turks at Kuchuk Kainarji on the Danube. The sultan ceded his rights over the Tartar principalities on the north coast of the Black Sea to the tsarina, admitted Russian ships to the Straits, and recognized Russia as the special protector of Christians in the Ottoman empire.

Catherine had only delayed, not altered, her plans with respect to Turkey. She decided to neutralize the opposition of Austria. She invited Joseph II to visit her in Russia, and the two sovereigns proceeded together on a tour of her newly won Black Sea provinces. Her favorite of the moment, Potemkin, constructed artificial one-street villages along their way and produced throngs of cheering and happy looking villagers to greet them, all of which enriched mankind with nothing except the phrase "Potemkin villages" to mean bogus evidence of a non-existent prosperity. At Kherson the two monarchs passed through a gate marked "The Road to Byzantium." "What I want is Silesia," said Joseph II, but the tsarina induced him to join in a war of conquest against Turkey. This war was interrupted by the French Revolution. Both governments reduced their commitments in the Balkans to await developments in western Europe. It became Catherine's policy to incite Austria and Prussia into a war with France, in the name of monarchy and civilization, in order that she might have a free hand in the Polish-Turkish sphere.[25] Meanwhile she contributed to killing off the nationalist and reforming movement among the Poles. In 1793 she arranged with Prussia for the second partition, and in 1795 with both Prussia and Austria for the third. She was the only ruler who lived to take part in all three partitions of Poland.

24 See map, p. 221.
25 See pp. 352-3.

The Polish kingdom was now extinct, and the Russian-Polish frontier set at about the line it was to follow in the 1950's. But Catherine's ideas were not yet exhausted, though her judgment seems to have failed her in the last months of her life. In 1796 she allowed her then favorite, Platon Zubov, to dispatch an army of 20,000 men on a mad expedition to conquer India by way of Persia. This force was immediately recalled after her death.

Catherine's foreign policy was purely expansionist and unscrupulous, and the net effect of her domestic policy, aside from a few reforms of detail, was to favor the half-Europeanized aristocracy and to extend serfdom among the people. Her own protestations of enlightenment tempt one to an ironical judgment of her career, but in her defense it may be observed that unscrupulous expansion was the accepted practice of the time, and that, domestically, probably no ruler could have corrected the social evils from which Russia suffered. If there was to be a Russian empire it had to be with the consent of the serf-owning gentry, which was the only politically significant class. As Catherine observed to Diderot on the subject of reforms: "You only write on paper, but I have to write on human skin, which is incomparably more irritable and ticklish." She had reason to know how easily tsars and tsarinas could be unseated and even murdered, and that the danger of overthrow came not from the peasants but from cliques of army officers and landlords.

She therefore yielded, but at least she never yielded her mind. She never said that slavery was a positive good. She never said that there were two or more worlds, subject to different moral codes or different laws of civilization. She never thought that the peculiar institutions of her own country should be cherished and elaborated as a contribution to human welfare. Ideas of this kind, in the following century, gained ground in both Europe and America, to justify conditions which the philosophy of the Enlightenment impatiently condemned. Catherine continued at least to recognize the standards of the Enlightenment as standards. Her mind became somewhat compartmentalized, if not hypocritical, with one part for the play of ideas and another part for the administration of Russia. But she seems not to have abandoned the hope that some day Russia might share in the one swelling stream of human progress. At least, in her later years, she gave careful attention to her favorite grandson, Alexander, closely supervising his education, which she planned on the western model. She gave him as a tutor the Swiss *philosophe*, La Harpe, who filled his mind with humane and liberal sentiments on the duties of princes. Trained by Catherine as a kind of ideal ruler, Alexander I was destined to cut a wide circle in the affairs of Europe, to defeat Napoleon Bonaparte, preach peace and freedom, and suffer from the same internal divisions and frustrations by which educated Russians seemed characteristically to be afflicted.

THE LIMITATIONS OF ENLIGHTENED DESPOTISM

Enlightened despotism, seen in retrospect, foreshadowed an age of revolution and even signified a preliminary effort to revolutionize society by authoritative action from above. People were told by their own governments that reforms were needed, that many privileges, special liberties, or tax-exemptions were bad, that the past was a source of confusion, injustice, or inefficiency in the present. The state rose up as more completely sovereign, whether acting frankly in its own interest or claiming to act in the interest of its people. All old and established rights were brought into question—rights of kingdoms and provinces, orders and classes, legal bodies and corporate groups. Enlightened despotism overrode or exterminated the Society of Jesus, the Parliament of Paris, the autonomy of Bohemia, and the independence of Poland. Customary and common law was pushed aside by authoritative legal codes. Governments, by opposing the special powers of the church and the feudal interests, tended to make all persons into uniform and equal subjects. To this extent enlightened despotism favored equality before the law. But it could go only a certain distance in this direction. The king was after all a hereditary aristocrat himself, and no government can be revolutionary to the point of breaking up its own foundations.

Even before the French Revolution enlightened despotism had run its course. Everywhere the "despots," for reasons of politics if not of principle, had reached a point beyond which they could not go. In France Louis XVI had appeased the privileged classes, in the Austrian empire Joseph's failure to appease them threw them into open revolt, in Prussia and in Russia the brilliant reigns of Frederick and Catherine wound up in an aggravation of landlordism for the mass of the people. Almost everywhere there was an aristocratic and even feudal revival. Religion also was renewing itself in many ways. Many were again saying that kingship was in a sense divine, and a new alliance was forming between "the throne and the altar." The French Revolution, by terrifying the old vested interests, was to accelerate and embitter a reaction which had already begun. Monarchy in Europe, ever since the Middle Ages, had generally been a progressive institution, acting along the line that Europe seemed destined to take, and in any case setting itself against the feudal and ecclesiastical powers. Enlightened despotism was the culmination of the historic institution of monarchy. After the enlightened despots, and after the French Revolution, monarchy became on the whole nostalgic and backward-looking, supported most ardently by the churches and aristocracies that it had once tried to subdue, and least of all by those who felt in themselves the surge of the future.

37. The American Revolution

Meanwhile, something new and portentous was injected into world affairs by the successful revolt of the main body of the British colonials, who in a revolutionary movement running from 1763 to 1789, and hence contemporary with enlightened despotism in Europe, managed to establish the republic of the United States of America. The American revolution was not a local event. Its effects were felt in Europe immediately, and ultimately by all peoples. Nor were its causes especially local, for it arose out of a situation characteristic of Europe at the time. There was much that was unique about the American revolution, but probably Americans exaggerate its uniqueness, and in the following paragraphs we shall try, while keeping the unique features in sight, to place events in America within the framework of a transatlantic civilization.

BRITAIN: SCOTLAND, IRELAND, AND INDIA

The British countries had their own way of passing through the Age of Enlightenment. Jacobite flurries aside, there was general contentment with the arrangements that followed the English revolution of 1688—it has often been remarked that nothing is so conservative as a successful revolution. British thought lacked the asperity of thought on the Continent. The writers who most resembled French *philosophes*, such as Hume and Gibbon, were innocuously moderate in their political ideas. Not until the time of the American revolution, when men like Thomas Paine and Thomas Jefferson came forward, were there any important radical writers. Nor was there any "despotism" in England, enlightened or otherwise. The young George III, who inherited the throne in 1760, did feel himself to be a "patriot king." He did wish to heighten the influence of the crown and to overcome the factionalism of parties.[26] But it was through Parliament that he had to work. He had to descend into the political arena himself, buy up or otherwise control votes in the Commons, grant pensions and favors and make promises and deals with other Parliamentary politicians. What he did in effect was to create a new faction, the "king's friends." This faction was in power during the ministry of Lord North from 1770 to 1782. It is worth noting that all factions were factions of Whigs, that the Tory party was practically defunct, that Britain did not yet have a two-party system, and that the word "Tory," as it came to be used by American revolutionaries, was little more than a term of abuse.

In Britain, Parliament was supreme, as in most Continental countries, the monarch. It had the power, as one facetious jurist put it, to do all things except change a man into a woman. The British Parliament was as sovereign as any European ruler, and indeed more so, since less that could be called feudalism remained in England than on the Continent. The powers of sovereignty were in any case exercised by ministers. Ministers in Britain, even a ministry of the "king's friends," had mainly to assure themselves of the backing of Parliament, whereas in the continental monarchies they had mainly to assure themselves of the backing of the ruler. But in all the leading countries ministers faced much the same problems. They all had to deal with the issues raised by the great war of the mid-century, in its two phases

---

[26] See p. 239.

of the Austrian Succession and Seven Years' War. Everywhere the solution adopted by governments was to increase their own central power. We have seen how the French government, in attempting to tap new sources of revenue, tried to encroach on the liberties of Brittany and other provinces and to subordinate the bodies which in France were called parliaments.[27] We have likewise seen how the Hapsburg government, also in an effort to raise more taxes, repressed local self-government in the empire and even abrogated the constitution of Bohemia.[28] The same tendency showed itself in the British system. The revocation of the charter of Bohemia in 1749 had its parallel in the revocation of the charter of Massachusetts in 1774. The disputes of the French king with the estates of Brittany or Languedoc had their parallel in the disputes of the British Parliament with the provincial assemblies of Virginia or New York.

The British empire in the middle of the century was decentralized and composite. Thirty-one governments were subordinate to Westminster, ranging from the separate kingdom of Ireland through all the crown and charter colonies to the various political establishments maintained in the East by the East India Company. The whole empire, with about 15,000,000 people of all colors in 1750, was less populous than France or the Austrian monarchy. The whole tract of the American mainland from Georgia to Nova Scotia compared in the number of its white population with Ireland or Scotland—or with Brittany or Bohemia—a figure of about two million being roughly applicable in each case.

Scotland proved a source of weakness in the War of the Austrian Succession. The Lowlanders were loyal enough, but the Highlanders revolted with French assistance in the Jacobite rising of 1745, and by invading England threatened to take the British government in the rear as it was locked in the struggle with France.[29] The Highlands had never really been under any government, even under the old Scottish monarchy before the union of 1707 with England. Social organization, in the Highland fastnesses, followed the primitive principle of physical kinship. Men looked to their chiefs, the heads of the clans, to tell them whom and when to fight. The chiefs had hereditary jurisdiction, often including powers of life and death, over their clansmen. A few leaders could throw the whole region to the Stuarts or the French. The British government, after 1745, proceeded to make its sovereignty effective in the Highlands. Troops were quartered there for years. Roads were pushed across the moors and through the glens. Law courts enforced the law of the Scottish Lowlands. Revenue officers collected funds for the treasury of Great Britain. The chiefs lost their old quasi-feudal jurisdiction. The old system of land tenure was broken up. The holding of land from clannish chiefs was ended. The clansman swayed by his chief was turned into the subject of the crown of Great Britain. He was turned also, in many cases, into an almost

[27] See pp. 303–6.
[28] See p. 307.
[29] See p. 239.

landless "crofter," while some of the chiefs, or their sons, emerged as landed
gentlemen of the English type. Fighting Highlanders were incorporated into
newly formed Highland regiments of the British army, under the usual discipline imposed by the modern state on its fighting forces. For thirty years
the Scots were forbidden to wear the kilt or play the bagpipes.

In Ireland the process of centralization worked itself out more slowly.
Ireland was a separate kingdom, with its own parliament, its own fiscal system, and its own debt. The kingdom was run by and for the Protestant
minority.[30] No Catholic could purchase land or hold public office. The established church, an Anglican communion, was maintained by tithes to which
the Catholic majority was obliged to contribute. Many landed estates were
owned by absentees who resided habitually in England. It was estimated in
1745 that the Irish sent out £628,000 a year in rents to absentee landlords, a
sum larger than all its commercial exports to England. Through a long series
of historical misfortunes the native Catholic Irish had fallen into a wretched-
ness scarcely paralleled in central or western Europe; perhaps nowhere west
of Poland and Turkey would one find, in the mid-eighteenth century, so
large a region in which the overwhelming majority suffered from such abject
poverty and systematic discrimination. The native Irish were generally pro-
French, and their historic tendency to favor the enemies of England was in
fact one reason why they were now treated as conquered people. In the mid-
century wars Ireland remained quiet. In the next French war, however, the
War of American Independence, the Protestant leaders of Ireland, with support from the Catholics, threatened armed rebellion against Great Britain.
The British, having lost America through obstinacy, tried liberality with Ireland, and in 1782 allowed a great increase of power to the Irish Parliament
at Dublin. But from this Parliament Catholics were still excluded, so that the
old grievances and unrest continued, and in the next war between France and
Britain, which began in 1793, the French repeatedly stirred up the Irish and
nearly landed a French revolutionary army in the island. The British then
turned to centralization. The Irish kingdom lost its separate identity. The
Irish parliament was abolished. Ireland was thereafter represented in the
Parliament at Westminster. These provisions were incorporated in the Act
of Union of 1801, creating the United Kingdom of Great Britain and Ireland, which lasted until 1922.

British establishments in India also felt the hand of Parliament increasingly upon them. At the close of the Seven Years' War the various British posts in and around Bombay, Madras, and Calcutta were unconnected
with each other and subordinate only to the board of directors of the Company in London. Company employees interfered at will in the wars and
politics of the Indian states, and enriched themselves by such means as they
could, not excluding graft, trickery, intimidation, rapine, and extortion.[31] In
1773 the ministry of Lord North passed a Regulating Act, of which the main

---

[30] See pp. 148, 153–4.
[31] See pp. 253–4.

purpose was to regulate, not Indians, but the British subjects in India, whom no Indian government could control. The Company was left with its trading activities, but its political activities were brought under Parliamentary supervision. The act gathered all the British establishments under a single governor-general, set up a new supreme court at Calcutta, and required the Company to submit its correspondence on political matters for review by the ministers of His Majesty's Government. Warren Hastings became the first British governor-general in India. He was so high-handed with some of the Indian princes, and made so many enemies among jealous Englishmen in Bengal, that he was denounced at home, impeached, and subjected to a trial which dragged on for seven years in the House of Lords. He was finally acquitted. After Clive, he was the main author of British supremacy in India. Meanwhile, in 1784, by a new India Act of that year, the post of Secretary of State for India, together with an India office, was created in the British ministry at home. The governor-general henceforth ruled the growing British sphere in India almost as an absolute monarch, but only as the agent of the ministry and Parliament of Great Britain.

The trend in the British world was to centralization. Despite the flutter of royalism under George III, it was to a centralization of all British territories under authority of the Parliament. What was happening in empire affairs, as in domestic politics in England, was a continuing application of the principles of 1689. The Parliamentary sovereignty established in 1689 was now, after the middle of the eighteenth century, being applied to regions where it had heretofore had little effect. And it was against the British Parliament, not the British king, that the Americans primarily rebelled. Some at the time, including Jefferson and Franklin in America and Burke in England, conceived plans by which the Americans, while remaining under the British crown, should possess a kind of parliament of their own co-ordinate with the Parliament of Great Britain. They sketched out the "dominion status" now enjoyed by Canada and Australia. What effect the adoption of such a federal or decentralizing scheme might have had has long been a subject of speculation. It was scarcely a practical possibility at the time. Not only was the trend, for good reason, toward greater centralization of the powers of government. It also seemed, before the revolution itself taught them otherwise, that the American colonials were incapable of responsible self-rule.

BACKGROUND TO THE REVOLUTION

The behavior of the Americans in the Seven Years' War was unsatisfactory by any standard.[32] The several colonial legislatures rejected the Albany Plan of Union drafted by Franklin and commended to them by the British officials. During the war it was the British regular army and navy, financed by taxes and loans in Great Britain, that drove the French out of America. The

[32] See p. 251.

war effort of the Anglo-Americans was desultory at best. Only three colonies contributed their quota of troops. "Elsewhere," in the words of two eminent American historians, "there was a woeful lack of co-operation. Requisitions of men and money were flouted. Commercial regulations were evaded. Trade with the enemy flourished." [33] After the defeat of the French the colonials had still to reckon with the Indians of the interior, who preferred French rule to that of their new British and British-colonial masters. Many tribes joined in an uprising led by Pontiac, a western chief, and they ravaged as far eastward as the Pennsylvania and Virginia frontiers. Again, the colonials proved unable to deal with a problem vital to their own future, and peace was brought about by officials and army units taking their orders from Great Britain.

The British government tried to make the colonials pay a larger share toward the expenses of the empire. The colonials had hitherto paid only local taxes. They were liable to customs duties, of which the proceeds went in principle to Great Britain; but these duties were levied to enforce the Acts of Trade and Navigation, to direct the flow of commerce, not to raise revenue; and they were seldom paid, because the Acts of Trade and Navigation were persistently ignored. American merchants, for example, commonly imported sugar from the French West Indies, contrary to law, and even shipped in return the iron wares which it was against the law for Americans to manufacture for export. Disregard of law was commonplace in the eighteenth century, when governments freely enacted general legislation without succeeding in or even caring about enforcement in particular cases—one is reminded of the French censorship or the British ban on Indian cloth. Yet the British Americans were possibly the least law-abiding of all the more civilized European peoples. Their illicit trade went on outside the revenue system. Receipts from customs duties fell short even of paying the salaries and other emoluments of the customs officials. The colonial in practice paid only such taxes as were approved by his own local legislature for local purposes. The Americans in effect enjoyed a degree of tax-exemption within the empire, and it was against this form of provincial privilege that Parliament began to move.

By the Revenue Act of 1764 (the "Sugar" Act), the British ministry, while reducing and liberalizing the customs duties payable in America, entered upon a program of actual and systematic collection. In the following year the ministry attempted to extend to British subjects in America a tax peaceably accepted by those in Great Britain and commonplace in most of Europe. This imposed on all uses of paper, as in newspapers and commercial and legal documents, the payment of a fee which was certified by the affixing of a stamp. The Stamp Act aroused violent and concerted resistance in the colonies, especially among the businessmen, lawyers, and editors who were the most articulate class. It therefore was repealed in 1766. In 1767 Parliament, clumsily casting about to find a tax acceptable to the Americans, hit

---

[33] S. E. Morison and H. S. Commager, *The Growth of the American Republic*, (New York: Oxford University Press, 1937), I., 9.

upon the "Townshend duties," which taxed colonial imports of paper, paint, lead, and tea. Another outcry went up, and the Townshend duties were repealed, except for the one on tea, which was kept as a token of the sovereign power of Parliament to tax all persons in the empire.

The colonials had proved stubborn, the government pliable but lacking in constructive ideas. The Americans argued that Parliament had no authority to tax them because they were not represented in it. The British replied that Parliament represented America as much as it represented Great Britain. If Philadelphia sent no actually elected deputies to the Commons, so this argument ran, neither did Manchester in England, yet both places enjoyed a "virtual representation," since members of the Commons did not in any case merely speak for local constituencies, but made themselves responsible for imperial interests as a whole. To this many Americans retorted that if Manchester was not "really" represented it ought to be, a belief shared by a growing number of Englishmen, for the movement broadened into a transatlantic reform movement, of which one aim was to regularize the erratic methods by which the House of Commons was recruited. Meanwhile the strictly Anglo-American question subsided after the repeal of the Stamp Act and the Townshend program. There had been no clarification of principle on either side. But in practice the Americans had resisted significant taxation, and Parliament had refrained from making any drastic use of its sovereign power.

The calm was shattered in 1773 by an event which proved, to the more dissatisfied Americans, the disadvantages of belonging to a global economic system in which the main policies were made on the other side of the ocean. The East India Company was in difficulties. It had a great surplus of Chinese tea,[34] and in any case it wanted new commercial privileges in return for the political privileges which it was losing by the Regulating Act of 1773. In the past the Company had been required to sell its wares at public auction in London; other merchants had handled distribution from that point on. Now, in 1773, Parliament granted the Company the exclusive right to sell tea through its own agents in America to American local dealers. Tea was a large item of business in the commercial capitalism of the time. The colonial consumer might pay less for it, but the intermediary American merchant would be shut out. The Company's tea was boycotted in all American ports. In Boston, to prevent its forcible landing, a party of disguised men invaded the tea ships and dumped the chests into the harbor. To this act of vandalism the British government replied by measures far out of proportion to the offense. It "closed" the port of Boston, thus threatening the city with economic ruin. It virtually rescinded the charter of Massachusetts, forbidding certain local elections and the holding of town meetings.

And at the same time, in 1774, apparently by coincidence, Parliament enacted the Quebec Act. The wisest piece of British legislation in these troubled years, the Quebec Act provided a government for the newly con-

---

[34] See p. 229.

quered Canadian French, granting them security in their French civil law
and Catholic religion, and laying foundations for the British empire that was
to come. But the act defined the boundaries of Quebec somewhat as the
French themselves would have defined them, including in them all territory
north of the Ohio river—the present states of Wisconsin, Michigan, Illinois,
Indiana, and Ohio. These boundaries were perfectly reasonable since the few
white men in the area were French, and since, in the age before canals or
railways, the obvious means of reaching the whole region was by way of the
St. Lawrence valley and the Lakes. The ability of frontiersmen to make the
laborious passage over the Alleghenies was quite unappreciated in London.
To the Americans the Quebec Act was a barrier to westward expansion, an
outrage, pro-French and pro-Catholic, and it was lumped with the closing of
an American port and the destruction of an American government as one of
the "Intolerable Acts" which must be resisted.

     And indeed the implications of Parliamentary sovereignty were now
apparent. The meaning of centralized planning and authority was now clear.
It was no longer merely an affair of taxation. A government that had to take
account of the East India Company, the French Canadians, and the British
taxpayers, even if more prudent and enlightened than Lord North's ministry
of 1774, could not possibly at the same time have satisfied the Americans of
the thirteen seaboard colonies. These Americans, since 1763 no longer afraid
of the French empire, were less inclined to forego their own interests in order
to remain in the British. British policies had aroused antagonism in the
coastal towns and in the backwoods, among wealthy land speculators and
poor squatter frontiersmen, among merchants and the workingmen who depended on the business of merchants. The freedom of Americans to determine their own conditions of political life was in question. Yet there were
few in 1774, or even years later, who were prepared to face the thought of
independence.

THE WAR OF AMERICAN INDEPENDENCE

     After the "Intolerable Acts" self-authorized groups met in the several
colonies, and sent delegates to a "continental congress" in Philadelphia. This
body adopted a boycott of British goods, to be enforced on unwilling Americans by local organizers of resistance. Fighting began in the next year, 1775,
when the British commander at Boston sent a detachment to seize unauthorized stores of weapons at Concord. On the way, at Lexington, in a brush
between soldiers and partisans or "minutemen," someone fired the "shot
heard round the world." The Second Continental Congress, meeting a few
weeks later, proceeded to raise an American army, despatched an expedition
to force Quebec into the revolutionary union, and entered into overtures with
Bourbon France.

     The Congress was still reluctant to repudiate the tie with Britain. But
passions grew fierce in consequence of the fighting. Radicals convinced

moderates that the choice now lay between independence and enslavement. It appeared that the French, naturally uninterested in a reconciliation of British subjects, would give help if the avowed aim of American rebels was to dismember the British empire. In January 1776 Thomas Paine, in his pamphlet *Common Sense*, made his debut as a kind of international revolutionary; he was to figure in the French Revolution and to work for revolution in England. He had come from England less than two years before, and he detested English society for its injustices to men like himself. Eloquent and vitriolic, *Common Sense* identified the independence of the American colonies with the cause of liberty for all mankind. It pitted freedom against tyranny in the person of "the royal brute of Great Britain." It was "repugnant to reason," said Paine, "to suppose that this Continent can long remain subject to any external power. . . . There is something absurd in supposing a Continent to be perpetually governed by an island. In no instance hath nature made the satellite larger than its primary planet; and as England and America, with respect to each other, reverse the common order of nature, it is evident that they belong to different systems. England to Europe; America to itself." *Common Sense* was read everywhere in the colonies, and its slashing arguments unquestionably spread a sense of proud isolation from the Old World. On July 4, 1776, the Congress adopted the Declaration of Independence, by which the United States assumed its separate and equal station among the powers of the earth.

The War of American Independence thereupon turned into another European struggle for empire. For two more years the French government remained ostensibly non-interventionist, but meanwhile poured munitions into the colonies through an especially rigged up commercial concern. Nine-tenths of the arms used by the Americans at the battle of Saratoga came from France. After the American victory in this battle the French government concluded, in 1778, that the insurgents were a good political risk, recognized them and signed an alliance with them, and declared war on Great Britain. Spain soon followed, hoping to drive the British from Gibraltar, and deciding that its overseas empire was more threatened by a restoration of British supremacy in North America than by the disturbing example of an independent American republic. The Dutch were drawn into hostilities after recognizing American independence. Other powers, Russia, Sweden, Denmark, Prussia, Portugal, and Turkey, irked at British employment of blockade and sea power in time of war, formed an "Armed Neutrality" to protect their commerce from dictation by the British fleet. The French, in a brief revival of their own sea power, landed an expeditionary force of 6,000 men in Rhode Island. Since the Americans suffered from the internal differences inseparable from all revolutions, and were in any case still unable to govern themselves to any effect, meeting with the old difficulties in raising both troops and money, it was the participation of regiments of the French army, in conjunction with squadrons of the French fleet, which made possible the defeat of the armed forces of the British empire and so persuaded the British government to recognize the independence of the United States. By the peace treaty of 1783, though the British were still in possession of New York and Savannah, and though the governments befriending the Americans would just as soon have confined them east of the mountains, the new republic obtained territory as far west as the Mississippi. Canada remained British. It received an English-speaking population by the settlement of over 60,000 refugee Americans who remained loyal to Great Britain.

SIGNIFICANCE OF THE REVOLUTION

The upheaval in America was a revolution as well as a war of independence. The cry for liberty against Great Britain raised echoes within the colonies themselves. The Declaration of Independence was more than an announcement of secession from the empire; it was a justification of rebellion against established authority. Curiously, although the American quarrel had been with the Parliament, the Declaration arraigned no one but the king. One reason was that the Congress, not recognizing the authority of Parliament, could separate from Great Britain only by a denunciation of the British crown; another reason was that the cry of "tyrant" made a more popular and flaming issue. Boldly voicing the natural right philosophy of the age, the Declaration held as "self-evident," *i.e.*, as evident to all reasonable men, that "all men are created equal, that they are endowed by their Creator with certain unalienable rights, that among these are life, liberty, and the pursuit of happiness." These electrifying words leaped inward into America, and outward to the world.

In the new states democratic equality made many advances, in different ways from one state to another. Businessmen, lawyers, and landowners who led the movement against England needed the support of numbers, and to obtain it were willing to make promises and concessions to the lower classes. Or the popular elements, workmen and mechanics, farmers and frontiersmen, often dissidents in religion, extorted concessions by force or threats. There was a good deal of violence, as in all revolutions; the new states confiscated property from the counter-revolutionaries, called Tories, some of whom were in addition tarred and feathered by infuriated mobs. The dissolution of the old colonial governments threw open all political questions. Persons who before had had no vote now voted for legislators and public officials. The principle was adopted, unknown to the parliamentary bodies of Europe, that every member of a legislative assembly should represent about the same number of citizens. All states north of Maryland took steps toward the extinction of slavery. Many quasi-feudal institutions, shared with Europe, disappeared. Quitrents, which corresponded to some of the manorial fees paid by farmers in England and Europe, disappeared in most of the new states. Primogeniture and entail, by which landed families aspiring to an aristocratic mode of life were kept in being, went down before the demands of democrats and small property-owners. Tithes were done away with, and the established churches, Anglican in the South, Congregationalist in New England, lost their privileged position in varying degree. But the revolution was not socially as profound as the revolution soon to come in France, or as the revolution in Russia in 1917. Property changed hands, but the law of property was modified only in detail. The inherited common law of England remained everywhere in effect. There had been no such thing in British America as a native nobleman or even a bishop; clergy and aristocracy had been incomparably less ingrained in American than in European society, and the rebellion against them was less devastating in its effect.

The main import of the American revolution remained political and even constitutional in a strict sense. The great fount of ideas was Locke. The American leaders were themselves part of the Age of Enlightenment, sharing fully in its humane and secular spirit. But probably the only non-British thinker by whom they were influenced was Montesquieu, and Montesquieu owed his popularity to his philosophizing upon English institutions. The American cast of mind went back before Montesquieu, back even before Locke, back to the English Puritan revolution of the 1640's.[35] At that time in England the sub-Parliamentary classes, Levellers and many radical sects, had insisted that every man ought to vote and that there should be some written constitution, some "agreement of the people," to protect man's natural or God-given rights from the encroachments of earthly powers. Such ideas had died out in England, where they were replaced by the idea of Parliamentary sovereignty. But older ideas remained alive in the English colonies, in which many English radicals of an earlier day had taken refuge. Five generations of life in America had sharpened the old insistence upon personal liberty and equality. When the dispute with Britain came to a head, the Americans found themselves arguing both for the historic and chartered rights of Englishmen and for the timeless and universal rights of man, both of which were held up as barriers against the inroads of Parliamentary sovereignty. The Americans came to believe, more than any other people, that government should possess limited powers only, and operate only within the terms of a fixed and written constitutional document.

All thirteen of the new states lost no time in providing themselves with written constitutions (in Connecticut and Rhode Island merely the old charters reaffirmed), all of which enshrined virtually the same principles. All followed the thought stated in the great Declaration, that it was to protect "unalienable" rights that governments were instituted among men, and that whenever government became destructive to this end the people had a right to "institute new government" for their safety and happiness. All the constitutions undertook to limit government by a separation of governmental powers. All appended a bill of rights, stating the natural rights of the citizens and the things which no government might justly do. None of the constitutions were as yet fully democratic; even the most liberal gave some advantage in public affairs to the owners of property.

Federalism, or the allocation of power between central and outlying

wwwwwwwwwwww

[35] See pp. 148–9.

governments, went along with the idea of written constitutions as a principal offering of the Americans to the world. Like constitutionalism, federalism developed in the atmosphere of protest against a centralized sovereign power. It was a hard idea for Americans to work out, since the new states carried over the old separatism which had so distracted the British. Until 1789 the states remained banded together in the Articles of Confederation. The United States was a union of thirteen independent republics. Disadvantages in this scheme becoming apparent, especially to the business and propertied interests, a convention met in 1787 and drew up the constitution which is today the world's oldest written instrument of government still in operation. In it the United States was conceived not merely as a league of states, but as a union in which individuals were citizens of the United States of America for some purposes, and of their particular states for others. Persons, not states, composed the federal republic, and the laws of the United States fell not merely on the states but on the people.

With the adoption of the new constitution in 1789 the revolutionary period in British America can be considered closed. But one other action of these years requires notice, the Northwest Ordinance of 1787. A Swiss historian, Eduard Fueter, once called it the most far-reaching piece of legislation ever enacted in America. It provided that new states, identical in all legal respects with the old, but excluding slavery, should be formed in the area north of the Ohio River. The Americans thereby proceeded to develop their western lands, not by a system of colonial subordination or of competitive expansion on the part of the original states (as might have happened), but on the principle of an elastic federalism in which the new areas, as they matured, should enjoy the rights and liberties won by war and revolution in the old. The great Mississippi valley was made ready for the coming inrush of Europeans, and "the colonization of the North American continent," in the words of Fueter, "was thus prepared by the United States in the very best way possible."

The consequences of the American Revolution can hardly be overstated. By overburdening the French treasury the American war became a direct cause of the French Revolution. Beyond that, it ushered in an age of predominantly liberal revolution which lasted through the European revolutions of 1848. The American doctrine, like most thought in the Age of Enlightenment, was expressed in universal terms of "man" and "nature." All peoples regardless of their own history could apply it to themselves, because, as Alexander Hamilton once put it, "the sacred rights of man are not to be rummaged for among old parchments or musty records. They are written, as with a sunbeam, in the whole volume of human nature, by the hand of Divinity itself, and can never be erased or obscured by mortal power." The Americans, in freeing themselves, had done what all men ought to do.

The revolt in America offered a dramatic judgment on the old colonial system, convincing some, in England and elsewhere, that the empires for which they had long been struggling were hardly worth acquiring, since colonies in time, in the words of Turgot, fell away from the mother country "like ripe fruit." The idea spread, since trade between Britain and America continued to prosper, that one could do business with a country without exerting political influence or control, and this idea became fundamental to the coming movement of economic liberalism and free trade. By coincidence, the book that became the gospel of the free trade movement, Adam Smith's *Wealth of Nations*, was published in England in the year 1776. The American example was pointed to by other peoples wishing to throw off colonial status—first by the Latin Americans, then by the peoples of the older British dominions, and finally, in the twentieth century, by those of Asia and Africa also. In Europe, the American example encouraged the type of nationalism in which subjugated nations aspire to be free. And at home the revolution did much to determine the spirit and method by which the bulk of the North American continent was to be peopled, and the attitudes for which the United States, when it became a leading power a century and a half later, was to stand before the world.

More immediately, the American example was not lost on the many Europeans who sojourned in the new states during and after the war. Of these the Marquis de Lafayette was the most famous, but there were many others: Thomas Paine, who returned to Europe in 1787; the future French revolutionist Brissot; the future Polish national leader Kosciusko; the future marshals of Napoleon, Jourdan and Berthier; the future reformer of the Prussian army Gneisenau. Contrariwise various Americans went to Europe, notably the aging Benjamin Franklin, who in the 1780's was incredibly lionized in the fashionable and literary world of Paris.

The establishment of the United States was taken in Europe to prove that many ideas of the Enlightenment were practicable. Rationalists declared that here was a people, free of past errors and superstitions, who showed how enlightened beings could plan their affairs. Rousseauists saw in America the very paradise of natural equality, unspoiled innocence, and patriotic virtue. But nothing so much impressed Europeans, and especially the French, as the spectacle of the Americans meeting in solemn conclave to draft their state constitutions. These, along with the Declaration of Independence, were translated and published in 1778 by a French nobleman, the Duke de La Rochefoucauld. They were endlessly and excitedly discussed. Constitutionalism, federalism, and limited government were not new ideas in Europe. They came out of the Middle Ages, and were currently set forth in many quarters, for example in Hungary, the Holy Roman Empire, and the Parliament of Paris. But in their prevailing form, and even in the philosophy of Montesquieu, they were associated with feudalism and aristocracy. The American revolution made such ideas progressive. The American influence, added to the force of developments in Europe, made the thought of the later Enlightenment more democratic. The United States replaced England as the model country of advanced thinkers. A school of radical reformers appeared in England itself. On the Continent there was less passive trust in the enlightened despotism of the official state. Confidence in self-government was aroused.

The American constitutions seemed a demonstration of the social con-tract. They offered a picture of men in a "state of nature," having cast off their old government, deliberately sitting down to contrive a new one, weigh-ing and judging each branch of government on its merits, assigning due powers to legislature, executive, and judiciary, declaring that all government was created by the people and in possession of a merely delegated authority, and listing specifically the inalienable rights of men—inalienable in that they could not conceivably be taken away, since men possessed them even if denied them by force. And these rights were the very same rights that many Europeans wanted secured for themselves—freedom of religion, freedom of press, freedom of assembly, freedom from arbitrary arrest at the discretion of officials. And they were the same for all, on the rigorous principle of equality before the law. The American example crystallized and made tangible the ideas that were strongly blowing in Europe, and the American example was one reason why the French, in 1789, began their revolution with a declara-tion of human rights and with the drafting of a written constitution.

And more deeply still, America became a kind of mirage or ideal vi-sion for Europe, a land of open opportunity and of new beginnings, free from the load of history and of the past, wistfully addressed by Goethe:

> *America, thou hast it better*
> *Than has our Continent, the old one.*

The United States for over a century, until great changes came within itself, and until a new revolutionary movement set in in Europe, stood out as the utopia of the common man, not only for the millions who migrated to it but for other millions who stayed at home, who often wished that their own countries might become more like it, and who would agree, with Lincoln, in calling it the last best hope of earth.

CHAPTER IX

The French Revolution

I N 1789 France fell into revolution, inaugurating an age of social upheaval and war that lasted for over a quarter of a century and raising ideas
and concepts of government that exercised a profound and continuing influence on the history of the European world. Unlike the Russian Revolution
of 1917, the French Revolution occurred in the most advanced country in
Europe. With a population of some 24,000,000, the French in 1789 were the
most numerous of all European peoples under a single government. They
may also have been the wealthiest, though not per capita. French exports
to Europe were greater than those of Great Britain. It is said that half the
goldpieces circulating in Europe were French. Paris was the center of the
intellectual movement of the Enlightenment. The French language was universally spoken in intellectual and aristocratic circles. The established classes
of Europe were in the habit of taking ideas from France, and therefore were
the more horrified and astounded when revolution broke out in that country.

38. Backgrounds

THE OLD REGIME: THE THREE ESTATES

Some remarks have already been made about the Old Regime, as the pre-revolutionary society came to be called after it disappeared, and about the failure of enlightened despotism in France to make any fundamental alteration in it.[1] The essential fact about the Old Regime was that it was still legally aristocratic and in many ways feudal. Everyone belonged legally to an "estate" or "order" of society. The First Estate was the clergy, the Second Estate the nobility, and the Third Estate included everyone else— from the wealthiest business and professional classes to the poorest peasantry and city workers. These categories were important in that the individual's legal rights and personal prestige depended on the category to which he belonged. Politically, they were obsolescent; not since 1614 had the estates assembled in an Estates-General of the whole kingdom, though in some provinces they had continued to meet as provincial bodies. Socially, they were obsolescent also, for the threefold division no longer corresponded to the real distribution of interest, influence, property, or productive activity among the French people.

Conditions in the church and the position of the clergy have been much exaggerated as a cause of the French Revolution. The church in France levied a tithe on all agricultural products, but so did the church in England; the French bishops often played a part in government affairs, but so did bishops in England through the House of Lords. The French bishoprics of 1789 were in reality no wealthier than those of the Church of England were found to be when investigated forty years later. In actual numbers, in the secular atmosphere of the Age of Enlightenment, the clergy, especially the monastic orders, had greatly declined, so that by 1789 there were probably not more than 100,000 Catholic clergy of all types in the entire population. But if the importance of the clergy has often been overemphasized, still it must be said that the church was deeply involved in the prevailing social system. For one thing, church bodies—bishoprics, abbeys, convents, schools, and other religious foundations—owned between five and ten per cent of the land of the country, which meant that collectively the church was the greatest of all landowners. Moreover, the income from church properties, like all income, was divided very unequally, and much of it found its way into the hands of the aristocratic occupants of the higher ecclesiastical offices. For while the mass of the parish clergy was of lower-class origin (more so than in the Church of England), the better positions were reserved for the nobles. Every bishop of Louis XVI's time was a nobleman—a state of affairs unknown before the eighteenth century. It need only be added that in the Age

wwwwwwwwwwwwwww

[1] See pp. 302–6.

of Enlightenment the church no longer expressed the ideas of many think-ing—and unthinking people.

The noble order, which in 1789 comprised about 400,000 persons, including women and children, had enjoyed a great resurgence since the death of Louis XIV in 1715.[2] The intendants, usually commoners a century before, were now usually nobles. Government service, higher church offices, army, parliaments, and most other public and semipublic honors were almost monopolized by the titled aristocracy in the time of Louis XVI, who, it will be recalled, had mounted the throne in 1774. Repeatedly, through parlia-ments, provincial estates, or the assembly of the clergy dominated by the noble bishops, the aristocracy had blocked royal plans for taxation and shown a desire to control the policies of state. At the same time the bourgeoisie, or upper crust of the Third Estate, had never been so influential. The fivefold increase of French foreign trade between 1713 and 1789 suggests the growth of the merchant class. As members of the bourgeoisie became stronger, more widely read, and more self-confident, they resented the distinctions enjoyed by the nobles. Some of these were financial: nobles were exempt from the most important direct tax, the *taille*, on principle, whereas bourgeois obtained exemption with more effort, but so many bourgeois enjoyed tax privileges that purely monetary self-interest was not primary in their psychology. The bourgeois resented the nobleman for his superiority and his arrogance. What had formerly been customary respect was now felt as humiliation. And they felt that they were being shut out from office and honors, and that the nobles were seeking more power in government as a class. The Revolution was the collision of two moving objects, a rising aristocracy and a rising bourgeoisie.

The common people, below the commercial and professional families in the Third Estate, were probably as well off as in most countries. But they were not well off compared with the upper classes. Wage earners had by no means shared in the wave of business prosperity. Between the 1730's and the 1780's the prices of consumers' goods rose about 65%, whereas wages rose only 22%. Persons dependent on wages were therefore badly pinched, but they were less numerous than today, for in the country there were many small farmers, and in the towns many small craftsmen, both of which groups made a living not by wages but by selling the products of their own labor at market prices. Yet in both town and country there was a significant wage-earning or proletarian element, which, though it had as yet no class-consciousness or philosophy, was to play a decisive part in the Revolution.

THE AGRARIAN SYSTEM OF THE OLD REGIME

Over four-fifths of the people were rural. The agrarian system had developed so that there was no serfdom in France, to be sure, as it was known in eastern Europe.[3] The relation of lord and peasant in France was

[2] See pp. 236–7.
[3] See pp. 29, 101–2, 174.

not the relation of master and man. The peasant owed no labor to the lord—except a few token services in some cases. The peasant worked for himself, either on his own land or on rented land; or he worked as a sharecropper (*métayer*); or he hired himself out to the lord or to another peasant.

The manor, however, still retained certain surviving features of the feudal age. The noble owner of a manor enjoyed "hunting rights," or the privilege of keeping game preserves, and of hunting on his own and the peasants' land. He usually had a monopoly over the village mill, bakeshop, or wine press, for the use of which he collected fees, called *banalités*. He possessed certain vestigial powers of jurisdiction in the manorial court, and certain local police powers, from which fees and fines were collected. These seigneurial privileges were of course the survivals of a day when the local manor had been a unit of government and the noble had performed the functions of government, an age that had long passed with the development of the centralized modern state.

There was another special feature to the property system of the Old Regime. Every owner of a manor (there were some bourgeois and even wealthy peasants who had purchased manors) possessed what was called a right of "eminent property" with respect to all land located in the manorial village. This meant that lesser landowners within the manor "owned" their land in that they could freely buy, sell, lease out, bequeath or inherit it; but they owed to the owner of the manor, in recognition of his "eminent property" rights, certain rents, payable annually, as well as transfer fees that were payable whenever the land changed owners by sale or death. Subject to these "eminent" property rights, land ownership was fairly widespread. Peasants directly owned about two-fifths of the soil of the country; bourgeois a little under a fifth. The nobility owned perhaps a little over a fifth, and the church somewhat under a tenth, the remainder being crown lands, wastelands, or commons. Finally, it must be noted that all property rights were subject also to certain "collective" rights, by which villagers might cut firewood or run their pigs in the commons, or pasture cattle on land belonging to other owners after the crops were in, there being usually no fences or enclosures.

All this may seem rather complex, but it is important to realize that property is a changing institution. Even today, in industrialized countries, a high proportion of all property is in land, including natural resources in and below the soil. In the eighteenth century property meant land even more than it does today. Even the bourgeois class, whose wealth was so largely in ships, merchandise, or commercial paper, invested heavily in land, and in France in 1789 enjoyed ownership of almost as much land as the nobility, and of more than the church. The Revolution was to revolutionize the law of property by freeing the private ownership of land from all the indirect encumbrances described—manorial fees, eminent property rights, communal village agricultural practices, and church tithes. It also was to abolish other older forms of property, such as property in public office or in masterships in the gilds, which had become useful mainly to closed and privileged groups. In final effect the Revolution established the institutions of private property

in the modern sense, and benefited, therefore, most especially the landowning peasants and the bourgeoisie.

The peasants not only owned two-fifths of the soil, but occupied almost all of it, working it on their own initiative and risk. That is to say, land
owned by the nobility, the church, the bourgeoisie, and the crown was divided up and leased to peasants in small parcels. France was already a country of small farmers. There was no "big agriculture" as in England, eastern
Europe, or the plantations of America. The manorial lord performed no economic function. He lived, not by managing an estate and selling his own
crops or cattle, but by receiving innumerable dues, quitrents, and fees. During the eighteenth century, in connection with the general aristocratic resurgence, there took place a phenomenon often called the "feudal reaction."
Manorial lords, faced with rising living costs, and acquiring higher living
standards because of the general material progress, collected their dues more
rigorously or revived old ones that had fallen into disuse. Leases and share-
cropping arrangements also became less favorable to the peasants. The
farmers, like the wage earners, were under a steadily increasing pressure. At
the same time the peasants resented the "feudal dues" more than ever, because they regarded themselves as in many cases the real owners of the land,
and the lord as a gentleman of the neighborhood who for no reason enjoyed a
status different from their own. The trouble was that much of the property
system no longer bore any relation to real economic usefulness or activity.

The political unity of France, achieved over the centuries by the monarchy, was likewise a fundamental prerequisite, and even a cause, of the
Revolution. Whatever social conditions might have existed, they could give
rise to nation-wide public opinion, nation-wide agitation, nation-wide policies, and nation-wide legislation only in a country already politically unified
as a nation. These conditions were lacking in central Europe. In France a
French state existed. Reformers did not have to create it, but only capture
and remodel it. Frenchmen in the eighteenth century already had the sense
of membership in a political entity called France. The Revolution saw a
tremendous stirring of this sense of membership and of fraternity, turning it
into a passion for citizenship, civic rights, voting powers, use and application
of the state and its sovereignty for the public advantage. At the very outbreak
of the Revolution people saluted each other as *citoyen* and shouted *vive la
nation!*

39. The Revolution of 1789

THE FINANCIAL CRISIS

The Revolution was precipitated by a financial collapse of the government. What overloaded the government was by no means the costly magnificence of the court of Versailles. Only five per cent of public expenditures

in 1788 was devoted to the upkeep of the entire royal establishment. What overloaded all governments was war costs, both current upkeep of armies and navies and the burden of public debt, which in all countries was due almost totally to the war costs of the past. In 1788 the French government devoted about a quarter of its annual expenditure to current maintenance of the armed forces, and about a half to the payment of its debts. British expenditures showed almost the same distribution. The French debt stood at almost four billion *livres*. It had been greatly swollen by the War of American Independence. Yet it was only half as great as the national debt of Great Britain, and less than a fifth as heavy per capita. It was less than the debt of the Dutch Republic. It was apparently no greater than the debt left by Louis XIV three quarters of a century before. At that time the debt had been lightened by repudiation. No responsible French official in the 1780's even considered repudiation, a sure sign of the progress in the interim of the bourgeois class, who were the main government creditors.

Yet the debt could not be carried, for the simple reason that the French budget did not balance. Taxes and other revenues fell short of necessary expenditures. This in turn was not due to national poverty, but to the tax exemptions and tax evasions of privileged elements, especially the nobles. We have already described how the most important tax, the *taille*, was generally paid only by the peasants—the nobles being exempt by virtue of their class privilege, and office holders and bourgeois obtaining exemption in various ways.[4] The church too insisted that its property was not taxable by the state; and its periodic "free gift" to the king, though substantial, was less than might have been obtained from direct taxation of the church's land. Thus, although the country itself was prosperous, the government treasury was empty. The social classes which enjoyed most of the wealth of the country did not pay taxes corresponding to their income, and, even worse, they resisted taxation as degrading.

A long series of responsible persons—Louis XIV himself, John Law, Maupeou, Turgot—had seen the need of taxing the privileged classes. Jacques Necker, a Swiss banker made director of the finances in 1777 by Louis XVI, made moves in the same direction, and, like his predecessors, was dismissed. His successor, Calonne, as the crisis mounted, came to even more revolutionary conclusions. In 1786 he produced a program in which enlightened despotism was tempered by a modest resort to representative institutions. He proposed, in place of the *taille*, a general tax to fall on all landowners without exception, a lightening of indirect taxes and abolition of internal tariffs to stimulate economic production, a confiscation of some properties of the church, and the establishment, as a means of interesting the propertied elements in the government, of provincial assemblies in which all landowners, noble, clerical, bourgeois, and peasant, should be represented without regard to estate or order.

This program, if carried out, might have solved the fiscal problem and

[4] See pp. 162, 302–3.

averted the Revolution. But it struck not only at privileges in taxation—noble, provincial, and others—but at the threefold hierarchic organization of society. Knowing from experience that the Parliament of Paris would never accept it, Calonne in 1788 convened an "assembly of notables," hoping to win its endorsement of his ideas. The notables insisted on concessions in return, for they wished to share in control of the government. A deadlock followed; the king dismissed Calonne and appointed as his successor Loménie de Brienne, the exceedingly worldly-wise archbishop of Toulouse. Brienne tried to push the same program through the Parliament. The Parliament rejected it, declaring that only the three estates of the realm, assembled in an Estates-General, had authority to consent to new taxes. Brienne and Louis XVI at first refused, believing that the Estates-General, if convened, would be dominated by the nobility. Like Maupeou and Louis XV, Brienne and Louis XVI tried to break the parliaments, replacing them with a modernized judicial system in which the law courts should have no influence over policy. This led to a veritable revolt of the nobles. All the parliaments and provincial estates resisted, army officers refused to serve, the intendants hesitated to act, noblemen began to organize political clubs and committees of correspondence. With his government brought to a standstill, and unable to borrow money or collect taxes, Louis XVI on July 5, 1788, promised to call the Estates-General for the following May. The various classes were invited to elect representatives and also to draw up lists of their grievances.

FROM ESTATES-GENERAL TO NATIONAL ASSEMBLY

Since no Estates-General had met in over a century and a half, the king asked all persons to study the subject and make proposals on how such an assembly should be organized under modern conditions. This led to an outburst of public discussion. Hundreds of political pamphlets appeared, many of them demanding that the old system by which the three estates sat in separate chambers, each chamber voting as a unit, be done away with, since under it the chamber of the Third Estate was always outnumbered. But in September 1788 the Parliament of Paris, restored to its functions, ruled that the Estates-General should meet and vote as in 1614, in three separate orders.

The nobility, through the Parliament, thus revealed its aim. It had forced the summoning of the Estates-General, and in this way the French nobility initiated the Revolution. The Revolution began as another victory in the aristocratic resurgence against the absolutism of the king. The nobles actually had a liberal program: they demanded constitutional government, guarantees of personal liberty for all, freedom of speech and press, freedom from arbitrary arrest and confinement. Many now were even prepared to give up special privileges in taxation; this might have worked itself out in time. But in return they hoped to become the preponderant political element in the state. It was their idea, not merely to have the Estates-General meet in

1789, but for France to be governed in all the future through the Estates-General, a supreme body in three chambers, one for nobles, one for a clergy in which the higher officers were also nobles, and one for the Third Estate.

This was precisely what the Third Estate wished to avoid. Lawyers, bankers, business men, government creditors, shopkeepers, artisans, working-men, and peasants had no desire to be governed by lords temporal and spiritual. Their hopes of a new era, formed by the philosophy of the Enlightenment, stirred by the revolution in America, rose to the utmost excitement when "good king Louis" called the Estates-General. The ruling of the Parliament of Paris in September 1788 came to them as a slap in the face—an unprovoked class insult. The whole Third Estate, turned on the nobility with detestation and distrust. The abbé Sieyès in January 1789 launched his famous pamphlet, *What is the Third Estate?*, declaring that the nobility was a useless caste which could be abolished without loss, that the Third Estate was the one necessary element of society, that it was identical with the nation, and that the nation was absolutely and unqualifiedly sovereign. Through Sieyès the ideas of Rousseau's *Social Contract* entered the thought of the Revolution. At the same time, even before the Estates-General actually met, and not from the books of *philosophes* so much as from actual events and conditions, nobles and commoners viewed each other with fear and suspicion. The Third Estate, which had at first supported the nobles against the "despotism" of the king's ministers, now ascribed to them the worst possible motives. Class antagonism poisoned the Revolution at the outset, made peaceful reform impossible, and threw many bourgeois without delay into a radical and destructive mood. And the mutual suspicion between classes, produced by the Old Regime and inflamed by the Revolution, has troubled France ever since.

The Estates-General met as planned in May 1789 at Versailles. The Third Estate, most of whose representatives were lawyers, boycotted the organization in three separate chambers. It insisted that deputies of all three orders should sit as a single house and vote as individuals; this procedure would be of advantage to the Third Estate, since the king had granted it as many deputies as the other two orders combined. For six weeks a deadlock was maintained. On June 13 a few priests, leaving the chamber of the First Estate, came over and sat with the Third. They were greeted with jubilation. On June 17 the Third Estate declared itself the "National Assembly." Louis XVI, under pressure from the nobles, closed the hall in which it met. The members found a neighboring indoor tennis court, and there, milling about in a babel of confusion and apprehension, swore and signed the Oath of the Tennis Court on June 20, 1789, affirming that wherever they foregathered the National Assembly was in existence, and that they would not disband until they had drafted a constitution. This was a revolutionary step, for it assumed virtually sovereign power for a body of men who had no legal authority. The king ordered members of the three estates to sit in their separate houses. He now somewhat tardily presented a reforming program of his own, too late to win the confidence of the disaffected, and in any case continuing the organization of French society in legal classes. The self-entitled National Assembly refused to back down. The king faltered, failed to enforce his commands promptly, and allowed the Assembly to remain in being. In the following days, at the end of June, he summoned about 18,000 soldiers to Versailles.

What had happened was that the king of France, in the dispute raging between nobles and commoners, chose the nobles. It was traditional in France for the king to oppose feudalism. For centuries the French monarchy had drawn strength from the bourgeoisie. All through the eighteenth century the royal ministers had carried on the struggle against the privileged interests. Only a year before, Louis XVI had been almost at war with his rebellious aristocracy. In 1789 he failed to assert himself. He lost control over the Estates-General, exerted no leadership, offered no program until too late, and provided no symbol behind which parties could rally. He failed to make use of the profound loyalty to himself felt by the bourgeoisie and common people, who yearned for nothing so much as a king who would stand up for them, as in days of yore, against an aristocracy of birth and status. He tried instead, at first, to compromise and postpone a crisis; then he found himself in the position of having issued orders which the Third Estate boldly defied; and in this embarrassing predicament he yielded to his wife, Marie Antoinette, to his brothers, and to the court nobles with whom he lived, and who told him that his dignity and authority were outraged and undermined. At the end of June Louis XVI undoubtedly intended to dissolve the Estates-General by military force. But what the Third Estate feared was not a return to the old theoretically absolute monarchy. It was a future in which the aristocracy should control the government of the country. There was now no going back; the revolt of the Third Estate had allied Louis XVI with the nobles, and the Third Estate now feared the nobles more than ever, believing with good reason that they now had the king in their hands.

THE LOWER CLASSES IN ACTION

The country meanwhile was falling into dissolution. The lower classes, below the bourgeoisie, were out of hand. For them too the convocation of the Estates-General had seemed to herald a new era. The grievances of ages, and those which existed equally in other countries than France, rose to the surface. Short run conditions were bad. The harvest of 1788 had been poor; the price of bread, by July 1789, was higher than at any time since the death of Louis XIV. The year 1789 was also one of depression; the rapid growth of trade since the American war had suddenly halted, so that wages fell and unemployment spread while scarcity drove food prices up. The government, paralyzed at the center, could not take such measures of relief as were customary under the Old Regime. The masses were everywhere restless. Labor trouble broke out; in April a great riot of workingmen devastated a wallpaper factory in Paris. In the rural districts there was much disorder. Peasants declared that they would pay no more manorial dues, and were likewise refusing taxes. In the best of times the countryside was troubled by vagrants, beggars, rough characters, and smugglers who flourished along the many tariff frontiers. Now the business depression reduced the income of honest peasants who engaged in weaving or other domestic industries in their homes; unemployment and indigence spread in the country; people were uprooted; and the result was to raise the number of vagrants to terrifying proportions. It was believed, since nothing was too bad to believe of the aristocrats (though it was not true), that they were secretly recruiting these "brigands" for their own purposes to intimidate the Third Estate. The economic and social crisis thus became acutely political.

The towns were afraid of being swamped by beggars and desperadoes. This was true even of Paris, the largest city in Europe except London. The Parisians were also alarmed by the concentration of troops about Versailles. They began to arm in self-defense. All classes of the Third Estate took part. The banker Laborde, whose career was noted in an earlier chapter,[5] and whose son sat in the assembly at Versailles, was one of many to provide funds. Crowds began to look for weapons in arsenals and public buildings. On July 14 they came to the Bastille, a stronghold built in the Middle Ages to overawe the city, like the tower of London in England. It was used as a place of detention for persons with enough influence to escape the common jails, but was otherwise in normal times considered harmless; in fact there had been talk, some years before, of tearing it down to make room for a public park. Now, in the general turbulence, the governor had placed cannon in the embrasures. The crowd requested him to remove his cannon, and to furnish them with arms. He refused. Through a series of misunderstandings, reinforced by the vehemence of a few firebrands, the crowd turned into a mob, which assaulted the fortress, and which, when helped by a handful of trained soldiers and five artillery pieces, persuaded the governor to surrender. The mob, enraged by the death of ninety-eight of its members, streamed in and murdered six soldiers of the garrison in cold blood. The governor was murdered while under escort to the Town Hall. The mayor of Paris met the same fate. Their heads were cut off with knives, stuck on the ends of pikes, and paraded about the city. While all this happened the regular army units on the outskirts of Paris did not stir, their reliability being open to question, and the authorities being in any case unaccustomed to firing on the people.

The capture of the Bastille, though not so intended, had the effect of saving the assembly at Versailles. The king, not knowing what to do, accepted the new situation in Paris. He recognized a citizens' committee, which had formed there, as the new municipal government. He sent away the troops that he had summoned, and commanded the recalcitrants among nobles and clergy to join in the National Assembly. In Paris and other cities a bourgeois

[5] See pp. 233-4.

or national guard was established to keep order. The Marquis de Lafayette, "the hero of two worlds," received command over the guard in Paris. For insignia he combined the colors of the city of Paris, red and blue, with the white of the house of Bourbon. The French tricolor, emblem of the Revolution, thus originated in a fusion of old and new.

In the rural districts matters went from bad to worse. Vague insecurity rose to the proportions of panic in the Great Fear of 1789, which spread over the country late in July in the wake of travelers, postal couriers, and others. The cry was relayed from point to point that "the brigands were coming," and peasants, armed to protect their homes and crops, and gathered together and working upon each other's feelings, often turned their attention to the manor houses, burning them in some cases, and in others simply destroying the manorial archives in which fees and dues were recorded. The Great Fear became part of a general agrarian insurrection, in which the peasants, far from being motivated by wild alarms, knew perfectly well what they were doing. They intended to destroy the manorial regime by force.

THE INITIAL REFORMS OF THE NATIONAL ASSEMBLY

The Assembly at Versailles could restore order only by meeting the demands of the peasants. To wipe out all manorial payments would deprive the landed aristocracy of most of its income. Many bourgeois also owned manors. There was therefore much perplexity. A small group of deputies prepared a surprise move in the Assembly, choosing an evening session from which many would be absent. Hence came the "night of August 4." A few liberal noblemen, by pre-arrangement, arose and surrendered their hunting rights, their *banalités*, their rights in manorial courts, and feudal and seigneurial privileges generally. What was left of serfdom and all personal servitudes were declared ended. Tithes were abolished. Other deputies repudiated the special privileges of their provinces. All personal tax privileges were given up. On the main matter, the dues arising from "eminent property" in the manors, a compromise was adopted. These dues were all abolished, but compensation was to be paid by the peasants to the former owners. The compensation was in most cases never paid. Eventually, in 1793, in the radical phase of the Revolution, the provision for compensation was repealed. In the end French peasant landowners rid themselves of their manorial obligations without cost to themselves. From the cocoon of the manor the French peasant democracy emerged intact, in contrast to what later happened in most other countries, where the peasants, when in turn liberated from manorial obligations, either lost part of their land or were crushed under instalment payments lasting many years.

The decree summarizing the resolutions of August 4 announced flatly that "feudalism was abolished." In its place the Assembly proceeded to map out the new order. The first step was to issue, on August 26, 1789, the Declaration of the Rights of Man and Citizen. This document affirmed the principles of the new state, which were essentially the rule of law, equal individual citizenship, and collective sovereignty of the people. "Men are born and remain," declared article I, "free and equal in rights." Man's natural rights were held to be "liberty, property, security, and resistance to oppression." Freedom of thought and religion were guaranteed; no one might be arrested or punished except by process of law; all persons were declared eligible for any public office for which they met the requirements. Liberty was defined as the freedom to do anything not injurious to others, which in turn was to be determined only by law. Law must fall equally upon all persons. Law was the expression of the general will, to be made by all citizens or their representatives. The only sovereign was the nation itself, and all public officials and armed forces acted only in its name. Taxes might be raised only by common consent, all public servants were accountable for their conduct in office, and the powers of government should be separated among different branches. Finally, the state might for public purposes, and under law, confiscate the property of private persons, but only with fair compensation. The Declaration, printed in thousands of leaflets, pamphlets, and books, read aloud in public places or framed and hung on walls, became the catechism of the Revolution in France, and translated into other languages it soon carried the same message to all of Europe.

Division began to appear, among those who had thus far led the Revolution, when, in September 1789, the Assembly began the actual planning of the new government. Some wanted a strong veto power for the king, and a legislative body in two houses, as in England. Others, the "patriots," wanted only a suspensive veto for the king and a legislative body of one chamber. Here again, it was suspicion of the aristocracy that proved decisive. The "patriots" were afraid that an upper chamber would bring back the nobility as a collective force, and they were afraid to make the king constitutionally strong, by giving him a full veto, because they believed him to be in sympathy with the nobles. He was, at the moment, hesitating to accept both the August

---

A Woman of the Revolution

BY JACQUES-LOUIS DAVID (FRENCH, 1748–1825)

Here is something of what historians mean by the "working class," and it may be compared with the representations of aristocracy and of the middle class already shown. The coarse garments and untended hair, the colorless lips, the lined forehead and the evidences of suffering in the eyes, all reveal a life of much labor and few amenities. The woman seems to be observing something with an interest mixed with suspicion, and her air of determination and even of defiance suggests the political mindedness aroused even in the poorest classes in time of revolution. David painted this portrait in 1795, a year after the Terror in France. He was himself an active revolutionary, a member of the Convention and of the Committee of General Security. It is rare to find portraits of people of this class of society done with so much realism, sympathy, and force. Courtesy of the Musée des Beaux-Arts, Lyon.

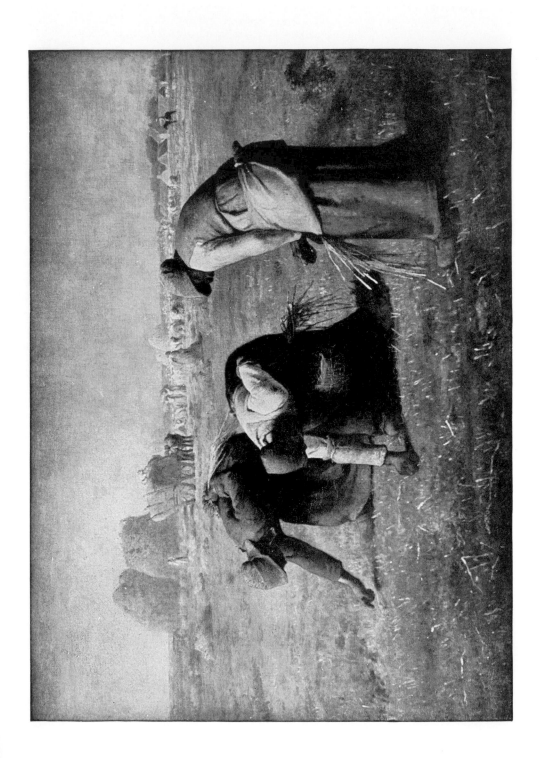

4th decrees and the Declaration of Rights. His brother, the Count of Artois, followed by many aristocrats, had already emigrated to foreign parts, and, along with these other émigrés, was preparing to agitate against the Revolution with all the governments of Europe. The patriot party would concede nothing, the more conservative party could gain nothing. The debate was interrupted again, as in July, by insurrection and violence. On October 4, a crowd of market women and revolutionary agitators, followed by the Paris national guard, took the road from Paris to Versailles. Besieging and invading the chateau, they obliged Louis XVI to take up his residence in Paris, where he could be watched. The National Assembly also shifted itself to Paris, where it too soon fell under the influence of radical elements in the city. The champions of a one-chamber legislative body and of a suspensive veto for the king won out.

The more conservative revolutionaries, if such they may be called, disillusioned in seeing constitutional questions settled by mobs, began to drop out of the Assembly. Men who on June 20 had bravely sworn the Oath of the Tennis Court now felt that the Revolution was falling into unworthy hands. Some even emigrated, forming a second wave of émigrés that would have nothing to do with the first. So the counter-revolution gathered strength. But those who wanted still to go forward, and they were many, began to organize in clubs. Most important of all was the Society of Friends of the Constitution, called the Jacobin club for short, since it met in an old Jacobin monastery in Paris. The dues were at first so high that only substantial bourgeois belonged; they were later lowered, but never enough to include persons of the poorest classes, who therefore formed lesser clubs of their own. The most advanced members of the Assembly were Jacobins, and used the club as a caucus in which to discuss their policies and lay their plans. More will soon be said of the Jacobins.

The Gleaners

BY JEAN-FRANÇOIS MILLET (FRENCH, 1814–75)

As an illustration of a social class this picture may be compared with the three preceding ones. When first exhibited in Paris in 1857 it raised an outcry. One irate critic found that "behind these three gleaning-women, against the leaden horizon, the pikes, riots and scaffolds of '93 are silhouetted." Millet denied any such political implication. The three women here are of the poorest of the French peasantry. Bowed with labor, reaching out with strong muscular hands, clutching their few stalks of grain, they are exercising a legal right, glanage, by which poor people were allowed to glean the fields after the owners had taken in their harvest. Glanage was one of the collective village rights, originally common to France, England, and most of Europe (pp. 336, 348, 423), which tended to disappear with the spread of modern private-property institutions into the country. Note how the fields in the picture are "open"; there has yet been no "enclosure" by walls or fences, though the land is privately owned, mainly by the more well-to-do peasants. Courtesy of the Louvre.

40. The Reorganization of France, 1789–91

THE CONTINUED REFORMS OF THE NATIONAL
(CONSTITUENT) ASSEMBLY

In the two years from October 1789 to September 1791 the National Assembly (or the Constituent Assembly, as it had come to be called because it was preparing a constitution) continued its work of simultaneously governing the country, devising a written constitution, and destroying in detail the institutions of the Old Regime. The old ministries, the old organization of government bureaus, the old taxes, the old property in office, the old titles of nobility, the old parliaments, the hundreds of regional systems of law, the old internal tariffs, the old provinces, and the old urban municipalities all went into the discard. Contemporaries, like Edmund Burke, were appalled at the thoroughness with which Frenchmen seemed determined to eradicate their national institutions. Why, asked Burke, should the French fanatics cut to pieces the living body of Normandy or Provence? The truth is that the provinces, like everything else, were impacted in the whole system of special privilege and unequal rights. All had to disappear if the hope of equal citizenship under national sovereignty was to be attained. In place of the provinces the Constituent divided France into eighty-three equal "departments." In place of the old towns, with their quaint old magistrates, it introduced a uniform municipal organization, all towns henceforth having the same form of government, varying only according to size. All local officials, even prosecuting attorneys and tax-collectors, were elected locally. Administratively the country was decentralized to the last degree in reaction against the bureaucracy of the Old Regime. No one outside Paris now really acted for the central government, and local communities enforced the national legislation, or declined to enforce it, as they chose. This proved ruinous when the war came, and although the "departments" created by the Constituent Assembly still exist, it has been traditional in France since the Revolution, as it was before, to keep local officials under strong control by ministers in Paris.

Under the constitution that was prepared, sometimes called the Constitution of 1791 because it went into effect at that date, the sovereign power of the nation was to be exercised by a one-chamber elected assembly, called the Legislative Assembly. The king was given only a suspensive veto power by which legislation desired by the Assembly could be postponed. In general, the executive branch, *i.e.*, king and ministers, was kept weak, partly in reaction against "ministerial despotism," partly from a well founded distrust of Louis XVI. In June 1791 Louis attempted, in the "flight to Varennes," to escape from the kingdom, join with émigré noblemen and seek help from foreign powers. He left behind him a written message in which he explicitly repudiated the Revolution. Arrested at Varennes in Lorraine, he was brought back to Paris and forced to accept his status as a constitutional monarch. The attitude of Louis XVI greatly disoriented the Revolution, for it made impossible the creation of a strong executive power, and left the country to be ruled by a debating society which under revolutionary conditions contained more than the usual number of hotheads.

Not all this machinery of state was democratic. In the granting of political rights the abstract principles of the great Declaration were seriously modified for practical reasons. Since most people were uneducated it was thought that they could have no reasonable political views. Since the small man was often a domestic servant or shop assistant it was thought that in politics he would be a mere dependent of his employer. The Constituent therefore distinguished in the new constitution between "active" and "passive" citizens. Both had the same civil rights, but only active citizens, those paying more than a stated amount of taxes, had the right to vote. The Constituent, rather liberally, included over half of all adult males in the category of active citizens. These, however, had limited political powers. Officials were not elected directly by the voters, but by electoral colleges which the voters elected—as the President of the United States is theoretically elected to this day. To be a member of an electoral college one had to meet a property qualification. Perhaps over half the active citizens could legally qualify as "electors." The active citizens, however, chose electors in a proportion of only one for each hundred active citizens, so that only about 50,000 electors actually functioned in 1790 and 1791. These men, generally the notables of their localities, designated the department officials and the deputies to the national Legislative Assembly. Affluent ex-nobles and prosperous peasants had rights corresponding to their wealth, but in some ways the new regime represented the rule of the bourgeoisie. Property was now, in the new legally equal society, the one legal distinction between man and man.

ECONOMIC POLICIES

Economic policies that were adopted had little to attract the lowest classes. The public debt had precipitated the Revolution, but the Revolutionary leaders, even the most extreme Jacobins, never disowned the debt of the Old Regime. The reason is that the bourgeois class, on the whole, were the people to whom the money was owed. To secure the debt, and to pay current expenses of government, since tax collections had become very sporadic, the Constituent Assembly as early as November 1789 resorted to a device by no means new in Europe, though never before used on so extensive a scale. It confiscated all the property of the church. Against this property, it issued negotiable instruments called *assignats*, first regarded as bonds and issued only in large denominations, later regarded as currency and issued in small bills. Holders of *assignats* could use them, or any money, to buy parcels of the former church lands. None of the confiscated land was given away; all was in fact sold at the highest possible prices, since the interest of the government was fiscal rather than social. The peasants, even when they had the money, could not easily purchase because the lands were sold at distant auctions or in large undivided blocks. The peasants were disgruntled, though they did acquire a good deal of the former church lands through middlemen. Peasant landowners were likewise expected, until 1793, to pay compensation for their old quitrents and many other manorial fees. And the landless peasants were aroused when the government, with its bourgeois ideas, encouraged the dividing up of the village commons and extinction of various collective village rights, in the interest of individual private property.

The Revolutionary bourgeoisie favored free economic individualism. It had had enough, under the Old Regime, of government regulation over the sale or quality of goods, and of privileged companies and other economic monopolies. Reforming economic thought at the time, not only in France but in England, where Adam Smith had published his epoch-making *Wealth of Nations* in 1776, held that organized special interests were bad for society, and that all prices and wages should be determined by free arrangement between the individuals concerned. The more prominent leaders of the French Revolution believed firmly in this freedom from control. The Constituent Assembly abolished the gilds, which were mainly monopolistic organizations of small business men or master craftsmen, interested in keeping up prices and averse to new machinery or new methods. There was also, in France, a rather highly organized labor movement. Since the masterships in the gilds had become practically hereditary (as a form of property and privilege), the journeymen had become lifelong wage workers. They had formed their own associations, or trade unions, called *compagnonnages*, outside the gilds.[6] Many trades were so organized—the carpenters, plasterers, paper workers, hatters, saddlers, cutlers, nail-makers, carters, tanners, locksmiths, and glass workers. Some were organized nationally, some only locally. All these journeymen's unions had been illegal under the Old Regime, but they had flourished nevertheless. They collected dues and maintained officers. They often dealt collectively with the gild masters or other employers, requiring the payment of a stipulated wage or amendment of working conditions. Sometimes they even imposed closed shops. Organized strikes were quite common. The labor troubles of 1789 continued on into the Revolution. Business fell off in the atmosphere of disorder. In 1791 there was another wave of strikes. The Assembly, in the Le Chapelier law of that year, renewed the old prohibitions of the *compagnonnages*. The same law restated the abolition of the gilds, and forbade the organization of special economic interests of any kind. All trades, it declared, were free for all to enter. All men, without belonging to any organization, had the right to work at any occupation or business they might choose. All wages were to be settled privately by the workman and his employer. This was not at all what the workingman, at that time or any other, really wanted. Nevertheless the provisions of the Le Chapelier law remained a part of French law for three quarters of a century. The embryonic trade unions continued to exist secretly, though with more difficulty than under the hit-and-miss law enforcement of the Old Regime.

[6] See pp. 99–100.

THE QUARREL WITH THE CHURCH

Most fatefully of all, the Constituent Assembly quarreled with the Catholic Church. The confiscation of church properties naturally came as a shock to the clergy. The village priests, whose support had made possible the revolt of the Third Estate, now found that the very buildings in which they worshiped with their parishioners on Sunday belonged to the "nation." The loss of income-producing properties undercut the religious orders and ruined the schools, including the 40,000 scholarships by which boys were assisted in getting an education before the Revolution. Yet it was not on the question of material wealth that the church and the Revolution came to blows. Members of the Constituent Assembly took the view of the church that the great monarchies had taken before them. The idea of separation of church and state was far from their minds. They regarded the church as a form of public authority, and as such subordinate to the sovereign power. They frankly argued that the poor needed religion if they were to respect the property of the more wealthy. In any case, having deprived the church of its own income, they had to provide for its maintenance. For the schools many generous and democratic projects of state-sponsored education were drawn up, though under the troubled conditions of the time little was accomplished. For the clergy the new program was mapped out in the Civil Constitution of the Clergy of 1790.

This document went far toward setting up a French national church. Under its provisions the parish priests and bishops were elected, the latter by the same 50,000 electors who chose other important officials. Protestants, Jews, and agnostics could legally take part in the elections, purely on the ground of citizenship and property qualifications. Archbishoprics were abolished, and all the borders of existing bishoprics were redrawn. The number of dioceses was reduced from over 130 to 83, so that one would be coterminous with each department. Bishops were allowed merely to notify the pope of their elevation; they were forbidden to acknowledge any papal authority in their assumption of office, and no papal letter or decree was to be published or enforced in France except with government permission. All clergy received salaries from the state, the average income of bishops being somewhat reduced, that of parish clergymen being raised. Sinecures, plural holdings, and other abuses by which noble families had been supported by the church were done away with. The Constituent Assembly (independently of the Civil Constitution) also prohibited the taking of religious vows and dissolved all monastic houses.

Some of all this was not in principle alarmingly new, since before the Revolution the civil authority of the king had designated the French bishops and passed on the admission of papal documents into France. French bishops, in the old spirit of the "Gallican liberties," were traditionally jealous of papal power in France.[7] Many were now willing to accept something like the Civil

---

[7] See pp. 49, 62–3, 82, 115, 163.

Constitution if allowed to produce it on their own authority. The Assembly refused to concede so much jurisdiction to the Gallican Church, and applied instead to the pope, hoping to force its plans upon the French clergy by invoking the authority of the Vatican. But the Vatican pronounced the Civil Constitution a wanton usurpation of power over the Catholic Church. Unfortunately, the Pope also went further, condemning the whole Revolution and all its works. The Constituent Assembly retorted by requiring all French clergy to swear an oath of loyalty to the constitution, including the Civil Constitution of the Clergy. Half took the oath and half refused it, the latter half including all but seven of the bishops. One of the seven willing to accept the new arrangements was Talleyrand, soon to be famous as foreign minister of numerous French governments.

There were now two churches in France, one clandestine, the other official, one maintained by voluntary offerings or by funds smuggled in from abroad, the other financed and sponsored by the government. The former, comprising the non-juring, unsworn or "refractory" clergy, turned violently counter-revolutionary. To protect themselves from the Revolution they insisted, with an emphasis quite new in France, on the universal religious supremacy of the Roman Pontiff. They denounced the "constitutional" clergy as schismatics who spurned the pope, and as mere careerists willing to hold jobs on the government's terms. The constitutional clergy, those taking the oath and upholding the Civil Constitution, considered themselves to be patriots and defenders of the rights of man; and they insisted that the Gallican Church had always enjoyed a degree of liberty from Rome. The Catholic laity were terrified and puzzled. Many were sufficiently attached to the Revolution to prefer the constitutional clergy; but to do so meant to defy the pope, and Catholics who persisted in defying the pope were on the whole those least zealous in their religion. The constitutional clergy therefore stood on shaky foundations. Many of their followers, under stress of the times, eventually turned against Christianity itself.

Good Catholics tended to favor the "refractory" clergy. The outstanding example was the king himself. He personally used the services of refractory priests, and thus gave a new reason for the revolutionaries to distrust him. Whatever chance there was that Louis XVI might go along with the Revolution was exploded, for he concluded that he could do so only by endangering his immortal soul. Former aristocrats also naturally preferred the refractory clergy. They now put aside the Voltairean levities of the Age of Enlightenment, and the "best people" began to exhibit a new piety in religious matters. The peasants, who found little in the Revolution to interest them after their own insurrection of 1789 and the consequent abolition of the manorial regime, also favored the old-fashioned or refractory clergy. Much the same was true of the urban working-class families, especially the women. The Constituent Assembly, and its successors, were at their wits' end what to do. Sometimes they shut their eyes at the intrigues of refractory clergy; the constitutional clergy then became fearful. Sometimes they hunted out and persecuted the refractories; in that case they only stirred up religious fanaticism.

The Civil Constitution of the Clergy has been called the greatest tactical blunder of the Revolution. Certainly its consequences were unfortunate in the extreme, and they spread to much of Europe. In the nineteenth century the church was to be officially anti-democratic and anti-liberal;[8] and democrats and liberals in most cases were to be violently and outspokenly anticlerical. The main beneficiary was the papacy. The French church, which had clung for ages to its Gallican liberties, was thrown by the Revolution into the arms of the pope. Even Napoleon, when he healed the schism a decade later, acknowledged powers in the papacy that had never been acknowledged by the French kings. These were steps in the process, leading through the proclamation of papal infallibility in 1870,[9] by which the affairs of the modern Catholic Church have become increasingly centralized at the Vatican. The authority of Rome has never been higher in the Catholic world than it is today.

With the proclamation of the constitution in September 1791, the Constituent Assembly disbanded. Before dissolving, it ruled that none of its members might sit in the forthcoming Legislative Assembly. This body was therefore made up of men who still wished to make their mark in the Revolution. The new regime went into effect in October 1791. It was a constitutional monarchy in which a unicameral Legislative Assembly chosen by the 50,000 top property owners of France was supreme. Designed as the permanent solution to France's problems, it was to collapse in ten months, in August 1792, as a result of popular insurrection four months after France became involved in war. A group of Jacobins, known as Girondists, for a time became the left or advanced party of the Revolution and in the Legislative Assembly led France into war.

41. The Revolution and Europe: The War and the "Second" Revolution, 1792

THE INTERNATIONAL IMPACT OF THE REVOLUTION

The European governments were long reluctant to become involved with France. They were under considerable pressure. On the one hand, pro-French and pro-Revolutionary groups appeared immediately in many quarters. The doctrines of the French Revolution, as of the American, were highly exportable: they took the form of a universal philosophy, proclaiming the rights of man regardless of time or place, race or nation. Moreover, depending on what one was looking for, one might see in the first disturbances

wwwwwwwwwwwww
[8] See pp. 484–5, 604.
[9] See p. 604.

in France a revolt of either the nobility, the bourgeoisie, the common people, or the entire nation. In Poland those who were trying to reorganize the country against further partition hailed the French example. The Hungarian landlords pointed to it in their reaction against Joseph II. In England, for a time, those who controlled Parliament complacently believed that the French were attempting to imitate them.

But it was the excluded classes of European society who were most inspired. The hard pressed Silesian weavers were said to hope that "the French would come." Strikes broke out at Hamburg, and peasants rebelled elsewhere. One English diplomat found that even the Prussian army had "a strong taint of democracy among officers and men." In Belgium, where the privileged elements were already in revolt against the Austrian Emperor, a second revolt broke out, inspired by events in France and aimed at the privileged elements. In England the newly developing "radicals," men like Thomas Paine and Dr. Richard Price, who wished a thorough overhauling of Parliament and the established church, entered into correspondence with the Assembly in Paris. Business men of importance, including Watt and Boulton, the pioneers of the steam engine, were likewise pro-French since they had no representation in the House of Commons. The Irish too were excited, and presently revolted. Everywhere the young men were aroused, the young Hegel in Germany, or in England the young Wordsworth, who later recalled the sense of a new era that had captivated so many spirits in 1789:

> Bliss was it in that dawn to be alive,
> But to be young was very heaven!

On the other hand the anti-Revolutionary movement gathered strength. Edmund Burke, frightened by the French proclivities of English radicals, published as early as 1790 his *Reflections on the Revolution in France.* For France, he predicted anarchy and dictatorship. For England, he sternly advised the English to accept a slow adaptation of their own English liberties. For all the world, he denounced a political philosophy that rested on abstract principles of right and wrong, declaring that every people must be shaped by its own national circumstances, national history and national character. He drew an eloquent reply and a defense of France from Thomas Paine in the *Rights of Man.* Burke soon began to preach the necessity of war, urging a kind of ideological struggle against French barbarism and violence. His *Reflections* were translated and widely read. In the long run his book proved an influential work in the history of thought. In the short run it fell on willing ears. The king of Sweden, Gustavus III, offered to lead a monarchist crusade. In Russia old Catherine was appalled; she forbade further translations of her erstwhile friend Voltaire, she called the French "vile riffraff" and "brutish cannibals," and she packed off to Siberia a Russian named Radishchev, who in his *Voyage from St. Petersburg to Moscow* pointed out the evils of serfdom. It is said that Russians were even forbidden to speak of the "revolutions of the heavenly spheres." The terrors were heightened by plaintive messages from Louis XVI and Marie Antoinette, and by the émigrés who kept bursting out of France, led as early as July 1789 by the king's own brother, the count of Artois. The émigrés, who at first were nobles, settled in various parts of Europe and began using their international aristocratic connections. They preached a kind of holy war. They bemoaned the sad plight of the king, but what they most wanted was to get back their manorial incomes and other rights. They hinted that Louis XVI himself was a dangerous revolutionary, and much preferred the unyielding Count of Artois.

In short, Europe was soon split by a division that overran all frontiers. The same was true of America also: in the United States the rising party of Jefferson was branded as Jacobin and pro-French, that of Hamilton as reactionary and pro-British; while in colonial Spanish America ideas of independence were strengthened, and the Venezuelan Miranda became a general in the French army. In all countries of the European world, though least of all in eastern and southern Europe, there were revolutionary or pro-French elements that were feared by their own governments. In all countries, including France, there were implacable enemies of the French Revolution. In all countries were people whose loyalties lay abroad. There had been no such situation since the Protestant Reformation, nor was there anything like it again until after the Russian Revolution of the twentieth century.

THE COMING OF THE WAR, APRIL 1792

Yet the European governments were slow to move. Catherine had no intention of becoming involved in western Europe. She only wished to involve her neighbors. William Pitt, the British prime minister, resisted the war cries of Burke. Son of the Earl of Chatham, prime minister since 1784, chief founder of the new Tory party, Pitt had a reforming program of his own; he had tried and failed to carry a reform of Parliament, and was now concentrating on a policy of orderly finance and systematic economy. His program would be ruined by war. He insisted that the domestic affairs of France were of no concern to the British government. The key position was occupied by the Hapsburg emperor, Leopold II, brother to the French queen. Leopold in effect answered Marie Antoinette's pleas for help by telling her to adjust herself to conditions in France. He resisted the furious demands of the émigrés, whom he understood perfectly, having inherited from Joseph II a fractious aristocracy himself.

Still, the new French government was a disturbing phenomenon. It openly encouraged malcontents all over Europe. It showed a tendency to settle international affairs by unilateral action. For example, it annexed Avignon at the request of local revolutionaries, but without the consent of its historic sovereign, the pope. Or again, in Alsace there had been much overlapping jurisdiction between France and Germany ever since the Peace of Westphalia.[10] The Constituent Assembly abolished feudalism and manorial

[10] See maps, pp. 128–9, 161, 304–5.

dues in Alsace as elsewhere in France. To German princes who had feudal rights in Alsace the Assembly offered compensation, but it did not ask their consent; and the German princes concerned, deprived by a revolutionary decree of rights guaranteed them by past treaties, appealed to the Holy Roman Emperor to protest the infringement of international understandings. Moreover, after the arrest of Louis XVI at Varennes, after his attempted flight in June 1791, it became impossible to deny that the French king and queen were prisoners of the revolutionaries.

In August Leopold met with the king of Prussia at Pillnitz in Saxony. The resulting Declaration of Pillnitz rested on a famous *if*: Leopold would take military steps to restore order in France if all the other powers would join him. Knowing the attitude of Pitt, he believed that the *if* could never materialize. His aim was mainly to rid himself of the French émigrés. These perversely received the Declaration with delight. They used it as an open threat to their enemies in France, announcing that they would soon return alongside the forces of civilized Europe, to punish the guilty and right the wrongs that had been done to them.

In France the upholders of the Revolution were alarmed. They were ignorant of what Leopold really meant, and took the dire menaces of the émigrés at their face value. The Declaration of Pillnitz, far from cowing the French, enraged them against all the crowned heads of Europe. It gave a political advantage to the then dominant faction of Jacobins, known to history as the Girondists. These included the *philosophe* Condorcet, the humanitarian lawyer Brissot, and the civil servant Roland and his more famous wife, Mme. Roland, whose house became a kind of headquarters of the group. They attracted many foreigners also, such as Thomas Paine and the German Anacharsis Cloots, the "representative of the human race." In December 1791 a deputation of English radicals, led by James Watt, son of the inventor of the steam engine, received a wild ovation at the Paris Jacobin club.

The Girondists became the party of international revolution. They declared that the Revolution could never be secure in France until it spread to the world. They contemplated a war in which French armies should enter neighboring countries, unite with local revolutionaries, overthrow the established governments, and set up a federation of republics. In their call for "a crusade of universal liberty," in which all peoples should rise against all tyrants, they were supported by the connivance of some who wished to curb the Revolution by holding it at the line of constitutional monarchy. This group, led by Lafayette, mistakenly believed that war might restore the much damaged popularity of Louis XVI, unite the country under the new government, and make it possible to put down the continuing Jacobin agitation. As the war spirit boiled up in France, the Emperor Leopold II died. He was succeeded by Francis II, a man much more inclined than Leopold to yield to the clamors of the old aristocracy. Francis resumed negotiations with Prussia. In France all who dreaded a return of the Old Regime listened more readily to the Girondists. Among the Jacobins as a whole, only a few, generally a handful of radical democrats, opposed the war. On April 20, 1792, without serious opposition, the Assembly declared war on "the king of Hungary and Bohemia."

THE "SECOND" REVOLUTION: AUGUST 10, 1792

The war intensified the existing unrest and dissatisfaction of the un-propertied classes. Both peasants and urban workers felt that the Constituent and the Legislative Assembly had served the propertied interests and had done little for them. Peasants were dissatisfied at the inadequate measures taken to facilitate land distribution; workers felt especially the pinch of soaring prices, which by 1792 had greatly risen. Gold had been taken out of the country by the émigrés; paper money, the *assignats*, was almost the sole currency, and the future of the government was so uncertain that it steadily lost value. Peasants concealed their food products rather than sell them for depreciating paper. Actual scarcity combined with the falling value of money to drive up the cost of living. The lowest income groups suffered the most. But dissatisfied though they were, when the war began they were threatened with a return of the émigrés and a vindictive restoration of the Old Regime, which at least for the peasants would be the worst of all possible eventualities. The working classes—peasants, artisans, mechanics, shopkeepers, wage workers—rallied to the Revolution but not to the revolutionary government in power. The Legislative Assembly and the constitutional monarchy lacked the confidence of large elements of the population.

In the summer of 1792 great masses of the French people, guided and roused by the bourgeois Jacobins—both Girondists and others even more radical like Robespierre, Danton, and the vitriolic journalist Marat—burst out in a passion of nationalist excitement, directed against the foreign powers that threatened to crush the Revolution by war, and also in a kind of furious class upheaval, in which the intention was to use the Revolution for the benefit of the working people. They turned against the king not only because he was identified with powers at war with France, but also because, in France itself, those who still supported him were using the monarchy as a defense against the lower classes. Republicanism in France was partly a rather sudden historical accident, in that France was at war under a king who could not be trusted, and partly a kind of lower-class or quasi-proletarian movement, in which, however, many bourgeois revolutionaries shared.

Feeling ran high during the summer of 1792. Recruits streamed into Paris from all quarters on their way to the frontiers. One detachment, from Marseilles, brought with them a new marching song, known ever since as the *Marseillaise*, a fierce call to war upon tyranny. The transient provincials stirred up the agitation in Paris. On August 10, 1792, the working class quarters of the city rose in revolt, supported by the recruits from Marseilles and elsewhere, stormed the Tuileries against resistance by the Swiss Guard, many of whom were massacred, and seized and imprisoned the king and the royal family. A revolutionary municipal government, or "Commune," was set up in Paris. Usurping the powers of the Legislative Assembly, it forced the abrogation of the constitution, and the election, by universal male suffrage, of a Constitutional Convention that was to govern France and prepare a new and more democratic constitution. The very word Convention was used in recollection of the American Constitutional Convention of 1787. Meanwhile hysteria, anarchy, and terror reigned in Paris; a handful of insurrectionary soldiers, declaring that they would not fight enemies on the frontiers until they had disposed of enemies in Paris, dragged about 1,100 persons—refractory priests and other counter-revolutionaries—from the prisons of the city and killed them after drumhead trials. These were the "September massacres."

For over two and a half years, since October 1789, there had been an abatement of popular violence. Now the coming of the war and the dissatisfaction of the lower classes with the course of events so far had led to new explosions. The insurrection of August 10, 1792, the "second" French Revolution, initiated the most advanced phase of the Revolution.

42. The Emergency Republic, 1792–5: The Terror

THE NATIONAL CONVENTION

The National Convention met on September 20, 1792; it was to sit for three years. It immediately proclaimed the Year One of the French Republic. The disorganized French armies, also on September 20, won a great moral victory in the "cannonade of Valmy," a battle that was hardly more than an artillery duel, but which induced the Prussian commander to give up his march on Paris. The French soon overran Belgium and the Left Bank of the Rhine. To reinforce its swarming armies the Convention called for an international people's revolution, enacting two "propaganda decrees." One announced that the French Republic would assist "all peoples who might wish to recover their liberty"; the other ordered French generals to confiscate property and repress counter-revolutionaries, i.e., all opposition, in the occupied countries. The Republic was realizing, in its own way, the old dream of Louis XIV for the expansion of France to its "natural boundary" on the Rhine.

The British and Dutch prepared to resist. Pitt, still insisting that the French might have any domestic regime that they chose, declared that Great Britain could not tolerate the French occupation of Belgium. The British and Dutch began conversations with Prussia and Austria, and the French declared war on them on February 1, 1793. Within a few weeks the Republic had annexed Savoy and Nice, as well as Belgium, and had much of the German Rhineland under its military government.[11] Meanwhile, in eastern Europe,

wwwwwwwwwwwww

[11] See map, p. 368.

while denouncing the rapacity of the French savages, the rulers of Russia and
Prussia came to an arrangement of their own, each appropriating a portion of
Poland in the second partition in January 1793.[12] The Austrians, excluded
from the second partition, became anxious over their interests in the East.
The infant French Republic, now at war with all Europe, was saved by the
weakness of the Coalition, for Britain and Holland had no land forces of
consequence, and Prussia and Austria were too jealous of each other, and
too pre-occupied with Poland, to commit the bulk of their armies against
France.

In the Convention all the leaders were Jacobins, but the Jacobins were
again splitting. The Girondists were no longer the most advanced revolutionary group as they had been in the Legislative Assembly. Beside the Girondists
appeared a new group, whose members preferred to sit in the highest seats in
the hall, and therefore were dubbed the "Mountain" in the political parlance
of the day. The leading Girondists came from the provinces; the leading
Mountaineers, though often of provincial origin, were representatives of the
city of Paris and owed much of their political strength to the radical and
popular elements in the city. After the revolution of August 10, 1792, and the
ensuing September massacres, which they had done much to precipitate, the
Girondists began to dilate on the horrors of mob rule. Before the war they
had been the most ardent war party; now they hesitated to create a strong
war government, fearing dictatorship by the radicals of Paris. They had been
among the first theoretical republicans; now, with the king deposed and imprisoned, they adopted various devices to delay his trial, and, once it began, to
obtain clemency in the sentence. The Convention put Louis XVI on trial for
treason in December 1792. On January 15 it unanimously pronounced him
guilty, but on the next day, out of 721 deputies present, only 361 voted for
immediate execution, a majority of one. Louis XVI died on the guillotine
forthwith. The 361 deputies were henceforth branded for life as regicides;
never could they allow, in safety to themselves, a restoration of the Bourbon
monarchy in France. The other 360 deputies were not similarly compromised;
their rivals called them Girondists, "moderatists," counter-revolutionaries.
All who still wanted more from the Revolution, or who feared that the slightest wavering would bring the Allies and the émigrés into France, now looked
to the Mountain wing of the Jacobins.

BACKGROUND TO THE TERROR

In the spring of 1793 the Allied armies drove the French from Belgium
and threatened to invade France. Counter-revolutionaries in France exulted.
Revolutionaries were terrified. Prices continued to rise, the currency fell, food
was harder to obtain, and the working classes were increasingly restless. The
working-class leaders were called *enragés*. They were small and unknown men,

---

[12] See pp. 220–2, 317.

outside the Convention. They demanded price controls, currency controls, rationing, legislation against the hoarding of food, requisitioning to enforce the circulation of goods, in short a kind of regulated economy. They denounced the bourgeoisie as profiteers and oppressors of the people. The Girondist wing of the Jacobins dismissed them as anarchists. The Mountain was willing to work with them, partly from sympathy with their ideas, and in any case to win mass support for the war. On May 31, 1793, the Commune of Paris, under *énragé* leadership, assembled a host of demonstrators and insurrectionists who invaded the Convention and forced the arrest of the Girondist leaders. Other Girondists fled to the provinces, including Condorcet, who, while in hiding, and before his suicide, found occasion to write his encomium on the *Progress of the Human Mind.*[13]

The Mountain now ruled in the Convention, but the Convention itself ruled very little. Not only were the foreign armies and the émigrés at the gates, bent on destroying the Convention as a band of regicides and social incendiaries. The authority of the Convention was widely repudiated in France itself. In the West, in the Vendée, the peasants had revolted against military conscription; they were worked upon by refractory priests, British agents and royalist emissaries of the count of Artois. The great provincial cities, Lyons, Bordeaux, Marseilles and others, had also rebelled, especially after the fugitive Girondists reached them. These "federalist" rebels demanded a more "federal" or decentralized republic. Like the Vendéans, with whom they had no connection, they objected to the ascendancy of Paris, having been accustomed to more regional independence under the Old Regime. These rebellions became counter-revolutionary, since all sorts of foreigners, royalists, émigrés and clericals streamed in to assist them.

But the Convention also lacked the support of revolutionaries, principally outside the assembly, who did not think it radical enough. The politically conscious working-class leaders, the *enragés*, local organizers, agitators and politicians preferred to short-cut parliamentary methods. They organized "revolutionary armies," semimilitary bands of men who scoured the country for food, searched the barns of peasants, and denounced suspects. They worked through the *communes*, or local municipal governments, in Paris and elsewhere, and also through the "popular societies," provincial clubs now affiliated with the Paris Jacobins.

As for the Convention, while it cannot be said ever to have had any commanding leaders, the program it followed for about a year was on the whole that of Maximilian Robespierre, himself a Jacobin but not one to go along with popular revolution or anarchy. Robespierre is one of the most argued about and least understood men of modern times. Persons accustomed to stable conditions dismiss him with a shudder as a bloodthirsty fanatic, dictator, and demagogue. Others have considered him an idealist, a visionary, and an ardent patriot whose goals and ideals were at least avowedly democratic. All agree on his personal honesty and integrity and on his revolutionary

[13] See pp. 299–300.

zeal. He was by origin a lawyer of northern France, educated with the aid of scholarships in Paris. He had been elected in 1789 to sit for the Third Estate in the Estates-General, and in the ensuing Constituent Assembly played a minor role, though calling attention to himself by his views against capital punishment and in favor of universal suffrage. During the time of the Legislative Assembly, in 1791–92, he continued to agitate for democracy and vainly pleaded against the declaration of war. In the Convention, elected in September 1792, he sat for a Paris constituency. He became a prominent member of the Mountain, and welcomed the purge of the Girondists. He had always kept free of the bribery and graft in which some others became involved, and for this reason was known as the Incorruptible. He was a great believer in the importance of "virtue." This term had been practically a technicality among the *philosophes:* both Montesquieu and Rousseau had held that republics depended upon "virtue," or unselfish public spirit and civic zeal, to which was added, under Rousseauist influence, a somewhat sentimentalized idea of personal uprightness and purity of life. Robespierre was determined, in 1793 and 1794, to bring about a kind of "republic of virtue," or democratic republic made up of good citizens and honest men.

THE PROGRAM OF THE CONVENTION, 1793–4: THE TERROR

The program of the Convention, which Robespierre helped to form, was to repress anarchy, civil strife, and counter-revolution at home, and to win the war by a great national mobilization of the country's people and resources. It would prepare a democratic constitution and initiate legislation for the lower classes, but it would not yield to the Paris Commune and other agencies of direct revolutionary action. To conduct the government, the Convention granted wide powers to a Committee of Public Safety, a group of twelve members of the Convention who were re-elected every month. Robespierre was an influential member; others were the youthful St. Just, the partially paralyzed Couthon, and the army officer Carnot, "organizer of victory."

To repress the "counter-revolution," the Convention and the Committee of Public Safety set up what is popularly known as the "Reign of Terror." Revolutionary courts were instituted as an alternative to the lynch-law of the September massacres. A Committee of General Security was created as a kind of supreme political police. Designed to protect the Revolutionary Republic from its internal enemies, the Terror struck at those who were in league against the Republic, and at those who were merely suspected of hostile activities. Its victims ranged from Marie Antoinette and other royalists to the former revolutionary colleagues of the Mountain, the Girondist leaders; and before the year 1793–4 was over, some of the old Jacobins of the Mountain who had helped inaugurate the program also went to the guillotine. The number of persons who lost their lives in the Terror, from the late summer of 1793 to July 1794, has often been exaggerated. By the standards of the twentieth century, in which governments have undertaken to extirpate whole classes or races, the Terror was fairly mild. Yet about 40,000 persons died in it; and additional hundreds of thousands were at one time or another arrested and held in custody. Most executions took place in the Vendée, at Lyons, and in other places in open rebellion, and were directed against persons in insurrection in time of war. The Terror showed no respect for, or interest in, the class origins of its victims. About eight per cent were nobles, but the nobles as a class were not molested unless suspected of political agitation. Fourteen per cent of the victims were classifiable as bourgeois, mainly of the rebellious southern cities. Six per cent were clergy, while no less than seventy per cent were of the peasant and laboring classes. The republic of "virtue" and of the Declaration of the Rights of Man was of course, in theory, to follow the Terror once the war and the emergency were over, but meanwhile, the Terror was inhuman at best and in some places atrocious, as at Nantes where two thousand persons were loaded on barges and deliberately drowned. The Terror left long memories in France of antipathy to the Revolution and to republicanism.

To conduct the government in the midst of the war emergency the Committee of Public Safety operated as a joint dictatorship or war cabinet. It prepared and guided legislation through the Convention. It gained control over the "representatives on mission," who were members of the Convention on duty with the armies and in the insurgent areas of France. It established the *Bulletin des loix*, so that all persons might know what laws they were supposed to enforce or to obey. It centralized the administration, converting the swarm of locally elected officials, left over from the Constituent Assembly, and who were royalists in some places, wild extremists in others, into centrally appointed "national agents" named by the Committee of Public Safety.

To win the war the Committee proclaimed the *levée en masse*, calling on all able-bodied men to rally to the colors. It recruited scientific men to work on armaments and munitions. The most prominent French scientists of the day, including Lagrange and Lamarck, worked for or were protected by the government of the Terror, though one, Lavoisier, "father of modern chemistry," was guillotined in 1794 because he had been involved in tax-farming before 1789. For military reasons also the Committee instituted economic controls, which at the same time met the demands of the *enragés* and other working-class spokesmen. The assignats ceased to fall during the year of the Terror. Thus the government protected both its own purchasing power and that of the masses. It did so by controlling the export of gold, by confiscating specie and foreign currency from French citizens, to whom it paid *assignats* in return, and by legislation against hoarding or the withholding of goods from the market. Food and supplies for the armies, and for civilians in the towns, were raised and allocated by a system of requisitions, centralized in a Subsistence Commission under the Committee of Public Safety. A "general maximum" set ceilings for prices and wages. It helped to check inflation during the crisis, but it did not work very well; the Committee believed, on principle, in a free market economy, and lacked the technical and administrative machinery to enforce thorough controls. By 1794 it was giving freer rein to private enterprise and to the peasants, in order to encourage production. It tried also to hold down wages, and in that respect failed to win the adherence of many working-class agitators.

In June 1793 the Committee produced, and had adopted by the Convention, a republican constitution which provided for universal male suffrage. But the new constitution was suspended indefinitely, and the government was declared "revolutionary until the peace," "revolutionary" meaning extra-constitutional or of an emergency character. In other ways the Committee showed intentions of legislating in behalf of the lower economic classes. The price controls and other economic regulations answered the demands of the *enragés*. The last of the manorial regime was done away with; the peasants were relieved of having to pay compensation for the obligations that had been abolished at the opening of the Revolution. Purchase of land by the peasants was made somewhat easier. There were even moves, in the Ventôse laws of March 1794, to confiscate the property of suspects (not merely of the church or convicted émigrés), and to give such property gratis to "indigent patriots"; but these laws were drafted in unworkable form, never received much support from the ruling Committee, and came to very little. The Committee busied itself also with social services and measures of popular uplift: it issued pamphlets to teach farmers to inprove their crops, selected promising youths to receive instruction in useful trades, opened a military school for boys of all classes, even the humblest, and certainly intended to introduce universal elementary education. It was at this time, also, that slavery was abolished in the French colonies, free Negroes having already received civic rights.

The Committee of Public Safety wished to concentrate the revolution in itself. It had no patience with unauthorized revolutionary violence. With a democratic program of its own, it disapproved of the turbulent democracy of popular clubs and local assemblies. In the fall of 1793 it arrested the leading *enragés*. Extreme revolutionism thereafter took the name of Hébertism, after Hébert, an officer of the Paris Commune. The Hébertists were a large and indefinable group, and included many members of the Convention. They indiscriminately denounced merchants and bourgeoisie. They were the party of extreme Terror; a Hébertist brought about the drownings at Nantes. Believing all religion to be counter-revolutionary, they launched the movement of Dechristianization. Even a Republican calendar was adopted by the Convention. Its main purpose was to blot out from men's minds the Christian cycle of Sundays, saints' days, and such holidays as Christmas and Easter. It counted years from the founding of the French Republic, divided each year into new months of thirty days each, and even abolished the week, which it replaced with the *décade*.[14] As a popular measure it somewhat misfired, for where the old Sunday was one day of rest in seven, the new *décade* gave only one in ten.

———————————

[14] Though not adopted until October 1793, the Revolutionary calendar dated the Year I of the French Republic from September 22, 1792. The names of the months, in order, were Vendémiaire, Brumaire, Frimaire (autumn); Nivôse, Pluviôse, Ventôse (winter) Germinal, Floréal, Prairial (spring); Messidor, Thermidor, Fructidor (summer).

Another form taken by Dechristianization was the cult of Reason which sprang up all over France at the end of 1793. In Paris the bishop resigned his office, declaring that he had been deluded; and the Commune put on ceremonies in the cathedral of Notre Dame, in which Reason was impersonated by an actress who was the wife of one of the city officials. But Dechristianization was severely frowned upon by Robespierre. He believed that it would alienate the masses from the Republic, and ruin such sympathy as was still felt for the Revolution abroad. The Committee of Public Safety, therefore, ordered the toleration of peaceable Catholics, and in June 1794 Robespierre introduced the "Worship of the Supreme Being," a kind of national and naturalistic cult, in which the Republic was declared to recognize the existence of God and the immortality of the soul. Robespierre hoped that both Catholics and agnostic anti-clericals could become reconciled on this ground. But Catholics were now beyond reconciliation, and the freethinkers, appealing to the tradition of Voltaire, regarded Robespierre as a reactionary and a mystery-monger, and were instrumental in bringing about his fall.

Meanwhile the Committee proceeded relentlessly against the Hébertists, whose main champions it sent to the guillotine in March 1794. The paramilitary "revolutionary armies" were repressed. The extreme Terrorists were recalled from the provinces. The revolutionary Paris commune was destroyed. Robespierre filled the municipal offices of Paris with his own appointees. This Robespierrist commune disapproved of strikes and tried to hold down wages, on the plea of military necessity; it failed to win over the ex-Hébertists and working-class spokesmen, who became disillusioned in the Revolution and dismissed it as a bourgeois movement. Probably to prevent just such a conclusion, and to avoid the appearance of deviation to the right. Robespierre and the Committee, after liquidating the Hébertists, also liquidated certain right-wing members of the Mountain who were known as Dantonists. Danton and his followers were accused of financial dishonesty and of dealing with counter-revolutionaries; the charges contained much truth, but were not the main reason for the executions.

By the spring of 1794 the French Republic possessed an army of 800,-000 men, the largest ever raised up to that time by a European power. It was a national army, representing a people in arms, commanded by officers who had been promoted rapidly on grounds of merit, and composed of troops who felt themselves to be citizens fighting for their own cause. Its intense political mindedness made it the more formidable, and contrasted strongly with the indifference of the opposing troops, some of whom were in fact serfs, and none of whom had any sense of membership in their own political systems. The Allied governments, each pursuing its own ends, and still distracted by Poland, where the third partition was impending, were unable to combine their forces against France. In June 1794 the French won the battle of Fleurus in Belgium. The Republican hosts again streamed into the Low Countries; in six months their cavalry rode into Amsterdam on the ice.

Military success made the French less willing to put up with the dictatorial rule and economic regimentation of the Terror. Robespierre and the

Committee of Public Safety had antagonized all significant parties. The proletarian radicals of Paris would not support him, and after the death of Danton the National Convention was afraid of its own ruling committee. A group in the Convention obtained the "outlawing" of Robespierre on 9 Thermidor (July 27, 1794); he was guillotined with some of his associates on the following day. Many who turned against Robespierre believed they were pushing the Revolution farther forward, as in destroying the Girondists the year before. Others thought, or said, that they were stopping a dictator and a tyrant. All agreed, to absolve themselves, in heaping all blame upon Robespierre. The idea that Robespierre was an ogre originated more with his former colleagues than with conservatives of the time.

THE THERMIDORIAN REACTION

The fall of Robespierre stunned the country, but its effects manifested themselves during the following months as the "Thermidorian reaction." The Terror subsided. The Convention reduced the powers of the Committee of Public Safety, and it closed the Jacobin club. Business men, landowning peasants, army suppliers, speculators in land and currency made their voices heard. Price control and other regulations were removed. Inflation resumed its course, prices again rose, and the disoriented and leaderless working classes suffered more than ever. Sporadic risings broke out, of which the greatest was the insurrection of Prairial in the Year Three (May 1795), when a mob all but dispersed the Convention by force. Troops were called to Paris for the first time since 1789. Insurrectionists in the working-class quarters threw up barricades in the streets. The army prevailed without much bloodshed, but the Convention arrested, imprisoned, or deported ten thousand of the insurgents. A few organizers were guillotined, including one Negro. The affair of Prairial gave a foretaste of nineteenth-century social revolution.

The triumphant element was the bourgeois class which had guided the Revolution since the Constituent Assembly and had not been really unseated even during the Terror. To the old solid bourgeois of the Old Regime new elements were now added, *parvenus* and *nouveaux riches*, speculators and profiteers, often noisy, ostentatious, and vulgar, and whose women, nicknamed the *merveilleuses*, were commonly overdressed or underdressed in the extreme. Young bourgeois often joined with former aristocrats in a "white terror" against the Jacobins. But the bourgeoisie, disreputable though a few of them were, had not lost faith in the Revolution. Democracy they associated with red terror and mob rule, but they still believed in individual legal rights and in a written constitution. Conditions were rather adverse, for the country was still unsettled, and although the Convention made a separate peace with Spain and Prussia, France still remained at war with Great Britain and the Hapsburg empire. But the bourgeois of the Convention were determined to make another attempt at constitutional government. They set aside the democratic constitution written in 1793 (and never used), and produced another, known as the Constitution of the Year III, which went into effect at the end of 1795.

43. The Constitutional Republic: The Directory, 1795–99

THE WEAKNESS OF THE DIRECTORY

The first formally constituted French republic, known as the Directory, lasted only four years. Its weakness was that it rested on an extremely narrow social base, and that it presupposed certain military conquests. The new constitution applied not only to France but also to Belgium, which was regarded as incorporated constitutionally into France, though the Hapsburgs had not yet ceded these "Austrian Netherlands," nor had the British yielded in their refusal to accept French occupation. The constitution of 1795 thus committed the Republic to a program of successful expansion. At the same time it restricted the politically active class. It gave almost all literate citizens the vote, but voters voted only for "electors," who had to be owners of so much real estate that they were only 20,000 in number, fewer than in 1791. The electors chose all important department officials and also the members of the national legislative assembly, which this time was divided into two chambers. The lower chamber was called the Council of Five Hundred, the upper, composed of 250 members, the Council of Ancients—"ancients" being men over forty. The chambers chose the executive, which was called the Directory (whence the whole regime got its name), and was made up of five Directors.

The government was thus theoretically in the hands of about 20,000 owners of land, rural and urban, but its real base was narrower still. In the reaction after Thermidor many people began to consider restoring the monarchy. The Convention, to protect its own members, ruled that two-thirds of the men initially elected to the Council of Five Hundred and Council of Ancients must be ex-members of the Convention. This interference with the freedom of the elections provoked serious disturbances in Paris, instigated by persons called royalists; but the Convention, having now accustomed itself to using the army, instructed a young general who happened to be in Paris, named Bonaparte, to put down the royalist mob. He did so with a "whiff of grapeshot." The constitutional republic thus made itself dependent on military protection at the outset. As it turned out, 506 *Conventionnels*, or almost all surviving members of the Convention, reappeared among the 741 elected to the new legislative chambers, in which therefore they had a comfortable majority. They were derisively called "perpetuals" by their opponents. The new republic, to its critics, seemed to be a storm-cellar for regicides. All the old faces reappeared in new positions.

The regime had enemies to both right and left. On the right, undisguised royalists agitated in Paris and even in the two councils. Their center was the Clichy club, and they were in continuous touch with the late king's brother, the count of Provence, whom they regarded as Louis XVIII (Louis XVI's son, who died in prison, being counted as Louis XVII). Louis XVIII had installed himself at Verona in Italy, where he headed a propaganda agency financed largely by British money. The worst obstacle to the resurgence of royalism in France was Louis XVIII himself. In 1795, on assuming the title, he had issued a Declaration of Verona, in which he announced his intention to restore the Old Regime and punish all involved in the Revolution back to 1789. It has been said, correctly enough in this connection, that the Bourbons "learned nothing and forgot nothing." Had Louis XVIII offered in 1795 what he offered in 1814, it is quite conceivable that his partisans in France might have brought about his restoration and terminated the war. As it was, the bulk of the French adhered, not exactly to the republic as set up in 1795, but more negatively to any system that would shut out the Bourbons, prevent a reimposition of the manorial system, and secure the new landowners, peasant and bourgeois, in the possession of the church properties which they had purchased.

The Left was made up of survivors of the working-class movement of 1793. Having no means of going through parliamentary channels, they turned to secretly plotting further revolution, most especially in the Conspiracy of Equals organized by "Gracchus" Babeuf. Babeuf, who had been a minor office-holder during the Terror, concluded from the failure of the *enragés* and the Hébertists that only drastic changes would be of benefit to the common man. He clearly conceived of the abolition of both private property and parliamentary government, and of replacing private enterprise with a thoroughgoing economic and social plan. For these ideas he is warmly acclaimed by modern communist writers. The government of the Directory accused the Babouvists of fomenting agrarian reform and insurrection, arrested them in 1796, and guillotined or deported them in 1797. Meanwhile it did nothing to relieve the distress of the lower classes, who showed little inclination to follow Babeuf, but who did suffer from the persistent ravages of scarcity and inflation.

THE POLITICAL CRISIS OF 1797

In March 1797 occurred the first really free election ever held in France under republican auspices. A third of the membership of the two councils was to be renewed. Some 216 "perpetuals" retired, of whom about 150 stood for re-election. Only thirteen were re-elected. The successful candidates were for the most part constitutional monarchists or at least vaguely royalist. A change of the balance within the Five Hundred and the Ancients, in favor of royalism, seemed to be impending. This was precisely what most of the republicans of 1793, including the regicides, could not endure, even though they had to violate the constitution to prevent it. Nor was it endurable, for other reasons, to General Napoleon Bonaparte.

Bonaparte had been born in 1769 into the minor nobility of Corsica, shortly after the annexation of Corsica to France. He had studied in French military schools and been commissioned in the Bourbon army, but would never have reached high rank under the conditions of the Old Regime. In 1793 he was a fervent young Jacobin officer, who had been useful in driving the British from Toulon, and who was consequently made a brigadier general by the government of the Terror. In 1795, as noted, he rendered service to the Convention by breaking up a demonstration of royalists. In 1796 he received command of an army, with which, in two brilliant campaigns, he crossed the Alps and drove the Austrians from north Italy. Like other generals he got out of control by the government in Paris, which was financially too harassed to pay his troops or to supply him. He lived by local requisitions in Italy, became self-supporting and independent, and in fact made the civilian government in Paris dependent on him, by sending it funds and booty. He developed a foreign policy of his own. His headquarters in Italy resembled the court of a sovereign prince. He established a "Cisalpine" Republic in the Po valley on the French model, and dreamed of reaching the Adriatic and the East. The Directory, on the whole, meant to return north Italy to the Austrians in compensation for Austrian recognition of the French conquest of Belgium. Bonaparte insisted that France hold its position in both Belgium and Italy. He therefore needed expansionist republicans in the government in Paris, and was perturbed by the elections of 1797.

The Austrians negotiated with Bonaparte because they had been beaten by him in battle. The British also, in conferences with the French at Lille, discussed peace in 1796 and 1797. The war had gone badly for England; a party of Whigs led by Charles James Fox had always openly disapproved it, and the pro-French and republican radicals were so active that the government suspended *habeas corpus* in 1794, and thereafter imprisoned political agitators at its discretion. In 1795 an assassin fired on George III, breaking the glass in his carriage. Crops were bad, and bread was scarce and costly; it was in the 1790's that Britain became permanently dependent on the importation of food. England too suffered from inflation, for Pitt at first financed the war by extensive loans, and a good deal of gold was shipped to the Continent to finance the Allied armies. In February 1797 the Bank of England suspended gold payments to private citizens. Famine threatened, the populace was restless, and there were even mutinies in the fleet. Ireland was in rebellion; the French came close to landing a republican army in it, and it could be supposed that the next attempt might be more successful. The Austrians, Britain's only remaining ally, were routed by Bonaparte, and at the moment the British could subsidize them no further. The British had every reason to make peace. Many were inclined to settle for colonial conquests, regarding the war as a renewal of the eighteenth-century struggle for empire. The conferees at Lille reached the point of considering an arrangement by which Britain should recognize the French annexation of Belgium, in return for the cession of Ceylon, the Cape of Good Hope, and Trinidad to Great Britain. These were, in truth, not French to cede; Ceylon and the

Cape were Dutch, and Trinidad Spanish; but France had conquered Holland, where it had set up a puppet Batavian Republic, and the Spanish monarchy had become allied with the French Republic through the old fear of Great Britain.

Prospects of peace seemed good in the spring of 1797, and were brightened by the royalist victories in the French elections. The peace party in France was numerous. It was the hope of peace that turned many people to royalism, for the king, if restored, could easily abjure the conquests of the republic. But the republicans in the government, most of them "perpetuals" from the Convention, could make peace with difficulty, if at all. They were constitutionally bound to retain Belgium; they were so unpopular that they needed the allurements of martial glory; they were financially so embarrassed that they were supporting their government in part by tribute from conquered countries; and in any case they had lost control over their own generals. Nor could the supreme question be evaded: Was peace dear enough to purchase by a return of the Old Regime, such as Louis XVIII had himself promised?

The coup d'état of Fructidor (September 4, 1797) resolved all these many issues. It was the turning point of the constitutional republic, and was decisive for all Europe. The Directory asked for help from Bonaparte, who sent one of his generals, Augereau, to Paris. While Augereau stood by with a force of soldiers, the councils annulled most of the elections of the preceding spring. Two Directors were purged; one of them, Lazare Carnot, "organizer of victory" in the Committee of Public Safety, and now in 1797 a strict constitutionalist, was driven into exile. On the whole, it was the old republicans of the Convention who secured themselves in power. Their justification was that they were defending the Revolution, keeping out Louis XVIII and the Old Regime. But to do so they had violated their own constitution and quashed the first free election ever held in a constitutional French republic. And they had become more than ever dependent on the army.

After the coup d'état the "Fructidorian" government raised its terms in the conferences with the British at Lille. The conferences broke up. With Austria a treaty was signed at Campo Formio on October 17, 1797, incorporating Bonaparte's ideas. It produced peace on the Continent, since only France and Britain remained at war, but a peace full of trouble for the future. By the treaty of Campo Formio Austria recognized the French-dominated Cisalpine Republic in Italy and the French annexation of Belgium and the Left Bank of the Rhine. In return, Bonaparte destroyed the thousand-year-old republic of Venice, keeping its Ionian Islands off the Greek coast as stepping stones to the East, and turning over Venice and the mainland of Venetia to Austria in compensation for its losses. The Left Bank of the Rhine, in the atomistic Holy Roman Empire, was occupied by a great many German princes who would now have to vacate. The treaty of Campo Formio provided that they should be compensated by church territories in Germany east of the Rhine, and that France should have a hand in arranging the redistribution. The German princes turned greedy eyes on the German bishops and abbots,

FRENCH REPUBLIC
1798

DEPENDENT REPUBLICS
1798

GERMAN CHURCH STATES
TO BE ABSORBED BY
OTHER GERMAN STATES

FRENCH REPUBLIC
AND ITS SATELLITES
1798-1799

By 1798 the revolutionary French Republic had annexed Belgium and the German Left Bank of the Rhine, and had created, with the aid of native sympathizers, a group of lesser revolutionary republics in the Netherlands, Switzerland and most of Italy. The map also shows the church-states of Germany which, by the treaty of Campo Formio, were to be absorbed by various German rulers under French auspices.

and the almost thousand-year-old Holy Empire, hardly more than a solemn form since the Peace of Westphalia, now sank to the level of a land rush or real estate speculation, while France became involved in the territorial reconstruction of Germany.

THE COUP D'ÉTAT OF 1799: BONAPARTE

After Fructidor the idea of maintaining the republic as a free or constitutional government was given up. There were more uprisings, more quashed elections, more purgings both to Left and Right. The Directory became a kind of ineffective dictatorship. It repudiated most of the *assignats* and the debt, but failed to restore financial confidence or stability. Guerilla activity flared up again in the Vendée and other parts of western France. The religious schism became more acute; the Directory took severe measures toward the refractory clergy.

Meanwhile Bonaparte waited for the situation to ripen. Returning from Italy a conquering hero, he was assigned to command the army in training to invade England. He concluded that invasion was premature, and decided to strike indirectly at England, and India, by a spectacular invasion of Egypt. In 1798, outwitting the British fleet, he landed a French army at the mouth of the Nile. Egypt was part of the Ottoman Empire, and the French occupation of it alarmed the Russians, who, as has been seen in connection with Catherine's "Greek project," [15] had their own designs on the Near East. The Austrians objected to the French re-arrangement of Germany. A year and a half after the treaty of Campo Formio Austria, Russia and Great Britain formed an alliance known as the Second Coalition. The republic was again involved in a general war. And the war went unfavorably, for in August 1798 the British fleet had cut off the French army in Egypt by winning the Battle of the Nile (or Aboukir), and in 1799 Russian forces, under Marshal Suvorov, were operating as far west as Switzerland and north Italy, where the Cisalpine Republic went down in ruin.

General Bonaparte's opportunity had come. He left his army in Egypt, and, again slipping through the British fleet, reappeared unexpectedly in France. He found that certain civilian leaders in the Directory were planning a change. They included Sieyès, of whom little had been heard since he wrote *What Is the Third Estate?* ten years before, but who had sat in the Convention, voted for the death of Louis XVI, and was in fact one of the "perpetuals." Sieyès' formula was now "confidence from below, authority from above"—what he now wanted of the people was acquiescence, and of the government, power to act. This group was looking about for a general, and their choice fell on the sensational young Bonaparte, who was still only thirty. Dictatorship by an army officer was repugnant to most republicans of the Five Hundred and the Ancients. Bonaparte, Sieyès and their followers resorted to force, executing the coup d'état of Brumaire (November 9, 1799),

[15] See pp. 316–17.

in which armed soldiers drove the legislators from the chambers. They proclaimed a new form of the republic, which Bonaparte decided to entitle the Consulate. It was headed by three consuls, with Bonaparte as the First Consul.

44. The Despotic Republic: The Consulate, 1799–1804

The next chapter takes up the affairs of Europe as a whole in the time of Napoleon Bonaparte, the purpose at present being only to tell how he closed, in a way, the Revolution in France.

It happened that the French Republic, in falling into the hands of a general, fell also to a man of such remarkable talents as are often denominated genius. Bonaparte was a short dark man, of Italian type, who would never have looked impressive in civilian clothing. He was temperamentally high-strung, yet could sleep at will; talkative or taciturn as his mood changed, and on occasion eloquent, as in the haranguing of troops. His manners were rather coarse; he lost his temper, cheated at cards, and pinched people by the ear in a kind of formidable play—he was "no gentleman." A child of the Enlightenment and the Revolution, he was entirely emancipated not only from customary ideas but from moral scruples as well. He regarded the world as a flux to be formed by his own mind. He had an exalted belief in his own destinies, which became more mystical and exaggerated as the years went on. He claimed to follow his "star." His ideas of the good and the beautiful were rather blunt, but he was a man of extraordinary intellectual capacity, which impressed all with whom he came in contact. "Never speak unless you know you are the ablest man in the room," he once advised his stepson, on making him viceroy of Italy, a maxim which, if he followed it himself, still allowed him to do most of the talking. His interests ran to solid subjects, history, law, military science, public administration. His mind was tenacious and perfectly orderly; he once declared that it was like a chest of drawers, which he could open or close at will, forgetting any subject when its drawer was closed, and finding it ready with all necessary detail when its drawer was opened. He had all the masterful qualities associated with leadership; he could dazzle and captivate those who had any inclination to follow him at all. Some of the most humane men of the day, including Goethe and Beethoven in Germany, and Lazare Carnot among the former Revolutionary leaders, at first looked on him with high approval. He inspired confidence by his crisp speech, rapid decisions, and quick grasp of complex problems when they were newly presented to him. He was, or seemed, just what many Frenchmen were looking for after ten years of upheaval.

GOVERNMENT UNDER THE CONSULATE

Under the Consulate France reverted to a form of enlightened despotism, and Bonaparte may be thought of as the last and most eminent of the enlightened despots. Despotic the new regime undoubtedly was from the start. Self-government through elected bodies was ruthlessly pushed aside. Bonaparte delighted in affirming the sovereignty of the people; but to his mind the people was a sovereign, like Voltaire's God, who somehow created the world but never thereafter interfered in it. He clearly saw, as Frederick the Great and Joseph II had seen more dimly, that a government's authority was greater when it was held to represent the entire nation. In the weeks after Brumaire he assured himself of a popular mandate by devising a written constitution and submitting it to a general referendum or "plebiscite." The voters could take it—or nothing. They took it by a majority officially reported as 3,011,007 to 1,562.

The new constitution set up a make-believe of parliamentary institutions. It gave universal male suffrage, but the citizens merely chose "notables"; men on the lists of notables were then appointed by the government itself to public position. It is curious how the conception of "notables" reappears in successive French regimes from 1789 to the revolution of 1848: the 50,000 electors provided for in the constitutional monarchy of 1791, the 20,000 electors of the constitutional republic, the "notables" of the Consulate, of whom probably not over 10,000 qualified for national office, the 100,000 voters allowed after 1815, and the 200,000 after 1830, were all roughly the same kind of people, men of property, education and standing, bourgeois or former nobles, or, as John Adams said in America, "the rich, the well born and the able." [16]

Under the Consulate even the notables had no powers of their own. They were merely available for appointment to office. They might sit in a Legislative Body, where they could neither initiate nor discuss legislation, but only mutely reject or enact it. There was also a Tribunate which discussed and deliberated, but had no enacting powers. There was a Conservative Senate, which had rights of appointment of notables to office ("patronage" in American terms), and in which numerous storm-tossed regicides found a haven. The main agency in the new government was the Council of State, imitated from the Old Regime; it prepared the significant legislation, often under the presidency of the First Consul himself, who always gave the impression that he understood everything. The First Consul made all the decisions and ran the state. The regime did not openly represent anybody, and that was its strength, for it provoked the less opposition. In any case, the political machinery just described fell rapidly into disuse.

Bonaparte entrenched himself also by promising and obtaining peace. The military problem, at the close of 1799, was much simplified by the attitude of the Russians, who, for reasons given in the following chapter, in effect withdrew from the war with France.[17] In the Italian theater Bonaparte had to deal only with the Austrians, whom he again defeated, by again crossing the Alps, at the battle of Marengo in June 1800. In February 1801 the Austrians

[16] See pp. 347, 364, 444, 456.
[17] See p. 378.

signed the treaty of Lunéville, in which the terms of Campo Formio were confirmed. A year later, in March 1802, peace was made even with Great Britain.

Peace was made also at home. Bonaparte kept internal order, partly by a secret political police, but more especially through a powerful and centralized administrative machine, in which a "prefect," under direct orders of the minister of the interior, ruled firmly over each of the departments created by the Constituent Assembly. The new government put down the guerillas in the west. Its laws and taxes were imposed on Brittany and the Vendée. Peasants there were no longer terrorized by marauding partisans. A new peace settled down on the factions left by the Revolution. Bonaparte offered a general amnesty, and invited back to France, with a few exceptions, exiles of all stripes from the first aristocratic émigrés to the refugees and deportees of the republican coups d'état. Requiring only that they work for him and stop quarreling with each other, he picked reasonable men from all camps. His Second Consul was Cambacérès, a regicide of the Terror, his Third Consul Lebrun, who had been Maupeou's colleague in the days of Louis XV.[18] Fouché emerged as minister of police; he had been a Hébertist and extreme terrorist in 1793, and had done as much as any man to bring about the fall of Robespierre. Before 1789 he had been an obscure bourgeois professor of physics. Talleyrand appeared as minister of foreign affairs; he had spent the Terror in safe seclusion in the United States, and his principles, if he had any, were those of constitutional monarchy. Before 1789 he had been a bishop, and was of an aristocratic lineage almost unbearably distinguished— no one who had not known the Old Regime, he once said, could realize how pleasant it had been. Men of this sort were now willing, for a few years beginning in 1800, to forget the past and work in common toward the future.

Disturbers of the new order the First Consul ruthlessly put down. Indeed, he concocted alarms to make himself more welcome as a pillar of order. On Christmas Eve, 1800, on his way to the opera, he was nearly killed by a bomb, or "infernal machine," as people then said. It had been laid by royalists, but Bonaparte represented it as the work of a Jacobin conspiracy, being most afraid at the moment of some of the old republicans; and over a hundred former Jacobins were again deported. Contrariwise, in 1804, he greatly exaggerated certain royalist plots against him, invaded the independent state of Baden, and there arrested the Duke of Enghien, who was related to the Bourbons. Though he knew Enghien to be innocent, he had him shot. His purpose now was to please the old Jacobins by staining his own hands with Bourbon blood; Fouché and the regicides concluded that they were secure so long as Bonaparte was in power.

THE SETTLEMENT WITH THE CHURCH

For all but the most convinced royalists and republicans, reconciliation was made easier by the establishment of peace with the Church. Bonaparte

[18] See p. 303.

himself was a pure eighteenth-century rationalist. He regarded religion as a convenience. He advertised himself as a Moslem in Egypt, as a Catholic in France, and as a freethinker among the professors at the Institute in Paris. But a Catholic revival was in full swing, and he saw its importance. The refractory clergy were the spiritual force animating all forms of counter-revolution. "Fifty émigré bishops, paid by England," he once said, "lead the French clergy today. Their influence must be destroyed. For this we need the authority of the pope." Ignoring the horrified outcries of the old Jacobins, in 1801 he signed a concordat with the Vatican.

Both parties gained from the settlement. The autonomy of the pre-revolutionary Gallican church came to an end. The pope received the right to depose French bishops, since before the schism could be healed both constitutional and refractory bishops had to be obliged to resign. The constitutional or pro-Revolutionary clergy came under the discipline of the Holy See. Publicity of Catholic worship, in such forms as processions in the streets, was again allowed. Church seminaries were again permitted. But Bonaparte and the heirs of the Revolution gained even more. The pope, by signing the Concordat, virtually recognized the Republic. The Vatican agreed to raise no question over the former tithes and the former church lands. The new owners of former church properties thus obtained clear titles. Nor was there any further question of Avignon, an enclave within France, formerly papal, annexed to France in 1790. Nor were the papal negotiators able to undermine religious toleration; all that Bonaparte would concede was a clause that was purely factual, and hence harmless, stating that Catholicism was the religion of the majority of Frenchmen. The clergy, in compensation for loss of their tithes and property, were assured of receiving salaries from the state. But Bonaparte, to dispel the notion of an established church, put Protestant ministers of all denominations on the state payroll also. He thus checkmated the Vatican on important points. At the same time, simply by signing an agreement with Rome, he disarmed the counter-revolution. It could no longer be said that the Republic was godless. Good relations did not, indeed, last very long, for Bonaparte and the papacy were soon at odds. But the concordat proved lasting.

THE REFORMS OF BONAPARTE

With peace and order established, the constructive work of the Consulate turned to the fields of law and administration. The First Consul and his advisers combined what they conceived to be the best of the Revolution and of the Old Regime. The modern state took on clearer form. It was the reverse of everything feudal. All public authority was concentrated in paid agents of government, no person was held to be under any legal authority except that of the state, and the authority of government fell on all persons alike. There were no more estates, legal classes, privileges, local liberties, hereditary offices, gilds, or manors. Judges, officials, and army officers re-

ceived specified salaries. Neither military commissions nor civil offices could
be bought and sold. Citizens were to rise in government service purely according to their abilities. This was the doctrine of "careers open to talent";
it was what the bourgeoisie had wanted before the Revolution, and a few
persons of quite humble birth profited also.

Another deep demand of the French people, deeper than the demand
for the vote, was for more reason, order, and economy in public finance and
taxation. The Consulate gave these also. Taxes were henceforth collected,
not by local persons who allocated quotas upon individual taxpayers at their
own discretion, but by professional collectors who were employed by the
central government and dealt directly with each individual taxpayer. There
were no tax exemptions because of birth, status, or special arrangement. Everyone was supposed to pay, so that no disgrace attached to payment, and
there was less evasion. In principle these changes had been introduced in
1789; after 1799 they began to work. For the first time in ten years the government really collected the taxes which it levied, and so could rationally
plan its financial affairs. Order was introduced also into expenditure, and
accounting methods were improved. There was no longer a haphazard assort-
ment of different "funds," on which various officials drew independently and
confidentially as they needed money, but a concentration of financial management in the treasury, and even in a kind of budget. An element of irresponsi-
bility remained because the Consulate never published any clear or candid
financial statements. But Bonaparte probably understood his own finances
better than any official of the Old Regime had ever done, even though they
remained a mystery to the public of his own time, and to historians since.
The Revolutionary gyrations in the value of money were also ended. Because
the Directory had shouldered the odium of repudiating the currency and
government bonds, the Consulate was able to establish a relatively sound
currency and secure national debt. To assist in government financing, one of
the banks of the Old Regime was revived and established as the Bank of
France.

Like all enlightened despots, Bonaparte codified the laws, and of all
law codes since the Romans the Napoleonic codes are the most famous. To
the three hundred legal systems of the Old Regime, and the mass of parliamentary and royal ordinances, were now added the thousands of laws enacted
but seldom implemented by the revolutionary assemblies. This jumble was
now collated, digested, condensed, and made consistent. Five codes emerged,
the Civil Code (often called simply the Code Napoleon), the codes of civil
and of criminal procedure, and the commercial and penal codes. The codes
made France legally and judicially uniform. They assured legal equality; all
French citizens had the same civil rights. They embodied the principle of
reason, for they held that custom, local practice or decision in earlier cases
was insufficient to make a rule actually lawful, and that positive law must
somehow correspond to a natural law of abstract and considered justice. They
formulated the new law of property, made landed property a more exclusively
private right than under the Old Regime, and set forth the law of contracts,

debts, leases, stock companies, and similar matters in such a way as to create the legal framework for an economy of private enterprise. They repeated the ban of all previous regimes on organized labor unions, and were severe with the individual workingman, his word not being acceptable in court against that of his employer—a significant departure from equality before the law. The criminal code was somewhat freer in giving the government the means to detect crime than in granting the individual the means of defending himself against legal charges. As for the family, the codes recognized civil marriage and divorce, but left the wife with very restricted powers over property, and the father with extensive authority over minor children. The codes reflected much of French life under the Old Regime. They also set the character of France as it has been ever since, socially bourgeois, legally equalitarian and administratively bureaucratic.

In France, with the Consulate, the Revolution was over. If its highest hopes had not been accomplished, the worst evils of the Old Regime had at least been cured. The beneficiaries of the Revolution felt secure. The country was a combination of peasant democracy and bourgeois paradise. Even former aristocrats were rallying. The proletarian movement, always weak because the number of true wage-earners was small, and repeatedly frustrated under all the Revolutionary regimes, now vanished from the political scene, to reappear as socialism thirty years later. What the Third Estate had most wanted in 1789 was now both codified and enforced, with the exception of parliamentary government, which after ten years of turmoil many people were temporarily willing to forego. Moreover, in 1802, the French republic was at peace with the papacy, Great Britain and all continental powers. It reached to the Rhine, and had dependent republics in Holland and Italy. So popular was the First Consul that in 1802, by another plebiscite, he had himself elected consul for life. A new constitution, in 1804, again ratified by plebiscite, declared that "the government of the republic is confided to an emperor." The Consulate became the Empire, and Bonaparte emerged as Napoleon I, Emperor of the French.

But France, no longer revolutionary at home, was revolutionary outside its borders. Napoleon became a terror to the patricians of Europe. They called him the "Jacobin." And the France which he ruled, and used as his arsenal, was an incomparably formidable state. Even before the Revolution it had been the most populous in Europe, perhaps the most wealthy, in the front rank of scientific enterprise and intellectual leadership. Now all the old barriers of privilege, tax exemption, localism, caste exclusiveness, and routine-mindedness had disappeared. The new France could tap the wealth of its citizens, and put able men into position without inquiring into their origins. Every private, boasted Napoleon, carried a marshal's baton in his knapsack. The French looked with disdain on their caste-ridden adversaries. The principle of civic equality proved not only to have the magnificent appeal of justice, but also to be politically useful, and the resources of France were hurled against Europe with a force which for many years nothing could check.

CHAPTER X

Napoleonic Europe

‚‚

ONAPARTE is the name of a French army officer and dictator. Napoleon is a name in the history of the European world. The French emperor came nearer than any man has ever come to imposing a political unity on the European continent, nearer even than the German conqueror Adolf Hitler, with whom it is both illuminating and misleading to compare him, for Napoleon ruled somewhat less by force than did the Germans in the early 1940's, and at the high point of his conquests he was diplomatically recognized by, and at peace with, all the great powers except Great Britain. Of his ascendancy of fifteen years, from 1799 to 1814, two stories are to be told. One is a story of international relations—of coalitions, wars and treaties, sea power and land power, shifts of alliances and rearrangements of frontiers, all reflecting the diverse interests of the states of Europe. The other is a story of internal development of the European peoples, for all were profoundly affected by the Napoleonic domination, either by reforms which Napoleon forced upon them, or by the means which they adopted to resist him.

It is convenient to think of the fighting from 1792 to 1814 as a "world war," as indeed it was, affecting not only all of Europe but places as remote as Spanish America, where the wars of independence began, or the interior of North America, where the United States purchased Louisiana in 1803 and attempted a conquest of Canada in 1812. But it is important to realize that this world war was actually a series of wars, most of them quite short, sharp and distinct. Only Great Britain remained continually at war with France, except for about a year of peace in 1802–1803. Never were the four great powers, Britain, Austria, Russia, and Prussia, simultaneously in the field against France until 1813.

The history of the Napoleonic period would be much simpler if the European governments had fought merely to protect themselves against the aggressive French. Each, however, in its way, was as dynamic and expansive as Napoleon himself. For some generations Great Britain had been building a commercial empire, Russia pushing upon Poland and Turkey, Prussia consolidating its territories and striving for leadership in north Germany. Austria was less aggressive, being somewhat passively preoccupied by the rise of Prussia and Russia, but the Austrians were not without dreams of ascendancy in Germany, the Balkans and the Adriatic. None of these ambitions ceased during the Napoleonic years. Governments, in pursuit of their own aims, were quite as willing to ally with Napoleon as to fight him. Only gradually, and under repeated provocation, did they conclude that their main interest was to dispose of the French emperor entirely.

45. The Formation of the French Imperial System

THE DISSOLUTION OF THE FIRST AND SECOND COALITIONS, 1792–1802

The conflicting purposes of the powers had been apparent from the beginning. Leopold of Austria, in issuing the Declaration of Pillnitz, in 1791, had believed a general European coalition against France to be impossible. When the First Coalition was formed in 1792, the Austrians and Prussians kept their main forces in eastern Europe, more afraid of each other and of Russia, in the matter of Poland, than of the French revolutionary republic. Indeed, the main accomplishment of the First Coalition was the extermination of the Polish state.[1]

In 1795 the French broke up the coalition. The British withdrew their army from the Continent. The Prussians made a separate peace; the French bought them off by recognizing them as "protectors" of Germany north of the river Main. Spain also made a separate peace in 1795. The world saw the spectacle, outrageous to all ideology or principle, of an alliance between Bourbon Spain and the republic which had guillotined Louis XVI and kept Louis XVIII from his monarchic rights. Spain simply reverted to the eight-

ᵛᵛᵛᵛᵛᵛᵛᵛᵛᵛᵛᵛᵛᵛᵛᵛ

[1] See pp. 354, 356–7.

eenth century pattern, in allying with France because of hostility to Great Britain, whose possession of Gibraltar, naval influence in the Mediterranean, and attitude toward the Spanish empire were disquieting to the Spanish government. When Austria signed the peace of Campo Formio in 1797 the First Coalition was totally dissipated, only British naval forces remaining engaged with the French.[2]

The Second Coalition of 1799 fared no better. Russia joined it because Bonaparte's expedition to Egypt introduced a western military force into the Near East.[3] The Russians had their own ambitions in the Mediterranean. A Russian fleet in 1799 passed through the Turkish straits and occupied the Ionian Islands off the coast of Greece, lately taken by Bonaparte from Venice.[4] The Russians set up a puppet republic of their own in the islands. They looked with interest also farther west to Malta, for the Knights of Malta had elected the tsar Paul, Catherine's son, their grand commander, hoping for his protection against France and Britain. But the British installed themselves in Malta (taking over from the French), and also defeated the French fleet in the battle of the Nile, cutting off the French army in Egypt.

The Russians now feared the British more than the French as rivals within the weakening Ottoman Empire. Veering around, they became anti-British and hence mildly pro-French. They recalled Suvorov's army from western Europe, being unable to agree with the Austrians, and in 1801 they joined in the Armed Neutrality to protect their shipping from search and seizure by British sea power. The acceptance by Austria of the peace of Lunéville in 1801 dissolved the Second Coalition. In 1802 Great Britain signed the peace of Amiens. For the only time between 1792 and 1814 no European power was at war with another—though the British, to be sure, were at war with some Indian princes, the Russians with some Caucasian tribesmen, and the French with Toussaint l'Ouverture, the Negro who was attempting to found an independent republic in Haiti.

PEACE INTERIM, 1802–3

Never had a peace been so advantageous to France as the peace of 1802. Austria had again agreed to the conditions of Campo Formio. The British, in the treaty of Amiens, accepted terms less favorable than those they had rejected five years before.[5] France retained Belgium and the Left Bank of the Rhine as integral parts of the Republic, and won recognition for its satellites, the Batavian Republic in Holland, the Helvetic Republic in Switzerland, the Ligurian Republic at Genoa, and the Cisalpine Republic in the Po valley. Britain agreed to withdraw from Malta, Minorca, Elba, Trinidad,

[2] See p. 367.
[3] See p. 369.
[4] See p. 367.
[5] See p. 366.

and the French Caribbean islands, and to retain only Dutch Ceylon.[6] The peace of Amiens was so repugnant to British war aims that probably it would not have lasted in any case. But Bonaparte gave it no chance. He used peace as he did war to advance his interests. He despatched a sizable army to Haiti, ostensibly to win back a rebellious French colony, but with the further thought (since Louisiana had been ceded back by Spain to France in 1800) of reviving the French colonial empire in America. He reorganized the Cisalpine Republic into an "Italian" Republic with himself as president. He reorganized the Helvetic Republic, making himself "mediator" of the Confederation of Switzerland. He reorganized Germany; that is to say, he and

[6] See maps, pp. 257 and 368.

NAPOLEONIC GERMANY

In the panel at the left are shown, by shading, territories of the Duchy of Würtemberg in 1800. Note how Würtemberg had "islands" of territory unconnected with its main mass, and "holes" or enclaves formed by smaller states enclosed within the mass of Würtemberg. Note, too, how Würtemberg, itself only fifty miles wide, was surrounded by a mosaic of tiny jurisdictions—free cities, counties, duchies, principalities, abbacies, commanderies, bishoprics, archbishoprics, etc.—all "independent" within the Holy Roman Empire. The right-hand panel shows the Kingdom of Würtemberg as consolidated and enlarged in the time of Napoleon. Similar consolidations all over Germany greatly reduced the number of states and added to the efficiency of law and government.

his agents closely watched the rearrangement of territory which the Germans themselves had been carrying out since 1797.

By the treaty of Campo Formio,[7] it will be recalled, German princes of the Left Bank of the Rhine, expropriated by the annexation of their dominions to the French Republic, were to receive new territories on the Right Bank. The result was a scramble called by patriotic German historians the "shame of the princes." The German rulers, far from opposing Bonaparte or upholding any national interests, competed desperately for the absorption of German territory, each bribing and fawning upon the French (Talleyrand made over 10,000,000 francs in the process) to win French support against other Germans. The Holy Roman Empire was fatally mauled by the Germans themselves. Most of its ecclesiastical principalities and forty-five out of its fifty-one free cities disappeared, annexed by their larger neighbors. The number of states in the Holy Empire was greatly reduced, especially of the Catholic states, so that it could be foreseen that no Catholic Hapsburg would again be elected Emperor. Prussia, Bavaria, Würtemberg, and Baden consolidated and enlarged themselves. These arrangements were ratified in February 1803 by the diet of the Empire. The enlarged German states now depended on Bonaparte for the maintenance of their new position.

FORMATION OF THE THIRD COALITION IN 1805

In these circumstances Britain refused to evacuate Malta; Bonaparte protested; and Britain declared war in May 1803. Bonaparte, his communications with America menaced by the British navy, and his army in Haiti decimated by disease and by rebellious Negroes, suspended his ideas for re-creating an American empire and sold Louisiana to the United States. Great Britain began to seek allies for a Third Coalition. In May 1804 Napoleon pronounced himself Emperor of the French to assure the hereditary permanency of his system, though he had no son. Francis II of Austria, seeing the ruin of the Holy Roman Empire, promulgated the Austrian Empire in August 1804. He thus advanced the long process of integrating the Danubian Monarchy. In 1805 Austria signed an alliance with Great Britain. The Third Coalition was completed by the accession of the Russian Tsar Alexander I, who, after Napoleon himself, was to become the most considerable figure on the European stage.

Alexander was the grandson of Catherine the Great, educated by her to be a kind of enlightened despot on the eighteenth-century model.[8] The Swiss tutor of his boyhood, La Harpe, later turned up as a moderate pro-French revolutionary in the Swiss cantons. Alexander became tsar in 1801, at the age of twenty-four, through a palace revolution which implicated him in the murder of his father Paul. He still corresponded with La Harpe, and he surrounded himself with a circle of liberal and zealous young men of various

[7] See pp. 367–8.
[8] See p. 318.

nationalities, of whom the most prominent was a Polish youth, Czartoryski. Alexander regarded the still recent partitions of Poland as a crime.[9] He wished to restore the unity of Poland with himself as its constitutional king. In Germany many who had first warmed to the French Revolution, but had been disillusioned, began to hail the new liberal tsar as the protector of Germany and hope of the future. Alexander conceived of himself as a rival to Napoleon in the destinies of Europe in an age of change. With a genuine concern for reform, constitutional government, international peace and the extension of modern enlightenment, he was an autocratic humanitarian, who wished mankind to owe its blessings to himself. Regarding the extension of his personal influence as identical with the progress of human freedom, he in effect carried over, in more seductive form, the expansionist program of Catherine and Peter. Moralistic, self-righteous, impressionable, and unstable, given to flights of religious mysticism and perhaps to brooding over his father's death, he puzzled and disturbed the statesmen of Europe, who generally saw, behind his humane and republican utterances, either the familiar specter of Russian aggrandizement or an enthroned leader of all the "Jacobins" of Europe.

Yet Alexander, more than his contemporaries, formed a conception of international collective security and the indivisibility of peace. He was shocked when Napoleon in 1804, to seize the Duke of Enghien, rudely violated the legal independence of Baden.[10] He declared that the issue in Europe was clearly between law and force—between an international society in which the rights of each member were secured by international agreement and an international organization, and a society in which no state was secure but all trembled before the rule of cynicism and conquest embodied in the French usurper.

Alexander was therefore ready to enter a Third Coalition with Great Britain. The war aims of the Third Coalition, though not accomplished, suggest what was at stake in the ten years that followed, and anticipated much of the final peace settlement of 1814. Alexander and William Pitt did not in truth commit themselves specifically to much. But Pitt did not reject Alexander's idea that, after the war, some kind of organized international body should enforce the peace. Alexander's interest in the "freedom of the seas," which in plain terms meant international controls on the use of British sea power in war time, aroused no corresponding interest in London. It was somewhat vaguely agreed that French ascendancy in Germany and Italy should cease; that the French should be driven from Belgium, and Belgium combined with Holland in a strong buffer state against France; and that Prussia should be strengthened on the Rhine. It was understood that England should receive territory overseas, and Alexander revealed some of his plans for reuniting Poland. The tsar pictured himself as the future arbiter of central Europe. On the Ottoman Empire and the Mediterranean he kept his

wwwwwwwwwwwww

[9] See pp. 218–23, 356–7.
[10] See p. 372.

ideas secret, but he hoped, after the destruction of Napoleon, to partition the Ottoman Empire, take over Constantinople, put Russian garrisons in Malta and Corfu (the chief of the Ionian Islands), and establish a league of Balkan states under Russian protection. The Anglo-Russian treaty, signed in April 1805, said little or nothing of these matters; but Britain undertook to pay Russia £1,250,000 for each 100,000 soldiers that the Russians raised.

THE THIRD COALITION, 1805–7: THE PEACE OF TILSIT

Napoleon meanwhile, since the resumption of hostilities in 1803, had been making preparations to invade England. He concentrated large forces on the channel coast, together with thousands of boats and barges, in which he gave the troops amphibious training in embarkation and debarkation. He reasoned that if his own fleet could divert or cripple the British fleet for a few days he could place enough soldiers in the defenseless island to force its capitulation. The British, sensing mortal danger, lined their coasts with lookouts and signal beacons and set to drilling a home guard. Their main defense was twofold: the Austro-Russian armies and the British fleet under Lord Nelson. The Russian and Austrian armies moved westward in the summer of 1805. In August Napoleon relieved the pressure upon England, shifting seven army corps from the channel to the upper Danube. On October 15 he surrounded an Austrian force of 50,000 men at Ulm in Bavaria, forcing it to surrender without resistance. On October 21 Lord Nelson, off Cape Trafalgar on the Spanish coast, caught and annihilated the main body of the combined fleets of France and Spain.

The battle of Trafalgar established the supremacy of the British navy for over a century—but only on the proviso that Napoleon be prevented from controlling the bulk of Europe, which would furnish an ample base for eventual construction of a greater navy than the British. And to control Europe was precisely what Napoleon proceeded to do. Moving east from Ulm he came upon the Russian and Austrian armies in Moravia, where on December 2 he won the great victory of Austerlitz. The broken Russian army withdrew into Poland, and Austria made peace. By the treaty of Pressburg Napoleon took Venetia from the Austrians, to whom he had given it in 1797, and annexed it to his kingdom of Italy (the former Cisalpine and Italian Republic), which now included a good deal of Italy north of Rome. Venice and Trieste soon resounded with the hammers of shipwrights rebuilding the Napoleonic fleet. In Germany, early in 1806, the French emperor raised Bavaria and Würtemberg to the stature of kingdoms, and Baden to a grand duchy. The Holy Roman Empire was finally, formally and irrevocably dissolved. In its place Napoleon began to gather his German client states into a new kind of Germanic federation, the Confederation of the Rhine, of which he made himself the "protector."

Prussia, at peace with France for ten years, had declined to join the Third Coalition. Napoleon held off the Prussians diplomatically, making them all sorts of promises, such as the cession of Hanover, which belonged to the king of England. But as Napoleon's program for controlling Germany became clear after Austerlitz the war party in Prussia became irresistible, and the Prussian government, outwitted and distraught, went to war with the French unaided and alone. The French smashed the famous Prussian army at the battles of Jena and Auerstädt in October 1806. The French cavalry galloped all over north Germany unopposed. The Prussian king and his government took refuge in the east, at Königsberg, where the tsar and the re-forming Russian army might protect them. But the terrible Corsican pursued the Russians also. Marching through western Poland and into East Prussia, he met the Russian army first at the sanguinary but indecisive battle of Eylau, and then defeated it on June 14, 1807, at Friedland. Alexander I was unwilling to retreat into Russia. He was unsure of his own resources; if the country were invaded there might be a revolt of the nobles, or even of the serfs—for people still remembered Pugachev's rebellion.[11] He feared also merely playing the game of the British. He put aside his war aims of 1804, and signified his willingness to negotiate with Napoleon. The Third Coalition had gone the way of the two before it.

The Emperor of the French and the Autocrat of All the Russias met privately on a raft in the Niemen river, not far from the border between Prussia and Russia, the very easternmost frontier of civilized Europe, as the triumphant Napoleon gleefully imagined it. The hapless Prussian king, Frederick William III, paced nervously on the bank. Bonaparte turned all his charm upon Alexander, denouncing England as the author of all the troubles of Europe, and captivating him by flights of Latin imagination, in which he set before Alexander a boundless destiny as Emperor of the East, intimating that his future lay toward Turkey, Persia, Afghanistan, and India. The result of their conversations was the treaty of Tilsit of July 1807, in many ways the high point of Napoleon's success. The French and Russian empires became allies, mainly against Great Britain. Ostensibly this alliance lasted for five years. Alexander accepted Napoleon as a kind of Emperor of the West. As for Prussia, Napoleon seems to have considered eradicating it entirely, but concluded by leaving it in existence, as a buffer between himself and Alexander, and at Alexander's earnest pleadings for his friend the king; but he continued to occupy Berlin with his troops, and he took away all Prussian territories west of the Elbe, combining them with others taken from Hanover to make a new kingdom of Westphalia, which became part of his Confederation of the Rhine.

THE CONTINENTAL SYSTEM AND THE WAR IN SPAIN

Hardly had the "peace of the continent" been re-established, on the foundation of a Franco-Russian alliance, when Napoleon began to have serious

---

[11] See p. 315.

trouble. He was bent on subduing the British who, secure in their island, seemed beyond his reach. Since the French naval disaster at Trafalgar, there was no possibility of invading England in the foreseeable future. Napoleon therefore turned to economic warfare. He would fight sea power with land power, using his political control of the Continent to shut out British goods and shipping from all European ports. He would destroy the British trade in exports to Europe, both exports of British products and the profitable British re-export of goods from America and Asia. Thereby, he hoped, he would ruin British commercial firms and cause a violent business depression, marked by overloaded warehouses, unemployment, runs on the banks, a fall of the currency, rising prices and revolutionary agitation, in which the British government, which would simultaneously be losing revenues from its customs duties, would find itself unable to carry the enormous national debt, or to borrow additional funds from its subjects, or to continue its financial subsidies to the military powers of Europe. This same strategy had been adopted by the republicans of 1793; they, too, had prohibited the importation into France of goods originating in the British empire. The same prohibition had been sporadically extended to regions conquered by the French. Napoleon simply made it more systematic and more universal. At Berlin, in 1806, after the battle of Jena, he issued the Berlin Decree, forbidding the importation of British goods into any part of Europe allied with or dependent on himself. He thus formally established the Continental System.

To make the Continental System effective Napoleon believed that it must extend to all continental Europe without exception. By the treaty of Tilsit, in 1807, he required both Russia and Prussia to adhere to it. They agreed to exclude all British goods; in fact, in the following months Russia, Prussia and Austria all declared war on Great Britain. Napoleon then ordered two neutral states, Denmark and Portugal, to adhere. Denmark was an important entrepôt to all central Europe, and the British, fearing Danish compliance, despatched a fleet to Copenhagen, bombarded the city for four days, and took captive the Danish fleet. The outraged Danes allied with Napoleon and joined the Continental System. Portugal, long a satellite of Britain, re-

---

The Shootings of the Third of May

BY FRANCESCO GOYA (SPANISH, 1746–1828)

French troops are here executing insurgents in the Spanish uprising of 1808. The tonsured figure with clasped hands is a priest; the rebels represent Catholic, royalist, and nationalist opposition to Napoleon. Goya has evoked here the raw facts of political domination. A row of disciplined men, impersonally obeying orders, in the name of an emperor hundreds of miles away, shoots down a huddled and helpless group of other men who refuse to accept the system. Against the somber background of Madrid, and in the dead of night, the lantern illuminates the gruesome target, lighting up faces and hands contorted by anguish, by despair and defiance, by terror and courage at the moment of death. Goya used many other scenes in Napoleonic Spain to depict the horrors of war. Courtesy of the Museo del Prado, Madrid.

fused compliance; Napoleon invaded it. To control the whole European coastline from St. Petersburg around to Trieste he now had only to control the ports of Spain. By a series of deceptions he got both the Bourbon Charles IV and his son Ferdinand to abdicate the Spanish throne. He made his brother Joseph king of Spain in 1808, and reinforced him with a large French army.

He thus involved himself in an entanglement from which he never escaped. The Spanish regarded the Napoleonic soldiers as godless villains who desecrated churches. Fierce guerillas took the field. Cruelties of one side were answered by atrocities of the other.[12] The British sent an expeditionary force of their small regular army, eventually under the Duke of Wellington, to sustain the Spanish guerillas; the resulting Peninsular War dragged on for five years. But from the beginning the affair went badly for Napoleon. In July 1808 a French general, for the first time since the Revolution, surrendered an army corps, without fighting, by the capitulation of Baylen. In August another French force surrendered to the British army in Portugal. And these events raised hopes in the rest of Europe. An anti-French movement swept over Germany. It was felt strongly in Austria, where the Hapsburg government, undaunted by three defeats, and hoping to lead a general German national resistance, prepared for a fourth time to go to war with France.

THE AUSTRIAN WAR OF LIBERATION, 1809

Napoleon summoned a general congress which met at Erfurt in Saxony in September 1808. His main purpose was to talk with his ally of a year, Alexander; but he assembled numerous dependent monarchs as well, by

wwwwwwwwwwwwwww

[12] See the painting by Goya reproduced in this book, *The Shootings of the Third of May*, facing p. 384.

Liberty Leading the People

BY EUGÈNE DELACROIX (FRENCH, 1798–1863)

Delacroix, a founder of the romantic school of painting, painted this picture soon after the July Revolution in Paris in 1830 (see p. 455). It well illustrates the idealistic conception of revolution which prevailed among revolutionaries before 1848, in sharp contrast to the "realistic," "scientific," or "materialistic" conception of revolution that set in after 1848 and was typified by Karl Marx. (See pp. 493–5, 496–500.) Revolution is shown as a noble and moral act. The figures express determination and courage, but show no sign of hatred or even anger. They are not a class (note how the costume varies from the top hat to the semi-nude); they are the People, affirming the rights of man. Liberty, holding the tricolor aloft, is a composed and even rational goddess. Romantic though the painter was, he represents the insurgents as realizing an abstract idea—Liberty or the Republic. It is to this idea that the half-recumbent and presumably wounded figure directs his gaze. Courtesy of the Louvre.

whose presence he hoped to overawe the tsar. He even had Talma, the leading actor of the day, play in the theater of Erfurt before "a parterre of kings." Alexander was unimpressed. He was hurt in a sensitive spot because Napoleon, a few months before, had made moves to recreate a Polish state, setting up what was called the Grand Duchy of Warsaw. He had found Napoleon unwilling, despite the grandiose language of Tilsit, really to support his expansion into the Balkans. In addition, Alexander was taken aside by Talleyrand, Napoleon's foreign minister. Talleyrand had concluded that Napoleon was overreaching himself, and said so confidentially to the tsar, advising him to wait. Talleyrand thus acted as a traitor, betraying the man whom he ostensibly served, and preparing a safe place for himself in the event of Napoleon's fall; but he acted also as an aristocrat of the pre-nationalistic Old Regime, seeing his own country as only one part of the whole of Europe, believing a balance among the several parts to be necessary, and holding that peace would be possible only when the exaggerated position of French power should be reduced. For France and Russia, the two strongest states, to combine against all other states was contrary to all principles of the older diplomacy.[13] What Napoleon, at Erfurt, most wanted from Alexander was his support in the impending war against Austria, which would catch him under the disadvantage of reverses in Spain. Almost in desperation, he promised the tsar to evacuate Poland and to recognize Russian annexation of the Danubian principalities. Alexander was unmoved; he hoped for more from the French emperor's fall. The Franco-Russian alliance, now tested, failed to hold.

Austria proclaimed a war of liberation in April 1809. Napoleon advanced rapidly along the familiar route to Vienna. The German princes, indebted to the French, declined to join in a general German war. Alexander stood watchfully on the sidelines. Napoleon won the battle of Wagram in July. In October Austria made peace. The short War of 1809 was over. The Danubian Monarchy, by no means as fragile as it seemed, survived a fourth defeat at the hands of the French without internal revolution or disloyalty to the Hapsburg house. From it, in punishment, Napoleon took considerable portions of its territory. Part of Austrian Poland was used to enlarge Napoleon's Grand Duchy of Warsaw, and parts of Dalmatia, Slovenia, and Croatia, on the south, were erected into a new creation which Napoleon called the Illyrian Provinces.[14] Both these moves, the one enlarging Napoleonic Poland, the other bringing Bonaparte within the edges of the Balkans, naturally worsened his relations with the tsar.

NAPOLEON AT HIS PEAK, 1809–11

Napoleon in 1809 successfully weathered a severe crisis, for the Austrians, had they resisted longer, might have been joined by the Russians and

---

[13] See pp. 135–6.
[14] See map, pp. 390–1.

by others. The next two years saw the Napoleonic empire at its peak. In Austria after the defeat of 1809 the conduct of foreign affairs fell to a man who was to retain it for forty years. His name was Clemens von Metternich. He was a German from west of the Rhine, whose ancestral territories had been annexed to the French Republic, but he had entered the Austrian service and even married the granddaughter of Kaunitz,[15] the old model of diplomatic *savoir faire*, of which Metternich now became a model himself. Austria had been repeatedly humiliated and even partitioned by Napoleon, most of all in the treaty of 1809. But Metternich was not a man to conduct diplomacy by grudges. Believing that Russia was the really permanent problem for a state situated in the Danube valley, Metternich thought it wise to renew good relations with France. He was quite willing to go along with Napoleon, whom he knew personally, having been Austrian ambassador to Paris before the short war of 1809.

The French emperor, who in 1809 was exactly forty, was increasingly concerned by the fact that he was childless. He had made an empire which he pronounced hereditary. Yet he had no son. Between him and his wife Josephine whom he had married in youth, and who was six years his senior, there had long since ceased to be affection or even fidelity on either side. He divorced her in 1809, though since she had two children by a first husband she naturally protested that Napoleon's childlessness was not her fault. He intended to marry a younger woman who might bear him offspring. He intended also to make a spectacular marriage, to extort for himself, a self-made Corsican army officer, the highest and most exclusive recognition that aristocratic Europe could bestow. He debated between Hapsburgs and Romanovs, between an archduchess and a grand duchess. Tactful inquiries at St. Petersburg concerning the availability of Alexander's sister were tactfully rebuffed; the tsar intimated that his mother would never allow it. The Russian alliance again showed its limitations. Napoleon was thrown into the arms of Metternich—and of Marie Louise, the buxom eighteen-year-old daughter of the Austrian emperor, and niece of another "Austrian woman," Marie Antoinette. They were married in 1810. In a year she bore him a son, whom he entitled the King of Rome.

Napoleon assumed ever more pompous airs of imperial majesty. He was now, by marriage, the nephew of Louis XVI. He showed more consideration to French noblemen of the Old Regime—only they, he said, knew really how to serve. He surrounded himself with a newly made hereditary Napoleonic nobility, hoping that the new families, as time went on, would bind their own fortunes to the house of Bonaparte. The marshals became dukes and princes, Talleyrand the Prince of Benevento, and the bourgeois Fouché, a Hébertist of '93, and more latterly a police official, was now solemnly addressed as the Duke of Otranto. In foreign affairs also the cycle had been run. With one significant exception all the powers of the successive coalitions

[15] See p. 249.

were allied with the French, and the Son of the Revolution now gravely referred to the Emperor of Austria as "my father."

46. The Grand Empire: Spread of the Revolution

THE ORGANIZATION OF THE NAPOLEONIC EMPIRE

Territorially Napoleon's influence enjoyed its farthest reach in 1810 and 1811, when it comprehended the entire European mainland except the Balkan peninsula. The Napoleonic domain was in two parts. Its core was the French Empire; then came thick layers of dependent states, which together with France comprised the Grand Empire. In addition, to the north and east were the "allied states," not under Napoleon's direct rule but under their traditional governments—the three great powers, Prussia, Austria, and Russia, and also Denmark and Sweden. The allied states were at war with Great Britain, though not engaged in positive hostilities; their populations were supposed to do without British goods under the Continental System, but otherwise Napoleon had no direct lawful influence upon their internal affairs.

The French Empire, as successor to the French Republic, included Belgium and the left Bank of the Rhine.[16] In addition, by 1810, it had developed two appendages which on a map looked like tentacles outstretched from it. When he proclaimed France an empire, and turned its dependent republics into kingdoms, Napoleon had set up his brother Louis as King of Holland; but Louis had shown such a tendency to ingratiate himself with the Dutch, and such a willingness to let Dutch business men trade secretly with the British, that Napoleon dethroned him and incorporated Holland into the French Empire. In his endless war upon British goods he found it useful to exert more direct control over the ports of Bremen, Hamburg, Lübeck, Genoa, and Leghorn; he therefore annexed directly to the French Empire the German coast as far as the western Baltic, and the Italian coast far enough to include Rome. Rome he desired for its imperial rather than its commercial value. Harking back to traditions as old as Charlemagne, he considered Rome the second city of his empire and entitled his son the "King of Rome"; and when Pope Pius VII protested, Napoleon took him prisoner and interned him in France. The whole French Empire, from Lübeck to Rome, was governed directly by departmental prefects who reported to Paris, and the eighty-three departments of France, created by the Constituent Assembly, had risen in 1810 to a hundred and thirty.

The dependent states, forming with France the Grand Empire, were of different kinds. The Swiss federation remained republican in form. The Illyrian Provinces, which included Trieste and the Dalmatian coast, were administered in their brief two years almost like departments of France. In

———————————————

[16] See pp. 364, 367-8.

Poland, since the Russians objected to a revived kingdom of Poland, Napoleon called his creation the Grand Duchy of Warsaw. The Duchy was composed of Polish fragments taken from Prussia in 1807 and from Austria in 1809, and it included most of the area within which the majority of the population was undeniably Polish. Napoleon gave the Duchy to his protégé the king of Saxony as grand duke. Among the most important of the dependent states in the Grand Empire were the German states organized into the Confederation of the Rhine. Too modestly named, the Confederation included all Germany between what the French annexed on the west and what Prussia and Austria retained on the east. It was a league of all the German princes in this region that were regarded as sovereign, and who now numbered only about twenty, the most important being the four newly made kings—of Saxony, Bavaria, Würtemberg, and Westphalia. Westphalia was an entirely new and synthetic state, made up of Hanoverian and Prussian territories and of various atoms of the old Germany. Its king was Napoleon's youngest brother Jerome. Westphalia was only one of the group of dependent states in which Napoleon placed a relative of his on the throne.

For Napoleon used his family as a means of rule. The Corsican clan became the Bonaparte dynasty. His brother Joseph from 1804 to 1808 functioned as king of Naples, and after 1808 as king of Spain. Louis Bonaparte was for six years king of Holland. Jerome was king of Westphalia. Sister Caroline became queen of Naples after brother Joseph's transfer to Spain; for Napoleon, running out of brothers (having quarreled with his remaining brother Lucien), gave the throne of Naples to his brother-in-law, Joachim Murat, a madcap cavalry officer who was Caroline's husband. In the "Kingdom of Italy," which in 1810 included Lombardy, Venetia and most of the former papal states, Napoleon himself retained the title of king, but set up his stepson, Eugene Beauharnais (Josephine's son) as Viceroy. "Uncle Joseph," Napoleon's mother's brother, became Cardinal Fesch. The mother of the Bonapartes, Letitia, who had brought up all these children under very different circumstances in Corsica, was suitably installed at the imperial court as Madame Mère. According to legend she kept repeating to herself, "If only it lasts!"; she outlived Napoleon by fifteen years.

NAPOLEON AND THE SPREAD OF THE REVOLUTION

In all the states under French domination the same course of events tended to repeat itself. First came the stage of military conquest and occupation by French troops. Then came the establishment of a native satellite

---

Europe, 1810 (map on following pages)

In 1810 Napoleon dominated the whole of the Continent of Europe except the Balkan peninsula. A British expeditionary force was fighting the French in Portugal, and the British controlled all the islands.

200 MILES

St. Petersburg

SCOTLAND

Edinburgh

NORTH

SEA

Riga

RUSSIAN

COURLAND

GREAT

BRITAIN

Moscow

Borodino

Vitebsk

Tilsit

Kovno

Smolensk

Königsberg

Vilna

Borisov

ENGLAND

K. OF
HOLLAND

Amsterdam

Warsaw

EMPIRE

Brest-
Litovsk

London

NAPOLEON'S
RUSSIAN CAMPAIGN

JUNE TO DECEMBER
1812

Plymouth

Dover

Antwerp

Brussels

Boulogne

ENGLISH   CHANNEL

Cherbourg

Amiens

CHANNEL IS.
(BR)

SEINE R.

Paris

Valmy

EUROPE
1810

Versailles

Fontainebleau

FRENCH

Nantes

Orléans

LOIRE R.

FRENCH
EMPIRE

GRAND
EMPIRE

ALLIED WITH
NAPOLEON

EMPIRE

Lyons

Rochefort

RHONE R.

Bordeaux

Avignon

GARONNE R.

Toulouse

Marseilles

Coruña

Galicia

CAPE
FINISTERRE

Burgos

EBRO R.

Saragossa

Oporto

DOURO R.

Almeida

Ciudad
Rodrigo

Barcelona

PORTUGAL

Madrid

Talavera

TAGUS R.

Lisbon

Ocaña

SPAIN

BALEARIC IS.
(SP.)

MINORCA

Elvas

Valencia

MAJORCA

Albuera

IVIZA

Baylen

Seville

ANDALUSIA

Cadiz

MED

TRAFALGAR ×

GIBRALTAR
(BR)

Algiers

Tangier

MOROCCO

ALGERIA
(TURK.)

TRM

government with the support of local persons who were willing to collaborate with the French and who helped in the drafting of a constitution specifying the powers of the new government and regularizing its relationships with France. In some areas these two stages had been accomplished under the Revolutionary governments before Napoleon came into power. In certain regions, in some of which French control began as late as 1808, no more than these two stages was ever really completed, notably in Spain, which was never pacified, and the Grand Duchy of Warsaw, which remained hardly more than an armed outpost against Russia. But Italy and Germany witnessed a third stage, that of sweeping internal reform and reorganization, modeled on Bonaparte's reforms in France, and hence derivatively on the French Revolution.[17] Belgium and the German territories west of the Rhine, annexed directly to France in the years before Napoleon's rise to power, may be said to have reached even a fourth stage and to have felt most strongly the impact of the French and of the Revolution.

Napoleon considered himself a great reformer and man of the Enlightenment. He called his system "liberal," and though the word to him meant almost the reverse of what it meant later to Liberals, he was possibly the first to use it in a political sense. He believed also in "constitutions"; not that he favored representative assemblies or limited government, but he wanted government to be rationally "constituted," *i.e.*, deliberately mapped out and planned, not merely inherited from the jumble of the past. Man on horseback though he was, he believed firmly in the rule of law. He insisted with the zeal of conviction on transplanting his Civil Code [18] to the dependent states. This code he considered to be based on the very nature of justice and human relationships, and to be applicable, therefore, to all countries with no more than minor adaptation. The idea that a country's laws must mirror its peculiar national character and history was foreign to his mind, for he carried over the rationalist and universalist outlook of the Age of Enlightenment. He thought that people everywhere wanted, and deserved, much the same thing. He undoubtedly believed in a unity of European civilization, to be furthered by a regime of uniform law in all countries under the authoritarian but impartial sanction of himself. He wrote to Jerome in 1807, on making him king of Westphalia:

You will find enclosed the constitution of your kingdom. . . . You must faithfully observe it. . . . What the peoples of Germany impatiently demand is that men who are not nobles, but who do have ability, should have an equal right to your favor and your employment, and that every kind of serfdom, or of feudal powers between the sovereign and the lowest class of his subjects, should be entirely done away with. The benefits of the Code Napoleon, public trial and the introduction of juries, will be so many distinctive features of your monarchy. . . . What people will want to return under the arbitrary Prussian rule, once it has tasted the benefits of a wise and liberal administration? The peoples of Germany, as of France, Italy and Spain, want equality and liberal ideas. For some years now I have man-

---

[17] See pp. 373–5.
[18] See pp. 374–5.

aged the affairs of Europe, and I am convinced that the cackling of the privileged classes was everywhere disliked. Be a constitutional king. Even if reason and the enlightenment of the age were not sufficient cause, it would be good policy for one in your position.

Nowhere does Napoleon better reveal himself—peremptory and dictatorial but not merely cynical, believing in certain reforms as an instrument of policy to rally support for himself, but also because they were obviously reasonable, just, and enlightened.

The same plan of reform was initiated, with some variation, in all the dependent states from Spain to Poland and from the mouth of the Elbe to the Straits of Messina. The reforms were directed, in a word, against everything feudal. They established the legal equality of individual persons, and gave governments more complete authority over their individual subjects. Legal classes were wiped out, as in France in 1789; the theory of a society made up of "estates of the realm" gave way to the theory of a society made up of legally equal individuals. The nobility lost its privileges in taxation, office-holding, and military command. Careers were "opened to talent."

The manorial system, bulwark of the old aristocracy, was virtually liquidated. Lords lost all legal jurisdiction over their peasants; peasants became subjects of the state, personally free to move, migrate or marry, and able to bring suit in the courts of law. The manorial fees, along with tithes, were generally abolished, as in France in 1789. But whereas in France the peasants escaped from these burdens without having to pay compensation, because they had themselves risen in rebellion in 1789 and because France passed through a radical popular revolution in 1793, in other parts of the Grand Empire the peasants were committed to payment of indemnities, and the former feudal class continued to receive income from its abolished rights. Only in Belgium and the Rhineland, incorporated with France under the Republic, did the manorial regime disappear without compensation as it did in France, leaving a numerous entrenched class of small landowning farmers. East of the Rhine Napoleon had to compromise with the aristocracy which he assailed. In Poland, the only country in the Grand Empire where a thoroughgoing serfdom had prevailed, the peasants received legal freedom during the French occupation; but the Polish landlords remained economically unharmed, since they owned all the land. Napoleon had to conciliate them, for there was no other effective class in Poland to which he could look for support. In general, outside of France, the assault upon feudalism was not socially as revolutionary as it had been in France. The lord was gone, but the landlord remained.

Everywhere in the Grand Empire the church lost its position as a public authority alongside the state. Church courts were abolished or restricted; the Inquisition was outlawed in Spain. Tithes were done away with, church property confiscated, monastic orders dissolved or severely regulated. Toleration became the law; Catholics, Protestants, Jews and unbelievers received the same civil rights. The state was to be based not on the idea of religious community but on the idea of territorial residence. With the nobility, or on economic matters, Napoleon would compromise; but he would not compromise with the Catholic clergy on the principle of a secular state. Even in Spain he insisted on these fundamentals of his system, a sure indication that he was not actuated by expediency only, since it was largely his religious program that provoked the Spanish populace to rebellion.

Gilds were generally abolished or reduced to empty forms, and the individual's right to work was generally proclaimed. Peasants, gaining legal freedom, might learn and enter any trade as they chose. The old town oligarchies and bourgeois patriciates were broken up. Towns and provinces lost their antique liberties and came under general legislation. Internal tariffs were removed, and free trade within state frontiers was encouraged. Some countries shifted to a decimal system of money; and the heterogeneous weights and measures which had originated in the Middle Ages, and of which the Anglo-American bushels, yards, ounces and pints are living survivals, yielded to the Cartesian regularities of the metric system. Ancient and diverse legal systems gave way to the Napoleonic codes. Law courts were separated from the administration. Hereditary office and the sale of office were done away with. Officials received salaries large enough to shield them from the temptations of corruption. Kings were put on civil lists, with their personal expenses separated from those of the government. Taxes and finances were modernized. The common tax became a land tax, paid by every landowner; and governments knew how much land each owner really owned, for they developed systematic registration of property and systematic methods of appraisal and assessment. Tax farming was replaced by direct collection. New methods of accounting and of collecting statistics were introduced.

In general, in all countries of the Grand Empire, some of the main principles of the French Revolution were introduced under Napoleon, with the notable exception that there was no self-government through elected legislative bodies. In all countries Napoleon found numerous natives willing to support him, mainly among the commercial and professional men, who were read in the writers of the Enlightenment, often anti-clerical, desirous of more equality with the nobility, and eager to break down the old localisms that interfered with trade and with the exchange of ideas. He found supporters also among many progressive nobles, and, in the Confederation of the Rhine, among the native rulers. His program appealed to a certain class of men everywhere, and in all parts of the Grand Empire was executed mainly by local persons. Repression went with it, though hardly on a scale to which the twentieth century has become accustomed. There were no vast internment camps, and Fouché's police was engaged more in spying and submitting reports than in the brutalizing of the disaffected. The execution of a single Bavarian bookseller, named Palm, became a famous outrage.

There was, in short, at first, a good deal of pro-Napoleonic feeling in the Grand Empire. The French influence (outside Belgium and the Rhineland) struck deepest in north Italy, where there were no native monarchist traditions, and where the old Italian city states had produced a strong and often anti-clerical burgher class. In south Germany also the French influence was profound. The French system had the least appeal in Spain, where Catholic royalist sentiment produced a kind of counter-revolutionary movement of independence. Nor did it appeal to agrarian eastern Europe, the land of lord and serf. Yet even in Prussia, as will be seen, the state was remodeled along French lines. In Russia, during the Tilsit alliance, Alexander gave his backing to a pro-French reforming minister, Speranski. The Napoleonic influence was pervasive because it carried over the older movement of enlightened despotism, and seemed to confer the advantages of the French Revolution without the violence and the disorder. Napoleon, it seemed to Goethe, "was the expression of all that was reasonable, legitimate and European in the revolutionary movement."

But the Napoleonic reforms were also weapons of war. As in France itself, so in Bavaria, Baden, or Italy, the state obtained more freedom in the use of its human and material resources. With the feudal barriers down, and equality enforced, the state raised taxes more abundantly and more quickly, and could recruit, train, officer, and equip its armies with regard only to military efficiency. All the dependent states were required by Napoleon to supply him with money and soldiers. Germans, Dutch, Belgians, Italians, Poles, and even Spaniards fought in his armies. In addition, the dependent states defrayed much of the cost of the French army, most of which was stationed outside France. This meant that taxes in France could remain low, to the general satisfaction of the propertied interests that had issued from the Revolution.

47. The Continental System: Britain and Europe

Beyond the tributary states of the Grand Empire lay the countries nominally independent, joined under Napoleon in the Continental System. Napoleon thought of his allies as at best subordinate partners in a common project. The great project was to crush Great Britain, and it was for this purpose that the Continental System had been established. But the crushing of Britain became in Napoleon's mind a means to a further end, the unification and mastery of all of Europe. This in turn, had he achieved it, would doubtless have merely opened the way to further conquests.

At the point where he stood in 1807 or 1810 the unification of Continental Europe seemed a not impossible objective. He cast about for an ideology to inspire both his Grand Empire and his allies. His problem was to breathe a spirit into a half-articulated body. It was to find some other basis than force, some common ground of consent and teamwork on which Europeans could combine. He held out the cosmopolitan doctrines of the eighteenth century, spoke endlessly of the enlightenment of the age, urged all peoples to work with him against the medievalism, feudalism, ignorance, and obscurantism by which they were still surrounded. And while appealing to the sense of modernity he dwelt also on the grandeur of Roman times. The

Roman inspiration reflected itself in the arts of the day. The massive "empire" furniture, the heroic canvasses of David, the church of the Madeleine in Paris, resembling a classical temple and converted to a Temple of Glory, the Arch of Triumph in the same city, begun in 1806, all evoked the atmosphere of far-spreading majesty in which Napoleon would have liked the peoples of Europe to live. His inclination to the Roman showed itself in the very terminology that he employed—his consuls, prefects, tribunate, and senate, his Legion of Honor, Cisalpine Republic, and Illyrian Provinces, and indeed the term "empire" itself. But Europe was not to be converted by archaism. To arouse a European feeling, Napoleon worked upon the latent hostility to Great Britain.

The British, in winning out in the eighteenth-century struggle for wealth and empire, had made themselves disliked in many quarters. There was the natural jealousy felt toward the successful, and resentment against the high-handedness by which success had been won and was maintained. Such feelings were present among almost all Europeans. For over a century the British Navigation Acts had been aimed against Continental shipping.[19] Beginning with the Seven Years' War, as their naval supremacy became established, the British also developed a theory of the use of sea power, or so at least it seemed to Europeans, though it was not the English habit to theorize on such matters, and the doctrine was only explicitly formulated much later by the American Admiral Mahan. The British held, in effect, that naval forces were characterized by extreme mobility and striking power, so that warships would be wastefully employed if one or two of them were stationed at every enemy port to blockade it; and that, instead, British war vessels should have the right to stop neutral vessels anywhere on the high seas, inspect their cargoes, and remove or destroy such as were contraband of war, contraband being defined by the British. Opponents contemptuously rejected these doctrines as mere theories of "paper blockade." They held that a country was truly and lawfully blockaded only in so far as warships patrolled its ports. Against the incipient doctrine of command of the sea, naturally entertained by the British since the British had the principal navy, the neutrals and lesser naval powers put forward the idea of "freedom of the seas," claiming extensive rights for neutrals to trade with all belligerents in time of war. The strength of anti-British sentiment was shown in the two leagues of Armed Neutrality of 1780 and 1801.[20]

BRITISH BLOCKADE AND NAPOLEON'S CONTINENTAL SYSTEM

It was believed that the British were really using their sea power to win a larger permanent share of the world's seaborne commerce for themselves. Nor, in truth, was this belief mistaken. The British, in the Revolu-

---

[19] See pp. 140, 148, 150.
[20] See pp. 327, 378.

tionary and Napoleonic wars, when they declared France and its allies in a state of blockade, did not expect either to starve them or to deprive them of necessary materials of war. Western Europe was still self-sufficient in food, and armaments were to a large extent produced locally, from simple materials like iron, copper, and saltpeter. Europe required almost nothing indispensable from overseas. The chief aim of the British blockade was not, therefore, to keep imports out of enemy countries; it was to keep the trade in such imports out of enemy hands. It was to kill off enemy commerce and shipping, in order, in the short run, to weaken the war-making powers of the enemy government by undermining its revenues and its navy, and in the long run to weaken the enemy's position in the markets of the world. Economic warfare was trade warfare. The British were willing enough to have British goods pass through to the enemy either by smuggling or by the mediation of neutrals. This in turn was because British exports had limited military value. Great Britain, through the Napoleonic wars, concentrated heavily on the production of civilian-type manufactures, notably on cotton yarn and cloth, then being revolutionized by the application of power machinery.[21] Export of cottons, woollens, pottery, and cutlery was of limited military significance, and the large re-export of colonial products—sugar, tobacco, tea, coffee, chocolate, dyestuffs, drugs, spices—had almost no military significance whatsoever. Hence, the more the British could sell to Europe the better.

As early as 1793 the French republicans had denounced England as the "modern Carthage," a ruthless mercantile and profit-seeking power which aspired to enslave Europe to its financial and commercial system. With the wars, the British in fact obtained a monopoly over the shipment of overseas commodities into Europe. At the same time, being relatively advanced in the industrial revolution, they could produce cotton cloth and certain other articles, by power machinery, more cheaply than other peoples of Europe, and so threatened to monopolize the European market for such manufactured goods. There was much feeling in Europe against the modern Carthage, especially among the bourgeois and commercial classes who were in competition with it. The upper classes were perhaps less hostile, not caring where the goods that they consumed had originated, but aristocracies and governments were susceptible to the argument that Britain was a money power, a "nation of shopkeepers" as Napoleon put it, which fought its wars with pounds sterling instead of blood, and was always in search of dupes in Europe.

It was on all these feelings that Napoleon played, reiterating time and again that England was the real enemy of all Europe, and that Europe would never be prosperous or independent until relieved of the incubus of British "monopoly." To prevent the flow of goods into Britain was no more the purpose of the Continental System than to prevent the flow of goods into France was the purpose of the British blockade. England could indeed, have been more readily starved than Europe; it had begun to depend habitually on

~~~~~~~~~~~~~~~~~~~

[21] See pp. 424–6.

imports of food. But Napoleon, to drain off British gold reserves, actually shipped food to his enemy. The purpose of the Continental System, as of the British blockade, was to destroy the enemy's commerce, credit, and public revenues by the destruction of his exports—and also to build up markets for oneself.

To destroy British exports Napoleon prohibited, by the Berlin Decree of 1806, the importation of British goods into the continent of Europe. Counted as British, if of British or British colonial origin, were goods brought to Europe in neutral ships as the property of neutrals. The British, in response, ruled by an "order in council" of November 1807 that neutrals might enter Napoleonic ports only if they first stopped in Great Britain, where the regulations were such as to encourage their loading with British goods. The British thus tried to move their exports into enemy territory through neutral channels, which was precisely what Napoleon intended to prevent. He announced, by the Milan Decree of December 1807, that any neutral vessel that had stopped at a British port, or submitted to search by a British warship at sea, would be confiscated upon its appearance in a Continental harbor.

With all Europe at war, virtually the only trading neutral was the United States, which could now trade with neither England nor Europe except by violating the regulations of one belligerent or the other. It would thus become liable to reprisals, and hence to involvement in war. President Jefferson, to avoid war, attempted a self-imposed policy of commercial isolation, which proved so ruinous to American foreign trade that the United States government offered to renew trade relations with whichever belligerent first removed its controls over neutral commerce. Napoleon offered to do so, on condition that the United States would defend itself against the enforcement of British controls. At the same time an expansionist party among the western Americans, ambitious to annex Canada, considered that with the British army engaged in Spain the time was ripe to complete the War of Independence by driving Britain from the North American mainland. The result was the Anglo-American war of 1812, which had few results, except to demonstrate the distressing inefficiency of military institutions in the new republic.

But the Continental System was more than a device for destroying the export trade of Great Britain. It was also a scheme—today it would be called a "plan"—for developing the economy of Continental Europe, around France as its main center. Before the wars, as has been seen, Europe had imported more from France than from Great Britain.[22] Now, by doing entirely without British goods, Europeans were to become economically more powerful and self-sufficient. The System carried over the older policies of mercantilist states of the past two hundred years. But where mercantilist governments had worked to create national economies in place of the old local economies,[23] the Continental System, if successful, would replace the

[22] See p. 228.
[23] See pp. 102-3.

national economies with an integrated economy for the Continent as a whole. It would create the framework for a European civilization. And it would ruin the British sea power and commercial monopoly; for a unified Europe, Napoleon thought, would itself soon take to the sea.

THE FAILURE OF THE CONTINENTAL SYSTEM

But the Continental System failed; it was worse than a failure, for it caused widespread antagonism to the Napoleonic regime. The dream of a united Europe, under French rule, was not sufficiently attractive to inspire the necessary sacrifice—even a sacrifice more of comforts than of necessities. As Napoleon impatiently said, one would suppose that the destinies of Europe turned upon a barrel of sugar. It was true, as he and his propagandists insisted, that Britain monopolized the sale of sugar, tobacco and other overseas goods, but people preferred to deal clandestinely with the British rather than go without them. The charms of America destroyed the Continental System.

British manufactures were somewhat easier than colonial goods to replace. Raw cotton was brought by land from the Levant through the Balkans, and the cotton manufactures of France, Saxony, Switzerland, and north Italy were stimulated by the relief from British competition. There was a great expansion of Danish woollens and German hardware. The cultivation of sugar beets, to replace cane sugar, spread in France, central Europe, Holland, and even Russia. Thus infant industries and investments were built up which, after Napoleon's fall, clamored for tariff protection. In general, the European industrial interests were well disposed toward the Continental System.

Yet they could never adequately replace the British in supplying the market. One obstacle was transportation. Much trading between parts of the Continent had always been done by sea; this coastal traffic was now blocked by the British. Land routes were increasingly used, even in the far away Balkans and Illyrian Provinces, through which raw cotton was brought; and improved roads were built through the Simplon and Mont Cenis passes in the Alps. No less than 17,000 wheeled vehicles crossed the Mont Cenis pass in 1810. But land transport, at best, was no substitute for the sea. Without railroads, introduced some thirty years later, a purely continental economy was impossible to maintain.

Another obstacle was tariffs. The idea of a Continental tariff-union was put forward by some of his subordinates, but Napoleon never adopted it. The dependent states remained insistent on their ostensible sovereignty. Each had widened its trading area by demolishing former internal tariffs, but each kept a tariff against the others. The kingdoms of Italy and Naples enjoyed no free trade with each other, nor did the German states of the Confederation of the Rhine. France remained protectionist; and when Napoleon annexed Holland and parts of Italy to France he kept them outside the French customs. At the same time Napoleon forbade the satellite states to raise high tariffs against France. France was his base, and he meant to favor French industry, which was much crippled by its loss of its Near Eastern and American markets. His program was for "France First" within Europe, and the Continental System, in one of its aspects, was a struggle of French manufacturers to capture Continental markets from the British.

Shippers, shipbuilders, and dealers in overseas goods, a powerful element of the older bourgeoisie, were ruined by the System. The French ports were idle, and their populations distressed and disgruntled. The same befell all ports of Europe where the blockade was strictly enforced; at Trieste, total annual tonnage fell from 208,000 in 1807 to 60,000 in 1812. Eastern Europe was especially hard hit. In the west there was the stimulus to new manufactures. The east, long dependent on western Europe for manufactured goods, could no longer obtain them from England legally, nor from France, Germany, or Bohemia because of the difficulties of land transport and the British control of the Baltic. Nor could the landowners of Prussia, Poland and Russia market their produce. The aristocracy of Eastern Europe, which was the principal spending and importing class, had additional reason to dislike the French and to sympathize with the British.

As a war measure against Britain the Continental System also failed. The British occupied practically all the islands, even those in sight of the French armies. The flow of goods into Europe was augmented when Napoleon, for his own convenience, issued licenses for the import of British products. It even came about that the French army wore overcoats made in England. Nevertheless, British trade with Europe was significantly reduced. But the loss was made up elsewhere because of British control of the sea. Exports to Latin America rose from £300,000 in 1805 to £6,300,000 in 1809. Here again the existence of the overseas world frustrated the Continental System. Despite the System, export of British cotton goods, rising on a continuous tide of the industrial revolution, more than doubled in four years from 1805 to 1809. And while part of the increase was due to mere inflation and rising prices, it is estimated that the annual income of the British people more than doubled in the Revolutionary and Napoleonic wars, leaping from £140,000,000 in 1792 to £335,000,000 in 1814.

48. The National Movements: Germany

THE RESISTANCE TO NAPOLEON: NATIONALISM

From the beginning, as far back as 1792, the French met with resistance as well as collaboration in the countries they occupied. There was resentment when the invading armies plundered and requisitioned upon the country, when the newly organized states were required to pay tribute of men and money, when their policies were dictated by French residents or ambassadors, and when the Continental System was used for the especial benefit of French manufacturers. Europeans began to feel that Napoleon was employing them merely as tools against England. And in all countries, including France itself, people grew tired of the peace that was no peace, the wars and rumors of war, the conscription and the taxes, the aloof bureaucratic government from on high, the obviously growing and insatiable appetite of Napoleon for power and self-exaltation. Movements of protest and independence showed themselves even within the Napoleonic structure. We have seen how the dependent states protected themselves by tariffs. Even the emperor's proconsuls tried to root themselves in local opinion, as when Louis Bonaparte, king of Holland, tried to defend Dutch interests against Napoleon's demands, or when Murat, king of Naples, appealed to Italian sentiment to secure his own throne.

Nationalism, as it was to be known in all the later history of Europe, developed as a movement of resistance against the forcible internationalism of the Napoleonic empire. It arose in protest against the Napoleonic idea, to which Napoleon himself was by no means faithful, of a European Continent united by uniform law and administration, with a Continental economic system of its own, a single foreign policy, and all its armies combined in a Grand Army under one command. Since the international system was essentially French, the nationalist movements were anti-French; and since Napoleon was an autocrat, they were anti-autocratic. The nationalism of the period was a mixture of the conservative and the liberal. Some nationalists, predominantly conservative, insisted on the value of their own peculiar institutions, customs, folkways, and historical development, which they feared might be obliterated under the French and Napoleonic system. Others, or indeed the same ones, insisted on more self-determination, more participation in government, more representative institutions, more freedom for the individual against the bureaucratic interference of the state. Both conservatism and liberalism rose up against Napoleon, destroyed him, outlasted him, and shaped the history of the following generations.

Nationalism was thus very complex, and appeared in different countries in different ways. In England the profound solidarity of the country exhibited itself; all classes rallied and stood shoulder to shoulder against "Boney"; and ideas of reforming Parliament or tampering with historic English liberties were resolutely put aside. It is possible that the Napoleonic wars helped England through a very difficult social crisis, for the industrial revolution was causing dislocation, misery, unemployment, and even revolutionary agitation among a small minority, all of which were eclipsed by the patriotic need of resistance to Bonaparte. In Spain, nationalism took the form of implacable resistance to the French armies that desolated the land. Some Spanish nationalists were liberal; a bourgeois group at Cadiz, rebelling against the French regime, proclaimed the Spanish constitution of 1812, modeled on the French constitution of 1791. But Spanish nationalism drew its greatest strength from sentiments that were counter-revolutionary, aiming to restore the clergy and the Bourbons. When the French government only a decade later, in 1822, sent a French army into Spain to protect the church and the Bourbons, it met with no serious resistance. Spain under Napoleon was a kind of Vendée within the Grand Empire—the Vendée, it will be recalled, being the region within France where Catholic and royalist peasants had risen up against the armies and the officials of the French Republic.[24] In Italy the Napoleonic regime was better liked, and national feeling was less anti-French than in Spain. Bourgeois of the Italian cities generally prized the efficiency and enlightenment of French methods, and often shared in the anti-clericalism of the French Revolution. The French regime, which lasted in Italy from 1796 to 1814, broke the habit of loyalty to the various duchies, oligarchic republics, papal states, and foreign dynasties by which Italy had long been ruled. Napoleon never unified Italy, but he assembled it into only three parts, and the French influence brought the notion of a politically united Italy within the bounds of reasonable aspiration. With the Poles Napoleon positively encouraged national feeling. He repeatedly told them that they might win a restored and united Poland by faithfully fighting in his cause. A few Polish nationalists, like the aging patriot Kosciuzsko, never trusted Napoleon, and some others, like Czartoryski, looked rather to the Russian tsar for a restoration of the Polish kingdom; but in general the Poles, for their own national reasons, were exceptionally devoted to the Emperor of the French, and lamented his passing.

THE MOVEMENT OF THOUGHT IN NAPOLEONIC GERMANY

By far the most momentous national movement took place in Germany. Napoleonic Germany was a seedbed that was to fertilize, fructify, and also to poison much of the later development of Europe. The Germans rebelled not only against the Napoleonic rule but against the century-old ascendancy of French civilization. They rebelled not only against the French armies but against the philosophy of the Age of Enlightenment. The years of the French Revolution and Napoleon were for Germany the years of its greatest cultural efflorescence, the years of Beethoven, Goethe and Schiller, of Herder, Kant, Fichte, Hegel, Schleiermacher and many others. German ideas fell in with all the ferment of fundamental thinking known as "romanticism," which was everywhere challenging the "dry abstractions" of the Age of Reason and about which more will be said in this and the following chapter. Germany became the most "romantic" of all countries and German influence spread throughout Europe. In the nineteenth century the Germans came to be widely regarded as intellectual leaders, somewhat as the French had been in the century before. And most of the distinctive features of German thought were somehow connected with nationalism in a broad sense.

Formerly, especially in the century following the peace of Westphalia,

[24] See p. 358.

the Germans had been the least nationally minded of all the larger European peoples.[25] They prided themselves on their world-citizenship or cosmopolitan outlook. Looking out from the tiny states in which they lived, they were conscious of Europe, conscious of other countries, but hardly conscious of Germany. The Holy Roman Empire was a shadow. The German world had no tangible frontiers; the area of German speech simply faded out into Alsace or the Austrian Netherlands, or into Poland, Bohemia, or the upper Balkans. That "Germany" ever did, thought, or hoped anything never crossed the German mind. There was scarcely even a developed language, for the speech habits of Berlin and Vienna were more different than those of London and New York today. The upper classes, becoming contemptuous of much that was German, took over French fashions, dress, etiquette, manners, ideas, and language, regarding them as an international norm of civilized living. Frederick the Great hired French tax-collectors and wrote his own books in French.

About 1780 signs of a change set in. Even Frederick, in his later years, predicted a golden age of German literature, proudly declaring that Germans could do what other nations had done. In 1784 appeared a book by J. G. Herder, called *Ideas on the Philosophy of the History of Mankind*. Herder was an earnest soul, a Protestant pastor and theologian who thought the French somewhat frivolous. He concluded that imitation of French ways, or of any foreign ways, made people shallow and artificial. He declared that German ways were indeed different from French, but not for that reason the less worthy of respect. All true culture or civilization, he held, must arise from native roots. It must arise also from the life of the common people, the *Volk*, not from the cosmopolitan and denatured life of the upper classes. Each people, he thought, meaning by a people a group sharing the same language, had its own attitudes, spirit, or genius. A sound civilization must express a national character or *Volksgeist*. And the character of each people was special to itself. Herder did not believe the nations to be in conflict, quite the contrary; he simply insisted that they were different. He did not believe German culture to be the best; many other peoples, notably the Slavs, later found his ideas applicable to their own needs. His philosophy of history was very different from Voltaire's. Voltaire and the *philosophes* had expected all peoples to progress along the same path of reason and enlightenment toward the same civilization. Herder thought that all peoples should develop their own genius in their own way, each slowly unfolding with the inevitability of plant-like growth, avoiding sudden change or distortion by outside influence, and all ultimately reflecting, in their endless diversity, the infinite richness of humanity and of God.

The idea of the *Volksgeist*, possibly the most significant single German idea of these agitated years, was reinforced from other and non-German sources, and soon passed to other countries in the general movement of romantic thought. Like much else in romanticism, it emphasized genius or

[25] See pp. 176–82.

intuition rather than reason. It stressed the differences rather than the similarity of mankind. It broke down that sense of human similarity which had been characteristic of the Age of Enlightenment,[26] and which revealed itself in French and American doctrines of the rights of man, or again in the law codes of Napoleon. In the past it had been usually thought that what was good was good for all peoples. Good poetry was poetry written according to certain classic principles or "rules" of composition, which were the same for all writers from the Greeks on down. Now, according to Herder and to romantics in all countries, good poetry was poetry that expressed an inner genius, either an individual genius or the genius of a people—there were no more "rules." Good and just laws, according to the older philosophy of natural law, somehow corresponded to a standard of justice that was the same for all men. But now, according to Herder and the romantic school of jurisprudence, good laws were those that reflected local conditions or national idiosyncrasies. Here again there were no "rules," except possibly the rule that each nation should have its own way.

Herder's philosophy set forth a cultural nationalism, without political message. The Germans had long been a non-political people. In the microscopic states of the Holy Empire they had had no significant political questions to think about; in the more sizable ones they had been excluded from public affairs. The French Revolution made the Germans acutely conscious of the state. It showed what a people could do with a state, once they took it over and used it for their own purposes. For one thing, the French had raised themselves to the dignity of citizenship; they had become free men, responsible for themselves, taking part in the affairs of their country. For another, because they had a unified state which included all Frenchmen, and one in which a whole nation surged with a new sense of freedom, they were able to rise above all the other peoples of Europe. Many in Germany were beginning to feel humiliation at the paternalism of their governments. The futilities of the Holy Roman Empire, which had made Germany for centuries the battlefield of Europe, now filled them with shame and indignation. They saw with disgust how their German princes, forever squabbling with each other for control over German subjects, disgraced themselves before the French to promote their own interests. The national awakening in Germany, which set in strongly after 1800, was therefore directed not only against Napoleon and the French, but also against the German rulers and many of the half-Frenchified German upper classes. It was democratic in that it stressed the superior virtue of the common people.

Germans became fascinated by the idea of political unity and national greatness, precisely because they had neither. A great national German state, expressing the deep moral will and distinctive culture of the German people, seemed to them the solution to all their problems. It would give moral dignity to the individual German, solve the vexatious question of the selfish petty princes, protect the deep German *Volksgeist* from violation, secure the

wwwwwwwwwwwww

[26] See p. 300.

Germans from conquest and subjection by outside powers. The nationalist philosophy remained somewhat vague, because in practice there was little that one could do. "Father" Jahn organized a kind of youth movement, and became the inventor of what might be termed political gymnastics, having his young men do calisthenics for the Fatherland; he led them on open-air expeditions into the country, where they made fun of aristocrats in French costume; and he taught them to be suspicious of foreigners, Jews, and internationalists, and indeed of everything that might corrupt the purity of the German *Volk*. Most Germans thought him too extreme. Others collected wonderful stories of the rich medieval German past. There was an anonymous anti-French work *Germany in Its Deep Humiliation*, for selling which the bookseller Palm was put to death. Others founded the Moral and Scientific Union, generally known as the *Tugendbund* or league of virtue or manliness, whose members, by developing their own moral character, were to contribute to the future of Germany.

The career of J. G. Fichte illustrates the course of German thought in these years. Fichte was a moral and metaphysical philosopher, a professor at the university of Jena. His doctrine, that the inner spirit of the individual creates its own moral universe, was much admired in many countries. In America, for example, it entered into the transcendental philosophy of Ralph Waldo Emerson. Fichte at first was practically without national feeling. He enthusiastically approved of the French Revolution, as did Jahn and Arndt. In 1793, with the Revolution at its height and many foreign observers turning against it, Fichte published a laudatory tract on the French Republic. He saw it as an emancipation of the human spirit, a step upward in the elevation of human dignity and moral stature. He accepted the idea of the Terror, that of "forcing men to be free"; and he shared Rousseau's conception of the state as the embodiment of the sovereign will of a people. He came to see the state as the means of human salvation. In 1800, in his *Closed Commercial State*, he sketched a kind of totalitarian system in which the state planned and operated the whole economy of the country, shutting itself off from the rest of the world in order that, at home, it might freely develop the character of its own citizens. When the French conquered Germany Fichte became intensely and self-consciously German. He took over the idea of the *Volksgeist*: not only did the individual spirit create its own moral universe, but the spirit of a people created a kind of moral universe as well, manifested in its language, arts, folkways, customs, institutions, and ideas.

At Berlin, in 1808, Fichte delivered a series of *Addresses to the German Nation*, declaring that there was an ineradicable German spirit, a primordial and immutable national character, more noble than that of other peoples (thus going beyond Herder), to be kept pure at all costs from all outside influence, either international or French. The German spirit, he held, had always been profoundly different from that of France and western Europe; it had never yet really been heard from, but would be some day. The French army commander then occupying the city thought the lectures too academic to be worth suppression. They had, in fact, few hearers; Fichte was considered a firebrand by most Germans; but they later regarded him as a national hero.

The movement of thought in Napoleonic Germany did not solve the political problem of the Germans themselves. It did rally feeling against the French. It laid the way for the fall of Napoleon. It raised up a democratic sentiment against the ruling dynasties of the Fatherland. It made Germans dream of a great united and awakened Germany of the future. And the same movement of ideas profoundly influenced, indirectly, the whole of Europe. The Germans became interested not only in their own national history, but in history itself as a fundamental method of thought, and they thus launched an intellectual revolution, through the philosophy of Hegel and by other means, which is described in a later chapter.[27]

REFORMS IN PRUSSIA

Politically, in the revolt against the French, the main transformations came in Prussia. Prussia after the death of Frederick the Great had fallen into a period of satisfied inertia, such as is likely to follow upon rapid growth or spectacular success. Then in 1806, at Jena-Auerstädt, the kingdom collapsed in a single battle. No great European power, until the somewhat comparable collapse of France in 1940, ever came so near extinction as Prussia in the following years. Its western and most of its Polish territories were taken away. It was relegated by Napoleon to its old holdings east of the Elbe. Even here the French remained in occupation, for Napoleon stationed his Ninth Corps in Berlin. But in the eyes of German nationalists Prussia had a moral advantage. Of all the German states it was the least compromised by collaboration with the French; for except for the Austrians, who in 1810 allied themselves with Napoleon by marriage, all the other German states were French satellites in the Confederation of the Rhine. Prussia, ruined by Napoleon, was an unwilling ally in his Continental System, and toward Prussia, as toward a haven, German patriots made their way. East-Elbian Prussia, formerly the least German of German lands, became the center of an all-German movement for national freedom. The years after Jena were decisive in the long historic process of the "Prussianizing" of Germany; but it is to be observed that neither Fichte nor Hegel, Gneisenau nor Scharnhorst, Stein nor Hardenberg, all rebuilders of Prussia, was a native Prussian.

The main problem for Prussia was military, since Napoleon could be overthrown only by military force. And as always in Prussia, the requirements of the army shaped the form taken by the state.[28] The problem was conceived to be one of morale and personnel. The old Prussia of Frederick, which had fallen ingloriously, had been mechanical, arbitrary, soulless; its people

wwwwwwwwwwwwww

[27] See pp. 439–40.
[28] See pp. 201–5, 311–12.

had lacked the sense of membership in the state, and in the army had had no hope of promotion, no patriotism, and no spirit. To produce this spirit was the aim of the army reformers, Scharnhorst and Gneisenau. Gneisenau, a Saxon, had served in one of the British "Hessian" regiments in the War of American Independence, during which he had observed the military value of patriotic feeling in the American soldiers. He was a close observer also of the consequences of the French Revolution. He wrote in 1807, blending ideas of the *Volksgeist* with ideas taken from the French:

> The Revolution has awakened all forces in the French and given to each force its proper sphere of action. Heroes rose to head the army, statesmen to the chief positions in administration. . . .
>
> What infinite power lies sleeping undeveloped and unused within the womb of the nation! Within the breasts of thousands there lives a great genius, but their lowly condition prevents its flowering. . . . Why did not the courts make use of the simplest and surest means, that of providing a career for this genius, wherever it may be, and of encouraging these talents and virtues, no matter from what class or rank they might come? . . .
>
> The Revolution has set in action the national energy of the entire French people, putting the different classes on an equal social and fiscal basis. . . . If the other states wish to establish the former balance of power, they must open up and use these same resources. They must take over the results of the Revolution, and so gain the double advantage of being able to place their entire national energies in opposition to the enemy and of escaping from the dangers of a revolution. . . .

Democracy, in the sense of legal equality and free opportunity, had proved itself not only just but useful. It had survival value. It made the state stronger; it strengthened the army. Democratic, in this sense, the new Prussia should therefore be. Prussia would learn from the enemy. It would adapt from the Revolution what it needed. And for two reasons: to destroy the enemy, and to prevent revolution in Prussia.

The reconstruction of the state, prerequisite to the reconstruction of the army, was initiated by Baron Stein and continued by his successor, Hardenberg. Like Metternich, Stein came from western Germany; he had been an imperial knight of the late Holy Empire, who from a bridge near his castle had beheld the domains of no less than eight German princes in one sweep of the eye. Stateless himself, he thought of Germany as a whole; he was long hostile to what he considered the barely civilized Prussia, but finally resorted to it as the hope of the future. Deeply committed to the philosophy of Kant and Fichte, he dwelt on the concepts of duty, service, moral character, and responsibility. He thought that the common people must be awakened to moral life, raised from a brutalized servility to the level of self-determination and membership in the community. This, he believed, required an equality more of duties than of rights.

Under Stein the old caste structure of Prussia came to an end. Property became interchangeable between classes; bourgeois were allowed to buy land and serve as officers in the army. The burghers, to develop a sense of citizenship and participation in the state, were given extensive freedom of self-government in the cities; the municipal system of Prussia, and later of

Germany, became a model for much of Europe in the following century. Stein had ideas for parliamentary institutions in Prussia as a whole, thinking they would strengthen the country, but he left office before acting upon them.

His most famous work was the "abolition of serfdom." It was naturally impossible, since the whole reform program aimed at strengthening Prussia for a war of liberation against the French, to antagonize the *Junkers* who commanded the army. Stein's ordinance of 1807 abolished serfdom only in that it abolished the "hereditary subjection" of peasants to their manorial lords.[29] It gave peasants the right to move and migrate, marry and take up trades without the lord's approval. If, however, the peasant remained on the land, he was still subject to all the old services of forced labor in the fields of the lord. Peasants enjoying small tenures of their own continued to be liable for the old dues and fees. By an edict of 1810, a peasant might convert his tenure into private property, getting rid of the manorial obligations, but only on condition that one-third of the land he had held should become the private property of the lord. In the following decades many such conversions took place, of which the result was that the estates of the *Junkers* grew considerably larger. The reforms in Prussia somewhat reduced the old patriarchal powers of the lords, and gave legal status and freedom of movement to the mass of the population, thus laying the foundation for a modern state and modern economy. But the peasants tended to become mere hired agricultural laborers; and the position of the *Junkers* was heightened, not reduced. Prussia avoided the Revolution. Stein himself, because Napoleon feared him, was obliged to go into exile in 1808, but his reforms endured.

49. The Overthrow of Napoleon: The Congress of Vienna

The situation at the close of 1811 may be summarized as follows. Napoleon had the mainland of Europe in his grip. Russia and Turkey were at war on the Danube, but otherwise there was no war except in Spain, where four years of fighting remained inconclusive. The Continental System was working badly. Britain was hurt by it only negatively, in that, without it, British exports to Europe would have risen rapidly in these years. Well launched in the industrial revolution, Great Britain was amassing a vast store of national wealth, accumulating the wherewithal to assist European governments financially against Napoleon. The peoples of Europe were increasingly restless, dreaming increasingly of national freedom. In Germany, especially, many awaited the opportunity to rise in a war of independence. But Napoleon could be overthrown only by the destruction of his army, with which neither British wealth nor British sea power, nor the European patriots and nationalists, nor the Prussian nor the Austrian armed forces were able to cope. All eyes turned to Russia. Alexander I had long been dissatisfied with his French alliance. He had obtained from it nothing but the annexation of

ᴡᴡᴡᴡᴡᴡᴡᴡᴡᴡᴡᴡᴡ
[29] See pp. 101–2.

Finland in 1809. He received no assistance from France in his war with Turkey; he saw Napoleon marry into the Austrian house; he had to tolerate the existence of a French-oriented Poland at his very door. The articulate classes in Russia, namely the landowners and serf-owners, loudly denounced the French alliance and demanded a resumption of open trade relations with England. An international clientele of émigrés and anti-Bonapartists, including Baron Stein, also gradually congregated at St. Petersburg, where they poured into the tsar's ears the welcome message that Europe looked to him for its salvation.

THE RUSSIAN CAMPAIGN AND THE WAR OF LIBERATION

On December 31, 1810, Russia formally withdrew from the Continental System. Anglo-Russian commercial relations were resumed. Napoleon resolved to crush the tsar. He concentrated the Grand Army in eastern Germany and Poland, a vast force of 700,000 men, the largest ever assembled up to that time for a single military operation. It was an all-European host. Hardly more than a third was French; another third was German, from German regions annexed to France, from the states of the Confederation of the Rhine, and in token forces from Prussia and Austria; and the remaining third was drawn from all other nationalities of the Grand Empire, including 90,000 Poles. Napoleon at first hoped to meet the Russians in Poland or Prussia. This time, however, they decided to fight on their own ground, and they needed in any case to delay until their forces on the lower Danube could be recalled. In June 1812 Napoleon led the Grand Army into Russia.

He intended a short, sharp war, such as most of his wars had been in the past, and carried with him only three weeks' supplies. But from the beginning everything went wrong. It was Napoleon's principle to force a decisive battle; but the Russian army simply melted away. It was his principle to live on the country, so as to reduce the need for supply trains; but the Russians destroyed as they retreated, and in any case, in Russia, even in the summer, it was hard to find sustenance for so many men and horses. Finally, not far from Moscow, Napoleon was able to join battle with the main Russian force at Borodino. Here again everything miscarried. It was his principle always to outnumber the enemy at the decisive spot; but the Grand Army had left so many detachments along its line of march that at Borodino the Russians outnumbered it. It was Napoleon's principle to concentrate his artillery, but here he scattered it instead; and to throw in his last reserves at the critical moment, but at Borodino, so far from home, he refused the risk of ordering the Old Guard into action. Napoleon won the battle, at a cost of 30,000 men, as against 50,000 lost by the Russians; but the Russian army was able to withdraw in good order.

On September 14, 1812, the French emperor entered Moscow. Almost immediately the city broke into flames. Napoleon found himself camping in a ruin, with troops strewn along a long line all the way back to Poland, and with a hostile army maneuvering stealthily near at hand. Baffled, he tried to negotiate with Alexander, who refused all overtures. After five weeks, not knowing what to do, and fearful of remaining isolated in Moscow over the winter, Napoleon ordered a retreat. Prevented by the Russians from taking a more southerly route, the Grand Army retired by the same way as it had come. The cold weather set in early, and was unusually severe. For a century after 1812 the retreat from Moscow remained the last word in military horror. Men froze and starved, horses slipped and died, vehicles could not be moved, and equipment was abandoned. Discipline broke down toward the end; the army dissolved into a horde of individual fugitives, speaking a babel of languages, harassed by bands of Russian irregulars, picking their way on foot over ice and snow, most of the time in the dark, for the nights are long in these latitudes in December. Of 611,000 who entered Russia 400,000 died of battle casualties, starvation and exposure, and 100,000 were taken prisoner. The Grand Army no longer existed.

Now at last all the anti-Napoleonic forces rushed together. The Russians pushed westward into central Europe. The Prussian and Austrian governments, which in 1812 had half-heartedly supplied troops for the invasion of Russia, switched over in 1813 and joined the tsar, Prussia quickly and eagerly, Austria more slowly and reluctantly, for Metternich was fearful of the rising Russian colossus, suspicious of the perfervid nationalism of Germany, and still willing to see Napoleon on the throne of a trimmed down France. Throughout Germany the patriots, often half-trained boys, marched off in the War of Liberation. Anti-French riots broke out in Italy. In Spain Wellington at last pushed rapidly forward; in June 1813 he crossed the Pyrenees into France. The British government, in three years from 1813 to 1815, poured £32,000,000 as subsidies into Europe, more than half of all the funds granted during the twenty-two years of the wars. An incongruous alliance of British capitalism and east-European agrarian feudalism, of the British navy and the Russian army, of Spanish clericalism and German nationalism, of divine-right monarchies and newly aroused democrats and liberals, combined at last to bring the Man of Destiny to the ground.

Napoleon, who had left his army in Russia in December 1812, and rushed across Europe to Paris, by sleigh and coach, in the remarkable time of thirteen days, raised a new army in France in the early months of 1813. But it was untrained and unsteady, and he himself had lost some of his genius for command. His new army was smashed in October at the battle of Leipzig, known to the Germans as the Battle of the Nations, the greatest battle in number of men engaged ever fought until the twentieth century. The allies drove Napoleon back upon France. But the closer they came to defeating him the more they began to fear and distrust each other.

THE RESTORATION OF THE BOURBONS

The coalition already showed signs of splitting. Should the allies, together or singly, negotiate with Napoleon? How strong should the France of the future be? What should be its new frontiers? What form of government should it have? There was no agreement on these questions. Alexander wanted to dethrone Napoleon and dictate peace in Paris, in dramatic retribution for the destruction of Moscow. He had a scheme for giving the French throne to Bernadotte, a former French marshal, now crown prince of Sweden, who as king of France would depend on Russian support. Metternich preferred to keep Napoleon or his son as French emperor, after clearing the French out of central Europe; for a Bonaparte dynasty in a reduced France would be dependent on Austria. The Prussian counsels were divided. The British declared that the French must get out of Belgium, and that Napoleon must go; they held that the French might then choose their own government, but believed a restoration of the Bourbons to be the best solution. The three continental monarchies had no concern for the Bourbons, and both Alexander and Metternich, if they could make France dependent respectively on themselves, were willing to see it remain strong to the extent of including Belgium. In November 1813 Metternich communicated to Napoleon a proposition known as the "Frankfurt proposals," by which Napoleon would remain French emperor, and France would retain its "natural" frontier on the Rhine. There was a chance of peace on this basis, for the allies could not shake off their old fear of Napoleon, the Prussians could be compensated elsewhere, and among the Russians many of the generals and others were impatient to go home. The British, their diplomatic influence reduced by the fact that they had few troops in Europe, faced the appalling prospect that the Continent would again make peace without them—and a peace in which France should again keep Belgium.

The British foreign minister, Viscount Castlereagh, arrived in person on the Continent in January 1814. He held a number of strong cards. For one thing, Napoleon rejected the Frankfurt proposals. He continued to fight, and the allies therefore continued to ask for British financial aid. Castlereagh skillfully used the promise of British subsidies to win acceptance of the British war aims. In addition, he found a common ground for agreement with Metternich, both Britain and Austria fearing the domination of Europe by Russia. Castlereagh's first great problem was to hold the alliance together, for without Continental allies the British could not defeat France. He succeeded, on March 9, 1814, in getting Russia, Prussia, Austria, and Great Britain to sign the treaty of Chaumont. Each power bound itself for twenty years to a Quadruple Alliance against France, and each agreed to provide 150,000 soldiers to enforce such peace terms as might be arrived at. For the first time since 1792 a solid coalition of the four great powers now existed against France. Three weeks later the allies entered Paris, and on April 4 Napoleon abdicated at Fontainebleau.

He was forced to this step by lack of support in France itself. Twenty years before, in 1793 and 1794, France had fought off the combined powers of Europe—minus Russia. It could not and would not do so in 1814. The country cried for peace. Even the imperial marshals advised the emperor's abdication. But what was to follow him? For over twenty-five years the French had had one regime after another. Now there were some who wished a republic, some who wished the empire under Napoleon's infant son, some who wished a constitutional monarchy, and some even who longed for the Old Regime. Talleyrand stepped into the breach. The "legitimate" king, he said, Louis XVIII, was after all the man who would provoke the least factionalism and opposition. The powers, likewise, had by this time concluded in favor of the Bourbons. A Bourbon king would be peaceable, under no impulse to win back the conquests of the republic and empire. He would also, as the native and rightful king of France, need no foreign support to bolster him up, so that the control of France would not arise as an issue to divide the victorious powers.

So the Bourbon dynasty was restored. Louis XVIII, ignored and disregarded for a whole generation, both by most Frenchmen and by the governments of Europe, returned to the throne of his brother and his fathers. He issued a "constitutional charter," partly at the insistence of the liberal tsar, and partly because, having actually learned from his long exile, he sought the support of influential people in France. The charter of 1814 made no concession to the principle of popular or national sovereignty. It was represented as the gracious gift of a theoretically absolute king. But in practice it granted what most Frenchmen wanted. It promised legal equality, eligibility of all to public office without regard to class, and a parliamentary government in two chambers. It recognized the Napoleonic law codes, the Napoleonic settlement with the church, and the redistribution of property effected during the Revolution. It carried over the abolition of feudalism and privilege, manorialism and tithes. It confined the vote, to be sure, to a very few large landowners; but for the time being, except for a few irreconcilables, France settled down to enjoy the blessings of a chastened revolution—and peace.

THE SETTLEMENT BEFORE THE VIENNA CONGRESS

It was with the government of the restored Bourbons that the powers, on May 30, 1814, signed a treaty. This document, the "first" treaty of Paris, confined France to its boundaries of 1792, those obtaining before the wars. The allied statesmen disregarded cries for vengeance and punishment, imposed no indemnity or reparations, and even allowed the works of art gathered from Europe during the wars to remain in Paris. It was not the desire of the victors to handicap the new French government on which they placed their hopes. Napoleon meanwhile was exiled to the island of Elba on the Italian coast.

To deal with other questions, the powers had agreed, before signing the Alliance of Chaumont, to hold an international congress at Vienna after defeating Napoleon. The recession of the French flood left the future of much of Europe—Belgium, Holland, Germany, Poland, Italy, Spain—fluid and uncertain. There were many other debatable questions also; the Russian annexation of Finland and ambitions on the Danube, the disintegration of the Spanish American empire, the British occupation of French, Dutch and Spanish possessions, the troublesome issue of the freedom of the seas.

Both Russia and Great Britain, before consenting to a general conference, specified certain matters that they would decide for themselves as not susceptible to international consideration. The Russians refused to discuss Turkey and the Balkans; they retained Bessarabia as the prize of their recent war with the Turks. They also kept Finland, as an autonomous constitutional grand duchy, as well as certain recent conquests in the Caucasus almost unknown to Europe. The British refused any discussion of the freedom of the seas. They also barred all colonial and overseas questions. The revolts in Spanish America were left to run their course. The British government simply announced to Europe which of its colonial and insular conquests it would keep and which it would return.

In Europe, the British remained in possession of Malta, the Ionian Islands and Heligoland. In America, they kept St. Lucia, Trinidad and Tobago in the West Indies, and reasserted their claims to the Pacific Northwest, or Oregon country, to which claims were also made by Russia, Spain and the United States. Of former French possessions, the British kept the island of Mauritius in the Indian Ocean. Of former Dutch territories, they kept the Cape of Good Hope and Ceylon, but returned the Netherlands Indies. During the Revolutionary and Napoleonic wars in Europe the British had also made extensive conquests in India, bringing much of the Deccan and the upper Ganges valley under their rule. The British emerged, in 1814, as the controlling power in both India and the Indian Ocean.

Indeed, of all the colonial empires founded by Europeans in the sixteenth and seventeenth centuries, and whose rivalry had been a recurring cause of war in the eighteenth, only the British now remained as a growing and dynamic system. The old French, Spanish, and Portuguese empires were reduced to mere scraps of their former selves; the Dutch still held vast establishments in the East Indies, but all the intermediate positions, the Cape, Ceylon, Mauritius, Singapore, were now British. Nor, in 1814, did any people except the British have a significant navy. With Napoleon and the Continental System defeated, with the industrial revolution bringing power machinery to the manufacturers of England, with no rival left in the contest for overseas dominion, and with a virtual monopoly of naval power, whose use they studiously kept free from international regulation, the British embarked on their century of world leadership, which may be said to have lasted from 1814 to 1914.

THE CONGRESS OF VIENNA, 1814–15

The Congress of Vienna assembled in September 1814. Never had such a brilliant gathering been seen. All the states of Europe sent representa-

---

Europe, 1815 (map on following pages)

Boundaries are those set by the Congress of Vienna in 1815. Outside the Balkans they remained basically unchanged until the Italian war of 1859, except that Belgium became independent and the separate kingdom of Poland disappeared in 1830–1 (p. 457). For the great crisis of the Congress of Vienna, the Polish-Saxon question, see panels 6 and 7 of the map on pp. 198–9.

EUROPE, 1815

500 MILES

tives; and many defunct states, such as the formerly sovereign princes and ecclesiastics of the late Holy Roman Empire, sent lobbyists to urge their restoration. But procedure was so arranged that all important matters were decided
by the four triumphant Great Powers. Indeed it was at the Congress of
Vienna that the terms great and small powers entered clearly into the diplomatic vocabulary. Europe was at peace, a treaty having been signed with the
late enemy; France also was represented at the congress, by none other than
Talleyrand, now minister to Louis XVIII. Castlereagh, Metternich, and Alexander spoke for their respective countries; Prussia was represented by Hardenberg. The Prussians hoped, as always, to enlarge the kingdom of Prussia.
Alexander was a question mark: he wanted Poland, he wanted constitutional
governments in Europe, he wanted some kind of international system of collective security. Castlereagh and Metternich, with support from Talleyrand,
were most especially concerned to produce a balance of power on the Continent. Aristocrats of the Old Regime, they applied eighteenth-century diplomatic principles to the existing problem. They by no means desired to restore the territorial boundaries obtaining before the wars. They did desire, as
they put it, to restore the "liberties of Europe," meaning the freedom of
European states from domination by a single power.[30] The threat of "universal monarchy," a term which diplomats still sometimes used to signify such a
system as Napoleon's, was to be offset by an ingenious calculation of forces,
a transfer of territory and "souls" from one government to another, in such a
way as to distribute and balance political power among a number of free and
sovereign states. It was hoped that a proper balance would also produce a
lasting peace.

The chief menace to peace, and most likely claimant for the domination of Europe, naturally seemed to be the late trouble-maker, France. The
Congress of Vienna, without much disagreement, erected a barrier of strong
states along the French eastern frontier. The historic Dutch Republic, extinct
since 1795, was revived as the Kingdom of the Netherlands, with the house of
Orange as a hereditary monarchy; to it was added Belgium, the old Austrian
Netherlands with which Austria had long been willing to part. It was hoped
that the combined Dutch-Belgian kingdom would be strong enough to discourage the perennial French drive into the Low Countries. On the south, the
Italian kingdom of Sardinia was restored, and strengthened by the incorporation of the defunct republic of Genoa, extinct since 1797. Behind the Netherlands and Sardinia, and further to discourage a renewal of French pressure
upon Germany and Italy, two great powers were installed. Almost all the
German Left Bank of the Rhine was ceded to Prussia. Prussia was to be, in
Castlereagh's words, a kind of "bridge" spanning central Europe, a bulwark
against both France in the west and Russia in the east. With the Rhineland
Prussia received, by international agreement, an accession of territory as significant as Silesia, which it had conquered in war, or the Polish territories,
which it had appropriated in the partitions. In Italy, again as a kind of sec-

---

[30] See pp. 135–6.

ondary barrier against France, the Austrians were firmly installed. They not only took back Tuscany and the Milanese, which they had held before 1796, but also annexed the extinct republic of Venice (as by the treaty of Campo Formio with Bonaparte in 1797); the Austrian Empire now included a Lombardo-Venetian kingdom in north Italy, which lasted for almost half a century. In the rest of Italy the Congress recognized the restoration of the pope in the papal States, and of former rulers in the smaller duchies; but it did not insist on a restoration of the Bourbons in the kingdom of Naples. There Napoleon's brother-in-law Murat, with support from Metternich, managed for a time to retain his throne. The Bourbons and Braganzas restored themselves respectively in Spain and Portugal, and were recognized by the Congress.

As for Germany, the Congress made no attempt to put together again the Humpty Dumpty of the Holy Roman Empire. The pleas of the former princelings went unheeded. The French and Napoleonic reorganization of Germany was substantially confirmed. The kings of Bavaria, Würtemberg, and Saxony kept the royal crowns that Napoleon had bestowed on them. The king of England, George III, was recognized as king, not "elector," of Hanover. The German states, now thirty-eight in number, including Prussia and Austria, were joined in a loose confederation in which the members remained virtually sovereign, and which did nothing to solve the Austro-Prussian dualism or rivalry. The Congress ignored the yearnings of German nationalists for a great unified Fatherland; Metternich especially feared nationalistic agitation; and in any case the nationalists themselves had no practical answer to concrete questions, such as the institutions of government and the frontiers that a united Germany should have. The Congress did declare, somewhat ineffectually, that in each of the German states there should be a representative legislative body.

THE POLISH-SAXON QUESTION

The question of Poland, reopened by the fall of Napoleon's Grand Duchy of Warsaw, brought the Congress almost to disaster. Alexander still insisted on undoing the crime of the partitions, which to his mind meant reconstituting the Polish kingdom with himself as constitutional king, in a merely personal union with the Russian empire. A similar arrangement was being initiated in the Grand Duchy of Finland, where Alexander reigned as a constitutional grand duke. To reunite Poland required that Austria and Prussia surrender their respective segments of the old Poland, most of which they had in any case lost to Napoleon. The Prussians were willing, with the proviso, which Alexander supported, that Prussia receive instead the whole of the kingdom of Saxony, which was considered available because the king of Saxony had been the last German ruler to abandon Napoleon. The issue presented itself as the Polish-Saxon question, with Russia and Prussia standing together to demand all Poland for Russia, and all Saxony for Prussia.

Such a prospect horrified Metternich. For Prussia to absorb Saxony would raise Prussia prodigiously in the eyes of all Germans, and it would greatly lengthen the common frontier between Prussia and the Austrian Empire. Furthermore, for Alexander to become king of all Poland, and incidentally the protector of an extended Prussia, would incalculably augment the influence of Russia in the affairs of Europe. Metternich found that Castlereagh shared these views. To Castlereagh it seemed that the main problem at Vienna was to restrain Russia. The British had not fought the French emperor only to have Europe fall to the Russian tsar. For months the Polish-Saxon question was debated, Metternich and Castlereagh exploring every device of argument to dissuade the Russo-Prussian combination from its expansionist designs. Finally they accepted the proffered assistance of Talleyrand, who shrewdly used this rift between the victors to bring France back into the diplomatic circle as a power in its own right. On January 3, 1815, Castlereagh, Metternich, and Talleyrand signed a secret treaty, pledging themselves to go to war if necessary against Russia and Prussia. So, in the very midst of the peace conference, war again reared its head; and, in the very deliberations of the victors, one party among them allied itself with the vanquished.

No sooner had news of the secret treaty leaked out than Alexander offered to compromise. In his mixed nature he was, among other things, a man of peace, and he agreed to content himself with a reduced Polish kingdom. The Congress therefore created a new Poland (called "Congress Poland," which lasted for fifteen years); Alexander became its king, and he gave it a constitution; it comprised much the same area as Napoleon's Grand Duchy, representing in effect a transfer of this region from French to Russian control. It reached two hundred and fifty miles farther west into Europe than had the Russian segment of the third partition of 1795. Some Poles still remained in Prussia, and some in the Austrian empire; Poland was not reunited. With the tsar thus content, Prussia too had to back down. It received about two-fifths of Saxony, the rest remaining to the Saxon king. The addition of both Saxon and Rhenish territories brought the Prussian monarchy into the most advanced parts of Germany. The net effect of the peace settlement, and of the Napoleonic wars, in this connection, was to shift the center of gravity of both Russia and Prussia farther west, Russia almost to the Oder, Prussia to the borders of France.[31]

With the solution of the Polish-Saxon question the main work of the Congress was completed. Other incidental matters were taken up. The Congress initiated international regulation of certain rivers. It issued a declaration against the Atlantic slave trade, which, however, remained ineffective, since the Continental powers were unwilling to grant the British navy free powers of search at sea, and the British were unwilling to put naval forces at the disposal of an international body. Committees of the Congress set to work to

wwwwwwwwwwww

[31] See maps on pp. 199, 213, 221.

draft the Final Act. And at this point the whole settlement was brought into jeopardy.

THE HUNDRED DAYS AND THEIR AFTERMATH

Napoleon escaped from Elba, landed in France on March 1, 1815, and again proclaimed the Empire. In the year since the return of the Bourbons discontent had been spreading in France. Louis XVIII proved to be a sensible man, but a swarm of unreasonable and vindictive émigrés had come back with him. Reaction and a "white terror" were raging through the country. Adherents of the Revolution rallied to the Emperor on his dramatic reappearance. Napoleon reached Paris, took over the government and army, and headed for Belgium. He would, if he could, disperse the pompous assemblage at Vienna. To the victors of the year before, and to most of Europe, it seemed that the Revolution was again stirring, that the old horror of toppling thrones and recurring warfare might not after all be ended. The opposing forces met in Belgium at Waterloo, where the Duke of Wellington, commanding an allied force, won a great victory. Napoleon again abdicated, and was again exiled, this time to distant St. Helena in the south Atlantic. A new peace treaty was made with France, the "second" treaty of Paris. It was more severe than the first, since the French seemed to have shown themselves incorrigible and unrepentant. The new treaty imposed minor changes of the frontiers, an indemnity of 700,000,000 francs, and an army of occupation.

The effect of the Hundred Days, as the episode following Napoleon's return from Elba is called, was to renew the dread of revolution, war, and aggression. Britain, Russia, Austria, and Prussia, after being almost at war with each other in January, again joined forces to get rid of the apparition from Elba, and in November 1815 they solemnly reconfirmed the quadruple alliance of Chaumont, adding a provision that no Bonaparte should ever govern France. They agreed also to hold future congresses to review the political situation and enforce the peace. No change was made in the arrangements agreed to at Vienna, except that Murat, who fought for Napoleon during the Hundred Days, was captured and shot, and an extremely unenlightened Bourbon monarchy was restored in Naples. In addition to the quadruple alliance of the great powers, bound specifically to enforce or amend the terms of the peace treaty by international action, Alexander devised a vaguer scheme which he called the Holy Alliance. Long attracted to the idea of an international order, appalled by the return of Napoleon, and influenced at the moment by the pietistic Baroness von Krüdener, the tsar proposed, for all monarchs to sign, a statement by which they promised to uphold Christian principles of charity and peace. All signed except the Pope, the Sultan and the Prince Regent of Great Britain. The Holy Alliance, probably sincerely meant by Alexander as a condemnation of violence, and at first not taken seriously by the others who signed it, and who thought it absurd to mix Christianity with politics, soon came to signify, in the minds of liberals, a kind of unholy alliance of monarchies against liberty and progress.

The peace of Vienna, including generally the treaty of Vienna itself, the treaties of Paris, and the British and colonial settlement, was the most far-reaching diplomatic agreement between the peace of Westphalia of 1648 and the peace of Versailles which closed the First World War in 1919. It had its strong points and its weak ones. It produced a minimum of resentment in France; the late enemy accepted the new arrangements. It ended almost two centuries of colonial rivalry; for sixty or seventy years no colonial empire seriously challenged the British. Two other causes of friction in the eighteenth century—the control of Poland and the Austro-Prussian dualism in Germany—were smoothed over for fifty years. With past issues the peace of 1815 dealt rather effectively; with future issues, not unnaturally, it was less successful. The Vienna treaty was not illiberal in its day; it was by no means reactionary, for the Congress showed little desire to restore the state of affairs in existence before the wars. The reaction that gathered strength after 1815 was not written into the treaty itself.

But the treaty gave no satisfaction to nationalists and democrats. It was a disappointment even to many liberals, especially in Germany. The transfer of peoples from government to government, without consultation of their wishes, opened the way under nineteenth-century conditions to a good deal of subsequent trouble. The peacemakers were in fact hostile both to nationalism and to democracy, the potent forces of the coming age; they regarded them, with reason, as leading to revolution and war. The problem to which they addressed themselves was to restore the balance of power, the "liberties of Europe," and to make a lasting peace. In this they were successful. They restored the European state-system, or system in which a number of sovereign and independent states existed without fear of conquest or domination. And the peace which they made, though some details broke down in 1830, and others in 1848, on the whole subsisted for half a century; and not for a full century, not until 1914, was there a war in Europe that lasted longer than a few months, or in which all the great powers were involved. No international disturbance comparable in magnitude to that created by the French Revolution and Napoleonic empire has ever been followed by such a protracted period of peace.

CHAPTER XI

Reaction vs. Progress, 1815-48

MERGING in 1815 from a generation of warfare, the European world proceeded to roll along the broad avenue of the nineteenth century, which, seen in retrospect, stands as the most remarkable period of material progress in the history of the human race. Post-war economic troubles there were, due to the sudden stopping of war production, to the readjustment of markets after the collapse of the Continental System, and to the enormously swollen government debts and inflated prices. These troubles were overcome. Europe was shaken by the wars, but not ruined. The injury to Europe produced by the wars of our own century was to be incomparably greater. One reason why Europe came out of the wars of 1792–1815 with relatively so little damage is that warfare was then incomparably less destructive. Another is that Europe was carried on the wave of an expanding economy. The economic expansion which had been going on for centuries was now, in the years around 1815, accentuated and accelerated by the phenomenon generally known as the Industrial Revolution.

The processes of industrialization in the long run were to revolutionize the lives of men everywhere. In the short run, in the generation following the peace of Vienna, the same processes had pronounced political effects. The Industrial Revolution, by greatly enlarging both the business and the wage-earning classes, doomed all attempts at "reaction," attempts, that is, to undo or check the consequences of the French Revolution. Industrialization made the flood of progress too powerful for conservatism to dam up. It hastened the growth of that world-wide economic system whose rise in the eighteenth century has already been observed. And since industrialization first took place in western Europe, one of its early effects was to widen the difference between eastern and western Europe, and so to weaken the efforts made, after the defeat of Napoleon, to organize a kind of international union of Europe.

50. The Industrial Revolution

On the whole, from the beginning of history until about 1800, the work of the world was done with hand tools. Since then it has been increasingly done by machines. Before about 1800 power was supplied by human or animal muscle, reinforced by levers or pulleys, and supplemented by the force of running water or moving air. Since then power has been supplied by the human manipulation of more recondite natural forces found in steam, electricity, the combustion of gases, and most recently within the atom. The process of shifting from hand tools to power machinery is what is meant by the Industrial Revolution. Its beginning cannot be dated exactly. It grew gradually out of the technical practices of earlier times. It is still going on, for in some countries industrialization is barely beginning, and even in the most highly developed it is still making advances. It will in all probability continue long into the future, until some distant time when Chinese peasants plow their fields with tractors or Bolivian Indians ride in some futuramic sort of pullmans. But the first country to be profoundly affected by industrialization was Great Britain, where its effects became manifest in the half-century following 1780.

It seems likely, despite the emphasis placed on revolutionary upheavals by historians, that people are habitually quite conservative. Working men do not put off their old way of life, move to strange and overcrowded towns, or enter the deadly rounds of mine and factory except under strong incentive. Well-to-do people, living in comfort on assured incomes, do not risk their wealth in new and untried ventures except for good reason. The shifting to modern machine production requires in any country a certain mobility of people and of wealth. Such mobility may be produced by state planning, as in the industrialization of the Soviet Union in recent times. In England a high degree of social mobility existed in the eighteenth century in consequence of a long historical development.

THE AGRICULTURAL REVOLUTION IN BRITAIN

The English revolution of 1688, confirming the ascendancy of Parliament over the king, meant in economic terms the ascendancy of the more well-to-do property-owning classes.[1] Among these the landowners were by far the most important, though they counted the great London merchants among their allies. For a century and a half, from 1688 to 1832, the British government was substantially in the hands of these landowners—the "squirearchy" or "gentlemen of England." The result was a thorough transformation of farming, an Agricultural Revolution without which the Industrial Revolution could not have occurred.

Many landowners, seeking to increase their money incomes, began experimenting with improved methods of cultivation and stock-raising. They made more use of fertilizers (mainly animal manure); they introduced new implements (such as the "drill seeder" and "horse-hoe"); they brought in new crops, such as turnips, and a more scientific system of crop rotation; they attempted to breed larger sheep and fatter cattle. An improving landlord, to introduce such changes successfully, needed full control over his land. He saw a mere barrier to progress in the old village system of open fields, common lands, and semi-collective methods of cultivation. Improvement also required an investment of capital, which was impossible so long as the soil was tilled by numerous poor and custom-bound small farmers.

The old common rights of the villagers were part of the common law. Only an act of Parliament could modify or extinguish them. It was the great landowners who controlled Parliament, which therefore passed hundreds of "enclosure acts," authorizing the enclosure, by fences, walls, or hedges, of the old common lands and unfenced open fields. Land thus came under a strict regime of private ownership and individual management. At the same time small owners sold out or were excluded in various ways, the more easily since the larger owners had so much local authority as justices of the peace. Ownership of land in England, more than anywhere else in central or western Europe, became concentrated in the hands of a relatively small class of wealthy landlords, who let it out in large blocks to a relatively small class of substantial farmers. This development, though in progress throughout the eighteenth century, reached its height during the Napoleonic wars.

One result was greatly to raise the productivity of land and of farm labor. Fatter cattle yielded more meat, more assiduous cultivation yielded more cereals. The food supply of England was increased, while a smaller percentage of the population was needed to produce it. Labor was thus released for other pursuits. Socially, the results were distressing. Oliver Goldsmith reflected upon them in *The Deserted Village*:

wwwwwwwwwwwwww

[1] See pp. 154–5.

Ill fares the land, to hastening ills a prey,
Where wealth accumulates, and men decay.
Princes and lords may flourish. . . .
But a bold peasantry, their country's pride,
When once destroyed, can never be supplied.

The yeomanry, or small landowners—the "bold peasantry"—disappeared as a class. The greater number of the English country people became wage laborers, working as hired men for the farmers and landlords, or spinning or weaving in their cottages for merchants in the towns. The English working man (and woman) was dependent on daily wages long before the coming of the factory and the machine. English working people became mobile; they would go where the jobs were, or where the wages were slightly higher. They became also available, in that fewer of them were needed on the land to produce food. Such conditions hardly obtained except in Great Britain. On the Continent agricultural methods were less productive, and the rural workers were more established on the soil, whether by institutions of serfdom as in eastern Europe, or by the possession of property or firm leaseholds as in France.[2]

INDUSTRIALISM IN BRITAIN: INCENTIVES AND INVENTIONS

Meanwhile, as the Agricultural Revolution ran its course in the eighteenth century and into the nineteenth, the British had conquered a colonial empire, staked out markets all over the Americas and Europe, built up a huge mercantile marine, and won command of the sea. The British merchant could sell more, if only more could be produced. He had the customers, he had the ships, and moreover he had the capital with which to finance new ideas. The profit motive prompted the search for more rapid methods of production. The old English staple export, woollen cloth, could be marketed indefinitely if only more of it could be woven. The possibilities in cotton cloth were enormous. The taste of Europeans for cottons had been already formed by imports from Asia. By hand methods Europeans could not produce cotton in competition with the East. But the market was endless if cotton could be spun, woven, and printed with less labor, *i.e.*, by machines. Capital was available, mobile and fluid, because of the rise of banking, credit, and stock companies. Funds could be shifted from one enterprise to another. Wealthy landowners could divert some of their profits to industry. If an invention proved a total loss, as sometimes happened, or if it required years of development before producing any income, still the investment could be afforded. Only a country already wealthy from commerce and agriculture could have been the first to initiate the machine age. England was such a country.

These conditions induced a series of successful inventions in the textile industry. In 1733 a man named John Kay invented the fly shuttle, by which

---

[2] See pp. 174-5.

only one man instead of two was needed to operate a loom. The resulting increase in the output of weaving set up a strong demand for yarn. This was met in the 1760's by the invention of the spinning jenny, a kind of mechanized spinning wheel. The new shuttles and jennies were at first operated by hand and used by domestic workers in their homes. But in 1769 Richard Arkwright patented the water-frame, a device for the multiple spinning of many threads. At first it was operated by water power, but in the 1780's Arkwright introduced the steam engine to drive his spinning machinery. Thus requiring a considerable installation of heavy equipment, he gathered his engines, frames, and workers into large and usually dismal buildings, called "mills" by the English, or "factories" in subsequent American usage. Mechanical spinning now for a time overwhelmed the hand weavers with yarn. This led to the development of the power loom, which became economically practicable shortly after 1800. Weaving as well as spinning was therefore done increasingly in factories. These improvements in the finishing process put a heavy strain on the production of raw cotton. An ingenious Connecticut Yankee, Eli Whitney, while acting as a tutor on a plantation in Georgia, in ten days produced a cotton gin, which by speeding up the removal of seeds greatly increased the output of cotton. The gin soon spread through the American South, where the almost decaying plantation economy was abruptly revived, becoming an adjunct to the Industrial Revolution in England. British imports of raw cotton multiplied fivefold in the thirty years following 1790. In value of manufactures, cotton rose from ninth to first place among British industries in the same years. By 1820 it made up almost half of all British exports.

The steam engine, applied to the cotton mills in the 1780's, had for a century been going through a development of its own.[3] Scientific and technical experiments with steam pressures had been fairly common in the seventeenth century, but what gave the economic impetus to invention was the gradual dwindling away of Europe's primeval stocks of timber. The wood shortage became acute in England about 1700, so that it was more difficult to obtain the charcoal needed in smelting iron, and smelters turned increasingly to coal. Deeper coal shafts could not be sunk until someone devised better methods of pumping out water. About 1702 Thomas Newcomen built the first economically significant steam engine, which was soon widely used to drive pumps in the coal mines. It consumed so much fuel in proportion to power delivered that it could generally be used only in the coal fields themselves. In 1763 James Watt, a technician at the University of Glasgow, began to make improvements on Newcomen's engine. He formed a business partnership with Matthew Boulton. Boulton, originally a manufacturer of toys, buttons, and shoe buckles, provided the funds to finance Watt's rather costly experiments, hand-made equipment, and slowly germinating ideas. By the 1780's the firm of Boulton and Watt was eminently successful, manufacturing steam engines both for British use and for the export trade.

At first, until further refinements and greater precision could be ob-

[3] See p. 271.

tained in the working of iron, the engines were so cumbersome that they could be used as stationary engines only, as in the new spinning mills of Arkwright and others. Soon after 1800 the steam engine was successfully used to propel river boats, notably on the Hudson in 1806, by Robert Fulton, who employed an imported Boulton and Watt engine. Experiments with steam power for land transportation began at the same time. As it was in the coal fields of England a century before that Newcomen's engine had been put to practical uses, so now it was in the coal fields that Watt's engine first became a "locomotive." Well before 1800 the mines had taken to using "rail ways," on which wagons with flanged wheels, drawn by horses, carried coal to canals or to the sea. In the 1820's steam engines were successfully placed on moving vehicles. The first fully satisfactory locomotive was George Stephenson's *Rocket*, which in 1829, on the newly built Liverpool and Manchester Railway, not only reached an impressive speed of sixteen miles per hour but met other more important tests as well. By the 1840's the era of railroad construction was under way in both Europe and the United States.

The Industrial Revolution in Great Britain in its early phase, down to 1830 or 1840, took place principally in the manufacture of textiles, with accompanying developments in the exploitation of iron and coal. The early factories were principally textile factories, and indeed mainly cotton mills; for cotton was an entirely new industry to Europe, and hence easily mechanized, whereas the long established woollen trade, in which both employers and workers hesitated to abandon their customary ways, was mechanized more slowly. The suddenness of the change must not be exaggerated. It is often said that the Industrial Revolution was not a revolution at all. As late as the 1830's only a small fraction of the British working people were employed in factories. But the factory and the factory system were even then regarded as the coming mode of production, destined to grow and expand, mighty symbols of the irresistible march of progress.

SOME SOCIAL CONSEQUENCES OF INDUSTRIALISM IN BRITAIN

The Britain that emerged fundamentally unscathed and in fact strengthened from the wars with Napoleon was no longer the "merrie England" of days of yore. The island was becoming crowded with people, as was the lesser island of Ireland. The combined population of Great Britain and Ireland tripled in the century from 1750 to 1850, rising from about 10,000,000 in 1750 to about 30,000,000 in 1850. The growth was distributed very unevenly. Formerly, in England, most people had lived in the south. But the coal and iron, and hence the steam power, lay in the Midlands and the north. Here whole new cities rose seemingly out of nothing. In 1785 it was estimated that in England and Scotland, outside of London, there were only three cities with more than 50,000 people. Seventy years later, the span of one lifetime, there were thirty-one British cities of this size.

Pre-eminent among them was Manchester in Lancashire, the first and

most famous of industrial cities of modern type. Manchester, before the coming of the cotton mills, was a rather large market town. Though very ancient,
it had not been significant enough to be recognized as a borough for representation in Parliament. Locally it was organized as a manor. Not until 1845 did
the inhabitants extinguish the manorial rights, buying them out at that time
from the last lord, Sir Oswald Mosley, for £200,000 or about a million dollars.
In population Manchester grew from 25,000 in 1772 to 455,000 in 1851. But
until 1835 there was no regular procedure in England for the incorporation
of cities. Urban organization was more backward than in Prussia or France.
Unless inherited from the Middle Ages, a city had no legal existence. It
lacked proper officials and adequate tax-raising and law-making powers. It was
therefore difficult for Manchester, and the other new factory towns, to deal
with problems of rapid urbanization, such as provision of police protection,
water and sewers, or the disposal of garbage.

POPULATION DENSITY
PERSONS PER SQUARE MILE
250 to 500   OVER 500   CITIES OVER 100 000

ABOUT **1700**   IN **1911**

Glasgow   Edinburgh

Newcastle
Sunderland

50 MILES

Manchester
Oldham
Halifax
Bradford
Preston   Leeds
Blackburn   Hull
Bolton
Liverpool
Sheffield
Nottingham
Derby   Norwich
Wolverhampton
Leicester
Birmingham

London

Cardiff   London

Southampton
Portsmouth   Brighton
Plymouth

ENGLAND BEFORE AND AFTER
THE INDUSTRIAL REVOLUTION
TRM

*In 1700 England, Scotland and Wales had only one city with a population
of more than 100,000. In 1911 they had nearly thirty. The area within the small
rectangle in the right-hand panel, roughly the Midlands, is almost exactly the area
of Massachusetts.*

The new urban agglomerations were drab places, blackened with the heavy soot of the early coal age, settling alike on the mills and the workers' quarters, which were dark at best, for the climate of the Midlands is not sunny. Housing for workers was hastily built, closely packed, and always in short supply, as in all rapidly growing communities. Whole families lived in single rooms, and since working-class women commonly worked all day in the factories, family life and common morals went to pieces. A police officer in Glasgow observed that there were whole blocks of tenements in the city each swarming with a thousand ragged children who had first names only, usually nicknames—like animals, as he put it.

The distressing feature of the new factories was that for the most part they required unskilled labor only. Skilled workers found themselves degraded in status. Hand weavers and spinners, thrown out of work by the new machines, either languished in a misery that was the deepest of that of any class in the Industrial Revolution, or else went off to a factory to find a job. The factories paid good wages by the standards for unskilled labor at the time. But these standards were very low, too low to allow a man to support his wife and children. This had generally been true for unskilled labor, in England and elsewhere, under earlier economic systems also. In the new factories the work was so mechanical that women and children as young as six years old were often preferred. They worked for less, and were often more adept at handling a bobbin. Most male workingmen objected indignantly to this situation; a few lived shamelessly by the spawning of large families.

Hours in the factories were long, fourteen a day or occasionally more; and though such hours were familiar to persons who had worked on farms, or at domestic industry in rural households, they were more tedious and oppressive in the more regimented conditions that were necessary in the mills. Holidays were few, except for the unwelcome leisure of unemployment, which was a common scourge, because the short-run ups and downs of business were very erratic during this period of bewildering expansion. A day without work was a day producing nothing to live on, so that even where the daily wage was relatively attractive the worker's real income was chronically insufficient. Workers in the factories, as in the mines, were almost entirely unorganized. They were a mass of recently assembled humanity without traditions or common ties. Each bargained individually with his employer, who, usually a small business man himself, facing a ferocious competition with others, often in debt for the equipment in his factory, or determined to save money in order to purchase more, held his "wages bill" to the lowest possible figure that he could manage.

The factory owners, the new "cotton lords," were the first industrial capitalists. They were often self-made men, who owed their position to their own intelligence, persistency, and foresight. They lived in comfort without ostentation or luxury, saving from each year's income to build up their factories and their machines. Hard working themselves, they thought that landed gentlemen were usually idlers and that the poor tended to be lazy. They were usually honest, in a hard and exacting way; they would make money by any means the law allowed, but not beyond it. They were neither brutal nor knowingly hard-hearted. They gave to charitable and philanthropic causes. They believed that they did "the poor" a favor by furnishing them with work and by seeing to it that they worked diligently and productively. Most of them disapproved of public regulation of their business, though a few, driven by competition to expedients that they did not like, such as the employment of small children, would have accepted some regulation that fell on all competitors equally. It was a cotton magnate, the elder Robert Peel, who in 1802 pushed the first Factory Act through Parliament. This act purported to regulate the conditions in which pauper children were employed in the textile mills, but it was a deadletter from the beginning, since it provided no adequate body of factory inspectors. The English at this time, alone among the leading European peoples, had no class of trained, paid, and professional government administrators; nor did they yet want such a class, preferring self-government and local initiative. To have inspectors for one's affairs smacked of Continental bureaucracy. The fact that the older methods of economic regulation were obsolescent, actually unsuited to the new age, had the effect of discrediting the idea of regulation itself. The new industrialists wanted to be let alone. They considered it unnatural to interfere with business, and believed that, if allowed to follow their own judgment, they would assure the future prosperity and progress of the country.

CLASSICAL ECONOMICS: "LAISSEZ-FAIRE"

The industrialists were strengthened in these beliefs by the emerging science of "political economy." In 1776 Adam Smith published his epochal *Wealth of Nations,* which criticized the older mercantilism, with its regulatory and monopolistic practices, and urged, though with moderation, that certain "natural laws" of production and exchange be allowed to work themselves out. Smith was followed by Thomas R. Malthus, David Ricardo, and the so-called Manchester School. Their doctrine was dubbed (by its opponents) *laissez-faire,* and in its elaborated form is still called the classical economics. It held, basically, that there is a world of economic relationships autonomous and separable from government or politics. The economic world, in this view, is regulated within itself by certain "natural laws," such as the law of supply and demand or the law of diminishing returns. All persons should follow their own enlightened self-interest; each knows his own interest better than anyone else; and the sum total of individual interests will add up to the general welfare and liberty of all. Government should do as little as possible; it should confine itself to preserving security of life and property, providing reasonable laws and reliable courts, and so assuring the discharge of private contracts, debts, and obligations. Not only business, but education, charity, and personal matters generally should be left to private initiative. There should be no tariffs; free trade should reign everywhere, for the economic system is world-wide, unaffected by political barriers or national differences. As for the workingman, according to classical economists before about 1850, he should not expect to make more than a bare minimum living; an "iron law of wages" brings it about that as soon as the worker receives more than a subsistence wage he breeds more children, who eat up the excess, so that he reduces himself, and the working class generally, again to a subsistence level. The workingman, if discontented, should see the folly of changing the system, for this *is* the system, the natural system—there is no other. Political economy as taught in grim Manchester was not without reason called the "dismal science."

For working people in England the Industrial Revolution was a hard experience. It should be remembered, however, that neither low wages, nor the fourteen-hour day, nor the labor of women and children, nor the ravages of unemployment were anything new. All had existed for centuries, in England and western Europe, as agricultural and commercial capitalism replaced the more self-sufficient economies of the Middle Ages. The factory towns were in some ways better places to live than the rural slums from which many of their people came. Factory routine was psychologically deadening, but the textile mills were in some ways not worse than the domestic sweatshops in which manufacturing processes had previously been carried on. The concentration of working people in city and factory opened the way to improvement in their condition. It made their misery apparent; philanthropic sentiment was gradually aroused among the more fortunate. Gathered in cities, workers obtained more knowledge of the world. Mingling and talking together they developed a sense of solidarity, class interest, and common political aims; and in time they became organized, establishing labor unions by which to obtain a larger share of the national income.

Britain after the fall of Napoleon became the workshop of the world. Though factories using steam power sprang up in France, Belgium, New England, and elsewhere, it was really not until after 1870 that Great Britain faced any industrial competition from abroad. The British had a virtual monopoly in textiles and machine tools. The English Midlands and Scottish Lowlands shipped cotton thread and steam engines to all the world. British capital was exported to all countries, there to call new enterprises into being. London became the world's clearinghouse and financial center. Progressive people in other lands looked to Britain as their model, hoping to learn from its advanced industrial methods, and to imitate its parliamentary political system. Thus more foundations of the nineteenth century were laid.

51. The Advent of the "Isms"

The combined forces of industrialization and of the French Revolution led after 1815 to the proliferation of doctrines and movements of many sorts. These broke out in a general European revolution in 1848. As for the thirty-three years from 1815 to 1848. there is no better way of grasping their long-run meaning than to reflect on the number of still living "isms" that arose at that time.

So far as is known the word "liberalism" first appeared in the English language in 1819, "radicalism" in 1820, "socialism" in 1832, "conservatism" in 1835. The 1830's first saw "individualism," "constitutionalism," "humanitarianism," and "monarchism." "Nationalism" and "communism" date from the 1840's. Not until the 1850's did the English-speaking world use the word "capitalism" (French *capitalisme* is much older); and not until even later had it heard of "Marxism," though the doctrines of Marx grew out of and reflected the troubled times of the 1840's.

The rapid coinage of political "isms" does not in every case mean that the ideas they conveyed were new. Men had loved liberty before talking of liberalism, and been conservative without knowing conservatism as such. The appearance of so many "isms" shows rather that people were making their ideas more systematic. They were being obliged to reconsider and analyze society as a whole. The social sciences were taking form. An "ism" (excluding such words as "hypnotism" or "favoritism") may be defined as the conscious espousal of a doctrine in competition with other doctrines. Without the "isms" created in the thirty-odd years after the Peace of Vienna it is impossible to understand or even talk about the history of the world since that event, so that a brief characterization of some of the most important is in order.

ROMANTICISM

One of the "isms" was not political. It was called "romanticism," a word first used in English in the 1840's to describe a movement then half a century old. Romanticism was primarily a theory of literature and the arts. Its great exponents included Wordsworth, Shelley, and Byron in England, Victor Hugo and Chateaubriand in France, Schiller and the Schlegels and many others in Germany. As a theory of art it raised basic questions on the nature of significant truth, on the importance of various human faculties, on the relation of thought and feeling, on the meaning of the past and of time itself. Representing a new way of sensing all human experience, it affected most thinking on social and public questions.

Possibly the most fundamental romantic attitude was a love of the unclassifiable—of moods or impressions, scenes or stories, sights or sounds or things concretely experienced, personal idiosyncrasies or peculiar customs which the intellect could never classify, box up, explain away, or reduce to an abstract generalization. The romantics, characteristically, insisted on the value of feeling as well as of reason. They were aware of the importance of the subconscious. They were likely to suspect a perfectly lucid idea as somehow superficial. They loved the mysterious, the unknown, the half-seen figures on the far horizon. Hence romanticism contributed to a new interest in strange and distant societies and in strange and distant historical epochs.

Where the *philosophes* of the Enlightenment had deplored the Middle Ages as a time of intellectual error, the romantic generation looked back upon them with respect and even nostalgia, finding in them a fascination, a colorfulness, or a spiritual depth which they missed in their own time. The "Gothic," which rationalists thought barbarous, had a strong appeal for romantics. A Gothic Revival set in in the arts, of which one example was the British Parliament buildings, built in the 1830's.

In medieval art and institutions, as in the art and institutions of every age and people, the romantics saw the expression of an inner genius. The idea of original or creative genius was in fact another of the most fundamental romantic beliefs. A genius was a dynamic spirit that no rules could hem in, one that no analysis or classification could ever fully explain. Genius, it was thought, made its own rules and laws. The genius might be that of the individual person, such as the artist, writer, or Napoleon-like mover of the world. It might be the genius or spirit of an age. Or it might be the genius of a people or nation, the *Volksgeist* of Herder, an inherent national character making each people grow in its own distinctive way, which could be known only by a study of its history, and not by ratiocination.[4] Here again romanticism gave a new impetus to study of the past. Politically, romantics could be found in all camps, conservative and radical. Let us turn to the more purely political "isms."

CLASSICAL LIBERALISM

The first Liberals, calling themselves by that name (though Napoleon used that word for his own system, as has been seen[5]), arose in Spain among certain opponents of the Napoleonic occupation. The word then passed to France, where it denoted opposition to royalism after the restoration of the Bourbons in 1814. In England many Whigs became increasingly liberal, as did even a few Tories, until the great Liberal party was founded in the 1850's. Nineteenth-century, or "classical," liberalism varied from country to country, but it showed many basic similarities.

Liberals were generally men of the business and professional classes, together with enterprising landowners wishing to improve their estates. They believed in what was modern, enlightened, efficient, reasonable, and fair. They had confidence in man's powers of self-government and self-control. They set a high value on parliamentary or representative government, working through reasonable discussion and legislation, with responsible ministries and an impartial and law-abiding administration. They demanded full publicity for all actions of government, and to assure such publicity they insisted on freedom of the press and free rights of assembly. All these political advantages they thought most likely to be realized under a good constitutional

wwwwwwwwwwwww

[4] See pp. 403–4.
[5] See p. 392.

monarchy. Outside of England they favored explicit written constitutions. They were not democrats; they opposed giving every man the vote, fearing the excesses of mob rule or of irrational political action. Only as the nineteenth century progressed did liberals gradually and reluctantly come to accept the idea of universal manhood suffrage. They subscribed to the doctrines of the rights of man as set forth in the American and French Revolutions, but with a clear emphasis on the right of property, and in their economic views they followed the British Manchester school or the French economist J. B. Say.[6] They favored *laissez-faire*, were suspicious of the ability of government to regulate business, wanted to get rid of the gild system where it still existed, and disapproved of attempts on the part of the new industrial laborers to organize unions. Internationally they advocated freedom of trade, to be accomplished by the lowering or abolition of tariffs, so that all countries might exchange their products easily with each other and with industrial England. In this way, they thought, each country would produce what it was most fitted for, and so best increase its wealth and standards of living. From the growth of wealth, production, invention, and scientific progress they believed that the general progress of humanity would ensue. They generally frowned upon the established churches and landed aristocracies as obstacles to advancement. They believed in the spread of tolerance and education. They were also profoundly civilian in attitude, disliking wars, conquerors, army officers, standing armies, and military expenditures. They wanted orderly change by processes of legislation. They shrank before the idea of revolution. Liberals on the Continent were usually admirers of Great Britain.

RADICALISM, REPUBLICANISM, SOCIALISM

Radicalism, at least as a word, originated in England, where about 1820 the Philosophical Radicals proudly applied the term to themselves. These Radicals in the 1820's included not only the few working-class leaders who were beginning to emerge but also many of the new industrial capitalists, who were still unrepresented in Parliament. They took up where such English "Jacobins" as Thomas Paine had left off a generation earlier, before the long crisis of the French wars had discredited all radicalism as pro-French.[7]

The Philosophical Radicals were a good deal like the French *philosophes* before the Revolution. They were followers of an elderly sage, Jeremy Bentham, who in prolific writings from 1776 to 1832 undertook to reform the English criminal and civil law, church, Parliament, and constitution. The English Radicals professed to deduce the right form of institutions from the very nature and psychology of man himself. They impatiently waved aside all arguments based on history, usage, or custom. They went to the "roots"

wwwwwwwwwwwwww

[6] See pp. 429–30.
[7] See pp. 352, 366.

of things. They wanted a total reconstruction of laws, courts, prisons, poor relief, municipal organization, rotten boroughs, and fox-hunting clergy. Their demand for the reform of Parliament was vehement and insistent. They detested the Church of England, the peerage, and the squirearchy. Many radicals would just as soon abolish royalty also; not until the long reign of Queen Victoria (1837–1901) did the British monarchy become undeniably popular in all quarters. Above all, radicalism was democratic; it demanded a vote for every adult Englishman. After the Reform Bill of 1832 the industrial capitalists generally turned into liberals, but the working class leaders remained radical democrats, as will be seen.

On the Continent radicalism was represented by militant republicanism. The years of the First French Republic, which to liberals and conservatives signified horrors associated with the Reign of Terror, were for the republicans years of hope and progress, cut short by forces of reaction. Republicans were a minority even in France; elsewhere, as in Italy and Germany, they were fewer still, though they existed. Mostly the republicans were drawn from intelligentsia such as students and writers, from working class leaders protesting at social injustice, and from elderly veterans, or the sons and nephews of veterans, to whom the Republic of '93, with its wars and its glory, was a living thing. Because of police repression, republicans often joined together in secret societies. They looked with equanimity on the prospect of further revolutionary upheaval, by which they felt that the cause of liberty, equality, and fraternity would be advanced. Strong believers in political equality, they were democrats demanding universal suffrage. They favored parliamentary government, but were much less primarily concerned with its successful operation than were the liberals. Most republicans were bitterly anticlerical. Remembering the internecine struggle between the church and the republic during the French Revolution, and still facing the political activity of the Catholic clergy (for republicanism was most common in Catholic countries), they regarded the Catholic Church as the implacable enemy of reason and liberty. Opposed to monarchy of any kind, even to constitutional monarchy, intensely hostile to church and aristocracy, conscious heirs of the great French Revolution, organized in national and international secret societies, not averse to overthrowing existing regimes by force, the more militant republicans were considered by most people, including the liberals, to be little better than anarchists.

Republicanism shaded off into socialism. Socialists generally shared the political attitudes of republicanism but added other views besides. The early socialists, those before the revolution of 1848, were of many kinds, but all had certain ideas in common. All of them regarded the existing economic system as aimless, chaotic, and outrageously unjust. All thought it improper for owners of wealth to have so much economic power—to give or deny work to the worker, to set wages and hours in their own interests, to guide all the labors of society in the interests of private profit. All therefore questioned the value of private enterprise, favoring some degree of communal ownership of productive assets—banks, factories, machines, land, and transportation.

All disliked competition as a governing principle, and set forth principles of harmony, coordination, organization, or association instead. All flatly and absolutely rejected the *laissez-faire* of the liberals and the political economists. Where the latter thought mainly of increasing production, without much concern over distribution, the early socialists thought mainly of a fairer or more equal distribution of income among all useful members of society. They believed that beyond the civil and legal equality brought in by the French Revolution a further step toward social and economic equality had yet to be taken.

One of the first socialists was also one of the first cotton lords, Robert Owen (1771–1858) of Manchester and the Scottish Lowlands. Appalled at the condition of the mill-hands, he created a kind of model community for his own employees, paying high wages, reducing hours, sternly correcting vice and drunkenness, building schools and housing and company stores for the cheap sale of workers' necessities. From such paternalistic capitalism in his early years he passed on to a long lifetime spent in crusading for social reforms, in which he was somewhat handicapped, not only by the opposition of industrialists, but by his unpopular radicalism in matters of religion.

Most of the early socialists were Frenchmen, spurred onward by the sense of an uncompleted revolution. One was a nobleman, the Count de Saint-Simon (1760–1825), who had fought in the War of American Independence, accepted the French Revolution, and in his later years wrote many books on social problems. He and his followers, who called themselves not socialists but Saint-Simonians, were among the first clear exponents of a planned society. They advocated the public ownership of industrial equipment and other capital, with control vested in the hands of great captains of industry or social engineers, who should plan vast projects like the digging of a canal at Suez, and in general coordinate the labor and resources of society to productive ends. Of a different type was Charles Fourier (1772–1837), a somewhat doctrinaire thinker who subjected all known institutions to a sweeping condemnation. His positive program took the form of proposing that society be organized in small units which he termed "phalansteries." Each of these he conceived to contain 1,620 persons, each doing the work suited to his natural inclination. Among the practical French no phalanstery was ever successfully organized. A number were established in the United States, still the land of Europe's utopian dream; the best known, since it was operated by literary people, was the Brook Farm "movement" in Massachusetts, which ran through a troubled existence of five years from 1842 to 1847. Robert Owen also, in 1825, had founded an experimental colony in America, at New Harmony, Indiana, on the then remote and unspoiled banks of the Wabash; it, too, lasted only about five years. Such schemes, presupposing the withdrawal of select spirits to live by themselves, really had little to say on the problems of society as a whole in an industrial age.

Politically the most significant form of antediluvian socialism—before the "deluge" of 1848—was the movement stirring among the working classes of Paris, a compound of revolutionary republicanism and socialism. The politically minded Paris workingmen had been republican since 1792. For them the Revolution, in the 1820's, 1830's, 1840's, was not finished but only momentarily interrupted. Reduced to political impotence, discriminated against in their rights in the law courts, obliged to carry identity papers signed by their employers, goaded by the pressures of industrialization as it spread to France, they developed a deep hostility to the owning classes of the bourgeoisie. They found a spokesman in the Paris journalist Louis Blanc, editor of the *Revue de progrès* and author of the *Organization of Work* (1839), one of the most constructive of the early socialist writings. He proposed a system of "social workshops," or state-supported manufacturing centers, in which the workers should labor by and for themselves without the intervention of private capitalists. Of this kind of socialism we shall hear more as the story unfolds.

As for "communism," it was at this time an uncertain synonym for socialism. A small group of German revolutionaries, mainly exiles in France, took the name for themselves in the 1840's. They would have been historically forgotten had they not included Karl Marx and Frederick Engels among their members. Marx and Engels consciously used the word in 1848 to differentiate their variety of socialism from that of such utopians as St. Simon, Fourier, and Owen. But the word "communism" went out of general use after 1848, to be revived after the Russian Revolution of 1917, at which time it received a new meaning.

NATIONALISM: WESTERN EUROPE

Nationalism, since it arose so largely in reaction against the international Napoleonic system, has already been discussed in the preceding chapter.[8] It was the most pervasive and the least crystallized of the new "isms." In western Europe—Britain, France, or Spain—where national unity already existed, nationalism was not a doctrine so much as a latent state of mind, easily aroused when national interests were questioned, but normally taken

〰〰〰〰〰〰〰〰〰〰

[8] See pp. 400–8.

Languages of Europe

There are three main European language-families—Germanic, Latin and Slav. It will be seen that they cover most of Europe. Language areas are shown as they were in the first part of the twentieth century, at which time they had not changed much in over five centuries. The map cannot show local complications which have been a leading source of political trouble—such as the overlapping of adjoining languages, bilingual areas and the existence of small language "pockets," as of Turkish in the Balkans, Greek in Asia Minor, Yiddish in Poland or German in scattered parts of eastern Europe. For the area within the diamond-shaped zone no map on the present scale can give a realistic idea; the reader must consult an atlas. In any case, during the past decades, many language-pockets have been wiped out through exchange, transportation or extermination of peoples.

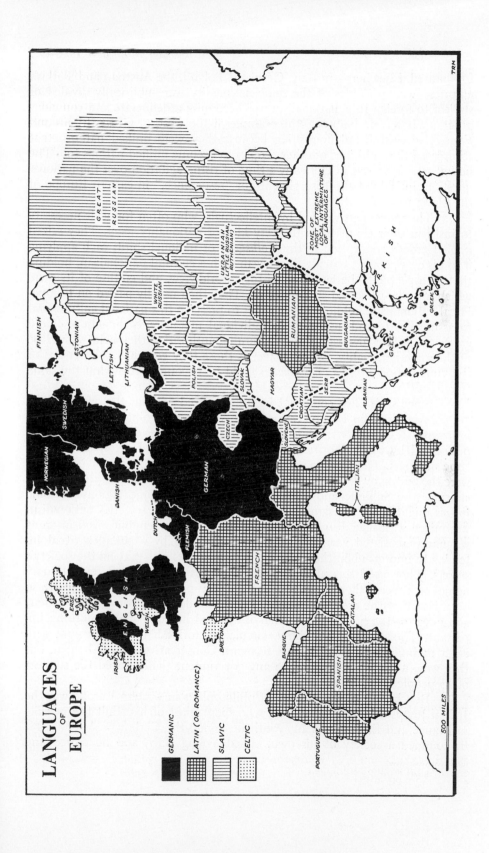

LANGUAGES
OF
EUROPE

GERMANIC

LATIN (OR ROMANCE)

SLAVIC

CELTIC

ZONE OF
MOST EXTREME
LOCAL INTERMIXTURE
OF LANGUAGES

GREAT RUSSIAN

FINNISH

ESTONIAN

LETTISH

LITHUANIAN

WHITE RUSSIAN

UKRAINIAN
(LITTLE RUSSIAN,
RUTHENIAN)

POLISH

SLOVAK

CZECH

MAGYAR

SLOVENE

CROATIAN

RUMANIAN

SERB

BULGARIAN

ALBANIAN

GREEK

GREEK

TURKISH

NORWEGIAN

SWEDISH

DANISH

DUTCH

FLEMISH

GERMAN

ENGLISH

IRISH

ERSE

WELSH

BRETON

FRENCH

ITALIAN

BASQUE

SPANISH

CATALAN

PORTUGUESE

500 MILES

TRM

for granted. Elsewhere—in Italy, Germany, Poland, the Austrian and Turkish empires—where peoples of the same nationality were politically divided or subject to foreign rule, nationalism was becoming a deliberate and conscious program. It was undoubtedly the example of the west, of Great Britain and France, successful and flourishing because they were unified nations, that stimulated the ambitions of other peoples to become unified nations too. The period after 1815 was in Germany a time of rising agitation over the national question, in Italy of the Risorgimento or "resurgence," in eastern Europe of the Slavic Revival.

The movement was led by intellectuals, who often found it necessary to instil in their compatriots the very idea of nationality itself. They seized upon Herder's conception of the *Volksgeist* or national spirit, each applying it to his own people.[9] Usually they began with a cultural nationalism, holding that each people had a language, history, world-view, and culture of its own, which must be preserved and perfected. They then usually passed on to a political nationalism, holding that in order to preserve this national culture, and to assure liberty and justice to its individual members, each nation should create for itself a sovereign state. Governing authorities, they held, should be of the same nationality, *i.e.*, language, as those they governed. All persons of the same nationality, *i.e.*, language, should be encompassed within the same state.

Since such ideas could not be fully realized without the overthrow of every government in Europe east of France, thoroughgoing nationalism was inherently revolutionary. Outspoken nationalists were discountenanced or persecuted by the authorities, and consequently formed secret societies in large numbers. The Carbonari, organized in Italy in the time of Napoleon, were the best known. There were many others, the *Veri Italiani*, the Apophasimenes, the Sublime and Perfect Masters, *etc.* In some regions Masonic lodges might serve the same purpose. In many of the societies nationalism was mixed with liberalism, socialism, or revolutionary republicanism in an as yet undifferentiated way. Members were initiated by a complex ritual intended to impress upon them the dire consequences of betraying the society's secrets. They used special grips and passwords and adopted revolutionary names to conceal their identity and baffle the police. They were usually so organized that the ordinary member knew the identity of only a few others, and never of the higher-ups, so that if arrested he could reveal nothing important. The societies kept busy, circulating forbidden literature and generally maintaining a revolutionary ferment. Conservatives dreaded them, but they were not really dangerous to any government that enjoyed the support of its people.

Best known of the nationalist philosophers in western Europe was the Italian Joseph Mazzini (1805–72), who spent most of his adult life in exile in France and England. In his youth he joined the Carbonari, but in 1831 he founded a society of his own, called Young Italy, and he edited and

[9] See pp. 403–4.

smuggled into Italy copies of a journal of the same name. Young Italy was soon imitated by other societies of similar aim, such as Young Germany. In 1834, from a base in Switzerland, Mazzini organized a kind of filibustering expedition against the kingdom of Sardinia, hoping that all Italy would rise and join him. Undeterred by its total failure, he continued to organize, to conspire, and to write. For Mazzini nationality and revolution were a holy cause in which the most generous and humane qualities were to find expression. He was a moral philosopher, as may be judged from the title of his most widely read book, *The Duties of Man,* in which he placed a pure duty to the nation intermediate between duty to family and duty to God. Mazzini sympathized with the national aspirations of all peoples, but his own feelings went out to his own Italian homeland, which he believed had a special mission to lead humanity against oppression. Mazzini was lionized by liberals in England; but being a republican he was distrusted by liberals in Italy, many of whom hoped to unify Italy without revolution, by federation of the existing monarchical and papal states under some kind of constitutional monarchy.

To the Germans, divided and frustrated, nationality became almost an obsession. It affected everything from folklore to metaphysics. *Grimm's Fairy Tales,* for example, was first published in 1812. It was the work of the two Grimm brothers, founders of the modern science of comparative linguistics, who traveled about Germany to study the popular dialects and in doing so collected the folk tales that for generations had been current among the common people. They hoped in this way to find the ancient, native, indigenous "spirit" of Germany, deep and unspoiled in the bosom of the *Volk.* The same preoccupation with nationhood revealed itself in the philosophy of Hegel (1770–1831), possibly the most stupendous of all nineteenth century thinkers.

To Hegel, with the spectacle of the Napoleonic years before him, it was evident that for a people to enjoy freedom, order, or dignity it must possess a potent and independent state. The state, for him, became the institutional embodiment of reason and liberty—the "march of God through the world," as he put it, meaning not an expansion in space through vulgar conquest, but a march through time and through the processes of history. Hegel conceived of reality itself as a process, an unfolding development, a growth having an inner logic and necessary sequence of its own. He thus broke with the more static and mechanical philosophy of the eighteenth century, with its fixed categories of unchangeable right and wrong. He became an evolutionary philosopher before the scientific theories of biological evolution were successfully framed. The pattern of change he held to be the "dialectic," or irresistible tendency of the mind to proceed by the creation of opposites. A given state of affairs (the "thesis") would in this view inevitably produce the conception of an opposite state of affairs (the "antithesis"), which would equally inevitably be followed by a reconciliation and a fusion of the two (the "synthesis"). Thus it could be thought that the very disunity of Germany, by producing the idea of unity, would inevitably bring about the creation of a German state.

The Hegelian dialectic was soon to be appropriated by Karl Marx to new uses, but meanwhile Hegel's philosophy, with other currents in Germany, made the study of history more philosophically meaningful than it had ever been before. History, the study of time process, seemed to be the very key with which to unlock the true significance of the world. Historical studies were stimulated, and the German universities became centers of historical learning attracting scholars from many countries. Most eminent of the German historians was Leopold von Ranke (1795–1886), founder of the "scientific" school of historical writing. Ranke, too, though intellectually scrupulous to the last degree, owed much of his incentive to his national feeling. His first youthful work was a study of the *Latin and Teutonic Peoples*; and one of his main ideas, throughout his long life, was that Europe owed its unique greatness to the co-existence and interplay of several distinct nations, which had always resisted the attempts of any one nation to control the whole. By the latter Ranke really meant France—the France of Louis XIV and Napoleon. The Germans, said Ranke in 1830, had a mission from God to develop a culture and a political system entirely different from those of the French. They were destined to "create the pure German state corresponding to the genius of the nation." Whether western constitutional, parliamentary, and individualist principles were suited to the national character of Germany seemed to Ranke very doubtful. The Germans, to free themselves spiritually from the French, became subtly and deeply counter-revolutionary, in that much of their most profound thought consisted in a critique of the French eighteenth-century Enlightenment and of the French Revolution and all its works.

In economics Friedrich List, in his *National System of Political Economy* (1841), came to much the same conclusion. He held that political economy as taught in England, far from being a valid science, was only a British national opinion. It was suited only to England. It was not an abstract truth, but a body of ideas developed in a certain historical stage in a certain country. List thus became a founder of the historical or institutional school of economics. The doctrine of free trade, he said, was designed to make England the world's industrial center by keeping other countries in the status of suppliers of raw material and food. But any country, he held, if it was to be civilized and develop its own national culture, must have cities, factories, industries and capital of its own. It must therefore put up high tariffs (at least temporarily, in theory) to protect itself from the British, since at the moment no one else could compete with the factories that were already humming in England. List, it should be remarked, had developed his ideas during a sojourn in the United States, where Henry Clay's "American system" was in fact a national system of political economy.

NATIONALISM: EASTERN EUROPE

In eastern Europe the Poles and the Magyars had long been active political nationalists, the Poles wishing to undo the partitions and re-establish their Polish state, the Magyars insisting on autonomy of their kingdom of Hungary within the Hapsburg empire.[10] But for the most part nationalism in eastern Europe long remained more cultural than political. Centuries of development had tended to submerge the Czechs, Slovaks, Ruthenians, Rumanians, Serbs, Croatians, Slovenians—and even the Poles and Magyars in lesser degree. Their upper classes spoke German or French, and looked to Vienna or to Paris for their ideas. The native languages had remained peasant languages, and the cultures peasant cultures, barely known to civilized Europeans. It seemed that many of these languages would disappear, as native Irish was disappearing before English.

But early in the nineteenth century the process began to reverse itself. Patriots began to demand the preservation of their historic cultures. They collected the folk tales and ballads; they studied the languages, composing grammars and dictionaries, often for the first time; and they took to writing books in their mother tongues. They urged their own educated classes to give up "foreign" ways. They wrote histories showing the famous exploits of their several peoples in the Middle Ages. A new nationalism stirred the Magyars; in 1837 a national Hungarian theater was established at Budapest. In what was to become Rumania a former Transylvanian peasant youth named George Lazar began as early as 1816 to teach at Bucharest. He lectured in Rumanian (to the surprise of the upper classes, who preferred Greek), telling how Rumania had a distinguished history back to the Roman emperor Trajan. As for the Greeks, they entertained visions of restoring the medieval Greek empire (known to Westerners as the Byzantine empire) in which persons of Greek language or Greek Orthodox religion should become the predominant people of the Balkans.

The most far-reaching of these east European movements was the Slav Revival. The Slavs included the Russians, Poles, and Ruthenians; the Czechs and Slovaks; and the South Slavs, consisting of the Slovenes, Croats, Serbs, and Bulgars. They had never had any especial consciousness of Slavdom. The Croatian Krizhanich, an early Pan-Slav of the seventeenth century, had found no response for his ideas.[11] The Napoleonic empire excited the sparsely strewn intellectuals of the Slavic world. Many were thrilled by the denouement of 1812–14, when the mighty emperor's armies had been destroyed in Slavic Russia, and a Russian tsar had ridden in triumph into Paris.

All branches of the Slavs began to come to life. In 1814 the Serb Vuk Karajich published a grammar of his native tongue and a collection of *Popular Songs and Epics of the Serbs*; he worked out a Serbian alphabet, translated the New Testament, and declared that the dialect of Ragusa should become the literary language of all South Slavs. He was opposed by the Serbian clergy, who preferred to have writing confined to Slavonic, a purely learned language, like Latin; but he found much support outside Serbia, including that of the brothers Grimm. The Czechs had always been a more advanced peo-

[10] On the Poles, see pp. 219–23, 402; on the Magyars, pp. 192, 247, 309–10.
[11] See p. 208.

ple than the Serbs, but educated Czechs were usually half Germanized. In
1836 the historian Palacky published the first volume of his *History of Bohemia*. It was designed to give the Czechs a new pride in their national past.
A widely instructed man, who knew German, French, and English, Palacky
first wrote his book in German, the common reading language of educated
Czechs. But he soon recast it into Czech, significantly re-entitling it a *History of the Czech People*. Among Poles the poet and revolutionary Adam
Mickiewicz may be mentioned. Arrested by the Russians in 1823 for membership in a secret society, he was soon allowed by the tsarist government to
pass into western Europe. From 1840 to 1844 he taught Slavic languages at
the Collège de France, using his lecture platform as a rostrum to deliver eloquent pleas for the liberation of all peoples and overthrow of autocracy. He
wrote epic poems on Polish historical themes, and continued to be active
among the revolutionary Polish exiles settled in France.

Russia itself, which Poles and Czechs regarded as very backward, was
slower to develop a pronounced national sense. Under the Tsar Alexander I
a Western or European orientation prevailed, but in Alexander's last years
and after his death the doctrines of Slavophilism began to spread. Russian
Slavophilism, or the idea that Russia possessed a way of life of its own, different from and not to be corrupted by that of Europe, was simply the application to Russia of the fundamental idea of the *Volksgeist*. Such views in Russia were at least as old as the opposition to the reforms of Peter the Great.[12]
In the nationalistic nineteenth century they crystallized more systematically
into an "ism," and they tended to merge into Pan-Slavism, which made substantially the same assertions for the Slavic peoples as a whole. But Pan-
Slavism, before 1848, was no more than embryonic.

OTHER "ISMS"

Liberalism, radical republicanism, socialism, and nationalism were
after 1815 the political forces driving Europe onward toward a future still
unknown. Of other "isms" less need be said. Conservatism, too, remained
strong. Politically, on the Continent, conservatism upheld the institutions of
absolute monarchy, aristocracy, and church, and opposed the constitutional
and representative government sought by liberals. As a political philosophy,
conservatism built upon the ideas of Edmund Burke, who had held that
every people must change its institutions by gradual adaptation, and that no
people could suddenly realize in the present any freedoms not already well
prepared for in the past.[13] This doctrine lacked appeal for those to whom
the past had been a series of misfortunes. Conservatism sometimes passed
into nationalism, since it stressed the firmness and continuity of national
character. But nationalists at this time were more often liberals or republi-

[12] See pp. 216–17, 313.
[13] See p. 352.

cans. "Monarchism" was conservative, and even reactionary. Gone was the enlightened despotism of the last century, when kings had boldly irritated their nobles and defied their churches. After the thunders of the French Revolution aristocracy and monarchy huddled together, and their new watchword was to maintain "the throne and the altar."

Deeper than other "isms," a feeling shared in varying ways by people of all parties, was the profound current of humanitarianism. It consisted in a heightened sense of the reality of cruelty inflicted upon others. Here the thought of the Age of Enlightenment suffered no reversal. Torture was gone, and even backward governments showed no inclination to restore it. Conditions in prisons, hospitals, insane asylums, and orphanages improved. People began to be moved by the misery of pauper children, chimney sweeps, women in the mines, and Negro slaves. Russian serf-owners and American slaveowners began to show psychological signs of moral doubt. To degrade a human being, use him as a work animal, torture him, confine him unjustly, hold him as a hostage for others, tear apart his family, and punish his relatives were regarded by Europeans as foreign to true civilization, something distant, "Turkish" or "Asiatic," like the castration of eunuchs, the impressment of janissaries, or the burning of widows. The Christian sense of the inviolability of the human person was now again, in a mundane way, beginning to relieve the sufferings of humanity.

52. The Dike and the Flood: Domestic

It is time now to resume the narrative of political events, broken off at the close of the last chapter with the peace settlement of 1814–15. The governments that defeated Napoleon wanted to assure themselves above all else that the disturbances of the past twenty-five years would not be renewed. In France the restored Bourbon king, Louis XVIII, aspired to keep his throne for himself and his successors. In Great Britain the Tory governing class hoped to preserve the old England that they had so valiantly saved from the clutches of Bonaparte. In Germany, Austria, Italy, and central Europe the chief aim of Metternich, who for another thirty-three years remained the master mind of these regions, was to maintain a system in which the prestige of the Hapsburg dynasty should be supreme. The aims of the tsar, Alexander, were less clear. He was feared by representatives of the other powers as a dreamer, a self-chosen world-savior, a man who said he wanted to bring Christianity into politics, a crowned Jacobin, and even a liberal. It became one of Metternich's chief hopes to convert Alexander to conservatism.

The arrangements made by the victorious powers were in some ways moderate, at least when the provocations they had undergone in the late wars are considered. Partly by the tsar's insistence written constitutions existed after 1814 in France and in Russian or "Congress" Poland. Some of the rulers of south German states allowed a measure of representative government. Even the king of Prussia promised a representative assembly for his kingdom, though the promise was not kept. But it was difficult to maintain any kind of stability. The forces of the political right, the privileged classes (or in France the former privileged classes) denounced all signs of liberalism as dangerous concessions to revolution. Those of the political left—liberals, nationalists, republicans—regarded the newly installed regimes as hopelessly reactionary and inadequate. Statesmen were jittery on the subject of revolution, so that they met every sign of agitation with attempts at repression, which though they might drive agitation temporarily underground really only made it worse by creating additional grievances. A vicious circle was set endlessly revolving. "Kings will be tyrants from policy when subjects are rebels from principle," as Edmund Burke had sagaciously remarked in 1790; but a less conservative observer might have put the idea in reverse form with equal truth: that subjects would be rebels from principle when governments were repressive by policy. Both statements describe what happened in the years immediately following the peace of Vienna.

REACTION AFTER 1815: FRANCE, POLAND

In France Louis XVIII in 1814 granted an amnesty to the regicides of 1793. But the regicides, like all republicans, found the France of 1814 an uncomfortable place to live in, exposed as they were to the unofficial vengeance of counter-revolutionaries, and in 1815 most of them rallied to Napoleon when he returned from Elba. This exasperated the royalist counter-revolutionaries beyond all measure. A brutal "white terror" broke out. Upper-class youths murdered Bonapartists and republicans, Catholic mobs seized and killed Protestants at Marseilles and Toulouse. The Chamber of Deputies chosen in 1815 (by the tiny electorate of 100,000 well-to-do landowners) proved to be more royalist than the king—*plus royaliste que le roi*. The king himself could not control the mounting frenzy of reaction, which he was sensible enough to realize would only infuriate the revolutionary element still further, as in fact happened. In 1820 a fanatical workingman assassinated the king's nephew, the Duke de Berry. Those who said that all partisans of the French Revolution were criminal extremists seemed to be justified. The reaction deepened, until in 1824 Louis XVIII died and was succeeded by his brother Charles X. Not only was Charles X the father of the recently murdered Duke de Berry, but for over thirty years he had been the acknowledged leader of implacable counter-revolution. As the Count of Artois, youngest brother of Louis XVI, he had been among the first to emigrate in 1789. He had always remained the leader of the émigrés during the Revolution, and was in fact the favorite Bourbon among the most obstinate ex-*seigneurs*, nobles, and churchmen. He regarded himself as hereditary absolute monarch by the grace of God, had himself crowned at Rheims with all the romantic pomp of ages past, and proceeded to stamp out not only revolutionary republicanism but liberalism and constitutionalism as well.

In Poland, it will be recalled, the Vienna settlement created a constitutional kingdom, with Alexander as king, joined in merely personal union with the Russian empire. The new machinery did not work very well. The Polish constitution provided for an elected diet, a very wide suffrage by the standards of the day, the Napoleonic civil code, freedom of press and religion and exclusive use of the Polish language. But the Poles discovered that Alexander, though favoring liberty, did not like to have anyone disagree with him. They could make little use of their much touted freedom in any actual legislation. The elected diet could not get along with the viceroy, who was a Russian. In Russia the serf-owning aristocracy viewed Alexander's idea of a constitutional kingdom in Poland with a jaundiced eye. They wanted no experimentation with liberty on the very borders of Russia. The Poles themselves played into the hands of their enemies. For the Poles were nationalist at least as much as they were liberal. They were dissatisfied with the boundaries accorded to Congress Poland. They dreamed of the vast kingdom that had existed before the First Partition, and so agitated the interminable question of the Eastern Border, laying claim to huge territories in the Ukraine and White Russia.[14] Alexander actually took steps to transfer parts of the Eastern Border to Poland; to him it made no difference, so long as he ruled both Poland and Russia, but it produced a violent reaction among the Russians. At the University of Vilna, in the Border region, the tsar himself encouraged the systematic study of Polish culture and history. He was dismayed when professors and students began to join secret societies. Some members of these societies were revolutionaries aiming at driving out Alexander, reuniting with Prussian and Austrian Poland, and reconstituting an independent Polish state. It was in the discovery and breaking up of one such society, the Philarets of Vilna, that Adam Mickiewicz was arrested in 1823. Reaction and repression now struck the University of Vilna.

REACTION AFTER 1815: THE GERMAN STATES, BRITAIN

In Germany those who had felt national stirrings during the Wars of Liberation were disillusioned by the peace treaty, which maintained the several German principalities about as Napoleon had left them, and purposely united them only in a loose federation or *Bund*. National ideas were most common in the numerous universities, where students and professors were more susceptible than most people to the doctrines of an eternal *Volksgeist* and a far-flung *Deutschtum*. National ideas, being a glorification of the German common people, carried with them a kind of liberal-democratic opposition to aristocrats, princes and kings. Students in many of the universities in 1815 formed college clubs, called collectively the *Burschenschaft*, which, as centers of serious political discussion, were to replace the older clubs devoted to drinking and dueling. The *Burschenschaft*, a kind of German youth move-

14 See map, p. 221.

ment, held a nation-wide congress at Wartburg in 1817. Students listened to rousing speeches by patriotic professors, marched about in "Teutonic" costume and burned a few reactionary books. This undergraduate performance was no immediate threat to any established state, but the nervous governments took alarm. In 1819 a theology student assassinated the German writer Kotzebue, known as an informer in the service of the tsar. The assassin received hundreds of letters of congratulation, and at Nassau the head of the local government barely escaped the same fate at the hands of a pharmacy student.

Metternich now chose to intervene. He had no authority in Germany except in that Austria was a member of the Germanic federation. He regarded all these manifestations of German national spirit, or of any demand for a more solidly unified Germany, as a threat to the favorable position of the Austrian empire and to the whole balance of Europe. He called a conference of the principal German states at Carlsbad in Bohemia; the frightened conferees adopted certain resolutions, proposed by Metternich, which were soon enacted by the diet of the *Bund*. These Carlsbad Decrees (1819) dissolved the *Burschenschaft* and the equally nationalistic gymnastic clubs (some of whose members thereupon joined secret societies); and they provided for government officials to be placed in the universities to watch them, and for censors to control the contents of books and of the periodical and newspaper press. The Carlsbad Decrees remained in force for many years, and they imposed a rather effective check on the growth of liberal and nationalist ideas in Germany, especially since they seem not to have been very strongly resisted by any substantial element of the population.

Metternich was unable to persuade the south German rulers to retract the constitutions they had granted. The rulers here, in Bavaria, Würtemberg and elsewhere, found that with representative government they could rally popular support as well as assimilate the numerous new territories that they had obtained from Napoleon. But in general, throughout Germany, after 1820, repression of new or unsettling ideas was the rule. Still more so was this true of the Austrian empire, which Metternich could more directly control. So manifold were the regulations governing Austrian intercourse with the outside world, so rigid was Metternich's stand against change or innovation of any kind, that Austria came to be known as the China of Europe.

Nor did Great Britain escape the dreary rounds of agitation and repression. As elsewhere, radicalism produced reaction, and vice versa. Britain after Waterloo was still a country of the old regime, but one afflicted by the most advanced social evils. In 1815, at the close of the wars, the landed classes feared an inrush of imported agricultural products and consequent collapse of farm prices and rentals. The gentry who controlled Parliament enacted a new Corn Law, raising the protective tariff on imports of grains to the point where importation became impossible unless prices were very high. Landlords and their farmers benefited, but wage-earners found the price of breadstuffs soaring out of reach. At the same time there was a post-war depression in industry. Wages fell and many were thrown out of work. These conditions naturally contributed to the spread of political radicalism, which looked first of all to a drastic reform of the House of Commons, in order that thereafter a radical program of social and economic legislation might be enacted.

A riot broke out in London in December 1816. In the following February the Prince Regent was attacked in his carriage. The government suspended *habeas corpus* and employed *agents provocateurs* to obtain evidence against the agitators. Industrialists of Manchester and the new factory towns, determined to force through the reform of Parliamentary representation, took the chance offered by the distress of the working classes to organize mass meetings of protest. At Birmingham a crowd elected a mock member of Parliament. At sprawling Manchester 80,000 people staged an enormous demonstration at St. Peter's Fields in 1819; they demanded universal male suffrage, annual election of the House of Commons and the repeal of the Corn Laws. Although perfectly orderly they were fired upon by soldiers; eleven persons were killed and about four hundred wounded, including a hundred and thirteen women. Radicals called this episode the Peterloo massacre in derisive comparison with the battle of Waterloo. The frightened government thanked the soldiers for their brave upholding of the social order. Parliament rushed through the Six Acts (1819), which outlawed "seditious and blasphemous" literature, put a heavy stamp tax on newspapers, authorized the search of private houses for arms, and rigidly restricted the right of public meeting. A group of revolutionaries thereupon plotted to assassinate the whole cabinet at a dinner; they were caught in Cato Street in London in 1820—whence the name "Cato Street Conspiracy." Five of them were hanged. Meanwhile, for publishing the writings of Thomas Paine, Richard Carlisle spent seven years in prison.

"Our example," wrote the Duke of Wellington to a Continental correspondent in 1819, "will be of value in France and Germany, and it is to be hoped that the world will escape from the general revolution with which we all seem to be threatened."

In summary, reactionary policies entrenched themselves everywhere in the years following the peace. The reaction was due only in part to memories of the French Revolution. It was due even more to the living fear of revolution in the present. This fear, though exaggerated, was no mere hallucination. Sensing the rising flood, the established interests desperately built dikes against it in every country. The same is true of international politics at the time.

53. The Dike and the Flood: International

At the Congress of Vienna the powers agreed to hold meetings in the future to enforce the treaty and take up new issues as they arose. A number of congresses of the Great Powers resulted, which are of significance as an experimental step toward international regulation of the affairs of Europe.

The congresses resembled, in a tentative and partial way, the League of Nations that arose after the First World War of 1914–18, or the United Nations that arose during and after the war of 1939–45. The powers had also, in 1815, in alarm after the return of Napoleon, subscribed to Alexander I's Holy Alliance, which became the popular term for the collaboration of the European states in the congresses.[15] The Holy Alliance, on the face of it a statement of Christian purpose and international concord, gradually became an alliance for the suppression of revolutionary and even liberal activity, following in that respect the trend of the governments which made it up.

THE CONGRESS OF AIX-LA-CHAPELLE, 1818

The first general post-war assemblage of the powers took place at the Congress of Aix-la-Chapelle (or Aachen) in 1818. The principal item on the agenda was to withdraw the allied army of occupation from France. The French argued that Louis XVIII would never be popular in France so long as he was supported by a foreign army. The other powers, since they all desired the French to forget the past and accept the Bourbons, withdrew their military forces without disagreement. They arranged also to have private bankers take over the French reparations debt (the 700,000,000 francs imposed by the second treaty of Paris); the bankers paid the allied governments and the French in due time paid the bankers. On a few other smaller matters international collective action proved successful. The Congress heard a request from the Elector of Hesse, who asked that he be granted the title of king, arguing that the title of Elector was meaningless since the dissolution of the Holy Roman Empire, and that the former Electors of Bavaria, Saxony, and Hanover now were kings. His request was refused. The Congress also considered a plea from Napoleon's mother, who urged that her sick son be allowed to return to Europe. It was decided to keep Napoleon at St. Helena.

The Tsar Alexander was still the most advanced internationalist of the day. He suggested at Aix-la-Chapelle a kind of permanent European union, and even proposed the maintenance of international military forces to safeguard recognized states against changes by violence. Governments if thus reassured against revolution, he argued, would more willingly grant constitutional and liberal reforms. But the others demurred, especially the British foreign minister Lord Castlereagh. The British declared themselves willing to make international commitments against specified contingencies, such as a revival of aggression on the part of France. But they would assume no obligations to act upon indefinite and unforeseeable future events. They reserved the right of independent judgment in foreign policy. Concretely, the Congress addressed itself to the problems of the Atlantic slave trade and of the recurring nuisance of the Barbary pirates. It was unanimously agreed that

ᴧᴧᴧᴧᴧᴧᴧᴧᴧᴧᴧᴧᴧᴧᴧᴧ

[15] See pp. 419–20.

both should be suppressed. To suppress them required naval forces, which only the British possessed in adequate amount, and it meant also that naval captains must be authorized to stop and search vessels at sea. The Continental states, always touchy on the subject of British sea power, refused to countenance any such uses of the British fleet. They feared for the freedom of the seas. As for the British, they would not even discuss placing British warships in an international naval pool, or putting British squadrons under the authority of an international body. Nothing therefore was done; the slave trade continued, booming illicitly with the endless demand for cotton; and the Barbary pirates were not disposed of until the French occupied and annexed Algeria some years later. The growth of international institutions was blocked by the separate interests of the sovereign states.

REVOLUTION IN SOUTHERN EUROPE: TROPPAU, 1820

Scarcely had the Congress of Aix-la-Chapelle disbanded when revolutionary agitation came to a crisis in southern Europe. It was not that revolutionary or liberal sentiment was stronger here than in the North, in the sense of having more followers, but rather that the governments in question, those of Spain, Naples, and the Ottoman Empire, were inefficient, ignorant, flimsy, and corrupt. In 1820 the governments of Spain and Naples collapsed with remarkable ease before the demonstrations of the revolutionaries. The kings of both countries reluctantly took oaths to the Spanish constitution of 1812, itself modeled on the French Revolutionary constitution of 1789–91.[16]

Metternich considered Italy, since the ejection of Napoleon, to be within the legitimate sphere of influence of the Austrian empire. He saw the insurrections as the first symptoms of a new revolutionary seizure against which Europe should be quarantined. It was a fact that revolutionary agitation was international, easily leaping across frontiers, because of the operations of secret societies and of political exiles, and because in any case the same ideas had been aroused in all countries by the French Revolution. Metternich therefore called a meeting of the Great Powers at Troppau, hoping to use the authority of an international congress to put down the revolution in Naples. The governments of Great Britain and France, not eager to play Austria's game, sent only observers to the congress. Metternich's main problem was, as usual, Alexander. What would be the attitude of the liberal tsar, the friend and patron of constitutions, toward the idea of a constitutional monarchy in Naples? At an inn in Troppau Metternich and Alexander met alone, and there held a momentous interview over the tea-cups. Metternich reviewed the horrors of revolutionism, the unwisdom of granting any concessions lest revolutionaries be encouraged. Alexander was already somewhat disillusioned by the ungrateful feelings of the Poles. He was troubled by rumors of disaffection among officers in his own army. He had always

~~~~~~~~~~~~~~~~~~

[16] See pp. 346–7.

believed that constitutions should be granted by legitimate sovereigns, not extorted from them by revolutionaries, as had happened in Naples. He allowed himself to be persuaded by Metternich. He declared that he had always been wrong, and that Metternich had always been right; and he announced himself ready to follow Metternich's political judgment. The triumph of the Austrian chancellor was complete. The radical tsar now turned reactionary.

Thus fortified, Metternich drew up a document, the protocol of Troppau, for consideration and acceptance by the five Great Powers. It held that all recognized European states should be protected by collective international action, and in the interests of general peace and stability, from internal changes brought about by force. The protocol read:

States belonging to the European alliance, which have undergone in their internal structure an alteration brought about by revolt, whose consequences may be dangerous to other states, cease automatically to be members of the alliance. [If such states] cause neighboring states to feel an immediate danger, and if action by the Great Powers can be effective and beneficial, the Great Powers will take steps to bring the disturbed area back into the European system, first of all by friendly representations, and secondly by force if force becomes necessary to this end.

The protocol was a statement of collective security against revolution. Neither France nor Great Britain accepted it. Castlereagh wrote to Metternich that if Austria felt her interests to be threatened in Naples she should intervene in her own name only. It was not the repression of the Neapolitan revolution that the Tories of 1820 objected to, so much as the principle of a binding international collaboration. Metternich could get only Russia and Prussia to endorse his protocol, in addition to Austria. These three, acting as the Congress of Troppau, authorized Metternich to despatch an Austrian army into Naples. He did so; the Neapolitan revolutionaries were arrested or put to flight; the incompetent and brutal Ferdinand I was restored as "absolute" king; the demon of revolution was seemingly exorcised. Reaction won out. But the Congress of Troppau, ostensibly a Europe-wide international body, had in effect functioned as an anti-revolutionary alliance of Austria, Russia, and Prussia. A gap opened between the three Eastern autocracies and the two western powers—even when the latter consisted of Tories and Bourbons.

SPAIN, SPANISH AMERICA, THE NEAR EAST: VERONA, 1822

Thousands of revolutionaries and liberals fled from the terror now raging in Italy. Many went to Spain, now dreaded by conservatives as the main seat of revolutionary infection. In addition, the Spanish Americans had set up independent revolutionary republics under the leadership of native revolutionists like Simón Bolívar, called The Liberator, José de San Martín, the Chilean Bernardo O'Higgins, and others long irritated by Spanish colonial rule and inflamed by the precepts of the Enlightenment and the examples of the American and French Revolutions. During the Napoleonic domination of Spain the Spanish American countries had seized the opportunity to launch rebellions. Now, in the years after 1815, the independence movement gathered momentum and succeeded everywhere. To regain his own absolute power and win back the rebellious colonies became the twin objectives of the Spanish king.

The Near East also seemed about to ignite in conflagration. Alexander Ypsilanti, a Greek who had spent his adult life in the military service of Russia, in 1821 led a band of armed followers from Russia into Rumania (still a part of Turkey), hoping that all Greeks and pro-Greeks in the Turkish empire would join him. He expected Russian support, since the penetration of Turkey by the use of Greek Christians had long been a pet project of Russian foreign policy. The possibility of a Turkish empire converted into a "Greek" empire and dependent on Russia was naturally unpleasant to Metternich. To deal with all these matters an international congress met at Verona in 1822.

Alexander, in shifting from liberal to reactionary views, had not changed his belief in the need of international government. Had pure power politics determined his decisions he would doubtless have favored Ypsilanti's Grecophile revolution. But he stood by the principle of international solidarity against revolutionary violence. He disowned Ypsilanti, who found less enthusiasm for Greek culture among the Rumanians and Balkan peoples than he had expected, and was soon defeated by the Turks. As for intervention to repress the Greek uprising, the question did not arise, since the Turkish government proved quite able for a time to handle the matter itself.

Further to advance the cause of international solidarity Alexander urged that the Congress of Verona mediate between Spain and its revolting colonies. This was a euphemistic way of suggesting military intervention in Spanish America, following the principle of the protocol of Troppau. The British objected. They had penetrated the Spanish empire commercially for over a century. During the Napoleonic wars they had increased their exports to Latin America twentyfold.[17] This advantage they intended to retain, and even the Tory government favored the break-up of the Spanish empire into independent states, with which free-trade treaties might be negotiated. Without at least benevolent neutrality from the British fleet no armed force could sail to America. The Spanish Americans therefore maintained their independence, thanks in part to the use made by the British of their sea power on this occasion.

The new republics received strong moral support from the United States also. In December 1823 President James Monroe, in a message to Congress, announced the "Monroe doctrine." It stated that attempts by European powers to return parts of America to colonial status would be viewed as an unfriendly act by the United States. The British foreign minister George Canning (who had just succeeded Castlereagh) boasted that he had "called the New World into existence to redress the balance of the Old." He

[17] See p. 400.

meant that he had enlisted United States diplomatic support for Britain against the Eastern powers on the Spanish American question. In reality, the United States government had outmaneuvered Canning. Canning had proposed that the British and United States governments issue a joint statement. President Monroe, at the advice of his secretary of state John Quincy Adams, decided instead to make a unilateral statement in the form of a message to Congress. They intended to aim their "doctrine" at Great Britain as well as at the continental states, since the British, with their command of the sea, were in fact the only power by which the independence of American states could in practice be threatened. The Monroe doctrine, in its original form, may also be thought of as a counterblast to the Metternich doctrine of the protocol of Troppau. Where the latter announced the principle of intervention against revolution, the Monroe doctrine announced that revolutions in America were outside the pale of attention by European powers.

The question of the revolution in Spain was settled in a different way. The Bourbon regime in France had no taste for a Spain in which revolutionaries, republicans, political exiles, and members of secret societies might be harbored. The French government proposed to the Congress of Verona that it be authorized to dispatch an army across the Pyrenees. The Congress welcomed the offer, and despite many dire predictions of ruin, arising from memories of Napoleon's disaster, a French army of 200,000 men moved into Spain in 1823. The campaign proved to be a military promenade through a cheering country. Not many Spanish liberals, constitutionalists or revolutionaries could be found. The mass of the people saw the invasion as a deliverance from Masons, Carbonari, and heretics, and shouted with satisfaction at the restoration of church and king. Ferdinand VII, unscrupulous and narrow-minded, repudiated his constitutional oath and let the vindictive ecclesiastics, grandees, and hidalgos have their way. The late revolutionaries were savagely persecuted, exiled, or jailed.

THE END OF THE CONGRESS SYSTEM

After the Congress of Verona no more such meetings were held. The attempt at a formal international regulation of European affairs was given up. In the broadest retrospect, the congresses failed to make progress toward an international order because, especially after Alexander's conversion to conservatism, they came to stand for nothing except preservation of the status quo. They made no attempt at accommodation with the new forces that were shaping Europe. It was not the policy of the congresses to forestall revolution by demanding that governments institute reforms. They simply repressed or punished all revolutionary agitation. They propped up governments that could not stand on their own feet. They supported the reactionary Bourbon monarchies of Spain and Naples, corrupt regimes that were too unsteady to hold up against small handfuls of revolutionaries, and which were becoming an offense to the moral conscience of the European world.

In any case the congresses never succeeded in subordinating the separate interests of the Great Powers. Perhaps Alexander's repudiation of Ypsilanti was a sacrifice of Russian advantage to international principle; but when the Austrian government intervened to crush the revolution in Naples, and when the French government crushed the revolution in Spain, though in both cases they acted with an international mandate, each was really promoting what it conceived to be its own interests. The interest of Great Britain was to pull away from the system entirely. As defined by Castlereagh and by Canning after him, it was to stand aloof from permanent international commitments, to preserve a free exercise of sea power and foreign policy, and to take a benevolent view toward revolution in other countries. Since France eventually pulled away also, the Holy Alliance ceased to be even ostensibly a European system, and became no more than a counter-revolutionary league between the three eastern autocracies. With a majority of the five Great Powers highly illiberal, the cause of liberalism in Europe was advanced by the collapse of the international system. At the same time the collapse of the system opened the way to the uncontrolled nationalism of the sovereign states. "Things are getting back to a wholesome state again," wrote George Canning in 1822; "Every nation for itself and God for us all!"

RUSSIA: THE DECEMBRIST REVOLT, 1825

Alexander I, "the man who defeated Napoleon," the ruler who had led his armies from Moscow to Paris, who had frightened the diplomats by the Russian shadow that he threw over the Continent, and who yet in his way had been the great pillar of constitutional liberalism and international order, died at Taganrog in 1825. His death was the signal for revolution in Russia. Officers of the Russian army, during the campaigns of 1812–15 in Europe, had become acquainted with many unsettling ideas. Secret societies were formed even in the Russian officer corps; their members held all sorts of conflicting ideas, some wanting a constitutional tsardom in Russia, some demanding a republic, some even dreaming of an emancipation of the serfs. When Alexander died it was for a time uncertain which of his two brothers, Constantine or Nicholas, should succeed him. The restless coteries in the army preferred Constantine, who was thought to be more favorable to innovations in the state. In December 1825 they proclaimed Constantine at St. Petersburg, having their soldiers shout "Constantine and Constitution!" The soldiers, it is said, thought that Constitution was Constantine's wife. But the fact was that Constantine had long before abdicated in favor of Nicholas, who was the rightful heir. The uprising, known as the Decembrist revolt, was soon put down. Five of the mutinous officers were hanged; many others were condemned to forced labor or interned in Siberia. The Decembrist revolt was the first manifestation of the modern revolutionary movement in Russia—of a revolutionary movement inspired by an ideological program, as distinguished from the elemental mass upheavals of Pugachev or Stephen Razin.

But the immediate effect of the Decembrist revolt was to clamp repression upon Russia more firmly. Nicholas I (1825–55) maintained an unconditional and despotic autocracy.

Ten years after the defeat of Napoleon the new forces issuing from the French Revolution seemed to be routed, and reaction, repression, and political immobility seemed everywhere to have prevailed. The dike—a massive dike—seemed to be containing the flood.

54. The Breakthrough of Liberalism in the West: Revolutions of 1830–2

The dike broke in 1830, nor in Western Europe was the stream thereafter stopped. The seepage, indeed, had already begun. By 1825 Spanish America was independent. The British and the French had pulled away from the congress system. The Greek nationalist movement against the Turks had broken out in the early 1820's.

With the defeat of Ypsilanti in 1821 the Greek nationalists turned somewhat away from the idea of a neo-Greek empire, and more toward the idea of independence for Greece proper, the islands and peninsulas where Greek was the predominant language. The Tsar Nicholas was more willing than Alexander to assist this movement. The governments of Great Britain and France were not inclined to let Russia stand as the only champion of Balkan peoples. Moreover, liberals in the West thought of the embattled Greeks as ancient Athenians fighting the modern oriental despotism of the Turkish empire.

The result was a joint Anglo-French-Russian naval intervention, which destroyed the Turkish fleet at Navarino Bay in 1827. Russia again, as often in the past, sent armies into the Balkans. A Russo-Turkish war and a great Near Eastern crisis followed, in the course of which the rival powers agreed in 1829 to recognize Greece as an independent kingdom. The Balkan states of Serbia, Wallachia, and Moldavia were also recognized as autonomous principalities within the badly shaken Ottoman Empire.[18] From the same crisis Egypt emerged as an autonomous region under Mohammed Ali, its first "khedive." Egypt, an Arabic country, in time became a center of Arabic nationalism, which cut down Ottoman power in the south as Balkan nationalism did in the north.

FRANCE, 1824–30: THE JULY REVOLUTION, 1830

It was in 1830, and first of all in France, that the wall of reaction really collapsed. Charles X became king in 1824.[19] In the next year the legislative

[18] See maps, pp. 414–15, 633.
[19] See p. 444.

Chambers voted an indemnity, in the form of perpetual annuities totaling 30,000,000 francs a year, to those who as émigrés thirty-odd years before had had their property confiscated by the Revolutionary state. Catholic clergy began to take over classrooms in the schools. A law pronounced the death penalty for sacrilege committed in church buildings. But the France of the restored Bourbons was still a free country, and against these apparent efforts to revive the Old Regime a strong opposition developed in the newspapers and in the Chambers. In March 1830 the Chamber of Deputies, in which the bankers Laffitte and Casimir-Périer led the "leftist" opposition, passed a vote of no-confidence in the government. The king, as was his legal right, dissolved the Chamber and called for new elections. The elections repudiated the king's policies. He replied on July 26, 1830, with four ordinances issued on his own authority. One dissolved the newly elected Chamber before it had ever met; another imposed censorship on the press; the third so amended the suffrage as to reduce the voting power of bankers, merchants, and industrialists and to concentrate it in the hands of the old-fashioned aristocracy; the fourth called for a new election on the new basis.

These July Ordinances produced on the very next day the July Revolution. The upper bourgeois class was of course desperate at being thus brazenly ousted from political life. But it was the republicans—the nucleus of revolutionary workingmen, students, and intelligentsia in Paris—that actually moved. For three days, from July 27 to 29, barricades were thrown up in the city, behind which a swarming populace defied the army and the police. Most of the army refused to fire. Charles X, in no mood to be made captive by a revolution like his long dead brother Louis XVI, precipitately abdicated and headed for England.

The revolutionary students and workingmen wished to proclaim a democratic republic. The bankers, merchants, and industrialists thought differently. They had been satisfied in general with the constitutional charter of 1814; it was only to the policies and personnel of the government that they had objected, and they wished now to continue with constitutional monarchy, somewhat liberalized, and with a king whom they could trust. A solution to the deadlock was found by the elderly Marquis de Lafayette, the aging hero of the American and the French Revolutions, who now came forward as symbol of national unity. Lafayette produced the Duke of Orleans on the balcony of the Paris Hotel de Ville, embraced him before a great concourse of people, and offered him as the answer to France's need. The duke was a collateral relative of the Bourbons; he had also, as a young man, fought in the republican army of 1792. The militant republicans accepted him, willing to see what would develop; and the Chamber on August 7 offered him the throne, on condition that he observe faithfully the constitutional charter of 1814. He reigned, until 1848, under the title of Louis-Philippe.

The regime of Louis-Philippe, called the Orleanist, bourgeois, or July monarchy, was viewed very differently by different groups in France and in Europe. To the other states of Europe and to the clergy and legitimists within France, it seemed shockingly revolutionary. The new king owed his throne to an insurrection, to a bargain made with republicans, and to promises made to a parliament. He called himself not King of France but King of the French, and he flew not the Bourbon lily but the tricolor flag of the Revolution. The latter produced an effect on the established classes not unlike that of the hammer and sickle of a later day. He cultivated a popular manner, wore sober dark clothing (the ancestor of the modern "business suit") and carried an umbrella. Though in private he worked stubbornly to maintain his royal position, in public he adhered scrupulously to the constitution.

The constitution remained substantially what it had been in 1814. The main political change was one of tone; there would be no more absolutism, with its notion that constitutional guarantees could be abrogated by a reigning prince. Legally the main change was that the Chamber of Peers ceased to be hereditary, to the chagrin of the old nobility, and that the Chamber of Deputies was to be elected by a somewhat enlarged body of voters. Where before 1830 there had been 100,000 voters, there were now about 200,000. The right to vote was still based on the ownership of a considerable quantity of real estate. About one-thirtieth of the adult male population (the top thirtieth in the possession of real property) now elected the Chamber of Deputies. The beneficiaries of the new system were the upper bourgeoisie—the bankers, merchants, and industrialists. The big property-owners constituted the *pays légal*, the "legal country," and to them the July monarchy was the consummation and stopping-place of political progress. To others, and especially to the radical democrats, it proved as the years passed to be a disillusionment and an annoyance.

REVOLUTIONS OF 1830: BELGIUM, POLAND, AND ELSEWHERE

The immediate effect of the three-day Paris revolution of 1830 was to set off a series of similar explosions throughout Europe. These in turn, coming after the collapse of the Bourbons in France, brought the whole peace settlement of 1815 into jeopardy. It will be recalled that the Congress of Vienna had joined Belgium with the Dutch Netherlands to create a strong buffer state against a resurgent France, and had also done what it could to prevent direct pressure of Russian power upon Central Europe by way of Poland.[20] Both these arrangements were now undone.

The Dutch-Belgian union proved economically beneficial, for Belgian industry complemented the commercial and shipping activity of the Dutch, but politically it worked very poorly, especially since the Dutch king had absolutist and centralizing ideas. The Belgians, though they had never been independent, had always stood stiffly for their local liberties under former Austrian rulers (and Spanish before them); now they did the same against the Dutch. The Catholic Belgians disliked Dutch Protestantism; those

---

[20] See pp. 416–18.

Belgians who spoke French (the Walloons) objected to regulations requiring the use of Dutch. About a month after the July revolution in Paris disturbances broke out in Brussels. The leaders asked only for local Belgian self-government, but when the king took arms against them they went on to proclaim independence. A national assembly met and drafted a constitution.

Nicholas of Russia wished to send troops to stamp out the Belgian uprising. But he could not get his forces safely through Poland. In Poland, too, in 1830, a revolution broke out. The Polish nationalists saw in the fall of the French Bourbons a timely moment for them to strike. They objected also to the appearance of Russian troops bound presumably to suppress freedom in western Europe. One incident led to another, until in January 1831 the Polish diet proclaimed the dethronement of the Polish king (*i.e.*, Nicholas), who thereupon sent in a large army. The Poles, outnumbered and divided among themselves, could put up no successful resistance. They obtained no support from the West. The British government was unsettled by agitation at home. The French government, newly installed under Louis-Philippe, had no wish to appear disturbingly revolutionary, and in any case feared the Polish agents who besought its backing as international firebrands and republicans. The Polish revolution was therefore crushed. "Congress" Poland disappeared; its constitution was abrogated, and it was merged into the Russian Empire. Thousands of Poles settled in western Europe, where they became familiar figures in republican circles. In Poland the engines of repression rolled. The tsar's government exiled some thousands to Siberia, began to Russify the eastern Border, and closed the Universities of Warsaw and Vilna. Since meanwhile it was too late for the tsar any longer to contemplate intervention in Belgium, it may be said that the sacrifice of the Poles contributed to the success of the west-European revolution of 1830, as it had done to that of the great French Revolution of 1789–95.[21]

It was true enough, as Nicholas maintained, that an independent Belgium presented great international problems. Belgium for twenty years before 1815 had been part of France. A few Belgians now favored reunion with it, and in France the republican left, which regarded the Vienna treaty as an insult to the French nation, saw an opportunity to win back this first and dearest conquest of the First Republic. In 1831, by a small majority, the Belgian national assembly elected as their king the son of Louis-Philippe, who, however, not wishing trouble with the British, forbade his son to accept it. The Belgians thereupon elected Leopold of Saxe-Coburg, a German princeling who had married into the British royal family and become a British subject. He was in fact the uncle of a twelve-year-old girl who was to be Queen Victoria. The British negotiated with Talleyrand, sent over by the French government (it was his last public service); and the result was a treaty of 1831 (confirmed in 1839) setting up Belgium as a perpetually neutral state, incapable of forming alliances and guaranteed against invasion

[21] See pp. 357, 362, and map on p. 221.

by all five of the Great Powers. The aim intended by the treaty of Vienna, to prevent the annexation of Belgium to France, was thus again realized in a new way. Internally Belgium presently settled down to a stable parliamentary system, somewhat more democratic than the July monarchy in France, but fundamentally offering the same type of bourgeois and liberal rule.

Revolutionary disturbances also took place in 1830 in Germany, Italy, Switzerland, Spain, and Portugal. To trace them in any detail is not necessary. In a word, a greater measure of liberalism was established in Switzerland; Spain entered a long period of tortuous parliamentary development confused by civil wars, which arose from a disputed succession to the throne; and in Italy and Germany the 1830 uprisings were quickly put down, showing only the continuance of a radical dissatisfaction still held in check by the authorities. It was in Great Britain that sweeping changes really came.

REFORM IN GREAT BRITAIN

The three-day Paris revolution of 1830 had direct repercussions across the Channel. The quick results following on working class insurrection gave radical leaders in England the idea that threats of violence might be useful. On the other hand, the ease and speed with which the French bourgeoisie gained the upper hand reassured the British middle classes, who concluded that they might unsparingly embarrass the government without courting a mass upheaval.

The Tory regime in England had in fact already begun to loosen up. A group of younger men came forward in the 1820's in the Tory party, notably George Canning, the foreign minister, and Robert Peel, son of one of the first cotton manufacturers.[22] This group was sensitive to the needs of British business and to the doctrines of liberalism.[23] They began to clear out the untended garden of antiquated laws. They abolished capital punishment for about a hundred different offenses. They introduced a professional police force in London in place of the old "watch"—it is after Robert Peel that London policemen are called "bobbies." They allowed an opening wedge for the organization of labor unions. They reduced tariff duties and liberalized the old Navigation Acts, permitting British colonies to trade with countries other than Britain. By repealing certain old statutes, they made it lawful for skilled workmen to emigrate from England, taking their skills with them to foreign parts, and for manufacturers to export machinery to foreign countries, even though English industrial secrets would thus be given away. By such measures they advanced the liberal conception of a freely exchanging international economic system; they moved toward freedom of trade. The Liberal Tories also attacked the legal position of the Church of England, advancing the modern conception of a secular or non-religious state. They repealed

wwwwwwwwwwww

[22] See p. 429.
[23] See pp. 432–3.

the old laws (which dated from the seventeenth century) forbidding dissenting Protestants to sit in Parliament or hold public office except through
the legal fiction of "occasional conformity" by which they pretended to be
Anglicans.[24] They even (and it was their hardest struggle) managed to carry
Catholic Emancipation, repealing the Test Act of 1673. Catholics in both
Great Britain and Ireland received the same rights as others; or rather, the
old Catholic-Protestant issue at last became immaterial for public life.

There were two things that the Liberal Tories could not do. They
could not question the Corn Laws, and they could not reform the House of
Commons. By the Corn Laws, the tariff on imported grain, raised to new
heights in 1815, the gentlemen of England protected their rent-rolls; and by
the existing structure of the House of Commons they governed the country,
expecting the working classes and the business interests to look to them as
natural leaders.

Never in the five hundred years of its history had the Commons been
so unrepresentative. No new borough had been created since the revolution
of 1688. The boroughs, or urban centers having the right to elect members of
Parliament, were heavily concentrated in southern England. With the Industrial Revolution, population was shifting noticeably to the north. The
new factory towns were unrepresented. Of the boroughs, many had decayed
over the centuries; some were quite uninhabited, and one was under the
waters of the North Sea. In a few boroughs real elections took place, but in
some of them it was the town corporation, and in others the owners of certain
pieces of real estate, that had the right to name members of Parliament. Each
borough was different, carrying over the local liberties of the Middle Ages.
Many boroughs were entirely dominated by influential persons called borough-
mongers by their critics. As for the rural districts, the "forty-shilling free-
holders" chose two members of Parliament for each county, in a convivial
assembly much influenced by the gentle-folk. It was estimated about 1820
that less than five hundred men, most of them members of the House of
Lords, really selected a majority of the House of Commons.

Some two dozen bills to reform the House of Commons had been introduced in the half-century preceding 1830. They had all failed to pass. In
1830, after the Paris revolution, the issue was again raised by the minority
party, the Whigs, who, having been out of office since before the French
Revolution, had good reason to favor a revision of the electoral procedures.
The Tory prime minister, the Duke of Wellington, the victor of Waterloo
and a most extreme conservative, so immoderately defended the existing
system that he lost the confidence even of some of his own followers. The
existing methods of election in England, he declared, were more perfect than
any that human intelligence could contrive at a single stroke. After this outburst a Whig ministry took over the government. It introduced a reform
bill. The House of Commons rejected it. The Whig ministry thereupon resigned. The Tories, fearing popular violence, refused to take the responsibility

[24] See pp. 150–3.

for forming a cabinet. The Whigs resumed office, and again introduced their reform bill. This time it passed the Commons, but failed in the House of Lords. An angry roar went up over the country. Crowds milled in the London streets, rioters for several days were in control at Bristol, the jail at Derby was sacked and Nottingham castle burned. Only the passage of the bill, it seemed, could prevent an actual revolution. Using this argument the Whigs got the king to promise to create enough new peers to change the majority in the House of Lords.[25] The Lords yielded rather than be swamped, and in April 1832 the bill became law.

The Reform Bill of 1832 was a very English measure. It adapted the English or medieval system, rather than following new ideas let loose by the French Revolution. On the Continent, where constitutions existed at all (as in France), the idea was that each representative should represent roughly the same number of voters, and that voters should qualify to vote by a flat uniform qualification, usually the payment of a stated amount of property taxes. The British held to the idea that members of the House of Commons represented boroughs and counties, in general without regard to size of population (with exceptions); in other words, no attempt was made to create equal electoral districts. The qualification for voting was enormously simplified, but it still remained rather complex. The franchise, or right to vote, depended on whether one lived in a borough or in a county. It was defined also very largely in terms of rents, because in England, with the high concentration of landownership in the old landowning class, many important people did not own any land at all.

In a borough, under the new law, a man could vote for a member of Parliament if he occupied premises for which he paid £10 annual rental. In a county (a rural area or a small town not considered a borough), a man could vote if he paid £10 annual rental for land held on a long-term sixty-year lease; but he had to pay as high as £50 rental for land occupied on a shorter-term lease in order to be eligible to vote. If he himself owned the land, he could vote if its annual rental value was £2 a year (the old forty-shilling freehold). Thus the vote was nicely distributed according to evidences of economic substance, reliability, and permanence. The total effect on the size of the electorate was to raise the number of voters in the British Isles from about half a million to about 813,000. Some persons actually lost their votes, namely the poorer elements in the handful of old boroughs which had been fairly democratic, like the borough of Westminster in greater London.

The most important thing was not the increased size of the electorate but its redistribution by region and by class. The Reform Bill reallocated the seats in the House of Commons. Fifty-six of the smallest older boroughs were abolished, their inhabitants thereafter voting as residents of their counties. Thirty other small boroughs kept the right to send only one burgess to Parliament instead of the historic two. The 143 seats thus made available were given to the new industrial towns. Here it was the £10-householders

---

[25] See note, p. 170.

who voted, *i.e.*, the middle classes—factory-owners and business men and their principal employees; doctors, lawyers, brokers, merchants, and newspaper people; relatives and connections of the well-to-do.

The Reform Bill of 1832 was more sweeping than the Whigs would have favored except for their fear of revolution. It was more conservative than the democratic radicals would have accepted, except for their belief that the suffrage might be widened in the future. Great Britain in 1830 was probably nearer to real revolution than any country of Europe—for the revolutions of 1830 on the Continent were in reality only insurrections and readjustments. In Britain a distressed mass of factory workers, and of craft workers thrown out of employment by factory competition, was led by an irate manufacturing interest, grown strong by industrial changes, and determined no longer to tolerate its exclusion from political life. Had these elements resorted to general violence a real revolution would have occurred. Yet there was no violent revolution in Britain. The reason probably lies first of all in the existence of the historic institution of Parliament, which, erratic though it was before the Reform Bill, provided machinery by which social changes could be legally accomplished. Conservatives, driven to the wall, would yield; they could allow a revision of the suffrage because they could expect to remain themselves in public life. Radicals, using enough violence to scare the established interests, did not thereafter face a blank wall; they could expect, once the breach was made, to carry some day a further democratization of Parliament, and with it their social and economic program by orderly legislation.

BRITAIN AFTER 1832

But the Reform Bill of 1832 was in its way a revolution. The new business interests, created by industrialization, took their place alongside the old aristocracy in the governing elite of the country. The aristocratic Whigs who had carried the reform bill gradually merged with formerly radical industrialists and with a few Liberal Tories to form the Liberal party. The main body of the Tories, joined by a few old Whigs and even a few former radicals, gradually turned into the Conservative party. The two parties alternated in power at short intervals from 1832 to the First World War, this being the classic period in Great Britain of the two-party system.

In 1833 slavery was abolished in the British empire. In 1834 a new Poor Law was adopted. In 1835 the Municipal Corporations Act, second only to the Reform Bill in basic importance, modernized the local government of English cities; it broke up the old local oligarchies and brought in uniform electoral and administrative machinery, enabling city dwellers to grapple more effectively with the problems of urban life. In 1836 the House of Commons allowed the newspapers to report how its members voted; a long step toward publicity of government proceedings was thus taken. Meanwhile an ecclesiastical commission reviewed the affairs of the Church of

England; financial and administrative irregularities were corrected, together
with the grosser inequalities between the income of upper and lower clergy,
all of which had made the Church formerly a kind of closed preserve for the
landed gentry.

The Tories, thus assaulted in their immemorial strongholds of local
government and the established church, carried a counteroffensive into the
strongholds of the new liberal manufacturing class, namely the factories and
the mines. Tories became champions of the industrial workers. Landed gentlemen, of whom the most famous was Lord Ashley, later seventh earl of
Shaftesbury, took the lead in publicizing the social evils of a rapid and even
ruthless industrialization. They received some support from a few humanitarian industrialists; indeed, the early legislation tended to follow practices
already established by the best or strongest business firms. A Factory Act of
1833 forbade the labor of children less than nine years old in the textile mills.
It was the first effective piece of legislation on the subject, for it provided for
paid inspectors and procedures for enforcement. An act of 1842 initiated
significant regulation in the coal mines; the employment under ground of
women and girls, and of boys under ten, was forbidden.

The greatest victory of the working classes came in 1847 with the Ten
Hours Act, which limited the labor of women and children in all industrial
establishments to ten hours a day. Thereafter men commonly worked only
ten hours also, since the work of men, women, and young people was too
closely coordinated for the men to work alone. The great Liberal, John Bright,
Quaker and cotton magnate, called the Ten Hours Act "a delusion practiced
on the working classes." To regulate the hours of labor was contrary to the
accepted principles of *laissez-faire*, economic law, the free market, freedom of
trade, and individual liberty for employer and workman. Yet the Ten Hours
Act stood, and British industry continued to prosper.

Gathering their strength, the Whig-liberal-radical combination established in 1838 an Anti-Corn Law League. Wage earners objected to the
Corn Laws because the tariff on grain imports kept up the price of food.
Industrial employers objected to them because, in keeping up food prices,
they also kept up wages and cost of production in England, thus working to
England's disadvantage in the export trade. Defenders of the Corn Laws
argued that protection of agriculture was necessary to maintain the natural
aristocracy of the country (most land being owned by peers and gentry, as
has been seen), but they also sometimes used more widely framed economic
arguments, affirming that Britain should preserve a balanced economy as between industry and farming, and avoid becoming too exclusively dependent
on imported food. The issue became a straight contest between the industrialists, acting with working-class support, and the aristocratic and predominantly Tory landowning interest. The Anti-Corn Law League, whose
headquarters were at Manchester, operated like a modern political party. It
had plenty of money, supplied by large donations from manufacturers and
small ones from laboring people. It sent lecturers on tour, agitated in the

newspapers, and issued a stream of polemical pamphlets and educational books. It held political teas, torchlight processions, and open-air mass meetings. The pressure proved irresistible, and received a final impetus from a famine in Ireland. It was a Tory government, headed by Sir Robert Peel, which in 1846 yielded before so vociferous a demand.

The repeal of the Corn Laws in 1846 stands as a symbol of the change that had come over England. It reaffirmed the revolutionary consequences of the Reform Bill of 1832. Industry was now a governing element in the country. Free trade was henceforth the rule. Great Britain, in return for the export of manufactures, became deliberately dependent on imports for its very life. It was committed henceforth to an international and even world-wide economic system. The first to undergo the Industrial Revolution, possessing mechanical power and methods of mass production, the British could produce yarn and cloth, machine tools and railroad equipment, more efficiently and more cheaply than any other people. In Britain, the workshop of the world, people would pour increasingly into mine, factory, and city, live by selling manufactures, coal, shipping, and financial services to the other peoples of the earth, and obtain raw cotton, rare ores, meat, cereals, and thousands of lesser but still vital necessities from the rest of the earth in exchange. The welfare of Britain depended on the maintenance of a freely exchanging world-wide economic system.

It depended also, more than ever, on British control of the sea, which was rarely mentioned by the civilian-minded Anti-Corn Law League, but which, firmly established in the long duel with Napoleon, was now an assumed postulate of economic discussion. No one understood this better than Lord Palmerston, a flamboyant Anglo-Irish Whig aristocrat, who by risky and audacious moves that alarmed his colleagues and threw Queen Victoria into consternation, came forward as the very British bulldog in defense of Britain's name. For example, in 1850 a Moroccan Jew known as Don Pacifico, who was a British subject, got into trouble in Greece because of certain debts owed to him by the Greek government. Though the claim was not above question, Palmerston unloosed the thunders of the British fleet. He sent a squadron to the Piraeus, the port of Athens, and forbade Greek vessels the use of their own harbor until the matter was settled. Criticized in Parliament, Palmerston made a stirring speech climaxed by the Latin phrase, *civis Romanus sum.* Just as in ancient times the Roman citizen everywhere commanded respect, so now, according to Palmerston, any British subject had behind him the might of the British navy anywhere in the world. On another occasion, in 1856, when Chinese authorities arrested a Chinese ship called the *Arrow,* which, though without due right, was flying the British flag, Palmerston again called on the navy, which proceeded to bombard Canton and precipitated the Second Anglo-Chinese war. In other connections, as a good mid-nineteenth-century liberal, Palmerston favored movements for national independence, including that of the Confederate States of America, expecting them to result in the further extension of free trade.

55. Triumph of the West-European Bourgeoisie

In both Great Britain and France (as also in Belgium) the revolutionary agitation of 1830–2 ushered in a period of ascendancy for the bourgeois
or propertied classes. The reigning liberal doctrine was the "stake in society"
theory: those should govern who have something to lose. In the France of the
July monarchy (1830–48) about one adult male in thirty could vote, in the
Britain of the first Reform Bill (1832–67) about one in eight. In Britain
virtually the whole middle class was now enfranchised, in France only the
most well-to-do. In Britain the continuation of the Tory landed interests in
politics somewhat blunted the edge of capitalist and managerial rule, resulting in the passage of significant legislation for the protection of industrial
labor. In France the aristocratic landed interest, weaker and less public
spirited than in England in any case, lost much of its influence by the revolution of 1830. France under Louis-Philippe was a more purely bourgeois country than Great Britain, and less was done to relieve the condition of labor.

In general, the decades following 1830 may be thought of as a kind of
golden age of the west-European bourgeoisie. The business man of Britain,
France, and Belgium, while he had established himself against the man of
birth, had as yet hardly to reckon politically with the man of toil. By its upholders the system was regarded as perfect and final. Two examples may be
given, François Guizot in France and Thomas Babington Macaulay in England, both active in the parliaments of their respective countries, both brilliant writers of history, both proud of the triumphs of modern civilization
and of the industrious and intelligent middle classes from which they came—
and both convinced that political democracy would lead to ruin.

The bourgeois era left its mark on Europe in many ways. For one
thing, western Europe continued to accumulate capital and build up its industrial plant. National income was constantly rising, but a relatively small
share went to the laboring class, and a relatively large share went to owners
of capital. This meant that less was spent on consumers' goods—housing,
clothing, food, recreation—and that more was saved and available for reinvestment. New stock companies were constantly formed, and the law of
corporations was amended, allowing for the extension of corporate enterprise
to new fields. The factory system spread from Britain to the Continent, and
within Britain from the textile industry to other lines of production. The
output of iron, a good index to economic advancement in this phase of
industrialism, rose about 300% in Great Britain between 1830 and 1848, and
about 65% in France between 1830 and 1845. (All the German states combined, at the latter date, produced about a tenth as much iron as Great
Britain, and less than half as much as France.) Railroad building set in in
earnest after 1840. In 1840 Samuel Cunard put four steamships in regular
transatlantic service. Much capital was exported; as early as 1839 an American
estimated that Europeans (mainly British) owned $200,000,000 worth of

stocks in American companies. Such investments financed the purchase of British and other goods, and helped to rivet together a world economic system, in which western Europe and especially England took the lead, with other regions remaining in a somewhat subordinate status.

THE FRUSTRATION AND CHALLENGE OF LABOR

The bourgeois age had the effect also of estranging the world of labor. The state in Britain and France was as near as it has ever been to what Karl Marx was soon to call it—a committee of the bourgeois class. Already in France people spoke worriedly of the *prolétaires*, those at the bottom of society, who had nothing to lose. Republicans in France, radical democrats in Britain, felt cheated and imposed upon in the 1830's and 1840's. They had in each country forced through a virtual revolution by their insurrections and demonstrations, and then in each country had been left without the vote. Some lost interest in representative institutions. Excluded from government they were tempted to seek political ends through extra-governmental, which is to say revolutionary or utopian, channels. Social and economic reforms seemed to the workingman far more important, as a final aim, than mere governmental innovations. The workingman was told by respected economists that he could not hope to change the system in his own favor. He was tempted therefore to destroy the system, to replace it utterly with some new system conceived mainly in the minds of thinkers. He was told by the Manchester School, and by its equivalent in France, that the income of labor was set by ineluctable natural laws, that it was best and indeed necessary for wages to remain low, and that the way to rise in the world was to get out of the laboring class altogether, by becoming the owner of a profitable business and leaving working people about where they were.[26]

The reigning doctrine emphasized the conception of a labor market. The workman sold labor, the employer bought it. The price of labor, or wage, was to be agreed upon by the two individual parties. The price would naturally fluctuate according to changes in supply and demand. When a great deal of a certain kind of labor was required the wage would go up, until new persons moved into the market offering more labor of this type, with the result that something like the old wage would again be established. When no labor was needed none should be bought, and persons who could not sell labor might then subsist for a time by poor relief. The New Poor Law of 1834 was especially repugnant to the British working classes. It corrected crying evils in the old system, which had pauperized and demoralized millions of people. But the new law followed the stern precepts of the dismal science; its main principle was to safeguard the labor market by making relief more unpleasant than any job. It granted relief only to persons willing to enter a workhouse, or poorhouse; and in these establishments the sexes were segre-

[26] See pp. 429–30, 433.

gated and life was in other ways made noticeably less attractive than in the outside world. The workers considered the new law an abomination. They called the workhouses "bastilles." They resented the whole conception of a labor market, in which labor was to be bought and sold (or remain unsold) like any other commodity.

There were two means of escape. One was to improve the position of labor in the market. This led to the formation of labor unions for control of the labor supply and collective bargaining with employers. Such unions, illegal in France, were barely legal in Great Britain after 1825, though it was still illegal in both countries to strike. The other means of escape was to repudiate the whole idea of a market economy and of the capitalist system. It was to conceive of a system in which goods were to be produced for use, not for sale; and in which working people should be compensated according to need, not according to the requirements of an employer. This was the basis of most forms of socialism.[27]

SOCIALISM AND CHARTISM

Socialism spread rapidly among the working classes after 1830. In France it blended with revolutionary republicanism. There was a revival of interest in the great Revolution and the democratic republic of 1793. Cheap reprints of the writings of Robespierre began to circulate in the working-class quarters of Paris. Robespierre was now seen as a people's hero. The socialist Louis Blanc, for example, who in 1839 published his *Organization of Work*, recommending the formation of "social workshops," also wrote a long history of the French Revolution, in which he pointed out the democratic ideals that had inspired the National Convention in 1793. In Britain, as befitted the different background of the country, socialistic ideas blended in with the movement for further parliamentary reform. This was advanced by the working-class group known as the Chartists, from the People's Charter which they drafted in 1838. Between the British Chartists and the French socialists there was considerable coming and going. One Chartist, the Irish-born journalist Bronterre O'Brien translated a French book on the "conspiracy of Babeuf" of 1796, which itself was a source and inspiration of the rising socialism of France.[28]

Chartism was far more of a mass movement than the French socialism of the day. Only a few Chartists were clearly socialists in their own minds. But all were anti-capitalistic. All could agree that the first step must be to win working-class representation in Parliament. The Charter of 1838 consisted of six points. It demanded (1) the annual election of the House of Commons by (2) universal suffrage for all adult males, through (3) a secret ballot and (4) equal electoral districts; and it called for (5) the abolition of

[27] See pp. 434–6.
[28] See p. 365.

property qualifications for membership in the House of Commons, which perpetuated the old idea that Parliament should be composed of gentlemen of independent income, and urged instead (6) the payment of salaries to the elected members of Parliament, in order that people of small means might serve. A convention composed of delegates sent by labor unions, mass meetings and radical societies all over the country met in London in 1839. "Convention" was an ominous word, with French revolutionary and even terrorist overtones; some members of this British convention regarded it as the body really representing the people, and favored armed violence and a general strike, while others stood only for moral pressure upon Parliament.

A petition bearing over a million signatures, urging acceptance of the Charter, was submitted to the House of Commons. The violent and revolutionary wing, or "physical force" Chartists, precipitated a wave of riots which were effectively quelled by the authorities. In 1842 the petition was again submitted. This time, according to the best estimate, it was signed by 3,317,702 persons. Since the entire population of Great Britain was about 19,000,000 it is clear that the Charter, whatever the exact number of signatures, commanded the explicit adherence of half the adult males of the country. The House of Commons nevertheless rejected the petition by 287 votes to 49. It was feared, with reason, that political democracy would threaten property rights and the whole economic system as they then existed. The Chartist movement gradually died down in the face of firm opposition by the government and the business classes, and weakened by the mutual fears and disagreements among its own supporters. It had not been entirely fruitless; for without popular agitation and the publicizing of working-class grievances, the Mines Act of 1842 and the Ten Hours Act of 1847 might not have been enacted. These measures in turn alleviated the distress of industrial workers and kept alive a degree of confidence in the future of the economic system. Chartism revived briefly in 1848, as will be seen in the next chapter; but in general, in the 1840's, British working people turned from political agitation to the forming and strengthening of labor unions, by which they could deal directly with employers without having to appeal to the government. Not until 1867 was the suffrage extended in Great Britain, and it took about eighty years to realize the full program of the Charter of 1838, except for the annual election of Parliament, for which there soon ceased to be any demand.

It is not easy to summarize the history of Europe between 1815 and 1848. Between all the forces set free by the French and Industrial Revolutions—liberalism, conservatism, nationalism, republicanism, democracy, socialism—no stabilization had been achieved. No international system had been created; Europe had rather fallen into two camps, composed of a west in which liberal conceptions moved forward, and an east in which three autocratic monarchies held sway. Western Europe favored the principles of nationality; governments in central and eastern Europe still opposed them. The west was growing collectively richer, more liberal, more bourgeois. Middle class people in Germany, central Europe, and Italy (as well as in Spain and Portugal) did not enjoy the dignities and emoluments that they enjoyed in Great Britain or France. But the west had not solved its social problem; its whole material civilization rested upon a restless and sorely tried working class. Everywhere there was repression, in varying degree, and everywhere apprehension, more in some places than in others; but there was also hope, confidence in the progress of an industrial and scientific society, and faith in the unfinished program of the rights of man. The result was the general Revolution of 1848.

1848: A Revolution That Misfired

FEARS haunting the established classes of Europe for thirty years came true in 1848. Governments collapsed all over the Continent. Remembered horrors appeared again, as in a recurring dream, in much the same sequence as after 1789 only at a much faster rate of speed. Revolutionaries milled in the streets, kings fled, republics were declared, and within four years there was another Napoleon. Soon thereafter came a series of wars.

Never before or since has Europe seen so truly universal an upheaval as in 1848. While the French Revolution of 1789 and the Russian Revolution of 1917 both had immediate international repercussions, in each of these cases a single country took the lead. In 1848 the revolutionary movement broke out spontaneously from native sources from Copenhagen to Palermo and from Paris to Budapest. Contemporaries sometimes attributed the universality of the phenomenon to the machinations of secret societies, and it is true that the faint beginnings of an international revolutionary movement existed before 1848; but the fact is that revolutionary plotters had little influence upon what actually happened, and the nearly simultaneous fall of governments is quite understandable from other causes. Many people in Europe wanted substantially the same things—constitutional government, the independence and unification of national groups, an end to serfdom and manorial restraints where they still existed. With some variation, there was a common body of ideas among politically conscious elements of all countries. Some of the powers that the new forces had to combat were themselves international, notably the Catholic Church and the far-spreading influence of the Hapsburgs, so that resistance to them arose independently in many places. In any case, only the Russian Empire and Great Britain escaped the revolutionary contagion of 1848, and the British received a very bad scare.

But the Revolution of 1848, though it shook the whole Continent, was lacking in basic driving strength. It failed almost as rapidly as it succeeded. Or, more accurately, it misfired. It hit some of its objectives, but missed others, and it set off long chains of direct consequences that were not aimed at. It was the unintended consequences of the Revolution of 1848 that were among the most far-reaching. Within the nationalist turmoil of Central Europe could be discerned the elements of pan-German and pan-Slavic nationalist ambitions. In the social turmoil appeared the first features of modern Marxism and of the contrary doctrines of Bonapartism and of nationalism as a bridge to overarch the gulf between classes.

56. Paris: The Specter of Social Revolution in the West

The July Monarchy in France was a platform of boards built over a volcano. Under it burned the repressed fires of the republicanism put down in 1830, which since 1830 had become steadily more socialistic.[1] Republicanism had its strength in Paris and a few other great cities. But the French political system was so centralized, the prefects instituted by Napoleon in the several departments were so accustomed to taking orders from the Ministry of the Interior, the whole French public was so much in the habit of following the ways of the capital, that Paris was in effect a kind of fuse that might explode the whole country.

Politics in the July Monarchy became increasingly more unreal. So few interests were represented in the Chamber of Deputies that the most basic issues were seldom debated. Even most of the bourgeois class had no representation. Graft and corruption were more common than they should have been, as economic expansion favored stockjobbing and fraud by business promoters and politicians in combination. A strong movement set in to give

―――――――――――

[1] See pp. 455-6, 465-6.

the vote to more people, instead of to only one man in thirty. Radicals wanted universal suffrage and a republic, but liberals asked only for a broadening of voting rights within the existing constitutional monarchy. The king, Louis-Philippe, and his prime minister, Guizot, instead of allying with the latter against the former, resolutely and obtusely opposed any change whatsoever.

THE "FEBRUARY" REVOLUTION IN FRANCE

Reformers, against the king's expressed wishes, planned a great banquet in Paris for February 22, 1848, to be accompanied by demonstrations in the streets. The government on February 21 forbade all such meetings. That night barricades were built in the working-class quarters. These consisted of paving-blocks, building stones, or large pieces of furniture thrown together across the narrow streets and intersections of the old city, and constituting a maze within which insurgents prepared to resist the authorities. The government called out the National Guard, which refused to move. The king now promised electoral reform, but republican firebrands took charge of the semi-mobilized working-class elements, which held a demonstration outside the house of Guizot. Someone shot at the guards placed around the house; the guards replied, killing twenty persons. The republican organizers put some of the corpses on a torch-lit cart and paraded them through the city, which, armed and barricaded, soon began to swarm in an enormous riot. On February 24 Louis-Philippe, like Charles X before him, abdicated and made for England. The February Revolution of 1848, like the July Revolution of 1830, had unseated a monarch in three days.

The constitutional reformers hoped to carry on with Louis-Philippe's young son as king, but the republicans, now aroused and armed, poured into the Chamber of Deputies and forced the proclamation of the Republic. Republican leaders set up a provisional government of ten men, pending election by all France of a Constituent Assembly. Seven of the ten were "straight" republicans, the most notable being the poet Lamartine. Three were "social" republicans, the most notable being Louis Blanc. A huge crowd of working-men appeared before the Hotel de Ville, or city hall, demanding that France adopt the new socialist emblem—the red flag. They were dissuaded by the eloquence of Lamartine, and the tricolor remained the republican standard.

Louis Blanc urged the Provisional Government to push through a bold economic and social program without delay. But since the "social" republicans were in a minority in the Provisional Government (though probably not among Paris republicans generally), Louis Blanc's ideas were very much watered down in the application. He wanted a Ministry of Progress to organize a network of "social workshops," the state-supported and collectivist manufacturing establishments that he had projected in his writings. All that was created was a Labor Commission, with limited powers, and a system of shops significantly entitled "national" rather than "social." The

National Workshops, as they are always called in English (though "workshop" suggests something more insignificant than Louis Blanc had in mind) were agreed to by the Provisional Government only as a political concession, and no significant work was ever assigned them to do, for fear of competition with private enterprise and dislocation of the economic system. Indeed, the man placed in charge of them admitted that his purpose was to prove the fallacies of socialism. Meanwhile the Labor Commission was unable to win public acceptance for the ten-hour-day, which the British Parliament had enacted the year before.

The National Workshops became in practice only an extensive project in unemployment relief. Men of all trades, skilled and unskilled, were set to work digging on the roads and fortifications outside of Paris. They were paid two francs a day. The number of legitimate unemployed increased rapidly, for 1847 had been a year of depression and the revolution prevented the return of business confidence; and a certain number of common idlers naturally presented themselves for remuneration, especially since there were soon too many men for the amount of "work" that was made available. There were 25,000 enrolled in the Workshops by the middle of March, 66,000 by the middle of April, and about 120,000 by the middle of June, by which time there were also in Paris 50,000 other unemployed men whom the bulging Workshops could no longer accommodate. In June there were probably almost 200,000 essentially idle but able-bodied men in a city of about a million people.

The Constituent Assembly, elected in April by universal suffrage throughout France, met on May 4. It immediately replaced the Provisional Government with a temporary executive board of its own. The main body of France, a land of provincial bourgeois and peasant landowners, was not socialist in the least. The new temporary executive board, chosen by the new Constituent Assembly in May, included no "social" republicans. All five of its members, of whom Lamartine was the head, were known as outspoken enemies of Louis Blanc. Blanc and the socialists could no longer expect even the grudging and insincere concessions that they had so far obtained.

The battle lines were now drawn, after only three months of revolution, somewhat as they had been drawn in 1792 after three years.[2] Paris was pitted against the country at large. Still the largest city on the Continent, Paris stood for a degree of revolutionary action that the rest of the country was not prepared to accept. Revolutionary leaders in Paris, in 1848 as in 1792, were unwilling to accept the processes of majority rule or slow parliamentary deliberation. But the crisis in 1848 was more acute than in 1792. A larger proportion of the Paris population were wage-earners. Under a system of predominantly merchant capitalism, in which machine industry and factory concentration were only beginning, they were tormented by the same evils as the more industrialized working classes of England. Hours were if anything longer, and pay less, in France than in Great Britain; insecurity and unem-

[2] See pp. 355-6.

ployment were at least as great; and the feeling that a capitalist economy held no future for the laboring man was the same. In addition, where the English workingman shrank from the actual violation of Parliament, the French workingman saw nothing very sacrilegious in the violation of elected assemblies. Too many regimes in France since 1789, including those preferred by the comfortable classes, had been based on insurrectionary violence for the French workingman to feel much compunction over using it for his own ends.

THE "JUNE DAYS" OF 1848

On the one hand stood the nationally elected Constituent Assembly. On the other, the National Workshops had mobilized in Paris the most distressed elements of the working class. Tens of thousands had been brought together where they could talk, read journals, listen to speeches, and concert common action. Agitators and organizers naturally made use of the opportunity thus presented to them. Men in the Workshops began to feel desperate, to sense that the social republic was slipping from them perhaps forever. On May 15 they attacked the Constituent Assembly, drove its members out of the hall, declared it dissolved, and set up a new provisional government of their own. They announced that a social revolution must follow the purely political revolution of February. But the National Guard, a kind of civilian militia, turned against the insurgents and restored the Constituent Assembly. The Assembly, to root out socialism, prepared to get rid of the National Workshops. It offered those enrolled in them the alternatives of enlistment in the army, transfer to provincial workshops, or being put out of Paris by force. The whole laboring class of the city began to resist. The government proclaimed martial law, the civilian executive board resigned, and all power was given to General Cavaignac and the regular army.

There followed the "Bloody June Days"—June 24–26, 1848—three days during which a terrifying class war raged in Paris. Over twenty thousand men from the Workshops took to arms (more would doubtless have done so had not the government continued to pay wages in the Workshops during the insurrection), and they were joined by other unnumbered thousands from the working-class districts of the city. Half or more of Paris became a labyrinth of barricades defended by determined men and equally stubborn women. Military methods of the time made it possible for civilians to shoot it out openly with soldiers; small arms were the main weapons, and armies had no armored vehicles or even any very devastating artillery. The soldiers found it a difficult operation, even several generals being killed, but after three days the outcome was in doubt no longer. Ten thousand persons had been killed or wounded. Eleven thousand insurgents were taken prisoner. The Assembly, refusing all clemency, decreed their immediate deportation to the colonies.

The June Days sent a shudder throughout France and Europe. Whether the battle in Paris had been a true class struggle, how large a portion of the laboring class had really participated (it was large in any case), how much they had fought for permanent objectives, and how much over the temporary issue of the Workshops—all these are secondary questions. It was widely understood that a class war had in fact broken out. Militant workers were confirmed in a hatred and loathing of the bourgeois class, in a belief that capitalism existed in the last analysis by the callous shooting of laboring men in the streets. People above the laboring class were thrown into a panic. They were sure that they had narrowly escaped a ghastly upheaval. The very ground of civilized living seemed to have quaked. After June, 1848, wrote a French-woman of the time, society was "a prey to a feeling of terror incomparable to anything since the invasion of Rome by the barbarians."

Nor were the signs in England much more reassuring. There the Chartist agitation was revived by the February Revolution in Paris.[3] "France is a Republic!" cried the Chartist Ernest Jones; the Chartist petition was again circulated, and was soon said to have six million signatures. Another Chartist Convention met, considered by its leaders to be the forerunner of a Constituent Assembly as in France. The violent minority was the most active; it began to gather arms and to drill. The old Duke of Wellington swore in 70,000 special constables to uphold the social order. Clashes occurred at Liver-pool and elsewhere; in London the revolutionary committee laid plans for systematic arson and organized men with pick-axes to break up the pavements for barricades. Meanwhile the petition, weighing 584 pounds, was carried in three cabs to the House of Commons, which estimated that it contained "only" two million signatures, and again summarily rejected it. The revolu-tionary menace passed. One of the secret organizers in London proved to be a government spy; he revealed the whole plan at the critical moment, and the revolutionary committee was arrested on the day set for insurrection. Most Chartists had in any case refused to support the militants. All now became discouraged. Tens of thousands emigrated to the United States. The net effect in Great Britain was somewhat as in France. Many of the upper and middle classes felt a sense of unthinkable dangers barely escaped. Soon, how-ever, since there was no actual revolution in Britain in 1848, at a time when the whole Continent was rocking, the prevailing outlook became a compla-cent satisfaction with the stability of British institutions. The belief that no change or improvement was necessary was entrenched more firmly. But the truculent minority of radical workingmen and journalists had a deeper sense of envenomed class-consciousness. The word "proletarian" was imported from France. "Every proletarian," wrote the Chartist editor of Red Revolution, "who does not see and feel that he belongs to an enslaved and degraded class is a fool."

The specter of social revolution thus hung over western Europe in the summer of 1848. Doubtless it was unreal; in all probability there could have been no successful socialist revolution at the time. But the specter was there, and it spread a sinking fear among all who had something to lose. This fear shaped the whole subsequent course of the Second Republic in France, and of

---

[3] See pp. 466–7.

the revolutionary movements that had by this time begun in other countries as well.

THE EMERGENCE OF LOUIS-NAPOLEON BONAPARTE

In France, after the June Days, the Constituent Assembly (keeping General Cavaignac as a virtual dictator) set about drafting a republican constitution. It was decided, in view of the disturbances just passed, to create a strong executive power in the hands of a president to be elected by universal suffrage. It was decided also to have this president elected immediately, even before the rest of the constitution was finished. Four candidates presented themselves: Lamartine, Cavaignac, Ledru-Rollin—and Louis-Napoleon Bonaparte. Lamartine stood for a somewhat vaguely moral and idealistic republic, Cavaignac for a republic of disciplined order, Ledru-Rollin for somewhat chastened "social" ideas. What Bonaparte stood for was not so clear. He was, however, elected by an avalanche of votes in December 1848, receiving over 5,400,000, to only 1,500,000 for Cavaignac, 370,000 for Ledru-Rollin and a mere 18,000 for Lamartine.

Thus entered upon the European stage the second Napoleon. Born in 1808, Louis-Napoleon Bonaparte was the nephew of the great Napoleon. His father, Louis Bonaparte, was at the time of his birth the king of Holland. When Napoleon's own son died in 1832 Louis-Napoleon assumed the headship of the Bonaparte family. He resolved to restore the glories of the Empire. With handfuls of followers he tried to seize power at Strasbourg in 1836 and at Boulogne in 1840, leading what the following century would know as *Putsches*. Both failed ridiculously. Sentenced to life imprisonment in the fortress of Ham, he had escaped from it as recently as 1846 by simply walking off the grounds dressed as a stonemason. He expressed advanced social and political ideas, had probably joined the Carbonari in his youth, and had taken part in the Italian revolutionary uprising of 1830. He wrote two books, one called *Napoleonic Ideas*, claiming that his famous uncle had been misunderstood and checkmated by reactionary forces, and one called the *Extinction of Poverty*, a somewhat anti-capitalistic tract like so many others of its time. But he was no friend of "anarchists," and the spring of 1848, at which time he was still a refugee in England, found him enrolled as one of Wellington's special constables to oppose the Chartist revolution. He soon returned to France. He was compromised neither by the June Days nor by their repression; he was supposed to be a friend of the common man and at the same time a believer in order; and his name was Napoleon Bonaparte.

For twenty years a groundswell had been stirring the popular mind. It is known as the Napoleonic Legend. Bored with the drab bourgeois monarchy, Frenchmen began to dream upon the past. Victor Hugo wrote poems, and Adolphe Thiers histories, in which the name of Napoleon gleamed like a waving sword. Peasants put up pictures of the emperor in their cottages, fondly imagining that it had been Napoleon who gave them the free ownership of their land. The completion of the Arch of Triumph in 1836 drove home the memory of imperial glories, and in 1840 the remains of the Emperor were brought from Saint Helena and majestically interred at the Invalides on the banks of the Seine. All this happened in a country where, government being in the hands of a few, most people had no political experience or political sense except what they had gained in revolution. When millions were suddenly, for the first time in their lives, asked to vote for president in 1848, the name of Bonaparte was the only one they had ever heard of. "How should I not vote for this gentleman," said an old peasant, "I whose nose was frozen at Moscow?"

So Prince Louis-Napoleon became president of the republic, by an overwhelming and indubitable popular mandate, in which an army officer, General Cavaignac, was his only even faintly successful rival. He soon saw the way the wind was blowing. The Constituent Assembly dissolved itself in May 1849, and was replaced by the Legislative Assembly provided for in the new constitution. It was a strange assembly for a republic. It may be recalled that in 1797 the first normal election in the First Republic had produced a royalist majority.[4] Now in the Second Republic, under universal suffrage, the result was the same. Five hundred of the deputies, or two thirds, were really monarchists, but they were divided into irreconcilable factions—the Legitimists, who favored the line of Charles X, and the Orleanists, who favored that of Louis-Philippe. One third of the deputies called themselves republicans. Of these, in turn, over two-thirds, or about 180, were socialists of one kind or another; and only about 70 were "straight" or old-fashioned republicans to whom the main issue was the form of government rather than the form of society itself. The fear that followed the June Days, together with a taxation policy by which peasants paid more taxes under the republic than under the July monarchy, had thrown the mass of the voters into the hands of the monarchists.

The president and the assembly at first combined to conjure away the specter of socialism, with which republicanism itself was now clearly associated. An abortive insurrection of June 1849 provided the chance. The Assembly, backed by the president, ousted thirty-three socialist deputies, suppressed public meetings, and imposed controls on the press. In 1850 it went so far as to rescind universal suffrage, taking the vote away from about a third of the electorate—naturally the poorest and hence most socialistic third. The Falloux law of 1850 put the schools at all levels of the educational system under supervision of the Catholic clergy; for, as M. Falloux said in the Assembly, "lay teachers have made the principles of social revolution popular in the most distant villages," and it was necessary "to rally around religion to strengthen the foundations of society against those who want to divide up property." The French Republic, now actually an anti-republican government, likewise intervened against the revolutionary republic established by Mazzini in the city of Rome. French military forces were sent to Rome to protect the pope; they remained there twenty years.

[4] See p. 365.

To the conservatives Bonaparte knew that he was virtually indispensable. They were sharply divided between two sets of monarchists—Legitimist and Orleanist—who so detested each other that each would accept any anti-socialist regime rather than yield to the other faction. Bonaparte's problem was to win over the radicals. He did so by urging in 1851 the restoration of universal suffrage, which he had himself helped to repeal in 1850. He now posed as the people's friend, the one man in public life who trusted the common man. He let it be thought that greedy plutocrats controlled the Assembly and hoodwinked France. He put his lieutenants in as ministers of War and of the Interior, thus controlling the army, the bureaucracy, and the police. On December 2, 1851, the anniversary of Austerlitz, he sprang his coup d'état. Placards appeared all over Paris. They declared the Assembly dissolved, and the vote for every adult Frenchman reinstated. When members of the Assembly tried to meet they were attacked, dispersed, or arrested by the soldiers. The country did not submit without fighting. One hundred and fifty persons were killed in Paris, and throughout France probably a hundred thousand were put under arrest. But on December 20 the voters elected Louis-Napoleon president for a term of ten years, by a vote officially stated as 7,439,216 to 646,737. A year later the new Bonaparte proclaimed the Empire, with himself as Emperor of the French. Remembering Napoleon's son, he called himself Napoleon III.

How the Empire functioned will be seen below. Not only was the republic dead. The republic as republicans understood it, an equalitarian, anti-clerical regime with socialist or at least anti-bourgeois tendencies, had been dead since June 1848. Feeble anyway, it was killed by its reputation for radicalism. Liberalism and constitutionalism were dead also. Bourgeois and property-owning monarchists were greater sticklers for constitutional liberalism than were the republicans or the Bonapartists, or than town laborers or rural peasants. But the monarchists, hopelessly divided between themselves, were now pushed aside. For the first time since 1815 France ceased to have any parliamentary life. It was ruled by a dictatorship, more demagogic, more calculating, more hollow, and more modern than any that the first Napoleon had ever imagined.

57. Vienna: The Nationalist Revolution in Central Europe and Italy

THE AUSTRIAN EMPIRE IN 1848

The Austrian empire of the Hapsburgs, with its capital at Vienna, was in 1848 the most populous European state except Russia, and its peoples, living principally in the three major geographical divisions of the empire, Austria, Bohemia, and Hungary, were of about a dozen recognizably different nationalities or language groups—Germans, Czechs, Magyars, Poles, Ruthenians, Slovaks, Serbs, Croats, Slovenes, Dalmatians, Rumanians, and Italians.[5] In some parts of the empire the nationalities lived in solid blocks, but in many regions two or more were interlaced together, the language changing from village to village, or even from house to house, in a way quite unknown in western Europe.

Germans, the leading people, occupied all of Austria proper and considerable parts of Bohemia, and were scattered also in small pockets throughout Hungary. The Czechs occupied Bohemia and the adjoining Moravia. The Magyars were the dominant group in the historic kingdom of Hungary, which contained a mixture of nationalities with a considerable number of Slavic peoples. Two of the most advanced parts of Italy also belonged to the empire— Venetia, with its capital at Venice, and Lombardy, whose chief city was Milan.

The Czechs, Poles, Ruthenians, Slovaks, Serbs, Croats, Slovenes, and Dalmatians in the empire were all Slavs; i.e., their languages were all related to one another and to the several forms of Russian. Neither the Magyars nor the Rumanians were Slavs. The Magyars, as national sentiment grew, prided themselves on the uniqueness of their language in Europe, and the Rumanians on their linguistic affiliations with the Latin peoples of the West. Rumanians, Magyars, and Germans formed a thick belt separating the South Slavs (in later years called Yugoslavs) from those of the north. Germans and Italians within the empire were in continual touch with Germans and Italians outside. The peoples of the empire represented every cultural level known to Europe. Vienna, where the Waltz King Johann Strauss was reigning, recognized no peer except Paris itself. Milan was a great center of trade. Bohemia had long had a textile industry of importance, which was beginning to be mechanized in the 1840's; but two hundred miles to the south a Croatian intellectual remarked, about the same time, that the first steam-engine he ever saw was in a picture printed on a cotton handkerchief imported from Manchester. In 1848, some denied that any such people as the Ruthenians existed at all. Nor was it clear exactly what groups made up the South Slavs. No such word as Yugoslavia or Czechoslovakia had been invented, and Rumania was a term used only by professors.

Thus the empire ruled from Vienna included, according to political frontiers established seventy years later, in 1918, all of Austria, Hungary, and Czechoslovakia, with adjoining portions of Poland, Rumania, Yugoslavia, and Italy. But the political authority of Vienna reached far beyond the borders of the empire. Austria since 1815 had been the most influential member of the German confederation, for Prussia in these years was content to look with deference upon the Hapsburgs. The influence of Vienna was felt throughout Germany in many ways, as in the enactment and enforcement of the Carlsbad decrees mentioned in the last chapter.[6] It reached also through the length

~~~~~~~~~~~~~~~~~~~~~~~

[5] See maps, pp. 188, 414–15, 437; and pp. 187–93, 245–9, 306–11, 386–7.
[6] See p. 446.

of Italy. Lombardy and Venetia were part of the Austrian empire. Tuscany, ostensibly independent, was governed by a Hapsburg grand duke. The kingdom of Naples or the Two Sicilies, comprising all Italy south of Rome, was virtually a protectorate of Vienna. The Papal States looked politically to Vienna for leadership, at least until 1846, when the college of cardinals elected a liberally minded Pope, Pius IX—the one contingency upon which Metternich confessed he had failed to reckon. In all Italy there was only one state ruled by a native Italian dynasty and attempting any consistent independence of policy—the kingdom of Sardinia (called also Savoy or Piedmont) tucked away in the northwest corner around Turin. Italy, said Metternich blandly, was only a "geographical expression," a mere regional name. He might have said the same of Poland, or even of Germany, though Germany was tenuously joined in the *Bund*, or loose confederation, of 1815.

These peoples since the turn of the century had all felt the flutters of the *Volksgeist*, persistent stirrings of a cultural nationalism, and among Germans, Italians, Poles, and Hungarians a good deal of political agitation and liberal reformism had been at work. Metternich, in Vienna, had discouraged such manifestations for over thirty years, ominously predicting that if allowed to break out they would produce the *bellum omnium contra omnes*—"the war of all against all." As a prophet he was not wholly mistaken, but if it is the business of statesmanship not merely to prophesy events but to control them it cannot be said that the regime of Metternich was very successful. The whole nationalities question was evaded. The fundamental problem of the century, the bringing of peoples into some kind of mutual and moral relationship with their governments—the problem of which nationalism, liberalism, constitutionalism, and democracy were diverse aspects—remained unconsidered by the responsible authorities of central Europe. All that Metternich offered was the idea that a reigning house, with an official bureaucracy, should rule benevolently over peoples with whom it need have no connection, and who need have no connection with each other. They were the ideas of the eighteenth century, dating from before the French Revolution, and best suited to an agricultural and localistic society.

Trouble in the Austrian realms was an old story. The Polish and Hungarian gentry had been nationalistic for generations. In Italy there had been brief and futile revolutions in 1820 and 1830. In 1846 a revolt broke out in Austrian Poland—Galicia. It was the Polish landowners who were the nationalists, but some of them were not wealthy, and in exile in Western Europe had picked up hazy "communistic" ideas. To win over the masses they promised emancipation of the serfs. But the serfs fought against the landlords, especially in eastern Galicia, where the lower classes were mainly not Polish but Ruthenian. A class war between lord and serf devastated Galicia. The Vienna government backed up the peasants, offered a bounty of ten florins to any peasant capturing a seditious landlord alive or dead, and hesitatingly made a few reforms to protect the serf against the lord. At least 162 landlords are known to have been killed by peasants, often with indescribable cruelty. Polish nationalism again faded out. In Russian Poland it was held down by police repression. This is the reason why in the almost universal rising of 1848 so little is heard of Poland.

THE MARCH DAYS

Elsewhere in the Austrian system, in March 1848, everything collapsed with incredible swiftness. At that time the diet of Hungary had been sitting for some months, considering constitutional reforms, and, as usual, debating further means of keeping German influence out of Hungary. Then came news of the February Revolution in Paris. The radical party in the Hungarian diet was aroused. Its leader, Louis Kossuth, on March 3 made an impassioned speech on the virtues of liberty. This speech was immediately printed in German and read in Vienna, where restlessness was also heightened by the news from Paris. On March 13 workingmen and students rose in insurrection in Vienna, manned barricades, fought off soldiers, and invaded the imperial palace. So flabbergasted and terrified was the government that Metternich, to the amazement of Europe, resigned and fled in disguise to England.

The fall of Metternich proved that the Vienna government was entirely disoriented. Revolution swept through the empire and through all Italy and Germany. On March 15 rioting began in Berlin; the king of Prussia promised a constitution. The lesser German governments collapsed in sequence. On the last day of March a Pre-Parliament met to arrange the calling of an all-German national assembly. In Hungary, aroused by Kossuth's national party, the diet on March 15 enacted the March Laws, by which Hungary assumed a position of complete constitutional separatism within the empire, while still recognizing the Hapsburg house. The harassed Emperor Ferdinand a few days later granted substantially the same status to Bohemia. At Milan between March 18 and 22 the populace drove out the Austrian garrison. Venice proclaimed itself an independent republic. Tuscany drove out its grand-duke and also set up as a republic. The king of Sardinia, Charles Albert (who, stimulated by the Paris revolution, had granted a constitution to his small country on March 4) declared war on Austria on March 23 and invaded Lombardy-Venetia, hoping to bring that area under the House of Savoy. Italian troops streamed up from Tuscany, from Naples (where revolution had broken out as early as January), and even from the Papal States (the new pope being in some sympathy with national and liberal aims) to join in an all-Italian war against the seemingly helpless Austrian government.

Thus in the brief span of these phenomenal March Days the whole structure based on Vienna went to pieces: the Austrian empire had fallen into its main components, Prussia had yielded to revolutionaries, all Germany was preparing to unify itself, and war raged in Italy. Everywhere constitutions had been wildly promised by stupefied governments, constitutional assemblies were meeting and independent or autonomous nations struggled into existence. Patriots everywhere demanded liberal government and national freedom —written constitutions, representative assemblies, responsible ministries, a more or less extended suffrage, restrictions upon police action, jury trial, civil liberty, freedom of press and assembly. And where it still existed—in Prussia, Galicia, Bohemia, Hungary—serfdom was declared abolished and the peasant masses became legally free from control by their local lords.

THE TURNING OF THE TIDE AFTER JUNE

The revolution, as in France, surged forward until the month of June, and then began to ebb. For its steady reflux there are many reasons. The old governments had been only stunned in the March Days, not really broken. They merely awaited the opportunity to take back promises extorted by force. The force originally imposed by the revolutionaries could not be sustained. The revolutionary leaders were not really very strong. Middle-class, bourgeois, property-owning, and commercial interests were nowhere nearly as highly developed as in western Europe. The revolutionary leaders were to a large extent writers, editors, professors and students, men of ideas rather than spokesmen for large positive interests. In Vienna, Milan, and a few other cities the working class was numerous and socialist ideas fairly common; but the workers were not as literate, organized, politically conscious, or irritated as in Paris or Great Britain. They were strong enough, however, to disquiet the middle classes; and especially after the specter of social revolution rose over western Europe, the middle-class and lower-class revolutionaries began to be afraid of each other. The liberated nationalities also began to disagree. The peasants, once emancipated, had no further interest in revolution. Nor were the peasants at this time conscious of nationality; nationalism was primarily a doctrine of the educated middle classes or of the landowning classes in Poland and Hungary. Since the old internationally minded aristocracy furnished the bulk of officers in the armies, and the peasants the bulk of the soldiers, the armies remained almost immune to nationalist aspirations. This attitude of the armies was decisive.

The tide first turned in Prague. The all-German national assembly met at Frankfurt-on-the-Main in May. Representatives from Bohemia had been invited to come to Frankfurt, since many Germans had always lived in Bohemia, and since Bohemia formed part of the confederation of 1815 as it had of the Holy Roman Empire before it. But the idea of belonging to a national German state, a Germany based on the principle that the inhabitants were Germans (which had not been the principle of the Holy Roman Empire or of the confederation of 1815) did not appeal to the Czechs in Bohemia. They refused to go to the all-German congress at Frankfurt. Instead, they called an all-Slav congress of their own. At Prague, in June 1848, this first Pan-Slav assembly met. Most of the delegates were from the Slav communities within the Austrian empire, but a few came from the Balkans and non-Austrian Poland. Only one Russian was present, the anarchist revolutionary Michael Bakunin. Slavs generally did not at this time look with favor upon Russia, the oppressor of Poles; nor did the tsarist government, under Nicholas I, think well of Pan-Slavism, seeing in it a subversive popular agitation.

The spirit of the Prague congress was that of the Slavic revival described in the last chapter;[7] the Czech historian Palacky was in fact one of its most active figures. The congress was profoundly anti-German, since the essence of the Slav revival was resistance to Germanization. But it was not profoundly anti-Austrian or anti-Hapsburg. A few extremists, indeed, maintained that Slavdom should be the basis of political regeneration, and that the world therefore had no place for an Austrian empire. But the great majority at the Prague congress were Austroslavs. Austroslavism held that the many Slavic peoples, pressed on two sides by the population masses of Russians and Germans, needed the Austrian empire as a political frame within which to develop their own national life. It demanded that the Slavic peoples be admitted as equals with the other nationalities in the Austrian empire, enjoying local autonomy and constitutional guarantees.

The Germans of Bohemia, the Sudeten Germans, were of course attracted to the Frankfurt Assembly. They were eager to be included in the unified Germany about to be formed. As the Bohemian Czechs would be a minority in a German Germany, so the Bohemian Germans would be a minority in a Czech Bohemia. Minorities questions are always also questions of frontiers. There was therefore friction among the mixed people of Bohemia, and in Prague, a bilingual city.

The German-Slav issue in the Austrian empire did not seem altogether insuperable. The March revolution produced not only projects for constitutions for the major parts of the empire, but also a project for a federal constitution for the empire as a whole. An assembly sitting at Kremsier in Moravia, and including delegates from almost all parts of the empire except Hungary and north Italy, finally after much heated argument produced a federal plan. By this Kremsier constitution the Germans of the empire, *i.e.*, some of the liberal Germans brought forward by the revolution, acknowledged the main principles of Austroslavism. The empire, as they saw it, should become a federation of equal nationalities. All persons should be assured in their right to have schools, law courts, and a public press in their own language. The empire should be decentralized, with wide powers given to local and municipal authorities. At the same time it should hold together as a federal system under a constitutional monarchy of the House of Hapsburg.

VICTORIES OF THE COUNTER-REVOLUTION, JUNE—DECEMBER

But the Emperor Ferdinand, and the advisors on whom he chose to rely, would have nothing to do with Kremsier constitutions and Austroslavism. These national schemes were also liberal, bristling with restrictions upon the powers of the state. All therefore were to be resisted. The first victory of the old government came at Prague. In that city a Czech insurrection broke out on June 12, at the time when the Slav congress was sitting, and made

~~~~~~~~~~~~~~~~~~

[7] See pp. 440–2.

worse by local animosities between Czechs and Germans. Windischgrätz, the local army commander, bombarded and subdued the city. The Slav congress dispersed. The Hapsburg army was in control.

The next victory of the counter-revolution came in north Italy in the following month. Only Lombardy-Venetia, of all parts of the empire, had declared independence from the Hapsburgs during the upheavals of March. The diminutive kingdom of Sardinia had supported them and had declared war on Austria. Italians from all over the peninsula had flocked in to fight; and until after the June Days in Paris it seemed not impossible that republican France might intervene, to befriend fellow revolutionaries, as in 1796. But in France no radical or expansionist revolution succeeded. In Italy the republicans and the king of Sardinia distrusted each other, a principal belief of republicans being that there should be no kings, and of kings that republicans were dangerously subversive. The troops sent from Naples were recalled to suppress the revolution there. The pope decided that he ought not to be participating in a war. The north Italians were left to themselves. Radetsky, the Austrian commander in Italy, overwhelmingly defeated the king of Sardinia at Custozza on July 25. The Sardinian king, Charles Albert, retreated into his own country. Lombardy and Venetia were restored with savage vengeance to the Austrian empire. In Vienna some of the German revolutionaries (for not all entertained the broad views of Kremsier) expressed a nationalistic delight at this new German suppression of Italian rebels. To some of them liberty meant liberty for Germans, and they failed to perceive that the victorious imperial army would soon be turned against themselves.

The third victory of the counter-revolution came in September and October. The Hungarian radical party of Louis Kossuth was liberal and even democratic in many of its principles, but it was a Magyar nationalist party above all else. Triumphant in the March Days, it completely shook off the German connection. It moved the capital from Pressburg near the Austrian border to Budapest in the center of Hungary. It changed the official language of Hungary from Latin to Magyar. Less than half the people of Hungary were Magyars, and Magyar is an extremely difficult language, quite alien to the Indo-European tongues of Europe. It soon became clear that one must be a Magyar to benefit from the new liberal constitution, and that the Magyars intended to denationalize and Magyarize all others with whom they shared the country. Slovaks, Rumanians, Germans, Serbs, and Croats violently resisted, each group determined to keep its own national identity unimpaired. The Croats, who had enjoyed certain Croatian liberties before the Magyar revolution, took the lead under the "ban" of Croatia, Jellachich. In September Jellachich raised a civil war in Hungary, leading a force of Serbo-Croatians, supported by the whole non-Magyar half of the population. Half of Hungary, alarmed by Magyar nationalism, now looked to the Hapsburgs and the empire to protect them. Emperor Ferdinand made Jellachich his military commander against the Magyars. Hungary dissolved into the war of all against all.

At Vienna the more clear-sighted revolutionaries now saw that Jellachich's army, if successful against the Magyars, would soon be turned against revolutionists in Vienna. They therefore rose in a second mass insurrection (the first since March) in October 1848. The emperor fled; never had the Viennese revolution gone so far. But it was already too late. The Austrian military leader Windischgrätz brought his intact forces down from Bohemia. He besieged Vienna for five days, and forced its surrender on October 31.

With the recapture of Vienna the upholders of the old order took heart. Counter-revolutionary leaders—large estate-holders, Catholic clergy, high-ranking army men—decided to clear the way by getting rid of the Emperor Ferdinand, considering that promises made in March by Ferdinand might be more easily repudiated by his successor. Ferdinand abdicated, and on December 2, 1848, was succeeded by Francis Joseph, a boy of eighteen, destined to live until 1916, and to end his reign in a crisis even more shattering than that in which he began it.

FINAL OUTBURST AND REPRESSION, 1849

For a time in the first part of 1849 the revolution in many places seemed to blaze more fiercely than ever. Republican riots broke out in parts of Germany. In Rome someone assassinated the reforming minister of Pius IX; the pope fled from the city, and a radical Roman Republic was proclaimed under three Triumvirs, one of whom was Mazzini, who hastened from England to take part in the republican upheaval. In north Italy Charles Albert of Sardinia again invaded Lombardy. In Hungary, after the revived Hapsburg authorities repudiated the new Magyar constitution, the Magyars, led by the flaming Kossuth, went on to declare absolute independence. But all these manifestations proved short-lived. German republicanism flickered out. Mazzini and his republicans were driven from Rome, and Pius IX was restored, by intervention of the French army.[8] The Sardinian king was again defeated by Radetsky at Novara on March 23, 1849. In Hungary the Magyars put up a terrific resistance, which the imperial army and the anti-Magyar native irregulars could not overcome. The Hapsburg authorities now renewed the procedures of the Holy Alliance. The new Emperor Francis Joseph invited the Tsar Nicholas to intervene. Over a hundred thousand Russian troops poured over the mountains into Hungary, soon defeated the Magyars, and laid the prostrate country at the feet of the court of Vienna. This was in August 1849.

The nationalist upheaval of 1848 in central Europe and Italy was now over. Reaction, or anti-revolutionism, became the order of the day. Things were not as they had been before 1848. That was impossible. The old governments and states were restored, but the attitude of those who governed was different. Pius IX, the "liberal pope" of 1846, resumed the papal throne disillusioned in his liberal ideas. The breach between liberalism and Roman Catholicism, which had opened wide in the first French Revolution, was

〰〰〰〰〰〰〰〰〰〰

[8] See p. 476.

made a yawning chasm by the revolutionary violence of Mazzini's Roman Republic and by the measures taken to repress it. Pius IX now reiterated the anathemas of his predecessors. He codified them in 1864 in the *Syllabus of Errors*, which warned all Catholics, on the authority of the Vatican, against everything that went under the names of liberalism, progress, and civilization. As for the nationalists in Italy, many were disillusioned with the fire-cracker methods of romantic republicans, and inclined to conclude that Italy would be liberated from Austrian influence only by an old-fashioned war between established powers.

In the Austrian empire, under Prince Schwarzenberg, the Emperor's chief minister, the main policy was now to oppose all forms of popular self-expression, with a sophistication, in view of the events of 1848, that Metternich had never known, and with a candid reliance on military force. Constitutionalism was to be rooted out, as well as all forms of nationalism—Slavism, Magyarism, Italianism, and also Germanism, which would draw the sentiments of Austrian Germans from the Hapsburg empire to the great kindred body of the German people. The regime came to be called the Bach system, after Alexander Bach, the minister of the interior. Under it, the government was rigidly centralized. Hungary lost the separate rights it had had before 1848. The ideal was to create a perfectly solid and unitary political system. Bach insisted on maintaining the emancipation of the peasants, which had converted the mass of the people from subjects of their landlords into subjects of the state. He drove through a reform of the legal system and law courts, created a free trading area of the whole empire with only a common external tariff, and subsidized and encouraged the building of highways and railroads. The aim, as in France at the same time under Louis-Napoleon, was to make people forget liberty in an overwhelming demonstration of administrative efficiency and material progress. But some, at that time, would not forget. A liberal said of the Bach system that it consisted of "a standing army of soldiers, a sitting army of officials, a kneeling army of priests, and a creeping army of informers."

58. Frankfurt and Berlin: The Question of a Liberal Germany

THE GERMAN STATES

Meanwhile, from May 1848 to May 1849, the Frankfurt Assembly was sitting at the historic city on the Main. It was attempting to bring a unified German state into being, one which should also be liberal and constitutional, assuring civil rights to its citizens, and possessing a government responsive to popular will as manifested in free elections and open parliamentary debate. The failure to produce a democratic Germany has been one of the overshadowing facts of modern times.

The convocation of the Frankfurt Assembly was made possible by the collapse of the existing German governments in the March Days of 1848. The existing governments, the thirty-eight states created in Germany by Napoleon and the Congress of Vienna, were the main obstacles in the way of unification. The reigning princes, and their ministers and upper civil servants, enjoyed a heightened political stature from political independence. The German states resisted the surrender of sovereignty to a united Germany just as national states in the next century were to resist the surrender of sovereignty to a United Nations. In another way Germany was a miniature of the political world. It consisted of both great and small powers. Its great powers were Prussia and Austria. Austria was the miscellaneous empire described above; Prussia included the Rhineland obtained in 1815, a central region around Berlin, and an eastern region inhabited by a mixture of Germans and Poles.[9] Neither of these great powers could submit to the other, or allow the other to dominate its lesser German neighbors. The small German powers, in turn, upheld their own independence in the balance between the two great ones.

This German "dualism," or polarity between Berlin and Vienna, had been somewhat abated under the common menace of the Napoleonic empire. Then from 1815 to 1848 the Prussian kings, Frederick William III and Frederick William IV, had adopted a deferential respectfulness toward the House of Austria. Sharing the ideology of conservatism, they had made no open issue of Metternich's influence in the lesser states. The whole German question had lain dormant, so far as the governments were concerned, nor did it agitate the old aristocracies. In Prussia the *Junkers*, the owners of great landed estates east of the Elbe, were singularly indifferent to the all-German dream. Their political feeling was not German but Prussian. They were making a good thing of Prussia for themselves, and could expect only to lose by absorption into Germany as a whole, for in Germany west of the Elbe the small peasant holding was the basis of society, and there was no landowning element corresponding to the *Junkers*. The rest of Germany reciprocated the sense of difference, looking upon Prussia as somewhat uncouth and eastern; but this feeling, too, had been abated in the time of Napoleon, when patriots from all over Germany enlisted in the Prussian service.[10]

BERLIN: FAILURE OF THE REVOLUTION IN PRUSSIA

Prussia was illiberal but not backward. Frederick William III repeatedly evaded his promise to grant a modern constitution.[11] His successor, Frederick William IV, who inherited the throne in 1840, and from whom much was at first hoped by liberals, proved to be a somewhat cloudy and neo-medieval romantic, equally determined not to share his authority with his subjects. At the same time the government, administratively speaking, was efficient, progressive, and fair. The universities and elementary school system

[9] See maps, pp. 198–9, 414–15.   [11] See p. 444.
[10] See p. 406.

surpassed those of Western Europe. In few places was literacy so high. The government followed in mercantilist traditions of evoking, planning, and supporting economic life.[12] In 1818 it initiated a tariff union, at first with tiny states (or enclaves) wholly enclosed within Prussia. This tariff union, or *Zollverein*, was extended in the following decades until by 1848 almost all Germany, outside of Austria and Bohemia, was joined in an economic union led by Prussia. Compared with the "China of Europe," the unmoving Austria of Metternich, Prussia seemed progressive and forward-looking.

On March 15, 1848, as noted above in passing, rioting and street-fighting broke out in Berlin. For a time it seemed as if the army would master the situation. But the king, Frederick William IV, a man of notions and projects, and erratically conscientious, called off the soldiers and allowed his subjects to elect the first all-Prussian legislative assembly. Thus though the army remained intact, and its *Junker* officers unconvinced, revolution proceeded superficially on its way. The Prussian assembly proved surprisingly radical, since it was dominated by anti-*Junker* lower-class extremists from East Prussia. These men had long been in touch with Polish revolutionaries and exiles. Their main belief was that the fortress of reaction was tsarist Russia—that the whole structure of Junkerdom, landlordism, serf-owning, and repression of national freedom depended ultimately on the armed might of the tsarist empire. The subsequent intervention of Russia in Hungary gave an indication of the truth of this diagnosis.

Prussian radicals, like those elsewhere, therefore hoped to smash the Holy Alliance by raising an all-German or even European revolutionary war against Russia. To precipitate it the Prussian radical party supported the claims of the Poles. The Berlin assembly granted local Polish self-government in Polish Prussia. But in Polish Prussia (West Prussia and Posen), as in Bohemia, Germans and Slavs had long lived side by side. The Germans in Posen refused to respect the authority of Polish officials. Prussian army units stationed in Posen supported the German element. As early as April 1848, a month after the "revolution," the army crushed the new pro-Polish institutions set up in Posen by the Berlin assembly. It was clear where the only real power lay. By the end of 1848, in Prussia as in Austria, the revolution was over. The king again changed his mind; and the old authorities, acting through the army, were again in control.

THE FRANKFURT ASSEMBLY

Meanwhile a similar story was enacted on the larger stage of Germany as a whole. The disabling of the old governments left what is known in modern parlance as a power vacuum. A self-appointed committee convoked a Pre-Parliament, which in turn arranged for the election of an all-German assembly. By-passing the existing sovereignties, voters throughout Germany sent delegates to Frankfurt to create a federated super-state. The strength

wwwwwwwwwwwwww

[12] See pp. 102–4, 307, 311–12.

and weakness of the resulting Frankfurt Assembly originated in this manner
of its election. The Assembly represented the moral sentiment of people at
large, the liberal and national aspirations of many Germans. It stood for an
idea. Politically it represented nothing. The delegates had no power to commit anybody to do anything. There was no one to whom they could issue
orders and expect compliance. Superficially resembling the National Assembly which met in France in 1789, the German National Assembly at Frankfurt was really in a very different position. There was no pre-existing national
structure for it to work with. There was no all-German king from whom
sovereignty could be wrested, and no all-German army or civil service for the
Assembly to take over. The whole history of the Frankfurt Assembly may be
summarized in the remark that, having no power of its own, it became dependent on the power of the very sovereign states that it was attempting to
supersede.

The Assembly met in May 1848. Its members with a handful of exceptions were not at all revolutionary. They were overwhelmingly professional
people—professors, judges, lawyers, government administrators, clergy both
Protestant and Catholic, and prominent business men. They wanted a liberal,
self-governing, federally unified and "democratic" though not equalitarian
Germany. Their outlook was earnest, peaceable, and legalistic; they hoped
to succeed by persuasion. Violence was abhorrent to them. They wanted no
armed conflict with the existing German states, even had they had the wherewithal to conduct it. They wanted no war with Russia. They wanted no general international upheaval of the working classes. The example of the June
Days in Paris, and of the Chartist agitation in Great Britain, coinciding with
the early weeks of the Frankfurt Assembly, increased the dread of that body
for radicalism and republicanism in Germany. The tragedy of Germany (and
hence of Europe) lies in the fact that this German revolution came too late,
at a time when social revolutionaries had already begun to declare war on the
bourgeoisie, and the bourgeoisie was already afraid of the common man. It is
the common man, not the professor or respectable merchant, who in unsettled times actually seizes firearms and rushes to shout revolutionary utterances
in the streets. Without lower class insurrection not even middle-class revolutions have been successful. The combination effected in France between
1789 and 1794, an unwilling and divergent combination of bourgeois and
lower-class revolutionaries, was not and could not be effected in Germany in
1848. One form of revolutionary power—controlled popular turbulence—the
Germans of the Frankfurt Assembly would not or could not use. Quite the
contrary: when radical riots broke out in Frankfurt itself in September 1848
the Assembly undertook to repress them. Having no force of its own, it appealed to the Prussian army. The Prussian army put down the riots, and
thereafter the Assembly met under its protection.

But the most troublesome question facing the Frankfurt Assembly was
not social but national. What, after all, was this "Germany" which so far existed only in the mind? Where was the line really to be drawn in space? Did
Germany include Austria and Bohemia, which belonged to the _Bund_ of 1815

and had in former days belonged to the Holy Roman *Reich?*[18] Did it include all Prussia, although eastern Prussia had lain outside the *Reich*, and did not now belong to the *Bund?* On the side toward Denmark, did it include the duchies of Schleswig and Holstein, which belonged to the Danish king, who was therefore himself, as ruler of Holstein, a member of the 1815 confederation? And if, as poets said, the Fatherland existed wherever the German tongue was spoken, what of the German communities in Hungary and Moravia, or along the upper Baltic and in the city of Riga, or in some of the Swiss cantons and the city of Zurich, or for that matter in Holland, which had left the Holy Empire only two hundred years before—not long as time is measured in Europe.

These last and most soaring speculations, though they had already been launched by a few bold spirits, were put out of mind by the men of the Frankfurt Assembly. The other questions remained. The men at Frankfurt, eager to create a real Germany, naturally could not offer one smaller than the shadow Germany that they so much deplored. Most therefore were Great Germans; they thought that the Germany for which they were writing a constitution should include the Austrian lands, except Hungary. This would mean that the federal crown must be offered to the Hapsburgs. Others, at first a minority, were Little Germans; they thought that Austria should be excluded, and that the new Germany should comprise the smaller states and the entire kingdom of Prussia. In that case the king of Prussia would become the federal emperor. Under Great German auspices, the Pre-Parliament had invited Bohemian delegates to come to Frankfurt, had met with the refusal from the Czechs described above, and had precipitated the calling of the Prague Assembly in reply. These manifestations of Slavism were annoying to the Germanists at Frankfurt. Nationally minded Germans, both moderate and radical, believed that the Slavs west of Russia were destined for assimilation to German culture, following the Sorbs, Wends, Polabs, Kashubes, and other extinct or nearly extinct Slavonic peoples. They would point to the United States, where the English-speaking element gradually assimilated all others. And in truth the civilizing influence of Germans in Eastern Europe was a historical fact, though German nationalists greatly idealized it.

The desire of the Frankfurt Assembly to retain non-German peoples in the new Germany, at a time when these peoples also were feeling national ambitions, was another reason for its fatal dependency upon the Austrian and Prussian armies. The Frankfurt Assembly applauded when Windischgrätz broke the Czech revolution. It expressed its satisfaction when Prussian forces put down the Poles in Posen. On this matter the National Assembly at Frankfurt and the Prussian assembly at Berlin did not agree. The men of Frankfurt, thinking the Prussians too radical and pro-Polish, and wanting no war with Russia, in effect supported the Prussian army and the *Junkers* against the Berlin revolution, without which the Frankfurt Assembly itself could never have existed.

[18] See maps, pp. 414–15, 523.

A still clearer case arose over Schleswig-Holstein. These duchies belonged to the Danish king. Schleswig, the northern of the two, had a mixed population of Danes and Germans. The Germans in Schleswig rebelled in March 1848; and the Danes, who also had a constitutional upheaval at the time, proceeded to incorporate Schleswig integrally into their modernized Danish state. When the Frankfurt Assembly met, it found that the Pre-Parliament had already declared an all-German war upon Denmark in defense of fellow Germans in Schleswig. Having no army of its own, the Frankfurt Assembly invited Prussia to fight the war; and the revolutionary Prussian government in Berlin was at first able to persuade the Prussian generals to initiate a campaign. Great Britain and Russia prepared to intervene to keep control of the mouth of the Baltic out of German hands. The Prussian army simply withdrew from the war. Its officers had no desire to antagonize Russia or to advance the interests of nationalist revolutionaries in Germany. The Frankfurt Assembly, humiliated and helpless, was obliged to accept the armistice concluded by the Prussian generals. Radical socio-nationalistic riots broke out against the *Junkers,* the tsar and the Frankfurt Assembly; and it was at this time that the Assembly called in Prussian forces for its own protection.

THE FAILURE OF THE FRANKFURT ASSEMBLY

By the end of 1848 the débacle was approaching. The nationalists had checkmated each other. Everywhere in central Europe, from Denmark to Naples and from the Rhineland to the Transylvanian forests, the awakening nationalities had failed to respect each other's aspirations, had delighted in each other's defeats, and by quarreling with each other had hastened the return of the old absolutist and non-national order. At Berlin and at Vienna the counter-revolution, backed by the army, was in the saddle. At this very time, in December, the Frankfurt Assembly at last issued a Declaration of the Rights of the German People. It was a humane and high-minded document, announcing numerous individual rights, civil liberties, and constitutional guarantees, much along the line of the French and American declarations of the eighteenth century, but with one significant difference—the French and Americans spoke of the rights of man, the Germans of the rights of Germans. In April 1849 the Frankfurt Assembly completed its constitution. It was now clear that Austria must be excluded, for the simple reason that the restored Hapsburg government refused to come in. The Danubian empire, as already seen, was as profoundly opposed to Germanism as to any other nationalistic movement. The Little Germans in the Assembly therefore had their way. The hereditary headship of a new German *Reich* or empire, a constitutional and federal union of German states minus Austria, was now offered to Frederick William IV, the king of Prussia.

Frederick William was tempted. The Prussian army officers and East-Elbian landlords were not. They had no wish to lose Prussia in Germany.

The king himself had his scruples. If he took the proffered crown he would still have to impose himself by force on the lesser states, which the Frankfurt Assembly did not represent and could not bind, and which were in fact still the actual powers in the country. He could also expect trouble with Austria. He did not wish war. Nor was it proper for an heir to the Hohenzollerns to accept a throne circumscribed with constitutional limitations, and representing the revolutionary conception of the sovereignty of the people. Declaring that he could not "pick up a crown from the gutter," he turned it down. It would have to be offered freely by his equals, the sovereign princes of Germany.

Thus all the work of the Frankfurt Assembly went for nothing. Most members of the Assembly, having never dreamed of using violence in the first place, concluded that they were beaten and went home. A handful of extremists remained at Frankfurt, promulgated the constitution on their own authority, urged revolutionary outbreaks, and called for elections. Riots broke out in various places. The Prussian army put them down—in Saxony, in Bavaria, in Baden. The same army drove the rump Assembly out of Frankfurt, and that was the end of it.

But the king of Prussia, like Caesar, really craved the crown he spurned. He devised a German union of his own, a federation of the German princes without Austria. A united Germany of any kind, even monarchist and conservative, was distasteful to Schwarzenberg's government at Vienna, and at least equally so to a mightier potentate, the Russian tsar. For centuries, indeed, the division of Germany had been basic to the whole political structure of Europe. At a conference at Olmütz in 1850 the three eastern monarchies reached an agreement: the king of Prussia would drop his German plan, and the loose confederation of 1815 would be restored. This incident, under the influence of Prusso-German writers of later years, passed into the history books as the "humiliation" of Olmütz.

In summary, Germany in 1848 failed to solve the problem of its unification in a liberal and constitutional way. Liberal nationalism failed, and a less gentle kind of nationalism soon replaced it. The German movement of 1848, like so much else in German history, in the long run contributed to a fateful estrangement between Germany and the west. Thousands of disappointed German liberals and revolutionaries migrated to the United States, which came to know them as the "Forty-eighters." They brought to the new country, besides a ripple of revolutionary agitation, a stream of men trained in science, medicine, and music, and of highly skilled craftsmen like silversmiths and engravers.

THE PRUSSIAN CONSTITUTION OF 1850

In Prussia itself the ingenious monarch undertook to placate everybody by issuing a constitution of his own, one that should be peculiarly Prussian. It remained in effect from 1850 to 1918. It granted a single parliament for all the miscellaneous regions of Prussia. The parliament met in two chambers. The lower chamber was elected by universal suffrage, not along the individualist or equalitarian principles of the West, but by a system that in effect divided the population into three estates—the wealthy, the less wealthy, and the general run of the people. Division was made according to payment of taxes. Those few big taxpayers who together contributed a third of the tax-returns elected a third of the deputies in the lower house. Middle-sized tax-payers elected another third; and all the numerous small people whose combined payments made up only a third of the total taxes elected only a third of the representatives. One large property-owner thus had as much voting power as hundreds of working people. Large property in Prussia in 1850 still meant mainly the landed estates of the East-Elbian *Junkers*, but as time went on it came to include industrial property in the Rhineland also. The *Junkers* likewise were not harmed by the final liquidation of serfdom. They increased the acreage of their holdings, as after the reforms of Stein; [14] and the former servile agricultural workers turned into free wage-earners economically dependent on the great landowners.

For 1850 the Prussian constitution was fairly progressive. If the mass of the people could elect no more than a third of the deputies, the mass of the British people, until 1867 or even 1884, could elect no deputies to Parliament at all. But the Prussian constitution remained in force until 1918. By the close of the nineteenth century, with democratic advances elsewhere, the electoral system in Prussia, remaining unchanged, had come to be reactionary and illiberal, giving the great landowners and industrialists an unusual position of special privilege within the state.

59. Consequences of the 1848 Movements: The New Toughness of Mind

THE RESULTS OF 1848

The Revolution of 1848 failed not only in Germany but also in Hungary, in Italy, and in France. The dreams of half a century, visions of a humanitarian nationalism, aspirations for liberalism without violence, ideals of a peaceful and democratic republican commonwealth, were all blasted in 1848. Everywhere the cry had been for constitutional government, but only in a few small states—Denmark, Holland, Belgium, Switzerland, Sardinia— was constitutional liberty more firmly secured by the Revolution of 1848. Everywhere the cry had been for the freedom of nations, to unify national groups or rid them of foreign rule; but nowhere was national liberty more advanced in 1850 than it had been two years before. France obtained universal suffrage in 1848, and kept it permanently thereafter; but it did not ob-

wwwwwwwwwwwww

14 See p. 408.

tain democracy; it obtained a kind of mass dictatorship under Louis-Napoleon Bonaparte. One accomplishment, however, was real enough. The peasantry was emancipated in the German states and the Austrian empire. Serfdom and manorial restraints were abolished, nor were they reimposed after the failure of the revolution. This was the most fundamental accomplishment of the whole movement. The peasant masses of central Europe were thereafter free to move about, find new jobs, enter a labor market, take part in a money economy, receive and spend wages, migrate to growing cities—or even go to the United States. But the peasants, once freed, showed little concern for constitutional or bourgeois ideas; and peasant emancipation in fact strengthened the forces of political counter-revolution.

Possibly the failure of the 1848 revolution frustrated the democratic development of Europe. Possibly its failure saved Europe from ruin. Had the more zealous revolutionists been more successful, there might indeed have been a spread of democratic institutions, but there might also have been war with Russia, turning into a general European war, inflamed class violence, and nationalistic strife. Possibly the balance of successes and failures gave Europe a half-century of respite for the constructive development of its civilization. The tradition of slow and unforced Parliamentary change was confirmed in England. Constitutionalism was established permanently in the small states of the west. The propertied classes of Europe—bourgeois, landlords, small landowning peasants—were secured. The 1850's initiated a period of rising prices and wages, of general economic prosperity as compared with the 1840's; the working classes quieted down, and revolutionary agitation subsided. But the Revolution of 1848 had deposited some deeply laid time-bombs—class hatred and national jealousy, pan-Germanism and pan-Slavism, a dictatorship in France betraying certain features later called "fascist," and last but not least the philosophy of Karl Marx.

REALISM AND REALPOLITIK

The most immediate and far-reaching consequence of the 1848 revolution was a moral reorientation. Idealism was discredited. Ideas themselves were seen in a new way. It had been proved insufficient to have only an idea (or "ideal") of Germany, or an idea of Austroslavism, or an idea of constitutional liberty, or of a socialized community, or of a free and equal republic. It had been shown that an idea could not be realized unless one had the means to achieve it. Emphasis therefore began to fall upon the means. It had been shown everywhere, but most clearly and unmistakably in Germany, that no political aim could be accomplished without power. People therefore became interested in power itself, in what it was, and how to obtain it.

Formerly men had prided themselves on being idealistic—on holding and working for ideas because they believed them to be right. Even conservatives of the old school, like Metternich and Wellington, believed in principle in the old order of things which they defended. Now, as the years passed after 1848, men prided themselves on being realistic, emancipated from illusions, willing to face facts as they were. Whether an idea was "right" became a somewhat irrelevant if not unanswerable question. The question was whether it was workable. A good idea was one that would succeed. The test was to be found in practical results. In any case, it now seemed, ideas had no especial validity in themselves. They were mere products, results of causes, outgrowths of social conditions. The question was not whether representative government was right or reasonable, suited to the nature of free and rational human beings. That was the old eighteenth-century way of thinking. The questions on representative government were, rather, what form of society it was suited for, what social classes demanded it, what they proposed to do with it, how they would advance their interests if they had it.

Everywhere after 1848 could be detected a new toughness of mind. It was an insistence on seeing facts, viewing things as they are rather than as they ought to be. In literature and the arts it was called "realism." Writers and painters broke away from romanticism, which they said colored things out of all relation to the real facts. They attempted to describe and reproduce life exactly as they found it, without intimation of a better or more noble world. More and more people came to trust science, not merely for an understanding of nature, but for insights into the true meaning of man and society. In religion the movement was toward skepticism, renewing the skeptical trend of the eighteenth century, which had been somewhat halted during the intervening period of romanticism. It was variously held, not by all but by many, that religion was unscientific and hence not to be taken seriously; or that it was a mere historical growth among peoples in certain stages of development, and hence irrelevant to modern civilization; or that one ought to go to church and lead a decent life, without taking the priest or clergyman too seriously, because religion was necessary to preserve the social order against radicalism and anarchy. To this idea the radical counterpart was of course that religion was a bourgeois invention to delude the people.

In basic philosophy the new mental toughness appeared as materialism, holding that everything mental, spiritual, or ideal, was an outgrowth of physical or physiological forces. It appeared as positivism, holding that to have reliable knowledge one should concentrate on concrete facts and avoid abstract ideas. Its great exponent was the French philosopher Auguste Comte. It appeared also as voluntarism, deriving from a profound work published as long ago as 1819, but ignored for thirty years, *The World as Will and Idea* by the German Arthur Schopenhauer. Schopenhauer, much influenced by the philosophy of India (which became known to Europe as the British empire advanced there) held that the underlying reality of the universe was will—a blind, instinctual, dynamic, driving will-to-live. Ideas formed in the mind, he thought, were rather shadowy representations, more or less useful, projected by this will for its own purposes. Schopenhauer himself taught that men could only be happy and at peace if the will-force was suppressed. But what the world learned from him was that thought and reason were offshoots of interests, urges, and drives. Since urges and interests were facts, would it not be "unrealistic" and "unscientific" to suppress them? And how would one know which facts to suppress and which to encourage, without going back to merely "idealistic" ideas of reason and right?

In politics the new toughness of mind was called by the Germans *Realpolitik*. This simply meant a "politics of reality." In domestic affairs it meant that people should give up utopian dreams, such as had caused the débacle of 1848, and content themselves with the blessings of an orderly, honest, hardworking government. For radicals it meant that people should stop imagining that the new society would result from goodness or the love of justice, and that social reformers must resort to the methods of politics—power and calculation. In international affairs it meant that governments should not be guided by ideology, or by any system of "natural" enemies or "natural" allies, or by any desire to defend or promote any particular view of the world; but that they should follow their own practical interests, meet facts and situations as they arose, make any alliances that seemed useful, disregard tastes and scruples, use any practical means to achieve their ends. The same men who, before 1848, had been not ashamed to express pacifist and cosmopolitan hopes now dismissed such ideas as a little soft-headed. War, which governments since the overthrow of Napoleon had successfully tried to prevent, was accepted in the 1850's as an obvious means sometimes necessary to achieve a purpose. It was not especially glorious; it was not an end in itself; it was simply one of the tools of the statesman. *Realpolitik* was by no means confined to Germany, despite its German name and although Bismarck became its most famous practitioner. Two other tough-minded thinkers, each in his way, were Louis-Napoleon Bonaparte and Karl Marx.

60. The Birth of Marxism

MARX AND ENGELS: THE COMMUNIST MANIFESTO, 1848

Marxism, which a century later was to command the assent of hundreds of millions in all parts of the world, first made its appearance in January 1848 with the publication of an obscure tract called *The Communist Manifesto*. It was written by two Germans, Karl Marx and Frederick Engels, for an organization that called itself the Communist League. Marx (1818–83), son of a lawyer in the Prussian Rhineland, was a democratic-radical newspaper man, who had studied law and philosophy. Engels (1820–95) was the son of a well-to-do German textile manufacturer who owned a factory at Manchester, which the young Engels went to England to manage. Marx and Engels met in Paris in 1844. There they began a collaboration in thinking and writing that lasted for forty years. In 1847 they joined the Communist League.

This League, which had also called itself the League of the Just, was a tiny secret group of revolutionaries, mainly Germans in exile in the more liberal western Europe. The League, according to Engels, was at first "not actually much more than the German branch of the French secret societies." It aspired to become international, and worked by tactics of infiltration. In 1840, for example, a group of German workingmen living in London had founded the German Workers' Educational Association. This society, wrote Engels later, was used by the League as a recruiting ground,

and since, as always, the Communists were the most active and intelligent members of the Association, it was a matter of course that its leadership lay entirely in the hands of the League. The League soon had several local sections, or, as they were still called, "lodges," in London. The same obvious tactics were followed in Switzerland and elsewhere. Where workers' associations could be founded, they were utilized in like manner. Where this was forbidden by law, one entered choral societies, gymnastic clubs and the like.

Though the *Manifesto* published in January 1848 passed quite unnoticed, and had no influence on the upheaval that soon occurred, members of the League agitated like those of other societies during the Revolution of 1848. They issued a set of "Demands of the Communist Party in Germany," which urged a unified indivisible German republic, democratic suffrage, universal free education, arming of the people, a progressive income tax, limitations upon inheritance, state ownership of banks, railroads, canals, mines, *etc.*, and a degree of large-scale, scientific, collectivized agriculture. It was such obscurely voiced radicalism that alarmed the Frankfurt Assembly. With the triumph of counter-revolution in Germany the Communist League was crushed. Engels returned to his factory at Manchester, and Marx also settled in England, spending the rest of his life in London, where, after long labors in the British Museum, he finally produced his huge work called *Capital*, of which the first volume was published in 1867.

Marxism played no real role in the Revolution of 1848. Not for another twenty years was Marxian socialism at all well known even to socialists. As a historical force Marxism set in in the 1870's. But it grew out of and exactly reflected the conditions of the 1840's. The main positions of Marxism were all mapped out in the *Communist Manifesto* and in contemporary studies which Marx and Engels made of the 1848 revolution. One of these, *Germany: Revolution and Counter-revolution*, first appeared as a series of dispatches to the *New York Tribune* in 1851 and 1852, for which Horace Greeley paid five dollars apiece. Another, *The Eighteenth Brumaire of Louis Bonaparte*, was also first published in 1852 in the United States, in a German-language paper called *Die Revolution*.

SOURCES AND CONTENT OF MARXISM

Marxism may be said to have had three sources, or to have merged three national streams: French revolutionism, the British Industrial Revolution, and German philosophy. Without the massive fact of the Great French

Revolution standing at the opening of the nineteenth century it is doubtful whether anyone would have developed so improbable a doctrine as the abrupt and total renovation of human affairs by The Revolution. But revolution had in fact occurred; it therefore might occur again. What the bourgeois class had done, the workers could do too. And Marxism along with all early forms of socialism pointed to the unredeemed promise of the French Revolution, the idea that social and economic equality would follow the civil and legal equality already won.[15] The revolutionary outbreaks of 1848, coming within a few weeks of the publication of the *Communist Manifesto*, naturally confirmed Marx and Engels in their beliefs, and the actual class war that shook Paris in the June Days was taken by them as a manifestation of a universal class struggle. But Marx was no mere insurrectionary schemer, like the "revolution-makers," as he contemptuously called them. His thought was a system for producing revolution, but it showed how the future revolution must come by the operation of vast impersonal forces.

Engels, a Manchester factory owner, possessed a personal knowledge of the new industrial and factory system in England. He was in touch with a few of the most radical Chartists, though he had no respect for Chartism itself as a revolutionary movement. In 1844 he published a revealing book on *The Condition of the Working Classes in England*. The depressed condition of labor, to which Marxism like all forms of socialism called emphatic attention, was an actual fact.[16] It was a fact that labor received a relatively small portion of the national income, and that much of the product of society was being reinvested in capital goods, which belonged as private property to private persons. Government and parliamentary institutions, also as a matter of fact, were in the hands of the well-to-do in both Great Britain and France. Religion was commonly held to be necessary to keep the lower classes in order. The churches at the time, as a matter of fact, took next to no interest in problems of the workers. At best, evangelical sects taught the poor that they must be patient. The family, as an institution, was in fact disintegrating among laboring people in the cities, through employment of women and children and the overcrowding in inadequate and unsanitary living quarters. All these facts were seized upon and dramatized in the *Communist Manifesto*: The worker is deprived of the wealth he has himself created! The state is a committee of the bourgeoisie for the exploitation of the people! Religion is a drug to keep the workingman quietly dreaming upon imaginary heavenly rewards! The worker's family, his wife and children, have been prostituted and brutalized by the bourgeoisie! It seemed to Marx and Engels that the uprooted workingman should be loyal to nothing—except his own class. Even country had become meaningless. The proletarian had no country. Workers everywhere had the same problems and faced everywhere the same enemy. Therefore "let the ruling classes tremble at a communist revolution. The proletarians have nothing to lose but their chains.

---

[15] See pp. 434–6, 466.
[16] See pp. 426–9, 465.

They have a world to win. Workingmen of all countries, unite!" So closed
the *Manifesto*.

It was from English sources that Marx also took over much of his
economic theory. From British political economy he adopted the subsistence
theory of wages, or Iron Law, which orthodox economists presently abandoned since wages did in fact begin to rise.[17] It held that the average workingman could never obtain more than a minimum level of living—of which
the corollary, for those who wished to draw it, was that the existing economic
system held out no future for the laboring class as a class. Marx likewise took
over from orthodox economists the labor theory of value, holding that the
value of any man-made object depended ultimately on the amount of labor
put into it—capital being regarded as the stored up labor of former times.
Orthodox economists soon discarded the labor theory of value, preferring the
theory that value is determined psychologically by satisfaction of human
wants or tastes. Marx, from the labor theory, developed his doctrine of surplus value. This was very intricate; but "surplus value" meant in effect that
the workingman was being robbed. He received in wages only a fraction of
the value of the product which his labor produced. The difference was "expropriated" by the bourgeois capitalists—the private owners of the factories
and the machines. And since workers never received in wages the equivalent
of what they produced, capitalism was constantly menaced by overproduction, the accumulation of goods that people could not afford to buy. Hence
it ran repeatedly into crises and depressions, and was obliged also to be constantly expanding in search of new markets. It was the depression of 1847,
according to Marx, that had precipitated the Revolution of 1848; and with
every such depression during the rest of his lifetime Marx hoped that the day
of the great social revolution was drawing nearer.

What brought all these observations together in a unified and compelling doctrine was the philosophy of dialectical materialism. By dialectic,
Marx meant what the German philosopher Hegel had meant,[18] that all things
are in movement and in evolution, and that all change comes through the
clash of antagonistic elements. The word itself, coming from the Greek,
meant originally a way of arriving at a higher conclusion through debate.
The implications of the dialectic, for both Hegel and Marx, were that all
history, and indeed all reality, is a process of development through time, a
single and meaningful unfolding of events, necessary, logical, and deter-
ministic; that every event happens in due sequence for good and sufficient
reason (not by chance); and that history could not and cannot happen any
differently from the way it has happened and is still happening today. This,
it need hardly be said, cannot be demonstrated on any basis of knowable fact.

Marx differed from Hegel in one vital respect. Whereas Hegel emphasized the primacy of "ideas" in social change, Marx gave emphasis to the
primacy of material conditions. By materialism, Marx meant that the basic

[17] See pp. 429–30, 595.
[18] See p. 439.

element in society is economic. It is not primarily by having ideas that men create the social world in which they live. On the contrary, their form of society, especially their economic institutions, predisposes them to have certain ideas. At bottom, it is the "relations of production" (technology, invention, natural resources, property-systems, *etc.*) that determine what kind of religions, philosophies, governments, laws, and moral values men accept. To believe that ideas precede and generate actualities was, according to Marx, the error of Hegel. Hegel had thought, for example, that the mind conceives the idea of freedom, which it then realizes in the Greek city state, in Christianity, in the French Revolution and in the kingdom of Prussia. Not at all, according to Marx: the idea of freedom, or any other idea, is generated by the actual economic and social conditions. Conditions are the roots, ideas the trees. Hegel had held the ideas to be the roots, and the resulting actual conditions to be the trees. Or as Marx and Engels said, they found Hegel standing on his head, and set him on his feet again.

Dialectical materialism, or Marxian dialectic, offered an explanation of everything that had ever happened or could happen on earth. It is known also as economic determinism, or as the materialist conception of history. As a philosophy of history, it raised the passing events of 1848 and of Marx's lifetime to a higher level of cosmic meaning. It gave Marxism the universal aspects of a religion. It made Marxian socialism into a dogma and a faith.

The picture of historical development offered by Marxism was somewhat as follows. Material conditions, or the relations of production, give rise to economic classes. Agrarian conditions produce a landholding or feudal class, but with changes in trade routes, money, and productive techniques a new commercial or bourgeois class arises. Each class, feudal and bourgeois, develops an ideology suited to its needs. Prevailing religions, governments, laws, and morals reflect the outlook of these classes. The two classes inevitably clash. Bourgeois revolutions against feudal interests break out—in England in 1642, in France in 1789, in Germany in 1848, though the bourgeois revolution in Germany proved abortive. Meanwhile, as the bourgeois class develops, it inevitably calls another class into being, its dialectical antithesis, the proletariat. The bourgeois is defined as the private owner of capital, the proletarian as the wage-worker who has lost everything but his own hands. The more a country becomes bourgeois, the more it becomes proletarian. The more production is concentrated in factories, the more the revolutionary laboring class is built up. Under competitive conditions the bourgeois tend to devour and absorb each other; ownership of the factories, mines, machines, railroads, *etc.* (capital) becomes concentrated into very few hands. Others sink into the proletariat. In the end the proletarianized mass simply takes over from the remaining bourgeois. It "expropriates the expropriators," abolishes the old private property in the means of production. The social revolution is thus accomplished. It is inevitable. A classless society results, because class arises from economic differences which have been done away with. The state and religion, being outgrowths of bourgeois interests, also disappear. For a time, until all vestiges of bourgeois interests have been rooted out, or until the danger of counter-revolution against socialism has been overcome, there will be a "dictatorship of the proletariat." After that the state will "wither away," since there is no longer an exploiting class to require it.

Meanwhile the call is to war. Bourgeois and proletarian are locked in a universal struggle. It is really war, and as in all war all other considerations must be subordinated to it. Periods of social calm are not peace; they are merely interludes between battles. The workers must not be allowed to grow soft or conciliatory, any more than an army should be allowed to forget its primary function of fighting. Workingmen and labor unions must be kept in a belligerent and revolutionary mood. They must never forget that the employer is their class enemy, and that government, law, morality, and religion are merely so much artillery directed against them. Morals are "bourgeois morals," law is "bourgeois law," government is an instrument of class power, and religion is a form of psychological warfare, a means of providing "opium" for the masses. The worker must not let himself be fooled; he must learn how to detect the class interest underlying the most exalted institutions and beliefs. In this piece of military intelligence, ferreting out the ways of the enemy, he will be helped by an understanding of dialectical materialism, and will receive aid from intellectuals especially trained in explaining it to him. Like all fighting forces, the workers need a disciplined solidarity. The individual must lose himself in the whole—in his class. It is a betrayal of his class for a worker to rise above the proletariat, to "improve himself," as the bourgeois says. It is dangerous for labor unions merely to obtain better wages or hours by negotiation with employers, for by such little gains the war itself may be forgotten, the worker may lose interest in his own ultimate emancipation by revolution and in the plight of his fellow workers with whom his gains have not been shared. It is likewise dangerous, and even treasonous, for workers to put faith in the state, to be content with democratic machinery or "social legislation," for the state, an engine of repression, can never be made into an instrument of welfare. Law is the will of the stronger (i.e., the stronger class); "right" and "justice" are thin emanations of class interest. We must hold, wrote Marx in 1875, to "the realistic outlook which has cost so much effort to instil into the party, but which has now taken root in it"; and we must not let this outlook be perverted "by means of ideological nonsense about 'right' and other trash common among the democrats and French Socialists."

THE APPEAL OF MARXISM: ITS STRENGTH AND WEAKNESSES

Marxism was a hard doctrine, with many advantages and many handicaps in the winning of adherents. One of its advantages was its claim to be scientific. Marx classified early and rival forms of socialism [19] as utopian: they

[19] See pp. 434–6.

rested on moral indignation, and their formula for reforming society was for
men to become more just, or for the upper classes to be converted to sympathy
for the lower. His own doctrine, Marx insisted, had nothing to do with
ethical ideas; it was purely scientific, resting upon the study of actual facts
and real processes, and it showed that socialism would be not a miraculous
reversal but a historical continuation of what was already taking place. He
also considered it utopian and unscientific to describe the future socialist
society in any detail. It would be classless, with neither bourgeois nor proletarian; but to lay any specific plans would be idle dreaming. Let the revolution come, and the socialism would take care of itself.

The dialectical philosophy was another great advantage in the spreading of Marx's ideas. It disintegrated the foundations on which the world
believed itself to be standing. State, church, law, morals became merely
"bourgeois." Everything became a phase or manifestation of something else.
Permanent things were made to look transient, and absolute things to look
relative, as in the great religions. But where in religion it was the idea of God
before which all else became transitory and relative, in Marxism it was the
idea of the everlasting class war. Class was the one enduring reality in a
world of flux—until the Revolution, at which time class, the motivating force
of all history, would suddenly cease to exist, a "utopian" element in Marxism
that has often been pointed out, but which has never had a discouraging
effect upon the winning of followers—rather the contrary. At the same time
the dialectical philosophy, while disintegrating the "bourgeoisie," integrated
the "proletariat." As Engels wrote:

Communism among the French and Germans, Chartism among the English, now
no longer appeared as matters of chance that could just as well not have occurred.
These movements now presented themselves as the movement of a modern oppressed class, the proletariat . . . , but distinguished from all earlier class struggles
by this one thing, that the present-day oppressed class, the proletariat, cannot
achieve its emancipation without emancipating society as a whole from division
into classes and therefore from class struggles. And communism now no longer
meant the concoction by means of the imagination of an ideal society as perfect as
possible, but the understanding of the nature and conditions . . . of the struggle
waged by the proletariat.

In short, Marxism was a strong compound of the scientific, the historical, the
metaphysical, and the apocalyptic.

But some elements of Marxism stood in the way of its natural propaga-
tion. The working people of Europe were not really in the frame of mind of
an army in battle. They hesitated to subordinate all else to the distant
prospect of a class revolution. They were not exclusively class-men, nor did
they behave as such. Enough of Christianity was still alive in them, and of
older natural-law ideas, to inhibit the belief that morality was a class weapon,
or right and justice "trash." They had national loyalties to country; they
could with difficulty associate themselves emotionally with a world proletariat
in an unrelenting struggle against their own neighbors.

The cure for the revolutionism of 1848 proved in time to be the admission of the laboring classes to a fuller membership in society. Wages generally rose after 1850, labor unions were organized, and by 1870 in the principal European countries the workingman very generally had a vote. Through their unions, workers were often able to get better wages and working conditions by direct pressure upon employers. Having the vote, they gradually formed working-class parties, and as they proceeded to act through the state they had less inclination to destroy it. Marx's word for such maneuvers was "opportunism." Opportunism, the tendency of working people to better themselves by dealing with employers and by obtaining legislation through existing government channels, was the most dangerous of all dangers to the Revolution. For in war people do not negotiate or pass laws; they fight. From Marxism the working classes absorbed much, including a watchful hostility to employers and a sense of working-class solidarity; but on the whole, as Marxism spread at the close of the nineteenth century it ceased to be really revolutionary.[20] Had the old Europe not gone to pieces in the twentieth-century wars, and had Marxism not been revived by Lenin and transplanted to Russia, it is probable that Marx's doctrines would have been domesticated into the general body of European thought, and that much less would be said about them in this book.

61. Bonapartism: The Second French Empire, 1852–70

We have seen how Louis-Napoleon Bonaparte, elected president of the republic in 1848, in 1852 made himself Emperor of the French with the title of Napoleon III.[21] Those willing to fight for the parliamentary and liberal institutions which he crushed in 1851 proved to be a helpless minority. There is no doubt that he became "dictator" on a wave of popular acclaim.

POLITICAL INSTITUTIONS OF THE SECOND EMPIRE

Indeed the dubious title of first modern dictator fits Napoleon III far better than it fits Napoleon I. The new Napoleon was not at all like his great uncle. He was no soldier, no administrator, and though intelligent enough he had no especial distinction or force of mind. He was a politician. He had led *Putsches* against the July monarchy, for which he had been imprisoned. The first Napoleon came to power in the course of a war which he had not started. The second Napoleon made himself dictator in time of peace, by playing on social fears in a country divided by an abortive revolution. The first Napoleon, it is hardly too much to say, never in his life condescended to make a public speech. Louis-Napoleon made them all the time;

[20] See pp. 594–6.
[21] See pp. 475–7.

the political rostrum was his natural habitat. Public opinion was more of a force in 1850 than in 1800. Louis-Napoleon recognized it as an opportunity, not merely as a nuisance. He appealed to the masses by promises and by pageantry; he cultivated, solicited, directed, and manufactured popular favor. He understood perfectly that a single leader exerts more magnetism than an elected assembly. And he knew that a Europe still shuddering over the June Days was hoping desperately for Order in France.

He gloried in modern progress. Toward the changes coming over Europe the monarchs of the old school usually showed an attitude of timidity and doubt if not positive opposition. Napoleon III boldly offered himself as the leader in a brave new world. Like his uncle, he announced that he embodied the sovereignty of the people. He believed, probably sincerely, that he had found a solution to the problem of mass democracy. In all the other great Continental states and in Great Britain, in 1852, universal suffrage was thought to be incompatible with intelligent government and economic prosperity. Napoleon III claimed to put them together. Like Marx and other "realists" after 1848 he held that elected parliamentary bodies, far from representing an abstract "people," only accentuated class divisions within a country. He declared that the regime of the restored Bourbons and the July monarchy had been dominated by special interests, that the republic of 1848 had first been violent and anarchic, then fallen into the hands of a distrustful assembly that robbed the laboring man of his vote, and that France would find in the Empire the permanent, popular and modern system for which it had been vainly searching since 1789. He affirmed that he stood above classes, and would govern equally in the interests of all. In any case, like many others after 1848, he held that forms of government were less important than economic and social realities. Like Marxism or the Bach system in Austria, the Bonapartism of Napoleon III put a low value on political freedom. It was as a leader in a great march toward material progress that the new Napoleon proposed himself to the French people. As he said at Bordeaux, while still "selling" the idea of the Empire:

We have immense territories to cultivate, roads to open, harbors to deepen, canals to dig, rivers to make navigable, railroads to complete. . . . That is how I interpret the Empire, if the Empire is to be restored. Such are the conquests I contemplate; and you, all of you who surround me, and who wish our country's good, you are my soldiers.

But in this great enterprise the government must be untroubled by party politics and the vacillations and reversals of elected assemblies.

The political institutions of the Second Empire were therefore authoritarian, modeled on those of the Consulate of the first Bonaparte. There was a Council of State, composed of experts who drafted legislation and advised on technical matters. There was an appointive senate with few significant functions. There was a Legislative Body elected by universal suffrage. The elections were carefully managed. The government put up an official candidate for each seat whom all office-holders in the district were required to support. Other candidates might offer themselves for election, but there could be no political meetings of any kind, and if the independent candidate put up posters he had to use a different kind of paper from the official candidate. Few ventured in these circumstances to differ with the government.

The Legislative Body had no independent powers of its own. It could not initiate legislation, but only consider what was submitted to it by the Emperor's will. It had no control over the budget, for the Emperor was legally free to borrow money as he saw fit. It had no power over the army or the foreign office or the making of war and peace. To publish speeches made in the legislative chamber was against the law. Any five members, by requesting a secret session, could exclude the public from the galleries. Parliamentary life sank toward absolute zero, and democracy meant that the citizen enjoyed the occasional pleasure of registering his approval of the regime. The newspapers were carefully muzzled, only those authorized by the government being permitted. Professorships of history and philosophy, which seem always to frighten dictatorial governments, were regulated or suppressed.

To captivate public attention and glorify the Napoleonic name the new Emperor set up a sumptuous court at the Tuileries. Balked in the ambition to marry into one of the great dynasties, Napoleon III chose as his empress a young Spanish beauty, Eugénie, who was destined to outlive the Empire by fifty years, dying in 1920. It was said to be a love-match—a sure sign of popularized royalty. The court life of the empire was brilliant, gay, luxurious, and showy beyond anything known at the time in St. Petersburg or Vienna. The note of pageantry was further struck in the embellishment of the city of Paris. Baron Haussmann, one of the most creative of city planners, gave Paris much of the appearance that it has today. He built roomy railway stations with broad approaches, and he constructed a system of boulevards and public squares offering long vistas ending in fine buildings or monuments, as at the Place de l'Opéra. The building program, like the expensive court, had the additional advantage of stimulating business and employment. And the cutting of wide avenues through the crooked streets and congested old houses would permit easier military operations against insurrectionists entrenched behind barricades, should the events of 1848 ever be repeated.

ECONOMIC DEVELOPMENTS UNDER THE EMPIRE

It was as a great social engineer that Napoleon III preferred to be known. In his youth he had tried to read the riddle of modern industrialism, and now, as emperor, he found some of his main backers in former Saint-Simonians, who called him their "socialist emperor." Saint-Simon, it may be recalled, had been among the first to conceive of a centrally planned industrial system.[22] But the Saint-Simonians of the 1850's shared in the new sense of being realistic, and their most signal triumph was the invention of invest-

[22] See p. 435.

ment banking, by which they hoped to guide economic growth through the concentration of financial resources. They founded a novel kind of banking institution, the *Crédit Mobilier*, which raised funds by selling its shares to the public, and with the funds thus obtained bought stock in such new industrial enterprises as it wished to develop. A land bank, or *Crédit Foncier*, was likewise established to lend funds to landowners for the improvement of agriculture.

The times were exceedingly favorable for expansion, for the discovery of gold in California in 1849, and in Australia soon afterwards, together with the newly organized credit facilities, brought a substantial increase in the European money supply, which had a mildly inflationary effect. The steady rise of prices and all money values encouraged company-promotion and investment of capital. Railway mileage, increasing everywhere in the Western world, increased in France from 3,000 to 16,000 kilometers in the 1850's. The demand for rolling stock, iron rails, auxiliary equipment, and building materials for stations and freight-houses kept the mines and factories busy. The railway network was rationalized, fifty-five small lines in France being merged into six big regional trunks. Iron steamboats replaced wooden sailing ships. Between 1859 and 1869 a French company built the Suez Canal, which it still owns, though the British government in 1875 became the principal stockholder.

Large corporations made their appearance, in railroads and banking first of all. In 1863 the law granted the right of "limited liability," by which a stockholder could not lose more than the par value of his stock, however insolvent or debt-burdened the corporation might become. This encouraged investment by persons of small means, and by capitalists large and small in enterprises of which they knew very little; thus the wealth and savings of the country were more effectively mobilized and put to work. Stocks and shares became more numerous and diversified. The Stock Exchange boomed. Financiers—those whose business was to handle money, credit, and securities—assumed a new eminence in the capitalistic world. A good many people became very rich, richer perhaps than anyone had ever been in France before. Real industrial growth went along with a sag in morals, a scramble for easy money, a frenzy of speculation, and a rather vulgar taste for ostentatious living—anticipating the age of the tycoons that began in the United States some twenty years later. The Second Empire, in this respect, was even more "bourgeois" than the July monarchy.

The emperor aspired also to do something for the workingman, within the limits of the existing system. The land bank was of some use to the more substantial peasants. Jobs were plentiful and wages good, by the ideas of the day, at least until the temporary depression of 1857. The emperor had a plan, as did some of the Saint-Simonians, for organizing forces of workers in military fashion and setting them to clear and develop uncultivated land. Not much was done in this direction. More was accomplished in the humanitarian relief of suffering. Hospitals and asylums were established, and free medicines were distributed. The outlines of a social-service state began somewhat vaguely to appear. Meanwhile the workers were building up unions. All combinations of workingmen had been prohibited during the French Revolution, and the Le Chapelier Law of 1791 was deemed to be still in force.[23] Gradually the ambiguous legal position of labor unions was clarified. In 1864 it even became legal for organized workingmen to go on strike. Large labor units, or unions, and large business units, or corporations, were thus legalized at the same time. Napoleon III hardly did enough for labor to rank as a working-class hero, but he did enough to be suspected as "socialistic" by many middle-class people of the day.

More recent dictatorships, bent like the Second Empire on a program of economic development, have usually been highly protectionist, unwilling to face open competition with the rest of the world. Napoleon III believed in freedom of international trade. He had a project for a tariff-union with Belgium, which some Belgians also supported. Belgium was already well industrialized, and a Franco-Belgian union, especially since Belgium had the coal which France lacked, would have formed a trading area of very great strength. But the plan was blocked by private interests in both countries, and strongly opposed by both Great Britain and the German Zollverein. The emperor then turned to an all-around reduction of import duties. Since the repeal of the Corn Laws in 1846 the free-traders were in power in England.[24] They were eager to abolish trade barriers between Britain and France. Napoleon III, overriding opposition in his Legislative Body, concluded a free trade treaty with Great Britain in 1860. He set aside 40,000,000 francs of government funds to assist French manufacturers to make adjustments in the face of British competition; but this sum was never spent in full, and it has hence been concluded that French industry was able to compete successfully with the more intensively mechanized industry of Britain. The Anglo-French treaty was accompanied by lesser trade agreements with other countries. It looked, in the 1860's, as if Europe might actually be about to enter the promised land of freedom of trade.

INTERNAL DIFFICULTIES AND WAR

But by 1860 the empire was running into trouble. It took a few years to overcome the depression of 1857. By his free trade policy the emperor made enemies among industrialists in certain lines. The Catholics did not like his policy in Italy.[25] After 1860 opposition mounted. The emperor granted more leeway to the Legislative Body. The 1860's are called the decade of the Liberal Empire—all such terms being relative. How the empire would have fared had purely internal causes been left free scope we shall never know. Louis-Napoleon actually ruined himself by war. His empire evaporated on the battlefield in 1870. But he was at war long before that.

[23] See p. 348.
[24] See p. 463.

[25] See p. 516.

"The empire means peace," he had assured his audiences in 1852: *l'empire, c'est la paix*. But war is after all the supreme pageantry (or was then); France was the strongest country of Europe, and the emperor's name was Napoleon. Less than a year and a half after the proclamation of the empire France was at war with a European state for the first time since Waterloo. The enemy was Russia, and the war was the Crimean War. Napoleon III did not alone instigate the Crimean War. Many forces in Europe after 1848 made for war; but Napoleon III was one of these forces. In 1859 the new Napoleon was fighting in Italy, from 1862 to 1867 in Mexico, and in 1870 in France itself, in a war with Prussia which he could easily have avoided. These wars form part of the story of the following chapter.[26]

It is enough to say here that in 1870 the Second Empire went the way of the First, into the limbo of governments tried and discarded by the French. It had lasted eighteen years, exactly as long as the July Monarchy, and longer than any other regime known in France, up to that time, since the fall of the Bastille. Not until the 1920's and '30's, when dictators sprouted all over Europe, did the world begin to suspect what Louis-Napoleon had really been, an omen of the future rather than a bizarre reincarnation of the past. It is only right to add that some, like Alexis de Tocqueville, suspected it even then.

[26] See pp. 511–13, 514–16, 525–6; for Mexico, see p. 624.

CHAPTER XIII

The Consolidation of
Large Nation-States,
1859-71

ONLY a dozen years, from 1859 to 1871, were enough to see the formation of a new German Empire, a unified kingdom of Italy, a Dual Monarchy of Austria-Hungary, drastic internal changes in tsarist Russia, the triumph of central authority in the United States, the creation of a united Dominion of Canada, and the revolutionizing and "Europeanization" of the Empire of Japan. All these disparate events reflected profound changes brought in by the railroad, steamship, and telegraph, which made the communication of ideas, exchange of goods, and movement of people over wide areas more frequent and easier than ever before. Politically, all represented the advancing principle of the nation-state.

62. Backgrounds: The Idea of the Nation-State

Before 1860 there were two prominent nation-states—Great Britain and France. Spain, united on the map, was internally so miscellaneous as to belong to a different category. Sweden, Denmark, Norway, Portugal, Switzerland, and the Netherlands were nation-states, but small and peripheral. The characteristic political organizations were small states comprising fragments of a nation, such as were strewn across the middle of Europe—Hanover, Baden, Sardinia, Tuscany or the Two Sicilies—and large sprawling empires made up of all sorts of peoples, distantly ruled from above by dynasties and bureaucracies, such as the Romanov, Hapsburg, and Ottoman domains.[1] Except for recent developments in the Americas the same mixture of small non-national states and of large non-national empires was to be found in most of the rest of the world.

Since 1860 or 1870 a nation-state system has prevailed. The consolidation of large nations became a model for other peoples large and small. In time, in the following century, other large peoples undertook to establish nation states in China, Hindu India, Pakistan, and Indonesia. Small and middle-sized peoples increasingly thought of themselves as nations, entitled to their own sovereignty and independence; the result, also accomplished in the following century, was the appearance of such states as Czechoslovakia, the Turkish republic, Eire, or Israel. Some of these sovereignties comprise fewer people than a large modern city. The idea of the nation-state has served both to bring people together into larger units and to break them apart into smaller ones. In the nineteenth century, outside the disintegrating Ottoman Empire, from which Greece, Serbia, Bulgaria, and Rumania became independent, and in which an Arabic national movement also began to stir, the national idea served mainly to create larger units in place of small ones. The map of Europe, from 1871 to 1918, was the simplest it has ever been before or since.[2]

About the idea of the nation-state and the movement of nationalism much has been said already in this book. Earlier chapters have described the ferment of national ideas and movements stirred up by the French Revolution and by the Napoleonic domination of Europe, the nationalist agitation and repression of the years after 1815, and the frustration and failure of patriotic aspirations in Germany, Italy, and Central Europe in the Revolu-

---

[1] See map, pp. 414–15.
[2] See map, pp. 528–9.

tion of 1848.[3] For many in the nineteenth century, nationalism, the winning of national unity and independence and the creation of the nation-state, became a kind of secular faith.

A nation-state may be thought of as one in which supreme political authority somehow rests upon and represents the will and feeling of its inhabitants. There must be a people, not merely a swarm of human beings. The people must basically will and feel something in common. They must sense that they belong—that they are members of a community, participating somehow in a common life; that the government is their government, and that outsiders are "foreign." The outsiders or foreigners are usually (though not always) those who speak a different language. The nation is usually (though not always) composed of all persons sharing the same speech. A nation may also possess a belief in common descent or racial origin (however mistaken), or a sense of a common history, a common future, a common religion, a common geographical home, or a common external menace. Nations take form in many ways. But all are alike in feeling themselves to be communities, permanent communities in which individual persons, together with their children and their children's children, are committed to a collective destiny on earth.

In the nineteenth century governments found that they could not effectively rule, or develop the full powers of state, except by enlisting this sense of membership and support among their subjects. The consolidation of large nation-states had two distinguishable phases. Territorially, it meant the union of pre-existing smaller states. Morally and psychologically it meant the creation of new ties between government and governed, the admission of new segments of the population to political life, through the creation or extension of liberal and representative institutions. This happened even in Japan and in tsarist Russia. National consolidation favored constitutional progress. Although there was considerable variation in the real power of the new political institutions and in the extent of self-government actually realized, parliaments were set up for the new Italy, the new Germany, the new Japan, the new Canada; and the movement in Russia was in the same direction. In Europe, some of the aims which the revolutionists of 1848 had failed to achieve were now realized by the established authorities.

They were realized, however, only in a series of wars. To create an all-German or an all-Italian state, as the revolutions of 1848 had already shown, it was necessary to break the power of Austria, render Russia at least temporarily ineffective, and overthrow or intimidate those German and Italian states which refused to surrender their sovereignty. In the United States, to maintain national unity as understood by President Lincoln, it was necessary to repress the movement for Southern independence by force of arms. For forty years after 1814 there had been no war between established powers of Europe. Then in 1854 came the Crimean War, in 1859 the Italian War, in 1864 the Danish War, in 1866 the Austro-Prussian War, in 1870 the

⁂

[3] See pp. 337, 351–3, 400–8, 436–58, 477–95.

Franco-Prussian War. Concurrently the Civil War raged in the United States. After 1871, for forty-three years there was again no war between European powers.

THE CRIMEAN WAR, 1854–6

Before moving on to the first of the national consolidation movements, the Italian, we must examine the Crimean War which, though seemingly remote and unconnected, helped to make possible the success of the European national movements. Its chief significance in the story of the present chapter is that it seriously weakened both Austria and Russia, the two powers most bent on preserving the peace settlement of 1815 and on preventing national changes; it provided also an opportunity for the presentation of Italian grievances to an international forum at the peace congress which ended the war. The war was significant in other ways too. It was the first war covered by newspaper correspondents. It was the first war in which women, led by Florence Nightingale, established their position as army nurses. It was the first war in centuries in which France and Great Britain were on the same side. France and Britain came together because they believed their interests in the eastern Mediterranean to be threatened by Russia.

The pressure of Russia upon Turkey was an old story. Every generation saw its Russo-Turkish war.[4] In the last Russo-Turkish war, to go back no further, that of 1828–9, the Tsar Nicholas I protected the independence newly won by Greece and annexed the left bank of the mouth of the Danube. Now, in 1853, Nicholas again made demands upon the still large but decaying Ottoman Empire, moving in on the two Danubian principalities, Wallachia and Moldavia (later to be known as Rumania), with military forces.[5] The dispute this time ostensibly involved the protection of Christians in the Ottoman Empire, including the foreign Christians at Jerusalem and in Palestine. Over these Christians the French also claimed a certain protective jurisdiction. The French had for centuries been the principal Western people in the Near East: they had often furnished money and advisers to the sultan, they carried on a huge volume of trade, they staffed and financed Christian missions, and they were continually talking of building a Suez canal. Napoleon III had especial reason to resent the Tsar Nicholas, who regarded him as a revolutionary adventurer. Napoleon III encouraged the Turkish government to resist Russian claims to protect Christians within Turkey. War between Russia and Turkey broke out late in 1853. In 1854 France joined the side of the Turks, as did Great Britain, whose settled policy was to uphold Turkey and the Near East against penetration by Russia. The two western powers were soon joined by a diminutive and somewhat ridiculous ally, which had no visible interest in the issues—the small mountain kingdom of

---

[4] See pp. 212–13; 316–17, 378, 381–2, 409, 451, 454.
[5] See maps, pp. 414–15, 633.

Sardinia, which entered the war solely for the purpose of raising the Italian question at the peace conference.

The British fleet successfully blockaded Russia in both its Baltic and Black Sea outlets. French and British armies invaded Russia itself, landing in the Crimean peninsula, to which all the important fighting was confined. The Austrian Empire had its own reasons not to wish Russia to conquer the Balkans and Constantinople, or to see Britain and France master the situation alone; Austria therefore, though not yet recovered from the upheaval of 1848–9, mobilized its armed forces at a great effort to itself and occupied Wallachia and Moldavia, which the Russians evacuated under this threat of attack by a new enemy. The Tsar Nicholas died in 1855, and his successor Alexander II sued for peace.

A congress of all the great powers made peace at Paris in 1856. By the treaty the powers pledged themselves jointly to maintain the "integrity of the Ottoman Empire." The Russian tide ebbed a little. Russia ceded the left bank of the mouth of the Danube to Moldavia, and gave up its claim to the special protection of Christians in the Turkish Empire. Moldavia and Wallachia (united as "Rumania" in 1858), together with Serbia, were recognized as self-governing principalities under protection of the European powers. It was agreed that Russia should maintain no warships on the Black Sea, and that the Danube should be an international river open to commercial shipping of all nations. The British, who had found it easy to blockade Russia, and were now mainly concerned with commercial prosperity and free trade, even relaxed their doctrine of sea power, agreeing that "free ships make free goods." What the Continent called the freedom of the seas, the rights of neutrals to trade in wartime, opposed by Britain in its struggle with Napoleon, was now written (temporarily) into international law. At the Congress of Paris all seemed harmonious. There seemed to be such a thing as Europe, undertaking collective obligations, protecting small states, rationally and peaceably conducting its affairs.

But trouble was in the making. Napoleon III needed glory. The Italians wanted some kind of unified Italy. The Prussians, who had done nothing in the Crimean War, and were only tardily invited to the Congress of Paris, feared that their status as a great power might be slipping away. Napoleon III, the Italian nationalists, the Prussians, all stood to gain by change. Change in central Europe and Italy meant a tearing up of the treaty of Vienna of 1815, long guarded by Metternich, and unsuccessfully challenged by the revolutionaries of 1848. Now, after the Crimean War, the forces opposing change were very weak. It was the Russian and Austrian empires that had stood most firmly for the status quo. It was the victory of counter-revolution in Vienna, with the aid of Russian intervention in Hungary, that had doomed the Revolution of 1848 not only in the Hapsburg empire but in Germany and Italy also. It was Russia and Austria, at Olmütz in 1850, that had forbidden the king of Prussia to create a German union according to his own notions. But Austria, though it had not fought, was badly strained by the effort of mobilization in the Crimean War. Russia was in defeat. The two powers which had most seriously attempted to uphold the Vienna settlement could do so no longer. The first proof came in Italy.

63. Cavour and the Italian War of 1859: The Unification of Italy

ITALIAN NATIONALISM: THE PROGRAM OF CAVOUR

In Italy, it will be recalled, there had long been about a half dozen sizable states, together with a few very small ones. They had all been over-thrown by Napoleon I, but were rearranged by the Congress of Vienna. In the northwest lay Sardinia, called also Savoy or Piedmont; its royal house was the only native Italian dynasty in Italy. East of it lay Lombardy, and east of that, Venetia. Since 1814 Lombardy and Venetia belonged to the Austrian empire. South of Lombardy, in the northwest corner of the "leg" of the peninsula, was the duchy of Tuscany with its capital at Florence. The smaller duchies of Modena, Parma, and Lucca filled the interstices between Tuscany and the northern states. Across the middle of the peninsula were spread the Papal States, the hereditary temporal possession of the Roman See. Further south, comprising half of all Italy, lay the large kingdom of Naples or the Two Sicilies, ruled since 1735 by a branch of the Bourbons. The governments of these states were generally content with their separate independence. But the governments were remote from their peoples.

There was a widespread disgust in Italy with the existing authorities, and a growing desire for a liberal national state in which all Italy might be embodied and which might resurrect the Italian grandeur of ancient times and of the Renaissance. This sentiment, the dream of an Italian *Risorgimento*, or resurgence, had been stirred up by the French Revolution and Napoleon, then transformed into a moral purpose by the writings of Mazzini.[6] Mazzini, it will be recalled, had exalted the cause of Italian national unity and invested it with almost a holy character, identifying it with the most generous, humane, and fraternal impulses. He had seen his hopes for a re-publican Italy elevated for a brief moment and then blasted in the general débacle of 1848. In the stormy events of 1848 the papacy had been frightened off by the radical romantic republicanism of Mazzini, Garibaldi, and other firebrands, and could no longer be expected to support the cause of Italian nationalism. And in the same events the kingdom of Sardinia had failed in its vow to oust Austria from the Italian peninsula without the aid of any outside great power.[7]

These lessons were not lost on the prime minister of Sardinia, which was ruled since 1848 as a constitutional monarchy and was now under King Victor Emmanuel. This prime minister of Sardinia after 1852 was Camillo

[6] See pp. 436–9.
[7] See pp. 480, 483, 484–5.

di Cavour, one of the shrewdest political tacticians of that or any age. Cavour was a liberal of Western type. He tried to make Sardinia a model of progress, efficiency, and fair government that other Italians would admire. He worked hard to plant constitutional and parliamentary practices in Sardinia. He favored the building of railroads and docks, the improvement of agriculture and emancipation of trade. He followed a strongly anticlerical policy, cutting down the number of religious holidays, limiting the right of church bodies to own real estate, abolishing the church courts—all without negotiation with the Holy See. A liberal and constitutional monarchist, a loyal servant of the house of Savoy, a wealthy landowner in his own right, he had no sympathy for the revolutionary and republican nationalism of Mazzini. To him it did not seem that Italy would be united by the methods of conspiracy and secret societies, by hortatory literature smuggled in from political exiles, or by the proclamation of idealistic radical republics, as in 1848, which alarmed the most influential people in the country.[8]

Cavour shared in that new toughness of mind described in the last chapter. He embraced a "politics of reality." He did not approve of republicans, but was willing to work with them surreptitiously. He did not idealize war, but was willing to make war to unify Italy under the Sardinian king. With unruffled calculation, he took Sardinia into the Crimean War, sending troops to Russia, for no reason except to win a place at the peace table and raise the Italian question at the Congress of Paris. It was evident to him that against one great power one must pit another, and that the only way to get Austria out of Italy was to use the French army. It became his master plan deliberately to provoke war with Austria, after having assured himself of French military support.

It was not difficult to persuade Napoleon III to collaborate. The Bonapartes looked upon Italy as their ancestral country, and Napoleon III, in his adventurous youth, had traveled in conspiratorial Italian circles and even participated in an Italian insurrection in 1831. Now, as emperor, in his role of apostle of modernity, he entertained a "doctrine of nationalities" which held the consolidation of nations to be a forward step at the existing stage of history. To fight reactionary Austria for the freedom of Italy would also mollify liberal opinion in France, which in other ways Napoleon was engaged in suppressing. The last note in persuasion was furnished by an Italian republican named Orsini, who in 1858, finding the French emperor too slow

[8] See pp. 484–5.

Nation Building, 1859–1867

In eight years from 1859 to 1867 Italy was unified (except for the city of Rome annexed in 1870), the Hapsburg government tried to solve its nationalities problem by creating a Dual Monarchy of Austria-Hungary, the United States affirmed its unity by defeating the southern secessionist movement, and the Dominion of Canada was formed to include all British North America except Newfoundland and Labrador, which were added in 1949.

NATION BUILDING
1859-1867

UNIFICATION
OF
ITALY
1859-1870

LOMBARDY
VENETIA
Turin
Milan
Venice
PIEDMONT
PARMA
MODENA
Florence
PAPAL
STATES
KINGDOM OF
SARDINIA
TUSCANY
ROME
NAPLES
SARDINIA
200 MILES
SICILY

FORMATION OF
DUAL MONARCHY
OF
**AUSTRIA-
HUNGARY**
1867

A U S T R I A
Vienna
Budapest
H U N G A R Y

NORTHWEST TERRITORIES
LABRADOR
NEWFOUNDLAND
BRITISH
COLUMBIA
ALBERTA
SASKAT-
CHEWAN
MANITOBA
QUEBEC
ONTARIO
MARITIME
PROVINCES
Ottawa

FORMATION OF
**DOMINION
OF
CANADA**
1867

600 MILES

**UNITED
STATES**
DEFEAT OF
SOUTHERN
SECESSIONIST
MOVEMENT
1861-1865

CONFEDERATE
STATES
OF AMERICA

TRM

to make up his mind, attempted to assassinate him with a bomb. Napoleon III reached a secret agreement with Cavour. In April 1859, Cavour tricked Austria into a declaration of war. The French army poured over the Alps.

There were two battles, Magenta and Solferino, both won by the French and Sardinians. But Napoleon III was now in a quandary. The Prussians began to mobilize on the Rhine, not wishing France to create an Italian sphere of influence for itself. In Italy, with the defeat of the Austrians, revolutionary agitation broke out all over the peninsula, as it had a decade before—and the French emperor was no patron of popular revolution. The revolutionaries overthrew or denounced the existing governments, and clamored for annexation to Sardinia. In France, as elsewhere, the Catholics, fearful that the pope's temporal power would be lost, upbraided the emperor for this godless and unnecessary war. The French position was indeed odd, for while the bulk of the French army fought Austria in the north, a detachment of it was still stationed in Rome, sent there in 1849 to protect the pope against Italian republicanism.[9] Napoleon III, in July 1859, at the height of his victories, stupefied Cavour. He made a separate peace with the Austrians.

The Franco-Austrian agreement gave Lombardy to Sardinia, but left Venetia within the Austrian empire. It offered a compromise solution to the Italian question, in the form of a federal union of the existing Italian governments, to be presided over by the pope. This was not what Cavour, or the Sardinians, or the more fiery Italian patriots wanted. Revolution continued to spread. Tuscany, Modena, Parma, and Romagna drove out their old rulers. They were annexed to Sardinia, after plebiscites or general elections in these regions had shown an overwhelming popular favor for this step. Since Romagna belonged to the Papal States the pope excommunicated the organizers of the new Italy. Undeterred, representatives of all north Italy except Venetia met at the Sardinian capital of Turin in 1860 in the first parliament of the enlarged kingdom. The British government hailed these events with enthusiasm, and Napoleon III also recognized the expanded Sardinian state, in return for the transfer to France of Nice and Savoy, where plebiscites disclosed enormous majorities for annexation to France.

THE COMPLETION OF ITALIAN UNITY

There were now, in 1860, a north Italian kingdom, the Papal States in the middle, and the kingdom of the Two Sicilies still standing in the south. The latter was being undermined by revolutionary agitation, as often in the past.[10] A Sardinian republican, Giuseppe Garibaldi, brought matters to a head. Somewhat like Lafayette, Garibaldi was a "hero of two worlds," who

[9] See p. 476.
[10] See pp. 449–50, 480.

had fought for the independence of Uruguay, lived in the United States, and been one of the Triumvirs in the short-lived Roman Republic of 1849. He now organized a group of about 1,150 personal followers—"Garibaldi's Thousand," or the Red Shirts—for an armed expedition to the south. Cavour, unable openly to favor such filibustering against a neighboring state, connived at Garibaldi's preparations and departure. Garibaldi landed in Sicily and soon crossed to the mainland. Revolutionists hastened to join him, and the government of the Two Sicilies, backward and corrupt, commanding little loyalty from its population, collapsed before this picturesque intrusion.

Garibaldi now prepared to push from Naples up to Rome. Here, of course, he would meet not only the pope but the French army, and the international scandal would reverberate throughout the globe. Cavour decided that so extreme a step must be averted, but that Garibaldi's successes must at the same time be used. Anticipating Garibaldi, a Sardinian army entered the Papal States, carefully avoiding Rome, and proceeded onward into Naples. The kingdom conquered from its king by Garibaldi, was now conquered from Garibaldi by the Sardinian army and the ingenuity of Cavour. The conquest was peaceful; for Garibaldi, though somewhat disposed to bargain, and though he vainly demanded Cavour's resignation, finally yielded. The chief of the Red Shirts, the foe of kings, consented to ride in an open carriage with Victor Emmanuel through the streets of Naples amid cheering thousands. Plebiscites held in the Two Sicilies showed an almost unanimous willingness to join with Sardinia. In the remainder of the Papal States, except for Rome and its environs, plebiscites were held also, with the same result. A parliament representing all Italy except Rome and Venetia met in 1861, and the Kingdom of Italy was formally proclaimed, with Victor Emmanuel II as king "by grace of God and the will of the nation." Venetia was added in 1866, as a prize for Italian aid to Prussia in a war against Austria, and Rome was annexed in 1870 after the withdrawal of French troops in the Franco-Prussian War of 1870.[11]

So Italy was "made," as the phrase of the time expressed it. It had been made by the long high-minded apostolate of Mazzini, the audacity of Garibaldi, the cold policy of Cavour, by war and insurrection, by armed violence endorsed by popular vote.

PERSISTENT PROBLEMS AFTER UNIFICATION

Very little was settled or ended by unification. Even territorially, the more pronounced nationalists refused to believe that Italian unity was completed. They looked beyond, to regions of mixed population where Italians were numerous or preponderant—to the Trentino, to Trieste, to certain Dalmatian islands, or to Nice and Savoy. They saw in these regions an *Italia irredenta*, "an unredeemed Italy," awaiting in its turn the day of incorpora-

[11] See pp. 522, 524, 526, 605.

tion. "Irredentism" even passed into the English language as a word signifiy-ing a vociferous demand, on nationalist grounds, for annexation of regions beyond one's own frontiers.

The occupation of Rome in 1870 by the Italian government opened the rift between church and state still wider. The pope, deprived of territories he had held for a thousand years, renewed his condemnations and chose to remain in life-long seclusion in the Vatican. His successors followed the same policy until 1929. Hence good Italian patriots were bound to be anti-clerical, and good Catholics were bound to look upon the Italian state with unfriendly eyes. The regional differences between northern and southern Italy did not disappear with unification. The north looked upon the agrarian south, the land of priest, landlord, and impoverished peasant, as disgracefully backward. Lawlessness in Sicily and Naples did not disappear with the over-throw of the Bourbons.

The new Italy was parliamentary but not democratic. At first the vote was only given to some 600,000 persons out of more than twenty million. Not until 1912 was the suffrage significantly broadened. Meanwhile parlia-mentary life, confined to a few, was somewhat unrealistic and frequently corrupt. With the mass of the population excluded from the vote, which in any case they were incapable of exercising, the revolutionary agitation con-tinued unabated after the unification. Garibaldi himself, in the 1860's, made two more attempts to seize Rome by violence. In general, the revolutionary movement shifted from the older republican nationalism to the newer forms of Marxian socialism, anarchism or syndicalism.

But the dream of ages was realized. Italy was one. The period that seemed so shameful to patriots, the long centuries that had elapsed since the Renaissance, were now terminated in the glories of a successful *Risorgi-mento*.

64. Bismarck: The Founding of a German Empire

To play upon the divisions among the Germans, keeping them in rivalry with each other and dependent upon outside powers, had been the policy of France ever since the Reformation, and of Russia since it began to take part in the affairs of Europe. The pulverization of the Germanic world was in fact a kind of negative prerequisite to the development of mod-ern history as we know it, for without it the economic and cultural leadership of Europe would hardly have become concentrated along the Atlantic sea-board, or a great military empire have arisen in Russia and spread along the Baltic and into Poland.

Gradually, as we have seen, the Germans became dissatisfied with their position. They became nationalistic.[12] Many German thinkers held that

∿∿∿∿∿∿∿∿∿∿∿∿∿∿

[12] See pp. 400–6, 439–40.

Germany was different from the West, destined some day to work out a peculiarly German way of life and political system of its own. To the Slavs the Germans felt immeasurably superior. German philosophy, as shown most clearly in Hegel, took on a certain characteristic tone. It pronounced individualism to be Western; it skipped lightly over individual liberty; it tended to glorify group loyalties, collectivist principles and the State. It made a great to-do about History, which in the thought of Hegel, and after him Marx, became a vast force almost independent of human beings. History was said to ordain, require, necessitate, condemn, justify, or excuse. What one did not like could be dismissed as a mere historical phase, opening into a quite different and more attractive future. What one did want, in the present or future, could be described as historically necessary and bound to come.

THE GERMAN STATES AFTER 1848

In 1848 a series of revolutions unseated the several governments of Germany. At the Frankfurt Assembly a group composed essentially of private citizens undertook to organize a united Germany by constitutional methods. They failed because they had no power. Hence after 1848 the Germans began to think in terms of power, developing a somewhat unbalanced admiration for *die Macht*. The men of Frankfurt failed also, perhaps, because they were insufficiently revolutionary. The Germans were a sober, orderly, and respectful people. They were still attached emotionally to their several states. What happened in Italy, a revolutionary extermination of all the old governments except that of Sardinia, could not happen in Germany.[13]

After the failure of the 1848 revolution German nationalists and liberals were confused. By 1850 the old states were restored—Austria and Prussia, the kingdoms of Hanover, Saxony, Bavaria, and Würtemberg, together with about thirty other states ranging in size down to the free cities of Hamburg and Frankfurt. The loose confederation of 1815, linking all these states together, was restored also.[14] But within this framework great economic and social changes were occurring. Between 1850 and 1870 the output of both coal and iron in Germany multiplied sixfold. In 1850 Germany produced less iron than France, in 1870 more. Germany was overcoming the economic and social lag which had characterized it for three hundred years. A *Zollverein*, or tariff union, initiated by Prussia in 1818 had come to include almost all Germany outside of Austria and Bohemia and provided a large measure of economic unity. The German cities were growing, bound together by railroad and telegraph, requiring larger supporting areas on which to live. Industrial capitalists and industrial workingmen were becoming more numerous. With the advantages of unity more obvious than ever, with the ideals of 1848 badly compromised, with an exaggerated respect for the state and for power,

[13] See pp. 485–91.
[14] See pp. 417, 491, 523.

and with a habit of accepting the successful event as the "judgment of his-tory," the Germans were ripe for what happened. They did not unify them-selves by their own exertions. They fell into the arms of Prussia.

PRUSSIA IN THE 1860's: BISMARCK

Prussia had always been the smallest and most precarious of the great powers. Ruined by Napoleon, it had risen again. It owed its international influence and internal character to its army. Actually it had fought rather fewer wars than other great powers, but, with its army in being, it had fol-lowed a program of expansion by conquest or diplomacy. The taking of Silesia in 1740, of parts of Poland in the 1770's and 1790's, of the Rhineland in 1815 by an international bargain were the highlights of Prussian growth.[15] After 1850 those who controlled the destinies of Prussia were apprehensive. Their state had been shaken by revolution. At Olmütz in 1850 they had to yield to the Austrian emperor and the tsar. In the Crimean War and at the Congress of Paris they were hardly more than spectators. Italy was unified without any Prussian saying yes or no. It seemed as if the hard won and still relatively recent position of Prussia might be waning. It likewise seemed easy to enlarge the army. Since 1815 the population of Prussia had grown from eleven to eighteen millions, but the size of the army had not changed. A mere enforcement of existing principles of conscription would therefore almost double the army. But this would require increased financial appropria-tions. After 1850 Prussia had a parliament.[16] It was a parliament, to be sure, dominated by the men of wealth; but some of the wealthy Prussians, notably the capital-owners of the Rhineland, were liberals who wished the parliament to have control over government policies. These men did not like professional armies, and considered the Prussian *Junkers*, from whom the officer corps was recruited, as their main rivals in the state. The parliament refused the neces-sary appropriations. The king and his war minister, Roon, were in despair. The army reforms, considered by them as necessary to the future of Prussia, could not be effected. The king at this juncture, in 1862, on von Roon's recommendation, appointed a new chief minister, Otto von Bismarck.

Bismarck was a *Junker* from old Brandenburg east of the Elbe. He cultivated the gruff manner of an honest country squire, though he was in fact an accomplished man of the world. Intellectually he was far superior to the rather slow-witted landlord class from which he sprang, and for which he often felt an impatient contempt, though he remained loyal to it. He shared in many *Junker* ideas. He advocated, and even felt, a kind of stout Protestant piety. He cared nothing for the world's opinion; criticism and denunciation left him morally untouched. He was in fact obstinate. He was not a nationalist. He did not look upon all Germany as his Fatherland. He

---

[15] See maps, pp. 198–9.
[16] See pp. 491–2.

was a Prussian. His social affinities, as with the *Junkers* generally, lay to the East with corresponding landowning elements of the Baltic provinces and Russia.[17] The west, including the bulk of Germany, he neither understood nor trusted; it seemed to him revolutionary, turbulent, freethinking, materialistic. Parliamentary bodies he considered ignorant and irresponsible as organs of government. Individual liberty seemed to him disorderly selfishness. Liberalism, democracy, socialism were repugnant to him. He preferred to stress duty, service, order, and the fear of God. The idea of forming a new German union developed only gradually in his mind, and then as an adjunct to the strengthening of Prussia. A real and complete German national union, one including the Germans of Austria and Bohemia, who were as German as any, was impossible in Bismarck's eyes. It would bring in another great power to dispute with Prussia. It might create a Catholic majority. It would strengthen south against north. In it the East Elbian *Junkers* would be outnumbered and lost.

Bismarck thus had his predilections, and even his principles. But no principle bound him, no ideology seemed to him an end in itself. He became the classic practitioner of *Realpolitik*. The time came when the *Junkers* thought him a traitor to his class, when even the king was afraid of him, when he outraged and then mollified the august House of Hapsburg, when he made friends with liberals, democrats, and even socialists, and in turn made enemies of them. First he made wars, then he insisted upon peace. Enmities and alliances were to him only matters of passing convenience. The enemy of today might be the friend of tomorrow. Far from planning out a long train of events, then following it step by step to a grand consummation, he seems to have been practical and opportunistic, taking advantage of situations as they emerged, and prepared to act in any one of several directions as events might suggest.

In 1862, as minister president, it was his job, or duty, to outface the liberals in the Prussian parliament. For four years, from 1862 to 1866, Bismarck waged this "constitutional struggle." The parliament refused to vote the proposed taxes. The government collected them anyway. The taxpayers paid them without protest—it was the orderly thing to do, and the collectors represented public authority. The limitations of Prussian liberalism, the docility of the population, the respect for officialdom, the belief that the king and his ministers were wiser than the elected deputies, all clearly revealed themselves in this triumph of military policy over the theory of government by consent. The army was enlarged, reorganized, retrained, and re-equipped. Bismarck fended off the showers of abuse from the liberal majority in the chamber. The liberals declared that the government's policy was flagrantly unconstitutional. The constitution, said Bismarck, could not have been meant to undermine the State. The government, said the liberals, was itself undermining Prussia, for the rest of Germany hoped to find in Prussia, as Italy had found in Sardinia, a model of political freedom. What the Germans

---

[17] See map, p. 175.

admired in Prussia, replied Bismarck coldly, was not her liberalism but her power. He declared that the Prussian boundaries as set in 1815 were unsound, that Prussia must be prepared to seize favorable opportunities for further growth.[18] And he added one of his most memorable utterances: "Not by speeches and majority votes are the great questions of the day decided—that was the great error of 1848 and 1849—but by blood and iron."

BISMARCK'S WARS: NORTH GERMAN CONFEDERATION, 1867

A favorable opportunity was not long in presenting itself. The Schleswig-Holstein question arose again. We have seen how it had arisen in 1848, and how even the mild men of Frankfurt had insisted, to the point of war, upon the incorporation of the two duchies into their German union.[19] Now in 1863 the story was repeated. The Danes, engaged in a process of national consolidation of their own, wished to make Schleswig an integral part of Denmark. The population of Schleswig was part Dane and part German. The diet of the German confederation, unwilling to see Germans thus annexed outright to Denmark, called for an all-German war upon the Danes, just as the revolutionary Frankfurt Assembly had done. Bismarck had no desire to support or strengthen the existing German confederation. He wanted not an all-German war but a Prussian war. To disguise his aims he acted jointly with Austria. In 1864 Prussia and Austria together went to war with Denmark, which they soon defeated. It was Bismarck's intention to annex both Schleswig and Holstein to Prussia, gaining whatever other advantages might present themselves from future trouble with Austria. He arranged a provisional occupation of Schleswig by Prussia, and of Holstein by Austria. Disputes soon arose over rights of passage, the keeping of internal order, and other problems with which occupying forces are commonly afflicted. While pretending to try to regulate these disputes he allowed them to ripen.

He now proceeded to discredit and isolate Austria. The British government was at the time following a policy of non-intervention in the affairs of the Continent. The Russian empire was in no position for action; it was divided internally by a reform program then at its height; it was in a mood of hostility to Austria because of events of the Crimean War, and well disposed toward Prussia and Bismarck, because Bismarck in 1863 took care to support it against an uprising of Russian Poles. To win over the new kingdom of Italy Bismarck held out the lure of Venetia. As for France, Napoleon III was embarrassed by domestic discontents and had his army committed to adventures in Mexico. In addition, Bismarck charmed him at a confidential interview at Biarritz, where vague oral intimations of French expansion were exchanged, and the two men seemed to agree to a needed modernization of the map of Europe. To weaken Austria within Germany, Bismarck presented

---

[18] See maps, pp. 199, 523.
[19] See p. 490.

THE GERMAN QUESTION, 1815-1871

Legend:
- GERMAN CONFEDERATION, 1815-1866
- PRUSSIA, 1815-1866
- ANNEXED TO PRUSSIA, 1866
- JOINED WITH PRUSSIA IN NORTH GERMAN CONFEDERATION, 1867
- SOUTH GERMAN STATES JOINED IN GERMAN EMPIRE, 1871
- ALSACE-LORRAINE, CEDED BY FRANCE TO GERMAN EMPIRE, 1871
- AUSTRIAN DOMINIONS EXCLUDED FROM GERMAN CONFEDERATION, 1866

BISMARCK'S GERMAN EMPIRE 1871

100 MILES

TRM

From 1815 to 1866 there were thirty-eight states in Germany (of which only the largest are shown) joined in the Confederation of 1815. At the Frankfurt Assembly in 1848 (see p. 489) two groups developed, the Great Germans who adhered to the idea of an all-German union, including the Austrian lands except Hungary; and the Little Germans who were willing to exclude Austria and her empire. Bismarck was a Little German but a Great Prussian. He (1) enlarged Prussia by conquest in 1866, (2) joined Mecklenburg, Saxony, etc., with his enlarged Prussia in a North German Confederation of 1867, (3) combined this in turn with Bavaria, Würtemberg, etc., to form the German Empire of 1871, (4) conquered Alsace-Lorraine from France, and (5) ejected Austria. The boundaries of Bismarckian Germany remained unchanged until 1918. See also maps, pp. 199, 414-15, 700-1.

himself as a democrat. He proposed a reform of the German confederation, recommending that it have a popular chamber elected by universal suffrage. He calculated that the mass of the German people were wedded neither to the well-to-do capitalistic liberals, nor to the existing government structures of the German states, nor to the House of Hapsburg. He would use "democracy" to undermine all established interests that stood in his way.

Meanwhile the occupying powers continued to quarrel over Schleswig-Holstein. Austria finally raised the matter formally in the German federal diet, one of whose functions was to prevent war between its members. Bismarck declared that the diet had no authority, accused the Austrians of aggression, and ordered the Prussian army to enter Holstein. The Austrians called for federal sanctions in the form of an all-German force to be sent against Prussia. The result was that Prussia, in 1866, was at war not only with Austria, but with all the other German states. The Prussian army soon proved its superiority. Trained to an unprecedented precision, equipped with the new needle-gun, by which the infantryman could deliver five rounds a minute, brought into the zone of combat by an imaginative strategy that made use of the new railroads, commanded by the skill of von Moltke, the Prussian army overthrew the Austrians at the Battle of Sadowa (or Königgrätz), and defeated the other German states soon thereafter. The Austro-Prussian, or Seven Weeks' War, was unexampled in its shortness. Bismarck hastened to make peace before the other European powers, which he had first hoodwinked and now stunned, could realize what had happened.

Prussia annexed outright, together with Schleswig-Holstein, the whole kingdom of Hanover, the duchies of Nassau and Hesse-Cassel and the free city of Frankfurt. Here the old governments simply disappeared before the axe of the "red reactionary." The German federal union disappeared likewise. In its place, in 1867, Bismarck organized a North German Confederation, in which the newly enlarged Prussia joined with twenty-one other states, all of which combined it greatly outweighed. The German states south of the river Main—Austria, Bavaria, Baden, Würtemberg, and Hesse-Darmstadt—remained outside the new organization, with no kind of union among themselves. Meanwhile the kingdom of Italy annexed Venetia.

For the North German Confederation Bismarck produced a constitution. The new structure, though a federal one, was much stronger than the now defunct Confederation of 1815. The king of Prussia became its hereditary head. Ministers were responsible to him. There was a parliament with two chambers. The upper chamber, as in the United States, represented the states as such, though not equally. The lower chamber, or Reichstag, was deemed to represent the people and was elected by universal suffrage. Such flirting with democracy seemed madness to both conservative *Junker* and liberal bourgeois. It was indeed a bold step, for only France at the time illustrated universal suffrage in Europe on a large scale, and in the France of Napoleon III neither old-fashioned conservatives nor genuine liberals could take much satisfaction. As for Great Britain, where voting rights were extended in this same year, 1867, they were still given to less than half the adult male population. Bismarck sensed in the "masses" an ally of strong government against private interests. He negotiated even with the socialists, who had arisen with the industrialization of the past decade, and who, in Germany at this time, were mainly followers of Ferdinand Lassalle. The Lassallean socialists, unlike the Marxian, believed it theoretically possible to improve working-class conditions through the action of existing governments. To the great annoyance of Marx, then in England (his *Capital* first appeared in 1867), the bulk of the German socialists reached an understanding with Bismarck. In return for a democratic suffrage they agreed to accept the North German Confederation. Bismarck, for his part, by making use of democratic and socialist sentiment, won popular approval for his emerging empire.

THE FRANCO-PRUSSIAN WAR, 1870

It was clear that the situation was not yet stable. The small south German states were left floating in empty space; they would sooner or later have to gravitate into some orbit or other, Austrian, Prussian, or French. In France there were angry criticisms of Napoleon III's foreign policy. French intervention in Mexico had proved a fiasco.[20] A united Italy had been allowed to rise on France's borders. And now, contrary to all principles of French national interest observed by French governments for hundreds of years, a strong and independent power was being allowed to spread over virtually the whole of Germany. Everywhere people began to feel that war was coming between France and Prussia. Bismarck played on the fears of France felt in the south German states. South Germany, though in former times it had often been a willing satellite to France, was now sufficiently nationalistic to consider such subservience to a foreign people disgraceful. To Bismarck it seemed that a war between Prussia and France would frighten the small south German states into a union with Prussia, leaving only Austria outside— which was what he wanted. To Napoleon III, or at least to some of his advisers, it seemed that such a war, if successful, would restore public approval of the Bonapartist empire. In this inflammable situation the responsible persons of neither country worked for peace.

Meanwhile a revolution in Spain had driven the reigning queen into exile, and a Spanish provisional government invited Prince Leopold of Hohenzollern, the king of Prussia's cousin, to be constitutional king of Spain. To entrench the Prussian royal house in Spain would naturally be distasteful to France. Three times the Hohenzollern family refused the Spanish offer. Bismarck, who could not control such family decisions, but who foresaw the possibility of a usable incident, deviously persuaded the Spanish to issue the invitation still a fourth time. On July 2, 1870, Paris heard that Prince Leopold had accepted. The French ambassador to Prussia, Benedetti, at the direction of his government, met the king of Prussia at the bathing resort of Ems,

[20] See p. 624.

where he formally demanded that Prince Leopold's acceptance be withdrawn. It was withdrawn on July 12. The French seemed to have their way. Bismarck was disappointed.

The French government then took a further step, hoping to win a resounding diplomatic triumph. Benedetti received further instructions: he should again approach the king at Ems, and demand that at no time in the future would a Hohenzollern become a candidate for the Spanish throne under any conditions. The king politely declined any such commitment, and telegraphed a full report of the conversation to Bismarck at Berlin. Bismarck, receiving the telegram, which became famous as the "Ems despatch," saw a new opportunity, as he put it, to wave a red flag before the Gallic bull. He condensed the Ems telegram for publication, so reducing and abridging it that it seemed to newspaper readers as if a curt exchange had occurred at Ems, in which the Prussians believed that their king had been insulted, and the French that their ambassador had been snubbed. In both countries the war party demanded satisfaction. On July 15, 1870, on these trivial grounds, and with the ostensible issue of the Spanish throne already settled, the irresponsible and decaying government of Napoleon III declared war on Prussia.

Again the war was short. Again Bismarck had taken care to isolate his enemy in advance. The British generally felt France to be in the wrong. They had been alarmed by French operations in Mexico, which suggested an ambition to recreate a French American empire. The Italians had long been awaiting the chance to seize Rome; they did so in 1870, when the French withdrew their troops from Rome for use against Prussia. The Russians had been awaiting the chance to upset the clause of the Peace of 1856 which forbade them to keep naval vessels in the Black Sea. They did so in 1870. It was Austria, defeated in 1866, that might most probably have combined with France in 1870 to stop the rise of Prussia. But Bismarck had purposely granted lenient terms to Austria in 1866. The Austrians detested Napoleon III for his part in Italian unification. The Austrian empire was undergoing an internal reorganization, in which the Magyars of Hungary obtained more influence in affairs of state. Since the days of Maria Theresa the military power of the empire had rested very largely on the Magyars, and the Magyars were now inclined to take the part of Bismarck and of Prussia, because the more the Hapsburg monarchy was pushed out of Germany, the better the position of the Magyars within it became.

So the War of 1870, like the others of the time, failed to become a general European struggle. Prussia was supported by the south German states. France had no allies. The French army proved to be technically backward compared with the Prussian. War began on July 15; on September 2, after the battle of Sedan, the principal French army surrendered to the Germans. Napoleon III was himself taken prisoner. On September 4 an insurrection in Paris proclaimed the Republic. The Prussian and German forces moved into France and laid siege to the capital. Though the French armies dissolved, Paris refused to capitulate. For four months it was surrounded and besieged.

THE GERMAN EMPIRE, 1871

With their guns encircling Paris, the crowned heads of Germany assembled at the small neighboring city of Versailles. The chateau and gardens of Versailles, since Louis XVI's unceremonious departure in October, 1789, had been little more than a vacant monument to a society long since dead. Here, in the most sumptuous room of the palace, the resplendent Hall of Mirrors, where the Sun King had once received the deferential approaches of German princes, Bismarck on January 18, 1871, caused the German Empire to be proclaimed. The king of Prussia received the hereditary title of German Emperor. To him the other German rulers (excepting, to be sure, the ruler of Austria, and those whom Bismarck had himself dethroned) took a vow of imperial allegiance. Ten days later the people of Paris, shivering, hungry, and helpless, opened their gates to the enemy. France had no government with which Bismarck could make peace. It was not at all clear what kind of government the country wanted. Bismarck insisted on the election of a Constituent Assembly by universal suffrage. He wished, as it were, to have the whole French nation sign his terms. He demanded that France pay the German Empire a war indemnity of five billion gold francs (then an enormous and unprecedented sum), and cede to it the border region of Alsace and most of Lorraine. Though the Alsatians spoke German, most of them felt as Frenchmen, having shared in the general history of France since the seventeenth century. There was strong local protest at the transfer to Germany, and the French never reconciled themselves to this cold-blooded amputation of their frontier. The peace dictated by Bismarck was embodied in the treaty of Frankfurt of May 10, 1871. Thereafter, as will be seen, the French Constituent Assembly gradually proceeded to construct the Third Republic.[21]

The consolidation of Germany transformed the face of Europe. It reversed the dictum not only of the Peace of Vienna but even of the Peace of Westphalia.[22] The German empire, no sooner born, was the strongest state on the continent of Europe. Rapidly industrialized after 1870, it became more potent still. Bismarck, by consummate astuteness, by exploiting the oppor-

[21] See pp. 577–8.
[22] See p. 130.

Europe, 1871   See following pages

From 1871 to 1914 Europe had fewer separate states, fewer land frontiers and a simpler political geography than at any other time in its history. Except for the voluntary separation of Norway and Sweden there were no changes in this period outside the Balkans, as shown in the insets. Here certain readjustments followed from the Russo-Turkish War and Congress of Berlin of 1878. In 1908 Austria annexed Bosnia. The Balkan Wars of 1912–13 resulted in the recession of the Ottoman frontier almost to the Straits, and in the corresponding enlargement of Greece and Serbia and creation of the independent kingdom of Albania.

EUROPE
1871

BALKANS
1878

AUSTRIA-HUNGARY

RUSS.

Belgrade

RUMANIA
(IND.)

DOBRUJA

BOSNIA
(MIL.OCC.)

SERBIA
(IND.)

DANUBE R.

BLACK
SEA

MONTE-
NEGRO
(IND.)

BULGARIA
(TRIB.)

E. RUMELIA
(AUT. PROV.)

ITALY

ALBANIA

MACEDONIA

OTTOMAN

Constantinople

1881

EMP.

(TURK.)

GREECE
(IND.)

NORWAY
AND
SWEDEN

Kristiania

Stockholm

SHETLAND IS.
(BR)

SCOTLAND

NORTH
SEA

DENMARK

Copenhagen

BALTIC

GERMAN
EMPIRE

HELIGOLAND
(BR)

Hamburg

Bremen

Berlin

Danz

IRELAND

Belfast

Dublin

Liverpool

ENGLAND

GREAT
BRITAIN

London

ODER R.

ENGLISH CHANNEL

Brussels

BELG.

Cologne

RHINE R.

Dresden

ELBE R.

NETH.

Amsterdam

SEINE R.

LUX.

Paris

Reims

Metz

Strasburg

Prague

Tours

LOIRE R.

Munich

FRANCE

SWITZ.

Vienna

Budo

Bordeaux

Lyons

RHONE R.

Milan

Venice

CROATIA
SLOVENIA

Turin

Bilbao

ADRIATIC

BOSN

Lisbon

TAGUS R.

Madrid

EBRO R.

Marseilles

CORSICA
(FR)

Rome

MONT.
NEGR.
(IN

PORTUGAL

SPAIN

Barcelona

SARDINIA

Naples

Seville

BALEARIC IS.
(SP.)

ITALY

Tangier

GIBRALTAR
(BR)

MEDITERRANEAN

Algiers

SICILY

Fez

MOROCCO

ALGERIA
(FR)

Tunis

TUNISIA
(TURK.)

MALTA
(BR)

TRM

500 MILES

ARCTIC OCEAN

NORTH CAPE

LAPPLAND

WHITE SEA

Archangel

FINLAND

LAKE LADOGA

Helsingfors

St. Petersburg

Riga

Vilna

EAST RUSSIA

Warsaw

POLAND

VISTULA R.

RUSSIAN

VOLGA R.

Moscow

Orenburg

URAL R.

EMPIRE

Kiev

AUSTRIA-HUNGARY

VOLGA R.

Astrakhan

DON R.

Rostov

HUNGARY

DNIESTER R.

BESSARABIA

PRUTH R.

Odessa

SEA OF AZOV

CRIMEA

CASPIAN SEA

Sevastopol

CAUCASIA

Baku

SERBIA (TRIB.)

RUMANIA (TRIB.)

DANUBE R.

DOBRUJA

BLACK SEA

OTTOMAN

BULGARIA

Sinope

MACEDONIA

Constantinople

Tabriz

PERSIA

DARDANELLES

AEGEAN SEA

EMPIRE

TIGRIS R.

Smyrna

Athens

EUPHRATES R.

MESOPOTAMIA

GREECE (IND.)

SYRIA

Bagdad

CRETE (TURK.)

SEA

CYPRUS (BR.)

ARABIA

BALKANS 1914

AUSTRIA-HUNGARY

RUSS.

Belgrade

RUMANIA

BOSNIA (ANNEXED 1908)

Sarajevo

SERBIA

DANUBE R.

1913

BLACK SEA

BULGARIA

E. RUMELIA 1885

MONTE-NEGRO

ITALY

1913

Constantinople

ALBANIA (IND.)

1913

1913

OTTOMAN EMP.

GREECE

tunities offered by a Europe in flux, and with no more fighting than that involved in a few weeks in three small wars, had brought about what European statesmen of many nationalities had long said should at all costs be prevented. He outwitted everybody in turn, including the Germans. The united all-German state that issued from the nationalist movement was a Germany conquered by Prussia. Prussia, with its annexations of 1866, embraced almost all Germany north of the Main. Within the empire it had about two-thirds of the area. In Prussia the liberals capitulated before Bismarck's unanswerable success. In 1867 the Prussian parliament passed an "indemnity act"; the gist of it was that Bismarck admitted to a certain highhandedness during the constitutional struggle, but that the parliament legalized the disputed tax collections *ex post facto*, agreeing to forgive and forget, in view of the victory over Austria and its consequences. Thus liberalism withered away before nationalism. The quick victory over France confirmed the same tendency. All nations respect the methods to which they attribute their successes, and to the Germans it seemed that one should be "realistic" and that an effective army is the mainstay of the state.

The German Empire received substantially the constitution of the North German Confederation. It was a federation of monarchies, each based in theory on divine or hereditary right. At the same time, in the Reichstag elected by universal suffrage, it rested on a kind of mass appeal and was in a sense democratic. Yet the country's ministers were responsible to the emperor and not to the elected chamber. Moreover, it was the rulers who joined the empire, not the peoples. There were no popular plebiscites as in Italy. Each state kept its own laws, government and constitution. The people of Prussia, for example, remained for Prussian affairs under the rather illiberal constitution of 1850,[23] while in affairs of the Reich, or empire, they enjoyed an equal vote by universal suffrage. The emperor, who was also the king of Prussia, had legal control over the foreign and military policy of the empire. The German Empire in effect served as a mechanism to magnify the role of Prussia, the Prussian army, and the East Elbian Prussian aristocracy in world affairs.

65. The Dual Monarchy of Austria-Hungary

THE HAPSBURG EMPIRE AFTER 1848

Bismarck united Germany, but he also divided it, for he left about a sixth of the Germans outside his German Empire. These Germans of Austria and Bohemia had now to work out a common future with the dozen other nationalities in the Danubian domain.

The clumsiness of the old Hapsburg multinational empire is clear

‑‑‑‑‑‑‑‑‑‑‑‑‑‑‑‑‑‑‑

[23] See pp. 491–2.

enough, but more impressive is its astonishing capacity to live and to survive. Prussia and France, in the 1740's, had tried unsuccessfully to dismember it. Smashed four different times by the French between 1796 and 1809, it outlived this crisis, and after 1815, under Metternich, it guided the counsels of Europe.[24] Broken up in 1848, restored by the intervention of Russia in 1849, dislocated by its effort at mobilization in 1855, attacked by Napoleon III in 1859 and by Bismarck in 1866, it still continued to hold together, and disappeared finally only in 1918 in the cataclysm of the First World War.[25] But the events of the 1850's and 1860's greatly altered its character.

The essential question, in a nationalist age, was how the Hapsburg government would react to the problems raised by national self-expression. The nationalities did not wish to destroy the empire. Among the Hungarians after 1848–49, only a handful of extreme radicals dreamed of a Hungary entirely independent. Most of them followed Francis Deak, desiring constitutional autonomy for Hungary but not denying the link with Vienna. Slav opinion, at the Slav Congress of Prague in 1848, went basically no further than Austroslavism.[26] The peoples of the empire, while increasingly insistent on certain national rights—such as a degree of local self-government, and schools, lawcourts, and administration in their own language—felt an underlying need for the larger political structure which the empire gave.

By Hapsburg, in this period, one means primarily Francis Joseph, who as emperor from 1848 to 1916 reigned even longer than his famous contemporary, Queen Victoria. Francis Joseph, like many others, could never shake off his own tradition. His thoughts turned on his House and on its rights. Buffeted unmercifully by the waves of change, he cordially disliked everything liberal, progressive, or modern. He allied himself with the Catholic hierarchy and the Vatican, which also, for decades after 1848, and for understandable reason, set itself bluntly against compromise with the new age. Personally, Francis Joseph was incapable of enlarged views, ambitious projects, bold decisions, or persevering action. And he lived in a pompous dream world, surrounded in the imperial court by great noblemen, high churchmen, and bespangled personages of the army.

Yet the government was not idle; it was, if anything, too fertile in devising new deals and new dispensations. Various expedients were tried after 1849, but none was tried long enough to see if it would work. For several years the ruling idea was centralization, to govern the empire through the German language and with German efficiency, maintaining the abolition of serfdom as accomplished in 1848 (and which required a strong official control over the landlords if it was to work in practice) and favoring the building of railroads and other apparatus of material progress.[27] This Germanic and bureaucratic centralization was distasteful to the non-German nationalities, and especially to the Magyars. It is important to say Magyars, not Hungarians, because the Magyars composed less than half the very mixed popu-

---

[24] See pp. 245–9, 366–7, 378, 382, 385–7, 443–52.
[25] See pp. 477–85, 512, 516, 522–4, 687.

[26] See pp. 481–2.
[27] See p. 485.

lation of Hungary within its then-existing borders. Nevertheless the Magyars, as the strongest of the non-German groups, and hence the most able to maintain a political system of their own, felt the Germanic influence as most oppressive. In the war of 1859 the Magyars sympathized with the Italians.

The war, which took away Lombardy, proved the inability of the empire to defend itself under existing conditions. The government concluded that it must solicit the support of its subjects. In 1860 a kind of federative scheme was adopted, but in 1861 this was dropped for a new form of centralization, one in which, alongside the old officialdom, there should be a parliament for the whole empire. In the parliament the nationalities were to be represented proportionately. But the Magyars boycotted the parliament. They declined to merge the separate identity of Hungary in any higher structure, either absolutist or parliamentary. After four years during which the machinery of state ground to a halt, the Vienna government opened negotiations with the Magyars. In 1866 the war with Prussia revealed the impossible handicaps under which the empire labored. In 1867 the Vienna authorities concluded an agreement with the Magyars, and one which lasted as long as the House of Hapsburg.

THE COMPROMISE OF 1867

The Compromise of 1867, commonly known as the *Ausgleich*, was essentially a bargain between the Germans of Austria-Bohemia and the Magyars of Hungary. It worked to the common disadvantage of the Slavs. Both Germans and Magyars looked upon the Slavs somewhat as whites in the United States at the time looked upon Negroes, seeing in them a people useful for labor, naturally slovenly, who had shown no aptitude for civilization except under tutelage. In fact the word "slave" in many languages (German *sklave*) had originated from the word "Slav." As Count Beust, the Austrian negotiator, put it in 1867, the idea of the Compromise was that each people, Germans and Magyars, should thereafter govern its own barbarians in its own way.

The Compromise created a Dual Monarchy, of a kind unparalleled in Europe. West of the river Leith was the Empire of Austria, east of it the Kingdom of Hungary. The two were now judged exactly equal. Each had its own constitution and its own parliament, to which in each country the governing ministry was henceforth to be responsible. The administrative language of Austria would be German, of Hungary, Magyar. Neither state might intervene in the other's affairs. The two were joined by the fact that the same Hapsburg ruler should always be emperor in Austria and king in Hungary. Yet the union was not personal only; for, though there was no common parliament, delegates of the two parliaments were to meet together alternately in Vienna and Budapest, and there was to be a common ministry for finance, foreign affairs and war. To this common ministry of Austria-Hungary both Austrians and Hungarians were to be appointed.

In effect, the Compromise treated Austria as a kind of German nation-state, and Hungary as a Magyar nation-state. It furnished each with parliamentary and constitutional organs, by which the leading nationality was made to feel a sense of participation in government. But the Germans formed less than half the people of Austria, as did the Magyars of Hungary. Austria included the Slovenes, Czechs, Poles, and Ruthenians (and a few Italians); Hungary the Slovaks, the Croats and Serbs, and the Transylvanians, who were essentially Rumanians.[28] All these peoples felt aggrieved.

In later years the Germans of Austria proved more liberal toward their minorities than did the Magyars, though never quite liberal enough to allay the discontents. In 1871 Francis Joseph even prepared to recognize the Czechs, agreeing to place Bohemia on the same footing as Hungary. He abandoned the idea in the face of protests from the Germans, especially the Sudeten Germans who lived in Bohemia and who wanted no Czechish state, and also of the Magyars, who feared that the autonomy of Bohemia would be an unsettling example to their own "barbarians." The idea of a Triple Monarchy thereafter never died, but neither did it ever come to life. The Slavs of the Dual Monarchy remained submerged. A man of Slavic birth could hold high office and enjoy the satisfactions of public activity only by adopting the German or Magyar language and culture. Thus frustrated, the Slavs were increasingly tempted to agree with their most radical nationalists.

The Germans of Austria, kept out of Germany by Bismarck, were kept out of Hungary by the Magyars. It was the Magyars who were the great beneficiaries of the Compromise. Somewhat as Bismarck's empire was a mechanism to magnify the rule of East Elbian Prussia, so the Dual Monarchy became a mechanism to enlarge the influence of the great Hungarian landowners. It was Hungary that adjoined the explosive Balkan peninsula. It was the ruling Magyars, stubbornly refusing concessions to the other peoples, and working through the joint ministry of Austria-Hungary, that transmitted into Europe the shocks originating in the Balkans.

Both Austria and Hungary, under the Dual Monarchy, were in form constitutional parliamentary states although the principle of ministerial responsibility was not consistently honored. Neither was democratic. In Austria, after much juggling with voting systems, a true universal manhood suffrage was instituted in 1907. In Hungary, when the First World War came in 1914, still only a quarter of the adult male population had the vote. Socially, the great reform of 1848, the abolition of serfdom, was not allowed to lead on to upsetting conclusions. The owners of great landed estates, especially in Hungary (but also in parts of the Austrian Empire) remained the unquestionably dominant class. They were surrounded by landless peasants, an agrarian proletariat, composed partly of lower classes of their own nationality, and partly of entire peasant peoples, like the Slovaks and Serbs, who had no educated or wealthy class of their own. National and social questions therefore came together. For some nationalities, and for none more than the Magyars, not

⁓⁓⁓⁓⁓⁓⁓⁓⁓⁓⁓

[28] See maps, pp. 437, 528–9.

only a national but a social and economic ascendancy was at stake. Landlordism became the basic social issue. A landowning class, educated and civilized, faced a peasant mass that was generally ignorant, rude, and left out of the advancing civilization of the day.

66. Liberalization in Tsarist Russia: Alexander II

TSARIST RUSSIA AFTER 1856

For Russia also the Crimean War set off a series of changes. The ungainly empire, an "enormous village" as it has been called, stretching from Poland to the Pacific, had proved unable to repel a localized attack by France and Great Britain, into which neither of the Western powers had put anything like its full resources. Alexander II (1855–81), who became tsar during the war, was no liberal by nature or conviction. But he saw that something drastic must be done. The prestige of western Europe was at its height. There the most successful and even enviable nations were to be found. The reforms in Russia therefore followed, at some distance, the European model.

Imperial Russia was a political organization very difficult to describe. Its own subjects did not know what to make of it. Some, called Westernizers in the mid-nineteenth century, believed Russia destined to become more like Europe. Others, the Slavophiles, believed Russia to be entrusted with a special destiny of its own, which imitation of Europe would only weaken or pervert.

That Russia differed from Europe at least in degree was doubted by nobody. The leading institution was the autocracy of the tsar. This was not exactly the absolutism known in the West. In Russia certain very old European conceptions were missing, such as the idea that spiritual authority is independent of even the mightiest prince, or the old feudal idea of reciprocal duties between king and subject.[29] The notion that men have rights, claims for justice at the hands of power, which no one in Europe had ever expressly repudiated, was in Russia a somewhat doctrinaire importation from the West. The tsardom did not rule by law; it ran the country by ukase, police action, and the army. The tsars, since Peter and before, had built up their state very largely by importing European technical methods and technical experts, often against strong objection by native Russians of all classes, upon whom the new methods were, when necessary, simply forced. More than any state in Europe, the Russian empire was a machine superimposed upon its people without organic connection—bureaucracy pure and simple. But as the contacts with Europe were joined, many Russians acquired European ideas of a kind in which the autocracy was not interested—ideas of liberty and fraternity, of

ᴡᴡᴡᴡᴡᴡᴡᴡᴡᴡᴡᴡᴡᴡᴡᴡ

[29] See pp. 12–13, 24.

a just and classless society, of individual personality enriched by mental culture and moral freedom. Many people, with such sentiments, found themselves chronically critical of the government and of Russia itself. The government, massive though it seemed, was afraid of such people. Any idea arising outside of official circles seemed pernicious, and the press and the universities were as a rule severely censored.

A second fundamental institution, which had grown up with the tsardom, was legalized bondage or serfdom. The bulk of the population were serfs dependent upon masters. Russian serfdom was more onerous than that found in east-central Europe until 1848.[30] It resembled the slavery of the Americas in that serfs were "owned"; they could be bought and sold, and used in other occupations than agriculture. Some serfs worked the soil, rendering unpaid labor service to the gentry. Others could be used by their owners in factories or mines, or rented out for such purposes. Others were more independent, working as artisans or mechanics, and even traveling about or residing in the cities, but from their earnings they had to remit certain fees to the lord, or return home when he called them. The owners had a certain paternalistic responsibility for their serfs, and in the villages the gentry constituted a kind of personal local government. The law, as in the American South, did little or nothing to interfere between gentry and servile mass, so that the serf's day-to-day fortunes depended on the personality or economic circumstances of his owner.

By the mid-nineteenth century both conservative and liberal Russians were agreeing that serfdom must some day end. Serfdom was in any case ceasing to be profitable; some two-thirds of all the privately owned serfs (*i.e.*, those not belonging to the tsar or state) were mortgaged as security for loans at the time of Alexander II's accession. Increasingly serfdom was recognized as a bad system of labor relations, making the *mujiks* into illiterate and stolid drudges, without incentive, initiative, self-respect, or pride of workmanship, and also very stupid soldiers for the army.

Educated Russians, full of Western ideas, were estranged from the government, from the Orthodox Church, which was an arm of the tsar, and from the common people of their own country They felt ill at ease in a mass of ignorance and obscurantism, and a pang of guilt at the virtual slavery on which their own position rested. Hence arose, at about the time under discussion, what may almost be called another Russian institution, the "intelligentsia." In Russia it was thought so remarkable to be educated, to have ideas, to subscribe to magazines or engage in critical conversation that the intelligentsia sensed themselves as a class apart. They were made up of students, university graduates, and persons who had a good deal of leisure to read. Such people, while not very free to think, were more free to think than to do almost anything else. The Russian intelligentsia tended to sweeping and all-embracing philosophies. They believed that intellectuals should play

---

[30] See pp. 209, 314–16.

a large role in society. They formed an exaggerated idea of the direct influence of thinkers upon the course of historical change. Their characteristic attitude was one of opposition. Some, overwhelmed by the mammoth immobility of the tsardom and of serfdom, turned to revolutionary and even terroristic philosophies. This only made the government more repressive. Russia became the land of intimidation, of violent and jarring ideas and lawless acts.

THE EMANCIPATION ACT OF 1861 AND OTHER REFORMS

Alexander II, on becoming tsar, attempted to enlist the support of the liberals among the intelligentsia. He gave permission to travel outside of Russia, eased the controls on the universities, and allowed the censorship to go relatively unenforced. Newspapers and journals were founded, and those written by Russian revolutionaries abroad, like the *Polar Star* of Alexander Hertzen in London, penetrated more freely into the country. The result was a great outburst of public opinion, which was agreed at least on one point, the necessity of emancipating the peasants. This was in principle hardly a party question. Alexander's father, Nicholas I, had been a noted reactionary, who abhorred western liberalism, and is memorable for having organized, as the "Third Section" of his chancellory, a system of secret political police until then unparalleled in Europe for its ruthlessness. Yet Nicholas I had taken serious measures to alleviate serfdom. Alexander II, basically conservative on Russian affairs, proceeded to set up a special branch of the government to study the question. The government did not wish to throw the whole labor system and economy of the country into chaos, nor to ruin the gentry class without which it could not govern at all. After many discussions, proposals, and memoranda, an imperial ukase of 1861 declared serfdom abolished and the peasants free.

By this great decree the peasants became legally free in the Western sense. They were henceforth subjects of the government, not subjects of their owners. It was hoped that they would be stirred by a new sense of human dignity. As one enthusiastic official put it shortly after emancipation: "The people are erect and transformed; the look, the walk, the speech, everything is changed." The gentry lost their old quasi-manorial jurisdiction over the villages. They could no longer exact forced and unpaid labor, or receive fees arising from servitude.

It is important to realize what the Act of Emancipation did and did not do. Roughly (with great differences from region to region) it allocated about half the cultivated land to the gentry and half to the former serfs. The latter had to pay redemption money for the land they received and for the fees and services which the gentry lost. The Russian aristocracy was far from weakened; in place of a kind of human property largely mortgaged anyway, they now had clear possession of some half the land, they received the redemption money, and were rid of obligations to the peasants.

The peasants, on the other hand, now owned some half the arable land in their own right—a considerable amount by the standards of almost any European country. They did not, however, possess it according to the principles of private property or independent farming that had become prevalent in Europe. The peasant land, when redeemed, became the collective property of the ancient peasant village or *mir*. The village, as a unit, was responsible to the government for payment of the redemption, and for collection of the necessary sums from its individual members. The village commune, in default of collection, might require forced labor from the defaulter or a member of his family; and it could prevent peasants from moving away from the village, lest those remaining bear the whole burden of payment. It could (as in the past) assign and reassign certain lands to its members for tillage, and otherwise supervise cultivation as a joint concern. To keep the village community intact, the government presently forbade the selling or mortgaging of land to persons outside the commune. This tended to preserve the peasant society, but also to discourage the investment of outside capital, with which equipment might be purchased, and so to retard agricultural improvement and the growth of wealth. Not all peasants within the village unit were equal. As in France before the Revolution, some had the right to work more land than others. Some were only day laborers. Others had rights of inheritance in the soil (for not all land was subject to reassignment by the commune), or rented additional parcels of land belonging to the gentry. These lands they worked by hiring other peasants for wages. These more substantial peasants, as agricultural entrepreneurs, resembled farmers of the "bourgeois" type found in France or the United States. None of the Russian peasants, however, after the emancipation, possessed full individual freedom of action. In their movements and obligations, as in their thoughts, they were restricted by their village communes as they had once been restricted by their lords.

Alexander II proceeded to overhaul and westernize the legal system of the country. With the disappearance of the lord's jurisdiction over his peasants a new system of local courts was needed in any case, but the opportunity was taken to reform the courts from bottom to top. The arbitrariness of authority and defenselessness of the subject were the inveterate evils. They were greatly mitigated by the edict of 1864. Trials were made public, and private persons received the right to be represented in court by lawyers of their own choosing. All class distinctions in judicial matters were abolished although in practice peasants continued to be subject to harsh disadvantages. A clear sequence of lower and higher courts was established. Requirements were laid down for the professional training of judges, who henceforth received stated salaries and were protected from administrative pressure. A system of juries on the English model was introduced.

While thus attempting to establish a rule of law, the tsar also moved in the direction of allowing self-government. He hoped to win over the liberals, and to shoulder the upper and middle classes with some degree of public responsibility. He created, again by an edict of 1864, a system of provincial and district councils called zemstvos. Elected by various elements, including the peasants in theory, the zemstvos went gradually into operation, and took up matters of education, medical relief, public welfare, food supply, and road maintenance in their localities. Their great value was in developing civic sentiment among those who took part in them. Many liberals urged a representative body for all Russia, a Zemsky Sobor or Duma, which, however, Alexander II refused to concede. After 1864 his policy became more cautious. A rebellion in Poland in 1863 inclined him to take advice from those who favored repression. He began to mollify the vested interests that had been disgruntled by the reforms, and to whittle down some of the concessions already granted. But the essence of the reforms remained unaffected.

REVOLUTIONISM IN RUSSIA

The autocrat who thus undertook to liberalize Russia barely escaped assassination in 1866, had five shots fired at him in 1873, missed death by a half-hour in 1880 when his imperial dining-room was dynamited, and in 1881 was to be killed by a bomb. The revolutionaries were not pleased with the reforms, which if successful would merely strengthen the existing order. Dissatisfied intelligentsia in the 1860's began to call themselves "nihilists": they believed in "nothing"—except science—and took a cynical view of the reforming tsar and his zemstvos. The peasants, saddled with heavy redemption payments, remained basically unsatisfied, and intellectuals toured the villages fanning this discontent. Revolutionaries developed a mystic conception of the revolutionary role of the Russian masses. They reminded the peasants of the vast rebellions of Stephen Razin and Pugachev, in which they saw a native Russian revolutionary tradition.[31] Socialists, after the failure of socialism in Europe in the revolution of 1848, came in many cases to believe, as Alexander Herzen wrote, that the true and natural future of socialism lay in Russia, because of the very weakness of capitalism in Russia and the existence of a kind of collectivism already established in the village commune.

More radical than Hertzen were the anarchist Bakunin and his disciple Nechaiev. In their *People's Justice* these two called for terrorism not only against tsarist officials but against liberals also. As they wrote in their *Catechism of a Revolutionist*, the true revolutionary "is devoured by one purpose, one thought, one passion—the revolution. . . . He has severed every link with the social order and with the entire civilized world. . . . Everything which promotes the success of the revolution is moral, everything which hinders it is immoral." Terrorism (which is really to say assassination) was rejected by many of the revolutionaries, especially by those who in the 1870's took up the scientific socialism of Karl Marx. To Marx it did not seem that frantic violence would advance an inevitable social process. But other groups,

〰〰〰〰〰〰〰〰〰〰

[31] See pp. 209–10, 315.

recognizing the inspiration of men like Bakunin and Nechaiev, organized secret terroristic societies. One of these, the People's Will, determined to assassinate the tsar. In an autocratic state, they held, there was no other road to justice and freedom.

Alexander II, alarmed by this underground menace, which of course did not escape the attention of the police, again turned for support to the liberals. The liberals, who were themselves threatened by the revolutionaries, had become estranged from the government by its failure to follow through with the reforms of the early sixties. Now, in 1880, to rally support, the tsar again relaxed the autocratic system. He abolished the dreaded Third Section or secret police set up by his father, allowed the press to discuss most political subjects freely, and encouraged the zemstvos to do the same. Further to associate representatives of the public with the government he proposed, not exactly a parliament, but two nationally elected commissions to sit with the council of state. He signed the edict to this effect on March 13, 1881, and on the same day was assassinated, not by a demented individual acting wildly and alone, but by the efforts of several hundred highly trained members of the People's Will.

Alexander III, upon his father's death, abandoned the project for elected commissions, and during his whole reign, from 1881 to 1894, reverted to a program of brutal resistance to liberals and revolutionaries alike. The new regime established by peasant emancipation, judicial reform, and the zemstvos was nevertheless allowed to continue. How Russia finally received a parliament in 1905 is explained below in the chapter on the Russian Revolution. At present it is enough to have seen how even tsarist Russia, under Alexander II, shared in a liberal movement that was then at its height. The abolition of serfdom, putting both aristocracy and peasant more fully on a money economy, opened the way for capitalistic development within the empire. And between the two confining walls of autocracy and revolutionism —equally hard and unyielding—European ideas of law, liberty, and humanity inserted themselves in a tentative way.

67. The United States: The American Civil War

The history of Europe, long interconnected with that of the rest of the world, by the early twentieth century became merged with it entirely. Similarly the development of non-European regions, long a collection of separate stories, was to fuse into a single world-wide theme, to which later chapters of this book are largely devoted. It is no great leap at this point to pass to a treatment of areas overseas (as seen from Europe), some of which underwent in the 1860's the same process of national consolidation, or attempted consolidation, already traced in Italy and Germany, Austria, Hungary, and the Russian Empire. In particular, foundations were laid for two new "powers" like those of Europe—the United States of America and the Empire of Japan. The huge Dominion of Canada was also established.

GROWTH OF THE UNITED STATES

As in the time of the American Revolution and Napoleon, the history of the United States in the nineteenth century reflected that of the European world of which it formed a part. The most basic fact, besides territorial expansion, was rapid growth. This was so obvious as to lead a French observer in the 1830's, Alexis de Tocqueville, to make a famous prediction: that within a century the United States would have a hundred million people, and would, along with Russia, be one of the two leading powers of the world. By 1860, with 31,000,000, the United States was almost as populous as France, and more so than Great Britain.

The growth in numbers was due to a prolific birth-rate, but also to the arrival of immigrants, who became prolific in their turn. The immigrants— except for an uncounted, because illegal, importation of Negro slaves—came entirely from Europe, and before 1860 almost entirely from Great Britain, Ireland, and Germany. The immigrants did not desire to surrender their native ways. The Catholicism of many of them, especially at a time when Catholicism was at odds with liberalism and republicanism in Europe, was unpopular and even abhorrent to many native Americans. What Europe would call a national question therefore developed. A secret, anti-foreign, native-American movement, calling itself the "Know-nothing" or "American" party, even entered briefly into national politics in the 1850's. It quickly collapsed, in the face of more burning issues, and with the refusal of most native Americans to believe themselves actually menaced.

It was of course true that the constant arrival of Europeans was transforming the United States. The transformation was in some ways indisputably for the better, as when educated Germans, in flight from counter-revolution after 1848, brought a knowledge of the sciences, medicine, music, and the most skilled mechanical arts which the new country greatly needed. In other ways it presented a true social problem, obliging peoples to live together without common tradition, and landing in the United States many who had been a problem at home. On the whole, it appears that the native Americans accepted the reshaping of their country more calmly than most Europeans would have done in similar circumstances. Few concessions were made. English was the language of the public schools, the police, law courts, local government, and public notices and announcements. Usually the immigrant had to know some English to hold a job. On the other hand no one was exactly forced to become "Americanized"—the new arrivals were free to maintain churches, newspapers, and social gatherings in their own tongues. The fact that the English, Scotch, and Irish already spoke English, and that the Germans readily learned it, alleviated the language issue. The immigrants did not constitute minorities in the European sense. They were more than willing to embrace American national attitudes as formed in the eighteenth century—the national traditions of republicanism and self-government, of individual liberty, free enterprise, and unbounded opportunity for self-improvement. The old America impressed itself on the new, being somewhat impressed itself in the process. In this sense a new nationality was being consolidated.

THE ESTRANGEMENT OF NORTH AND SOUTH

But at the same time the nation was falling to pieces. North and South became completely estranged. The Industrial Revolution had contrary effects on the two regions. It turned the South into an economic associate of Great Britain. The South became the world's chief producer of raw cotton for the Lancashire mills. The Southerners, living by the export of a cash crop, and producing virtually no manufactures, wished to purchase manufactured goods as cheaply as possible. Hence they favored free trade, especially with Great Britain. In the North, the Industrial Revolution led to the building of factories. Northern factory owners, usually backed by their workmen, demanded protection from the inflow of British goods, with which no other country at the time could easily compete. The North therefore favored a high tariff which the South declared to be ruinous.

More fundamental was the difference in the status of labor. As the demand for raw cotton reached astronomical magnitudes the South fell more deeply under the hereditary curse of the Americas—the slave and plantation system.[32] In the nineteenth century slavery increasingly revolted the moral conscience of the white man's world. It was abolished in the British colonies in 1833, in the French colonies in 1848, in the Latin American republics at different dates in the first half of the century. Similarly, serfdom was abolished in the Hapsburg possessions in 1848, and in Russia in 1861. The American South could not, and after about 1830 no longer even wished to shake the system off. The South was the Cotton Kingdom whose "peculiar institution" was unfree labor of Negroes. Whites were hurt by the system as well as blacks. Few free men could prosper alongside a mass of subservient and virtually uncompensated labor. The incoming Europeans settled overwhelmingly in the North, the South remaining more purely "Anglo-Saxon"—except that in its most densely peopled areas some half of the people were of African descent.

In the movement westward, common to North and South, the pressure in the South came mainly from planters wishing to establish new plantations, in the North from persons hoping to set up small farms and from business men bent on building railroads and creating markets. As once France and Great Britain had fought for control beyond the Alleghenies so now North and South fought for control beyond the Mississippi. In 1846 the United States made war upon Mexico by methods at which Bismarck would

[32] See pp. 229–30.

not have blushed. The North widely denounced the war as a piece of Southern aggression, but was willing enough to take the ensuing conquests, which comprised the region from Texas to the Pacific. The first new state created in this region, California, prohibited slavery. Since 1820 the United States had held together precariously by the "Missouri Compromise," under which new states, as set up in the West, were admitted to the Union in pairs, one "slave" and one "free," so that a rough equality was maintained in the Senate and in the presidential electoral vote. With the creation of California this balance of power was upset in favor of the North, so that in return, by the "compromise of 1850," the North agreed to enforce the laws on runaway slaves to the satisfaction of the South. But the new strictness toward fugitive slaves ran against mounting sentiment in the North. Attempts to arrest Negroes in the free states and return them to slavery aroused abolitionist sentiment to a higher pitch. The abolitionists, a branch of the humanitarian movement then sweeping the European world, and somewhat resembling the radical democrats who came forward in Europe in 1848, demanded the immediate and total extermination of slavery, without concession, compromise, or compensation for the property interests of the slave owners. Abolitionists denounced the Union itself as the unholy accomplice in a social abomination.

By 1860 a sense of "sectionalism" had developed in the South not different in principle from the nationalism felt by many peoples in Europe. In their proud insistence on states' rights and constitutional liberties, their aristocratic and warlike codes of ethics, their demand for independence from outside influence and for freedom in ruling their own subject people, the Southern whites suggested nothing in Europe so much as the Magyars of the Austrian empire. They now wondered whether their way of life could be safely maintained within the union which they had helped to create. They sensed Northerners as outsiders, unsympathetic, foreign, hostile, and the South as potentially an independent and distinct nation. They were aware that within the Union they were increasingly a minority; for where in 1790 North and South had been approximately equal, by 1860 the North had outrun the South in population, in part because of the stream of migration from Europe. The incipient nationalism of the South was of the type of the small nation struggling against the great empire. In the North, nationalism was a sentiment in favor of maintaining the whole existing territory of the United States. Northerners by 1860, with a few exceptions, refused to admit that any state of the Union could withdraw, or secede, for any reason.

In 1860 the new Republican party elected Abraham Lincoln president. It advanced a program of free Western lands for small farmers, a higher tariff, transcontinental railroad building, and economic and capitalistic development on a national scale. The new party's radical wing, to which Lincoln himself did not belong, was vehemently abolitionist and anti-Southern in sentiment. Southern leaders, after the election of Lincoln, brought about the solemn withdrawal of their states from the United States of America, and the creation of a Confederate States of America reaching from Virginia to Texas. Lincoln ordered the armed forces to defend the territory of the United States, and the resulting Civil War, or war of Southern independence, lasting for four years, and involving battles as great as those of Napoleon, was the most harrowing struggle of the nineteenth century with the possible exception of the Tai-ping rebellion in China.[33]

European governments, while never recognizing the Confederacy, were partial to the South. The United States stood for principles still considered revolutionary in Europe, so that, while the European working classes generally favored the North, the upper classes were willing enough to see the North American republic end in collapse and failure. In addition, Great Britain and France saw in the break-up of the United States the same advantages that they had formerly seen in the break-up of the Spanish empire.[34] In the Confederate States the British, and the French to a lesser degree, expected to find another free trade country, supplying western Europe with raw materials and buying its manufactures, in short not a competitor, like the North, but a complementary partner to the industry of the Old World. It was likewise during the American Civil War that a French army sent by Napoleon III invaded Mexico to create a puppet empire under an Austrian archduke.[35] Thus the only serious attempt to ignore the Monroe Doctrine, violate the independence of Latin America, and revive European colonialism in the Americas occurred at the time when the United States was in dissolution.

But the North won the war and the Union was upheld. The Mexicans rid themselves of their unwanted emperor. The Tsar Alexander II sold Alaska to the United States. The war ended the idea of the Union as a confederation of member states from which members might withdraw at will. In its place triumphed the idea that the United States was a national state, composed not of member states but of a unitary people irrevocably bound together. This doctrine was written explicitly into the Fourteenth Amendment to the constitution, which pronounced all Americans to be citizens not only of their several states but of the United States, and forbade any state to "deprive any person of life, liberty or property without due process of law"—"due process" to be determined by authority of the national government. The new force of central authority was felt first of all in the South. President Lincoln, using his war powers, issued the Emancipation Proclamation in 1863, abolishing slavery in areas engaged in hostilities against the United States. The Thirteenth Amendment in 1865 abolished slavery everywhere in the country. No compensation was paid to the slave-owners, who were therefore ruined. The legal authority of the United States was thus used for an annihilation of individual property rights without parallel (outside of modern communism) in the history of the Western world; for neither the nobility in the French Revolution, nor the Russian serf-owners in 1861, nor the slave-owners of the West Indies in the nineteenth century, nor the owners of businesses nationalized by twentieth-century socialists in western Europe had to face such a total and overwhelming loss of property values as the slave-owners of the American South.

~~~~~~~~~~~~~~~~~~

[33] See p. 652.   [34] See pp. 171, 451.   [35] See p. 624.

AFTER THE CIVIL WAR:

RECONSTRUCTION; INDUSTRIAL GROWTH

The assassination of Lincoln in 1865 by a fanatical Southern patriot strengthened those radical Republicans who said that the South must be drastically reformed. With the old Southern upper class completely ruined, Northerners of many types poured into the defeated country. Some came to represent the federal government, some to dabble in local politics, some to make money, and a great many out of democratic and humanitarian impulses, to teach the debased ex-slaves the elements of reading and writing or of useful trades. Negroes in the South voted, sat in legislatures, occupied public office. This period, called Reconstruction, may be compared to the most advanced phase of the French Revolution, in that "radical republicans" undertook to press liberty and equality upon a recalcitrant country, under conditions of emergency rule, and under the auspices of a highly centralized national government with a mobilized army. The Southern whites strenuously objected, and the Northern radicals discredited themselves and gradually lost their zeal. Reconstruction was abandoned in the 1870's, and, by what Europeans would call a counter-revolution, the Southern whites gradually regained control.

The Northern business interests—financiers, bankers, company promoters, railway builders, manufacturers—expanded greatly with the wartime demand for munitions and military provisioning. They received protection by the Morrill tariff of 1861. In the next year, partly as a war measure, the Union Pacific Railroad was incorporated, and in 1869, at a remote spot in Utah, the last spike was driven in the first railroad to span the American continent. The Homestead Act, providing farms to settlers on easy conditions, and the granting of public lands to certain colleges (ever since called "land-grant colleges"), largely for the promotion of agricultural sciences, encouraged the push of population and civilization into the West. Vast tracts of land were given by the government to subsidize railway building. With the destruction of the Southern slaveholders, who before the war had counter-balanced the rising industrialists, it was now industry and finance that dominated national politics in the increasingly centralized United States. The Fourteenth Amendment, for many years, was mainly interpreted not to protect the civil rights of individual persons, but the property rights of business corporations against restrictive legislation by the states. The shift of political power from the states to the federal government accompanied and protected the shift of economic enterprise from local businesses to far-flung and continent-embracing corporations. As in France under Napoleon III, there was a good deal of corruption, fraud, speculation, and dishonestly or rapaciously acquired wealth; but industry boomed, the cities grew and the American mass market was created. On Fifth Avenue in New York, and in other Northern cities, rose the pretentious and gaudy mansions of the excessively rich.

In short, the American Civil War, which might have reduced English-speaking America to a scramble of jealously competing minor republics, resulted instead in the economic and political consolidation of a large nation-state, liberal and democratic in its political principles, and committed enthusiastically to private enterprise in its economic system.

68. The Dominion of Canada, 1867

North of the United States, at the time of the Civil War, lay a number of British provinces unconnected with one another, and each in varying degree dependent on Great Britain. The population had originated in three great streams. One part was French, settled in the Saint Lawrence valley since the seventeenth century. A second part was made up of descendants of United Empire Loyalists, old seaboard colonists who, remaining faithful to Britain, had fled from the United States during the American Revolution.[36] They were numerous in the Maritime Provinces and in Upper Canada, as Ontario was then called.[37] A third part consisted of recent immigrants from Great Britain, men and women of the working classes who had left the home country to improve themselves in America.

The French firmly resisted assimilation to the English-speaking world around them. Their statute of freedom was the Quebec Act of 1774, which had been denounced as "intolerable" by the aroused inhabitants of the Thirteen Colonies, but which put the French civil law, French language and French Catholic Church under the protection of the British Crown.[38] The French looked with apprehension upon the stream of immigrants, English-speaking and Protestant, which began to flow into Canada about 1780 and thereafter never stopped. There was constant irritation between the two nationalities.

The British government tried various expedients. In 1791 it created two provinces in the Saint Lawrence and Great Lakes region—a Lower Canada to remain French, and an Upper Canada to be English. They received the same form of government as that enjoyed by the Thirteen Colonies before their break from the empire. Each colony, that is, had a locally elected assembly with certain powers of taxation and law-making, subject to veto by the British authorities, as represented either by the governor or by the London government itself. For many years there was no objection to these arrangements. The War of 1812, in which the United States embarked on the conquest of Canada, aroused a national sentiment among both French and English in that country, together with a willingness to depend politically upon Great Britain for military security. But the internal political differences continued. In Lower Canada the French feared the English-speaking minority. In Upper Canada the old aristocracy of United Empire Loyalists, who had carved the province from the wilderness, hesitated to share control with the

---

[36] See p. 328.   [37] See map, p. 515.   [38] See pp. 325–6.

new immigrants from Great Britain. Between the provinces there were grievances also, since Lower Canada stood in the way of Upper Canada's outlet to the sea. In 1837 a superficial rebellion broke out in both provinces. It was put down virtually without bloodshed.

LORD DURHAM'S REPORT

In Great Britain at this time the reforming Whigs were busily renovating many ancient English institutions.[39] Some of them had definite views on the administration of colonies. In general, they held that it was not necessary to control a region politically in order to trade with it. This was an aspect of the free trade doctrine, separating economics from politics, business from power. The Whig reformers were rather indifferent to empire, unconcerned with military, naval, or strategic considerations. A few even thought it natural for colonies, when mature, to drop away entirely from the mother country. Whigs, liberals, and radicals all wished to economize on military expenditure, to relieve British taxpayers by cutting down British garrisons overseas.

After the Canadian insurrection of 1837 the Whig government sent out the Earl of Durham as governor. Durham, one of the framers of the parliamentary Reform Bill of 1832, published his views on Canadian affairs in 1839. Durham's Report has ever since been regarded as one of the classic documents in the rise of the British Commonwealth of Nations. He held that in the long run French separatist feeling in Canada should be extinguished, and all Canadians brought to feel a common citizenship and national character. He therefore called for the re-uniting of the two Canadas into one province. To consolidate this province he proposed an intensive development of railways and canals. In political matters he urged the granting of virtual self-government for Canada and the introduction of the British system of "responsible government," in which the elected assembly should control the executive ministers in the province, the governor becoming a kind of legal and ceremonial figure like the king in Great Britain.

Most of Durham's Report was accepted immediately, and a united Canada was given the machinery of self-government in 1840. The British army was withdrawn. The Canadians undertook to maintain their own military establishment, still regarded as necessary, since the era of the famous undefended frontier between Canada and the United States had not yet dawned. The Webster-Ashburton treaty of 1842 put an end to the long dispute over the Maine border. But as late as 1866 the Canadians had to repel armed invaders from the United States, when several hundred Irish Americans, members of the Fenians, an Irish republican secret society, staged a Garibaldi-like attempt to detach Canada from the British empire. Local Canadian forces proved sufficient to this threat.

The principle of responsible government was established in the late

[39] See pp. 461–2.

1840's, the governors of Canada allowing the elected assembly to adopt policies and appoint or remove ministers as it chose. Responsible government, still confined to internal matters, worked satisfactorily from the beginning. But one feature of the new plan, the union of the two Canadas, began to produce friction as the English-speaking immigration continued. The French were afraid of being outnumbered in their own country. Many Canadians therefore turned to the idea of a federation, in which the French and English areas might each conduct its own local affairs, while remaining joined for larger purposes in a superior government.

FOUNDING OF THE DOMINION OF CANADA

Federalism in Canada was thus partly a decentralizing idea, aimed at satisfying the French element by a re-division into two provinces, and in part a plan for a new centralization or unification, because it contemplated bringing all the provinces of British North America into union with the Saint Lawrence and Great Lakes region, to which alone the term Canada was then applied. While British North Americans discussed federation the Civil War was disrupting the United States. In the face of this unpleasant example, the British North Americans formed a strong union in which all powers were to rest in the central government except those specifically assigned to the provinces. The federal constitution, drafted in Canada by Canadians, was passed through the British Parliament in 1867 as the British North America Act. British advice prevailed in one significant matter; for where the Canadians had decided to call their union the Kingdom of Canada, the British government suggested instead the term Dominion, to spare the well-known sensibilities of the United States on the matter of "kingdoms" in the Americas. The British North America Act of 1867 constitutionally established the Dominion of Canada.

The new Dominion received a common parliament, in which the majority party controlled a responsible ministry according to British principles of cabinet government. The original provinces were Quebec and Ontario, formed from the old Canada, and Nova Scotia and New Brunswick, which joined on the understanding that a railroad be built to connect them with Quebec. The old Hudson's Bay Company, founded in 1668, transferred its rights of government over the vast Northwest to the Dominion in 1869. From these territories the province of Manitoba was created in 1870 and British Columbia in 1871. To link them solidly with the rest of the Dominion the Canadian Pacific Railway was completed in 1885. It made possible the development of the prairies, where the provinces of Saskatchewan and Alberta were added in 1905.

The Dominion of Canada, though not large in population, possessed from the beginning a significance beyond the mere number of its people. It was the first example of successful devolution, or granting of political liberty, within one of the European colonial empires. It embodied principles which

Edmund Burke and Benjamin Franklin had vainly recommended a century before to keep the Thirteen Colonies loyal to Great Britain. The Dominion after 1867 moved forward from independence in internal matters to independence in such external affairs as tariffs, diplomacy and the decisions of war and peace. It thus pioneered in the development of "Dominion status," working out precedents later applied in Australia (1901), New Zealand (1907), the Union of South Africa (1910), and in the 1920's, temporarily, in Ireland. By the middle of the twentieth century the same idea, or what may be called the Canadian idea, was even applied to the world-wide problem of colonialism as it affected non-European peoples, notably in India, Pakistan, Ceylon, and Indonesia.

More immediately, in America, the founding of the Dominion, a solid band of self-governing territory stretching from ocean to ocean, stabilized the relations between British North America and the United States, The United States regarded its northern borders as final. The withdrawal of British control from Canadian affairs furthered the United States conception of an American continent entirely free from European political influence. The founding of the Dominion and the purchase of Alaska, coming in the same year, rounded out the Monroe Doctrine to the north. The Dominion of Canada filled up politically, in a way more than satisfactory to the United States, the huge territorial vacuum lying between the inhabited regions of North America and the Arctic Sea.

69. Japan and the West

The Japanese, when they allowed the Westerners to discover them, were a highly civilized people living in a complex society. They had many large cities, they enjoyed the contemplation of natural scenery, they went to the theater, and they read novels. With their stylized manners, their fans and their wooden temples, their lacquer work and their painting on screens, their tiny rice fields and their curious and ineffectual firearms, they seemed to Europeans to be the very acme of everything quaint. This feeling is immortalized in *The Mikado* of Gilbert and Sullivan, first performed in 1885. Not long thereafter the idea of Japanese quaintness, like the idea of the Germans as an impractical people given mainly to music and metaphysics, had to be revised. The Europeans, in "opening" Japan, opened up more than they knew.

In 1853, the American Commodore Perry forced his way with a fleet of naval vessels into Yedo Bay, insisted upon landing, and demanded of the Japanese government, somewhat peremptorily, that it engage in commercial relations with the United States and other Western powers. In the next year the Japanese began to comply, and in 1867 an internal revolution took place,

of which the most conspicuous consequence was a rapid Westernizing of
Japanese life and institutions. But if it looked as if the country had been
"opened" by Westerners, actually Japan had exploded from within.

BACKGROUND: TWO CENTURIES OF ISOLATION, 1640–1854

For over two centuries Japan had followed a program of self-imposed
isolation. No Japanese was allowed to leave the islands, or even to build a
ship large enough to navigate the high seas. No foreigner, except for handfuls
of Dutch and Chinese, was allowed to enter. Japan remained a sealed book to
the west. The contrary is not quite so true, for the Japanese knew rather more
about Europe than Europeans did about Japan. The Japanese policy of seclusion was not merely based upon ignorance. Initially, at least, it was based
on experience.

The first Europeans—three Portuguese in a Chinese junk—are
thought to have arrived in Japan in 1542. For about a century thereafter there
was considerable coming and going. The Japanese showed a strong desire to
trade with the foreigners, from whom they obtained clocks and maps, learned
about printing and shipbuilding, and took over the use of tobacco and potatoes. Thousands also adopted the Christian religion as preached to them by
Spanish and Portuguese Jesuits. Japanese traveled to the Dutch Indies and
even to Europe. The Japanese in fact proved more receptive to European
ideas than other Asiatic peoples. But shortly after 1600 the government began
to drive Christianity underground; in 1624 it expelled the Spaniards, in 1639
the Portuguese, and in 1640 all Europeans except for a few Dutch merchants
who were allowed to remain at Nagasaki under strict control. From 1640 to
1854 these few Dutch at Nagasaki were the only channel of communication
with the West.[40]

The reasons for self-seclusion, as for its abandonment later, arose from
the course of political events in Japan. The history of Japan showed an odd
parallel to that of Europe. In Japan, as in Europe, a period of feudal warfare
was followed by a period of government absolutism, during which civil peace
was kept by a bureaucracy, an obsolescent warrior class was maintained as a
privileged element in society, and a commercial class of native merchants
grew wealthier, stronger and more insistent upon its position.

When the first Europeans arrived the islands were still torn by the
wars and rivalries of the numerous clans into which the Japanese were organized. Gradually one clan, the Tokugawa, gained control, taking over the office
of "shogun." The shogun was a kind of military head who governed in the
name of the emperor, and the hereditary Tokugawa shogunate, founded in
1603, lasted until 1867. The early Tokugawa shoguns concluded from a good
deal of evidence that the Europeans in Japan, both merchants and mission-

---

[40] See p. 138.

aries, were engaged in feudal or inter-clan politics, and even aspiring to dominate Japan by helping Christian or pro-European Japanese to get into power. The first three Tokugawa shoguns, to establish their own dynasty, to pacify and stabilize the country, and to keep Japan free from European penetration, undertook to exterminate Christianity and adopted the rigid policy of non-intercourse with the rest of the world.

Under the Tokugawa Japan enjoyed peace, a long peace, for the first time in centuries. The Tokugawa shoguns completed the detachment of the emperor from politics, building him up as a divine and legendary being, too august and too remote for the hurly-burly of the world. The emperor remained shut in at Kyoto on a modest allowance furnished by the shoguns. The shoguns established their own court and government at Yedo (later called Tokyo); and as Louis XIV brought nobles to Versailles, or Peter the Great forced his uncouth lords to build townhouses in St. Petersburg, so the shoguns required the great feudal chieftains and their men-at-arms to reside at least part of the year in Yedo.

The shoguns administered the country through a kind of military bureaucracy or dictatorship. This formidable instrument of state watched over the great lords (called daimyo), who, however, retained a good deal of feudal authority over their subjects in the regions most distant from Yedo. The great lords and their armed retainers (the samurai), having no further fighting to occupy them, turned into a landed aristocracy which spent a good deal of its time in Yedo and other cities. As a leisure class, they developed new tastes and standards of living, and hence needed more income, which they obtained by squeezing the peasants, and which they spent by buying from the merchants.

The merchant class greatly expanded by catering to the government and the gentry. Japan in the seventeenth century passed on to a money economy. Many lords fell seriously into debt to the merchants. Many samurai, like lesser nobles in France or Poland at the time, were almost ridiculously impoverished, hard pressed to keep up appearances, with nothing except social status to distinguish them from commoners. The law, as in Europe under the Old Regime, drew a sharp line between classes. Nobles, merchants, and peasants were subject to different taxes, and were differently punished for different offenses. What was a crime for a commoner would be excusable for a samurai; or what in a samurai would be a punishable breach of honor would be accepted in a common person. The samurai had the right to carry two swords as a mark of class and could in theory cut down an impudent commoner without arousing further inquiry. In practice the shoguns repressed violence of this kind, but there was much less development of law and justice than in the European monarchies of the Old Regime. Economically the merchants and artisans prospered. By 1723 Yedo was a city with 500,000 people, by 1800 with over 1,000,000; it was larger than London or Paris, and twenty times as large as the largest city in the United States. After 1800 some merchants were able to purchase the rank of samurai for money. The old class lines were beginning to blur.

Though deliberately secluded, the economic and social life of Japan was thus by no means static. The same is true of its intellectual life. Buddhism, the historic religion, lost its hold on many people during the Tokugawa period, so that Japan in its way underwent, like the West, a "secularization" of ideas. As a code of personal conduct there was a new emphasis on Bushido, the "way of the warrior," a kind of non-religious moral teaching which exalted the samurai virtues of honor and loyalty. With the decline of Buddhism went also a revival of the cult of Shinto, the "way of the gods," the ancient indigenous religion of Japan; which held, among much else, that the emperor was veritably the Son of Heaven. There was much activity in the study and writing of history, arousing, as in Europe, an acute interest in the national past. History, like Shinto, led to a feeling that the shoguns were usurpers and that the emperor, obscurely relegated to Kyoto, was the true representative of everything highest and most lasting in the life of Japan.

Meanwhile, through the crack left open at Nagasaki, Western ideas trickled in. The shogun Yoshimune in the mid-eighteenth century permitted the importation of Occidental books, except those relating to Christianity. A few Japanese learned Dutch, and began to decipher Dutch books on anatomy, surgery, astronomy, and other subjects. In 1745 a Dutch-Japanese dictionary was completed. For European manufactures also—watches, glassware, velvets, woolens, telescopes, barometers—there came to be an eager demand, satisfied as much as possible by the methodical Dutch. Nor were the Japanese wholly uninformed about politics in the West. While the most assiduous Westerner could learn nothing of the internal affairs of Japan, an educated Japanese could, if he wished, arrive at some idea of the French Revolution, or know who was president of the United States.

THE OPENING UP OF JAPAN

When Perry in 1853 made his unwanted visit he therefore had many potential allies within Japan. There were nobles, heavily in debt, unable to draw more income from agriculture, willing to embark upon foreign trade and to exploit their property by introducing new enterprises. There were penurious samurai, with no future in the old system, ready and willing to enter upon new careers as army officers or civil officials. There were merchants hoping to add to their business by dealing in Western goods. There were scholars eager to learn more of Western science and medicine. There were patriots fearful that Japan was becoming defenseless against Western guns. Spiritually the country was already adrift from its moorings, already set toward a course of national self-assertion, restlessly susceptible to hazily understood new ideas. Under such pressures, and from downright fear of a bombardment of Yedo by the Americans, which if it would not subdue Japan would at least ruin the declining prestige of the shogunate, the shogun Iesada in 1854 signed a commercial treaty with the United States. Similar treaties were soon signed with the Europeans.

In the following years were sown the seeds of much later misunderstanding between Japan and the West. The whites in those days—European and American—were somewhat trigger-happy in the discharge of naval ordnance against backward peoples. The Japanese, a proud and elaborately civilized nation, soon found that the whites considered them backward. They found, for example, as soon as they learned more of the West by reading and travel, that the treaties they signed in the 1850's were not treaties between equals as understood in the West. These first treaties provided that Japan should maintain a low tariff on imports, and not change it except with the consent of the foreign powers. To give outsiders a voice in determining tariff policy was not the custom among sovereign states of the West. The early treaties also provided for extraterritoriality. This meant that Europeans and Americans residing in Japan were not subject to Japanese law, but remained under the jurisdiction of their respective homelands as represented by consular officials. Such extraterritorial provisions had long been established in Turkey, and were currently taking root in China.[41] Europeans insisted upon them in countries where European principles on property, debt or security of life and person did not prevail. At the same time, of course, no civilized state ever permitted a foreign power to exercise jurisdiction within its borders. Extraterritoriality was a mark of inferiority, as the Japanese soon discovered.

A strong anti-foreign reaction developed after 1854. It was at first led by certain nobles of the western islands, the lords of Choshu and Satsuma, who had never been fully subordinated to the shogun at Yedo, and who now dreamed of overturning the Tokugawa shogunate and leading a national revival with the emperor as its rallying point. Their first idea was to check Western penetration (as two and a half centuries before) by driving the Westerners out. But in 1862 some Englishmen unintentionally violated a small point of Japanese etiquette. One of them was killed. The British government demanded punishment for the offending Japanese who were followers of the lord of Satsuma. The shogun proved unable to arrange this, and the British navy thereupon itself sailed up and bombarded the capital of Satsuma. In the same year the lord of Choshu, who commanded the straits of Shimonoseki with some ancient artillery, ordered it to fire on passing vessels. The British, French, Dutch, and United States governments immediately protested, and, when the embarrassed shogun proved unable to discipline Choshu, despatched an allied naval force to Shimonoseki. The forts and shipping of Choshu were destroyed, and an indemnity of three million dollars was imposed. These incidents were remembered in Japan long after they were forgotten in Europe and the United States. It was likewise remembered that the Western powers, discovering that the shogun was not the supreme ruler of the country, sent a naval expedition to Kyoto itself, and required the emperor to confirm the treaties signed by the shogun, and to reduce import duties, under threat of naval bombardment.

ᴧᴧᴧᴧᴧᴧᴧᴧᴧᴧᴧᴧᴧ

[41] See pp. 186, 653.

THE MEIJI ERA (1868–1912): THE WESTERNIZATION OF JAPAN

The lords of Choshu and Satsuma now concluded that the only way to deal with the West was to adopt the military and technical equipment of the West itself. They would save Japan for the Japanese by learning the secrets of Western power. First they forced the resignation of the shogun, whose prestige had long been undermined anyway, and who had now discredited himself first by signing undesirable treaties with the West and then failing to protect the country from outrage. The last shogun abdicated in 1867. The reformers declared the emperor restored to his full authority. It was their intention to use the plenitude of imperial power to consolidate and fortify Japan for its new position in the world. In 1868 a new emperor inherited the throne; his name was Mutsuhito, but according to Japanese custom a name was given to his reign also, which was called Meiji. The Meiji era (1868–1912) was the great era of the Westernization of Japan.

Japan turned into a modern national state. Feudalism was abolished, most of the great lords voluntarily surrendering into the emperor's hands their control over samurai and common people. "We abolish the clans and convert them into prefectures," declared one imperial decree. The legal system was reorganized, and equality before the law introduced, in the sense that all persons became subject to the same rules regardless of class. In part with the hope of getting rid of extraterritoriality, the reformers recast the criminal law along Western lines, deleting the bizarre and cruel punishments which Europeans considered barbaric. A new army was established, modeled mainly on the Prussian. The samurai in 1871 lost his historic right to carry two swords; he now served as an army officer, not as the retainer of a clannish chief. A navy, modeled on the British, followed somewhat later. Control of money and currency passed to the central government, and a national currency, with decimal units, was adopted. A national postal service began to function, and above all a national school system, which soon brought a high rate of literacy to Japan. Buddhism was discouraged, and the property of Buddhist monasteries was confiscated. Shinto was the cult favored by the government. Shinto gave a religious tincture to national sentiment, and led to a renewed veneration of the imperial family. In 1889 a constitution was promulgated. It confirmed the civil liberties then common in the West, and provided for a parliament in two chambers, but it stressed also the supreme and "eternal" authority of the emperor, to whom the ministers were legally responsible. In practice, in the new Japan, the emperor never actively governed. He remained aloof, as in the past; and political leaders, never fully responsible to the parliament, tended to govern freely in what they conceived to be the interests of the state.

Industrial and financial modernization went along with and even preceded the political revolution. In 1858 the first steamship was purchased from the Dutch. In 1859 Japan placed its first foreign loan, borrowing five million yen by a bond issue floated in England. In 1869 the first telegraph connected Yokohama and Tokyo. The first railroad, between the same two cities, was completed in 1872. In 1870 appeared the first spinning machinery. Foreign trade, almost literally zero in 1854, was valued at $200,000,000 a year by the end of the century. The population rose from 33,000,000 in 1872 to 46,000,-000 in 1902. The island empire, like Great Britain, became dependent on exports and imports to sustain its dense population at the level of living to which it aspired.

The Westernization of Japan still stands as the most remarkable transformation ever undergone by any people in so short a time. It recalls the Westernizing of Russia under Peter over a century before, though conducted somewhat less brutally, more rapidly, and with a wider consent among the population. For Japan, as formerly for Russia, the motive was in large measure defense against Western penetration, together with an admiration for Western statecraft and an ambition to become a "power." [42] What the Japanese wanted from the West was primarily science, technology, and organization. They were content enough with the innermost substance of their culture, their moral ideas, their family life, their arts and amusements, their religious conceptions, though even in these they showed an uncommon adaptability. Essentially it was to protect their internal substance, their Japanese culture, that they took over the external apparatus of Western civilization. This apparatus—science, technology, machinery, arms, political and legal organization—was the part of Western civilization for which other peoples generally felt a need, which they hoped to adopt without losing their own spiritual independence, and which therefore, though sometimes rather scornfully dismissed as materialistic, became the common ground for the interdependent world-wide civilization that emerged at the close of the nineteenth century.

In brief, to conclude a long chapter, the world between 1850 and 1870, revolutionized economically by the railroad and steamship, was revolutionized politically by the formation of large and consolidated nation-states. These states at the time all embodied certain liberal and constitutional principles, or at least the machinery of parliamentary and representative government. But the whole earth had also become an arena in which certain mighty beings, called nations or powers, were to act. The Great Powers in 1871 were Great Britain, Germany, France, Austria-Hungary, and Russia. Britain had produced a daughter nation in Canada. Whether Italy was to be a Great Power was not yet clear. No one knew what Japan would do. All agreed that the United States would one day play a large role in international politics, but the time was not yet.

ᴧᴧᴧᴧᴧᴧᴧᴧᴧᴧᴧᴧᴧᴧᴧᴧ

[42] See pp. 205–18.

European Civilization, 1871-1914

▼▼▼▼▼▼▼▼▼▼▼▼▼▼▼▼▼▼▼▼▼▼▼▼▼▼▼▼▼▼▼▼▼▼▼▼▼▼▼

HALF a century elapsed between the period of national consolidation described in the last chapter and the outbreak of the First World War in 1914. In this half-century Europe in many ways reached the climax of the modern phase of its civilization, and also exerted its maximum influence upon peoples outside of Europe. The present chapter will attempt a description of European civilization in these years, the next chapter an account of the world-wide ascendancy which Europe enjoyed at the time.

For Europe and the European world the years 1871 to 1914 were marked by hitherto unparalleled material and industrial growth, by international peace, by the advance of constitutional, representative, and democratic government, and by continued faith in science, reason, and progress. But in these very years, in politics, economics, and basic thinking there were forces operating to weaken and undermine the liberal premises and tenets of this European civilization. Most of the present chapter will be devoted to the continuing triumphs of liberalism, but the signs of its transformation and wane will be pointed out too.

70. The "Civilized World"

EUROPEAN CIVILIZATION: MATERIALISTIC AND
NON-MATERIALISTIC IDEALS

With the extension of the nation-state system Europe was politically more divided than ever. Its unity lay in the sharing by all Europeans of a similar way of life and outlook, which existed also in such "European" countries as the United States, Australia, and New Zealand. Europe and its offshoots constituted the "civilized world." Other regions—Africa, China, India, the up-country of Peru—were said to be "backward." (They are today more politely referred to as "underdeveloped.") Europeans were extremely conscious and inordinately proud of their civilization in the half century before 1914. They believed it to be the well-deserved outcome of centuries of progress. Feeling themselves to be the most advanced branch of mankind in the important areas of human endeavor, they assumed that all peoples should respect the same social ideals—that so far as they were unwilling or unable to adopt them they were backward, and that so far as they did adopt them they became civilized in their turn.

These ideals of civilization were in part materialistic. If Europeans considered their civilization to be better in 1900 than in 1800, or better in 1900 than the ways of non-Europeans at the same time, it was because they had a higher standard of living, ate and dressed more adequately, slept in softer beds, and had more satisfactory sanitary facilities. It was because they possessed ocean liners, railroads, and street cars, and after about 1880 telephones and electric lights. But the ideal of civilization was by no means exclusively materialistic. Knowledge as such, correct or truthful knowledge, was held to be a civilized attainment—scientific knowledge of nature, in place of superstition or demonology; geographical knowledge, by which civilized people were aware of the earth as a whole with its general contours and diverse inhabitants. The ideal was also profoundly moral, derived from Christianity, but now secularized and detached from religion. An Englishman, Isaac Taylor, in his *Ultimate Civilization* published in 1860, defined this moral ideal by listing the contrasting "relics of barbarism" which he thought were due to disappear—"Polygamy, Infanticide, Legalized Prostitution, Capricious Divorce, Sanguinary and Immoral Games, Infliction of Torture, Caste and Slavery." The first four of these had been unknown to the approved customs of Europe at least since the coming of Christianity. Torture went out of use about 1800, even in the illiberal European states; and legalized caste and slavery in the course of the nineteenth century. But there were few non-European peoples, in 1860, among whom two or three of Taylor's "relics" could not be found.

There are certain other indices, more purely quantitative, worked out by sociologists to show the level of advancement of a given society. One of these is the death rate, or number of persons per thousand of population who die each year. In England, France, and Sweden the "true" death rate (or death-rate regardless of the proportion of infants and old people, who are most susceptible to death) is known to have fallen from about 25 before 1850, to 19 in 1914 and 18 in the 1930's. Indeed, before the Second World War, it stood seemingly stabilized at about 18 in all countries of northwestern Europe, the United States, and the British Dominions. Death rates in countries not "modern" run over 40 even in favorable times. A closely related index is infant mortality, which fell rapidly after 1870 in all countries affected by medical science. Thus a woman under civilized conditions had to go through pregnancy and childbirth less often to produce the same number of surviving children. Another index is life-expectancy, or the number of years of age which a person has an even chance of attaining. In England the expectation of life at birth rose from 40 years in the 1840's to 59 in 1933. In India in 1931 it was less than 27 years. Still another index is the literacy rate, or proportion of persons above a certain age (such as ten) able to read and write. In northwestern Europe by 1900 the literacy rate approached 100. In some countries it still does not rise very far above zero. A further basic index is the productivity of labor, or amount produced by one worker in a given expenditure of time. This is difficult to compute, especially for earlier periods for which statistical data are lacking. In the 1930's, however, the productivity of a farmer in Denmark was over ten times that of a farmer in Albania. All northwestern Europe was above the European average in this respect with the exception of Ireland, whereas Ireland, Spain, Portugal, Italy, and all eastern Europe were below it.

The essence of civilized living doubtless is in the intangibles, in the way in which men use their minds, and in the attitudes they form toward others or toward the conduct and planning of their own lives. The intangibles, however, are not always agreed upon by persons of different culture or ideology. On the quantitative criteria there is less disagreement; all men, with few exceptions, wish to lower the death-rate, raise the literacy rate, and increase the productivity of human exertion. Even if we apply quantitative or sociological indices alone, we can say that after 1870 there was in fact, and not merely in the opinion of Europeans, a civilized world of which Europe was the center.

THE "ZONES" OF CIVILIZATION

Or rather, a certain region of Europe was the center. For there were really two Europes, an inner zone and an outer. A Frenchmen writing in the 1920's, describing the two Europes that had risen since 1870, called the inner zone the "Europe of steam," and bounded it by an imaginary line joining Glasgow, Stockholm, Danzig, Trieste, Florence, and Barcelona. It included not only Great Britain but Belgium, Germany, France, northern Italy, and the western portions of the Austrian empire. Virtually all heavy European industry was located in this zone. Here the railway network was thickest. Here was concentrated the wealth of Europe, in the form both of a high living standard and of accumulations of capital. Here likewise were almost all the laboratories and all the scientific activity of Europe. Here, in the same zone, lay the strength of constitutional and parliamentary government, and of liberal, humanitarian, socialistic, and reformist movements of many kinds. In this zone the death rate was low, life expectancy high, conditions of health and sanitation at their best, literacy almost universal, productivity of labor very great. To the same zone, for practical purposes, belonged certain regions of European settlement overseas, especially the northeastern part of the United States.

The "outer zone" included most of Ireland, most of the Iberian and Italian peninsulas, and all Europe east of what was then Germany, Bohemia, and Austria proper. The outer zone was agricultural, though the productivity of agriculture, per farm worker or per acre, was far less than in the inner zone. The people were poorer, more illiterate and more likely to die young. The wealthy were landlords, often absentees. The zone lived increasingly after 1870 by selling grain, livestock, wool, or lumber to the more industrialized inner zone, but was too poor to purchase many manufactured products in return. To obtain capital it borrowed in London or Paris. Its social and political philosophies were characteristically imported from Germany and the west. It borrowed engineers and technicians from the first zone to build its bridges and instal its telegraph systems, and sent its youth to universities in the first zone to study medicine or other professions. Many areas of European settlement overseas, for example in Latin America and the southern part of the United States, may also be thought of as belonging to this outer zone.

A Summer Sunday on Grande Jatte Island

by Georges Seurat (French, 1859–91)

This picture of sunny calm, painted in 1886, suggests something of the well-being brought to a great many people by the European civilization of the late nineteenth century. Whether boating, or idly fishing, or quietly sitting and watching, or strolling alone or in pairs or in families with their children, the figures seem to live in a peaceable world which a later age of war, speed and mechanical amusements has made to seem far away. Technically this is one of the most remarkable pictures ever painted. The artist, an impressionist, created it without the use of lines by filling the canvas with thousands of minute dots of the primary colors, which so blur and mix in the eye as to produce the forms and hues of nature. As a result it seems to be a picture of light itself, with an actual shimmer on the water, an astonishing "grassiness" in the grass, with shadows that seem to be real shadows, and distant figures looking really distant as if seen through the intervening air. Courtesy of the Art Institute of Chicago.

Beyond the European world lay a third zone, the immense reaches of Asia and Africa, all "backward" by the standards of Europe, with the exception of the recently Europeanized Japan, and all destined, with the exception of Japan, to become heavily dependent upon Europe after 1870. Much of the world's history since 1870 could be written as the story of relations among these three zones; but it is necessary in all human things to guard against formulas that are too simple.

71. Basic Demography: The Increase of the Europeans

EUROPEAN AND WORLD POPULATION GROWTH, 1650–1950

All continents except Africa grew enormously in population in the three centuries following 1650, but it was Europe that grew the most. It is highly probable that the proportion of Europeans in the world's total reached its maximum for all time between 1850 and the Second World War. Estimates are given in the table below, beginning with 1650. (Experts believe that before 1650 the greater population masses had long been either stationary or increasing very slowly.)

The causes of sudden rise in world population after 1650 are not known. Some of them must obviously have operated in Asia as well as Europe. All students agree in attributing the increase to falling death rates rather than to increasing birth rates. Populations grew because more people lived longer, not because more were born. It is probable that a better preservation of civil order reduced death rates in both Asia and Europe. In Europe the organized sovereign states, as established in the seventeenth century, put an end to a long period of civil wars, stopping the chronic violence and marauding, with the accompanying insecurity of agriculture and of family life, which were more deadly than wars fought by armies between govern-

---

The Belt-Conveyor

BY DIEGO RIVERA (MEXICAN, 1886–   )

In 1931 the Detroit Institute of Arts, wishing to have a large court decorated by mural paintings, commissioned the Mexican Diego Rivera to do the work. Rivera was already known as the greatest living muralist, and for his Marxist social opinions. His Detroit murals raised great indignation; he was accused of spreading a Communist Manifesto on the walls. But, while Rivera's conception of the capitalist United States can hardly be called flattering, it is the machine age as such that these murals most vividly portray. The fragment reproduced here shows part of the assembly line in an automobile plant, with workers of various races working speedily and as a team, while white-collar visitors in the background somewhat stupidly watch and marvel. No one has succeeded better than Rivera in the painting of machinery, which he renders with a mixture of faithful realism and artistic heightening, conveying the sense of automatism, movement, and power. Courtesy of the Detroit Institute of Arts.

Estimated Population of the World *

	1650	1750	1850	1900	1950
	millions				
Europe	100	140	266	401	540
United States & Canada	1	1	26	81	160
Total "Europeans"	101	141	292	482	700
Latin America	12	11	33	63	145
Oceania-Australasia	2	2	2	6	12
Africa	100	95	95	120	175
Asia	330	479	749	937	1,200
Grand Total	545	728	1,171	1,608	2,232
	percentages				
Europe	18.3	19.2	22.7	24.9	24.3
United States & Canada	.2	.1	2.3	5.1	7.2
Total "Europeans"	18.5	19.3	25.0	30.0	31.5
Latin America	2.2	1.5	2.8	3.9	6.5
Oceania-Australasia	.4	.3	.2	.4	.5
Africa	18.3	13.1	8.1	7.4	7.8
Asia	60.6	65.8	63.9	58.3	53.7
Grand Total	100.0	100.0	100.0	100.0	100.0

* Figures for 1650–1900 are from A. N. Carr-Saunders, *World Population*, p. 42, Oxford, 1936. For dates after 1850 the population of Australasia, and a large proportion of that of Latin America, are to be considered as European, so that in 1950, for example, instead of the 700,000,000 given in the table for "Europeans," we should reckon on some such figure as 750,000,000.

ments. Similarly, the Tokugawa kept peace in Japan, and the Manchu dynasty brought a long period of order to China. The British rule in India, and that of the Dutch in Java, by curbing famine and violence, allowed the populations to mount very rapidly. Only in Africa, where the slave trade is thought to have removed twenty million persons of the child-bearing ages in two or three centuries, and where slave raiding led to inter-tribal warfare and the disruption of Negro cultures, did the growth of population fail to keep pace with the world's average. The fate of the American aborigines was somewhat the same, but they were never very numerous.

In Europe, sooner than in Asia, other causes of growth were at work beyond the maintenance of civil peace. They included the liberation from certain endemic diseases, beginning with the subsiding of bubonic plague in the seventeenth century and the conquest of smallpox in the eighteenth; the improvement of agricultural output, beginning notably in England about 1750; the improvement of transportation, which, by road, canal, and railroad, made localized famine a thing of the past since food could be moved into areas of temporary shortage; and, lastly, the development of machine industry, which allowed large populations to subsist in Europe by trading with peoples overseas.

Consequently, while it seems that the death rate fell in Asia as well as in Europe after 1650, it fell much more substantially in Europe, and since the European birth rate long remained at a high level, the result was a tremendous swelling of population. Asia increased over threefold in population between 1650 and 1950, but Europe increased over fivefold, and the total number of Europeans, including the descendants of those who migrated to other continents, increased more than sevenfold. In 1650 there were more than four non-Europeans for every European. In 1950 there were only two non-Europeans for each person of European descent. The ascendancy in modern times of European civilization, or roughly of the white races, has been due in some measure to a merely quantitative advantage.

STABILIZATION OF EUROPEAN POPULATION

This advantage of numbers began to be lost in the middle of the twentieth century. As early as 1910 it was possible to anticipate that the population of Europe, especially of western Europe, or, more accurately, of the most advanced "inner zone," would soon cease to expand, because the children being born about 1910, who would become the parents of 1940, were not sufficiently numerous to maintain growth at the birth rates which then existed. It now seems likely that eastern Europe will become more populous in proportion to western Europe, that by the year 2000 the Soviet Union will outnumber the combined countries of the old "inner zone," and that the colored peoples will pull ahead of whites in their rate of growth.

Stabilization and decline of European population followed from a fall in the birth rate. We have seen how the persistence of high birth rates, while death rates fall, accounts for a long period of rapid expansion. But European birth rates began to fall about 1880. As early as 1830 they began noticeably to drop in France, with the result that France, long the most populous European state, was surpassed in population by Russia in the eighteenth century, by Germany about 1870, by the British Isles about 1895 and by Italy about 1930. France, once thought to be decadent for this reason, was in fact only the leading country in a population cycle through which all modernized countries seem to pass. The birth rate, which had fallen below 30 per thousand in France in the 1830's, fell to that level in Sweden in the 1880's, in England in the 1890's, and in Germany, Bohemia, and the Netherlands between 1900 and 1910. After the First World War, it fell below 30 in Italy, Spain, and eastern Europe, leaving in 1939 only the Soviet Union with a birth rate above 30 per thousand.

The reduced birth rate is not a mere dry statistical item, nor does it affect populations merely in the mass. It is one of the indices of modern civilization, first appearing in that inner European zone in which the other indices were also highest, and thence spreading outward in a kind of wave. Concretely, a low birth rate means that families average about two children, where in former times, or today under conditions not "modern," families are commonly found to consist of ten children or even more. The low birth rate means the small family system, than which few things are more fundamental to modern life. The principal means used to hold down the birth rate, or to limit the family, is the practice of contraception. But the true causes, or reasons why parents wish to limit their families, are deeply embedded in the codes of modern society.

The French peasants after the Revolution, many of them owners of land, and obliged by the Napoleonic Code to divide inheritances among their children, soon began to limit themselves to two or three children, in order that each child (by inheritance, marriage, and dowries) might remain in as high an economic and social status as its parents. It was thus economic security and the possession of a social standard that led to the reduced birth rate in France. In the great cities of the nineteenth century, in which standards of life for the working classes often collapsed, the effect was at first an unthinking proliferation of offspring. But life in the city, under crowded conditions of housing, also set a premium on the small family. There were many amusements in the city which people with many children could with difficulty enjoy. After about 1880 child labor became much less frequent among the working classes. When children ceased to earn part of the family income parents tended to have fewer of them. About the same time governments in the advanced countries began to require universal compulsory schooling. The number of years spent in education, and hence in economic dependency upon parents, grew longer and longer, until it became common even for young adults to be still engaged in study. Each child represented many years of expense for its parents. The ever rising idea of what it was necessary to do for one's children, and the desire of parents to give them every possible ad-vantage in a competitive world, were probably the most basic causes of voluntary limitation of the family. Hardly less basic was the desire to lighten the burdens upon mothers. The small family system, together with the decline of infant mortality, since they combined to free women from the interminable bearing and tending of infants, probably did more than anything else to improve the position of civilized women.

Most causes for the falling birth rate may be summarized under the idea of welfare. It is in those countries, in those periods, and in those classes of society in which well-being and living standards have been relatively high that the birth rate fell and still falls. The small family is also the sign of a society that looks mainly to the well-being of individuals. It is for the sake of individual parents, especially mothers, and of individual children and their preparation and opportunity in life, that the number of children is held to two or three. Before 1914 liberalism and individualism were in the ascendant, and no government attempted to check the fall in the birth rate by legislation. But the small family system produced a fateful paradox. Even an average of three children for each married pair is barely enough to maintain a population without decline. Those societies in which individual welfare is most highly prized, by the very means they take to promote it, become smaller than the societies which value mass and collective strength. It must be added that what people consider to be welfare easily passes into self-indulgence, and that some of the most civilized persons have few children, or none at all, for the most grossly selfish reasons. It is possibly because of this moral issue (and because a group which limits the family beyond a certain point declines in number) that the Roman Catholic Church prohibits most forms of birth control to its members.

But the effects of the small family system upon total population became manifest only slowly. More people lived on into the middle and older age groups, and the fall of the birth rate was gradual, so that in all the leading countries except France (which reached its peak about 1910) total numbers continued to rise until 1940 or 1950. The persistent note was one of superabundant increase. In five generations, between 1800 and 1930, some 200,000,000 Europeans grew into 700,000,000.

GROWTH OF CITIES AND URBAN LIFE

Where did so many people go? Some stayed in the rural areas where most people had always lived. Rural populations in the "inner zone" became more dense, turning to the more intensive agriculture of truck gardening or dairy farming, leaving products like wool and cereal grains to be raised elsewhere and then imported. But it is estimated that of every seven persons added to the western European population only one stayed on the land. Of the other six, one left Europe altogether, and five went to the growing cities.

The modern city is mostly the child of the railroad, for with the railroads it became possible for the first time to concentrate manufacturing in large towns, to which bulky goods such as foods and coal could now be moved in great volume. The growth of cities between 1850 and 1914 was phenomenal. In England two-thirds of the people lived in places of 20,000 or less in 1830; in 1914 two-thirds lived in places of 20,000 or more; and since 1914 the change in this respect has been slight.[1] Germany, the historic land of archaic towns carried over from the Middle Ages, after 1870 rivaled England in modern industrial urbanization. Where in 1840 only London and Paris had a million people, the same could be said by 1914 of Berlin, Vienna, St. Petersburg, and Moscow.[2] Some places, like the English Midlands and the Ruhr valley in Germany, became a mass of contiguous smaller cities, vast urban agglomerations divided only by municipal lines.

The great city set the tone of modern society. City life was impersonal and anonymous; people were uprooted, less tied to home or church than in the country. They lacked the country person's feeling of deference for aristocratic families. They lacked the sense of self-help characteristic of older rural

---

[1] See map, p. 427.

[2] And, outside Europe, of New York, Chicago, Philadelphia, Rio de Janeiro, Buenos Aires, Calcutta, Tokyo, and Osaka. Forty years later the list of the world's largest cities was almost the same, with the addition of Shanghai.

communities. The hungry, the jobless, the miserable could expect little comfort from neighbors. To correct minor nuisances or to rescue people in emergencies one relied on the police—an epileptic, for example, could lie in a busy street without attracting much notice. It was in the city that the daily newspaper press, which spread rapidly in the wake of the telegraph after 1850, found its most habitual readers. The so-called "yellow" or sensational press appeared about 1900. Articulate public opinion was formed in the cities, and city people were on the whole disrespectful of tradition, receptive to new ideas, having in many cases deliberately altered their own lives by moving from the country or from smaller towns. That socialism spread among the industrial masses of European cities is hardly surprising. It is less often realized that some of the more blatant nationalism that arose after 1870 was stimulated by city life, for people felt increasingly detached from all institutions except the state. At the same time city life, by its greater facilities for schooling, reading, and discussion, made for a more alert and informed public opinion of an enlightened kind.

MIGRATION FROM EUROPE, 1840–1940

During the same period in which the cities were rising, approximately 60,000,000 people left Europe altogether, of whom possibly a fifth sooner or later returned. This Atlantic Migration—aptly so called, because all crossed the ocean except those who moved from European to Asiatic Russia—towers

MIGRATION FROM EUROPE [a]
1846–1932

FROM:		
	Great Britain and Ireland	18,000,000
	Italy	10,100,000
	Russia [b]	9,200,000
	Austria-Hungary	5,200,000
	Germany	4,900,000
	Spain	4,700,000
	Portugal	1,800,000
	Sweden	1,200,000
	Norway	850,000
	Poland [c]	640,000
	France	520,000
	Denmark	390,000
	Finland	370,000
	Switzerland	330,000
	Holland	220,000
	Belgium	190,000
	Total	58,610,000

[a] Carr-Saunders, *op. cit.*, pp. 49 and 56.
[b] Including 7,000,000 from European to Asiatic Russia up to 1914 only. It is thought that 3,000,000 went from European to Asiatic parts of the U.S.S.R. between 1926 and 1939. Subsequent movement is unknown.
[c] 1920–32 only.

above all other historical migrations in magnitude, and possibly also in significance, for it was the means by which earlier colonial offshoots of Europeans were transformed into new Europes alongside the old. All parts of

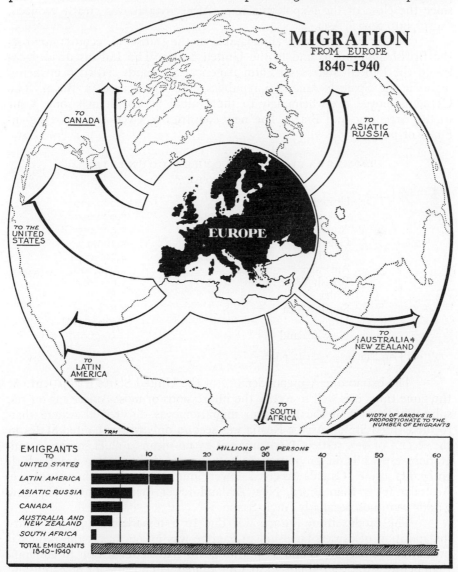

Over 60,000,000 people left Europe in the century preceding the Second World War, distributing themselves as shown in the diagram above. (See figures on p. 566.) About half went to the United States. This huge wave of settlement built up, outside of Europe, populous "European" countries which produced foods and raw materials for Europe and borrowed capital and bought manufactures from Europe, thus helping to support the increasingly dense European population and to build up a world-wide economic system.

Europe contributed, as is shown in the table on p. 564, which comprises the years from 1846 to 1932. Before 1846 the movement had scarcely begun, though over a million immigrants had entered the United States at that time since the close of the Napoleonic wars. After 1932 it was greatly reduced, except into Soviet Asia.

The British and Irish (inseparable in the statistical records) went to the British Dominions and to the United States. The Italians divided between the United States and Latin America. Spaniards settled overwhelmingly in the Spanish American republics, and Portuguese in Brazil. The Germans moved overwhelmingly to the United States, though some went to the Argentine and Brazil. The new countries received the following influxes of people:

IMMIGRATION INTO OTHER COUNTRIES
FROM EUROPE *

TO:	United States	34,000,000
	Asiatic Russia (to 1914 only)	7,000,000
	Argentina	6,400,000
	Canada	5,200,000
	Brazil	4,400,000
	Australia	2,900,000
	British West Indies	1,600,000
	Cuba	860,000
	South Africa	852,000
	Uruguay	713,000
	New Zealand	594,000

* Carr-Saunders, *op. cit.*, p. 49.

The extraordinary preponderance of the United States is apparent. At the same time, it is well to rectify the impressions of most Americans on the subject. Almost half the European migration was directed elsewhere than to the United States. Asiatic Russia was second only to the United States in the receipt of new settlers. Germany was by no means a chief source of emigration, especially in proportion to total national population from which emigrants came. Canada received fewer immigrants than the Argentine, Australia fewer than Brazil, New Zealand fewer than Uruguay. The new worlds were not peculiarly Anglo-Saxon.

The exodus from Europe was due to a remarkable and temporary juxtaposition of causes. Hardship in Europe was by no means the principal one; after the Second World War Europeans had better reason to emigrate than before 1914, yet did not do so. One fundamental cause, or precondition, was that before 1914 the new countries welcomed immigration. Hands were wanted to farm the land, build houses, dig in the mines. This was least true of Australia and New Zealand, which preferred to limit themselves to English-speaking settlers, and which also pioneered as social democracies, becoming models, even before 1900, of legislation to protect the working classes. One result was that no inrush of outsiders to compete for jobs at low wages was

desired. A similar combination of national preferences and labor protectionism led to laws restricting immigration in the United States in 1921 and
1924. Thereafter immigrants could enter only under quotas, and the quotas
were lowest for Eastern and Southern Europe from which most emigration
was then forthcoming.

In Europe there were many conditions propelling emigrants outward.
Physically, the steamship made it easier and cheaper to cross the sea, and
the railroad helped people to get to the ports, as well as to distribute themselves after landing in the new countries. Economically, people in the mass
could for the first time afford a long journey. People migrated to improve
their material circumstances; but the great crests in the wave of emigration
coincided with crests in the business cycle in Europe, when jobs in Europe
were plentiful and wages at their highest. Of the opposite case, of actual
flight from economic ruin or starvation, the emigration from Ireland after
1846 is the best example. After the revolutions of 1848 a certain number left
Europe for political reasons, and, later on, to avoid compulsory military service. The best example of flight from actual persecution is that of the Jews
of Russia and Russian Poland, of whom a million and a half moved to the
United States in the fifteen years preceding the First World War.

But perhaps most basic in the whole European exodus was the underlying liberalism of the age. Never before (nor since) had people been legally
so free to move. Old laws requiring skilled workmen to stay in their own
countries were repealed, as in England in 1824.[3] The old semi-communal
agricultural villages, with collective rights and obligations, holding the individual to his native group, fell into disuse except in Russia. The disappearance
of serfdom allowed the peasant of Eastern Europe to change his residence
without obtaining a lord's permission.[4] Governments permitted their subjects to emigrate, to take with them their savings of shillings, marks, kronen,
or lire, and to change nationality by becoming naturalized in their new
homes. The rise of individual liberty in Europe, as well as the hope of enjoying it in America, made possible the great emigration. For so huge a mass
movement the most remarkable fact is that it took place by individual initiative and at individual expense. Individuals and family groups (to borrow the
metaphor of one authority) detached themselves atom by atom from the
mass of Europe, crossed the seas on their own, and reattached themselves
atom by atom to the accumulating mass of the New World.

72. The World Economy of the Nineteenth Century

How did the swelling population of Europeans manage to feed itself?
How, in fact, did it not merely feed itself but enjoy an incomparably higher

---

[3] See p. 458.
[4] See pp. 481, 492–3.

standard of living in 1900 than in 1800? By science, industry, transportation. And by organization—in business, in finance, and in labor.

INDUSTRIAL ADVANCES

The same inventiveness in science and technology that led to the use of steam power, the growth of the textile, iron and coal industries, and revolutionary improvements in transportation in the early part of the nineteenth century[5] led from the 1870's on to the tapping of new sources of power, the expansion of industries already mechanized, and the emergence of entire new industries, all of which set the pattern for the continuing technological growth of the twentieth century. The steam engine itself was refined and improved and by 1914 still predominated over all other power machinery, but the internal combustion (or gasoline) engine, the Diesel engine and, above all, electricity with its tremendous advantages over all other sources of power had made their appearance. Vastly improved and more economical processes for refining iron ore magnified the demand for coal and iron, and made possible a great expansion in the production of steel, the key product of the new industrial age; aluminum and other metal alloys soon rivaled steel. New chemical and synthetic fabric industries, industrial research laboratories, the manufacture and use of precision instruments, the development of mass-production and assembly-line techniques, the growth in heavy industry, that is, of machines to make machines, and the availability of all kinds and quantities of consumer goods all entered into the expanding economy of the late nineteenth century. Railroad mileage multiplied rapidly, and new inventions facilitated communications not only from house to house but from continent to continent. The automobile and automotive industries became important, and later the airplane and aeronautical industries; these in turn meant that oil became one of the most coveted of natural resources. In this new phase of the industrial revolution machine industry spread geographically, from Britain, Belgium and France outward to Italy, Russia, Japan, and, most notably, to Germany and the United States. To use steel alone as a criterion, in 1871 Germany was producing annually three-fifths as much steel as Britain; by 1890 she was ahead; by 1914 she was producing twice as much as Britain but at the same time only half as much as the new industrial giant, the United States. American steel output was now greater than that of Germany, Britain, and France combined. Britain, the pioneer in mechanization, was being outstripped in both the old world and the new.

FREE TRADE AND THE EUROPEAN "BALANCE OF PAYMENTS"

It was Britain in the mid-nineteenth century, then the workshop of the world, that had inaugurated the movement toward free trade. It will be

[5] See pp. 424–6.

recalled that in 1846, by the repeal of the Corn Laws, the British embarked upon a systematic free trade policy, deliberately choosing to become dependent upon overseas imports for their food.[6] France adopted free trade in 1860.[7] Other countries soon followed. It is true that by 1880 there was a movement back to protective tariffs, except in Britain, Holland, and Belgium. But the tariffs were impediments rather than barriers, and until 1914 the characteristic of the economic system was the extreme mobility of goods across political frontiers. Politically, Europe was more than ever nationalistic; but economic activity, under generally liberal conditions in which business was supposed to be free from the political state, remained predominantly international and globe-encircling. Only the First World War of 1914, the world depression of 1929, and the Second World War of 1939 led to a positive blocking of international exchange.

Broadly speaking, the great economic accomplishment of Europe before 1914 was to create a system by which the huge imports used by industrial Europe could be acquired and paid for. All European countries except Russia, Austria-Hungary, and the Balkan states imported more than they exported. It was the British again that had led in this direction. Britain had been a predominantly importing country since the close of the eighteenth century. That is to say, despite the expanding export of cotton manufactures and other products of the Industrial Revolution, Britain consumed more goods from abroad than it sent out. Industrialization and urbanization in the nineteenth century confirmed the same situation. Between 1800 and 1900 the value of British exports multiplied eightfold, but the value of imports into Great Britain multiplied tenfold, and in the decade before 1914 the British had an import surplus of about three-quarters of a billion dollars a year. Great Britain and the industrial countries of Europe together (roughly Europe's "inner zone"), at the beginning of the twentieth century, were drawing in an import surplus, measured in dollars, of almost two billion dollars every year (the dollar then representing far more goods than it came to do later). The imports into Europe's inner zone consisted in raw materials for its industries and in food and amenities for its people.

How were the imports paid for? How did Europe enjoy a favorable "balance of payments" despite an unfavorable balance of trade in commodities? Export of European manufactures paid for some imports, and even most, but not all. It was the so-called "invisible exports" that made up the difference, that is, shipping and insurance services rendered to foreigners, and interest on money lent out or invested, all bringing in foreign exchange. Shipping and insurance were important. An Argentine merchant in Buenos Aires, to ship hides to Germany, might employ a British vessel; he would pay the freight charges in Argentine pesos, which might be credited to the account of the British shipowner in an Argentine bank; the British shipowner would sell the pesos to someone, in England or elsewhere in Europe,

------

[6] See p. 463.
[7] See p. 506.

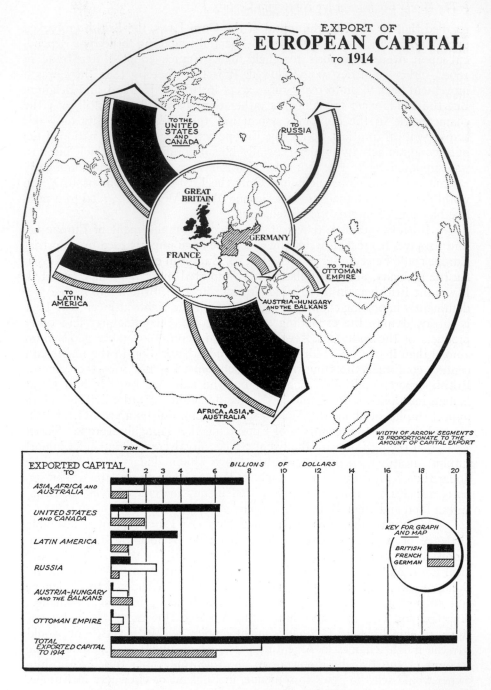

EXPORT OF
EUROPEAN CAPITAL
TO 1914

WIDTH OF ARROW SEGMENTS
IS PROPORTIONATE TO THE
AMOUNT OF CAPITAL EXPORT

EXPORTED CAPITAL
TO

BILLIONS OF DOLLARS

ASIA, AFRICA AND
AUSTRALIA

UNITED STATES
AND CANADA

LATIN AMERICA

RUSSIA

AUSTRIA-HUNGARY
AND THE BALKANS

OTTOMAN EMPIRE

TOTAL
EXPORTED CAPITAL
TO 1914

KEY FOR GRAPH
AND MAP

BRITISH
FRENCH
GERMAN

In 1914 the British, French and Germans held upwards of $30,000,000,-
000 in foreign and colonial loans and investments, distributed as shown on the

who needed them to buy Argentine meat. The far-flung British merchant marine thus earned a considerable amount of the food and raw materials needed by Britain. To insure themselves against risks of every conceivable kind people all over the world turned to Lloyds of London. With the profits drawn from selling insurance the British could buy what they wished. Governments or business enterprises borrowed money in Europe, and mainly in England; the interest payments, putting foreign currencies into European and British hands, constituted another invisible export by which an excess of imports could be financed. But the lending of money to foreigners is only part of a larger phenomenon, the export of capital.

THE EXPORT OF EUROPEAN CAPITAL

The migration of millions of Europeans had the effect of creating new societies, basically European in character, which both purchased manufactures from Europe and produced the food, wool, cotton, and minerals that Europe needed. It could not have had this effect if Europe had exported people only, especially people of such small means as most emigrants were. Europe also exported the capital necessary to get the new settlers and the new worlds into production.

The export of capital meant that an older and wealthier country, instead of using its whole annual income to raise its own standard of living, or to add to its own capital by expanding or improving its houses, factories, machinery, mines, transportation, *etc.*, diverted some of its income to expanding or improving the houses, factories, machinery, mines and transportation of foreign countries. It meant that British, French, Dutch, Belgian, Swiss, and eventually German investors in the desire to increase their income bought the stocks of foreign business enterprises and the bonds of foreign businesses and government; or they organized companies of their own to operate in foreign climes; or their banks granted loans to banks in New York or Tokyo, which then lent the funds to local users. Capital arose in Europe to some extent from the savings of quite small people, especially in France, where peasants and modest bourgeois families were notably thrifty. But most capital accumulated from savings by the well-to-do. The owners of a business concern, for example, instead of spending the concern's income by paying higher wages, took a portion of it in profits or dividends, and instead of

---

map. Dutch investments, especially in the Netherlands Indies, together with Swiss, Belgian and Scandinavian holdings, would add several billion dollars more. Proceeds from such investments helped Europeans to pay for the excess of their imports over exports. New and undeveloped countries were built up by capital borrowed from Europe. British capital predominated in the overseas world, while the less advanced regions of Eastern Europe and the Near East were financed mainly from Germany and France. Most of the investment shown on this map was lost or expended in the First World War. See pp. 691, 698.

spending all this on their own living, reinvested part of it in domestic or foreign enterprises. The gap between rich and poor was thus one cause of the rapid accumulation of capital, though the accumulation of capital, in the nineteenth century, produced in turn a steady rise of living standards for the working classes. In a sense, however, the common man of western Europe, by foregoing the better housing, diet, education, or pleasures which a more democratic society might have planned for him, made possible the export of capital and hence the financing and building up of other regions of the world.

The British were the chief exporters of capital, followed at some distance by the French, and at the close of the century by the Germans. As early as the 1840's half the annual increase of wealth in Great Britain was going into foreign investments. By 1914 the British had $20,000,000,000 in foreign investments, the French about $8,700,000,000, the Germans about $6,000,000,000. A quarter of all the wealth owned by the inhabitants of Great Britain consisted in 1914 in holdings outside the country. Almost a sixth of the French national wealth lay in investments outside of France. All three countries had given hostages to fortune, and fortune proved unkind, for in the First World War the British lost about a quarter of their foreign investments, the French about a third, the Germans all.

These huge sums, pouring out from Europe's inner zone for a century before 1914, at first went mainly to finance the Americas and the less affluent regions of Europe.[8] No country except Great Britain completely built its railways with its own resources. In the United States the railway system was built very largely with capital borrowed from England. In central and eastern Europe British companies often constructed the first railways, then sold out to native operating companies or to governments which subsequently ran them. In the Argentine Republic the British not merely financed and built the railways, but continued thereafter to operate and own them. In addition, up to 1914 the British sold about 75,000,000 tons of coal a year to South America to keep the railways going, not to mention items for replacement and upkeep of equipment. Docks, warehouses, mines, plantations, processing and manufacturing establishments all over the world were similarly built up with capital drawn from Europe. European capital also helped emigrants in the new countries to live in civilized fashion. In the United States, for example, state and local governments very commonly sold their bonds in Europe, to build roads, pave streets, or construct school systems for the westward-moving population. A few of these American bonds proved a partial or total loss to European investors. On the whole, by 1914, the United States had paid back a good deal of its indebtedness. Even so, in 1914, Americans still owed about four billion dollars to Europeans—a sum three times as large as the national debt of the United States at the time.

〰〰〰〰〰〰〰〰

[8] The penetration of European capital into Asia and Africa, after about 1890, is considered in the following chapter.

AN INTERNATIONAL MONEY SYSTEM: THE GOLD STANDARD

The international economy rested upon an international money system, based in turn upon the almost universal acceptance of the gold standard. England had adopted the gold standard in 1816, when the pound sterling was legally defined as the equivalent of 113 grains of fine gold. Western Europe and the United States adopted an exclusively gold standard in the 1870's. A person holding any "civilized" money—pounds, francs, dollars, marks, *etc.*—could turn it into gold at will, and a person holding gold could turn it into any money. The currencies were like so many different languages all expressing the same thing. All had substantially the same value, and until 1914 the exchange rates between currencies remained highly stable. It was assumed that no civilized country's currency ever "fell"; such things might happen in Turkey or China, or in the French Revolution, but not in the world of practical men, modern progress, and civilized affairs.

The important currencies were all freely exchangeable. A Frenchman, selling silks to a German, and hence receiving German marks, could turn the marks into francs, pounds sterling, or dollars. That is, he was not obliged to buy from Germany or spend his money in Germany, but could use the proceeds of his German sale to buy French, British, or American goods or services as he chose. Trade was multilateral. A country needing imports from another country, such as American cotton, did not have to sell to that country to obtain them; it could sell its own goods anywhere and then import according to its needs. Thus Europe, which as time went on sold fewer manufactures to the United States, was still able to buy from the United States by selling manufactures to Brazil or the Dutch East Indies; and Americans correspondingly could buy Brazilian coffee or East Indian rubber by selling to Europe.

It was the acceptance of the gold standard, and the fact that all important countries possessed a sufficient share of gold to support their currencies, that made possible so fluid an interchange. At the same time the gold standard had less wholesome effects. It was hard on countries that lacked gold. And it produced a gradual fall of prices, especially between 1870 and 1900, because (until the gold discoveries in South Africa, Australia, and Alaska in the 1890's) the world's production of gold lagged behind the expanding production of industrial and agricultural goods. Persistently declining prices were a hardship to those who habitually worked with borrowed money —many farmers, many business men, and debtor nations as a whole. A famous speech of William Jennings Bryan in the United States in 1896, declaring that mankind should not be "crucified upon this cross of gold," expressed a restlessness that was world-wide. But falling prices were an advantage to the wage-earning class, which generally improved its position in these years, and also to the wealthy, the owners and lenders of capital, the bankers and financiers, who so long as prices were falling were repaid in money of more value than that which they had lent.

The center of the global economic and financial system was London. The London banks came forward in consequence of the defeat of Napoleon, the older financial centers in Amsterdam having been ruined in the Revolutionary and Napoleonic wars. It may be recalled also that the victors in 1815 imposed upon France an indemnity of 700,000,000 francs, which in 1818 was taken over by a syndicate of private bankers; the London banks played a leading part in this affair, and so developed their connections with many government treasuries.[9] In the Crimean War of 1854–6, with England at war with Russia, the London banks floated loans for the Russian government—so independent were business and politics then thought to be. The early adoption of the gold standard in England meant that many people, British and foreign, kept their funds in the form of sterling on deposit in London, where quantities of available capital therefore accumulated.

The banks, too, grew up in the financing of the British export trade, itself borne on the tide of the Industrial Revolution. A small Lancashire manufacturer, for example, might receive an order for a gross of scissors from an unknown merchant in Trieste. He would draw a bill or "sight draft" against the Trieste merchant, and take this bill to a financial institution known as an acceptance house. The acceptance house, which in the course of its business had acquired a microscopic knowledge of the credit of thousands of individuals and firms in all parts of the world, would then "discount" the bill, giving cash to the Lancashire manufacturer and collecting from the Trieste merchant through international banking channels. In this way the bank took a burden off the British manufacturer, and extended short-term credit to foreigners for the purchase of British goods. Many acceptance houses gradually went into the business of long-term foreign lending also. London became the apex of a pyramid which had the world for its base. It was the main center of exchange of currencies, the clearinghouse of the world's debts, the depository from which all the world borrowed, the banker's bank, the insurance man's resort for re-insurance, as well as the world's shipping center and the headquarters of many international corporations.

A WORLD MARKET: UNITY, COMPETITION—AND INSECURITY

Never had the earth been so unified economically, with each region playing its due role in a global specialization. Western Europe, and in 1870 mainly Great Britain, was the world's industrial workshop. Other parts of the earth supplied its many needs. Stanley Jevons, an English economist, wrote in awestruck tones as early as 1866:

The several quarters of the globe are our willing tributaries. The plains of North America and Russia are our cornfields; Chicago and Odessa our granaries; Canada and the Baltic our forests; Australia contains our sheep farms, and in South

---

[9] See p. 448.

America are our herds of oxen. Peru sends her silver, and the gold of California and Australia flows to London; the Chinese grow tea for us; and coffee, sugar and spice arrive from the East Indian plantations. Spain and France are our vineyards, and the Mediterranean our fruit garden; our cotton grounds, which formerly occupied the southern United States, are now everywhere in the many regions of the earth.

To a degree only less than Great Britain the rest of Europe's "inner zone" could have made the same boast before the First World War.

A true world market had been created. Goods, services, money, capital, people moved back and forth almost without regard to national boundaries. Articles were bought and sold at uniform world prices. Dealers in wheat, for example, followed prices in Minneapolis, Liverpool, Buenos Aires, and Danzig as reported by telegraph and cable from day to day. They bought where it was cheapest, and sold where it was dearest. In this way the world's wheat supply was distributed roughly according to need or ability to pay. The working man of Milan, if the Italian crop was poor and prices high, was fed from another source. On the other hand, the Italian wheat grower would in this case feel the pinch of world competition. The world market, while it organized the world into a unified economic system, at the same time brought distant regions into competition for the first time. The producer—whether business man, factory employee, farmer, or coffee planter—had no secure outlet for his product, as had generally been true in the past. He was in competition not only with the man across the street or down the road, but with the world.

The creation of an integrated world market, the financing and building up of countries outside of Europe, and the consequent feeding and support of Europe's increasing population were the great triumphs of the nineteenth-century system of unregulated capitalism. The system was intricate, with thousands and even millions of individuals and business firms supplying each other's wants without central planning. But it was extremely precarious, and the position of most people in it was exceedingly vulnerable. Region competed against region, and person against person. A fall of grain prices in the American Middle West, besides ruining a few speculators, might oblige the Prussian or Argentine wheat grower to sell at a price at which he could not live. A factory owner might be driven out of business if his competitor successfully undersold him, or if a new commodity made his own product obsolete. The workingman, hired only when needed by an employer, faced unemployment when business slackened, or the permanent disappearance of his job by the next labor-saving invention. The system went through cycles of boom and depression. It rested on expansion and on credit; but sometimes people could not pay their debts, so that credit collapsed, and sometimes expansion failed to keep pace with expectations, and anticipated profits proved to be losses. To combat the essential insecurity of private capitalism, all manner of devices were resorted to. Governments adopted protective tariffs on the one hand and social insurance and welfare legislation on the other; trade unionism and socialist movements grew;

business mergers took place. These and other measures, to which we shall return, signalized the gradual decline in the years after 1880 of nineteenth-century, unregulated, *laissez-faire* capitalism.

CHANGES IN ORGANIZATION: BIG BUSINESS

A great change came over capitalism itself about 1880 or 1890. Formerly characterized by a very large number of very small units, small businesses run by individuals, partnerships, or small companies, it was increasingly characterized by large and impersonal corporations. The attractions of the "limited liability" corporation as a form of business organization and as a means of encouraging investment arose from laws, enacted by most countries in the nineteenth century, which limited the individual investor's personal loss in the event of a bankruptcy to the amount of his shares of stock in the enterprise. The corporation, in its modern form appearing first with the railroads, became the usual form of organization for industry and commerce. As machinery grew more complicated only a large pool of capital could finance it. And as corporations grew in size and number, relying on the sale of stock and the issue of bonds, the influence of banking and financial circles was enhanced. Financiers, using not so much their own money as the savings of others, had a new power to create or to extinguish, to stimulate, discourage, or combine corporate enterprises in various industries. Industrial capitalism brought finance capitalism with it.[10]

Corporate organization made it possible to concentrate economic processes under unified management. In retail commerce, large department stores appeared about 1890 in the United States and France. In industry, steel offers a good example. Steel became in any case a big business when heavy blast furnaces were introduced. It was not safe for the steel business, or for the blast furnaces, to rely for iron and coal on independent producers who might sell to whomsoever they pleased. The steel works therefore began to operate mines of their own, or to buy out or otherwise reduce coal and iron mines to subsidiary status. Some, to assure their markets, began to produce not merely steel but steel manufactures as well—steel ships, railway equipment, naval and military ordnance. Thus entire processes from mining to finished product became concentrated in a "vertical" integration. By "horizontal" integration concerns at the same level combined with each other to reduce competition and to protect themselves against fluctuations in prices and in markets. Some fixed prices, some agreed to restrict production, some divided up markets among themselves. They were called trusts in the United States, cartels in Europe. They were common in many of the new industries at the close of the century, such as chemicals, aluminum, and oil. In steel such combinations produced the great interests of Krupp in Germany, Schneider-Creusot in France, Vickers-Armstrong in Great Britain. It was in the United States that such big business developed furthest, headed by "captains" of

――――――――――――――

[10] See pp. 505, 544.

industry and "titans" of finance. Andrew Carnegie, by origin a poor Scotch immigrant boy, produced more steel than all England; in 1901 he sold out to an even more colossal organization, the United States Steel Corporation, formed by the financier J. P. Morgan. It was in the United States, too, that concern over monopoly and the power of big business in general was felt most strongly; anti-trust legislation, beginning with the Sherman Act of 1890, was enacted but never with any substantial effect.

Many of the new combinations were beneficial in making the ups and downs of business less erratic, and so providing more stable prices and more continuous and secure employment. Generally they reduced the costs of production; but whether the savings went into higher profits, higher wages, or lower prices depended on numerous factors. Some trusts were more greedy than others, or confronted with only weakly organized or unorganized labor. In any case, for good or ill, decisions rested with management and finance. A new kind of private power had arisen, which its critics loved to call "feudal." Since no economic system had ever been so centralized up to that time, never in fact had so few people exercised so much economic power over so many. The middle class, with the rise of great corporations, came typically to consist of salaried employees; the salaried man might spend a lifetime with the same company, and feel toward it, in its disputes with labor or government, a loyalty not unlike that of a lord's retainer in feudal times. The laboring class was less amenable; labor attempted to organize unions capable of dealing with increasingly gigantic employers. It also after about 1880 played an increasingly decisive role in the politics of all advanced nations.

73. The Advance of Democracy: Third French Republic, United Kingdom, German Empire

In the years under consideration the machinery of democratic self-government was being established and extended in western Europe and even in central and southern Europe. Political life was increasingly marked by movements toward constitutional government, representative assemblies, responsible ministries, the guarantee of individual liberties, and, most notably in this period, the democratic extension of the vote to the working class— the adoption of universal manhood suffrage, which in turn meant the creation of mass political parties. In response to a variety of pressures governments also found themselves more and more assuming responsibility for the social and economic problems created by industrialism. The welfare state in its modern form was taking shape.

FRANCE: THE ESTABLISHMENT OF THE THIRD REPUBLIC

In France the democratic republic was not easily established, and its troubled early years left deep cleavages within the country. It will be recalled that in September 1870, when the empire of Napoleon III revealed its help-lessness in the Franco-Prussian War, insurrectionaries in Paris, as in 1792 and 1848, again proclaimed the Republic.[11] A provisional government of national defense sought desperately to continue the war, but the cause was hopeless. By January 1871, a bitter siege of Paris came to an end and an armistice was signed. Bismarck, insisting that only a properly constituted government could make peace, permitted the election, by universal male suffrage, of a National Assembly which was to consider his peace terms and draft a constitution for the new French state. When the elections were held in February, it was found, as in 1848 (and, indeed, 1797), that republicanism was so distrusted by the French people as a whole, and most especially in the provinces and rural areas, that a free election brought monarchist elements into power.[12] Republicanism was still thought to be violent—bellicose in its foreign policy, turbulent in its political workings, unfriendly to the church, and socialistic or at least equalitarian in its views of property and private wealth. The new Assembly contained only about two hundred republicans out of more than six hundred deputies.

But the Paris republicans, who had defended France when Napoleon III failed to do so, who for four months had been besieged, starved and frozen by the Germans, and who still refused to make peace on the harsh terms imposed by Bismarck and about to be accepted by the Assembly, refused to recognize the latter's authority. A civil war broke out between the National Assembly, now sitting at Versailles, and the city of Paris, where a revolutionary municipal council or "Commune" was set up. Paris, so lately attacked by German soldiers, was now attacked by French.

The Paris Commune, which lasted from March to May 1871, seemed to be another explosion of social revolution. Actually, it was in essence a revival of the Jacobinism of 1793. It was fiercely patriotic and republican, anti-German, opposed to wealthy bourgeois, aristocrats and clergy, in favor of government controls upon prices, wages and working conditions, but still not socialist in any sweeping or systematic way. Among its leaders, however, filtered in a few of the new international revolutionary socialists, who saw in a Jacobin or democratic republic a step toward their new order. Marx in England, and others elsewhere, hopefully read into the Commune the impending doom of the bourgeoisie. This was precisely what more conservative elements feared. To many of the French middle and peasant class, and to people like them all over Europe, it seemed that the "Communards" were wild and savage destroyers of nineteenth-century civilization. The fighting in Paris was atrocious beyond anything known in any preceding French revolution. The Communards, in final desperation, burned a number of public buildings and put to death the Archbishop of Paris, whom they held as a hostage. The forces of the National Assembly, when finally triumphant, were determined to root out the inveterate revolutionism of Paris. Some 330,000

[11] See p. 527.
[12] See pp. 365, 476.

persons were denounced, 38,000 arrested, 20,000 put to death, and 7,500 deported to New Caledonia. The Third Republic was born in an atmosphere of class hate and social terror.

The form of government for the new regime still had to be established. The monarchist majority in the Assembly was itself evenly divided between those who favored a restoration of the Bourbon family and those who favored the Orleanist. In the end, even after they were reconciled, the Bourbon candidate alienated everyone by his stiff insistence on a return to the white flag of the Bourbons. The monarchists checkmated each other. Meanwhile, after extended discussion of various constitutional projects, the Assembly adopted in 1875, not a constitution, but certain constitutive laws. By a margin of one vote, a resolution indirectly amounting to the establishment of a republic was passed. The new laws provided for a president, a parliament in two chambers, and a council of ministers, or cabinet, headed by a premier. The Senate was to be elected by a complicated and indirect system of election, the Chamber of Deputies, by universal, direct, manhood suffrage.

Within two years, in 1877, the role of the president, the ministers, and the parliament was further clarified as a result of an unsuccessful attempt by an early president, Marshal MacMahon, to dismiss a premier of whom he did not approve but who had the backing of the Chamber. MacMahon proceeded to dissolve the Chamber and to hold new elections, but the example of Napoleon III's transformation of the Second Republic into a personal dictatorship was still fresh. The elections vindicated the principle of parliamentary primacy and of the responsibility of the premier and his cabinet to the legislature, a responsibility which in France meant generally but not exclusively to the lower house. The true executive in republican France was to be the premier and his cabinet, themselves held strictly to account by a majority of the legislature. Unfortunately, that majority, in a parliament where a dozen or so parties were represented, was always difficult to form and could be created only by unstable, temporary, shifting party alliances, coalitions, or *blocs*. No president, and indeed no premier, could henceforth dissolve the chamber in order to hold new elections and consult the country as could be done in Britain. Actually, under the Third Republic the substantial machinery of state—ministries, prefectures, law courts, police, army, all under highly centralized control—was carried over virtually untouched as in all upheavals since the time of Napoleon I. France in the nineteenth century, so volatile in appearance, in effect underwent less revolutionary reorganization than any other leading country of Europe.

THE TRIALS OF THE THIRD FRENCH REPUBLIC

Yet the Third Republic was precarious. The government had changed so often since 1789 that all forms of government seemed to be transitory. Questions which in other countries were only party questions became in France questions of "regime"—monarchy versus republic. Many people, especially those influenced by the upper classes, the Catholic clergy, and the professional army officers, continued to feel a positive aversion to the republic. On the other hand, the unmerciful and vindictive repression of the Commune made many middle-class people sympathetic to the republicans. Many turned republican simply because no other form of government established itself, or because it was the form of government that divided the country the least. As republicanism took in wider elements of society, it became less revolutionary and less fearsome. In 1879, for the first time, republicans won control of the government in the Third Republic. They proved mild indeed, in the light of memories of 1871, 1848, or 1793. In the 1880's their radicalism hardly went further than the founding of a democratic and compulsory school system at government expense and the passage of anti-clerical legislation intended to curb church influence in the schools.

For over a quarter of a century, however, republican energies had to be expended in defense of republican institutions in order to ensure the survival of the regime. An initial crisis arose in 1886-9, when General Boulanger gathered around him an incongruous following which included not only Bonapartists, monarchists, and aristocrats but also extreme radical republicans who wished a war of revenge against Germany and workingmen disgruntled over their general lot. Boulanger became a popular figure and seemed for a moment about to seize power as a dictator. But the menace collapsed in a comical failure as the general lost heart at the crucial hour and fled into exile. Meanwhile, in the 1880's and 1890's scandals and revelations of corruption in high quarters provided ammunition for the anti-republicans. A president's son-in-law was discovered trafficking in Legion of Honor decorations, a disclosure that strengthened Boulanger's following. A number of deputies and senators were implicated in the failure of the Panama Canal venture, which had gone bankrupt because of dishonesty and mismanagement. For a time, however, especially after the Boulanger fiasco, it seemed that unsympathetic French Catholics would rally to the republic as the established form of government, which they were urged to do by French prelates and by Pope Leo XIII in 1892. The hope that the recalcitrant would accept the republic was shattered by the Dreyfus Affair which in the late 1890's rocked the country, and indeed the world.

In 1894 Captain Dreyfus, an army officer who happened to be Jewish in religion, the first of his faith to be admitted to the army's general staff corps, was found guilty of treason by a military court and deported to Devil's Island. Evidence accumulated showing his innocence, and indicating that another officer, an aristocrat, a Catholic, and a royalist, was the true traitor. The country was split into two camps. The army and most of the "best" people refused to reopen the Dreyfus case because they wished to disgrace the whole republican regime. The partisans of Dreyfus stubbornly upheld him, both because they believed in justice and because they wished to discredit their adversaries. In 1899 he was pardoned, and in 1906, fully exonerated. In the aftermath of the Dreyfus Affair the republicans launched a counteroffensive, putting through a series of laic laws by 1905 that "sepa-

rated" church and state, thereby abolishing the close relationship established
by Napoleon's concordat a hundred years earlier. They proceeded also to
purge the army of officers disloyal to the republic.

THE STRENGTH AND WEAKNESS OF THE REPUBLIC

The Third Republic, when the war came in 1914, a test which it was
successfully to meet, had lasted over twice as long as any French regime since
1789. Born unwanted and accidentally, though it still had its enemies, it now
commanded the loyalty of the overwhelming mass of the French people.
What it had done, since 1870, was to domesticate democratic republicanism
in Europe. Republicanism, one of the most militant of revolutionary movements down to 1870, had been shown in France to be compatible with
order, law, parliamentary government, economic prosperity, and a mutual
tolerance between classes, to the extent at least that they no longer butchered
each other in the streets. Industrial workers were in many ways less well off
than in England or Germany, but there were fewer of them; and for most
people France in these years was a pleasant country, full of painters, writers,
scholars, and scientists, full of bankers, bourgeois and well-established farmers, a country living comfortably and unhurriedly on the savings of generations, and one in which, in a close-knit family group, the average man could
plan securely for his own and his children's future.

But the very comforts and values of *bourgeois* France were not those
that would equip it for leadership in the modern age of technology and
industrial power. Though substantial economic progress was made, the
country lagged behind Germany in industrial development; the French *entrepreneur* showed little inclination to take the business risks needed for
industrial growth. Politically, the fragmentation of political parties, itself a
democratic reflection of a divided public opinion, and the distrust for historic reasons of a strong executive power led to the rise and fall of numerous
short-lived ministries—no fewer than fifty in the years between 1871 and
1914. Ministerial instability was to be a chronic symptom of French parliamentary life both before and after 1914; continuity of government policy
was, however, generally maintained because of stability in certain key ministries and because of the permanent civil service.

French labor was to remain a steady source of discontent. Although
French workingmen received a modicum of labor legislation in the two
decades after 1890, they continued to feel frustrated at the failure to establish a "social republic." Socialist representation in the Chamber grew. However, the most important single party of the republic, the Radicals, or Radical Socialists, were in actuality radical republicans—patriotic, anti-clerical,
spokesmen for the small shopkeepers and the lesser propertied interests; they
drew the line at the advanced social legislation that labor expected from them,
and on occasion their leaders even took positive steps to prevent unionization and to suppress strikes. Since some of these Radicals had started out as

socialists, the distrust of French workingmen for all politicians and even for political processes was intensified. But the difficulties of the republic went deeper. The political energies of the republican statesmen had gone into liquidating the past, into curbing the political strength of the monarchists, the church and the army; by the turn of the century, even before these older issues were fully resolved, the republic was compelled to meet the challenge of labor and of other industrial, social, and international issues that were to try it sorely. The Third Republic was to weather the crisis of the First World War but not that of the Second.

THE BRITISH CONSTITUTIONAL MONARCHY

The British constitutional monarchy in the half-century before 1914 was the great exemplar of reasonable, orderly, and peaceable self-government through parliamentary methods. For over sixty years, spanning two-thirds of the nineteenth century, Victoria reigned (1837–1901) and gave her name to a distinguished era of material progress, literary accomplishment, and political stability. The two great parties, Liberal and Conservative, the heirs roughly of the Whigs and Tories, took form in the 1850's, the former producing its great leader in William E. Gladstone, the latter, a series of leaders of whom the most colorful was Benjamin Disraeli.

The advance toward an equalitarian political democracy in Britain was more cautious and slower than in France. The Reform Bill of 1832 had granted the vote to about an eighth of the adult male population. The democratic Chartist agitation of the 1830's and '40's came to nothing.[13] In 1867, in response to continued demand for a wider suffrage, the Second Reform Bill was passed, Conservatives as well as Liberals outdoing one another in an effort to satisfy the country and to win new political strength for their own party. The Bill, adopted under Disraeli's Conservative ministry, extended the suffrage to include over a third of the adult males of the United Kingdom, reaching down far enough to include most workingmen in English cities. A Conservative critic called it a "leap in the dark." In 1884, under Liberal auspices, the suffrage was again broadened, this time to include over three-quarters of all adult males, but still omitting many agricultural wage-laborers, servants living with employers, and such people as unmarried grown sons who lived in the homes of their parents. Although the franchise was now broad, it could not yet be equated with universal manhood suffrage. Not until 1918 did Great Britain adopt universal manhood suffrage, as generally understood; and at that time women over thirty were given the vote too.

Despite the extension of the suffrage, the leadership of the country at the turn of the century was still in the hands of the upper and wealthier classes. Until 1911 the government paid no salaries to members of the House of Commons, who therefore, in both great parties, were usually gentlemen

ᴧᴧᴧᴧᴧᴧᴧᴧᴧᴧᴧᴧᴧᴧᴧᴧᴧ

[13] See pp. 466–7, 474.

with private incomes, possessing the same family background and education. An attitude of sportsmanship and good feeling was characteristic of British politics. The two parties alternated in power at regular intervals, each indulgent toward the other, carrying over and developing rather than reversing the policies of its predecessor in office. Both parties sought support where they could find it, the Liberals leaning somewhat more on the industrial and commercial interests, the Conservatives on the landed aristocracy, both seeking and succeeding in winning their share of the new working-class vote.

The Liberals were usually the more willing to pioneer, the first of the four ministries of Gladstone being especially notable in this respect. Gladstone in this first ministry (1868–74) developed the principle of state-supported public education for all classes, introduced the secret ballot, definitely legalized labor unions, eliminated the purchase and sale of commissions in the army (a form of property in office), and by abolishing religious tests enabled persons not members of the Church of England to graduate from Oxford and Cambridge. The Conservative party, less sensitive to pressure from business interests for a *laissez-faire* policy in economic matters and continuing the tradition of earlier Tory reformers, took the initiative in further labor legislation; the existing acts regulating conditions in mines and factories were extended and codified under Disraeli's second ministry (1874–80).

BRITISH POLITICAL CHANGES AFTER 1900

Around the turn of the century important changes were discernible on the British political scene. Labor emerged as an independent political force, the Labor party itself being organized shortly after 1900.[14] The rise of labor had a deep impact upon the Liberal party, and indeed upon liberalism itself. With many persons insisting that protective measures be taken to counteract the poor health, low income, and economic insecurity of the British working people, the Liberals abandoned their traditional position of *laissez-faire* and sponsored a policy of government intervention and social legislation in behalf of the workingman. The Liberals, though they acted in part for humanitarian reasons, were not unaware that with the emergence of the Labor party workingmen who customarily had voted for them might readily transfer their allegiance.

In control of the government from 1906 to 1916, with Herbert Asquith as prime minister and David Lloyd George as chancellor of the exchequer during most of this time, the Liberals put through a spectacular program of social welfare. Sickness, accident, old-age, and a degree of unemployment insurance were adopted, and a moderate minimum wage law was enacted. Labor exchanges, or employment bureaus, were set up over the country. Restrictions on strikes and other trade union activities were removed. To meet the costs of the new program as well as of other government expenditures,

᠆᠆᠆᠆᠆᠆᠆᠆᠆᠆᠆᠆᠆᠆᠆

[14] See p. 592.

Lloyd George's budget of 1909 called for progressive income and inheritance taxes: the wealthier the taxpayer, the higher the rate at which he was taxed. He was in effect advancing the then novel idea of using taxation to modify the extremes of wealth and poverty. It was a "war budget," he said, intended "to wage war against poverty." Its fiscal measures were directed primarily at the landed aristocracy, and it aroused great opposition, especially in the House of Lords, where the contest over the budget led eventually to a further constitutional curtailment of the power of the upper house. The Parliament Act of 1911 deprived the Lords of all veto power in money matters and of all but a two-year delaying veto on action of the Commons in other legislation. At this time, too, the government voted to pay salaries to members of the House of Commons, making it possible for workingmen and others without independent incomes to take seats in Parliament. This last measure was enacted to get around a court ruling, the Osborne Judgment of 1909, that trade unions could not pay the salaries of workingmen elected to Parliament.

The Liberal party seemed to be turning into a party of labor; certainly it was embracing a program of positive state intervention in social and economic matters that the older liberalism, nurtured on the doctrines of *laissez-faire* and the Manchester school, would not have accepted. With the Liberals actively seeking the support of labor and altering much in their traditional program, the Conservatives in the twentieth century tended to become the party of industry as well as of landed wealth and to replace the Liberals as the champions of economic liberalism and *laissez-faire*. In the next generation, after the First World War, the Conservatives were to remain one of the two major parties of the country; the Liberals were to be far outstripped by the Labor party.

Meanwhile, despite its gains, labor was not pacified. Real wages showed a tendency to fall after 1900, and great coal and railway strikes broke out in 1911 and 1912. The British capacity to survive crises without violence, while still conspicuous, was being strained. An even more serious threat came from Ireland.

THE IRISH QUESTION

Britain suffered from one of the worst minorities questions in Europe —the Irish question. After 1801 Britain was known as the United Kingdom of Great Britain and Ireland, Ireland having been incorporated into the United Kingdom as a defensive measure against Napoleon.[15] The Irish objected to the union with England, and the Irish representatives who sat in Parliament were generally obstructionist in their tactics. The Irish had many substantial grievances too numerous to mention, but among which two were conspicuous. The Irish peasant was defenseless against his landlord, far more

―――――――――――――――

[15] See pp. 322, 366.

so, for example, than the French peasant before 1789; and the Irish people, though predominantly Catholic, were obliged to pay tithes to the established Church of Ireland (an Anglican sister-church to the Church of England), which also owned a good deal of the land.

Gladstone, in his first ministry, disestablished the Church of Ireland. He also initiated measures to protect the Irish farm tenant. By 1900, under Conservative auspices, the Irish tenant was being assisted by the British government to buy out his landlord—often an Englishman or an Anglicized and absentee Irishman. The Irish also wanted home rule, or a parliament of their own. Gladstone, in trying to give it to them in 1886, split his Liberal party, part of which went along with the Conservatives, not wishing political division of the British Isles. Home rule was finally granted to Ireland in 1914. But the Ulstermen, Presbyterians of north Ireland, objected vehemently to inclusion in an autonomous Ireland, in which they would be outnumbered by the Catholics of the south. The latter, however, insisted with equal vehemence on the inclusion of Ulster, not wishing a political division of Ireland.

The Ulstermen, backed by British Conservatives, started arming and drilling to resist the act of Parliament that authorized home rule. Great Britain, in 1914, was about to see a civil war on its own doorstep. It suffered from something of the insoluble nationalistic disputes that afflicted Austria-Hungary. During the First World War home rule was suspended, and after considerable violence on both sides Catholic Ireland (Eire) in 1922 received Dominion status, but eventually, after the 1930's dissolved all ties with Britain. Ulster remained in the United Kingdom. Thus both the United Kingdom and Ireland itself were "partitioned."

BISMARCK AND THE GERMAN EMPIRE, 1871–90

The German Empire, as put together by Bismarck in 1871 with William I, King of Prussia, as Kaiser, was a federation of monarchies, a union of twenty-five German states, in which the weight of absolutist Prussia, the Prussian army, and the Prussian landed aristocracy was preponderant. It developed neither the strong constitutionalism of England nor the democratic equality that was characteristic of France. To win popular support for his projects, Bismarck had exploited existing democratic and socialist sentiment and allowed members of the Reichstag, the lower chamber, to be elected by universal manhood suffrage.[16] Remaining chancellor of the united empire for some twenty years, from 1871 to 1890, he usually tried to have a majority in the Reichstag on his side, but he recognized no dependence on a majority in principle, holding to the absolutist doctrine that it was the emperor and his chancellor who were to govern the country. Moreover, power of the lower house to initiate legislation was severely restricted, and the upper chamber,

wwwwwwwwwwwwwwww

[16] See pp. 524–5, 530.

representing the princes and not the people, had considerably more legislative power. Despite the nature of the empire, the Prussian conservatives, the East Elbian *Junker* landlords, were at first by no means enthusiastic over Bismarck's unified Germany.[17] They opposed his democratic concessions and were horrified when in 1872 he undertook to extinguish what was left of their manorial jurisdiction over their peasants.

Bismarck in the 1870's therefore leaned not on the Conservatives but on the National Liberals. With their aid he put through a number of economic and legal measures designed to consolidate the unity of the new empire. Bismarck's first serious conflict developed with the Catholic Church. At the very time that he was bent on subordinating all groups within the state to the sovereign power of the new empire, the Church had spoken out. In 1864 in the "Syllabus of Errors," it denounced the encroachment of all governments on educational and church affairs; in 1870 the new dogma of papal infallibility made it incumbent on Catholics to accept unreservedly the pope's pronouncements in matters of faith and morals.[18] To many, the implication was that the new empire could not count on the undivided loyalty of its Catholic citizens. To defend Catholic interests and those of the south German states where Catholicism predominated, Catholic elements had organized the strong Center party, which now upheld the Church pronouncements. In 1871 Bismarck launched the so-called *Kulturkampf*, or "battle for modern civilization." The Liberals joined in eagerly. Like nineteenth-century liberals elsewhere (Gladstone's campaign against Anglican influence and the French laic laws have just been mentioned), they were strongly anticlerical and disapproved of the influence of organized churches in public and private life. Laws were put through imposing restrictions upon Catholic worship and education, the Jesuits were expelled, and many Catholic bishops throughout Germany were arrested or went into exile. But Bismarck gradually concluded that the anti-Catholic legislation was fruitless, that he had overestimated the danger to the state of organized Catholicism, and realized that he needed the support of the Center party for other parts of his program.

In 1879, with the support of the Center and Conservative parties but to the dismay of many of his erstwhile Liberal allies, Bismarck abandoned free trade and adopted a protective tariff that provided needed revenues for the government and gave satisfaction both to agricultural and industrial interests. Meanwhile, with the country's rapid and spectacular industrial expansion, the German working class had been growing and, to the alarm of Bismarck, socialism had been spreading among the German masses.

The German Social Democratic party had been founded in 1875 by a fusion of Marxian socialists and the reformist followers of Ferdinand Lassalle on an essentially moderate program which Marx had denounced. But even a moderate socialism was mistrusted by Bismarck. He shared in the European horror at the recent Paris Commune, he feared socialism as an-

---

[17] See pp. 486, 520–1
[18] See p. 604.

archy, and he knew that socialism was in any case republican, and in that alone a potentially revolutionary movement in an empire of monarchies. Two radical attempts on the emperor's life (in neither case by Social Democrats) provided him with all the excuse he needed. In 1878, having already made peace with the Catholics, he set out to exterminate socialism. Anti-socialist laws from 1878 to 1890 prohibited socialist meetings and socalist newspapers. For twelve years socialism was driven underground. But repression was not his only weapon; he turned also to another tactic. Bismarck sought to persuade the workers to place their faith in him and the German Empire rather than in Marx and the prophets of socialism. To that end, in the 1880's, he initiated an extensive program of social legislation. Workmen were insured by the state against sickness, accident, and old age. "Our democratic friends," said Bismarck, "will pipe in vain when the people see princes concerned with their well-being." In social insurance imperial Germany was, from whatever motives, years ahead of more democratic England and France.

Bismarck failed to kill socialism. The number of socialists elected to the Reichstag was greater in 1890 than in 1878—for Bismarck's anti-socialist campaign, in deference to the then current standards of civilized government, never suppressed the voter's freedom to vote as he chose. It seems, however, that Bismarck by the later 1880's was more apprehensive than ever of social revolution that would destroy his empire, and contemplated some kind of coup d'état in which the Reichstag would be throttled. He never reached this point because in 1890, at the age of seventy-five, he was obliged by the new emperor William II to retire.

THE GERMAN EMPIRE AFTER 1890: WILLIAM II

William I died in 1888 and was succeeded by his son Frederick III who, incurably ill, died some three months after his accession. Frederick's son, William II, the last King of Prussia and the last German Kaiser, began his reign (1888–1918) as a young man of twenty-nine, full of startling ideas about his personal power and privileges. He was uncomfortable in the presence of an elder statesman who had made the German Empire, who had been his grandfather's aide and adviser, and whom he regarded partly with veneration and partly as an old fogy. William soon quarreled with Bismarck over continuation of the anti-socialist laws and over matters of foreign affairs. When Bismarck forbade his ministers to meet with the emperor on policy matters unless he were present, William resolved that he, and not Bismarck, would rule the empire, and in 1890 he ordered Bismarck to resign, "dropping the pilot," in the celebrated phrase. Under the four chancellors who succeeded Bismarck, it was William who dominated policy.

After 1890 Germany embarked upon what was termed a "new course." In foreign affairs this meant a more aggressive and ambitious colonial, naval, and diplomatic policy. In domestic affairs it meant a more conciliatory attitude toward the masses. The anti-socialist laws were dropped, and the system of social security legislation was enlarged and extended. But no democratic adjustment seemed possible. William II believed in the divinely ordained prerogatives of the House of Hohenzollern, and the empire still rested on the absolutism of the federated princes, on the *Junkers*, the army, and the new industrial magnates. But the Social Democrats, the Progressive party and other democratic forces were growing in strength. They demanded, for Prussia, a reform of the illiberal constitution of 1850,[19] and for the Reich, real control over the federal chancellor by the majority party in the Reichstag. In the election of 1912 the Social Democrats, who, despite their Marxist program, had become increasingly reformist and parliamentary in their outlook, reached a new high by polling four and a quarter million votes, about one-third of the total, and by electing 110 members to the Reichstag, in which they now formed the largest single party. Even had war not come in 1914, it is clear that the imperial Germany created by Bismarck was moving toward a constitutional crisis in which political democracy would be the issue.

DEMOCRATIC DEVELOPMENTS ELSEWHERE

Of political developments in other European states before 1914, something has already been said in the preceding chapter. Italy had become a constitutional monarchy in the 1860's and completed its unification by the forceful seizure of Rome in 1870.[20] Despite parliamentary forms, Italian political life in substance was characterized by unstable, opportunistic maneuvers and alliances manipulated by party chieftains. The quarrel with the papacy over the seizure of papal territories remained unsettled; poverty and illiteracy, especially in the agrarian south, were grievous problems, and strikes and radical unrest mounted in the industrial cities. Still some progress was made in overcoming illiteracy, labor legislation was enacted to relieve social distress, and the machinery of democracy was broadened. In 1912 the electorate was tripled, in what amounted almost to universal manhood suffrage, although few of the newly enfranchised hastened to exercise their voting privilege.

In the Dual Monarchy of Austria-Hungary, created by the Compromise of 1867, Austria and Hungary were each in form constitutional parliamentary states.[21] In theory, the Emperor-King, Francis Joseph in these years, ruled through ministries responsible to the legislature in each state. However, in the important sphere of matters affecting the empire as a whole, such as foreign affairs and military questions, there was less parliamentary restraint on the Emperor. Here he had virtually final authority; moreover, in all matters he still had broad powers to govern by decree, which he exercised. As in Germany, the tide of socialism was held back both by repressive laws and by social insurance and benevolent legislation. The most serious problem in the empire remained not socialism but agitation by the various subject

---

[19] See pp. 491–2.   [20] See pp. 516–18.   [21] See pp. 532–4.

nationalities, the Czechs and other Slavic peoples. Political democracy took a different course in Austria than in Hungary. In the former, partly as an effort to placate nationalist sentiment, universal male suffrage was introduced in 1907. In the latter it was bitterly and successfully resisted by the Magyars, who saw in it a weapon that could be employed by the Slavs to contest and destroy their preponderance.

Of other countries it need only be said here that the political forms of democracy showed signs of advancing everywhere. In these years universal manhood suffrage was adopted in Switzerland in 1874, in Belgium in 1893 (though plural voting was still permitted), in the Netherlands in 1896; and in these same years in Denmark, Sweden, and Norway (the latter was peacefully separated in 1905 from Sweden); and in southern Europe, besides Italy, in Spain, Greece, Bulgaria, and Serbia. Although both Spain and Portugal were beset by civil wars in this period, constitutional forms were eventually adopted in both countries, universal male suffrage being introduced in Spain in 1890 and a liberal suffrage in Portugal under a republic in 1911. Even tsarist Russia, after the Revolution of 1905, received a Duma, or national parliament, elected on a wide franchise but on an indirect and undemocratic class basis, and with narrow powers.[22]

Thus, among states west of the Russian Empire, only Hungary and Rumania confined the vote to a minority of the population on the eve of the First World War. Women voted in certain Western states of the United States, in Australia, New Zealand, and Norway. In 1918 woman suffrage was introduced with certain restrictions in Great Britain; in 1920 it became general in the United States through constitutional amendment. Use of the secret or "Australian" ballot, palladium of the small voter's electoral freedom, also spread very widely in the decades after 1880. In Australia and New Zealand, and in the Scandinavian states political democracy was coupled with considerable social legislation. The progress of representative and democratic institutions did not in all cases mean an end to the rule of monarchs, landed aristocrats, and other minority interests. Of the major powers, it was mainly in the United States, Britain, and France that democratic and popular control seemed to be an increasing reality; but in almost all Europe, and in many outlying areas peopled by European descendants, liberal, constitutional, and democratic government was also advancing, and before 1914 it seemed that such government must some day emerge everywhere.

74. The Advance of Democracy: Socialism and Labor Unions

The artisan and laboring classes had never viewed with much pleasure the rise of capitalism or of "bourgeois" liberalism. They had always been doubtful of free competition, unrestrained private enterprise, the Manchester

School, *laissez-faire*, the laws of supply and demand, the free market for goods and labor, the idea of an economy independent of states and governments. These were the ideas of middle-class liberals, not of radical democrats. Popular leaders had opposed them in the French Revolution in 1793. The English Chartists had been outspokenly anti-capitalistic, and on the Continent the ideas of socialism had been spreading. In 1848 there was a strong movement among the working classes for a "social" republic, and, though the social revolution failed in 1848, the force of it was enough to terrify the possessing classes and shape the philosophy of Karl Marx.[23] With the advent of the ballot, workers pressed for social legislation and used their political power to gain a greater measure of social democracy.

But in addition, before and after obtaining the ballot, working people resorted to other devices for the improvement of their position. Against the owners of capital, who controlled the giving of jobs, there were two principal lines of action. One was to abolish the capitalists, the other to bargain with them. The former led to socialism, the latter to the formation of labor unions. Socialism, in logic, meant the extinction of the private employer as such.[24] Trade unionism, in logic, meant that the workingman had every reason to keep his employer prosperously in business in order that bargaining with him might produce more results. The working-class movement thus contained an internal contradiction which was never completely resolved.

Middle-class and educated people who took up the workers' cause, the "intellectuals" of the movement—Karl Marx, Frederick Engels, Louis Blanc, Ferdinand Lassalle, and thousands of less famous names—tended more to socialism than to unionism. They thought of society as a whole, they saw the economic system as a system, they thought of the future in long-run terms, and their time scale allowed generously for whole historical epochs to come and go. The actual workingman, put to work at an early age, barely educated if at all, with the waking hours of his adult life spent on a manual job, was inclined to keep his attention more on unionism than on socialism. To earn a shilling more every week beginning next week, to be spared the nervous strain and physical danger of constant exposure to unprotected machinery, to have fifteen minutes every day more for lunch, were likely to seem more tangible and important than far-reaching but distant plans for a reconstructed society. The worker looked on the intellectual as an outsider, however welcome; the intellectual looked on the worker as shortsighted and timid, however much in need of help.

After the failures of 1848 the socialist and trade union movements diverged for a generation. The 1850's, compared with the hungry forties, were a time of full employment, rising wages, and increasing prosperity for all classes. Workingmen set to organizing unions, socialist thinkers to perfecting their doctrines.

[23] See pp. 465–8, 471–5, 496.
[24] See pp. 434–5, 466.

THE TRADE UNION MOVEMENT AND RISE OF BRITISH LABOR

Organizations of wage-workers, or labor unions in the modern sense (as distinguished from medieval craft gilds), had long maintained a shadowy and sporadic existence, as in the old French journeymen's associations.[25] But they had always been extra-legal, frowned upon or actually prohibited by governments. French revolutionaries in the Le Chapelier act of 1791, British Tories in the Combination Act of 1799, had been as one in forbidding workers to unite. It was the rise of "bourgeois" liberalism, so insensitive to the worker in most ways, that first gave legal freedom to labor unions. The British unions received a tacit recognition from the Liberal Tories in 1825, and explicit recognition from Gladstone's Liberal ministry in 1871. French unions were recognized by Napoleon III in 1864, then restrained in the reaction caused by the Commune, then fully legalized in 1884. In Germany Bismarck negotiated with labor leaders to find support against the vested interests that stood in his way.

The prosperity of the 1850's favored the formation of unions, for workingmen can always organize most easily when employers are most in need of their services. The craft union—or union of skilled workers in the same trade, such as carpenters—was at first the typical organization. It was most fully developed in England, where a "new model" unionism was introduced by the Amalgamated Society of Engineers (*i.e.*, machinists) in 1851. It was the policy of the "new model" union officials to take the unions out of politics, to forget the semi-socialism of the Chartists, to abandon Robert Owen's grandiose idea of "one big union" for all workers, and to concentrate on advancing the interests of each separate trade. The new leaders proposed to be reasonable with employers, avoid strikes, accumulate union funds, and build up their membership. In this they were very successful; the unions took root; and the two governing parties in England, reassured by the unexpected moderation of working class spokesmen, combined to give the town workman the vote in 1867.

In the 1880's, and especially with the great London dock strike of 1889, which closed the port of London for the first time since the French Revolution, unions of unskilled workers began to form. Industrial unionism, or the joining in one union of all workers in one industry, such as coal or transportation, regardless of the skill or job of the individual worker, began to take shape at the same time. In some cases the older skilled unions joined with unskilled laborers who worked beside them. Thus gradually arose, for example, the Transport Workers Union, which half a century later was to give a Foreign Secretary to the government in the person of Ernest Bevin. By 1900 there were about 2,000,000 union members in Great Britain, compared with only 850,000 in Germany and 250,000 in France.

[25] See pp. 99–100, 348, 506.

It was largely because the British workingman was so far advanced in trade-unionism, and so successful in forcing collective bargaining upon his employer, that he was much slower than his Continental counterpart in forming a workers' political party. By the 1880's, when avowed socialists were already sitting in French, Belgian, and German parliaments, the only corresponding persons in Britain were a half-dozen Lib-Labs, as they were called, laboring men elected on the Liberal ticket. The British Labor party was formed at the turn of the century by the joint efforts of trade union officials and middle-class intellectuals. Where on the Continent the labor unions were often led, and even brought into being, by the socialist political parties, in Britain it was the labor unions that brought into being, and subsequently led, the Labor party. Hence for a long time the Labor party was less socialistic than working-class parties on the Continent. Its origin and rapid growth was due in large measure to a desire to defend the unions as established and respectable institutions. The unions were threatened in their very existence by a ruling of the British courts in 1901, the Taff Vale decision, which held a union financially responsible for business losses incurred by an employer during a strike. The shortest and most orderly strike, by exhausting a union's funds, might ruin the union. Steps had already been taken toward the creation of a Labor organization; the Taff Vale decision unified all ranks and precipitated the formation of the party. In the election of 1906 the new Labor party sent twenty-nine members to Parliament, which thereupon overruled the Taff Vale decision by new legislation. The social legislation put through Parliament in the decade that followed by the Liberal party government, in good part under pressure from labor, has already been described.[26]

EUROPEAN SOCIALISM AFTER 1850

As for socialism, which had so frightened the middle and upper classes in 1848, it seemed in the 1850's to go into abeyance. Karl Marx, after issuing the *Communist Manifesto* with Engels in 1848, and agitating as a journalist in the German revolution of that year, withdrew to the secure haven offered by England and spent the rest of his life in London, where, after years of painstaking research in the British Museum, he published the first volume of his *Capital* in 1867. This work, of which the two succeeding volumes were published after his death, gave body, substance, and argument to the principles announced in the *Manifesto*.[27] Marx, during more than thirty years in London, scarcely mixed with the labor leaders then building up the English unions. Hardly known to the English, he associated mainly with political exiles and temporary visitors of numerous nationalities.

In 1864 there took place in London the first meeting of the International Working Men's Association, commonly known as the First Interna-

ᐱᐱᐱᐱᐱᐱᐱᐱᐱᐱᐱᐱᐱᐱᐱᐱ

[26] See pp. 583–4.
[27] See pp. 497–8.

tional. It was sponsored by a heterogeneous group, including the secretary of the British carpenters' union, Robert Applegarth; the aging Italian revolutionary, Mazzini; and Karl Marx. With the union officials absorbed in union business, leadership in the Association gradually passed to Marx, who used it as a means of publicizing the ideas about to appear in his *Capital*. At subsequent annual congresses, at Geneva, Lausanne, Brussels, Basel, Marx built up his position. He made the Mazzinians unwelcome, and he denounced the German Lassalleans for their willingness to cooperate with Bismarck, arguing that it was not the business of socialists to cooperate with the state but to seize it. His sharpest struggle was with the Russian Bakunin. With his background in tsarist Russia, Bakunin believed the state to be the cause of the common man's afflictions; he was hence an "anarchist," holding that the state should be attacked and abolished. To Marx anarchism was abhorrent; the correct doctrine was that the state—tsarist or bourgeois—was only a product of economic conditions, a tool in the class struggle, a weapon of the propertied interests, so that the true target for revolutionary action must be not the state but the capitalistic economic system. Marx drove Bakunin from the International in 1872.

Meanwhile members of the First International watched with great excitement the Paris Commune of 1871, which they hoped might be the opening act of a European working-class upheaval. Members of the International infiltrated into the Commune, and the connection between the two, though rather incidental, was one reason why the French bourgeois repressed the Commune with such terrified ferocity. But the Commune actually killed the First International. The Commune had been bloody and violent; it had been an armed rebellion against the democratically elected National Assembly of France. Marx praised it as a stage in the international class war. He even saw in it a foretaste of what he was coming to call the "dictatorship of the proletariat." He thus frightened many possible followers away. Certainly British trade unionists, sober and steady men, could have nothing to do with such doings or such doctrines. The First International faded out of existence after 1872.

But in 1875, at the Gotha conference, Marxian and Lassallean socialists effected enough of a union to found the German Social Democratic party, whose growth thereafter, against Bismarck's attempts to stop it, has been already seen. About 1880 socialist parties sprouted up in many countries. In Belgium, highly industrialized, a Belgian Socialist Party appeared in 1879. In the industrial regions of France some workingmen were attracted to Jules Guesde, a self-taught worker, former Communard, and now a rigid Marxist, who held it impossible to emancipate the working class by compromise of any sort; others followed the "possibilist" Dr. Brousse, who thought it possible for workers to arrive at socialism through parliamentary methods; still others supported Jean Jaurès, who eloquently advocated social reform and the defense of republican institutions. Not until 1905 did the socialist groups in France form a unified Socialist party. In England, in 1881, H. M. Hyndman founded a Social Democratic Federation on the German model and with a Marxist program; it never had more than a handful of members. In 1883 two Russian exiles in Switzerland, Plekhanov and Axelrod, who had just been converted to Marxism, founded the Russian Social Democratic Party, from which the communism of the following century was eventually to be derived. The socialist parties all came together to establish an international league in 1889, known as the Second International, which thereafter met every three years and lasted until 1914.

REVISIONIST AND REVOLUTIONARY SOCIALISM, 1880–1914

The new socialist parties of the 1880's were all Marxist in inspiration. Marx died in 1883. Marxism or "scientific socialism," by the force of its social analysis, the mass of Marx's writings over forty years, and an attitude of un-yielding hostility to competing socialist doctrines, had become the only widely current form of systematic socialism that there was. Strongest in Germany and France, Marxism was relatively unsuccessful in Italy and Spain, where the working class, less industrialized anyway, more illiterate, unable to place its hopes in the ballot, and habituated to an excitable insurrectionism in the manner of Garibaldi, turned more frequently to the anarchism preached by Bakunin.

Nor was Marxism at all successful in England; the worker stood by his trade unions, and middle-class critics of capitalism followed the Fabian Society, established in 1883. The Fabians (so called from the ancient Roman general Fabius Cunctator, the "delayer," or strategist of gradual methods) were very English and very un-Marxist. George Bernard Shaw, H. G. Wells, and Sidney and Beatrice Webb were among early members of the Society. For them socialism was the social and economic counterpart to political democracy, as well as its inevitable outcome. They held that no class conflict was necessary or even existed, that gradual and reasonable and conciliatory measures would in due time bring about a socialist state, and that improvement of local government, or municipal ownership of such things as waterworks and electric lighting, were steps toward this consummation. The Fabians, like the trade union officials, were content with small and immediate satisfactions. They joined with the unions to form the Labor party. At the same time, by patient and detailed researches into economic realities, they provided a mass of practical information on which a legislative program could be based.

The Marxist or social democratic parties on the Continent grew very rapidly. Marxism turned into a less revolutionary "parliamentary socialism"— except indeed for the Russian Social Democratic party, since Russia had no parliamentary government. For the growth of socialist parties meant that true workingmen, and not merely intellectuals, were voting for socialist candidates for the Reichstag, Chambre des Députés, or whatever the lower house of parliament might be called; and this in turn meant that the psychology and influence of labor unions within the parties was increased. The workers, and their union officials, might in theory consider themselves locked in an enormous struggle with capital; but in practice their aim was to get more for themselves out of their employers' business. They might believe in the internationalism of the worker's interests; but in practice, acting through the parliaments of national states, they would work for orderly legislation benefiting the workers of their own country only—social insurance, factory regulation, minimum wages, or maximum hours. Nor was it possible to deny, by the close of the century, that Marx's anticipations (based initially on conditions of the 1840's) had not come true, at least not yet; the bourgeois was getting richer, but the proletarian was not getting poorer. Real wages—or what the wage-earner's income would actually buy, even allowing for the losses due to unemployment—are estimated to have risen about 50% in the industrialized countries between 1870 and 1900. The increase was due to the greater productivity of labor through mechanization, the growth of the world economy, the accumulation of capital wealth, and the ever stronger pressure of organized labor upon employers.

Repeatedly, but in vain, the Second International had to warn its component socialist parties against collaboration with the bourgeoisie. Marxism began in the 1890's to undergo a movement of revisionism, led in France by Jean Jaurès, socialist leader in the Chamber of Deputies, and in Germany by Eduard Bernstein, social democratic member of the Reichstag and author in 1898 of *Evolutionary Socialism*, an important tract setting forth the new views. The revisionists held that the class conflict might not be absolutely inevitable, that capitalism might be gradually transformed in the workers' interest, and that now that the workers had not only the vote, but a political party of their own, they could obtain their ends through democratic channels, without revolution and without any dictatorship of the proletariat. Most socialists or social democrats followed the revisionists.

This tendency to "opportunism" [28] among Marxists drove the really revolutionary spirits into new directions. Thus there arose revolutionary syndicalism, of which the main intellectual exponent was a Frenchman, Georges Sorel. Syndicalism is simply the French word for trade-unionism (*syndicat*, a union), and the idea was that the workers' unions might themselves become the supreme authoritative institutions in society, replacing not only property and the market economy, but government itself. The means to this end was to be a stupendous general strike, in which all workers in all industries should simultaneously stop work, thus paralyzing society and forcing acceptance of their will. Syndicalism made most headway where the unions were weakest, as in Italy, Spain, and France, since here the unions had the least to lose and were most in need of sensational doctrines to attract members. Its strongest base was in the French General Confederation of Labor, founded in 1895.

Among orthodox Marxists there was also a revival of Marxian fundamentals in protest against revisionism. In Germany Karl Kautsky arraigned

[28] See p. 502.

the revisionists as compromisers who betrayed Marxism for petty-bourgeois ends. In 1904 he and other rigorists prevailed upon the Second International to condemn the political behavior of the French Socialist Alexandre Millerand in accepting a ministerial post in a French cabinet. Socialists might use Parliament as a forum, the International ruled, but Socialists who entered the government itself were unpardonably identifying themselves with the enemy bourgeois state. Not until the First World War did Socialists henceforth join the cabinet of any European country. In the Russian Social Democratic party the issue of revisionism came to a head in 1903, at a party congress held in London—for the Russian Marxists were mainly exiles. Here a group led by Lenin demanded that revisionism be stamped out. Lenin won a majority, at the moment at least, and hence the uncompromising Marxists were called Bolsheviks (from the Russian word for majority), while the revisionist or conciliatory Russian Marxists, those willing to work with bourgeois liberals and democrats, were subsequently known as Mensheviks or the "minority" group.[29] But in 1903 the Russian Marxists were considered very unimportant.

In general, in Europe's "inner zone," by the turn of the century, most people who called themselves Marxists were no longer actively revolutionary. As revolutionary republicanism had quieted down in the Third French Republic, so revolutionary Marxism seemed to have quieted down into the milder doctrines of social democracy. What would have happened except for the coming of war in 1914 cannot be known; possibly social revolutionism would have revived, since real wages no longer generally rose between 1900 and 1914, and considerable restlessness developed in labor circles, punctuated by great strikes. But in 1914 the working class as a whole was in no revolutionary mood. Workers still sought a greater measure of social justice, but the social agitation so feared or hoped for in 1848 had subsided. There seem to have been three principal reasons: capitalism had worked well enough to raise the worker's living standard above what he could remember of his father's or grandfather's; the worker had the vote, and so felt that he participated in the state, could expect to benefit from the government, and had little to gain by its overthrow; and, thirdly, he had his interests watched over by organized and increasingly powerful unions, by which a larger share in the national income could be demanded and passed on to the worker.

75. Science, Philosophy, the Arts, and Religion

FAITH IN SCIENCE

Faith in the powers of natural science has been characteristic of modern society for three hundred years, but never has there been a time when this faith spread to so many people, or was held so firmly, so optimistically

---

[29] See p. 712.

and with so few qualms or mental reservations as in the half-century preceding the First World War. Science lay at the bottom of the whole movement of industrialization; and if science became positively popular after about 1870, in that persons ignorant of science came to look upon it as an oracle, it was because it manifested itself to everybody in the new wonders of daily life. Hardly had the world's more civilized regions digested the railroad, the steamship, and the telegraph when a whole series of new inventions already alluded to had begun to unfold itself. Medicine ran a tongue-twisting alphabetical gamut from anaesthetics to X rays. Chemistry discovered new fertilizers, and from coal tar alone produced a bewildering array ranging from artificial food flavors to high explosives. With the latter the first great tunnels were built, the Mont Cenis in 1873, the Simplon in 1906—both in the Alps; and great new canals, the Suez in 1869, the Kiel in 1895, the Panama in 1914. Electricity revolutionized all indoor and outdoor lighting. The telephone appeared in the 1870's. The invention of the internal combustion engine, to which electricity was a prerequisite, gave the world automobiles, airplanes, and submarines in the two decades before 1914. The moving picture and the radio likewise modestly presented themselves. In thirty years following 1875 the number of patents tripled in the United States, quadrupled in Germany, and multiplied in all the civilized countries; for the scientific and technical advance was as completely international (though confined mainly to the "inner zone") as any movement the world has ever seen. Never had the rush of scientific invention been so fundamentally useful, so helpful to the constructive labors and serious problems of mankind, and in that sense human.

In more basic scientific thinking important changes set in about 1860 or 1870. Up to that time, generally speaking, the underlying ideas had been those set forth by Isaac Newton almost two centuries before.[30] The law of universal gravitation reigned unquestioned, and with it, hardly less so, the geometry of Euclid and a physics that was basically mechanics. The ultimate nature of the universe was thought to be regular, orderly, predictable, and harmonious; it was also timeless, in that the passage of ages brought no change or development. By the end of the epoch considered here, that is by 1914, the old conceptions had begun to yield on every side.

THE IMPACT OF EVOLUTION

In impact upon general thinking the greatest change came in the new emphasis upon biology and the life sciences. Here the great symbolic date is the publication by Charles Darwin of the *Origin of Species* in 1859. Evolution, after Darwin, became the order of the day. Evolutionary philosophies, holding that the way to understand anything was to understand its development, were not new in 1859. Hegel had introduced the evolutionary conception into metaphysics; and he and Marx, into theories of human society.[31]

[30] See pp. 269–73.
[31] See pp. 439, 498–502.

The idea of progress, taken over from the Age of Enlightenment, was a kind of evolutionary philosophy; and the great activity in historical studies, under romantic and nationalistic auspices, had made people think of human affairs in terms of a time-process.[32] In the world of nature, the rise of geology after 1800 had opened the way to evolutionary ideas, and venturesome biologists had allowed themselves to speculate on an evolutionary development of living forms. What Darwin did was to stamp evolution with the seal of science, marshaling the evidence for it and offering an explanation of how it worked. In 1871, in his *Descent of Man*, he applied the same hypotheses to human beings.

By evolution, Darwin meant that species are mutable; that no species is created to remain unchanged once and for all; and that all species of living organisms, plant and animal, microscopic or elephantine in dimensions, living or extinct, have developed by successive small changes from other species that went before them. An important corollary was that all life was interrelated and subject to the same laws. Another corollary was that the whole history of living things on earth, generally held by scientists in Darwin's time to be many millions of years, was a unified history unfolding continuously in a single meaningful process of evolution.

Darwin thought that species changed, not by any intelligent or purposeful activity in the organism, but essentially by a kind of chance. Individual organisms, through the play of heredity, inherited slightly different characteristics, some more useful than others in food-getting, fighting, or mating; and the organisms that had the most useful characteristics tended to survive, so that their characteristics were passed on to offspring, until the whole species gradually changed. Certain phrases, not all of them invented by Darwin, summed up the theory. There was a "struggle for existence" resulting in the "survival of the fittest" through "natural selection" of the "most favored races"—races meaning not human races but the strains within a species. The struggle for existence referred to the fact that, in nature, more individuals were born in each species than could live out a normal life span; the "fittest" were those individual specimens of a species having the most useful characteristics, such as fleetness in deer or ferocity in tigers; "natural" selection meant that the fittest survived without purpose in themselves or in a Creator; the "favored races" were the strains within a species having good survival powers.

Darwin's ideas precipitated a great outcry. Scientists rushed to defend and churchmen to attack him. The biologist T. H. Huxley became the chief spokesman for Darwin—"Darwin's bulldog." He debated with, among others, the Bishop of Oxford. Darwin was denounced, with less than fairness, for saying that men came from monkeys. It was feared that all grounds of human dignity, morality, and religion would collapse. Darwin himself remained complacent on this score; under civilized conditions, he said, the social and cooperative virtues were useful characteristics assisting in survival, so that "we

---

[32] See pp. 290, 299–300, 403, 439–40.

may expect that virtuous habits will grow stronger, becoming perhaps fixed by inheritance." Much of the outburst against Darwin was somewhat trivial, nor were those who attacked him generally noted for spiritual insight; yet they were not mistaken in sensing a profound danger.

That Darwinism said nothing of God, Providence, or salvation was not surprising; no science ever did. That evolution did not exactly square with the first chapter of Genesis was disturbing but not fatal; much of the Old Testament was already regarded as symbolic, at least outside certain fundamentalist circles. Even the idea that man and the animals were of one piece was not ruinous; the animal side of human nature had not escaped the notice of theologians. The novel and upsetting effect of evolutionary biology was to change the conception of nature. Nature was no longer a harmony, it was a scene of struggle, "nature red in tooth and claw." Struggle and elimination of the weak were natural, and as means toward evolutionary development they might even be considered good. There were no fixed species or perfected forms, but only an unending flux. Change was everlasting; and everything seemed merely relative to time, place, and environment. There were no norms of good and bad; a good organism was one that survived where others perished; adaptation replaced virtue; outside of it there was nothing "right." The test was, in short, success; the "fit" were the successful; and here Darwinism merged with that *toughness* of mind, or *Realpolitik*, which came over Europe at the same time from other causes.[33]

Such at least were the implications if one generalized from science, carrying over scientific findings into human affairs, and the prestige of science was so great that this is precisely what many people wished to do. With the popularization of biological evolution, a school known as Social Darwinists actively applied the ideas of the struggle for existence and survival of the fittest to human society. Social Darwinists were found all over Europe and the United States. Their doctrines were put to various uses, to show that some peoples were naturally superior to others, such as whites to blacks, or Nordics to Latins, or Germans to Slavs (or vice versa) or non-Jews to Jews; or that the upper and middle classes, comfortable and contented, deserved these blessings because they had proved themselves "fitter" than the shiftless poor; or that big business in the nature of things had to take over smaller concerns; or that some states, such as the British or German Empire, were bound to rise; or that war was morally a fine thing, proving the virility and survival value of those who fought.

ANTHROPOLOGY, PSYCHOLOGY, THE NEW PHYSICS

The newer life sciences, such as anthropology and psychology, developed very rapidly in the latter part of the nineteenth century. Their effect upon the civilization of the day was not unlike that of Darwinism. Both ac-

[33] See pp. 493–5.

cepted biological evolution. Both, as the price of being truly scientific, eschewed standards of right and wrong and set themselves to finding out and explaining the mere facts of human behavior.

Anthropology set itself the task of studying the physical and cultural characteristics of all branches of mankind. Physical anthropologists became interested in the several human "races," some of which they considered might be "favored" in the Darwinian sense, that is superior in inheritance and survival value. It was often concluded, even by scientists at the time, that the whites were the most competent race, and among the whites the Nordics, Teutons, or Germans and Anglo-Saxons. The public, more or less exaggerating such ideas, became more race-conscious than Europeans had ever been before. On the other hand the cultural anthropologists, surveying all manner of primitive or complex societies with scientific disinterest, seemed sometimes to teach a more deflating doctrine. Scientifically, it seemed, no culture or society was "better" than any other, all being adaptations to an environment, or merely a matter of custom—of the *mores*, as people said in careful distinction from "morals." The effect was again a kind of relativism or skepticism— a negation of values, a belief that right and wrong were matters of social convention, psychological conditioning, mere opinion, or point of view. We are describing, let it be repeated, not the history of science itself but the effects of science upon European civilization at the time.

The impact of anthropology was felt keenly in religion too. Sir James Frazer (1854–1941) in his multi-volumed *The Golden Bough* could demonstrate that some of the most sacred practices, rites, and ideas of Christianity were not unique but could be found among primitive societies, and that, moreover, only the thinnest of lines divided magic from religion. Anthropology, Darwinian evolution, and other developments went far to upset traditional religious beliefs.

Psychology, as a science of human behavior, led to thoroughly upsetting implications about the very nature of man. It was launched in the 1870's as a natural science by the German physiologist Wilhelm Wundt (1832– 1920), who based his work on laboratory experiments with animals. The Russian Ivan Pavlov (1849–1936), also working with animals, conducted a famous series of experiments in which he "conditioned" dogs to salivate automatically at the ringing of a bell once they had become accustomed over a period of time to associate the sound with the serving of their food. Pavlov's observations were important; they implied that a great part of animal behavior, and presumably human behavior, could be explained on the basis of conditioned responses. In the case of humans these would be responses which men have become trained to make automatically by virtue of their environment and upbringing, and that they do not make through choice or conscious reasoning. Most significant of all the developments in psychology was the work of Sigmund Freud (1856–1939) and those inspired by him. Freud, a Viennese physician, came to the conclusion that certain forms of mental disturbance like hysteria could be traced to earlier completely forgotten episodes of a patient's life, perhaps even to his infancy. From this Freud began to explore the drives, frustrations, and repressions within the mind itself that influence every individual's behavior without his even being aware of it. Freud and the new schools of psychology all laid great stress on the unconscious. Revealing the wide areas of human behavior that lie outside conscious control, they showed the ways in which man was not a rational being; they suggested in essence that man was not primarily a rational being at all.

The revolutionary conclusions of the nineteenth and early twentieth centuries, initiated in biology and the life sciences, had their counterpart in mathematics and physics. By 1914, a mathematics of four dimensions, inconceivable to the layman, was commonplace to mathematicians. Discoveries in magnetism, electricity, and radiation made physics unimaginable to the ordinary person, who had formerly been able to imagine the hard round bodies of Newtonian physics clearly enough. With the "quantum theory," signalized by Planck's hypothesis in 1900, it appeared that neither cause and effect nor time and space were present in the sub-atomic world. With the work of Albert Einstein (1879–1955), beginning soon after 1900, it appeared that time and space were interdependent, that matter and energy were interchangeable according to a formula that he gave, and that no such thing as absolute motion could be discovered. Even Newton's "law of universal gravitation" no longer applied within the atom, nor indeed to the cosmos as a whole. All this was popularly called "relativity." From it was to develop the whole realm of nuclear physics and the tapping of the atom's energy. But physics really became too specialized for the layman to grasp, or for history to record.

TRENDS IN PHILOSOPHY AND THE ARTS

The step from pure science to philosophy is a long one, but one that many were prepared to take. Not only was the faith in science widespread but it was widely held that science was the only means of certain knowledge, and that anything unknowable to science must remain unknowable forever—a doctrine called agnosticism, or the acknowledgment of ignorance. Herbert Spencer (1820–1903) in England and Ernst Haeckel (1834–1919) in Germany were widely read popularizers of agnosticism; both also pictured a universe governed by Darwinian evolution. For Spencer especially, all philosophy could be unified, organized, and co ordinated through the doctrine of evolution; this doctrine he applied not only to all living things but to sociology, government, and economics as well. The evolution of society, he felt, was toward the increasing freedom of the individual, the role of governments being merely to maintain freedom and justice; they were not to interfere with natural, social, and economic processes, nor to coddle the weak and unfit. Yet, like Darwin himself, Spencer believed that altruism, charity, and good will as individual ethical virtues were themselves useful and laudable products of evolutionary development.

These latter views were not shared by another of the serious writers of the age, also much influenced by evolutionary ideas, the German philosopher Friedrich Nietzsche (1844–1900). More a philosopher of art than of science, and drawing from many intellectual currents of the century, Nietzsche was an unsystematic and unclear thinker to whom it is easy to do less than justice. It is evident, however, that his opinion of mankind was a low one, and that from a background of evolutionary thinking he developed some kind of doctrine of a Superman, a noble being who, in a final triumph of world history, should issue from, lead, dominate, and dazzle the multitude. Qualities of humility, patience, brotherly helpfulness, hope and love, in short the specifically Christian virtues, Nietzsche described as a slave morality concocted by the weak to disarm the strong. Qualities of courage, love of danger, intellectual excellence, and beauty of character he considered much better. Such views, for better or worse, were actually a new form of paganism. Nietzsche was neither much read nor much respected by his contemporaries, who considered him unbalanced or even insane; but he nevertheless, as a philosopher should, expressed with unshrinking frankness many ideas implied in the outlook of his day.

In works of creative imagination—pure literature and the fine arts—the dawn of the twentieth century showed many signs of a troubled day. Some writers, like Zola in France or Ibsen in Scandinavia, turned to the portrayal of social problems, producing a realistic literature dealing with industrial strife, strikes, prostitution, divorce, or insanity. Freudian and other views of psychology slowly made themselves felt in works of fiction; the new novels were often more lifelike than the old, but they added little to one's faith in human nature. The arts followed the intellectual developments of the age, reflecting prevalent attitudes of relativism, irrationalism, social determinism, and interest in the subconscious. On the other hand, never had artist and society been so far apart. The painter Gauguin, an extreme case, fled to the South Seas, went primitive, and reveled in the stark violence of tropical colors. Never had there been a civilization with so little understanding between artist and public, to the great disadvantage of both; for the artist, sensing an indifferent public, often became absorbed in technicalities of his art or mere capricious self-expression, and the public, having no sense of living art, often let its imagination be governed by insignificant or merely inherited books or pictures. Art at its extreme fringe became as incomprehensible as physics, and the average man was deprived of a means (as old as the cave paintings of the Stone Age) of perceiving, seizing, and enjoying the world about him.

It was apparent that the arts by 1900 suffered from the extreme specialization of the modern world. The artist was not thought of as a collective spokesman or creator of something for common use. Like the mathematician, philosopher, historian, doctor, business man, or politician, he was thought of as a specialist plying his own trade and pursuing his own concerns. Society was divided into busy groups almost unknown to one another, unable to communicate except on superficial matters, and hence in the long run less able to sympathize, to understand, or to work in common.

THE CHURCHES AND THE MODERN AGE

Religion, too, was displaced. It was now a long time since almost everyone had looked to religion for guidance. But religion was more threatened after 1860 or 1870 than ever in the past, because never before had science, or philosophies drawing upon science, addressed themselves so directly to the existence of life and of man. Never before had so many of the fundamental premises of traditional religion been questioned or denied. Darwinian evolution had challenged the traditional picture of Creation, and anthropologists had questioned the uniqueness of the most sacred Christian tenets. There developed also the textual, or "higher," criticism of the Bible, an effort to apply to the Scriptures the techniques of scholarship long applied to secular documents, and to reconstruct a naturalistic, historical account of ancient religious times. The movement, going back at least to the seventeenth century,[34] now took on significant proportions and was applied both to the Old Testament and the New. In the case of the Old Testament the patient scrutiny of style and language cast doubt on the validity of certain prophecies; and in the New the inconsistencies of the several Gospel sources were made patent. The German theologian David Friedrich Strauss (1808–74), one such critical scholar, was the author of a widely discussed *Life of Jesus*, in which many miraculous and supernatural episodes were reverently but firmly explained away as "myth." The sensitive French historian and man of letters Ernest Renan (1823–92) in a somewhat similar vein wrote on the origins of Christianity and on the life of ancient Israel. The ordinary person's long-established articles of faith were being further undermined. Moreover, the whole tenor of the time, its absorption in material progress, likewise kept people away from church; and the wholesale uprooting, the movement from country to city, often broke religious ties.

The Protestant churches were less successful than the Catholic in protecting their membership from the disintegrating effects of the age. Church attendance among Protestants became increasingly casual, and the doctrines set forth in sermons seemed increasingly remote. Protestant laymen traditionally trusted their own private judgment, and regarded their clergy as their own agents, not as authoritative teachers placed above them. Protestants also had always set especial emphasis on the Bible as the source of religious belief; and as doubts accumulated on the literal truth of Biblical narratives there seemed no other source on which to rely.

Protestants tended to divide between modernists and fundamentalists. The fundamentalists, as they were called in the United States, in an effort to

---

[34] See p. 280.

defend the literal word of Scripture were often obliged to deny the most indubitable findings of science. The modernists were willing enough to be scientific and to interpret much of the Bible as allegory, but they could with difficulty recapture any spirituality or urgent feeling of Christian truth. Most Protestant churches were slow to face the social problems and wholesale injustices produced by the economic system, though a group of "Christian socialists" developed, notably within the Church of England. And as education and the care of orphans, aged, sick, and insane persons passed to the state, Protestant groups had less to do in the relief of suffering and upbringing of the young. Protestantism, to the regret of many Protestants, became increasingly a customary observance by people whose minds were elsewhere. Not until the middle of the twentieth century could a strong Protestant revival be discerned, with a reaffirmation of basic doctrines by thinkers like Karl Barth and Reinhold Niebuhr, and a movement on the part of divergent Protestant churches to combine.

The Roman Catholic Church proved more resistant to the trends of the age. We have seen how Pope Pius IX (1846–78), after being driven from Rome by republicans in 1848, gave up his inclinations to liberalism.[35] In 1864, in the *Syllabus of Errors*, he denounced as erroneous a long list of widely current ideas, including the faith in rationalism and science, and he vigorously denied that the head of the Church "should reconcile and align himself with progress, liberalism, and modern civilization." The *Syllabus* was in form a warning to Catholics, not a matter of dogma incumbent upon them to believe. In dogma, the Immaculate Conception of the Virgin Mary was announced as dogmatic truth in 1854; this ended an old dispute within the church, and reaffirmed in a skeptical age certain distinctive features of Catholic worship.

Pius IX also convened an ecumenical church council (the first since the Council of Trent, nor has there been one since) which met at the Vatican in 1870. The Vatican Council proclaimed the dogma of papal infallibility, which holds that the Pope, when speaking *ex cathedra* on matters of faith and morals, speaks with a final and supernatural authority which no Catholic may question or reject. The Vatican Council, and the acceptance of papal infallibility by Catholics (except for a few dissidents like the Old Catholics in Germany who soon became unimportant), was only the climax of centuries of development within the church. In brief, as the world grew more national, Catholicism became more international. As state sovereignty and secularism grew, Catholic clergy looked increasingly to the spiritual powers of Rome. Much in the past three hundred years had made Catholics distrustful of their own governments or of non-Catholics in their midst—the Protestantism and the state churches of the sixteenth century, the Jansenist movement of the seventeenth, the anti-clericalism of enlightened despotism in the eighteenth, the hostility to the church shown by the French Revolution, and by liberalism, republicanism, and socialism in the nineteenth century. The net effect

᠁᠁᠁᠁᠁᠁᠁

[35] See pp. 484–5.

was to throw Catholics into the arms of the Holy See. Ultramontanism, the unconditional acceptance of papal jurisdiction, prevailed over the old Gallican and other national tendencies within the church.

In 1870, while the six hundred prelates of the Vatican Council were sitting, the new Italian state unceremoniously entered and annexed the city of Rome.[36] The pope's temporal power thus disappeared. It is now widely agreed that with the loss of local temporal interests the spiritual hold of the papacy on Catholics throughout the world has been enhanced. The popes long refused, however, to recognize the loss of Rome; and each pope in turn, from 1870 to 1929, adopted a policy of self-imprisonment in the Vatican grounds. By the Lateran treaty of 1929 the papacy finally recognized the Italian state, and Italy conceded, along with much else, the existence of a Vatican City about a square mile in area, as an independent state not legally within Italy at all. The papacy thus gained that independence from national or secular authority deemed necessary by Catholics to the performance of its role.

Pius IX's successor, Leo XIII (1878–1903), carried on the counteroffensive against irreligion, and instituted a revival of medieval philosophy as represented by Thomas Aquinas.[37] But Leo XIII is chiefly remembered for formulating Catholic social doctrine, especially in the encyclical *Rerum Novarum* ("of modern things") of 1891, to which subsequent pontiffs have adhered, and from which various movements of Catholic socialism are derived. *Rerum Novarum* upheld private property as a natural right, within the limits of justice; but it criticized capitalism for the poverty, insecurity, and even degradation in which many of the laboring classes were left. It declared that much in socialism was Christian in principle; but it criticized socialism in so far as (like Marxism) it was materialistic and anti-religious. The pope therefore recommended that Catholics, if they wished, form socialist parties of their own, and that Catholic workingmen form labor unions under Catholic auspices. Since the 1830's there had been individual Catholics and Catholic clergy who were socialists, or at least severe critics of the then emerging social order; these were encouraged by the encyclical of 1891, and Catholic (or Christian, as they were often called) socialist parties and labor unions began to appear at the turn of the century. The Roman church thus undertook to free itself from dependency upon capitalism. At the same time it took steps to insure that a future society, if socialistic, might be Catholic also.

The next pope, Pius X (1903–14), stamped out "modernism," or the belief that the church should modify its basic doctrines, to make them consistent with modern science. Modernism in this sense, defined as heresy in 1907, has disappeared among Catholics; but, since much of modern science is declared to be irrelevant to spiritual truth, Catholics have generally been able to embrace such scientific ideas as they wished. The church, as an organ-

[36] See p. 526.
[37] See pp. 37–8.

ized institution, undertook to emancipate itself from science as it did from capitalism and from non-Catholic socialism, marking out instead a way of its own, and never surrendering its ancient position, much battered by the secularism of modern times, that all worldly concerns should be subordinated to a spiritual authority, transmitted from Christ himself, and exercised by a Catholic hierarchy headed by the bishop of Rome.

As for Judaism, the Jews were a small minority, but their condition had always been a kind of barometer reflecting changes in the atmosphere of Europe as a whole. In the nineteenth century the basic trend was toward "emancipation" and "assimilation." Science and secularism had the same dissolving effect upon Orthodox Judaism as upon traditional Christianity. Reform Judaism grew up as the Jewish counterpart to "modernism" in other faiths. Individual Jews increasingly gave up their old distinctive Jewish way of life. In society at large, the prevalence of liberalism allowed them to act as citizens and to enter business or the professions like everybody else. Jews were thus freed from old legal discriminations that had been imposed on them for centuries.

Toward the end of the century two tendencies, counter to assimilation, became evident. One originated with Jews themselves, some of whom feared an assimilation that would lead to a loss of Jewish identity and perhaps even the disappearance of Judaism itself. Some Jews therefore (like other peoples with similar fears) launched a nationalist movement of their own. Jewish nationalism expressed itself in Zionism; the first international Zionist congress met at Basel in 1897. Zionists hoped to establish a Jewish state in Palestine, in which Jews from all the world might find refuge. Since the Jews had not had an independent kingdom in Palestine since 586 B.C., nor even a dependent kingdom since A.D. 100, this must be accounted the most extreme of the nineteenth-century nationalist revivals.

The other counter-tendency, a barrier to assimilation, was the rise of anti-Semitism, noticeable in many quarters by 1900. Racialistic theories, dislike for Jewish competitors in business and the professions, socialist scorn for Jewish capitalists like the Rothschilds, upper-class fears of Jewish revolutionaries like Karl Marx, together with a growth of ethnical nationalism, which held that France should be purely French and Latin, Germany purely German and Nordic, or Russia purely Russian and Slav, all combined to raise an anti-Semitic hue and cry. In Russia there were actual pogroms, or massacres of Jews. In France the Dreyfus case, dragged out from 1894 to 1906, revealed unsuspected depths of anti-Semitic fury. Many Jews were forced by such hostility into a new sense of Jewish identity. Many, wishing civic assimilation yet despairing of obtaining it, began to sympathize with the Jewish nationalist movement, looking to Zionism and a Jewish renascence as a way to maintain their own dignity. Others insisted that Judaism was a religious faith, not a nationality by itself; that Jews and non-Jews within the same country shared in exactly the same nationality, citizenship, and political and social outlook. Liberals and democrats were of the same opinion. On the integration of Jews into the larger community the traditions of the Enlightenment, the American and French Revolutions, the empire of Napoleon I, and the liberalism of the nineteenth century all agreed.

76. The Waning of Classical Liberalism

The net effect of the political, economic, and intellectual trends described above seemed twofold in nature: there was a continued advance of much that was basic to liberalism and at the same time a weakening of the grounds on which liberalism had firmly rested ever since the seventeenth and eighteenth centuries. A third effect might be noted too: even where the essentials of liberalism persisted, its program and doctrines underwent important changes; liberalism persisted but the classical type of liberalism was in eclipse.

Classical liberalism, the liberalism in its heyday in the nineteenth century, went back at least as far as John Locke in the seventeenth century and the *philosophes* of the eighteenth, and found its highest nineteenth-century expression in the writings of men like John Stuart Mill and in the political outlook of men like William Gladstone. Classical liberalism had as its deepest principle the liberty of the individual person.[88] Man, each man or specimen of mankind, according to liberals, was or could become a free-standing human being. He was not a class-man, nor a race-man, nor a church-man, nor a nation-man, nor a state-man. Morally, he was independent of all such things; he did not owe his nature or being to any of them; he did not have such-and-such ideas because he belonged to such-and-such a group. He was capable of the free use of reason, or of thinking things out independently of his particular interests, prejudices, or subconscious drives. And, since this was so, people of different interests could reasonably and profitably discuss their differences, make compromises, and reach solutions by peaceable agreement. It was because they thought all men potentially reasonable that liberals favored education. They opposed all imposition of force upon the individual, from physical torture to mental indoctrination. In religion, liberals thought each individual should adopt any faith or no faith as he chose, and that churches and clergy should play little or no part in public affairs. In politics, they thought that governments should be constitutional and limited in power, with individuals governing themselves through their chosen representatives, with issues presented, discussed, and decided by the use of intelligence, both by the voters in election campaigns and by elected deputies in parliamentary debate. The will of a majority, or larger number of individuals, was taken as decisive, with the understanding that the minority might become a majority in its turn through individual changes of opinion. At first

~~~~~~~~~~~~~~~~~~~~~~

[88] See pp. 432–3.

distrustful of democracy, fearing the excesses of popular rule, and eager to limit political power and the suffrage to the propertied classes, in the course of the nineteenth century liberals had accepted the democratic principle of universal manhood suffrage. In economics, liberals thought of the whole world as peopled by individuals doing business with one another—buying and selling, borrowing and lending, hiring and firing—without interference from governments and without regard to religion or politics, both of which were thought to impose superficial differences upon the underlying uniformity of mankind. The practical consequences of liberalism were toleration, constitutionalism, *laissez-faire*, free trade, and an international or non-national economic system. It was thought that all peoples would progress to these same ends.

There never was a time, even in one country, when all liberal ideas were simultaneously triumphant. Pure liberalism has never existed except as a doctrine. Advancing in one way, liberalism would be blocked or reversed in another. On the whole, Europe before 1914 was predominantly liberal. But signs of the wane of liberalism set in clearly about 1880; many have already been mentioned in this chapter.

THE DECLINE OF NINETEENTH-CENTURY LIBERALISM:

ECONOMIC TRENDS

The free economy produced many hardships. The workingmen tossed by the ups and downs of a labor market, the producer tossed by those of a world commodity market, alike clamored for protection against exposure. A severe depression in 1873 sent prices and wages into collapse. European farmers, both small French farm owners and big *Junker* landlords of East Germany, demanded tariff protection: they could not compete with the American Middle West or the steppes of South Russia, both opened up by rail and steamship, and both of which after 1870 poured their cereals at low prices into Europe. The revival of tariffs, and decline of free trade, very marked in Europe about 1880, thus began with the protection of agricultural interests. Industry soon demanded the same favors. In Germany the *Junkers* and the rising Rhineland industrialists joined forces in 1879 to extort a tariff from Bismarck. The French in 1892 adopted a high tariff to shelter both manufacturing and agricultural interests. The United States, rapidly industrializing, also put up protective tariffs beginning in the 1860's, the earliest of all.

The industrial revolution was now definitely at work in other countries than Great Britain. There was an increasing resistance to buying manufactures from England, selling only raw materials and foodstuffs in return. Everywhere there was a revival of the arguments of the German economist Friedrich List, who a half-century before, in his *National System of Political Economy* (1840), had branded free trade as a system mainly advantageous to the British, and declared that no country could become strong, independent, or even fully civilized if it remained a semi-rustic supplier of unfinished goods.[39] With Germany, the United States, and Japan manufacturing for export, a nationalist competition for world markets set in, contributing also to the drive for colonies and the phenomena of imperialism described in the next chapter. The new imperialism was another sign of the waning of liberalism, which had been largely indifferent to colonies.

In all these respects the division between politics and economics, postulated by liberals, began to fade. A kind of neo-mercantilism arose, recalling the attempts of governments in the seventeenth and eighteenth centuries to subordinate economic activity to political ends. A better term is economic nationalism, which became noticeable by 1900, though still only a faint anticipation of what it was to become after the First World War. Nations struggled to better themselves by tariffs, by trade rivalries, and by internal regulation, without regard to the effect upon other nations. And for the individual worker or business man also, in purely economic matters, it now made a great difference to what nation he belonged, by what government he was backed, and under what laws he lived.

It was of course to protect themselves against insecurity and abuse as individuals that workers formed labor unions. It was likewise to protect themselves against the uncertainties of uncontrolled markets that business interests began to merge, to concentrate in large corporations, or to form monopolies, trusts, or cartels. The rise of big business and organized labor undermined the theory and practice of individual competition to which classical liberalism had been attached. Organized labor, socialist parties, the effects of universal suffrage, and a sensitivity to social distress all obliged political leaders to intervene increasingly in economic matters. Factory codes became more detailed and better enforced. Social insurance, initiated by Bismarck, spread to other countries. Governments regulated the purity of food and drugs. The social service state developed, a state assuming responsibility for the social and economic welfare of the mass of its own subjects. The "new" liberalism, that of the Liberals in England of the David Lloyd George era, of the Republican President Theodore Roosevelt and the Democratic President Woodrow Wilson in the United States, accepted the enlarged role of the government in social and economic matters. Both Theodore Roosevelt and Wilson, and others, sought also to re-establish economic competition by government action against monopolies and trusts. The new liberals were generally less well disposed toward business than toward workingmen and the depressed classes, seeing in the amelioration of their lot a vindication of the basic humanitarian concern of liberalism with the dignity and worth of the individual person. The welfare state, remote as it was from the conceptions of the older liberalism, seemed to be the direction taken by the new liberals. Others, liberal and otherwise, viewed with concern the growing power of governments and centralized authority, and were apprehensive for individual liberties.

~~~~~~~~~~~~~~~~~~~~

[39] See p. 440.

THE DECLINE OF THE OLDER LIBERALISM:

INTELLECTUAL CURRENTS AND EVENTS OF THE AGE

Liberalism, both old and new, was undermined also by many developments in the field of thought described earlier in this chapter—Darwinian
evolution, the new psychology, trends in philosophy and the arts. Paradoxi-
cally, this great age of science found that man was not a rational animal. Darwinian theory implied that man was merely a highly evolved organism whose
faculties were merely adaptations to an environment. Psychology seemed
to teach that what was called reason was often only rationalization, or a
finding of alleged "reasons" to justify material wants or emotional and unconscious needs, and that conscious reflection dominated only a narrow part of
human behavior. Ideas themselves were said to be the products of conditioning. There were English ideas or Anglo-Saxon ideas, or bourgeois or progressive or reactionary ideas. Politically, it began to be felt that parties or nations
with conflicting interests could never reasonably agree on a program common
to both, since neither could ever get beyond the limitations of its own outlook. It became common to dismiss the arguments of an adversary without
further thought, and without any expectation that thought could overcome
difficulties. This insidious "anti-intellectualism" was destructive to liberal
principles. If, because of prior conditioning, it was impossible for anyone to
change his mind, then there was no hope of settling matters by persuasion.

From the view that man was not essentially a rational being, which
in itself was only a scientific attempt at a better understanding of human
behavior, it was but a short step deliberately to reject reason and to emphasize and cultivate the irrational, to stress the will, intuition, impulse, and
emotion, and to place a new value on violence and conflict. A philosophy of
"realism," a kind of unrealistic faith in the constructive value of struggle and
a tough-minded rejection of ideas and ideals, spread. It was not new. Marxism,
since the 1840's, had taught that class war, latent or open, was the motivating power of history. Schopenhauer earlier in the century had written that
the underlying reality of the universe was a blind, instinctual, dynamic will
to survive.[40] In this age Nietzsche rejected the ordinary virtues in favor of
courage and daring; the Social Darwinists glorified the successful and the
dominant in all phases of human activity as the "fit" in the perpetual struggle for existence. Other thinkers embraced a frank irrationalism. Among these
may be mentioned Georges Sorel, the philosopher of syndicalism, who, in
his *Reflections on Violence* in 1908, declared that violence was good irrespective of the end accomplished (so much did he hate existing society), and
that workingmen should be kept alert in the class war through believing in
the "myth" of a future general strike, even though such a strike, with its
attendant débacle of bourgeois civilization, was in fact known to be only a

[40] See p. 494.

"myth." The function of thought, in this philosophy of the social myth, was to keep people agitated and excited and ready for action, not to achieve any correspondence with rational or objective truth. Such ideas passed into the fascism that followed the First World War.

Thus, the end of the nineteenth century, the greatest age of peace in Europe's history, abounded in philosophies glorifying struggle. Men who had never heard a shot fired in anger solemnly announced that world history moved forward by violence and antagonism. They said not merely that struggle existed (which would have been a purely factual statement) but that struggle was a positive good through which progress was to be accomplished. The popularity of struggle was due not only to the intellectuals but in part to actual historical events. People remembered that before 1871 certain weighty questions had been settled by force, that the movements of social revolution in 1848 and in the Paris Commune of 1871 had been put down by the military, and that the unity of Italy and Germany, as well as of the United States, had been confirmed by war. In addition, after 1871, all Continental European states maintained large standing armies, the largest ever maintained until then in time of peace.

In economic and political matters, even in England, the homeland of liberalism, there were numerous signs between 1900 and 1914 that the older liberalism was on the wane. Joseph Chamberlain led a movement to return to tariff protection (to repeal, so to speak, the repeal of the Corn Laws); it failed at the time, but was strong enough to disorient the Conservative party in 1906. The Liberal party abandoned its traditional *laissez-faire* policy in sponsoring the labor legislation of the years following 1906. The new Labor party required its members in Parliament to vote as directed by the party, thus initiating a system of party solidarity, eventually copied by others, that hardened the lines of opposition, denied that individuals should freely change sides, and hence reduced the practical significance of parliamentary discussion. The Irish nationalists had long used unparliamentary methods; in 1914, when Parliament at last enacted Irish home rule, the anti-Irish and Conservative interests prepared to resist parliamentary action by force. The suffragettes, as women pioneering for woman suffrage were called, despairing of ever getting the men to listen to reason, resorted to amazingly "un-English" and unreasonable arguments. They chained themselves to public buildings, smashed the store fronts in Bond Street, threw acids into mailboxes, and broke porcelains in the British Museum; when arrested they went on hunger strikes threatening self-starvation, to which the police replied by "forcible feeding" through tubes lowered into the ladies' stomachs. And in 1911 and 1912 great railway and coal strikes disclosed the sheer power of organized labor.

Still, it is the persistence of liberalism rather than its wane that should be emphasized at the close of a chapter on European civilization before 1914. Tariffs existed, but goods still circulated freely in world trade. Nationalism was heightened, but there was nothing like totalitarianism. Racialistic ideas were in the air, but at least in Europe and America, as among whites, they had little political importance. Anti-Semitism was sometimes vocal; but all governments except the Russian protected the rights of Jews, and the years from 1848 to 1914 were in fact the great period of Jewish integration into general society. The *laissez-faire* state was disappearing, but social legislation continued the humanitarian strain that had always been the essence of liberalism. A few advanced revolutionaries preached social catastrophism, but social democrats and laboring men were overwhelmingly revisionist, loyal to parliamentary procedures and to their existing states. Doctrinaires exalted the grim beauty of war, but all governments down to 1914 tried to prevent war among the great powers. And there was still a supreme faith in progress.

CHAPTER XV

Europe's World
Supremacy

〜〜〜〜〜〜〜〜〜〜〜〜〜〜〜〜〜〜〜〜〜〜〜〜〜

77. Imperialism: Its Nature and Causes

78. The Americas

79. The Dissolution of the Ottoman Empire

80. The Partition of Africa

81. Imperialism in Asia: The Dutch, the British, and the Russians

82. Imperialism in Asia: China and the West

83. The Russo-Japanese War and Its Consequences

A CENTURY ago the great segments of mankind still lived apart. China was a world in itself, India a world, Negro Africa a world, Islam a world, penetrating, to be sure, each of the three others. Europe and its American offshoot formed the Western world. Each of these several worlds had developed its own way of life, most deeply differentiated by the religion it had long ago adopted, in the millennium running from Confucius and Buddha through Jesus to Mohammed. Within each of these worlds there was much coming and going—Moslems, for example, could move from Morocco to the East Indies—but each world remained mysterious and unknown to the others. It was the European white men who first brought them all into an interconnected society.

European civilization, as described in the last chapter, spread to and influenced all the earth, especially after about 1870. The large nation-states, whose consolidation was traced in the chapter before last, gained empires for themselves in Africa, Asia, and the islands of the sea. In opposition to these empires, non-European and subject peoples began to assert ideas learned from Europe—ideas of liberty, democracy, independence, nationalism, sovereignty, and of an anti-capitalism that might pass easily into socialism. They brought into Asia, and more slowly into Africa, the substance of the European revolutions of 1789 and 1848. European history broadened out into the history of the world.

The emergence of an interrelated world civilization was obviously a fact of momentous import. But the process was barely begun, and it created innumerable dislocations and difficulties. Tribal societies and complex old civilizations were alike penetrated by the West. Modern science, modern weapons of warfare, modern machine industry, modern communications, modern capitalism and wage-labor, modern forms of taxation, law-enforcement, and debt-collecting, modern practices in medicine and sanitation (along with certain "modern" diseases such as syphilis or alcoholism) were suddenly pressed in an overwhelming mass upon bewildered peoples who for generations could neither resist them, adjust to them, nor control them.

All peoples were drawn into a world economy and a world market. But it was the Europeans who reaped the reward in the form of rising material standards of living. In India, China, or Africa the native industries often suffered, and many people found it harder than ever to subsist even at a low level. The building of railways in China, for example, threw boatmen, carters, or innkeepers out of work. In India, the hand spinners and weavers of cotton could not compete in their own villages with the machine-made products of Lancashire. In parts of Africa, Negro tribes which had lived by owning herds of cattle, moving from place to place to obtain grazing lands, found white farmers or plantation or mine owners occupying their country, and were often forced by the white man's law to give up their migratory habits. Peoples of all races began to produce for export—rubber, raw cotton, jute, copra, tin, gold—and hence were exposed to the rise and fall of world prices. A depression tended to become a world depression, dragging all down alike.

Neither the world economy, nor the world market, nor the international investment of capital or movement of people, nor the spread and exchange of scientific or technical or military or medical ideas, absolutely presupposed any one kind of political system or domination by any one part of the world. Presumably, the tendencies toward a world-wide civilization will continue despite all political changes. In the period from 1870 to 1914 they went along with imperialism, which may be briefly defined as the government of one people by another. European imperialism (including that of the United States and Japan) was the first phase in the spread of the industrial and scientific civilization which originated in Europe's "inner zone." [1] That it

---

[1] See pp. 557–9.

was not the last phase became clear as the twentieth century unfolded. The
subordinated peoples, forcibly introduced to the West by imperialism, came
to feel a need for modernizing and industrializing their own countries, and
for the aid of European or American science, skill and capital; but they wished
to get rid of imperialists, govern themselves, and control the conditions under
which modernization and borrowing should take place. The present chapter
deals only with the imperialist phase.

77. Imperialism: Its Nature and Causes

European civilization had always shown a tendency to expand. In the
Middle Ages Latin Christendom spread by conquest and conversion to include the whole area from Spain to Finland. Then came the age of overseas
discoveries and the founding of colonial empires, whose struggles filled the
seventeenth and eighteenth centuries, and of which the Europeanization of
the Americas was the most far-reaching consequence. At the same time European culture spread among the upper classes of Russia. The defeat of
Napoleon left only one of the old colonial empires standing in any strength,
namely the British. For sixty years after 1815 there were no significant colonial rivalries. In many circles there was an indifference to overseas empire.
Under principles of free trade, it was thought unnecessary to exercise political
influence in areas in which one did business. Actually, in these years, the
French moved into Algeria, the British strengthened their Indian empire, the
Dutch developed Java and the neighboring islands more intensively, and the
Western powers "opened" Japan and began to penetrate China. But there
was no overt conflict among Europeans, and no systematic program, doctrine
or "ism."

Rather suddenly, about 1870 or 1880, colonial questions came again to
the fore. In the short space of two decades, by 1900, the advanced countries
partitioned most of the earth among themselves. A world map by 1900
showed their possessions in some eight or ten colors.

THE NEW IMPERIALISM

The new imperialism differed both economically and politically from
the colonialism of earlier times. The older empires had been maritime and
mercantile. The European trader, in India, Java, or Canton, had simply purchased the wares brought to him by native merchants as produced by native
methods. He operated on a kind of cash-and-carry basis. European governments had had no territorial ambitions beyond the protection of way stations
and trading centers. To these generalizations America had been an exception;
it had neither native states which Europeans respected, nor native industries
in which Europeans were interested, and Europeans therefore developed ter-

ritorial claims, and invested capital and brought in their own methods of production and management, most especially in the then booming sugar islands of the West Indies.[2]

Under the new imperialism Europeans were by no means content simply to purchase what native merchants provided. They wanted goods of a kind or in a quantity that pre-industrial handicraft methods could not supply. They moved into the "backward" countries more thoroughly. They invested capital in them, setting up mines, plantations, docks, warehouses, factories, refineries, railroads, river steamships, banks. They built offices, homes, hotels, clubs, and cool mountain resorts suitable for white men in the tropics. Taking over the productive life of the country, they transformed large elements of the local population into the wage employees of foreign owners, and so introduced the class problems of industrial Europe in a form accentuated by racial difference. Or they lent money to native rulers—the Khedive of Egypt, the Shah of Persia, the Emperor of China—to enable them to hold up their tottering thrones, or simply to live with more pleasure and magnificence than they could pay for from their usual revenues. Europeans thus developed a huge financial stake in governments and economic enterprises outside the pale of Western civilization.

To secure these investments, and for other reasons, in contrast to what had happened under the older colonialism, the Europeans now aspired to political and territorial domination. Some areas became outright "colonies," directly governed by white men. Others became "protectorates": here the native chief, sultan, bey, rajah, or prince was maintained and guaranteed against internal upheaval or external conquest. A European "resident" or "commissioner" usually told him what to do. In other regions, as in China or Persia, where no single European state could make good its claims against the others, they arranged to divide the country into "spheres of influence," each European power having advisory privileges, and investment and trade opportunities within its own sphere. The sphere of influence was the vaguest of all forms of imperial control; supposedly, it left the country independent.

An enormous differential opened up, about 1875, between the power of European and non-European states. Queen Elizabeth had dealt with the Great Mogul with genuine respect. Even Napoleon had pretended to regard the Shah of Persia as an equal. Then came the industrial revolution in Europe, iron and steel ships, heavier naval guns, more accurate rifles. Democratic and nationalistic movements produced large and solid European peoples, united in the service of their governments as no "backward" people ever was. Seemingly endless wealth, with modern administration, allowed governments to tax, borrow and spend almost without limit. The civilized states loomed as enormous power-complexes without precedent in the world's history. At the same time it so happened that all the principal non-European empires were in decay. They were receiving a minimum of support from their own subjects. As in the eighteenth century the disintegration of the Mogul

---

[2] See pp. 229–30.

empire had enabled the British to take over in India,[3] so in the nineteenth century the decrepitude of the Sultan of Turkey, the Sultan of Zanzibar, the Shah of Persia, the Emperor of China, and the Shogun of Japan made European intervention easy. Only the Japanese were able to revolutionize their government in time to ward off imperialist penetration. Even the Japanese, thanks to early treaties, remained unfree to determine their own tariff policy until after 1900.[4]

So great was the difference in the sheer mechanics of power that usually a mere show of force allowed the white men to impose their will. A garrison of only 75,000 white troops long held India for the British. Numerous sporadic little wars were constantly fought—Afghan wars, Burmese wars, Zulu wars—which passed unnoticed by Europeans in the home country and were no more like true war than the operations of the United States Army against the Indians of the western plains. The Spanish-American War of 1898 and the Boer War of 1899 were also wars of colonial type, fought between entirely unequal parties. Often a show of naval strength was enough. It was the classic age of the punitive or minatory bombardment. We have seen how the American Commodore Perry threatened to bombard Tokyo in 1854.[5] In 1856 the British consul at Canton, to punish acts of violence against Europeans, called upon the local British admiral to bombard that Chinese city. In 1863 the British bombarded Satsuma, and in 1864 an allied force including Americans bombarded Choshu—precipitating revolution in Japan.[6] Similarly, Alexandria was bombarded in 1882 and Zanzibar in 1896. The usual consequence was that the local ruler signed a treaty, reorganized his government, or accepted a European (usually British) adviser.

INCENTIVES AND MOTIVES

Behind this aggressiveness lay many pressures. Europeans could not maintain, for themselves in Europe, the style of life to which they had become accustomed, except by bringing the rest of the world within their orbit. But many other needs felt in Europe drove men into distant and savage places. Catholic and Protestant groups sent growing numbers of missionaries to regions increasingly remote and wild. The missionaries sometimes got into trouble with the natives; sometimes they were killed; and while the missionaries themselves might regard these as normal risks, and even disapprove of political intervention, public opinion in the home countries, soon learning of such events by ocean cable, might clamor for political action to suppress such vestiges of barbarism. Similarly, science required scientific expeditions for geographical exploration, or for botanical, zoölogical, or mineral discoveries or for astronomical or meteorological observations. Wealthy persons travelled more, now that travel was so easy; they hunted tigers or elephants,

---

[3] See pp. 253–5, 322–3.   [4] See p. 552.   [5] See pp. 548, 551.
[6] See pp. 463, 552–4.

or simply went to see sights. It seemed only reasonable, at the close of the nineteenth century, that all civilized persons wherever they might choose to go should enjoy the security of life and limb and the orderly procedures that only European supervision could provide. It must be remembered that many peoples, only half a century ago, were in fact more savage than they are today.

Economically, European life required material goods, many of which only tropical regions could supply. Even the working classes now drank tea or coffee every day. After the American Civil War Europe relied for its cotton increasingly on Africa and the East. Rubber and petroleum became staple needs. The lowly jute, which grew only in India, was used to make burlap, twine, carpets, and the millions of jute bags employed in commerce. The lordly coconut tree had innumerable common uses, which led to its intensive cultivation in the Dutch Indies. Various parts of it could be eaten, or manufactured into bags, brushes, cables, ropes, sails, or doormats, or converted into copra and coconut oil, which in turn went into the making of candles, soap, lard, margarine, cocoa butter, or chocolate.

Industrial countries also attempted to sell their own products, and one of the reasons given by imperialists, in support of imperialism, was the urgent necessity of finding new markets. The industrialization of Germany, the United States, Japan, and other countries, after about 1870, meant that they competed with each other and with Great Britain for foreign trade. The slowly declining price level after 1873 meant that a business firm had to sell more goods to turn over the same amount of money. Competition was more intense. The advanced countries raised tariffs to keep out each other's products. It was therefore argued that each industrial country must develop a colonial empire dependent on itself, an area of "sheltered markets," as the phrase went in England, in which the home country would supply manufactured goods in return for raw materials. The idea was to create a large self-sufficient trading unit, embracing various climates and types of resources, protected if necessary from outside competition by tariffs, guaranteeing a market for all its members, and wealth and prosperity for the home country. This phase of imperialism is often called neomercantilism, since it revived in substance the mercantilism of the eighteenth and earlier centuries.[7]

Purely financial considerations also characterized the new imperialism. Money invested in "backward" countries, by the close of the nineteenth century, brought a higher rate of return than if invested in the more civilized ones. For this there were many reasons, including the cheap labor of non-European regions, the heavy and unsatisfied demand for non-European products, and the greater risk of losses in half-unknown areas where European ideas of law and order did not prevail. By 1900 Western Europe and the northeastern United States were equipped with their basic industrial apparatus. Their railway networks and first factories were built. Opportunities for investment in these countries became stabilized. At the same time, these

[7] See pp. 102–4, 225–31.

countries themselves accumulated capital seeking an outlet. In the mid-century most exported capital was British-owned. By the close of the century more French, German, American, Dutch, Belgian, and Swiss investors were investing or lending outside their own borders. In 1850, most exported capital went to build up Europe, the United States, Canada, Australia, or the Argentine—the white man's world. By 1900 more of it was going to the backward regions. This capital (unlike much of the capital exported in the 1950's, which was usually furnished by governments) was the property of small private savers or of large banking combinations. Investors preferred "civilized" political control over the parts of Asia, Africa, or Latin America in which their railroads, mines, plantations, government loans, or other investments were situated. Hence the profit motive, or desire to invest "surplus" capital, promoted imperialism.

This analysis was put forward by critics like the English socialist J. A. Hobson, who wrote an influential book on imperialism in 1903, and later by Lenin, in his *Imperialism the Highest Stage of World Capitalism*, written in 1916. They ascribed imperialism primarily to the accumulation of surplus capital and condemned it on socialist grounds. Argued Hobson especially, if more of the national income went to workers as wages, and less of it to capitalists as interest and dividends, or if wealthy people were more heavily taxed and the money used for social welfare, there would be no surplus of capital and no real imperialism. Since the working class, if this were done, would also have more purchasing power, it would also be less necessary to look endlessly for new markets outside the country. But the "surplus-capital" explanation of imperialism was not entirely convincing. That investors and exporters were instrumental in the rise of imperialism was of course very true. That imperialism arose essentially from the capitalists' pressure to invest abroad was more doubtful. Perhaps even more basic was Europe's need for imports—only by enormous imports could Europe sustain its dense population, complex industry, and high standard of living. It was the demand for such imports—cotton, cocoa, coffee, copper, or copra drawn from "the colonies"—that made investment in the colonies financially profitable. Moreover, non-Europeans themselves often asked for the capital, glad though the European lenders were to lend it at high rates; in 1890 this might mean merely that a shah or sultan wanted to build himself a new palace, but the need of non-Europeans for Western capital was basic, nor was it to decline as the world became more democratic. Lastly, the imperialism of some countries, notably Russia and Italy, which had little capital and few modern-type capitalists of their own, could not reasonably be attributed to pressure for lucrative foreign investments.

For the British, however, the capitalistic incentive was of great importance. We have seen how the British, in 1914, had $20,000,000,000 invested outside of Great Britain, a quarter of all their wealth.[8] About half, or $10,000,-000,000, was invested in the British empire. Only a tenth of French foreign

ᴧᴧᴧᴧᴧᴧᴧᴧᴧᴧᴧᴧᴧ

[8] See p. 572.

investments was in French colonies. French investment in the colonial world
in general, however, including Egypt, Suez, South Africa, and Asia in addition to the French colonies, amounted to about a fifth of all French foreign
investments. Only an infinitesimal fraction of German foreign investment in
1914 was in German colonies, which were of slight value. A fifth of German
foreign investments, however, was placed in Africa, Asia, and the Ottoman
Empire. These sums are enough to suggest the pressures upon the European
governments to assert political influence in Africa, Turkey, or China.

In addition, French investors (including small bourgeois and even
affluent peasants) had in 1914 a huge stake in the Russian Empire. Russia,
an imperial power with respect to adjoining countries in the Balkans and
Asia, occupied an almost semi-colonial status with respect to western Europe.
The tsardom in its last twenty years, not unlike the Ottoman sultanate or
the Manchu dynasty, was kept going by foreign loans, predominantly French.
The French in 1914 had lent over $2,000,000,000 to Russia, more than to all
colonial regions combined. For these huge outlays the motivation was at least
as much political as economic. The French government often urged French
banks to buy Russian bonds. The aim was not merely to make a profit for
bankers and savers, but to build up and hold together a military ally against
Germany.

Politics went along with economics in the whole process of imperialist
expansion. National security, both political and economic, was as important
an aim as the accumulation of private wealth. So, too, was the growing concern in many quarters over the economic security and welfare of the working classes. The ideas of the British statesman Joseph Chamberlain (1836–
1914) illustrated how these motives entered into imperialist thinking.

Chamberlain, father of Neville Chamberlain who was to be prime
minister of Britain in the years just prior to the Second World War, began as
a Birmingham manufacturer, the type of man who a generation before would
have been a staunch free-trader and upholder of *laissez-faire*. Discarding the
old individualism, he came to believe that the community should and could
take better care of its members, and, in particular, that the British community
(or empire) could advance the welfare of Britons. As mayor of Birmingham,
he introduced a kind of municipal socialism, including civic ownership of
utilities. As colonial secretary from 1895 to 1903, he preached Britain's need
for a great empire in an age of rising international competition—"a great self-
sustaining and self-protecting empire" as he said in 1896—a world-wide
British trading area whose resources would be developed by British capital,
and which would give a secure source of raw materials and food, secure markets for exports, and a secure level of profits, wages, and employment.

Chamberlain saw with misgivings the tendencies toward independence
in Canada, New Zealand, and the Australian Commonwealth. For these Dominions he favored complete self-government, but he hoped that, once assured of virtual independence, they would re-knit their ties with each other
and with Great Britain. Such a re-integration of the empire he called "imperial federation." Britain and its Dominions, in Chamberlain's view, should

pool their resources first of all for military defense, but also for economic well-being. The Dominions had already levied tariffs against British manufactures in order to build up their own. Chamberlain, to favor British exports, urged the Dominions to charge a lower duty on British wares than on the same wares coming from foreign countries. To have something in return to offer the Dominions Chamberlain even proposed that Great Britain adopt a protective tariff, so that it might then favor Canadian or Australian goods by imposing on them a lower rate. His plan was to bind the empire together by economic bonds, making it a kind of tariff union, or system of "imperial preference." Since Britain imported mainly meat and cereals from the Dominions, Chamberlain was obliged to recommend a tariff even upon these— to "tax the people's food," repudiating the very ark of the covenant of Free Trade upon which the British economy had rested for half a century.[9] The proposal was rejected. Chamberlain died in 1914, his goal unaccomplished. But after the First World War the British empire, or Commonwealth of Nations, followed closely along the lines he had mapped out.[10]

Whether the economic welfare and security of the European working classes was advanced by imperialism is still debated. It is probable that the working man in western Europe did benefit from imperialism. Socially conservative imperialists were joined in this belief by thinkers of the extreme Left. Marx himself, followed by Lenin, thought that the European worker obtained higher real wages through the inflow of low-priced colonial goods. To Marxists this was unfortunate, for it gave European workers a vested interest in imperialism, made the European proletariat "opportunistic" (*i.e.*, unrevolutionary), and blocked the formation of a true international world proletariat of all races.

Another imperialist argument much heard at the time held that European countries must acquire colonies to which surplus population could migrate without altogether abandoning the native land. It seemed unfortunate, for example, that so many Germans or Italians emigrating to the United States should be lost to the fatherland. This argument was purely specious. No European country after 1870 acquired any colony to which European families in any numbers wished to move. There were not, and never have been, in all tropical Africa, India, and the Far East, more than handfuls of Europeans, almost all transients. The millions who still left Europe, up to 1914, persisted in heading for the Americas, where in the circumstances no European colony could be founded.[11]

The competitive nature of the European state system introduced other almost exclusively political elements. The European states had to guard their security against each other. They had to keep some kind of balance among themselves, in the overseas world as in Europe. Hence, as in the scramble for Africa, one government often hurriedly annexed territory simply for fear that

[9] See pp. 463, 568–9.
[10] See p. 783.
[11] See map, p. 565.

another might do so first. Or again, colonies came to have an intangible but
momentous value in symbolism and prestige. To have colonies was a normal
criterion of greatness. It was the sign of having arrived as a Great Power.
Britain and France had had colonies for centuries. Therefore the new powers
formed in the 1860's—Germany, Italy, Japan, and in a sense the United States
—had to have colonies also.

IMPERIALISM AS CRUSADE

Imperialism arose from the commercial, industrial, financial, scientific,
political, journalistic, intellectual, religious, and humanitarian impulses of
Europe compounded together. It was an outthrust of the whole white man's
civilization. It would bring civilization and enlightened living to those who
still sat in darkness. Faith in "modern civilization" had become a kind of
substitute religion. Imperialism was its crusade.

So the British spoke of the White Man's Burden, the French of their
mission civilisatrice, the Germans of diffusing *Kultur*, the Americans of the
blessings of Anglo-Saxon protection. Social Darwinism and popular anthropology taught that white races were "fitter" or more gifted than colored.[12]
Others argued, more reasonably, that the backwardness of non-Europeans
was due to historical and hence temporary causes, but that for a long period
in the future the civilized whites must keep a guardianship over their darker
protégés. In the psychology of imperialism there was much that was not unworthy. Young men of good family left the pleasant lands of Devonshire or
Poitou, where, for them, all was temperate, ordered, clean, calm, and con-
genial, to spend long and lonely years in hot and savage places, sustained by
the thought that they were advancing the work of humanity. It was a good
thing to bring clearer ideas of justice to barbaric peoples, to put down slave-
raiding, torture, and famine, to combat degrading superstitions or fight the
diseases of neglect and filth. But these accomplishments, however real, went
along all too obviously with self-interest and were expressed with unbearable
complacency and gross condescension to the larger part of the human race.
As Rudyard Kipling wrote in 1899:

> *Take up the White Man's burden—*
> *Send out the best ye breed—*
> *Go bind your sons to exile,*
> *To serve your captives' need;*
> *To wait in heavy harness,*
> *On fluttered folk and wild—*
> *Your new-caught sullen peoples,*
> *Half devil and half child.*

[12] See pp. 599, 600.

78. The Americas

After the general considerations above, let us turn to each of the earth's great regions in turn.

In America the break-up of the Spanish empire in the first quarter of the nineteenth century, during and after the Napoleonic wars, left the vast tract from Colorado to Cape Horn very unsettled. Most of the people were Indian or a mixture of Indian and white (*mestizo*), with clusters here and there of pure European stock, which the nineteenth-century immigration was greatly to increase. Both the white and the Indian population, except in inaccessible spots, were Spanish in culture, language, and religion, or Portuguese in Brazil.[13] The disappearance of Spanish control, and the political unpreparedness of the native upper classes, left a large number of flaccid and shifting republics, chronically engaged in border disputes with one another. Fortunately for these republics, at the time of independence in the 1820's, European imperialism was at a low ebb. We have seen how the Congress of Verona considered ways of returning them to Spain, and how, in 1823, the United States, itself still no tower of strength, boldly announced the Monroe Doctrine, declaring that no European power should contemplate the reestablishment of colonies in the Americas.[14] For many years no European power recognized the Monroe Doctrine. As George Canning, the British foreign minister, noted in 1823, "the doctrine, if such it can be called . . . is absolutely unacceptable to my government and to France." It was British policy, however, largely for commercial reasons, to keep outside influence out of Spanish America. British sea power therefore gave the new republics a chance to grow. Nor was the Monroe Doctrine much liked by the Spanish Americans, who noted that it proclaimed no bar against the ambitions of the United States. And it was by the United States that one of the new republics was first threatened from the outside.

THE UNITED STATES AND MEXICO

Mexico, on becoming independent of Spain, reached almost to the Mississippi and the Rocky Mountains. Hardly was it independent when land-seekers from the United States swarmed over its northeastern borders. They brought with them Negro slaves, to grow the cotton so voraciously demanded in industrial England. The Mexican Republic did not allow slavery. The newcomers proclaimed their own republic, which they called Texas. Agitation developed for annexation to the United States. Mexico objected, but in 1845 the United States annexed Texas. A war followed, in which Mexico lost to

wwwwwwwwwwwwww

[13] See pp. 93–4.
[14] See pp. 450–2.

the United States not only Texas but the whole region from Texas to the California coast. As is usual in such affairs, the loser preserved a longer memory than the winner. It soon seemed only natural in the United States to possess these regions; in Mexico many decades had to pass before the wound was healed. Mexico had lost half its territory within the first generation of its independence. It was argued at the time that the United States had far better facilities than Mexico for civilizing the region.

The next threat to Mexico came from Europe. A certain pretender to government in Mexico, named Miramón, backed by Mexican churchmen and landowners, contracted large loans in Europe on exorbitant terms, the European lenders rightly estimating his credit to be highly unsound. He soon collapsed, though not before seizing certain British properties at the British legation. His successor, the liberal Juarez (a pure-blooded Indian, at least racially "non-European"), repudiated the Miramón loan. European bondholders demanded satisfaction from their governments. The United States was paralyzed by the Civil War. Great Britain, France, and Spain, which had never recognized the Monroe Doctrine, in 1861 sent combined military forces to Vera Cruz. The British proposed seizure of the customs houses in Mexican ports, and appropriation of the customs revenues to pay off the debt (an expedient introduced in China three years before); but the French had more ambitious designs. Unknown both to the British, who wanted only to collect debts, and to the Spanish, who dreamed of setting up a new Bourbon monarchy in Mexico, the Emperor Napoleon III had a secret project for establishing a French satellite state in Mexico, which French capital and exports might subsequently develop. He planned to create a Mexican empire with the Austrian archduke Maximilian as its figurehead emperor. The British and Spanish disapprovingly withdrew their forces. The French army proceeded into the interior. Maximilian reigned for some years, but Napoleon III gradually concluded that conquest of Mexico was impossible, or too expensive. It further appeared, by 1865, that the United States was not going to collapse after all, as expected and even hoped for by the European governing classes. The United States protested strongly to the French government. The French withdrew, Maximilian was captured and shot, and Juarez and the Mexican liberals came back to power.

United States pressure, before 1870, had thus in turn both despoiled and protected the adjoining part of Latin America. This ambivalent situation became characteristic of the New World. As the United States became a great power the Monroe Doctrine became an effective barrier to European territorial ambitions. Latin America never became subject to imperialism as completely as did Asia and Africa. On the other hand, the United States became the imperialist power feared above all others south of the border. It was the *Yanqui* menace, the Colossus of the North.

In the 1870's in the course of its turbulent politics, both natives of Mexico and foreign residents were obliged to pay forced loans to rival leaders. The State Department at Washington demanded that American citizens be reimbursed by the Mexican government. The double standard characteristic of imperialism—one standard for civilized and one for uncivilized states—became clear in the exchange of notes. The Mexican government, now under Porfirio Diaz, attempted to lay down the principle that "foreigners locating in a country accepted the mode of life of the people . . . and participated not only in the benefits of such residence but also in the adversities. Foreigners should enjoy the same guarantees and the same legal protection as natives, but no more." The Mexicans observed that the United States had never recognized the claims of foreigners for losses sustained in its Civil War. The United States, under President Hayes, held on the other hand that citizens of advanced states, operating in more primitive regions, should continue to enjoy the security of business and property characteristic of their home countries. The United States sent troops to the border in 1877, and when the Mexicans objected the Secretary of State remarked on "the volatile and childish character of these people and their incapacity to treat a general question with calmness and without prejudice." Mexico retorted that the United States had "disregarded all the rules of international law and practice of civilized nations and treated the Mexicans as savages, as Kaffirs of Africa."

It was, in fact, a principle of international law, in the nineteenth century, that civilized states might not intervene in each other's affairs but had the right of intervention in backward countries. In the dispute of 1877 the United States classified Mexico as backward, "volatile and childish." What the Mexicans objected to was being treated like "savages and Kaffirs." They differed on which of the two standards should apply.

UNITED STATES IMPERIALISM IN THE 1890'S

The 1890's saw a crescendo of imperialism both in Europe and in the United States. In 1895, in a resounding restatement of the Monroe Doctrine, President Cleveland forbade the British to deal directly with Venezuela in a boundary dispute affecting British Guiana. The British were obliged to accept international arbitration. When, however, the adjacent Colombia faced a revolution in the Isthmus of Panama the United States supported the revolutionaries, and, consulting nobody, recognized Panama as an independent republic. Here the United States leased and fortified a Canal Zone, and proceeded to build the Panama Canal. Panama became in effect what Europeans would call a protectorate of the United States.

Meanwhile what was left of the old Spanish American empire, confined to Cuba and Puerto Rico, was agitated by revolutionary disturbances looking to independence. Sympathies in the United States lay with the revolutionaries. Every sign of the new imperialism showed itself unmistakably. Americans had fifty million dollars invested in Cuba. They bought the bonds issued by Cuban revolutionaries in New York. Cuban sugar, whose production was interfered with by political troubles, was necessary to the famed American standard of living. An orderly and amenable Cuba was vital to American strategic interests in the Caribbean, in the soon to be built Canal, and in the

Pacific. The barbarity of the Spanish authorities was deplored as an outrage to modern civilization. The newspapers, especially the new "yellow" press, roused the American public to a fury of moral indignation and imperial self-assertion. The climax came when an American warship, the *Maine*, sank under mysterious circumstances in Havana harbor.

The United States easily won the ensuing war with Spain in 1898. Puerto Rico was annexed outright, as were the Philippine Islands on the other side of the world. Cuba was set up as an independent republic, subject to the Platt Amendment, a series of provisions by which the United States obtained the right to oversee Cuba's relations with foreign powers, and to intervene in Cuba in matters of "life, property, individual liberty" and "Cuban independence." Thus the United States obtained another protec-torate in the Caribbean. The right of intervention in Cuba was exercised several times in the following two decades, until the growth of Cuban na-tionalism and subsiding of American imperialism led to abrogation of the Platt Amendment in 1934. Later, after the Second World War, the Philip-pines formally received independence, in 1946, and Puerto Rico moved to-ward greater autonomy.

It was under President Theodore Roosevelt, the peppery "hero of San Juan hill," that the imperial greatness of the United States was most em-phatically trumpeted. He announced in 1904 that weakness or misbehavior "which results in a general loosening of the ties of civilized society may . . . require intervention by some civilized nation," and that the Monroe Doc-trine might force the United States "to the exercise of an international police power." In the following year Santo Domingo fell into such financial dis-order that European creditors were alarmed. To forestall any pretext for European intervention, the United States sent a financial administrator to Santo Domingo, reformed the economy of the country, and impounded half the customs receipts to pay its debts. Roosevelt declared—it came to be known as the "Roosevelt corollary" to the Monroe Doctrine—that, since the United States would not permit European states to intervene in America to collect debts, it must itself assume the duty of intervention to safeguard the investments of the civilized world. The Monroe Doctrine, initially a negative warning to Europe, now stood with the new corollary as a positive notice of supervision of all America by the United States. A quarter of a century of "dollar diplomacy" followed, in which the United States repeatedly inter-vened, by military or other means, in the Caribbean and Mexico. But the Roosevelt corollary, like the Platt Amendment, created so much bad feeling in Latin America that the Washington government finally repudiated it. Gradually, the United States substituted what came to be known in the 1930's as the "good neighbor" policy, which was designed to respect the sov-ereignty of the Latin American countries, to treat them as equals of the United States, and to encourage joint, or Pan-American, solutions to com-mon problems.

The story of the Hawaiian Islands was as typical of the new imperial-ism as any episode in the history of any of the European empires. Known originally to outsiders as the Sandwich Islands, these spots of land long enjoyed isolation in the vastnesses of the mid-Pacific. The growth of navigation in the nineteenth century introduced them to the world. Sailors, whalers, missionaries, and vendors of rum and cloth filled Honolulu by 1840. The native ruler, confused and helpless in the new situation, almost accepted a British protectorate in 1843, and in 1875 did accept a virtual protectorate by the United States, which guaranteed Hawaiian independence against any third party, obtained trading privileges, and acquired Pearl Harbor as a naval base. American capital and management entered the islands. They created huge sugar and pineapple industries, entirely dependent on export to, and investment by, the United States. In 1891, when Queen Liliuokalani came to the throne, she tried to check Westernization and Americanization. The American interests, endangered by her nativist policies, overthrew the queen and set up an independent republic, which soon sought annexation to the United States. It was the story of Texas re-enacted. For several years the issue hung in the balance because of lingering disapproval in the United States for such strong-arm methods. But with Japan revealing imperial designs in 1895, the rush of other powers into China, the Spanish-American War, acquisition of the Philippines and plans for the Panama Canal, the United States "accepted its destiny" in the Pacific, and annexed the Hawaiian republic by treaty in 1898.

The United States, as the twentieth century opened, possessing a broad sphere of influence in America, strategic and economic outposts in the Pacific, an active policy in the Far East, and a growing navy, was one of the Great Powers of the World. Canada formed an autonomous Dominion within the British empire. Latin America, while exposed to the indignities of dollar diplomacy, was spared the outright conquest or subjugation to which competitive imperialism reduced most of the rest of the world.

79. The Dissolution of the Ottoman Empire

THE OTTOMAN EMPIRE IN THE 1850'S

Of all parts of the non-European world, the Ottoman, or Turkish, Empire was the nearest to Europe, and with it Europeans had for centuries had close relations. It had for long extended from Hungary and the Balkan peninsula to the south Russian steppes and from Algeria to the Persian Gulf. The empire was not at all like a European state. Immense in extent, it was a congeries of religious communities. Most of its people were Moslem, including both orthodox Moslems and such reform sects as Druses and Wahabis; some were Jews who had always lived in the Near East; many were Christian, principally Greek Orthodox. The Turks were the ruling class and Islam the dominant religion. Only Moslems, for example, could serve in the army; non-Moslems were known as *raya*, the "flock" or "herd"—they paid the taxes.

Persons of different religion lived side by side, each under the laws, courts, and customs of his own religious group. Religious officials—patriarchs, bishops, rabbis, imams, ulemas—were responsible to the Turkish government for their own people, over whom therefore they had a great deal of authority.[15]

Western Europeans had their own special rights. Roman Catholic clergy, living mainly in Palestine, looked to the pope in religion and to France for a mundane protector. Western merchants enjoyed the regime of the "capitulations," or special rights granted by the Ottoman government in numerous treaties going back to the sixteenth century. By the capitulations Turkey could not levy a tariff of more than 8% on imported goods. Europeans were exempt from most taxes. Cases involving two Europeans, civil or criminal, could be settled only in a court held by a European consul under European law. Disputes between a European and an Ottoman subject were adjudicated in Turkish courts, but only in the presence of a European observer.

The Ottoman Empire, in short, completely lacked the European idea of nationalism or national unity. It lacked the European idea of sovereignty, and a uniform law for all its peoples. It lacked the European idea of the secular state, or of law and citizenship separated from religion. And it had fallen behind Europe in scientific, mechanical, material, humanitarian, and administrative achievements.

Turkey was the "sick man of Europe," and its long decline constituted the Eastern Question. Since the loss of Hungary in 1699 the Ottoman Empire had entered on a long process of territorial disintegration. That the empire lasted another two centuries was due to the European balance of power. The first partition of Poland, in 1772, had been contrived to keep the Russians from overrunning Turkey, and the empire had survived the Napoleonic wars only because the Russians, British, and French deadlocked each other's designs upon it.[16] But by the 1850's the empire was falling away at the edges. Russia had advanced in the Crimea and the Caucasus. Serbia was autonomous, Greece independent, and Rumania recognized as a self-governing principality. The French occupied Algeria. A native Arab dynasty, the Sauds, of the Wahabi reform sect, ruled over much of Arabia. A former Turkish governor of Egypt, Mohammed Ali, had established his family as hereditary "khedives" in the Nile valley.[17] Notwithstanding these changes, the Ottoman Empire in the 1850's was still huge. It encompassed not only the Turkish or Anatolian peninsula (including Armenia and territory south of the Caucasus) but also the central portion of the Balkan peninsula from Constantinople to the Adriatic where many Christians of Slavic nationality lived, Tripoli (Libya) in North Africa, and the islands of Crete and Cyprus. Egypt and Arabia, though autonomous, were still under the nominal suzerainty of the sultan.

The Crimean War of 1854–6 opened a new phase in Ottoman history

[15] See pp. 184–7.
[16] See pp. 219–20, 316–17, 378, 386.
[17] See p. 454.

as in that of Europe.[18] We have seen how this war was followed by the consolidation of great nation-states in Europe, and how even the United States, Canada, and Japan consolidated or modernized themselves at the same time. The Turks tried to do the same between 1856 and 1876.

In the Crimean War the Turks were on the winning side, but the war affected them as it affected Russia, the loser. Exposing their military and political weakness, it pointed up the need of reorganization. The outcome of the war was taken to prove the superiority of the political system of England and France. It was therefore on Western lines that Turkish reformers wished to remodel. It was not merely that they wished to defend themselves against another of the periodic wars with Russia. They wished also to avoid being periodically saved from Russia by the West, a process which if continued could lead only to French or British control of Turkey.

ATTEMPTS AT REFORM AND REVIVAL, 1856–76

In 1856 the Ottoman government issued the Hatt-i Humayun, the most far-reaching Turkish reform edict of the century. Its purport was to create an Ottoman national citizenship for all persons in the empire. It abolished the civil authority of religious hierarchs. Equality before the law was guaranteed, as was eligibility to public office without regard to religion. The army was opened to Christians and Moslems alike, and steps were even taken to include both in non-segregated military units. The edict announced a reform of taxes, security of property for all, abolition of torture, and reform of prisons. It promised to combat the chronic evils of graft, bribery, and extortion by public officials.

For twenty years there were serious efforts to make the reform decree of 1856 a reality. Western and liberal ideas circulated freely. Newspapers were founded. Writers called for a national Turkish revival, threw off the old Persian style in literature, composed histories of the Ottomans, translated Montesquieu and Rousseau. Foreign loans entered the country. Railroads joined the Black Sea and the Danube. Abdul Aziz (1861–76), the first sultan to travel in Europe, visited Vienna, London, and the great Paris world's fair of 1867.

Very powerful resistance developed against such radical changes, more radical indeed than anything that the great French Revolution had attempted, since the essential character of the empire was to be reversed. The most obstinate resistance came not from conservative Turks but from the religious leaders whose authority over their own communities was being taken away. The patriarch of Constantinople, for example, controlled the enormous properties of the Greek church (seven-eighths of the land in the Rumanian provinces), and since, under the old Ottoman regime, excommunication meant virtual outlawry, he also possessed an unlimited power over all Greek

---

[18] See pp. 511–13.

Christians. The religious heads, Christian, Jewish, and Moslem, had every reason to prefer the old regime to the new conception of a secular state, individual freedom, or Ottoman nationality. Many Christians in the empire, however, at odds with their own higher clergy, cooperated with the Turkish reformers to reduce clerical control. But basically, the Christians were beginning to think of themselves as belonging to a nationality rather than to a religion—as Bulgars, Rumanians, Greeks, Serbs, or Armenians. As such, they had no interest in a reformed Ottoman Empire. They even blocked proposals made in 1872 to federalize the empire with local autonomy for the Balkan peoples. On the other hand, the best efforts of the Turkish reformers miscarried. There were too few Turks with skill or experience in the work required. Abdul Aziz took to spending his borrowed money somewhat too freely for purposes of the harem. In 1874 the Ottoman government, having recklessly overborrowed, repudiated half its debt.

A new and more determined reformer, Midhat Pasha, goaded by opposition and desperate at the weight of inertia, deposed Abdul Aziz in 1876 and set up Abdul Hamid II as sultan in his place. The new sultan at first briskly went along with the reform movement, proclaiming a new constitution in 1876. It declared the Ottoman Empire to be indivisible, and promised personal liberty, freedom of conscience, freedom of education and the press, and parliamentary government. The first Turkish parliament met in 1877. Its members earnestly addressed themselves to reform. But they reckoned without Abdul Hamid, who in 1877 revealed his true intentions. He got rid of Midhat, packed off the parliament and threw away the constitution.

REPRESSION AFTER 1876

Abdul Hamid reigned for thirty-three years, from 1876 to 1909. For all this time he lived as a terrified animal, fighting back blindly and ferociously against forces that he could not understand. Once when a consignment of dynamos reached the Turkish customs it was held up by fearful officials, because the contents were declared to make several hundred revolutions per minute. Again, chemistry books for use in the new American college were pronounced seditious, because their chemical symbols might be a secret cipher. The sultan sensed that tampering with the old Ottoman way would lead to ruin. He dreaded any moves to check his own whim or power. He was thrown into a panic by Turkish reformers and Westernizers, who became increasingly terroristic in the face of his opposition. Driven away by Abdul Hamid, some tens of thousands of Young Turks, the men of the reform era before 1876, or their sons and successors, lived in exile in Paris, London, or Geneva, plotting their return to Turkey and vengeance upon Abdul the Damned. The sultan was frightened also by agitation among his non-Turkish subjects. Nationalist zealots, Armenians, Bulgars, Macedonians, or Cretans, constantly taunted and defied the Ottoman authorities, even precipitating the slaughter of their own people to dramatize their sufferings in the eyes of Europe. The Bulgarian massacres of 1876, the Armenian massacres of 1894, horrible butcheries of thousands of peasants by Ottoman troops, came as a shock to a Europe unused to such violence, and were blamed entirely on the allegedly exceptional barbarity of the terrible Turk. Lastly, and with good reason, Abdul Hamid lived in a creeping fear of the designs of the imperialist European powers upon his dissolving empire.

A thoroughly reformed, consolidated, and modernized Ottoman Empire was the last thing that European governments desired. They might wish for humanitarian reforms in Turkey, for more efficiency and honesty in Turkish government and finance, and even for a Turkish parliamentary system. Such demands were eloquently expressed by liberals like Gladstone in England. But no one wanted what Turkish reformers wanted, a reinvigorated Ottoman Empire that could deal with Europe politically as an equal.

THE RUSSO-TURKISH WAR OF 1877–8: THE

CONGRESS OF BERLIN

In Russia, since the time of Catherine II, many had dreamed of installing Russia on the shores of the Bosporus.[19] Constantinople they called Tsarigrad, the Imperial City, which Orthodoxy was to liberate from the infidel. Crusading motives, in a nationalist and imperialist age, reappeared anew in the form of Pan-Slavism. The first Pan-Slav congress, in 1848, had been a phenomenon of revolution, liberal in its aims, confined to the Western Slavs including the Poles, and hence anti-tsarist and anti-Russian.[20] Twenty years later Pan-Slavism was preached by leading Russians, including the novelist Dostoievski, the poet Tyutchev, and the publicist Danilevsky. Danilevsky's *Russia and Europe*, published in 1871, predicted a long war between Europe and Russia, to be followed by a grand federation of the East, in which not only all Slavs, but Greeks, Hungarians, and parts of Asiatic Turkey would be included under Russian control. This type of Pan-Slavism was favored and patronized by the Russian government; it diverted attention from internal and revolutionary troubles. As for the Slav peoples of the Ottoman Empire, they were willing to use Russian Pan-Slavism, not especially because they approved of it, but as a means of combating their Turkish rulers. Insurrection against the Turks (and pro-Turkish Slavs) broke out in Bosnia in 1875, in Bulgaria in 1876. In 1877 Russia declared war on Turkey. Russia was again on the move against the Ottoman Empire, for the sixth time in a hundred years.

The British, who had fought Russia over Turkey in 1854, were prepared to do so again. A number of recent developments added to their apprehension. The Suez Canal was completed in 1869. It was within the ter-

[19] See p. 511, note 4.
[20] See pp. 481–2.

ritory of the Ottoman Empire. It restored the Near East to its ancient position as a crossroads of world trade. The British also took alarm when Russia, in 1870, in the confusion of the Franco-Prussian war, repudiated a clause in the treaty of 1856 and began to build a fleet on the Black Sea. In 1874 Benjamin Disraeli, a Conservative and an imperialist, became prime minister of Great Britain. By a sudden coup in the following year he was able to buy up, from the almost bankrupt Khedive of Egypt, 44% of the shares of the Suez Canal Company. In 1876, in a dramatic affirmation of imperial splendor, he had Queen Victoria take the title of Empress of India. British commercial and financial interests in India and the Far East were growing, and the Suez Canal, of which the British government was now the principal stockholder, was becoming the "lifeline" of empire. But the Ottoman state, and hence the whole Near East, was now collapsing before the Russians, whose armies advanced rapidly through the Balkans in 1877, reached Constantinople, and forced the Turks to sign a treaty, the treaty of San Stefano. By this treaty Turkey ceded to Russia Batum and Kars on the south side of the Caucasus mountains, gave full independence to Serbia and Rumania, promised reforms in Bosnia, and granted autonomy to a new Bulgarian state, whose boundaries were to be very generously drawn, and which everyone expected to be dominated by Russia. England seethed with a popular clamor for war against Russia. The outcry gave the word "jingoism" to the language:

> We don't want to fight, but by jingo, if we do,
> We've got the men, we've got the ships, we've
>   got the money too.

It now appeared that the weakness of Turkey, its inability to fend off foreigners from its borders, would precipitate at least an Anglo-Russian and possibly a general European war. But war was averted by diplomacy. Bismarck assembled a congress of all the European great powers at Berlin. Once again Europe attempted to assert itself as a unity, to restore life to the much battered Concert of Europe by dealing collectively with the common problem presented by the Eastern Question. The immediate need was to mediate

---

The Dissolution of the Ottoman Empire

Beginning in 1699, with the loss of Hungary to the House of Austria, the Ottoman Empire entered upon a long process of territorial disintegration which lasted for over two hundred years. Dates shown are those at which territories dropped away. In general, regions lost from 1699 to the fall of Napoleon, 1812–1815, were annexed directly by Austria and Russia. European territories lost in the nineteenth century emerged as independent states, owing to the rise of nationalism and the balance among the great European powers. In the Arabic world, reaching from Algeria to the Persian Gulf, regions lost before the First World War were absorbed into European colonial empires; those lost in the First World War (1918) were at first mostly assigned to France and Britain as mandates, but after the Second World War emerged as independent Arabic states. During the First World War Britain, France, Italy, Russia and Greece took steps to partition Turkey proper, but a Turkish nationalist movement blocked these designs and established a Turkish republic (pp. 678, 768).

between the Russians and Turks and to placate the British. To prevent any single power from gaining unequal advantage, and to win the acceptance of all powers for the arrangements agreed to, it was deemed necessary to give something to all, or almost all. The congress in effect initiated a partition of the Ottoman domain. It kept peace in Europe at the expense of Turkey. The European balance now both protected and dismembered Turkey at the same time.

The Russians were persuaded at Berlin to give up the treaty of San Stefano that they had imposed on the Turks, but they still obtained Batum and Kars and won independence for the Serbs and Rumanians. Montenegro, too, was recognized as an independent state. They compromised on Bulgaria, which was divided into three zones with varying degrees of autonomy, all still nominally within the Ottoman Empire. Austria-Hungary was authorized by the congress to "occupy and administer" Bosnia (but not annex it) in the interests of civilization and in compensation for the spread of Russian influence in the Balkans. To the British (Disraeli boasted he brought home "peace with honor") the Turks ceded Cyprus, a large island not far from the Suez Canal. The French were told that they might expand from Algeria into Tunisia. To the Italians (who counted least) it was more vaguely hinted that some day, somehow, they might expand across the Adriatic into Albania. As Bismarck put it, "the Italians have such a large appetite and such poor teeth." Germany took nothing. Bismarck said he was the "honest broker," with no interest except in European peace.

The treaty of Berlin of 1878 dispelled the immediate threat of war. But it left many continuing problems for later statesmanship to deal with, problems which, because they were not dealt with successfully, became a principal cause of the First World War thirty-six years later. Neither the Balkan nationalists nor the Russian Pan-Slavs were satisfied. The Turks, both reactionaries like Abdul Hamid and the revolutionary Young Turks in exile, were indignant that peace had been made by further dismemberment of their territory. The demonstrated weakness of Turkey was a constant temptation not only to Russians, Austrians, Serbs, Bulgars, Greeks, and Armenians, but also to the British, French, Italians, and finally the Germans, who found imperialist penetration into its nominal borders irresistibly easy. In the years before 1914 German influence grew. Germans and German capital entered Turkey, projecting, and partially completing, a great Berlin to Bagdad railway to be accompanied by the exploitation of Near Eastern natural resources. The railroad was all but completed before 1914 despite the protests and representations of the Russians, the French, and particularly the British, who saw in it a direct threat to their empire in India.

Abdul Hamid, whose reign began with the Russian war and the Berlin congress, not unreasonably regarded all the nationalistic agitation against him as inspired by foreign imperialists. He repressed all agitation with unblushing despotism and unabashed brutality. He held his empire together by playing the Europeans against one another, for which they accused him of

Oriental duplicity. He both lost and gained from the influence of foreign capital. In 1881, overcome with war debts, he had virtually to hand over the whole taxation system of his empire to the agents of foreign bankers, but on the other hand the bondholders, mainly French, could not willingly see the total collapse of a sultan to whom they had lent so much money. He tried also to combat nationalism and revolutionism by a religious revival. He re-asserted the dormant powers of the Ottoman sultan as caliph, or commander of the faithful, the universal spiritual head of all Islam. He hoped to rouse a militant neo-Islam against the common menace of the so-called Christian world. But although waves of Pan-Islamism, of neo-Moslem and anti-Christian feeling were in fact stirring all Islam at this time, neo-caliphism appealed to very few. Arabs and Persians, the learned doctors at Mecca, the Moslems of India and the East Indies remained unstirred by a caliph who was also the Turkish sultan. Nevertheless, Abdul Hamid for thirty years hung on to his empire, except in North Africa.

EGYPT AND NORTH AFRICA

For Egypt, technically autonomous within the Ottoman Empire, the 1850's and 1860's were a time of progress in the Western sense as they had been for the Empire as a whole. The Egyptian government modernized its administration, court system, and property law, cooperated with the French in building the Suez Canal, encouraged shipping on the Red Sea, and let British and French interests construct railroads. Between 1861 and 1865, while the American South was unable to export raw cotton, the annual export of Egyptian cotton rose from 60,000,000 to 250,000,000 pounds. Egypt more than Turkey was drawn into the world market, and the khedive more than the sultan became a Western type of man. The khedive Ismail built himself a fine new opera house in Cairo, where, in 1871, two years after the opening of the Suez Canal, Verdi's *Aïda*, written at the khedive's request, was resoundingly performed for the first time.

Such improvements cost a good deal of money, borrowed in England and France. The Egyptian government was soon in financial straits, only temporarily relieved by the sale of Canal shares to Disraeli. By 1879 matters reached the point where Western banking interests forced the abdication of Ismail and his replacement by Tewfik, who, with a childlike fascination for the new Western marvels, soon let himself become thoroughly enmeshed by his creditors. This led to nationalistic protests within Egypt, headed by Colonel Arabi. In a pattern repeated in many parts of the colonial world, especially in Manchu China, the nationalists opposed both the foreigners and their own government, charging it with being a mere front for foreign interests. Arabi's movement, nationalistic and religious, neo-Moslem and anti-foreign, led to riots in Alexandria, where Europeans had to flee aboard British and French shipping in the harbor. A British squadron then unceremoniously bombarded Alexandria. British troops (the French, though invited to take part, refused) disembarked in 1882 at Suez and Alexandria, defeated Arabi, and took Tewfik under their protection. The military intervention of 1882 was said by the British to be temporary, but British troops remained there for a long time, through two world wars and far into the twentieth century.

Egypt became a British protectorate. The British protected the khedive from discontent within his own country, from the claims of the Ottoman Porte, and from the rival attentions of other European powers. The British resident from 1883 to 1907, an exceptionally capable administrator named Evelyn Baring, the first Earl of Cromer, reconstructed the economy of the country, reformed its taxation, eased the burdens on the peasants and raised their productivity, encouraged the growth of raw materials wanted by England, and assured regular payment of interest to British, French and other holders of Egyptian bonds.

The French strenuously objected when the British stayed on so long in Egypt. It had long been the French who had the greatest investments in the Near East, and Near Easterners who were at all Westernized—Egyptian, Syrian, Turkish—overwhelmingly preferred the French language and culture to the English. The French, harboring deep suspicion of British designs in Egypt, compensated themselves by building a North African empire farther west. They developed Algeria, assumed a protectorate over Tunisia and began to penetrate Morocco. Upon these French advances the British, and soon the Germans, looked with unmitigated disfavor. Rivalry for the spoils of the Ottoman Empire thus created enmity among the Great Powers, and constituted a fertile source of the war scares, fears and diplomatic maneuvers that preceded the First World War. These are related in the following chapter.

The dissolution of the Ottoman Empire became indistinguishable from the whole chronic international crisis before 1914. It is enough to say here, to keep the fate of the Ottoman Empire in focus, that Abdul Hamid's frantic policies came to nothing and that the Young Turks won control of the Ottoman government in 1908. They forced the restoration of the constitution of 1876 and introduced many reforms. In the midst of the revolutionary disturbances of 1908 Bulgaria proclaimed its full independence and Austria annexed Bosnia. In the Turco-Italian War of 1911–12 Italy took Libya and the Dodecanese Islands from the Turks. In two successive Balkan Wars (1912–13) Turkey lost nearly all its territory in Europe to Bulgaria, Serbia, Greece, and Albania, the latter becoming an independent state in 1912. Finally, when all Europe became involved in war in 1914, Russia again declared war on Turkey and the Turks came into the war on the side of Germany, whose political and economic influence in the Empire had been steadily growing. During the war, with British aid, the Arabs detached themselves from the empire, becoming eventually independent Arab states. Egypt, too, ended all connections with the Empire. In 1923 a Turkish Republic was proclaimed. It was confined to Constantinople and the Anatolian peninsula, where the bulk of the true Turkish people lived. The new republic proceeded to undergo a thorough nationalist and secular revolution.[21]

80. The Partition of Africa

South of Mediterranean Africa lay the Sahara, and south of that lay Black Africa, the Dark Continent for Europeans. For centuries Europeans knew only its coasts—the Gold Coast, Ivory Coast, Slave Coast—to which from an inexhaustible interior had come shackled processions of captive slaves, as well as the swelling waters of enormous rivers, like the Nile and the Congo, whose sources in the dim hinterland were a subject of romantic speculation. The population was Negro, except that Arabic-speaking whites were found on the east coast, and in the southern part of the continent (at the time of the founding of the Union of South Africa in 1910) about 1,100,-000 Europeans lived along with about 5,000,000 blacks. The Negroes, agricultural or pastoral, without writing or enduring political states, were at a cultural level resembling that of the Germans as known to the Romans fifteen hundred years before.

THE OPENING OF AFRICA

Missionaries, explorers, and individual adventurers first opened this world to Europe. The historic pair, Livingstone and Stanley, well illustrate the drift of events. Long before the imperialist age, in 1841, the Scotsman David Livingstone arrived in southeast Africa as a medical missionary. He gave himself to humanitarian and religious work, with a little occasional trading, and much travel and discovery, but without political or true economic aims. Exploring the Zambesi river, he was the first white man to look upon the Victoria Falls. Fully at home in inner Africa, safe and at friends with its native people, he was quite content to be let alone. But the hectic forces of modern civilization sought him out. Word spread in Europe and America that Dr. Livingstone was lost. The New York *Herald*, to manufacture news, sent the roving journalist H. M. Stanley to "find" him, which he did in 1871. Livingstone soon died, deeply honored by the natives. Stanley was a man of the new era. Seeing vast possibilities in Africa, he went to Europe to solicit backers. In 1878 he found a man with the same ideas, who happened to be a king, Leopold II, King of the Belgians.

Leopold, for all his royalty, was at heart a promoter. China, Formosa, the Philippines, and Morocco had in turn attracted his fancy, but it was the central African basin of the Congo that he decided to develop. Stanley was exactly the man he was looking for, and the two founded at Brussels, with a

⌇⌇⌇⌇⌇⌇⌇⌇⌇⌇⌇⌇⌇⌇⌇⌇

[21] See pp. 767–9.

few financiers, an International Congo Association in 1878. It was a purely private enterprise; the Belgian government and people had nothing to do with it. All Africa inland from the coasts was considered to be, like America in the time of Columbus, a *terra nullius*, without government and claimed by nobody, wide open to the first civilized persons who might arrive. Stanley, returning to the Congo in 1882, in a year or two concluded treaties with over five hundred chiefs, who in return for a few trinkets or a few yards of cloth, put their crude marks on the mysterious papers and accepted the blue-and-gold flag of the Association.

Since the Dark Continent was still innocent of internal frontiers, no one could tell how much ground the Association might soon cover by these methods. The German explorer Karl Peters, working inland from Zanzibar, was signing treaties with the chiefs of east Africa. The Frenchman Brazza, departing from the west coast, and distributing the tricolor in every village, was claiming on the Congo river itself a territory larger than France. The Portuguese aspired to join their ancient colonies of Angola and Mozambique into a trans-African empire, for which they required a generous portion of the interior. Britain supported Portugal. In every case the home governments in Europe were still hesitant over involvement in the African wilds, but they were pushed on by small organized minorities of colonizing enthusiasts, and they faced the probability that if they missed the moment it would be too late.

Bismarck, who personally thought African colonies an absurdity, but was sensitive to the new pressures, called another conference at Berlin in 1885, this time to submit the African question to international regulation. Most European states, as well as the United States, attended. The Berlin conference attempted to do two things: to set up the territories of the Congo Association as an international state, under international auspices and restrictions; and to draft an international code governing the way in which European powers wishing to acquire African territory should proceed.

The Congo Free State, which in 1885 took the place of the International Congo Association, was not only an international creation but embodied, in principle, what was to be known in the next century as international trusteeship for backward peoples. The Berlin conference specified that the new state should have no connection with any power, including Belgium. It delegated the government to Leopold. It drew the boundaries, making the Congo Free State almost as large as the United States east of the Mississippi, and it added certain specific provisions: the Congo river was internationalized, persons of all nationalities should be free to do business in the Congo state, there should be no tariff levied on imports, and the slave trade should be suppressed. Leopold in 1889 reassembled the signatory powers in a second conference, held at Brussels. The Brussels conference took further steps to root out the slave trade, which remained a stubborn though declining evil, because the Moslem world was several generations behind the Christian in abolishing slavery. The Brussels conference also undertook to protect native rights, correct certain glaring abuses, and reduce the traffic in liquor and firearms.

This attempt at internationalism failed, because Europe had no international machinery by which the hard daily work of executing general agreements could be carried out. Leopold went his own way in the Congo. His determination to make it commercially profitable led him to unconscionable extremes. Europe and America demanded rubber, and the Congo was at the time one of the world's few sources of supply. The Congo people, among the least advanced of the Negroes, and afflicted by the disease and enervation of a lowland equatorial climate, could be made to tap enough rubber trees only by inhuman severity and compulsion. The trees themselves were destroyed without thought of replacement. Leopold, by ravaging its resources and virtually enslaving its people, was able to draw from the Congo a princely income to be spent in Brussels, but he could never make the enterprise self-supporting. Consumed with debt, he borrowed another twenty-five million francs from the kingdom of Belgium, agreeing that Belgium should inherit the Congo on his death if the debt was unpaid. In 1908, the reluctant Belgians thus found themselves heirs to some "tropical gardens" to which they had been consistently indifferent. The Free State became the Belgian Congo, and under Belgian administration the worst excesses of Leopold's regime were removed.

The Berlin conference of 1885 had also laid down, for expansion in Africa, certain rules of the game—a European power with holdings on the coast had prior rights in the back country; occupation must not be on paper only, through drawing lines on a map, but must consist in real occupation by administrators or troops; and each power must give proper notice to the others as to what territories it considered its own. A wild scramble for "real occupation" quickly followed. In fifteen years the entire continent was parcelled out. The sole exceptions were Ethiopia and, technically, Liberia, founded in 1822 as a colony for emancipated American slaves and virtually a protectorate of the United States ever since.

Everywhere a variant of the same process was repeated. First, somewhere in the wilderness, would appear a handful of white men, bringing their inevitable treaties—sometimes printed forms. To get what they wanted, the Europeans commonly had to ascribe powers to the chief which by the customs of the tribe he did not possess—powers to convey sovereignty, sell land, or grant mining concessions. Thus the Africans were baffled at the outset by foreign legal conceptions. Then the Europeans would build up the position of the chief, since they themselves had no influence over the people. This led to the widespread system of "indirect rule," by which colonial authorities acted through the existing chiefs and tribal forms. There were many things that only the chief could arrange, such as security for isolated Europeans, porter services, or gangs of workmen to build roads or railroads.

Labor was the overwhelming problem. For pure slavery Europeans now had an abhorrence, and they exterminated it wherever they could. But the African, so long as he lived in his own native way, did not react like the free wage-earner postulated in civilized business and economics. He had little sense of individual gain, and almost no use for money. Generally he did not work very hard according to European ideas; work, continuous and laborious work, was in many African societies left to the women. The result was that Europeans all over Africa resorted to forced labor. For road building, systems like the French *corvée* before the Revolution reappeared.[22] Or the chief would be required to supply a quota of able-bodied men for a certain length of time, and frequently he did so gladly, to raise his own importance in the eyes of the whites. More indirect methods were also used. The colonial government might levy a hut-tax or a poll-tax, payable only in money, to obtain which the native would have to seek a job. Or the new government, once installed, might allocate so much land to Europeans as private property (another foreign conception) that the local tribe could no longer subsist on the lands that remained to it. Or the whole tribe might be moved to a reservation, like Indians in the United States. In either case, while the women tilled the fields or tended the stock at home, the men would move off to take jobs under the whites for infinitesimal pay. The men then lived in "compounds," away from family and tribal kindred; they became demoralized or even degenerate; and the labor they gave, unintelligent and unwilling, would scarcely have been tolerated in any more civilized community. In these circumstances everything was done to uproot the African, and nothing was done to Westernize him. The old tribal or village society collapsed, and nothing replaced it.

Conditions improved with the twentieth century, as traditions of enlightened colonial administration were built up. Colonial officials even came to serve as buffers or protectors of the natives against the white man's interest. Throughout, it was part of the ethos of imperialism to put down slavery, tribal warfare, superstition, disease, and illiteracy. Slowly a Westernized class of African Negroes grew—chiefs and the sons of chiefs, Catholic priests and Protestant ministers, warehouse clerks and government employees. Young men from Nigeria or Uganda appeared as students at Oxford, the University of Paris, or Howard University in the United States, which as the Negro world became aware of itself emerged as the world's leading Negro institution of learning. Westernized Africans usually resented both exploitation and paternalism. They showed signs of turning nationalistic, like corresponding persons in the Ottoman Empire or Asia. If they wanted Westernization, it was at a pace and for a purpose of their own. As the twentieth century progressed, nationalism in Africa grew more vocal and more intense.

FRICTION AND RIVALRY BETWEEN THE POWERS

Meanwhile, in the fifteen years from 1885 to 1900, the Europeans in Africa came dangerously near to open blows. The Portuguese annexed huge domains in Angola and Mozambique. The Italians took over two barren tracts, Italian Somaliland and Eritrea on the Red Sea. They then moved inland, in quest of more imposing possessions, to conquer Ethiopia and the

[22] See p. 306.

headwaters of the Nile. Some 80,000 Ethiopians, however, slaughtered and routed 20,000 Italians in pitched battle at Adowa in 1896. It was the first time that native Africans successfully defended themselves against the whites, and it discouraged invasion of Ethiopia by the Italians (or other Europeans) for forty years. Italy and Portugal, like the Congo Free State and Spain (which retained a few vestiges of former days) were able to enjoy sizable holdings in Africa because of mutual fears among the principal contenders. The principal contenders were Great Britain, France, and Germany. Each preferred to have territory held by a minor power rather than by one of its significant rivals.

The Germans were late comers in the colonial race, which Bismarck entered with reluctance. By the 1880's all the usual imperialist arguments were heard in Germany, though most of them, such as the need of new markets, of outlets for emigration, or for the investment of capital, had little or no application in tropical Africa. The Germans established colonies in German East Africa, and in the Cameroons and Togo on the west coast, not to mention an unpleasant desert called German Southwest Africa. It did not escape the notice of German imperial planners that some day the Congo and the Portuguese colonies might be joined with German East Africa and the Cameroons in a solid German belt across the African heartland. The French controlled most of west Africa, from Algeria across the Sahara and the Sudan to various points on the Guinea coast. They also occupied Obok on the Red Sea, and after the Italian defeat in 1896 their influence in Ethiopia grew. French planners therefore dreamed of a solid French belt across Africa from Dakar to the Gulf of Aden. The French government in 1898 despatched Captain J. B. Marchand with a small party eastward from Lake Chad, to hoist the tricolor far away on the upper Nile, in the southern part of the Sudan, which no European power as yet "effectively" occupied.

The two presumptive east-and-west belts, German and French, were cut (presumptively) by a north-and-south belt, projected in the British imperial imagination as an "Africa British from the Cape to Cairo." From the Cape of Good Hope Cecil Rhodes pushed northward into Rhodesia. Kenya and Uganda in the mid-continent were already British. In Egypt, a British protectorate since 1882, the British began to support old Egyptian claims to the upper Nile. The first venture proved a disaster, when in 1885 a British officer, "Chinese Gordon," leading an Egyptian force, was killed by aroused Moslems at Khartoum. In the following decade British opinion turned imperialist in earnest. Another British officer, General Kitchener (with a young man named Winston Churchill under his command) again started southward up the Nile, and defeated the local Moslems in 1898 at Omdurman. He then pushed on further upstream. At a place called Fashoda he met Marchand.

The ensuing Fashoda Crisis brought Britain and France to the verge of war. Already at odds over Egypt and Morocco,[23] the two governments used the encounter at Fashoda to force a showdown. It was a test of strength, not

[23] See pp. 635–6.

only for their respective plans for all Africa, but for their relative position in all imperialist and international issues. Both at first refused to yield. The British virtually threatened to fight. The French, fearful of their insecurity against Germany in Europe, at last decided not to take the risk. They backed down, and recalled Marchand from Fashoda. A wave of hatred for the British swept over France.

The British no sooner won this Pyrrhic victory than they became involved in more unpleasantness at the other end of the African continent. In 1890 Cecil Rhodes had become prime minister of the Cape Colony. He was a principal sponsor of the Cape-to-Cairo dream. Two small independent neighboring republics, the Transvaal and the Orange Free State, stood in his way. Their people were Afrikaners—Dutch who had originally settled the Cape in the seventeenth century, then after 1815, when England annexed the Cape of Good Hope, had made the "great trek" to escape from British rule. The Boers, as the English called them, from the Dutch word for "farmer," were simple, obstinate, and old-fashioned. They thought Negro slavery not ungodly, and disliked promoters, fortune-hunters, footloose adventurers, mining-camp people, and other Uitlanders.

The discovery of diamonds and gold in the Transvaal brought the issue to a head. British capital and British people poured in. The Transvaal refused to pass legislation needed by the mining corporations and their employees. In 1895 Rhodes, attempting to precipitate revolution in the Transvaal, sent a party of armed irregulars, under Dr. Jameson, over its borders. This Jameson Raid was a failure, but in Europe a great cry went up against British bullying of a small inoffensive republic. The German Emperor, William II, despatched a famous telegram to Paul Kruger, president of the Transvaal, congratulating him on his driving off the invaders "without having to call for the support of friendly powers"—*i.e.*, Germany. Three years later the British empire went to war with the two Boer republics. It took another three years to subdue them. Once conquered and brought within the British empire they were left with their self-governing institutions, and in 1910 they were joined with the predominantly English colonies of Natal and Cape Colony into the Union of South Africa, which received a semi-independence along the lines of the Dominion of Canada.

The Fashoda crisis and the Boer War, coming in rapid succession, revealed to the British the bottomless depths of their unpopularity in Europe. All European governments and peoples were pro-Boer; only the United States, involved at the time in a similar conquest of the Philippines, showed any

---

Africa, 1914

The map shows the recognized holdings of the Powers in 1914. The inset suggests the directions of political pressure about 1898. These pressures led to the Fashoda crisis in 1898 and the Boer war in 1899. In 1898 the British and German governments held secret discussions on the possible partitioning of the Portuguese colonies, which, however, never came to pass since the British greatly preferred to have the Portuguese colonies remain in the hands of Portugal.

AFRICA
1914

1000 MILES

LINES OF
POLITICAL
PRESSURE
ABOUT 1898

BRITISH
FRENCH
GERMAN

30°N

30°W
TROPIC OF
CANCER

MADEIRA IS.
(PORT.)

CANARY IS.
(SP.)

RIO DE ORO
(SP.)

Tangier
FRENCH
MOROCCO
GIBRALTAR (BR.)

ALGERIA

Algiers

TUNISIA

MALTA
(BR.)

MEDITERRANEAN SEA

LIBYA
(ITL.)

Alexandria

Cairo

SUEZ CANAL

Dakar
GAMBIA
(BR.)
SENEGAL
(FR.)

PORTUGUESE
GUINEA

SIERRA
LEONE
(BR.)

LIBERIA

FRENCH
WEST AFRICA

NIGER R.

SAHARA

FRENCH SUDAN

LAKE CHAD

AFRICA R.

EQUATOR

IVORY
COAST
(FR.)
GOLD COAST
(BR.)

TOGO
(GER.)

NIGERIA
(BR.)

FRENCH
EQUATORIAL
AFRICA

KAMERUN
(GER.)

RIO MUNI
(SP.)
Libreville

FRENCH

Congo R.

0°

Congo R.

BELGIAN
CONGO

LAKE TANGANYIKA

ANGLO-
EGYPTIAN

EGYPT

NILE R.

RED SEA

ARABIA

ADEN

Omdurman
Khartoum
SUDAN
Fashoda
WHITE NILE

BLUE NILE

ERITREA
(ITL.)

Agrwo
ADI
TANA

Addis
Ababa

FRENCH
SOMALILAND

BRITISH
SOMALILAND

Okok

UGANDA

ETHIOPIA

ITALIAN
SOMALILAND

ANGOLA
(PORT.)

LAKE
VICTORIA

GERMAN
EAST
AFRICA
(TANGANYIKA)

BRITISH
EAST
AFRICA

ZANZIBAR (BR.)

INDIAN OCEAN

WALFISCH
BAY (BR.)

GERMAN
SOUTHWEST
AFRICA

BECHUANA
LAND

RHODESIA

NYASA
LAND

VICTORIA
FALLS

ZAMBEZI R.

LAKE
NYASA

MOZAMBIQUE
(PORT.)

TROPIC OF
CAPRICORN

60°E

Cape Town
CAPE OF
GOOD HOPE

CAPE COLONY

ORANGE
FREE STATE

TRANS-
VAAL

NATAL

UNION OF
SOUTH
AFRICA

MADAGASCAR

BRITISH

FRENCH

GERMAN

ITALIAN

TRM

sympathy for the British. The British, after the Boer War, began to rethink their international position, as will soon be seen.

As in the case of the Ottoman Empire, rivalry between the Great Powers over the spoils of Africa embittered international relations and helped prepare the way for the First World War. The rivalry over Morocco involving France and Germany entered into the general pre-war crisis, and will be related in the following chapter. As for Africa as a whole, there was little territorial change after the Boer War, although in 1911 Italy took Libya, in North Africa, from the Turks. In 1914 the Germans were excluded from their short-lived empire. Had the Germans won the First World War, the map of Africa would probably have been greatly revised, but since they lost it the only change was to assign the German colonies, under international mandate, to the French and British empires. With this change, and except for the conquest of Ethiopia by Italy in 1935, a conquest which did not survive the Second World War, and the formal acquisition of independence by Libya in 1951, the map of Africa long remained what the brief years of partition had made it.

81. Imperialism in Asia: The Dutch, the British, and the Russians

THE DUTCH EAST INDIES AND BRITISH INDIA

British India and the Dutch East Indies, in the half century before the First World War, were the world's ideal colonies. They illustrated the kind of empire that all imperialists would have wished to have, and a glance at them suggests the goal toward which imperialism was logically moving.

Whereas all countries of western Europe showed a surplus of imports, receiving more goods from the rest of the world than they sent out, India and Indonesia invariably, year after year and decade after decade, showed a surplus of exports, sending out far more goods than they took in. This export surplus was the hallmark of the developed colonial area, geared closely into the world market, with low purchasing power for the natives, and kept going by foreign investment and management. Both regions, in addition, were so large as to have a good deal of internal business—commerce, insurance, banking, transportation—which never appeared in the statistics for world trade, but which, being dominated by Europeans, added immeasurably to their profits. Both had rich and varied natural resources, tropical in character, so that they never competed with the products of Europe—though India even before 1914 showed tendencies to industrialization. In both regions the people were adept and quick to learn. But they were divided by religion and language, so that, once conquered, they were relatively easy for the whites to govern. Neither region before the First World War had any self-government at the highest levels. Both were ruled by a civil service, honest and high-minded by its own lights, in which the most illustrious, most influential, and best paying positions were reserved for the whites. Hence upper-class families in England and the Netherlands valued their empires as fields of opportunity for their sons—somewhat as they had formerly valued an established church. In both India and Indonesia the governments were more or less benevolent despotisms, which, by curbing warfare, plague, and famine, at least allowed the population to grow in numbers. Java, with 5,000,000 people in 1815, had 48,000,000 in 1942. India's population in the same years probably grew from less than 200,000,000 to almost 400,000,000. Finally, as the last virtue of a perfect colony, no foreign power directly challenged the British in India, or the Dutch in their islands.

The Dutch in 1815 occupied little more than the island of Java itself.[24] In the following decades the British moved into Singapore, the Malay peninsula and north Borneo, and made claims to Sumatra; the French in the 1860's appeared in Indo-China; the Germans in the 1880's annexed eastern New Guinea and the Marshall and Solomon islands. Ultimately it was the mutual jealousy of these three that preserved the Dutch position. The Dutch, however, took initiative themselves. To forestall occupation by other Europeans, and to put down native pirates and find raw materials that the world demanded, the Dutch spread their rule over the whole three-thousand-mile extent of the archipelago. They created an empire, in place of the old chain of trading posts concerned only with buying and selling. Revolts were suppressed in 1830, 1849, 1888; not till the twentieth century were northern Sumatra or the interior of Celebes brought under control. For some decades the Dutch exploited their huge empire by a kind of forced labor, the "culture system," in which the authorities required farmers to deliver, as a kind of tax, stated amounts of stated crops, such as sugar or coffee. After 1870 a freer system was introduced. The Dutch also, as an important matter of policy, favored instruction in the Malay and Javanese languages, not in Dutch. This preserved the native cultures from Westernizing disintegration, but at the same time meant that Western ideas of nationalism and democracy entered more slowly. The strongest resistance to Dutch imperialism (as later to the equally foreign doctrines of Marxism) came from the Mohammedanism of the people. By 1914, thanks to Western steamship lines, 20,000 Indonesians a year were making the pilgrimage to Mecca. Pan-Islamism, the idea that all Islam should stand united against the Christians (an idea that Abdul Hamid used in vain by reasserting the caliphate), made rapid progress in Indonesia.

In India, in 1857, the British faced a dangerous rebellion, commonly called the Indian Mutiny, as if it had been a revolt of undisciplined soldiers only. The Indian army, with its sepoys, was the only organization through which Indians could exert any collective pressure. The proportion of sepoys in the Army was high in 1857 (about five-sixths) because British units had been withdrawn for the Crimean war, and for action in China. Many Indians, outside the army, had been restless for decades. Rulers had been conquered and dethroned. Landowners had lost their property and been replaced by new

〰〰〰〰〰〰〰〰〰〰

[24] See p. 138.

ones more friendly to the British. Religious sentiments were inflamed. The British too obviously regarded Indian beliefs as repulsive: they had outlawed suttee, or widow-burning, suppressed the Thugs, a small sect of holy assassins, and one British officer even declared that in ten years the government would abolish caste. The Moslems were agitated by Wahabi fundamentalism. Mysterious propaganda circulated over India. It infiltrated the sepoys, announcing to Moslem soldiers that certain newly issued cartridges were greased with the fat of a pig, and to Hindus that the same cartridges were greased with the fat of a cow. Since for Hindus the cow was sacred, and for Moslems to touch

This small map shows almost half the surface of the earth. All the most important parts of the British Empire are visible except Canada and the United Kingdom itself. All shores of the Indian Ocean are shown to be British, except for French Madagascar, the politically weak Portuguese, Italian and Dutch colonies, and the Arabian and Persian coasts, in which British influence was strong. It is easy to see why the Mediterranean and the Suez Canal, leading from Europe into this half-world, were called the lifeline of the British Empire.

pork was profane, much agitation was produced. The sepoys mutinied in the Ganges valley; and with them the other injured interests, including the far-faded Great Mogul and his court, rose against the British.

The British put down the rebellion, aided by the fact that western and southern India took no part in it. But the uprising persuaded the British to a radically new course of policy, pursued basically until the end of the Indian Empire almost a century later. The British East India Company and the Mogul Empire were both finally and forever done away with. British authorities ruled directly. But the British concluded that they must rule India with and through the Indians themselves, not against them. This in practice meant a collaboration between the imperial power and the Indian upper classes. The British began to shelter Indian vested interests. They supported the Indian landlords, and became more indulgent toward Indian "superstition." Where before 1857, when they conquered an Indian state, they had simply abolished it and incorporated its territories, after the Mutiny they kept the remaining Indian states as protectorates. States existing in 1857, such as Hyderabad and Kashmir and over two hundred others, with their galaxy of rajahs and maharajahs, carried on to the end of British rule in 1947. It was largely to provide a fitting summit for this mountain of Indian royalty that Queen Victoria was proclaimed Empress of India in 1877.

India had been a considerable manufacturing country by pre-industrial standards. Indian merchants had once been important throughout the Indian Ocean, and before 1800 Indian exports to Europe had included many textiles and other finished goods.[25] The native crafts collapsed before modern industrialism reinforced by political power. "India," observed a British expert in 1837, "can never again be a great manufacturing country, but by cultivating her connection with England she may be one of the greatest agricultural countries in the world." Free trade (made possible by military superiority, usually overlooked by the economists) turned Britain into the world's workshop and India into a supplier of raw materials. Indian exports, in the latter part of the nineteenth century, consisted increasingly in raw cotton, tea, jute, oilseeds, indigo, and wheat. The British shipped their manufactures in return. Business in India boomed; India came to have the densest railway-network outside of Europe and North America. It is important to note, however, as a commentary on dealing with poor countries, that Britain in 1914 did far more trading with the 6,000,000 high-standard white people of Australia and New Zealand than with the 315,000,000 impoverished people of India.

The British, in contrast to the Dutch, decided in 1835 to favor instruction in English, not in the native languages. The historian Macaulay, one of the commission to make this recommendation, branded the Indian languages as vehicles of barbarous and unenlightened ideas—a bar to progress. The British also, after the Mutiny, admitted Indians to the civil service and to governors' councils—sparingly indeed, but more than the Dutch in Indonesia. There were also many Indian business men. A class of Westernized

[25] See pp. 228-9

Indians grew up, speaking perfect English, and often educated in England. They demanded more of a role in the affairs of their country. In 1885 the predominantly Hindu Indian National Congress was organized; in 1906, the All India Moslem League. Moslem separatism, while favored by the British and sometimes even blamed upon them, was natural to India and exploited by some Indian leaders. Nationalism spread. It became increasingly anti-British, and radical nationalism turned also against the Indian princes, capitalists, and business men, as accomplices in imperialism, and so took on the color of socialism. In the period of the First World War, under nationalist pressure, the British granted more representation to Indians, especially in provincial affairs, but the movement toward self-rule was never fast enough to overcome the basic anti-British feeling of the Indian peoples.

CONFLICT OF RUSSIAN AND BRITISH INTERESTS

While no outsider yet threatened the British in India, British statecraft discerned in the northern sky a large cloud which was clearly approaching. The Russian empire had occupied northern Asia since the seventeenth century.[26] About 1850 Russian pressure on inner Asia was resumed. It was a type of imperialism in which neither the demand for markets, nor for raw materials, nor for the investment of capital, counted for much. In these matters Russia was itself semi-colonial with respect to the West. The Russians had, like the Westerners, a sense of spreading their type of civilization; but Russian expansion was distinctively political in that most of the initiative came from the government. Russia was an ice-bound empire, craving "warm water ports." It was a land-locked empire, so that whichever way it turned it moved toward one ocean or another. The ocean was the domain of the Westerners, and in particular the British. In the large picture, Russia pushed by land against the Ottoman Empire, Persia, India, and China, all of which the British (and others) reached by sea. In 1860, on the shores of the Sea of Japan, the Russians founded Vladivostok, the farthest-flung of all Slavic cities, whose name meant Lord of the East. But their advance in the mid-century was mainly in the arid and thinly settled regions of western Asia. The British had already fought two Afghan wars to keep Afghanistan as a no-man's land between Russia and India. In 1864 the Russians took Tashkent, in Turkestan. A decade later they touched India itself, but were kept away by an Anglo-Russian agreement, which allotted a long tongue of land to Afghanistan, and so separated the Indian and Russian empires by twenty miles—the new frontier, in the high Pamirs, on the Roof of the World, was to be sure, scarcely adapted to military operations.

Russian advances in Turkestan, east of the Caspian, increased the pressure on Persia, which had long felt the same pressure west of the Caspian, where cities like Tiflis and Baku, now Russian, had once been Persian. If

[26] See p. 207.

Tiflis and Turkestan could fall to the Russian empire, there was no reason why Persia should not do so next—except that Persia had a scacoast, and so might also be available for occupancy by the British. In 1864 a British company completed the first Persian telegraph, as part of the line from Europe to India. Other British investments and interests followed. Oil became important about 1900. In 1890, to bolster the Persian government against Russia, the British granted it a loan—taking the customs in Persian Gulf ports as collateral. In 1900 the Russian government granted the same favor, making its own loan to Persia, and appropriating as security all Persian customs except those of the Gulf. Russian ships appeared in the Persian Gulf in 1900, a demonstration soon countered by a state visit to Persia of the Viceroy of India, Lord Curzon. Clearly Persia was losing control of its own affairs, falling into zones, turning ripe for partition. A Persian nationalist revolution, directed against all foreigners and against the subservient government of the shah, broke out in 1905 and led to the assembly of the first parliament, but hardly settled the question of Persian independence. In 1907 the British recognized a Russian "sphere of influence" in northern Persia, the Russians a British sphere in the south.[27]

Imperial ambitions had deepened the hostility between Great Britain and Russia, with disputes over Persia and the Indian borderlands adding fuel to the quarrel they had long waged over the Ottoman Empire. We have seen how the struggle for Africa had at the same time estranged Britain from France, and indeed from all Europe.

82. Imperialism in Asia: China and the West

CHINA BEFORE WESTERN PENETRATION

But the biggest bone of imperialist contention was offered by China. On this bone every Great Power without exception tried to bite. The Manchu

[27] See p. 665.

Imperialism in Asia, 1840–1914

Boundaries and possessions are as of 1914. During these years the British and Dutch filled out their holdings in India and the East Indies, in each case moving outward from establishments founded long before. The Russians, who had long occupied Siberia, pressed southward in Central Asia, founded Vladivostok in 1860, and penetrated Manchuria at the close of the century. The French built an empire in Indo-China, while the United States acquired the Philippines, and the Germans, as late comers, were confined to miscellaneous parts of the Western Pacific. The Japanese won control of Korea and replaced the Russians as the chief outside influence in Manchuria. Meanwhile all obtained special rights and concessions in China. A bid for such concessions by Italy was refused.

IMPERIALISM IN ASIA, 1840-191[...]

RUSSIAN

EUROPE ASIA

OTTOMAN EMP.

ARCTIC

St. Petersburg · Archangel

Moscow

Samara · Tobolsk

Constant-inople

BLACK SEA

Astrakhan

Tomsk

Omsk

TRANS-SIBERIAN

Cairo

EGYPT · Jerusalem · Mosul

SUEZ CANAL

CASPIAN SEA · 1846

Baku · 1873

1873

LAKE BALKHASH

1854

Bagdad

Teheran

RUSSIAN SPHERE 1907

1881 1884 · Merv

1885

1864 · Tashkent

1860-65

1876

TURKESTAN

BOKHARA 1868

1895

Kashgar

SINKIANG

Basra

PERSIA

BRITISH SPHERE 1907

PERSIAN GULF

Kabul

AFGHAN-ISTAN

KASHMIR 1846

TIB[...]

Mecca

A R A B I A

OMAN

YEMEN

Karachi

BALUCH-ISTAN 1883

PUNJAB

INDUS

Delhi

MALAYA

NEPAL

BRAHMAPUTRA

GANGES

Aden (BR., 1839)

60°E

Diu (PORT.)

Bombay

I N D I A · Calcutta

B R I T I S H

Hyderabad

Goa (PORT.)

Yanaon (FR.)

BAY OF BENG[...]

Madras

Pondicherry (FR.)

Karikal (FR.)

CEYLON

AND[...]

EQUATOR

S N D I A

20°N

40°N

60°E

CRITICAL AREA
1895-1905

JEHOL

MANCHURIA

Mukden

Kinchow

GREAT WALL

Peking

LIAOTUNG PEN.

Tientsin

Taku

GULF OF CHILI

Dairen
Port Arthur

(LEASE TO {RUSSIA, 1898 / JAPAN, 1905}

KOREA

GRAND CANAL

CHINA

Chifu

Wei-hai-wei (BR., 1898)

YELLOW SEA

Tsinan

SHANTUNG

Kiaochow (GER., 1898)

Tsingtao

150 MILES

1000 MILES

TRM

ALASKA PURCHASED
BY UNITED STATES
FROM RUSSIA
1867

BERING
SEA

ALEUTIAN IS. (USA., 1867)

OCEAN

120°E

60°N

KAMCHATKA

NORTH

EMPIRE

SEA OF
OKHOTSK

PACIFIC

LENA R.

Yakutsk

SAKHALIN

KURILE
ISLANDS
(JAP., 1875)

40°N

LAKE
BAIKAL

Chita

AMUR
PROVINCE
1858

Khabarovsk

KARAFUTO
(JAP., 1905)

Irkutsk

AMUR R.

MARITIME
PROVINCE
(RUSS., 1868)

OCEAN

MANCHURIA

OUTER
MONGOLIA
(AUT. 1912,
RUSS. SPHERE)

Urga

Harbin

Vladivostok
1860

SEA
OF
JAPAN

Tokyo

INNER
MONGOLIA

Mukden

KOREA
(JAP., 1905,
1910)

JAPANESE
EMPIRE

JEHOL

CHINA

Peking
Tientsin

Port Arthur
(JAP., 1905)

Kiao-chow
(GER., 1898)

EAST CHINA

20°N

HUANG HO

Nanking

Shanghai
(BR., 1842)
Ningpo
1842

SEA

Chungking

Hankow
Foochow
1842

RYUKYU ISLANDS

MARIANAS IS.
(GER., 1899)

YANGTSE R.

Amoy

FORMOSA
(JAP., 1895)

SOUTH

GUAM
(USA., 1898)

YÜNNAN

KWANGSI
(FR. SPHERE)

Canton
(BR., 1842)

PESCADORES, (JAP., 1895)

RMA
52, 1885)

Hong Kong (BR., 1842)
Macao (PORT., 1557)

YAP

CAROLINE I.S.

52.
007

1826

Hanoi

Kwang-chow
(LEASE TO FR.
1898)

HAINAN

PHILIPPINE IS.
(USA., 1898, 1899)

PACIFIC

CAROLINE IS.
(GER., 1899)

PALAU IS.

MEKONG R.

SIAM

Bangkok

FRENCH
INDO-CHINA
1884, 1907

SOUTH

CHINA

Manila

MALAY STATES
(BR., 1000, 1824)

Saigon

SEA

BR.
N. BORNEO
1888

OCEAN

KAISER
WILHELMSLAND
(GER., 1884)

SARAWAK
1888

NEW
GUINEA

Singapore
(BR., 1819)

BORNEO

CELEBES

SUMATRA

Batavia

DUTCH

EAST

TIMOR

(PORT.
1859)

Darwin

AUSTRALIA

120° E

dynasty held a suzerainty over the whole area affected by Chinese civilization, from the mouth of the Amur river (as far north as Labrador) to Burma and Indo-China (as far south as Panama), and from the ocean westward into Mongolia and Tibet. In the old Chinese view China was the world itself, the Middle Kingdom between the upper and nether regions. The Europeans were outlandish barbarians. A few had trickled through to China since the European Middle Ages. But the Chinese people persistently wanted nothing to do with them.

China was moving into an upheaval of its own even before Western influence became of any importance. For two thousand years the country had seen dynasties come and go in a kind of cycle. The Manchu dynasty in the nineteenth century was clearly nearing its end. It was failing to preserve order or to curb extortion. About 1800 a White Lotus Society revolted and was suppressed. In 1813 a Heavenly Reason Society attempted to seize Peking. In the 1850's a Moslem rebellion set up a temporary independent state in the southwest. Greatest of all the upheavals was the Tai-ping Rebellion of 1850, in which as many as twenty million people, approximately the population of Great Britain at the time, are thought to have perished. Except that some fragmentary Christian ideas, obtained from missionaries, were expressed by some of the Tai-pings, the rebellion was due entirely to Chinese causes. The rebels attacked the Manchus, who had come from Manchuria two centuries before, as corrupt foreigners ruling over China. Their grievances were poverty, extortion, rack-renting, and absentee landlords. The Tai-pings at first set up a state in south China, and their armies were at first disciplined, but the fighting lasted so long that both the Tai-ping leaders and the Manchu commanders sent against them got out of control, and much of the country sank into chronic banditry and disorder. It was in this period that China's war lords, men controlling armed forces but obeying no government, took their rise. The Manchus managed to put down organized Tai-ping resistance after fourteen years, with some European assistance, led by the British General Gordon, the "Chinese Gordon" who later died at Khartoum. But it is clear that Chinese social confusion, agrarianism, and nationalism (the latter at first only anti-Manchu) antedated the impact of European imperialism. They were to remain after the Europeans had come and gone.

Into this distracted China the Europeans began to penetrate about 1840. It became their policy to extort concessions from the Manchu empire, but at the same time to defend the Manchu empire against internal opposition, as was shown by the exploits of Gordon. This was because they needed some kind of government in China with which they could make treaties, legalizing their claims, and binding upon the whole country.

THE OPENING OF CHINA TO THE WEST

The modern phase of Chinese relations with the West was inauspiciously opened by the Opium War of 1841. We have already observed how, though Europeans wanted Chinese products, the Chinese had no interest in buying European products in return. Trade therefore was difficult, and the British East India Company had for decades solved the problem of getting Chinese tea for Europe by shipping Indian-grown opium in return, since opium was one available commodity for which a Chinese demand existed.[28] When the Chinese government attempted to control the inflow of opium the British government went to war. Fifteen years later, in 1857, Britain and France combined in a second war upon China, to force the Chinese to receive their diplomats and deal with their traders. The Chinese proving contumacious, 17,000 French and British soldiers entered Peking and deliberately burned the emperor's very extensive Summer Palace, an appalling act of vandalism from which soldiers brought back so much loot—vases, tapestries, porcelain, enamels, jades, wood-carvings—as to set a fashion in Europe and America for Chinese art.

From the first of these wars arose the treaty of Nanking (1842), from the second, the treaties of Tientsin (1857), whose terms were soon duplicated in still other treaties signed by China with other European powers and with the United States. The resulting complex of interlocking agreements imposed certain restrictions on China, or conferred certain rights upon foreigners, which came to be known as the "treaty system." To the British in 1842 the Chinese ceded Hong Kong outright. They opened over a dozen cities, including Shanghai and Canton, to Europeans as "treaty ports." In these cities Europeans were allowed to make settlements of their own, immune to all Chinese law. Europeans traveling in the Chinese Empire remained subject only to their own governments, and European and American gunboats began to police the Yangtse river. The Chinese likewise paid large war indemnities, though it was they themselves who suffered most of the damages. They agreed to levy no import duty over 5%, and so became a free trade market for European products. To administer and collect the customs a staff of European experts was introduced. Money from the customs, collected with a new efficiency, on a swelling volume of imports, went in part to the British and French in payment of the indemnities, but part remained with the Manchu government, which, as noted, the Europeans had no desire to overthrow.

ANNEXATIONS AND CONCESSIONS

While China was thus permeated at the center like an aging cheese, by extraterritorial and other insidious privileges for Europeans, whole slabs of it were cut away at the outer rim. The Russians moved down the Amur river, established their Maritime Province and founded Vladivostok in 1860. The British annexed Burma in 1886. The French in 1883 assumed a protectorate over Annam despite Chinese protests; they soon combined Annam and other states into a sizable empire in French Indo-China. The Japanese,

[28] See pp. 229, 325.

now sufficiently Westernized to behave like Europeans in such matters, in 1876 recognized the independence of Korea. These outlying territories had never, it is true, been integral parts of China proper; but it was with China that they had had their most important political and cultural relations, and to the Chinese Emperor that they had paid tribute.

Japan, whose modernization has been described already, lost little time in developing an imperialistic urge.[29] An expansionist party already looked to the Chinese mainland and to the south. Japanese imperialism first revealed itself to the rest of the world in 1894, when Japan went to war with China over disputes in Korea. The Japanese soon won, equipped as they were with modern weapons, training and organization. They obliged the Chinese to sign the treaty of Shimonoseki in 1895, by which China ceded Korea, Formosa and the Liaotung Peninsula. The latter was a tongue of land reaching down from Manchuria to the sea; at its tip was Port Arthur. Manchuria was the northeastern part of China itself.

This sudden Japanese triumph precipitated a crisis in the Far East. No one had realized how strong Japan had become. All were astounded that a people who were not "European," *i.e.*, white, should show such aptitude for modern war and diplomacy. It was to be supposed that Japan had designs on Manchuria.

Now it so happened that Russia, not long before, in 1891, had begun to build the Trans-Siberian Railway, whose eastern terminus was to be Vladivostok, the Lord of the East. Manchuria extended northward in a great hump between central Siberia and Vladivostok. The Russians, whether or not they ever dominated Manchuria themselves, could not allow its domination by another Great Power. It happened also that Germany was at this time looking for a chance to enter the Far Eastern arena, and that France had formed an alliance with Russia, whose good will it was eager to retain.[30]

Russia, Germany, and France therefore registered an immediate joint demurrer with the Tokyo Foreign Office. They demanded that Japan give up the Liaotung Peninsula. The Japanese hesitated, they were indignant, but they yielded. The Liaotung went back to China; Korea and Formosa were retained.

In China many alert people were humiliated at the defeat by the Japanese whom they had despised. The Chinese government, at last facing the inevitable, began madly to plan Westernization. Huge loans were obtained from Europe—the customs being pawned as security, following the pattern well established in Turkey, Persia, and Santo Domingo. But the European powers did not wish China to become consolidated too soon. Nor had they forgotten the sudden apparition of Japan. The result was a frantic scramble for further concessions in 1898.

It seemed in 1898 as if the Chinese empire in its turn would be partitioned. The Germans extorted a ninety-nine-year lease on Kiaochow Bay,

ᴧᴧᴧᴧᴧᴧᴧᴧᴧᴧᴧᴧᴧᴧᴧᴧ

[29] See pp. 548–54.
[30] See p. 662.

plus exclusive rights in the Shantung peninsula. The Russians took a lease on the Liaotung Peninsula from which they had just excluded Japan; they thus obtained Port Arthur, and rights to build railroads in Manchuria to interlock with their Trans-Siberian system. The French took Kwangchow, and the British Wei-hai-wei, in addition to confirming their sphere of influence in the Yangtse Valley. The Italians demanded a share, but were refused. The United States, fearing that all China might soon be parcelled out into exclusive spheres, announced its policy of the Open Door. The idea of the Open Door was that China should remain territorially intact and independent, and that powers having special concessions or spheres of influence should maintain the 5% Chinese tariff and allow business men of all nations to trade without discrimination. The British supported the Open Door, as a means of discouraging actual annexations by Japan or Russia, which, as the only Great Powers adjacent to China, were the only ones that could despatch real armies into its territory. The Open Door was a program, not so much of leaving China to the Chinese, as of assuring that all outsiders should find it literally "open."

If the reader will imagine what the United States would be like if foreign warships patrolled the Mississippi as far as St. Louis, if foreigners came and went throughout the country without being under its laws, if New York, New Orleans, and other cities contained foreign settlements outside its jurisdiction, but in which all banking and management were concentrated, if foreigners determined the tariff policy, collected the proceeds and remitted much of the money to their own governments, if the western part of the city of Washington had been burned (the Summer Palace), Long Island and California annexed to distant empires (Hong Kong and Indo-China) and all New England were coveted by two immediate neighbors (Manchuria), if the national authorities were half in collusion with these foreigners and half victimized by them, and if large areas of the country were the prey to bandits, guerillas, and revolutionary secret societies conspiring against the helpless government and occasionally murdering some of the foreigners—then he can understand how observant Chinese felt at the end of the last century, and why the term "imperialism" came to be held by so many of the world's peoples in abomination.

One Chinese secret society, its name somewhat literally translated as the Order of Literary Patriotic Harmonious Fists, and so dubbed the Boxers by the amused Westerners, broke out in insurrection in 1899. The Boxers pulled up railway tracks, fell upon Chinese Christians, besieged the foreign legations, and killed about three hundred foreigners. The European powers, joined by Japan and the United States, sent a combined international force against the insurgents, who were put down. The victors imposed still more severe controls on the Chinese government and inflicted an indemnity of $330,000,000. Of this the United States received $24,000,000, of which, however, in 1924, it cancelled the balance that was still due. On the other hand, as a consequence of the Boxer Rebellion, the Manchu officials strove desperately to strengthen themselves by Westernization, while at the same time the

NORTHEAST CHINA
AND ADJOINING REGIONS
1895-1914

SPHERES OF INFLUENCE ABOUT 1900
RUSSIAN   BRITISH   GERMAN

300 MILES

This area has long been one of the world's trouble zones. Note how Vladivostok is shut off from the ocean by the Japanese islands and Korea, and almost shut off from the mass of Russia by the intervening bulk of Manchuria. Manchuria, which began to be industrialized about 1900, became an object of dispute between China, to which it belonged historically, the Russian Empire, to which it had strategic value and offered an access to the open ocean, and the Japanese Empire, which found in it an outlet for commercial and military expansion and a buffer against Russia. Manchuria was dominated by Russian interests from 1898 to 1905, by Japanese interests from 1905 to 1945, and again by Russian interests revolutionary movement in China, aiming at expulsion of Manchus and foreigners alike, spread rapidly throughout the country, especially in the South, under the leadership of Sun Yat-sen.

83. The Russo-Japanese War and Its Consequences

Meanwhile Russia and Japan opposed each other's intrigues in Manchuria and Korea. The Japanese felt a need for supplying their new factories with raw materials and markets on the Asiatic mainland, for employment for their newly Westernized army and navy, for recognized status as a Great Power in the Western sense. The Russian government needed an atmosphere of crisis and expansion to stifle criticism of tsarism at home; it could not abide the presence of a strong power directly on its East Asian frontier; it could use Manchuria and Korea to strengthen the exposed outpost of Vladivostok, which was somewhat squeezed against the sea, and land-locked by Japanese waters. The Russians had obtained a concession from China to build the Chinese Eastern Railway to Vladivostok across the heart of Manchuria. A railway, in Manchuria, implied special zones, railway guards, mining and timber rights, and other auxiliary activities. The Japanese saw the fruits of their successful war of 1895 against China greedily enjoyed by their rival. In 1902 Japan signed a military alliance with Great Britain. We have seen how the British were alarmed by their diplomatic isolation after Fashoda and the Boer War, and how for many years, in the Far East, the Middle East, and the Near East, they had been expecting to have trouble with Russia. The Anglo-Japanese military alliance lasted twenty years.

War broke out in 1904, undeclared, by Japanese naval attack on Russian installations at Port Arthur. Both sides sent large armies into Manchuria. The battle of Mukden, in the number of men engaged, which was 624,000, was the largest battle which human experience had thus far witnessed. Military observers were present from all countries, anxiously trying to learn what the next war in Europe would be like. The Russians sent their Baltic fleet around three continents to the Far East, but to the world's amazement the Russian fleet was met and destroyed at Tsushima Strait by the new and untested navy of Japan. Russian communications by sea were thereby broken, and since the Trans-Siberian Railway was unfinished, and since the Japanese also won the battle of Mukden, Russia was beaten.

---

after 1945. Korea was dominated by Japan after her victories over China in 1895 and over Russia in 1905. With Japan's defeat in the Second World War, Korea was promised independence but was divided at the 38th parallel into a Russian occupation zone to the north and an American zone to the south. After the bloody but indecisive Korean War (1950–53, see pp. 870–2) the country remained divided at roughly the same parallel with a Russian and Chinese Communist-sponsored regime in the north and a Western-sponsored regime in the south.

At this point the president of the United States, Theodore Roosevelt, stepped upon the scene. With an outpost in the Philippines and growing interests in China, it was to the American advantage to have neither side win too overwhelming a victory in the Far East. The most imperially minded of all American presidents offered his mediation, and plenipotentiaries of the two powers met at Portsmouth, New Hampshire. By the treaty of Portsmouth, in 1905, Japan recovered from Russia what it had won and lost in 1895, namely Port Arthur and the Liaotung Peninsula, a preferred position in Manchuria, which remained nominally Chinese, and a protectorate in Korea, which remained nominally independent, although a few years later, in 1910, it was annexed by Japan. Japan also received from Russia the southern half of the island of Sakhalin. Much of what Russia lost to Japan in 1905 was regained forty years later, at the end of the Second World War.

The Russo-Japanese war was the first war between Great Powers since 1870. It was the first war fought under conditions of developed industrialism. It was the first actual war between Westernized powers to be caused by competition in the exploitation of backward countries. Most significant of all (except for the Ethiopian rout of the Italians), it was the first time that a colored people had defeated a white people in modern times. Asiatics had shown that they could learn and play, in less than half a century, the game of the Europeans.

The Japanese victory set off long chains of repercussions in at least three different directions. For one thing, the Russian government, frustrated in its foreign policy in East Asia, shifted its attention back to Europe, where it resumed an active role in the affairs of the Balkans. This contributed to a series of international crises in Europe, of which the result was the First World War. Secondly, the tsarist government was so weakened by the war, both in prestige and in actual military strength, and opinion in Russia was so disgusted at the clumsiness and incompetency with which the war had been handled, that the various underground movements were able to come to the surface, producing the Revolution of 1905. This in turn was a prelude to the great Russian Revolution twelve years later, of which Soviet communism was the outcome. Thirdly, news of Japan's victory over Russia electrified those who heard of it throughout the non-European world. The fact that Japan was itself an imperialist power was overlooked in the excited realization that the Japanese were not white. Only half a century ago the Japanese, too, had been "backward"—defenseless, bombarded, and bulldozed by the Europeans. The moral was clear. Everywhere leaders of subjected peoples concluded, from the Japanese precedent, that they must bring Western science and industry to their own countries, but that they must do it, as the Japanese had done, by getting rid of control by the whites, supervising the process of modernization themselves, and preserving their own native national character. Nationalist revolutions began in Persia in 1905, in Turkey in 1908, in China in 1911. In India and Indonesia many were stirred by the Japanese achievement. In the face of rising agitation, the British admitted an Indian to the Viceroy's executive Council in 1909, and in 1916 the Dutch created a People's Council, to include Indonesian members, in the Indies. The self-assertion of Asians was to grow in intensity after the First World War.

The Japanese victory, and Russian defeat, can therefore be seen as steps in three mighty developments, the First World War, the Russian Revolution, and the Revolt of Asia. These three together put an end to Europe's world supremacy, and almost to European civilization; or at least they so transmuted them as to make the world of the twentieth century far different from that of the nineteenth, and, at least for Europeans of the prosperous classes, less easy to live in.

CHAPTER XVI

The First World War

WHEN a traveler has wandered off his course it is easy for him, if he has a good map and if the country is well marked with road signs, to retrace his steps, find the point where he went astray, and resume the route to his destination. It would not be so easy if he had no map, if there were no signs, and if he could never under any circumstances go backward.

Somewhere before 1914 Europe went off its course. Europeans believed themselves to be heading for a kind of high plateau, full of a benign progress and more abundant civilization, in which the benefits of modern science and invention would be more widely diffused, and even competitive struggle worked out somehow for the best. Instead, Europe stumbled in 1914 into disaster. It is not easy to see exactly where Europe went astray, at what point, that is, the First World War became inevitable, or (since the human mind does not know what is truly inevitable) so overwhelmingly probable that only the most Olympian statesmanship could have avoided it. History is

not as exact as a map, its road signs are read differently by different people—
and the traveler can never go backward.

84. The International Anarchy

After 1870 Europe lived in a repressed fear of itself. The great questions of the mid-century had been settled by force. The German Empire was
only the strongest and most obvious of the new structures which armed power
had reared. Never had the European states maintained such huge armies in
peacetime as at the beginning of the twentieth century. One, two, or even
three years of compulsory military service for all young men became the rule.
In 1914 each of the Continental Great Powers had not only a huge standing
army but millions of trained reserves among the civilian population. Few
people wanted war; all but a few sensational writers preferred peace in Europe, but all took it for granted that war would come some day. In the last
years before 1914 the idea that war was bound to break out sooner or later
probably made some statesmen, in some countries, more willing to unleash it.

RIVAL ALLIANCES: TRIPLE ALLIANCE VS. TRIPLE ENTENTE

Political diagnosticians, from Richelieu to Metternich, had long
thought that an effective union of Germany would revolutionize the relationships of Europe's peoples. After 1870 their anticipations were more than confirmed. Once united (or almost united), the Germans entered upon their
industrial revolution. Manufacturing, finance, shipping, population grew
phenomenally. In steel, for example, of which Germany in 1865 produced
less than France, by 1900 Germany produced more than France and Great
Britain combined. Germans felt that they needed and deserved a "place in the
sun," by which they vaguely meant some kind of acknowledged supremacy
like that of the British. Neither the British nor the French, the leaders of
modern Europe since the seventeenth century, could share wholeheartedly in
such German aspirations. The French had the chronic grievance of Alsace
and Lorraine, annexed to Germany in 1871. The British as the years passed
saw German salesmen appear in their foreign markets, selling goods often at
lower prices and by what seemed ungentlemanly methods; they saw Germans
turn up as colonial rivals in Africa, the Near East, and the Far East; and they
watched other European states gravitate into the Berlin orbit, looking to the
mighty German Empire as a friend and protector to secure or advance their
interests.[1]

Bismarck after 1871 feared that in another European war his new German Empire might be torn to pieces. He therefore followed, until his retire-

ᴧᴧᴧᴧᴧᴧᴧᴧᴧᴧᴧᴧᴧᴧᴧ
[1] See map, "Anglo-German Industrial Competition," p. 663.

ment in 1890, a policy of peace. We have seen him as the "honest broker" at the Berlin Congress of 1878, helping to adjudicate the Eastern Question, and again offering the facilities of Berlin in 1885 to regulate African affairs. To isolate France, divert it from Europe, and keep it embroiled with Britain, he looked with satisfaction on French colonial expansion. He took no chances, however; in 1879 he formed a military alliance with Austria-Hungary, to which Italy was admitted in 1882. Thus was formed the Triple Alliance, which lasted until the First World War. Its terms were, briefly, that if any member became involved in war with two or more powers its allies should come to its aid by force of arms. To be on the safe side, Bismarck signed a "re-insurance" treaty with Russia also; since Russia and Austria were enemies (because of the Balkans), to be allied to both at the same time took considerable diplomatic finesse. After Bismarck's retirement his system proved too intricate, or too lacking in candor, for his successors to manage. The Russo-German agreement lapsed. The French, faced by the Triple Alliance, soon seized the opportunity to form their own alliance with Russia, the Dual Alliance of 1894. In its time this was regarded as politically almost impossible. The French Republic stood for everything radical, the Russian Empire for everything reactionary and autocratic. But ideology was thrown to the winds, French capital poured into Russia, and the tsar bared his head to the Marseillaise.

The Continent was thus divided by 1894 into two opposed camps, the German-Austrian-Italian against the Franco-Russian. For a time it seemed that this rigid division might soften. Germany, France and Russia co-operated in the Far Eastern crisis of 1895.[2] All were anti-British at the time of Fashoda and the Boer War.[3] The Kaiser, William II, outlined tempting pictures of a Continental league against the global hegemony of England and her empire.

Much depended on what the British would do. They had long prided

~~~~~~~~~~~~~~~~~~~

[2] See p. 654.
[3] See pp. 640–4.

Anglo-German Industrial Competition

This diagram really shows two things: first the huge increase in world trade in the last fifteen years before the First World War, shared in by all countries; and second, the fact that German exports grew far more rapidly than British. The exports of both countries together, as shown on the diagram, multiplied no less than threefold in these fifteen years. The increase, while due in small part to a slight rise of prices, was mainly due to a real increase in volume of business.

If the reader will compare the shaded bands within the large arrows he will see that, for the countries shown, British exports about doubled but those of Germany multiplied many times. In 1913 total German exports about equalled the British, but German exports to the United States and Russia greatly exceeded the British. Note how the Germans even gained in exports to British India, where the liberalism of British policy freely admitted competitive goods.

In merchant marine, though the Germans doubled their tonnage, the British continued to enjoy an overwhelming lead.

ANGLO-GERMAN
INDUSTRIAL-COMPETITION

AS SHOWN BY
BRITISH AND GERMAN EXPORTS
TO SPECIFIED COUNTRIES IN
1898 AND 1913

TO THE
UNITED STATES

TO RUSSIA

TO CHINA

GREAT
BRITAIN

TO BRITISH
INDIA

GERMANY

TO THE
ARGENTINE

EXPORTS
TO   HUNDRED MILLIONS OF DOLLARS

UNITED STATES

BRITISH INDIA

RUSSIA

ARGENTINE

CHINA

KEY FOR GRAPHS
AND MAP

BRITISH   1898
           1913
GERMAN   1898
           1913

TOTAL EXPORTS
TO
ALL COUNTRIES,
FOREIGN AND
COLONIAL,
1898 & 1913

MERCHANT
MARINE   MILLIONS OF TONS

GREAT
BRITAIN

GERMANY

themselves on a "splendid isolation," going their own way, disdaining the kind of dependency that alliance with others always brings. Fashoda and the Boer War came as a shock. British relations with France and Russia were very bad. Some in England, including Joseph Chamberlain, therefore thought that a better understanding with Germany was to be sought. Arguments of race, in this exceedingly race-conscious age, made Englishmen and Germans feel akin.[4] But politically it was hard to co-operate. The Kaiser's Kruger Telegram of 1896 was a studied insult.[5] Then in 1898 the Germans decided to build a navy.

A new kind of "race" now entered the picture, the naval competition between Germany and Great Britain. British sea power for two centuries had been all too successful. The American Admiral Mahan, teaching at the Naval War College, and taking his examples largely from British history, argued that sea power had been the foundation of Britain's greatness, and that in the long run sea power must always choke off and ruin a power operating on the land. Nowhere were Mahan's books read with more interest than in Germany. The German naval program, mounting rapidly after 1898, in a few years became a source of concern to the British, and by 1912 was felt as a positive menace. The Germans insisted that they must have a navy to protect their colonies, secure their foreign trade, and "for the general purposes of their greatness." The British held with equal resolution that England, as a densely populated industrial island, dependent even for food upon imports, must at all costs control the sea in both peace and war. They adhered stubbornly to their traditional policy of maintaining a navy as large as the next two combined. The naval race led both sides to enormous and increasing expenditures. In the British it produced a sense of profound insecurity, driving them as the years passed ever more inescapably into the arms of Russia and France.

Slowly and cautiously the British emerged from their diplomatic isolation. In 1902 they formed a military alliance with Japan against their common enemy, Russia.[6] The decisive break came in 1904, from which may be dated the immediate series of crises issuing in the World War ten years later.

In 1904 the British and French governments agreed to forget Fashoda and the accumulated bad feeling of the preceding twenty-five years. The French recognized the British occupation of Egypt, and the British recognized the French penetration of Morocco. They also cleared up a few lesser colonial differences, and agreed to support each other against protests by third parties. There was no specific alliance; neither side said what it would

------

[4] The will of Cecil Rhodes, who died in 1902, illustrates this point. Rhodes left most of his fortune (£6,000,000) to establish scholarships at Oxford: two from each state in the United States, as an Anglo-Saxon country, three from each of eighteen British colonies, and fifteen from Germany. The German Rhodes Scholarships were suspended from 1914 to 1930 and again after 1938. The same feeling that Germans were racially akin was common in the United States also; a prominent example would be Theodore Roosevelt.

[5] See p. 642.
[6] See p. 657.

do in the event of war; it was only a close understanding, an *entente cordiale.* The French immediately tried to reconcile their new friend to their ally, Russia. After defeat by Japan the Russians proved amenable. The British, increasingly uncertain of German aims, proved likewise willing. In 1907 Britain and Russia, the inveterate adversaries, settled their differences in an Anglo-Russian Convention. In Persia, the British recognized a Russian sphere of influence in the north, the Russians a British sphere in the south and east. By 1907 England, France, and Russia were acting together. The older Triple Alliance faced a newer Triple Entente, the latter somewhat the looser, since the British refused to make any formal military commitments.

THE CRISES IN MOROCCO AND THE BALKANS

The Germans, who already felt encircled by the alliance of France and Russia, naturally watched with concern the drift of England into the Franco-Russian camp. The Entente Cordiale was barely concluded when the German government decided to test it, to find out how strong it really was, or how far the British would really go in support of France. The French, now enjoying British backing, were taking over more police powers, concessions, and loans in Morocco. In March 1905 William II disembarked from a German warship at Tangier, where he made a startling speech in favor of Moroccan independence. To diplomats everywhere this carefully staged performance was a signal: Germany was attempting not primarily to keep France out of Morocco, nor even to reserve Morocco for itself, but to break up the new understanding between France and England. The Germans demanded and obtained an international conference at Algeciras (at which the United States was represented), but the conference, which met in 1906, supported the French claims in Morocco, only Austria voting with Germany. The German government had thus created an incident, and been rebuffed. The British, disturbed by German diplomatic tactics, stood by the French all the more firmly. French and British army and naval officers now began to discuss common plans. Distrust of Germany also inclined the British to bury the hatchet with Russia in the next year. The German attempt to break the Entente simply made it more solid.

In 1911 came a second Morocco crisis. A German gunboat, the *Panther,* arrived at Agadir "to protect German interests." It soon developed that the move was a hold-up: the Germans offered to make no further trouble in Morocco if they could have the French Congo. The crisis passed, the Germans obtaining some trifling accessions in Africa. But a member of the British cabinet, David Lloyd George, made a rather inflammatory speech on the German menace.

Meanwhile a series of crises rocked the Balkans. Here at the opening of the twentieth century the situation was very confused. The Ottoman Empire, in an advanced state of dissolution, still held a band of territory from Constantinople westward to the Adriatic.[7] South of this band lay an independent Greece. North of it, on the Black Sea side, lay an autonomous Bulgaria and an independent Rumania. In the center and west of the peninsula, north of the Turkish belt, was the small, land-locked independent kingdom of Serbia, adjoined by Bosnia-Herzegovina, which belonged legally to Turkey but had been "occupied and administered" by Austria since 1878. Within the Austro-Hungarian empire, adjoining Bosnia on the north, lay Croatia and Slovenia.

Serbs, Bosnians, Croats, and Slovenes all spoke basically the same language, the main difference being that Serbs and Bosnians wrote with the eastern or Cyrillic alphabet, the Croats and Slovenes with the western or Roman. With the Slav revival and general growth of nationalism these peoples came to feel that they were really one people, for which they took the term South Slavs or Yugoslavs. We have seen how, when the Dual Monarchy was formed in 1867, the Slavs of the Hapsburg empire were kept subordinate to the German Austrians and to the Magyars. By 1900 the most radical Slav nationalists within the empire had concluded that the Dual Monarchy would never grant them equal status, that it must be broken up, and that all South Slavs should form an independent state of their own. Concretely, this meant that an element of the Austro-Hungarian population, namely the Croatian and Slovenian nationalists, wished to get out of the empire and join with Serbia across the border. Serbia became the center of South Slav agitation. The Serbs conceived of their small kingdom as the Sardinia of a South Slav Risorgimento, the nucleus around which a new national state could be formed, at the expense of Austria-Hungary, which, to repeat, contained Croatia-Slovenia within its own frontiers, and "occupied" Bosnia.

This brew was brought to a boil in 1908 by two events. First, the Young Turks, whose long agitation against Abdul Hamid has been noted, managed in that year to carry through a revolution.[8] They obliged the sultan to restore the liberal-parliamentary constitution of 1876. They showed, too, that they meant to stop the dissolution of the Ottoman Empire, by taking steps to have delegates from Bulgaria and Bosnia sit in the new Ottoman parliament. Secondly, Russia, its foreign policy in the Far East ruined by the Japanese war, turned actively to the Balkan and Turkish scene. Russia, as always, wanted control at Constantinople. Austria wanted full annexation of Bosnia, the better to discourage Pan-Yugoslav ideas. But if the Young Turks really modernized and strengthened the Ottoman Empire, Austria would never get Bosnia, nor the Russians Constantinople.

The Russian and Austrian foreign ministers, Isvolsky and Aehrenthal, at a conference at Buchlau in 1908 came to a secret agreement: they would call an international conference, at which Russia would favor Austrian annexation of Bosnia, and Austria would support the opening of the Straits to Russian warships. Austria, without waiting for a conference, proclaimed the annexation of Bosnia without more ado. This infuriated the Serbs, who had

---

[7] See maps, pp. 528–9, 633, and 437.
[8] See pp. 630–1.

marked Bosnia for their own. Meanwhile, that same year, the Bulgarians and
the Cretans broke finally with the Ottoman Empire, Bulgaria becoming fully
independent, Crete uniting with Greece. Isvolsky was never able to realize
his plans for Constantinople. His partners in the Triple Entente, Britain and
France, refused to back him; the British in particular were evasive on plans
for opening the Straits to the Russian fleet. The projected international conference was never called. In Russia itself public opinion knew nothing of
Isvolsky's secret deal. The known fact in Russia was that the Serbs, the little
Slav brothers of Russia, had had their toes rudely stepped on by the Austrians
by the annexation of Bosnia.

This "first Balkan crisis" presently passed. The Russians, weakened by
the Japanese war and by recent revolution,[9] accepted the Austrian *fait accom-
pli.* Russia protested, but backed down. Austrian influence in the Balkans
seemed to be growing. And South Slav nationalism was frustrated and inflamed.

In 1911 Italy declared war on Turkey, from which it soon conquered
Tripoli and the Dodecanese Islands. With the Ottomans thus embarrassed,
Bulgaria, Serbia, and Greece joined forces in their own war against Turkey,
hoping to annex certain Balkan territories to which they believed they had a
right. Turkey was soon defeated, but the Bulgarians claimed more of Macedonia than the Serbs would yield, so that the first Balkan war of 1912 was
followed in 1913 by a second, in which Serbia, Greece, Rumania, and Turkey
turned upon and defeated Bulgaria. Albania also, a mountainous region on
the Adriatic, mainly Moslem, and known as the wildest place in all Europe,
was the subject of angry discord. The Serbs occupied part of it in the two
Balkan wars, but the Greeks also claimed a part, and it had also on several
occasions been vaguely promised to Italy.[10] Russia supported the Serbian
claim. Austria was determined to shut off the Serbs from access to the sea,
which they would obtain by annexation of Albanian territory. An agreement
of the Great Powers, to keep the peace, conjured up an independent kingdom
of Albania. This confirmed the Austrian policy, kept Serbia from the sea, and
aroused vehement outcries in both Serbia and Russia. But Russia again
backed down. Serbian expansionism was again frustrated and inflamed.

The third Balkan crisis proved to be the fatal one. It was fatal because
two others had gone before it, leaving feelings of exasperation in Austria,
desperation in Serbia, and humiliation in Russia.

THE SARAJEVO CRISIS AND THE OUTBREAK OF WAR

On June 28, 1914, a young Bosnian revolutionary, a member of the
Serbian secret society called "Union or Death," and commonly known as the
Black Hand, acting with the knowledge of certain Serbian officials, assassi-

---

[9] See pp. 714–17.
[10] See p. 634; and see map, pp. 528–9.

nated the heir to the Hapsburg empire, the Archduke Francis Ferdinand, in the streets of Sarajevo, the Bosnian capital, in the Austrian empire. The world was shocked at this terroristic outrage, and at first sympathized with the protests of the Austrian government. Francis Ferdinand, who would soon have become emperor, was known to favor some kind of transformation of Austria-Hungary, in which a more equal place might be given to the Slavs; but the reformer who makes a system work is the most dangerous of all enemies to the implacable revolutionary, and it is perhaps for this reason that the archduke was killed by the Black Hand.

The Austrian government was determined to make an end to the South Slav separatism that was gnawing its empire to pieces. It decided to crush the independence of Serbia, the nucleus of South Slav agitation, though not to annex it, since there were now thought to be too many Slavs within the empire already. The Austrian government consulted the German, to see how far it might go with the support of its ally. The Germans, issuing their famous "blank check," encouraged the Austrians to be firm. The Austrians, thus reassured, despatched a drastic ultimatum to Serbia, demanding among other things that Austrian officials be permitted to collaborate in investigating and punishing the perpetrators of the assassination. The Serbs counted on Russian support, even to the point of war, judging that Russia could not again yield in a Balkan crisis, for the third time in six years, without losing its influence in the Balkans altogether. The Russians in turn counted on France; and France, terrified at the possibility of being some day caught alone in a war with Germany, and determined to keep Russia as an ally at any cost, in effect gave a blank check to Russia. The Serbs rejected the critical item in the Austrian ultimatum as an infringement on Serbian sovereignty, and Austria thereupon declared war upon Serbia. Russia prepared to defend Serbia, and hence to fight Austria. Expecting that Austria would be joined by Germany, Russia rashly mobilized its army on the German as well as the Austrian frontier. Since the power which first mobilized had all the advantages of a rapid offensive, the German government demanded an end to the Russian mobilization on its border, and, receiving no answer, declared war on Russia on August 1, 1914. Convinced that France would in any case enter the war on the side of Russia, Germany also declared war on France on August 3.

The German decisions were posited on a reckless hope that Great Britain might not enter the war at all. England was bound by no formal military alliance. Even the French did not know for certain, as late as August 3, whether the British would join them in war. The British clung to scraps of their old proud isolation; they hesitated to make a final choice of sides; and as the Foreign Secretary, Sir Edward Grey, repeatedly explained, in England only Parliament could declare war, so that the Foreign Office could make no binding promise of war in advance. It has often been said that, had the German government known as a positive fact that England would fight, the war might not have come. Hence the evasiveness of British policy is made a contributing cause of the war. In reality, the probability that England would fight was so great that to underestimate it, as the Germans did, was an act of supreme and even criminal folly. The British were deeply committed to France, especially through naval agreements. As the German High Seas Fleet grew, the British had been obliged to concentrate naval forces in the North Sea. They had therefore had to withdraw forces from the Mediterranean. In 1914, by agreement with France, the French fleet was concentrated in the Mediterranean, watching over British interests, while the British fleet attended to French interests in the north. The French Channel coast was therefore open to German naval attack, unless the British defended it. Sir Edward Grey accepted this moral obligation, but what swept the British public was the invasion of Belgium. So huge was the German army hurled against France that it could deploy and maneuver only by crossing Belgium. When the Belgians protested, the Germans invaded anyway, violating the treaty of 1839 which had guaranteed Belgian neutrality. England declared war on Germany on August 4.

The mere narration of successive crises does not explain why the chief nations of Europe became locked in combat over the murder of an imperial personage within a few days. Among more obvious general causes, the alliance system may be singled out. Europe was divided into two camps. Every incident tended to become a test of strength between the two. A given incident, such as German intervention in Morocco, or the assassination of Francis Ferdinand, could not be settled on its own merits, merely by the parties concerned; however it was dealt with, one of the two camps was deemed to have lost or gained, and hence to have lost or gained in influence in other incidents, of perhaps greater purport, that would arise in the future. Each power felt that it must stand by its allies whatever the specific issue. This was because all lived in the fear of war, of some nameless future war in which allies would be necessary. The Germans complained of being "encircled" by France and Russia, and dreaded the day when they might be crushed by a war on two fronts; they were obliged to hold to their one ally, Austria-Hungary, which was in turn able to sell its support at its own price. The French dreaded a coming conflict with Germany, which in forty years had far surpassed France in population and industrial strength; they were obliged to cling to their ally Russia, which therefore could oblige the French to yield to Russian wishes. As for Russia and Austria, they were both tottering empires. Especially after 1900, the tsarist regime suffered from endemic revolutionism, and the Hapsburg empire from chronic nationalistic agitation. Authorities in both empires became desperate. Like the Serbs, they had little to lose, and were therefore reckless. It was Russia that drew France and hence England into war in 1914, and Austria that drew in Germany. Seen in this light, the tragedy of 1914 is that the most backward or politically bankrupt parts of Europe, through the alliance system, dragged the more advanced parts automatically into ruin.

The German Empire, too, faced an internal crisis. The Social Democrats became the largest party in the Reichstag in 1912. Their sentiments were anti-militarist and anti-war. But the German imperial government recognized no responsibility to a majority in the chamber. Policy was determined by men of the old unreconstructed upper class, in which army and navy interests were very strong. The perplexities they faced at home, their feeling that their position was being undermined by the Social Democrats, may have made them less unwilling to view war as a way out. And while it is not true that Germany started the war, as its enemies in 1914 popularly believed, it must be granted that its policies had for some years been rather peremptory, arrogant, devious and obstinate. In a broad sense, the failure of Europe to assimilate the consolidated industrial Germany which arose after 1870 was a distant and basic cause of the war.

The alliance system was only a symptom of deeper trouble. In a word, the world had an international economy but a national polity. Economically, each European people now required habitual contact with the world as a whole. Each people was to that extent dependent, and insecure. Industrial countries were especially vulnerable, relying as they did on import of raw materials and food, and on export of goods, services or capital in return. There was, however, no world state to police the world-wide system, assuring participation in the world economy to all nations under all conditions. Each nation had to take care of itself. Hence came much of the drive for imperialism, in which each Great Power tried to stake out part of the world-system for itself. And hence also came the quest for allies and for binding alliances. The alliances, in a world that was in the strict sense anarchic (and seemed likely to remain so), were a means by which each nation attempted to bolster up its security; to assure that it would not be cut off, conquered or subjected to another's will; to obtain some hope of success in the competitive struggle for use of the world's goods.

85. The Marne and the New Face of War

THE SCHLIEFFEN PLAN AND BATTLE OF THE MARNE, 1914

The First World War lasted over four years, from 1914 to the end of 1918, the United States entering with effective result in the last year. Germany and its allies were called the Central Powers, while the Entente governments were termed the Allies.

At first a short war, as in 1870, was universally expected. The German General Staff had its plans ready for a two-front struggle against France and Russia. The disadvantage of fighting on two fronts was offset by the possession of interior lines, which allowed the rapid shuttling of troops from one front to the other. The German war plan, called the Schlieffen Plan, rested upon this fact. Since it was foreseen that Russia would be the slower of the two enemies in developing its full power, the plan called for holding the eastern front defensively in the early stages, to permit concentration of maximum forces in the West for a quick, sharp victory over France, after which Russia could be disposed of at leisure. In the West the German armies were to swing in a great wheeling movement. The hub of the wheel was near the Swiss border; the moving wing, the German right, was to march rapidly through Belgium into northern France, catch the French army on its left, and roll the whole French force backwards against the Swiss frontier. The Schlieffen plan required that the German right wing be kept very strong. By this

Land fighting in the First World War was confined to the areas shown by the two darker types of horizontal shading. The huge battles on the Western Front, which in expenditure of manpower exceeded those of the Second World War in the West, for four years swayed back and forth over the small area indicated, less than a hundred miles wide.

plan the German commander Moltke declared in May 1914 that he could crush France in six weeks.

On August 3, 1914, the Germans launched 78 infantry divisions in the West. They were opposed by 72 French divisions, 5 British and 6 Belgian. The Germans swept irresistibly forward. The Schlieffen plan seemed to be moving like clockwork. Then a hitch occurred: the Russians were fulfilling the terms of their alliance; the ten billion francs invested by Frenchmen in Russia now paid its most significant dividend. The Russians pushed two armies into Germany, penetrating into East Prussia. Moltke, becoming nervous, withdrew forces from the German right wing in France, on August 26, for service in the east. The Germans moved on, but the striking arm was weakened. Joffre, the French commander, regrouping his forces, with strong support from the relatively small British contingent, and at exactly the right moment, ordered the counterattack. The ensuing Battle of the Marne, fought from September 5 to 12, changed the whole character of the war. The Germans were obliged to retreat. The hope of felling France at a single blow was ended. Both sides now hurled themselves into a "rush to the sea" to control the French Channel ports. Here too the Germans failed, so that French and British communications remained uninterrupted. For these reverses the great victories meanwhile won by the Germans in the east, though of gigantic proportions (the battles of Tannenberg and the Masurian Lakes, at which 225,000 Russians were captured) were in the long run an insignificant consolation.

THE WAR OF POSITION

In the west the war of movement now settled into a war of position. The armies on the western front became almost immobile. The units of horse cavalry, the uhlans, hussars, and lancers that had pranced off to war in high spirits, disappeared from the field. Since motor transport was still new (the armies had trucks, but no self-propelled guns, and no tanks until very late in the war), the basic soldier more than ever was the man on foot. Airplanes were used for reconnaissance, artillery observation, and occasional bombing; not till the last months of the war did concentrated bombing of rear areas begin. The Germans raided London many times with Zeppelins, long cigar-shaped airships, but did little damage. Hostilities were confined to the front, and on the whole it was only soldiers who were killed or wounded.

The queen of battles was the machine gun. Against it infantry could advance only after elaborate preparations. Infantry on both sides dug into trenches, long zigzag slits higher than a man's head, which soon formed connected mazes from Switzerland to the North Sea. Dugouts, or caves where men might sleep or eat, communicated with the trenches. And between hostile trenches lay No Man's Land, and in front of its trenches, to protect them from attackers, each side set up thick entanglements of barbed wire, on which assailants could be impaled, and then easily bayoneted or shot. Before infantry could attack it was necessary to break up the barbed wire, silence the machine guns, and disarrange the enemy's trenches and dugouts. This was a task for heavy artillery, of which altogether unprecedented quantities came to be used. If the wind was right, an attack might also be prepared by the discharge of poison gases, first used by the Germans in the spring of 1915; but the vagaries of wind, the quick adoption of gas masks, and its ineffectiveness against guns and entrenchments made gas an indecisive weapon. An artillery preparation preceded every advance. At the Somme, in 1916, the Allies placed 2,000 heavy cannon behind a ten-mile front, and the preliminary bombardment lasted continuously for seven days and nights. If the destruction by shellfire was sufficient, the infantry might struggle forward five or ten miles, using bayonets and hand-grenades in addition to fire, and often wearing gasmasks, but it would soon find the enemy again entrenched, and be unable to go farther, because the indispensable artillery moved forward far more slowly than the foot soldier. Only when the British introduced the tank in the last months of the war, was an answer found to the problem posed by the machine gun.

Such conditions gave every advantage to the defensive. Attack was laborious, costly in lives, and at best achieved small results. With opposing forces dug in in continuous lines almost face to face, there was little opportunity for slashing action by small units. Vast armies had to be employed as heavy masses; it was a war of the battering ram rather than the stiletto. Each side nevertheless attempted repeatedly to achieve a breakthrough. But the defending line seldom broke; even when it did, the defenders could pour in reserves faster than the attackers could advance, because, where an advancing force had to find its way slowly through country wrecked by artillery, a retreating force could use Western Europe's superb network of roads and railroads, which aviation as yet scarcely disturbed. Battle therefore was unprofitable, but casualties were enormous, and they came wholesale in tremendous holocausts. More men were used and killed on the western front in the First World War than in the Second.

86. The Deadlock of 1915–16: Naval, Diplomatic, Military

NAVAL BLOCKADE AND NAVAL WARFARE

After the Battle of the Marne it became evident that the war would be a long one. For a long war no power had made any plans. In a long war Germany and the Central Powers were at a disadvantage, because they were exposed to the slow effects of blockade by sea. Naval blockade was a deadly weapon, if only one could wait, and so long as Russia and France, by remaining unconquered, prevented Germany from exploiting the resources of Europe and Asia. To the Allies, on the other hand, a long war gave an advantage; their control of the sea allowed them to import food, as usual, from Canada, Australia, and the Argentine, and munitions from the United States. A long war also gave time to the Allies to develop their manpower. The French had virtually all their manpower in readiness in 1914; but the British, who in 1914 could send only five divisions to the Continent, required two years to produce a mass army. The British long resisted conscription, which they considered, even in wartime, ill suited to their free institutions. For over a year they relied on volunteers, but by the beginning of 1916 they too turned to compulsory service, and by the spring of that year they had an army of 70 divisions. Moreover, of course, had the war not been a long one, the United States would never have entered it, nor, once entered, would it have had time to raise, train, equip, and transport its forces.

The British and French lost no time in developing the naval blockade. International law at the time placed goods headed for a country at war into two classes. One class was called "contraband"; it included munitions and certain listed raw materials which might be used in the manufacture of military equipment. The other class, including foodstuffs and raw cotton, was defined as non-contraband. A country was supposed, by international law, to be able to import non-contraband goods even in war time. Contraband goods could be stopped by a blockading power; if on an enemy ship, the whole ship and cargo could be seized, but if on a neutral ship it had to be proved from the ship's papers, before confiscation, that the contraband goods were destined for the enemy. These terms of wartime law had been set forth as recently as 1909 at an international conference held in London. The purpose was to make it impossible for a sea power (that is, the British) to starve out an enemy in wartime, or even to interfere with normal civilian production. The jealousy of Continental Europe for British sea power was an old story.

Such law, if observed, would make the blockade of Germany entirely ineffective, and the Allies did not observe it. To starve out the enemy and ruin his economy was precisely their purpose. Economic warfare took its place alongside armed attack as a military weapon—as in the days of Napoleon.[11] The Allies announced a new international law. The distinction between contraband and non-contraband was gradually abolished. The British navy (aided by the French) proceeded to stop all goods of whatever character destined for Germany or its allies. Neutrals, among whom the Americans, Dutch, and Scandinavians were the ones mainly affected, were not allowed to make for German ports at all. Neutrals could still, of course, import into their own countries. Goods destined for resale to Germany therefore moved into Rotterdam and Copenhagen. It was, in fact, largely to use these cities as ports of entry that the Germans refrained from occupying Denmark and the Netherlands in the First World War. The Allies retorted by placing Denmark and the Netherlands under strict quotas, allowing them only the kind and quantity of imports that they had customarily received before the war. They even attempted to prevent the Netherlands and Scandinavia from selling their own domestic products to Germany. The Germans, for example, feeling the food shortage, took to buying large amounts of Norwegian fish. But the Norwegian fishing fleet depended on British coal, and its canning industry on

[11] See pp. 396–400.

imported tin. The British, by rationing coal and tin for Norway, soon checked the flow of fish into Germany. The whole system was enforced by requiring neutral vessels to stop at Gibraltar or other Allied points, have their cargoes and papers examined, and obtain clearance. Thus all sea-borne imports into Germany were prevented, and imports into Germany's neutral neighbors were controlled.

The United States protested vehemently against these regulations. It defended the rights of neutrals. It reasserted the distinction between contraband and non-contraband, claimed the right to trade with other neutrals, and upheld the "freedom of the seas." Much mutual bad feeling resulted between the American and British governments in 1915 and 1916. But when the United States entered the war it adopted the Allied position *in toto*, and its navy joined in enforcing exactly the same regulations. International law was in fact changed. In the Second World War the very words "contraband" and "freedom of the seas" were never heard.

The Germans also attempted to blockade England. A few isolated German cruisers were able for some time to destroy British shipping in the several oceans of the world. But the Germans relied mainly on the submarine, against which the preponderant British naval power at first seemed helpless. The submarine was an unrefined weapon; a submarine commander could not always tell what kind of ship he was attacking, nor could he remove passengers, confiscate cargo, escort the vessel, nor indeed do much except sink it. Citing British abuses of international law in justification, the German government in February 1915 declared the waters surrounding the British Isles to be a war zone, in which Allied vessels would be torpedoed and neutral vessels would be in grave danger. Three months later the liner *Lusitania* was torpedoed off the Irish coast. About 1,200 persons were drowned, of whom 118 were American citizens. The *Lusitania* was a British ship; it carried munitions of war manufactured in the United States for Allied use; and the Germans had published ominous warnings in the New York papers that Americans should not take passage upon it. Americans then believed that they should be able to sail safely, on peaceable errands, on the ship of a belligerent power in wartime. The loss of life shocked the country. President Wilson informed the Germans that another such act would be considered "deliberately unfriendly." The Germans, to avoid trouble, refrained for two years from making full use of their submarines. For two years the Allies enjoyed an only partly impeded use of the sea.

Allied access to the sea was confirmed by the one great naval engagement of the war, the Battle of Jutland. The German admirals, especially when deprived of the full use of their submarine arm, became restless to see their newly built navy skulking behind mine-fields on the German shores. The High Seas Fleet could not presume to challenge the superior British Grand Fleet, posted watchfully at Scapa Flow. It hoped, however, to decoy smaller formations of British ships in turn, destroy them one by one, and perhaps eventually obtain enough of a naval balance in the North Sea to loosen the British blockade, by which Germany was slowly being strangled. In May 1916 the Germans believed that they had trapped a squadron of British cruisers, under Admiral Beatty, into a surprise engagement with the High Seas Fleet. The British, however, whose intelligence services were excellent, knew the German plan. Beatty was really, at great risk to himself, luring the Germans into a trap. The Germans found too late that the entire Grand Fleet of 151 ships under Admiral Jellicoe was bearing down upon them. They tried to withdraw, but Jellicoe maintained contact. For several hours the two navies, whose rivalry had been a main cause of the war, enjoyed their one opportunity to inflict destruction upon each other. But Jellicoe, who has been called the one man who could have lost the war in a single day, was too prudent to jeopardize his enormous command, and all it stood for, without good reason. The Germans were able to break off and withdraw into mined waters. They had lost less tonnage and fewer men than the British. They had proved themselves to be dangerously proficient in naval combat. But their fleet never came out again. The British retained command of the sea.

DIPLOMATIC MANEUVERS AND SECRET AGREEMENTS

With the war on land virtually deadlocked, both sides looked about for new allies, to open up new fronts, or add even the small increment of strength that might turn the balance. Germany and Austria-Hungary were soon joined by the Ottoman Empire, whose enemy was Russia, and by Bulgaria, which considered itself outraged by Serbia in the Balkan war of 1913. The most important new prospect was Italy, which, although formally a member of the Triple Alliance, had long ago drifted away from it, and took no part in the crisis of 1914. Both sides solicited the Italian government, which was willing to bargain imperturbably with both. The Italian public was divided. Probably most people wanted to stay at peace, which was recommended both by Catholic and by Socialist leaders. Extreme nationalists saw in the war a chance to obtain their *irredenta*, the border regions in which Italians lived, but which had not been incorporated in the time of Cavour.[12] The Italian government opened negotiations with Austria-Hungary, offering to refrain from attacking Austria if the Trentino and south Tyrol were ceded. The negotiations with Austria were used also to frighten the Allies, which in the end Italy joined on terms very advantageous to itself. By the secret treaty of London of 1915, between England, France, Russia, and Italy, it was agreed that if the Allies won the war Italy should receive the Trentino, the south Tyrol, Istria and the city of Trieste and some of the Dalmatian Islands; that, if Turkey were partitioned, Italy should receive Adalia in Asia Minor; and that if England and France took over Germany's African colonies, Italy should receive territorial increases in Libya and Somaliland. The treaty of London, in short, carried on the most brazen pre-war practices of territorial expansionism. It must be remembered that the Allies were desperate. Italy,

[12] See pp. 517–18.

thus bought, and probably against the will of most Italians, opened up a front against Austria-Hungary.

Each side tampered with minorities and discontented groups living within the domains of the other. The Germans promised an independent Poland, to embarrass Russia. They stirred up local nationalism in the Ukraine. They raised up a pro-German Flemish movement in Belgium. They persuaded the Ottoman sultan, as caliph, to proclaim the holy war in North Africa, hoping that irate Moslems would drive the British from Egypt and the French from Algeria. This had no success. German agents worked in Ireland, and one Irish nationalist, Sir Roger Casement, landed in Ireland from a German submarine, precipitating the Easter Rebellion of 1916, which was suppressed by the British.

To Americans the most amazing of similar activities was the famous Zimmermann telegram. In 1916 an American military force had crossed the Mexican border in pursuit of bandits, against protests by the Mexican government. Relations between the United States and Germany were also deteriorating. In January 1917 the German state secretary for foreign affairs, named Zimmermann, despatched a telegram to the German minister at Mexico City, telling him what to say to the Mexican president. He was to say this: that if the United States went to war with Germany, Germany would form an alliance with Mexico and if possible Japan, enabling Mexico to get back its "lost territories." These latter referred to the region conquered by the United States from Mexico in 1848—Texas, New Mexico, and Arizona (California was not mentioned by Zimmermann, who was no doubt somewhat vague on the exact history and location of these Alsace-Lorraines of America). Zimmermann's telegram was intercepted and decoded by the British, and passed on by them to Washington. Printed in the newspapers, it was not relished in the United States.

The Allies were more successful in appealing to nationalist discontent, for the obvious reason that the most active national minorities were within the lands of their enemies. They were able to promise restoration of Alsace-Lorraine to France without difficulty. They promised independence to the Poles, though with some difficulty as long as the tsarist monarchy stood. They gave a haven, though as yet no official recognition or support, to various "committees" of émigrés who, fleeing mainly from Austria-Hungary during the war, set up national councils—a Czech national council in Moscow, and a more important one in London, to which Masaryk and Beneš belonged; a Yugoslav national council in London; a Polish national council in Paris, led by the great pianist Paderewski. These councils worked to have independence for their respective nations included in the Allied war aims. They drew much of their support and funds from the United States, to which millions of Poles, Czechs, Slovaks, and South Slavs had emigrated in the preceding thirty years. Czechs in the Austrian army deserted in great numbers to the Russians, and South Slavs fought with great reluctance except against the Italians, so that national discontent from the beginning undermined the military power of the Austrian monarchy.

The Allies made plans for a final partition of the Ottoman Empire. The British aroused Arab hopes for independence. The British Colonel T. E. Lawrence led an insurrection in the Hejaz against the Turks; and the emir Hussein of Hejaz, with British support, in 1916 took the title of King of the Arabs, with a kingdom reaching from the Red Sea to the Persian Gulf. Zionists saw in the impending Ottoman collapse the opportunity to realize their dream for Palestine.[13] Since Palestine was an Arabic country (and had been for over a thousand years) the Zionist program conflicted with British plans to sponsor Arab nationalism. Nevertheless, in the Balfour note of 1917, the British government promised to support the idea of a Jewish "homeland" in Palestine.

Nor was the very center of the Ottoman Empire overlooked. In the first months of the war the Russians brought up the eternal question of the Turkish Straits. Russia in 1915 bore the brunt of the German attack; the Western Allies needed the respite thus given them, and feared that Russia might if unsatisfied make a separate peace. Britain and France themselves, in 1915, were attacking the Straits at the Dardanelles.[14] They therefore had to reassure their Russian ally as to their ultimate intentions. By a secret agreement of March 1915 the British and French accepted the Russian terms. Russia, after the war, was to annex Constantinople, together with the Bosporus, Sea of Marmora and Dardanelles—i.e., the entire Straits. The Western powers thus abandoned a policy to which they had clung stubbornly for generations—many Russians, indeed, doubted whether, if the Allies emerged victorious, they would ever live up to the bargain. As for the rest of Turkey, another agreement of 1916, made at the time when Hussein became king in Arabia, divided it into spheres of influence: Mesopotamia was to go to Britain, Syria and southeastern Asia Minor to France, Armenia and Kurdistan to Russia. Adalia and Smyrna were reserved for Italy.

Meanwhile the British and French easily conquered the German colonies in Africa. Early in the war the British foreign secretary, Sir Edward Grey, revealed to Colonel House, President Wilson's personal emissary, that it was not the intention of the Allies for Germany ever to get its colonies back.

In China, too, the third important area of imperialist competition, the war accelerated the tendencies of preceding years. The Japanese saw their own opportunity in the self-slaughter of the Europeans. Japan had also been allied to Britain since 1902. In August 1914 Japan declared war on Germany. It soon overran the German concessions in China, and the German islands in the Pacific, the Marshalls and Carolines. In January 1915 Japan presented its Twenty-One Demands on China, a secret ultimatum most of which the Chinese were obliged to accept. Japan thereby proceeded to turn Manchuria and north China into a kind of exclusive protectorate.

All these developments, whether accomplished facts or secret agreements, affecting Europe, Asia, or Africa, became very troublesome later on

13 See p. 606.
14 See pp. 679–80.

at the peace conference. They continued to be the most unsettling tendencies of European politics before the war. It does not appear that the Allies, until driven by Woodrow Wilson, gave any thought to means of controlling anarchic nationalism or of preventing war in the future. As for the Germans, their war aims were also expansionist, and included acquisitions in Eastern Europe, colonial readjustments and the annexation or subordination of Belgium, to obtain more direct access to the Atlantic. Wilson, though his personal sympathies lay with England and France, saw politically little to choose between the warring alliances, and in his public utterances spoke as if they were Tweedledum and Tweedledee. Both sides were indignant that he saw no difference between them. In 1916 he attempted to mediate, entering into confidential discussions with both; but both still hoped to win on their own terms, so that negotiation was fruitless. Wilson judged that most Americans wished to remain uninvolved, and in November 1916 was re-elected to a second term, on the popular cry that "he kept us out of war." He urged a true neutrality of thought and feeling. As late as January 1917, three months before going to war, he called for a "peace without victory," one in which neither side should be altogether crushed.

CAMPAIGNS OF 1915–16

Meanwhile the fighting dragged on. The Germans and Austro-Hungarians, early in 1915, began the operation which they hoped would put Russia out of the war. Some expressed misgivings, remembering the fate of Napoleon. They were reassured by the German General Hoffmann: "If Napoleon had had the railroad, telephone, motor convoy, telegraph, and airplane he would still be in Moscow today." The offensive opened with much promise. On the eastern front the western conditions of immobility did not obtain. The front was too long to be thoroughly entrenched, and the Russians lacked machine guns and heavy artillery. The attackers pressed on into Lithuania and White Russia. The Russian losses were of truly Asiatic proportions— 2,000,000 killed, wounded or captured in 1915 alone. But at the end of the year the Russian army was still fighting. Peace could not be imposed.

On the western front, in 1915, the Allies tried to take advantage of German concentration in the east. They too mounted an offensive, but they could not pierce the German lines. With 250,000 Allied casualties (almost twice as many as those of the German defenders) the campaign was a failure.

In January 1915 Winston Churchill, First Lord of the Admiralty, proposed that Britain use its control of the sea to select its own point of attack. He recommended an onslaught at the Dardanelles. It was at first thought that purely naval action would suffice, so that no forces need be diverted from France. The battleships were to demolish the fortifications with their great guns, then push through the narrow passage (only a mile wide) and seize Constantinople. Thus the deadlock in France would be circumvented, Turkey driven out of the war, aid brought to Serbia, the Balkan front built up, and communications opened with Russia—all at small cost. There was some opposition to the plan, especially by the French, and by some British naval officers, who objected to such a dispersion of effort from the main theater; but the opposition was overruled. The fleet, after initial successes, reached the narrowest part of the strait. After a naval bombardment of five days it was decided that army units must land to clean out the Turkish forts on the peninsula of Gallipoli. First one division was sent, and ultimately five—as many as the British had been able to send against the Germans in the preceding August. German officers supervised the defense of the Turkish forts. The most terrific pounding by both army and navy was of no use. Repeatedly the British refused to withdraw, fearing loss of prestige throughout the Moslem world. In the end, all told, 450,000 men were poured into the Dardanelles. There were 145,000 Allied killed and wounded. After almost a year the enterprise was given up as a failure. Poor coordination, between British and French and between army and navy, ruined a plan which if more vigorously prosecuted in its early stages might have been successful. Since in the end it consumed a huge outlay of Allied men and material, as well as time, the only person to express satisfaction was Falkenhayn, chief of the German High Command.

For 1916 both sides turned again to France as the scene of their main effort. The Allies planned a great offensive along the river Somme while the Germans prepared one in the neighborhood of Verdun. The Germans disconcerted the Allies by moving first. Verdun occupied a salient in the French line, protruding in such a way that it could be shelled and assaulted from several directions. Falkenhayn selected it for attack because he believed that the French would defend it to the last ditch. His aim was not to find a weak spot, break through, restore mobile warfare and obtain a quick decision—all these he had given up as impossible in the West. His aim was to pick a strong spot, hammer at it incessantly, draw in wave after wave of French reserves, and methodically slaughter them. He expected to inflict five casualties for every two he lost, and so to bleed his adversary slowly to death. It was a strategy of pure attrition. Verdun was a piece of flypaper on which the French army would be caught.

The Germans attacked Verdun in February 1916. The French commander, Joffre, put in General Pétain to defend it, but resisted letting his main reserves become committed, holding as many as he could for the coming offensive in the Somme. Pétain and his troops, held to minimum numbers, thus had to take the full weight of the German army. The battle of Verdun lasted six months, it drew the horrified admiration of the world, and it became a legend of determined resistance ("they shall not pass"), until the Germans finally abandoned the attack because they sustained almost as many casualties as the French—330,000 to 350,000—so that their purpose was baffled.

While the inferno raged at Verdun (and a month after the battle of Jutland) the Allies opened their offensive in the Somme on July 1. The outlook seemed good. The Germans were still involved at Verdun. The Russians, according to plan, had attacked in the East, showing surprising strength after the disasters of 1915, so that three German divisions had already been withdrawn from France. During the summer of 1916 the Central Powers were to lose almost 400,000 men in Russia. In the Somme, the Allies brought up unheard of amounts of artillery, and the newly trained British army was present in force. The idea was to break through the German line simply by stupendous pressure; on both sides, Allied and German, the art of generalship had perforce sunk to an all-time low. Despite a week-long artillery bombardment the British lost 60,000 men on the first day of the attack. In a week they had advanced only a mile along a six-mile front. In a month they had advanced only two miles and a half. As at Verdun, the superiority of the defensive was again demonstrated. The Battle of the Somme, lasting from July to October, cost the Germans about 500,000 men, the British 400,000 and the French 200,000. Nothing of any value had been gained. It was, indeed, at the Somme that the British first used the tank, an armored vehicle with caterpillar tracks that could crush through barbed wire, lunge over trenches and smash into machine-gun nests; but the tanks were introduced in such small numbers, and with such skepticism on the part of many commanders, that they had no effect on the battle.

Meanwhile in 1916 the Italians held off repeated Austrian blows. The Germans and Austro-Hungarians overran Serbia, despite ill-coordinated efforts of an Allied expeditionary force to defend it. They also overran Rumania, which somewhat inopportunely entered the war on the side of the Allies in the hope of enlarging its territories. On the Eastern front, in 1916, the Russians lost another million men, but 1916 was not a good year for the Germans. In the west, Verdun and the Somme were both signal failures for those who planned them, and proved again the superiority of the defensive. At sea, the naval blockade continued. Germany and its allies controlled Central Europe from the North Sea to the Turkish Straits. There was no fighting on the soil of Germany or Austria-Hungary. But they were a beleaguered fortress, cut off from the sea, hemmed in by Russians, Italians, French, and British. The deadlock was confirmed for both sides, and the slow murderous futility of the war of attrition became more apparent.

As of the end of 1916, it is hard to see how the First World War would have turned out, had not two new sets of forces been brought in.

87. The Collapse of Russia and the Intervention of the United States

THE WITHDRAWAL OF RUSSIA: REVOLUTION AND THE

TREATY OF BREST-LITOVSK

The first victim of the First World War, among governments, was the Russian Empire. As the Russo-Japanese War had led to the Revolution of 1905 in Russia, so the more ruinous war in Europe led to the far greater

Revolution of 1917. The story of the Russian Revolution is told in the follow-ing chapter. It is enough to say here, as part of the history of the war, that war offered a test that the tsarist government could not meet. Bungling, dis-honest, and secretive, incapable of supplying the materiel required for mod-ern fighting, driving hordes of peasants into battle in some cases even with-out rifles, losing men by the millions yet offering no goal to inspire sacrifice, the tsarist regime lost the loyalty of all elements of its people. In March 1917 the troops in St. Petersburg mutinied, while strikes and riots desolated the city. The Duma, or Russian parliament, used the occasion to press its de-mands for reform. On March 15 Nicholas II abdicated. A Provisional Gov-ernment took over, made up of liberal noblemen and middle-class leaders, generally democrats and constitutionalists, with at first only one socialist. The Provisional Government remained in office from March to November 1917. Its members, who shared in the liberalism of western Europe, believed that a liberal and parliamentary regime could not succeed in Russia unless the German Empire were defeated. They took steps, therefore, to prosecute the war with a new vigor. In July 1917 an offensive was opened in Galicia, but the demoralized Russian armies again collapsed.

The mass of the Russian people were wearied of a war in which they were asked to suffer so much for so little. Nor did the Russian peasant or workingman feel any enthusiasm for the Westernized intellectuals and pro-fessional men who manned the Provisional Government. The ordinary Rus-sian, so far as he had any politics, was drawn to one or another of numerous forms of socialism, Marxist and non-Marxist. The Russian Marxist party, the Social Democrats, was divided between Menshevik and Bolshevik factions, the latter being the more extreme. The Bolshevik leaders had for some time lived as exiles in western Europe. Their principal spokesman, V. I. Lenin, with a few others, had spent the war years in Switzerland. In April 1917 the German government offered safe passage to Lenin through Germany to Rus-sia. A railway car full of Bolsheviks, carefully "sealed" to prevent infection of Germany, was thus hauled by a German train to the frontier, whence it passed on to St. Petersburg, or Petrograd, as the city was re-named during the war. The aim of the Germans in this affair, as in the sending of Roger Case-ment to Ireland in a submarine, was of course to use a kind of psychological warfare against the enemy's home front. It was to promote rebellion against the Provisional Government, and thus at last to eliminate Russia.

The position of the Provisional Government became rapidly more un-tenable, from many causes, until by November 1917 the situation was so confused that Lenin and the Bolsheviks were able to seize power. The Bol-sheviks stood for peace with Germany, partly to win popular favor in Russia, and partly because they regarded the war impartially as a struggle between capitalist and imperialist powers, which should be left to exhaust and destroy each other for the benefit of socialism. On December 3, 1917, a peace confer-ence opened between the Bolsheviks and the Germans at Brest-Litovsk. Meanwhile the peoples within the western border of the old Russia—Poles, Ukrainians, Bessarabians, Estonians, Latvians, Finns—with German backing, proclaimed their national independence. The Bolsheviks, since they would not or could not fight, were obliged to sign with Germany a treaty to which they vehemently objected, the treaty of Brest-Litovsk of March 3, 1918. By this treaty they acknowledged the "independence," or at least the loss to Russia, of Poland, the Ukraine, Finland, and the other new states of the Baltic coast, Estonia, Latvia, and Lithuania.

For the Germans the treaty of Brest-Litovsk represented their maximum success during the First World War. Not only had they neutralized Russia; they also now dominated eastern Europe through puppets placed at the head of the new independent states. They relieved the effects of the naval blockade by drawing considerable quantities of foodstuffs from the Ukraine, though less than they expected. A certain number of German troops remained in the East to preserve the new arrangements. But it was no longer a two-front war. Masses of the German army were shifted from east to west. The High Command, now under Hindenburg and Ludendorff, prepared to concentrate for a last blow in France to end the war in 1918.

The year 1918 was essentially a race to see whether American aid could reach Europe soon enough, in sufficent amount, to offset the added strength which Germany drew from the collapse of Russia. In March of that year the Germans, beginning with gas attacks and a bombardment by 6,000 artillery pieces, opened a formidable offensive before which the French and British both recoiled. On May 30, 1918, the Germans again stood at the Marne, thirty-seven miles from Paris. At this time there were only two American divisions in action, though the United States had been at war over a year. At this point in the story there are therefore two open questions: how the United States entered the war, and the length of time required for the build-up of its forces overseas.

THE UNITED STATES AND THE WAR

We have seen how President Wilson clung persistently to neutrality. The American people were divided. Many had been born in Europe, or were the children of immigrants. Those of Irish origin were anti-British; those of German origin were often sympathetic to Germany. On the other hand, since the time of the Spanish-American and Boer Wars, a noticeable current of friendliness to the English had been running, more than ever before in American history. The sale of war materials to the Allies, and the purchase of the bonds of Allied governments, had given certain limited though influential circles a material interest in an Allied victory. The idealism of the country was on the side of England and France, so far as it was not isolationalist. An Allied victory would clearly advance the cause of democracy, freedom, and progress far more than a victory of the German Empire. On the other hand, England and France were suspected of somewhat impure motives, and they were allied with the Russian autocracy, the reactionary and brutal government of the tsar.

The fall of tsarism made a great impression. Democratic and progressive men now came forward even in Russia. No one had ever heard of Lenin, or foreseen the Bolshevik revolution. It seemed in the spring of 1917 that Russia was struggling along the path that England, France, and America had already taken. An ideological barrier had dropped away, and the demand for American intervention to safeguard democracy became more insistent.

The Germans gave up the attempt to keep the United States out. Constricted ever more tightly by the blockade, and failing to get a decision on land, the German government and High Command listened more readily to the submarine experts, who declared that if given a free hand they could force British surrender in six months. It was the chief example in World War I of the claim that one branch of the service could win the war alone. Civilian and diplomatic members of the government objected, fearing the consequences of war with the United States. They were overruled; it was a good example of the way in which, in Germany, the army and navy had taken the highest policy into their hands. It was decided to reopen unrestricted submarine warfare on February 1, 1917. It was foreseen that the United States would declare war, but it was believed that this would make no immediate difference. The Germans in 1917 estimated (correctly) that between the time when the United States entered a European war and the time when it could take part with its own army a time-lag of about a year must intervene. Meanwhile, the planners said, in six months they could force Britain to accept defeat, after which neither the United States nor any other power could fight in Europe. Their error was in exaggerating the role of the submarine.

On January 31, 1917, the Germans notified Wilson of the resumption of unrestricted submarine attacks. They announced that they would sink on sight all merchant vessels found in a zone around the British Isles or in the Mediterranean. Wilson broke off diplomatic relations, and ordered the arming of American freighters. Meanwhile the publication of the Zimmermann telegram had convinced many Americans of German aggressiveness. German secret agents had been at work in America, fomenting strikes and causing explosions in factories engaged in the manufacture of munitions for the Allies. Americans regarded the activity of these "spies" as an interference with their rights as neutrals. Wilson at last concluded that Germany was a menace. He seems to have felt, not so much that it menaced the actual military security of the United States, as that it menaced everything that was right, lawful, decent, and progressive in modern civilization. He did not think in material terms. Even to protect commerce, in his view, was not a matter of material self-interest or profit; it was a matter of principle, of protecting the right of neutral nations to go about their affairs, normally, safely, and lawfully, even though other nations happened to be at war. Having made his decision Wilson saw a clear-cut issue between right and wrong. The American people now saw it in the same way, and Wilson obtained a rousing declaration of war from Congress, on April 2, 1917, with a speech notable for its eloquence and solemnity:

It is a fearful thing to lead this great peaceful people into war, into the most terrible and disastrous of all wars, civilization itself seeming to be in the balance. But the right is more precious than peace, and we shall fight for the things which we have always carried nearest our hearts—for democracy, for the right of those who submit to authority to have a voice in their own Government, for the rights and liberties of small nations, for a universal dominion of right by such a concert of free peoples as shall bring peace and safety to all nations and make the world itself at last free.

The United States went to war "to make the world safe for democracy."

At first the German submarine campaign realized and even exceeded the predictions of its sponsors. In February 1917 the Germans sank 540,000 tons of shipping, in March 578,000 tons, in April, as the days grew longer, 874,000 tons. Something akin to terror, with difficulty concealed from the public, seized on the government in London. Britain was reduced to a mere six-weeks' reserve of food. Gradually counter-measures were developed—mine-barrages, hydrophones, depth-charges, airplane reconnaissance, and most of all the convoy. It was found that a hundred or more freighters together, though all had to steam at the pace of the slowest, could be protected by a sufficient concentration of warships to keep submarines away. The United States navy, which, unlike the army, was of considerable size and ready for combat, supplied enough additional force to the Allies to make convoying and other anti-submarine measures highly effective. By the end of 1917 the submarine was no more than a nuisance. For the Germans the great plan produced the anticipated penalty without the reward—its net result was only to add America to their enemies.

On the western front in 1917, while the Americans desperately got themselves ready for the war they had entered, the French and British continued to hold the line. The French, finding in General Nivelle a commander who still believed in the breakthrough, launched an offensive so unsuccessful and so bloody that mutiny spread through the French army. Pétain then replaced Nivelle; he restored discipline to the exhausted and disillusioned soldiers, but he had no thought of further attack. "I am waiting for the Americans and the tanks," he said. The British then assumed the main burden. For three months late in 1917 they fought the dismal battle of Passchendaele. They advanced five miles, near Ypres, at a cost of 400,000 men. At the very end of 1917 the British surprised the Germans with a raid by 380 tanks, which penetrated deep into the German lines but then had to withdraw, since no reserve of fresh infantry was at hand to exploit their success. Meanwhile the Austro-Hungarians, strongly reinforced by German troops, overwhelmed the Italians at the disastrous battle of Caporetto. The Central Powers streamed into northern Italy, but the Italians, with British and French reinforcements, were at last able to hold the line. The net effect of the campaigns of 1917, and of the repulse of the submarine at the same time, was to re-emphasize the stalemate in Europe, incline the weary Allies to await the Americans, and give the Americans what they most needed—time.

The Americans made good use of the time that was given them. Conscription, democratically entitled selective service, was adopted immediately after the declaration of war. The United States Army, whose professionals in 1916 numbered only 130,000, performed the mammoth feat of turning over 3,500,000 civilians into soldiers. With the Navy, the United States came to have over four million in its armed services (which may be compared with over twelve million in the Second World War). Aid flowed to the Allies. To the loans already made through private bankers were added some ten billion dollars lent by the American government itself. The Allies used the money mainly to buy food and munitions in the United States. American farms and factories, which had already prospered by selling to the Allies during the period of neutrality, now broke all records for production. Civilian industry was converted to war uses; radiator factories turned out guns, and piano factories airplane wings. Every possible means was employed to build up ocean shipping, without which neither American supplies nor American armies could reach the theater of war. Available shipping was increased from a million to ten million tons. Civilian consumption was drastically cut. Eight thousand tons of steel a year were saved in the manufacture of women's corsets, and 75,000 tons of tin in the making of children's toy wagons. Every week people observed Meatless Tuesday, and sugar was rationed. Daylight-saving time, invented in Europe during the war, was introduced to save coal. By such means the United States made enormous stocks available for its Allies as well as itself, though for some items, notably airplanes and artillery ammunition, the American armies, when they reached France, drew heavily on British and French manufactures.

THE FINAL PHASE OF THE WAR

The Germans, as we have seen, victorious in the east, opened a great final offensive in the west in the spring of 1918, hoping to force a decision before American participation turned the balance forever. To oppose it, a new unity of command was at last achieved, for the first time, when a French general, Ferdinand Foch, was made commander-in-chief of all Allied forces in France, with the national commanders subordinate to him, including Pershing for the Americans. In June the Germans first made contact with American troops in significant force, meeting the Second Division at Chateau-Thierry. The German position was so favorable that civilians in the German government thought it opportune to make a last effort at a compromise peace. The military, headed by Hindenburg and Ludendorff, successfully blocked any such attempts; they preferred to gamble on one final throw. The German armies reached their farthest advance on July 15 along the Marne. There were now nine American divisions in the Allied line. Foch used them to spearhead his counterattack. By July 18 the badly overstrained Germans began to falter. Over 250,000 American troops were now landing in France every month. The Allied offensive which opened in September, with American troops in the

Argonne occupying an eastern sector, proved more than the Germans could withstand. The German High Command notified its government that it could not win the war. The German foreign office made peace overtures to President Wilson. An armistice was arranged, and on November 11, 1918, firing ceased on the western front.

Since Germany's allies had surrendered during the preceding weeks, the war, or at least the shooting war in western Europe, was now over. The horror it brought to individual lives cannot be told by statistics, which drily report that almost ten million men had been killed, and twenty million wounded. Each of the European great powers (except Italy) lost from a million to two million in killed alone. The United States, with some 330,000 casualties of all types (of whom 115,000 died) lost in the entire war fewer men than the main combatants had lost in such a single battle as Verdun or Passchendaele.[15] American assistance was decisive in the defeat of Germany. But it came so late, when the others had been struggling for so long, that the mere beginnings of it were enough to turn the scale. On the date of the armistice there were two million American soldiers in France, and another million were on the way. But the American army had really been in combat only four months. During the whole year 1918, out of every hundred artillery shells that were fired by the three armies, the French fired 51, the British 43 and the Americans only 6.

88. The Collapse of the Austrian and German Empires

The war proved fatal to the German and Austro-Hungarian empires, as to the Russian. The subject Hapsburg nationalities, or the "national councils" representing them in the Western capitals, obtained increasing recognition from the Allies, and in October declared their independence. The last Austrian emperor, Charles I, abdicated on November 12, and on the next day Austria was proclaimed a republic, as was Hungary in the following week. Before any peace conference could convene, the new states of Czechoslovakia, Yugoslavia, an enlarged Rumania, a republican Hungary, and a miniature republican Austria were in existence by their own action.

The German Empire stood solid until the closing weeks. Liberals, democrats, and socialists had put off their demands for the duration of the war. It was the High Command itself that precipitated the débacle. In the last years of the war dictatorial powers had become concentrated in the hands of General Ludendorff, and in September 1918 only he and his closest military associates realized that the German cause was hopeless. On September 29, at supreme headquarters at Spa in Belgium, Ludendorff informed the

---

[15] Of the 115,000 American deaths only 50,000 represented men killed in battle, the remainder representing mainly deaths by disease. The great influenza epidemic of 1918, which swept over civilians and military alike, in all parts of the world, probably accounted for 25,000 deaths in the American army.

Kaiser that Germany must ask for peace. He urged that a new government be formed at Berlin, reflecting the majority in the Reichstag, on democratic parliamentary principles. William II was astonished. Ludendorff could not wait. A sharp exchange passed between them on September 30:

"Is the new government not yet formed?" asked Ludendorff.

"I am not a magician," said the Emperor.

"We must have a new government immediately, so that the peace offer can be despatched today."

"You should have told me that two weeks ago," said the All Highest.

Ludendorff, in calling for immediate peace negotiations, seems to have had two ideas in mind. First, he might win time to re-form his armies and prepare a new offensive. But if worst came to worst, if collapse became unavoidable, then the civilian or democratic elements in Germany would be the ones to sue for peace.

The liberal Prince Max of Baden was found to head up a cabinet in which even socialists were included. In October various reforms were enacted, the Bismarckian system was ended, Germany became a liberal constitutional monarchy. For Ludendorff the changes were not fast enough. What was happening was essentially simple. The German military caste, at the moment of Germany's crisis, was more eager to save the army than to save the empire. The army must never admit surrender; that was an affair for small men in business suits. Emperor, High Command, officers, and aristocrats were unloading frantically upon civilians.

President Wilson unwittingly played into their hands. Speaking now as the chief of the Allied coalition, the one to whom peace overtures were first made, he insisted that the German government must become more democratic. It may be recalled how Bismarck, after defeating France in 1871, demanded a general election in France before making peace.[16] Wilson, unlike Bismarck, really believed in democracy; but in a practical way his position was the same. He wanted to be sure that he was dealing with the German people itself, not with a discredited elite. He wanted it to be the real Germany that applied for and accepted the Allied terms. In Germany, as realization of the military disaster spread, many people began to regard the Kaiser as an obstacle to peace. Or they felt that Germany would obtain better terms if it appeared before the Allies as a republic. Even the officer corps, to halt the fighting before the army disintegrated, began to talk of abdication. Sailors mutinied at Kiel on November 3, and councils of workers and soldiers were formed in various cities. The socialists threatened to withdraw from the cabinet (*i.e.*, go into revolutionary opposition and end the representative nature of the new government) unless William II abdicated. A general strike, led by minority socialists and syndicalists, began on November 9. "Abdication," Prince Max told the Emperor, "is a dreadful thing, but a government without the socialists would be a worse danger for the country." William II abdicated on November 9, and slipped across the frontier into Holland, where

wwwwwwwwwwwww

[16] See p. 527.

despite cries to try him as a "war criminal" he lived quietly until 1942. Germany was proclaimed a republic on the same day. Two days later the war stopped.

The fall of the empire in Germany, with the consequent adoption of the republic, did not arise from any basic discontent, deep revolutionary action, or change of sentiment in the German people. It was an episode of the war. The republic (soon called the Weimar Republic) arose because the victorious enemy demanded it, because the German people craved peace, because they wished to avoid forcible revolution, and because the old German military class, to save its face and its future strength, wished at least temporarily to be excused. When the war ended the German army was still in France, its discipline and organization still apparently unimpaired. No hostile shot had been fired on German soil. It was said later, by some, that the army had not been defeated, that it had been "stabbed in the back" by a dissolving civilian home front. This was untrue; it was the panic-stricken Ludendorff who first cried for "democracy." But the circumstances in which the German republic originated made its later history, and hence all later history, very troubled.

89. The Economic and Social Impact of the War

EFFECTS ON CAPITALISM: GOVERNMENT-REGULATED

ECONOMIES

European society was forced by the First World War into many basic changes that were to prove more lasting than the war itself. First of all, the war profoundly affected capitalism as previously known. Essential to the older capitalism (or economic liberalism, or free private enterprise) had been the idea that government should leave business alone, or at the most regulate certain general conditions under which business men went about their affairs. Before 1914 governments had increasingly come into the economic field. They had put up tariffs, protected national industries, sought for markets or raw materials by imperialist expansion, or passed protective social legislation to benefit the wage-earning classes. During the war all belligerent governments controlled the economic system far more minutely. Indeed, the idea of the "planned economy" was first applied in the First World War. For the first time (with such rare and archaic precedents as the French dictatorship of 1793) [17] the state attempted to direct all the wealth, resources and moral purpose of society to a single end.

Since no one had expected a long war, no one had made any plans for industrial mobilization. Everything had to be improvised. By 1916 each government had set up a system of boards, bureaus, councils and commissions to

[17] See pp. 360–1.

coordinate its war effort. The aim was to see that all manpower was effectively utilized, and that all natural resources within the country, and all that could possibly be imported, were employed where they would do the most good. In the stress of war free competition was found to be wasteful, and undirected private enterprise too uncertain and too slow. The profit motive came into disrepute. Those who exploited shortages to make big profits were stigmatized as "profiteers." Production for civilian use, or for mere luxury purposes, was cut to a minimum. Business men were not allowed to set up or close down factories as they chose. It was impossible to start a new business without government approval, because the flotation of stocks and bonds was controlled, and raw materials were made available only as the government wished. It was equally impossible to shut down a business engaged in war production; if a factory was inefficient or unprofitable the government kept it going anyway, making up the losses, so that in some cases management came to expect government support. Here too the tests of competition and profitableness were abandoned. The new goal was coordination or "rationalization" of production in the interests of the country as a whole. Labor was discouraged from protesting against hours or wage rates, and the big unions generally agreed to refrain from strikes. For the upper and middle classes it became embarrassing to show their comforts too openly. It was patriotic to eat meagerly and to wear old clothes. War gave a new impetus even to the idea of economic equality, if only to enlist rich and poor alike in a common cause.

Military conscription was the first step in the allocation of manpower. Draft boards told some men to report to the army, granting exemptions to others to work safely in war industries. Given the casualty rates at the front, state determination over individual life could hardly go farther. With the insatiable need for troops, drawing in men originally exempted or at first rejected as physically inadequate, great numbers of women poured into factories and offices, though not yet (as in the Second World War) into women's branches of the armed forces. Women took over many jobs which it had been thought only men could do. Since their invasion proved to be permanent, the labor force of all countries was enlarged, women's place in society was revolutionized, the institution of marriage and the relations of husband and wife were transformed, and the lives, liberty, and outlook of millions of individual women were turned outwards from the home. Governments did not directly force men or women to drop one job and take another. There was no systematic labor conscription. But by influencing wage scales, granting draft exemptions, forcing some industries to expand and others to contract or stand still, and propagandizing the idea that work in an arms factory was patriotic, the state shifted vast numbers of workers to war production. Impressed or "slave" labor was not used in the First World War nor were prisoners of war obliged to give labor service, though there were some abuses of these rules of international law by the Germans, who were possibly the least scrupulous and certainly the most hard pressed.

Governments controlled all foreign trade. It was intolerable to let private citizens ship off the country's resources at their own whim. It was equally intolerable to let them use up foreign exchange by importing unneeded goods, or to drive up prices of necessities by competing with one another. Foreign trade became a state monopoly, in which private firms operated under strict licenses and quotas. Even neutrals were affected, as when the Netherlands Overseas Trust was set up to monopolize and administer the rigid quota of imports allowed to enter Holland through the Allied blockade. The greatest of the exporting countries was the United States, whose annual exports rose from two to six billion dollars between 1914 and 1918. The endless demand for American farm and factory products naturally drove up prices, which, however, were fixed by law in 1917, for the most important items, before reaching the level to which free competition would have naturally driven them.

As for the European Allies, which even before the war had exported less than they imported, and were now exporting as little as possible, they could make purchases in the United States only by enormous loans from the American government. British and French citizens, under pressure from their own governments, sold off their American stocks and bonds, which were bought up by Americans. The former owners received pounds sterling or francs from their own governments, which in return took and spent the dollars paid by the new American owners. In this way the United States ceased to be a debtor country (owing some $4,000,000,000 to Europeans in 1914), and became the world's leading creditor country, to which by 1919 Europeans owed about $10,000,000,000. Europe's "dollar shortage," or inability to find means of payment for all the American goods that it needed, was to become a chronic problem of the twentieth century.

The Allies controlled the sea, but they never had enough shipping to meet rising demands, especially with German submarines taking a steady though fluctuating toll. Each government set up a shipping board, to expand shipbuilding at any cost, and to assign available shipping space to whatever purposes—troop movements, rubber imports, foodstuffs—the government considered most urgent in view of over-all plans. Control and allocation eventually became international, in the Interallied Shipping Council of which the United States was a member after entering the war. In England and France, where all manufactures depended on imports, government control of shipping and hence of imports was itself enough to give control over the whole economy.

Germany, denied access to the sea, and also to Russia and western Europe, was obliged to adopt unprecedented measures of self-sufficiency. The oil of Rumania and grain of the Ukraine, which became available late in the war, were poor substitutes for the world trade on which Germany had formerly depended. The Germans went hungrier than other belligerents. Their government controls became more thorough and more efficient, producing what they called "war socialism." In Walter Rathenau they found an organizer with genius. He was an industrialist, son of the head of the German electrical trust, and a man of bold and forward-looking ideas. One of the first to foresee a long war, he was put in charge of the mobilization of raw materials. Early in the war it seemed that Germany might be soon defeated by

lack of nitrogen, necessary to make explosives. Rathenau sweepingly requisitioned every conceivable natural source, including the very manure from the
farmers' barnyards, until German chemists succeeded in extracting nitrogen
from the air. The German chemical industry developed many other substitute products, such as synthetic rubber. Rathenau mobilized German production by organizing War Companies, one for each line of industry. Each
company was a kind of trust, representing the various business firms engaged
in one industry. Under government supervision, each War Company strove
for maximum production, fixed common prices, allotted raw materials to
member firms and individual plants, and determined how much each mine or
factory should produce. The War Companies represented the negation of
competition, the triumph of the trend toward trusts and monopolies that
had gone on in Europe and America since 1890.

Rathenau thought his War Companies a good halfway house between
private corporations and government bureaus, and believed that something
like them might be instituted permanently after the war. In his book, *Of
Things to Come,* he sketched a future for industrial society, one in which the
waste of competition and profit-seeking should be done away with, with
management and labor organized together in each industry, to plan and divide up the work and assure a fair return for all. His ideas had considerable
influence outside of Germany after the war and passed into ideas of the
corporative state. In Germany the war killed for good, for almost everybody,
the faith in a freely competitive private capitalism.

The other belligerent governments also replaced competition between
individual firms and factories with coordination. "Consortiums" of industrialists in France allocated raw materials and government orders within each
industry. The War Industries Board, under Bernard Baruch, did the same in
the United States. In Britain, similar methods became so efficient that by
1918, for example, the country produced every two weeks as many shells as
in the whole first year of the war, and turned out seventy times as much
heavy artillery.

INFLATION, INDUSTRIAL CHANGES, CONTROL OF IDEAS

No government, even by heavy taxes, could raise all the funds it needed
except by printing paper money, selling huge bond issues, or obliging banks
to grant it credit. The result, given heavy demand and acute shortages, was
rapid inflation of prices. Prices and wages were regulated, but were never
again so low as before 1914. The hardest hit by this development were those
whose money income could not easily be raised—people living on "safe" investments, those drawing annual salaries, professional people, government
employees. These classes had been one of the most stabilizing influences in
Europe before the war. Everywhere the war threatened their status, prestige,
and standard of living. The huge national debts meant higher taxes for years
to come. The debt was most serious when it was owed to a foreign country.

During the war the Continental Allies borrowed from Britain, and they and the British both borrowed from the United States. They thereby mortgaged their future. To pay the debt, they were bound for years to export more than they imported—or, roughly, to produce more than they consumed. It may be recalled that in 1914 every advanced European country habitually imported more than it exported.[18] That fact, basic to the European standard of life, was now threatened with reversal.

Moreover, with Europe torn by war for four years, the rest of the world speeded up its own industrialization. The productive capacity of the United States increased immensely. The Japanese began to sell in China, in India, in South America the cotton textiles and other civilian goods which these countries for the time being could not obtain from Europe. The Argentine and Brazil, unable to get locomotive parts or mining machinery from England, began to manufacture them themselves. In India the Tata family, a group of wealthy Parsees controlling $250,000,000 worth of native Indian capital, developed numerous manufacturing enterprises, one of which became the largest iron and steel works in the British empire. With Germany entirely out of the world market, with Britain and France producing desperately for themselves, and with the world's shipping commandeered for war uses, the position of western Europe as the world's workshop was undermined. After the war Europe found new competitors in its own traditional business. The economic foundations of the nineteenth century had slipped away. The Age of European Supremacy was in its twilight.

All the belligerent governments during the war attempted to control ideas as they did economic production. Freedom of thought, respected everywhere in Europe for half a century, went into the discard. Propaganda and censorship became more effective than any government, however despotic, had ever been able to devise. No one was allowed to sow doubt by raising any basic questions.

It must be remembered that the facts of the pre-war crises, as related above, were then largely unknown. People were trapped in a nightmare whose causes they could not comprehend. Each side wildly charged the other with having started the war from pure malignance. The long attrition, the fruitless fighting, the unchanging battlelines, the appalling casualties were a severe ordeal to morale. Civilians, deprived of their usual liberties, working harder, eating dull food, seeing no victory, had to be kept emotionally at a high pitch. Placards, posters, diplomatic white papers, schoolbooks, public lectures, solemn editorials, and slanted news reports conveyed the message. The new universal literacy, the mass press, the new moving pictures, proved to be ideal media for the direction of popular thinking. Intellectuals and professors advanced complicated reasons, usually historical, for loathing and crushing the enemy. In Allied countries the Kaiser was portrayed as a demon, with glaring eyes and abnormally bristling mustaches, bent on the mad project of conquest of the world. In Germany people were taught to dread the day when

[18] See p. 569.

Cossacks and Senegalese Negroes should rape German women, and to hate England as the inveterate enemy which inhumanly starved little children with its blockade. Each side convinced itself that all right was on its side, and all wrong, wickedness, and barbarity on the other. An inflamed opinion helped to sustain men and women in such a fearsome struggle. But when it came time to make peace the rooted convictions, fixed ideas, profound aversions, hates, and fears became an obstacle to political judgment.

90. The Peace of Paris, 1919

The late Ally, Russia, was in the hands of Bolsheviks, ostracized like a leper colony, and taking no part in international relations. The late German and Austro-Hungarian empires were already defunct, and more-or-less revolutionary regimes struggled to establish themselves in their places. New republics already existed along the Baltic coast, in Poland and in the Danube basin, but without effective governments or acknowledged frontiers. Europe east of France and Italy was in a state approaching chaos. Western Europe was wrenched out of all resemblance to its former self. In these circumstances the victors assembled in Paris, in the bleak winter of 1919, to reconstruct the world. During 1919 they signed five treaties, all named after Paris suburbs—St. Germain with Austria, Trianon with Hungary, Neuilly with Bulgaria, Sèvres with Turkey (1920), and most especially, with Germany, the Treaty of Versailles.

The world looked with awe and expectation to one man—the President of the United States. Wilson occupied a lone eminence, enjoyed a universal prestige. Victors, vanquished, and neutrals admitted that American intervention had decided the conflict. Everywhere people who had been long tried, confused, bereaved, were stirred by Wilson's thrilling language in favor of a higher cause, of a great concert of right in which peace would be forever secure and the world itself at last free. Wilson reached Europe in January 1919, visiting several Allied capitals. He was wildly acclaimed, and almost mobbed, greeted as the man who would lead civilization out of its wasteland.

THE FOURTEEN POINTS AND THE TREATY OF VERSAILLES

Wilson's views were well known. He had stated them in January 1918 in his Fourteen Points—principles upon which, after victory, peace was to be established. The Fourteen Points demanded an end to secret treaties and secret diplomacy (or in Wilsonian language, "open covenants openly arrived at"); freedom of the seas "alike in peace and in war"; removal of barriers and inequalities in international trade; reduction of armaments by all powers; colonial readjustments; evacuation of occupied territory; self-determination of nationalities and a redrawing of European boundaries along national lines;

and, last but not least, an international political organization to prevent war. On the whole, Wilson stood for the fruition of the democratic, liberal, progressive, and nationalist movements of the century past, for the ideals of the Enlightenment, the French Revolution, and of 1848. As Wilson saw it, and as many believed, the World War should end in a new type of treaty. There was thought to be something sinister about peace conferences of the past, for example the Congress of Vienna of 1815.[19] The old diplomacy was blamed for leading to war. It was felt that treaties had too long been wrongly based on a politics of power and the balance of power, or on unprincipled deals and bargains made without regard to the people concerned. Democracy having defeated the Central Powers, people hoped that a new settlement, made in a democratic age, might be reached by general agreement in an atmosphere of mutual confidence. There was a real sense of a new era.

Wilson had had some difficulty, however, in persuading the Allied governments to accept his Fourteen Points. The French declared that something about making Germany pay for war damages must be added. The British vetoed the freedom of the seas "in peace and war"; it was naval rivalry that had estranged them from Germany, and they had fought the war, in a basic sense, to preserve British command of the sea. But with these two reservations the Allies expressed their willingness to follow Wilson's lead. With the same two reservations, the Germans who asked for the armistice believed that peace would be made along the lines of the Fourteen Points. The socialists and democrats now trying to rule Germany thought also that, having thrown out the Kaiser and gotten rid of the warlords, they would be treated by the victors with some moderation, and that a new democratic Germany would re-emerge into the place in the world which they considered to be due it.

Twenty-seven nations assembled at Paris in January 1919, but the full or plenary sessions were unimportant. Matters were decided by conferences among the Big Four—Wilson himself, Lloyd George for England, Clemenceau for France, Orlando for Italy. The conjunction of personalities was not a happy one. Wilson was sternly and stubbornly righteous, Lloyd George a fiery and changeable Welshman, Clemenceau an aged patriot, the "tiger of France," who had been not exactly young in the War of 1870 (he was born in 1841); Orlando a passing phenomenon of Italian politics. None of them was especially equipped for the task in hand. Clemenceau was a pronounced nationalist, Lloyd George had always been concerned with domestic reforms, Orlando was by training a professor like Wilson, and Wilson, a former college president, lacked concrete knowledge or intimate feeling for peoples other than his own. However, they democratically represented the governments and peoples of their respective countries, and thus spoke with an authority denied to professional diplomats of the old school.

Wilson first fought a hard battle for a League of Nations, a permanent international body in which all nations, without sacrificing their sovereignty,

---

[19] See pp. 413–20.

should meet together to discuss and settle disputes, each promising not to
resort to war. Few European statesmen had any confidence in such a League.
But they yielded to Wilson, and the charter of the League of Nations was
written into the treaty with Germany. In return, Wilson had to make concessions to Lloyd George, Clemenceau, Orlando, and the Japanese. He was
thus obliged to compromise the idealism of the Fourteen Points. Probably
compromise and bargaining would have been necessary anyway, for such general principles as national self-determination and colonial readjustment invariably led to difference of opinion in concrete cases. Wilson allowed himself to believe that, if a League of Nations were once established and operating, faults in the treaty could be corrected at leisure by international discussion later on.

The great demand of the French at the peace conference was for security against Germany. On this subject the French were almost rabid. The
war in the west had been fought entirely (except for part of Belgium) on
their soil. To trim Germany down more nearly to French size, they proposed
that the part of Germany west of the Rhine be set up as an independent state
under Allied auspices. Wilson and Lloyd George objected, sagely observing
that the resulting German resentment would only lead to another war. The
French yielded on this point, but only on condition that they obtain their
security in another way, namely by a promise from both Britain and the
United States to join them immediately if they were again attacked by the
Germans. An Anglo-French-American guarantee treaty, with these provisions,
was in fact signed at Paris. France obtained the Saar coalfields, which were
complementary to the iron ones of Lorraine, and the right to administer the
Saar territory until 1935, when a plebiscite was to be held. Lorraine and
Alsace were returned to France. It was agreed to have Allied troops occupy
the Rhineland for fifteen years to assure German compliance with the treaty.

In the east the Allies wished to set up strong buffer states against Bolshevism in Russia. Sympathies with Poland ran very high. Those parts of the
former German Empire that were inhabited by Poles, or by mixed populations of Poles and Germans—Posen and West Prussia—were assigned to the
new Polish state. This gave Poland a corridor to the sea, but at the same time
cut off the bulk of Germany from East Prussia.[20] Danzig, an old German
town, became a free city, belonging to no country. Memel also was internationalized; it was soon seized by Lithuania. Upper Silesia, a rich mining country, went to Poland after a disputed plebiscite. In Austria and among the
Sudeten Germans of Bohemia, now that there was no longer a Hapsburg
empire (whose existence had blocked an all-German union in 1848 and in
the time of Bismarck)[21] a feeling developed for annexation to the new German republic. But the feeling was unorganized, and in any case the Allies
naturally refused to make Germany bigger than it had been in 1914. Austria
remained a dwarf republic, and Vienna a former imperial capital cut off from

[20] See maps, pp. 700–01 and 221, panel 4.
[21] See pp. 487–91, 520–5.

its empire—a head severed from its body, and scarcely more capable of sustaining life. The Bohemian Germans became disgruntled citizens of Czechoslovakia.

Germany lost all its colonies. Wilson and the South African General Smuts, to preserve the principle of internationalism against raw conquest, brought it about that the colonies were actually awarded to the League of Nations, which in turn, under "mandates," assigned them to various powers for administration. In this way France and Great Britain divided the best of the African colonies; the Belgian Congo received a slight enlargement; and the Union of South Africa took over German Southwest Africa. Italy got nothing. Japan received the mandate for German Pacific islands north of the equator, Australia for German New Guinea and the Solomon Islands. New Zealand for German Samoa. The Japanese claimed rights over the German concessions in China. The Chinese at the Paris conference tried to get all special concessions and extraterritorial rights in China abolished.[22] No one listened to such proposals. By a compromise, Japan received about half the former German rights. The Japanese were dissatisfied. The Chinese walked out of the conference.

The Allies took over the German fleet, but the German crews, rather than surrender it, solemnly scuttled it at Scapa Flow. The German army was limited to 100,000. Since the Allies forbade conscription, or the annual training of successive groups of young civilians, the army became exclusively professional, the officer class retained political influence in it, and the means used by the Allies to demilitarize Germany served if anything the contrary purpose. The treaty forbade Germany to have any heavy artillery, aviation, or submarines. Wilson saw his plan for universal disarmament applied to Germany alone.

The French, even before the armistice, had stipulated that Germany must pay for war damages. The other Allies made the same demand. Wilson, at the conference, was stupefied at the size of the bills presented. The Belgians suggested, for their own share, a sum larger than the entire wealth of all Belgium according to officially published Belgian statistics. The French and British proposed to charge Germany with the entire expenses, including war pensions, incurred by them during the war. Wilson observed that "total" reparation, while not strictly unjust, was absolutely impossible, and even Clemenceau noted that "to ask for over a trillion francs would lead to nothing practical." The insistence on enormous reparations was in fact largely emotional. No one knew or considered how Germany would pay, though all dimly realized that such sums could only be made up by German exports, which would then compete with the Allies' own economic interests. The Germans, to avoid worse, even offered to repair physical damages in Belgium and France, but were brusquely refused on the ground that the Belgians and French would thereby lose jobs and business. No total at all was set for reparations in the treaty; it was made clear that the sum would be very large, but it

[22] See p. 653.

was left for a future commission to determine. The Allies, maddened by the war, and themselves loaded with fantastic debts to the United States, had no desire in the matter of reparations to listen to economic reason, and regarded the reparations as simply another means of righting a wrong, and of putting off the dangers of a German revival. As a first payment on the reparations account the treaty required Germany to surrender most of its merchant marine, make coal deliveries, and give up all property owned by German private citizens abroad. This last proviso ended Germany's pre-war career as an exporter of capital.

It was with the specific purpose of justifying the reparations that the famous "war guilt" clause was written into the treaty. By this clause Germany explicitly "accepted the responsibility" for all loss and damage resulting from the war "imposed upon them (the Allies) by the aggression of Germany and her allies." The Germans themselves felt no such responsibility as they were now obliged formally to accept. They considered their honor as a people to be impugned. The "war-guilt" clause gave a ready opening to agitators in Germany, and made even moderate Germans regard the treaty as something to be escaped from as a matter of self-respect.

The Treaty of Versailles was completed in three months. The absence of the Russians, the decision not to give the Germans a hearing, and the willingness of Wilson to make concessions in return for obtaining the League of Nations, made it possible to dispose of intricate matters with considerable facility. The Germans, when presented with the completed document in May 1919, refused to sign. A government crisis ensued in Berlin. No German wished to damn himself, his party or his principles, in German eyes, by putting his name to a document which all Germans regarded as outrageous. A combination drawn from the Social Democrat and Catholic parties finally consented to shoulder the hateful burden. Two abashed and unknown men, with the plain names of Müller and Bell, appeared at the Hall of Mirrors at Versailles, and signed the treaty for Germany in the presence of a large concourse of Allied dignitaries.

The other treaties drafted by the Paris conference, in conjunction with the Versailles Treaty, laid out a new map for eastern Europe, and registered the recession of the Russian, Austrian, and Turkish empires. Seven new independent states now existed: Finland, Estonia, Latvia, Lithuania, Poland, Czechoslovakia, and Yugoslavia. Rumania was enlarged by adjoining areas formerly Hungarian and Russian; Greece was enlarged at the expense of Turkey. Austria and Hungary were now small states, and there was no connection between them. The Ottoman Empire presently disappeared: Turkey emerged as a republic confined to Constantinople and Asia Minor, Syria and Lebanon went to France as mandates of the League of Nations, Palestine and Iraq to Great Britain on the same basis.[23] The belt of states from Finland to

----

[23] The secret treaty of 1915 (p. 678) promising the Straits to Russia lapsed with the Revolution, neither the Bolsheviks nor the Allies recognizing an agreement made with the tsarist government.

Rumania was regarded as a *cordon sanitaire* (sanitary zone) to prevent the westward expansion of communism. The creation of Yugoslavia realized the aims of the South Slav or Pan-Serb movement which had set off the fatal crisis of 1914. The fact, however, that Italy received Trieste and some of the Dalmatian islands (in keeping with the secret treaty of 1915) left the more ambitious Yugoslavs discontented.

SIGNIFICANCE OF THE PARIS PEACE SETTLEMENT

The most general principle of the Paris settlement was to recognize the right of national self-determination, at least in Europe. Each people or nation, as defined by language, was in principle set up with its own sovereign and independent national state. Nationalism triumphed in the belief that it went along naturally with liberalism and democracy. It must be added that the peacemakers at Paris had little choice in this matter, for the new states had already declared their independence. Since in eastern Europe the nationalities were in many places intermixed, and since the peacemakers did not contemplate the actual movement and exchange of populations to sort them out, each new state found alien minorities living within its borders, or could claim that people of its own kind still lived in neighboring states under foreign rule. There were Hungarians in Czechoslovakia, Ruthenians in Poland, Poles in Lithuania, Bulgars in Rumania—to cite only a few examples. Hence minority problems and irredentism troubled eastern Europe, as they had before 1914. Eventually it was the complaint of Germans in Czechoslovakia that they were an oppressed minority, together with the irredentist demand of Germany to join these outlying brothers to the Fatherland, that touched off the Second World War somewhat as similar agitation among South Slavs had touched off the First.[24]

The treaty of Versailles was designed to put an end to the German menace. It was not a successful treaty. The wisdom of it has been discussed without end, but a few comments can safely be made. For practical purposes,

∿∿∿∿∿∿∿∿∿∿∿∿∿∿∿∿
[24] See pp. 823–6.

Europe, 1923   See following pages

The map shows European boundaries between the two World Wars. They are as established by the treaty of Versailles of 1919, the other treaties of the Peace of Paris, the settlement of the Irish troubles, the outcome of the Russo-Polish war of 1920, the termination of the Greek-Turkish war and the end of Allied intervention in Russia and in Turkey. By comparison with the language map on p. 437, it may be seen to what extent these boundaries set up various nationalities as independent states. The boundaries here shown began to collapse in 1938 with the Munich conference, by which Germany annexed the adjoining Sudeten areas. On the Polish question, which precipitated the Second World War, see also panel 4 of the map on p. 221.

EUROPE
1923

AREAS LOST BY
GERMANY

AREAS LOST BY
RUSSIA

AREAS LOST BY
OTTOMAN EMPIRE

ARCTIC

Reykjavik
ICELAND
(DEN.)

FAEROE IS.
(DEN.)

NORWAY

SWEDE

Oslo

Stock

SCAPA
FLOW

*NORTH
SEA*

DENMARK

GERMAN
WEIMAR REPU

Da

Edinburgh

ULSTER

IRISH
FREE
STATE

Dublin

GREAT
BRITAIN

Liverpool

Hamburg

Bremen

Berlin

POLISH
CORRIDOR

ATLANTIC

London

Amsterdam

NETH.

RUHR

Cologne

Weimar

Dresden

ENGLISH CHANNEL

Brussels

BELG

Prague

CZE

OCEAN

Paris

Versailles

Metz

LUX.

RHINE

SAAR

Frankfurt

Stuttgart

Strasburg

Munich

DANUBE R.

Vienna

AUSTRIA

Bu

FRANCE

Geneva

SWITZ

Bordeaux

Locarno

Trent

Trieste

Fiume

Bilbao

Marseilles

Florence

Zara
(IT.)

ADRIATIC SEA

PORTUGAL

Madrid

SPAIN

Barcelona

CORSICA
(FR.)

ITALY

Rome

Lisbon

Seville

BALEARIC IS.
(SP.)

SARDINIA
(IT.)

Naples

Cadiz

GIBRALTAR
(BR.)

Tangier

SP. MOROCCO

Algiers

MED

SICILY

MOROCCO
(FR.)

ALGERIA
(FR.)

TUNISIA
(FR.)

MALTA
(BR.)

TRM

500 MILES

with respect to Germany, the treaty was either too severe or too lenient. It was too severe to conciliate, and not severe enough to destroy. Possibly the victors should have dealt more moderately with the new German republic, which professed their own ideals, as the monarchical victors over Napoleon, in 1814, had dealt moderately with the France of the restored Bourbons, regarding it as a regime akin to their own. As it was, the Allies imposed upon the German Republic about the same terms that they might have imposed upon the German Empire. They innocently played the game of Ludendorff and the German reactionaries; it was the Social Democrats and liberals who bore the "shame" of Versailles. The Germans from the beginning showed no real intention to live up to the treaty. On the other hand, the treaty was not sufficiently disabling to Germany to destroy its economic and political strength. Even the degree of severity that it incorporated soon proved to be more than the Allies were willing to enforce. The treaty-makers at Paris in 1919, working hastily and still in the heat of war, under pressure from press and propaganda in their own countries, drafted a set of terms which the test of time showed that they themselves did not in the long run wish to impose. As the years passed many people in Allied countries declared various provisions of the Versailles Treaty to be unfair or unworkable. The loss of faith by the Allies in their own treaty only made easier the task of those German agitators who demanded its repudiation. The door was opened for Adolf Hitler.

Even at the beginning the Allies showed doubts. Lloyd George, in the last weeks before signature, tardily called for certain amendments, though in vain; for in 1919 British opinion shifted somewhat from fear of Germany to the fear of Bolshevism, and already the idea of using Germany as a bulwark against communism was expressed. The Italians disliked the whole settlement from the beginning; they observed that the spoils of Africa and the Near East went only to France and Great Britain. The Chinese were also dissatisfied. The Russians, when they re-entered the international arena some years later, found a situation that they did not like, and had had no part in making. They objected to being faced with a *cordon sanitaire* from Finland to Rumania, and soon remembered that most of this territory had once belonged to the Russian Empire.

The United States never ratified the Treaty of Versailles at all. A wave of isolationalism and disgust with Europe spread over the country; and this feeling, together with some rational criticism of the terms, and a good deal of party politics, caused the Senate to repudiate Wilson's work. The Senate likewise refused to make any advance promises of military intervention in a future war between Germany and France, and hence also declined to ratify the Anglo-French-American guarantee treaty on which Wilson had persuaded Clemenceau to rely. The French considered themselves duped, deprived both of the Rhineland and of the Anglo-American guarantee. They raised more anguished cries over their insecurity. This led them to try to hold Germany down while it was still weak, in turn raising many further complications.

The League of Nations was established at Geneva. Its mere existence marked a great step beyond the international anarchy before 1914. Wilson's vision did not die. But the United States never joined; Germany was not admitted until 1926, or Russia until 1934. The League could handle and despatch only such business as the Great Powers were willing to allow. It was associated with a west-European ascendancy that no longer corresponded to the facts of the world situation. Its charter was part of the Versailles treaty, and many people in many countries, in both sides in the late war, saw in it, not so much a system for international adjudication, as a means for maintaining a new *status quo* in favor of Britain and France.

The First World War dealt a last blow to the ancient institutions of monarchy and aristocratic feudalism. Thrones toppled in Turkey, in Russia, in Austria-Hungary, in the German Empire and the individual German states; and with the kings went the courtly retainers and all the social preeminence and special advantage of the old landed aristocracies. The war was indeed a victory for democracy, though a bitter one. It carried further a process as old as the French and American revolutions. But for the basic problems of modern civilization, industrialism and nationalism, economic security and international stability, it gave no answer.

CHAPTER XVII

The Russian Revolution

91. *Backgrounds*

92. *The Revolution of 1905*

93. *The Revolution of 1917*

94. *The Union of Soviet Socialist Republics*

95. *Stalin: The Five-Year Plans and the Purges*

96. *The International Impact of Communism, 1919–39*

NO LESS powerful than the First World War as a force shaping the twentieth century has been the revolution in Russia, of which the decisive step was the seizure of power by Lenin in November 1917. The Russian Revolution of 1917 can be compared in its magnitude only with the French Revolution of 1789. Both originated from deep-lying and distant causes, and both made their repercussions felt in many countries for many years. The present chapter will set forth the revolutionary process in Russia over half a century. We shall begin with the old regime before 1900, pass through the two revolutions of 1905 and 1917, and survey the Union of Socialist Soviet Republics down to 1939, at which time a new order had been consolidated under Joseph Stalin, a form of "planned economy" successfully realized, and the last of the true revolutionaries, or Old Bolsheviks, either silenced or put to death.

The comparison of the Russian revolution to the French is enlightening in many ways. Both aimed at liberation, the one from feudalism, the other from capitalism. Neither was a strictly national movement dealing with

merely domestic troubles; both addressed their appeal to all men regardless
of creed or color. Both attracted followers in all countries. Both became international. Both aroused a strong reaction on the part of those in all countries whose view of life was endangered. Both showed the same pattern of
revolutionary politics: a relative unity of opinion so long as the problem was
to overthrow the old regime, followed by disunity and conflict over the
founding of the new, so that one set of the original revolutionaries eliminated
others, until a small, organized and determined minority (Jacobin democrats
in 1793, Bolshevik communists in 1918) suppressed all opposition in order to
defend or advance the revolutionary cause; and in short order (within a
matter of months in France, years in Russia), many of the dominant revolutionary party were themselves suppressed or liquidated.

The differences are equally deserving of notice. Relatively speaking,
or compared in general civilization with other European countries, Russia in
1900 was in the rear, and France in 1780 in most ways in the lead. Nor is the
difference merely relative. Illiteracy was probably more widespread in Russia
in 1900 than in France in 1780. The last tsar, Nicholas II, was horsewhipped
as a young man by his own father, Alexander III; the last tsarina, Alexandra,
was a superstitious woman much given to consultation with necromancers.
The private life of Louis XVI and Marie-Antoinette was less primitive. Moreover, the French Revolution of 1789 broke out in time of peace, whereas both
in 1905 and in 1917 revolution came in Russia in conjunction with an unsuccessful war. This may signify that under modern conditions an established
government has little to fear from revolution in peacetime. On the other
hand, the French Revolution led to a series of European wars. Russia after
its Revolution (largely because Europe was exhausted in 1918) fought no
major foreign war until 1941, when the German Adolf Hitler invaded the
Soviet Union.

In France, to pursue the contrast, the revolution just "happened," in
that ordinary people from many walks of life unexpectedly found themselves
in a revolutionary situation, and even the Jacobin dictatorship was improvised
by men who had spent their lives thinking of other things. In Russia bands
of professional revolutionaries worked for the revolution long in advance, and
the dictatorship of the Bolsheviks realized the plans and preparations of
twenty years. In France the revolution was followed by a reaction in which
émigrés returned, dispossessed classes reappeared in politics, and even the
Bourbons were restored. The Russian revolution effectively wiped out its
opposition; no once discredited class ever came back, few émigrés returned,
no Romanovs regained their throne. The Russian Revolution was in this sense
more immediately successful. Yet it may be that the effects of the French
Revolution were deeper and more subtle.

It has just been said that professional revolutionists worked for revolution in Russia. They did not, however, "cause" it. Lenin and the Bolsheviks
did not bring about the Russian Revolution. They captured it after it had
begun. They boarded the ship in midstream. The Russian Revolution, like all
great revolutions, originated in a totality of previous history.

91. Backgrounds

RUSSIA AFTER 1881: REACTION AND PROGRESS

We have seen in earlier chapters how the tsarist autocracy arose, how it ruled as a machine superimposed upon its subjects, how the upper class became Westernized while the masses sank further into serfdom, and how an intelligentsia developed, divorced both from the work of government and the activities of the people.[1] It has been explained in Chapter XIII how Alexander II freed the serfs in 1861, and created provincial and district councils or zemstvos, elected mainly by landowners, which attended to such matters as roads, schools and hospitals.[2]

In 1881 Alexander II was assassinated by members of the People's Will. His son, Alexander III (1881–94), tried to stamp out revolutionism and to silence even peaceable criticism of the government. Revolutionaries and terrorists were driven into exile. The People's Will as an organized group became extinct. Jews were subjected to pogroms, by far the worst of any (hitherto) in modern times. For the first time the empire adopted a program of systematic Russification. Poles, Ukrainians, Lithuanians, Caucasians, the scattered German communities, the various Moslem groups, all faced the prospect of forcible assimilation to the Great Russian culture. The philosopher and chief official of this movement was Pobiedonostsev, procurator of the Holy Synod, or layman head, under the tsar, of the Russian Orthodox Church. Pobiedonostsev saw in the West something alien and doomed. Drawing on such old enemies of the French Revolution as Edmund Burke, he attacked Western rationalism and liberalism in his writings, declared that Slavs had a peculiar national character of their own, and dreamed of turning Holy Russia into a kind of churchly community, in which a disciplined clergy should protect the faithful from the insidious influences of the West.

This is not, however, what happened. In the closing decades of the nineteenth century Russia became more than ever before a part of European civilization. Almost overnight it presented Europe with great works of literature and music that Europeans could understand. The Russian novel became known throughout the Western world. All could read the novels of Tolstoy (1828–1910) without a feeling of strangeness; and if the characters of Turgeniev (1818–83) and of Dostoievsky (1821–81) behaved more queerly, the authors themselves were obviously within the great European cultural family. The melodies of Tchaikovsky (1840–93) and songs of Rimsky-Korsakov (1844–1908) became familiar throughout Europe and America; if they sometimes seemed hauntingly wild, distant, or sad, they still betrayed no more than the usual amount of national idiosyncrasy. Russians also contributed to

[1] See pp. 205–18, 313–18, 534–6.
[2] See pp. 536–8.

the sciences, notably chemistry. They were considered to be especially talented in the more abstruse intellectual exercises, such as higher mathematics, physics, or chess.

Russia also, from the 1880's, began to pass through the industrial revolution and take its place as an integral part of the world economic system. European capital entered the country, financing railways, mines, and factories (as well as government and the army) until by 1914 Europeans had about the same amount invested in Russia as in the United States, some four billion dollars in each case.[3] In 1897, under the reforming ministry of Count Witte, Russia adopted the gold standard, making its currency readily convertible with all others. In the quarter-century between 1888 and 1913 the Russian railway mileage more than doubled, the miles of telegraph wires multiplied fivefold, the number of post-offices trebled, and the number of letters carried by the mails multiplied seven times. Russian exports rose in value from 400,000,000 rubles in 1880 to 1,600,000,000 in 1913. Imports, though smaller, grew more rapidly, quintupling in the same period. They consisted of such items as tea and coffee, and of the machines and industrial goods made in Western Europe. Never after the Revolution did the Soviet Union conduct as much foreign trade as the Russian Empire on the eve of the First World War. This was because the Soviet Union, to keep control over its own economic system, depended as little as possible on outside markets and sources of supply.

Industrialization, in Russia as in all countries, brought an increase both of the business and the wage-earning classes, or, in socialist terminology, of the bourgeoisie and the proletariat. Though growing, they were still not numerous by standards of the West. Factory workers, laboring for eleven or more hours a day, for low wages under hard conditions, were in somewhat the same position as in England or France before 1850.[4] Unions were illegal, and strikes prohibited. Nevertheless, great strikes in the 1890's called attention to the misery of the new industrial workers. As for the Russian business and capitalist class, it was relatively the weaker because of several features in the situation. Ownership of much of Russia's new industrial plant was in foreign hands. Much was owned by the tsarist government itself; Russia already had the largest state-operated economic system in the world. Moreover, in Russia (unlike the United States at the time) the government itself was a heavy borrower from Europe; hence it was less dependent financially on its own people, and more able to maintain an absolutist regime.

Nevertheless, the rising business and professional classes, reinforced by enterprising landowners, were strong enough to form a liberal segment of public opinion, which emerged in 1903 as the Constitutional Democrat party (the K.D.'s or "Cadets"). Many of those who were active in the provincial zemstvos also became Constitutional Democrats. They were liberals, progressives, or constitutionalists in the Western sense, thinking less about the

---

[3] See pp. 570, 572, 620.
[4] See pp. 428, 465-8, 471-5.

troubles of factory workers and peasants than about the need of a nationally elected parliament to control the policies of state.

Russia remained predominantly agricultural. Its huge exports were mainly farm and forest products. The peasants formed four-fifths of the population. Free from their former lords since 1861, they lived in their village communes or *mirs*.[5] In most communes the land was divided and re-divided among peasant households by agreement of the village community, nor could anyone leave without communal permission. The peasants still carried a considerable burden. Until 1906 they paid redemption money arising from the Emancipation of 1861. They also paid high taxes, for the government defrayed the interest on its foreign loans from taxes raised at home. The constantly rising export of cereals (also used to pay off debts contracted by Russia in the West) tended to keep food from the farmer's table; many a peasant raised the best wheat for sale, and ate black bread himself. The farm population, in short (as in other countries in similar stages of their development), bore a considerable share of the costs of industrialization.

Under such pressures, and because of their crude methods of cultivation, the peasants were forever demanding more land. "Land hunger" was felt both by individual families and by the *mirs*. The Emancipation had turned over roughly half the land to peasant ownership, individual and collective; and in the following half-century the peasants added to their share by buying from non-peasant owners. The *mirs* were by no means obsolescent. They were in fact flourishing; they acquired far more land by purchase than did individual buyers, and perhaps half or more of the peasants valued communal security above the uncertain pleasures of private property. The exceptions were the minority of more enterprising and wealthier peasants, later called the *kulaks*. Such a one was Leon Trotsky's father, who, a hard-working, rude, and illiterate man, owned or leased the equivalent of a square mile of land, employed scores of field hands at harvest time, and permanently maintained a large domestic staff. That such a "big farmer" could afford so many employees suggests the poverty in which the bulk of the peasants lived. Not all of the well-to-do peasants were as affluent as Trotsky's father, but the big farmers stood out conspicuously from the mass, by whom they were not liked.

THE EMERGENCE OF REVOLUTIONARY PARTIES

The peasants were the ancient source of revolutionary disturbance in Russia. Fables about Pugachev and Stephen Razin circulated in peasant legend.[6] After the Emancipation the peasants continued to believe that they had some kind of rights in *all* the land of former estates on which they had formerly been serfs—not merely in the portion that had been allotted to peasant possession. They demanded (and obtained) credit from the government to

[5] See p. 537.
[6] See pp. 209–10, 315.

buy from the big landowners or former masters. Their land hunger could not be appeased. They remained jealous of the landed aristocrat's very existence. In Russia, as elsewhere in Europe, and unlike the United States, the rural population was divided into two sharply distinct classes, on the one hand the peasants of all types, who worked the soil, and on the other the gentry who resided upon it. The two never intermarried. They differed not merely economically, but in speech, dress, and manners, and even in the looks of their faces and hands. But in the last three decades of the nineteenth century the Russian peasants were notably quiet, insurrectionism seemingly having subsided.

The other traditional source of revolutionary disturbance lay among the intelligentsia.[7] It is hard for most Americans to imagine a society in which many of the best and purest spirits become violent revolutionaries, yet this is the kind of society that Russia was under the tsars. Revolutionary intelligentsia (as distinguished from those who were simply liberal or progressive) yearned for a catastrophic overthrow of the tsardom. Since the days of the Decembrists [8] they had formed secret organizations, comprising a few hundreds or thousands of members, engaged in outwitting the tsarist police, by whom they were bafflingly interpenetrated. For example, at a Bolshevik party Congress held in 1913, out of twenty-two delegates present, no less than five, unknown to the others, were government spies.

The revolutionary intelligentsia, since there was normally little that they could do, spent their time in vehement discussion and interminable refinement of doctrine. By 1890 the terrorism and nihilism of the 1870's were somewhat passé. The great question was where these willing officers of a revolutionary movement could find an army. Disputation turned upon such topics as whether the peasants or the new factory workers were the true revolutionary class, whether the peasants were potentially proletarian or incurably petty bourgeois, whether Russia was bound to experience the same historical process as the West, or whether it was different; and, specifically, whether Russia had to go through capitalism or might simply skip the capitalist stage in reaching the socialist society.

Most of the revolutionary intelligentsia were "populists." Some had once belonged to the now broken People's Will. Some continued to approve of terrorism and assassination as morally necessary in an autocratic country. They generally had a mystical faith in the vast inchoate might of the Russian people, and since most Russians were peasants, the populists were agrarians interested in peasant problems and peasant welfare. They believed that a great native revolutionary tradition existed in Russia, of which the peasant rebellion of Pugachev, in 1773, was the chief example. The populists were Slavophiles; they believed that Russia was different from Europe, and better.[9] They put faith in the peasant commune or *mir*, which they called "naively

[7] See pp. 535–6.
[8] See p. 453.
[9] See pp. 442, 534, 631.

socialistic," seeing in it a basic institution that had saved the Russians from self-seeking Western individualism, and upon which a more developed socialism might be built. They read and respected Marx and Engels; indeed, a populist first translated the *Communist Manifesto* into Russian; but they regarded Marxism as suited to the conditions of western Europe. They did not believe that an urban proletariat was the only true revolutionary class. They did not believe that capitalism, by creating such a proletariat, had inevitably and logically to precede socialism. They said that, in Russia, the horrors of capitalism could be skipped. They addressed themselves to the plight of the farmer and the evils of landlordism, favored strengthening the *mir* and equalizing the shares of all peasants in it, and, since they did not have to wait for the prior triumph of capitalism in Russia, they thought that revolution might come quite soon. This populist sentiment crystallized in the founding in 1901 of the Social Revolutionary party. Agrarian populism, rather than Marxism or communism, has remained the chief spontaneous form of radicalism in Eastern Europe ever since.

Two populists, Plekhanov and Axelrod, fleeing to Switzerland in the 1870's, there became converted to Marxism. In 1883 they founded in exile the organization from which the Russian Social Democratic or Marxist party was to grow. A few Marxists began to declare themselves (though not publicly) in Russia itself. When the youthful Lenin met his future wife Krupskaya in 1894, she already belonged to a circle of argumentative Marxists. The fact that the peasants in the 1890's were disappointingly quiescent, while machine industry, factory labor, and strikes were developing rapidly, turned many of the revolutionary intelligentsia, though only a minority, from populism to Marxism. To Plekhanov (1857–1918) and Axelrod (1850–1928) were added, as younger leaders, Lenin (1870–1924), Trotsky (1879–1940), Stalin (1879–1953) and others.

Of these it was Lenin who, after Marx, was to be claimed by communism as a father. Lenin was a short almost rotund man, with a small man's bounding quickness and intense, penetrating gaze. High cheekbones and somewhat slanting eyes showed an Asiatic strain on the paternal side; Russian friends at first said that he looked "like a Kalmuck." His hair receded in early youth, leaving a massive forehead, behind which a restless mind was inexhaustibly at work. Even in his twenties he was called the Old One. He was of upper middle-class origin, son of an inspector of schools who rose in the civilian bureaucracy to a rank equivalent to major-general. His boyhood was comfortable and even happy, until the age of seventeen, when his elder brother, a student at St. Petersburg, became somewhat incidentally involved in a plot to assassinate Alexander III, for which he was put to death by order of the tsar himself. Because of the blot on the family record it became impossible for Lenin to continue with his law studies. He soon joined the ranks of professional revolutionaries, having no other occupation, and living precariously from the party funds, which came mainly from the donations of well-to-do sympathizers.

Arrested as a revolutionary, he spent three years of exile in Siberia. Here the tsarist government treated educated political prisoners with an indulgence not later shown by the Soviet regime. Lenin and most of the others lived in cottages of their own, or boarded with natives. No labor was required of them. They borrowed books from Europe; met and visited with one another; debated, played chess, went hunting, meditated, and wrote. They chafed, however, at being cut off from the mainstream of Russian political life back home. Lenin, his term over, proceeded in 1900 to western Europe, where except for short secret trips to Russia he remained until 1917. His intellectual vigor, irresistible drive, and shrewdness as a tactician soon made him a force in the party. Genius has been called the faculty for everlasting concentration upon one thing. Lenin, said his one-time close associate Axelrod, "for twenty-four hours of the day is taken up with the revolution, has no thoughts but thought of revolution, and even in his sleep dreams of nothing but revolution."

In 1898 the Marxists in Russia, spurred on by émigrés, founded the Social Democratic Labor party. They were not more revolutionary than the larger group of Social Revolutionaries. They simply had a different conception of the revolution. First of all, as good Marxists, they regarded the revolution as an international movement, part of the dialectical process of world history in which all countries were involved. Russia for them was no different from other countries, except that it was less advanced. They expected the world revolution to break out first in western Europe. They particularly admired the German Social Democratic party, the largest and most flourishing of all the parties that acknowledged the fatherhood of Marx.[10]

Where, in Russian terms, the populist Social Revolutionaries were Slavophiles, the Social Democrats were Westernizers. Indeed, most of the leaders lived in Europe. They held that Russia must develop capitalism, an industrial proletariat, and the modern form of class struggle before there could be any revolution. Seeing in the urban proletariat the true revolutionary class, they looked upon all peasantry with suspicion, ridiculed the *mir* and abhorred the Social Revolutionaries. "Marxism," said Lenin, "has forever shaken itself loose from the nonsensical patter of the populists and anarchists to the effect that Russia can escape a capitalist development." (Russian Marxists were on this point more Marxist than Marx and Engels, both of whom, when urged, refused to pronounce on the merits of the *mir*, or on the need of capitalism as a precondition to socialism in Russia.) Like Marx himself, the Russian Marxists disapproved of sporadic terrorism and assassination. For this reason, and because their doctrine seemed somewhat academic and their revolution rather conditional and far in the future, the Marxists were for a time actually favored by the tsarist police, who regarded them as less dangerous than the Social Revolutionaries.

〰〰〰〰〰〰〰〰〰〰

[10] See pp. 586–7, 593, 595.

THE SPLIT IN THE SOCIAL DEMOCRATS, 1903:

BOLSHEVIKS AND MENSHEVIKS

The Russian Marxists held a second party congress in Brussels and London in 1903, attended by both émigrés like Lenin and delegates from the underground in Russia, and by both Social Democrats and members of lesser organizations. The purpose of the congress was to unify all Russian Marxism, but in fact it split it forever. The two resulting factions called themselves Bolsheviks, or majority men, and Mensheviks or minority men. Lenin was the main author of the split, and hence the founder of Bolshevism. Although he obtained his majority after one participating organization, the Jewish Bund, had seceded in indignation, and by calling for surprise votes on tactical issues, and although after 1903 it was usually the Mensheviks who had the majority, Lenin clung proudly and stubbornly to the term Bolshevism, with its favorable connotation of a majority in his support. For a number of years after 1903 the Social Democrats remained at least formally a single Marxist party, but they were irreconcilably divided into two wings. In 1912 the Bolshevik wing organized itself as a separate party.

Bolshevism, or Leninism, originally differed from Menshevism mainly on matters of organization and tactics. Russian Marxists referred to each other as "hards" and "softs." The "hards" were attracted to Lenin, the "softs" repelled by him. Lenin believed that the party should be a small revolutionary elite, a hard core of reliable and zealous workers. Those who wished a larger and more open party, with membership for mere sympathizers, became Mensheviks. Lenin insisted upon a strongly centralized party, without autonomy for national or other component groups. Lenin demanded strong authority at the top, by which the central committee would determine the doctrine (or "party line") and control personnel at all levels of the organization. The Mensheviks favored a greater degree of influence by the membership as a whole. Lenin thought that the party would strengthen itself by purges, expelling all who developed deviations of opinion. The Mensheviks favored covering up or bridging over all but the most fundamental disagreements. The Mensheviks came to recommend cooperation with liberals, progressives, and bourgeois democrats. Lenin regarded such cooperation as purely tactical and temporary, never concealing that in the end the Bolsheviks must impose their views through a dictatorship of the proletariat. The Mensheviks, in short, came to resemble the Marxists of western Europe, so far as that was possible under Russian conditions.[11] Lenin stood for the rigid reaffirmation of Marxian fundamentals, dialectical materialism and irreconcilable class struggle.

If we ask what Leninism added to the original Marxism,[12] the answer

[11] See pp. 594–6.
[12] See pp. 495–502.

is not easy to find. Lenin accepted Marx's governing ideas: that capitalism exploited the workers, that it necessarily produced and preceded socialism, that history was logically predetermined, that class struggle was the law of society, that existing forms of religion, government, philosophy, and morals were weapons of the ruling class. He did, however, develop and transform into a first-rank element of Marxism certain theories of "imperialism" and of the "uneven development of capitalism" that had been propounded in only general terms by Marx and Engels. In the Marxist-Leninist view, "imperialism" was exclusively a product of monopoly capitalism, that is, capitalism in its big-business, "highest," and "final" stage, which develops differently and at different times in each country. Monopoly capitalism is bent on exporting surplus capital and investing it in underdeveloped areas for greater profits.[13] The unceasing drive for colonies and markets in a world already almost completely partitioned leads inevitably to international "imperialist" wars for the "redistribution" of colonies, as well as to intensified national colonial struggles for independence; both provide new revolutionary opportunities for the proletariat. In other respects, Lenin roundly denounced all who attempted to "add" anything to the fundamental principles of Marx. Nothing infuriated him so much as revisionist efforts to tone down the class struggle, or hints that Marxism might in the last analysis perhaps find room for some kind of religion. He wrote in 1908:

Marx's theory is the objective truth. Following the path of this theory, we will approach the objective truth more and more closely, while if we follow any other path we cannot arrive at anything except confusion and falsehood. From the philosophy of Marxism, cast of one piece of steel, it is impossible to expunge a single basic premise, a single essential part, without deviating from objective truth, without falling into the arms of bourgeois-reactionary falsehood.[14]

Lenin was a convert. He discovered Marxism; he did not invent it. He found in it a theory of revolution which he accepted without reservation as scientific, and on which he was more outspokenly dogmatic even than Marx himself. His powers of mind, which were very great, were spent in demonstrating how the unfolding events of the twentieth century confirmed the analysis of the master.

But it was by his powers of will that Lenin was most distinguished, and if Leninism contributed little to Marxism as a theory it contributed a great deal to it as a movement. Lenin was an activist. He was the supreme agitator, a field commander in the class war, who could dash off a polemical pamphlet, dominate a party congress, or address throngs of workingmen with equal ease. Beside him, Marx and Engels seem almost to be mere recluses or sociologists. Marx and Engels had preferred to believe that the dictatorship of the proletariat, when it came, would represent the wishes of the great majority in a

---

[13] See pp. 618–19.

[14] David Shub, *Lenin* (New York, 1948), p. 69. Many other quotations in the present chapter are taken from Mr. Shub's biography, and many are from B. D. Wolfe, *Three Who Made a Revolution* (New York, 1948).

society in which most people had become proletarians. Lenin more frankly foresaw the possibility that the proletarian dictatorship might represent the conscious wishes of a small vanguard, and might have to impose itself on great masses by an unshrinking use of force.

Above all, Lenin developed Marx's idea of the role of the Party. He drew on the rich experience of pre-Marxist revolutionaries in Russia—the mysterious use of false names, invisible ink, secret ciphers, forged passports, and hidden rendezvous—the whole conspiratorial wonderland which, when it existed to a lesser degree in the West before 1848, drew Marx's scorn and laughter. Lenin's conception of the party was basically Marx's, reinforced by his own experience as a Russian. The party was an organization in which intellectuals provided leadership and understanding for workers, who could not see for themselves. For trade unionism, concerned only with the day-to-day demands of workingmen, Lenin had even less patience than Marx. "The unconscious growth of the labor movement," he wrote, "takes the form of trade unionism, and trade unionism signifies the mental enslavement of the workers to the bourgeoisie." The task of intellectuals in the party, the elite or experts, was to make the trade unions and the working-class "conscious" and hence revolutionary. Armed with "objective" knowledge, known to be correct, the party leadership naturally could not listen to the subjective opinions of others—the passing ideas of laboring men, of peasants, of mistaken party subordinates, or of other parties pretending to know more than Marx himself. The idea that intellectuals supply the brains and workers the brawn, that an elite leads while the toilers meekly follow, is understandable enough in view of the Russian background, which had created on the one hand a painfully self-conscious intelligentsia, and on the other a repressed working-class and peasantry deprived of all opportunity for political experience of their own. It was one of the most distinctive traits of Leninism and one of the most foreign to the democratic movement of the West.

Leninism accomplished the marriage of Russian revolutionary traditions with the Western doctrine of Marxism. It was an improbable marriage, whose momentous offspring was to be communism. But at the time, when Bolshevism first appeared in 1903, it had little or no effect. A real revolution broke out in Russia in 1905. It took the revolutionary émigrés almost entirely by surprise.

92. The Revolution of 1905

BACKGROUND AND REVOLUTIONARY EVENTS

The almost simultaneous founding at the turn of the century of the Constitutional Democrat, Social Revolutionary, and Social Democrat parties was clearly a sign of mounting dissatisfaction. None of these was as yet a party in the Western sense, organized to get men elected to office, for there were no elections in Russia above the provincial zemstvo level. All three parties were propaganda agencies, made up of leaders without followers, intellectuals who followed respectively the liberal, agrarian or Marxian lines of thought. All, even the liberal Constitutional Democrats, were watched by the police and obliged to do most of their work underground. At the same time, after 1900, there were signs of growing popular unrest. Peasants were trespassing on lands of the gentry, and even rising in local insurrections against landlords and tax-collectors. Factory workers sporadically refused to work. But with these popular movements none of the new parties had formed any solid links.

The government refused to make concessions of any kind. The tsar, Nicholas II, who had mounted the throne in 1894, was a man of narrow outlook. To the Little Father all criticism seemed merely childish. Tutored in his youth by Pobiedonostsev,[15] he regarded all ideas questioning autocracy, Orthodoxy, and Great Russian nationalism as un-Russian. That persons in the government should be controlled by interests outside the government— the mildest liberalism or most orderly democracy—seemed to the tsar, the tsarina, and the leading officials to be a monstrous aberration. Autocracy, for them, was the best and only, as it was the God-given, form of government for Russia.

The chief minister, Plehve, and the circles at court, hoped that a short successful war with Japan would restore sympathy for the government. The war went so badly that its effect was the reverse.[16] Critics of the regime (except for the handful of the most internationalist Marxists) were sufficiently patriotic to be ashamed at the ease with which Russia was defeated by an upstart and Asiatic power. As after the Crimean War, there was a general feeling that the government had exposed its incompetence to all the world. Liberals believed that its secret methods, its immunity to criticism or control, had made it sluggish, torpid, obstinate, and inefficient, unable either to win a war or to lead the economic modernization that was taking place in Russia. But there was little that the liberals could do.

The police had recently allowed a priest, Father Gapon, to go among the St. Petersburg factory workers and organize them, hoping thus to counter the propaganda of revolutionaries. Father Gapon took up their grievances in all seriousness. They believed, as simple peasants only recently transplanted to the city, that if only they could reach the ear of the Little Father, the august being high above all hard capitalists and stony officials, he would hear their complaints with shocked surprise, and rectify the evils that afflicted Russia. They drew up a petition, asking for an eight-hour day, a minimum daily wage of one ruble (fifty cents), a repudiation of bungling bureaucrats, and a democratically elected Constituent Assembly to introduce representative government into the empire. Unarmed, peaceable, respectful, singing "God save the Tsar," a crowd of two hundred thousand—men, women, and children—gath-

[15] See p. 706.
[16] See p. 657.

ered before the tsar's Winter Palace one Sunday in January 1905. But the
tsar had fled, and his officials were afraid. Troops marched up and shot down
the demonstrators in cold blood, killing several hundred.

"Bloody Sunday" in St. Petersburg snapped the moral bond upon
which all stable government rests. The horrified workers saw that the tsar
was not their friend. The autocracy stood revealed as the force behind the
hated officials, the tax collectors, the landlords, and the owners of the industrial plants. A wave of political strikes broke out. Social Democrats (more
Mensheviks than Bolsheviks) appeared from the underground or from exile
to give revolutionary direction to these movements. Councils or "soviets" of
workers were formed in Moscow and St. Petersburg. The peasants, too, in
many parts of the country spontaneously began to erupt, overrunning the
lands of the gentry, burning manor houses and doing violence to their owners.
Social Revolutionaries naturally tried to take this movement in charge. The
liberal Constitutional Democrats, professors, engineers, business people, lawyers, leaders in the provincial zemstvos founded forty years before, tried also
to seize leadership or at least use the crisis to force the government's hand.
All agreed on one demand—that there should be more democratic representation in the government.

The tsar yielded grudgingly, and as little as possible. In March 1905
he promised to call to office men "enjoying the confidence of the nation." In
August (after the ruinous battle of Tsushima) he agreed to call a kind of
Estates General, for which peasants, landowners, and city people should vote
as separate classes. Still the revolution raged unchecked. The St. Petersburg
Soviet, or workers' council, led mainly by Mensheviks (Lenin had not yet
reached Russia), declared a great general strike in October. Railroads stopped,
banks closed, newspapers ceased to appear, and even lawyers refused to go to
their offices. The strike spread to other cities and to the peasants. With the
government paralyzed, the tsar issued his October Manifesto. It promised a
constitution, civil liberties, and a Duma to be elected by all classes alike, with
powers to enact laws and control the administration.

The tsar and his advisers intended to divide the opposition by releasing
the October Manifesto, and in this they succeeded. The Constitutional Democrats, with a Duma promised, allowed themselves to hope that social problems could henceforth be dealt with by parliamentary methods. Liberals were
now afraid of revolutionaries; industrialists feared the strength shown by labor
in the general strike, and landowners demanded a restoration of order among
the peasants. Aroused peasants and workingmen were not yet satisfied; the
former still wanted more land and less taxation, the latter a shorter working
day and a living wage. The several branches of revolutionary intellectuals
worked upon the continuing popular agitation, hoping to carry matters forward until the tsarist monarchy was abolished and a socialist republic established with themselves at its head. They believed also (and correctly) that the
October Manifesto was in any case a deception, which the tsar would refuse
to adhere to as soon as revolutionary pressure was removed. The Soviets

continued to seethe, local strikes went on, soldiers mutinied at Kronstadt and sailors in the Black Sea fleet.

But the government was able to maintain itself. With the middle-class liberals now inactive or demanding order, the authorities arrested the members of the Petersburg Soviet. Peace was hastily made with Japan, and reliable troop units were recalled from the Far East. The revolutionary leaders fled back to Europe, or again went underground or were caught and sent to prison or to Siberia; executions were carried out in the countryside.

THE RESULTS OF 1905: THE DUMA

The chief apparent result of the Revolution of 1905 was to make Russia, at least ostensibly, into a parliamentary type of state, like the rest of Europe. The promised Duma was convoked. For ten years, from 1906 to 1916, Russia had at least the superficial attributes of a semi-constitutional monarchy. The year 1905 was Russia's 1789, with its 1793 held for twelve years in abeyance.

But Nicholas II soon showed that he did not intend to yield much. He drew the teeth of the new Duma before the creature could even be born, by announcing in advance, in 1906, that it would have no power over foreign policy, the budget, or government personnel. His attitude toward constitutional monarchy continued until 1917 to be entirely negative; the one thing that tsarism would not allow was any real participation in government by the public. Within this "public" the two extreme fringes were equally impervious to liberal constitutionalism. On the right, stubborn upholders of pure autocracy and the Orthodox Church organized the Black Hundreds, terrorizing the peasantry and urging them to boycott the Duma. On the left, in 1906, the Social Revolutionaries and both the Bolshevik and Menshevik wings of the Social Democrats likewise refused to recognize the Duma, urged workers to boycott it, and refused to put up any candidates for election.

The short-lived first Duma was elected in 1906 by a system of indirect and unequal voting, in which peasants and workers voted as separate classes, and with proportionately far less representation than was granted to the landlords. In the absence of socialist candidates, workers and peasants voted for all sorts of people, including the liberal Constitutional Democrats (the "Cadets"), who obtained a sweeping majority. The Cadets, when the Duma met, found themselves still fighting for the bare principle of constitutional government. They demanded true universal suffrage and the responsibility of ministers to a parliamentary majority. The Tsar's response was to dismiss the Duma after two months. The Cadets fled to Viborg in autonomous Finland, which the tsarist police generally let alone. It is significant that these constitutional liberals and democrats, in council at Viborg, again appealed for a general strike and non-payment of taxes—that is, for mass revolution. But real revolutions are not easy to start, and nothing happened.

A second Duma was elected in 1907, with the government trying to control the elections through suppression of party meetings and newspapers, but since Social Revolutionaries and Mensheviks now consented to take part some eighty-three socialists were elected. The Cadets, now afraid of the revolutionary left, and concluding that constitutional progress must be gradual, showed a willingness to cooperate with the government, which, however, denouncing and arresting some fifty socialists as revolutionaries bent only on destruction, again abruptly put an end to the Duma itself. A third Duma, elected after an electoral change that gave an increased preponderance of representation to the landed propertied class and guaranteed a conservative majority for the government, managed to hold several sessions between 1907 and 1912; so, similarly, did a fourth Duma from 1912 to 1916. The deputies, by following the lead of the government, by addressing themselves only to concrete issues, by losing themselves in committee work, and by avoiding the basic question of where supreme power lay, kept precariously alive a modicum of parliamentary institutions in the tsarist empire.

THE STOLYPIN REFORMS

Some officials believed that the way to checkmate the revolutionaries, and strengthen the hold of the monarchy, was for the government, while keeping all controls in its own hands, to attract the support of reasonable and moderate people by a program of reforms. One of these was Peter Stolypin, whom the tsar retained as his principal minister from 1906 to 1911. It was Stolypin who dissolved the first two Dumas. But it was not his policy merely to stand still. His aim was to build up the propertied classes as friends of the state. He believed, perhaps rightly, that a state actively supported by widespread private property had little to fear from doctrinaire intellectuals, conspirators, and émigrés. As he said in a speech to the Third Duma in 1908: "The government has placed its wager, not on the needy and the drunken, but on the sturdy and the strong—on the sturdy individual proprietor who is called upon to play a part in the reconstruction of our Tsardom."

Stolypin therefore favored and broadened the powers of the provincial zemstvos, in which the larger landowners took part in administering local affairs. For the peasantry he put through legislation more sweeping than any since the Emancipation.

Seeing in the *mir* the source of communal agrarian restlessness, Stolypin hoped to replace this ancient institution with a regime of private individual property. He abolished what was left of the redemption payments for which the *mirs* had been collectively responsible. He allowed each peasant to sell his share of the communal rights and to leave the commune at will. He authorized peasants to buy land freely from the communes, or from each other, or from the gentry. He thus favored the rise of the class of "big farmers," the later *kulaks*, men who obtained control of large tracts, worked them with hired help, and produced cash crops for the market. These were "the sturdy and the strong" upon whom Stolypin pinned his hopes. At the same time, by allowing peasants to sell out and leave the *mir* (it would generally be the worst farmers or most improvident persons who did so) he hastened the formation of a migratory wage-earning class, which would either seek work from the big farmers or go off to take jobs in the city.[17] The creation of a mobile labor force, and of a food supply raised by big farmers for the market, would thus advance the industrialization of Russia.

The Stolypin policy was highly successful. Nor did it create a small class of *kulaks* only; it seemed to be leading to a widespread peasant proprietorship, as in France. Between 1907 and 1916 6,200,000 families out of 16,000,000 who were eligible applied for legal separation from the *mir*. At the time of the Bolshevik revolution the peasants owned over three-quarters of the arable land. Almost nowhere else did actual dirt farmers own so much. There was indeed no mistaking the trend toward individual property and independent farming. But the results of the Stolypin program must not be exaggerated. The *mir* was far from broken. A vast majority of peasants were still involved in the old system of common rights and communal restrictions. The land shortage was still acute in the agricultural areas where yields were highest. Land hunger and poverty continued in the countryside. There were *kulaks*, to be sure, to be resented and envied, but the largest landed proprietors were still the gentry.

Stolypin was not left long to carry on his program. The tsar gave him only an unwilling support. Reactionary circles disliked his tampering ways and his Western orientation. Social Revolutionaries naturally cried out against dissolution of the communes. Even Marxists, who should in theory have applauded the advance of capitalism in Russia, feared that Stolypin's reforms might do away with agrarian discontent. "I do not expect to live to see the revolution," said Lenin in these years. Stolypin's wife and children were killed by a bomb; and he himself was shot dead at a theater in Kiev, in the presence of the tsar and tsarina, in 1911. The assassin, one of the terrorist wing of the Social Revolutionaries, is thought also to have been a secret agent of the reactionary police. It may be added that Stolypin's predecessor, Plehve, and about a dozen other high officials within the past few years had died by assassins' hands.

But all in all, violent and half barbaric though it still was, the Russian Empire on the eve of the First World War was apparently moving in a Western direction. Its industries were growing, its railways expanding, its exports almost half as great in value as those of the United States. It had a parliament, if not a parliamentary government. Private property and individualist capitalism were spreading to new layers of the people. There was a guarded freedom of the press, illustrated, for example, by the legal and open establishment of the Bolshevik party paper, *Pravda*, in St. Petersburg in 1912. It is not possible to say how far this development might have gone, for it was menaced on both the right and the left, by obstinate and obscurantist reac-

~~~~~~~~~~~~~~~~~~

[17] See pp. 408, 423–4, 493.

tionaries upholding the absolute tsardom, and by revolutionaries whom nothing but the end of tsardom and wholesale transformation of society could appease. But both extremes were discouraged. The desperation of extreme reactionaries in the government, the feeling that they might in any case soon lose their position, perhaps made them the more willing to precipitate a European war by armed support of Serbian nationalists. As for the revolutionary parties, and especially the Bolsheviks, they were losing in membership on the eve of the war, their leaders lived year after year in exile, dreaming of the great days of 1905 which stubbornly failed to repeat themselves, and sometimes pessimistically admitting, as Lenin did, that there might be no revolution in their time.

93. The Revolution of 1917

END OF THE TSARDOM: THE REVOLUTION OF MARCH 1917

War again put the tsarist regime to a test that it could not meet. In this war, more "total" than any had ever been, willing co-operation between government and people was indispensable to success. This essential prerequisite the tsarist empire did not have. National minorities, Poles, Jews, Ukrainians, Caucasians, and others, were disaffected. As for the socialists, who in every other European parliament voted for the war credits, the dozen otherwise disunited socialists in the Duma refused to do so, and were promptly jailed.[18] The ordinary workingman and peasant marched off with the army, but without the sense of personal conviction felt by common people in Germany and the West. More decisive was the attitude of the middle class. Because they patriotically wished Russia to win, the glaring mismanagement of the government was the more intolerable to them. The disasters with which the war opened in 1914, at Tannenberg and the Masurian Lakes, were followed by the advance of the Central Powers into Russia in 1915, at the cost of two million Russian soldiers killed, wounded, or captured.[19]

At the war's outbreak middle-class people, as in all countries, offered their assistance to the government.[20] The provincial zemstvos formed a union of all zemstvos in the empire to facilitate the mobilization of agriculture and industry. Business groups at Petrograd (St. Petersburg lost its Germanic name at this time), formed a Commercial and Industrial Committee to get the factories into maximum production. The government distrusted these signs of public activity arising outside official circles. On the other hand, organized in this way, middle-class people became conscious of their own strength and more critical of the bureaucracy. Some officials in the war ministry itself

ᴧᴧᴧᴧᴧᴧᴧᴧᴧᴧᴧᴧᴧᴧᴧᴧᴧᴧ

[18] See p. 747.
[19] See pp. 672, 679.
[20] See pp. 689–92.

were known to be at heart pro-German, reactionaries who feared the liberalism of England and France, with which Russia was allied.

Life at court was bizarre even for Russia. The tsarina Alexandra, by origin a German woman, looked upon all Russians outside her own circle with contempt, incited her husband to play the proud and pitiless autocrat, and took advice from a self-appointed holy man, the bearded and weird Rasputin. She was convinced that Rasputin possessed supernatural and prophetic powers, because he had apparently cured her young son, the tsarevitch, of hemophilia. Rasputin, by his influence over her, had a voice in appointments to high office. All who wished an audience with the imperial pair had to go through him. Patriotic and enlightened persons of all classes vainly protested. In these circumstances, and given the military defeats, the union of zemstvos and other such war-born bodies complained not merely of faults of administration but of fundamental conditions in the state. The government responded by holding them at arm's length. The tsarist regime, caught in a total war, was afraid of the help offered by its own people.

During the war the Duma was suspended. It was known that reactionaries—inspired by the tsarina, Rasputin, and other sinister forces—expected that a victory in the war would make it possible to kill liberalism and constitutionalism in Russia. The war thus revived all the basic political issues that had been latent since the Revolution of 1905. The union of zemstvos demanded the assembly of the Duma. The Duma met in November 1916, and, conservative though it had always been, expressed loud indignation at the way affairs were conducted. Among all elements of the population dissatisfaction with the course of the war and the government's ineptitude mounted. In December Rasputin was assassinated. The tsar began to consider repression, and again adjourned the Duma. Machine guns were issued to the police. Members of the Duma, and of the new extra-governmental bodies, concluded that the situation could be saved only by force. It is when moderate persons, normally concerned with their own business, come to such conclusions that revolution becomes a political possibility. The shift of moderates and liberals, their need of a coup d'état to save themselves from reactionaries, likewise raised the long failing prospects of the minority of professional revolutionaries.

Again it was the workers of Petrograd who precipitated the crisis. Food had become scarce, as in all the belligerent countries. But the tsarist administration was too clumsy and too demoralized by graft to institute the controls that had become usual elsewhere, such as maximum prices and ration cards. It was the poorest who felt the food shortage most keenly. On March 8, 1917 food riots broke out, which soon developed, doubtless with the help of revolutionary intellectuals, into political insurrections. Crowds shouted, "Down with the tsar!" Troops within the city refused to fire on the insurgents; mutiny and insubordination spread from unit to unit. Within a few days, on the model of 1905, a Soviet of Workers' and Soldiers' Deputies had been organized in Petrograd.

Middle-class leaders, with the government now helpless, demanded dismissal of the ministry and formation of a new one commanding the confidence of a majority of the Duma. The Duma set up an executive committee to take charge until the situation clarified. There were now two new authorities in the city: one, the Duma committee, essentially moderate, constitutionalist, and relatively legal; the other, the Petrograd Soviet, representing revolutionary forces arising by spontaneous upsurge from below. The Petrograd Soviet (or workers' "council") was to play in 1917 a role like that of the Paris Commune of 1792, constantly pushing the supposedly higher and more nation-wide authority to the left. The Soviet became the public auditorium and administrative center of the working-class upheaval. Since it was generally socialist in its outlook, all the factions of doctrinaire socialists—Social Revolutionaries, Mensheviks, Bolsheviks—tried to win it over and utilize it for their own ends.

The Petrograd Soviet and the Duma committee, by an agreement of March 14, set up a Provisional Government under Prince Lvov. The Duma liberals, as a concession to the Soviet, admitted one socialist to the new government, Alexander Kerensky, a moderate, legal-minded Social Revolutionary, and they furthermore consented to demand the abdication of Nicholas II. The tsar was then at the front. He tried to return to his palace near Petrograd, but the imperial train was stopped and turned back by troops. The army, fatefully, was taking the side of the revolution. The very generals in the field, unable to vouch for the loyalty of their men, advised abdication. Nicholas consented; his brother the grand duke declined to succeed him; and on March 17, 1917, Russia became a republic.

THE BOLSHEVIK REVOLUTION OF NOVEMBER 1917

The Provisional Government, following the best precedents of European revolutions, called for elections by universal suffrage to a Constituent Assembly, which was to meet late in the year and prepare a constitution for the new regime. It tried also to continue the war against Germany. In July an offensive was mounted but the demoralized armies were quickly routed. Pending final decision by the Constituent Assembly, the Provisional Government promised wholesale redistribution of land to the peasants, but took no action. Meanwhile, the peasants, driven by the old land hunger, were already overrunning the rural districts, burning and looting. At the front the armies melted away; many high officers refused to serve the republic, and masses of peasant soldiers simply turned their backs and went home, unwilling to be absent while farmlands were being handed out. The Petrograd Soviet, opposing the Provisional Government, called for speedy termination of the war, and, fearing reactionary officers, issued on March 14 its Order No. 1, entrusting command within the army to committees elected by both officers and men. Discipline collapsed.

The revolution was thus already well advanced when Lenin and the other Bolsheviks arrived in Petrograd in the middle of April.[21] They immediately took sides with the Petrograd Soviet against the Provisional Government, and with similar soviets that had sprung up in other parts of the country. A Bolshevik-led uprising in July was put down, and Lenin for a time had to flee to Finland, but as a bid for popular support the Provisional Government put the socialist Kerensky at its head, in place of Prince Lvov. Kerensky's middle position was next threatened from the right. A general at the front, Kornilov, led a force of cavalry to Petrograd to restore order. Many liberals and Constitutional Democrats wished him success. Kornilov was defeated, Bolsheviks temporarily rallying with other socialists, and insurrectionary soldiers in the city offering armed resistance. Radicals denounced liberals as accomplices in Kornilov's counter-revolution; and with the liberals thus discredited, Kerensky formed a government composed entirely of non-Bolshevik socialists. Meanwhile the food shortage was worse than ever, with transport disarranged and the farm population in turmoil, so that workers in the city listened more willingly to the most extreme speakers.

The Bolsheviks adapted their program to what the most aroused elements in a revolutionary people seemed to want. Lenin concentrated on four points: first, immediate peace with the Central Powers; second, redistribution of land to the peasants; third, transfer of factories, mines and other industrial plants from the capitalists to committees of workers in each plant; and, fourth, recognition of the soviets as the supreme power instead of the Provisional Government. Lenin, though a rigid dogmatist on abstract questions, was a flexible and bold tactician; and his program in 1917 was dictated more by the immediate situation in Russia than by considerations of theoretical Marxism. What was needed was to win over soldiers, peasants, and workers by promising them "peace, land and bread." With this program, and by infiltration and parliamentary stratagems, and by their accuracy as political prophets—predicting the Kornilov counter-revolution and "unmasking" the trend of middle-way liberals to support it—the Bolsheviks won a majority in the Petrograd Soviet and in soviets all over the country.

Lenin thereupon raised the cry, "All power to the Soviets!" to crush Kerensky and forestall the coming Constituent Assembly. Kerensky, to broaden the base on which he stood, and unable to wait for the Constituent Assembly, convoked a kind of pre-parliament representing all parties, labor unions, and zemstvos. Lenin and the Bolsheviks boycotted this pre-parliament. Instead they called an all-Russian congress of soviets.

Lenin now judged that the hour had come for the seizure of power. The Bolsheviks themselves were divided, many like Zinoviev and Kamenev opposing the move, but Lenin was backed by Trotsky, Stalin, and a majority of the party central committee. Troops garrisoned in Petrograd voted to support the soviets, which the Bolsheviks now controlled. On the night of November 6-7, 1917, the Bolsheviks took over telephone exchanges, railway stations, and electric lighting plants in the city. A warship turned its guns on

21 See pp. 710-14.

the Winter Palace, where Kerensky's government sat. The latter could find no armed defenders except a few Constitutional Democrats. The hastily assembled congress of soviets pronounced the Provisional Government defunct, and named in its place a "council of people's commissars," of which Lenin became the head. Trotsky was named "commissar for foreign affairs," Stalin, "commissar for nationalities." Kerensky fled, eventually reaching New York, where he lived for many years.

Thus was accomplished the Bolshevik or November Revolution.[22] But the long awaited Constituent Assembly remained to be dealt with. It met in January 1918. Thirty-six million persons had voted for it. Of these, 9,000,000 had voted for Bolshevik deputies, showing that the Bolshevik program, launched less than a year before by a small band of émigrés, had a widespread mass appeal. But almost 21,000,000 had voted for Kerensky's party, the agrarian-populist, native Russian, peasant-oriented Social Revolutionaries. However, said Lenin, "to hand over power to the Constituent Assembly would again be compromising with the malignant bourgeoisie." The Assembly was broken up on the second day of its sessions; armed sailors despatched by the people's commissars simply surrounded it. The dissolution of the Constituent Assembly was a frank repudiation of majority rule in favor of "class rule"—to be exercised for the proletariat by the Bolsheviks. The dictatorship of the proletariat was now established. Two months later, in March 1918, the Bolsheviks renamed themselves the Communist Party.

THE NEW REGIME: THE CIVIL WAR, 1918–22

In these same months the Communists, or Bolsheviks, made the peace of Brest-Litovsk with Germany, surrendering to Germany control over the Baltic provinces, Poland and the Ukraine. The conquests of two centuries were thus abandoned; not since the days of Peter the Great had the Russian frontier been so far from central Europe. To Lenin it made no difference. He was convinced that the events that he had just mastered in Russia were the prelude to a general upheaval; that the war, still raging in the west, would bring all Europe to the inevitable proletarian or Marxist revolution; that Imperial Germany was therefore doomed, and that Poles, Ukrainians, and others would soon emerge, like the Germans themselves, as free socialist peoples. In any case, it was largely by promising peace that Lenin had won enough backing to overthrow Kerensky, who on this deep popular demand had delayed too long, waiting for England and France to release Russia from its treaty obligations as an Ally. But real peace did not come, for the country sank immediately into civil war.

Not only old tsarist reactionaries, and not only liberals, bourgeois,

---

[22] Also known as the October Revolution, since according to the Julian calendar, used in Russia until 1918, the events described took place in October.

zemstvo men, and Constitutional Democrats, but all types of anti-Leninist socialists as well, Mensheviks and Social Revolutionaries, scattered in all directions to organize resistance against the regime of soviets and people's commissars. They found followers among the peasants and obtained aid from the western Allies.

As for the new regime, the oldest of its institutions was the Party, founded as a wing of the Social Democrats in 1903, the next oldest were the soviets, dating from 1905 and 1917, and then came the council of people's commissars set up on the day of the coup d'état. The first institution founded under the new order was a political police, an Extraordinary All-Russian Commission of Struggle against Counter-revolution, Speculation and Sabotage, commonly known from its Russian initials as the Cheka, and in later years, without basic change of methods or purpose, under the successive names of the OGPU, the NKVD and the MVD. It was established on December 7, 1917. In January 1918 the Red Army was founded, with Leon Trotsky as war commissar and virtually its creator. In July a constitution was promulgated.

In social policy the Bolsheviks at first adopted no long-range plans, contenting themselves with a mixture of principle and expediency known as "war communism." They soon nationalized some nine hundred of the largest industrial enterprises. The pressing problem was to find food, which had ceased to move through any normal channels. The peasants, very much as in the French Revolution under similar conditions—worthless money, insecure property titles, unruly hired men, armed marauding, and a doubtful future— were producing less food than usual, consuming it themselves, or hoarding it on their own farms. The response of the government and city workers was also much as in 1793. The new government levied requisitions, required the peasants to make stated "deliveries," and invited labor unions to send armed detachments into the country to procure food by force. Since it was naturally the big farmers who had the surplus, these came into disrepute as starvers of the people. Class war broke out, rabid, ferocious, and elemental, between farmers who feared that their very subsistence as well as their property would be taken away, and city people, often supported by hungry agricultural laborers, who were driven to desperation by famine. Many peasants, especially the larger farmers, therefore rallied to anti-Bolshevik political leaders.

Centers of resistance developed on every side. In the Don valley a small force assembled under Kornilov and Denikin, with many army officers, gentry landowners, and expropriated business people taking part in it. The Social Revolutionaries gathered followers on the middle Volga. At Omsk a disaffected group proclaimed the independence of Siberia. As a military organization the most significant was a force of some 45,000 Czechs, who had deserted or been captured from the Austro-Hungarian armies, and had then been organized as a Czech Legion to fight on the side of Russia and the Allies. After the November revolution and the peace of Brest-Litovsk, these Czechs decided to leave Russia by way of the Trans-Siberian railroad, return to Europe by sea, and resume fighting on the Western front. When Bolshevik officials undertook to disarm them they allied with the Social Revolutionaries on the Volga.

The Allied governments believed that Bolshevism was a temporary madness that with a little effort could be stopped. They wished also to bring Russia back into the war against Germany. So long as the war in Europe lasted, they could not reach Russia by the Black or Baltic sea. A small Allied force took Murmansk and Archangel in the North. But for Allied military intervention the best opening was in the Far East, through Vladivostok. The Japanese, who had declined military aid to their Allies in any other theater, received this proposal with enthusiasm, seeing in the ruin of the Russian Empire a rare opportunity to develop their sphere of influence in East Asia. It was agreed that an interallied military force should land at Vladivostok, cross Siberia, join with the Czechs, break up Bolshevism and fall upon the Germans in eastern Europe. For this ambitious scheme Britain and France could supply no soldiers, engaged as they were on the western front; the force turned out to be American and Japanese, or rather almost purely Japanese, since Japan contributed 72,000 men, and the United States only 8,000. They landed at Vladivostok in August 1918.

The civil war lasted until 1920, or even later in some places. It became a confused melee in which the Bolsheviks struggled against dissident Russians and against foreign intervention. They fought in the Ukraine first against the Germans, and then against the French, who occupied Odessa as soon as the war ended in Europe. They reconquered the Ukraine, Armenia, Georgia, and Azerbaijan, which had declared their independence; put to flight a hundred thousand "Whites" under Wrangel in the South; and fought off Admiral Kolchak, who, with a White army in Siberia, proclaimed himself ruler of all Russia. In 1920, the Bolsheviks carried on a war with the new republic of Poland, which was scarcely organized when it set out to recover the huge Ukrainian and White Russian territories that had been Polish before 1772.[23] British, French, and American troops remained at Archangel until the end of 1919, the Japanese at Vladivostok until the end of 1922.

But the anti-Bolshevik forces could never unite. The anti-Communist Russians represented every hue of the political spectrum from unregenerate tsarists to left-wing Social Revolutionaries. Many of the rightist anti-Bolsheviks openly antagonized the peasants by proceeding to restore expropriated landed estates in areas they reoccupied; many engaged in vindictive reprisals in a kind of "white terror." The Allies themselves could not agree; the French sent troops to the Ukraine and gave aid to the Poles, but the British and Americans wanted to be rid of all military entanglements as soon as the armistice with Germany was signed. Leon Trotsky, on the other hand, forged in the crucible of the civil wars the hard and solid metal of the Red Army, recruiting it, organizing it, restoring its discipline, equipping it as best he could, assigning political commissars to watch it, and assuring that trustworthy officers occupied its high command. The Bolsheviks could point to

﹏﹏﹏﹏﹏﹏﹏﹏﹏

[23] See map, p. 221.

the foreign intervention and appeal to national patriotism. By 1922 the Bol-shevist-Communists had established themselves up to the frontiers of the former tsarist empire in every direction except on the European side. There the band of Baltic states in the *cordon sanitaire* remained independent; Ru-mania had acquired Bessarabia, the new Rumanian frontier reaching now almost to Odessa; and Poland, as a result of the war of 1920, retained a fron-tier farther east than the Allies themselves had intended. Russia had lost thousands of square miles of territory and buffer areas acquired over the cen-turies by the tsars. They were to remain lost until the Second World War. But peace was won and the regime stood.

It was during these civil wars that the Red Terror broke out in Russia. Like the famous Terror in France in 1793, it was in part a response to civil and foreign war. Before the Bolshevik Terror, the old Jacobin Terror paled. They differed as the cruelty and violence endemic in the old Russia differed from the more humane or law-abiding habits of western Europe. Thousands were shot merely as hostages (a practice unknown to Europe for some cen-turies); and other thousands without even the summary formalities of revolu-tionary tribunals. The Cheka was the most formidable political police that had yet appeared. The Bolshevik Terror was aimed at the physical extermina-tion of all who opposed the new regime. A bourgeois class background would go far to confirm the guilt of the person charged with conspiring against the Soviet state. As a chief of the Cheka said: "The first questions you should put to the accused person are, To what class does he belong, what is his origin, what was his education, and what is his profession? These should determine the fate of the accused. This is the essence of the Red Terror." But a working-class background made little difference. In 1918 a young woman named Fanny Kaplan shot at Lenin and wounded him. She deposed that she had favored the Constituent Assembly, that her parents had emigrated to America in 1911, that she had six working-class brothers and sisters; and that she had intended to kill Lenin. She was of course executed, and a massacre followed in Petrograd. When the sailors at Kronstadt, who were among the first ad-herents won by the Bolsheviks, rose in 1921, objecting to domination of the soviets by the Party (threatening a kind of leftist renewal of the revolution, like the Hébertists who had opposed Robespierre) they were branded as petty-bourgeois and shot down by the thousands. The Terror decimated the revolutionists themselves quite as much as the bourgeoisie; it was to continue to do so long after the Revolution was secured.

The Terror succeeded in its purpose. Together with the victories of the Red Army, it established the new regime. Those "bourgeois" who survived took on the protective coloration of "toilers." No bourgeois as such ever again presumed to take part in the politics of Russia. Mensheviks and other social-ists fleeing to Europe told appalling stories of the human toll taken by Lenin. Horrified European socialists repudiated communism as an atrocious, Byzantine, Asiatic perversion of Marxism. But, at whatever cost, Lenin and his followers were now able to start building the socialist society as they un-derstood it.

94. The Union of Soviet Socialist Republics

GOVERNMENT: THE NATIONALITIES AND FEDERALISM

With the end of the civil wars and foreign intervention, and with the termination of the war with Poland, it became possible in 1922 to establish the Union of Soviet Socialist Republics. Its first members were four in number: the Russian Soviet Federated Socialist Republic, the Ukrainian Soviet Socialist Republic, the White Russian Soviet Socialist Republic and the Transcaucasian Soviet Socialist Republic.[24] In the new Union, which geographically replaced the old Russian Empire, the name Russia was not officially used. The guiding conception was a blend of the national and the international: to recognize nationality by granting autonomy to national groups, while holding these groups together in a higher union, and making it possible for new groups to enter regardless of historic frontiers. In 1922 the expectation of world revolution was still alive. The constitution, in its preamble, pronounced the founding of the U.S.S.R. to be "a decisive step by way of uniting the workers of all countries into one World Soviet Socialist Republic." It made the union, in principle, fluid and expansible, declared that any member republic might secede (none ever has) and that newly formed soviet socialist republics might join. When, in connection with the Second World War, the U.S.S.R. took back territories detached from tsarist Russia after the First World War—Bessarabia from Rumania, Karelia from Finland, parts of White Russia and the Ukraine from Poland, and Estonia, Latvia, and Lithu-

[24] There are today fifteen soviet republics in the U.S.S.R. The original Russian federal S.S.R. was subsequently somewhat reduced to allow certain Central Asian peoples to have soviet republics of their own, and the Transcaucasian federal S.S.R. was dissolved into its three components, so that by the constitution of 1936 the S.S.R.'s were eleven in number, to which five more were added in 1940; the Karelo-Finnish S.S.R. lost this status in 1956. The component republics with their populations in 1940 were as follows:

Russian S.F.S.R.	109,000,000
Ukrainian S.S.R.	40,000,000
White Russian (Byelorussian) S.S.R.	10,000,000
Armenian S.S.R.	1,250,000
Georgian S.S.R.	3,500,000
Azerbaijan S.S.R.	3,200,000
Uzbek S.S.R.	6,300,000
Turkmen S.S.R.	1,200,000
Tadjik S.S.R.	1,500,000
Kazakh S.S.R.	6,100,000
Kirghiz S.S.R.	1,500,000
Added in 1940:	
Karelo-Finnish S.S.R.	500,000
Moldavian S.S.R.	3,500,000
Lithuanian S.S.R.	2,900,000
Latvian S.S.R.	2,000,000
Estonian S.S.R.	1,100,000
Total U.S.S.R. in 1940	195,000,000

ania after two decades of independence—these territories were sovietized and added to the Union as republics on a footing of legal equality with the old ones.

The federal principle in the U.S.S.R. was designed to answer the problem of nationalism. The tsardom, in its last decades, had tried to deal with this problem by systematic Russification. The nationalities had resisted, and nationalist discontent had been one of the forces fatally weakening the empire. Nationalism, or the demand that national groups should have their own political sovereignty, had not only broken up the Austro-Hungarian empire but "Balkanized" central and eastern Europe. In 1922 the U.S.S.R., occupying a sixth of the world's land area, was adjoined on the west by a Europe which in one twenty-seventh of the world's land surface contained twenty-seven independent states.

A hundred languages were spoken in the Soviet Union, and fifty distinct nationalities were recognized within its borders. Many of these were extremely small, splinter groups or isolated communities left by the ebb and flow of mankind in inner Asia over thousands of years. Many were very primitive, without political consciousness. All recognized nationalities received a cultural autonomy, or the right to use their own language, have their own schools, wear their own dress, and follow their own folkways without interference. Indeed, the Soviet authorities favored the growth of cultural nationalism. Some fifty languages were reduced to writing for the first time, and the new regime encouraged the singing of national songs, performance of dances, and collection of folklore. Administratively the nationalities were put on various levels, with varying degrees of separate identity according to their size, degree of civilization, or importance. Some constituted only regional areas; others became "autonomous republics" within one of the federated soviet republics; others, the most important, were component republics of the Union. An example of the second category was Birobijan in the Far East, administratively an autonomous Jewish republic within the R.S.F.S.R. Politically, by the new Soviet constitution of 1936, an upper house of the U.S.S.R. legislative body was created, called a Soviet (or council) of Nationalities, to which each Union republic sent twenty-five delegates, each "autonomous" republic eleven, and each regional area five. Armenia with a million people

---

The Union of Soviet Socialist Republics   See following pages

The U.S.S.R. is over 5,000 miles long, and covers one-sixth of the land area of the globe, including 42% of Europe and 43% of Asia, though the conventional distinction between Europe and Asia is not officially recognized in the Soviet Union. It is the only state which immediately adjoins so many important political regions—Europe in the west, the Near and Middle East in the south, China along a long frontier, Japan across a narrow sea, and the United States on the side toward Alaska and the Aleutian islands. The Union has fifteen member republics, of which the Russian is by far the largest. Most of it lies farther north than Lake Superior, but around Tashkent, in the latitude of New York and Chicago, cotton and citrus fruits are grown.

UNION OF SOVIET SOCIALIST

AREAS ANNEXED SINCE 1939

SPITZBERGEN (NOR.)

FRANZ JOSEF LAND

SEVERNAYA IS.

ARCTIC

BARENTS SEA

NORTH CAPE

NOVAYA ZEMALAYA

KARA SEA

NORWAY

SWEDEN

FINLAND

KARELO-FINNISH S.S.R.

Murmansk

Kara

Salekhard

Igarka

SOVIET

Viborg

ESTONIAN S.S.R.

Berlin

BALTIC SEA

LATVIAN S.S.R.

LITHUANIAN S.S.R.

Leningrad

RUSSIAN MOUNTAINS

POLAND

Warsaw

Minsk

WHITE RUSSIAN S.S.R.

Moscow

Kirov

Samarovo

Gorki

Molotov

Sverdlovsk

Tobolsk

Kiev

Kazan

Tomsk

UKRAINIAN S.S.R.

MOLDAVIAN S.S.R.

RUMANIA

Kuibyshev

VOLGA R.

Omsk

Novosibirsk

Odessa

Magnitogorsk

URAL R.

Sevastopol

Stalingrad

Rostov

Istanbul

BLACK SEA

Astrakhan

KAZAK S.S.R.

Semipalatinsk

Ankara

GEORGIAN S.S.R.

ARAL SEA

LAKE BALKHASH

TURKEY

Batum

ARMENIAN S.S.R.

CASPIAN SEA

TURKESTAN

SYRIA

Baku

AZERBAIJAN S.S.R.

UZBEK S.S.R.

Tashkent

Alma Ata

KIRGIZ S.S.R.

TURKMEN S.S.R.

JORDAN

IRAQ

Teheran

Ashkhabad

TADJIK

SAUDI ARABIA

IRAN

AFGHANISTAN

KASHMIR

DVINA R.

OB R.

REPUBLICS

ALASKA
(USA)

BERING STR.

ST. LAWRENCE I.
(USA)

BERING
SEA

60°N

NOVO
SIBIRSK
IS.

120°E

ARCTIC CIRCLE

KOMANDORSKIE
IS.

KAMCHATKA

Anadyr

Verkhoyansk

Khatanga

KOLYMA R.

Petropavlovsk

LENA R.

REPUBLIC

Okhotsk

SEA OF
OKHOTSK

Yakutsk

SOCIALIST

SAKHALIN

KURILE ISLANDS
(FROM JAPAN)
1945

Nikolaevsk

FEDERATED

Vitim

KARAFUTO
(FROM JAPAN)
1945

YENISEI R.

Kirensk

AMUR R.

HOKKAIDO

Tygda

Biro-
bijan

Khabarovsk

eneseisk

LAKE
BAIKAL

AMUR R.

KUZNETSK
BASIN

Chita

MANCHURIA

alinsk

Harbin

Irkutsk

Vludivostok

TANNU
TUVA
1944

JAPAN

40°N

Ulan
⊙ Bator

Mukden

SEA OF
JAPAN

ALTAI MTS.

MONGOLIAN
REPUBLIC

JEHOL

KOREA

INNER MONGOLIA

Peiping

Duiren
Port Arthur

SINKIANG

INNER MONGOLIA

CHINA

Shanghai

EAST
CHINA
SEA

TIBET

1000 MILES

120°E

TRM

thus had as many delegates to this council as Russia proper, with its hundred million. In practice, the Russian S.F.S.R., with over half the population and three quarters of the territory of the Union, predominated over the others. When to the Russian were added the Ukrainian (or Little Russian) and White Russian republics, whose people were not very different from the Great Russians, the overwhelmingly Russian and Slavic character of the Union became more marked.

The federal structure, while not disturbing the essential unity of the whole, assured by the great Slavic preponderance, gave a dignity, self-respect, and sense of equal co-operation to the numerous minorities, all of which, before the annexations of 1940, were in any case less civilized than the Russians. To be sure, there seemed to be little substance to the formal claim that each constituent republic was sovereign, had the right to secede, and had the right to conduct its own foreign affairs, on the basis of which the Soviets demanded sixteen, and received three, votes in the United Nations when it was formed in 1945. Moreover, separatism did not wholly die down, remaining especially alive in the Ukraine. In the Second World War, four autonomous republics and one autonomous region were officially dissolved, apparently for separatist as well as collaborationist activities. Yet on the whole the U.S.S.R. was free from internal nationalistic agitation, and it is often said (even by those who are critical of other aspects of the controversial Soviet Union) that the U.S.S.R. within the framework of the over-all Soviet system seemed to have found a constructive solution to its nationalities question, and is the best example afforded by the twentieth century of a multinational state.

GOVERNMENT: PARALLELISM OF STATE AND PARTY

Government in the Union, and in each component republic, followed a pattern worked out during the Revolution and written into the constitution of 1922 and the later constitution promulgated in 1936. Its chief feature was a system of parallelism. On the one hand was the State; on the other, paralleling the State but technically not part of it, was the Party. There was a close interlocking relationship between the two.

On the side of the State, the distinctive institution was the council or soviet. Here elections took place, and authority proceeded from the bottom upward to the top. Under the constitution of 1922 only "toilers" had the right to vote. Surviving bourgeois, private traders, "persons using the labor of others to make a profit," as well as priests, were excluded from the suffrage. An indirect system of elections prevailed. In each village and town the voters chose a local soviet; the local soviet elected delegates to a provincial soviet, which in turn sent delegates to a soviet of the republic (Russian or other); the soviets of these republics sent delegates to a Union-wide Congress of Soviets, the supreme law-enacting body of the country. Soviets at all levels chose executive officials; the Congress of Soviets chose the Council of People's Commissars, or ministry.

In the constitution of 1936 a more direct democratic procedure was introduced—for the State side of the parallelism. Voters henceforth directly elected members of the higher soviets, a secret ballot was adopted, and no class was any longer denied the vote. A bicameral parliament was created, with an upper chamber, the Soviet of Nationalities mentioned above, and a lower chamber, a Soviet of the Union, in which there was one representative for every 300,000 persons in the whole country. The Supreme Soviet, with its two chambers, chose a smaller body, a Presidium, to function while the chambers were not in session. The chairman of the Presidium served as "president," or nominal head, of the U.S.S.R. The Presidium supervised the Council of People's Commissars or Council of Ministers, as it came to be called after 1946, which the Supreme Soviet continued to elect. The chairman of the Council of Ministers was in western terms the premier or prime minister. On the State side, as set forth in the constitution, especially the constitution of 1936, the government was in many aspects highly democratic.

Alongside the State, at all levels and in all localities, was the Party. Only one party was allowed, namely the Communist, though non-party members might be elected to the soviets or to other official positions. In the Party, authority began at the top and proceeded downward. At its apex stood the Central Committee, whose members varied in number from time to time, but were usually about seventy. The Central Committee did its work through an executive Secretariat headed by a general secretary and through an Orgburo and a Politburo, sub-committees handling respectively matters of party organization and party policy. The Central Committee itself, or an inside group within it, and especially the general secretary, determined the membership of the Committee and of its sub-committees. It likewise assigned, transferred, and gave orders to party members through the successive lower levels of its organization. Although party congresses met about every two years before the Second World War, they generally simply registered decisions already made by the Central Committee. Actually it was the Politburo of about a dozen men that dominated the Central Committee.[25] Power and authority flowed downward and outward, as in an army, or as in a highly centralized government agency or large private corporation in the West, except that the Party was not subject to any outside control. Discipline was likewise enforced in ways not used in liberal countries, the fearsome machinery of the Cheka (OGPU, NKVD, MVD) being available for use in extreme cases against Party members as well as those outside.

The number of Party members, men and women, rose to about two million by 1930, three million by 1940, and six million by 1950, normally comprising two or three per cent of the adult population. The Leninist ideal of a small, compact, and manageable party, made up of faithful and zealous workers who willingly carried out orders, the ideal on which the Bolsheviks had

᠕᠕᠕᠕᠕᠕᠕᠕᠕᠕᠕᠕᠕᠕

[25] In 1952–3 a number of technical changes were introduced, among which were the abolition of the Orgburo and Politburo and the transfer of their functions to a new, somewhat larger Presidium of the Central Committee; the Secretariat was also enlarged.

separated from the Mensheviks in 1903, continued to characterize the Communist Party in the Soviet Union. Old Bolsheviks, those who had been members in the lean years before 1917, long continued to occupy the seats in the
Politburo and other important party positions. The problem, once it was clear
that the Revolution had come to stay, was to prevent an inrush of careerists,
persons who simply wished to belong to the new governing elite, old Mensheviks, Social Revolutionaries, or even former bourgeois now flying Communist
colors. A party of two million members, though small in contrast to the population of the U.S.S.R., still represented an enormous growth for the party
itself, in which for each old member (who had joined before 1917) there were
hundreds of new ones. To preserve Party unity under the new conditions
strict uniformity was enforced. Members made an intensive study of the principles of Marxism-Leninism, embraced dialectical materialism as a philosophy
and even a kind of religion, learned how to take orders without question or
compunction, and to give authoritative leadership, assistance, or explanations
of policy to the mass of non-party members among whom they worked. The
bottom of the party structure consisted in small nuclei or cells. In each factory, in each mine, in each office, in each class at the universities and technical schools, in each labor union, in each at least of the larger villages, one,
two, or a dozen of the local people (factory workers, miners, office workers,
students, *etc.*, as the case might be) belonged to the Party, and imparted
Party views and Party momentum to the whole.

The function of the Party, in Marxist terms, was to carry out the dictatorship of the proletariat. It was to lead the people as a whole to the realization of socialism, and, in day-to-day affairs, to coordinate the ponderous
mechanism of government and make it work. Party members were present at
all levels. The same men sat, in the Party, in the Politburo of the Central
Committee, and, in the State, in the Council of People's Commissars. At
the next lower level, in the soviets of the Union and of the component republics, Party members were numerous. Lower down, Party members became
more rare. In a small rural soviet there might be no one belonging to the Party
at all; the village councilmen would receive instructions, exhortations, or "pep
talks" from itinerant Party members. In any event, throughout the whole
structure, the Party decided what the State should do.

The role of the Party in the U.S.S.R. has been called, at its best, a
"vocation of leadership." Those joined it who were willing to work hard, to
devote themselves to Party matters day and night, to absorb and communicate the Party policy (or "line"), to go where they were sent, to attend meetings, speak up, and remain until all others had left for home, to perceive and
explain the significance of small passing events for the future of Russia or the
world revolution, to master intricate technical details of farming, manufacturing, or the care of machinery, so that others would look to them willingly for
advice. The Party was a specially trained elite whose members were in constant touch with each other. It was the thin stream of life blood which, circulating through all the diverse tissues of the U.S.S.R.—the multitudinous republics, soviets, bureaus, army, industrial and other enterprises owned under

socialism by the state—kept the whole complex body unified, organic, functioning, and alive.

To the country as a whole the party undoubtedly represented the vocation of leadership. The corollary was that more than ninety-five out of a hundred persons were condemned to be followers, and while it is perhaps true (as apologists for the system have said) that under any system true leadership is exercised by a tiny fraction of people, the difference between Communist and non-Communist in the U.S.S.R. became a clear matter of social status. As the years passed, by the 1930's, many Communists in the U.S.S.R. were less of the type of revolutionary firebrand than of the successful and the efficient man or woman in any social system. They represented the satisfied, not the dissatisfied. Sometimes they enjoyed material privileges, such as access to the best jobs, better housing, special food coupons, or priorities on trains. They worked faithfully for recognition and promotion in the Party. They developed a bourgeois concern for the advantages of their own children. They became a new vested interest. Within the Party, members had to be not so much leaders as followers. A homogeneous and monolithic organization was desired, presenting a solid front to the far more numerous but unorganized outsiders. Within the Party, from time to time, a great deal of difference of opinion and open discussion was tolerated (indeed, since there was only one Party all political questions were intra-Party disputes), but in the end the entire membership had to conform. The Party favored a certain initiative of action, and a certain fertility of mind in inventing ways to get things done, but it did not favor, and in fact repressed, originality, boldness, or freedom of thought.

THE NEW ECONOMIC POLICY, 1921–7

By 1920 "war communism," as we have seen, had hopelessly antagonized the peasants, who, it was estimated, were cultivating only 62% as much land as in 1914.[26] This fact, together with a severe drought and the breakdown of transportation, produced a great famine. Four or five million people died. The ravages of eight years, of the World War, the Revolution, the civil wars, the Terror, had left the country in ruins, its productive facilities thrown back by decades as compared with the point reached in 1914. The rising of the Kronstadt sailors in 1921 revealed profound disillusionment in the revolutionary ranks themselves. Lenin concluded that socialization had advanced too fast. He openly advocated a compromise with capitalism, a strategic retreat. The New Economic Policy, or Nep, adopted in 1921, lasted until 1927. Most of the decade of the 1920's saw a relaxation of tempo for most people in the U.S.S.R.

Under the Nep, while the state controlled the "commanding heights" of the economy, maintaining state ownership of the basic productive indus-

[26] See p. 725.

tries, it allowed a great deal of private trading for private profit. The basic problem was to restore trade between town and country. The peasant would produce nothing beyond the needs of his own subsistence unless he could exchange his surplus for city-made wares such as clothing or tools. The city people had to be fed from the country if they were to turn out factory products or even continue to live in the city. Under the Nep, peasants were allowed to sell their farm products freely. Middlemen were allowed to buy and sell farm products and manufactured articles at will, to whom they pleased, at market prices, and at a profit to themselves. The Nep therefore favored the big individualist farmer or *kulak*. Indeed, rural changes initiated before 1914 were still at work; [27] peasant families consolidated millions of acres as private property in 1922, 1923, and 1924. Correspondingly, other peasants became "proletarians," wage-earning hired hands. The Nep also favored the sprouting of a new-rich commercial class, neo-bourgeois who ate expensive dinners in the cafés of Moscow, and whose very existence seemed to explode the dream of a classless society. Under the Nep the worst damages of war and revolution were repaired. But there was no real progress, for in 1928 Russia was producing only about as much grain, raw cotton, cattle, coal, and oil as in 1913, and far less than it presumably would have produced (given the rate of growth before 1913) had there been no revolution.

STALIN AND TROTSKY

Lenin died in 1924 prematurely at the age of fifty-four. His embalmed remains were put permanently on view in the Kremlin; Petrograd was renamed Leningrad; a leader cult was built up around his name and image; the Party presented him as a deified equal of Marx himself; and it became necessary for all schools of Communist thought to claim unflinching fidelity to the Leninist tradition. Actually, in his own lifetime, the old Bolsheviks had never regarded Lenin as infallible. They had often differed with him and with each other. After his death his old companions and contemporaries, men in their prime, carrying on the feuding habits of the émigré days, fought with each other for control of the Party in Lenin's name. They disputed over Lenin's intentions. Had he secretly thought of the Nep as a permanent policy? If not, how would he have modified it, and, most especially, how soon? Quietly, behind the scenes, as secretary of the Party, without much attention to broader problems, a hitherto relatively modest member named Joseph Stalin, of whom Lenin had never had an enthusiastic opinion, was drawing all the strings of Party control into his own hands. More openly and vociferously Leon Trotsky, who as war commissar in the critical years had been only less conspicuous than Lenin himself, raised the basic issues of the whole nature and future of the movement.

Trotsky, in 1925 and 1926, inveighed against the lassitude that had

ΛΛΛΛΛΛΛΛΛΛΛΛΛΛ

[27] See pp. 718–19.

descended upon socialism.[28] The Nep with its tolerance of bourgeois and *kulaks* excited his contempt. He developed his doctrine of "permanent revolution," an incessant drive for proletarian objectives on all fronts in all parts of the world. He stood forth as the exponent of world revolution, which many in the Party were beginning to discard in favor of first building socialism in one country. He denounced the tendency to bureaucratic ossification in the Party, and urged a new movement of the masses to give it life. He called for more forceful development of industry, and for the collectivization of agriculture, which had figured in Communist manifestos ever since 1848.[29] Above all, he demanded immediate adoption of an over-all Plan, a central control and operation of the whole economic life of the country.

Trotsky failed to carry the Party with him. He was charged with Leftist deviationism, machinations against the Central Committee, and inciting to public discussion of issues outside the Party. Stalin wove his web. At a Party Congress in 1927 854,000 members dutifully voted for Stalin and the Central Committee, and only 4,000 for Trotsky. Trotsky was first exiled to Siberia, then banished from the U.S.S.R.; he lived first in Turkey, then France, then Mexico, writing and propagandizing for the Permanent Revolution, stigmatizing developments in the U.S.S.R. as "Stalinism," a monstrous betrayal of Marxism-Leninism, organizing an underground against Stalin as he had done in former days against the tsar. He was murdered in Mexico in 1940 under mysterious circumstances, presumably by Soviet agents or sympathizers.

95. Stalin: The Five-Year Plans and the Purges

ECONOMIC PLANNING

Hardly had the Party expelled Trotsky when it appropriated certain fragments of his program. In 1928 it launched the First Five-Year Plan, aimed at rapid industrialization and the collectivization of agriculture. "Planning," or the central planning of a country's whole economic life by government officials, was to become the distinctive feature of Soviet economics, and the one which was to have the greatest influence in the rest of the world.

In retrospect, it seems strange that the Communists waited ten years before adopting a Plan. The truth seems to be that the Bolsheviks had only confused ideas of what to do after their seizure of power. Marxism for the most part gave only general hints. Marxism was primarily an analysis of existing or bourgeois society. It was also a theory of class war. But to portray any details of a future society, or specify what should be done after the class war

ᴀᴀᴀᴀᴀᴀᴀᴀᴀᴀᴀᴀᴀᴀᴀᴀᴀᴀᴀ

[28] For communists, though not for socialists, the terms "communism" and "socialism" are almost interchangeable, since Russian Communists regard their own system as true socialism, and all other socialism as opportunistic, reactionary, or false. Communism is also defined, in the U.S.S.R., as a future state of society toward which socialism, *i.e.*, Soviet socialism, is the intermediate stage.

[29] See p. 496.

had been won by the proletariat, was according to Marx and Engels sheer utopian fantasy. The bourgeoisie, to be sure, would be destroyed; there would be "social ownership of the means of production," and no "exploitation of man by man"; everyone would work, and there would be neither leisure class nor unemployment. This was not much to go on in the operation of a modern industrial system.

One great constructive idea had been mapped out, most clearly by Engels. *Within* each private enterprise, Engels had observed, harmony and order reigned; it was only *between* private enterprises that capitalism was chaotic. In the individual factory, he noted, the various departments did not compete with each other; the shipping department did not purchase from the production department at prices fluctuating according to daily changes in supply and demand; the output of all departments was planned and coordinated by management. In a larger way, the great capitalist mergers and trusts, controlling many factories, prevented blind competition between them, assigned specific quotas to each, anticipated, coordinated, and stabilized the work of each plant and each person by an over-all policy. With the growth of large corporate enterprise, observed Engels, the area of economic life under free competition was constantly reduced, and the area brought under rational planning was constantly enlarged. The obvious next step, according to Engels and other socialists, was to treat *all* the economic life of a country as a single factory with many departments, or a single enormous monopoly with many members, under one unified, vigorous and far-seeing management.

During the First World War the governments of belligerent countries had in fact adopted such centralized controls.[30] They had done so not because they were socialistic, but because in time of war people were willing to give up their usual liberties and willing to do as they were told by the government, and because all else was subordinated to a single overwhelming and undisputed social purpose—victory. The "planned society" therefore made its first actual (though incomplete) appearance in the First World War. It was partly from socialist doctrine as exemplified by Engels, partly from experience of the War, and in even larger measure from the irresistible pressure to meet the continuing chronic problems of the country by raising its productive level that Stalin and the Party in Russia gradually developed the idea of a Plan. The war experience was especially valuable for the lessons it gave on technical questions of economic planning, such as what kind of bureaus to set up, what kind of forecasts to make, and what kind of statistics to collect.

In the U.S.S.R. it was decided to plan for five years into the future, beginning with 1928. The aim of the plan was to strengthen and enrich the country, to lay the groundwork for a true workers' society, and overcome the Russian reputation for backwardness. As Stalin said in a speech in 1929:

We are advancing full steam ahead along the path of industrialization to Socialism, leaving behind the age-long Russian "backwardness." We are becoming

ᜠᜠᜠᜠᜠᜠᜠᜠᜠᜠᜠᜠᜠᜠᜠᜠᜠ
[30] See pp. 689–92.

a country of metal, a country of automobiles, a country of tractors. And when we have put the U.S.S.R. in a motor car and the *muzhik* in a tractor . . . we shall see which countries may then be "classified" as backward and which as advanced.

The First Five-Year Plan was declared fulfilled in 1932, and a Second Five-Year Plan was launched, lasting until 1937. The Third was interrupted by war, the Fourth (1946–50) was devoted to post-war recovery. A Fifth and a Sixth Five-Year Plan followed in the 1950's, declaring their objective to be the "surpassing" of the per capita industrial output of the capitalist countries.

The First Five-Year Plan (like its successors) was administered by a supreme agency called the Gosplan. Within the frame of general policy set by the Party, the Gosplan determined how much of every article the country should produce, how much of the national effort should go into the formation of capital and how much into producing articles for daily consumption, what wages all classes of workers should receive, and at what prices all goods should be exchanged. At the bottom level, in the individual factory, the local management drew up its "requirements," or estimates of what it would need, in raw material, machinery, trained workers, plant facilities and fuel, if it was to deliver the planned quantity of its product at a stated date. These estimates were passed up the planning ladder (or, thousands of such estimates up thousands of ladders) until they reached the Gosplan, which, balancing them against each other and against other needs as seen at the top, determined how much steel, coal, *etc.* should be produced, and in what qualities and grades; how many workers should be trained in technical schools, and in what particular skills; how many machines should be manufactured, and how many spare parts; how many new freight cars should be constructed, and which lines of railway track needed repair, and how, where, when, and to whom the steel, coal, technicians, machines, and rolling stock should be made available. The Plan, in short, undertook to control, by conscious management, the flow of resources and manpower which under free capitalism was regulated by shifts in demand and supply, through changes in prices, wage levels, profits, interest rates, or rent.

The system was exceedingly intricate. It was not easy to have the right number of ball bearings, for example, arrive at the right place at the right time, in exact correspondence to the amounts of other materials or to the number of workers waiting to use them. Sometimes there was overproduction, sometimes underproduction. The Plan was often amended as it was applied in action. Countless reports, check-ups, and exchanges of information were necessary. A huge class of white-collar office workers came into existence to handle the paper-work. But the Plan achieved its aim.

The primary objective of the First Five-Year Plan was to build up the heavy industry, or capital wealth, of the U.S.S.R. The aim was to industrialize without the use of foreign loans.[31] Russia in 1928 was still chiefly an agri-

---

[31] The Bolsheviks had repudiated the entire debt of the tsarist empire. Their credit in capitalist countries was therefore not good, so that, in addition to fearing dependence upon foreign lenders, they were in any case unable to borrow large sums.

cultural country. The world offered hardly any case of a country shifting from agriculture to industry without borrowing capital from abroad. Great Britain, the original home of the Industrial Revolution, was the best example, although even there, in the eighteenth century, a great deal of capital invested in England was owned by the Dutch. An agricultural country could industrialize from its own resources only by drawing upon agriculture itself. An Agricultural Revolution had been prerequisite to an Industrial Revolution in England.[32] By enclosure of land, the squeezing out of small independent farmers and the introduction of scientific cultivation, under the auspices of a growing class of wealthy landowners, England had both increased its production of food and released many of the rural population to find employment in industry. The First Five-Year Plan called for a similar agricultural revolution in Russia, without benefit to landlords and under the auspices of the state.

THE COLLECTIVIZATION OF AGRICULTURE

The Plan provided for the collectivization of agriculture. It set up collective farms, averaging a few thousand acres apiece, which were considered to be the property not of the state but of the peasants collectively who resided on them. Individual peasants were to pool their privately owned fields and livestock in these collectives. Those peasants who possessed fields or stock in considerable amount, the prosperous peasants or *kulaks*, resisted surrendering them to the new collectives. The *kulaks* were therefore liquidated as a class. Zealous detachments of Communists from the cities often used more violence that the Plan envisaged; poor peasants turned upon rich ones; hundreds of thousands of *kulaks* and their families were killed, and many more transported to labor camps in remote parts of the Soviet Union. The trend that had gone on since Stolypin and indeed since the Emancipation, building up a class of property-owning, labor-hiring, and "bourgeois" peasants, was now abruptly reversed. Politically, the obstinate obstruction of individualistic farmers was removed, and the peasantry was converted into a class more nearly resembling the proletariat of Marxian doctrine, a class of people who as individuals owned no capital and employed no labor, and so were better able to feel the advantages of a proletarian state. The year 1929, not 1917, was the great revolutionary year for most people in Russia.

Collectivization was accomplished at the cost of village class war in which the most capable farmers perished, and at the cost also of a wholesale destruction of livestock. The big farmers slaughtered their horses, cattle, pigs, and poultry rather than give them up. Even middling and small farmers did the same, caring nothing about animals that were no longer their own, or naively expecting that under collectivism the state would soon furnish a new supply. The ruinous loss of animals was the worst unforeseen calamity of the

[32] See pp. 423-4.

First Five-Year Plan. For years, meat, dairy products, leather, animal fats, and horse power were in short supply. Agricultural disorder, together with two summers of bad weather, was followed in 1932 by temporary but deathly famine in southeast Russia.

By introducing thousand-acre units in place of very small ones, collectivization made it possible to apply capital to the soil. Formerly the average peasant had been far too poor to buy a tractor, and his fields too tiny and dispersed for him to use one, so that only a few rare *kulaks* had employed any machinery. In the course of the First Five-Year Plan hundreds of Machine Tractor Stations were organized throughout the country. Each, in its region, maintained a force of tractors, harvesting combines, expert agronomists, *etc.*, which were despatched from one collective farm to another by local arrangement. The application of capital increased the output per peasant. It was also much easier administratively for higher authorities to get control over the agricultural surplus (products not consumed by the village itself) from a single collective farm than from numerous small and unorganized peasants. Each collective was assigned a quota on which it contracted in advance to make delivery. Members of the collective could sell in a free market any products they raised beyond this quota; but meanwhile the government knew the quantity of agricultural produce it could count on, either to feed the cities and other regions that did not produce their own food, or for export in the world market to pay for imports of machinery from the West. For various reasons, both technical and administrative, in the six years from 1927 to 1933 the marketable surplus in grains almost doubled, and more than doubled in cotton, flax and wool. Simultaneously, the villages needed less labor, so that between 1926 and 1939 twenty million people moved from country to city.

Collectivization of agriculture was therefore a great success for the purpose for which it was intended. Unfriendly critics have observed that it threw the peasant back into something like the *mir*, condemning him to the rounds of communal living, robbing him of the chance to make any decisions of his own. By obliging peasants to make "deliveries" below market prices, it even revived some features of the type of serfdom and forced labor that had prevailed a century before over most of Eastern Europe. It is probable, however, that in Russia half or more of the peasantry was glad to retain the communalism of the *mir*. It seems likely, too, that by 1939 a great many of the rural people were better housed and better fed than they had been before the Revolution. *Kulaks* who might have remembered better conditions had not survived.

THE GROWTH OF INDUSTRY

With the agricultural base thus revolutionized, industrialization went rapidly forward. At first there was considerable dependence on the capitalist countries. Engineers and other technicians from western Europe and the United States took service in the Soviet Union. Much machinery was at first imported. But the world-wide depression that set in about 1931, bringing a catastrophic fall of agricultural prices, meant that foreign-made machines became more costly in terms of the cereals that were the chief Soviet export. The international situation also deteriorated. Both Japan and Germany in the 1930's showed an increasing hostility to the U.S.S.R. The Second Five-Year Plan, launched in 1932, differed from the first in its greater determination to cut down imports and achieve national self-sufficiency, especially in the heavy industry that was basic to war production.

No ten years in the history of any Western country ever showed such a rate of industrial growth as the decade of the first two Plans in the Soviet Union. In Great Britain industrialization had been gradual; in Germany and the United States it had been more rapid, and in each country there had been decades in which output of coal or iron doubled; but in the U.S.S.R., from 1928 to 1938, production of iron and steel expanded four times, and that of coal three and a half times. In 1938 the U.S.S.R was the world's largest producer of farm tractors and railway locomotives. Four-fifths of all its industrial output came from plants built in the preceding ten years. Two plants alone, at the new cities of Magnitogorsk in the Urals and Stalinsk a thousand miles farther east, produced as much iron and steel as the whole Russian Empire in 1914. The U.S.S.R. was second only to the United States in gross industrial output.

The Plans called for a marked development of industry east of the Urals, and so brought a modernization of life for the first time to inner Asia, in a way comparable only to the movement of machine industry into the once primitive Great Lakes region of the American Middle West. Pittsburghs, Clevelands, and Detroits rose in the old Turkestan and Siberia. Copper mines were opened in the Urals and around Lake Balkash, lead mines in the Far East and in the Altai Mountains. New grain producing regions were developed in Siberia and in the Kazakh S.S.R., whence grain was shipped westward to Russia proper, or southward to the Uzbek S.S.R., which was devoted mainly to cotton. Tashkent, the Uzbek capital, formerly a remote town of bazaars and caravans, grew to be a city of over half a million, a center of cotton culture, copper mining and electrical industries, connected with the North by the newly built Turksib railway. The Kuznetsk basin, two thousand miles inland from every ocean, was found to possess coal deposits of high grade. Kuznetsk coal and the iron ores of the Urals became complementary, though separated by a thousand miles, somewhat like Pennsylvania coal and Minnesota iron in the United States. The opening of all these new areas, requiring the movement of food to Uzbekstan in exchange for cotton, or of Ural iron to the new Kuznetsk cities, demanded a revolution in transportation. The railroads in 1938 carried five times as much freight as in 1913.

These astounding developments were enough to change the relative economic strength of the world's peoples with respect to one another. It was significant that inner Asia was for the first time turning industrial. It was significant, too, that although the U.S.S.R. had less foreign trade than had the Russian Empire, it had more trade than the old Russia with its Asian neighbors, with which it formed new and close connections. The Russia that went to war with Germany in 1941 proved to be a different antagonist from the Russia of 1914. Industrialization in the Urals and in Asia enabled the U.S.S.R. (with a good deal of Allied assistance) to survive the German occupation and destruction of the older industrial areas in the Don valley. The new "socialist fatherland" proved able to absorb the shock.

At the same time, the degree of industrialization of the U.S.S.R. should not be exaggerated. It was phenomenal because it started from so little. In efficiency, as shown by output per worker employed, the U.S.S.R. continued to lag behind the West. In intensity of modernization, as shown by output of certain items in proportion to the whole population, it also lagged. Per capita of its huge population, in 1937, the U.S.S.R. produced less coal, electricity, cottons, woollens, leather shoes, or soap than did the United States, Britain, Germany, France, or even Japan, and less iron and steel than any of them except Japan. Production of paper is revealing because paper is used in so many "civilized" activities—in books, newspapers, magazines, correspondence, placards, maps, pictures, charts, business and government records, and household articles and amenities. Where the United States about 1937 produced 103 pounds of paper per person, Germany and Great Britain each 92, France 51, and Japan 17, the U.S.S.R. produced only 11.

SOCIAL COSTS AND SOCIAL EFFECTS OF THE PLANS

Industrialization in Russia, as formerly in other countries, was put through at great sacrifice on the part of the people. It was not merely that *kulaks* lost their lives, or that others, whose numbers have never been known except to Soviet authorities, were found to be enemies of the system and sent off to correctional labor camps. All were required to accept a program of austerity and self-denial, going without the better food, housing, and other consumers' goods that might have been produced, in order that the capital wealth and heavy industry of the country might be built up. As much as a third of the national income was re-invested in industry every year—twice as much as in the England of 1914, though probably not more than in the England of 1840. The Plan required hard work, and low wages. People looked to the future, to the time when, the basic industries having been built, better housing, better food, better clothing, and more leisure would follow. Morale was sustained by propaganda. One of the chief functions of Party members was to explain why sacrifices were necessary. In the late 1930's life began to ease; food rationing was abolished in 1935, and a few more products of light industry, such as dishes and fountain pens, began to appear in Soviet retail stores. But the need for war preparations, as the world again approached chaos, again drove back the vision of the Promised Land.

Socialism, as realized in the Plans, did away with some of the evils of unrestrained free enterprise. There was no unemployment. There was no cycle of boom and depression. There was no such misuse of women and children as in the early days of industrialism in the West. There was no absolute want or pauperization, except for political undesirables, and except for temporary conditions of famine. There was a minimum below which no one was supposed to fall. On the other hand, there was no economic equality. Marxism, indeed, had never seen equality of income as a virtue. While there was no handful of very rich people, as in the West (where the income of the rich came from property), the differences in wages and salaries were as great as in Europe or the United States. Managers, engineers, and intellectual workers received the highest pay. People with large incomes, by buying government bonds or accumulating personal possessions, could build up little fortunes for themselves and their children. They could not, however, under socialism, own any industrial capital.

Competition persisted. In 1935 a miner named Stakhanov greatly increased his daily output of coal by devising improvements in his methods of work. He also greatly increased his wages, since Soviet workers were paid at piece rates. His example proved contagious; workers all over the country began to break records of all kinds. The government publicized their achievements, called them Stakhanovites and "labor heroes," and pronounced the movement to be "a new and higher stage of socialist competition." In labor circles in the United States such straining to increase output would be called a speed-up, and piecework wages had long been anathema to the organized labor of all countries. Nor was management free from competitive pressure. A factory manager who failed to show a profit upon which the Plan counted, or who failed to meet his quota of output, might lose not only his job but his social status or even his life. Poor management was often construed as sabotage. Poor use of the men and resources allocated to a factory was considered a betrayal of Soviet workers and a waste of the property of the nation. The press, not otherwise free, freely denounced whole industries or individual executives for failures to meet the Plan.

The sense of competition or emulation, the feeling that everybody was busily toiling and struggling to create a socialist fatherland, was perhaps the most distinctive achievement of the new system. Workers had a real belief that the new industrial wonders were their own. The sense of participation, of belonging, which democracy had given to the average man in the West in political matters, was widely felt in the U.S.S.R. in economic matters also. People rejoiced at every new advance as a personal triumph. It became a national pastime to watch the mounting statistics, the fulfilling of quotas or hitting of "targets." Newspaper readers read no comic strips; they read eagerly of the latest doings (or misdoings) on the economic front. Never had there been such unalloyed delight in material and mechanical progress, not even in America in the Gilded Age. No class difference was felt between labor and management. There was apparently little envy, since differences of income, being socialistic, were regarded as necessary and fair. In creating this solidarity, this widely shared willingness to contribute, this trust in one's economic superiors and pride in collective accomplishment, the U.S.S.R. offered one of its most serious challenges to the private enterprise and private capitalism of the West.

How real this feeling was, how much of it was spontaneous, and how much was inculcated by a watchful and dictatorial government, are questions on which there has been much difference of opinion. There is no doubt that solidarity was purchased at the price of totalitarianism.[33] The government supervised everything. There was no room for skepticism, eccentricity of thought, or any basic criticism that weakened the will to achieve. As in tsarist times, no one could leave the country without special permission, which was given far more rarely than before 1914. There was only one Party. There were no free labor unions, no free press, no freedom of association, and at best only an irritable tolerance for religion. Art, literature, and even science became vehicles of political propaganda. Dialectical materialism was the official philosophy. Conformity was the ideal, and the very passion for solidarity made for fear and suspicion of all who might go astray. As for the number of people sacrificed to the Juggernaut, liquidated bourgeois, liquidated *kulaks*, purged Party members, disaffected persons sentenced to long terms in labor camps, not even an approximate estimate can be made, but it certainly reached many millions over the years.

THE PURGE TRIALS OF THE 1930'S

In 1936 socialism was judged to have proved so successful that a new constitution for the U.S.S.R. was proclaimed. It enumerated, as rights of Soviet citizens, not merely the usual civil liberties of Western democracy but the rights to steady employment, rest, leisure, economic security, and a comfortable old age. All forms of racism were condemned. It reorganized the soviet republics and granted a democratic system of voting, as explained above.[34] The new constitution was favorably commented upon in the West, where it was hoped that the Russian Revolution, like former revolutions, had at last turned into more peaceable and quiet channels. It soon became apparent, however, that the Communist Party remained the sole governing group in the country. And the Party was racked by internal troubles.

It was natural that the complex and multifarious operations of the Five-Year Plans should produce divergences of opinion among the men who carried them out. The Party elders, however, were engaged not merely in discussions of policy but in the older game of the seizure of power. On the Right, led by Bukharin, was a group that believed in more gradual methods of collectivizing the peasants. More important was the element described as Leftist. Its mastermind and rallying point was the exiled Trotsky. Probably there was some kind of secret Trotskyist machine within the U.S.S.R. and within the Party. Possibly, as was later charged, some Trotskyists had intrigued with some Germans to overthrow and replace Stalin; it seems less inherently improbable when we recall that it was the Germans who had

[33] See also on totalitarianism, Fascist, Nazi, and Soviet, pp. 811–15.
[34] See p. 733.

shipped Lenin to Russia in 1917. As early as 1933 the Party underwent a drastic purge, in which a third of its members were expelled. In 1934 Serge Kirov, an old friend and revolutionary companion of Stalin since 1909, now a member of the Central Committee and of its Politburo, was assassinated in his office. The Party, horrified, struck back at its unknown enemies by a revival of terror, executing 103 persons before the assassin, who proved to be a Party member, was apprehended.

Then came a series of sensational trials. In 1936 sixteen Old Bolsheviks were brought to trial. Some, like Zinoviev and Kamenev, had been expelled from the Party in 1927 for supporting Trotsky and subsequently, after the proper recantations, had been readmitted. Now they were charged with the murder of Kirov, with plotting the murder of Stalin, and with having organized, in 1932, under Trotsky's inspiration, a secret group to disorganize and terrorize the Central Committee. To the amazement of the world, all the accused made full confession to the charges in open court. All blamed themselves as unworthy and erring reprobates. All were put to death. In 1937, after similar trials, seventeen other Old Bolsheviks met the same fate; and in 1938 Bukharin and the Rightists, charged with wanting to restore bourgeois capitalism and conspiring with Trotsky to revolutionize the U.S.S.R., were likewise executed. The same confessions and self-accusations followed in almost every case. How these confessions were obtained in open court, from men apparently in full possession of their faculties and bearing no sign of physical harm, has remained one of the great mysteries of modern statecraft. In addition to these public trials, in 1937, in a secret court-martial, Marshal Tukhachevski and seven other ranking generals were accused of Trotskyism and of conspiring with the Germans and Japanese, and were put to death. The victims of all these purges included, among other high officials, one ex-Premier, several vice-Premiers, two former chiefs of the Communist International, the chief of the General Staff, and no fewer than two heads of the secret police who had originally gathered the evidence for the trials of many of the others. Meanwhile, in 1937 and 1938, severe purges of Trotskyists and others were made in the Party's lesser rank-and-file, the administration, the schools, and the army.

By these famous "purge trials" Party discipline was enforced. It is likely that a real danger of renewed revolution was averted. Had the tsarist government dealt as summarily with Bolsheviks as Bolsheviks dealt with one another there could have been no November Revolution. Stalin rid himself by the trials of all possible rivals for his own position. He disposed of the embarrassment of having men about him who could remember the old days, who could quote Lenin as a former friend, or belittle the reality of 1937 by recalling the dreams of 1917. After 1938 there were virtually no Old Bolsheviks left. Or, to put a different light on the matter, it may be said that a new Party and a new leadership had emerged. The aging but still explosive professional revolutionaries were now dead. A younger group, products of the new order, successful men of affairs, practical, constructive, and impatient of "agitators," were operating what was now an established system.

96. The International Impact of Communism, 1919–39

SOCIALISM AND THE FIRST WORLD WAR

Marxism had always been international in its outlook. To Marx, and the early Marxists, existing states (like other institutions) owed their character to the class struggle. They were committees of the bourgeoisie to govern the proletariat. National states were regarded as frameworks, destined to be dismantled and pass away in the course of inevitable historic processes. After Marx's death, as Marxist parties grew in numbers, and as the states of western Europe became more democratic, most people who called themselves Marxists actually accepted the national state, seeing in it a means by which the workingman's lot could be gradually improved. This view was part of the movement of "revisionism," or what more rigorous Marxists called "opportunism." [35] In the First World War national loyalty proved its strength. The socialist parties in the Reichstag, the French chamber, and other parliamentary bodies voted for war credits without hesitation. Socialist workingmen reported for mobilization like everyone else. In Germany socialists said that the reactionary Russian tsardom must be resisted; in France, that the Germans menaced all Frenchmen alike. In general, all political parties, including the socialists, declared a moratorium on party politics during the war.

Small minorities of socialists in every country, however, refused to accept the war. Marxian socialism had long taught that workingmen of all nations were bound by the supreme loyalty of class, that their real enemies were the capitalists of their own countries, that international wars were capitalist and "imperialist" quarrels, and that class struggle was the only kind of warfare that the proletarian should accept. These socialists denounced the action of the socialist majorities as a sellout to capitalism and imperialism. They met in international conferences with each other and with socialists from the neutral countries. Active among them were Lenin and other Russian Social Democrats then in Switzerland. "The only task for socialists," wrote Lenin in 1914, "is to convert the war of peoples into a civil war." The minority or antiwar socialists met at the small Swiss town of Zimmerwald in 1915, where they drew up a "Zimmerwald program," calling for immediate peace without annexations or indemnities. This had no effect on most socialists in the belligerent countries. The Zimmerwald group itself soon began to split. Most Zimmerwalders regarded peace, or the repudiation of the war, as their aim. But a "Zimmerwald Left" began to develop, inspired mainly by Lenin and the Russian émigrés. This faction made its aim not peace but revolution. It hoped that the war would go on until it caused social revolution in the belligerent countries.

Then in April 1917, with the German Imperial Government wishing

[35] See pp. 502, 594–6.

them *bon voyage*, Lenin and the other Bolsheviks went back to Russia and accomplished the November Revolution. Lenin, until his death in 1924, believed that the Russian Revolution was only a local phase of a world revolution—of *the* revolution of strict Marxian doctrine. Russia, for him, was the theater of currently most active operations in the international class war. Because he expected proletarian upheaval in Germany, Poland, the Danube valley, and the Baltic regions, he accepted without compunction the treaty of Brest-Litovsk. He took no pride in Russia; he was no patriot or "social-chauvinist," to use his own term. In the founding of the U.S.S.R. in 1922 he saw a nucleus around which other and greater soviet republics of any nationality might coalesce. "Soviet republics in countries with a higher degree of civilization," he wrote, "whose proletariat has greater social weight and influence, have every prospect of outstripping Russia as soon as they start upon the road of proletarian dictatorship."

The First World War was in fact followed by revolutions in Germany and eastern Europe. With the German and Austro-Hungarian empires wrecked, socialists and liberals of all descriptions strove to establish new regimes. Among socialists the old differences persisted, between Social Democrats favoring gradual, non-violent and parliamentary methods, and a more extreme (and smaller) group which saw in post-war disintegration a chance to realize the international proletarian revolution. The first group looked upon the Bolshevik revolution with horror. The second looked upon it with admiration. The first group included not only trade union officials and practical socialist politicians, but such pre-war giants of Marxian exegesis as Karl Kautsky and Eduard Bernstein. Even Kautsky, who had upheld pure Marxism against the revisionism of Bernstein, could not stomach the methods of Lenin. The mass of European socialists, with their fiercest leaders removed, were to remain characterized by relative moderation. Marxist in principle, they were in fact more than ever wedded to gradual, peaceable and parliamentary methods.

In the second group, the sifted residue of uncompromising Leninist neo-Marxists, who accepted the Bolshevik revolution, were Karl Liebknecht and Rosa Luxemburg. Organizing the Spartacist [36] movement in Germany, they attempted, in January 1919, to overthrow the majority-socialist government in Germany, as Lenin had overthrown the Provisional Government in Russia in November 1917. In the second group also was Bela Kun, who had turned Bolshevik during a sojourn in Russia, and who set up and maintained a soviet regime in Hungary for several months in 1919.

Lenin and the Bolsheviks, though absorbed in their own revolution, gave all possible aid to the fringe of Left socialists of Europe. They sent large sums of money to Germany, to Sweden, to Italy. When the Bolshevik Radek was arrested in Berlin he was found to have a plan for proletarian revolution in all Central Europe in his possession. The Party considered sending Russian troops to Hungary to support Bela Kun. But the chief instrument of

‿‿‿‿‿‿‿‿‿‿‿‿‿‿‿

[36] See p. 759 and note.

world revolution, created in March 1919, was the Third or Communist International.

THE FOUNDING OF THE THIRD INTERNATIONAL

The Second International, which since its foundation in 1889 had met every two or three years until 1914, held its first post-war meeting at Berne in 1919.[37] It represented socialist parties and labor organizations of all countries. The Berne meeting was stormy, for a small minority vehemently demanded "revolution as in Russia, socialization of property as in Russia, application of Marxism as in Russia." Overruled at Berne, they repaired to Moscow, and there founded a new International in conjunction with the Russian Communist Party, and with Lenin and the Russians dominating it completely. It was Lenin's hope, by founding a new International of his own, to discredit moderate socialism and to claim for the Communists the true line of succession from the First International of Karl Marx. The First International, he declared, had laid the foundations for proletarian struggle, the Second had broadened it, the Third "took over the work of the Second International, cut off its opportunistic, social-chauvinist, bourgeois and petty-bourgeois rubbish, and began to carry into effect the dictatorship of the proletariat."

The first congress of the Third International in 1919 was somewhat haphazard, but at the second, in 1920, the extreme Left parties of thirty-seven countries were represented. The Russian party was supposedly only one component. Actually, it supplied most of the personnel and most of the funds; the Bolshevik Zinoviev was its first president, remaining in this office until his disgrace as a Trotskyist in 1927. The Third or Communist International— the Comintern—was in part a spontaneous rallying of Marxists from all countries who accepted the Bolshevik Revolution as the true fruition of Marxism, and so were willing to follow the Russian lead; but, even more, it was the creation and weapon of the Bolsheviks themselves, by which to disgrace and isolate the moderate socialists and effectuate world revolution. Of all enemies the Communists hated the socialists most, reserving for them even choicer epithets than they bestowed upon capitalists and imperialists, because Communists and socialists were competing for the same thing, the leadership of the world's working class.

Parties adhering to the Comintern were obliged to drop the old name "socialist" and call themselves Communist. They were obliged to accept strong international centralization. Where the Second International had been a loose federation, and its congresses hardly more than forums, the Third International put strong powers in the hands of its Executive Committee, whose orders the Communist parties of all countries had to obey. Since there was a kind of interlocking directorate by which members of the Central Committee of the Party in Russia sat also as members of the Execu-

∿∿∿∿∿∿∿∿∿∿∿∿∿∿∿

[37] See pp. 594–5.

tive Committee of the Third International, the top Communists in Russia had, in the Comintern, an "apparatus" by which they could produce desired effects in many countries—the use of party-members to penetrate labor unions, foment strikes, propagandize ideas, or interfere in elections.

The second congress of the International, in 1920, endorsed a program of Twenty-One Points, written by Lenin. These included the requirements that each national party must call itself Communist, repudiate "reformist" socialism, propagandize labor unions and get Communists into the important union offices, infiltrate the army, impose an iron discipline upon members, require submission of each party worker to his national committee and to the orders of the international Executive, use both legal channels and secret underground methods, and expel promptly any member not hewing to the party line. Making no pretense of respect for parliamentary democracy, the second congress ruled that "the only question can be that of utilizing bourgeois state institutions for their own destruction." As for the labor movement, Lenin wrote that "the struggle against the Gomperses, the Jouhaux, the Hendersons [38] . . . who represent an *absolutely similar* social and political type as our Mensheviks . . . must be waged without mercy to the end." The Comintern was not an assemblage of humanitarians engaged in welfare work; it was a weapon for revolution, organized by revolutionaries who knew what revolution was.

For several years the U.S.S.R., using the Comintern or more conventional diplomatic channels, promoted world revolution as best it could. Communists from many countries went to Russia for indoctrination. Native-born or Russian agents proceeded to the Dutch Indies, to China, to Europe, to America. Until 1927 the Chinese revolutionists welcomed assistance from Moscow; the Russian, Borodin, became an adviser in their affairs. In 1924, in England, publication of the "Zinoviev letter," in which, at least allegedly, the Comintern urged British workers to provoke revolution, led to a great electoral victory for the Conservative party. The Bolshevik menace, real and imagined, produced everywhere a strong reaction. It was basic to the rise of fascism described in the following chapters.

In 1927, with the suppression of Trotskyism and world-revolutionism in Russia, and with the concentration under Stalin on a program of building socialism in one country, the Comintern entered upon a period of inaction. About 1935, as fascist dictators became more noisily bellicose, the U.S.S.R. turned to a policy of international collective security, and the Comintern instructed all Communist parties, each in its own country, to enter into coalitions with socialists and advanced liberals, in what were called "popular

‸‸‸‸‸‸‸‸‸‸‸‸‸‸‸‸‸‸

[38] Samuel Gompers (1850–1924), began as a cigar maker, president of the American Federation of Labor, 1886–1924; Léon Jouhaux (1879–1954), began as a factory worker, secretary-general of the French General Confederation of Labor, 1909–47, resigned in 1947 to found a new labor organization in opposition to Communism; Arthur Henderson (1863–1935), began as an ironmoulder's apprentice, chairman of the Parliamentary Labor Party, 1908–10, 1914–17, Member of Parliament, 1903–31, Secretary of State for Foreign Affairs, 1929–31.

fronts," to combat fascism and reaction. During the Second World War (in 1943), as a gesture of good-will to Great Britain and the United States, the U.S.S.R. abolished the Comintern entirely, but it reappeared in 1947 under a new name, the Communist Information Bureau or Cominform. In the revolutionary unrest that followed the Second World War, as in similar circumstances after the First World War, the Communist offensive was resumed.

Outside Russia (as, indeed, in it) the number of actual "card-carrying" members of Communist parties remained very small. They were a tiny minority from which no people had anything to fear. Even in Russia, only the accumulated effects of war, revolution, and disaster had made possible Lenin's seizure of power. What others had to fear was war and disaster, not Communism as such.

It was not through the Comintern that the U.S.S.R. exerted its greatest influence on the world. It exerted its influence by the massive fact of its very existence. By 1939 it was clear that a new type of economic system had been created. However one judged the U.S.S.R., no one could dismiss its socialism as visionary or impracticable. An alternative to free enterprise and capitalism had been brought into being. Marxism was not merely a theory; there was an actual society, embracing a sixth of the globe, which called itself Marxist. In every country those who were most critical of capitalist institutions compared them unfavorably to those of the Soviet Union. Many believed, or hoped, that something like Soviet results might be obtained without the use of Soviet methods, which were dismissed as typically Russian, a deplorable heritage from the Byzantine empire and the tsars. With the appearance of an extreme Communist Left, socialism and socialist ideas seemed in contrast to be middling and respectable. Everywhere in the 1930's the idea of "planning" began to find favor. Everywhere workers obtained more security against the fluctuations of capitalism. The so-called "backward" peoples, especially in Asia, were particularly impressed by the achievement of the U.S.S.R., which had shown how a backward country could develop a scientific industrial civilization without falling under the influence of foreign capital or foreign guidance.

Those in the 1930's who hoped to profit from the Soviet experience were not generally communist, and had no intention of following the dictates of Moscow. Wholly accepting neither Russian Communism nor historic Western capitalism, they hoped to combine the best attributes of both. Even to say this much is to suggest the tremendous implications of the Russian Revolution. Before 1917 no one in Europe or Asia had thought that anything was to be learned from Russia. Twenty years later even critics of the U.S.S.R. feared that it might represent the wave of the future. Its sheer power was soon demonstrated in the Second World War. While undeniably violent and terroristic, and ruthless in its disregard for individual persons and individual liberties, the U.S.S.R., in its prestige, its ideas, its anti-imperialist appeal to many of the earth's peoples, was a force on which all had to reckon.

CHAPTER XVIII

The Apparent Victory
of Democracy

‌‌‌‌‌‌‌‌‌‌‌‌‌‌‌‌‌‌‌‌‌‌‌‌‌‌‌‌

97. The Advance of Democracy after 1919
98. The German Republic and the Spirit of Locarno
99. The Revolt of Asia
100. The Great Depression: Collapse of the World Economy

W E HAVE followed events in Russia down to about the year 1939, but have left the story of Europe and the rest of the world at the signing of the peace treaties of 1919. We must deal now with the period of just twenty years that elapsed between the formal close of the First World War in 1919 and the outbreak of the Second World War in 1939. In these twenty years the world made a dizzy passage from confidence to disillusionment and from hope to fear. It went through a few years of superficial prosperity, abruptly followed by unparalleled economic disaster. For a time, in the 1920's, democracy seemed to be almost everywhere advancing; then, in the 1930's, the new phenomenon of totalitarianism began to spread. Let us first examine the apparent triumphs of democracy in the 1920's, turn next to the devastating world-wide effects of the great depression that began in 1929, and then, in the following chapter, trace the painful decade of the 1930's.

97. The Advance of Democracy after 1919

GAINS OF DEMOCRACY AND SOCIAL DEMOCRACY

The first years following the war were troubled. Even the victors faced serious difficulties in reconversion from war to peace. Men demobilized from the huge armies found themselves unemployed and psychologically restless. Farms and factories geared to maximum production during the war faced a sudden disappearance of markets. They produced more than could now be sold, so that the war was followed by a sharp post-war depression, which, however, had run its course by 1922. Basically, the economic position even of the victors was seriously damaged, for the war had disjointed the world of 1914, in which industrial western Europe had lived by exchange with eastern Europe and with overseas countries.

The war, President Wilson had said, had been fought to make the world safe for democracy. Political democracy now made advances everywhere. The new states that emerged from the war all adopted written constitutions and universal manhood suffrage. Democracy made advances even in countries that had long been in large measure democratic. The last steps toward universal manhood suffrage were taken in Great Britain in 1918. The most conspicuous innovation was the enfranchisement of women. Women now voted in Britain, the United States, Germany and in most of the smaller states of Europe. The United States Senate, by constitutional amendment of 1913, was elected directly by the voters instead of by state legislatures, as formerly. Proportional representation—a system of marking and counting ballots in such a way as to make the elected legislature exactly reflect the strength of all parties—was introduced in the new German republic, in some of the smaller states, and, in a way, in France. It was thought more democratic for all minorities, even small ones, to be able to differentiate themselves and be represented freely and accurately in a parliament. The referendum, initiative, and recall were widely discussed and in many countries adopted. The "referendum" permitted referral to the electorate of measures passed by a legislature. The "initiative" was a process by which voters might initiate legislation without waiting for the legislature, the "recall" a process by which voters might depose unfit public servants without awaiting the expiration of an elective term.

In most European countries the successors of the old pre-war socialists gained in strength. With the Left of the old socialists generally seceding, calling themselves communists, and affiliated with each other and with Moscow in the Communist International, the European socialists or social democrats were preponderantly a party of peaceable or revisionist Marxism, entirely willing to carry on the class conflict by parliamentary and legislative methods. Labor unions, with new self-confidence gained from the role they had played in the war, grew in membership, prestige, and importance.

Social legislation which before the war would have seemed radical was now enacted in many places. An eight-hour legal working day became common, and government-sponsored insurance programs against sickness, accident, and old age were either adopted or extended; an act of 1930, in France, insured almost ten million workers. An air of progressive democracy pervaded Europe and the European world. The social service, or welfare, state, already under way in the late nineteenth century, was becoming more firmly established.

Only in Italy in the early post-war years did democracy receive a sharp setback. Italy had been a parliamentary state since the days of Cavour, but it had never been democratic. After the war the Italians held their first elections under universal manhood suffrage. But Italian democracy was abruptly ended. In 1922 an agitator named Benito Mussolini, leading a movement which he called Fascism, killed off the Italian parliament.[1] He became the first of the personal dictators of post-war Europe. Fascist Italy, in the 1920's, was the chief exception in what seemed in general to be a rising tide of democracy.

THE NEW STATES OF CENTRAL AND EAST-CENTRAL EUROPE

In central and east-central Europe—in Germany, in the territory of the former Austro-Hungarian empire, and in the western fringe of former tsarist Russia—entirely new states and new governments struggled to establish themselves. The new states included, besides republican Germany, the four successor states to the Hapsburg empire—Austria, Hungary, Czechoslovakia, and Yugoslavia; and the five states that had broken away from the Russian empire—Poland, Finland, Estonia, Latvia, and Lithuania.[2] The other small states in eastern Europe, Rumania, Bulgaria, Greece, and Albania, had already been independent before 1914; their boundaries underwent some modification and their governments considerable reorganization after the war. The Turkish Republic is considered elsewhere.[3]

The new states were to a large extent accidents of the war. Nowhere, except possibly in Poland, did they represent a deeply felt, long-maturing, or widespread revolutionary sentiment. Only an infinitesimal number of Germans in 1914 would have voted for a republic. Even among the nationalities of Austria-Hungary in 1914 few persons would have chosen the complete break-up of the Hapsburg empire. The republicans, moderate socialists, agrarians, or nationalists who now found themselves in power had to improvise governments for which there had been little preparation. They had to contend with reactionaries, monarchists, and members of the old aristocracy. They had also to deal with the real revolutionaries, who, inspired by Lenin's success, hoped to bring about the dictatorship of the proletariat. A communist revolt broke out in Germany in 1919 but was quickly suppressed;

~~~~~~~~~~~~~~~~~~~~~~
[1] See pp. 800–3.
[2] See map, pp. 700–1.
[3] See pp. 767–9.

soviet regimes were actually set up but soon crushed in Hungary and in the German state of Bavaria; and as late as 1923 there was a communist uprising in the German state of Saxony.

The new states all embodied the principle of national self-determination, which held that each nationality should enjoy political sovereignty—one nation, one government. But people in this region were and always had been locally intermixed.[4] Each of the new states therefore included minority nationalities; for, with the exception of an exchange of populations between Greece and Turkey, arranged in 1923, there was no thought of the actual physical removal of "alien" groups. Poland and Czechoslovakia were the most composite of the new states. Each of these two possessed, in particular, among its several minorities, a considerable population of disaffected Germans. The new states also disputed with each other over places of mixed nationality to which two or more laid claim. Poland and Lithuania clashed over the largely Jewish city of Vilna, Poland and Czechoslovakia over the Teschen district, Poland and Russia went to war because the Poles claimed the far-spreading boundaries of 1772;[5] Austria and Hungary quarreled over the border province of Burgenland, Hungary and Rumania over Transylvania, Yugoslavia and Italy over Fiume, Rumania and Czechoslovakia over Bukovina, which was mainly Ukrainian; and the Greeks invaded what was left of Turkey. Each of these incidents was "settled," but in each case one party continued to nurse a grievance.

Nevertheless, despite economic and nationalist troubles, the new states and governments attempted at the outset to make themselves democratic. Except for the German republic they were all relatively small. All the newly created states were republics except Yugoslavia, which was under the older Serbian dynasty. Hungary started out in 1918 as a republic, but the attempt of Bela Kun to found a Hungarian Soviet Republic in 1919 brought back the counter-revolutionaries who restored the Hapsburg monarchy in principle, though they were prevented by foreign pressure from restoring the king in person. Hungary emerged in 1920 as a monarchy with a perennially vacant throne, under a kind of dictatorship exercised by Admiral Horthy. All smaller states of Europe, including Hungary, possessed at least the external apparatus of democracy until the 1930's; that is, they had constitutions, parliaments, elections, and a diversity of political parties. If civil liberty was sometimes violated, the right to civil liberty was not denied; and if the elections were sometimes rigged, they were at least in principle supposed to be free.

ECONOMIC PROBLEMS OF EASTERN EUROPE: LAND REFORM

The whole east-European zone was predominantly agricultural. For centuries, as has often been seen in the preceding pages, this zone had been a

[4] See map, p. 437.
[5] See map, p. 221.

region of large landed estates, which supported on the one hand a wealthy landowning aristocracy of almost feudal outlook, and on the other an impoverished mass of agricultural workers with little or no property of their own. The landed aristocracy had been the chief support of the Austro-Hungarian empire, and an important pillar of the old order in the tsarist empire and in eastern Prussia. The mass of the rural population, through all this region, had been free from serfdom, or released from subjection to manorial landlords, only since the middle of the preceding century.[6] The middle class of business and professional men was small except in Austria and Bohemia, the western portion of Czechoslovakia. In general, the whole region was conscious of lagging behind western Europe, not only in industry, factories, railroads, and great cities, but also in literacy, schooling, reading habits, health, death rates, length of life, and material standard of living.[7]

The new states set out to modernize themselves, generally on the model of the West. They introduced democratic and constitutional ideas. They put up protective tariffs, behind which they tried to develop factories and industries of their own. But the new national boundaries created difficulties. Where Europe in 1913 had had 6,000 miles of frontiers, after the war it had almost 10,000, and all the increase was in Eastern Europe. Goods circulated much less easily. Protected industries in the old agricultural regions produced inefficiently and at high cost. Old and established industries, in Austria, Czechoslovakia, and western Poland, cut off by the new frontiers and new tariffs from their former markets, fell upon hard times. The working class of Vienna lived in misery, because Vienna, a city of two million persons, formerly the capital of an empire of fifty millions, was now the capital of a republic of six millions. In Czechoslovakia the German minority, the Sudetens, complained that in hard times the German business men and workers, because of government policies, always suffered more than their Czech counterparts. Economically, the carving up of eastern Europe into a dozen independent states was self-defeating.

The greatest of reforms undertaken by the new east-European states was the reform of land ownership. Although it far from solved basic economic problems in the area, it did have substantial effect on the pattern of land distribution. The whole traditional agrarian base of society was overturned. The work of the Revolution of 1848, which, in the Hapsburg lands, had liberated the peasants but left them landless, was now carried a step further. The example of the Russian Revolution gave a powerful stimulus, for in Russia in 1917 peasants had driven off landlords, and communists and communist sympathizers won a hearing among discontented and propertyless peasants from Finland to the Balkans. Not until 1929, it should be recalled, did the Soviet Union embark on the collectivization of agriculture; until then, communism appeared to favor the small individual farmer. But it may be said with equal truth that the model for agrarian reform lay in the West, especially in France, the historic land of the small peasant proprietor.

᠁᠁᠁᠁᠁᠁

[6] See p. 493 and map, p. 175.
[7] See p. 558.

Land reform worked out differently in different countries. In the Baltic states the big properties belonged almost entirely to German families, the "Baltic barons," descendants or at least successors to the medieval Teutonic Knights.[8] In Estonia, Latvia, and Lithuania, the nationalist dislike for Germans thus made it easier to liquidate landlords. Small farms here became the rule. In Czechoslovakia over half the arable land was transferred from large to small owners; here again, the fact that many great landowners had been German, in some cases since the days of the Thirty Years' War,[9] made the operation in a sense more palatable, though it inflamed the German minority in Bohemia. In Rumania and Yugoslavia the break-up of large estates, though considerable, was less thorough. In Finland, Bulgaria, and Greece the issue hardly arose, since small landownership was already common.

Land reform had least success in Poland and Hungary. In both countries, indeed, reforms were announced. A Polish law of 1925 promised to redistribute some 5,000,000 acres to some hundreds of thousands of families, and the Hungarian republic of 1919 actually began to divide up the great estates. But in both Poland and Hungary the landed magnates were exceptionally strong and well rooted. They had been the leaders, literally for centuries, of the nationalist movement in their respective countries. In both countries, in the 1920's, nationalistic sentiment appealed to more people than did social reform. The Poles, consumed with a desire to restore the immense Poland that had existed before the partitions of the eighteenth century, became involved at first in an actual war with Soviet Russia, and thereafter supported a dictatorial and reactionary government which made no attempt to carry out the laws of 1925. The Hungarians were frightened by Bela Kun into a fear of all lower-class movements, and all Hungarians, rich and poor, felt a sense of national outrage at the treaty of Trianon, which had cut to pieces the former Apostolic Kingdom of St. Stephen. After ten years' talk, in 1930, a third of the cultivated land in Hungary still belonged to a few hundred families.

After the land reforms, political parties of peasants or small landholders became the chief democratic force within the various states on the western border of Russia. Often they inclined to socialism, especially since capitalism was to them a foreign thing. On the other hand, the great landowners, the former aristocrats of the pre-war empires, whether already expropriated or merely threatened with expropriation, were confirmed in a reactionary outlook, frightened by the neighboring communism of Russia but equally opposed to democracy, disposed to favor what was soon to be known generically as fascism. The land reforms did not solve basic economic problems. The new small farms were very small, frequently no more than ten acres. The peasant owners lacked capital, agricultural skill, and knowledge of the market. Farm productivity did not rise. In place of old differences between landlord and tenant there developed new differences between the more

wwwwwwwwwwwwww

[8] See p. 41.
[9] See pp. 123–4, 192.

comfortable peasant and the proletarian hired man—between the *kulak* and the toiler, in communist parlance. The continuance of relative poverty, the obstinacy of reactionary upper classes, the new stresses and strains among the peasants themselves, the economic distortions produced by numerous tariff walls, the lack of any sustained tradition of self-government, all helped to frustrate the democratic experiments so hopefully launched in the 1920's and to produce a situation of which German Nazis in the 1930's, and Russian Communists in the 1940's, were to take advantage.

98. The German Republic and the Spirit of Locarno

The keystone of Europe was Germany. Germany, too, had its revolution in 1918. But it was a revolution without revolutionaries, a negative revolution caused more by the disappearance of the old than by any vehement arrival of the new. The Emperor and the High Command of the army, in the last weeks of the war, had bowed themselves out of the picture, leaving it to others to face defeat and humiliation.[10] For a time, after November 1918, the men in charge of affairs were mainly Social Democrats. The Social Democrats were Marxists, but their Marxism was the tamed, toned down, and revisionist Marxism that had prevailed for twenty years before the advent of Lenin. They were trade union officials and party managers. They could look back, in 1918, on decades spent in developing labor organizations and building up the Social Democratic party, which in 1912 had become the largest single party in the Reichstag.[11] Now, in 1918, they were a cautious and prudent group, essentially conservative, more anxious to preserve what they had already achieved than to launch audacious new social experiments. Before 1917 the Social Democrats considered themselves well to the Left. But the Bolshevik revolution in Russia, and the emergence of a pro-Bolshevik or communist element in Germany, put the Social Democrats in the middle. The middle is an awkward spot, especially in disturbed times; the communists regarded the Social Democrats as reactionaries, despicable traitors to the working-class movement; whereas the true reactionaries, recruited from old monarchists, army officers, *Junker* landowners, and big business groups, saw in Social Democracy, or professed to see in it, a dangerous flirtation with Bolshevism.

The middle group in Germany, the Social Democrats reinforced by the Catholic Center party and others, were more afraid of the Left than of the Right. They were appalled, in 1918 and 1919, by the stories brought out of Russia, not merely by fugitive bourgeois or tsarist aristocrats, but by refugee Social Democrats, Mensheviks, and anti-Leninist Bolsheviks, men whom all socialists had long known and trusted in the Second International. In

---

[10] See pp. 687–9.
[11] See pp. 588, 594–5.

January 1919 the Spartacists,[12] led by Karl Liebknecht and Rosa Luxemburg, attempted to bring about a proletarian revolution in Germany, like that in Russia. Lenin and the Russian Bolsheviks lent their aid. For a time, there seemed to be a possibility that Germany might go communist, that the Spartacists might succeed in imposing a dictatorship of the proletariat. But the Social Democratic Provisional Government crushed the Spartacist uprising, turning for that purpose to demobilized army officers and volunteer vigilantes recruited from the disbanding army. The Spartacist leaders Liebknecht and Luxemburg were shot by the police. The events of "Spartacus Week" widened a chasm between Social Democrats and communists which was not to be bridged even in Hitler's concentration camps.

Shortly after, elections were held for a National Constituent Assembly. No single party received a majority but the Social Democrats were returned as the leading party; these two results were to characterize all elections in republican Germany until 1932. Coalition government always was to be necessary. It was not the Social Democrats for the most part, however, who formed governments but the Catholic Center party principally with parties further to the Right. Now in 1919 a coalition of Social Democrats, Center party and liberal Democrats were predominant in the Assembly. After several months of deliberations at the city of Weimar, in July 1919, a constitution was adopted establishing a democratic republic. The Weimar republic (as the regime in Germany from 1919 to the advent of Hitler in 1933 is called) was soon threatened ominously from the Right. In 1920 a group of disaffected army officers staged a *Putsch*, or armed revolt, put the republican government to flight, and attempted to place a puppet of their own, one Dr. Kapp, at the head of the state. The Berlin workers, by turning off public utilities, stopped the Kapp *Putsch* and saved the republic. But the Weimar government never took sufficiently firm measures to put down private armed bands led by reactionary or outspokenly anti-democratic agitators. One of these was soon to be Adolf Hitler, who as early as 1923 staged an abortive revolt in Munich.[13] Nor, being democratic and liberal, did it ever deny the rights of election to the Reichstag, and of free speech in the Reichstag and in public, either to communists or to anti-democratic reactionaries.

The Weimar republic was in principle highly democratic. The constitution embodied all the devices then favored by the most advanced democrats, not only universal suffrage including the vote for women, but proportional representation and the initiative, referendum, and recall.[14] But except for the legal eight-hour day and a few other such safeguards to the workers' welfare (and traditional demands of organized labor) the republic of which the Social Democrats were the main architects in its formative years was remote from anything socialistic. No industries were nationalized. No property changed hands. No land laws or agrarian reforms were undertaken, as in the

‸‸‸‸‸‸‸‸‸‸‸‸‸‸‸

[12] So named from Spartacus, a Roman slave who led a slave revolt in south Italy in 72 B.C.

[13] See p. 807.

[14] See p. 753.

new states of eastern Europe; the East Elbian *Junkers* remained untouched in their landed estates. There was almost no confiscation even of the property of the former Kaiser and other ruling dynasties of Bismarck's federal empire. The very statues of emperors, kings, princes and grand dukes were left standing in the streets and squares. Officials, civil servants, police agents, professors, schoolteachers of old imperial Germany remained at their respective duties. The army, though limited by the Versailles treaty to 100,000 men, remained the old army in miniature, with all its essential organs intact, and lacking only in mass. The soldiers were peasant youths enlisted for long terms and soon formed to German and Prussian military traditions. The officers were predominantly of the old aristocratic families—as always.

Never had there been a revolution so mild, so reasonable, so tolerant. There were no terror, no fanaticism, no stirring faith, no expropriation, no émigrés. There had in truth been no revolution at all, in the sense in which France, England, the United States, Russia, and other countries, either recently or in the more distant past, had experienced revolutions.

THE GERMAN DEMOCRACY AND VERSAILLES

The supreme question, for Europe and the world, was how Germany would adjust itself to the post-war conditions. How would the Germans accept the new internal regime of democracy? How would they accept the new German frontiers and other provisions of the treaty of Versailles? These two questions were unfortunately interconnected. The Weimar republic and the treaty of Versailles were both products of the defeat of Germany in the war. There were many in Germany who favored democracy, notably the numerous Social Democrats, and many more possibly could have been won over to it, given time and favorable conditions. But no one, not even the Social Democrats, accepted the treaty of Versailles or the new German frontiers as either just or final. If "democracy" in Germany meant the perpetual acceptance of the treaty without amendment, or if it meant economic distress or hardship which could either reasonably or unreasonably be explained as consequences of the treaty, then "democracy" would lose such appeal as it had for the Germans.

The German republicans, we have seen, protested against the Versailles treaty before signing, and signed only under pressure.[15] The Allies continued the war-time naval blockade after the armistice, until the Germans accepted the treaty; this confirmed, in German ears, the argument that the treaty of Versailles was a *Diktat*, a dictated peace, Carthaginian, ruthless and vengeful. The "war-guilt" clause, while it perhaps on the one hand satisfied a peculiar Anglo-American sense of morality, on the other hand offended a peculiar German sense of honor. Neither the reparations demanded of them, nor the new frontiers, were accepted by the Germans as settled. Reparations they regarded as a perpetual mortgage on their future. They generally ex-

‸‸‸‸‸‸‸‸‸‸‸‸‸‸

[15] See p. 698.

pected, some day, to revise their eastern frontier, get back at least the Polish corridor, and incorporate Austria. In Austria, now purely German, no longer joined with Slavs and Hungarians, there was through the 1920's a strong movement for union with Germany. But plans for union, even for a tariff union, were blocked by the Allies.

The French lived in terror of the day when Germany would recover. Their plans for their own security, and for the collective security of Europe against a German revival, had been disappointed. They had been unable to detach the Rhineland from Germany. The United States Senate had refused to ratify the treaty, signed at Paris by Wilson, by which the United States was to guarantee France against German invasion in the future.[16] Both Britain and the United States showed a tendency to isolation, to pull away from the Continent, to get back to "normalcy," to work mainly for a restored trade in which a strong Germany would be a large customer. The League of Nations, of which the United States was not a member, and in which every member nation had a veto, offered little assurance of safety to a people so placed as the French. The French began to form alliances, against a potentially resurgent Germany, with Poland, Czechoslovakia, and other east-European states. They insisted also on German payment of reparations. The amount of reparations, left unstated in the treaty, was fixed by a Reparations Commission in 1921 at 132 billion gold marks. This sum, the equivalent of $35,000,000,000, was soon pronounced by various Western economists to be more than Germany could possibly contrive to pay.

The Weimar government in these circumstances looked to Russia, which had been no party to the Versailles treaty and claimed no reparations. The Soviet government meanwhile, concluding from the failure of proletarian revolution in Germany and Hungary that the time was not ripe for the sovietizing of Europe, prepared to enter into normal diplomatic relations with established governments. Germany and Russia, despite ideological repugnance, thus signed the treaty of Rapallo in 1922. In the following years the Soviet Union obtained needed manufactures from Germany, and German factories and workingmen were kept busy by orders from Russia. The German army despatched officers and technicians to give instruction to the Red army. Obliged by the treaty of Versailles to restrict its activities, the German army was in fact able, through its work in Russia, and through a number of subterfuges at home, to maintain a high standard of training, planning, technical knowledge, and familiarity with new weapons and equipment. The good understanding between Germany and Russia naturally caused apprehension in the West.

REPARATIONS, THE GREAT INFLATION OF 1923, RECOVERY

The French, baffled in the attempt to collect reparations, and assisted by the Belgians, in 1923 sent units of the French Army to occupy the indus-

[16] See pp. 696, 702.

trial sites of the Ruhr valley. The Germans responded by general strikes and passive resistance. To sustain the workmen in this patriotic idleness the Weimar government paid them benefits, grinding paper money off the printing presses for this purpose. Germany, like other belligerent countries, had suffered from inflation, *i.e.*, rising prices, during and after the war; neither the imperial government nor the Weimar statesmen had been willing to impose heavier taxes to offset inflation. But what now swept Germany was different from ordinary inflation. It was of catastrophic and utterly ruinous proportions. Paper money became literally worthless. By the end of 1923 it took over four trillion paper marks to equal a dollar.

This inflation brought far more of a social revolution than the fall of the Hohenzollern empire had ever done. Debtors paid off debts in worthless money. Creditors received baskets full of meaningless paper. Salaries even when raised lagged behind the soaring cost of living. Annuities, pensions, proceeds of insurance policies, savings accounts in the banks, income from bonds and mortgages—every form of revenue which had been arranged for at some time in the past, and which often represented the economy, foresight and personal planning of many years—now turned to nothing. The middle class was pauperized and demoralized. Middle-class people were now materially in much the position of day-workers and proletarians. Their whole view of life, however, made it impossible for them to identify themselves with the laboring class or to accept its Marxist or socialist ideologies. They had lost faith in society itself, in the future, in the old burgher codes of self-reliance and rational planning of their own lives in an understandable world. A kind of moral void was created, with nothing for middle-class people to believe in, hope for, or respect.

The inflation, however, by wiping out all outstanding indebtedness within the country, made it possible, once the losses were written off and accepted, to start up economic production afresh. The United States was persuaded to play a reluctant role. The United States, in these years, demanded payment of the huge war debts owed to it by the Allies.[17] The Allies—Britain, France, Belgium—insisted that they could not pay debts to the United States unless they collected reparations from Germany. In 1924 the Dawes Plan, named for the American Charles G. Dawes, was instituted in Germany to assure the flow of reparations. By the Dawes Plan the French evacuated the Ruhr, the sum of reparations was cut down, and arrangements were made for the German republic to borrow abroad. A good deal of American private capital was invested in Germany in the following years, both in German government bonds and in German industrial enterprises. Gradually, so at least it seemed, Germany was put on its feet. For four or five years the Weimar republic even enjoyed a bustling prosperity, and there was a good deal of new construction in roads, housing, factories, and ocean liners. But the prosperity rested in good measure on foreign loans, and the great depression that began in 1929 reopened all the old questions.

〰〰〰〰〰〰〰〰

[17] See pp. 691, 693, 697-8.

THE SPIRIT OF LOCARNO

These years of economic prosperity were years also of relative international calm. No issue, in truth, was dealt with fundamentally. The universal German hatred for the treaty of Versailles elicited no concessions from the Allies. Conceivably, had the Allies been willing at this time to amend the treaty by international agreement, they might have taken wind from the sails of nationalistic rabble-rousers in Germany and so spared themselves much later grief. It may be, however, that no possible concession would have sufficed. The great problem was to prevent a German overthrow of the treaty structure by violence, especially in eastern Europe where the Germans regarded the new frontiers as basically subject to reconsideration. After the Ruhr incident, and adoption of the Dawes Plan, a group of moderate and peace-loving men shaped the foreign policy of the principal countries—Gustav Stresemann in Germany, Édouard Herriot and Aristide Briand in France, Ramsay MacDonald in England.

The charter of the League of Nations provided for international sanctions against potential aggressors. Like the system of congresses after the Peace of Vienna, the League was supposed to assure peaceable compliance with the peace treaties, or their modification without resort to force.[18] No one expected the League, by any authority of its own, to prevent war between Great Powers, but the League achieved various minor pacifications in the 1920's, and in any case its headquarters at Geneva offered a convenient meeting place in which statesmen could talk. In 1924 Ramsay MacDonald, then prime minister of the Labor government in England, brought forward his Geneva Protocol. This provided for compulsory arbitration of international disputes, called for joint military action by members of the League of Nations against an aggressor, and explicitly defined the aggressor as the power unwilling to accept arbitration. Opinion in England was hesitant to make such a guarantee for Europe as a whole. The British overseas Dominions, each of which was free to form its own foreign policy, feared entanglement in Europe. Britain preferred to go along with its own Dominions. The Conservative British government that followed MacDonald declined to sign the Geneva Protocol, which was abandoned.

In its place, in 1925, the European powers signed a number of treaties at Locarno. These marked the highest point in international good will reached between the two World Wars. Germany signed treaties with France and Belgium guaranteeing their respective frontiers unconditionally. It signed arbitration treaties with Poland and Czechoslovakia—not guaranteeing these frontiers as they stood, but undertaking to attempt changes in them only by international discussion, agreement, or arbitration. France signed treaties with Poland and Czechoslovakia promising military assistance in the event that they should be attacked by Germany. France thus developed its system

[18] See pp. 447–53.

of a Little Entente to balance German power in the East. Great Britain "guaranteed"—*i.e.*, promised military aid in the event of violation—the frontiers of Belgium and France against Germany. It did not give an equivalent guarantee with respect to Czechoslovakia or Poland. The British took the view that their own basic security would be threatened by German expansion westward, but not by German expansion to the east. It was on the borders of Czechoslovakia and Poland, fourteen years later, that the Second World War began. Had the British gone along with France in 1925 in guaranteeing these two countries against violence, and then stuck to the guarantee, it is possible that the Second World War could have been prevented. On the other hand, no war ever depends on any single decision; it is the accumulation of many decisions that matters.

In 1925 people talked with relief of the "spirit of Locarno." In 1928 international harmony was again strengthened when the French foreign minister Briand and the United States Secretary of State Frank B. Kellogg arranged for the Pact of Paris. Ultimately signed by over sixty nations, it condemned recourse to war for the solution of international controversies. Although no measures of enforcement were provided and a number of reservations were added before certain countries signed, the Pact solemnly affirmed the will of the nations to renounce war as an instrument of national policy. Meanwhile, the idea of general disarmament, pledged by Wilson in his Fourteen Points, was kept alive by a number of conferences. Some agreement was reached by the powers on naval construction at the Washington Conference of 1921–2 and at subsequent, less successful, meetings at Geneva and London. Agreement on land disarmament was more difficult to arrive at; a League of Nations preparatory commission began consultations in 1925, but no general disarmament conference was held until 1932; by then the atmosphere had changed.

In the mid-1920's the outlook was indeed full of hope. At Locarno, Germany had of its own volition (and not by the *Diktat* of Versailles) accepted its borders both east and west, to the extent of abjuring violence and unilateral action even in the east. In 1926 Germany joined the League of Nations. Germany was a going concern as a democratic republic. Democracy seemed to work, as well as could be expected, in most of the new states of eastern Europe—the *cordon sanitaire* against Communist Russia, which itself had halted its post-war revolutionary offensive. The world was again prosperous, or seemed to be so. World production was at or above the pre-war level. In 1925 the world's production of raw materials, it was estimated, was 17% greater than in 1913. World trade, by 1929, measured in hard money—gold —had almost doubled since 1913. The war and the post-war troubles were remembered as a nightmare escaped from. It seemed that, after all, the world had been made safe for democracy.

But complacency was shattered by the great world depression, by the growth of a malignant nationalism in Germany, due in some part to the depression, and by the assertion of a new militancy in Japan, which also was not unrelated to the depression. But let us turn first to the post-war years in Asia.

99. The Revolt of Asia

RESENTMENTS IN ASIA

The peoples of Asia had never been satisfied with the position in which the great European expansion of the nineteenth century had placed them.[19] Increasingly they condemned everything associated with "imperialism." In this respect there was little difference between countries actually governed by Europeans as parts of European empires, such as British India, the Netherlands Indies, French Indo-China (or the American Philippines), and countries which remained nominally independent under their own governments, such as China, Persia, and the Ottoman Empire. In the former, as political consciousness awakened, there was objection to the monopoly of Europeans in the important offices of government. In the latter, there was objection to the special rights and privileges enjoyed by Europeans, the widespread impounding of customs revenues to pay foreign debts, the capitulations in Turkey, the extraterritorial rights in China, the spheres of influence in Persia which divided the country between British and Russians.

By imperialism, in either case, aroused Asiatics meant a system whereby the affairs of their own country were conducted, its resources exploited, its people employed, for the benefit of foreigners, Europeans or white men. They meant the system of absentee capitalism, by which the plantations, docks or factories before their eyes, and on which they themselves labored, were the property of owners thousands of miles away whose main interest in them was a regular flow of profits. They meant the constant threat that an alien civilization would disintegrate and eat away their own ancient cultures. They meant the nuisance of having to speak a European language, or the calamity of having to fight wars originated by Europeans. And they meant the airs of superiority assumed by white men, the race-consciousness exhibited by all whites, though perhaps most of all the British and Americans, the color line that was everywhere drawn, the attitudes varying between contempt and condescension, the relation of native "boy" and European "sahib." Imperialism to them signified the gentlemen's clubs in Calcutta to which no Indian was ever admitted, the hotels in Shanghai from which Chinese were carefully kept out, the park benches in various cities on which no "native" could ever sit. In deeper psychology, as well as in economics and in politics, the revolt of self-conscious Asians was a rebellion against social inferiority and humiliation.

The revolt against the West was generally ambivalent or two-sided. It was a revolt against Western supremacy, but at the same time, in most cases, those who revolted meant to learn from and imitate the West, in order that, by taking over Western science, industry, organization, and other sources of

~~~~~~~~~~~~~~~~~~~~

[19] See pp. 613–22, 631–7, 644–59.

Western power, they might preserve their own identity and emerge as the West's equals.

The crisis in Asia had broken out with the Russo-Japanese War, when an Asian people, in 1905, defeated a great European power for the first time.[20] In 1906 revolution began in Persia, leading to the assembly of the first majlis, or parliament. In 1908 the Young Turks staged a successful revolution in Constantinople, and summoned a parliamentary assembly to represent all regions then in the Ottoman Empire. In 1912 the revolutionists in China, led by Sun Yat-sen, overthrew the Manchu dynasty and proclaimed the Chinese Republic. In each case the rebels charged their old monarchs—shah, sultan, emperor—with subservience to Western imperialists. In each case they summoned national assemblies on the prevailing democratic model of Europe, and they proposed to revive, modernize and Westernize their countries to the degree necessary to avoid domination by the West.

IMPACT OF THE FIRST WORLD WAR AND THE

RUSSIAN REVOLUTION

In the World War almost all the Asiatic peoples were somehow involved. The Ottoman Empire, allied with Germany, immediately repudiated all the capitulations or special legal rights of Europeans. Persia attempted to remain neutral, and to get rid of the partition made in 1907 between British and Russian spheres, but it became a battleground of British, Russian and Turkish forces. China, which joined the Allies, attempted at the peace conference to have the extraterritorial rights in China abolished. We have seen how this request of the Chinese republic was refused, and how the Allies, instead, transferred many of the pre-war German concessions to the Japanese.[21] The dependent regions of Asia, the Dutch, French and British possessions, were stimulated economically by the war.[22] The Netherlands Indies, though remaining neutral, increased its output of foodstuffs, oil, and raw materials. India developed its steel industry and textile manufactures, and contributed over a million soldiers, combat and service troops, to the British cause. All the dependent regions were stirred by Woodrow Wilson's call to make the world safe for democracy. By this they understood gaining more democracy, or at least more national independence, for themselves.

The home governments made concessions. They were naturally afraid to go too far; they insisted that their subject peoples were not yet capable of self-government; they had huge investments at stake; and the whole world economy depended on the continuing production of tropical and sub-tropical countries. But they did compromise. In 1916 the Dutch created a legislative assembly to advise the governor-general of the Indies; half its members were

[20] See pp. 657–9.
[21] See p. 697.
[22] See p. 693.

elected from native races. In 1917 the British agreed to a measure of self-government in India; an Indian legislative assembly was set up with 140 members, of whom 100 were elected, and in the provinces of British India the number of elected representatives and of native Indian officials was increased. The French in 1922 provided for a somewhat similar assembly in Indo-China. Thus all three imperial powers, at about the same time, began to experiment with consultative bodies whose membership was partly elective, partly appointive, and partly native, partly European. The United States introduced an elected assembly in the Philippine Islands in 1916.

The Russian Revolution added a new stimulus to unrest in Asia. The Bolsheviks denounced not only capitalism but also imperialism. In Marxist-Leninist ideology imperialism was an aspect of capitalism.[23] Colonial peoples also tended to identify the two, not so much for Marxist reasons as because modern capitalism was a foreign or "imperialist" phenomenon in colonial countries, where the ownership and the management of large enterprises were both foreign. Nationalism in Asia, the movement for independence or for more equality with the West, thus easily shaded off into socialism and the denunciation of capitalistic exploitation. The Bolsheviks were quick to see the advantages for themselves in this situation. As it became clear that the world revolution, as expected by Lenin, would not soon come to pass in Europe, the Russian communists turned to Asia as the theater in which world capitalism might be attacked by a great flanking movement. In September 1920 a "congress of oppressed Eastern peoples" assembled at Baku, on the coast of the Caspian Sea. Zinoviev, head of the Communist International, called for war upon "the wild beasts of British capitalism." Not much was accomplished at the conference. But a few extremists from Asian countries in the following years sojourned in Moscow, and a few communists despatched from Moscow stirred up the discontents which existed, quite without Russian instigation, all over Asia.

The post-war situation in Asia was thus extremely fluid. Men who were not communists hailed communism as a liberating force. Anti Westerners declared that their countries must Westernize. Nationalism overshadowed all other isms. In the Indian National Congress rich Indian capitalists consorted with socialist leaders, with whom they were held together in relative harmony so long as the common enemy was the British.

THE TURKISH REVOLUTION: KEMAL ATATURK

The most immediately successful of the revolutionary movements was the one in Turkey. The Young Turks at first, in 1908, had meant to prevent the further dissolution of the Ottoman Empire.[24] This proved to be impossible. In the Balkan wars of 1912–13 the Ottoman power was almost totally

[23] See p. 713.
[24] See pp. 630, 666.

excluded from the Balkan peninsula. In the World War, in which the Turks were on the losing side, the Arabs with a great deal of British assistance broke away. After the war the Greeks invaded the Anatolian peninsula. They dreamed of a Great Greece embracing both sides of the Aegean. Europeans still regarded Turkey as the sick man of Europe, the Ottoman state as doomed to extinction, and the Turkish people as barbarous and incompetent. The Allies had agreed in 1915 to partition Turkey; and after the war the Western powers favored the Greek invasion, Italian and French forces occupied parts of Anatolia, and Italians, French and British undertook to take Constantinople from Turkish rule, though its disposition remained uncertain. (It had been promised to Russia in 1915, before the Bolshevik revolution.[25]) In these circumstances a powerful army officer named Mustapha Kemal rallied Turkish national resistance. Gradually, and with aid from Soviet Russia, the Turks drove the Greeks and the Western Allies away. They affirmed their hold on the Anatolian peninsula, and on both shores of the Straits, including Constantinople.[26]

The Nationalists, under the energetic drive of Mustapha Kemal, now put through a revolution scarcely paralleled in any country at any time. They abolished the sultanate and the caliphate, since the Sultan had somewhat compromised himself with foreigners, and was also, as caliph or commander of the faithful, a religious functionary for all Islam and hence a conservative influence. The Turkish Republic was promulgated in 1923.

Where the Ottoman Empire had been a composite organization made up of diverse religious communities, among which the Moslems were the ruling group, the Turkish Republic was conceived as a national state in which the "people," i.e., the Turkish people, were sovereign. Universal suffrage was introduced, along with a parliament, a ministry and a president with strong powers. Non-Turks in Asia Minor now became "foreign" in a way they had not been before. Chief among these were the Greeks. About 1,400,000 Greeks either fled or were officially transported from Asia Minor to Greece, and, in exchange, some 400,000 Turks residing in northern Greece were transported to Turkey. The exchange of populations caused great hardship, it uprooted the Greek element that had lived in Asia Minor since 1000 B.C., and it overwhelmed the impoverished Greek kingdom by obliging it suddenly to absorb a mass of destitute refugees, who were a quarter as numerous as the population of Greece itself. But it enabled the Turkish Republic to acquire a homogeneous population. And it ended minority disputes between Greece and Turkey, and so in the long run stabilized the new situation.

For the first time in any Moslem country the spheres of government and religion were sharply distinguished. The Turkish republic affirmed the total separation of church and state. It declared religion to be a private belief, and it tolerated all religions. Government was reorganized on secular and non-religious principles stemming from the French Revolution. The law of

[25] See p. 678.
[26] See map, p. 633.

the Koran was thrust aside. The new law was modeled on the Swiss Code, the most recently codified European legislation, itself derived from the Code Napoleon.

Mustapha Kemal urged women to put aside the veil, to come out of the harem, to vote, and to occupy public office. He made polygamy a crime. Men he required by law to discard the fez. He fought against the fez as Peter the Great had fought against the beard, and for the same reason, seeing in it the symbol of conservative and backward habits. The hat, "headgear of civilization," correspondingly became the symbol of progress. The people shifted to Western dress. The Western alphabet became mandatory; literate Turks had to learn to read again, and illiteracy was reduced. The Western calendar and the metric system were adopted. Turks were required to assume hereditary family surnames, like Westerners; Kemal himself took the name Ataturk, or Great Turk. The capital was moved from Constantinople (renamed Istanbul) to Ankara. The republic put up a high tariff. In 1933 it adopted a five-year plan for economic development. The Turks, having shaken off foreign influence, were determined not to become again dependent on Western capital or capitalism. The five-year plan provided for mines, railroads and factories mainly under government ownership. At the same time, while willing to accept Russian aid against the Western powers, the republic had no patience with communism, which it suppressed. The Turks wanted a modern Turkey—by and for the Turks.

Persia experienced a similar revolution, somewhat less drastic. The old concessions, capitulations and spheres were done away with, and the Persian government renegotiated its oil contracts, asserting more control over foreign corporations, and receiving a larger return from them in taxes and royalties. In 1935, to emphasize its break with the past, Persia took the name of Iran.

THE NATIONAL MOVEMENT IN INDIA: GANDHI AND NEHRU

India at the close of the World War was on the verge of revolution against British rule.[27] Discontented Indians looked for leadership to Mohandas K. Gandhi, the Mahatma, or Holy One, who in the following decades, though hardly typical of modern Asia, attained a world-wide eminence as the spokesman of subjected peoples. Gandhi had been educated in England in the 1890's, and had practiced law in South Africa, where he became aware of racial discrimination as a world-wide problem. In India, after 1919, he led a movement for self-government, for economic and spiritual independence from Great Britain, and for greater tolerance within India itself both between Hindus and Moslems and between upper-caste Hindus and the depressed outcastes and untouchables. The weapons he favored were those of the spirit only; he preached non-violence, passive resistance, civil disobedience, and the boycott. He took to self-imposed fasts and hunger-strikes to break the firm-

‸‸‸‸‸‸‸‸‸‸‸‸‸‸‸‸

[27] See pp. 644-8, 658.

ness of British jailers, and later of Indians themselves. He and his most loyal followers, as the troubles mounted, refused to be elected or take part in the partially representative institutions that the British cautiously introduced, and also boycotted the British economic position in India, by refusing to buy or use goods imported from England. The latter touched the British in a sensitive spot. Before the World War half of all exports of British cotton cloth had gone to India. By 1932 this proportion fell to a quarter. Gandhi turned against all industrialism, even the mechanized industry that was growing up in India itself. He put aside Western costume, took to using a spinning wheel and living on goat's milk, urged Indian peasants to revive their old handicrafts, and appeared on solemn occasions clad in no more than a homespun loin-cloth. By the high level of his principles Gandhi made himself an inspiration to many groups which differed on more mundane matters. Even in the West he was regarded as one of the great religious teachers of all time.

India was very much divided within, and the British maintained that because of these divisions the ending of British rule would precipitate anarchy. There were Hindus and Moslems, between whom clashes and terrorist outrages were chronic. (Gandhi was himself murdered in 1948 by an anti-Moslem Hindu fanatic.) There were the hundreds of oriental potentates of the native states. There were Indian capitalists, like the Tata family, and growing masses of proletarians produced by Indian industrialization.[28] There were the higher castes and the outcastes, and there were hundreds of millions of peasants living in a poverty unimaginable in the West. In politics, there were those who demanded full independence, boycotted the British, and spent years in jail, as did Gandhi and his more practically-minded but devoted follower, Jawaharlal Nehru; and there were the moderates who believed that they might best advance the welfare of India by accepting government office, cooperating with the British and working for Dominion status within the British Empire. Marxism exerted a strong appeal, not indeed on the spiritual and pacific Gandhi, but on Nehru and even many of the less radical leaders. In the 1920's the Soviet Union stood in their eyes for the overthrow of imperialism; in the 1930's it pointed the way by its adoption of Five-Year Plans. For a people wishing to raise itself by its own bootstraps, to move from poverty to industrial strength and higher living standards without loss of time, and without dependence on foreign capital and capitalism, the Soviet Union with its economic planning seemed to offer a more appropriate model and more practical lessons than the rich democracies of the West, with their centuries of gradual progress behind them.

The twenty years between world wars were years of repeated disturbance, of rioting and repression, of sporadic violence despite the exhortations of Gandhi, of conferences and round tables, reforms and promises of reform, with a drift in the 1930's toward more participation of Indians in the affairs of the Indian Empire. Independence was not won until after the Second World War; with it took place a partition of the Indian sub-continent

[28] See p. 693.

into two new nations, a predominantly Hindu India and a predominantly Moslem Pakistan.[29]

In the Netherlands Indies, where the nationalist movement was less developed than in India,[30] the inter-war years were more quiet. A serious rebellion, in which communists took part, broke out in 1922 but was suppressed by the Dutch. The peoples of the archipelago were almost as diverse as those of India. Only the Dutch empire had brought them politically together. Opposition to the Dutch gave them a common program. In 1937 the legislative council petitioned for the grant of Dominion status within ten years. After a good deal of trouble the Dutch conceded independence, as in the case of the British and India, after the Second World War.[31]

THE CHINESE REVOLUTION: THE THREE PEOPLE'S PRINCIPLES

The Chinese revolution had opened in 1911 with the overthrow of the Manchu dynasty, which itself had belatedly begun to introduce Westernizing reforms. The Chinese republic was proclaimed, but the first immediate result was the establishment in Peking of a military dictatorship exercised by General Yuan Shih-kai, who had been a close adviser to the Manchus and who, until his death in 1916, never ceased to cast covetous eyes on the now empty imperial throne itself. In the south the veteran revolutionary Dr. Sun Yat-sen reorganized the Kuomintang (National People's, or Nationalist party), successor to the pre-revolutionary network of underground societies of which he had been the chief architect. Sun, elected the first president of the republic by a revolutionary provisional assembly, resigned within a few months in favor of General Yuan, who he mistakenly believed would unite the country under a parliamentary regime. Subsequently, in the confusion that followed the struggle for power in Peking after Yuan's death in 1916, Sun was proclaimed president of a rival government in the south at Canton, which exercised a nominal power over the southern provinces. Not until 1928 could any government have any basis for claiming actual rule over China—and even then, there were important exceptions. For most of these years the country was virtually in the hands of contending war lords, each of whom pocketed the customary taxes in his own locality, maintained his own army, and recognized no superior authority.

It was Sun Yat-sen who best expressed the ideas of the Chinese revolution. Born in 1867 and educated under American influence in the Hawaiian Islands, he had received a medical degree at Hong Kong, had traveled extensively about the world, studied Western ideas, lectured to Chinese audiences in America, collected money for his conspiracies against the Manchus and had returned from Europe to take part in the revolution. Shortly before his

〰〰〰〰〰〰〰〰〰

[29] See p. 854.
[30] See p. 645.
[31] See p. 854.

death in 1925 Sun gathered the lectures which he had been expounding for years into a book, *The Three People's Principles*. The book sheds much light on the revolt of China, and of all Asia, against the supremacy of the West.

The three people's principles, according to Sun Yat-sen, were democracy, nationalism, and livelihood. Livelihood meant social welfare and economic reform—a more equitable distribution of wealth and land, a gradual end to poverty and unjust economic exploitation. By nationalism Dr. Sun meant that the Chinese who had always lived mainly in the clan and family had now to learn the importance of the nation and the state. They were in fact a great nation, he thought, the world's most cultured, and had once prevailed from the mouth of the Amur to the East Indies. But they had never been cohesive; they had enjoyed too much liberty, each doing as he pleased, and for this reason the Westerners had been able to assault and invade them, occupy their cities, impose one-sided treaties and extort humiliating rights and concessions. True freedom was freedom within an organized whole. The Chinese had been "a sheet of loose sand"; they must now "break down individual liberty and become pressed together into an unyielding body like the firm rock which is formed by the addition of cement to sand."

By democracy Sun Yat-sen meant the sovereignty of the people. Like Rousseau, he gave little attention to voting, elections, or parliamentary processes. Western democracy he thought in many ways old-fashioned. "Let us not, as we pursue democracy, copy the West; let us make a clear distinction between sovereignty and ability." He meant that, while the people were sovereign, the able should govern. He thought that government must be conducted by experts in government, and criticized the West for neglecting this maxim.

Dr. Sun felt a warm sympathy for Lenin. All countries except Russia were governed by capitalists, he declared shortly before his death. Yet he was by no means a doctrinaire Marxist; he thought Marxism inapplicable to China, and argued that the Chinese must take Marxism as they took all other Western ideas, avoiding slavish imitation, using, adapting, amending, rejecting as they saw fit. He insisted that Marxism was unsuited to China because China had no native capitalism in any Marxist or Western sense. The "capitalists" in China, he said, were owners of land, and especially the owners of land in the cities, such as Shanghai, where the coming of Westerners had raised land values to dizzy heights. Hence if China could get rid of imperialism it would take a long step toward getting rid of capitalism also; it could set about an equalization of landowning and a confiscation by the state of unearned rents. Since China, he observed, had no true capitalists the state itself must undertake capitalist and industrial development. He acknowledged that it would need loans of foreign capital and the services of foreign managers and technicians. This simply added another reason why the Chinese state, to maintain control, must be strong.

With Sun Yat-sen, in short, democracy easily shaded off into a theory of benevolent and constructive dictatorship; Marxism, communism, socialism, "livelihood," the planned society, welfare economics, and anti-foreign and anti-imperialist sentiment were all mixed together.

The first aim of Sun Yat-sen and of the revolutionists in China was to shake off the "treaty system" which had bound China to outside interests since 1842.[32] In this respect the Paris peace conference had been disappointing; the Chinese not only failed to obtain the abolition of Western privileges and extraterritorial rights but could not block the retention by Japan of many of the former German concessions which the Japanese had taken over during the war. Like the United States, China never accepted the treaty of Versailles.[33] After the war the Western powers remained obdurately attached to their treaty rights, especially the British, who had the greatest stake in investments in China. At the Washington Conference of 1921–2, convened to consider naval disarmament and the general situation in the Pacific, the question of foreign withdrawal from China appeared on the agenda; it was dismissed with a reaffirmation of the "open door" policy,[34] a nine-power guarantee of the territorial integrity of China, and a few promises for the future.

Disappointed in the attempt to liberate China from foreign interests and frustrated in the effort to impose unity and effective government on the country as a whole, Sun and the Kuomintang turned to Russia. They declared the Russian and Chinese revolutions to be two aspects of the same worldwide movement of liberation. Members of the Chinese Communist party, which had been organized in 1921, were now in 1924 allowed to join the Kuomintang. The latter accepted Russian communist advisers, notably the veteran revolutionist Borodin, whom Sun Yat-sen had known years before in the United States.[35] The Soviet Union, following its strategy of outflanking world capitalism by penetrating Asia, sent military equipment, army instructors, and party organizers into China. It also surrendered the Russian concessions and extraterritorial rights acquired in China by the tsars. The Chinese policy of friendliness to Russia began to produce the hoped for effects; the British, to draw China from Russia, gave up a few of their lesser concessions at Hankow and other cities.

The Kuomintang, its armies reorganized and strengthened, now displayed a fresh vitality and after 1924 launched a military and political offensive, planned by the ever active Russian advisers, supported by the Chinese Communists, and headed by Chiang Kai-shek who soon succeeded to the leadership of the Kuomintang upon Sun's death in 1925. Chiang's main objectives were to compel the independent war lords and the regime still holding office in Peking to accept the authority of a single Nationalist government. By the end of 1928 Chiang's armies had swept northward, occupied Peking (renaming it Peiping, or "Northern Peace"), and transferred the new govern-

[32] See p. 653.
[33] See p. 697.
[34] See pp. 655, 764.
[35] See p. 750.

ment to Nanking. Chiang now exercised at least nominal control over most of China, although effective control was still limited by the recalcitrance of many provincial war lords and by another factor soon to be described. The outside powers, acknowledging the accomplishments of the Kuomintang, extended diplomatic recognition to the Nanking government and conceded its right to organize and run the country's tariff and customs affairs; they also partially surrendered their extraterritorial privileges, and pledged to abolish them completely in the near future.

But during these events, and while a measure of national unity was being forged in the country, a new division had emerged. The Kuomintang had begun to split internally between a right wing, made up mainly of Chinese financiers, merchants, and officeholders who were more nationalist than socially minded, and a left wing made up of pro-Russians, communists, semi-communists, agrarian radicals, and dissatisfied students and intellectuals. The Russians also, after Stalin's victory over Trotsky in 1927, had turned from world revolution and begun to concentrate upon socialization in Russia; they withdrew from the ideological offensive in China.

In 1927 an open break occurred between the Kuomintang and its left wing. The background was not altogether clear; but in the course of the northern military campaign, and particularly in the seizure of Nanking, popular disturbances and excesses including the killing of a number of foreigners had taken place, allegedly fomented by the Communists. These radical disturbances, it would seem, frightened and alienated the wealthier and more conservative element in the Kuomintang, and so jeopardized Chiang's chief source of financial assistance for his government and army. Chiang himself, also, had never apparently considered the alliance with either the Communists or the Russians as anything more than one of convenience. Now Chiang took decisive action. Communists, and Russian advisers, were forthwith purged from the Kuomintang; many were executed; Borodin and others fled to Moscow; and a Communist-led uprising in Canton was forcefully suppressed. A number of armed Communist groups fled to the safety of the mountain regions in the south and joined other guerilla contingents; in that way the Chinese Red Army was formed; among its leaders were Mao Tsetung, a former librarian, teacher, newspaper editor, and union organizer, and Chu Teh who had held high rank in the Kuomintang armies and who had traveled and studied in Germany and elsewhere in Europe.

Chiang, with the renewed financial and moral support of the Kuomintang bankers, thereupon resumed the northern offensive whose success by 1928 has been described. But the original revolutionary impulse of the Kuomintang was now very much dissipated. Made up of men who feared social upheaval and who often regarded their own maintenance in power as their chief problem, it exercised a kind of one-party dictatorship over most of China under Chiang's leadership. Chiang, it must be said, himself recognized mounting popular dissatisfaction with the reluctance or inability of the Kuomintang to initiate deep-seated reforms. But Chiang was still busy consolidating the regime; after 1931 he had to contend with Japanese aggression; and he had conceived a deadly hatred for Communists and those who actively agitated for revolutionary reform.

The Communists, operating now in southeast China, fed on popular discontent and drew support from the poor peasantry by a systematic policy of expropriation and distribution of large landed estates as well as by intensive propaganda. They succeeded in fighting off Chiang's armies and even in winning over part of his troops. They organized a network of local soviets and in 1931 proclaimed a Chinese Soviet Republic in the southeast. When after many years the Nationalist armies succeeded in dislodging them, they undertook in 1935 an amazing five-thousand-mile fighting retreat over near insuperable terrain to north-central China around Yenan, closer, it was said, to Soviet supply lines and in a position to outflank the Japanese invaders. Here they entrenched themselves again, fought off the Nationalist armies, and built up a strong popular following among the rural masses. With the Japanese invasion of north China well under way they abandoned their revolutionary offensive and pressed Chiang to end the civil war and to create a united front against the Japanese aggressor. Chiang, torn between his desire to destroy the Communists and to stave off the Japanese conquest of the country, had his decision made for him by the failure of his military campaigns against the Communists and by the pressure brought to bear upon him by his subordinates (he was even temporarily kidnapped in 1936). By 1937 an alliance was formed between the Kuomintang and the Communists; the Chinese Red Army was placed under Nationalist control and disposition; a united China would face the Japanese. The uneasy alliance between Kuomintang and Communists was not to last even until the defeat of the common Japanese foe in the Second World War.

JAPAN: MILITARISM AND AGGRESSION

The nationalist movement in China caused apprehension in Japan whose rise as a modern power has already been traced.[36] The Japanese, at least since the Sino-Japanese war of 1895, had looked upon the huge disintegrating area of China as a field for expansion of their own interests, in this scarcely differing from Europeans, except that they were closer to the scene. During the World War they had presented their Twenty-One Demands on China, taken over the German concessions in Shantung, and sent troops into eastern Siberia.[37] During the war the industrialization of Japan proceeded apace; Japan captured many markets while the Europeans were locked in the struggle; and after the war the Japanese remained one of the chief suppliers of textiles for the rest of Asia. The Japanese could produce at lower prices than the Europeans, prices at which the penniless masses of Asia were more able to buy. Densely packed in their mountainous islands, they sustained their stand-

[36] See pp. 548–54.
[37] See pp. 678, 697, 726.

ard of living by importing raw materials and selling manufactures. But the Chinese nationalists hoped to erect a protective tariff; it was for this reason, among others, that they denounced the treaty system, which for almost a century had bound China to international free trade. The Chinese, like the Turks, hoped to industrialize and Westernize their own country behind a high tariff wall, which would shut out Japanese manufactures as well as others.

During the 1920's the civilian, liberal, Western-oriented element in Japan remained in control of the government. In 1925 universal manhood suffrage was adopted. It was still the fashion in Europe and America to view the Japanese with sympathetic approval, as the most progressive of all non-Europeans, the one Asian people who had ably learned to play its part in the advancing world-wide civilization. But there was another facet to Japan. The constitution of 1889 and parliamentary operations were but a façade that concealed political realities. Only in Japan of all modern countries did a constitutional law prescribe that the war and navy ministers must be active generals or admirals, making it possible for the military to control the formation of all cabinets. The diet itself had sharply restricted powers. Ministers governed in the name of the supreme and sacred authority of the Emperor, to whom they were alone responsible. Economically, the government's sponsorship of industrial growth had resulted in a tremendous concentration of economic power in the hands of four family trusts known collectively as the Zaibatsu. The business interests and the civilian political leaders all looked to an expanding empire and growing markets, but the most restless element in Japan drew its strength from the nationalist revival which, even before the "opening" of Japan in 1854, had cultivated Shinto, emperor-worship and the way of the warrior as a new and modern view of life.[38] This element was recruited in large part from the old clansmen and samurai, whom the "abolition of feudalism" had uprooted from their accustomed ways, and who in many cases found no satisfying field of effort in the new regime. Many of these men now served as officers in the army. Often they were abysmally ignorant of the outside world. Often they regarded the West as decadent. They dreamed of the day when Japan would dominate all East Asia.

About 1927 this group began to hold ministries in the Japanese government, and to turn Japanese policy into increasingly aggressive and militaristic attitudes toward China. In 1931 Japanese army units stationed in Southern Manchuria (where the Japanese had been since defeat of the Russians in 1905), alleging the mysterious murder of a Japanese officer at Mukden, began to seize Chinese arsenals and spread northward over all Manchuria. In 1932, charging the Chinese with economic warfare against Japan (Chinese boycotts were in fact damaging the Japanese export trade materially), the Japanese landed 70,000 troops at Shanghai. They soon withdrew, preferring to concentrate at this stage on the occupation of the northern part of China. They

[38] See pp. 551, 553.

declared Manchuria to be an independent state under an emperor picked by themselves, renaming it Manchukuo.

After the Manchurian invasion the Chinese appealed to the League of Nations. The League sent a commission to Manchuria. The Commission, called the Lytton Commission, found Japan at fault for disturbing the peace. The small powers in the League generally cried for military sanctions, but the great powers, knowing that they would be the ones to bear the burden of military intervention against Japan, and in any case inclined to see no threat to their own immediate security, forced the League to adopt a compromise proposed by the Lytton Commission, so that, in effect, the Japanese remained in occupation of Manchuria and northeast China. The League also adopted a resolution, formulated originally by the American Secretary of State Henry L. Stimson, that no conquests achieved by force of arms in violation of existing agreements should receive diplomatic recognition; it was equally ineffectual. But the world at this time was also stunned by economic depression. Each government was preoccupied with its own internal social problems. The League, in the first clear test to be raised by a great power, failed to assure security to a member-state, in this case China, or to prevent open and undisguised aggression, in this case by Japan. The latter defiantly announced its withdrawal from the League. The Chinese remained in a state of war with Japan (not yet declared, and termed by the Japanese an "incident") from 1931 until 1945, a renewed large-scale invasion of China taking place in 1937. In a sense the Second World War began as early as 1931 with the Japanese seizure of Manchuria. One tributary of the torrent had begun to flow.

100. The Great Depression: Collapse of the World Economy

The capitalist economic system was a delicate and interlocking mechanism, in which any disturbance was rapidly transmitted with accelerating impact through all the parts.[39] For many basic commodities prices were determined by the free play of supply and demand in a world-wide market. There was much regional division of labor; large areas lived by producing a few specialized articles for sale to the world as a whole. A great deal of production, both local and international, especially in the 1920's, was financed by credit, which is to say by promises of repayment in the future. The system rested upon mutual confidence and mutual exchange—on the belief of the lender, creditor, or investor that he would get his money back, on the belief of the borrower that he could pay his debts, on the ability of farms and factories to market their products at prices high enough to bring a net return, so that farmers and factory people might purchase the output of other factories and farms, and so on round and round in countless circles of mutual interdependence, and throughout the world as a whole.

ⁿⁿⁿⁿⁿⁿⁿⁿⁿⁿⁿⁿⁿ

[39] See pp. 568–77, 608–9, 692–3.

THE PROSPERITY OF THE 1920'S AND ITS WEAKNESSES

The five years after 1924 were a period of prosperity, in that there was a good deal of international trade, building and development of new industries. The automobile, for example, still an oddity in 1914, became an article of mass production after the war; and its widespread use increased the demand for oil, steel, rubber, and electrical equipment, caused the building or re-building of tens of thousands of miles of roads, and created whole new secondary occupations for thousands of men as truckdrivers, garage mechanics, or filling-station attendants. Similarly the mass consumption of radios and moving pictures had repercussions in all directions. The ensuing expansion was most phenomenal in the United States, but almost all countries enjoyed it in greater or lesser degree. "Prosperity" became a mystic term, and some thought that it would last indefinitely, that the secret of human plenty and of progress had been found, and that science and invention were at last realizing the hopes of ages.

But there were weaknesses in this prosperity, various imperfections in this or that gear or valve of the mechanism, flaws which, under stress, were to bring the whole intricate structure to a halt. The expansion was largely financed by credit, or borrowing. Laboring people received less than a balanced share; wages lagged behind profits and dividends, so that mass purchasing power, even when inflated by installment buying (another form of credit) could not absorb the vast output that it was technically possible to produce. And throughout the world the whole decade of the 1920's was a time of chronic agricultural depression, so that farmers could neither pay their debts nor purchase manfactures to the degree required for the smooth functioning of the system.

During the war wheat fields under cultivation in Europe were reduced by a fifth. The world price of wheat went up, and farmers in the United States, Canada, and elsewhere increased their acreage. Often, to acquire land at high prices, they gave mortgages which in later years they were unable to

---

Classic Landscape

BY CHARLES SHEELER (AMERICAN, 1883–   )

The force of this picture lies in its severe abstraction. Charles Sheeler's work has dealt with characteristic American subjects, and the subject here is also American, being the River Rouge plant of the Ford Motor Company; but all local or national color has been removed, so that what results is a picture of pure industrialism, a symbol of the scientific civilization which peoples in all parts of the world in the twentieth century would like to possess. It is a picture of the good side of the modern world (for the bad side see the following page), portraying the order, economy, precision, cleanliness, and rationality of a developed technology. The absence of human beings is to be remarked: in modern industry the non-human is the orderly; it is only when the human equation is added that industrialism becomes a problem. Courtesy of Mrs. Edsel B. Ford.

repay. After the war Europe restored its own wheat production, and Eastern Europe re-entered the world market. Agriculture was increasingly mechanized. Where, in the nineteenth century, one man could cut ten times as much grain with a single horse-drawn reaper as with a scythe, and where, before 1914, he could cut fifty times as much with a combined reaper and binder, he could again increase his output fivefold after the war, by using a tractor-drawn harvester-thresher combine. At the same time dry farming opened up new land, and agronomic science increased the yield per acre. The result of all these numerous developments was a superabundant output of wheat. But the demand for wheat was what economists call "inelastic." By and large, within the area of the Western World, people already ate as much bread as they wanted, and would buy no more; and the undernourished masses of Asia, who in pure theory could have consumed the excess, could not pay even low costs of production or transportation. The world price of wheat fell incredibly. In 1930 a bushel of wheat, in terms of gold, sold for the lowest price in four hundred years.

Wheat-growers in all continents were faced with ruin. Growers of many other crops faced the same dismal prospect. Cotton and corn, coffee and cocoa all collapsed. Brazilian and African planters were caught by overproduction and falling prices. In Java, where not only had the acreage in sugar been extended, but the unit yield of sugar from the cane had multiplied ten times under scientific cultivation over the past century, the bottom dropped out of prices in the world market. There were indeed other and more profitable forms of agricultural production—for example in oranges and eggs, of which world consumption was steadily growing. But the coffee planter could not shift to eggs, nor the Iowa farmer to oranges. Not to mention the requirements of climate, the ordinary farmer or peasant lacked the capital, the special knowledge, or the access to refrigerated transportation that these newer branches of agriculture demanded. For the one thing that the average farmer or peasant knew how to do—grow wheat and other cereals—the new wonderful world of science and machinery had too little place.

The Survivor

BY GEORGE GROSZ (AMERICAN, 1893–   )

George Grosz, born in Germany, came to the United States in 1932 to avoid the Nazis. He painted this powerful picture in 1945 at the close of the Second World War. It suggests what is meant by the collapse of civilization. The hideous figure crawling out of the wreckage, according to the artist's own explanation, is insane with fear. He is starving, filthy, abandoned, and alone. In his teeth he desperately clasps a knife, which he will use to fight another terrified survivor, should he meet one, or to hunt for and cut up food. Note the symbolism of a broken swastika in the arrangement of the man's body and the debris. The picture is of course meant to be repulsive, to show the depths to which humanity can be degraded, and so shock people into constructive action. The question of the twentieth century is whether this picture or the preceding one shall prove the truer prophecy. Courtesy of the Artist.

The acute phase of the great depression, which began in 1929, was made much worse by this chronic background of agricultural distress, since there was no reserve of purchasing power on the farms. Contrariwise the farmer's plight became even worse when the city people, struck by depression in industry, cut down their expenditures for food. Agricultural depression, rather than industrial depression, was at the bottom of widespread troubles in the inter-war years throughout Eastern Europe and the colonial world.

THE CRASH OF 1929 AND THE SPREAD OF ECONOMIC CRISIS

The depression, in the strict sense, began as a stock-market and financial crisis. Prices of stocks had been pushed upward by years of continuing expansion and high dividends. At the beginning of 1929 prices on the European stock exchanges began to weaken. But the real crisis, or turning point, came with the crash on the New York Stock Exchange in October 1929. Here values had been driven to fantastic heights by excessive speculation. Not only professional speculators, but quite ordinary people, in the United States, as an easy way to make a good deal of money, bought stock with borrowed funds. Sometimes, trading on "margin," they "owned" five or ten times as much stock as the amount of their own money put into it; the rest they borrowed from brokers, and the brokers borrowed from banks, the purchased stock in each case serving as collateral. With money so easy to obtain, people pushed up stock prices by bidding against each other, and enjoyed huge fortunes on paper; but if prices fell, even a little, the hapless owners would be obliged to sell their stock to pay off the money they had borrowed. Hence, the weakening of values on the New York Stock Exchange set off uncontrollable tidal waves of selling, which drove stock prices down irresistibly and disastrously. In a month stock values dropped by forty per cent, and in three years, from 1929 to 1932, the average value of fifty industrial stocks traded on the New York Stock Exchange dropped from 252 to 61. In these same three years five thousand American banks closed their doors.

The crisis passed from finance to industry, and from the United States to the rest of the world. The export of American capital came to an end. Americans not only ceased to invest in Europe, but sold the foreign securities that they had. This pulled the foundations from under the post-war revival of Germany, and hence indirectly of much of Europe. Americans, their incomes falling, ceased to buy foreign goods; from Belgium to Borneo people saw their American markets slip away, and prices tumbled. In 1931 the failure of a leading Vienna bank, the *Creditanstalt*, sent a wave of shivers, bankruptcies, and business calamities over Europe. Everywhere business firms and private people could not collect what was owed them, or even draw on money that they thought they had in the bank. They could not buy, and so the factories could not sell. Factories slowed down or closed entirely. Between 1929 and 1932, the latter year representing the depth of the depression, world production is estimated to have declined by 38%, and the world's international trade fell by two-thirds. In the United States the national income fell from 85 to 37 billion dollars.

Unemployment, a chronic disease ever since the war, now assumed the proportion of pestilence. In 1932 there were 30,000,000 unemployed persons statistically reported in the world; and this figure did not include the further millions who could find work only for a few hours in the week, or the masses in Asia or Africa for whom no statistics were to be had. The worker's wages were gone, the farmer's income now touched bottom; and the decline of mass purchasing power forced more idleness of machinery and more unemployment. Men in the prime of life spent years out of work. Young men could not find jobs or establish themselves in an occupation. Skills and talents of older people grew rusty, young people found no opportunity to learn. Millions were reduced to living, and supporting their families, on the pittances of charity, doles, or relief. Great modern cities saw an outburst of sidewalk-art, in which, at busy street corners, jobless able-bodied men drew pictures on the pavement with colored chalk, in the hope of attracting a few sixpences or dimes. People were crushed in spirit by a feeling of uselessness; months and years of fruitless job-hunting left them demoralized, bored, discouraged, embittered, frustrated, and resentful. Never had there been such waste, not merely of machinery which now stood still, but of the trained and disciplined labor force on which all modern societies were built. And people chronically out of work naturally turned to new and disturbing political ideas.

REACTIONS TO THE CRISIS

Optimists at the time, of whom President Herbert Hoover in the United States was one, declared that this depression, though a severe one, was basically only another periodic low point in the business cycle, or alternation of expansion and contraction, which had ebbed and flowed in the Western World for over a century. Prosperity, they plaintively said, was "just around the corner." Others felt that the crisis represented the breakdown of the whole system of capitalism and free private enterprise. These people, in many cases, looked for signs of the future in the planned economy then being introduced in Soviet Russia. There was something in both views. After 1932, in part for purely cyclical reasons—because the depression cut down indebtedness, and reduced the costs of doing business—it again became possible to produce and sell. World steel production, for example, which had stood at 121 million tons in 1929, and then collapsed to 50 million in 1932, by 1936 again reached 122 million. (To what degree revival was due to armament building is debated.) On the other hand, the great depression did put an end to the old economic system in the old sense. Even if such a stricken economy had internal powers of full recuperation after a few years, still people would not stand for such terrifying insecurity in their personal lives. The horrors of mass unemployment were long remembered.

All governments took steps to provide work and incomes for their people. All, in one way or another, strove to free themselves from dependency on the uncertainties of the world market. The interlocking world economy collapsed both from the depression itself and from the measures adopted to cure it. The most marked economic consequence of the depression was a strong movement toward economic nationalism—toward greater self-sufficiency within the sphere which each government could hope to control.

The internationalism of money, the gold standard, and the free convertibility of currencies one into the other were gradually abandoned. Countries specializing in agricultural exports were among the first to be pinched. Agricultural prices were so low that even a large quantity of exports failed to produce enough foreign currency to pay for needed imports; hence the exporting country's currency fell in value. The currencies of Argentina, Uruguay, Chile, Australia, and New Zealand all depreciated in 1929 and 1930. Then came the turn of the industrial countries. England, as the depression went on, could not sell enough exports to pay for imports. It had to pay for imports in part by sending gold out of the country; thus the gold reserve supporting the pound sterling declined, and people who had pounds sterling began to convert their pounds into dollars or other currencies for which they thought the gold basis was more secure. This was known, in the poetic language of economics, as the "flight from the pound." In 1931 Great Britain went off the gold standard, which is to say that it devaluated the pound. The Briton or foreigner holding pounds sterling now could not get gold at all; he could use his sterling to buy British goods, or he could convert it to dollars or francs at depreciated rates. A pound was now worth a smaller number of dollars, or, contrariwise, fewer dollars (francs, marks, pesos, *etc.*) sufficed to buy a pound sterling. Hence other peoples were better able to buy British goods; one purpose of devaluation was in fact to restore Britain's export trade. But after Britain devaluated, some twenty-odd other countries, to protect their own exports and their own industries, did the same. Hence somewhat the same relative position re-appeared. Even the United States, which possessed most of the world's gold supply, abjured the gold standard and devaluated the dollar in 1933. The purpose was mainly to help American farmers, for with dollars cheaper in terms of foreign currencies, foreigners could afford to buy more American agricultural products. But it became harder for foreigners to sell to the United States.

Hence the depression, adding its effects to those of the World War and post-war inflation, led to chaos in the international monetary exchanges. Governments manipulated their currencies to uphold their sagging exports. Or they imposed definite exchange controls: they required that foreigners from whom their own people purchased, and to whom they thus gave their own currency, should use this currency to buy from them in return. Trade, which had been multilateral, became increasingly "bilateral." That is, where a Brazilian importer of steel, for example, had formerly bought steel wherever he wished, at such price or of such quality as he preferred, he now had to obtain steel, often regardless of price or precise quality, from a country to which Brazil had sold enough of its own products to make payment possible.

Sometimes, notably in the relations between Germany and East European countries in the 1930's, bilateralism degenerated into actual barter. The Germans would exchange a certain number of cameras with Yugoslavia in return for a certain number of pigs. In such cases the very conception of a market disappeared.

Currency control was one means of keeping one's own factories from idleness, by holding or capturing export markets in time of depression. Another way of keeping one's own factories going (or farms, or mines, or quarries) was to shut out competitive imports by the old device of protective tariffs. The United States, hit by depression in 1929, enacted the unprecedentedly high Hawley-Smoot tariff in 1930. Other countries, equally or more distressed, now could sell less to America, and hence buy less American goods. Other countries likewise raised their own tariffs, in the desperate hope of reserving national markets for their own people. Even Great Britain, citadel of free trade in the nineteenth century, turned to protectionism. It likewise revived and adopted Joseph Chamberlain's old idea of an imperial tariff-union, when in 1932, by the Ottawa agreements, Britain and the British Dominions adopted a policy of having lower tariffs against one another than against the world outside.[40] Thus the British manufacturers strove to hold a privileged market in the empire, and the harassed wheat-growers of Canada, or wool-growers of Australia, tried to assure themselves of a reliable outlet in Great Britain.

Even tariffs were not always enough. Quotas or quantitative restrictions were adopted in many states. By this system a government said in effect, not merely that goods brought into the country must pay a high tariff duty, but that above a certain amount no goods could be brought in at all. Increasingly both importers and exporters worked under government licenses, in order that a country's entire foreign trade could be centrally planned and managed. Such methods approached those of the Soviet Union, which asserted a government monopoly of all foreign trade, exported only in order to finance imports, and determined, without the bother of tariffs, the exact quantity of imported commodities that it would take.

Thus the world economy disintegrated into fiercely competing national economic systems. In the oceanic wreckage of the great depression, each state tried to create an island of economic security for its own people. Even before the great depression the new states of Eastern Europe, and such other new states as the Turkish republic, had surrounded themselves with tariffs in order to make themselves more modern, industrial, Western or up-to-date. This process, by depriving the older industrial countries of former markets, had in fact been one cause of depression. Now, with the depression, old and established industrial countries also retreated within their own borders. There were, indeed, attempts to break down the rising barriers, to unfreeze a world economy that was congealing into separate national blocks. An International Monetary and Economic Conference met at London in

ᴧᴧᴧᴧᴧᴧᴧᴧᴧᴧᴧᴧᴧᴧᴧᴧᴧ

[40] See pp. 620–1.

1933. It attempted to open the clogged channels of world trade; but it ended in failure because each national delegation was afraid to entrust its people to the ups and downs of a world market. Plans to stabilize the exchange rates of various currencies were especially blocked by the attitude of the United States. One sequel to the failure of the London Conference was an aggravation of the old war debts-reparations issue.[41] After the Conference there was a general default on war debt payments to the United States by the wartime Allies; German reparations payments to these countries had already been all but totally abolished the year before. The United States in the retaliatory Johnson Act of 1934 now denied to the defaulting wartime Allies the right to float bonds in the American security market. Since the vast lending and purchasing power of the United States made it the world's economic center of gravity, the actions taken by the United States at this time reinforced the trend to economic nationalism everywhere else. The decade that had opened with Woodrow Wilson's dream of international economic cooperation ended with an unprecedented intensification of economic rivalry and national self-centeredness; it was but one of the many promises of the twentieth century to be blasted by the Great Depression.

〰〰〰〰〰〰〰〰〰〰

[41] See pp. 691, 697–8, 761–2.

Democracy and Dictatorship

I N T H E 1920's, people in a general way had believed that the twentieth century was realizing all those goals summed up in the idea of progress; in the 1930's, they began to fear that "progress" was a phantom, to speak the word self-consciously with mental quotation marks, and to be content if only they could prevent a relapse into positive barbarization and a new world war.

The Great Depression ushered in the nightmare of the 1930's. Everywhere the demand was for security. Each nation tried to live economically, so far as possible, within itself. Each, increasingly regulating, controlling, guiding, planning or rescuing its own economic system, tried to be as little influenced as possible by the unpredictable behavior of other countries, or by the free rise and fall of prices in an uncontrolled world market. On the one hand, where democratic institutions were strong, well established, and flexible, this trend advanced the principles of the welfare state and social democracy; it protected the individual against the worst evils of unemployment and destitution and committed itself to protecting him from future catastrophes. But on the other hand the same economic trend became one aspect of the totalitarianism which spread alarmingly in the 1930's. For democracy was said to be suited only to wealthy countries. Unemployed people, especially where democracy was not established or taken for granted, cared far more for economic help, or for promises of economic help, than for any theory of how persons wielding public power should be selected. The cry was for a leader, someone who would act, make decisions, assume responsibilities, get results. Even in the United States this feeling contributed to the popularity of Franklin D. Roosevelt, who became president in 1933; in other countries it opened the way for true dictators, unscrupulous and ambitious political adventurers whose purposes, to put it mildly, were less benign than the American Roosevelt's and whose final solution to all problems, economic and political, it turned out, was war.

101. The United States: Depression and New Deal

Profound changes took place in the United States, where the stock market crash of 1929 had precipitated the great economic collapse. In 1932 national income had dropped to less than half of what it had been in 1929; twelve to fourteen million were unemployed; there was despair in all quarters. The Republican President Herbert Hoover, elected in 1928 at the floodtide of prosperity, was identified in the public mind with the hard times. Hoover viewed with disfavor any large-scale government intervention, convinced that the business cycle that had brought the depression would in turn bring prosperity, and that once business confidence was restored recovery would begin. Eventually his administration did act, proposing for the world economy a one-year suspension of payments on all intergovernmental debts, and at home giving financial assistance to banks and railroads, expanding credit facilities, and helping to save the mortgages of some farmers and small home owners. But further Hoover would not go; he opposed anything like immediate direct federal relief to the jobless; some twelve to fourteen thousand veterans seeking payment of their wartime bonuses to tide them over the bad times were ejected from Washington; unemployment, business failures, and farm foreclosures continued. In the election of 1932 the millions of unemployed workers, disheartened urban lower middle classes, and distressed farmers swept the Republican administration from office and elected the first Democratic president since Woodrow Wilson. The new president was Franklin Delano Roosevelt. The combination of recovery, relief, and reform legislation that he inaugurated is known as the New Deal.

The new president embarked on a program of improvisation and experimentation, but with such despatch and vigor as to generate at once an electric enthusiasm. Within a short time an impressive array of legislation was put through the Congress. The program of assistance to farmers, small home owners, and industry started under the Hoover administration was expanded so that it was no longer recognizable.

The government provided financial assistance for the relief of the unemployed and sponsored a broad public works program to absorb the jobless; at first it gave loans to the states for such construction projects as housing, roads, bridges and schools; later it organized a direct federal program of works projects. To meet the financial crisis, the banks were temporarily closed and then reopened under stricter supervision. The dollar was taken off the gold standard and devaluated in order to generate a moderate and controlled inflation, designed especially to help the farmers compete in foreign markets. The economic program of the New Deal was, at least at first, intensely nationalistic; we have noted how at the London Economic Conference in 1933 Roosevelt refused to tie the American currency to any international stabilization proposals. In agriculture the government gave subsidies to farmers who would curtail farm production, even going so far as to subsidize the destruction of crops and livestock, so that ruinous surpluses which had been one cause of the agricultural distress might be eliminated. It was a paradox, to be sure, for the government to reduce acreage and destroy agricultural products while city populations were in want. But the administration was endeavoring not only to cope with the immediate situation but also to meet the deep-seated agricultural crisis which antedated the depression. Subsequently, farmers received subsidies for devoting part of their land to soil-conserving crops. A Civilian Conservation Corps also promoted conservation and reforestation, and relieved unemployment by giving jobs to almost three million young people. For industry a National Recovery Administration (the NRA) encouraged business firms to set up voluntary "codes of fair competition" and to decide on prices and production; in return they accepted certain regulations and made concessions to labor.

The purpose of these relief and rehabilitation measures was to set the ailing capitalist system on its feet again. The basic approach was to create purchasing power and to stimulate private industry; the major technique was government spending, or "deficit financing" as it was called, along the lines of the theory, advanced by the British economist John Maynard Keynes, that if private investment funds are idle, government funds must be employed to encourage industrial activity and to increase purchasing power until such time as private funds are flowing again. It was to get money into circulation and to "prime the pump" of industrial production that the government undertook its huge borrowing and spending program. Unorthodox as "deficit financing" was, it seemed then, and even later, the only direct or active method of meeting, or preventing, economic collapse in a capitalist system. In all these recovery and reform measures the federal government assumed a role that it had hitherto played only in wartime. Alphabetically designated agencies proliferated; the federal payroll grew; the government debt mounted —between 1932 and 1940 it had more than doubled.

From the beginning, longer-range reform measures were initiated in addition to the recovery measures. A Securities and Exchange Commission was created to regulate the issuance of stock and to supervise the operations of the stock exchange; the aim was to prevent over-speculation and the recurrence of a crash such as that of 1929. Bank deposits were guaranteed by federal insurance so that depositors would never again lose their lifetime savings. A Tennessee Valley Authority served as a pilot program in flood control, regional economic development, and cheap public power production— a yardstick, it was said, for the private utility companies.

Increasingly, after 1935, the government seemed to shift toward an emphasis on regulation and reform. Sound economic recovery had not been achieved; there were still at least five million persons who could not find jobs in private industry. The NRA had not worked to the satisfaction of either labor or industry; it seemed only to have accentuated the concentration of economic power in the hands of bigger business firms. At first it had aroused enthusiasm, but no one was greatly concerned when the Supreme Court in 1935 declared it unconstitutional on technical grounds. Business men who at first had been responsive to the government's leadership were now increasingly resisting the government's regulation of finance and industry. Ambitious demagogues, not unlike those in Europe who at this very moment were building totalitarian dictatorships out of the chaos of the depression, were active—the Louisiana Senator Huey Long, the Catholic radio-priest Father Charles E. Coughlin, the rabble-rousing Gerald L. K. Smith, and others. Many liberals and intellectuals, always skeptical of the permanence of prosperity and disrespectful toward the worship of material success in the 1920's, viewed with admiration the Soviet "experiment," then in the midst of the industrial expansion of its second Five-Year Plan.

The tempo of New Deal reform after 1935 quickened, and moved in the direction of aiding labor and the little man. A broad national Social Security Act in 1935 provided for unemployment, old age, and disability insurance. The United States followed in the footsteps of imperial Germany, Britain, and other European countries which had had such legislation since before the First World War. Pioneer in democracy, America had hitherto not shown much tendency to advance in social legislation; nor had there ever been much demand for it even from labor ranks. Now, except for some details, the new program came to command almost universal respect. A Fair Labor Standards Act established forty hours as a maximum normal work week and set a minimum hourly wage; child labor was abolished. With the passage of a third measure, the National Labor Relations (or Wagner) Act, the American industrial scene was virtually transformed. For the first time the unions found the federal government and the law solidly aligned on their side in the campaign to organize labor. In the United States, far more effectively than in other industrial countries, employers had succeeded, in the 1920's and earlier, in preventing unionization by a variety of methods ranging from welfare paternalism to brute violence. Moreover, organized labor itself had not been enterprising. The American Federation of Labor, set up in 1886, had generally confined itself to the organization of skilled workers into craft-wide unions.

Under the new act, which guaranteed the right of workers to set up and bargain through unions of their own choice, company unions were outlawed and employers were forbidden to interfere with union organization or to discriminate against union members. Under its aegis the AF of L was revitalized and a new vigorous organization came into being, the Congress of Industrial Organizations (CIO), organizing workers on an industry-wide basis and reaching down to unskilled workers in such industries as automobile, steel, textile, maritime, and rubber. Millions never before organized, including women workers and Negroes, became part of powerful labor unions with expanding treasuries. Total union membership rose from about 4 million in 1929 to 9 million by 1940; in the 1950's it was over 15 million. Militant and conscious of its new strength but hardly touched by revolutionary ideology, American labor chose not to create a third party but to operate within the traditional two-party system.

Other reforms were introduced too. A program of slum clearance and low-cost housing made a start toward providing adequate housing. Aid was given to the tenant farmer and the sharecropper. All this was undertaken to help those whom the President described in 1937 as "one-third of a nation ill-nourished, ill-clad, ill-housed." If the New Deal did not feed, clothe, and house them, it at least demonstrated that the national community cared.

In keeping with the same reform orientation after 1935, a tax revision bill, called by its opponents a "soak the rich" scheme, arranged for steeply graduated income taxes, levies on corporate profits, and the plugging of various corporate tax-evasion loopholes. The New Deal later tried also to reverse the trend toward the concentration of economic power, which it had itself stimulated under the NRA, by an investigation into monopoly and monopoly practices, and a trust-busting campaign.

Government spending and renewed confidence in the soundness of the country's institutions did create a slow, gradual, and partial recovery. In mid-1937, however, a recession occurred, *i.e.*, business activity slid backward, when government spending slowed down; the recession did not end until 1938 when government spending was resumed. National income reached 71 billions by 1939, double what it had been at the depth of the depression, but still short of 1929. Despite substantial recovery, business activity did not once reach the high water mark of June 1929. Resistance from the business community itself may have played a part. The rising public debt, anti-business pronouncements by the government, heavier corporate and income taxes, and the many concessions to labor undoubtedly frightened off business investments and led to what was called a "sit-down strike" of capital. Some claimed even that wage rates had gone up too sharply, adding to production costs and therefore discouraging business expansion. The New Deal did much to help the patient get back on his feet. But he was not yet the same man. The New Deal did not end the depression. Complete recovery, the elimination of unemployment, the full use (and expansion) of the nation's productive capacity had to wait upon the huge war expenditures, by which depression spending was to be dwarfed. By 1938 or so the New Deal was over; the administration turned its attention from domestic reform to the gathering storm in Europe and the Far East.

The changes had been great under what some called the Roosevelt Revolution. Carrying forward a process that went back at least to the Theodore Roosevelt era, but enlarging the role of the federal government as no previous administration had done, the New Deal transformed the non-interventionist state into a social service or welfare state. The government had imposed controls on business, entered business itself, used its powers to redistribute wealth, and established a broad social security system. Labor's power and political influence had grown. The basic premise that seemed to emerge from the New Deal, the responsibility of public authority for the social and economic welfare of the people, was clearly established. Here perhaps was the real essence of the New Deal. After it no party would wish to question or could question certain innovations—the regulation of the stock exchange, social security, wages and hours legislation, the existence of the unions, protection to the farmer, the need for government watchfulness over the economy to prevent any new collapse, including even the willingness to spend government funds to prevent such a collapse. The Republican party, when it later returned to power in 1952, retained and even extended these various reforms. It was a tacit admission, despite fulminations at the time, that the New Deal had not aimed at destroying the system of capitalism but at rehabilitating and strengthening it by regulation and reform.

The New Deal, however, had engendered violent feelings, which lingered on. Roosevelt, himself of patrician and well-to-do background, denounced the "economic royalists"; in turn he was called a "traitor to his class," and even worse. Despite vociferous opposition, in the election of 1936 Roosevelt won all but two states in the most decisive victory in modern American history; and he was subsequently re-elected in 1940 and 1944 (during the wartime emergency, to be sure, and with increasingly smaller majorities) for a totally unprecedented four terms. Such an occurrence was later barred for the future by a constitutional amendment of 1951. Roosevelt battled with the Supreme Court as David Lloyd George had with the British House of Lords. When the Supreme Court declared certain measures unconstitutional, for various technical reasons but generally on the grounds that they exceeded the constitutional powers of the executive and of the federal government, the New Dealers denounced the Court as acting not as a judicial body but as a policy-making agency, and one insensitive to the emergency facing the country. Roosevelt made plans to reorganize and "pack" it, *i.e.*, enlarge the bench and fill the new vacancies; gradually, however, the Court itself softened in its hostility, and death and retirement made it possible for Roosevelt to appoint new justices sympathetic to the New Deal in their outlook. His conflict with the Court was the closest Roosevelt came to tampering with any of the fundamental constitutional structure of the country; even then he was only carrying forward a long tradition of conflict between executive and judiciary, and he intended to secure his aim only through proper legislative channels.

No one could be neutral about Roosevelt. By some it was argued that he had created an enormous, regulatory, governmental bureaucracy, expensive and cumbersome, a positive threat to the freedom and self-reliance of the individual citizen; that taxation had become unfair and oppressive and served to choke initiative and enterprise; that labor had come to overshadow the American economy. To some, like Hoover, the New Deal was a "vast casualty to liberty." But not even his bitterest foes could deny that he had gained and retained power through untrammeled free elections and an unaltered two-party system. Nor could anyone deny his great popularity with the masses of the American people; nor deny that he restored their confidence in the American democracy and the American system of private enterprise at a time when both were in a state of collapse. Despite its waste and inconsistencies, its costliness and unorthodox financial policies, its enlargement of the executive power and expansion of the governmental bureaucracy, the New Deal represented a bold and humanitarian way of meeting the greatest crisis the American republic had ever faced short of the challenge of arms; it preserved and reaffirmed American faith in its democratic system—and that at a time when democracy was succumbing almost everywhere else.

102. Trials and Adjustments of Democracy in Britain and France

BRITISH POLITICS: THE 1920'S AND THE DEPRESSION

Britain, like the United States, even in the troubles of the depression, remained firmly attached to representative institutions and democratic principles. The Great Depression aggravated and intensified Britain's older economic difficulties. More dependent on overseas markets than any other people, the British until 1914 had managed to hold their lead, exporting industrial products and capital, selling insurance and other services, and importing foodstuffs. But in the years before 1914 the British were increasingly losing their markets because of a combination of circumstances, among which had to be included the emergence of strong, economically aggressive industrial powers, the growth of tariff barriers, the development of native textile and other industries in India and elsewhere in the East, the substitution of new textile products for British cottons and woolens, and the substitution of new sources of fuel for British coal. The losses were accelerated by the economic disruption of the First World War, the disappearance of many investments, and the post-war disorganization and impoverishment of markets, though British trade for about a year enjoyed a short-lived boom caused by pent-up demands that could not be satisfied during the war. Exports were hurt too by the general rise in tariffs after the war and the customs barriers raised in the new small states of Europe. Increasingly, after 1918, Britain lived in a world no longer dependent on, or eager for, her manufactures. Britain's very historical primacy as the pioneer industrial country was also a handicap. The British had antiquated machinery and techniques that were easily improved upon by the younger industrial countries starting afresh.

The net result of all this was that in the inter-war years, even in times of relative prosperity for the rest of the world, Britain was in depression and suffered severely from unemployment. The unemployment insurance adopted in 1911 was called heavily into play. By 1921 over two million unemployed were receiving benefit payments, contemptuously called the "dole" by those who disliked it. Unemployment insurance, an expanded old-age pension system, medical aid, government subsidized housing and other social welfare measures helped to relieve economic distress and to prevent any drastic decline in the living standards of British workingmen. The welfare state was well under way in Britain before the Labor party took office after the Second World War.

The labor unions made a strenuous effort to retain wage gains and other concessions won in wartime. Industry, hard pressed itself, resisted. This situation reached a climax in 1926 in the coal mining industry, which was in a particularly bad plight; government subsidies had not helped and even conservative investigators had recommended some form of amalgamation and public management. A strike by the coal miners led to a "general strike" supported by the other British unions; about half of the six million organized workingmen in Britain left their jobs as a token of their sympathy and solidarity. But the government declared a state of emergency and made use of army and navy personnel and middle class volunteers to man essential services. The strike ended in failure, and even in a set-back for the trade unions, which were put under stricter control by the Trades Disputes Act of 1927, a measure that declared all such general or sympathy strikes illegal and placed other restrictions on labor. It remained in effect until repealed after the Second World War. But neither the unions nor the Labor party was seriously harmed.

After the election of 1922, the Labor party, founded at the beginning of the century,[1] replaced the Liberal party as the second of the two great parties of the country and faced the Conservatives as the Official Opposition. It was not easy to explain the decline in fortunes of the Liberals. Apart from internal dissension over the issue of continuing the wartime coalition of all parties which led to an open schism, and the partial abandonment of free trade by Lloyd George's coalition government in 1921 which alienated some Liberals, there was perhaps a deeper explanation. The transformation of the Liberals before the war into a party sponsoring labor reform and active government intervention in economic matters has been described.[2] Now, after the war, they were outdistanced by a Labor party which could more consistently and more actively champion both labor legislation and bolder measures to offset Britain's perilous economic state. The Labor party, moreover, which had been no more than a loose federation of trade union and socialist organizations before the war, tightened its organizational structure

[1] See p. 592.
[2] See pp. 583–4.

and for the first time in 1918, bridging the gap between the trade unionists and the socialists, committed itself to a program of socialism. But it was a program of gradualist, democratic socialism operating through customary British parliamentary and political procedures and hence able to gain and retain the good will of large sections of the middle classes.

Twice, in 1924 and in 1929, Labor governed the country with Ramsay MacDonald as prime minister, in each case as a coalition government with Labor dependent on the support of the Liberals for its majority. In 1924 the Laborites proved their moderation; their administration went no further than an extension of unemployment relief and the inauguration of housing and public works projects; indeed the Labor government acted rather firmly in the face of a series of strikes which broke out. Its overthrow was precipitated by its diplomatic recognition of the Soviet Union and the pledge of a loan to the Soviets for the purchase of British goods. Defeat was ensured by the pre-election publication of the so-called "Red (or Zinoviev) letter" purporting to be secret instructions to British labor groups from the head of the Communist International urging preparations for a Communist uprising in Britain.[3] The document is now fairly well established as a forgery, but the Conservatives successfully exploited the situation and easily won the election of 1924.

In the election of May 1929, however, Labor's representation almost doubled, and the Conservative representation dropped proportionately. MacDonald again became prime minister of a Labor-dominated coalition government. Thus the Wall Street crash and the world-wide depression broke while the Labor party government was in office. The effects of the depression were quickly felt. Unemployment, which had hovered about the million mark in 1929, soon was approaching the three million figure. The government expended large sums to supplement the unemployment insurance payments. Gold was flowing out of the country; tax receipts were declining; the public debt was growing. Alarmed at the mounting deficit, MacDonald took the advice of a committee of financial experts and made plans to introduce a severe economy policy, even to the extent of reducing the "dole" payments. The Labor party was outraged; some of the Labor ministers in his cabinet refused to support him. He and those ministers who went along with him were read out of the party. MacDonald thereupon formed an all-party coalition cabinet known as the National government. In an election in 1931 the new coalition won an overwhelming victory, the Conservative members of the coalition alone winning a majority of the seats in Parliament. MacDonald continued to head the National Government. A Conservative-dominated coalition cabinet remained in office thereafter until it was broadened during the Second World War to include the official Labor party too. Thus, as in the United States, the depression led to the ousting by the voters of those in office. The new government, though Conservative in essence, represented an effort to maintain national unity in the face of the economic emergency, within the framework of the British parliamentary democracy. Not a single seat in Parliament in

[3] See p. 750.

this depression election went to either the Communists or to a British Fascist party organized by Sir Oswald Mosley.

The National government coped with the depression in part along the retrenchment lines already mentioned, first under MacDonald, then successively after 1935 under Stanley Baldwin and Neville Chamberlain. When the economy measures were adopted, protest demonstrations were held in the larger cities and a group of sailors even "mutinied" in protest against their pay cuts; but these were passing events. In addition to the retrenchment policy which led to relatively successful budget-balancing, the government made some efforts to encourage industry to reorganize and rationalize production. Mainly, the government concentrated on the kind of economic nationalist measures that have already been described—the abandonment of the gold standard and devaluation of the pound in 1931, the curtailment of free trade and the adoption of protectionism in 1932; along with the latter went the system of "imperial preferences" adopted at Ottawa, providing advantageous treatment for British manufactures in the Dominions and for Dominion agricultural products in Britain.[4] As in the United States, despite some recovery from the depths of the depression, none of the measures taken brought full recovery or full employment. Unemployment persisted until military conscription and an expanded armament program absorbed the jobless. The Labor party, recovering from its rout in 1931, remained a vigorous opposition, pressing for the nationalization of key industries and broader social insurance coverage.

BRITAIN AND THE COMMONWEALTH: IMPERIAL RELATIONS

To the older British empire, India, the crown colonies, protectorates, and spheres of influence, the post-war settlement added a number of League of Nations mandates. British rule in its various forms extended to almost a half-billion people, a fourth of the earth's population and land surface. It was principally in Ireland, Egypt, India, and Palestine that the British faced complex imperial problems after the First World War. In Palestine, where the British exercised a League of Nations mandate, Arabs and Jews fought with each other and with Britain. In Egypt, in 1922, Britain formally ended the protectorate it had established forty years earlier, but many questions, especially the status of the Sudan, remained unresolved. In India the agitation for national independence, as we have seen, grew more intense. In these areas nothing resembling a solution was arrived at until after the Second World War. In Ireland the independence movement largely accomplished its ends.

The Irish question had disoriented English politics for forty years.[5] Irish home rule, authorized by Parliament in 1914, had been deferred for the duration of the war. Irish nationalists, during the war, had accepted German

[4] See pp. 781–4.
[5] See pp. 584–5, 611, 677.

support and had risen in rebellion in 1916. After the war, in 1919 and 1920, the Irish Nationalist or Sinn Fein party fought a small but savage war of independence against the British forces known as "Black and Tans." The British blocked independence, but in 1922 recognized the Irish Free State, granting it the same free and separate position as the Dominion of Canada. Ulster, where Presbyterians of Scotch origin had lived for three centuries, preferred to remain outside the Free State, and continued to be joined in the United Kingdom of Great Britain and Northern Ireland. Politics in the Free State (or Eire) remained unsettled, for the Irish generally demanded the annexation of Ulster, conducted tariff wars with a Britain from which they were now cut off, strove to revive Celtic in place of the English language, and fell into disputes in which Irish moderates were pitted against Irish republicans. The latter perpetrated an occasional assassination or other outrage, and insisted on severance of the last formal ties with the British Crown, which eventually took place in 1949.

As for the Dominions, the political status of these areas of white settlement overseas was now more clearly defined than ever before. The Dominions—Canada, Australia, New Zealand, and the Union of South Africa—had long pursued their own policies, even levying tariffs against British goods. They had all joined loyally with Great Britain in the First World War, but all were stirred by a nationalism of their own, and desired their virtual independence to be regularized and promulgated to the world. An imperial conference of 1926 defined "Dominion status," which was corroborated by the Statute of Westminster of 1931. The Dominions became legally equal with each other and with Great Britain. All alike were "autonomous communities within the British Empire, equal in status, in no way subordinate one to another in any aspect of their domestic or external affairs, though united by a common allegiance to the crown, and freely associated as members of the British Commonwealth of Nations." This meant that each of the countries concerned conducted its own affairs in its own way through a parliament and ministry of its own choosing, with the king or his governor-general playing a merely nominal role, as had long been the practice in Great Britain. No act passed by the British parliament could apply to a Dominion save by the Dominion's own consent. It was the decision of the Commonwealth ministers as much as that of the British cabinet itself that forced the abdication of Edward VIII in 1936 when he insisted on marriage to a twice divorced woman of American birth, an alliance which it was held would tarnish the prestige of the Crown. Despite independent policies in economic matters and even in foreign affairs, the bonds between the Dominions and Britain were firm; the support of the Dominions in the Second World War was to be vital in Britain's survival.

FRANCE: THE 1920'S AND THE COMING OF THE DEPRESSION

When the depression came to France agitation of fascist type made more headway than in any other great democratic country. Earlier, in the

1920's, France was preoccupied with recovery from the physical destruction of the war, the instability of public finances, and the fear of a resurgent Germany. Immediately after 1919, and for most of the 1920's, the government was run by coalitions of parties of the conservative Right, *i.e.*, parties supported by the business and financial interests and by many peasants, parties well disposed toward the army and Church, and interested, above all else, in economy and stability in domestic affairs. For about two years, from 1924 to 1926, the Radical Socialists were in control; this party of the center (though always in France designated as "Left"), was spokesman for the lower middle classes, the small business men, and many of the less conservative peasants; it advocated progressive social legislation so long as that did not involve increased taxes. Despite its name, a carry-over from an earlier era, it was firmly committed to private enterprise and private property; it was staunch in its defense of individual liberties and was fervently anti-clerical; sometimes, it seemed, its anti-clericalism was a substitute for any more positive program. Given its generally ambivalent outlook, the Radical Socialist party could govern in coalition with either the Right or with the Socialists to the Left. The Socialists were important in the Chamber but were considerably weakened by the secession in 1920 of the more radical members to form a French Communist party. Both Left and Right in France shaded off into anti-democratic groups that were basically hostile to the parliamentary republic as such. These included the Communists on the Left, who sat in Parliament and took part in all elections; and on the extreme Right, royalists of the *Action Française* and other anti-republican organizations, which operated principally outside the Chamber as militant and noisy pressure groups.

The outstanding figure of the moderate conservative Right was Raymond Poincaré; it was he who sent troops into the Ruhr in 1923 when the Germans failed to pay reparations; and it was he who "saved" the franc. The reparations question was extremely important for French finances. The country had undertaken a large-scale reconstruction program to repair the wartime devastation of northern and eastern France, and had counted upon the defeated enemy to pay. When German reparations were not paid as anticipated, the public debt mounted, a balanced budget became an impossibility, and the franc declined precipitously. Other factors, too, contributed to French financial difficulties, among them, the huge war expenditures, heavy wartime investment losses notably in Russia, and an outmoded taxation program which invited widespread evasion. Finally, after 1926, when the financial crisis reached a climax, a "national union" ministry under Poincaré took firm action; it inaugurated many new taxes, tightened tax collection somewhat, cut down drastically on government expenditures in order to balance the budget, and eventually stabilized the franc at about one-fifth of its pre-war value. The internal debt was thus in effect largely repudiated, to the despair of many bondholders, but the threat of a runaway inflation like that of the Weimar republic and national bankruptcy were avoided. From 1926 to 1929 the country prospered. Industry grew; it was still, to be sure, predominantly small-scale and concerned mainly with luxury items, but the war had stimulated heavy industry and mass production; and Alsace and Lorraine were again French. New factories, replacing those destroyed in the war, were modern and up-to-date. The index of industrial production rose; tourists flocked in. As in many other countries, workingmen did not share proportionately in the prosperity of the 'twenties. The unions received a sharp setback when, immediately following the war, a series of strikes of major proportions ended in failure; the unions were also divided between a Communist and non-Communist national confederation; collective bargaining in the country was virtually unknown. The workers were not mollified by a social insurance program adopted by a reluctant Parliament, which went into effect in 1930.

The Great Depression came later to France than to other industrial countries, partly because the French economy was more evenly balanced between industry and agriculture. After 1930 the effects of the depression were felt, not to the same extent, to be sure, as in the United States or Germany, but still in a telling way. Trade declined. Unemployment and part-time employment increased; at the worst period, in 1935, about one and a half million were unemployed; perhaps half of those employed worked part-time. Industrial production, which in 1930 was 40 per cent above the pre-war level, sank by 1932 back to the 1913 figure. The government displayed the usual pattern of unstable, shifting, short-lived ministries; in 1933 no fewer than five ministries rapidly succeeded one another (there were some forty all told in the twenty inter-war years). In 1932 an election had enlarged the Radical Socialist representation. The cabinets formed by the Radical Socialists were mainly dependent on the parties of the Right; fearful of inflation, they clung to the gold standard and followed a policy of retrenchment and economy. Meanwhile, in Germany Adolf Hitler had become Chancellor in 1933; all France's domestic difficulties were intensified by mounting international tension.

DEPRESSION FERMENT AND THE POPULAR FRONT

It was in the uneasy years of the depression that the latent hostility to the Republic always present in the country came to the surface. Fascist-type "leagues" appeared in open imitation of Italian and German fascist organizations; the most prominent was the *Croix de Feu* organized by Colonel de La Rocque, boasting some 30,000 members and obtaining funds from certain wealthy industrialists. The same elements that had been anti-republican, anti-democratic, or monarchist since the Great Revolution, and which had rallied behind Boulanger and denounced Dreyfus,[6] now grew more strident in their attacks on the Republic, denouncing its instability and its impotence.

In 1934 it seemed for a moment that the opportunity awaited by the anti-republican elements had come. A political and financial scandal, of the

vvvvvvvvvvvvvvv

[6] See pp. 579–81.

kind familiar in pre-war French public life, broke over the country. A financial manipulator and adventurer with excellent political connections, Stavisky by name, induced the municipal authorities at Bayonne to launch a flotation of worthless bonds. Faced with exposure, he fled and then apparently committed suicide; the sensationalist press encouraged the rumor that he had been shot by the police to prevent the implication of high-ranking politicians. A clamor went up accusing the government of involvement in the financial scandal. Where elsewhere such an affair would have called merely for turning the rascally incumbents out of office, in France it supplied ammunition for those who demanded the guillotining of the constitutional regime itself; the Republic was equated with corruption and venality.

The agitation reached a climax in the riots of February 1934. A mob of fascist tendency assembled in the Place de la Concorde, threatened the Chamber, and battled with the police; a number of persons were killed and wounded. French liberals and democrats, organized labor, and the Socialist party were outraged by the threat to the republic. The Communists were hostile to the fascist groups but were unfriendly to the government too; soon, guided by the Comintern, they sensed the danger to themselves and to the Soviet Union in the event of a French fascist triumph, and joined with the anti-fascists. As elsewhere, in the 1930's they emerged from their sectarian revolutionary isolation, became intensely patriotic, and grew considerably in prestige, influence, and appeal. An impressive labor-sponsored general strike was held a week after the riots. Shortly thereafter, the Radical Socialists, Socialists, and Communists drew together in a political coalition that came to be known as the Popular Front, of the kind that was being organized, or advocated, in many countries in the 1930's. It campaigned on a pledge to defend the republic against fascism, to take measures against the depression, and to introduce labor reforms. In the spring of 1936 it won a decisive victory at the polls. The French Socialists for the first time in their history became the leading party in the Chamber; their chief, Léon Blum, long an eloquent spokesman for democratic and reformist socialism, became premier of a coalition cabinet of Socialists and Radical Socialists; the Communists, who had increased their representation in the Chamber from 10 to 72 seats, did not join the cabinet but pledged their support.

THE POPULAR FRONT AND AFTER

Blum's Popular Front ministry, although it lasted little more than a year, put through a program of legislation unprecedented in French parliamentary annals. In part, this was due to the Popular Front election program; in part it was due to unforeseen events, for the tremendous enthusiasm generated by the victory led to a spontaneous nation-wide wave of "sit-down strikes," which did not subside until Blum pledged a number of immediate reforms.

Through Blum's mediation, industry at once awarded a blanket wage increase to all workers and promised to cooperate with social legislation passed by Parliament. Parliament in short order passed laws providing for a forty-hour week, vacations with pay, and a collective bargaining law. As in the case of the Wagner Act in the United States, the encouragement now given to collective bargaining led to the nation-wide signing of collective contracts for the first time in the country's history; similarly, the government protection and encouragement given to union organizing led to an enormous growth in trade union membership, which grew from about one to five million in about a year. Labor's strength was increased also by a reunification of the Communist and non-Communist labor confederations. Other legislation was important too. Steps were taken to nationalize the armaments and aviation industry; the fascist armed leagues were, at least in theory, dissolved; the Bank of France was reorganized and placed under government control to break the power of the "two hundred families." Machinery was established for the arbitration of labor disputes. Aid was given to farmers through price fixing and government purchases of wheat. As in the United States all these measures aimed at both recovery and reform; Blum spoke openly of his program as a "French New Deal." Like the American program, it was intended to create mass purchasing power, absorb the unemployed, and stimulate industry. No large-scale public works program was launched, however, nor was "deficit financing" resorted to; and the Blum government was too dependent on its middle class Radical Socialist allies to introduce any fundamental, or "structural," reforms. Still, French workers and the little man took heart: the "social republic" again seemed a possibility. But French conservatives, and the quasi-fascists to their Right, cried revolution; they uttered dark predictions that a French Lenin would follow Blum. They did not conceal their sullen resentment at what had come to pass: the fate of Catholic France was in the hands of a Leftist, a Socialist, and a Jew. Even salvation by a warrior from outside the country, one who had demonstrated his anti-Bolshevism, would be preferable. They envied the protection given to established interests by Mussolini; and there were those who muttered "better Hitler than Léon Blum"; they plotted and awaited their opportunity.

In all truth the Popular Front reform program, long overdue as it was, came to France at a time when the sands were rapidly running out. While France had a forty-hour week, German arms plants were operating at full capacity. In the shadow of Nazi remilitarization a rearmament program had to be undertaken at the very same time as reform; even moderates argued that the country could not afford both. Opposition from many quarters hindered success. French employers balked at cooperating in the new reforms and tried to pass on rising production costs to the consumer. Labor was disgruntled at the rise in prices that canceled out their wage gains. Both employers and labor applied the forty-hour week in such a manner that plants were shut down for two days a week instead of operating in shifts, as the law had intended. Nothing could check the flight of gold from the country. Industrial production hardly rose; even in 1938, when it had shown substantial recovery in other countries, it was only five per cent higher in France than at the depth

of the depression. The Communists attacked the Blum government for refusing aid to the hard-pressed Spanish Popular Front government across the
Pyrenees; Blum, following the lead of Britain and fearing involvement, resisted. In 1937, after a year in office, the Blum government was overthrown
by the Senate, which refused to grant it emergency financial powers. The
Popular Front coalition rapidly disintegrated. By mid-1938 the Radical Socialists had abandoned their allies on the Left, and under Edouard Daladier
formed a conservative ministry, whose attention was increasingly occupied by
the international crisis. Little remained of the Popular Front, or indeed of
the strength of labor, which declined rapidly and exhausted itself further by
a general strike in 1938 in protest against nullification of the forty-hour week;
the strike was broken by the government and was followed by retaliatory
legal measures. For the French workingman, 1936 had gone the way of other
"great years"; the comfortable classes had been thrown into panic by the
social turmoil; internal division and class hatreds had grown sharper. Yet the
French democracy, the Third Republic itself, had been successfully preserved
and its domestic enemies repulsed, at least for a time.

103. Totalitarianism: Italian Fascism

Though they shade into each other imperceptibly, it is well to distinguish dictatorship from totalitarianism. Dictatorship, an old phenomenon
in history, has commonly been regarded as a mere expedient, designed for
emergencies, and believed to be temporary; at most, it is a theory of government. Totalitarianism, as it arose after the World War, was not merely a
theory of government but a theory of life and of human nature. It claimed to
be no expedient, but a permanent form of society and civilization, and so far
as it appealed to emergency for justification, it regarded life itself as an everlasting emergency. Let us first review the pertinent events in Italy and Germany, return next to the general ideas of totalitarianism, and then, in the
final section of the chapter, trace the story of totalitarian foreign aggression
and crises which in 1939 again led to a world war.

The belief widely held in the 1920's, that democracy was generally advancing, was not deeply disturbed by the failure of Russia or Turkey or China
to develop effective parliaments or liberal institutions. These were backward
countries, in the throes of revolution; some day, when conditions quieted
down, it could be supposed, they would move forward to democracy as known
in the West. The first jarring exception to the apparent victory of democracy
was furnished by Italy, a country that was part and parcel of civilized Europe,
one which since 1861 had accepted parliamentary liberalism, but where, as
early as 1922, Benito Mussolini seized control of the government and proclaimed *Fascismo*.

Mussolini, born in 1883, the son of a blacksmith, was a fiery and pug-
nacious character, who before the war had followed the career of professional

revolutionary, left-wing socialist, and radical journalist. He had read and digested such works as Sorel's *Reflections on Violence* and Nietzsche's writings.[7] During the war he turned intensely nationalist, clamored for intervention on the side of the Allies, and demanded the conquest from Austria of *Italia irredenta*, the "unredeemed" Italian lands to the north and across the Adriatic. In the war he rose to the rank of corporal. In March 1919 he organized, mainly from demobilized and restless ex-soldiers, his first fighting band or *Fascio di Combattimento*. *Fascio* meant a bunch or bundle, as of sticks; it called to mind the Latin *fasces*, or bundles of rods, carried by the lictors in ancient Rome as a symbol of state power—for Mussolini loved to conjure up ancient glories.

In 1919 Italian glories were dim. Italy had entered the war on the side of the Allies quite frankly for territorial and colonial spoils; the secret treaty of London in 1915 promised the Italians certain Austrian lands and a share in German and Turkish possessions. During the war Italian arms did not especially shine; Italian troops were routed at Caporetto in 1917. Yet Italy lost over six hundred thousand lives in the war, and the Italian delegates came to the peace conference confident that their sacrifices would be recognized and their territorial aspirations satisfied. They were rapidly disappointed. Wilson refused to honor the provisions of the London secret treaty and other demands of the Italians. Britain and France displayed no eagerness to side with Italy. The Italians received some of the Austrian territories promised to them, but they were given no part of the former German or Turkish possessions as mandates.

After the war Italy, like other countries, suffered from the burden of wartime debt and from acute post-war depression and unemployment. Social unrest spread. In the countryside land seizures took place, not in any significant proportions but enough to spread concern among landowners; tenant farmers refused to pay rents; peasants burned crops and destroyed livestock. In the cities great strikes broke out in heavy industry and in such vital services as transportation. Some of the strikes turned into sit-down strikes, the workers refusing to leave the plants; demands were raised even for worker control of the factories. Moderate socialist and labor leaders disavowed all such extremism, but left-wing socialists who, as elsewhere, had turned communist and joined the Third International, fanned the existing discontents. Meanwhile, armed bands of young men, most prominent of whom were the Blackshirts or Fascists, brawled with communists and ordinary workingmen in the streets. By the late summer of 1920 the strikes and the agrarian unrest had subsided, although violence in the streets persisted.

During the months of turmoil the government itself refrained from any bold action. The Italian parliamentary system in the pre-war years had never functioned impressively nor commanded widespread esteem; now respect for parliament and the weak, shifting post-war coalition ministries sank even lower. In 1919 the first post-war election had been held, the first election

[7] See pp. 602, 610–11.

in Italy under conditions of universal manhood suffrage and proportional representation. The Socialists and a new Catholic Popular, or Christian Socialist, party made an impressive showing. In 1921, in the wake of the post-war disturbances, new elections were held. Liberals and democrats, moderate socialists, and the Catholic Popular party were all returned in large numbers. Mussolini's Fascist movement won thirty-five of the five-hundred-odd seats. Despite this less than impressive showing (the best ever made by the Fascists in a totally free election), the Fascist ranks had been swelling, in the backwash, as it were, of the post-war unrest. Although the social agitation had died down, burning itself out on its own, and there had in actuality never been any real threat of a soviet-style revolution, the propertied classes had gone through a great fright; they found comfort in the Fascist movement and were not unwilling to lend it financial support. Mussolini and the Fascists had at first gone along with the radical tide; they had not disapproved the factory seizures; they had inveighed against plutocracy and war profiteers, and called for a high levy on capital and profits. But Mussolini, never one to sacrifice opportunity to save principles or doctrine, had soon come forward with his Fascists as the upholders of national law and order, and hence property; he pledged battle "against the forces dissolving victory and nation." The propertied interests gave financial aid to the self-styled bulwark against Bolshevism; patriots and nationalists of all classes rallied to it; and the lower middle class, pinched by economic inflation and, as elsewhere, unable to find protection or solace in labor unions or socialist movements, joined too. The black-shirted upholders of national order meanwhile proceeded methodically to administer beatings (and doses of castor oil) to communists and alleged communists, to socialists and Christian socialists, and to ordinary persons who did not support them; nor did they refrain from arson and murder. Vigilante squadrons, the *squadristi*, broke up strikes, demolished labor union headquarters, and drove from office duly elected socialist and communist mayors and town officials. Mussolini reinforced his claim as paladin of law, authority, and order by declaring his loyalty to King and Church; a few years earlier he had been a rabid republican and anti-clerical.

In October 1922 took place the "March on Rome." The Blackshirts mobilized for a threatened coup and began to converge from various directions on the capital; Mussolini remained at a safe distance in Milan. The liberal-democratic coalition cabinet had viewed the events of the past two years with disapproval but at the same time with the undeniable satisfaction that the Blackshirts were serving something of a useful national purpose by suppressing trouble makers on the left. Now they made belated but ineffectual gestures to save the situation by an effort to have martial law declared; the king refused to approve. The cabinet resigned and Mussolini was named premier. It was all quite legal, or almost so. Indeed Italy was still in form a constitutional and parliamentary government. Mussolini even created a coalition ministry and received from parliament no more than a year's grant of full emergency powers to restore order and introduce reforms.

But soon it was clear in whose hands power rested. Before the expiration of his emergency powers Mussolini forced through Parliament a law providing that any party securing the largest number of votes in an election should automatically receive two-thirds of the seats in the legislature. This was Mussolini's solution to the instability of coalitions and blocs in parliamentary governments like those of Italy and France, and indeed most other Continental democracies, where a single party hardly ever enjoys a majority. The two-thirds law was not even necessary. In the 1924 elections, aided by government control of the electoral machinery and use of the *squadristi*, but still in relatively uncontrolled elections in which some twenty different opposition parties appeared, the Fascists received well over three-fifths of the total vote. The Fascist party was in overwhelming control of the Chamber.

Within a few years after 1924 Mussolini reduced the Italian parliament to a nonentity, curtailed universal suffrage, put the press under censorship, destroyed the labor unions and deprived labor of the right to strike, and abolished all other political parties. A secret police was established and special tribunals set up to try opponents of the regime; a new official Fascist militia replaced the *squadristi*—it continued to employ many of the old methods.

Fascism in the 1920's was an innovation which the rest of the world was slow to understand. In 1924 (when dissenters were still allowed in the parliament) the socialist deputy Matteotti publicly exposed hundreds of cases of armed Fascist violence, and of fraud and chicanery in elections. He was soon murdered by Fascists. For a government in civilized Europe to dispose of its critics by assassination was something of a novelty. Mussolini strutted, stuck out his jaw, and glared ferociously; he jumped through flaming hoops to show his virility, and had his chief subordinates do likewise; to the rest of Europe this seemed an odd way of demonstrating fitness for public office. He denounced democracy as historically outmoded, and declared that it accentuated class struggle, split people into countless minority parties, and led to selfishness, futility, evasion, and empty talk. In place of democracy he preached the need of vigorous action, under a strong leader; he himself took the title of Leader or *Duce*. He denounced liberalism, free trade, *laissez-faire*, and capitalism, along with Marxism, materialism, socialism, and class-consciousness which he said were the evil offspring of liberal and capitalistic society. In their place he preached national solidarity and state-management of economic affairs, under the same Leader's far-seeing and audacious vision. And in fact Mussolini seemed to bring a kind of efficiency to easy-going Italy; as the saying went, at least he made the trains run on time.

Mussolini introduced, at least in theory, the syndical, or corporative state. This had been discussed in both left- and right-wing circles for many years. Left-wing syndicalism, especially before the First World War, looked to revolutionary labor unions to expropriate the owners of industry and then to assume the direction of political and economic life. A more conservative syndicalism was endorsed and encouraged by the Catholic Church, with which, as has been noted in a previous chapter, Mussolini made his peace with the signing of the Lateran accord in 1929.[8] The latter type looked nostalgically toward a revival of the medieval gilds, or "corporations," in which master and journeymen, employer and employees, had labored side by side in a golden age of collaboration and social peace. The Fascist corporative system really resembled neither, because in it the hand of the state was writ large, something which none of the older corporative doctrines had anticipated. It went through a number of complicated stages, but as it finally emerged by the 1930's it provided for the division of all economic life into twenty-two major areas, for each of which a "corporation" was established. In each corporation representatives of labor, employers, and government (or party) exercised the authority to determine working conditions, wages, prices, and industrial policies; and in a national council these representatives were supposed jointly to devise plans for Italy's economic self-sufficiency. In each case the role of government was decisive and the whole structure was under the jurisdiction of Mussolini's Minister of Corporations. As a final step, these corporative economic chambers were integrated into the government proper so that in 1938 the old Chamber of Deputies was superseded by a Chamber of Fasci and Corporations representing the corporations and the Fascist party, its members selected by the government and not subject to popular ratification.

None of this was democratic, but this was an improvement over democracy, the Fascists asserted. A legislature in an advanced economic society, they said, should be an economic parliament; it should represent not political parties and geographical constituencies but economic occupations. Organization along such lines would do away with the anarchy and class conflict engendered by free capitalism, which only sap the strength of the national state. Real authority in any event rested with the government—the Head of the Government, who settled most matters by decree. In point of fact, social unrest and class conflict were "ended," not by the corporative system as such, but by the prohibition of strikes and lockouts and the abolition of independent labor unions. The corporative system represented the most extreme form of state control over economic life within a framework of private enterprise and a relatively capitalistic economy, that is, one in which ownership rested in private hands. It was the Fascist answer to western-style democracy and to Soviet proletarian dictatorship. Fascism, said Mussolini, is the "dictatorship of the State over many classes cooperating."

When the depression struck, none of Italy's economic controls availed very much. Mussolini was eager to lay upon the world depression the blame for Italy's continuing economic ills. He turned to a vigorous program of public works and to increasing economic self-sufficiency. A "battle of wheat" was launched as a campaign to increase food production; progress was made in reclaiming swamp areas in central Italy and in developing hydroelectric power as a substitute for the coal which Italy lacked. Throughout the Fascist era no fundamental reform took place in the position of the peasants. The

ᴠᴠᴠᴠᴠᴠᴠᴠᴠᴠᴠᴠᴠᴠ

[8] See p. 605.

existing structure of society, which in Italy meant social extremes of wealth and poverty, remained unaltered. Fascism failed to provide either the economic security or the material well-being for which it had demanded the sacrifice of individual freedom. But it undeniably substituted a widespread psychological exhilaration, a feeling that Italy was undergoing a heroic national revival; and after 1935 to support that feeling Mussolini turned increasingly to military and imperialist adventures.

Fascism came to be regarded in other countries as a possible alternative to democratic or parliamentary government, as an actual corrective to troubles whose reality no one could deny. All communists hated it, and so did all socialists, labor leaders, moderate leftists, and idealistic liberals; wealthier or established people, because of fear of Bolshevism, made more allowances in its favor. In east-European countries, often highly nationalistic, or influenced by disgruntled landowners, or simply unused to settling questions by majority vote, Fascism made a considerable appeal. In the Latin countries, in Spain, Portugal, and France, Mussolini's corporative state found champions and admirers. Sometimes, in Europe and elsewhere, intellectuals spun refined respectable theories about the new order of discipline and authority, forgetting how Mussolini himself with unusual candor had written, "Fascism was not the nursling of a doctrine worked out beforehand with detailed elaboration; it was born of the need for action."

104. Totalitarianism: Germany's Third Reich

It was in Germany that Mussolini found his aptest pupil. Born in Austria in 1889, Adolf Hitler was too young to have done much before the war. He was not an intellectual, like the pre-war journalist Mussolini. He was never a socialist, but he fell into a restless and somewhat ignorant type of radicalism. Son of a small government employee, orphaned at an early age, he came at nineteen to the great metropolis of Vienna, without friends, money, or means of making a living, often going hungry, or sleeping in what Americans would call flop-houses, a good example of uprooted humanity which the preceding half-century had thrown pell-mell into huge industrial cities. The young Hitler did not like what he saw in Vienna: neither the trappings of the Hapsburg court, nor the noblemen of eastern Europe who rode by in their carriages, nor the mixed nationalities of the Danubian empire, nor the Vienna workingman's attachment to international Marxism, nor above all the Jews, who thanks to a century of liberal influences had become assimilated to the German culture, and now occupied many distinguished positions in business, law, medicine, and journalism in the city. He became exceedingly race-conscious, like many others in many countries at the time,[9] but to the youthful Hitler it gave a special satisfaction to think of himself as a

[9] See pp. 599, 600, 606, 622, 664, 765.

pure German of the good old German stock. It has often been observed that pride in race is the last consolation of those who have little else to be proud of. Hitler became violently anti-Semitic, and he also disliked aristocracy, capitalism, socialism, cosmopolitanism, internationalism, and "hybridization."

His aversion for Austria led him to move to the south German state of Bavaria in 1912. Here he followed such trades as carpentry and house-painting. In the war he served in the German army. Like Mussolini, he rose no further than corporal. It is probable that in the more democratic American army both Hitler and Mussolini, who were both of lower middle-class families, would have received commissions and enjoyed promotion. For Hitler, as for Mussolini, and for countless others, the war was a thrilling, noble, and liberating experience. The average man, in modern society, led a pretty dull existence. Peace, for many, was a drab routine from which war was an exciting emancipation. Human atoms, floating in an impersonal and unfriendly world, they were stirred by the nationalism which the war aroused into a sense of belonging to, believing in, fighting for something greater than themselves, but which was yet their own. When peace returned, they felt a moral letdown.

After the war the demobilized Hitler, with no future, and no place in society to which to return, drifted back to Bavaria. Bavaria in 1919 was a main focus of the communist offensive in central Europe; a Bavarian Soviet Republic even existed for about three weeks, until crushed by the predominantly Social Democratic German federal government. But the Communist threat made Bavaria a busy center of all kinds of counter-revolutionary agitation—anti-communist, anti-socialist, anti-republican, and anti-democratic. A transposition in fact occurred after the World War, by which south Germany, always in the past more liberal than the north, became the seat of a disgruntled illiberalism, while Prussia became the main pillar of German democracy because of the large working-class population in Berlin and the Ruhr. Bavaria in particular swarmed with secret societies led by discontented army officers or others who fitted with difficulty into the new regime. One tiny group pretentiously called itself the German Workers' Party, and in this "party," in 1919, Adolf Hitler received membership card number seven. In 1920 it renamed itself the National Socialist German Workers' Party, though Hitler at this time, it is said, would have preferred the term Social Revolutionary. Thus were born the Nazis, so called from the Germany way of pronouncing the first two syllables of *National*.

In earlier pages we have noted the beginnings of the Weimar republic and the burdens it was compelled to bear from the start—the Versailles peace, reparations, the catastrophic inflation of 1923.[10] Something has been said also of the failure of the republicans to inaugurate the kind of deep social changes that might have democratized the political and social structure of German society and thereby strengthened republican forces. For five years

wwwwwwwwwwwww

[10] See pp. 760–2.

after the war, violence remained sporadic in Germany. Communist agitation continued; but more dangerous, because they attracted more sympathy among the Germans, were the maneuvers of monarchist and anti-republican organizations, which maintained armed bands and threatened uprisings like the Kapp *Putsch* of 1920.[11] One such private "army" was the Brownshirts or Storm Troopers maintained by the Nazis. Such bands even resorted to assassination. Thus Walter Rathenau was murdered in 1922; he had organized German production during the war, and in 1922 he was foreign minister, but he had democratic and internationalist inclinations—and was a Jew. Another victim was Matthias Erzberger, a leading moderate politician of the Catholic Center party—he had helped "betray" the army by signing the armistice.

In 1923, when reparations payments were not forthcoming, the French army occupied the Ruhr. A clamor of national indignation swept over Germany. Hitler and the National Socialists, who since 1919 had obtained a considerable following, denounced the Weimar government for shameful submission to the French. They judged the moment opportune for seizing power, and at the end of 1923, in imitation of Mussolini's march on Rome the year before, the Brownshirts staged the "beer-hall *Putsch*" in Munich. Hitler jumped on the platform, fired a revolver at the ceiling and shouted that the "national revolution has broken out." But the police suppressed the disturbance, and Hitler was sentenced to five years in prison. He was released after a year, since the Weimar democrats believed in freedom of speech. In prison he wrote his book, *Mein Kampf* or *My Struggle*, a turbid stream of personal recollection, racialism, nationalism, collectivism, theories of history, Jew-baiting, and political comment. The former corporal was not alone in his ideas; no less a person than General Ludendorff, who had distinguished himself in the war,[12] and after the war became one of the most grotesquely unbalanced of the old officer class, gave his warm support to Hitler and even took part in the beer-hall *Putsch*.

Beginning in 1924, with the French out of the Ruhr, reparations adjusted, a new and stable currency adopted, and loans from foreign countries, mainly America, Germany began to enjoy an amazing economic revival. National Socialism lost its appeal, the party lost members, Hitler was regarded as a charlatan and his followers as a lunatic fringe. All seemed quiet. Then came the great depression in 1929. Adolf Hitler, who without the depression might have faded out of history, was made by the circumstances attending the depression in Germany into a figure of Napoleonic proportions.

No country suffered more than Germany from the world-wide economic collapse. Foreign loans abruptly ceased or were recalled. Factories ground to a halt. There were six million unemployed. The middle class had not really recovered from the great inflation of 1923;[13] when struck again, after so brief a respite, they lost all faith in the economic system and in its

[11] See p. 759.
[12] See pp. 687–8.
[13] See pp. 761–2.

future. The communist vote steadily mounted; the great middling masses, who saw in communism their own death warrant, and who are extremely numerous in any highly developed society, looked about desperately for someone to save them from Bolshevism. The depression also stirred up the universal German loathing for the treaty of Versailles. Many Germans explained the ruin of Germany by the post-war treatment it had received from the Allies—the constriction of its frontiers, the loss of its colonies, markets, shipping and foreign investments, the colossal demand for reparations, the occupation of the Ruhr, the inflation, and much else.

Any people in such a trap would have been bewildered and resentful. But the way out chosen by the Germans was perhaps distinctively German, arising from deeper attitudes formed by German experience in the past centuries. Democracy—the agreement to obtain and accept majority verdicts, to discuss and compromise, to adjust conflicting interests without wholly satisfying or wholly crushing either side—was hard enough to maintain in any country in a true crisis. In Germany democracy was itself an innovation, which had yet to prove its value, which could easily be called un-German, an artificial and imported doctrine, or even a foreign system foisted upon Germany by the victors in the late war.

Hitler inflamed all such feelings by his propaganda. He denounced the treaty of Versailles as a national humiliation. He denounced the Weimar democracy for producing class struggle, division, weakness and wordy futility. He called for "true" democracy in a vast and vital stirring of the people, or *Volk*, behind a Leader who was a man of action. He declared that Germans, pure Germans, must rely only on themselves. He inveighed against Marxists, Bolsheviks, communists, and socialists, throwing them all together in a deliberate beclouding of the issues; but he claimed to favor the right kind of socialism for the little man, *i.e.*, the doctrine of the National Socialist German Workers' Party. He ranted against unearned incomes, war profits, the power of the great trusts and chain stores, land speculators, interest slavery, and unfair taxes. Above all, he denounced the Jews. Jews, like others, were found in all political camps. To the Left, Jewish capitalists were anathema. To the Right, Jewish revolutionaries were a horror. In anti-Semitism Hitler found a lowest common denominator upon which to appeal to all parties and classes. The thoughtless and the ignorant, who comprehended nothing of economics or social forces, found it easy enough to identify a Jew; and on being told that the Jews caused the country's troubles, they experienced a new sense of political understanding. At the same time the Jews were a small minority (only 600,000 in all Germany), so that in an age of mass politics it was safe enough to antagonize them.

In the election of 1930 the Nazis won 107 seats in the Reichstag; in 1928 they had won only twelve. The Communist representation rose from 54 to 77. The depression went on, hopelessness and desperation became deeper. Frequent elections had to be held because no workable majority was possible in the Reichstag; none of the elections helped break the deadlock. In July 1932 the Nazis won 230 seats, and were now by far the largest single party, though because of the multiplicity of parties they fell well short of a majority. In another election, in November 1932, the Nazis, though still well out in front, showed some loss of strength, dropping to 196 seats. The Communist vote had risen progressively to a peak of 100 in November 1932.

After the relative setback of November 1932 Hitler feared that his moment was passing. But certain conservative, nationalist, and anti-republican elements—old aristocrats, Junker landowners, army officers, Rhineland steel magnates and other industrialists—had conceived the idea that Hitler could be useful to them. From such sources came a portion of Nazi funds. This group of big men, mainly of the small Nationalist party, imagined that they would be able to control Hitler, and hence control the wave of mass discontent of which in such large measure he had made himself the leader; they were little disturbed by his anti-capitalist program.

Since 1930 there had been a succession of chancellors, who had been governing largely by decree under emergency constitutional powers. Now when General von Schleicher and his cabinet resigned, the Nationalist leaders prevailed upon President Hindenburg to name Hitler chancellor of a coalition cabinet. On January 30, 1933, by entirely legal means, Adolf Hitler became chancellor (or prime minister) of the German republic; other positions in the new cabinet were occupied by the Nationalists, with whom the Nazis were to share the power. But to share power was not their aim. Hitler called for another election. A week before election day the Reichstag building caught fire. The Nazis, who had set the fire themselves, blamed it on the communists. They raised up a terrific Red scare, suspended freedom of speech and press, and set loose the Brownshirts to bully the voters. Even so, in the election, the last election in fifteen years in which Germans were to enjoy even a semblance of freedom, the Nazis won only 44 per cent of the vote. Hitler, however, trumpeting a national emergency, was voted dictatorial powers by a pliant Reichstag from which the Communist deputies had been excluded. The Nazi Revolution now began.

Hitler called his new order the Third Reich. He declared that, following on the First Reich or Holy Roman Empire, and the Second Reich or empire founded by Bismarck, the Third Reich carried on the long process of true-German history, of which, he said, it was the organic outgrowth and natural culmination. The Third Reich, he prophesied, would last a thousand years.

Like Mussolini, Hitler took the title of Leader, or, in German, the *Führer*. He claimed to represent the absolute sovereignty of the German People. Jews were considered un-German. Democracy, parliamentarianism, and liberalism were stigmatized as "Western" and together with communism labeled as "Jewish." The new "racial science," whose high priest was Alfred Rosenberg, classified Jews as non-Aryan,[14] and included as Jewish anyone who had had one Jewish grandparent. The Nuremberg laws of 1935 deprived Jews of all citizenship rights and forbade intermarriage between Jews and non-

[14] See note p. 4.

Jews. Jews under the Third Reich were beaten up, hounded, driven from public office, ruined in private business, fined as a community, put to death, or allowed to flee the country after being stripped of all their possessions. The anti-Semitism of some fanatics descended to positive bestiality; it foreshadowed the wartime physical extermination of millions of German and East-European Jewry.

The new order was thought of as absolutely solid, or monolithic, like one huge single slab of rock in which no particle had any separate structure. Germany ceased to be federal; the old states such as Prussia and Bavaria were abolished, so that the historic process of German unification was carried forward. All political parties except the National Socialists were destroyed. The National Socialist party was itself violently purged in 1934, when a great many of the old Brownshirt leaders, those who represented the more social-revolutionary wing of the movement, were accused of plotting against Hitler and were summarily put to death. A secret political police, the Gestapo (*Geheime Staatspolizei*), together with People's Courts, and a system of permanent concentration camps in which thousands were detained without trial or sentence, suppressed all ideas at variance with the Leader's. Law itself was defined as the will of the German People operating in the interests of the Nazi state. Churches both Protestant and Catholic were "coordinated" with the new regime; their clergy were forbidden to criticize its activities, international religious connections were discountenanced, and efforts were made to keep children out of religious schools. The government encouraged anti-Christian pagan movements, in worship of the old Teutonic gods, but nothing was sponsored so much as worship of Nazism and its Führer. A Nazi Youth Movement indoctrinated the rising generation in the new concepts. Schools and universities became agencies of propaganda.

Labor unions also were "coordinated": they were replaced by a National Labor Front. Strikes were forbidden. Under the "leadership principle" employers were set up as small-scale Führers in their factories and industries, and given extensive control subject to the closest government supervision. An extensive public works program was launched, reforestation and swamp-drainage projects were organized, housing and super-highways were built. A vast rearmament program absorbed the unemployed and within a short time unemployment had significantly declined. Even under Nazi statistics labor's share in the national income was reduced, but workingmen had jobs; and an organization called Strength through Joy attended to the needs of people with small incomes, providing entertainment, vacations, and travel for many who could never otherwise afford them.

The government assumed increasing controls over industry, while leaving ownership in private hands. In 1936 it adopted a Four-Year Plan of economic development under the supervision of Hermann Göring. All countries after the great depression tended to economic nationalism, but Nazi Germany set up the goal of autarchy and self-sufficiency—absolute independence from foreign trade. German chemists developed artificial rubber, plastics, synthetic textiles, and many other substitute products to enable the country to do without raw materials imported from overseas. Germany took advantage of its position as the chief market on which East Europeans were dependent. Mixing political threats with ordinary business, the Nazis bartered for Polish wheat, Hungarian lumber, or Rumanian oil, often giving in return such articles as it was convenient for Germany to dispose of, rather than those that the east Europeans wanted. For Europe as a whole one of the basic economic problems, especially after the World War, was that while the Continent was economically a unit dependent on exchange between diverse regions, politically it was cut to pieces by tariff restrictions, currency differences and hot-house industries artificially nurtured by nationalist ambition. The Nazis claimed to have a solution for this problem in a network of bilateral trade agreements assuring all neighboring peoples an outlet for their products. But it was a solution in which Germans were to be the most industrial, most advanced, most powerful and most wealthy, and other Europeans relegated to permanently inferior status. And what could not be accomplished under trade agreements and economic penetration could be accomplished by conquest and war. Within a few years after 1933 the Nazi Revolution had turned Germany into a huge disciplined war machine, its internal foes liquidated or silenced, its munitions plants going full blast, its mesmerized masses roaring their approval in giant demonstrations, ready to follow the Führer in storming new Valkyrian heights. "Today Germany," went an ominous Nazi phrase, "tomorrow the whole world."

TOTALITARIANISM: SOME ORIGINS AND CONSEQUENCES

Totalitarianism was a many-sided thing. It had appeared first with the Bolshevik Revolution, for in the denial of individual liberty the Soviet regime did not differ from the most extreme anti-Soviet or fascist totalitarianism as manifested in Germany. There were at first important differences in principle. Theoretically, the proletarian dictatorship was temporary; it did not glorify the individual Leader-Hero; and it was not nationalistic, for it rested on a principle of world-wide class struggle in all nations alike. It adopted a democratic sounding constitution and paid at least lip service to the idea of a bill of rights. Its constitution officially condemned racism, and it did not deliberately and consciously cultivate an ethics of war and violence. But as time passed, Soviet totalitarianism became harder to distinguish from others. The Soviet dictatorship and one-party state seemed as permanent as any political system; the hollowness of the constitution and bill of rights became more apparent; a leader cult developed around the person of Stalin; and the emphasis became more nationalistic, falling less on the workers of the world and more on the glories of the Soviet Fatherland.

Totalitarianism, as distinct from mere dictatorship, though it appeared rather suddenly after the First World War, was no historic freak. It was an outgrowth of a good deal of development in the past. The state was an institution that had continuously acquired new powers ever since the Middle

Ages; step by step, since feudal times, it had assumed jurisdiction over law courts and men at arms, imposed taxes, regulated churches, guided economic policy, operated school systems, and devised schemes of public welfare. The First World War had continued and advanced the process.[15] The twentieth-century totalitarian state, mammoth and monolithic, claiming an absolute domination over every department of life, now carried this old development of state sovereignty to a new extreme. For centuries, for example, the state had clashed with the church; from Philip the Fair of France in 1303, down through Henry VIII, the enlightened despots, the French Revolutionaries, Napoleon, Mazzini, Bismarck, the list was a long one of those who had come into conflict with the Christian churches. The twentieth-century dictators did the same. In addition, however, they were in most cases not merely anti-clerical but explicitly anti-Christian, offering, or rather imposing, a "total" philosophy of life.

This new philosophy drew heavily upon a historic nationalism which it greatly exaggerated. It derived in part from the organic theory of society, which held that society (or the nation or state) was a kind of living organism within which the individual person was but a single cell. The individual, in this theory, had no independent existence; he received life itself, and all his ideas, from the society, people, nation, or culture into which he was born and by which he was nurtured. In Marxism, the absolute subordination of the individual to his class came to much the same thing. The individual was a microscopic cell, meaningless outside the social body. He was a little particle within a monolithic slab. He was but clay to be molded by the imprint of his group. It made little sense, given such theories, to speak of the individual's "reason" or "freedom," or to allow individuals to have their own opinions (which were formed for them by environment), or to count up individual opinions to obtain a merely numerical majority. Valid ideas were those of the group as a whole, of the people or nation (or, in Marxism, the class) as a solid block. Even science was a product of specific societies: there was a "Nazi science" which was bound to differ in its conclusions from democratic, bourgeois, Western, or "Jewish" science; and for the Soviets there was a Soviet science, consistent with dialectical materialism, and better equipped to see the truth than the decadent bourgeois, capitalistic or "fascist" science of the non-Soviet world. All art, too—music, painting, poetry, fiction, architecture, sculpture—was good art in so far as it expressed the society or nationality in which it grew. The avowed philosophy of totalitarian regimes (like much modern thought) was basically subjective. Whether an idea was held to be true depended on whose idea it was. Ideas of truth, or beauty, or right were not supposed to correspond to any outer or objective reality; they had only to correspond to the inner nature, interests, or point of view of the people, nation, society, or class that entertained such ideas. The older concepts of reason, natural law, natural right, and the ultimate alikeness of all mankind, or

[15] See pp. 689–94.

of a common path of all mankind in one course of progress, disappeared.[16]

The totalitarian regimes did not simply declare, as a dry finding of social science, that peoples' ideas were shaped by environment. They set about shaping them actively. Propaganda became a principal branch of government. Propaganda was hardly new; but in the past, and still in the democratic countries, it had been a piecemeal affair, urging the public to accept this or that political party, or to buy this or that brand of coffee. Now, like all else, it became "total." Propaganda was monopolized by the state, and it demanded faith in a whole view of life and in every detail of this co-ordinated whole. Formerly the control of books and newspapers had been mainly negative; under Napoleon or Metternich, for example, censors had forbidden statements on particular subjects, events or persons. Now, in totalitarian countries, control of the press became frighteningly positive. The government manufactured thought. It manipulated opinion. It re-wrote history. Writers were required to present whole ideologies, and books, newspapers, magazines, and the radio diffused an endless and overwhelming cloud of words. Loudspeakers blared in the streets, gigantic blown-up photographs of the Leader looked down in public places. The propaganda experts were sometimes fanatics; but often they were cynics like Dr. Goebbels in Germany, too intelligent to be duped by the rubbish with which they duped their country.

The very idea of truth evaporated. No norm of human utterance remained except political expediency—the wishes and self-interest of the men in power. No one could learn anything except what the government wanted him to know. No one could escape the omnipresent official doctrine, the insidious penetration of the very recesses of his mind by ideas planted by outsiders for their own purposes. People came to accept, and even to believe, the most extravagant statements when they were endlessly repeated, year after year. Barred from all independent sources of information, having no means by which any official allegation could be tested, the peoples of totalitarian countries became increasingly in fact, and not merely in sociological theory, incapable of the use of reason.

Racialism, more characteristic of Nazi Germany than of totalitarianism in general, was a further exaggeration, or degradation, of older ideas of nationalism and national solidarity. It defined the nation in a tribal sense, as a biological entity, a group of persons possessing the same physical ancestry and the same or similar physical characteristics. Anti-Semitism was the most venomous form of racialism in Europe. While a latent hostility to Jews had always been present in the Christian world, modern anti-Semitism had little to do with Christianity. It arose in part from the fact that, in the nineteenth century, with the general removal of religious disabilities, the Jews entered into general society and many of them achieved positions of prominence, and nowhere more so than in Germany, so that from the point of view of any individual non-Jew they could be represented as dangerous competitors in busi-

---

[16] See pp. 281–4, 287–8, 290, 299, 555–7.

ness or the professions. But most of all, anti-Semitism was inflamed by propagandists who wished people to feel their supposed racial purity more keenly, or to forget the deeper problems of society that could best be corrected by raising and stabilizing the incomes of the depressed classes.

For totalitarianism was an escape from the realities of class conflict. It was a way of pretending that differences between rich and poor were of minor importance. Typically, a totalitarian regime came into power by stirring up class fears, then remained in power, and represented itself as indispensable, by declaring that it had settled the class problem. Thus Mussolini, Hitler, and certain lesser dictators, before seizing office, pointed alarmingly to the dark menace of Bolshevism; and, once in power, declared that all classes stood shoulder to shoulder in slab-like solidarity behind the Leader. Nor were events in Russia altogether different. The Bolsheviks in 1917, armed with the ideas of Karl Marx, aroused the workers against capitalists, landlords, middle-class people, and rich peasants; then, once in power, and after extensive liquidations, they declared that the classless society had arrived, that no true social classes any longer existed, and that all Soviet citizens stood solidly behind a regime from which, they said, all good citizens benefited equally. Only the democracies admitted that they suffered from internal class problems, from maladjustments between rich and poor or between favored and unfavored groups in society.

The dictatorships blamed their troubles on forces outside the country. They accused dissatisfied persons of conspiring with foreigners or refugees— with being the tools of Trotskyism, imperialism, or international Jewry. Or they talked of the struggle between rich nations and poor nations, the "have" and the "have-not" countries, and thus transformed the problem of poverty into an international struggle. In the distinction between "have" and "have-not" countries there was, of course, more than a grain of truth; in more old-fashioned language some countries (in fact the European democracies, plus the United States and the British Dominions of the 1930's) had "progressed" farther than others. It is probable that any propaganda is more effective if partly true. But when the totalitarians blamed their troubles on other countries, and transformed the conflict between "have" and "have-not" into a struggle between nations, they gave the impression that war might be a solution for social ills.

Violence, the acceptance and even glorification of violence, was indeed the characteristic most clearly distinguishing the totalitarian from the democratic systems. We have seen how a cult of violence, or belief that struggle was beneficial, had arisen before the First World War.[17] The war itself habituated people to violence and direct action. Lenin and his followers showed how a small group could seize the helm of state under revolutionary or chaotic conditions. Mussolini in 1922 taught the same lesson, with further refinements; for the Italy in which he seized power was not at war, and it was merely the threat or possibility of revolution, not revolution itself, that pro-

᠕᠕᠕᠕᠕᠕᠕᠕᠕᠕᠕᠕

[17] See pp. 610–11.

vided him with his opportunity. In the 1920's, for the first time since the seventeenth century, some of the most civilized parts of Europe, in time of peace, saw private armies marching about the country, bands of uniformed and organized ruffians, Blackshirts or Brownshirts, who manhandled, abused and even killed law-abiding citizens with impunity. Nor would anyone in the 1920's have believed that, by the 1930's, Europe would see the re-introduction of torture.

The very ethics of totalitarianism was violent and neo-pagan. It borrowed from Nietzsche and other pre-war theoreticians, who, safe and civilized, had declared that men should live dangerously, avoid the flabby weakness of too much thought, throw themselves with red-blooded vigor into a life of action. The new regimes all instituted youth movements. They appealed to a kind of juvenile idealism, in which young people believed that by joining some kind of squad, donning some kind of uniform and getting into the fresh air they contributed to a great moral resurgence of their country. Young men were taught to value their bodies but not their minds, to be tough and hard, to regard mass gymnastics as patriotic demonstrations, and camping trips as a preparation for the world of the future. Young women were taught to breed large families without complaint, to be content in the kitchen, and to look with awe upon their virile mates. The body-cult flourished while the mind decayed. Especially in National Socialism the ideal was to turn the German people into a race of splendid animals, pink-cheeked, Nordic, and upstanding. Contrariwise, euthanasia was adopted for the insane, and was proposed for the aged. Later, in the Second World War, when the Nazis overran Poland, they committed Jews to the gas chambers, destroying some four million human beings by the most scientific methods. Animals were animals; one bred the kind one wanted, and killed the kind one did not.

THE SPREAD OF DICTATORSHIP

The trend to dictatorship or totalitarianism spread over Europe in the 1930's. By 1939 only ten out of twenty-seven European countries remained democratic, in the sense that different political parties honestly competed for office, and that citizens within generous limits thought and acted as they pleased. They were Great Britain and France; Holland, Belgium, and Switzerland; Czechoslovakia and Finland; and the three Scandinavian countries. The Soviet Union still exemplified the dictatorship of the proletariat, and all other European countries possessed more or less dictatorial regimes somewhat vaguely called, with more or less accuracy, "fascist."

The promise of the early 1920's that constitutional and democratic government would flourish had been thwarted. The weakness or absence of a parliamentary or democratic tradition, low education and literacy standards, the hostility of reactionary elements, the fear of Bolshevism, and the dissatisfaction of existing national minorities, all of which were coupled with economic strains, some resulting from the great depression, others going deeper and further back, contributed to the collapse of the new representative institutions. Apart from the avowedly totalitarian regimes of Italy and Germany, the new dictatorships and authoritarian systems rested generally on a combination of personal and military power. To name but a few, this was true of Spain under General Franco (soon to be referred to again); Poland under Marshal Pilsudski, Smigly-Rydz and a clique of generals and colonels; Hungary under a series of aristocratic counts and General Gömbös; Greece under General Metaxas; and Yugoslavia, Bulgaria, and Rumania under their respective kings. In Austria, Dollfuss and then Von Schuschnigg created a so-called "Christian Socialist" or clerical-fascist dictatorship in part to counter the threat of the native Nazi movement sponsored from Berlin before Austria's annexation in 1938. In many respects the dictatorships of Latin America under a diversity of *caudillos* and military juntas, in both origin and character, resembled the European dictatorships.

The authoritarian regimes were all alike in the repression of individual liberties, in the banning of opposition parties, and in the abolition or nullification of parliamentary institutions. Many borrowed features of the corporative state, outlawing independent labor organizations and forbidding strikes; many like Hungary, Rumania, and Poland instituted anti-Semitic legislation. None went so far in the total coordination of all political, economic, intellectual, and biological activities in a revolutionary mass-based dictatorship as did Hitler's Third Reich.

The acceptance and glorification of violence, it has been noted, was the feature most clearly distinguishing the totalitarian from the democratic systems. War in the Nazi and Fascist ethics was a noble thing, and the love of peace a sign of decadence. (The Soviet regime, while by its own theory it regarded war with non-Soviet powers as inevitable some day, did not preach it as a positive moral good.) The exaltation of war and struggle, the need of maintaining national solidarity, the habit of blaming foreign countries for social troubles, together with the considerable armaments program in which totalitarian states engaged, plus the personal ambition and egotistical mania of individual dictators, made the decade of the 1930's a time of recurrent international crises, of which the last one led to war.

105. The Weakness of the West: Again to War

Peace in the abstract, the peace which is the mere absence of war, does not exist in international relations. Peace is never found apart from certain conditions; it means peaceable acceptance of given conditions, or peaceable and orderly transformation of conditions by negotiation and agreement. The conditions, in the 1930's, were basically those laid down by the Paris peace conference of 1919—the states recognized, the frontiers drawn, the terms agreed to, at the close of the First World War.[18] In the 1930's neither Ger-

[18] See pp. 694–703.

many nor Italy nor Japan was content with these conditions; they were "revisionist" or dissatisfied powers; and they were willing to hazard war itself to make a change. Great Britain, France, and the United States were satisfied powers, expecting no benefit from change in the conditions; but on the other hand they had lost faith in the conditions, and were unwilling to risk war for the sake of upholding them. They had made a treaty in 1919 which a dozen years later they were unwilling to enforce. They stood idly by, as long as they could, while the dissatisfied powers tore to pieces the states recognized, the frontiers drawn, and the terms agreed to at the Peace of Paris. From the Japanese invasion of Manchuria in 1931 to the outbreak of European war in 1939, force was used by those who wished to upset international order, but never by those who wished to maintain it.

THE PACIFISM AND DISUNITY OF THE WEST

While dictators stormed, the Western democracies were swayed by a profound pacifism, which may be defined as a somewhat doctrinaire insistence on peace regardless of consequences. Many people now believed, especially in England and the United States, that the First World War had been a mistake, that little or nothing had been gained by it, that they had been deluded by war-time propaganda, that wars were really started by armaments manufacturers, that Germany had not really caused the war of 1914, that the treaty of Versailles was too hard on the Germans, that vigorous peoples like the Germans or Italians needed room for expansion, that democracy was after all not suited to all nations, that it took two to make a quarrel, and that there need be no war if one side resolutely refused to be provoked—a whole system of pacific and tolerant ideas in which there was perhaps the usual mixture of truth and misunderstanding. Taunted by enemies, the Western democracies behaved like Ferdinand the Bull, who "would not fight and be fierce no matter what they did," and who, in the story, because he would not fight, was allowed to go home and "just smell the flowers" and be "very happy." Unfortunately the Western democracies found pacifism less rewarding.

The pacifism of the West had other roots, most evident in France. One million, four hundred thousand Frenchmen had died in World War I; half of all French males between the ages of 20 and 32 in 1914 had been killed. To the French it was inconceivable that such a holocaust should be repeated. French strategy was therefore defensive, and sparing of manpower. If war came, the French expected to fight it in the elaborate fixed fortifications, called the Maginot Line, which they built on their eastern frontier facing Germany, from the Swiss to the Belgian border; to its north the Ardennes forest was to be a barrier to any invader. Moreover, as we have seen, during and after the depression France was torn by internal class conflict; and fascist and quasi-fascist agitation made progress.[19] Many Frenchmen of the

〰〰〰〰〰〰〰〰〰

[19] See pp. 797–800.

Right, historically unsympathetic to the republic and seeing, or claiming to
see, in such movements as the Popular Front the threat of social revolution,
did not conceal their admiration for Mussolini or even for Hitler. Abandoning their traditional role as ardent nationalists, they would do nothing to oppose the dictators. On the other hand, the Left, which gloried in France's
revolutionary and republican traditions, looked with sympathy upon the Soviet Union. France was ideologically too divided in the 1930's to possess any
firm foreign policy, and all elements took false comfort from the supposed impregnability of the French Chinese Wall.

A similar situation, in less degree, prevailed in Great Britain and the
United States. The loss and bloodshed of World War I were remembered. It
was well known that another world war would be even more horrible; there
was an unspeakable dread of the bombing of cities. Typical of the time was
the Oxford oath, by which British university students, in 1933, vowed that
they would never take up arms for their country under any conditions; the
movement spread to college students in the United States. The pull between
Left and Right was felt in England and America. In the 1930's, when any
international action seemed to favor either the U.S.S.R. on the one hand, or
Hitler and Mussolini on the other, it was hard to establish any foreign policy
on a firm basis of national unity. In Britain some members of the upper
classes were overtly sympathetic to the fascist dictators, or at least saw in
them a bulwark against communism. The government itself tried to be non-
committal; it believed that some means of satisfying or appeasing the more
"legitimate" demands of the dictators might be found. Neville Chamberlain, prime minister after 1937, became the principal architect of the appeasement policy.

The United States government, despite President Roosevelt's repeated
denunciation of the aggressors, followed in practice a policy of rigid isolation.
Neutrality legislation, enacted by a strong isolationist bloc in congress in the
years 1935 to 1937, forbade loans, export of munitions, and use of American
shipping facilities to any belligerent once the President had recognized a state
of war in a given area. It was then believed, by many, that the United States
had been drawn into the First World War by such economic involvement.
From this American neutrality legislation the aggressors of the 1930's were
to derive great benefit, but not the victims of their aggression.

As for the men who ruled the U.S.S.R., they were revisionist and dissatisfied in that they did not accept the new frontiers of Eastern Europe nor
the territorial losses incurred by Russia in the First World War. They resented the *cordon sanitaire* created in 1919 against the spread of Bolshevism,
the ring of small states on their borders from Finland to Rumania, which
were almost without exception vehemently anti-Soviet. They had no fond-
ness for the international status quo nor had they abandoned their long-range
revolutionary objectives. But, as communists and as Russians, they were obsessed by fear of attack and invasion. Their Marxist doctrine taught the inherent hostility of the entire capitalist world; the intervention of the Western
Allies in the Revolution and civil wars confirmed their Marxist theory. And

long before the Bolshevik Revolution, in the days of Napoleon and earlier, the fertile Russian plains had tempted ambitious conquerors. Resentful and suspicious of the whole outside world, now in the 1930's the men in the Kremlin were alarmed primarily by the signs of aggressive intentions in Germany. Hitler, in *Mein Kampf* and elsewhere, had declared that he meant to obliterate Bolshevism and subordinate large stretches of Eastern Europe to Germany.

The Soviets became interested in collective security, in international action against aggression. In 1934 they joined the League of Nations. They instructed communist parties to work with socialists and liberals in popular fronts.[20] They offered assistance in checking fascist aggressors. But too many people fled from the Soviet embrace with a shudder. They distrusted Soviet motives; or they were convinced that the purges and trials of the 1930's had left the Soviets weak and undependable as allies; or they felt that the fascist dictators might be diverted eastward against the Soviets, and so spare the Western democracies. Here again, though the Russians were ostensibly willing, no effective coalition against aggression could be formed. Events in the 1930's took their course, noted Winston Churchill, as if the Soviets did not even exist.

THE MARCH OF NAZI AND FASCIST AGGRESSION

Adolf Hitler perceived these weaknesses with uncanny genius. Determined to wreck the whole treaty system, he devised a tactics of gradual encroachment which played on the hopes and fears of the democratic peoples. He inspired in them alternating tremors of apprehension and sighs of relief. He would rage and rant, arouse the fear of war, take just a little, declare that it was all he wanted, let the former Allies wildly hope that he was now satisfied and that peace was secure; then rage again, take a little more, and proceed through the same cycle.

Each year he precipitated some kind of emergency, and each time the French and British saw no alternative except to let him have his way. In 1933, soon after seizing power, he took Germany out of the League of Nations and out of the International Disarmament Conference then taking place. In 1934 the Nazis of Austria staged a *Putsch*, assassinated the Austrian chancellor, Dollfuss, and demanded the union of Austria with Germany. The Western powers did nothing. It was Mussolini who acted. He had no desire to see Germany installed at the Brenner Pass, and mobilized large Italian forces on the frontier; he thus discouraged Hitler from intervening openly in Austria, and so preserved the independence of Austria for four more years. In 1935 Hitler announced the repudiation of those clauses in the Versailles treaty by which Germany remained disarmed; he began to build up the German army and navy without concealment. France, England and Italy pro-

᎖᎖᎖᎖᎖᎖᎖᎖᎖᎖᎖᎖᎖᎖᎖

[20] See pp. 750-1.

tested at such arbitrary and one-sided denunciation of an international treaty, but nothing happened. Indeed, Great Britain entered into a naval agreement with Germany, to the consternation of the French. That same year, 1935, a plebiscite was conducted in the Saar by the League of Nations as arranged under the Versailles treaty. Although Nazi agitation was intense, the results undoubtedly reflected the popular sentiment with accuracy. The Saar voted for reunion with the *Reich*.

In 1936, denouncing the Locarno pacts,[21] Hitler re-occupied the Rhineland; *i.e.*, he sent German troops into the German territory west of the Rhine which by the treaty of Versailles was supposed to be a demilitarized zone. There was much feeling in France for war, and at this time Hitler might have been fairly easily defeated, for German military preparations had only begun and German officers carried orders instructing them to withdraw at any sign of resistance. But France was divided, and Britain would not risk war to keep German troops from occupying German soil. In the next year, 1937, Nazi agitation flared up in Danzig, which the treaty of Versailles had set up as a free city; by the end of the year Danzig was virtually incorporated into Germany. In March 1938 German forces moved into Austria, and the union of Austria and Germany was at last consummated. In September 1938 came the turn of Czechoslovakia and the Munich crisis. To understand it we must first pick up other threads in the story.

Mussolini, too, had his ambitions, and required sensational foreign triumphs to magnetize the Italian people. Since 1919 the Italians had been dissatisfied with the peace arrangements. They had received nothing of the former Turkish territories and former German colonies which had been liberally parcelled out, as mandates, to Great Britain, France, Belgium and Japan, and even to South Africa, Australia and New Zealand.[22] They had never forgotten the humiliating defeat of Italian forces by Abyssinia at Adowa in 1896.[23] Ethiopia, as Abyssinia was now called, remained the only part of Negro Africa (with the exception of Liberia) that was still independent.

In 1935 Italy went to war with Ethiopia. The League of Nations pronounced the Italian action an unwarranted agression, and imposed sanctions on Italy, by which members of the League were to refrain from selling Italy either arms or raw materials—oil was excepted. The British even gathered large naval forces in the Mediterranean to enforce the verdict of the League. But in France there was sympathy for Mussolini in important quarters, and in England there was the fear that if sanctions became too effective, by refusal of oil or by closure of the Suez Canal, Italy might be irritated into a general war. Mussolini was thus able to defeat Ethiopia in 1936, and to combine it with Italian Somaliland and Eritrea in an Italian East African Empire. The Ethiopian Emperor Haile Selassie made futile pleas for further action at Geneva. The League of Nations again failed, as in the case of the occupation of

ᴧᴧᴧᴧᴧᴧᴧᴧᴧᴧᴧᴧᴧᴧᴧᴧᴧᴧ

[21] See pp. 763–4.
[22] See pp. 697, 702, 801.
[23] See pp. 640–1.

Manchuria by Japan, to provide machinery for disciplinary action against a wayward Great Power.[24]

THE SPANISH CIVIL WAR, 1936-39

Hardly had the Ethiopian crisis been disposed of, to the entire satisfaction of the aggressor, when an even more serious crisis broke out in Spain. In 1931, after a decade of political disturbance, a rather mild revolution had driven out Alfonso XIII, the last Bourbon, and brought about the establishment of a democratic Spanish republic. Old hostilities within the country came increasingly to a head. The new republican government undertook a program of social and economic reform. To combat the ancient entrenched power of the Church, anti-clerical legislation was enacted: church and state were separated, the Jesuit order was dissolved and its property confiscated, the schools were removed from clerical control. The old movement for Catalonian independence was somewhat mollified by the grant of considerable local autonomy. To placate the peasantry the government began to break up some of the larger landed estates and to redistribute the land. The government's program was never pushed vigorously enough to satisfy extremist elements who manifested their dissatisfaction in strikes and uprisings particularly in industrial Barcelona and the mining areas of the Asturias; but it was radical enough to antagonize the great property-owners and the churchmen. After 1933 the government fell increasingly into the hands of Rightist and conservative parties, who ruled through ineffective and unpopular ministries. An insurrection of the miners in the Asturias was put down with much brutality. Continuing agitation for complete Catalonian independence was re pressed. In February 1936 new elections were held. All elements of the Left —republicans, socialists, syndicalists, anarchists, communists—joined in a Popular Front against monarchists, clericals, army officers, and other adherents of the old regime. They won a decisive victory at the polls. Thereupon, in July 1936, an army general named Francisco Franco led an insurrection against the republican government. The parties of the Left united in resistance and the whole country fell into civil war. It was a considerable war, in which 700,000 men were killed in battle, and was attended by extreme cruelties on both sides. For nearly three years the republican or loyalist forces held their own before finally succumbing to the insurgents led by Franco, who then established an authoritarian, fascist-type rule over the exhausted country.

Spain provided a rehearsal for the greater struggle soon to come. The republican government could legitimately have looked forward to the purchase of arms abroad to suppress the rebellion, but Britain and France were resolved not to let the war expand into a general conflict. They forbade the shipment of war materials to the republican government; even the French

[24] See p. 777.

Popular Front government put obstacles in the way of aid to the hard-pressed Spanish Popular Front. The United States extended its neutrality legislation to cover civil wars and placed an embargo on the export of arms to Spain despite much pressure in the country for support to the loyalists. At British and French instigation twenty-seven nations, including all the major European powers, agreed not to intervene or take sides. But the non-intervention policy proved a fiasco. Germany, Italy, and the Soviet Union intervened anyway. The former two supported Franco and denounced the republicans as the tools of Bolshevism, while the U.S.S.R. supported the republic and stigmatized the rebels under Franco as the agents of international fascism. Germans, Italians, and Russians sent military equipment to Spain, testing out their own armaments in actual battle. The fascist bombings of Madrid and Barcelona, the first air bombings of civilians in history, horrified the democratic world. The Germans and Italians sent troops (the Italians over 50,000); the Soviets if only for geographical reasons could not do likewise, but thousands of persons of leftist or liberal sympathy, from the United States and from European countries, went to Spain as individuals to serve with the loyalist republican forces. Spain thus became the battlefield of contending ideologies. The Spanish civil war split the world into fascist and anti-fascist camps.

Its first effect was to bring Germany and Italy together. Mussolini had at first, like others, feared the revival of a militant Germany. He had been the one who outfaced Hitler when the latter threatened to absorb Austria in 1934. The Ethiopian war, Italian ambitions in Africa, and a clamorous Italian demand for ascendancy in the Mediterranean, the *mare nostrum* of the ancient Romans, estranged Italy from France and Britain. In 1936, soon after the outbreak of the Spanish war, Mussolini and Hitler came to an understanding, which they called the Rome-Berlin Axis, the diplomatic axle around which they hoped the world might turn. Japan soon subscribed to the same agreement, which was now called the Anti-Comintern Pact, because the three powers agreed to oppose communism and the Communist International. Each, thus furnished with allies, was able to push its demands with more success. We have seen how Germany in 1938 absorbed the very Austria which in 1934 Italy had denied it.

And in 1937 Japan, using as a pretext the firing upon Japanese troops at the Marco Polo Bridge near Peiping launched a new full-scale invasion of China. Within a short time despite valiant and united resistance from the Chinese forces, both Kuomintang and communist, the invader controlled most of China. The Chinese fought on from the hinterland, obtaining equipment and supplies by difficult and devious routes. The League again ineffectually condemned the Japanese action. The United States refrained from applying its neutrality legislation, since no war was officially declared. This made possible the extension of loans to the Chinese government, but it also made possible the purchase by the Japanese of vitally needed scrap iron, steel, oil, and machinery from American industrial firms. In all ways the Japanese profited from the tension in the white man's world; and in 1938 the tension in Europe was rapidly mounting.

THE MUNICH CRISIS: THE CLIMAX OF APPEASEMENT

By annexing Austria Hitler added about six million Germans to the Reich. Another three million Germans lived in Czechoslovakia.[25] All those who were adults in 1938 had been born under the Hapsburg empire. They had never, since 1918, been contented with their new position as a minority in a Slavic state, and they had long complained against various forms of subtle discrimination. There were Polish, Ruthenian and Hungarian minorities also, and since even the Slovaks felt a certain separatism from the Czechs there was in truth no preponderant national majority of any kind. The fact that Czechoslovakia had one of the most enlightened minorities policies in Europe, enjoyed the highest living standard east of Germany, and was the only country in Central Europe in 1938 that was still democratic, only demonstrated the difficulty of maintaining a multinational state under the most favorable of conditions.

Czechoslovakia was strategically the keystone of Europe. It had a firm alliance with France, which had repeatedly guaranteed to defend it against German attack. With Rumania and Yugoslavia it formed the Little Entente, upon which France relied to maintain the existing boundaries in that part of Europe. It had a well-trained army, important munitions industries and strong fortifications against Germany, which, however, were located in precisely that border area where the population was almost exclusively German. When Hitler annexed Austria—since Vienna is further east than Prague—he enclosed Czechoslovakia in a vise. From the German point of view it could now be said that Bohemia-Moravia, which was almost one-third German anyway, formed a bulge protruding into the German Reich.

The Sudetens, or Germans of Czechoslovakia, whether Nazis or not, fell under the influence of agitators whose aim was less to relieve their grievances than to promote National Socialism. Hitler fomented their demands for union with Germany. In May 1938 German troops almost crossed the border. Hitler held back, in the face of Czechoslovak mobilization and of clear warnings from Russia and France. The May incident seemed to show that Hitler, if resolutely opposed, might be stopped. Its main effect, however, was to intensify the fear of war in France and England, which instead of rejoicing in having prevented aggression, were appalled by their narrow escape from war; the French were nervous, and the British government, in the following months, strove to hold back France from a firm stand that might precipitate war. In September 1938 Hitler again loudly declared that the plight of Germans in Czechoslovakia was intolerable and must be corrected. The Czechs offered to accept arbitration as provided in the Locarno treaty of 1925. The French and British rejected arbitration, fearing that it would not be enough to satisfy Hitler. The Soviets urged a firm stand; the Western powers were afraid both of the Soviets and of a firmness that might mean

---

[25] See pp. 441–2, 482, 533, 696–7, 699, and map, pp. 700–01.

war. They could not be sure whether Hitler was bluffing. He might, if opposed, back down; but it seemed equally likely, or indeed more so, that he was entirely willing to fight.

In these circumstances, after several other conferences, the British prime minister, Neville Chamberlain, and the French premier, Edouard Daladier, repaired to Munich, where they were received by Hitler, reinforced by his ally Mussolini. The Soviet Union was excluded. Hitler's browbeating and apparently hysterical outbursts left his auditors bewildered. Chamberlain and Daladier accepted his terms. They put enormous pressure on the Czech government to yield, to sign its own death warrant in cold blood. France, urged on by England in a pacific course that it was only too willing to follow, repudiated its treaty obligation to protect Czechoslovakia, ignored the Russians who were willing to stop German expansion by force of arms at this point, and abandoned its whole system of a Little Entente in the East. It was agreed at Munich that Germany should annex the adjoining fringe of Bohemia in which the majority of the people were Germans. This fringe contained the mountainous approaches and the fortifications, so that its loss left Czechoslovakia militarily defenseless. After solemn guarantees, by all concerned, of the integrity of what remained of Czechoslovakia, the conference disbanded. Chamberlain and Daladier were received with cheers at home. Chamberlain happily reported that he had brought "peace in our time." Again the democracies sighed with relief, hoped that Hitler had made his last demand, and told themselves that, with wise concessions, there need be no war.

The Munich crisis, with its death sentence to Czechoslovakia, revealed the helpless weakness into which the West had fallen. There was, in fact, little that the French and British could do, at Munich, other than to accept Hitler's terms. They lagged far behind Germany in military preparedness. They were impressed by the might of the German army and air force. Bolder men than Daladier and Chamberlain, knowing the state of their own armed forces, would have declined to risk a quarrel. Their minds for years had been focused on domestic problems of economic revival. They loved peace, and would buy it at a high price, not daring to believe that they were dealing with a blackmailer whose price would be always raised. They suffered, too, from another moral uncertainty: by the very principle of national self-determination, accepted by the victors after World War I, Germany had a right to all that it had hitherto demanded. Hitler, in sending German troops into the German Rhineland, in annexing Austria, stirring up Danzig, incorporating the Bohemian Germans, had only asserted the right of the German people to have a sovereign German state. Moreover, if Hitler could be diverted eastward, enmeshed ultimately in a war with Russia, then communism and fascism might mutually destroy each other—so one might hope. Possibly it was one of Hitler's motives, in the Munich crisis, to isolate Russia from the West and the West from Russia. If so, he succeeded well enough.

In the weeks following Munich the Poles and Hungarians brought forth their demands on hapless Czechoslovakia. The Poles seized the Teschen district; and Hungary, with German and Italian approval, took 5,000 square

miles of Slovakia. France and Britain were not consulted, and did not seriously protest.

THE END OF APPEASEMENT

The final disillusionment came in March 1939. Hitler marched into
Bohemia-Moravia, the really Czech part of Czechoslovakia, which he transformed into a German protectorate. Exploiting Slovak nationalism, he declared Slovakia "independent." Czechoslovakia, merely trimmed down at
Munich, now disappeared from the map. Having promised to take only a
bite, Hitler swallowed the whole thing. He soon seized Memel from Lithuania and raised demands for the Polish Corridor. A horrible realization now
spread in France and Britain. It was clear that Hitler's most solemn guarantees were worthless, that his designs were not limited to Germans, but
reached out to all Eastern Europe and beyond, that he was essentially insatiable, that he could never be appeased. In April 1939 his partner in aggression,
Mussolini, took over Albania.

The Western powers now began to make military preparations. Britain, changing its East European policy at the eleventh hour, now gave a
guarantee to Poland—under the worst possible circumstances, the military
bastion of Czechoslovakia having been already surrendered, and the Soviet
Union alienated from the West by its exclusion at Munich.

Desperately, in the summer of 1939, the British and French tried to
form an anti-German alliance with Russia. Poland and the Baltic states were
unwilling to allow Soviet armies within their borders, even for the purpose
of defending them against the Germans. The Anglo-French negotiators,
clinging to a few shreds of international propriety, refused to throw Poland
and the Baltic states to Stalin in the way in which they had just thrown
Czechoslovakia to Hitler. Since the Poles, in 1920, had conquered more territory than the Allies had meant them to have,[26] pushing their eastern border
well into White Russia, almost to Minsk, the Anglo-French scruples seemed
to the Soviets unnecessarily delicate. The Russians did not wish the Germans
to launch an attack on them from a point as far east as Minsk. They thought,
too, with good reason, that what the French and British really wanted was for
Russia to take the brunt of the Nazi attack. And they considered it an affront
that the British sent a Foreign Office career official as negotiator to Moscow
when the prime minister himself had thrice flown personally to treat with
Hitler. Waving aside Anglo-French pleas, the Soviets signed a treaty of non-
aggression and friendship with Hitlerite Germany instead. In a secret protocol it was agreed that in any future territorial rearrangement, Russia and Germany would divide Poland and the Baltic states between them.

The Nazi-Soviet Pact of August 23, 1939 stupefied the world. Communism and Nazism, supposed to be ideological opposites, had come to-

[26] See p. 727, and map, p. 221.

gether. A generation more versed in ideology than in power politics was
dumbfounded. The pact was recognized as the signal for war. The Germans,
reassured by it, invaded Poland on September 1. On September 3 Great
Britain and France declared war on Germany. The second European war in a
generation, soon to be a world war, had begun.

CHAPTER XX

The Cataclysm: The Second World War and Its Aftermath

CATACLYSM, according to Webster's dictionary, is "any violent change involving sudden and extensive alterations of the earth's surface; hence, any upheaval, especially a social or political one." A cataclysm in nature, as we may imagine it, is a time when volcanoes erupt, earthquakes rumble, old mountain systems are broken down, new peaks and ranges thrust themselves upward, the very coastlines assume new shapes, living creatures flee from destruction, old forms of life become extinct, and new forms of life, at first unnoticed, enter upon careers in which they are later to flourish. The human world has been in the grip of such a cataclysm since 1914. The First World War, the post-war troubles, the Russian, Chinese, Turkish, and other revolutions, the great depression, the parade of the dictators, the Second

World War, the second crop of revolutionary changes and post-war troubles, are all part of the same process of readjustment, which has already altered the very coastlines of human society beyond recognition, which is not yet over, and for which "cataclysm" is not too strong a word.

106. The Years of Axis Triumph

NAZI EUROPE, 1939–40: THE POLISH CAMPAIGN

AND THE FALL OF FRANCE

The Second World War opened with the assault on Poland. German forces totaling over a million men, spearheaded by armored divisions and supported by the massed air power of the *Luftwaffe*, rapidly overran western Poland and subdued the ill-equipped Polish armies. The outcome of the campaign, a spectacular, perfectly executed example of *Blitzkrieg*, or lightning warfare, was clear within the first few days; organized resistance ended within a month. The Germans undertook at once the integration of their Polish conquest into the *Reich*.

Simultaneously, in the East, the Russians, acting under the secret clauses of the German-Soviet pact, moved into the eastern half of Poland two weeks after the German invasion; the territory occupied was roughly equivalent to that lost to Poland in 1920. The Russians proceeded also to establish fortified bases in the Baltic states—Estonia, Latvia, and Lithuania. Finland alone resisted Soviet demands. The Finns refused to cede border territories sought by the Russians or to yield military rights within their country. The Soviets insisted; Leningrad, the second major city of the U.S.S.R., lay only twenty miles from the Finnish frontier. When negotiations foundered in November, 1939, the Soviets attacked. Finnish resistance was valiant and at first effective, but the small country was no match for the U.S.S.R., even though the latter used only limited forces in the war. Western democratic sympathies were with the Finns; the British and French sent equipment and supplies, and even planned an expeditionary force. Russia was expelled from the League of Nations for the act of aggression—the only power ever to be so expelled. By March 1940 the fighting was over. The Finns had to yield somewhat more territory to the U.S.S.R. than originally demanded; the Soviets, out of a part of their acquisition, the Karelian isthmus in the Leningrad area, created a new constituent soviet republic.

Meanwhile all was deceptively quiet in the West. The pattern of 1914, when the Germans reached the Marne in the first month of hostilities, failed to repeat itself. Unlike 1914, the opening phase of the war was one of position from the start. The French sat behind their Maginot Line; the British had few troops; the Germans did not stir from behind their Siegfried Line, or West Wall, in the Rhineland. Hardly any air action took place. It was called the "phony war." The two great Western democracies still clung to their peacetime outlook. The mad hope still lingered that somehow a real clash might even yet be averted. During this same strange winter, a cold and bitter one, the Germans put their forces through special training, whose purpose became apparent in the spring.

In April and May, 1940, the Germans suddenly occupied Norway, Denmark, and the Netherlands and delivered their main attack in Belgium. Nothing could stand against their armored divisions and the dive bombers that roared above them. These tactics, though they had been used in Poland, took the French and British by surprise. Soon, skirting the northern end of the Maginot Line, which had never been extended to the sea, the German mechanized divisions drove through the Ardennes forest, deep into northern France, and raced toward the Channel ports. British and Belgian forces, and some French divisions, were cut off from the main French armies and fell back upon Dunkirk. The Belgians capitulated. The British could hope only to salvage their broken forces. In the week ending June 4 an epic evacuation of some 330,000 British and French troops was effected from the beaches of Dunkirk with the help of all kinds of British vessels manned in part by civilian volunteers and under air-force cover. The precious equipment of the shattered army was all but totally abandoned.

The German forces drove relentlessly southward. Paris itself was occupied on June 13, Verdun two days later; by June 22 France had sued for peace and an armistice had been signed. Hitler danced with glee.

France, obsessed by a defensive military psychology, its armies unprepared to operate in the open country, lacking an adequate air force, its government divided, its people split into hostile and suspicious factions, had fallen into the hands of a group of men of whom some were defeatist and some pro-Nazi. The fall of France left the world aghast. Everyone knew that France was no longer its former self, but it had still been considered a Great Power, and its collapse in one month seemed inconceivably epoch-making. A small group of Frenchmen, fleeing to England, established a Free French movement under General Charles de Gaulle. The British made the bitter decision to destroy the major part of the French fleet anchored in the Algerian harbor of Oran to prevent its falling into enemy hands.

France itself under the terms of the armistice was occupied in its northern half by the Germans. The Third Republic, its capital now at Vichy in the unoccupied southern half, was transformed by vote of a confused and stunned parliament into a totalitarian regime headed by the eighty-five-year-old Marshal Pétain and the cynical and unscrupulous politician Pierre Laval. The republic was dead; the very slogan *Liberty, Equality, and Fraternity* was banned from official use. Pétain, Laval, and others proceeded to collaborate with the Nazis and to integrate an authoritarian France into the Nazi new order in Europe.

Mussolini attacked France in June 1940, as soon as it was clear that Hitler had defeated it. Shortly thereafter, he invaded Greece and moved against the British in Africa. The Duce tied his own destinies, for good or ill, to those of the Führer. Since the Germans were emphatically the senior partner in this combination, since they were on good terms with Franco in Spain, and since Russia was benevolently neutral, they now dominated the entire European continent. History seemed to repeat itself, in the distant and unreal way which is the only way in which it ever repeats. The Germans controlled almost exactly the same geographical area as Napoleon. Organizing a new "continental system," they planned, exploited, and coordinated the resources, industry, and labor of Europe. They garrisoned virtually the whole of it with their own soldiers, creating what they called *Festung Europa*, the Fortress of Europe. In every country they had their sympathizers, collaborators or "quislings"—Vidkun Quisling, who had organized a Norwegian fascist party in 1933, and was premier of Norway from 1942 to 1945, was typical of the group.

But Hitler never commanded the following of Napoleon. It is significant that he never remotely approached Napoleon in raising an international army to fight his battles. Instead, by what the West called slave labor, he impressed millions of Frenchmen, Poles, Czechs, and others, prisoners of war or civilians, to work under close control in his war industries. It was one of the largest forcible displacements of population in all history. No liberating reforms, political, social, legal, like those of Napoleon and the French Revolution, followed in the wake of Hitler's armies. A generation reared to mistrust the fabricated atrocity tales of the First World War painfully became aware of the very real German horrors of the Second—hostages rounded up and shot in reprisal for resistance; a whole village like Lidice in Czechoslovakia razed to the ground and its inhabitants killed or deported; concentration camps converted into mass extermination centers, with gas chambers and crematory ovens, at Maidanek, Treblinka, Dachau, Buchenwald, Auschwitz, and elsewhere, where "inferior" peoples could be systematically liquidated. Before the war was over, in the areas of Nazi domination, at least five or six million human beings were so destroyed; the largest proportion were East-European Jewry, but Poles, Russians, Czechs, and other peoples were included as well. All this was done in the effort to "Germanize" Europe, to make it work and sacrifice for the greater glory of the *Herrenvolk*, the master race. Genocide, the attempted destruction of whole ethnic groups or peoples, was the greatest of the Nazi sins against mankind.

THE BATTLE OF BRITAIN AND THE AMERICAN

ARSENAL OF DEMOCRACY

In 1940, as in 1807, only Great Britain remained at war with the conqueror of Europe. After Dunkirk the British awaited the worst, momentarily expecting invasion. Winston Churchill, who had replaced Chamberlain as prime minister in May 1940 during the military débacle, rose to the summit of heroic leadership in adversity. To Parliament and the British people he promised nothing but "blood, toil, tears, and sweat." He pledged implacable war against "a monstrous tyranny, never surpassed in the dark, lamentable catalogue of human crime." To the American democracy across the Atlantic he appealed "Give us the tools, and we will finish the job." The United States began to respond.

Since 1939, and even before, the American government had been anything but neutral. Opinion was excitedly divided. One group, called isolationist, opposed any involvement in the European war, believing either that Europe was hopeless, or that the United States could not save it, or that the Germans would win anyway before America could act, or that Hitler, even if victorious in Europe, constituted no danger to the United States. Another group, the interventionists, urged immediate aid to the Allies, believing that Hitler was an actual menace, that fascism must be destroyed, or that the Nazis, if they subjected all Europe, would soon begin to tamper with the American republics. President Roosevelt was an interventionist, convinced that American security was endangered; he tried to rally national opinion by declaring that the United States might openly assist the Allies without itself fighting, by using "measures short of war." His Republican opponent in 1940, Wendell Willkie, took an identical stand.

The neutrality legislation of the mid-1930's was amended in November 1939, when the ban on the sale of arms was repealed. Britain and the British Empire the President described as "the spearhead of resistance to world conquest"; the United States was to be "the great arsenal of democracy." Both were fighting for a world, he said, in which the Four Freedoms were to be secure—freedom of speech, freedom of worship, freedom from want, and freedom from fear. In June 1940, immediately after Dunkirk, the United States sent a small initial shipment of arms to Britain. A few months later the United States gave the British fifty over-age destroyers in return for the right to maintain American bases in Newfoundland, the Bermudas, and the British Caribbean islands. In 1941 it adopted Lend-Lease, a policy of providing arms, raw material, and food to powers at war with the Axis. At the same time, in 1940 and 1941, the United States adopted conscription, built up its army and air force, and projected a two-ocean navy. Plans for joint hemisphere defense were developed with the Latin American republics. To protect its shipping it secured bases in Greenland and Iceland, and convoyed Allied shipping as far as Iceland. In October 1941 German submarines sank an American destroyer. It is likely that the Germans, as in 1917, would have eventually provoked war with the United States to stop the flow of aid to their enemies even had war not come from another quarter.

Meanwhile, after the fall of France, the Germans stood poised for the invasion of Britain. But they had not calculated on such rapid and easy successes in Europe and they had no immediately practical plans for the invasion. The Battle of Britain, which went on for months and reached its climax in the autumn of 1940, took the form of an air offensive. Never until then had any bombing been so severe. But the Germans were unable to win control of the air over Britain. Gradually the British Royal Air Force fought off the bombers with more success; new radar devices helped detect the approach of enemy planes. Although Coventry was wiped out, and the life and industry of other cities badly disrupted, and thousands of people killed (14,000 in London alone), still the productive activity of the country carried on. Nor, contrary to the predictions of most theorists of air power, did the bombings break the morale of the civilian population.

In the winter of 1940–1 the Germans began to shift their weight to the east. For Hitler had already decided, like Napoleon before him, that before finishing off with England he must dispose of Russia.

THE NAZI INVASION OF RUSSIA: THE RUSSIAN FRONT, 1941–2

The Nazi-Soviet alliance of 1939 which had precipitated the war, like the alliance between Napoleon and Alexander I, was never a warm or harmonious understanding. Both parties, foreseeing war with each other, probably entered it mainly to gain time. The Soviets gained space as well, pushing their borders westward. The two soon began to dispute over Eastern Europe. The Soviets, with their Nazi ally preoccupied by the war, hoped to win more influence in the Baltic, in the Balkans, and even at Constantinople. They had already occupied eastern Poland and the three Baltic states, and won territory from Finland. In June 1940, to the chagrin of the Germans, they had quietly sovietized and converted the three Baltic states into member republics of the U.S.S.R. The old German land-owning class, the famous "Baltic barons," who had lived there for centuries, were uprooted and were returned to German soil. At the same time the Soviets seized from Rumania the Bessarabian province which they had lost in the First World War; it became the sixteenth soviet republic. The Russians were expanding toward the Balkans, the historic area of Russian interest.

This the Germans viewed with dismay. They, and especially Hitler, wished to reserve Eastern Europe for themselves as a counterpart to industrial Germany. Hitler moved to bring the Balkans under German control. By early 1941 he had blackmailed, or by territorial concessions cajoled, Rumania, Bulgaria, and Hungary into joining the Axis; they became Axis lesser partners, and were occupied by German troops; this happened also with Yugoslavia despite initial resistance by the army and population. Greece too was subjugated, the Germans coming to the rescue of Mussolini's hard-pressed troops. Hitler thus barred Russian expansion in the Balkans, and made them part of the Nazi new order. And now, to realize his ambition of subduing Britain, to end the threat from the East, and to gain the wheat harvests of the Ukraine and the oil wells of the Caucasus, the core of the Eurasian "Heartland," Hitler was ready to move. After mutual deception that had continued since the pact of 1939, on June 22, 1941, he invaded Russia.

The war, which for two years had been only sporadic combat, now began in earnest. In the latter half of 1941 the queer war in Europe turned into the Second World War.

The German army, supplemented by Finnish, Rumanian, Hungarian, and Italian contingents, threw three million men into Russia along a vast two-thousand mile front. One swift moving battle melted into another. The Russians resisted but gave way. By the autumn of 1941 the Germans had over-run White Russia and most of the Ukraine. In the north, Leningrad was in a state of siege; in the south, the Germans had entered the Crimean peninsula and were besieging Sebastopol. And toward the center of the vast front, the Germans stood, exhausted, but apparently victorious, within twenty-five miles of Moscow. But the overconfident German forces had not calculated on the quality of Russian resistance, nor were they prepared to fight in the bitter Russian winter, which suddenly came upon them. A counter-offensive, launched by the Russians in the winter of 1941, saved Moscow. Hitler, dis-gusted and impatient with his subordinates, took over direct command of military operations; he shifted the main attack to the south and began a great offensive in the summer of 1942 directed toward the oil fields of the Caucasus. Sebastopol soon fell; the siege of Stalingrad began.

1942, THE YEAR OF DISMAY: RUSSIA, NORTH AFRICA,

THE PACIFIC

A year after the invasion, in the fateful summer of 1942, the German line reached from beleaguered Leningrad in the north, past the western out-skirts of Moscow, past Stalingrad southward to the Caucasus mountains; the Germans were within a hundred miles of the Caspian Sea. But the Russians had traded space for time. Though the industrial Don basin and the food-producing Ukraine were overrun, and deliveries of Caucasus oil rendered hazardous and uncertain, still the Russians continued to fight; industries were shifted to the new Ural and Siberian cities; and neither the Soviet economy nor the Soviet government was yet struck in a vital spot. A "scorched earth" policy, in which the retreating Russians destroyed crops and livestock and guerilla units wrecked industrial and transportation facilities, guaranteed that Russian resources would not fall into the hands of the conqueror, advancing though he was.

Simultaneously, late in 1942 the Axis also was moving forward in North Africa. Here the desert campaigns had started in September 1940 with an Italian eastward offensive mounted from Libya, which succeeded in crossing over into Egypt. The stakes here too were high—control over Suez and the Mediterranean. At the height of the battle of Britain, Churchill had made the decision to send vitally needed supplies and men to the Near East.

Europe, 1942   See following pages
The map shows Europe at the height of Axis military successes during World War II, just before the Soviet victory at Stalingrad and the Western in-vasion of North Africa. Austria, the Sudetenland, Bohemia-Moravia, Poland, and Alsace-Lorraine were all joined to Hitler's Reich. The Atlantic coast from southern France to northern Norway was under German military occupation, as was much of Russia almost to the Caspian Sea. Southern Europe from Vichy France to Rumania was occupied or allied. The whole was called Festung Europa—the Fortress of Europe.

EUROPE
1942

NORTH CAPE

OCEAN

500 MILES

HITLER'S "EMPIRE"

ALLIED WITH GERMANY

OCCUPIED BY THE AXIS

AT WAR AGAINST THE AXIS

RELATIONS BETWEEN THE AXIS AND VICHY FRANCE WERE GOVERNED BY THE ARMISTICE OF JUNE, 1940, BUT GERMANY OCCUPIED THE WHOLE OF FRANCE IN NOVEMBER, 1942

Murmansk

WHITE SEA

Archangel

FINLAND

LAKE ONEGA

LAKE LADOGA

Helsinki

Leningrad

SOVIET

ESTONIA

Riga

LATVIA

VOLGA R.

Moscow

Kuibyshev

LITHUANIA

Smolensk

Tula

●●●●● DEC., 1941
FARTHEST AXIS PENETRATION
••••• NOV., 1942

EAST RUSSIA

BYELO-RUSSIA

SUWALKI

UNION

arsaw

POLAND

Kiev

Kharkov

Stalingrad

VOLGA R.

Astrakhan

UKRAINE

DONETZ R.

DON R.

ARY

DNIESTER

BESSARABIA

Rostov

Maikop

CASPIAN SEA

Grozny

HUNGARY

RUMANIA

Sevastopol

Yalta

TRANSCAUCASIA

Baku

grade

Bucharest

BLACK SEA

Batum

RBIA

Sofia

BULGARIA

Istanbul

(TURK.)

Tabriz

grade

Ankara

IRAN

RBIA

GREECE

TURKEY

Athens

SYRIA

Bagdad

CYPRUS (BR.)

IRAQ

LEBANON

CRETE

PALESTINE

TRANS-JORDAN

SAUDI ARABIA

NEAN SEA

To the delight, and surprise, of the British a counter-offensive against vastly superior numbers swept the Italians out of Egypt and by early 1941 the British moved deep into Libya. Shortly thereafter the British overran Ethiopia and ended entirely Mussolini's short-lived East African empire; the Italian navy suffered reverses as well. But in North Africa fortunes were fickle. A German elite force, the Afrika Korps under General Rommel, reorganized the Axis armies and in the spring of 1941 attacked in Libya. The British, their forces depleted by transfers that had been made to the Greek front, were driven back to the Egyptian frontier. Then, a few months later, in a second successful offensive, the British once more advanced into Libya. Again fortunes shifted. By mid-1942 Rommel had repulsed the British and penetrated Egypt. The British took up a stand at El Alamein, seventy miles from Alexandria, their backs to the Suez. Here they held the Germans.

But it seemed in 1942 that the Axis armies, breaking through the Soviet Caucasus and across the isthmus of Suez in North Africa, might enclose the whole Mediterranean and Near East in a gigantic vise, and then, moving farther east, join forces with their allies the Japanese, who were at this time penetrating into the Indian Ocean.

For the Pacific situation in the latter half of 1941 had also exploded. It was Japan that finally drew the United States into war.

The Japanese, in 1941, had conducted a war against China for ten years. In the second war in Europe, as in the first, Japanese expansionists saw a propitious moment to assert themselves throughout the Far East. In 1940 they had cemented their alliance with Germany and Italy in a new three-power pact; the following year they had concluded a neutrality treaty with Russia. From the Vichy French government the Japanese obtained a number of military bases and other concessions in Indo-China, and began the occupation of that area. Belatedly, the United States placed an embargo on the export of such materials as scrap iron and steel to Japan. Hesitating to precipitate any all-out drive of the Japanese toward the Dutch East Indies and elsewhere, the United States government still sought some definition of Japanese aims in the Southeast Pacific. The new Japanese prime minister General Hideki Tojo, a staunch champion of the Axis, publicly proclaimed that the influence of Britain and the United States was to be totally eliminated from the Orient, but he agreed to send representatives to Washington for negotiations. At the very time that the Japanese representatives in Washington were carrying on conversations with the American Secretary of State Cordell Hull, on December 7, 1941, without warning, the Japanese launched a heavy air raid on the American naval base at Pearl Harbor in Hawaii and began to invade the Philippines. Simultaneously, they launched attacks on Guam, Midway, Hong Kong and Malaya. The Americans were caught off guard at Pearl Harbor; close to 2,500 were killed; the fleet was crippled; and the temporary disablement of the American naval forces allowed the Japanese to roam at will in the western Pacific. The United States, and Great Britain, declared war on Japan on December 8. Three days later Germany and Italy declared war on the United States as did the Axis puppet states.

The Japanese, working overland through Malaya, soon captured Singapore, a British naval base long fabulous for its supposed impregnability, the veritable Gibraltar of the East. The sinking by air of the mighty British battleship *Prince of Wales*, a feat often pronounced by naval experts to be impossible, added to the general consternation. In 1942 the Japanese conquered the Philippines, Malaya, and the Netherlands Indies. They invaded New Guinea and threatened Australia; they moved into the Aleutians. They streamed into the Indian Ocean, occupied Burma, and seemed about to invade India. Everywhere they found ready collaborators among enemies of European imperialism. They held up the idea of a Greater East Asia Co-Prosperity Sphere under Japanese leadership, in which the one clear element was that the European whites should be ejected. Meanwhile, as noted, the Germans stood at the Caucasus and almost at the Nile. And in the Atlantic, even to the shores of the United States and the American republics, German submarines were sinking Allied ships at an unprecedented and disastrous rate. The Mediterranean was unusable. For the Soviet-Western alliance, 1942 was the year of dismay. Despite Allied naval victories, the late summer and autumn of 1942 was the blackest period of the war. Few realized, wrote the United States Chief of Staff General George C. Marshall some years later, how "close to complete domination of the world" were Germany and Japan and "how thin the thread of Allied survival had been stretched."

107. The Western-Soviet Victory

PLANS AND PREPARATIONS, 1942–3

But by January 1942 twenty-six nations, including the three Great Powers, Britain, the United States, and the U.S.S.R., and representing Europe, Asia, and both Americas, were aligned against the Axis, a combination to which President Roosevelt gave the name the United Nations. Each pledged to use all its resources to defeat the Axis and never to make a separate peace. The Grand Alliance against the Axis aggressors, which could not be created in the 1930's, had at last been consummated.

The two Atlantic democracies, the United States and Great Britain, pooled their resources under an organization called the Combined Chiefs of Staff. Never had any two sovereign states formed so intimate a coalition. In contrast with the First World War an over-all strategy was in effect from an early date. It was decided that Germany was the main enemy, against which it was necessary to concentrate first. For the time being the Pacific war was relegated to the background. Australia became the chief base for operations against the Japanese. The American General Douglas MacArthur who had left the doomed American garrison in the Philippines under military orders, assumed command in the southwest Pacific; Admiral Chester Nimitz was in command of the Pacific naval forces. A separate organization was established for the China-Burma-India theater. The American navy and air force soon brought Japanese southward expansion to a halt and frustrated Japanese efforts to cut off supply lines to Australia; impressive naval victories were won in the spring of 1942 in the battle of the Coral Sea and at Midway, the only relief to the over-all gloom of that period. In the summer American forces landed at Guadalcanal in the Solomon Islands. A long ordeal of "island-hopping" with inadequate forces began.

In Europe it was decided to concentrate first on the air bombardment of Germany. The Russians, dissatisfied, called for a true "second front," an invasion by ground forces that would relieve the pressure of the three hundred German divisions that were ruining their country. Suspicious of the West as ever, doubly suspicious since the Munich conference of 1938, in which they saw a Western attempt to deflect the Germans into an attack on Russia, they regarded the failure to establish a second front as new evidence of anti-Soviet feeling. Throughout the war, they took what aid they could get, but never learned to like or trust their Allies.

But the United States, in 1942, was not ready to undertake land action by a direct assault on *Festung Europa*. Although in the Second World War, as in the First, more than two years elapsed between the outbreak of war in Europe and the intervention of the United States, and although in the second war American military preparations began much sooner, the United States in 1942 was still involved in the cumbersome processes of mobilization, converting industry to the production of war materials for itself and its Allies, imposing controls on its economy to prevent a runaway inflation, and giving military training to its profoundly civilian-minded people, of whom over twelve million eventually served in the armed forces—over three times as many as in the First World War. In any case, for a year after the United States entered the war, German submarines enjoyed enough control of the Atlantic to make large shipments of troops too risky. In effect, they blockaded the American army in the United States. The American and British navies gradually won the battle of the Atlantic; the submarine menace was reduced to tolerable proportions by the first part of 1943. It was decided to begin the assault upon Germany, from Great Britain as a base, with a massive and prolonged air bombardment of its factories and cities. Since not everything could be shipped across the Atlantic at the same time, this meant the deferment of land invasion until 1944. The embattled Russians were dissatisfied; their suspicions were aroused again; they professed to doubt whether the Western Allies meant ever really to face the German army at all.

THE TURNING OF THE TIDE, 1942–3: STALINGRAD,

NORTH AFRICA, SICILY

Meanwhile, at the end of 1942 the tide began to turn. In November an Anglo-American force effected a surprise invasion of Algeria and Morocco in an amphibious operation of hitherto unparalleled proportions. The Allies, despite ideological misgivings in some quarters, gambled on cooperation with the Vichy French governor Admiral Darlan, who assisted them in assuming control but was soon thereafter assassinated. On the Continent, after the North African landings, the Germans took over control of unoccupied France as well; they were frustrated, however, in the effort to obtain possession of the remainder of the French fleet by the action of French crews which scuttled the ships at Toulon. In North Africa the invading forces under the command of General Dwight D. Eisenhower fought their way eastward into Tunisia. Meanwhile the British forces under General Montgomery, having held the Germans at El Alamein in June 1942, had already launched their third (and final) counter-offensive in October, even before the invasion; they now pushed the Germans westward from Egypt until a large German force was crushed between the two Allied armies and destroyed in Tunisia. By May 1943 Africa was cleared of Axis forces. Mussolini's dream of an African empire had been thwarted; the Mediterranean was open; the threat to Egypt and the Suez canal was ended.

At the same time it became clear, in the winter of 1942–3, that the Germans had suffered a catastrophic reversal in Russia in the titanic battle of Stalingrad. In August 1942 massive German forces began an all-out assault on Stalingrad, the vital key to all transport on the lower Volga; by September they had penetrated the city itself. Stalin, who from the start of the war personally commanded military operations in Russia, ordered his namesake city held at all costs; Russian soldiery and the civilian population took a desperate stand. After weeks of house to house fighting the Germans had taken most of the city when suddenly the Russians began a great counter-attack, led by General Zhukov; twenty-two German divisions were forced to capitulate; over 330,000 Germans were lost. The Russians followed up their victory with a new counter-offensive, a great westward drive that netted them wholesale advances and regained for them what they had initially lost in the first year of the war. After Stalingrad, despite some setbacks, the Russians were on the offensive for the remainder of the war. Stalingrad was a turning point not only in the history of the war but in world history as well.

American equipment meanwhile all through 1943 was arriving in Russia in prodigious quantities. The terms of Lend-Lease were liberally extended to the Soviets; a stream of American planes, guns, vehicles, clothing, and food made its way laboriously to Russia through the Arctic Ocean and through the Persian Gulf. Machinery and equipment were sent for the Soviet arms plants, which were themselves tremendously increasing their output. Anglo-American bombing was crippling the German aviation industry at home. The Allied contribution to the Soviet war effort was indispensable but Russian human losses were tremendous. It was not forgotten in later years by the Russians that they lost more men in the battle of Stalingrad than the United States lost in battle during the entire war in all theaters combined.

With contemporary American successes in the Solomon Islands at the end of 1942 and the slow throttling of German submarines in the Atlantic, the beginning of the year 1943 brought new hope for the Allies in all quarters.

In a spectacular campaign of July-August 1943, the British, Canadians, and Americans conquered the island of Sicily. Mussolini immediately fell; the twenty-one-year-old Fascist regime came to an end. Some months later, the Duce, as he attempted to flee the country, was seized, shot, and strung up like a slaughtered pig by anti-Fascist Italians. The new Italian government under Marshal Badoglio, in August 1943, tried to make peace. The German army then occupied Italy. The Allies, having crossed to the Italian mainland, attacked from the south. In October the Badoglio government declared war on Germany, and Italy was recognized by the Allies as a "co-belligerent." But the Germans stubbornly blocked the advance of the Allies to Rome despite new Allied landings and beachheads. The Italian campaign turned into a long and disheartening stalemate because the Western Allies, concentrating troops in Great Britain for the approaching cross-Channel invasion, could never spare enough for the Italian front.

THE ALLIED OFFENSIVE, 1944–5: FROM NORMANDY

TO VICTORY IN EUROPE AND THE PACIFIC

Festung Europa, especially along its western approaches, the coasts of Holland, Belgium, and France, bristled with every kind of fortification that German scientific and military ingenuity could devise. A seaborne attack upon Europe was an operation of wholly unprecedented kind. It differed from the earlier amphibious attacks on Algeria, Sicily, or the Pacific islands in that the defender in Europe, in the very part of Europe where the road and railway network was thickest, could immediately rush overwhelming reserves to the spot attacked—except in so far as feinting tactics kept him uncertain, air power destroyed his transport, or the Russians held the bulk of his forces in the East. Precise and elaborate plans had been worked out. Ten thousand aircraft were to provide aerial protection, scores of warships were to bombard the coast, four thousand ships were to carry the invading troops and their supplies across the Channel, artificial harbors were to be created where none existed.

The invasion of Europe began before dawn on June 6, 1944. The spot selected was the coast of Normandy directly across the Channel from England. An unparalleled combination of forces, British, Canadian and American, land, sea, and air, backed up by huge accumulations of supplies and reserves of men assembled in Great Britain, and the whole under the unified command of the American General Eisenhower, assaulted the French coast, established a beachhead and maintained a front. The Allies poured in their strength, over 130,000 men the first day, a million within a month. The Germans were at first thrown back more easily than had been expected. By August Paris was liberated, by September the Allies crossed the frontier of Germany itself. In France, Italy, and Belgium the resistance movements, which had grown up in secret during the later years of German occupation,

now came into the open, drove out German officials and pro-German collaborators. In Germany itself an underground group in July 1944 attempted
assassinate Hitler and stop the war; it failed, and was wiped out by the
Gestapo.

In August, in another amphibious operation, the Allies landed on the
French Mediterranean coast and swept up from southern France to join the
Allied forces advancing against stiffening resistance. At one point, momentarily, the Allied offensive suffered a serious reversal. A sudden German drive,
launched under Hitler's direct personal orders in December 1944 against
thinly held American lines on the Belgian sector in the Ardennes, created
a "bulge" in the advancing armies and caused heavy losses and confusion. But
the Allies rallied. Neither Hitler's Ardennes counter-offensive nor the use of
new destructive weapons rained on Britain, jet propelled flying bombs and
rockets, availed the Germans. The Western allies pushed on and smashed
through the heavily fortified Siegfried line. The last natural obstacle, the
Rhine, was crossed when in March 1945 American forces by a stroke of luck
discovered an undestroyed bridge at Remagen; they poured troops over it and
established a bridgehead—the first troops to cross the Rhine in combat since
Napoleon's armies. Subsequent crossings took place to the north. Soon the
Allies were accepting wholesale surrenders in the Ruhr valley.

Meanwhile the Russian armies had swept through the Baltic states,
White Russia, the Ukraine, and Poland and forced the capitulation of Ru-
mania, Finland, and Bulgaria. Early in 1945 they had entered East Prussia,
Czechoslovakia, and Hungary, and had begun their final drive into Germany.
Soon they were at the gates of Berlin. The Allies offered no terms to Hitler,
nor to any Germans. They demanded unconditional surrender, and the Ger-
mans fought on until May 1945. By that time the Russians pouring in from
Poland and Hungary, and the American, British, Free French, and British
Empire forces coming from the West and from Italy, began to meet along
the Elbe river and in Bohemia and Austria. By Allied agreement a Russian
Army took Berlin. Hitler perished in the ruins of his capital. There was no
German government left to offer surrender; a German admiral went through
the formalities. By May 8, 1945, the war in Europe was over.

In the Pacific, against Japan, operations had dragged on for three years,
hampered by the strategic decision to concentrate against Germany first.
Slowly, from points in the Solomon Islands, the easternmost fringe of the
Indonesian archipelago, American forces, at first very small, worked their
way in a northwesterly direction toward far-away Japan. They had to fight in
turn for Guadalcanal, for New Guinea, for the reconquest of the Philippines.
They had to fight for the Japanese islands and atolls in the mid-Pacific (taken
by Japan from the Germans after the First World War, and converted into
powerful naval bases), the Gilbert Islands, the Marshalls, the Carolines, the
Marianas. In October 1944 they won a great naval victory at the battle of
Leyte Gulf. Finally, in one of the war's greatest and final battles, they won
the island of Okinawa, only three hundred miles from Japan itself. Okinawa
was captured just as the Germans collapsed in Europe. From the new Allied

WORLD WAR II
PACIFIC THEATER

JAPANESE EMPIRE 1940
OCCUPIED AREAS JUNE, 1942
AT WAR AGAINST JAPAN AUG. 7, 1945

NORTH POLE

ARCTIC OCEAN

CANADA

SOVIET UNION

ALASKA

Seattle

SINKIANG

⑤ SOVIET UNION ENTERS WAR AUG. 8, 1945

MONGOLIA

BERING SEA

UNITED STATES

San Francisco

TIBET

SAKHALIN

MANCHUKUO

KARAFUTO

ATTU KISKA

ALEUTIANS

Dutch Harbor

INDIA

CHINA

Peiping

Vladivostok

Chungking

KOREA

BURMA

Shanghai

Hiroshima

JAPAN

ATOMIC BOMBS DROPPED ON HIROSHIMA AND NAGASAKI, AUG., 1945
JAPAN SURRENDERS SEPT. 2, 1945

⑥

① JAPAN ATTACKS PEARL HARBOR DEC. 7, 1941

THAILAND

Canton

Nagasaki

Tokyo

Pearl Harbor

Hong Kong

OKIN-AWA

FORMOSA

MIDWAY

INDO-CHINA

P A C I F I C   O C E A N

HAWAIIAN IS. (USA)

④ U.S. FORCES RE-OCCUPY THE PHILIPPINES OCT. 1944

IWO JIMA

② GREATEST JAPANESE EXPANSION JUNE, 1942

Manila

PHILIPPINE IS.

Singapore

LEYTE

MARIANA IS.

SAIPAN TINIAN

WAKE

BORNEO

GUAM

YAP

PALAU

JAVA

CELEBES

ENIWETOK

KWAJALEIN

CAROLINE

TRUK

MARSHALL IS.

ISLANDS

HOWLAND I. (USA)

Hollandia

NEW GUINEA

GILBERT IS.

Port Moresby

SOLOMON IS.

GUADALCANAL

③ U.S. FORCES LAND ON GUADALCANAL AUG. 7, 1942

TUTUILA (USA)

AUSTRALIA

CORAL SEA

NEW HEBRIDES (BR. & FR.)

FIJI IS. (BR.)

→ SUPPLY LINES
→ ALLIED LAND OR NAVAL ATTACKS
⤍--- ALLIED AIR THRUSTS
⤍······ SOVIET THRUSTS INTO MANCHURIA AND KOREA

Sydney

NEW ZEALAND

TRM

These two maps show the global character of the war, and the central position of the United States with respect to the European and Pacific theaters. The legends in the small boxes, designated by numerals, summarize the successive stages of the war in both hemispheres. In 1942, with the Germans reaching as far east as Egypt and Stalingrad, and the Japanese as far west as Burma, the great danger to the Soviet-Western alliance was that these two might join forces, dominate southern Asia, control the oil resources of the Persian Gulf, and stop the flow of Western supplies to the Soviet Union from this direction. The almost simultaneous Soviet-Western successes, late in 1942, at Stalingrad and El Alamein, and

WORLD WAR II
ATLANTIC THEATER

Legend:
- ■ HITLER'S "EMPIRE"
- ▦ ALLIED WITH GERMANY
- ▨ OCCUPIED BY THE AXIS
- ⠿ AT WAR AGAINST THE AXIS

① HITLER INVADES POLAND SEPT. 1, 1939

⑥ GERMANY SURRENDERS MAY, 8, 1945

④ GREATEST AXIS EXPANSION DEC. 1941–NOV., 1942

② FRANCE SURRENDERS JUNE 22, 1940

⑤ ALLIES INVADE NORTH AFRICA NOV. 8, 1942 NORMANDY COAST JUNE 6, 1944

③ UNITED STATES BASES–DESTROYER DEAL SEPT. 2, 1940 ENACTS LEND LEASE MAR. 11, 1941 ENTERS THE WAR DEC. 8, 1941

NORTH POLE

SOVIET UNION — Murmansk · Kuibyshev · Moscow · Stalingrad

GREENLAND (DEN.) — ICELAND — NORWAY — SWEDEN — DEN. — GER. — IRAN — TURKEY — SUEZ CANAL

CANADA

UNITED STATES

UNITED KINGDOM — FRANCE — ITALY — El Allamein — EGYPT

PORT. SPAIN — TUNISIA — Oran — LIBYA

CUBA — PANAMA CANAL — VENEZUELA

AZORES (PORT.) — Casablanca — ALGERIA (FR.) — FR. MOROCCO

CANARY IS. (SP.)

A T L A N T I C   O C E A N

CAPE VERDE IS. (PORT.) · Dakar

FRENCH WEST AFRICA — FRENCH EQUATORIAL AFRICA

BRAZIL

← LEND LEASE SUPPLY LINES

◄ ALLIED THRUSTS

TRM

in the invasion of Morocco-Algeria and of Guadalcanal proved to be the turning point of the war. In 1943 the German submarine campaign in the Atlantic was defeated, so that American troops and supplies could move more freely to Europe. The invasion of Normandy in June, 1944, with continuing Soviet pressure from the east, brought about German surrender in May, 1945. Meanwhile, in the Pacific, American occupation of the islands and re-occupation of the Philippines prepared the way for the surrender of Japan, consummated by two atomic bombs in August, 1945.

bases that had been won, from Saipan, from Iwo Jima, and from Okinawa, and from aircraft carriers a heavy bomber offensive was launched against Japan, such as had devastated Germany in the preceding two years, shattering Japanese industry and destroying the remnants of the Japanese navy. The American army prepared to shift combat troops from the European theater to the Far East. The stage was being set for a full-scale invasion of Japan itself.

Then, on August 6, 1945, an atomic bomb, prepared in utmost secrecy by American and British scientists, hit the city of Hiroshima, with a population of 200,000 people, which it destroyed by a single explosion with the loss of over seventy thousand lives. Two days later, the Soviet Union, which had pledged itself to enter the conflict in the East within three months after the surrender of Germany, declared war on Japan and invaded Manchuria. On August 9 an even more powerful atomic bomb struck Nagasaki. The Japanese made peace at once. On September 2, 1945, the formal terms of surrender were signed. The Emperor remained at the head of the state, but the Japanese islands were placed under the rule of a United States army of occupation.

The Second World War of the twentieth century was over. The same cold impersonal statistics that had recorded ten million killed in the First World War now reported some fifteen million military deaths and at least that many civilian fatalities. Russian military deaths were estimated at six million, German at three million, Japanese at one and a quarter million. British and British Empire losses were about 500,000, American military deaths at something over 300,000. The death figures would have been greater except that one of every two soldiers seriously wounded was saved by new sulfa and penicillin drugs and by blood plasma transfusions. None of these military statistics could be more than approximate and no one could begin to estimate the complete toll of human lives lost in the war, directly or indirectly, from the bombings, the mass-extermination and deportation policies of the Germans, the post-war famines and epidemics. Perhaps the losses came to thirty-five or forty million, but at such figures the human mind retreats and human sensitivities are dulled. It is enough to say that peace had come.

THE FOUNDATIONS OF THE PEACE

The foundations of the peace had been laid, it was thought, during a number of major wartime Allied conferences. In August 1941 Roosevelt and Churchill had met at sea off the coast of Newfoundland and had drawn up the Atlantic Charter. There were meetings in 1943 at Casablanca, at Cairo, and at Teheran (in the latter Stalin participated for the first time); and in the final phase of the war, in February 1945, at Yalta, and in July 1945, at Potsdam, in the environs of shattered Berlin.

The Atlantic Charter, issued jointly by Roosevelt and Churchill at their first meeting, resembled in spirit the Fourteen Points of Woodrow Wilson. It pledged that sovereign rights and self-government would be restored to all who had been forcibly deprived of them, that all nations would have equal access to world trade and world resources, that all peoples would work together to achieve improved living standards and economic security. The post-war peace, it promised, would assure for men in all lands freedom from fear and want, and would guarantee an end to force and aggression in international affairs. Here, and in the Four Freedoms enunciated earlier by President Roosevelt, the ideological basis of the peace was proclaimed. At the 1943 conferences and through other consultations the Allies endeavored to concert their military plans and resolved to accept nothing less than the unconditional surrender of the Axis powers. The two conferences that arrived at the most important political decisions were the meetings at Yalta and at Potsdam.

The Yalta meeting in February 1945 took place when the Allies were close to final victory—closer, events disclosed, than anyone at the time realized. The three Allied statesmen met at an old tsarist Crimean summer resort on the Black Sea, rejoiced in their common triumphs, and took the measure of one other. There were differences, but agreements were reached, at least in principle, on Poland and Eastern Europe, Germany, the war in the Far East, and the projected post-war international organization, the United Nations.

The discussion of Poland and Eastern Europe raised the most serious difficulties. Stalin's armies, having driven the Nazi forces to within thirty miles of Berlin, were in control of Poland and almost all Eastern and Central Europe. The Russians remembered these areas as anti-Soviet, and Poland particularly as the perpetrator of aggression against Soviet territory in 1920 and as the ancient corridor of attack upon Russia. Neither Roosevelt nor Churchill had fought the war against the Nazis to leave Russia the undisputed master of all Eastern Europe and able to impose a totalitarian political system on all this vast area. Churchill had even during the war urged that an invasion be launched through southern Europe so that the Balkans might be liberated by Western armies, but his proposition had been voted down largely on the grounds of military expediency. At Yalta, Roosevelt and Churchill did what they could; they extracted from Stalin a number of promises. All the liberated states were to be permitted provisional governments "broadly representative of all democratic elements in the population," *i.e.*, not consisting merely as in the case of the provisional government of Poland already established, of authorities subservient to the Soviets. They pressed Stalin to pledge also the "earliest possible establishment through free elections of governments responsive to the will of the people." The pledge was a verbal concession that cost the Russian leader little; he rejected the suggestion of international supervision over future elections.

A number of territorial changes were also agreed to, pending final settlement at the post-war peace conference. It was agreed that the eastern boundary of Poland should be set roughly at the Curzon line, the frontier contemplated by the Allies in 1919 before the Poles conquered territory to its east. The Poles were to be compensated, in the north and west, at the expense of Germany. On this and on other matters relating to Germany there was a large area of accord; the three were united in their hatred of German Nazism and militarism. Germany was to be disarmed and divided into four occupation zones, to be administered by the big three powers and by France—the latter at the insistence of Britain. There was vague talk of dismembering Germany, of undoing the work of Bismarck, but the difficulties of such a step were understood. Reparations, it was stipulated, would go to those countries that had borne the main burden of the war and suffered the heaviest losses; the reparations would help also to destroy future German war potential; details were to be worked out later.

The plan for a post-war international organization, to be called the United Nations, was as dear to Roosevelt as the League had been to Woodrow Wilson. It was agreed that the big powers, the permanent members of the new organization's Security Council, would have a veto power on decisions. The Soviets pressed for more than one vote in the new organization, arguing that their constitution gave sovereign rights to each of their sixteen republics and that the British Dominions would each have a seat. It was agreed not to contest their claim for three seats. To Roosevelt this was a small concession; the American President rejoiced that an international organization was to come into being, that the Soviets were to participate, and that international affairs were never again to be run by big-power alliances and intrigues.

Critical agreements were reached on the Far East. Here political and military decisions were inextricably linked. In April 1941 the Soviets had concluded a non-aggression treaty with Japan and had remained neutral in the Pacific war despite their historic interests in the Far East. Given the magnitude of the war effort on the European front, no one pressed the Soviets to enter the Pacific war. It was agreed to wait at least until the Germans were on the verge of defeat. Now, at Yalta, it was hoped by the most important American military advisers that Russia could be persuaded to join the war against the Japanese. Though Japan was badly battered and its morale sinking, it was still estimated that Japanese resistance would last some eighteen months after Germany's fall; and a bloody invasion of the Japanese homeland was projected. The atomic bomb was in an advanced state of preparation but had not yet been tested. Russian participation, it was felt, would pin down the Japanese armies on the Chinese mainland and save Allied lives. Stalin agreed to enter the war against Japan, but he sought compensation; Russian "public opinion," the Soviet dictator averred, would demand it. It was stipulated that the U.S.S.R. would enter the war against Japan "two or three months" after Germany had surrendered. In return, the Soviets were to have restored to them territories and rights which tsarist Russia had lost to Japan forty years before in the Russo-Japanese war of 1904–5—the southern half of Sakhalin Island, and in Manchuria special concessions at the warm-water port of Dairen and at the naval base of Port Arthur, as well as joint control with China over the Manchurian railroads leading to these ports; in addition, the Soviets were to receive the Kurile Islands, which had not been Russian before. The sovereignty of China over

Manchuria was affirmed but China was not party to any of the agreement. The territorial concessions to the Soviets in the Far East implied nothing less than that the Western powers seemed to be sanctioning the replacement of Japanese imperialism by Russian imperialism in the crucial area of northeast China, and without China having any voice in the matter at all. The concessions were the price to be paid for Soviet assistance against the Japanese, assistance then considered indispensable for the final defeat of Japan. What really exasperated so many in later years was that Russia's entry into the war, as pledged, was not of the slightest military consequence; it came two days after the atomic bomb had been dropped. The concessions in the Far East need not have been made. But the wisdom of hindsight is indeed only one kind of wisdom.

At Yalta mutual suspicion and hostility were in abeyance, because the Western allies appreciated the Soviet war effort against the Germans, and were hopeful that wartime harmony would produce post-war cordiality, especially if all the participating personalities remained alive to assure it. Churchill was somewhat less certain of the future and would have preferred a franker recognition and definition of spheres of influence, but such a policy was held to be old-fashioned. Yet the spirit of the Atlantic Charter had at least in some ways been contravened. Like the Versailles treaty of 1919, the decisions at Yalta would not have been so disappointing had the ideals not been set so high.

At Potsdam, in July 1945 after the German collapse, the Big Three met again. A new American president, Harry S. Truman, represented the United States; President Roosevelt had died in April, on the eve of final victory. Churchill, in the midst of the conference, was replaced by the new British prime minister Clement Attlee after the Labor Party's victory at the polls. Stalin still represented Russia. By now, disagreements between the Western allies and the Soviets had deepened, not only over Poland, Eastern Europe, and the Balkans, but over German reparations and other matters. But comprehensive agreements were announced on the post-war treatment of Germany, on German disarmament, demilitarization, "denazification," and the punishment of war criminals. Pending the final peace treaty, German territory east of the Oder and Neisse rivers was committed to Polish administration. Poland thus extended its territorial boundaries about a hundred miles westward as compensation for Russian westward expansion at Polish expense. German East Prussia was similarly divided between Russia in the north and Poland in the south. The transfer of the German population in these areas was to be effected in an orderly and humane fashion; but hundreds of thousands were soon driven from their homes or fled within a few months.

It was agreed at Potsdam that peace treaties would be signed as soon as possible with the former German satellite states. Eighteen months later, after considerable difficulty because of the widening chasm between the Soviets and the West, a peace conference was held at Paris and in 1947 treaties were signed with Italy, Rumania, Hungary, Bulgaria, and Finland. All these states paid reparations and agreed to certain territorial adjustments.

In 1951 a peace treaty was signed with Japan—but not by the Soviets or the nations over which they had influence. And over a decade after the close of hostilities no final peace treaty had been signed with Germany, a Germany divided into two. For the wartime coalition had fallen tragically apart, and with it the dreams and aspirations of those who had fought the Second World War to a resounding triumph over one kind of aggression and one kind of attempted world domination.

108. Transformation and Revolution in Post-War Europe and Asia

The Second World War left the world in a worse state of shock and disorder than the First. Physical destruction was incomparably greater. In the First World War trench warfare had thoroughly destroyed limited regions. In the Second World War the ground fighting made a ruin of western Russia, and the air bombing reduced whole cities, especially in Germany, to piles of debris. The so-called "strategic" bombing had blighted the productive industry and the transport facilities of the Continent. Goods even if produced could not be moved; millions of refugees from bombed out cities or from hostile political regimes sought miserably for an asylum. More people died of starvation or cold, in civilized Europe in 1945 and 1946, than at any time in generations or even in centuries.

REVOLUTIONARY CHANGE IN CENTRAL AND EASTERN EUROPE

The Second World War, like the First, was followed by a wave of revolution. There was nothing quite so epochal as the replacement of tsardom by communism in Russia, but the advance of communism in Europe and Asia was, if anything, even more stupendous. Where communism in 1918 was chaos, in 1945 it was the way of life of an organized Great Power. There had been communist scares all over Eastern and Central Europe in 1919. In 1945 communism with Soviet backing materialized with real effect.

In Eastern and Central Europe, most of it occupied by Russian troops in the sweep of military operations at the end of the war, in one country after another, the native agrarian or peasant parties were pushed aside by communists, who, by dictatorial methods, set up "people's republics" closely bound to the Soviet Union. The Baltic states, Estonia, Latvia, and Lithuania, had already been sovietized in 1940. After 1944 came the turn of Rumania, Bulgaria, Hungary, Poland, Albania, Yugoslavia and finally, in 1948, of Czechoslovakia. Virtually the entire area considered in 1919 as a protective buffer zone against bolshevism fell under Russian domination. An "iron curtain" was said to have descended roughly along the old Elbe-Trieste line, of which much has been said in previous pages of this book. Finland, Austria, and Greece alone escaped, the Greeks only after a fierce civil war in which anti-communist forces, aided by the British occupation army, defeated the communists and restored the Greek monarchy. Elsewhere, as after the First World War, monarchies fell—in Italy, and in the new people's republics of Bulgaria, Rumania, Yugoslavia, and Albania. It was not to be expected that the revolutionary regimes would retain their royalty.

Almost everywhere the same pattern of events tended to repeat itself. Soviet military power made it possible for native revolutionaries to establish the new governments, not entirely unlike the course of events when the armies of the French Revolution and Napoleon swept over Europe and created a chain of client and satellite states. The Western-Soviet coalition had agreed during the war that the power or powers emancipating an area from the enemy would temporarily exercise full political control. In that way, the Western powers controlled political events in Italy without consultation with the Soviets. In Eastern and Central Europe the Soviets set up native provisional governments, which functioned under the watchful eye of the Red Army and of Soviet political overseers. They all but ignored the governments-in-exile in London representing the fallen regimes of the pre-war period; under Western pressure, at Yalta and elsewhere, the Soviets eventually gave some representation to these quarters, but it was only nominal. The provisional governments were set up as "united front" governments, *i.e.*, several political parties, including non-revolutionary parties, participated; they were generally pledged to the protection of private property and civil rights. Communists were in a minority in the new governments, but they occupied the key ministries of Interior and Justice, and thereby controlled the police and the courts. All elements alleged to be "fascist" or to have collaborated with the Nazis were barred from political life and from voting. The truth was that many of the nationalist and Rightist political elements so excluded had been guilty of fascist sympathies and even of collaboration, but it was equally true that the definition of "fascist" and even of "reactionary" made it possible to include many who were merely anti-communist. In the elections that were then held, the suppression of opposition candidates and the disfranchisement of political "undesirables" made a mockery of the pledge at Yalta to hold free and unfettered elections in these areas; this the United States and Great Britain pointed out in strong but ineffectual protests.

From all these maneuvers, the new "people's republics" formally emerged with constitutions modeled more or less on the Soviet 1936 pattern, even to the point of concessions to existing national minorities along Soviet federalist lines. With the establishment of the new governments repression tightened still further, and the communists took full control. The leaders of the opposition political parties, especially of the agrarian or peasant parties, took flight or were in other ways effectively silenced; Mikolajczyk fled Poland; Petkov was hanged in Bulgaria; scores in these countries and elsewhere were imprisoned. As a fitting climax, there then appeared the old Soviet story of purges, arrests, confessions, and executions among the highest-ranking satellite communists themselves once they fell from grace—among them the

Rumanian woman revolutionary Ana Pauker, the Pole Gomulka, the Hungarian Rajk, and the Czechoslovak leaders Clementis and Slansky. The new regimes, like other revolutionary orders, clashed with the church; high-ranking prelates of the Catholic church, Cardinal Mindszenty in Hungary, Archbishop Stepinac in Yugoslavia, others in Poland and elsewhere, were denounced, brought to public trial and imprisoned. Given the censorship and rigid control over communications with the outside world, no one could know with any certainty what social and economic changes were taking place in all these countries. It seemed apparent, however, that following Soviet lines, industry was being nationalized, economic planning and controls were being introduced, and landholding changes inaugurated. Under projects similar to the Soviet Five-Year plans, considerable industrialization was reported, notably in Poland. The landholding changes were greater than those in the period after the First World War. The large centuries-old landed estates of the former Junkers in East Prussia (now divided between the U.S.S.R. and Poland), of the remaining "Baltic barons" in the Baltic states, of the Magyar magnates in Hungary and of the Polish gentry seemed ended, with what benefits for the peasantry no one could yet say. Where landholding was already widespread, as in Rumania, some of the wealthier *kulak* elements were being dispossessed. Collectivization was not at first pushed; the time was not yet. The agrarian face of Central and Eastern Europe was being transformed; the apparent triumph of communism in these areas was the greatest single change in Europe in the post-war years.

The policies of the new regimes were coordinated through a new Communist International, created in 1947 and given the singularly innocuous name of Cominform, or Communist Information Bureau. It was essentially a revival of the Comintern dissolved by Stalin in 1943 as a gesture of ideological wartime harmony with the West; it became now the chief center of the propaganda war against the West. The relationship of the people's republics to the Soviets was formalized also by a network of military alliances and trade agreements. Before long the largest share of Soviet foreign trade in the post-war years was with its satellites. Of all the new communist regimes, Yugoslavia alone, freed from the Nazis largely by its own army, made a remarkable show of resistance to Soviet control. Tito, as the Yugoslav communist leader Joseph Broz was called, in a clear and perhaps symbolic demonstration of the centrifugal power of nationalism and national economic self-interest even in the tightly woven Soviet international order, openly defied Moscow. The Cominform first excommunicated and anathematized the heretic in 1948 and then in the 1950's sought to woo him back to the fold.

As for developments in the U.S.S.R. itself, they did not differ basically from the developments of the 1930's. Post-war five-year plans were launched, the country's fourth in 1946, and a fifth and sixth subsequently. The aim was to repair the tremendous devastation wrought by the war and then to increase the country's industrial potential. By the 1950's there seemed little doubt that the U.S.S.R. had been rehabilitated—it claimed to be producing twice as much steel and coal as in 1940; and so far as the statistics could be believed, it was expanding industrially at a rate not matched either by the United States or by Western Europe. Agriculture remained the weakest sector of the economy; here serious problems pressed in crop production and in livestock. In the five-year plans emphasis was still primarily on heavy industry; and despite a few concessions, living standards for the ordinary workingman in the socialist fatherland—consumer goods and services, and housing—remained poor by Western standards. Rigid control over intellectual life persisted; the orientation for a time after the war was vehemently nationalistic and xenophobic; deviations in economics, in music, in genetics were condemned on grounds of "cosmopolitanism," *i.e.*, internationalism. For a time it seemed forgotten that Marx and Engels were both West Europeans. The Soviets also claimed a leadership in all technological inventiveness, denying even that the Russia of Peter the Great ever had to be "Europeanized" by borrowings from the West.

In 1953, Russia's twentieth-century Peter the Great died. Even Stalin's victims and opponents could not deny his massive accomplishments—the industrialization of Russia, the defense in the Fatherland War, the successful promotion of Russian national interests and of international communism in the post-war world. At the same time it was Stalin's suspicions of the West and his inflexibility that had undoubtedly contributed to the poisoning of the post-war international atmosphere. After his death something more of a collective leadership seemed to be emerging in the Party and in the state, showing signs of a willingness to soften some aspects of the older tyrant's reign of almost thirty years but not to abandon any of the essential features of Soviet totalitarianism. By 1956 Nikita Khrushchev had established himself as top leader. Malenkov, who at first seemed in control, had faded into the background; Beria, head of the secret police, had been executed The power struggle in the post-Stalin era was not ended.

END OF THE COLONIAL EMPIRES IN ASIA:

INDIA AND INDONESIA

The revolt of Asia reached a veritable flood tide in the years immediately after 1945. The old colonial system, battered after the First World War, could be said to have collapsed after the Second. During the fighting the Japanese had sedulously stirred up old Asian resentments at the white man's rule and fanned Asian hopes of independence from the West. After the war Europeans could rule in Asia only at prohibitive military cost, if indeed at all; and they could rule only in contradiction of their own professed ideals of self-government. In the troubled waters of Asia, Moscow-oriented communists operated too, and with vastly greater success than in the 1920's. The wave of anti-imperialist unrest appeared now also in other areas—in Negro Africa where it was directed mainly against the British; in Moslem North Africa where in Algeria, Tunisia, and Morocco it was aimed at the expulsion of the French; and in the Middle East.

THE WORLD, 1955

On a small map of the world in 1955 the most readily visible changes, as compared to a map of the world before the Second World War, are the break-up of the British, French, and Dutch empires in Asia, and the peripheral expansion of the Soviet Union to include the former Baltic states and the southern part of the island of Sakhalin. India, Pakistan, and Ceylon became independent of Britain while remaining in the British Commonwealth; Burma became independent but outside the Commonwealth. French Indo-China turned into the republic of Viet-Nam and the kingdoms of Laos and Cambodia. The Netherlands Indies became the independent Republic of Indonesia. The Philippines also became independent.

China went communist, with the Nationalist government confined to the island of Formosa. Korea, formerly Japanese, became legally independent, though divided. The former Japanese Pacific islands were turned over to United States administration under a United Nations trusteeship. In the Near East Israel emerged as an independent state, while in Africa the conversion of the former Anglo-Egyptian Sudan into an independent republic portended further changes in that continent. In the Western hemisphere the Second World War brought no similar changes, but Newfoundland and its dependency, Labrador, became part of Canada in 1949.

British rule in India came to a dramatic but peaceful end in 1947. The drive for self-government and independence had gathered momentum in the 1930's and had resulted in numerous concessions. In the Second World War, as in the First, India rendered substantial aid to the British. To rally the Indian war effort and to counteract Japanese propaganda, which demanded "Asia for the Asiatics," the British promised Dominion status, to take effect at the war's end. In 1947, this was granted; the Indian Empire was dissolved and the British sovereign gave up the title of Emperor. Because many Moslems were unwilling to live in an India dominated by Hindus, the unity of India was lost in the winning of independence. The Indian sub-continent was partitioned. A Dominion of India was created, mainly Hindu, with some 360 million inhabitants, and a Dominion of Pakistan, mainly Moslem, with some 75 million inhabitants. Because of the Moslem distribution in the old Indian Empire, Pakistan had to be established in two disconnected parts separated by a thousand miles of Indian territory. Independence resulted, as the British had warned, in bloody riots between the Indian religious communities, forcible mass expulsions, and the deaths of thousands; but the uglier features of the communal tension soon subsided.

Both India and Pakistan retained a connection with the British Commonwealth of Nations, Pakistan remaining a Dominion. India, soon after independence, rejected Dominion status, i.e., even a nominal connection with the British crown, and became a republic; Nehru and other Indian nationalists had spent too many of their adult years in British prisons to continue allegiance to the crown. In a tribute, however, to the flexibility of British institutions, and to the gracefulness with which the British finally departed, India agreed to remain associated with the British Dominions in the Commonwealth of Nations and to consult and act with them on matters of common concern. Pakistan, while retaining Dominion status, moved also toward the establishment of a republic. Of the other integral parts of the older Indian Empire that became independent after the war, Burma chose to go its separate way, but Ceylon became another British Dominion. Since the new members of the Commonwealth lacked the tie of sentiment that bound white New Zealanders or Canadians to Great Britain, and since India insisted upon being a republic, the whole nature of the Commonwealth, or association of free communities under the British crown, became even more intangible than in the definition of 1926.

Another former great empire in the East, the Netherlands Indies, also came to an end. In 1949, after much dissension and actual hostilities, the Dutch recognized Indonesia with its sixty million peoples as an independent republic joined in a tenuous union with the Dutch crown; five years later, by mutual agreement, all connection with the Dutch crown was ended. With the British gone from India and the Dutch from the East Indies, and with the United States in 1946 granting full independence to the formerly Spanish Philippines, the old colonial empires dating from the early modern centuries were vanishing. Portugal alone stubbornly clung to a few enclaves on the mainland of India as a token of its former imperial grandeur in the great age of Western exploration and discovery.

REVOLUTIONARY CHANGE IN ASIA: CHINA AND INDO-CHINA

It was perhaps in China that the most momentous Asian events of the early post-war years occurred. By 1949 a communist China had come into being. The uneasy alliance between Kuomintang and communists established in 1937 could not hold together even through the war years, to the dismay of American advisers who sought a unified war effort against the Japanese. As the Pacific war neared its end, Chiang Kai-shek offered the Chinese communists minority representation in his government on condition that the Chinese Red Army be scaled down and be incorporated into the Kuomintang forces. The communists rejected the proposal; they demanded instead the convocation of a popular constitutional assembly and insisted on an equitable allotment of military supplies to their own independent army, which in fact in many areas had been fighting more actively against the Japanese than the Nationalists. When Japan suddenly surrendered, the communists poured into the northern Chinese provinces and made contact with the Russians who had moved into Manchuria. The U.S.S.R., however, at this juncture pledged itself to respect the sovereignty of the Kuomintang government, and also to evacuate Manchuria; in return the Kuomintang government confirmed the privileges and concessions promised the Russians at Yalta.

Mao Tse-tung and the other communist leaders meanwhile refused to accept Kuomintang political control over the country as a whole; they insisted on retaining autonomy in the northern provinces they had conquered and on keeping their army intact. In the autumn of 1945 heavy fighting broke out. A truce mediated by the American General Marshall temporarily halted hostilities. But with the eventual withdrawal of the U.S.S.R. from Manchuria in the spring of 1946, many months after it had pledged to do so and after it had removed Manchurian industrial assets as reparations, Kuomintang and communists came again into open warfare over control of the important border province. As Marshall noted, the communists were quite willing to plunge the country into civil war to achieve their ends; and, as he noted also, in the Kuomintang, despite the promulgation of a constitution in 1946 and the holding of elections, political power remained concentrated in the hands of an unprincipled inner group bent on repressing all opposition, even non-communist. To many it seemed a deep tragedy that the anti-communist forces in China, and elsewhere in Asia, were themselves far from democratic.

In the fighting from 1946 to 1949 the Nationalists lost ground almost steadily. Their morale declined; corruption, inflation, and economic chaos spread; the population at large revealed no inclination to support them and showed actual hostility. Despite large sums amounting to almost two billion dollars given the Kuomintang by the United States, the Nationalists seemed to lack the ability or the will to resist. On the other hand the Chinese Red Army, equipped with captured Japanese arms, receiving various kinds of aid from the Soviets, indirectly obtaining American supplies through mass surrenders and sale by corrupt Kuomintang officials, and moderating their propaganda so as to attract wide sections of the population, pressed forward victoriously, routing the Kuomintang armies in the north and then occupying the Nationalist capital at Nanking. By the end of 1949 resistance had ended on the mainland. Chiang withdrew his shattered forces to the island of Formosa where in subsequent years he regrouped and reorganized them with American aid and awaited the day of retribution.

The Chinese communist leaders, of whom Mao Tse-tung and Chou En-lai were most prominent, proceeded to consolidate communist control in the new Chinese People's Republic. The capital was re-established in the ancient northern city of Peiping. For the first time since the Revolution of 1912, and indeed for over a century before, for good or for ill, a unified central government seemed in control of all China. The Chinese communists openly leaned on Russian experience. A Soviet-type constitution was promulgated. Five-year plans were projected for the industrialization of the country; the socialization of industry was begun and steps taken first toward the re-distribution of the land and then toward its collectivization. The familiar apparatus of Soviet totalitarianism appeared—mass arrests and executions, a secret police, censorship and indoctrination, and party purges. To the new regime the U.S.S.R. ostentatiously surrendered its privileges and concessions in Manchuria. In 1950 the Chinese communists openly intervened in the Korean War, as will be related below. In 1951, pressing old claims of Chinese suzerainty, the Chinese communist republic occupied Tibet; the proletarian revolution thus passed to the land of the Dalai Lamas.

The Chinese communists, reviving the doctrines of Sun Yat-sen, and reinforcing them with Marxist-Leninist teachings, denounced Western capitalism and imperialism. No matter what else the future held, it was certain that the day of European privilege in China was over. As to the Soviets, despite the close relations maintained with Moscow, it remained a question whether the Chinese communists were not sufficiently nationalistic, and primarily Chinese, to oppose Soviet influence as they had opposed European. The emergence of a potential industrial and military power of almost five hundred million people, under strong unified control, posed grave future problems for the U.S.S.R. as well as for the non-Soviet world.

Western domination seemed at an end, too, in the former French colonial union of French Indo-China but not until after a decade of political turmoil and over seven and a half years of full-scale war between French armies and communist-led nationalist forces known as the Viet Minh. In 1954 when the fighting halted, the state of Viet Nam, which was the area most seriously contested, was partitioned into a somewhat more populous communist-sponsored section in the north and a native non-Communist government in the south. The French, who had suffered almost continued reversals throughout the war despite substantial American financial aid, prepared to withdraw from Viet Nam and from the other two states of Indo-China as well, Laos and Cambodia. The leader of the Viet Minh nationalist forces was the able, Russian-trained communist Ho Chi Minh. In Indo-China, and elsewhere, the active leadership of native nationalist independence movements was seized and held by communists. The French could claim that they were bent not on preserving old colonial privileges but on stemming the tide of world communism. There was substance to the argument, but the advance of communism in Asia (as distinct from its advance in Eastern and Central Europe) seemed closely linked to genuine native discontents and to popular revolutionary sentiments of nationalism and anti-colonialism. In all the revolutionary explosions in Asia, Western political ideas of sovereignty, independence, and freedom were compounded with racial hatred of European whites and Marxist denunciations of imperialism and capitalism. Without inquiry into what might follow, native nationalists in Asia showed a willingness to accept communist leadership in the determination to end Western imperialist control.

Meanwhile, in China, in India, in Indonesia, the new regimes faced the desperate problems of overpopulation and mass poverty. Having made promises and aroused hopes, they had to find rather better answers to these problems than the imperial authorities had ever offered. With less experience in government, they were obliged to deliver more. Otherwise, instability in the Far East would hardly cease.

THE NEAR AND MIDDLE EAST

In the Near and Middle East, where the Turkish Revolution after the First World War had quickened political awareness, communism made relatively little headway, but nationalism grew in intensity, as did the self-consciousness of the Moslem world as a political entity. The Moslem world took in more than the Middle East. Its main body stretched from Morocco on the Atlantic Ocean to Pakistan on the Indian Ocean, taking in all the Arab states, and stretching northward to Iran on the borders of the Soviet Union. The vital importance of the Middle East in world affairs lay in its possession of the richest oil reserves of the world as well as in its strategic location. Like other areas, the Middle East wanted to share in Western material advances but resisted Western political control. In Iran, anti-Western elements, after successfully resisting Soviet pressures, nationalized the country's oil resources and came close to the complete expropriation and expulsion of the predominantly British oil interests. A compromise in 1954 permitted the foreign oil companies to continue to work the oil wells with Western skill and equipment but gave a larger share of the royalties to the country itself. In Egypt, nationalist political leaders, after successfully forcing the withdrawal of British troops from their country, pressed with success to expel British forces even from the Suez Canal zone; in 1954, with some emergency provisions for returning, the British were forced to accede. The life line of the old British Empire was no longer secure; but the old British Empire itself was gone.

Of all the Moslem peoples the Arabs were the most vehemently nationalist. Syria and other Arab states, which had emerged from the old Turkish empire at the end of the First World War as European mandated areas, came out of the second as independent countries. The leading Arab states, Egypt, Saudi Arabia, Iraq, Syria, Jordan, and some others, though far from united on all issues, drew together in the Arab League to act jointly in international affairs and to advance Arab interests. The Arab League openly fomented Arab independence movements in French North Africa and was active elsewhere. The Arabs were aroused most by the post-war triumph of Zionism. The homeless survivors of European Jewry, assisted by Jewish organizations in America, sought out Palestine as a place of refuge. The Arabs did not feel that they should bear the brunt of Europe's persecution of the Jews. The Zionist leaders, once the British mandate was terminated, proclaimed the republic of Israel in 1948 and then in a short war defeated sizeable invading Arab armies. In the process of setting up the Israeli state almost a million Arabs were dispossessed. To all Arabs Zionism seemed like a new form of Western invasion of their region. The Israelis maintained that their new state would serve as a bridgehead for Western scientific, technological, and democratic advances in an economically underdeveloped, semi-feudal area. The Arabs remained unconvinced and threatened a renewal of open war.

109. The Democracies after 1945

In the domestic affairs of the Western countries there was again, as after the First World War, a decisive victory of democracy. It was an indubitable triumph for democracy to rid the world of the two chief fascist dictators. The experience with fascism even had a purging effect in the democratic countries; after Adolf Hitler, vehemently anti-rational philosophies lost ground in America and Western Europe. While democratic processes were continued and expanded, pre-war trends toward the welfare state were also accelerated. The memories of the great depression, the sacrifices made in the war, the desire to provide protection against economic insecurity of all kinds led to extended social security legislation and other reform measures.

THE UNITED STATES AND GREAT BRITAIN

For the United States, and indeed for much of the world, the most important single fact in the post-war years was the continuing productivity of the American economic system. The American economy, after recovering substantially from the Great Depression during the New Deal years, and expanding enormously to meet military needs during the Second World War, continued after 1945 to surpass its previous records. War damage in most other industrial countries made United States leadership in this respect greater than ever. For example, income per capita in the United States in 1938 was only a little higher than in Great Britain, Sweden, or Switzerland, the next wealthiest countries. In 1948 it was about twice as high. This situation, in which trained manpower was productive and in demand, favored the continuing solution in the United States of old problems of poverty and discrimination. It made possible also, through the Marshall Plan and other devices mentioned below, a program of material aid to other countries, especially in Europe, without which they could not so readily have overcome the ravages of the war. The United States hoped thus to strengthen democratic governments abroad, while keeping its industries busy and employment high at home. On the other hand, the economic ascendancy of the United States produced difficult problems. Able to export profusely, yet unwilling or not needing to import in the same proportion, the United States by its very productivity tended to unbalance the world exchanges. There was a chronic "dollar shortage"; that is, other countries could with difficulty find means to earn the dollars to buy American goods, and found themselves frustrated when they asked for "trade, not aid" in their relations with the United States. In addition, the superior wealth of the United States often made it hard for people in other countries to take a sympathetic view of American policies or of the American way of life.

President Truman, coming into office on Roosevelt's death, and reelected in 1948, attempted in his Fair Deal to continue the New Deal of his predecessor; but in the atmosphere of post-war prosperity and expanding production, attempts to extend government housing programs, public power control, and health insurance were checkmated. Wartime economic controls were rapidly weakened or dropped. A new labor-management-relations act, adopted under Republican auspices, curtailed what were described as unfair industrial practices of the labor unions, banning even the closed shop. When the Republican Party took over the presidency in the 1950's under the wartime hero Dwight D. Eisenhower, the orientation was more toward that of the business community but few fundamental steps were taken to nullify the changes inaugurated by the New Deal; in the 1950's social security coverage was even extended and legal minimum wages were raised. The United States remained the vigorous champion of free private enterprise, but the responsibility of the government for the state of the economy as a whole and the readiness to take government action to prevent the recurrence of anything like the crash of 1929 was recognized by both parties.

All purely domestic developments in the United States seemed overshadowed by the country's new world-wide international commitments, by its anxiety over the intentions and deeds of the U.S.S.R. and international communism, and by its concern with internal subversion and disloyalty. After the First World War, under the leadership of the then Attorney General A. Mitchell Palmer, raids had taken place on radical organizations, there had been deportations of alien radicals, and other similar developments. Now a much more extensive and longer-range program of curbing radical organizations and activities was established. By some the security program was declared too moderate and too mild. By others it was argued that the toleration of dissent, long the hallmark of American freedom, was more threatened than ever before. The United States continued also to grapple with its peculiarly "American dilemma," the question whether the American democracy could assimilate its thirteen million Negro citizens, or at least accord to them full political and civil equality. The problem was made more urgent by the new American leadership in world affairs, which made it desirable for the United States to appear in a favorable light to that majority of the world's population which was not white. The expansion of wartime and post-war economic opportunities for Negroes, changes initiated by wartime executive orders and Supreme Court rulings, and the determination of the great majority of the American people to work toward a peaceful solution held promise for the future; but the problem persisted.

In Britain the war was hardly over when the voters unseated Winston Churchill and put in a Labor government instead. Once the center of high capitalism, Great Britain for a while became the world's chief exemplar of a parliamentary socialism. The Labor party, ruling for the first time in history with a majority of its own, put through a broad social program in the six years between 1945 and 1951. Insisting that in an ailing economy the country's basic industries could not be left to the unplanned anarchy of capitalism and unrestrained competitive struggle for profit, it nationalized, i.e., brought under public ownership and control, while giving compensation to the former private owners, an important segment of the British economy, including the Bank of England, the coal mines, such public utilities as electricity and gas, the communications and transportation industries, and iron and steel production. Since only a relatively small proportion of all British industry was thus nationalized, what emerged was not socialism but a kind of mixed economy. Even in the private branches of the economy, however, steps were taken to influence the direction and extent of private investment; the national interest supplemented the enlightened self-interest of private enterprise and the profit motive. Simultaneously, the existing program of social insurance, inherited from the Liberal reforms of 1906–14, was greatly expanded and re-vamped. This had been promised earlier by the war-time coalition government along the lines of the recommendations made in the Beveridge Report on social insurance in 1942. The aim was to guarantee full employment in a free society and to provide social security for all "from the cradle to the grave." Not only was insurance coverage extended for unemployment, old age, and other contingencies but a comprehensive free medical and health service was inaugurated also. Taxes meanwhile were more steeply graduated.

All of this program, government ownership of key industries and close government control over the economy as a whole, the extensive social security program, and the use of taxation to redistribute wealth combined to build up the welfare state, by some called an oppressive, regimented, bureaucratic state and the road to a new serfdom, and by others, a demonstration that political democracies could protect the social and economic welfare of their citizenry and thereby insure an even greater devotion to democratic processes. The only constitutional change effected under the Labor government was the act passed in 1949 to reduce from three years to one the power of the House of Lords to delay legislation. Restrictions on labor activities dating from the general strike of 1926 were repealed. When in 1951 the Conservatives were returned to control of the House of Commons, in an election in which Labor still received a majority of the popular vote, they checked the nationalization program, and took steps to de-nationalize the iron and steel and trucking industries, but made no fundamental changes in the broad structure of social and medical insurance.

Both parties in Britain had to cope with the country's deteriorating international economic position. Britain was in an even worse state after the Second World War than after the First because most of its foreign holdings, amounting to some forty billion dollars before the war, had to be liquidated in the course of the war for military purposes; in addition, a large part of the British merchant marine had been lost. For Britain, still dependent on imports for its food and raw materials, this loss of interest on its investments and of income from its shipping services cut into the country's "invisible exports" and increased its adverse "balance of payments." The disappearance of a universally convertible currency such as the gold standard had provided, created obstacles to multilateral trade and aggravated the situation still further. Adopting a stern austerity program at home under the slogan "export or die," Britain girded to expand its exports and to compete in an increasingly difficult world market. With American financial aid and the intensified export drive, and with the post-war European economic cooperation program, the British position improved, but it remained vulnerable to the vicissitudes of international trade.

FOURTH FRENCH REPUBLIC

France's Fourth Republic inherited most of the troubles of the Third. The constitutional structure of the new republic differed only in detail from that of the older. One change was the extension of the suffrage to women. Again a multi-party system with unstable majorities and short-lived cabinets, a National Assembly jealous of its prerogatives, and a widespread suspicion of a strong executive characterized the French democracy. Again the perennial threat to the republic itself emerged. General de Gaulle was suspected in many quarters, not without some justification, of harboring anti-parliamentary, corporative, and even Bonapartist intentions. His claim that the Gaullist *Rally of the French People* was "above parties" confirmed these suspicions. Still when it would have been fairly easy for the general to seize power, in

1945 and 1946, he voluntarily relinquished even the presidency, apparently awaiting a more decisive call from the people. Another threat emerged from the extreme Left where the communists, largely on the record of their undeniably heroic role in the wartime resistance movement (after 1941), emerged for a time as the leading party in the country. A fourth of the electorate voted for candidates of the Communist party in France (as in Italy), but this seemed to represent the maximum which under existing circumstances communism in Western Europe was able to reach. Against communism on the Left and Gaullism on the Right, a "Third Force" coalition emerged in 1947, created largely by the Socialists and the Popular Republicans, a new Catholic progressive party that had grown out of the resistance movement. But the coalition had too many internal differences to thrive; cabinets still fell in France over the issue of state aid to church schools. By the early 1950's, however, the immediate threat from the extreme parties had subsided. In general, in the first post-war decade the country traveled full cycle from a Leftist orientation at the beginning to one in which the Center and Rightist parties dominated the political scene; even the once moribund moderate Radical party was again playing a key role in the 1950's.

From the first post-war phase something of a mixed economy emerged; important industries were nationalized and social insurance of various kinds was extended. But the spirit of enthusiasm and regeneration which was carried forward from the resistance movement into the first few years soon died down. In the more recent period few basic reforms could be introduced. Occasionally bold voices called for innovations to increase productivity and for fiscal reforms to end tax evasion. The Monnet plan, with American financial aid, helped to modernize French industry, but the economy still remained characterized by relatively small, inefficient, family-type industrial firms and small agricultural units. This was hardly the equipment for a great power in the twentieth century. Labor unrest persisted, aggravated by post-war inflation; great strikes took place in 1947, 1948, and in the 1950's, fomented in part by French communists for political reasons and in part motivated by old and genuine grievances. All internal problems were aggravated by the strain of trying to preserve the old French empire. In theory, colonial rule was thoroughly democratized in the French Union, as the empire was called after the war. Important steps were taken toward granting self-government and autonomy, but the reforms did not satisfy colonial revolutionaries in North Africa, Madagascar, and Indo-China. France, too, like all Western countries, had to contend with its problems in the strained atmosphere of post-war international relations.

DEMOCRACY IN THE FORMER AXIS COUNTRIES:

ITALY, GERMANY, AND JAPAN

In the former Axis countries democracy made headway also; to what degree the victory of democracy was real or apparent was a critical question.

In Italy, after twenty-one years under Mussolini, democratic processes were resumed. The Savoy monarchy was voted out of existence in 1946 and a republic took its place; the suffrage was extended to women. Communism emerged as a strong force in Italian political life, successfully exploiting existing economic and social grievances, of which there were many in Italy. The government was in the hands of Center coalitions, dominated largely by the Christian Democratic party, a Catholic party with a relatively advanced reform program. Steps were taken toward breaking up the larger landed estates, especially in the south, and toward redistributing the land; but poverty, land hunger, and unrest persisted, both in countryside and city.

Of Germany's part in international relations more will be noted below; something must be said here of German internal developments. Post-war Germany was divided into two separate parts. In East Germany, a German Democratic Republic followed the general pattern of the iron curtain people's republics in Eastern and Central Europe. In West Germany, democratic processes were inaugurated. A constitutional convention, meeting in 1948–9 with the encouragement of the Western occupying powers, established the Federal Republic of Germany, its capital in the Rhineland city of Bonn. The liberals and democrats of Bonn were resolved to create an enduring German democracy, something which the liberals and democrats at Frankfurt had failed to do a century before, in 1848–9, and which the men of Weimar had likewise failed to do in 1919. During the occupation, in 1947, the Allied authorities formally dissolved the old state of Prussia, of which much has had to be said in this history; the spirit of Prussian militarism and authoritarianism was thus to be exorcised from the German body politic; on this, Western and Soviet authorities were in agreement. The occupying powers cooperated also in the international trial held at Nuremberg in 1946 of twenty-two major Nazi leaders for crimes against humanity and world peace. The evidence of evil deeds was massive and incontrovertible, although there were misgivings in many quarters about the unprecedented step of punishing the leaders of a defeated enemy. Similar trials were held in Japan and gave rise to similar criticisms. The "denazification" program, carried out by Allied occupation authorities, each in its own way in its own zone, and by German courts under Allied supervision, had mixed and, for the long run, indeterminable results. In general, the attitude prevailed in the former Allied countries that collective or mass guilt for Nazi misdeeds ought not to be stressed; the sins of the Nazis were not to be visited on the German people as a whole. Economically, some effort was made during the occupation to break up the larger industrial combinations and cartels that had served as handmaidens to the Nazi war effort; but the decartelization program seemed neither thorough nor effective.

By 1954 the German Federal Republic had regained all but complete sovereignty and independence. The Western powers retained only the right to station troops in Germany for their European military structure, which the Germans were encouraged to join. The political fortunes of the new republic rested largely in the hands of the moderate and centrist Christian Democrats, in good part because of the skill of the able statesman Konrad Adenauer. The largest opposition party was that of the moderate Social Democrats. The outstanding achievement of West Germany was its spectacular industrial recovery and expansion; industrial production in the early 1950's was three-fifths greater than it had been before the war in the same territorial area. The German Federal Republic was a going concern, virtually sovereign, and a coveted ally of the Western powers, but Germany as a whole remained divided. Liberals and democrats in West Germany and communists in East Germany were at one in their determination to reunite their divided nation some day.

In Japan, as in Germany, the victorious Allies, especially the Americans, used military occupation as a means of inculcating democracy, with results that subsequent history had yet to disclose. A new constitution promulgated in 1946 ended the divine right rule of the Emperor and transformed him into a constitutional sovereign. Under the firm hand of General Douglas MacArthur the full political machinery of democratic government was established; women voted; local self-government was encouraged. Labor unions grew in size and became active even to the point where restrictions were soon placed on their activities among government workers. The large industrial and banking combinations known collectively as the Zaibatsu were ordered dissolved although there were signs that new forms of economic concentration were taking their place. A sweeping program of land re-distribution was inaugurated; unfortunately, many peasants lacked the means to purchase the holdings offered them, and there was much resistance to the program from the larger landowners. Although the moderate socialists, the Social Democrats, emerged as an important party, political control remained largely in the hands of conservative groups drawn from the upper social classes that had long ruled Japan. Japan, like Germany, profited from the tension between the Soviet and the Western world. In the peace treaty signed in 1951, to which the Soviets were not a party, no reparations were exacted nor were any drastic limitations on armaments imposed. Japanese sovereignty was re-established although the United States by treaty retained military rights in Japan. Japan, like Germany, ten years after the close of the war, was beginning, with the encouragement of the Western powers, to rearm.

PERSISTENT PROBLEMS

Broadly speaking, the Second World War created no wholly new problems for mankind, but it greatly aggravated certain basic problems that had troubled the world for over a century, making them both more difficult and more urgent. Three can be singled out—the problem of science, the problem of industrialism, and the problem of national sovereignty. They were aspects of the one and only super-problem, the moral question of man's fate: how could the human person, man, woman or child—the being said by some to be made in the image of God and by others to have a natural right to be happy

—live out his life, and realize his humanity in a world where science, industrialism, and national sovereignty pressed upon him from every side?

The problem of science was dramatized by the atomic bomb. The world shuddered at the instantaneous destruction of Hiroshima. With the war ending on this note, and with post-war improvements of atomic and hydrogen bombs, it was realized that a third world war would be unimaginably more awful. The use of inter-continental guided missiles, radio controls, proximity fuses, and probably biological warfare could be foreseen. Man, it was said, now possessed the means to annihilate not only his civilization but the very existence of human life on the planet. This thought, which possibly would not have perturbed St. Augustine, was appalling to a world which had set its highest values on social progress. And in truth, the reflective person wondered more than ever before how he himself or members of his family might meet their deaths, or what sufferings they might be called upon to endure.

The problem of science was not new. Science, with its partner, invention, had for a long time transformed the methods used in both industry and war. Observant people had long known that science could be applied either constructively or destructively, that knowledge was power, that the intelligence was the instrument of the will. It was the magnitude of destructive possibilities that made people formerly indifferent now see and worry over the problem. Scientists themselves rushed forward, after the first atomic explosion, to affirm the need of a moral regeneration. They insisted that science was neutral, that it was free from blame for the horror of Hiroshima, that scientific investigation must remain free, that the trouble lay only in the uses to which scientific knowledge was put. Never since the days of Galileo had scientists been so embarrassed, or so aroused over moral and social issues. Somehow science, or the exaggerated reliance on science, had misfired. The dream of those prophets of a scientific civilization, Bacon and Descartes, the idea that accumulation of scientific knowledge would automatically bring more human welfare, had taken on the ghastly distortions of a nightmare.

One answer was that there must be more social science. With better understanding of society and of human behavior, it seemed, men need not use physical science to kill each other. It was certainly true that the more fully society was understood, the better for all concerned. But in social science, too, lay the same kind of danger. From the scientific understanding of human behavior it was a short step to the scientific control of human behavior. We have seen how, in totalitarian states, governments not merely accepted the fact that people were shaped by environment but undertook to monopolize the environment and do the shaping themselves. A society in which science was pursued as one of many interests was one thing. A purely "scientific" society was another. In the latter, people might simply be manipulated by experts. Prophets of a scientific civilization had formerly drawn alluring pictures of a New Atlantis. Now, in the mid-twentieth century, prognosticators were more likely to portray a drab and mechanized world of the future, in which a ruling elite governed by scientific "techniques," using plenty of carbon paper and long-distance telephones, poring over statistical reports, card indexes, photographs and fingerprints, advised by social psychologists, public opinion pollsters, and propaganda technicians, and exercising a new technocratic despotism with the help of the police.

The problem of science in short passed over into the political problem. It was not science, but the practical uses of science, and the question of who should determine its practical uses, that created the difficulty. Scientific understanding of nuclear fission produced the atomic bomb, not because of anything in the nature of science or of nuclear fission, but because of something in the nature of human society and the clash of human wills.

The problem of industrialism and of security in an industrial society was likewise aggravated by the war. Industrialism produced a high degree of division of labor. Specialization reigned among persons within the same small community, and among the great regions of the earth. Each was dependent on continuing interchange with others. Each person, moreover, could perform his task only with the use of a great deal of capital. Railroad workers had to have a railroad; the farmer had to have access to a tractor; even the musician, after composing a symphony, could not hear it played unless someone paid a hundred performers' wages. These modern facts of life led to a great deal of difficulty. There were theoretically two opposite social poles. At one, represented by the U.S.S.R., all capital was owned by the state and supplied to workers as needed, and all interchange was planned out in detail by public authorities in advance. At the other pole, best represented by the United States, capital was owned by private persons, who chose the channels of investment and hence determined the availability of jobs, and interchange took place through the mechanism of the market. Neither system was in practice logically pure, but the difference remained pronounced. The drawback in the Soviet system was its lack of freedom, in the American system its lack of stability or of economic security. Americans spent a good deal more time trying to correct the lack of security than the Soviets did in trying to correct the lack of freedom.

The Second World War ruined the industrial system in one of the world's chief industrial areas. The dense European population could support itself only by an industry and exchange that now broke down. The war damage, chiefly bomb damage, destroyed the capital accumulation of generations—housing, paved streets, utilities plants, foundries, factories. And the ruin of freight yards, rolling stock, and bridges brought the interchange of commodities to a standstill. Town was cut off from country. City people dispersed to live with their country cousins, or reverted to primitive methods of hunting for food and fuel. In a year or two the worst local devastation was repaired. The basic problem remained. Industrial Europe was unable to exchange with agricultural Eastern Europe or with the world. The Continent as a whole was left in the position in which the First World War left Vienna. Europe was a world metropolis, a kind of huge continental city, now cut off from the trading area with which it had exchanged. It was a former world

capital in danger of becoming a slum. It lived by large and uninterrupted imports for which it could no longer afford to pay. It could not pay because in
the second war, as in the first, Europeans lost most of their overseas investments, and overseas countries built up their own industries and had less need
of those of Europe. Europe's capacity to manufacture for export was also
injured by the war. At the same time, as an advanced industrial region,
Europe had a politically awakened population. Europeans would not starve
or suffer in mute resignation. The European economy, at the very time when
its own productivity was badly impaired, had to carry a rising burden of social
services and maintain the welfare state.

One of the chief post-war questions was therefore the rescue of Europe,
or, in practical politics, who Europe's "rescuer" was to be. There were only
two candidates for this honor, the U.S.S.R. and the United States. Europeans
did not relish the prospect of being rescued by either. Communism most
Europeans regarded as slavery. Dependency even on the benefactions of the
United States they feared as a wild gamble; remembering the depression of
1929, and how all Europe had then gone down after the cessation of American loans, they had no desire to be dependent upon American capitalism.
They were obliged, however, to choose. Not all chose in the same way; many
countries were divided internally between pro-Soviet and pro-American elements. The former swelled the post-war communist movement. The latter,
unfortunately, included some people who, before or during the war, had
shown favor for Hitler and Mussolini.

Thus the problem of a ruined industrialism, of a society unable to
produce with efficiency, yet obliged to produce enough to satisfy a civilized
population, led like the problem of science straight into the thick of political
questions. Nor was Europe the only center of trouble. Throughout Asia,
especially in India and Java, the conditions of a world-wide industrialism had
helped to build up dense populations. The new governments, in India and
Pakistan, or in the Republic of Indonesia, or in communist China, had to
feed and satisfy these great multitudes of people. They believed that only by
industrializing could they raise their living standards. They needed machinery, loans, advisers; they looked in part to Europe, in part to the Soviet
Union, and in part to the United States. Imperialism in Asia was dead, but
the need of Asians for assistance was still alive, and in the furnishing of assistance there was bound to be a certain competition.

Was the modern world really One World, or was it not? The answer
was both yes and no. It was one world in the sense that it required a good
deal of mutual exchange, and in the sense that political repercussions traveled over it rapidly. But it was far from homogeneous. Half a dozen great cultures and hundreds of little ones clung to their identity. All admired the
steam turbine, and stood in awe of atomic fission, but beyond the material
level their schemes of values widely diverged. None wished to be subordinated to another, or to lose its own way of life in the gray vagueness of a
uniform world civilization. Here lay the root of the problem of national
independence.

In the Second World War, as in the First, the President of the United States had taken the initiative in planning a post-war international organization to prevent war in the future. A conference of all anti-Axis powers, held at San Francisco in 1945, established the United Nations on the basis of wartime cooperation. The United Nations, like the League of Nations which it superseded, had numerous organs of which two were central: a General Assembly in which all recognized sovereign states, however small, were considered equal; and a Security Council made up of the states regarded as great powers—the United States, Great Britain, France, China, and the Soviet Union—plus six elected members chosen by the Assembly. Each great power enjoyed a veto. The Security Council could act on important matters only if the great powers were unanimous.

Since only a great power could bring about a great war, and since any great power bent on war would obviously veto any measures aimed against it, it was clear that the United Nations could not prevent a great war if one were actually imminent. Hence many people criticized the provision in the United Nations charter for a great-power veto. They declared that it recognized the very national sovereignty which led to international war, and they urged some kind of world state in its place, which should have the authority to put down violence anywhere in the world as the national state put down violence within its own borders. It was certain, however, that the veto was necessary. The U.S.S.R. demanded it most frankly, but no other great power would have consented to enter the United Nations without this safeguard to its own freedom of action. Or, in practice, without the veto, one or more great powers would withdraw, and the U.N. would become a mere alliance against non-members. In the following years even small peoples—notably the Dutch in Indonesia and the Zionists in their new republic of Israel—refused to abide by judgments of the United Nations. It seemed likely that no people possessing a state of its own was yet willing, in a matter considered vital, to forego its independence. Yet in the grave international tension that marked the post-war years the United Nations stood as a testimonial to the human hope for international cooperation and peace.

110. The Clash of Worlds

The war in effect left only two great powers still standing in any strength, the United States and the Soviet Union. Since the seventeenth century the world has normally had some half a dozen great powers. That there were now only two made a great difference. The characteristic of a two-state system, not found in a multiple-state system, is that each super-power knows positively in advance who its only dangerous enemy can be. In such a situation all diplomatic delicacy breaks down. All measures that either power takes for its own security seem to be provocations to the other. Each likewise tends to make allies of the middling and lesser states. And every move by a middling or lesser state, even if entirely spontaneous, since it is bound to favor one of the super-powers in one way or another, is suspected by the other super-power of being instigated by its rival as a hostile act. After the war the United States and the U.S.S.R. fell into this unpleasant dualistic relationship.

THE "COLD WAR"

We have noted already the state of affairs at the close of hostilities. Russian armies occupied Eastern Europe as far west as the river Elbe; American, British, and French armies held the remainder of Germany, most of Austria, and all of Italy. The movement of ground armies during the fighting had determined the spheres of influence after the peace. In addition, the Soviets at the last moment had declared war on Japan and moved into Manchuria and Korea. Soon, in the months that followed, they lent aid to separatists in northern Iran, pressed the Turks for joint control of the Turkish Straits, favored the communists in Greece, forced a communist government upon Poland and other countries of Eastern Europe, and called for an active offensive of the communist parties of war-torn Western Europe. All this time they actively supported also the revolutionary offensive in Asia, aiding the Chinese communists, supporting the communist-led rebels in Indo-China and elsewhere, and establishing a puppet communist regime in North Korea.

It was not possible for anyone (even in Russia) to know what the men in the Kremlin really believed or intended. Probably, as confirmed Marxist-Leninists, they considered a clash between the U.S.S.R. and the Western powers to be bound to come at some indefinite future date. Probably they were disturbed by American possession of the atomic bomb. Probably they felt that the fluid post-war situation gave a chance to establish an outer buffer zone favorable to Russia, a program on which they had already embarked in their alliance with Germany in 1939, which had allowed them to absorb eastern Poland and the Baltic States—or to re-absorb them, since these regions had been Russian for over a century before 1918. Probably also they saw in the aftermath of the Second World War, as they had seen in the aftermath of the First World War, an opportunity to advance the international Marxist revolution in Europe and in Asia.

The U.S.S.R. rejected a plan put forward by the United States, and accepted by other powers, to put the manufacture of atomic weapons under international supervision and control. Disarmament in the past had always failed because some disarmed and some did not. The United States proposal therefore carried a condition: that the international control body, to prevent the manufacture of atomic bombs by national governments, should have the right to send inspectors at will into all countries, and to enforce sanctions, regardless of the veto, against any country found guilty of unauthorized uses of atomic power. To the Soviets the idea of having foreigners freely examine their new society had always been repugnant. They declared that inspection would violate national sovereignty. They questioned the good faith of the American proposal. Preferring to rely on themselves, they proceeded with their own atomic research, as did the United States. The atomic armaments race, universally dreaded, thus began. In 1949 it became apparent that the U.S.S.R. was equipped to conduct atomic warfare.

The Soviet Union, to protect its interests in an international body where the majority was consistently against it, made increasingly frequent use of its veto in the United Nations. Action by the U.N. did result in Soviet withdrawal from Iran, after sundry Soviet objections. But the United States, finding the U.N. unworkable as a check on communist expansion, began to develop a positive national policy of its own to "contain" communist expansion. In 1947, by the "Truman doctrine," it supplied military equipment and professional military advisers to Greece and Turkey. It announced a policy of assisting all peoples to prevent forcible capture of their governments by minority parties.

The Soviets denounced the American "warmongers." With the United States arming Greece and Turkey, with American carriers able to sail the length of the Mediterranean or lie off the coast of Murmansk, with American air bases established or easy to establish in the Near and Middle East, with the Americans in occupation of southern Korea and Japan, and virtually annexing Okinawa, and with the bulk of the United States lying across the North Pole from the vital centers of the Soviet Union, and the American capacity for long-range bombardment already sufficiently demonstrated, the Soviets not unnaturally felt encircled. Soviet suspicions dating from Munich, and even from the civil war of 1918–19, were inflamed. From 1946 on, relations between the two super-powers went from bad to worse. After 1946 what came to be known as the "cold war" spread. One of its highlights was the "battle of Berlin," when in 1948 the Soviets, in retaliation for currency reform introduced by the Western occupying powers, cut off all rail, water, and road routes to the sectors of Berlin under Western control. The Western powers, notably the United States, responded with a mass "air lift," daily flying in thousands of tons of cargo to prevent starvation among the Berlin populace; eventually, after many months, the blockade was lifted. Meanwhile, the United States and the Western European powers proceeded with their plans for the defense of Europe and the U.S.S.R. drew its satellites closer together.

THE WAR IN KOREA

The cold war turned to actual fighting in Asia. In June 1950, to the consternation of the Western world, the Soviet-sponsored regime of North Korea crossed the thirty-eighth border parallel and launched an attack on the republic in the south established under the aegis of the United Nations. During the Second World War it had been agreed that Korea, once a source of imperialist rivalry between Japan and Russia and since 1905 under Japanese rule, would become free and independent; for purely temporary occupation purposes Soviet troops were to occupy the northern part of Korea down to the thirty-eighth parallel and United States troops the area south of that parallel. In the months after the end of the Pacific war the U.S.S.R. created a puppet government on the order of the European "people's republics," proceeded to Sovietize its occupation zone, and trained a large native army. The Soviets put obstacles in the way of an American proposal to hold elections for all Korea under U.N. international supervision; the elections were held, but only in South Korea. By early 1949, however, both the U.S.S.R. and the United States had withdrawn their occupation troops from their respective zones.

In June 1950 came the attack; it was hard to believe that the move was not incited or encouraged by the larger communist powers, the U.S.S.R. and the newly established Chinese People's Republic—possibly by the latter alone. Undoubtedly the attackers calculated on a quick victory because of their superior forces and gambled that the outside world would do no more than lodge a moral protest, as in the Japanese invasion of Manchuria in 1931. But President Truman, initiating the firmest action ever taken under international auspices against overt aggression in the twentieth century, called upon the United Nations to take prompt military measures against the aggressor and committed American combat units to the fighting. For many weeks, however, in the summer of 1950, the United Nations forces under the command of General MacArthur were compelled to retreat and faced a real danger of expulsion from the peninsula. A successful amphibious landing at Inchon changed the picture. The U.N. forces hurled the communist armies northward and then, in a momentous decision, crossed the thirty-eighth parallel itself in hot pursuit, driving rapidly toward the Yalu river, the boundary line between Korea and the Manchurian province of communist China. At that juncture, in November 1950, the Chinese People's Republic entered the actual fighting; hundreds of thousands of Chinese communist troops supported by Russian-made jet airplanes again drove the U.N. forces southward in what looked like a repetition of the early phase of the war; but the U.N. forces held; they fought their way back to the thirty-eighth parallel, and even slightly to its north. A controversy developed in the United States when President Truman relieved General MacArthur of his command over irreconcilable differences about the conduct of the war. President Truman and his advisers, along with Britain and the majority of the nations in the U.N., were determined to punish the North Korean act of aggression but they were resolved also not to permit the conflict to develop into a third world war, which they feared might happen if Manchuria or other parts of China were bombed, a course of action being urged by both MacArthur and the south Korean President Syngman Rhee. The American people were stunned, hurt, and infuriated by the worst military reverses in their history; many wanted to punish communist China, but most saw the wisdom, or feasibility, of restricting the fighting. The MacArthur controversy faded away. In July 1951 a cease-fire agreement ended large-scale fighting. But truce negotiations dragged on for two full years, principally over the exchange and repatriation of prisoners of war, while sporadic fighting continued. In July 1953 a truce was signed. It had been an extensive war; fifteen nations had participated along with the United States in the U.N. combat forces; counting both sides, a total of over two million men were estimated dead, wounded, or missing; the United States suffered some 25,000 battle deaths, about half as many as in the First World War.

Politically, conditions reverted to what they had been before 1950. Korea was again divided roughly at the same parallel. The North Korean government, the Chinese People's Republic, and the U.S.S.R. persisted in rejecting international supervision of free elections for the entire country. To Western eyes a flagrant act of aggression had been checked; to the Soviet world the great capitalist power, the United States, had been prevented from reasserting Western imperialist supremacy in the East. The truth was that the United States, in the Korean war, and in its efforts to create regional security pacts in the East, found little enthusiasm among the larger non-communist Asian powers—India, Indonesia, Burma. Most of them disliked communism but refused to be involved in war; most distrusted the West; and in the years of Asian revolution the United States, although the least involved of all the great powers in nineteenth-century Asian imperialism, was held in many Asian quarters, by virtue of its new leadership in the Western world, to be the symbol of Western oppression and exploitation, a picture assiduously cultivated by the Soviets.

THE STRUGGLE FOR EUROPE

The other great object of rivalry in the post-war years was Europe. Europe, the main protagonist of this long history, was in ruins in 1945. But it was not yet negligible; its combined population exceeded that of either of the super-powers, and even in ruins it possessed one of the world's leading industrial plants. Europe was divided by its many national frontiers, and by social cleavages between economic classes. Short of catastrophe, Europe would not go communist. In France and Italy, to be sure, a quarter of the people voted the communist ticket, and communists held important positions in labor unions, but the number of those actually desirous of a communist society was not large. Nor was the number large of those who wished to be remodeled according to the economy or culture of the United States. Europe, like the world's other great aggregates, wanted to preserve its identity and at least its spiritual independence. But between the programs of the two super-powers there was this difference: the Soviets had more to gain by chaos in Europe, and the United States had more to gain by its rebuilding. The United States immediately after the war sent billions of dollars' worth of goods to relieve the distress of Europe and then embarked on an even more extensive recovery program. Its motives were much discussed and even impugned. In effect, the Americans thus satisfied their humanitarian impulse, found markets for their own industries (at the American taxpayers' expense), and reduced the drift of working-class Europeans into the communist camp.

The key to the rebuilding of Europe was Germany. The Ruhr was still Europe's industrial heartland. The question of Germany had contributed heavily to the post-war tension between the Soviets and the West. The former Allies had at first agreed to occupy Germany jointly. They agreed that Germany should pay reparations, especially to Russia, which had suffered most heavily from German attack. Gradually the American government, to make Europe self-supporting and less dependent on American aid, came to favor the economic reconstruction of Germany. The Russians became apprehensive. The Russians wished to use Germany to rebuild the Soviet Union. The Americans wished to use it to rebuild Europe. They did not wish to pour aid into Germany to have it drained off as reparations to the U.S.S.R. Joint administration of Germany broke down. As we have noted, the Russians reaffirmed their hold on eastern Germany; the Americans, British, and French went their own way in the West. Each side competed for the good will of the late enemy. Each accused the other of partitioning the country in violation of their agreements. By the partition, for it was a partition in fact, the West got control of the German industrial heartland, to the great disadvantage of Russia. But the Russians, by controlling the more agricultural eastern Germany, along with all eastern Europe, also held strong cards against the West; for in the long run the economic welfare of Europe required the restoration of interchange between western factories and eastern farms. The Germans, meanwhile, in the division between the victors, saw the chance to reassert their own national identity and restore their own importance.

The American Secretary of State, General Marshall, announced in 1947 what came to be called the Marshall Plan. By this plan the huge grants to Europe were continued, but they were no longer regarded as stop-gap relief. American aid was henceforth to be so apportioned among various countries, and so coordinated with each country's policies and with joint policies of European countries acting together, as to enable Europe to stand on its own feet and play its own part in international trade. American officials urged Europeans to reduce their tariff barriers and currency controls against each other. They declared that only by creating a free and Europe-wide internal market could Europeans obtain the advantage of mass production and lower costs such as prevailed in the United States.

The results of the Marshall Plan and of the movement toward European economic cooperation were impressive. The trend after the First World War toward high tariffs and economic rigidity, the United States taking the lead, had culminated in the great depression and with it had come a further intensification of economic nationalism. With the Marshall Plan the trend was reversed. There was now a freer movement of world trade and an almost complete liberalization of trade between the participating Western European countries. A European "payments union" provided a channel for the conversion of currencies. A "coal and steel community" established in 1952 made it possible for the Western European countries to pool their coal and steel resources. Industrial production, even apart from armaments, rose significantly. The Marshall Plan was in a sense revolutionary; it had proposed nothing less than that a wealthy country like the United States should use its economic resources to revive its competitors; it was an act of creative generosity and of economic statesmanship, a recognition of the mutual interdependence of all members of the world-wide economy. For Asia and other underdeveloped areas, where the problem was not to revive a sick industrial economy but to create industry, the American Point Four program of long-range capital investment and a similar British Commonwealth Colombo Plan were counterparts to the Marshall Plan for Europe. Communism would be combated in Europe and in Asia, under this theory, by removing its breeding grounds of poverty and want; it was a long-range program; the verdict would rest with generations still unborn.

Politically, too, Europe moved toward joint action. By the Brussels treaty of 1948, Britain, France, the Netherlands, Belgium, and Luxembourg established a rather loose federation called the Western Union with a "Council of Europe" serving as a consultative parliament. They began to make common military plans—the unspecified but only enemy being the U.S.S.R. By the North Atlantic Treaty, in 1949, the United States agreed to supply equipment for European rearmament and guaranteed Western Europe against invasion. In 1954, after other plans for a European defense community had failed, partly because of French misgivings over rearming Germany and partly because of British reluctance to accept Continental commitments indefinitely, a new organization, the Western European Union, began to mature. The Brussels organization was enlarged to include the German Federal Republic, which was authorized to create its own national army under the overall command of the North Atlantic Treaty Organization; provisions were made to control the manufacture of munitions in Germany and on the Continent. Under the same agreement Britain pledged not to withdraw its forces from the continent. British, like American, isolationism seemed ended; European unity was growing.

The U.S.S.R. could not be expected to view with equanimity the creation of a new super-power on its own western border—for a super-power, the equal of any, is what a restored and unified Europe would be. Any power, not merely the Soviet Union, would object to such consolidation among its neighbors. The American desire to unify Europe thus seemed to Russia another hostile act. But the likelihood of any real European unity was far from established. The European governments showed no haste to surrender their national sovereignty and independence. Their combined military planning was unavoidably indefinite. In the event of war, though much would depend on the circumstances in which war might come, Europe would still suffer from uncured social diseases; many of its soldiers would sympathize with the Soviet Union.

More than ten years after the end of the Second World War great international issues remained unresolved: the fate of Central and Eastern Europe, a final peace treaty with Germany, the reunification of Germany and the settlement of Germany's eastern borders, a final treaty with Japan, the reunification of Korea, the status of China, the easing of mutual apprehension over national armaments and over international military structures, and the appalling dread of atomic warfare—and all these problems were interrelated, each to the other. There were signs that the political leaders of the U.S.S.R. who had taken over after Stalin's death might be more conciliatory; they seemed willing to pick up again the broken threads of the peace negotiations and disarmament proposals. There were signs, too, in the United States that not all compromise and conference was to be shunned as appeasement. At Geneva, in 1955, the American President Eisenhower, along with British and French leaders, met face to face with the heads of the Russian state in a friendlier atmosphere than any since the war. But the Geneva spirit did not seem destined to prevail; the hopes of a troubled humanity were shattered once more. And whatever the international climate, it seemed certain that the revolutionary ferment in the mid-twentieth-century world, in Europe, in Asia, in Africa and elsewhere, would not cease. Pandora's box would not be closed so easily.

Europe, the homeland of modern and of Western civilization, faced a whole series of impossible dilemmas. It might be torn to pieces by the ideological tug between the Soviet Union and the United States. In war between these two, it might be occupied by the former and bombed into extinction by the latter. If it unified itself, it would antagonize Russia. If it did not unify, it might be left as a backwater, historically outmoded by the growth of super-powers, as the thriving cities of medieval Germany and Renaissance Italy had been historically outmoded by the rise of national states. A European union without Germany was helpless; with Germany, no matter what the safeguards, it might come to be dominated entirely by the Germans. If a European union should one day become an effective political entity, and if the newly awakened great Asian aggregates some day became effective political entities also, then there might again be half a dozen "great powers" in the world; and the globe as a whole might recapitulate the modern history of Europe. A new balance of power might be possible; or the world super-powers might contend in open warfare as the European great powers had contended in their heyday.

Against all the frightening eventualities of the post-war world one hope lay in international organization, in the actual or in an improved United Nations. Organization was important, but in the end it was only a mechanism. Just as parliaments did not work in countries where people wished each other's ruin, so international organization did not work where nations feared each other's designs upon their very existence. The world needed smoothly functioning mechanisms, but above all it needed confidence. Confidence is a matter of mind and spirit. Of all things, once lost, it was the hardest to create.

*   *   *

So the cataclysm carried on. But even a cataclysm, as already intimated, is not a time of downfall only. Mountains crumble, but others are thrust up. Lands vanish, but others rise from the sea. So it is with the social cataclysm of our times. Old landmarks are worn down. The British Empire and the gold standard pass away. The ascendancy of Europe, of the West, of the white races nears its close; all these must learn to negotiate with others, not to rule them. Upper- and middle-class people lose their former ease of life; but times are better for miners and the few remaining domestic servants. Everywhere there is what those of the old school regard as a new crudeness, a disregard for amenities, from the conduct of diplomacy to the writing of novels; but both diplomacy and fiction grapple boldly with real problems. Never has war been so scientifically destructive, and it is certain that another world war would blight some centers of civilization; but it would be parochial to suppose that no civilization anywhere would survive. Individual lives are fragile. But man as such is a tough animal, and a very widespread one. To close this book on a note of placidity would indeed be foolish, but so would it be to close it on a note of universal doom. It is entirely possible that if everybody in the world could vote on the question, provided only that literally everybody were included, as many or more would say that the land is rising as that it sinks.

Appendixes, Bibliography,

& Index

Chronological

TABLE ONE: TO 1519

Europe as a Whole: Political and Social	Europe as a Whole: Thought and Letters	British Isles
	500–300 B.C. Classical Greek civilization	
146 B.C. Greeks conquered by Rome	427–347 B.C. Plato	
31 B.C. Roman Empire	384–322 B.C. Aristotle	
288–337 Emperor Constantine	106–43 B.C. Cicero	
	2nd century: Ptolemy and Galen	43–410 Roman Empire in Britain
5th century: Germanic migrations	354–432 Saint Augustine	
476 Roman Empire in West ends		
7th century: spread of Islam		596 Conversion of Anglo-Saxons
800 Coronation of Charlemagne		
9th century: Norse and Magyar invasions		871–99 Alfred the Great
1054 Schism of West and East	1033–1109 Anselm	
1073–85 Pope Gregory VII (Hildebrand)	1079–1142 Abelard	1066 Norman conquest
1095 First Crusade	12th century: coming of Arabic and Greek science	
12th century: rise of towns		
1189 Third Crusade		12th century: development of the monarchy in England
1198–1216 Pope Innocent III	12th–13th century: universities, scholasticism	
13th century: rise of parliaments	1215 Fourth Lateran Council	1215 Magna Carta
1294–1303 Pope Boniface VIII	1225–74 Thomas Aquinas	
		1295 Model Parliament
1347 Black Death		
1378–1417 Schism of the West	1384 John Wycliffe died	1337–1453 Hundred Years' War
1414–15 Council of Constance		1381 Wat Tyler's rebellion
1453 Roman Empire in East ends	1438 Printing	
	15th century: the Renaissance at its height	1455–85 Wars of the Roses
	1452–1519 Leonardo	
1492 Discovery of America	1466–1536 Erasmus	1485–1603 *The Tudors*
1497 Portuguese reach India	1469–1527 Machiavelli	1485–1509 Henry VII

Tables

~~~~~~

TABLE ONE: TO 1519

WESTERN EUROPE	CENTRAL EUROPE	EASTERN EUROPE
		6th–4th century B.C. Greek city states
		3rd century B.C. Hellenistic Age begins
31 B.C.–476 Roman Empire	31 B.C.–476 Roman Empire in western and southern Germany	31 B.C.–1453 Roman Empire in East
		330 Constantinople founded
496 Conversion of Franks		
	568 Founding of Venice	
711 Moslems in Spain		10th century: conversion of Swedes, Poles, Hungarians to Rome; Russians to Constantinople
732 Moslem defeat at Tours		
768–814 Charlemagne	768–814 Charlemagne	
987–1792 *Capetian monarchy in France*	962–1806 *Holy Roman Empire*	1001–1918 *Kingdom of Hungary*
	1056–1106 Emperor Henry IV	1054 Schism of East and West
	1075–1122 Investiture struggle	
12th century: development of the monarchy in France		12th century: Teutonic Knights in Prussia
1208 Albigensian Crusade	13th century: failure of the Empire to organize Germany and Italy	13th century: conversion of East Baltic peoples to Rome
1303–1417 Papacy at Avignon		1236 Tartars in Russia
1337–1453 Hundred Years' War	1356 Golden Bull	1389 Turks in Balkan Peninsula
1412–31 Joan of Arc	1420–31 Hussite Wars	
1461–89 Louis XI of France	1438–1918 *Hapsburg Emperors*	
1479–1516 Ferdinand and Isabella of Spain		1453 Turks take Constantinople; end of Byzantine Empire
1494 French invasion of Italy		1480 Ivan ends Tartar control over Russia
1515–47 Francis I of France	1519–56 Charles V	

TABLE TWO: 1519–1618

Europe as a Whole: Political and Social	Europe as a Whole: Thought and Letters	BRITISH ISLES
1517 Beginnings of Reformation	1517 Luther's 95 Theses	
1519–56 Charles V		
1519–1648 Hapsburg supremacy		1521 Henry VIII's *Defense of Seven Sacraments*
1519–22 Magellan circumnavigates globe		
1529 Turks besiege Vienna		
	1530 Loyola's *Spiritual Exercises*	
1531 First stock exchange at Antwerp	1534 Luther's German Bible	1534 Act of Supremacy
	1536 Calvin's *Institutes*	1536–9 Dissolution of Monasteries
		1539 Six Articles
1540 Founding of Jesuits		
1541–64 Calvin at Geneva	1543 Copernicus' *Revolutions of Heavenly Orbs* and Vesalius' *Structure of the Human Body*	
1545–63 Council of Trent		1547–53 Edward VI
		1553–8 Mary
1555 Peace of Augsburg		
1556–98 Philip II of Spain		1558–1603 Elizabeth
		1559 J. Knox and the Reformation in Scotland
	1561–1626 Francis Bacon	
		1563 The 39 Articles
	1564–1642 Galileo	
		1569 Norfolk's rebellion
1571 Defeat of Turks at Lepanto		
	1576 Bodin's *Republic*	
		1577 Alliance with Netherlands
	1580 Montaigne's *Essays*	
	1582 Gregorian Calendar	
1588 Spanish Armada	1596–1650 Descartes	1588 Spanish Armada
		1603–1714 *The Stuarts*
		1603–25 James I
1607 English found Virginia		
	1611 King James' Bible	
1612 Dutch found New York		

TABLE TWO: 1519–1618

WESTERN EUROPE	CENTRAL EUROPE	EASTERN EUROPE
1515–47 Francis I of France	1519–56 Charles V Emperor	
1516 Concordat of Bologna		
		1520–66 Suleiman the Magnificent
	1521 Luther banned	
	1526 Charles V at war with Turks	1526 Turks occupy Hungary
	1529 Turks besiege Vienna	
		1535 First French capitulations in Turkey
1536 Franco-Turkish alliance against Charles V		
	1546–7 Schmalkaldic War	
1547–59 Henry II of France		1547–84 Ivan the Terrible, first Tsar of Russia
		1553 English in White Sea
	1555 Peace of Augsburg	
1556–98 Philip II of Spain	1556–64 Ferdinand I	
1559–89 Weakness of monarchy in France		
1562–98 Wars of Religion in France		
	1564–76 Maximilian II	
1566 Netherlands revolt begins		1571 Defeat of Turks at Lepanto
1572 Massacre of St. Bartholomew		1574 Turks take Tunis
1574–89 Henry III	1576–1612 Rudolf II	
1589–1792 *Bourbons in France*		
1589–1610 Henry IV		
1598 Edict of Nantes		
	1608 Protestant Union	1604–13 Time of troubles in Russia
	1609 Catholic League	
1610–43 Louis XIII		
	1612–19 Matthias	1613–45 Michael Romanov, Tsar
	1618 Thirty Years' War	

TABLE THREE: 1618–1714

Europe as a Whole: Political and Social	Europe as a Whole: Thought and Letters	BRITISH ISLES
	1561–1626 Francis Bacon 1564–1642 Galileo 1596–1650 Descartes	1603–1714 *Stuarts* 1603–25 James I
1618–48 Thirty Years' War		
17th century: English, French, Dutch in America; Dutch in South Africa and Indonesia	1623–62 Pascal 17th century: flowering of English, French, and Dutch literature	1625–49 Charles I
		1637 Ship money case 1640–60 Long Parliament
	1642–1727 Isaac Newton	1642–8 Puritan rebellion and Civil War
1648 Peace of Westphalia		
		1649 Execution of Charles I 1649–58 Rule of Cromwell 1649–53 Commonwealth 1653–60 Protectorate
	1660's Beginnings of scientific societies	1660 Restoration 1660–85 Charles II
1661–1715 Age of Louis XIV		
		1670's Rise of Whigs and Tories 1673 Test Act
1683 Turks threaten Vienna		
		1685–88 James II
	1687 Newton's *Principia*	
		1688 "Glorious Revolution"
1689–97 War of League of Augsburg		
		1688–1702 William and Mary
	1690 Locke's *Treatises on Government; Human Understanding* 1697 Bayle's *Dictionary*	
1701–14 War of Spanish Succession		
		1702–14 Anne
1713–14 Treaties of Utrecht and Rastadt		1707 Union of England and Scotland

TABLE THREE: 1618–1714

WESTERN EUROPE	CENTRAL EUROPE	EASTERN EUROPE
1610–43 Louis XIII of France	1618–48 Thirty Years' War	*1613–1917 Romanovs in Russia*
	1619 Emperor Ferdinand II	1613–45 Tsar Michael
	1620 Battle of White Mountain	Romanov
1624–42 Richelieu		
1629 Peace of Alais	1629 Edict of Restitution	17th century: spread of
1635 France in Thirty Years' War		serfdom in Russia and Eastern Europe
1642–61 Mazarin	1640–88 Frederick William, Great Elector of Brandenburg	
1643–1715 Louis XIV of France		
1648 Peace of Westphalia	1648 Peace of Westphalia	
	17th and 18th centuries: decline in Central Europe	
1652–74 Three Anglo-Dutch Wars		
1659 Peace of Pyrenees		
1665–1700 Charles II of Spain		
1667–68 Louis XIV's War of Devolution		1667 Russian church reforms: Old Believers
		1670 Revolt of Stephen Razin in Russia
1672–8 Louis XIV's Dutch war		
		1682–1725 Peter the Great
	1683 Turks threaten Vienna	1683 Turks threaten Vienna
		1683–1718 Hapsburg victories over Turks
1689–1714 Later wars of Louis XIV		
	1697–1733 Augustus of Saxony King of Poland	1697–1718 Charles XII of Sweden
		1699 Austro-Turkish Peace of Karlowitz
1700–1931 Bourbons in Spain	*1701–1918 Hohenzollern kings in Prussia*	
1700–1746 Philip V of Spain	1701–13 Frederick I of Prussia	

TABLE FOUR: 1714–1815

Europe as a Whole: Political and Social	Europe as a Whole: Thought and Letters	BRITISH ISLES
1713–14 Treaties of Utrecht and Rastadt	18th century: Age of Enlightenment	1714–1837 *Hanoverians* 1714–27 George I
		1720 South Sea Bubble 1721 Walpole's ministry 1727–60 George II 1739 War of Jenkins' Ear
1733–8 War of Polish Succession 1740–8 War of Austrian Succession 1740–89 Enlightened Despotism	1740–89 Enlightenment at its peak 1740–60 Voltaire at his height	
	1748 Montesquieu's *Spirit of Laws* 1751–68 French *Encyclopedia*	1745 Jacobite Rebellion
1756 Diplomatic Revolution 1756–63 Seven Years' War		1760–1820 George III
1763 Treaties of Paris and Hubertusburg	1761 Rousseau's *Social Contract*	1769 Watt's steam engine 1769 Arkwright's water-frame
1778–83 War of American Independence	1776 Adam Smith's *Wealth of Nations*	1776 American Revolution
1789 French Revolution begins	1784 Herder's *Philosophy of History of Mankind* 1790 Burke's *Reflections on the French Revolution* 1790's Spread of French revolutionary ideas	1782–1806 Ministries of the Younger Pitt
1792–1815 Revolutionary and Napoleonic Wars 1792–7 War of First Coalition	Beginnings of romanticism	1793–1814 War with France
1798–1801 War of Second Coalition		1798 Rebellion of Ireland 1801 Union of Great Britain and Ireland
1803–05 War of Third Coalition 1804–14 "Grand Empire"	1804 ff. Napoleonic codes	1802–3 Peace of Amiens
1806–12 Continental System		
1809–11 Napoleon at height 1812 Napoleon's invasion of Russia 1813 Leipzig 1814–15 Congress of Vienna 1815 Waterloo		1808–13 Peninsular War in Spain 1814 Alliance of Chaumont

TABLE FOUR: 1714–1815

WESTERN EUROPE	CENTRAL EUROPE	EASTERN EUROPE
1715–74 Louis XV of France	1711–40 Charles VI of Austria	1682–1725 Peter the Great
1715–23 Regency in France	1713–40 Frederick William I of Prussia	
1720 Mississippi Bubble	1713–40 Pragmatic Sanction	1721 Russo-Swedish Treaty of Nystadt
		1739 Austro-Turkish Peace of Belgrade
18th century: "Old Regime" in France	1740–86 Frederick II of Prussia	
	1740–80 Maria Theresa of Austria	
	1740–5 Silesian Wars	
	1756 Hapsburg-Bourbon Alliance	
	1756–63 Seven Years' War	1762–96 Catherine II of Russia
		1768–74 Russo-Turkish War
		1772 First Partition of Poland
		1773–4 Pugachev rebellion
1774–93 Louis XVI of France		1774 Russo-Turkish Treaty of Kuchuk Kainarji
	1780–90 Joseph II of Austria	
	1780's Cultural revival of Germany	
		1787–92 Russo-Turkish War
1789 French Revolution begins		
1792 First French Republic established		1793 Second Partition of Poland
1793–4 The Terror		1795 Third Partition of Poland
1795–99 Directory	1797 Treaty of Campio Formio	
1799 Bonaparte's coup	1798–1814 French predominance	1796–1801 Paul I of Russia
1799–1804 Consulate		
		1801–25 Alexander I of Russia
1804–14 Napoleon I: The Empire	1806 End of Holy Roman Empire	1806–12 Russo-Turkish War
	1806 Confederation of the Rhine	1807 Franco-Russian Alliance
1807 Peace of Tilsit		
		1812 Napoleon's invasion of Russia
1814 Restoration of Bourbons	1813–14 German War of Liberation: Leipzig	
1815 Hundred Days; Waterloo		

TABLE FIVE: 1815–1871

World as a Whole	Europe as a Whole	BRITISH ISLES
1806–25 Latin American independence	1814–15 Congress of Vienna	1760–1820 George III 1760–1830 Beginnings of modern industry 1815 Higher Corn Laws
	1818 Congress of Aix-la-Chapelle 1820 Congress of Troppau 1822 Congress of Verona	1819 Peterloo
1823 Monroe Doctrine		
	1830 Revolutions	
		1832 First Reform Bill
	1833 Lyell's *Principles of Geology*	
1841 Anglo-Chinese (Opium) War 1842–58 "Treaty System" in China		1837–1901 Victoria 1838–48 Chartism 1842 Mines Act 1846 Repeal of Corn Laws 1847 Ten Hours Act
	1848 Revolutions: Marx and Engels' *Communist Manifesto*	1850–73 Golden age of British capitalism
1854–68 Westernizing of Japan 1857 Indian Mutiny	1854–56 Crimean War	
	1859 Austro-Italian War	
1860 Russians found Vladivostok 1861–5 American Civil War 1863–7 French in Mexico	1859 Darwin's *Origin of Species*	
	1864–76 First International 1866 Austro-Prussian War 1867 Marx's *Capital*	
1867 Dominion of Canada		
	1870 Franco-Prussian War 1871–1918 German Empire	1867 Extension of suffrage 1870–4 Gladstone's first ministry

TABLE FIVE: 1815–1871

WESTERN EUROPE	CENTRAL EUROPE	EASTERN EUROPE
1814–30 Restored Bourbons in France 1814–24 Louis XVIII of France	1814–48 Influence of Metternich	1801–25 Alexander I of Russia
	1819 Carlsbad Decrees	
1824–30 Charles X of France		1825 Decembrists in Russia 1825–55 Nicholas I of Russia 1828–9 Russo-Turkish War 1829 Independence of Greece
1830 Revolution in France and Belgium 1830–48 July Monarchy in France: Louis Philippe	1830 Revolutionary flurries	1830 Revolution in Poland
1848 Revolution: Second French Republic	1848 Revolution: Frankfurt Assembly 1848–1916 Francis Joseph of Austria	
1852 Napoleon III: Second French Empire	1852–90 Bismarck active	1853 Russo-Turkish War 1854–6 Crimean War 1855–81 Alexander II of Russia
	1859–70 Unification of Italy	1858 Formation of Rumania
1860 Free trade with England		
1860–70 Liberal Empire		1861 Emancipation of Russian serfs
1870–1940 Third Republic in France 1871 Paris Commune	1866–71 Unification of Germany 1867 Dual Monarchy in Austria-Hungary	1870's Populism and Nihilism in Russia

TABLE SIX: 1871–1919

World as a Whole	Europe as a Whole	BRITISH ISLES
	1871 Darwin's *Descent of Man*	
	1878 Congress of Berlin, Austro-German Alliance	1874–80 Disraeli's ministry
1880–1914 Height of imperialism	1880's Socialist parties founded: revisionism	
	1882 Triple Alliance	
1883–93 French in Indo-China		
		1884 Extension of suffrage
1885 Berlin Conference on Africa		
1885–98 Partition of Africa		
	1889 Second International	
	1894 Franco-Russian Alliance	
1895–8 Far Eastern crisis		
1898 Fashoda crisis, Spanish-American War		
1899–1902 Boer War	1900 Freud's *Interpretation of Dreams*	1899–1902 Boer War
1902 Anglo-Japanese Alliance		
1904 Russo-Japanese War	1904 Anglo-French Entente	
	1905 Einstein's relativity theory	
	1905 Morocco crisis	
		1906–11 Social insurance and Parliamentary reform
1907 Anglo-Russian division of Persia	1907 Triple Entente	
	1908 Bosnian crisis	
1911 Chinese Revolution	1911 Agadir crisis	
	1912–13 Balkan crisis	
1914–18 First World War	1914–18 First World War	1914 Ulster Crisis
		1916 Battle of Jutland
1917 United States enters War		1916–22 Irish troubles
		1918 Universal suffrage
1919 Peace of Versailles	1919 Peace of Versailles	

TABLE SIX: 1871–1919

WESTERN EUROPE	CENTRAL EUROPE	EASTERN EUROPE
	1871–1918 German Empire	
	1871–83 *Kulturkampf* 1878–90 Bismarck's Anti-Socialist laws	1877 Russo-Turkish War 1878 Autonomy of Bulgaria; independence of Serbia
	1883–9 Bismarck's social insurance laws	1881 Assassination of Alexander II
1889 Boulanger in France 1894–1906 Dreyfus affair in France	1888–1918 William II of Germany	
	1898–1914 German naval race with England	
1901–05 Laic laws separate church and state in France 1900ff. Growth of democracy: universal suffrage in Netherlands 1896, etc.	1900ff. Growth of democracy: universal suffrage in Austria 1907, etc.	1903 Bolshevik-Menshevik split 1904 Russo-Japanese War 1905 Revolution in Russia
		1908 Bosnian crisis 1908 Young Turk Revolution
1914 Battle of Marne 1916 Verdun and the Somme 1918 Armistice	1914 Assassination of Francis Ferdinand 1918 Fall of German and Austro-Hungarian Empires	1912–13 Balkan Wars 1914 Battle of Tannenberg 1917 Fall of Tsardom: Bolshevik Revolution

TABLE SEVEN: 1919–

World as a Whole	Europe as a Whole	BRITISH ISLES
		1918 Universal suffrage
1919 Peace of Versailles	1919 Peace of Versailles	
	1919 Spread of democracy	
1922–9 "Prosperity Decade"	1922–43 Fascism in Italy	1922 Irish Free State
1923 Turkish Republic	1923 Ruhr crisis	
	1925 Locarno Pacts	
		1926 General Strike
		1926 Definition of Domin-
1929–33 Great Depression	1930–3 Depression	ion status
1931–2 Manchuria Crisis	1930's Decline of Parliamen-	1930–3 Depression
1931–45 Japanese in China	tarism; rise of dictators	1931 Britain leaves gold
1933–45 F. D. Roosevelt's	1933–45 Hitler in Germany	standard
presidency	1933 Germany leaves League	1932 Britain adopts Empire
1933 Failure of World	of Nations and rearms	tariff protection
Economic Conference		
1935–6 Ethiopian crisis		
1936–9 Spanish Civil War	1936–9 Popular fronts	1936 Edward VIII abdicates
	1937 Rome-Berlin-Tokyo	
1938 Munich crisis	Axis	
1939–45 Second World	1939 Nazi-Soviet Pact	
War	1940–4 German domination	1940 Battle of Britain
1940–5 Japan aims at	of Europe	
"Greater East Asia"		
1941 U.S.S.R., U.S.A. enter		
War		
1944 Allies invade Europe		
1945 Yalta conference		1945–51 Labor government
1945 First atomic bomb	1945 Death of Hitler	in power
1945 Russians in Manchuria	1946 *De facto* split of East	
1945 United Nations	and West	
1947 British leave India	1947 Marshall Plan, Truman	
1948 Israel established	Doctrine	
1949 Dutch leave Indonesia	1949 Council of Europe	
1949 Communist victory in	1949 North Atlantic Pact	
China		
1950–3 Korean War		
1951 Japanese peace treaty		1951 Return of Conserva-
		tives: Churchill, Eden
		1952 Elizabeth II
1954 Hydrogen bomb per-	1954 Western European	
fected	Union	

TABLE SEVEN: 1919–

WESTERN EUROPE	CENTRAL EUROPE	EASTERN EUROPE
		1917 Bolshevik Revolution
	1918 Fall of German and Austro-Hungarian Empires	
		1919–23 Greek-Turkish War
	1919–33 Weimar Republic	1920–43 Third International
		1920–2 Russo-Polish War
		1921–8 N.E.P. in Russia
	1922–43 Mussolini in power in Italy	1922 Founding of U.S.S.R.
	1923 French occupy Ruhr	1922 Russo-German treaty of Rapallo
	1923 Inflation in Germany	
	1924 Dawes Plan	1924 Death of Lenin
		1927 Expulsion of Trotsky
		1928–33 First Five-Year Plan
1930–3 Depression	1930–3 Depression	
1931–2 Spanish Revolution		
	1933–45 Hitler in power	
1934 Stavisky riots in Paris	1934 First Austrian crisis	1934 U.S.S.R. joins League of Nations
1936–9 Spanish Civil War	1936 Germany re-militarizes Rhineland	1936–7 Purge trials in U.S.S.R.
1936–7 Popular Front in France	1938 Germany annexes Austria	
	1939 Germany subjects Czechoslovakia	1939–41 Nazi-Soviet Pact
1940 Fall of France		1939–40 Russo-Finnish War; Soviets expand in Baltic
1940–4 German occupation of Western Europe		
		1941 Germans invade Russia
	1941–4 Allies bomb Germany	1942 Battle of Stalingrad
	1943 Allies invade Italy	
1944 Allies land in France		
		1945–8 Communist satellites in Eastern Europe
1946 Fourth French Republic	1946 Italian Republic	
	1947 Peace treaties with Italy, Hungary, etc.	1947 Cominform
	1949 *De facto* partition of Germany	
		1951–5 Fifth Five-Year Plan; atomic advances
		1953 Death of Stalin
	1955 West Germany virtually sovereign	

Rulers and Regimes

IN PRINCIPAL EUROPEAN COUNTRIES
SINCE 1500

I

HOLY ROMAN EMPIRE

Hapsburg Line

MAXIMILIAN I	1493–1519
CHARLES V	1519–56
FERDINAND I	1556–64
MAXIMILIAN II	1564–76
RUDOLPH II	1576–1612
MATTHIAS	1612–19
FERDINAND II	1619–37
FERDINAND III	1637–57
LEOPOLD I	1658–1705
JOSEPH I	1705–11
CHARLES VI	1711–40

Charles VI was succeeded by a daughter, Maria Theresa, who as a woman could not be elected Holy Roman Emperor. French influence in 1742 secured the election of

Bavarian Line

CHARLES VII   1742–5

On Charles VII's death the Hapsburg control of the Emperorship was resumed.

Lorraine Line

FRANCIS I   1745–65 (husband of Maria Theresa)

Hapsburg-Lorraine Line

JOSEPH II	1765–90 (son of Francis I and Maria Theresa)
LEOPOLD II	1790–2
FRANCIS II	1792–1806

The Holy Roman Empire became extinct in 1806.

II

AUSTRIAN DOMINIONS

The rulers of Austria from 1438 to 1740, and at least titular Kings of Hungary from 1526 to 1740, were the same as the Holy Roman Emperors. After 1740:

Hapsburg Line (through female heir)

MARIA THERESA	1740–80
JOSEPH II	1780–90
LEOPOLD II	1790–2
FRANCIS II	1792–1835

In 1804 Francis II took the title of Emperor, as Francis I of the Austrian Empire. Austria was declared an "empire" because Napoleon proclaimed France an empire in that year, and because the demise of the Holy Roman Empire could be foreseen.

FERDINAND I	1835–48
FRANCIS JOSEPH	1848–1916
CHARLES I	1916–18

The Austrian Empire became extinct in 1918.

III

BRITISH ISLES

Tudor Line

Kings of England and Ireland

HENRY VII	1485–1509
HENRY VIII	1509–47
EDWARD VI	1547–53
MARY I	1553–8
ELIZABETH	1558–1603

In 1603 James VI of Scotland, a great-great-grandson of Henry VII, succeeded to the English throne.

Stuart Line

Kings of England and Ireland, and of Scotland

JAMES I	1603–25
CHARLES I	1625–49

Republican Interregnum

THE COMMONWEALTH	1649–53
THE PROTECTORATE	
OLIVER CROMWELL, LORD PROTECTOR	1653–8
RICHARD CROMWELL	1658–60

Restored Stuart Line

CHARLES II	1660–85
JAMES II	1685–8

In 1688 James II was forced out of the country, but Parliament kept the crown in a female branch of the Stuart family, calling in Mary, the daughter of James II, and her husband William III of the Netherlands.

WILLIAM III	1689–1702,
AND MARY II	1689–94
ANNE	1702–14

In 1707, through the Union of England and Scotland, the royal title became King (or Queen) of Great Britain and Ireland. The Stuart family having no direct Protestant heirs, the throne passed in 1714 to the German George I, Elector of Hanover, a great-grandson of James I.

Hanoverian Line

Kings of Great Britain and Ireland

GEORGE I	1714–27
GEORGE II	1727–60
GEORGE III	1760–1820
GEORGE IV	1820–30
WILLIAM IV	1830–7

William IV having no heirs, the British throne passed in 1837 to Victoria, a grand-daughter of George III. In Hanover no woman could rule, and an uncle of Victoria inherited. Though the British family has continued in direct descent from George I, it has dropped the title of Hanoverian and is now known as the House of Windsor. From 1877 to 1947 the British rulers bore the additional title of Emperors of India.

VICTORIA	1837–1901
EDWARD VII	1901–10
GEORGE V	1910–36
EDWARD VIII	1936
GEORGE VI	1936–52
ELIZABETH II	1952–

IV

FRANCE

Valois Line

LOUIS XI	1461–83	HENRY II	1547–59
CHARLES VIII	1483–98	FRANCIS II	1559–60
LOUIS XII	1498–1515	CHARLES IX	1560–74
FRANCIS I	1515–47	HENRY III	1574–89

In 1589 the Valois line became extinct, and the throne passed to Henry of Bourbon, a remote descendant of French kings of the fourteenth century.

Bourbon Line

HENRY IV	1589–1610
LOUIS XIII	1610–43
LOUIS XIV	1643–1715
LOUIS XV	1715–74
LOUIS XVI	1774–92

The Republic

CONVENTION	1792–5
DIRECTORY	1795–9
CONSULATE	1799–1804

The Empire

NAPOLEON I, EMPEROR OF THE FRENCH AND KING OF ITALY, 1804–14

Restored Bourbon Line

LOUIS XVIII   1814–24

(Royalists count a Louis XVII, 1793–5, and date the reign of Louis XVIII from 1795.)

CHARLES X   1824–30

The Revolution of 1830 gave the throne to the Duke of Orleans, descendant of Louis XIII.

Orleans Line

LOUIS-PHILIPPE   1830–48

The Second Republic

1848–52

The Second Empire

NAPOLEON III, EMPEROR OF THE FRENCH, 1852–70

The Third Republic

1870–1940

Vichy Regime

1940–4

Provisional Government

1944–6

The Fourth Republic

1946–

---

v

PRUSSIA (and GERMAN EMPIRE)

A continuous Hohenzollern Line ruled until 1918.

Electors of Brandenburg and Dukes of Prussia

GEORGE WILLIAM	1619–40
FREDERICK WILLIAM, the "Great Elector"	1640–88
FREDERICK III	1688–1713

In 1701 Frederick III was permitted by the Holy Roman Emperor to entitle himself King in Prussia, as Frederick I.

Kings of Prussia

FREDERICK I	1701–13	FREDERICK WILLIAM II	1786–97
FREDERICK WILLIAM I	1713–40	FREDERICK WILLIAM III	1797–1840
FREDERICK II, the "Great"	1740–86	FREDERICK WILLIAM IV	1840–61
		WILLIAM I	1861–88

In 1871 William I took the title of German Emperor.

German Emperors

WILLIAM I	1871–88
FREDERICK III	1888
WILLIAM II	1888–1918

The German Empire became extinct in 1918. It was succeeded by the

Weimar Republic

1919–33

(an unofficial title for what was still called the *Deutsches Reich*, a phrase not easy to translate accurately)

The Third Reich

1933–45

(an unofficial title for the *Deutsches Reich* under Adolf Hitler)

Military Government in 1945 by the United States, U.S.S.R., Great Britain, and France, eventuating in 1949 in a *German Federal Republic* in the West and a *German Democratic Republic* in the East, separated by a merely *de facto* line.

VI

SARDINIA (and KINGDOM OF ITALY)

In 1720 Victor Amadeus II, Duke of Savoy, took the title of King of Sardinia, having acquired the island of that name.

Kings of Sardinia

VICTOR AMADEUS II	1720–30
CHARLES EMMANUEL III	1730–73
VICTOR AMADEUS III	1773–96
CHARLES EMMANUEL IV	1796–1802
VICTOR EMMANUEL I	1802–21
CHARLES FELIX	1821–31
CHARLES ALBERT	1831–49
VICTOR EMMANUEL II	1849–78

In 1861 Victor Emmanuel II took the title of King of Italy.

Kings of Italy

VICTOR EMMANUEL II	1861–78
HUMBERT I	1878–1900
VICTOR EMMANUEL III	1900–46

In 1936 Victor Emmanuel III took the title of Emperor of Ethiopia, which became meaningless with British occupation of Ethiopia in 1941. In 1946 the Kingdom of Italy became extinct and was succeeded by the

Italian Republic

1946–

VII

SPAIN

FERDINAND AND ISABELLA	1479–1504/16

Isabella died in 1504, but Ferdinand lived until 1516, whereupon the Spanish thrones were inherited by his grandson Charles, who became Charles V of the Holy Roman Empire, but was known in Spain as Charles I.

Hapsburg Line

CHARLES I	1516–56
PHILIP II	1556–98
PHILIP III	1598–1621
PHILIP IV	1621–65
CHARLES II	1665–1700

With Charles II the Spanish Hapsburg line became extinct, and the throne passed to the French Bourbon, grandson of Louis XIV of France and great-grandson of Philip IV of Spain.

Bourbon Line

PHILIP V	1700–46
FERDINAND VI	1746–59
CHARLES III	1759–88
CHARLES IV	1788–1808

Bonaparte Line

JOSEPH (brother of Napoleon) 1808–13

Restored Bourbon Line

FERDINAND VII	1813–33
ISABELLA II	1833–68
ALFONSO XII	1868–85
ALFONSO XIII	1885–1932

In 1931 a republican revolution unseated Alfonso XIII.

Spanish Republic

1932–6

Spanish Civil War

1936–9

Regime of Francisco Franco

1939–

VIII

RUSSIAN EMPIRE

Grand Dukes of Moscow

IVAN III, the "Great"	1462–1505
BASIL III	1505–33
IVAN IV, the "Terrible"	1533–84

In 1547 Ivan IV took the title of Tsar of Russia

Tsars of Russia

IVAN IV, the "Terrible"	1547–84
THEODORE I	1584–98
BORIS GODUNOV	1598–1605

Time of Troubles

1604–13

Romanov Line

MICHAEL	1613–45	ELIZABETH	1741–62
ALEXIS	1645–76	PETER III	1762
THEODORE II	1676–82	CATHERINE II, the "Great"	1762–96
IVAN V AND PETER I	1682–9	PAUL	1796–1801
PETER I, the "Great"	1689–1725	ALEXANDER I	1801–25
CATHERINE I	1725–7	NICHOLAS I	1825–55
PETER II	1727–30	ALEXANDER II	1855–81
ANNA	1730–40	ALEXANDER III	1881–94
IVAN VI	1740–1	NICHOLAS II	1894–1917

In 1917 the tsardom became extinct.

Provisional Government

1917

Communist Revolution

1917–22

Union of Soviet Socialist Republics

1922–

Bibliography[1]

THE following reading lists, comprising almost two thousand titles, are intended for the convenience of non-professional students of modern history. Classification follows the plan of chapters in the present book. No title is intentionally repeated; to find books on most topics it will therefore be advisable to look in several places. All works in foreign languages are excluded. Excluded also, in principle (there are a few exceptions), are textbooks, articles in periodicals, and primary source materials. Many biographies and memoirs are listed, but no effort has been made to provide comprehensive lists.

Works of General Coverage

BIBLIOGRAPHIES. There are literally hundreds of thousands of books on historical subjects. It is a difficult art to find the titles and names of authors of those one wants on a particular topic, but the following works—some of which include critical comments on the books—can be helpful: A guide to historical literature (1931), edited for the American Historical Association by G. M. Dutcher and others; J. Ragatz, A bibliography for the study of European history, 1815 to 1939 (1942 and later supplements) and The literature of European imperialism, 1815–1939 (1944); A. Bullock and A. J. P. Taylor, Select list of books on European history, 1815–1914 (1949); S. J. Case and others, A bibliographical guide to the history of Christianity (1931); R. J. Kerner, Slavic Europe: a selected bibliography in the western European languages, comprising history, languages and literatures (1918); E. M. Coulter and M. Gerstenfeld, Historical bibliographies: a systematic and annotated guide (1935); and the annual International bibliography of the historical sciences (1930 ff.). For United States history the most convenient bibliography is O. Handlin and others, Harvard guide to American history (1954). Historical fiction may be located through guides published by E. A. Baker (1914), J. Nield (1929), and through the more recent Fiction catalogue (1950 and supplements).

BRIEFER REFERENCE WORKS. W. L. Langer, An encyclopedia of world history: ancient, medieval, and modern, chronologically arranged (1948), is a vast table of dates and important events, useful in showing the factual framework of the history of various countries and periods. A similar service is performed by S. H. Steinberg, Historical tables, 58 B.C.–A.D.

---

[1] The Bibliography in the original edition was the work of Fredrick Aandahl, Jr. It has been revised and brought up to date for the present edition.

1945 (1947). Other convenient reference tools include *Webster's biographical dictionary* (1948); J. Thomas, *Universal pronouncing dictionary of biography and mythology* (1930); H. E. Smith, *Columbia dictionary of modern European literature* (1947); *The Columbia encyclopedia* (1950, 1953 supplement), and R. B. Morris, *Encyclopedia of American history* (1953).

MANY-VOLUMED ENCYCLOPEDIAS. Among the most useful are the *Encyclopaedia Britannica* [for many historical purposes the 11th edition (1910–11) is more helpful than the current]; *Encyclopaedia of the social sciences* (1930–5); *Encyclopaedia of religion and ethics* (1908–27); *Dictionary of national biography* (1885–1949), on notable Britons; *Dictionary of American biography* (1928–36); *The Jewish encyclopedia* (1901–06); *The Catholic encyclopaedia* (1907–14, and supplement, 1922); and *Encyclopaedia of Islam* (1913–36).

HISTORICAL ATLASES. The following are the most useful: W. R. Shepherd, *Historical atlas* (1911, 1929), of which a new edition is projected; *Muir's historical atlas—mediaeval and modern* (1947); and C. G. Robertson and J. G. Bartholomew, *An historical atlas of modern Europe from 1789 to 1922* (1924). Announced for early publication are E. W. Fox and H. S. Deighton, *Atlas of European history*; and R. R. Palmer and others, *Atlas of world history*. Two convenient and economical atlases for student use are J. H. Breasted and others, *European history atlas* (10th ed., 1954); and *Hammond's historical atlas* (1953). Geographical information may be conveniently located in *Webster's geographical dictionary* (1949) and in *Lippincott's new gazeteer* (1952).

COLLECTIONS OF SELECTED SOURCE MATERIALS AND SOURCE PROBLEMS. The following works are designed for use in college courses in history and social sciences: Columbia University, *Introduction to contemporary civilization in the West* (2 vols., 1946, rev. 1954); T. C. Mendenhall and others, *Select problems in historical interpretation, 800–1715*, and *1715–present* (2 vols., 1948, and in briefer form, under different titles, 1952); R. P. Stearns, *Pageant of Europe: sources and selections from the Renaissance to the present day* (1947); G. H. Knoles and R. K. Snyder, *Readings in Western civilization* (1951, rev. 1954); F. L. Baumer, *Main currents of Western thought: readings in Western European intellectual history from the middle ages to the present* (1952); and K. M. Setton, H. R. Winkler, and others, *Great problems in European civilization* (1954).

Among more specialized collections are D. O. Wagner, *Social reformers: Adam Smith to John Dewey* (1934); D. B. Henning and others, *Crises in English history, 1066–1945* (1949); and W. H. Dunham and S. Pargellis, *Complaint and reform in England, 1436–1714* (1938). For nineteenth- and twentieth-century history there are J. F. Scott and A. Baltzly, *Readings in European history since 1814* (1931); Baltzly and A. W. Salomone, *Readings in twentieth century European history* (1950); W. C. Langsam, *Documents and readings in the history of Europe since 1918* (1951); and A. L. Funk, *Source problems in twentieth century history* (1953). Among collections similar to the above, for United States history there are H. S. Commager, *Documents of American history* (5th ed., 1949); L. M. Hacker and H. M. Zahler, *The shaping of the American tradition* (1947); and the Amherst college series, *Problems in American civilization* (1949 ff.).

HISTORICAL SERIES FOR SUPPLEMENTARY READING IN COLLEGE COURSES. Brief volumes on selected topics, especially suitable for undergraduate reading, are to be found in the following series: the "Berkshire studies in European history" (1927 ff.), ed. by R. A. Newhall and others; the Cornell University "Narrative essays in the history of our tradition from its origins in ancient Israel and Greece to the present" (1950 ff.), ed. by E. W. Fox; "Teach yourself history" (1948 ff.), a British series, ed. by A. L. Rowse, very successfully using a biographical approach to lure the general reader to historical topics; and the "Anvil" series (1955 ff.), ed. by L. L. Snyder, consisting of commentary and selected readings on a variety of topics. H. Ausubel has brought together an excellent collection of periodical articles on various topics in *The making of modern Europe* (2 vols., 1951) and, with R. L. Schuyler, in *The making of English history* (1952). The Columbia University source book of readings is paralleled by thoughtful essays in *Chapters in Western civilization* (2 vols., 1946, rev. 1954). A number of series of shorter biographies are currently being published: "Brief lives," by The Macmillan Company; "Lives in brief," by Alfred A. Knopf, Inc.; and "Twentieth century lives," by Charles Scribner's Sons. An older biographical series is the "Heroes of the Nations" (52 vols., 1890–1919).

HISTORICAL MANUALS AND HISTORIOGRAPHY. Among recommended manuals on methods of research and on the writing of history are A. Nevins, *The gateway to history* (1938); S. Kent, *Writing history* (1941), very practical for the beginning student; L. R. Gottschalk, *Understanding history* (1950); G. J. Renier, *History: its purpose and method* (1950); G. J. Garraghan, *A guide to historical method* (1946); C. Gustavson, *A preface to history* (1955); and the older but still useful C. V. Langlois and C. Seignobos, *Introduction to the study of history* (1904). M. Bloch, *The historian's craft* (1953) is a perceptive essay for advanced students, while A. L. Rowse, *The use of history* (Teach yourself history, 1946), is a stimulating introduction. The great historians of the past and the evolution of history are discussed in H. E. Barnes, *A history of historical writing* (1938); J. T. Shotwell, *The history of history* (1939); and J. W. Thompson (with B. J. Holm), *A history of historical writing* (2 vols., 1942).

THEORY OF HISTORY. The historical manuals listed above all provide some introduction to the philosophy and theory of history, and generally have useful bibliographies. In addition, there are extensive bibliographies on the role and nature of historical studies in the Social Science Research Council's Bulletin 54, *Theory and practice in historical study* (1946), and Bulletin 64, *Social sciences in historical study* (1954). Among the leading works on the philosophy of history, all relatively advanced, are M. Mandelbaum, *The problem of historical knowledge* (1938); N. Berdyaev, *The meaning of history* (1936, 1949); J. R. Strayer (ed.) *The interpretation of history* (1943); R. G. Collingwood, *The idea of history* (1946); M. R. Cohen, *The meaning of human history* (1947); H. Butterfield, *Christianity and history* (1949); R. Niebuhr, *Faith and history: a comparison of Christian and modern views of history* (1949).

What may be called "theoretic" or "pattern" histories, recounting the human story in order to show how it follows a certain scheme or system, are generally regarded with distrust by historians, who are not convinced by the evidence offered. During the past generation the most important such grand-scale interpretations are A. J. Toynbee, *A study of history* (10 vols., 1934–54) [abridgment of first 6 vols., 1947, ed. by D. C. Somervell under same title] and O. Spengler, *Decline of the West* (2 vols., 1920–2, 1945), a more pessimistic view. Such works are to be distinguished from that of H. A. L. Fisher, *A history of Europe* (3 vols., 1935–6; 2 vols., 1949), the most notable effort in recent years, by a single author, to tell the whole Western story from the Greeks to the twentieth century in a purely historical way. Recent brief, provocative studies include H. J. Muller, *The uses of the past: profiles of former societies* (1952); S. B. Clough, *The rise and fall of civilization: an inquiry into the relationship between economic development and civilization* (1951); S. Barr, *The pilgrimage of Western Man* (1949), a fascinating account; and P. L. Ralph, *The story of our civilization* (1954).

LARGE SETS AND MANY-VOLUMED COLLABORATIVE WORKS. It is often convenient to refer to the *Cambridge Modern History* (13 vols., 1902–12—with a complete revision now in progress), authoritative but usually dry, with numerous contributors writing for each volume, each on his specialty. A valuable series by American scholars on Europe since 1250, not yet complete, is "The rise of modern Europe" (1936 ff.) [also known as the "Langer series," for its editor, W. L. Langer]; each volume contains a rich bibliography for the years covered; the individual volumes are described below in the appropriate chapters. Other important historical series are "The history of civilization (1924 ff.), major studies on a wide range of topics; "United Nations series" (1940 ff.); "Oxford history of England" (1934 ff.); and E. Eyre (ed.), *European civilization, its origin and development* (7 vols., 1934–9), a work under Catholic auspices by many contributors, some of them non-Catholic. Remarkable as the work of a single author, in 40 volumes in the English translation, is L. von Pastor's *History of the popes . . .* (1891–1953).

GENERAL ECONOMIC HISTORIES AND STUDIES. Of many general economic accounts the following are most useful: H. Heaton, *Economic history of Europe* (1936, 1948); S. B. Clough and C. W. Cole, *Economic history of Europe* (1941, 1952); M. Dobb, *Studies in*

the development of capitalism (1946); N. S. B. Gras, *Business and capitalism: an introduction to business history* (1939); and E. Lipson, *The growth of English society: a short
economic history* (1949). Many other works on economic history may be found in other
parts of this bibliography. General accounts of rural and agrarian history include H. D.
Irvine, *The making of rural Europe* (1923); N. S. B. Gras, *History of agriculture in Europe
and America* (1925); and A. W. Griswold, *Farming and democracy* (1948). Among studies of price and wage history there are J. E. T. Rogers, *Six centuries of work and wages: the
history of English labour* (1884, 1949); W. Beveridge, *Prices and wages in England from
the 12th to the 19th century* (1939 ff.); and N. W. Posthumus, *Inquiry into the history of
prices in Holland* (Vol. I, 1946).

POLITICAL AND LEGAL THOUGHT. Some important works not included elsewhere are
G. H. Sabine, *A history of political theory* (1937); F. Watkins, *The political tradition of
the West: a study in the development of modern liberalism* (1948); A. Cobban, *Dictatorship: its history and theory* (1939, 1943); J. A. Hawgood, *Modern constitutions since 1787*
(1939).

MILITARY HISTORY. *Makers of modern strategy: military thought from Machiavelli to
Hitler* (1944), ed. by E. M. Earle and others, is a good general guide to modern military
problems. A. Vagts, *A history of militarism: romance and realities of a profession* (1937),
from feudal times; B. H. Liddell Hart, *The decisive wars of history: a study in strategy*
(1929); and J. F. C. Fuller, *Decisive battles: their influence upon history and civilization*
(2 vols., 1940) and *A military history of the Western world* (1954 ff.) are other significant
works.

ARTS AND LETTERS. No attempt is made here to open up this enormous field, but the
following are suggested: H. Gardner, *Art through the ages* (1926, 1948); K. Nef, *An outline of the history of music* (1935); and B. F. Fletcher, *A history of architecture on the
comparative method, for students, craftsmen, and amateurs* (1896, 1948).

GENERAL HISTORY OF IDEAS. Three works on this subject are so useful as to deserve
special mention: B. Russell, *A history of Western philosophy and its connection with political and social circumstances from the earliest times to the present day* (1945); J. H.
Randall, *Making of the modern mind: a survey of the intellectual background of the present
age* (1926, 1940); and C. Brinton, *Ideas and men: the story of Western thought* (1950),
which for the post-medieval period has been published in paperback form as *The shaping
of the modern mind* (1953).

MISCELLANEOUS. Finally, on certain unclassifiable but usually important subjects, readers
may wish to turn to Mary R. Beard, *Woman as a force in history: a study in traditions and
realities* (1946); Miriam Beard, *A history of the business man* (1938); E. P. Prentice,
Hunger and history: the influence of hunger on human history (1939); R. N. Salaman,
The history and social influence of the potato (1949); K. Chorley, *Armies and the art of
revolution* (1943); C. Brinton, *The anatomy of revolution* (1938); H. Nicolson, *Diplomacy* (1939) and *The evolution of diplomatic method* (1955); S. Giedion, *Mechanization
takes command* (1948); and A. M. Carr-Saunders and P. A. Wilson, *Professions: their
organization and place in society* (1928).

Chapter I. The Rise of Europe

PREHISTORIC TIMES. For anthropology, archaeology, and prehistory the following very
readable books are suggested: A. L. Kroeber, *Anthropology* (1923, 1948); C. Kluckhohn,
Mirror for man (1949); V. G. Childe, *What happened in history* (1942, 1948) and *The
dawn of European civilization* (1925, 1947); C. Ceram, *Gods, graves, and scholars* (1951);
and W. Howells, *Back of history* (1954). Geographical influences on history are discussed
in D. S. Whittlesey, *Environmental foundations of European history* (1949); L. P. V.

Febvre, A geographical introduction to history (1925); N. J. G. Pounds, An historical and political geography of Europe (1947); and G. East, An historical geography of Europe (1935).

ANCIENT TIMES. W. Durant's volumes, Our Oriental heritage (1935), The life of Greece (1939), and Caesar and Christ: a history of Roman civilization and of Christianity from their beginnings to A.D. 325 (1944), are excellent accounts for the general reader. They should be compared with the more thorough studies of M. I. Rostovtzeff, A history of the ancient world (2 vols., 1926, 1930), and other writings. Two Berkshire studies, E. R. Goodenough, The Church in the Roman Empire (1931), and R. F. Arragon, The transition from the ancient to the medieval world (1936), and a brilliant little book by A. H. M. Jones, Constantine and the conversion of Europe (1949), in the Teach yourself history series, are also useful.

GENERAL WORKS ON THE MIDDLE AGES. Among the best introductory accounts are S. Painter, A history of the middle ages, 284–1500 (1953) and his briefer Medieval society (1953) in the Cornell University series; J. R. Strayer and D. C. Munro, The middle ages, 395–1500 (1942); and J. L. Lamonte, The world of the middle ages: a reorientation of medieval history (1949), which centers around Constantinople in the period A.D. 330–1453. W. Durant continues his earlier volumes with The age of faith (1950). C. W. Previte-Orton in the Shorter Cambridge medieval history (2 vols., 1952) has condensed for the general reader the multivolumed Cambridge medieval history. Excellent portraits of medieval life may be found in G. G. Coulton's Medieval panorama (1938) and his other works, and in E. Power, Medieval people (1924).

Intellectual developments are discussed with great insight in F. B. Artz, The mind of the middle ages, 200–1500 (1954) and in the older work by H. O. Taylor, The medieval mind: a history of the development of thought and emotion in the Middle Ages (2 vols. 1911, 1925–7). Among advanced works on medieval philosophy and political theory are studies by E. Gilson, O. F. von Gierke, R. W. and A. J. Carlyle, and P. Vinogradoff. Medieval geographical knowledge is well summarized in a series of lectures (A. P. Newton, ed.), Travel and travellers of the Middle Ages (1926).

Economic developments are discussed in the provocative little books of H. Pirenne, Economic and social history of medieval Europe (1936) and Medieval cities: their origins and the revival of trade (1925, 1939). The gilds and other organizations are discussed in P. Boissonnade, Life and work in medieval Europe from the 5th to the 15th century (1927). Two volumes have so far appeared in the Cambridge Economic History of Europe, valuable but of a technical and specialized nature: The agrarian life of the Middle Ages (1941) and Trade and industry in the Middle Ages (1952).

Various topics on Islam and on the contacts between Western Europe and the East are presented in Pirenne's challenging Mohammed and Charlemagne (1939); P. K. Hitti, History of the Arabs (1943); D. O'Leary, How Greek science passed to the Arabs (1949); G. E. von Grunebaum, Medieval Islam: a study in cultural orientation (1946), which compares the Islamic with the Byzantine and Christian civilizations; and in two excellent books by H. A. R. Gibb, Mohammedanism: an historical survey (1949), in the Home University Library, and Islamic society and the West (1951). For the Byzantine world there is the compact and readable summary by C. Diehl, History of the Byzantine empire (1925), and Byzantine portraits (1927). N. H. Baynes, The Byzantine Empire (1946) is a useful short account which may be supplemented by the essays in Byzantium: an introduction to East Roman civilization (1948), ed. by Baynes and H. Moss. A. A. Vasiliev has written a comprehensive History of the Byzantine Empire, 324–1453 (1952).

The following works deal with various regions and institutions during the Middle Ages: J. Bryce, The Holy Roman Empire (1864, 1909); G. Barraclough, Origins of modern Germany (1947); A. Tilley (ed.), Medieval France (1922); S. Painter, French chivalry: chivalric ideas and practices in mediaeval France (1940) and his brief Rise of the feudal monarchies (1951) in the Cornell University series; Ch. Petit-Dutaillis, The feudal monarchy in France and England, from the 10th to the 13th century (1933, 1949); G. O. Sayles, Medieval foundations of England (1948); G. L. Haskins, The growth of English representative government (1948); and C. H. McIlwain, The High Court of Parliament and its supremacy (1910). Two recent lively biographical accounts are A. R. Kelly, Eleanor *of Aquitaine and the four kings* (1950) and E. F. Jacob, *Henry V and the invasion of France* (Teach yourself history series, 1950).

THE FORMATION OF EUROPE. In addition to works listed above, notably those of Pirenne, the following should be consulted for divergent points of view on the relative importance of the various factors which produced medieval Europe: C. Dawson, *The making of Europe: an introduction to the history of European unity* (1937); S. Katz, *The decline of Rome and the rise of medieval Europe* (1955), a brief introductory account in the Cornell University series; H. St. L. B. Moss, *The birth of the Middle Ages, 395–814* (1935), which suggests that there was more continuity than catastrophe; F. Lot, *The end of the ancient world and the beginnings of the Middle Ages* (1931); and A. Dopsch, *The economic and social foundations of European civilization* (1923, 1937), which differs from Lot in its conclusions. Two important studies of the intellectual side of the early Middle Ages are *Thought and letters in Western Europe*, A.D. *500–900* (1931) by M. L. W. Laistner, and E. K. Rand, *Founders of the Middle Ages* (1941). Two well-written biographies are R. Winston, *Charlemagne: from the hammer to the cross* (1954), and E. S. Duckett, *Alcuin, friend of Charlemagne* (1951).

THE HIGH MIDDLE AGES: SECULAR CIVILIZATION. Much of the relative stability of the later medieval period can be attributed to the gradual development of vassalage. A handy introduction to this most complex subject is C. Stephenson, *Medieval feudalism* (1942). Other useful guides to economic topics of this period are two Berkshire studies: N. Neilson, *Medieval agrarian economy* (1936), and S. Baldwin, *Business in the Middle Ages* (1937). Many of the economic histories cited elsewhere should also be consulted.

   Three notable contributions to the knowledge of medieval secular culture are those of C. H. Haskins: *Normans in European civilization* (1915), *The Renaissance of the 12th century* (1927), and *The rise of universities* (1923). The last may be supplemented by the more elaborate study by H. Rashdall, *Universities of Europe in the Middle Ages* (1895, new 3 vol. ed., 1936).

THE MEDIEVAL CHURCH. The classic expression of the view that the spiritual unity of medieval Europe made possible a deeply satisfying sense of harmony is Henry Adams, *Mont-Saint-Michel and Chartres* (1912, 1936). C. Dawson, *Medieval religion* (1934) also stresses the close communion between European culture and Christian religion in the Middle Ages, as does J. J. Walsh, *The thirteenth, the greatest of centuries* (1943). Other important works include R. F. Wright, *Medieval internationalism: the contribution of the medieval Church to international law and peace* (1930); W. E. Lunt, *Papal revenues in the Middle Ages* (2 vols., 1934); and S. R. Packard, *Europe and the Church under Innocent III* (1927). A. S. Turberville, *Medieval heresy and the Inquisition* (1920, 1932) is a more popular and less trenchant treatment of the general subject to which Henry Charles Lea devoted great learning and energy. S. Baldwin, *The organization of medieval Christianity* (1929), a Berkshire study, and M. W. Baldwin, *The medieval church* (1953), in the Cornell University series, are good brief introductions.

   The Crusades may be approached through the Berkshire study, R. A. Newhall, *The Crusades* (1927), and the detailed and colorful S. Runciman, *A history of the Crusades* (3 vols., 1951–4). The first of five volumes of a collaborative, scholarly *History of the Crusades* (K. M. Setton, gen. ed.) has appeared, *The first hundred years* (M. W. Baldwin, ed., 1955). For all aspects of the expansion of Christianity the works of K. S. Latourette are indispensable, especially his *History of Christianity* (1953) and his longer *History of the expansion of Christianity* (7 vols., 1937–45).

Chapter II. The Revolution in the Christian Church

   Among the most valuable general accounts of the late medieval and transitional centuries are E. P. Cheyney, *The dawn of a new era, 1250–1453* (1936); M. Gilmore, *The world of humanism, 1453–1517* (1952) [both in the Langer series]; W. K. Ferguson, *The Renaissance* (1940), a Berkshire study; H. S. Lucas, *The Renaissance and Reformation* (1934); and V. H. H. Green, *Renaissance and Reformation* (1952).

THE DECLINE OF THE CHURCH. The growing restlessness within the confines of the Church is well illustrated by the following works: P. Hughes, *The revolt against the Church* (*Aquinas to Luther*) (1947), the third volume of *A history of the Church* (1934 ff.), an outstanding Catholic account; F. F. Jacobs, *Essays in the Conciliar Epoch* (1943); G. J. Jordan, *The inner history of the Great Schism in the West* (1930); and J. N. Figgis, *Studies of political thought from Gerson to Grotius* (1923), a classic study of the difficulties of "peaceful reform" within the Church. J. Huizinga, *The waning of the Middle Ages, a study of the forms of life, thought, and art in France and the Netherlands in the XIVth and XVth centuries* (1924) is a brilliant work. Two national heresies of the 14th century may be studied in J. Herben, *Hus and his followers* (1926), a popular account; B. Workman, *John Wyclif: a study of the English medieval church* (2 vols., 1926); and the briefer K. B. McFarlane, *John Wycliffe and the beginnings of English nonconformity* (1953), in the Teach yourself history series. Superstitions and religious folklore may be approached through the strange books of M. Summers, *The history of witchcraft and demonology* (1926) and *The geography of witchcraft* (1927), and checked against the more scholarly account of G. L. Kittredge, *Witchcraft in Old and New England* (1929). C. G. Loomis, *White magic: an introduction to the folklore of Christian legend* (1948) explores human thinking in the 12th and later centuries on miracles and unexplainable occurrences. Some of the works cited for Chapter VII trace the relations between ideas of magic and the development of science.

THE RENAISSANCE IN ITALY. Besides the general accounts cited for the beginning of this chapter, the Renaissance may be approached through G. C. Sellery, *The Renaissance: its nature and origins* (1950), and the colorfully written fifth volume in W. Durant's story of civilization, *The Renaissance: a history of civilization in Italy from 1304 to 1576 A.D.* (1953). The origins and development of the concept "Renaissance" are masterfully explored in W. K. Ferguson, *The Renaissance in historical thought: five centuries of interpretation* (1948), in which he examines, among other things, the classical account of the Italian Renaissance by J. A. Symonds (7 vols., 1875–86) and J. Burckhardt (1860, new ed., 1944), both of which stressed the originality and uniqueness of Italy. Among more specialized studies there are A. C. Krey's study of Florence, *A city that art built* (1936); F. Schevill, *History of Florence from the founding of the city through the Renaissance* (1936) and *The Medici* (1949); G. F. Young, *The Medici* (1910); R. De Roover, *The Medici Bank* (1948); H. Wölfflin, *The art of the Italian Renaissance* (1903); and F. C. Lane, *Venetian ships and shipping of the Renaissance* (1934). Machiavelli may be approached through studies by H. Butterfield (1940) and J. M. Whitfield (1947), while G. Mattingly has written *Renaissance diplomacy* (1955).

THE RENAISSANCE OUTSIDE ITALY. P. S. Allen, *The age of Erasmus* (1914) is a good introduction to the Northern Renaissance. P. Smith, *Erasmus: a study of his life, ideals, and place in history* (1923) is an excellent biography. Briefer and very spirited is M. M. Phillips, *Erasmus and the Northern Renaissance*, Teach yourself history series (1950). G. M. Trevelyan, *Illustrated English social history* (4 vols., 1949 ff.) begins with a discussion of Chaucer's England and the influence of the Continental Renaissance. The relations between banking and culture in Germany and elsewhere are shown in R. Ehrenberg, *Capital and finance in the age of the Renaissance: a study of the Fuggers and their connections* (1928), and in J. Strieder, *Jacob Fugger the Rich* (1931). A. Hyma, *The Christian Renaissance: a history of the "Devotio moderna"* (1924) questions the view that the Italian Renaissance brought on the Reformation.

PROTESTANTISM. Besides the general accounts listed above, brief introductory treatments are available in G. L. Mosse, *The Reformation* (1952), a Berkshire study, and E. H. Harbison, *The age of Reformation* (1955), in the Cornell University series. Other general accounts include H. J. Grimm, *The Reformation era* (1954); R. H. Bainton, *The Reformation of the sixteenth century* (1952); and the older but still valuable P. Smith, *The age of the Reformation* (1920). Smith has also written sympathetic biographies of Luther and Erasmus and an unsympathetic one of Calvin. For the immediate political background, see W. L. McElwee, *The reign of Charles V, 1516–1558* (1936), or the larger work of K. Brandi, *The Emperor Charles V: the growth and destiny of a man and of a world em-*

pire (1939). Among important biographical accounts of Luther and his times are those by H. Boehmer (1925, trans. 1946); H. Grisar (1926, trans. 1930), a Catholic account; E. G. Schwiebert (1950); and the vivid and scholarly R. Bainton, *Here I stand: a life of Martin Luther* (1950).

Among the best accounts of Calvin and his influence are J. T. McNeill, *The history and character of Calvinism* (1954), and biographical studies by W. Walker (1906), G. Harkness (1931), and J. MacKinnon (1936).

The course of the Reformation in England may be examined through two brief and able accounts, T. M. Parker, *The English Reformation to 1558* (1950), in the Home University Library; and F. E. Hutchinson, *Cranmer and the English Reformation* (Teach yourself history series, 1951). More advanced treatment is available in H. M. Smith, *Henry VIII and the Reformation* (1948), F. M. Powicke, *The Reformation in England* (1941), and A. F. Pollard, *Henry VIII* (1902, 1913).

The various forms of Protestantism are placed in the broad historical perspective of Christian tradition in E. Troeltsch's masterpiece, *The social teachings of the Christian churches* (2 vols., reissued 1949), and in his *Protestantism and Progress: a historical study of the relation of Protestantism to the modern world* (1912). Other notable studies are J. W. Allen, *History of political thought in the 16th century* (1928); R. H. Murray, *Political consequences of the Reformation* (1926); R. M. Jones, *Spiritual reformers of the 16th and 17th centuries* (1914); and Richard H. Niebuhr, *The social sources of denominationalism* (1929).

One of the most debated questions concerning the Reformation has been that of the relation between economic change and religious doctrine. M. Weber, *The Protestant ethic and the spirit of capitalism* (1904, reissued 1948), opened the controversy, and three of the most distinctive later points of view are presented in R. H. Tawney, *Religion and the rise of capitalism: a historical study* (1926, 1947), a brilliant work; J. Brodrick, *The economic morals of the Jesuits* (1934); and A. Hyma, *Christianity, capitalism, and communism* (1937). P. Fox, *Reformation in Poland: some social and economic aspects* (1924), and G. K. Brown, *Italy and the Reformation to 1550* (1933), deal with the spread of Protestantism into areas where it did not become predominant; and W. Haller, *The rise of Puritanism* (1938), describes "the way to the New Jerusalem" according to various English divines in the period 1570–1643.

CATHOLICISM REFORMED AND REORGANIZED. Important general accounts include B. J. Kidd, *The Counter-Reformation, 1550–1600* (1933), and P. Janelle, *The Catholic Reformation* (1949). Among other studies there are H. Jedin, *Papal Legate at the Council of Trent: Cardinal Seripando* (1947), C. Hess, *The Capuchins: a contribution to the history of the Counter-Reformation* (2 vols., 1929), C. Roth, *The Spanish Inquisition* (1937), and G. H. Putnam, *Censorship of the Church of Rome* (2 vols., 1906–07), a study of the *Index*, together with some material on the effect of Protestant and state censorship.

Of the large literature on the Jesuits, the following may be mentioned: P. Dudon, *St. Ignatius of Loyola* (1933, 1949); T. J. Campbell, *The Jesuits, 1534–1921* (2 vols., 1921); H. Boehmer, *The Jesuits* (1914, 1928); R. Fülöp-Miller, *The power and the secret of the Jesuits* (1930); and A. H. Rowbotham, *Missionary and mandarin: the Jesuits at the court of China* (1943), as one example of the overseas activities of the order. Jesuit activities in the Latin American colonies are described in some of the books listed for Chapter III.

Chapter III. The Wars of Religion

C. Oman, *The sixteenth century* (1936), is primarily a political and military history, but it also includes some discussion of religious and cultural topics. The same author has written *A history of the art of war in the 16th century* (1937). A well-planned, conservative general treatment of European power politics after the French invasion of Italy is C. Petrie, *Earlier diplomatic history, 1492–1713* (1949).

THE OPENING OF THE ATLANTIC. Brief introductory accounts include C. E. Nowell, *The great discoveries and the first colonial empires* (1954), in the Cornell University series, and J. E. Gillespie, *History of geographical discovery* (1933), a Berkshire study. W. C. Abbott,

The expansion of Europe (2 vols., 1918) and the briefer J. H. Parry, *Europe and a wider world, 1415–1715* (1949), both emphasize the effects of overseas activity upon the internal development of Europe. W. P. Webb, a student of American frontier expansion, has written a challenging book on the implications of European expansion, *The great frontier* (1952). Other important works include C. R. Beazley, *The dawn of modern geography* (3 vols., 1905–06); P. Sykes, *History of exploration* (2nd ed., 1935), beginning with ancient times; A. P. Newton (ed.), *The great age of discovery* (1932); J. A. Williamson, *Maritime enterprise 1485–1558* (1913) and the more compact *Europe overseas* (1925); J. B. Brebner, *The explorers of North America, 1492–1806* (1933); and II. H. Hart, *Sea route to the Indies* (1950).

Portuguese maritime and colonial enterprises are recounted in E. Prestage, *The Portuguese pioneers* (1933); C. R. Beazley, *Prince Henry the Navigator* (1895); H. M. Stephens, *Albuquerque* (1892, 1897); and in two fascinating books by E. Sanceau, *The land of Prester John* (1944), about Portuguese interest in Abyssinia, and *Knight of the Renaissance: a biography of D. João de Castre, soldier, sailor, scientist, and Viceroy of India, 1500–1548* (1949). G. Freyre, *Brazil: an interpretation* (1945), is the best short account in English, and an important special point is discussed in A. Marchant, *From barter to slavery: the economic relations of Portuguese and Indians in the settlement of Brazil, 1500–1580* (1942).

SPAIN IN EUROPE AND OVERSEAS. R. B. Merriman, *Rise of the Spanish empire in the old world and in the new* (4 vols., 1918–34), traces the evolution of Spanish policy and expansion from the early Middle Ages to the death of Philip II. A very readable and reliable shorter survey is R. T. Davies, *The golden century of Spain, 1501–1621* (1937, 1954). E. D. Salmon, *Imperial Spain* (1931), is a Berkshire study. S. E. Morison, *Admiral of the Ocean Sea* (2 vols., 1942), is the standard life of Columbus, and S. Zweig, *Conqueror of the seas* (1938), is a readable biography of Magellan, as is C. M. Parr, *So noble a captain* (1953). An important analysis is E. J. Hamilton, *American treasure and the price revolution in Spain, 1501–1650* (1934), which should be used in conjunction with the author's other writings.

C. H. Haring, *The Spanish empire in America* (1947), is more reliable than Salvador de Madariaga, *Rise of the Spanish American Empire* (1947). A picturesque account is F. A. Kirkpatrick, *The Spanish conquistadores* (1934, 1949). An interesting argument that absolutism in the empire in effect destroyed constitutionalism in Spain is presented in J. H. Parry, *The Spanish theory of empire in the 16th century* (1940). L. Hanke, *The Spanish struggle for justice in the conquest of America* (1949), questions some of the older views on the role of the Inquisition. A defense of Spanish colonial administration based upon the literature of the time is offered in I. A. Leonard, *Books of the brave* (1949). The question of Spanish treatment of subject peoples in Latin America is discussed in L. B. Simpson, *The encomienda in New Spain: forced native labor in the Spanish colonies, 1492–1550* (1929), and in F. Tannenbaum, *Slave and citizen: the Negro in the Americas* (1947), where it is argued that in Latin America (unlike North America) there was some recognition of the "moral personality" of the slave.

THE COMMERCIAL REVOLUTION AND MERCANTILISM. The general economic histories cited at the beginning of this bibliography should also be consulted. L. B. Packard's Berkshire study, *The commercial revolution, 1400–1776* (1927), is a good introduction. On the emergence of capitalism, H. E. Sée, *Modern capitalism: its origin and evolution* (1928), may be compared with F. L. Nussbaum, *History of the economic institutions of modern Europe* (1933), which is based largely on the work of the German historian W. Sombart. On mercantilism, E. Hecksher has written the most authoritative work, *Mercantilism* (2 vols., 1935); two briefer works are J. W. Horrocks, *A short history of mercantilism* (1925), and P. Buck, *The politics of mercantilism* (1942), the latter drawing some comparisons to 20th-century totalitarianism. E. S. Furniss, *The position of the laborer in a system of nationalism: a study in the labor theories of the later English mercantilists* (1920) is a thoughtful study.

The characteristic economic institutions of the period are described in the following: G. Renard and G. Weulersse, *Life and work in modern Europe: the 15th to the 18th centuries* (1926); D. Hannay, *The great chartered companies* (1926); G. Unwin, *Indus-*

trial organization in the 16th and 17th centuries (1904) and *Gilds and companies of London* (1909, 1925); and S. Kramer, *The English craft gilds: studies in their progress and decline* (1927). M. Beard's *History of the business man*, cited earlier, has some colorful accounts of this period.

NETHERLANDS. P. Geyl, *The revolt of the Netherlands, 1555–1609* (1932), seeks to show that the split between Belgium and Holland originated not in language or religion but in the fortunes of war; the sequel, *The Netherlands divided, 1609–48* (1936), describes the extreme particularism that grew up in the separated provinces. C. V. Wedgwood, *William the Silent* (1944), is an excellent, laudatory biography, and R. B. Merriman, *Six contemporaneous revolutions* (1938), relates events in the Netherlands to similar stirrings elsewhere in 17th-century Europe.

ELIZABETHAN ENGLAND. A general picture of the period can be obtained from the following: C. Read, *The Tudors: personalities and practical politics in 16th century England* (1936), A. L. Rowse, *Queen Elizabeth and her subjects* (1935), and *The England of Elizabeth: the structure of society* (1950); S. T. Bindoff, *Tudor England* (1952); J. D. Mackie, *The earlier Tudors, 1485–1558* (1952); G. R. Elton, *The Tudor revolution in government* (1953); and J. B. Black, *The reign of Queen Elizabeth, 1558–1603* (1936). The best biography is J. E. Neale, *Queen Elizabeth* (1934); two other good brief biographies of Elizabeth are those by M. Waldman (1952) and D. B. Chidsey (1955). There is a well-written biography of Mary Tudor by H. F. M. Prescott (rev., 1953). C. Read, *Mr. Secretary Walsingham and the policy of Queen Elizabeth* (3 vols., 1925), is a remarkably full account of the determination and execution of English policy.

On the naval and imperial side, three works by J. A. Williamson may be recommended: *The age of Drake* (1938, 1946), *The ocean in English history* (1941), and *Sir Francis Drake* (1951). D. Quinn has written *Raleigh and the British empire* (1947), in the Teach yourself history series. Some religious connections of English expansionism are pointed out in L. B. Wright, *Religion and Empire: the alliance between piety and commerce in English expansion, 1558–1625* (1943).

Important social and economic features of the period are treated in R. H. Tawney, *Agrarian problem in the 16th century* (1912), on the changing position of the peasantry; in L. B. Wright, *Middle class culture in Elizabethan England* (1935); and in the volumes of Trevelyan cited above.

DISINTEGRATION AND RECONSTRUCTION OF FRANCE. The religious and dynastic turmoil in 16th-century France is discussed in the following works: F. C. Palm, *Calvinism and the religious wars* (1932), a Berkshire study, and his fuller study, *Politics and religion in 16th century France* (1927); J. W. Thompson, *Wars of Religion in France, 1559–1576* (1909, 1914); H. M. Baird's numerous sympathetic volumes (1879–95) on the Huguenots, together with A. J. Grant's able little study, *The Huguenots* (1934); P. Van Dyke, *Catherine de Médicis* (2 vols., 1922); J. E. Neale, *The age of Catherine de Medici* (1943); H. Bremond, *A literary history of religious thought in France from the wars of religion down to our own times* (3 vols., 1928 ff.); and W. F. Church, *Constitutional thought in 16th century France* (1941).

The revival of France is described in Q. Hurst, *Henry of Navarre* (1938), in the hyper-patriotic A. Bailly, *The cardinal dictator: a portrait of Richelieu* (1936), which rejoices in Richelieu as a successful Machiavellian, and in C. V. Wedgwood's better balanced *Richelieu and the French monarchy* (1949), in the Teach yourself history series.

THE THIRTY YEARS' WAR. Apart from the general histories of the 17th century listed below for Chapter IV, the following books are suggested: S. R. Gardiner, *The Thirty Years' War* (1897), not entirely superseded by the excellent C. V. Wedgwood, *The Thirty Years' War* (1938). See also F. Watson, *Wallenstein: soldier under Saturn* (1938), and N. Ahnlund, *Gustav Adolf the Great* (1932, 1940). A fine account of the philosopher Leibniz's efforts to reconcile the various hostile factions of Christianity after a century of warfare is contained in G. J. Jordan, *The reunion of the churches* (1929).

Chapter IV. The Establishment of West-European Leadership

EUROPE IN THE SEVENTEENTH CENTURY. There are many more good general accounts of this century than of the preceding one; two notable syntheses are D. Ogg, *Europe in the 17th century* (1925, 1948), which is concerned primarily with affairs on the Continent, and G. N. Clark, *The seventeenth century* (1929, 1947), organized topically and centered about France. An interesting brief introduction is M. Beloff, *The age of absolutism, 1660–1815* (1954), in the Home University Library. Three volumes in the Langer series provide excellent coverage for the period: C. J. Friedrich, *The age of the baroque, 1610–1660* (1952); F. L. Nussbaum, *The triumph of science and reason, 1660–85* (1953); and J. B. Wolf, *The Emergence of the great powers, 1685–1715* (1951). W. F. Reddaway, *History of Europe, 1610–1715* (1948), may also be recommended.

Three other works of general character which bear on this period are R. B. Mowat, *A history of European diplomacy, 1451–1789* (1928); A. T. Mahan, *The influence of sea power on history, 1660–1783* (1890, 1906); and E. Barker, *The development of public services in Western Europe, 1660–1930* (1944).

THE DUTCH REPUBLIC AND EMPIRE. On Dutch overseas explorations and colonization, see H. W. Van Loon, *Golden book of the Dutch navigators* (1916); A. Vandenbosch, *Dutch East Indies: its government, problems and politics* (1934), relating earlier periods to the 20th century; A. Hyma, *The Dutch in the Far East: a history of the Dutch commercial and colonial empire* (1942); and the extensive E. S. DeKlerck, *History of the Netherlands East Indies* (2 vols., 1938). Three other important studies of Dutch activities in the Far East are J. S. Furnivall, *Netherlands India: a study of plural economy* (1939), covering in detail the period from 1600; and B. H. M. Vlekke, *Nusantara: a history of the East Indian archipelago* (1943) and his simpler narrative, *The story of the Dutch East Indies* (1945). Holland's place in European politics is discussed in specialized studies by G. Edmundson (1911), M. C. Trevelyan (1930), and G. N. Clark (1923). The imperial rivalry of England and Holland in Malaya and India is outlined in S. A. Khan, *The East India trade in the 17th century in its political and economic aspects* (1923). V. Barbour has written *Capitalism in Amsterdam in the 17th Century* (1950).

THE RISE OF BRITAIN. The most interesting general book on this period is still G. M. Trevelyan, *England under the Stuarts* (1904, 1947); two other general histories of high quality are G. Davies, *The early Stuarts, 1603–60* (1937), and G. N. Clark, *The later Stuarts, 1660–1714* (1934), both being volumes in the Oxford History of England. The English background to settlement in America is ably sketched in W. Notestein, *The English people on the eve of colonization, 1603–1630* (1954), a volume in the "New American Nation Series." Religious questions are given full consideration in R. G. Usher, *The reconstruction of the English church* (2 vols., 1910); and in W. K. Jordan, *The development of religious toleration in England* (4 vols., 1932–40), which traces changing laws and attitudes from Elizabethan to Restoration times. Three monographs, F. C. Dietz, *English public finance, 1558–1641* (1932), showing the financial dilemma faced by the Crown; G. N. Clark, *The wealth of England from 1496 to 1760* (1947); and L. A. Harper, *The English Navigation Laws: a 17th century experiment in social engineering* (1939), should be added to the economic studies cited elsewhere.

L. von Ranke and S. R. Gardiner's older histories of seventeenth-century England are justly regarded as classics, and from them the reader can still profit. H. R. Trevor-Roper presents an unsympathetic picture of an unbending autocrat in his not-quite-fair *Archbishop Laud, 1573–1645* (1940), which may be contrasted with J. H. Hexter's *The reign of King Pym* (1941), where it is held that the parliamentary leader Pym was really a moderate between monarchists and anti-monarchists. C. V. Wedgwood's discriminating *Strafford, 1593–1641* (1935, 1949), is a revisionist biography fairly sympathetic to Charles I's adviser. Miss Wedgwood's *Velvet studies* (1946), *Oliver Cromwell* (1939, 1947), and *The king's peace, 1637–1641* (1955), all merit attention. C. Firth, *Oliver Cromwell and the rule of the Puritans in England* (1900, 1925), is still the best biography, and there are other valuable ones by S. R. Gardiner, J. Morley, and J. Buchan. B. Willey, *The seventeenth century background: studies in the thought of the age in relation to poetry and religion* (1934, 1949), D. M. Wolfe, *Milton in the Puritan Revolution* (1941), and F. E. Hutchinson, *Milton and the English mind* (1946), in the Teach yourself history series, show something of the effect of political turmoil upon the English imagination.

Much of the present interest in Stuart and Commonwealth England is directed to the emergence and clarification during that period of some recognizably modern political and social problems, on which the following offer various points of view: G. P. Gooch, *English democratic ideas in the 17th century* (1898; ed. by H. J. Laski, 1927); M. James, *Social policy and problems during the Puritan Revolution* (1930); W. Schenk, *The concern for social justice in the Puritan Revolution* (1948), stressing religious rather than economic compulsions as basic in Puritan thought; E. Bernstein, *Cromwell and communism: socialism and democracy in the great English revolution* (1930), by a leading revisionist socialist; T. C. Pease, *The Leveller Movement* (1916); M. Ashley, *John Wildman, plotter and postmaster: a study of the English republican movement in the seventeenth century* (1947); and C. Firth, *Cromwell's army: a history of the English soldier during the Civil Wars, the Commonwealth, and the Protectorate* (1905). A. S. P. Woodhouse (ed.), *Puritanism and liberty, being the Army Debates (1647–49) from the Clarke manuscripts* . . . (1938), includes some very important material on the 17th-century ideas of democracy.

For the English Restoration period, D. Ogg's *England in the reign of Charles II* (2 vols., 1934), is standard, if somewhat Whiggish; a briefer Tory counterpart is A. Bryant, *King Charles II* (1932, 1949), which makes the best possible case for Charles's relations with Louis XIV. F. C. Turner, *James II* (1948), is fair and factual. Various special topics are covered in A. A. Seaton, *The theory of toleration under the Later Stuarts* (1911); J. Pollock, *The Popish Plot* (1903, 1945); D. Mathew, *The social structure in Caroline England* (1948); H. G. Plum, *Restoration Puritanism* (1943); A. Bryant, *Samuel Pepys* (3 vols., 1933–9); and J. H. Wilson, *Court wits of the Restoration* (1948).

G. M. Trevelyan's brilliant little book, *The English Revolution 1688–1689* (1939), argues that the immediate result of the revolution was to strengthen conservatism for the 18th century but that the long-run consequences made the revolution a turning point in history. The same author's *England under Queen Anne* (3 vols., 1930–4), vividly portrays the succeeding age. For foreign and military affairs, it should be supplemented by W. S. Churchill, *Malborough, his life and times* (4 vols., 1933–8). H. D. Traill, *William III* (1888, 1926), is still useful, but there is need for a good modern biography. J. Clapham, *The Bank of England* (2 vols., 1944), covers the period 1694–1944.

THE FRANCE OF LOUIS XIV. The age of French predominance in Europe may be approached through the stimulating book of A. Guérard, *The life and death of an ideal: France in the classical age* (1928), and also through the following: L. B. Packard, *The age of Louis XIV* (1929), an excellent Berkshire study; M. Ashley, *Louis XIV and the greatness of France* (1948), in the Teach yourself history series; D. Ogg, *Louis XIV* (1933); and C. Petrie, *Louis XIV* (1940). Older guides to the period are J. B. Perkins, *France under Mazarin* (2 vols., 1886) and *France under Louis XIV* (2 vols., 1897). Other studies include P. R. Doolin, *The Fronde* (1935); H. M. Baird, *The Huguenots and the revocation of the Edict of Nantes* (2 vols., 1895); and G. H. Dodge, *The political theory of the Huguenot dispersion* (1947).

On the development of French economy and empire, see C. W. Cole, *Colbert and a century of French mercantilism* (2 vols., 1939), also his earlier volume and a sequel which carries the story to 1700; E. C. Lodge, *Sully, Colbert, and Turgot: a chapter in French economic history* (1931); and H. I. Priestley, *France overseas through the Old Regime: a study of European expansion* (1939). S. L. Mims, *Colbert's West Indian policy* (1912), may be compared to G. H. Guttridge, *The colonial policy of William III in America and the West Indies* (1922).

Chapter V: The Transformation of Eastern Europe

P. Roberts, *The quest for security, 1715–1740* (1947), in the Langer series, presents a not entirely convincing thesis of a conservative reaction based on ideas of corporatism; further study and reassessment is necessary of the 18th-century remodeling of earlier ideas and institutions. A. Sorel, *The Eastern Question in the 18th century* (1898), is narrower than the title suggests, but it gives something of the author's general interpretation of 18th-century diplomacy. A more complete account is J. A. R. Marriott, *The Eastern Ques-*

tion: *an historical study in European diplomacy* (1917, 1940). S. H. Cross, *Slavic civiliza-tion through the ages* (1948), R. W. Seton-Watson, *German, Slav and Magyar* (1916), and O. Halecki, *Borderlands of Western Civilization: a history of East-Central Europe* (1952) are helpful introductions to the complex political and social structure of Central Europe. R. N. Bain, *Slavonic Europe: a political history of Poland and Russia from 1147 to 1796* (1908), is an older study; a briefer and better organized account is S. Konovalov, *Russo-Polish relations: an historical survey* (1945).

POLAND. A well-balanced history covering the years 1697–1935 is volume II of *The Cambridge History of Poland* (1941), ed. by W. F. Reddaway and others. R. H. Lord, *The Second Partition of Poland* (1915), is an important study. Also useful are D. B. Horn, *British public opinion and the First Partition of Poland* (1945), and three biographies: O. Laskowski, *Jan III Sobieski* (*King of Poland*), *1629–1696* (1941); R. N. Bain, *The last king of Poland and his contemporaries* (1909), on Stanislaus II; and M. M. Gardner, *Kosciuszko* (1920).

OTTOMAN EMPIRE. On the earlier period, see P. Wittek, *The rise of the Ottoman Empire* (1938); S. N. Fisher, *The foreign relations of Turkey, 1481–1512* (1948); and G. W. F. Stripling, *Ottoman Turks and Arabs, 1511–1574* (1942). R. B. Merriman, *Suleiman the Magnificent, 1520–1566* (1944), though not fully abreast of the latest scholarship in the field, is probably the best general introduction for Western readers. It should be supplemented by A. H. Lybyer, *Government of the Ottoman empire in the time of Suleiman the Magnificent* (1913), and by N. Sousa [Susa], *The capitulatory regime of Turkey, its history, origin, and nature* (1933), which explains the special status of various Christian and other minorities in the Turkish empire. B. H. Sumner, *Peter the Great and the Ottoman Empire* (1949), describes some of the early relations of Turkey with Russia.

AUSTRIA AND THE HAPSBURGS TO 1740. H. W. Steed and others, *A short history of Austria-Hungary and Poland* (1914), and L. P. Leger, *History of Austro-Hungary* (1889), are general narratives. P. Frischauer, *The imperial crown: the story of the rise and fall of the Holy Roman and the Austrian empires* (1939), is a more interesting work, primarily biographical in nature, on the House of Hapsburg to the death of Leopold II in 1792. The same author has also written a lively but not entirely adequate biography of the picturesque Austrian general: *Prince Eugene, 1663–1736: a man and a hundred years of history* (1934). The efforts of the Hapsburgs to overcome the divisive effects of the Reformation and the Thirty Years' War are described in H. F. Schwarz, *The Imperial Privy Council in the 17th century* (1943). H. Marczali, *Hungary in the 18th century* (1910), is a fairly detailed study.

PRUSSIA TO 1740. J. A. R. Marriott and C. C. Robertson, *The evolution of Prussia* (1915, 1946), and S. B. Fay, *The rise of Brandenburg-Prussia to 1786* (1937), a Berkshire study, are the two most convenient introductions in English. C. T. Atkinson, *Germany 1715–1815* (1908), is a standard account of military and political history. The economic aspects of the Prussian state-building process are analyzed in G. F. von Schmoller, *The mercantile system and its historical significance* (1884, 1896), which may be supplemented by A. Small, *The cameralists* (1909). On the earlier Hohenzollerns, see C. E. Maurice, *The life of Frederick William: the Great Elector of Brandenburg* (1926); F. Schevill, *The Great Elector* (1947); and R. Ergang, *The Potsdam Führer: Frederick William I, father of Prussian militarism* (1941).

RUSSIA TO 1725. Among the better general histories of Russia are those of B. H. Sumner (1943), B. Pares (1926, rev. 1953), V. O. Kluchevsky (5 vols., 1911–31), G. Vernadsky (1929, rev. 1954), and M. T. Florinsky (2 vols., 1953). G. P. Fedotov, *The Russian religious mind* (1946), sketches the early interplay of pre-Christian paganism, Byzantinism, and Russian political forms. F. Nowak, *Medieval slavdom and the rise of Russia* (1930) is a useful introduction in the Berkshire series. M. N. Pokrovsky, *History of Russia from earliest times to the rise of commercial capitalism* (1931), is a Marxist account, and J. Kucharzewski, *The origins of modern Russia* (1948), presents a generally hostile Polish view. There are vivid popular narratives by H. Lamb, *The march of Muscovy: Ivan the Terrible and the growth of the Russian empire, 1400–1648* (1948) and *The city and the Tsar: Peter the Great and the move to the West, 1648–1762* (1948). H. von Eckhardt, *Ivan the Terrible* (1949), depicts Ivan as a great national hero, but is not entirely uncritical. The older *Peter the Great* (2 vols., 1884), by E. Schuyler, is a detailed history; an excellent brief account is B. H. Sumner, *Peter the Great and the emergence of Russia* (1950), in the Teach yourself history series. R. N. Bain's various studies on Russia and Sweden are inadequate, but there are few other books to recommend except general histories of the two countries. Military and diplomatic special topics are discussed in studies by R. C. Anderson (1910) and J. F. Chance (1909). Russian expansion is discussed in R. J. Kerner, *The urge to the sea: the course of Russian history* (1942), which emphasizes the significance of trade routes, and in F. A. Golder, *Russian expansion on the Pacific, 1641–1850* (1914).

Chapter VI. The Struggle for Wealth and Empire

GLOBAL ECONOMY AND COLONIAL EMPIRES. W. L. Dorn, *Competition for Empire, 1740–1763* (1940), in the Langer series, is particularly good on the relation of the European state system to the overseas expansion and rivalry of the time. Special aspects are taken up in C. H. Wilson, *Anglo-Dutch commerce and rivalry in the 18th century* (1941), and C. L. Lokke, *France and the colonial question: a study of contemporary French opinion, 1763–1801* (1932). E. Williams has written an interesting study, *Capitalism and slavery* (1944).
    Several of the books on European overseas expansion listed for Chapter IV also discuss the 18th century. To these must be added the excellent C. E. Carrington, *The British overseas: exploits of a nation of shopkeepers* (1950) and H. Furber, *John Company at work: a study of European expansion in India in the late 18th century* (1948). For the general reader the following, though not confined to the eighteenth century, may be recommended: E. Thompson and G. T. Garratt, *Rise and fulfillment of British rule in India* (1934), and P. Woodruff [Mason], *The men who ruled India* (2 vols., 1954). Among biographical studies there are A. M. Davies, *Clive of Plassey, a biography* (1939); P. Moon, *Warren Hastings and British India* (1947), in the Teach yourself history series; the sympathetic biography of Hastings by K. Feiling (1954); and H. Dodwell, *Dupleix and Clive, the beginning of empire* (1920). More specialized and advanced studies include those by C. H. Philips (1940), W. Dalgleish (1933), G. B. Malleson (1868, 1893), F. B. Eldridge (1945); and the fifth volume, covering the years 1497–1858, of the Cambridge history of India (6 vols., 1922 ff.).
    The numerous volumes by Francis Parkman on the French regime in Canada are classics of 19th-century historiography; the standard 20th-century account is G. M. Wrong, *The rise and fall of New France* (2 vols., 1928) and his various other writings. The works of Priestley and Cole, cited for Chapter IV, should also be consulted on French policy before and after Colbert. Also recommended are M. Bishop, *Champlain: the life of fortitude* (1949); two studies by N. M. Crouse, *French pioneers in the West Indies, 1624–1664* (1940) and *The French struggle for the West Indies, 1665–1713* (1944); R. Pares, *War and trade in the West Indies* (1936), on the war of 1739; and J. O. McLachlan, *Trade and peace with old Spain, 1667–1750, a study of the influence of commerce on 18th century diplomacy* (1940).

THE BRITISH EMPIRE BEFORE THE AMERICAN REVOLUTION. A good geographical introduction, written from the point of view of geography as the "pivot" of history, is H. J. Mackinder, *Britain and the British seas* (1902, 1914). W. B. Willcox, *Star of empire: a study of Britain as a world power, 1485–1945* (1950), fills in the narrative from Henry VII to George VI and analyzes the main forces involved. Various studies by G. L. Beer, C. M. Andrews, and H. L. Osgood of the Old Colonial System and of mercantilism in operation are valuable for the 16th, 17th, and 18th centuries. For the mid-18th century these are complemented by the more recent L. H. Gipson, *The British Empire before the American Revolution* (8 vols. to date, 1936–54), based primarily on English sources. Another important large-scale treatment is the *Cambridge history of the British Empire* (8 vols. in 7, 1929–40). J. R. Seeley, *The expansion of England* (1883, 1895), is an interesting little essay. C. G. Robertson, *Chatham and the British Empire* (1948), and J. A. Williamson,

Cook and the opening of the Pacific (1948), are two excellent studies in the Teach yourself history series. J. R. Muir, *The life and achievements of Captain James Cook* (1939), is more biographical than the Williamson book. M. G. Lawson, *Fur: a study in English mercantilism, 1700–1775* (1943); R. G. Albion, *Forests and sea power: the timber problem of the Royal Navy, 1652–1862* (1926); and J. S. Corbett, *England in the Seven Years' War* (2 vols., 1907), illustrate other aspects.

BRITISH SOCIETY AND POLITICS BEFORE THE REVOLUTIONARY ERA. W. E. H. Lecky, *A history of England in the 18th century* (8 vols., 1878–90), is an interpretative and rather full history of 18th-century England and Ireland. B. Williams, *The Whig supremacy, 1714–1760* (1939), topically arranged, is a good general guide. The doctrines of John Locke are related to the Whig period by P. Larkin in *Property in the 18th century* (1930). Other recommended books on personalities and events include J. Morley, *Walpole* (1889); F. S. Oliver, *The endless adventure* (3 vols., 1930–5), a reflective assessment of English politics in Walpole's time and later; B. Williams, *Life of William Pitt, Earl of Chatham* (2 vols., 1913); the briefer J. H. Plumb, *Chatham* (1953); and L. Kronenberger, *Kings and desperate men: life in 18th century England* (1942).

A more institutional and descriptive approach is taken by A. James Henderson, *London and the national government, 1721–1742* (1945); L. B. Namier, *The structure of politics at the accession of George III* (2 vols., 1929); E. Porritt, *The unreformed House of Commons* (2 vols., 1903); A. S. Turberville, *The House of Lords in the 18th century* (1927); and W. T. Laprade, *Public opinion and politics in 18th century England* (1936).

On social and economic conditions, the following monographs are instructive: E. B. Chancellor, *The 18th century in London: an account of its social life and arts* (1920), with excellent contemporary illustrations; D. George, *London life in the 18th century* (1925), packed with interesting details; E. W. Gilboy, *Wages in 18th century* (1934); D. Marshall, *The English poor in the 18th century* (1926), on the administrative difficulties of dealing with poverty; M. G. Jones, *The charity school movement of the 18th century: a study of 18th century puritanism in action* (1938); and B. Rodgers, *Cloak of charity: studies in 18th century philanthropy* (1949). Other relevant books are listed below in connection with the Industrial Revolution (Chapter XI).

N. Sykes, *Church and state in England in the 18th century* (1934), covers institutional aspects of the Church of England. M. L. Edwards, *John Wesley and the 18th century* (1933), is primarily concerned with Wesley's social and political influence. H. Townsend, *The claims of the Free Churches* (1949), is a detailed account of how the "left wing Puritanism" of earlier centuries affected religious thought and action in the 18th and 19th centuries.

DIPLOMACY AND WAR IN EUROPE. In addition to various titles listed above for this chapter and for Chapter V and below for Enlightened Despotism, the following books deal with eighteenth-century European international relations: A. Sorel, *Europe under the Old Regime* (1947), a translation of the introduction to his classic study of Europe and the French revolution (8 vols., Paris, 1895–1904), on the 18th-century balance of power; C. Petrie, *Diplomatic history 1713–1933* (1946), opinionated but generally reliable; V. Valentin, *The German people: their history and civilization from the Holy Roman Empire to the Third Reich* (1946), which places the 18th century reshaping of Germany in a wider historical context; R. Lodge, *Great Britain and Prussia in the 18th century* (1923); A. W. Ward, *Great Britain and Hanover: some aspects of the personal union* (1899); J. F. Chance, *The alliance of Hanover, a study of British foreign policy in the last years of George I* (1923); C. T. Atkinson, *A history of Germany, 1715–1815* (1908), stressing political and military developments; and H. W. V. Temperley, *Frederick the Great and Kaiser Joseph: an episode of war and diplomacy in the 18th century* (1915), on the period 1763–79.

The relations of Britain and France are examined in the Berkshire study, A. H. Buffington, *The second hundred years' war, 1689–1815* (1929), and in the following specialized accounts: A. M. Wilson, *French foreign policy during the administration of Cardinal Fleury, 1726–43* (1936); H. Richmond, *The Navy in the war of 1739–1748* (3 vols., 1920); and S. Conn, *Gibraltar in British diplomacy in the 18th century* (1942).

Chapter VII. The Scientific View of the World

The most useful general guide to intellectual history from medieval Christendom to the 18th century is J. H. Randall, *The making of the modern mind* (1926, 1940); it is less satisfactory for the 19th and 20th centuries. The introductory comments and selections in F. L. Baumer's anthology, *Main currents of Western thought*, and C. Brinton's *Ideas and men*, both cited earlier, are also of considerable value. Other works cited in the introductory section concern various aspects of the history of thought; to these may be added W. E. H. Lecky, *History of the rise and influence of the spirit of rationalism in Europe* (2 vols., 1865, rev. 1872), on the declining sense of the miraculous and the secularization of politics; P. Smith, *A history of modern culture* (2 vols., 1930–34), a useful but rather heavy review of the years 1543–1776; and J. M. Robertson, *Short history of free thought, ancient and modern* (2 vols., 1906, rev. 1936), especially for the period before the 18th century.

THEORETICAL FOUNDATIONS OF SCIENCE. The fundamental reorientation of thinking about nature in early modern times has probably had far more influence on later times than any of the specific inventions or technical advances of the period. E. A. Burtt, *The metaphysical foundations of modern philosophical science* (1925, 1948), is a searching examination of the ideas of scientists from Copernicus to Newton. Other books exploring the theoretical foundations of science include: E. W. Strong, *Procedures and metaphysics* (1936); J. B. Conant, *On understanding science: an historical approach* (1947) and *Science and common sense* (1951); F. S. Marvin (ed.), *Science and civilization* (1923); R. G. Collingwood, *The idea of nature* (1945); and H. Butterfield, *The origins of modern science, 1300–1800* (1949). A. N. Whitehead, *Science and the modern world* (1925), is indispensable.

GENERAL HISTORIES OF SCIENCE. The twilight zone between the natural and the supernatural is explored in: L. Thorndike's monumental *History of magic and experimental science* (6 vols., 1923–41), for the period to the 16th century; the briefer C. J. Singer, *From magic to science* (1928), also primarily medieval in scope; K. Seligmann, *The mirror of magic* (1948), from antiquity to the 18th century; and R. Eisler, *The royal art of astrology* (1946). The most useful general work is W. C. D. Dampier, *A history of science and its relations with philosophy and religion* (1929, 1949). Other serviceable studies are W. T. Sedgwick and H. W. Tyler, *A short history of science* (1917, 1927); C. J. Singer, *A short history of science to the 19th century* (1941); F. S. Taylor, *A short history of science and scientific thought* (1949); and the well-executed *A short history of science and scientific thought, with readings from the great scientists from the Babylonians through Einstein* (1939), also issued under the title *The march of mind*, by F. S. Taylor. G. Sarton, *Introduction to the history of science* (3 vols., 1927–48), is a modern classic on the period to the 14th century; some of the author's more general ideas are presented in his *The life of science: essays in the history of civilization* (1948). H. T. Pledge, *Science since 1500: a short history of mathematics, physics, chemistry, and biology* (1939, 1947), is an excellent technical account.

Some standard histories of specific sciences are the following: J. Jeans, *The growth of physical science* (1948); Albert Einstein and L. Infeld, *The evolution of physics: the growth of ideas from early concepts to relativity and quanta* (1938), which is arranged more logically than chronologically; E. Whittaker, *From Euclid to Eddington: a study of conceptions of the physical world* (1949); W. W. Bryant, *History of astronomy* (1907); M. Davidson, *The stars and the mind: a study of the impact of astronomical development on human thought* (1948), interestingly written for the general reader; J. M. Stillman, *The story of early chemistry* (1924); T. M. Lowry, *Historical introduction to chemistry* (1926, 1936); and C. J. Singer, *The story of living things: a short account of the evolution of the biological sciences* (1931).

MEDICINE. Two encyclopedic factual works: F. H. Garrison, *Introduction to the history of medicine* (1913, 1929), and C. C. Mettler, *History of Medicine* (1947), are valuable for reference. A. Castiglioni, *A history of medicine* (1927, 1949), is well illustrated and covers a wide range of subjects. R. H. Shryock, *The development of modern medicine* (1947), and B. J. Stern, *Society and medical progress* (1941), discuss some of the prob-

lems of getting new ideas adopted. There are other good surveys of medical history by
W. Libby, M. Neuberger, W. Osler, A. H. Buck, C. G. Cumston, C. J. Singer, and D. Guthrie. H. W. Haggard has written the interesting, popular account, *Devils, drugs, and doctors*
(1929). H. Zinsser, *Rats, lice, and history* (1935), gives a vivid picture of the influence of
epidemics since ancient times, a subject studied also in F. Prinzing, *Epidemics resulting
from wars* (1916).

SCIENCE IN THE SEVENTEENTH CENTURY. On the organization of scientific activity and
the spread of new ideas, see the following: M. Ornstein, *The role of scientific societies in
the 17th century* (1928); H. Brown, *Scientific organizations in 17th-century France, 1620–
1680* (1934); H. Lyons, *The Royal Society, 1660–1940* (1944); D. Stimson, *Scientists and
amateurs: a history of the Royal Society* (1948) and *The gradual acceptance of the Copernican theory of the universe* (1917); and A. E. Shipley, *The revival of science in the 17th
century* (1906).
    The following bear on the wider implications of the new science: A. Wolf, *A his-
tory of science, technology, and philosophy in the 16th and 17th centuries* (1935) and
. . . *in the 18th century* (1939); R. K. Merton, "Science, technology, and society in 17th
century England" in volume 4 of *Osiris* (1938); G. N. Clark, *Science and social welfare
in the age of Newton* (1937); and the stimulating but not always accurate L. Mumford,
Technics and civilization (1934).

BIOGRAPHIES. H. Kesten, *Copernicus and his world* (1945); A. Armitage, *Copernicus: the
founder of modern astronomy* (1938); J. A. Gade, *The life and times of Tycho Brahe*
(1947); and C. Baumgardt, *Johannes Kepler: life and letters* (1951) describe the discoveries
and importance of the pioneer astronomers. Both F. H. Anderson, *The philosophy of
Francis Bacon* (1948), and B. Farrington, *Francis Bacon: philosopher of industrial science*
(1949), are more concerned with Bacon's ideas and impact than with the story of his life.
F. S. Taylor, *Galileo and the freedom of thought* (1938), is a dispassionate, carefully documented work. E. S. Haldane, *Descartes, his life and times* (1905), is primarily biographical,
and S. H. Mellone, *The dawn of modern thought: Descartes, Spinoza, Leibniz* (1930), explains the Cartesian system and its influence for the general reader. For Pascal, see
M. Bishop, *Pascal: the life of genius* (1936). Two other leading 17th-century scientists are
ably placed in their intellectual setting in L. T. More, *The life and works of the Honourable
Robert Boyle* (1944), and in A. E. Bell, *Christian Huygens and the development of science
in the 17th century* (1947). For Newton, the accounts by S. Brodetsky (1927), and
J. W. N. Sullivan (1938), and the short biography by E. N. Andrade (1954) are recommended.

HISTORICAL AND GEOGRAPHICAL SCIENCES IN THE 17TH CENTURY. The developing conceptions and techniques of historical writing are discussed in the various manuals and histories listed at the beginning of this bibliography. A satisfactory biography of the leading
early rationalist is H. Robinson, *Bayle the sceptic* (1931); E. A. Beller and M. du P.
Lee, Jr. have carefully edited *Selections from Bayle's Dictionary* (1952). T. K. Cheyne,
Founder of Old Testament criticism (1893), describes the work of several pioneers of
methodical Biblical criticism. For the development of the "auxiliary sciences" of history, see
in addition to the general histories of history, J. J. Bond, *Handy-book of rules and tables
for verifying dates with the Christian era* (1869); G. F. Hill, *Coins and medals* (1920);
and A. Philip, *The calendar: its history, structure, and improvement* (1921). The following
illustrate various aspects of geography and cartography: R. E. Dickinson and O. J. R.
Howarth, *The making of geography* (1933); L. C. Wroth, *Early cartography of the Pacific*
(1944); L. A. Brown, *The Story of Maps* (1949); and R. V. Tooley, *Maps and map-
makers* (1949), on the 15th through 19th centuries.

LAW, POLITICAL THEORY, AND NATURAL LAW. W. Seagle, *The quest for law* (1941), is a
general treatment of various stages and aspects of the formulation of law and jurisprudence.
G. P. Gooch's two works, *The history of English democratic ideas in the 17th century*
(1898; ed. by H. J. Laski, 1927) and *Political thought from Bacon to Halifax* (1914,
1923), are basic. J. N. Figgis, *The divine right of kings* (1896, 1922), and F. D. Wormuth,
The royal prerogative, 1603–49 (1939), are both concerned primarily with English consti-

tutional developments, as is Wormuth's *The origins of modern constitutionalism* (1949).

Some of the fundamental abstractions of early modern political theory are analyzed in these works: O. von Gierke, *Natural law and the theory of society, 1500–1800* (2 vols., 1934), which includes an important lecture by E. Troeltsch; J. W. Gough, *The social contract: a critical study of its development* (1936); E. Barker's introduction to his edition, *Social contract: essays by Locke, Hume, and Rousseau* (1947); D. G. Ritchie, *Natural rights: a criticism of some political and ethical conceptions* (1894, 1916); and C. G. Haines, *The revival of natural law concepts* (1930), concerned especially with some American ideas of natural law.

W. A. Dunning, *A history of political theories from Luther to Montesquieu* (1905), F. J. C. Hearnshaw (ed.), *The social and political ideas of some great thinkers of the 16th and 17th centuries* (1926), and similar volumes for other periods ed. by Hearnshaw contain helpful short summaries and criticisms. The following are also useful: L. Strauss, *The political philosophy of Hobbes: its basis and genesis* (1936); J. Gibson, *Locke's theory of knowledge and its historical relations* (1917); R. I. Aaron, *John Locke* (1937); S. P. Lamprecht, *The moral and political philosophy of John Locke* (1918); and W. S. M. Knight, *The life and works of Hugo Grotius* (1925).

Chapter VIII. The Age of Enlightenment

THE *Philosophes* AND THE ENLIGHTENMENT. Two French scholars have written indispensable studies: D. Mornet, *French thought in the 18th century* (1929); and P. Hazard, *The European mind: the critical years, 1680–1715* (1935, trans. 1953), a study of the "crisis of the European conscience," and his later work, *European thought in the eighteenth century: from Montesquieu to Lessing* (1946, trans. 1954). A. O. Lovejoy, *The great chain of being* (1930), sketches the idea of a coherent universe from Plato's time to the 18th century. A brief introduction to the thought of the age is provided in F. E. Manuel, *The age of reason* (1951), in the Cornell University series; and in L. L. Snyder, *The age of reason* (1955), in the Anvil series. A valuable survey is R. B. Mowat, *The age of reason* (1934); and an advanced interpretative essay is E. Cassirer, *The philosophy of the Enlightenment* (trans. 1951). G. R. Havens, *The age of ideas* (1955) is a popularized account. C. Becker has attempted a striking reconstruction of the 18th-century mind in *The Heavenly city of the 18th century philosophers* (1932). On a crucial aspect of the age, see J. B. Bury, *The idea of progress: an inquiry into its origin and growth* (1920, 1932), and C. Frankel, *The faith of reason: the idea of progress in the French Enlightenment* (1948).

L. Stephen, *History of English thought in the 18th century* (2 vols., 1876, 1902 ed. reprinted 1949), analyzes deism, moral philosophy, and political economy. M. Roustan, *The pioneers of the French Revolution* (1926), offers a sturdy defense of the *philosophes* as critics of the old regime and as original thinkers. Political thought is discussed fully in K. Martin, *French liberal thought in the 18th century* (1929; rev. ed. J. P. Mayer, 1954). Other political studies include C. E. Vaughan, *The political writings of Rousseau* (1915) and *Studies in the history of political philosophy before and after Rousseau* (2 vols., 1925); H. J. Laski, *Political thought in England from Locke to Bentham* (1920); and A. M. Osborn, *Rousseau and Burke: a study of the idea of liberty in 18th-century political thought* (1940). On economic thought, H. Higgs has written *The physiocrats* (1897, 1952), and M. Beer, *An inquiry into physiocracy* (1939); these may be read in connection with books on Adam Smith listed in Chapter XI. New views on the methods and importance of historical study are explained in J. B. Black, *The art of history: a study of four great historians of the 18th century* (1926) [on Voltaire, Hume, Robertson, and Gibbon]. The 17th-century literary quarrel is discussed in R. F. Jones, *Ancients and moderns: a study of the background of the battle of the books* (1936).

The following books are good on various leading thinkers of the Enlightenment: H. N. Brailsford, *Voltaire* (1935), which may be compared with A. Noyes, *Voltaire* (1936), and N. L. Torrey, *The spirit of Voltaire* (1938); A. Sorel, *Montesquieu* (1888); E. Cassirer, *The Question of Jean-Jacques Rousseau* (1954), with introduction by P. Gay; C. W. Hendel, *Jean-Jacques Rousseau: moralist* (2 vols., 1934); A. Cobban, *Rousseau and the modern state* (1934); A. L. Lindsay, *Kant* (1934, 1946); D. M. Low, *Edward Gibbon* (1937); H. P. Adams, *The life and writings of Giambattista Vico* (1935), on the leading Italian philosopher of the Enlightenment; and C. Van Doren, *Benjamin Franklin* (1938).

In addition to the books on British church problems suggested for Chapter VI, the following concern various aspects of 18th-century religion: J. M. Creed and J. S. Boys Smith, *Religious thought in the 18th century* (1934), a collection of extracts and short biographies, primarily of English writers; C. E. Elwell, *The influence of the Enlightenment on the Catholic theory of education in France, 1750–1850* (1944); and S. Todsvig, *Emanuel Swedenborg: scientist and mystic* (1948).

FRANCE UNDER THE OLD REGIME (POLITICAL AND ECONOMIC). In many ways the best starting place is Alexis de Tocqueville's study of the state of French society before 1789 (1856), the latest translation of which has appeared as *De Tocqueville's L'ancien régime* (1947). Two spirited defenders of the Old Regime are the conservative historians F. Funck-Brentano and P. Gaxotte, who have written *The old regime in France* (1929) and *Louis XV and his times* (1934), respectively. H. Sée, *Economic and social conditions in France during the 18th century* (1927), gives a more detached analysis of the various institutions of the period. D. Dakin, *Turgot and the ancien régime in France* (1939); J. M. S. Allison, *Lamoignon de Malesherbes, defender of the French monarchy* (1938); S. T. McCloy, *Government assistance in 18th century France* (1946); A. Bachman, *Censorship in France from 1715 to 1750: Voltaire's opposition* (1934); P. H. Beik, *A judgment of the Old Regime: being a survey by the Parlement of Provence of French economic and fiscal policies at the close of the Seven Years' War* (1944); and F. L. Ford, *Robe and sword: the regrouping of the French aristocracy after Louis XIV* (1953), are useful studies, mostly rather technical. Other books on 18th-century France are listed for Chapter IX, on the Revolution proper.

ENLIGHTENED DESPOTISM. L. Gershoy, *From despotism to revolution, 1763–1789* (1944), in the Langer series, is the most useful general account of European civilization in the generation before the outbreak of the French Revolution. G. Bruun, *Enlightened despots* (1929) is an excellent Berkshire study.

Frederick the Great has attracted many biographers: W. F. Reddaway, *Frederick the Great and the rise of Prussia* (1904), still useful; F. J. P. Veale, *Frederick the Great: his life and place in history* (1935), sympathetic; P. Gaxotte, *Frederick the Great* (1941); and G. P. Gooch, *Frederick the Great: the ruler, the writer, the man* (1947), a rather favorable view, drawn in considerable part from Frederick's own words. C. V. Easum has written *Prince Henry of Prussia, brother of Frederick the Great* (1942). The best general account of German political fragmentation and cultural stirrings is W. H. Bruford, *Germany in the 18th century: the social background of the literary revival* (1935). Frederick's development of the Prussian bureaucracy is described by W. L. Dorn in Vols. 46 and 47 of the *Political Science Quarterly* (New York, 1931, 1932).

Hapsburg affairs between 1740 and 1792 are recounted in the following books: J. F. Bright, *Maria Theresa* (1897) and *Joseph II* (1897), companion volumes stressing political and diplomatic affairs; C. L. Morris, *Maria Theresa, the last conservative* (1937), anecdotal and feminine; S. K. Padover, *The revolutionary emperor: Joseph the Second, 1741–90* (1934), arguing that Joseph was the typical "enlightened despot"; M. C. Goodwin, *The papal conflict with Josephinism* (1938); W. C. Langsam, *Francis the Good: the education of an emperor, 1768–1792* (1949); E. M. Link, *The emancipation of the Austrian peasant, 1740–1798* (1949); and R. J. Kerner, *Bohemia in the 18th century* (1932). Enlightened Despotism in Russia is well portrayed in A. Kornilov, *Modern Russian history from the age of Catherine the Great to the end of the 19th century* (1917, 1943); in G. S. Thomson, *Catherine the Great and the expansion of Russia* (1947), in the Teach yourself history series; and in G. P. Gooch, *Catherine the Great and other studies* (1954). There are biographies of Catherine by K. Waliszewski (1894), K. Anthony (1925), and G. Kaus (1935), and a study by G. Soloveytchik, *Potemkin: a picture of Catherine's Russia* (1938).

THE AMERICAN REVOLUTION AND ITS EUROPEAN IMPLICATIONS. Recent attempts to show what was distinctive in the North American civilization of the 18th century include: R. B. Perry, *Puritanism and democracy* (1944), on the convergence of puritanism and the Enlightenment: L. B. Wright, *The Atlantic frontier: colonial American civilization, 1607–1763* (1947); M. Savelle, *Seeds of liberty: the genesis of the American mind* (1948); C. Rossiter,

Seedtime of the Republic: the origin of the American tradition of political liberty (1953); and M. Kraus, *The Atlantic civilization: eighteenth century origins* (1949). R. L. Schuyler, *The fall of the old colonial system: a study in British free trade, 1770–1870* (1945), should be read in conjunction with books listed above on mercantilism and empire. *The debate on the American Revolution 1761–83* (1949), a collection of source materials ed. by M. Beloff, discusses the Revolution within the context of the British Empire. Two excellent little volumes in the Amherst studies present a sampling of conflicting interpretations: J. C. Wahlke (ed.), *The causes of the American Revolution* (1950), and E. Latham (ed.), *The Declaration of Independence and the Constitution* (1949).

   J. C. Miller, *Origins of the American Revolution* (1943) and *Triumph of freedom, 1775–1783* (1948), and J. R. Alden, *The American Revolution, 1775–1783* (1954), provide lively narratives and up-to-date interpretations. C. L. Becker, *The Declaration of Independence: a study in the history of political ideas* (1922, 1942), is an interesting little study. G. H. Guttridge, *English Whiggism and the American Revolution* (1942); H. Butterfield, *George III, Lord North, and the people, 1779–80* (1949); and C. R. Ritcheson, *British politics and the American Revolution* (1954), relate the events in America to British internal politics. A. L. Burt, *The United States, Great Britain, and British North America, from the Revolution to the establishment of peace after the War of 1812* (1940), is informative on the period 1775–1818.

   Relations between France and America are discussed in B. Fäy, *The revolutionary spirit in France and America* (1927); in W. Stark, *America, ideal and reality: the United States of 1776 in contemporary European philosophy* (1947); and in the various books (1935–50) by L. Gottschalk on Lafayette during the revolutionary era. Professor Gottschalk has also given a short expression of his views in *The place of the American Revolution in the causal pattern of the French Revolution* (1948). These special studies should also be noted: C. D. Hazen, *Contemporary American opinion of the French Revolution* (1897); E. S. Corwin, *French policy and the American alliance of 1778* (1916); and S. F. Bemis, *The diplomacy of the American Revolution* (1935).

Chapter IX. The French Revolution

GENERAL TREATMENTS. Books on the Old Regime have been listed in the preceding chapter. A fine introductory summary of the Revolutionary period, from a point of view rather critical of the Revolution, is C. Brinton, *A decade of revolution, 1789–99* (1934), in the Langer series, which is paralleled by the brief Berkshire study, L. Gershoy, *The French Revolution, 1789–99* (1932). Standard accounts of somewhat wider scope are Gershoy, *The French Revolution and Napoleon* (1933); L. Gottschalk, *The era of the French Revolution, 1715–1815* (1929); and J. M. Thompson, *The French Revolution* (1943). G. Salvemini, *The French Revolution 1788–1792* (1905, rev. and trans. 1954), is of somewhat more limited value. P. Farmer, *France reviews its revolutionary origins* (1944), is a usable guide to the highly controversial French historiography of the period, of which the following represent a wide coverage: H. Taine, *The French Revolution* (3 vols., 1878–85), by a 19th-century critic of French society; F. V. A. Aulard, *The French Revolution, a political history, 1789–1804* (4 vols., 1901, 1910), by a strong defender of the French republican tradition; the slightly ironic L. Madelin, *The French Revolution* (1911, 1928); A. Mathiez, *The French Revolution* (1928), and its sequel, *After Robespierre, The Thermidorean reaction* (1931), two studies by a great authority sympathetic to Robespierre and the Jacobin cause; and P. Gaxotte, *The French Revolution* (1932), an aggressively counter-revolutionary view. G. Lefebvre, *The coming of the French Revolution* (1947), is an excellent, well-balanced analysis of the forces that brought on the Revolution. J. H. Stewart has gathered together the most important Revolutionary documents in *A documentary survey of the French Revolution* (1951).

THE REIGN OF TERROR. Most of the general works listed above give close consideration to the motives, course, and effects of the Terror, and in addition the following books illustrate important phases of it: A. Mathiez, *The fall of Robespierre and other essays* (1927); R. R. Palmer, *Twelve who ruled: the Committee of Public Safety during the Terror* (1941); W. B. Kerr, *The Reign of Terror, 1793–94: the experiment of the democratic republic, and the rise of the bourgeoisie* (1927); D. M. Greer, *The incidence of the Terror during the French Revolution: a statistical interpretation* (1935), a very revealing study of who was actually executed, and by what procedures; and J. B. Sirich, *Revolutionary committees in the departments of France, 1793–94* (1943), on the relations between Paris and the country during the Terror. J. M. Thompson has an excellent brief study in the Teach yourself history series, *Robespierre and the French Revolution* (1953).

THE WAR. Various aspects are discussed in J. Clapham, *The causes of the war of 1792* (1899), which finds that most of the parties involved share responsibility for bringing on the war; S. Wilkinson, *The French army before Napoleon* (1915); A. T. Mahan, *The Influence of sea power upon the French Revolution and Empire, 1793–1812* (2 vols., 1893); R. W. Phipps, *The armies of the First French Republic and the rise of the marshals of Napoleon I* (5 vols., 1926–39); G. Ferrero, *The gamble: Bonaparte in Italy, 1796–1797* (1939); and P. G. Elgood, *Bonaparte's adventure in Egypt* (1931).

VARIOUS DEVELOPMENTS WITHIN FRANCE. For the mood of France in 1789, see—in addition to the Lefebvre book listed above—B. F. Hyslop, *French nationalism in 1789 according to the general cahiers* (1934) and *A guide to the general cahiers of 1789, with texts of unedited cahiers* (1936); E. F. Henderson, *Symbol and satire in the French Revolution* (1912); C. B. Rogers, *The spirit of revolution in 1789* (1949), which very effectively surveys the popular songs to show the unrest and sentiment among the sub-literary class; and S. Herbert, *The fall of feudalism in France* (1921), on the demands and gains of the peasants. J. B. Morton, *The Bastille falls, and other studies of the French Revolution* (1936), describes some of the dramatic episodes between 1789 and the fall of Robespierre; and S. E. Harris, *The assignats* (1930), shows that the paper money was a fairly effective instrument of war finance. On the complicated party structure and rivalries, the general works listed above should be consulted, but three important monographs may also be mentioned: C. Brinton, *The Jacobins: an essay in the new history* (1930), which sees the Revolution as a kind of religion; R. M. Brace, *Bordeaux and the Gironde, 1789–1794* (1947), for concrete details on middle class participation and misgivings; and D. Thomson, *The Babeuf plot: the making of a republican legend* (1947), on a leftist group crushed by the Directory. F. L. Nussbaum, *Commercial policy in the French Revolution: a study of the career of G. J. A. Ducher* (1923), explains how, under the Committee of Public Safety, the Revolution turned from economic liberalism to a revived mercantilism. On religion and the Revolution see, besides the older works by W. H. P. Jervis (1872, 1882) and W. M. Sloane (1901), F. V. A. Aulard, *Christianity and the French Revolution* (1927), and C. S. Phillips, *The church in France, 1789–1848* (1929).

BIOGRAPHIES. On Sieyès, the constitution-maker, see J. Clapham, *The Abbé Sieyès: an essay in the politics of the French Revolution* (1912), and G. G. Van Deusen, *Sieyès: his life and his nationalism* (1932). J. M. Thompson, *Leaders of the French Revolution* (1932), gives sketches of the outstanding personalities which may be filled out by using the following biographies: the somewhat sensational A. Vallentin, *Mirabeau* (1948), which does not entirely supersede L. Barthou, *Mirabeau* (1913); H. Wendel, *Danton* (1935); E. S. Scudder, *Prince of the blood* (1937), a life of Philippe Egalité; J. C. Dawson, *Lakanal the regicide* (1948), on an earnest reformer and his program; D. L. Dowd, *Pageant-master of the Republic: Jacques-Louis David and the French Revolution* (1948), a good picture of art and propaganda during a period of rapid changes; E. Ellery, *Brissot de Warville* (1915); J. S. Schapiro, *Condorcet and the rise of liberalism* (1934), on the ideas of the leading Girondist philosopher and his unsinkable optimism; L. R. Gottschalk, *Jean-Paul Marat: a study in radicalism* (1927); E. N. Curtis, *Saint-Just, colleague of Robespierre* (1935); and H. Dupre, *Lazare Carnot, republican patriot* (1940), on the "organizer of victory." The best-rounded biography of the most prominent figure on the Committee of Public Safety is J. M. Thompson, *Robespierre* (2 vols., 1935), and the following are also useful: R. S. Ward, *Maximilien Robespierre: a study in deterioration* (1934); R. Korngold, *Robespierre, first modern dictator* (1937) [also issued as *Robespierre and the fourth estate* (1941)]; J. M. Eagan, *Maximilien Robespierre, nationalist dictator* (1938); and F. Sieburg, *Robespierre, the incorruptible* (1938).

EFFECTS OF THE REVOLUTION OUTSIDE FRANCE. G. P. Gooch, *Germany and the French Revolution* (1920), and his subsequent work, *Studies in German history* (1948), are valuable. Various studies on Goethe and other intellectual leaders of the time should be consulted, as should the books on the revival of Germany cited in Chapter X. H. W. Van Loon, *The fall of the Dutch Republic* (1913, 1924) and *The rise of the Dutch Kingdom, 1795–1813* (1915), give a running account of events in the Netherlands through the 18th century. The situation in Italy may be seen in C. Giglioli, *Naples in 1799* (1903). In addition to the general histories of the United States on this period, covering such topics as the diplomatic complications, the positions of Jefferson, Paine, Gouverneur Morris, etc., there is a useful detailed study, *American commerce as affected by the wars of the French Revolution and Napoleon, 1793–1812* (1932) by A. C. Clauder. For effects in Haiti and the Negro world, see C. L. R. James, *The Black Jacobins: Toussaint l'Ouverture and the San Domingo Revolution* (1938).

Of the sizable literature on British relations with revolutionary France, the following titles are suggested: *The Cambridge history of British foreign policy, 1783–1919* (3 vols., 1922–3), ed. by A. W. Ward and G. P. Gooch; W. T. Laprade, *England and the French Revolution, 1789–97* (1909); W. P. Hall, *British radicalism, 1791–97* (1912); A. Cobban, *Edmund Burke and the revolt against the 18th century: a study of the political and social thinking of Burke, Wordsworth, Coleridge, and Southey* (1929); H. N. Brailsford, *Shelley, Godwin, and their circle* (1913); *Burke's politics: selected writings and speeches of Edmund Burke on reform, revolution, and war* (1949), ed. by R. J. S. Hoffman and P. Levack; *The debate on the French Revolution, 1789–99* (1949), ed. by A. Cobban; P. A. Brown, *The French Revolution in English history* (1918); and H. W. Meikle, *Scotland and the French Revolution* (1912).

Chapter X. Napoleonic Europe

The most convenient general survey in English of Europe in the age of Napoleon is G. Bruun, *Europe and the French Imperium, 1799–1814* (1938), in the Langer series. H. L. Hutton has edited excerpts from Albert Sorel's diplomatic history under the title, *Napoleon and the French Revolution, 1799–1814* (1928). A remarkable historical *tour de force* has been achieved by the Dutch historian Pieter Geyl in his *Napoleon, for and against* (1949), a brilliant interpretation of what French historians since 1815 have said about Napoleon. *Napoleon's memoirs* (2 vols.), as dictated by him at St. Helena, were reissued in 1945 for the first time since their publication in 1823, and should of course be used with caution. *Napoleon self-revealed in 300 selected letters* (1934), ed. by J. M. Thompson, gives the man's own words, and A. M. Broadley, *Napoleon in caricature, 1795–1821* (2 vols., 1910), shows how contemporary artists, mostly English, treated him. An interesting popular account is F. M. H. Markham, *Napoleon and the awakening of Europe* (1954), in the Teach yourself history series.

Of the innumerable biographies of Napoleon, some of the more noteworthy are the following: J. H. Rose, *Life of Napoleon I* (2 vols., 1902) and *The personality of Napoleon* (1912); F. M. Kircheisen, *Napoleon* (1932), a very factual abridgment of his monumental nine-volume work in German; A. Fournier, *Napoleon the First, a biography* (1903); H. A. L. Fisher, *Napoleon* (1913), a brief, well-balanced account; J. M. Thompson, *Napoleon Bonaparte* (1952), the most recent comprehensive account; J. Bainville, *Napoleon* (1932), by an able French royalist; O. Aubry, *Napoleon, soldier and emperor* (1938), the romanticized appreciation of a fervent admirer; S. Wilkinson, *Rise of General Bonaparte* (1930), a fine description of Napoleon's military education and early career; T. A. Dodge, *Napoleon, a history of the art of war* (4 vols., 1904–07), which may be supplemented by H. T. Parker, *Three Napoleonic battles* (1944); E. V. Tarlé, *Bonaparte* (1937), a Soviet view of unusual interest, emphasizing economic influences; and for a recent American popular narrative, F. Pratt's two volumes, *The road to empire* (1939) and *The empire and the glory: Napoleon Bonaparte 1800–1806* (1949). L. Madelin, *The consulate and the empire* (2 vols., 1934–6), is eulogistic of Napoleon.

Other studies of Napoleonic France include E. Heckscher, *The continental system: an economic interpretation* (1922); F. E. Melvin, *Napoleon's navigation system: a study of trade control during the continental blockade* (1919); H. C. Deutsch, *The genesis of Napoleonic imperialism* (1938); H. H. Walsh, *The concordat of 1801* (1933); and

S. Zweig, *Joseph Fouché, the portrait of a politician* (1930), a fascinating study. The significance of the Napoleonic Code may be approached through J. B. Brissaud, *History of French private law* (1912) and *History of French public law* (1915); H. Cachard, *The French civil code* (1930); and G. W. Stumberg, *Guide to the law and legal literature of France* (Library of Congress, 1931). Biographical studies of Talleyrand have been written by, among others, A. D. Cooper (1932), C. Brinton (1936), É. Dard (1937), and L. Madelin (1948).

BRITAIN IN THE TIME OF NAPOLEON. The concluding chapters of C. G. Robertson, *England under the Hanoverians* (1911), are still useful as a general introduction. On a much larger scale there are the even more patriotic British volumes of A. Bryant, *The years of endurance, 1793–1802* (1942), *The Years of victory, 1802–1812* (1944), and *The age of elegance, 1812–1822* (1950). J. H. Rose's many studies of the period, notably *William Pitt and the national revival* (1911), *William Pitt and the Great War* (1911), and *The indecisiveness of modern war* (1927), illuminate many general and special problems of the period. Among other useful monographs are G. S. Graham, *Sea power and British North America, 1783–1820: a study in British colonial policy* (1941); A. Cunningham, *British credit in the last Napoleonic war* (1910); A. Hope-Jones, *Income tax in the Napoleonic wars* (1939), W. F. Galpin, *The grain supply of England during the Napoleonic period* (1925); H. F. B. Wheeler and A. M. Broadley, *Napoleon and the invasion of England: the story of the Great Terror* (2 vols., 1908); and C. Oman [Lenanton], *Napoleon at the Channel* (1942), which has also appeared as *Britain against Napoleon* (1944). Miss Oman has also written a biography of Nelson (1946), as have J. K. Laughton (1904), G. L. Browne (1891), C. S. Forester (1929), and many others. A. T. Mahan, *The life of Nelson, the embodiment of the sea power of Great Britain* (1897), W. James, *The durable monument* (1948), and R. Grenfell, *Nelson the sailor* (1949), are critical and sometimes technical studies by naval officers. P. Guedalla and R. Aldington have each written good popular biographies of Wellington (1931, 1943, respectively).

GERMANY IN THE TIME OF NAPOLEON. Most of the following works deal with German and Prussian nationalism: R. Aris, *History of political thought in Germany from 1789–1815* (1936); E. N. Anderson, *Nationalism and the cultural crisis in Prussia, 1806–1815* (1939), essays on leading personalities and their activities; E. F. Henderson, *Blücher and the uprising of Prussia against Napoleon, 1806–1815* (1911); R. R. Ergang, *Herder and the foundations of German nationalism* (1931); F. McEachran, *The life and philosophy of Johann Gottfried Herder* (1939); A. G. Pundt, *Arndt and the nationalist awakening in Germany* (1935); H. C. Engelbrecht, *Johann Gottlieb Fichte: a study of his political writings* (1933); and W. C. Langsam, *The Napoleonic wars and German nationalism in Austria* (1930). Two challenging interpretations of the German mind, written during the First World War, are J. Dewey, *German philosophy and politics* (1915), and G. Santayana, *Egotism in German philosophy* (1916, 1940). [See the books suggested for Chapter XI for a number of other studies on nationalism.]

    Greater emphasis on political, diplomatic, and military history is given in the following works: J. Seeley, *Life and times of Stein, or Germany and Prussia in the Napoleonic age* (3 vols., 1878), in many ways a general history of the period; G. S. Ford, *Stein and the era of reform in Prussia, 1807–1815* (1922); C. de Grunwald, *Napoleon's nemesis: the life of Baron Stein* (1936); H. A. L. Fisher, *Studies in Napoleonic statesmanship: Germany* (1903); H. Rosinski, *The German army* (1939, 1944—the two editions contain different material), a history from Frederick the Great to Hitler; and W. O. Shanahan, *Prussian military reforms, 1786–1813* (1945), on the Prussian Revival and the War of Liberation. The able and cynical Gentz has been the subject of a good older biography by P. F. Reiff (1912) and of two recent ones: P. R. Sweet, *Friedrich von Gentz, defender of the old order* (1941), and G. Mann, *Secretary of Europe, the life of Friedrich Gentz, enemy of Napoleon* (1946).

OTHER COUNTRIES IN NAPOLEONIC TIMES. The classic account of the unsuccessful American efforts to avoid involvement in the maritime war between France and Britain is H. Adams, *History of the United States of America* [during the administrations of Jefferson and Madison] (9 vols., 1889–91; 3 vols. reprinted, 1929), which may be supplemented by later diplomatic histories and by L. M. Sears, *Jefferson and the embargo* (1927). Other ramifications in the Western hemisphere during the revolutionary era are shown in two excellent studies by W. Spence Robertson: *The life of Miranda* (2 vols., 1929) and *France and Latin American independence* (1939). On Napoleonic influences in other countries, there may also be mentioned these three books: A. A. Lobanov-Rostovsky, *Russia and Europe, 1789–1825* (1947); E. Tarlé, *Napoleon's invasion of Russia, 1812* (1942), an excellent account by a leading Soviet historian; and G. B. McClellan, *Venice and Bonaparte* (1931). On Italy, see also the work of R. M. Johnston cited under "republicanism" in Chapter XI.

WARTIME DIPLOMACY AND THE CONGRESS OF VIENNA. Excellent guides are H. Butterfield, *The peace tactics of Napoleon, 1806–1808* (1929); P. F. Shupp's more monographic *The European Powers and the Near Eastern question, 1806–1807;* C. K. Webster, *The foreign policy of Castlereagh, 1812–1815: Britain and the reconstruction of Europe* (1931); C. S. B. Buckland, *Metternich and the British Government from 1809 to 1813* (1932) and his shorter parallel study on Gentz (1933); and L. I. Strakhovsky, *Alexander I of Russia: the man who defeated Napoleon* (1947). F. D. Scott, *Bernadotte and the fall of Napoleon* (1935), deals mostly with Bernadotte in Sweden.

C. K. Webster, *The Congress of Vienna, 1814–1815* (1919), is a technical manual of diplomacy, whereas G. Ferrero, *The reconstruction of Europe: Talleyrand and the Congress of Vienna, 1814–1815* (1941), and H. Nicolson, *Congress of Vienna: a study in allied unity, 1812–1822* (1946), are works for the general reader.

Chapter XI. Reaction vs. Progress

GENERAL HISTORIES BEGINNING ABOUT 1815. The resettling of European institutions after the great French outburst marked the beginning of a new historical era in many countries. E. Fueter, *World history, 1815–1920* (1920), an exceptionally clear exposition written with Swiss detachment, and C. D. Hazen, *Europe since 1815* (2 vols., 1924), an American view, are notable for their objectivity. There are numerous national and topical histories commencing with the Congress of Vienna.

British history in the 19th century and after (1782–1919) (1922, 1937), by G. M. Trevelyan, is a beautifully written general account, and E. Halévy's classic *History of the English people in the 19th century* (6 vols., 1912 ff., 1949 ff.), a work of unusual breadth and imagination, is becoming available to English readers in its entirety. Three other important works of general nature are C. R. Fay, *Great Britain from Adam Smith to the present day, an economic and social survey* (1928, 1932); R. W. Seton-Watson, *Britain in Europe, 1789–1914: a survey of foreign policy* (1937); and D. C. Somervell, *English thought in the 19th century* (1929, 1947). An interesting brief survey is D. Thomson, *England in the nineteenth century* (1950).

Political and economic issues and alignments in 19th-century France are clearly set forth in J. B. Wolf, *France, 1815 to the present* (1940); J. P. T. Bury, *France 1814–1940: a history* (1949); S. B. Clough, *France, a history of national economics, 1789–1939* (1939); and R. H. Soltau, *French political thought in the 19th century* (1931). J. Clapham, *The economic development of France and Germany, 1815–1914* (1921, 1936), is an instructive comparative study. H. Kohn has edited *Making of the modern French mind* (1955) in the Anvil series.

Treitschke's history of Germany in the 19th century (7 vols., 1915–19), the English version of H. G. von Treitschke's arch-Prussian account (1879–94) of events to 1848, is very informative both about the subject and about its author. Roughly the same years are covered in the more detached J. G. Legge, *Rhyme and revolution in Germany: a study in German history, life, literature, and character, 1813–1850* (1918). E. Vermeil, *Germany's three Reichs: their history and culture* (1945), is a French interpretation, while *The growth of modern Germany* (1946), by R. Pascal, is a sociological approach. A. J. P. Taylor's *The course of German history: a survey of the development of Germany since 1815* (1946), although varying in tone between the sarcastic and the sardonic, is based on considerable shrewd analysis; it is not, however, as good as his less paradoxical *The Habsburg monarchy, 1809–1918* (1943, 1948 revision changes some of the conclusions). Two reliable recent histories of Germany are R. Flenley, *Modern German history* (1953), and K. S. Pinson, *Modern Germany: its history and civilization* (1954). Much of G. A. Craig, *The Politics of the Prussian Army, 1640–1945* (1955), deals with the nineteenth century. Other useful works include H. B. Clarke, *Modern Spain, 1815–1898* (1906); R. Dyboski, *Outlines of Polish history* (1925), especially on the rise of Polish nationalism in the 19th century; A. J. B. Whyte, *The evolution of modern Italy, 1715–1920* (1944), which seeks to show the place of the Risorgimento in the general history of modern Italy; R. Albrecht-Carrié, *Italy from Napoleon to Mussolini* (1950); and E. S. Forster, *A short history of modern Greece, 1821–1940* (1941).

INDUSTRIAL REVOLUTION AND BRITISH SOCIETY. *An economic history of Europe since 1750* (1937), by W. Bowden, M. Karpovich, and A. P. Usher, and *A history of mechanical inventions* (1929, 1954), by Usher, place the predominantly British story of early modern industrialization in its European setting. P. Mantoux, *The industrial revolution in the 18th century: an outline of the beginnings of the modern factory system in England* (1906, 1937), is still fundamental, and the small book by T. S. Ashton, *The industrial revolution, 1760–1830* (1948), presents the results of modern research clearly and interestingly. J. Clapham's *An economic history of modern Britain*, the standard work on its subject, consists of three volumes: *The early railway age, 1820–1850* (1926); *Free trade and steel, 1850–1886* (1932); and *Machines and national rivalries (1887–1914), with an epilogue (1914–1929)* (1938). J. L. and B. Hammond, *The rise of British industry* (1926), is a useful shorter survey.

Changes in British rural society are analyzed in Lord Ernle [R. E. Prothero], *English farming, past and present* (1912, 1936 additions by A. D. Hall); W. H. R. Curtler, *The enclosure and redistribution of our land* (1920), mostly on Tudor and Stuart times; H. C. Taylor, *Decline of landowning farmers in England* (1904); W. Hasbach, *History of the English agricultural labourer* (1894, 1920); and J. L. and B. Hammond, *The village labourer, 1760–1832, a study in the government of England before the Reform Bill* (1911, 1948), an indignant argument that the common people were exploited by the governing classes.

The following books illustrate some of the major changes experienced by urban people and institutions, particularly in England: H. Heaton, *The Yorkshire woollen and worsted industries from the earliest times up to the industrial revolution* (1920); T. S. Ashton and J. Sykes, *The coal industry of the 18th century* (1929); *Iron and steel in the industrial revolution* (1924), also by Ashton; A. P. Wadsworth and J. de L. Mann, *The cotton industry and industrial Lancashire, 1600–1780* (1931); W. H. B. Court, *The rise of the Midland industries, 1600–1838* (1938); and A. Redford, *Labour migration in England, 1800–1850* (1926). Professor Redford has also written *An economic history of England, 1760–1860* (1947) and *Manchester merchants and foreign trade, 1794–1858* (1934). There is a large and controversial literature on the effects of industrial change upon the well-being of the British working classes; on this subject J. L. and B. Hammond contribute two other vehement books, *The town labourer, 1760–1832: the new civilization* (1918) and *The skilled labourer, 1760–1832* (1919), which may be compared with the less emphatic M. C. Buer, *Health, wealth, and population in the early days of the industrial revolution* (1926). An extreme revisionist viewpoint minimizing the evil effects of early industrialism is set forth in the collection of essays ed. by F. A. von Hayek, *Capitalism and the historians* (1954).

For the political implications behind the growth of an industrial civilization, the reader may turn to G. D. H. Cole and R. Postgate, *The British people, 1746–1946* (1947), and Cole, *British working class politics, 1832–1914* (1941), both written from a Labor point of view; E. L. Woodward, *The age of reform, 1815–1870* (1938), a solid volume of the Oxford History of England; M. Hovell, *The Chartist movement* (1918, 1925); J. L. and B. Hammond, *The age of the Chartists, 1832–1854* (1930), of which their *The bleak age* (1934, 1947) is a shorter version; and R. J. Cruikshank, *Charles Dickens and early Victorian England* (1949), a colorful and well-illustrated study of the novelist and the people he wrote about. The widening functions of government are analyzed in E. W. Cohen, *The growth of the British civil service, 1780–1939* (1941); S. and B. Webb, *English local government: English Poor Law history* (2 vols.; in 3, 1927–9); and A. Redford, *A history of local government in Manchester* (3 vols., 1939–40). D. G. Barnes, *A history of the English Corn-Laws, from 1660–1846* (1930), explains one hotly disputed issue of the age.

E. Halévy's modern classic, *The growth of philosophic radicalism* (1901–04; 3 vols. in 1, 1949), gives an excellent account of Jeremy Bentham and of James and John Stuart Mill; a work of comparable scope and merit is L. Stephen, *The English Utilitarians* (3 vols., 1900). Among the biographies of thinkers and reformers of the age are M. Packe on John Stuart Mill (1954), and G. D. H. Cole on William Cobbett (1924) and Robert Owen (1930); other biographies of Owen by F. Podmore (1924) and M. Cole (1953); and G. M. Trevelyan, *Lord Grey of the Reform Bill* (1920, 1929). G. Wallas, *The life of Francis Place, 1771–1854* (1898, 1925), an excellent portrayal of a pioneer trades unionist, may profitably be compared with two studies of more conservative reformers: C. Driver, *Tory radical: the life of Richard Oastler* (1946), and B. Blackburn, *Noble lord: the Seventh Earl of Shaftesbury* (1949). M. W. Thomas, *The early factory legislation* (1948), is a valuable legislative and administrative study dealing with the years 1802–53.

Some useful works on the religious and humanitarian movements of the time are F. W. Cornish, *The English church in the 19th century* (2 vols., 1910); W. B. Selbie, *English sects: a history of Nonconformity* (1912); I. Grubb, *Quakerism and industry before 1800* (1930); W. J. Warner, *The Wesleyan movement in the industrial revolution* (1930); L. Radzinowicz, *A history of English criminal law: the movement for reform, 1750–1833* (1948); W. M. Law, *British slavery and its abolition, 1823–38* (1926); and F. J. Klingberg, *The anti-slavery movement in England* (1926).

FRANCE AFTER NAPOLEON. G. L. Dickinson, *Revolution and reaction in modern France* (1892, 1927), is a thoughtful older interpretation of France from the 1790's to the Franco-Prussian War, to be compared with G. Elton, *The revolutionary idea in France, 1789–1871* (1923), and J. Plamenatz, *The revolutionary movement in France, 1815–1871* (1952). The continuity of French economic development from 1789 and the consequent readjustments of class structures are analyzed in F. B. Artz, *France under the Bourbon Restoration, 1814–1830* (1931). The more anecdotal J. Lucas-Dubreton, *The Restoration and the July Monarchy* (1929), successfully pictures both the forces and the actors of the time. J. M. S. Allison has written various studies of 19th-century France, of which the widest in scope is his *Monsieur Thiers* (1932), describing French politics in the years 1824–73. Two useful studies of conservative ideas and activities are C. T. Muret, *French royalist doctrines since the Revolution* (1933), and N. E. Hudson, *Ultra-royalism and the French Restoration* (1936).

THE "ISMS" AND SOCIAL THOUGHT—GENERAL. Among a number of excellent works of literary criticism stressing 19th-century social thought are G. Brandes, *Main currents in 19th century thought* (6 vols., 1872 ff., 1901–06); C. Brinton, *Political ideas of the English romanticists* (1926); J. Barzun, *Romanticism and the modern ego* (1943); and B. Croce, *European literature in the 19th century* (1924). Other notable studies of the interplay of ideas and politics include H. Marcuse, *Reason and revolution: Hegel and the rise of social theory* (1941); G. O. Griffith, *Interpreters of man: a review of secular and religious thought from Hegel to Barth* (1943); and T. Whittaker, *Reason: a philosophical essay with historical illustrations: Comte, Mill, Schopenhauer, Vico, Spinoza* (1934). C. Brinton, *English political thought in the 19th century* (1933, 1950), may be supplemented by H. Cecil, *Conservatism* (1912). On conservative and nationalist implications of "scientific" history, see T. H. von Laue, *Leopold Ranke, the formative years* (1950). D. Thomson, *Equality* (1949), and A. Rosenberg, *Democracy and socialism: a contribution to the political history of the past 150 years* (1939), both explore some of the problems posed by the French Revolution for the 19th and 20th centuries. P. Viereck, *Metapolitics: from the Romantics to Hitler* (1941), and R. D'O. Butler, *The roots of National Socialism* (1942), are two of the best attempts to explain Nazism in historical terms—a procedure which can of course be quite unfair to the men of the 19th century. E. Golob, *The "isms": a history and evaluation* (1954), is useful but less comprehensive than the title would imply.

NATIONALISM. The vast literature on this subject may best be approached through the following general treatments: C. J. H. Hayes, *Essays on nationalism* (1926) and *The historical evolution of modern nationalism* (1931, 1948); H. Kohn, *The idea of nationalism: a study in its origins and background* (1944), from Hebraic and Hellenic times to the late 18th century, and his briefer *Prophets and peoples: studies in 19th century nationalism* (1946); L. L. Snyder, *The meaning of nationalism* (1954); and B. C. Shafer, *Nationalism: myth and reality* (1955), the latter probably the best statement of our present scholarly understanding of nationalism. H. Kohn has edited *Nationalism: its meaning and history* (1955), a volume of readings and commentary in the Anvil series. Other important studies on na tionalism include E. Barker, *National character and the factors in its formation* (1927); S. W. Baron, *Modern nationalism and religion* (1947); H. M. Chadwick, *Nationalities of Europe: the growth of national ideologies* (1945); E. H. Carr, *Nationalism and after* (1944); F. Hertz, *Nationality in history and politics* (1944); and A. Cobban, *National self determination* (1948). On language, the following are suggested: J. Vendryes, *Language: a linguistic introduction to history* (1925, 1949); K. Vossler, *The spirit of language in civilization* (1932); and F. Bodmer, *The loom of language* (1944).

The following works are suggestive of developments outside the major Western countries of Europe: *The rise of nationality in the Balkans* (1917) and a short essay, *The historian as a political force in Central Europe* (1922), both by R. W. Seton-Watson; W. M. Gewehr, *The rise of nationalism in the Balkans, 1800–1930* (1931), a Berkshire study; S. B. Clough, *A history of the Flemish movement in Belgium: a study in nationalism* (1930); O. J. Falnes, *National romanticism in Norway* (1933); and H. Kohn, *Pan-Slavism: its history and ideology* (1953).

REPUBLICANISM. H. A. L. Fisher, *The republican tradition in Europe* (1911), discusses developments from the fall of the ancient Roman republic to 1910. The influence of republican agitation upon European conservative thought and diplomacy is clearly traced in the books of E. L. Woodward: *French revolutions* (1934), a general political narrative of France 1789–1871; *Three studies in European conservatism: Metternich, Guizot, the Catholic Church in the 19th century* (1930); and *War and peace in Europe, 1815–1870, and other essays* (1931). Italian republicanism is discussed in the biographies of Mazzini, cited below in Chapter XIII, as well as in R. M. Johnston, *The Napoleonic empire in Southern Italy and the rise of the secret societies* (2 vols., 1904), and in M. C. W. Wicks, *The Italian exiles in London, 1816–1848* (1937). In a class by itself is the fascinating book by T. Frost, *The secret societies of the European Revolution, 1776–1876* (2 vols., 1876), chapters on a score of subversive groups.

LIBERALISM. The fundamental work on this subject is G. de Ruggiero, *The history of European liberalism* (1927), a comparative analysis of English, French, German, and Italian liberalism based upon careful definitions and keen insight. L. T. Hobhouse, *Liberalism* (1911), is a valuable little companion to the sections on England, and J. H. Hallowell, *The decline of liberalism as an ideology* (1943), argues on the basis of German experience that liberalism is lost if it is separated from ideas of absolute truth and value. B. Croce, *History of Europe in the 19th century* (1933), is a philosophical treatment of the idea of "liberty" from about 1815 to 1918. Three books that all throw doubt on the more optimistic assumptions of classical liberalism are R. Olden, *The history of liberty in Germany* (1946); J. P. Mayer, *Prophet of the mass age: a study of Alexis de Tocqueville* (1939); and J. J. Saunders, *The age of revolution: a survey of European history since 1815* (1947). J. S. Schapiro, *Liberalism and the challenge of fascism: social forces in England and France, 1815–1870* (1949), deals with the concurrent growth of liberal and anti-liberal ideas. But the most provocative book of all on this subject is doubtless H. J. Laski's, *The rise of European liberalism* (1936, 1947), which presents the story as one of the gradual taming of a revolutionary doctrine.

SOCIALISM. Among the most useful general surveys are H. W. Laidler, *Social-economic movements* (1944); P. Taft, *Movements for economic reform* (1950); T. Kirkup, *History of Socialism* (rev., 1920); N. I. Mackenzie, *Socialism: a short history* (1949); and the older W. Sombart, *Socialism and the social movement* (1909). A. Gray, *The Socialist tradition: Moses to Lenin* (1946), is a witty, penetrating, and essentially unsympathetic account.

G. D. H. Cole has published two volumes of a projected comprehensive history, *Socialist thought: the forerunners, 1789–1850* (1953) and *Socialist thought: Marxism and anarchism, 1850–1890* (1954). An invaluable bibliography as well as useful essays are available in the Princeton University symposium, D. D. Egbert, S. Persons, and T. Bassett (eds.), *Socialism and American life* (2 vols., 1952), a good part of which is concerned with the European setting; Vol. II is entirely devoted to a descriptive and critical bibliography of socialism. E. H. Carr, *Studies in Revolution* (1950) is a series of incisive essays on earlier and later socialists. M. Beer has written an extensive survey of "social struggles" since antiquity (5 vols.; English trans., 1922–5), while W. B. Guthrie has sketched early socialist developments in *Socialism before the French Revolution* (1907). B. Russell, *Freedom versus organisation, 1814–1914* (1934, 1949), shows the dilemma of liberalism during a period of rapid economic change. Some useful studies of pre-Marxian anti-capitalism are A. J. Booth, *Saint-Simon and Saint-Simonism: a chapter in the history of socialism in France* (1871); E. M. Butler, *The Saint-Simonian religion in Germany: a study of the Young Germany movement* (1926); D. W. Brogan, *Proudhon* (1934); and H. de Lubac, *The un-Marxian socialist: a study of Proudhon* (1948). British reform activities, including those of Robert Owen, are referred to above, at the beginning of this chapter, and additional literature on Marxism will appear below.

ECONOMIC THOUGHT. Clear explanations of the development of economic ideas are given in C. Gide and C. Rist, *History of economic doctrines from the physiocrats to the present day* (1913, 1948); E. Roll, *A history of economic thought* (1939, 1955); E. Whittaker, *A history of economic ideas* (1940); and A. Gray, *Development of economic doctrine* (1931). E. Ginzberg, *The house of Adam Smith* (1934), an illuminating and original essay on Smith's moral and economic ideas, does not entirely supersede J. Rae's authoritative biography (1895). Much of Smith's influence can be seen in *Free trade and other fundamental doctrines of the Manchester School* (1903), ed. by F. W. Hirst, an indispensable collection of speeches and writings. An interesting contrast may be noted between this work and *The life of Friedrich List and selections from his writings* (1909) by M. E. Hirst, a study of the German advocate of economic nationalism.

INTERNATIONAL POLITICS AFTER THE CONGRESS OF VIENNA. *Reaction and Revolution, 1814–1832* (1934) by F. B. Artz, in the Langer series, a well-conceived analysis of European reconstruction and reorientation, is the most useful general guide, and the Berkshire study, A. J. May, *The age of Metternich, 1814–1848* (1933), is a convenient introduction. W. A. Phillips, *The confederation of Europe: a study of the European Alliance, 1813–1823, as an experiment in the international organization of peace* (1914, 1920), and H. G. Schenk, *The aftermath of the Napoleonic wars: the Concert of Europe—an experiment* (1947), are concerned with diplomatic and ideological aspects, respectively. *Conservatism revisited: the revolt against revolt, 1815–1949* (1949), by P. Viereck, is an interesting attempt to rehabilitate the reputations of the post-1815 conservatives, especially Metternich, on whom there are also sympathetic biographies by A. Herman (1932) and H. du Coudray (1935).

British foreign affairs may be followed through some of the books cited earlier, and in closer detail through C. K. Webster, *The foreign policy of Castlereagh, 1815–1822: Britain and the European alliance* (1925); H. Temperley, *The foreign policy of Canning, 1822–1827: England, the Neo-Holy Alliance, and the New World* (1925); H. C. F. Bell, *Lord Palmerston* (2 vols., 1936); P. Guedalla, *Palmerston, 1784–1865* (1927, 1942); and W. H. Dawson, *Richard Cobden and foreign policy: a critical exposition* (1926).

The situation arising from the interest of European Powers in Latin America is excellently presented in D. Perkins, *Hands off! a history of the Monroe Doctrine* (1941), and in his more detailed earlier works on the same subject. C. K. Webster, *Britain and the independence of Latin America, 1812–1830* (1944); W. P. Cresson, *The Holy Alliance: the European background of the Monroe Doctrine* (1922); and A. P. Whitaker, *The United States and the independence of Latin America, 1800–1830* (1941), present other important aspects. An interesting introduction to the subject, in the Teach yourself history series, is J. B. Trend, *Bolivar and the independence of Spanish America* (1948).

Three other important stirrings in the same period are described in C. W. Crawley, *The question of Greek independence* (1930); J. H. Brady, *Rome and the Neapolitan Revolution of 1820–21, a study in papal neutrality* (1937); and A. G. Mazour, *The first Russian revolution, 1825: the Decembrist Movement, its origins, development, and significance* (1937).

Chapter XII. 1848: A Revolution That Misfired

The far-reaching influence of the events of 1848 in European history and the impulse to rethink old problems on the basis of more recent experience has led in the past
decade to the publication of innumerable articles and books, including the following:
F. Fejtö, *The opening of an era: 1848; an historical symposium* (1948), arguing that 1848
was the decisive moment in the history of the middle class; A. Whitridge, *Men in crisis:
the revolutions of 1848* (1949), studies of leading personalities in various countries; J. East-
wood and P. Tabori, *'48, the year of revolutions* (1948), a journalistic survey garnished
with *Punch* cartoons; G. Woodcock, *A hundred years of revolution: 1848 and after* (1948);
and R. J. Cruikshank, *Roaring century, 1846–1946* (1946), colorful sketches from the
files of the London *Daily Mail*. P. Robertson has written with great skill and verve *Revolutions of 1848: a social history* (1952).

REVOLUTIONS IN VARIOUS COUNTRIES. C. E. Maurice, *The revolutionary movement of
1848–49 in Italy, Austria-Hungary, and Germany, with some examination of the previous
thirty-three years* (1887), one of the first objective attempts to see the revolutions as a
related whole, is still very helpful, as is R. Schlesinger, *Federalism in Central and Eastern
Europe* (1945), primarily concerned with the problems of various nationalities living close
together. In addition to more general histories of each country, the following works are
recommended:
On France: J. Marriott, *The French revolution of 1848 in its economic aspect*
(2 vols., 1913), presenting the ideas of Louis Blanc and Émile Thomas; *The right to work*
(1919), a separate printing of the introduction to the same work; and two tracts by Karl
Marx: *The class struggles in France* [1848–50] (1851, 1934) and *The Eighteenth Brumaire
of Louis Bonaparte* (1852, 1898). An excellent monograph is D. C. McKay, *The national
workshops: a study in the French Revolution of 1848* (1933).
On Italy: G. F. H. and J. Berkeley, *Italy in the making* (3 vols., 1932–40), on the
period 1815–48, somewhat anecdotal and concerned primarily with the position of the
upper classes; G. M. Trevelyan, *Garibaldi's defense of the Roman Republic, 1848–9* (1907,
1949), a moving narrative, and also Trevelyan's *Manin and the Venetian revolution of
1848* (1923); A. J. P. Taylor, *The Italian problem in European Diplomacy, 1847–1849*
(1934); and K. R. Greenfield, *Economics and liberalism in the Risorgimento: a study in
nationalism in Lombardy, 1814–1848* (1934).
On Hapsburg lands: J. Redlich, *Emperor Francis Joseph of Austria* (1929), an
excellent biography; J. Blum, *Noble landowners and agriculture in Austria, 1815–1848: a
study in the origins of the peasant emancipation of 1848* (1948); A. Schwarzenberg, *Prince
Felix zu Schwarzenberg, Prime Minister of Austria, 1848–1852* (1947); and C. Sproxton,
Palmerston and the Hungarian revolution (1919). Metternich's career and fall are recounted in books listed above.
On Germany and the Frankfurt Assembly: V. Valentin, *1848: chapters of German
history* (1940), a somewhat fragmentary abridgment of the author's larger study in German; L. B. Namier, *1848: the revolution of the intellectuals* (1946), sharply critical of the
Frankfurt Assembly; Karl Marx and Friedrich Engels, *Revolution and counter-revolution,
or Germany in 1848* (1896, 1919), a challenging appraisal based on the authors' articles in
the *New York Tribune*, 1851–2. The impact of the failure of 1848 upon German society
is cogently demonstrated in E. Kohn-Bramstedt, *Aristocracy and the middle-classes in
Germany: social types in German literature, 1830–1900* (1937).

MARX AND THEORETICAL MARXISM. Of the numerous lives of Marx and his associates, the
following list is merely a representative sampling: M. Beer, *The life and teaching of Karl
Marx* (1921, 1935); E. H. Carr, *Karl Marx* (1938); F. Mehring, *Karl Marx: the story of
his life* (1918, 1948); O. Rühle, *Karl Marx: his life and work* (1929, 1943); L. Schwarz-
schild, *The Red Prussian: the life and legend of Karl Marx* (1947), very unfavorable to
Marx; I. Berlin, *Karl Marx: his life and environment* (1948); C. J. S. Sprigge, *Karl Marx*
(1949); G. Mayer, *Friedrich Engels: a biography* (1920, 1936), showing that Engels
played a far greater role in the team of Marx and Engels than was previously realized; and
D. Footman, *Ferdinand Lassalle: romantic revolutionary* (1946), a colorful picture of the

early Social Democrat's personality that by no means supersedes the earlier biographies by E. Bernstein (1893), W. H. Dawson (1899), and G. Brandes (1925).

On the theoretical foundations and concrete manifestations of socialism, there is of course an enormous and highly controversial literature, to which the books cited under socialism for Chapter XI and those cited below for Chapter XIV offer a certain amount of guidance. The obvious starting place is in the writings of Marx and Engels themselves, and to these a convenient introduction is E. Burns, *A handbook of Marxism* (1935), which also includes extracts from Lenin and Stalin. G. D. H. Cole, *The meaning of Marxism* (1948), is based on his earlier *What Marx really meant* (1934). Other valuable interpretations and criticisms appear in B. Croce, *Historical materialism and the economics of Karl Marx* (1914); S. Hook, *Towards the understanding of Karl Marx* (1933); and M. M. Bober, *Karl Marx's interpretation of history* (1927, 1948). H. J. Laski has written widely and incisively on socialism, and some of his keenest observations appear in his centennial edition, *The Communist Manifesto, socialist landmark: a new appreciation written for the Labour party* (1948), which also contains the original text and prefaces by Marx and Engels. S. Hook has edited *Marx and the Marxists: the ambiguous legacy* (1955), commentary and readings in the Anvil series.

Three widely different books, all of which have the merit of placing Marx and his ideas in a broader intellectual context, are J. Barzun, *Darwin, Marx, Wagner: critique of a heritage* (1941), which points out resemblances in the basic assumptions and conclusions of the three men; E. Wilson, *To the Finland Station: a study in the writing and acting of history* (1940), an imaginative discussion of the way in which socialists and others interpreted the past to influence the present; and K. R. Popper, *The open society and its enemies* (2 vols., 1945), a challenging philosophical interpretation.

Napoleon III and Bonapartism. A good political narrative is R. Arnaud, *The Second Republic and Napoleon III* (1930), and a more sympathetic view of the Emperor as a great European appears in O. Aubry, *The Second Empire* (1940). F. A. Simpson, *The rise of Louis Napoleon* (1909, 1925) and *Louis Napoleon and the recovery of France, 1848–1856* (1923, 1930), are interesting and well-written accounts, much more reliable than the livelier *Second Empire: Bonapartism, the Prince, the President, the Emperor* (1922, 1937) by P. Guedalla. A readable and informative work is J. M. Thompson, *Louis Napoleon and the Second Empire* (1954). Three thoughtful interpretations appear in *Bonapartism* (1908, 1914) by H. A. L. Fisher; and in *Reflections on the Napoleonic legend* (1924) and *Napoleon III* (1943), both by A. Guérard. Other studies include A. L. Dunham, *The Anglo-French treaty of commerce of 1860 and the progress of the industrial revolution in France* (1930), and C. S. Phillips, *The church in France, 1848–1907* (1936). In his provocative *Liberalism and the challenge of fascism* (1949), cited in Chapter XI, J. S. Schapiro sees Louis Napoleon as a "herald of fascism."

Chapter XIII. The Consolidation of Large Nation-States

Realism and nationalism, 1852–1871 (1935), by R. C. Binkley, in the Langer series, is a valiant effort to clarify that rather indeterminate segment of European history which followed the revolutions of 1848. One of the first attempts to view the period 1848–1918 as a whole, mainly diplomatic in emphasis, is A. J. P. Taylor, *The struggle for mastery in Europe, 1848–1918* (1954), in the new Oxford History of Modern Europe series. Some salient features of the Crimean War are treated in H. Temperley, *England and the Near East: the Crimea* (1936); V. J. Puryear, *England, Russia, and the Straits Question, 1844–1856* (1931); and G. B. Henderson, *Crimean War diplomacy, and other historical essays* (1947). A dramatic episode of the war is recounted in C. B. F. Woodham-Smith, *The reason why* (1953). Other useful works of somewhat wider scope are: E. A. Pratt, *The rise of rail-power in war and conquest, 1833–1914* (1916); G. Butler and S. Macoby, *The development of international law* (1928); and J. P. Baxter, *The introduction of the iron-clad warship* (1933). Other treatments of the Crimean War period will be found in the national histories of the various belligerents and of Austria. Books on nationalism are cited in Chapter XI.

Unification of Italy. In addition to the works cited for the two foregoing chapters, the following books are suggested: W. R. Thayer, *The life and times of Cavour* (2 vols.,

1911); A. J. Whyte, *The political life and letters of Cavour, 1848–1861* (1930); two studies by G. M. Trevelyan, *Garibaldi and the Thousand* (May 1860) (1909, 1920), and *Garibaldi and the making of Italy* (June–November 1860) (1911, 1920); O. Griffith, *Mazzini: prophet of modern Europe* (1932); and S. Barr, *Mazzini: portrait of an exile* (1935). An informative special study is L. M. Case, *Franco-Italian relations, 1860–1865* (1932).

BISMARCK AND THE FOUNDING OF THE SECOND REICH. W. O. Henderson, *The Zollverein* (1939), is an excellent study of the economic basis for unification, as is the more specialized A. H. Price, *The evolution of the Zollverein* (1949). H. Friedjung, *The struggle for supremacy in Germany, 1859–1866* (1897, 1935), is an outstanding diplomatic and military account by an Austrian historian. Other studies of the period include C. W. Clark, *Franz Joseph and Bismarck: the diplomacy of Austria before the war of 1866* (1934); L. D. Steefel, *The Schleswig-Holstein question* (1932); R. H. Lord, *The origins of the war of 1870* (1924); and H. Oncken, *Napoleon III and the Rhine: the origin of the war of 1870–71* (1928).

E. Eyck's full new biography of Bismarck (3 vols., 1941–4) is not yet translated, but a summary of Eyck's conclusions, *Bismarck after fifty years* (1950), is available. C. G. Robertson, *Bismarck* (1919), may be compared with A. J. P. Taylor's study (1955); and for this period there is also F. Darmstaedter, *Bismarck and the creation of the Second Reich* (1949). *Germany, 1815–1890* (3 vols., 1916–18), by A. Ward and S. Wilkinson, is valuable as a factual narrative.

AUSTRIA AND HUNGARY. A. J. P. Taylor's *The Habsburg monarchy*, cited at the beginning of Chapter XI, presents the clearest and best-connected account. O. Jaszi, *The dissolution of the Habsburg monarchy* (1929), though difficult reading, is very rewarding. Especially useful on domestic developments is A. J. May, *The Hapsburg monarchy 1867–1914* (1951). The works of R. W. Seton-Watson, including *Racial problems in Hungary* (1908) and *The Southern Slav Question in the Habsburg monarchy* (1911), are still indispensable. Although mostly concerned with 20th-century developments, E. Wiskemann's *Czechs and Germans: a study of the struggle in the historic provinces of Bohemia and Moravia* (1938), is an intelligent and well-balanced account.

THE RUSSIA OF ALEXANDER II. M. Karpovich, *Imperial Russia, 1801–1917* (1932), is a handy sketch in the Berkshire series, and S. Graham, *Tsar of freedom: the life and reign of Alexander II* (1935), is a sympathetic biography. The place of the peasant emancipation in Russian history is discussed in G. Pavlovsky, *Agricultural Russia on the eve of the Revolution* (1930), and in G. T. Robinson's excellent *Rural Russia under the old regime: a history of the landlord-peasant world and a prologue to the peasant revolution of 1917* (1930, 1949). Also useful are F. H. Skrine, *The expansion of Russia, 1815–1900* (1903), and three studies of intellectual unrest in Tsarist Russia: D. Hecht, *Russian radicals look to America, 1825–1894* (1947), and E. H. Carr's books, *The romantic exiles: a 19th century portrait gallery* (1933, 1949) and *Michael Bakunin* (1937).

THE UNITED STATES AND CANADA. J. G. Randall, *Civil War and Reconstruction* (1937), and A. Craven, *The coming of the Civil War* (1942), may be mentioned among the many general accounts of the age of Lincoln and Lee. Standard works on the European implications of the American struggle include J. M. Callahan, *Diplomatic history of the Southern Confederacy* (1901); E. D. Adams, *Great Britain and the American Civil War* (2 vols., 1925); and D. Jordan and E. J. Pratt, *Europe and the American Civil War* (1931), a study of European opinion which finds sympathy for the North predominant.

The growth of Canadian self-government within an imperial framework is discussed in general in D. G. Creighton, *Dominion of the North, a history of Canada* (1944), and more specifically in C. W. New, *Lord Durham* (1929), and C. P. Stacey, *Canada and the British army 1846–1871: a study in the practice of responsible government* (1936). A. Siegfried, *The race question in Canada* (1907), interprets the principal internal problem, whereas external affairs are discussed in J. B. Brebner, *North Atlantic triangle: the interplay of Canada, the United States and Great Britain* (1945), and in G. Glazebrook, *Canadian external relations: an historical study to 1914* (1942).

JAPAN AND THE WEST. G. B. Sansom's two books, *Japan: a short cultural history* (1931, 1943) and *The Western World and Japan* (1950), describe Japanese civilization before and during the 19th century, respectively. An excellent brief account is E. O. Reischauer, *Japan, past and present* (1946). A thoughtful survey of ideas and institutions is I. O. Nitobé, *Japan: some phases of her problems and development* (1931), in "The Modern World" series. P. J. Treat, *Japan and the United States, 1853–1921, revised and continued to 1928* (1928), and his related other works, and E. H. Norman, *Japan's emergence as a modern state* (1940), are also recommended.

Chapter XIV. European Civilization: 1870–1914

An indictment of the late 19th century (and by implication of the age that followed) is C. J. H. Hayes, *A generation of materialism, 1871–1900* (1941), in the Langer series, arguing that liberalism, tainted by materialism and nationalism, opened the way for destructive totalitarianism, and that only the Church under Pope Leo XIII was able to withstand the corruption of modernism. This thesis may be compared with several of the books cited under liberalism in Chapter XI.

BASIC DEMOGRAPHY. A. M. Carr-Saunders, *World population: past growth and present trends* (1936), is a careful interpretative study. Other important studies, include H. P. Fairchild, *People: the quantity and quality of population* (1939); R. E. Dickinson, *The West European city: a study in urban geography* (1951); W. E. Moore, *Economic demography of Eastern and Southern Europe* (1945); D. Kirk, *Europe's population in the interwar years* (1946); and F. Lorimer, *The population of the Soviet Union: history and prospects* (1946).

Population movements in modern times are interpreted in the massive volumes by W. F. Willcox and others, *International migrations* (2 vols., 1929, 1931); in J. Isaac, *Economics of migration* (1947); and in H. Jerome, *Migration and business cycles* (1926). Other important studies of modern migrations include T. G. Taylor, *Environment, race, and migration* (1927, 1937); S. C. Johnson, *A history of emigration from the United Kingdom to North America, 1763–1912* (1913); M. L. Hansen, *The Atlantic migration 1607–1860, a history of the continuing settlement of the United States* (1940); R. F. Foerster, *The Italian immigration of our times* (1919); and W. D. Forsyth, *The myth of open spaces: Australian, British, and world trends of population and migration* (1942).

THE WORLD ECONOMY. Various general economic histories have been suggested in the introductory section and for several foregoing chapters. In addition, the following more special works are recommended: H. M. Hyndman, *Commercial crises of the 19th century* (1892); P. W. L. Ashley, *Modern tariff history: Germany, United States, France* (1905, 1920); G. W. Edwards, *The evolution of finance capitalism* (1938); C. Wright and C. E. Fayle, *A history of Lloyd's* (1928), on the great English marine insurance center; and J. Clapham, *The Bank of England, a history* (2 vols., 1945), on the Bank since its founding in 1694.

Economic studies of more directly analytical and interpretative character include L. H. Jenks, *The migration of British capital to 1875* (1927, 1938), and H. Feis, *Europe, the world's banker, 1870–1914: an account of European foreign investment and the connection of world finance with diplomacy before the war* (1930); and also four penetrating studies of economic concentration and control: G. R. Carter, *The tendency toward industrial combination* (1913), on British experience; B. C. Hunt, *The development of the business corporation in England, 1800–1867* (1936); D. L. Burn, *The economic history of steelmaking, 1867–1939: a study in competition* (1940); and H. Levy, *The new industrial system: a study of the origin, forms, finance, and prospects of concentration in industry* (1936). There is also a large and growing literature on the problem of cartels.

FRANCE, 1870–1914. The general histories cited at the beginning of Chapter XI should be consulted. *The development of modern France, 1870–1939* (1940), also published as *France under the Republic*, by D. W. Brogan, presents an excellent general narrative and interpretation, and D. Thomson's briefer *Democracy in France* (1946, rev. 1952) is also quite useful, particularly on politics. Other general treatments are R. W. Hale, *Demo-*

cratic France: the Third Republic from Sedan to Vichy (1941), and J. P. Mayer, *Political thought in France from the Revolution to the Fourth Republic* (1943, 1949). An interesting monograph is J. A. Scott, *Republican ideas and the liberal tradition in France, 1870–1914* (1951).

The tumultuous beginnings of the Third Republic are discussed from various points of view in Karl Marx, *The civil war in France* (1871, 1921); E. S. Mason, *The Paris Commune: an episode in the history of the socialist movement* (1930); F. Jellinek, *The Paris Commune of 1871* (1937); F. H. Brabant, *The beginnings of the Third Republic in France: a history of the National Assembly, February–September 1871* (1940); and J. P. T. Bury, *Gambetta and the national defence: a republican dictatorship in France* (1936).

M. Josephson, *Zola and his time: the history of his martial career in letters* (1928), is a fascinating tale of a remarkable man; it gives an excellent account of the Dreyfus case, on which also D. C. McKay has edited *The Dreyfus case, by the man—Alfred Dreyfus— and his son Pierre Dreyfus* (1937). Other accounts of the Dreyfus affair are those by J. Kayser (1931), R. F. Byrnes (1950), G. Chapman (1955), and N. Halasz (1955). *Clemenceau and the Third Republic* (1948) by J. H. Jackson, in the Teach yourself history series, and G. Bruun, *Clemenceau* (1943), deal with a slightly later period.

ITALY. B. Croce, *A history of Italy, 1871–1915* (1929); A. W. Salomone, *Italian democracy in the making: the political scene in the Giolittian era, 1900–1914* (1945); and the volumes by R. Albrecht-Carrié and by A. J. B. Whyte listed at the beginning of Chapter XI are recommended.

GERMANY, 1870–1914. The volumes on Germany cited at the beginning of Chapter XI and on Bismarck in the preceding chapter are also to be consulted. W. H. Dawson, *The German Empire, 1867–1914, and the unity movement* (2 vols., 1919), is still the best-balanced general account in English. Important economic and institutional studies include T. Veblen, *Imperial Germany and the industrial revolution* (1915, 1939); W. F. Bruck, *Social and economic history of Germany, 1888–1938* (1938); H. Levy, *Industrial Germany: a study of its monopoly organizations and their control by the state* (1935); A. Gerschenkron, *Bread and democracy in Germany* (1943), on the agrarian basis of Junker power; L. W. Muncy, *The Junker in the Prussian administration under William II, 1888–1914* (1944); F. Lilge, *The abuse of learning: the failure of the German university* (1948); and R. Emerson, *State and sovereignty in modern Germany* (1928), a valuable study in political theory and jurisprudence.

How the diplomacy of the two decades after the Franco-Prussian war centered about Bismarck is shown with masterly clarity by W. L. Langer in *European alliances and alignments, 1871–1890* (1931, 1950), against which should be set J. V. Fuller, *Bismarck's diplomacy at its zenith* (1922), much more critical of the Chancellor's statecraft. J. Andrássy, *Bismarck, Andrássy and their successors* (1927), is also useful.

GREAT BRITAIN, 1870–1914. R. C. K. Ensor, *England, 1870–1914* (1936, 1949), provides the best general account of the period, although it is stronger on domestic than on foreign affairs. Recommended also are R. J. Evans, *The Victorian age, 1815–1914* (1950), and G. M. Young, *Victorian England: portrait of an age* (1954). H. M. Lynd, *England in the Eighteen Eighties: toward a social basis for freedom* (1945), is an interesting attempt to apply the "Middletown" technique of sociological investigation to history. H. Ausubel has edited a useful volume of readings, *The late Victorians* (1955), in the Anvil series.

Almost every major figure in British life in this period has been the subject of at least one biography. Among the most interesting biographies or books taking a biographical approach to developments of the era are L. Strachey, *Queen Victoria* (1921) and *Eminent Victorians* (1918, 1933); A. Cecil, *Queen Victoria and her prime ministers* (1952); R. Fulford, *Queen Victoria* (1951). On Gladstone: the older work of J. Morley (3 vols., 1903); W. P. Hall, *Mr. Gladstone* (1931); J. L. Hammond and M. R. D. Foot, *Gladstone and liberalism* (1953), in the Teach yourself history series; P. Magnus, *Gladstone: a biography* (1955). On Disraeli: the older work by W. F. Monypenny and G. E. Buckle (6 vols., 1913–20), and later accounts by A. Maurois (1928), and H. Pearson (1951). D. C. Somervell has written *Disraeli and Gladstone, a duo-biographical sketch* (1927).

Recommended also are W. Irvine, *The universe of G. B. S.* (1949) on Bernard Shaw; and
M. Cole (ed.), *The Webbs and their work* (1949).

Informative economic studies, apart from those listed elsewhere in this chapter, are
B. H. Brown, *The tariff reform movement in Great Britain, 1881–1895* (1944), and A. L.
Bowley, *Wages and income in the United Kingdom since 1860* (1938). G. Dangerfield,
The strange death of liberal England (1935), is a searching study of tensions in English
society between 1910 and 1914.

The perennial Irish question is discussed in J. O'Connor, *History of Ireland, 1798–
1924* (2 vols., 1926); J. E. Pomfret, *The struggle for land in Ireland, 1800–1923* (1930);
and in the excellent brief J. C. Beckett, *A short history of Ireland* (1952).

SOCIALIST MOVEMENT AND SOCIALIST PARTIES. General histories of socialism are listed for
Chapter XI, and works on Marx and theoretical Marxism for Chapter XII. On the modern
translation of Marxist ideas into institutional form, S. F. Markham, *A history of socialism*
(1931), and S. Graves, *A history of socialism* (1939), provide good general surveys.
M. Beer's *Fifty years of international socialism* (1937) is an interesting personal account
and his *History of British socialism* (1912, 1948), a comprehensive study. Bernard Shaw's
Intelligent woman's guide to socialism, capitalism, sovietism, and fascism (1928, 1949)
and B. Russell, *Proposed roads to freedom: socialism, anarchism, and syndicalism* (1919),
are provocative books. G. M. Stekloff's *History of the First International* (1928) is an
orthodox Marxian treatment; on its successor organization there is J. Lenz, *Rise and fall of
the Second International* (1932) and the informative account by J. Joll, *The Second International, 1889–1914* (1955).

Other useful studies include S. Bernstein, *The beginnings of Marxian socialism in
France* (1933), on the period roughly 1860–80; H. R. Weinstein, *Jean Jaurès: a study of
patriotism in the French socialist movement* (1936); J. H. Jackson, *Jean Jaurès: his life
and work* (1943); C. E. Raven, *Christian socialism, 1848–54* (1920); *Christian social reformers of the 19th century* (1927), ed. by H. Martin; M. R. Grennan, *William Morris:
medievalist and revolutionary* (1946); and G. D. H. Cole, *Fabian socialism* (1943).
P. Gay has written an excellent study of Bernstein and revisionism in *The dilemma of
democratic socialism: Eduard Bernstein's challenge to Marx* (1952). R. C. K. Ensor's
anthology of socialist writings, *Modern Socialism* (1910) is useful.

LABOR MOVEMENT AND LABOR UNIONS. An indispensable classic treatment is S. Perlman,
Theory of the labor movement (1928, 1949). W. A. McConagha, *The development of
the labor movement in Great Britain, France, and Germany* (1942), is a good general
survey, as is W. Galenson (ed.), *Comparative labor movements* (1952). J. Kuczynski's
Labor conditions in Western Europe, 1820 to 1935 (1937), *A short history of labor conditions in Great Britain and the Empire, 1750 to the present day* (1942), and his other
books written from a Marxian viewpoint argue the thesis that the position of the workers
has deteriorated markedly under industrial capitalism. An alternative to socialism and
capitalism is outlined in F. Hall and W. P. Watkins, *Co-operation: a survey . . . of the
co-operative movement in Great Britain and Ireland* (1934). S. and B. Webb, *History of
trade unionism* (1894, 1920), is a classic of modern economic history. The most complete
account of British labor developments is G. D. H. Cole, *A short history of the British
working class movement* (1947); other good studies are F. Williams, *Magnificent journey:
rise of the trade unions* (1955), and R. M. Rayner, *The story of trade unionism from the
Combination Acts to the General Strike* (1929). An excellent account of French trade
union development is V. R. Lorwin, *The French labor movement* (1954). Other studies
of Continental developments are M. R. Kelso, *The French labor movement during the
last years of the Second Empire* ('1936); L. L. Lorwin, *Syndicalism in France* (1912,
1914); P. T. Moon, *The labor problem and the Social Catholic movement in France: a
study in the history of social politics* (1921); W. H. Dawson, *Social insurance in Germany,
1883–1911* (1912); M. R. Carroll, *Unemployment insurance in Germany* (1929, 1930);
W. S. Sanders, *Trade unionism in Germany* (1916); and E. Anderson, *Hammer or anvil:
the story of the German working-class movement* (1945), mostly on the period after 1914.

THE NEW MOVEMENT IN SCIENCE. Histories of science and general considerations of its
place in the modern world are listed above for Chapter VII. To them may be added
E. Zimmer, *The revolution in physics* (1936); C. T. Chase, *The evolution of modern*

physics (1947), a good popular history; A. Findlay, *A hundred years of chemistry* (1937); and I. Galdston (ed.) *Social medicine: its derivations and objectives* (1949). A good brief introduction to Darwin is P. B. Scars, *Charles Darwin: the naturalist as a cultural force* (1950). On the impact of evolution, W. Irvine has written the entertaining *Apes, angels, and Victorians: the story of Darwin, Huxley, and evolution* (1955). Einstein may be approached through L. Infeld, *Albert Einstein: his work and its influence on our world* (1950), and L. Barnett, *The universe and Dr. Einstein* (1952). F. Wittels, *Freud and his time* (1931, 1948), is one of the best-balanced studies of Sigmund Freud; it may be compared with the comprehensive biography by E. Jones not yet completed (2 vols. to date, 1953, 1955). B. P. Babkin has written the interesting *Pavlov: a biography* (1949).

SOCIAL THOUGHT. The relations between science and social thought and other subjects are elucidated in considerable detail in J. T. Merz, *A history of European thought in the 19th century* (4 vols., 1897–1914). Other notable general works on the period include E. Barker, *Political thought in England from Herbert Spencer to the present day* (1915, 1947); H. E. Barnes (ed.), *An introduction to the history of sociology* (1948); E. Wilson, *Axel's castle: a study of the imaginative literature of 1870–1930* (1931); G. P. Gooch, *History and historians in the 19th century* (1913, 1949); E. Neff, *The poetry of history: the contribution of literature and literary scholarship to the writing of history since Voltaire* (1947); and R. Hofstadter, *Social Darwinism in American thought, 1860–1915* (1944). Three specialized studies are W. Irvine, *Walter Bagehot* (1939), on the English political economist and writer on evolution; H. Alpert, *Emile Durkheim and his sociology* (1939), on a leading French systematizer; and J. P. Mayer, *Max Weber and German politics: a study in political sociology* (1944). H. A. Reyburn, *Nietzsche: the story of a human philosopher* (1948), may be compared with C. Brinton, *Nietzsche* (1941), and G. A. Morgan, *What Nietzsche means* (1941). R. Humphrey has written *Georges Sorel: prophet without honor* (1951).

RACISM, INTEGRAL NATIONALISM, AND THEORIES OF VIOLENCE. The later development of totalitarianism is dealt with in connection with Chapter XIX. In *The pragmatic revolt in politics: syndicalism, fascism and the constitutional state* (1928), W. Y. Elliot presents the general problem of the revolt against rationalism in politics since the time of Sorel. Other provocative studies along similar lines are H. W. C. Davis, *Political thought of Heinrich von Treitschke* (1915); P. W. Massing, *Rehearsal for destruction: a study of political anti-semitism in imperial Germany* (1949); J. Barzun, *The French race: theories of its origins and their social and political implications prior to the Revolution* (1932); and W. C. Buthman, *The rise of integral nationalism in France, with special reference to the ideas of Charles Maurras* (1939).

CATHOLICISM SINCE 1870. An acute delineation of the place of organized religion in human society is J. N. Figgis, *Churches in the modern state* (1914). On one branch of Christian socialism see D. O. Wagner, *Church of England and social reform since 1854* (1930). More specifically on the Catholic church are the study by E. L. Woodward cited for Chapter XI; C. C. Eckhardt, *The papacy and world affairs, as reflected in the secularization of politics* (1937); L. P. Wallace, *The papacy and European diplomacy 1869–1878* (1948); and C. Butler, *The Vatican Council: the story told from inside in Bishop Ullathorne's letters* (2 vols., 1930).

Other studies of modern Catholicism include P. K. Guilday (ed.), *The Catholic philosophy of history* (1936); G. D. Smith (ed.), *The teaching of the Catholic church: a summary of Catholic doctrine* (2 vols., 1949), an authoritative Catholic view; G. P. McEntee, *The Social Catholic movement in England* (1927); R. Fülöp-Miller, *Leo XIII and our times: might of the church-power in the world* (1937) [also published as *The power and secret of the papacy*]; J. A. Ryan and F. J. Boland, *Catholic principles of politics* (1940); and W. Gurian (ed.), *The Catholic church in world affairs* (1954).

Chapter XV. Europe's World Supremacy

IMPERIALISM IN GENERAL. Inquiry into the theoretical nature of imperialism has been stimulated by two books: J. A. Hobson's *Imperialism: a study* (1902, 1948), an incisive critique by an English self-styled "economic heretic," and V. I. Lenin's *Imperialism, the highest stage of capitalism* (1916, 1939). A full and well-balanced discussion of imperialism in all aspects is contained in W. L. Langer, *The diplomacy of imperialism, 1890–1902* (2 vols., 1935). Other important studies of actual motives and alleged justifications for imperialist activity include L. C. Robbins, *The economic causes of war* (1939); E. Staley, *War and the private investor: a study in the relations of international politics and international investment* (1935); E. M. Winslow, *The pattern of imperialism: a study in the theories of power* (1948); P. T. Moon, *Imperialism and world politics* (1926); R. Maunier, *The sociology of colonies: an introduction to the study of race contact* (2 vols., 1949); and J. A. Schumpeter *Imperialism and social classes* (1955).

Imperial activities of the leading European powers (except Russia—discussed under Chapter XVII) are described in the following books: P. Knaplund, *The British Empire, 1815–1939* (1941); J. L. Garvin, *The life of Joseph Chamberlain* (3 vols., 1932–4); W. L. Strauss, *Joseph Chamberlain and the theory of imperialism* (1942); M. E. Townsend, *The rise and fall of Germany's colonial empire, 1884–1918* (1930); T. F. Power, Jr., *Jules Ferry and the renaissance of French imperialism* (1944); H. I. Priestley, *France overseas: a study of modern imperialism* (1938); S. H. Roberts, *History of French colonial policy, 1870–1925* (2 vols., 1929); and C. Hollis, *Italy in Africa* (1941).

THE AMERICAS. On the expansion of the United States, A. K. Weinberg, *Manifest destiny* (1935), is the standard general work. Other phases of American foreign policy are treated in the regular diplomatic histories and in M. W. Williams, *Anglo-American Isthmian diplomacy 1815–1915* (1916); J. W. Pratt, *Expansionists of 1898* (1936) and *America's colonial experiment* (1950); W. Millis, *The martial spirit* (1931), an ironic discussion of the Spanish-American war; and H. and M. Sprout, *The rise of American naval power, 1776–1918* (1939). D. Dawson, *The Mexican adventure* (1935), is a careful and objective account of Napoleon III's fiasco during the 1860's; and F. Tannenbaum's *Mexico: the struggle for peace and bread* (1950), provides a running narrative of Mexican history, with a detailed examination of 20th-century events. *Latin America and the industrial age* (1944), by J. F. Rippy, may be added to the works on South and Central America previously cited.

THE OTTOMAN EMPIRE. W. Miller, *The Ottoman Empire and its successors, 1801–1927* (1913, 1936), and J. A. R. Marriott, *The Eastern question* (1917, 1940), are standard older accounts. W. W. White, *The process of change in the Ottoman empire* (1937), is a useful study, and may be supplemented by N. Sousa, *The capitulatory regime of Turkey* (1933). Other valuable studies of the Ottoman Empire and its components, especially during the 19th century, are H. Dodwell, *The founder of modern Egypt: a study of Muhammad Ali* [Mehemet Ali] (1931); L. Ostroróg, *The Angora reform* (1928), the best account of 19th-century Turkish nationalism; D. C. Blaisdell, *European financial control in the Ottoman empire* (1929); and the outstanding account by H. Kohn, *A history of nationalism in the East* (1929).

More directly on the diplomatic status of Turkey in modern times are the following works: F. E. Bailey, *British policy and Turkish reform: a study in Anglo-Turkish relations, 1826–1853* (1942), and F. S. Rodkey, *The Turco-Egyptian question in the relations of England, France, and Russia, 1832–1841* (1924), both on the background of the Crimean War [discussed in Chapter XIII]; R. W. Seton-Watson, *Disraeli, Gladstone, and the Eastern Question* (1935); W. N. Medlicott, *The Congress of Berlin and after: a diplomatic history of the Near Eastern settlement, 1878–1880* (1938); E. M. Earle, *Turkey, the Great Powers, and the Bagdad railway* (1923); and M. K. Chapman, *Great Britain and the Bagdad railway* (1948).

THE BALKANS. The following may be added to the works already mentioned: C. Sforza, *Fifty years of war and diplomacy in the Balkans* (1941); J. A. Levandis, *The Greek foreign debt and the Great Powers, 1821–1898* (1944); T. W. Riker, *The making of Roumania: a study of an international problem, 1856–1866* (1931); and C. E. Black, *The establishment of constitutional government in Bulgaria* (1943).

AFRICA. Good introductory accounts are H. H. Johnston, *The opening up of Africa* (1911), and H. L. Hoskins, *European imperialism in Africa* (1930), in the Berkshire series, which may be compared with H. A. Wieschhoff, *Colonial policies in Africa* (1944).

B. Williams has written *Botha, Smuts, and South Africa* (1948) in the Teach yourself history series. W. E. B. Du Bois, *The world and Africa* (1947), presents ideas and historical materials not readily accessible elsewhere; it may be read in connection with R. L. Buell, *The native problem in Africa* (2 vols., 1928), and J. A. Noon, *Labor problems of Africa* (1944). Some important monographs are M. M. Knight, *Morocco as a French economic venture: a study of open door imperialism* (1937); R. Rudin, *Germans in the Cameroons, 1884–1914: a case study in modern imperialism* (1938); and S. E. Crowe, *The Berlin West-African conference, 1884–1885* (1942). There are biographies of Leopold by L. de Lichtervelde (1929) and L. Bauer (1935); and of Cecil Rhodes by B. Williams (1921) and A. Maurois (1953).

ASIA. Japan is discussed mainly in Chapter XIII, and Asiatic problems in general after 1918 are treated in Chapter XVIII.

J. Pratt, *The expansion of Europe in the Far East* (1947) and *China and Britain* (1944), are general discussions by a leading expert. An excellent comprehensive account is P. H. Clyde, *The Far East: a history of the impact of the West on eastern Asia* (1948, 1952). O. and E. Lattimore, *The making of modern China: a short history* (1944), is a good straightforward history designed for American readers. European relations with China are taken up in T. W. Overlach, *Foreign financial control in China* (1919); M. Collis, *Foreign mud: being an account of the opium imbroglio in Canton in the 1830's and the Anglo-Chinese war that followed* (1947); and N. A. Pelcovits, *Old China hands and the Foreign Office* (1948).

Sino-American relations are discussed in J. K. Fairbank, *The United States and China* (1948), and F. R. Dulles, *China and America: the story of their relations since 1784* (1946). C. Day, *The policy and administration of the Dutch in Java* (1904), may be added to the list of books on the Netherlands East Indies under Chapter IV. Other useful surveys of Asiatic developments with direct European implications are T. W. Wallbank, *India: a survey of the heritage and growth of Indian nationalism* (1948), a Berkshire study; C. Robequain, *The economic development of French Indo-China* (1944); and J. F. Cady, *The roots of French imperialism in Eastern Asia* (1954).

In addition to the works on Russian foreign policy cited in the chapters that follow, there may be mentioned here A. Lobanov-Rostovsky, *Russia and Asia* (1933); B. H. Sumner, *Tsardom and imperialism in the Far East and the Middle East, 1880–1914* (1942), a short sketch; and F. Thiess, *The voyage of forgotten men* (1947), the story of the Russian fleet that eventually was defeated at Tsushima by the Japanese.

Chapter XVI. The First World War

R. J. Sontag, *European diplomatic history, 1871–1932* (1933), is an excellent summary of the years covered. It may be compared with A. J. P. Taylor's *Struggle for mastery in Europe, 1848–1918*, cited in Chapter XIII. A brief introduction is B. E. Schmitt, *Triple alliance and triple entente* (1934), in the Berkshire series. N. Angell's *The great illusion: a study of the relation of military power in nations to their economic and social advantage* (1911) [rewritten as *The great illusion, 1933* (1933)], is a masterly dissection of political mythology. The indefatigable Winston S. Churchill has written one of the best and most outspoken general accounts of the period in his *The world crisis* (5 vols., 1923–9), a work of unfailing interest.

POLITICAL BACKGROUND OF THE WAR OF 1914. Nothing more can be done here than to call attention to some of the main general works on this much-vexed subject. Almost every major statesman, every diplomatic incident, and every shift in policy has been the subject of a book or an article.

Among the most important comprehensive treatments are S. B. Fay, *The origins of the World War* (1928, 2 vols. in 1, 1930); B. E. Schmitt, *The coming of the War, 1914* (2 vols., 1930); the innumerable writings of G. P. Gooch; P. Renouvin, *The immediate origins of the war* (1928); N. Mansergh, *The coming of the First World War: a study in the European balance, 1878–1914* (1949); and L. Albertini, *The origins of the war of 1914* (2 vols. in trans., 1952–3).

Among more specific books, the following are concerned primarily with the Allied powers: A. F. Pribram, *England and the international policy of the European Great Powers, 1871–1914* (1929, 1941); G. Michon, *The Franco-Russian alliance, 1891–1917* (1929); E. M. Carroll, *French public opinion and foreign affairs, 1870–1914* (1931); and J. E. Tyler, *The British army and the Continent, 1904–1914* (1938). The position of the Central Powers is discussed in E. Brandenburg, *From Bismarck to the World War: a history of German foreign policy, 1870–1914* (1927); E. M. Carroll, *Germany and the Great Powers, 1866–1914: a study in public opinion and foreign policy* (1938); A. F. Pribram, *Austrian foreign policy, 1908–1918* (1923); A. von Wegerer, *A refutation of the Versailles war guilt thesis* (1930); Count von Montgelas, *The case for the Central Powers: an impeachment of the Versailles verdict* (1925); and R. W. Seton-Watson, *Sarajevo* (1926). *The diplomacy of the Balkan wars, 1912–1913* (1938), by E. C. Helmreich, discusses Southeast-European antecedents of the wider 1914–18 war.

Anglo-German relations are discussed in H. Kantorowicz, *The spirit of British policy and the myth of the encirclement of Germany* (1931), a defense of British policy by a German expatriate; R. J. Sontag, *Germany and England: background of conflict, 1848–1894* (1938); P. R. Anderson, *The background of anti-English feeling in Germany, 1890–1902* (1939); and R. J. S. Hoffman, *Great Britain and the German trade rivalry, 1875–1914* (1933).

The naval race and various attempts to stop it are discussed in the volumes by Churchill already cited, in the memoirs of Tirpitz, Grey, Fisher, Haldane, and other participants, and in the following works: A. J. Marder, *The anatomy of British sea power* (1940); A. J. Woodward, *Great Britain and the German navy* (1935); and A. S. Hurd and H. Castle, *German sea-power: its rise, progress, and economic basis* (1913).

S. F. Bemis, *A diplomatic history of the United States* (1935, 1942), and T. A. Bailey, *A diplomatic history of the American people* (1940, 1946), and numerous other works suggested in these two books, may be consulted on the involvement of the United States in the First World War.

One should also consult the official publications of the various belligerents, most of whom later released large sections of their diplomatic correspondence, sometimes for objective, and sometimes for tendentious purposes.

MILITARY: STRATEGIC AND OPERATIONAL. Here again the available material is staggering. Two authors who have succeeded in organizing the subject into manageable shape are C. R. M. Cruttwell, with his *History of the Great War, 1914–1918* (1934), and B. H. L. Hart, with his *The real war 1914–1918* (1930) and *The war in outline* (1936). Another instructive account is F. Maurice, *Lessons of Allied co-operation: naval, military and air, 1914–1918* (1942). The most complete history in English of operations in various theaters during all the years of the war is the official British *History of the Great War based on official documents by the historical section of the Committee of Imperial Defence* (many volumes, 1920–1949 ff.).

ECONOMIC AND SOCIAL IMPACT OF THE WAR. [The Russian Revolution is discussed in Chapter XVII, and the German Revolution together with the longer-range effects of the First World War in Chapter XVIII.] On this general subject there is the multi-volumed, outstanding Carnegie Endowment series, *Economic and social history of the World War* (1921 ff.), under the general editorship of J. T. Shotwell. Representative titles include J. A. Salter, *Allied shipping control: an experiment in international administration* (1921); W. Beveridge, *British food control* (1928); F. W. Hirst, *Consequences of the war to Great Britain* (1934); A. Fontaine, *French industry during the war* (1926); *The Netherlands and the World War, studies in the war history of a neutral* (4 vols., 1923–28); S. O. Zagorsky, *State control of industry in Russia during the war* (1928); A. Mendelssohn-Bartholdy, *The war and German society: the testament of a liberal* (1938); A. Emin, *Turkey in the World War* (1930); E. Heckscher and others, *Sweden, Norway, Denmark, and Iceland in the World War* (1930); J. Redlich, *Austrian war government* (1929); and D. Mitrany, *The effect of the war in Southeastern Europe* (1936).

PEACE OF VERSAILLES. K. F. Nowak, *The collapse of Central Europe* (1924); F. Maurice, *The armistices of 1918* (1943); and H. R. Rudin, *Armistice, 1918* (1944), present the preliminaries of the Conference at Paris. H. Nicolson, *Peacemaking, 1919* (1933, 1939), and G. B. Noble, *Policies and opinions at Paris, 1919* (1935), describe the intellectual climate in which the momentous decisions were reached. H. W. V. Temperley, *A history of the peace conference of Paris* (6 vols., 1920–4), is a massive technical study, comparable to the official papers published by various governments from time to time on the conference and related topics, whereas F. S. Marston, *The peace conference of 1919* (1944), is a brief and readable guide intended to be of service to peacemakers after the Second World War.

Other valuable studies include A. Luckau, *The German delegation at the Paris peace conference* (1941); F. Deák, *Hungary at the Paris peace conference* (1942); S. Bonsal, *Suitors and suppliants: the little nations at Versailles* (1946); R. Albrecht-Carrié, *Italy at the Paris peace conference* (1938); I. Morrow, *The peace settlement in the German-Polish borderlands* (1936); A. Cobban, *National self-determination* (1944); and P. Birdsall, *Versailles twenty years after* (1941), a reassessment based on two decades of exacerbated controversy. One of the most hotly disputed issues was of course reparations, and on this J. M. Keynes's *The economic consequences of the peace* (1920) has been the most influential single book. *The Carthaginian peace—or the economic consequences of Mr. Keynes* (1946), by Étienne Mantoux, is a vigorous reply to Keynes. C. Bergmann, *The history of reparations* (1927), is a scholarly presentation of a German point of view, and in *The end of reparations* (1931), H. Schacht manages to vindicate his own policy. A wider point of view is found in A. L. Bowley, *Some economic consequences of the Great War* (1930).

BIOGRAPHIES. There are innumerable biographies, which vary widely in quality, of the civil and military figures of the period. Some of the better biographies are G. M. Trevelyan, *Grey of Fallodon* (1937); G. Wright, *Poincaré and the French presidency* (1943); L. B. Namier, *In the margin of history* (1939), on some "men who floundered into the war"— Bülow, Hötzendorf, Tisza, Andrassy, and others; K. Tschuppik, *Ludendorff: the tragedy of a military mind* (1932); R. S. Baker, *Woodrow Wilson: life and letters* (8 vols., 1927–39); M. Thomson, *David Lloyd George: the official biography* (1948); T. Jones, *Lloyd George* (1951); and also on Lloyd George, F. Owen, *Tempestuous Journey* (1955). T. E. Lawrence, *Seven pillars of wisdom: a triumph* (1926, 1935), on the revolt of the Arabs against the Turks, is a fascinating story of desert warfare and political intrigue.

Chapter XVII. The Russian Revolution

RUSSIA BEFORE 1917. Many books on modern Russia are listed for Chapters V and XIII, and some material on Russian imperialism and on the First World War is listed for Chapters XV and XVI. *The spirit of Russia* (2 vols., 1919), by T. G. Masaryk, is a profound and difficult work of extraordinary value. E. H. Carr, *Dostoevsky* (1821–1881), *a new biography* (1931); E. J. Simmons, *Leo Tolstoy* (1946); and W. H. Bruford, *Chekhov and his Russia: a sociological study* (1948), are other literary treatments of high merit, particularly helpful in giving Western readers some notion of 19th-century society and the enduring Russian character. Valuable also is R. Hare, *Pioneers of Russian social thought* (1951). H. Kohn has edited selections from the most important Russian writers in the years 1815 to 1917 in *The mind of modern Russia* (1954).

In addition to the books listed for Chapter XIII, economic and institutional topics are discussed in P. I. Liashchenko, *History of the Russian national economy to the 1917 revolution* (1949), independent-minded even though written in the Soviet Union; G. Pavlovsky, *Agricultural Russia on the eve of the Revolution* (1930); L. A. Owen, *The Russian peasant movement, 1906–1917* (1937); and J. S. Curtiss, *Church and state in Russia: the last years of the Empire, 1900–1917* (1940).

The political situation in late Tsarist Russia is best approached through H. Seton-Watson, *The decline of imperial Russia, 1855–1914* (1952), and through the various general histories cited for Chapter V. To these may be added G. Kennan, *Siberia and the exile system* (2 vols., 1891); B. H. Sumner, *Russia and the Balkans, 1870–1880* (1947), an outstanding analysis offering much more than the title suggests; A. Levin, *The Second Duma* (1940); and M. T. Florinsky, *The end of the Russian empire* (1931), one of several Russian studies in the Carnegie series [described in Chapter XVI].

THE REVOLUTION OF 1917 AND THE ESTABLISHMENT OF THE U.S.S.R. Good biographical introductions for the general reader are B. D. Wolfe, *Three who made a revolution: a biographical history* [Lenin, Trotsky, Stalin] (1948); C. Hill, *Lenin and the Russian*

Revolution (1947), in the Teach yourself history series; and the lives of Lenin by C. Vernadsky (1931) and D. Shub (1948). I. Deutscher has written two outstanding books: *Stalin: a political biography* (1949) and *The prophet armed: Trotsky, 1879–1921* (1954).

On the utterly controversial subject of the Revolution, the following general works are suggested: W. H. Chamberlin, *The Russian Revolution, 1917–1921* (2 vols., 1935); B. Pares, *The fall of the Russian monarchy: a study of the evidence* (1939), and other writings; and G. Vernadsky, *The Russian Revolution, 1917–1931* (1932), a Berkshire study. The most comprehensive account written from the sources is the as yet unfinished work of E. H. Carr, excellent but frankly sympathetic to Lenin, *A history of Soviet Russia* (4 vols. to date, 1950–4), which now carries the story through 1924.

Accounts by participants include V. M. Chernov, *The great Russian Revolution* (1936), by one who played a minor role; L. Trotsky, *The history of the Russian Revolution* (2 vols., 1932, 1937), who has also written his autobiography (1930) and a number of bitter but informative books on Stalin and his influence; A. Kerensky, *The catastrophe: Kerensky's own story of the Russian Revolution* (1927), and other books; and innumerable pronunciamentos by both Lenin and Stalin. *The Bolshevik revolution 1917–1918: documents and materials* (1934), a publication of the Hoover War Library, is a valuable source collection.

External relations in the crucial years 1917–20 are discussed in the following works: J. W. Wheeler-Bennett, *The forgotten peace: Brest-Litovsk, March 1918* (1939); L. I. Strakhovsky, *Intervention at Archangel* (1944); J. A. White, *The Siberian intervention* (1950); G. Stewart, *The White Armies of Russia: a chronicle of counter-revolution and Allied intervention* (1933); J. T. Shotwell and M. M. Laserson, *Poland and Russia, 1919–1945* (1945), a Carnegie study; and S. Konovalov, *Russo-Polish relations* (1945). Important documents and other source materials are printed in *Intervention, civil war, and communism in Russia, April–December 1918* (1936), ed. by J. Bunyan.

SOVIET FOREIGN RELATIONS. [The best places to turn for reasonably reliable and up-to-date guidance are the *Foreign Affairs Bibliographies*, described under Chapter XVIII, and the regular periodicals devoted to international affairs. Most of the books dealing with Soviet relations with Europe after 1920 will be found in the chapters that follow.] Two important and highly controversial accounts covering the whole period to the end of the Second World War are E. H. Carr's brief interpretation, *The Soviet impact on the Western world* (1947), and F. L. Schuman's lengthy narrative and analysis, *Soviet politics at home and abroad* (1946), which manage to put about as good a construction on Russian policy as is feasible. Other longer studies include M. Beloff, *The foreign policy of Soviet Russia, 1929–1941* (2 vols., 1947–9), a solid and dispassionate narrative; L. F. Fischer, *The Soviets in world affairs . . . 1917–29* (1930, 1951); and D. J. Dallin, *Soviet Russia's foreign policy, 1939–1942* (1942) and *Soviet Russia and the Far East* (1948). Other useful studies are H. L. Moore, *Soviet Far Eastern policy, 1931–1945* (1945); P. Tomkins, *American-Russian relations in the Far East* (1949); T. A. Taracouzio, *War and peace in Soviet diplomacy* (1940); and M. N. Roy, *Revolution and Counter-revolution in China* (1930, 1946).

U.S.S.R.—INTERNAL CONDITIONS. D. J. Simmons (ed.), *U.S.S.R.: a concise handbook* (1947), a convenient reference work of uneven quality, is in many respects the best introduction to this often obscure and always inconclusive question. R. Thompson has brought up to date and revised (usually in a more critical direction) S. N. Harper's excellent *The government of the Soviet Union* (1938, 1949), which to a large extent is paralleled by J. Towster's authoritative *Political power in the U.S.S.R., 1917–1947: the theory and structure of government in the Soviet state* (1948). Other important studies include A. Rosenberg, *A history of Bolshevism from Marx to the first Five Years' Plan* (1934); B. Moore, Jr., *Soviet politics: the dilemma of power* (1950); and M. Fainsod, *How Russia is ruled* (1953). The *History of the Communist Party of the Soviet Union (Bolsheviks), short course* (1939), is the official Stalinist version prepared by a commission of the Central Committee of the party.

Economic developments are discussed in a wider intellectual and cultural context in J. Maynard's sympathetic *Russia in flux* (1948). More technical description and evaluation appears in A. Baykov, *The development of the Soviet economic system: an essay on the experience of planning in the U.S.S.R.* (1946), the standard account; S. S. Balzak and others, *Economic geography of the U.S.S.R.* (1940, 1949), containing both facts and ideology; M. Dobb, *Soviet economic development since 1917* (1948), a pro-Soviet view; H. Schwartz, *Russia's Soviet economy* (1950, 1954); N. Jasny, *The socialized agriculture of the U.S.S.R.* (1949); G. Bienstock and others, *Management in Russian industry and agriculture* (1944); and A. Arakelian, *Industrial management in the U.S.S.R.* (1949), the translation of a work which appeared in Moscow in 1947.

Other important matters are taken up in D. F. White, *Growth of the Red Army* (1944); P. B. Anderson, *People, church and state in modern Russia* (1944); J. S. Curtiss, *The Russian church and the Soviet state, 1917–1950* (1953). R. Schlesinger, *Soviet legal theory: its social background and development* (1946); and A. Y. Vyshinsky (ed.), *The law of the Soviet state* (1948) and *The teachings of Lenin and Stalin on Proletarian revolution and the state* (1948).

U.S.S.R.—IDEOLOGY AND CULTURE. The following works are suggested: D. P. Mirsky, *A history of Russian literature* (1949); E. J. Simmons, *Outline of modern Russian literature, 1880–1940* (1943); J. Kunitz (ed.), *Russian literature since the Revolution* (1948), a vast anthology; N. Berdiaev [Berdyaev], *The origin of Russian Communism* (1937); R. Schlesinger, *The spirit of post-war Russia: Soviet ideology, 1917–1946* (1947); J. Somerville, *Soviet philosophy: a study of theory and practice* (1946); and G. S. Counts and N. Lodge, *The country of the blind: the Soviet system of mind control* (1949), on the political restrictions on intellectual activities. There are in addition a number of journalistic accounts, memoirs by ambassadors, and frankly polemical works of uneven quality.

WORLD COMMUNISM. On the transformation of earlier socialism and Marxism into communism, a number of excellent studies are available in addition to books listed in Chapters XI, XII, and XIV. Among them are M. Salvadori, *The rise of modern communism* (1952), a Berkshire study; R. N. C. Hunt, *Theory and practice of communism* (1950) and *Marxism: past and present* (1954); J. Plamenatz, *German Marxism and Russian communism* (1954); and R. Schlesinger, *Marx: his time and ours* (1950), the latter written from a Marxian viewpoint. E. H. Carr's *Studies in revolution* (1950), cited earlier, presents thoughtful essays ranging from Saint-Simon to Stalin. Personal testimonies of the impact of communism may be found in A. Balabanoff, *My life as a rebel* (1938) and R. H. Crossman (ed.), *The God that failed* (1950). F. Borkenau, *The Communist International* (1938) and *European communism* (1953), are informative, relatively unexcited accounts by a former Comintern agent. M. Ebon, *World communism today* (1948), is a moderate factual description. L. L. Lorwin has written *The International Labor Movement* (1953).

Chapter XVIII. The Apparent Victory of Democracy

THE WORLD SINCE 1919: GENERAL. [Books on international relations between the two wars and on internal developments in the major countries outside Asia are listed in the following chapter.] Practically indispensable for serious study of the forces and events of the 20th century are *Foreign affairs bibliography: a selected and annotated list of books on international relations, 1919–1932* (1933), ed. by W. L. Langer and H. F. Armstrong, and *. . . 1932–1942* (1945), ed. by R. G. Woolbert, two carefully compiled works including altogether about 15,000 titles and short descriptions of books on such topics as disarmament, mandates, domestic affairs in various countries, etc., for which space is lacking in the present bibliography. Publications since 1942 are listed as they appear in the current issues of the quarterly *Foreign Affairs*, and will provide the basis for a future cumulative volume. G. P. Gooch, *Bibliography of European history, 1918–1939* (1940), should also be consulted.

Among useful general introductory surveys of the first half of the twentieth century are H. Holborn, *The political collapse of Europe* (1951); A. Siegfried, *Europe's crisis* (1935); H. Kohn, *The twentieth century* (1949); J. S. Schapiro, *The world in crisis* (1950); F. P. Chambers, C. P. Harris, and C. C. Bayley, *This age of conflict* (1943, 1950); C. E. Black and E. C. Helmreich, *Twentieth-century Europe* (1950); and D. Thomson's brief *World history from 1914 to 1950* (1951). Q. Howe has completed two of the projected three volumes of A *world history of our times* (1949, 1953), an interesting account by a high level journalist. In addition to the document source books by Langsam and by Funk cited in the introductory section, there may be added L. L. Snyder, *The world in the twentieth century* (1955) and *Fifty major documents of the twentieth century* (1955), both in the Anvil series.

THE REVOLT OF ASIA. [See also the discussion of Imperialism under Chapter XV.] *Most of the world: the peoples of Africa, Latin America, and the East today* (1949), ed. by R. Linton, is a comprehensive survey giving an impressive indication of the magnitude of such world problems as food, population, standard of living, etc.

Recommended books on Turkey include H. N. Howard, *The partition of Turkey, 1913-1923* (1931); A. J. Toynbee, *The Western Question in Greece and Turkey: a study in the contact of civilizations* (1922); D. E. Webster, *The Turkey of Atatürk: social process in the Turkish reformation* (1939); H. E. Allen, *The Turkish transformation: a study in social and religious development* (1935); and M. W. Thornburg and associates, *Turkey: an economic appraisal* (1949).

Stirrings in the Middle East are discussed in D. Warriner, *Land and poverty in the Middle East* (1948); H. A. R. Gibb, *Modern trends in Islam* (1947), with emphasis on intellectual changes; A. H. Hourani, *Syria and Lebanon* (1946); G. Lenczowski, *Russia and the West in Iran, 1918-1948* (1949); R. N. Frye, *Iran* (1953), a Berkshire study; and H. L. Hoskins, *The middle east* (1954). Developments on the Indian sub-continent may be approached through D. R. Gadgil, *The industrial evolution of India in recent times* (1924, 1944); K. J. Shridharani, *The Mahatma and the world* (1946); T. W. Wallbank, *India* (1948), in the Berkshire series, and the same author's *India in the new era: a study of the origin and development of the Indian Union and Pakistan* (1951); K. L. Mitchell, *India without fable* (1942); W. N. Brown, *The United States and India and Pakistan* (1953); and T. G. Spear, *India, Pakistan, and the West* (1952). Nehru's autobiography, *Toward freedom* (1941), his *Glimpses of world history* (1942) and other writings make absorbing reading, as does Gandhi's *Autobiography: the story of my experiments with truth* (1948).

The ferment in the Far East is discussed in O. Lattimore, *The situation in Asia* (1949); E. H. Jacoby, *Agrarian unrest in South-east Asia* (1949), on the economic changes leading to political revolution; B. Lasker, *Asia on the move: population pressure, migration, and resettlement in Eastern Asia under the influence of want and war* (1945) and *Peoples of Southeast Asia* (1944). The historical background of southeast Asia is sketched in B. Harrison, *South-east Asia: a short history* (1954). On areas outside China, the following may be suggested: R. K. Reischauer, *Japan: government and politics* (1939); A. Tiedemann, *Modern Japan: a brief history* (1955), commentary and readings, in the Anvil series; J. S. Furnivall, *Netherlands India: a study of plural economy* (1939, 1944); C. Wolf, *The Indonesian story: the birth, growth, and structure of the Indonesian Republic* (1948); and E. J. Hammer, *The struggle for Indochina* (1954). On the Chinese Revolution and on the dramatic developments that accompanied the emergence of communism in China, the following are suggested: E. Snow, *Red star over China* (1937, 1944); A. Jacoby and T. H. White, *Thunder out of China* (1946); B. I. Schwartz, *Chinese communism and the rise of Mao* (1951); H. Feis, *The China tangle* (1953); J. K. Fairbank, *The United States and China* (1948); K. S. Latourette, *The American record in the Far East* (1952); and W. W. Rostow and others, *The prospects for Communist China* (1954).

THE DEPRESSION: COLLAPSE OF THE WORLD ECONOMY. The great depression and some of its effects are examined in the following books: P. Einzig, *The world economic crisis, 1929-1931* (1931); M. J. Bonn, *The crumbling of empire: the disintegration of world economy* (1938); G. E. Hubbard, *Eastern industrialisation and its effect on the West* (1930); H. W. Arndt, *The economic lessons of the Nineteen Thirties* (1944); E. Hexner, *International cartels* (1945); H. V. Hodson, *Slump and recovery, 1929-1937* (1938); *Monetary policy and the depression* (1933), by the Royal Institute of International Affairs; W. A. Brown, *The international gold standard reinterpreted, 1914-1934* (1940); V. P. Timoshenko, *World agriculture and the depression* (1933); and *The course and control of inflation: a review of monetary experience in Europe after World War I* (1946), a League of Nations publication. W. K. Galbraith has written a vivid history and analysis in *The* great crash: 1929 (1955) as well as a provocative study of the nature of contemporary economic life in *American capitalism: the concept of countervailing power* (1952).

Chapter XIX. Democracy and Dictatorship

THE WELFARE STATE AND AMERICAN NEW DEAL. On the general concept of the welfare state, these books may be especially recommended: J. M. Keynes, *The end of laissez-faire* (1927); J. A. Schumpeter, *Capitalism, socialism, and democracy* (1942); G. Soule, *A planned society* (1934), and other writings; and B. Wooton, *Freedom under planning* (1945). F. A. von Hayek, in *The road to serfdom* (1944) and other writings subjects the welfare state to an unsympathetic appraisal. A. Sturmthal, *The tragedy of European labor, 1918–1939* (1943, 1951), is a penetrating study criticizing labor in the inter-war period as too narrow in vision to be politically effective.

The immense and growing literature on the New Deal in the United States may best be approached though D. W. Brogan, *The era of Franklin D. Roosevelt* (1950), by an acute British writer; B. Rauch, *History of the New Deal, 1933–1938* (1944); C. A. and M. R. Beard, *America in Midpassage* (1939); and B. Mitchell, *Depression decade: from New Era through New Deal, 1929–1941* (1947). Many memoirs have already appeared, among them those of Eleanor Roosevelt (1939), Frances Perkins (1946), Harold L. Ickes (1943), Cordell Hull (1948), and James L. Byrnes (1947). Of special interest also, mainly on the war period, is R. E. Sherwood, *Roosevelt and Hopkins* (1948). A selection of conflicting interpretations of the New Deal is conveniently presented in the Amherst study, *The New Deal: revolution or evolution?* (1949), ed. by E. C. Rozwenc.

GREAT BRITAIN SINCE 1919. R. Graves and A. Hodge, *The long week-end: a social history of Great Britain, 1918–1939* (1940), gives a fine picture of moods and trends. Something of the impact of the 1914–18 war upon British culture and economy is revealed in A. Siegfried, *Post-war Britain, a French analysis* (1924), and A. C. Pigou, *Aspects of British economic history, 1918–1925* (1947); there are also some relevant volumes in the Carnegie series described under Chapter XVI. Something of the internal political structure may be seen in H. J. Laski's searching *Parliamentary government in England: a commentary* (1938). There are biographies of Stanley Baldwin by G. M. Young (1952), of Ramsay MacDonald by G. E. Elton (1939), and of Neville Chamberlain by K. Feiling (1946). On post-1945 developments, two interesting accounts written from a Labor viewpoint are F. Williams, *Socialist Britain* (1949), and C. R. Attlee, *The Labour party in perspective— and twelve years later* (1937, 1949). They may be compared with Q. Hogg, *The case for conservatism* (1947).

On the British Commonwealth of Nations, there are the authoritative works of A. B. Keith, such as *The dominions as sovereign states* (1938) and other books; and two excellent general surveys: E. A. Walker, *The British Empire: its structure and spirit* (1943), and G. E. Elton, *Imperial Commonwealth* (1946). R. G. Trotter, *The British Empire-Commonwealth* (1932), is a brief introduction in the Berkshire series. K. C. Wheare has written the informative *The statute of Westminster and dominion status* (1938). An important special situation is discussed in H. Harrison, *Ireland and the British* (1937).

FRANCE SINCE 1919. Histories of the Third Republic as a whole appear under Chapter XIV, and to these may be added E. J. Knapton, *France since Versailles* (1952), in the Berkshire series; R. H. Soltau, *French parties and politics, 1871–1930* (1931); A. Siegfried, *France: a study in nationality* (1930); W. R. Sharp, *The government of the French Republic* (1938); W. L. Middleton, *The French political system* (1933); and C. J. H. Hayes, *France: a nation of patriots* (1930). There are studies of French labor by M. R. Clark (1930), D. J. Saposs (1931), H. W. Ehrmann (1947), and V. R. Lorwin (1954), the latter two of outstanding quality. Other monographic studies include M. K. Wise, *Requisition in France and Italy: the treatment of national private property and services* (1944); K. A. Doukas, *The French railroads and the state* (1945); J. Colton, *Compulsory labor arbitration in France, 1936–1939* (1951); and on currency and financial problems, studies by R. H. Rogers (1929), E. L. Dulles (1929), and M. Wolfe (1951).

On the stormy events of the 1930's and the fall of France, the following are recommended: A. Werth, *The twilight of France, 1933–1940* (1942) and other writings by this able journalist; C. A. Micaud, *The French Right and Nazi Germany*, 1933–1939 (1943); A. Géraud [Pertinax], *The gravediggers of France: Gamelin, Daladier, Reynaud, Pétain, and Laval* (1944); A. Maurois, *Tragedy of France* (1940); M. Bloch, *Strange defeat: a statement of evidence written in 1940* (1949), by a distinguished historian who reports on what he saw; and L. Blum, *For all mankind* (1946), a moving testimony of faith written while a prisoner of Vichy. A. Rossi analyzes the role of the communists in the opening phase of the war in *A communist party in action* (1949). P. Farmer has written a judicious appraisal of the Pétain government in *Vichy: political dilemma* (1955), which supplements D. Pickles, *France between the Republics, 1940–1945* (1946).

The establishment and early years of the Fourth Republic are best approached through the following excellent studies: G. Wright, *The reshaping of French democracy* (1948); E. M. Earle (ed.), *Modern France: problems of the Third and Fourth Republics* (1951); D. C. McKay, *The United States and France* (1951); F. Goguel, *The Fourth Republic* (1952); D. Pickles, *French politics: the first years of the Fourth Republic* (1953); P. Williams, *Politics in post-war France* (1954); and H. Luethy, *France against herself* (1954).

TOTALITARIANISM, PARTICULARLY NAZISM. [Communism is discussed mainly in Chapter XVII, and Italian fascism is discussed separately in this chapter, as are various other works on Germany.]

The following general works are suggested as giving some insight into totalitarian attitudes and institutions: A. Cobban, *Dictatorship: its history and theory* (1939); E. Fromm, *Escape from freedom* (1941), a psychological inquiry into the reasons for widespread submission to tyranny; H. Arendt, *The origins of totalitarianism* (1951); G. W. F. Hallgarten, *Why dictators?* (1954); S. Neumann, *Permanent revolution* (1942); C. B. Hoover, *Dictators and democracies* (1937); S. Chakhotin, *The rape of the masses: the psychology of totalitarian political propaganda* (1940), a work to be used with caution; P. Drucker, *The end of economic man: a study of the new totalitarianism* (1939); and J. Barzun, *Race: a study in modern superstition* (1937).

More specifically on the German experience (in addition to several important books listed for earlier chapters) are: W. M. McGovern, *From Luther to Hitler: the history of Fascist-Nazi political philosophy* (1941), a work that is less than fair to the earlier Germans; P. Viereck, *Metapolitics, from the Romantics to Hitler* (1941); R. D. O'Butler, *The roots of national socialism, 1783–1933* (1941); L. L. Snyder, *German nationalism: the tragedy of a people* (1952); and R. H. Bowen, *German theories of the corporative state* (1947).

On the Nazi era itself, recommended works include S. H. Roberts, *The house that Hitler built* (1938); C. B. Hoover, *Germany enters the Third Reich* (1933); K. Heiden, *A history of National Socialism* (1935) and *Der Fuehrer: Hitler's rise to power* (1944), two important studies; F. L. Neumann, *Behemoth: the structure and practice of National Socialism* (1942), in many respects the best description and analysis; R. A. Brady, *The spirit and structure of German fascism* (1937), comparable to Neumann in scope and merit; F. L. Schuman, *The Nazi dictatorship* (1935); and A. Kolnai, *The war against the West* (1938), an exposé of Nazi ideology. A. L. C. Bullock has written an excellent biography of the Führer, *Hitler: a study in tyranny* (1952); and H. R. Trevor-Roper has written *The last days of Hitler* (1947). The proceedings of the Nuremberg war crimes trials have been published as *Nazi conspiracy and aggression* (8 vols., 1946).

GERMANY SINCE 1919. [Nazism as an organized movement is discussed above under "Totalitarianism."] In F. Meinecke's *The German catastrophe: reflections and recollections* (1946, 1950), a great German historian—who had held aloof from Hitlerism—analyzes the modern history of his country. His book may be compared with the chapters in H. Kohn (ed.), *German history: some new German views* (1954).

Narratives of the Weimar Republic and its fall include S. W. Halperin, *Germany tried democracy: a political history of the Reich from 1918 to 1933* (1946), probably the best-balanced account; A. Rosenberg's two important studies, *The birth of the German Republic, 1871–1918* (1931) and *A history of the German republic* (1936); G. Scheele, *The Weimar Republic: overture to the Third Reich* (1947); A. Brecht, *Prelude to silence: the end of the German republic* (1944); R. T. Clark, *The fall of the German republic: a political study* (1935); and L. M. Fraser, *Germany between two wars: a study of propaganda and war guilt* (1945), written partially for purposes of German re-education. R. Fischer, *Stalin and German communism: a study in the origins of the state party* (1948), is a revealing "inside story" to 1929. The two leading personalities of the Weimar Republic are discussed in A. Vallentin, *Stresemann* (1931), H. W. Gatzke, *Stresemann and the rearmament of Germany* (1954), and J. W. Wheeler-Bennett, *Wooden titan: Hindenburg in twenty years of German history, 1914–1934* (1936).

Important special topics are discussed in F. M. Watkins, *The failure of constitutional emergency powers under the German Republic* (1940); P. Kosok, *Modern Germany: a study of conflicting loyalties* (1933); J. B. Holt, *German agricultural policy, 1918–1934* (1936); F. Wunderlich, *Labor under German democracy: arbitration, 1918–1933* (1940); S. D. Stirk, *The Prussian spirit: a survey of German literature and politics, 1914–1940* (1941); R. Sasuly, *I. G. Farben* (1947); S. Kracauer, *From Caligari to Hitler: a psychological history of the German film* (1947); J. W. Wheeler-Bennett, *Nemesis of power* (1954), on the German army; and H. Rothfels, *The German opposition to Hitler* (1948), a useful introduction to an interesting and controversial subject. The second German republic may be studied in S. Neumann, *Germany: promise and perils* (1950); J. P. Warburg, *Germany: key to peace* (1953); and H. Morgenthau (ed.), *Germany and the future of Europe* (1951). On the eastern zone there is available the useful study by J. P. Nettl, *The Eastern zone and Soviet policy in Germany, 1945–1950* (1951).

ITALY SINCE 1919. Most of the following books discuss both the theory and the practice of Italian fascism: A. Rossi [pseudonym], *The rise of Italian fascism, 1918–1922* (1938), by a well-informed anti-fascist; G. Megaro, *Mussolini in the making* (1938); H. W. Schneider, *Making the Fascist state* (1928) and later works; H. Finer, *Mussolini's Italy* (1935); G. A. Borgese, *Goliath: the march of Fascism* (1937); G. Salvemini, *Under the axe of fascism* (1936), and on the Ethiopian conquest, *Prelude to World War II* (1954); M. H. H. Macartney and P. Cremona, *Italy's foreign and colonial policy, 1914–1937* (1938); C. T. Schmidt, *The plough and the sword* (1938) and *The corporate state in action: Italy under fascism* (1939); J. Meenan, *The Italian corporative system* (1945); and H. L. Matthews, *The fruits of fascism* (1943). On the new Italian republic, see M. Grindrod, *The new Italy* (1947); H. S. Hughes, *The United States and Italy* (1953); M. Einaudi and F. Goguel, *Christian Democracy in Italy and France* (1952); and M. Einaudi and others, *Communism in Western Europe* (1951).

SPAIN SINCE 1919. *Politics, economics, and men of modern Spain, 1808–1946* (1946), by A. Ramos Oliveira, despite its title, deals mostly with the period 1931–9. The underlying issues in Spain's turbulent past are brought out most clearly and perspicaciously in C. Brenan, *The Spanish labyrinth: an account of the social and political background of the Civil War* (1943). Other helpful books are N. J. Padelford, *International law and diplomacy in the Spanish civil strife* (1939); J. A. del Vayo, *Freedom's battle* (1940), by a leading Republican official; F. Borkenau, *The Spanish cockpit* (1937); H. Feis, *The Spanish story: Franco and the nations at war* (1948); and C. Foltz, Jr., *The masquerade in Spain* (1948). An interesting comparison may be made between the narratives by the American and British ambassadors in Madrid during the Second World War: C. J. H. Hayes, *Wartime mission in Spain, 1942–1945* (1945), and S. Hoare, *Complacent dictator* (1947); and both may be compared with C. Bowers, *My mission to Spain* (1954), the American ambassador during the civil war.

OTHER EUROPEAN DEVELOPMENTS. A variety of important topics is dealt with in the following books: H. Seton-Watson, *Eastern Europe between the wars, 1918–1941* (1945), an outstanding impartial and topical treatment; C. A. Gulick, *Austria from Habsburg to Hitler* (2 vols., 1948), a fully documented and detailed account sympathetic to the Austrian socialists; M. MacDonald, *The Republic of Austria, 1918–1934: a study in the failure of democratic government* (1946), a fine constitutional analysis; C. A. Macartney, *Hungary and her successors: the treaty of Trianon and its consequences, 1919–1937* (1937) and *Problems of the Danube Basin* (1942); A. Basch, *The Danube Basin and the German economic sphere* (1944); J. S. Roucek, *Balkan politics: international relations in No Man's Land* (1948); *Southeastern Europe: a political and economic survey* (1939), by the Royal

Institute of International Affairs; R. West, *Black lamb and grey falcon: a journey through Yugoslavia* (2 vols., 1941), a sensitive and discriminating description; E. Monroe, *The Mediterranean in politics* (1938); M. Boveri, *Mediterranean cross-currents* (1938); and W. F. Reddaway, *Problems of the Baltic* (1940). Perhaps the best introduction to the changes in Eastern Europe after 1945 is H. Seton-Watson, *The East-European revolution* (1950). The comprehensive historical survey of the area east of the Elbe by O. Halecki has been cited in Chapter V.

INTERNATIONAL AFFAIRS BETWEEN THE WARS. Recommended surveys include G. M. Gathorne-Hardy, *A short history of international affairs, 1920–1939* (1934, 1942), a well-proportioned and accurate general guide; E. H. Carr, *The twenty years' crisis, 1919–1939* (1939), a shrewd interpretation; and R. M. Rayner, *A twenty years' truce, 1919–1939* (1945). Of special value are the studies for the inter-war years edited for the Royal Institute of International Affairs by A. Toynbee and others, *Survey of international affairs* (1920 ff.) and the accompanying *Documents on international affairs*; a survey has been issued to cover the years 1939–46 (1954) and the volumes have been resumed also for the post-1946 period.

On the League of Nations, there are innumerable studies published by the League itself, and the following general accounts may also be mentioned: F. P. Walters, *A history of the League of Nations* (2 vols., 1952); J. T. Shotwell and M. Salvin, *Lessons on security and disarmament from the history of the League of Nations* (1949); W. E. Rappard, *The quest for peace since the World War* (1940); and A. Zimmern, *The League of Nations and the rule of law* (1936). S. R. Smith, *The Manchurian crisis, 1931–1932: a tragedy in international relations* (1948), is a discriminating study of the League's most disastrous defeat. There are some thoughtful chapters in F. Gilbert and G. A. Craig (eds.), *The diplomats, 1919–1939* (1953).

The uncertainties of the Western Powers are shown in A. Wolfers, *Britain and France between two wars: conflicting strategies of peace since Versailles* (1940); R. W. Seton-Watson, *Britain and the dictators: a survey of post-war British policy* (1938) and *From Munich to Danzig* (1939); and W. M. Jordan, *Great Britain, France, and the German problem, 1918–1939* (1943). The diplomacy leading up to the Second World War is treated also in the following: E. Wiskemann, *The Rome-Berlin Axis* (1949) and *Undeclared war* (1939); F. L. Schuman, *Europe on the eve: the crises of diplomacy, 1933–1939* (1939), a bitter indictment of appeasement; G. E. R. Gedye, *Betrayal in Central Europe* (1939); L. B. Namier, *Diplomatic prelude, 1938–1939* (1948), a painstaking and revealing examination of the formal diplomacy preceding the outbreak of hostilities; the same author's *Europe in decay: a study in disintegration, 1936–1940* (1950); and J. W. Wheeler-Bennett, *Munich: prologue to tragedy* (1948). Most of the nations involved have issued official or semiofficial explanations, documents, or apologies for their policies, and much intensive research is now being devoted to the period, so that further revelations may be expected. The German Foreign Office archives captured during the Second World War are being edited by an international group of distinguished historians as *Documents on German foreign policy, 1918–1945* (1949 ff.).

Chapter XX. The Cataclysm: The Second World War and Its Aftermath

THE SECOND WORLD WAR. The following are some of the more notable attempts to cover all the major theaters: W. S. Churchill, *The Second World War* (6 vols., 1948–53), a full-dress treatment by a historian with unrivaled opportunities; J. F. C. Fuller, *The Second World War, 1939–1945: a strategical and tactical history* (1948); W. P. Hall, *Iron out of Calvary: an interpretative history of the Second World War* (1946); R. W. Shugg and H. A. De Weerd, *World War II: a concise history* (1946); and E. McInnis, *The war* (6 vols., 1940–6). Many volumes have also appeared of the detailed official histories sponsored by the various armed services and more will be forthcoming. Wartime diplomacy is discussed in the latter volumes of Churchill's history, other memoirs, and in C. Wilmot, *The struggle for Europe* (1952). Conflicting interpretations of Yalta are conveniently brought together in the Amherst study ed. by R. F. Fenno, Jr., *The Yalta conference* (1955).

THE POST-WAR WORLD. Many works bearing on developments since 1945 in the major countries of Europe and Asia are listed in the three preceding chapters. Although no attempt can be made to include here any specialized studies of the world since 1945, there may be some point in asking the reader to consider the titles and contents of these books: B. Ward, *The West at bay* (1948) and *Faith and freedom* (1954); E. Fischer, *The passing of the European age: a study of the transfer of Western civilization and its renewal in other continents* (1943, 1948); V. Bush, *Modern arms and free men: a discussion of the role of science in preserving democracy* (1949); S. E. Harris, *The European Recovery Program* (1948); V. M. Dean, *Europe and the United States* (1950); W. S. and E. S. Woytinsky, *World population and production: trends and outlook* (1953); F. S. C. Northrop, *The meeting of East and West* (1946) and *The taming of the nations* (1952); R. Aron, *The century of total war* (1954); G. F. Kennan, *American diplomacy, 1900–1950* (1951) and *Realities of American foreign policy* (1954); H. S. Hughes, *An essay for our times* (1950); C. Brinton, *The temper of Western Europe* (1953); and A. J. Toynbee, *Civilization on trial* (1948) and *The world and the West* (1953).

Index

‸‸‸

DATES given after names of rulers and popes are the years of reigns or pontificates; those given for all others are the years of birth and death.

PRONUNCIATION is indicated where it is not obvious. With foreign words the purpose is not to show their exact pronunciation in their own language but to suggest how they may be acceptably pronounced in English. Fully Anglicized pronunciations are indicated by the abbreviation *Angl.* Pronunciation is shown by respelling, not by symbols, except that the following symbols are used for vowel sounds not found in English:

ø Indicates the sound of ö as in Königsberg. To form this sound, purse the lips as if to say *o,* and then say *ay* as in *ate.*

U indicates the sound of the French *u,* or of German *ü.* To form this sound, purse the lips as if to say *oo,* and then say *ee* as in *eat.*

aN, oN, uN, iN indicate the sounds of the French nasal vowels. Once learned, these are easily pronounced, roughly as follows: For aN, begin to pronounce the English word *on,* but avoid saying the consonant *n* and "nasalize" the *ah* sound instead. For oN, do the same with the English *own;* for uN, with the English prefix *un-;* for iN, with the English word *an.*

zh indicates the sound of *s* in the word *treasure.* This sound is common in English, though never found at the beginning or end of a word. *igh* always indicates the so-called "long *i*" as in *high.* The vowel sound of *hoot* is indicated by *oo,* that of *hood* by *ŏŏ.*

Compared with English, the European languages are highly regular in their spelling, in that the same letters or combinations of letters are generally pronounced in the same way.

A NOTE ON THE TYPE

This book was set on the Linotype in ELECTRA, designed by W. A. Dwiggins. The Electra face is a simple and readable type suitable for printing books by present-day processes. It is not based on any historical model, and hence does not echo any particular time or fashion. It is without eccentricities to catch the eye and interfere with reading—in general, its aim is to perform the function of a good book printing-type: to be read, and not seen.

The book was composed, printed, and bound by Kingsport Press, Inc., Kingsport, Tennessee. Typography by Sidney R. Jacobs; binding design by Charles E. Skaggs.

A NOTE ON THE TYPE

This book was set on the Linotype in ELECTRA, designed by W. A. Dwiggins. The Electra face is a simple and readable type suitable for printing books by present-day processes. It is not based on any historical model, and hence does not echo any particular time or fashion. It is without eccentricities to catch the eye and interfere with reading— in general, its aim is to perform the function of a good book printing-type: to be read, and not seen.

The book was composed, printed, and bound by Kingsport Press, Inc., Kingsport, Tennessee. Typography by Sidney R. Jacobs; binding design by Charles E. Skaggs.

Since first publ
tory of the M
widely rec
b

ROBE   born in
                           mi

POPULATION
DENSITY
PERSONS
PER SQUARE MILE

UNDER 5
5-100
101-250
OVER 250

ASIA, 1955

THE DARKER AREAS ARE THE STATES
RECOGNIZED AS INDEPENDENT
AFTER WORLD WAR II

1000 MILES

TRM